STATE ARCHIVES OF ASSYRIA

VOLUME VI

FRONTISPIECE. *Bronze lion-weight (665.7 g) inscribed 2/3 of a royal mina. From Nimrud.* BM 91230.

LEGAL TRANSACTIONS OF THE ROYAL COURT OF NINEVEH PART I

TIGLATH-PILESER III THROUGH ESARHADDON

Edited by
THEODORE KWASMAN
and
SIMO PARPOLA

Illustrations
edited by
JULIAN READE

HELSINKI UNIVERSITY PRESS
1991

Publication of this volume was made possible in part by a grant
from the Research Council for the Humanities of
the Academy of Finland

Set in Times
Typography and layout by Teemu Lipasti
The Assyrian Royal Seal emblem drawn by Dominique Collon from original
Seventh Century B.C. impressions (BM 84672 and 84677) in the British Museum
Ventura Publisher format by Robert M. Whiting
Electronic pasteup by Laura Kataja

Helsinki University Press
Vuorikatu 3 A 2, SF-00100 Helsinki, Finland
Tel. 358-0-701 9077, Tfx. 358-0-175 368

ISBN 951-570-001-9 (Whole Series, Paperback)
ISBN 951-570-002-7 (Whole Series, Hardbound)
ISBN 951-570-092-2 (Volume 6, Paperback)
ISBN 951-570-093-0 (Volume 6, Hardbound)

STATE ARCHIVES OF ASSYRIA

Published by the Neo-Assyrian Text Corpus Project
of the Academy of Finland
in co-operation with
Deutsche Orient-Gesellschaft

VOLUME VI

Theodore Kwasman and Simo Parpola

LEGAL TRANSACTIONS OF THE ROYAL COURT OF NINEVEH, PART I

Tiglath-Pileser III through Esarhaddon

HELSINKI UNIVERSITY PRESS

FOREWORD

The basic manuscript of this volume was prepared by Theodore Kwasman and Simo Parpola and is the result of both scholars' longstanding interest in this corpus. The specific contributions of the individual authors are set forth in more detail in the Preface.

Our thanks are due to the Trustees of the British Museum and to the Musée du Louvre for permission to publish illustrative material in their keeping and to I.L. Finkel of the Department of Western Asiatic Antiquities of the British Museum for last-minute collations.

We thank the Olivetti (Finland) Corporation for continuing technical support and the Finnish Ministry of Education for generous subsidies to help offset the costs of publication, and we express our gratitude to the Academy of Finland for renewing its financial support for the continuation of the Project.

Helsinki, June 1991 Robert M. Whiting

PREFACE

The present volume is the fruit of a lengthy collaboration between the two editors going back in part to spring 1976, when Kwasman spent several months in Helsinki working on the ADD texts with Parpola. At that time, we computerized practically all the texts published in ADD I on the basis of new transliterations based principally on the Johns copies but systematically taking into consideration also the collations by Ungnad published in AR. A printout of the transliterations and complete word and reverse word indices were generated from this material and made available to Kwasman in summer 1976, while the text files themselves were incorporated in what was gradually to evolve into the present SAA database.

In summer 1978, Parpola thoroughly collated a sizeable portion (about 300) of the texts at the British Museum. The results of this collation were published in a condensed form, omitting many drawings of collated passages, in Assur 2/5 (1979), pp. 109-197, and incorporated in the database by Parpola in spring 1984. Portions of the corpus not yet included in the database were computerized by Raija Mattila in 1986.

In the meantime, Kwasman continued working on the texts on his own, collating the texts and making a number of important joins in the course of several study trips to the British Museum. His Ph.D. dissertation on the corpus (NALK) was completed in early 1988, making it possible for him to accept, in November 1987, an invitation from Parpola to act as a co-editor of the present volume.

Since about 2/3 of the texts (with the exception of the dates and the witness lists) had just been translated in NALK, it was agreed that the translations in the volume would be based, as far as possible, on NALK, while the transliterations would, as usual, be based on the Project database. Accordingly, the translations in NALK were scanned and computerized by Laura Kataja in the fall of 1989, and the witness lists left untranslated in NALK were machine-translated by a computer programme written by Parpola in spring 1990. The two sets of translations were subsequently combined and sent for editing to Kwasman, who had earlier (in summer 1988) received a revised printout of the whole corpus as well as improved indices generated from it.

In early December 1990, Kwasman briefly visited Helsinki to discuss the order and selection of texts included in the volume and other editorial matters. Following Kwasman's departure, Parpola paid a one-week visit to the British Museum collating close to 200 texts included in the volume.

In detail, the editorial work on this volume and the responsibility for its individual parts was distributed as follows between the two editors:

The Introduction in its entirety is by Parpola.

The transliterations essentially are the result of joint work. The readings in NALK have been carefully checked against the database and all new readings based on collation have been included insofar as possible. Doubtful readings have been recollated, and cases where readings in NALK could not be accepted are briefly justified in the critical apparatus.

The translations are, as explained above, largely based on Kwasman's work in NALK but have been thorougly scrutinized and edited by Parpola. The translations of all witness lists and dates, as well as the normalization of personal names throughout the volume, are based on Parpola's work and have been scrutinized and edited by Kwasman. Texts not included in NALK were largely translated by Parpola.

The headings to the texts were supplied jointly by the two editors.

The bibliographical data in the critical apparatus were largely provided by Kwasman; the other parts of this section are largely the work of Parpola.

The order of texts in the volume and the selection of texts to be included is basically the work of Parpola.

The meanings of the words included in the glossary were basically supplied by Kwasman during his visit to Helsinki. Otherwise the glossary and all the indices included in the book are the work of Parpola.

Most of the drawings of seal and fingernail impressions published in the present volume were made by Parpola in the course of his work at the British Museum in July-August 1978 and December 1990. Twenty-two impressions not drawn by Parpola (those of nos. 5, 7, 17, 19, 45, 56, 60, 69, 74, 76, 77, 118, 126, 132, 136, 141, 154, 203, 218, 256, 305, and 625) were drawn for the volume by Dominique Collon of the British Museum; seven further impressions (those of nos. 63, 73, 75, 181, 204, 286 and 292) could be reproduced from the unpublished University of Munich dissertation of Suzanne Herbordt by the kind permission of the author. I.L. Finkel of the British Museum collated 34 tablets and contributed a drawing of one seal impression (no. 181). We wish to extend our thanks to these colleagues and the entire staff of the Department of Western Asiatic Antiquities for assistance rendered to us during the study of the texts.

The previously unpublished fragment K 16094 included in the volume was identified by Parpola and is published here by the kind permission of the Trustees of the British Museum.

The checking of the transliterations against the readings in NALK was chiefly done by Jukka Hartikainen and Katalin Miklóssy of the Project staff. Corrections to the database were entered by Laura Kataja and Jukka Hartikainen. Katalin Miklóssy inked drawings of seal and fingernail impressions for optical scanning.

Galley proofs were read by members of the Editorial Committee, J. N. Postgate, F. M. Fales and R. M. Whiting, who contributed several improvements and eliminated a number of mistakes.

June, 1991 Theodore Kwasman Simo Parpola

CONTENTS

INTRODUCTION

The bulk of the texts edited in the present volume have seen three major editions previously. C. H. W. Johns's fundamental *Assyrian Deeds and Documents* (ADD) from the turn of the century made practically the entire legal corpus from Nineveh available to scholars in cuneiform copy, and in addition presented many of the texts in (summary) English translation along with extensive commentaries.[1] For all its merits, this editio princeps is, of course, longe since outdated, and the need of a more comprehensive critical edition was already felt early. In 1913, Josef Kohler and Arthur Ungnad published their *Assyrische Rechtsurkunden* (AR), a full edition of the entire Neo-Assyrian legal corpus known at the time, giving the texts in transliteration and German translation along with an index of personal names and an analysis of the corpus from the legal point of view. This edition, superb for its time, is still very useful today, but later additions to the corpus as well as advances in Neo-Assyrian studies have rendered it too obsolete in the course of times.[2] Specifically, a critical English edition has been a desideratum for a long time. The need of such an edition was somewhat alleviated, yet by no means removed, by the appearance of Kwasman's *Neo-Assyrian Legal Documents in the Kouyunjik Collection of the British Museum* (NALK, 1988), which presents about two-thirds of the corpus in English translation and a new transliteration based on extensive museum work.

Apart from its obvious significance to the study of the legal practices in the Assyrian empire, the Ninevite legal corpus is a most important historical source in other respects as well. It derives from the palace area of the Assyrian capital at the apex of its power and largely relates to business conducted by the ruling class of the empire; practically every document in the corpus is closed by a list of witnesses, many of whom belonged to the ruling elite itself, and, in sharp contrast to other contemporary texts, practically all them are (or once were) precisely dated by day, month and eponym year. It is obvious that such a body of texts is of paramount importance to the study of the prosopography, chronology and socio-economic history of the period.

Though the importance of the corpus was recognized quite early, the unique prosopographical and historical information it contains is still far from having been fully exploited.[3] The reason for this is largely to be sought in the organization and constitution of the available editions. In both ADD and AR, the texts are arranged according to their legal and juridical content, which of course is ideal for the legal historian but completely obscures the chronological and archival structure of the corpus. Using these editions in more generally oriented research has proved extremely cumbersome and time-consuming, since texts related from the archival point of view are widely separated from each other and no adequate indices are included in the editions.[4]

In NALK, an attempt was made to arrange the material by archives and thus to bring associated texts more adequately together. However, since the overwhelming majority of the 'archives' (as defined in NALK)[5] consist of one or two (duplicate) texts only, and since the order in which the 'archives' are presented is alphabetical by archive holder, not chronological, the situation is not significantly improved.[6] It is hoped that the present volume, which presents the texts in a new, differently organized critical edition, will make the important evidence they contain better accessible and easier to use in historical research.

The Nature of the Nineveh Legal Archive

The legal texts from Nineveh belong as a major subgroup to a larger whole, the corpus of Neo-Assyrian legal documents, which, in addition to the Ninevite texts, consists of hundreds of similar documents retrieved from other Assyrian sites.[7] Formally there is no distinction between the texts from the other sites and the Nineveh texts, many of which were in fact drawn up outside Nineveh. An excellent introduction to the Neo-Assyrian legal corpus as a whole has been recently provided by J. N. Postgate in his *Fifty Neo-Assyrian Legal Documents* (1976), pp. 1-72,[8] and there is no need to repeat this information here.

By contrast, there has been no adequate discussion of the Nineveh legal corpus as a whole, even though certain aspects of the corpus have been treated by various scholars.[9] This introduction accordingly seems the perfect place for a brief description and discussion of the most important features and characteristics of the corpus. For the sake of clarity, discussion will be limited to the barest essentials.

The Archival Background of the Texts

The bulk of the Nineveh legal texts, as indeed the bulk of all texts discovered in Niniveh, were excavated at a time when Near Eastern archaeology still was in its infancy and no accurate methodology for the documentation of the finds made had yet been developed. As a result, we now lack essential information about the exact findspots of the excavated tablets. For the overwhelming majority of them, the only available indication about their provenance is "from Kuyunjik" (the acropolis of Nineveh), and sometimes even this general provenance remains doubtful despite the inclusion of a tablet in the "Kuyunjik Collection."[10] This is of course most unfortunate, especially since a knowledge of the findspot often is of decisive importance in determining the archival context and function of a legal text.

Of the texts included in the present volume, the (approximate) provenance of the following four can be established from the published excavation reports:

No. 88 (DT 12 = ADD 317, 'archive' or dossier of Ahi-ṭalli, harem governess, dated 687 B.C.): SW Palace of Sennacherib.[11]

No. 111 (K 76 = ADD 229, dossier of Se'-madi, village manager of the crown prince, dated 680 B.C.): SW Palace, "Chamber of Records."[12]

No. 114 (BM 134582 = Iraq 32 12, fragment dated 702): Chol, i.e. "flat area within the curve of the river and city outer walls."[13]

No. 217 (Sm 921 = ADD 378, dossier of Mannu-ki-Arbail, cohort commander, c. 673 B.C.): Library of the SW Palace.[14]

In addition, the provenance of two further documents to be edited in Pt. II can be similarly established:

Sm 957 = ADD 128 (corn loan dated 665 B.C.): SW Palace.

K 296 = ADD 642 (dossier of Iddin-Iya, priest of Ninurta, from the postcanonical [i.e., post-648] period): SW Palace, "Chamber of Records."

This is not much, but provides some extremely valuable clues to the archival background of the whole corpus.

As can be seen, practically all the texts in the above list originate from the palace of Sennacherib in the SW corner of the mound of Kuyunjik (Figs. 1 and 2), constructed in 703-694 B.C. and occupied throughout the 7th century; the dates on the tablets (687, 680, *673, 665, post-648) neatly reflect the occupational history of the palace. Three of them are explicitly said to have been found in the "Chambers of Records" (the royal library, rooms XL and XLI of the palace) among thousands of other archival texts and pieces of literature. It is also explicitly stated in the excavator's report that many more similar documents were found in these rooms.[15] This means that many more texts included in the present volume must have been deposited in the royal library. It is possible, with the help of the archival connections shown in the above list, to pinpoint at least some of these with reasonable confidence.

If tablets from the dossiers of Ahi-ṭalli, Se'-madi and Mannu-ki-Arbail were kept in the royal library, it is reasonable to suppose that the rest of their dossiers too (which all together make up about 8.5% of the present volume) was kept there. Furthermore, considering that the Ahi-ṭalli dossier belongs to a larger set of transactions of the "central city" harem of Nineveh (nos. 81-99), which in all probability was located within the SW Palace, it stands to reason that the other harem documents too were preserved with this dossier.[16] Similarly, one can speculate that if the dossiers of a village manager (Se'-madi) and a cohort commander (Mannu-ki-Arbail) could be kept in the royal library, then at least some of the other similar dossiers (e.g., that of Bahianu, nos. 60-80)[17] should derive from the same place. In fact, it is likely that most of the major dossiers in the present volume dating from the reigns of Sennacherib and his successors were deposited in the "Chambers of Records." However, there is no way of conclusively proving that this was the case, because it is certain that many documents in the corpus originate from elsewhere.

A major portion of the tablet finds in Nineveh was made in the Palace of Assurbanipal (actually, the old "Succession Palace" where Sennacherib had exercised his duties as crown prince under his father Sargon, restored by Assurbanipal in 648-645 B.C.) at the north end of the Kuyunjik mound (Fig. 2). It is likely that most if not all the documents from the reigns of Sargon II and earlier kings included in this volume (nos. 1-33) were found in that palace.[18] Moreover, as the example of no. 114 in the above list shows, the corpus also includes stray finds from various parts of the citadel and even outside the citadel proper.[19] Many of the isolated documents included in the "Varia" sections of the present volume probably originate in various departmental archives of the palace administration, dispersed in the various public

FIG. 1. *View of Kuyunjik from the north-east (1933), with walls of Nineveh, fields and river Tigris beyond.*
R.A.F. PHOTOGRAPH.

FIG. 2. *Air view of Kuyunjik (1932). Most texts were found in the south-west palace of Sennacherib (lower left), with some from the north palace of Assurbanipal (upper right).*
R.A.F. PHOTOGRAPH.

buildings of the citadel including the above-mentioned two palaces; some, like no. 114, may even derive from private houses or refuse dumps.[20]

However that may be in individual cases, it can be regarded as certain that the overwhelming majority of the tablets making up the Nineveh legal corpus were documents of court officials associated with the North and SW palaces of Kuyunjik and kept in the central archives of these palaces.

The Chronological Structure of the Corpus

The chronological structure of the Nineveh legal corpus, as recovered from the dated tablets, is illustrated in Table I. As can be seen, the corpus covers the reigns of eight successive kings (the 'postcanonical' texts including, besides texts from the latter part of Assurbanipal's reign, also ones from the reigns of his sons Aššur-etel-ilani and Sin-šarru-iškun) and spans a period of some 135 years, from 747 B.C. down to the fall of Nineveh (612 B.C.). This long period of time is not at all, however, evenly covered by the corpus. Only about 7% of the texts date from the reigns of the first three kings, a period of 42 years (some 30% of the total time range of the corpus), and there are only two isolated texts from the reign of Shalmaneser V. Only from year 702 on do the numbers of texts per year gradually start to increase (Table II). This is clearly related to the construction history of the SW Palace of Sennacherib (which appears to have be habitable from 703 on even though the building in its entirety was not finished until 694), and strongly supports the conclusion drawn above that the majority of the texts derive from this palace.

The majority of the 8th century texts, from the North Palace, are from the

TABLE I. *The Chronological Structure of the Nineveh Legal Corpus*

Reign	number of texts	% of whole corpus	% of datable texts
Tiglath-Pileser III	11	1.4	2.3
Shalmaneser V	2	0.3	0.4
Sargon II	21	2.6	4.3
Sennacherib	162	20.1	32.5
Esarhaddon	110	13.6	22.6
Assurbanipal (Pt. I)	44	5.5	9.0
Total (Pt. I)	350	43.5	71.1
Assurbanipal (Pt. II)	66	8.2	13.5
Assurbanipal Total	(110)	(13.6)	(22.6)
Post-canonical Texts	76	9.5	15.4
Undatable with Known Central Person	54	6.7	
Undatable with Unknown Central Person	258	32.1	
Total (Pt. II)	454	56.5	28.9
GRAND TOTAL	804	100.0	100.0

TABLE II. *The Chronological Distribution of Datable Legal Texts from Nineveh*

Year	Text no.
747	17
742	1
739	18
737	2
734	19, 21
729	5, 22
727	23
723	24
717	10, 25
716	—
715	12
714	—
713	6
712	—
711	26
710	13, 28, 29, 30
709	31, 34
708	—
707	32
706	33
705	—
704	60
703	—
702	113, 114, 115
701	—
700	35, 61, 116, 117
699	119, 120
698	100, 102, 118, 121, 122, 123, 124, 125
697	126, 127
696	62, 128, 129, 130
695	36, 63, 131, 132
694	37, 38, 39, 81, 83, 84, 103, 133, 134, 135, 136
693	40, 41, 64, 97, 137, 138, 139
692	42, 65, 85, 141, 142, 143, 144, 145, 146
691	—
690	104, 105, 147, 148
689	149
688	66, 67, 68, 69, 106, 150
687	88, 151, 152, 153, 154, 155, 156, 157, 158, 159, 160
686	70, 89, 107, 161, 162, 163, 164, 166, 167, 168, 169
685	71, 72, 170, 171, 172, 173, 174, 175
684	43, 44, 59, 73, 74, 177
683	90, 108, 178, 179, 180, 181, 182, 183, 186
682	45, 75, 76, 77, 98, 187, 188, 189, 190, 191, 192
681	46, 47, 91, 110, 193, 194, 195, 196, 197
680	48, 111, 201, 202, 203, 221, 222, 257, 258, 259, 260, 261, 262, 263, 264
679	204, 206, 223, 224, 247, 265, 268, 269, 270
678	207, 208, 255, 271
677	225, 267, 272
676	210, 211, 212, 213, 214, 215, 226, 239, 240, 273, 274
675	227, 229, 230, 232, 275, 276
674	233, 241, 242, 243, 252, 277, 278, 279
673	216, 280, 281
672	234, 244, 245, 282, 283
671	235, 284, 296, 297, 298, 299
670	236, 237, 286, 287, 289, 290, 291, 300, 301, 302, 303
669	292, 293, 304, 305, 306
668	307, 308
667	309, 310
666	311, 312, 313, 314, 315, 316, 317
665	318, 319
664	320, 321, 323, 324
663	325, 327, 328
660	329, 330, 331

reign of Sargon II, and it actually seems that many if not all of the earlier texts in the corpus also derive from archives belonging to officials of this king or his son Sennacherib. They will have been brought to Nineveh from Calah by these officials at the time the latter moved his staff and permanent residence to the North Palace about 715 B.C.[21]

Central Persons

As already intimated above, from the archival point of view the corpus is composed of two types of legal documents. A large part (in fact, the majority) of them are connected to other documents of the corpus through an individual centrally involved in the transaction, who also appears in the same or similar capacity in the other documents. Such individuals, who mostly figure in the deeds as either purchasers or creditors, are referred to in this volume as *central persons*, and the dossiers of documents associated with them will be called 'archives,' however inappropriate this term might be in this usage. The central persons figuring in the present volume and the sizes of their respective archives are surveyed in Table III. As can be seen, some of them are quite large, comprising more than 20 (in one case, more than 50) texts or fragments.

A most interesting fact immediately emerges from a study of the table. The persons figuring in it represent different professions, but professions largely interconnected with each other and reduceable to a few major classes or types. We have, first of all, a group of four royal charioteers whose dossiers, counted together, alone account for 1/4 of the texts included in this volume. Next, there are the dossiers of the harem governesses and village managers already discussed, which probably belong together, and counted together account for another 1/4 of the volume. This leaves us with the dossiers of four prominent individuals whose professions are largely unknown, but who include at least one cohort commander and a person (Silim-Aššur) promoted to a high state office under Assurbanipal.

Thus the central persons represented in the present volume can be reduced to two basic types: persons involved in the administration of the harem located in the SW Palace, and charioteers and military officers attached to the service of the king and the crown prince. This basic division also holds for the central persons of the later dossiers to be included in Part II of this edition. That documents relating to the administration of the harem should be kept in the royal archives seems natural, but the presence of dossiers of royal charioteers and military officers on the same premises (and not their own private archives) requires an explanation.

We suggest that the persons concerned constituted a special case because of the potential danger they posed to the safety of the king. Royal charioteers and commanders of the royal bodyguard had unique access to the person of the king, and it was therefore essential that the latter could absolutely count on their loyalty. This was secured by money, gifts, favours and privileges poured upon the individuals concerned. On the other hand, it was also essential to make sure that the wealth accumulating to these persons did not swell to such proportions that it in itself started posing a threat to the state.

TABLE III. *Central Persons*

Royal Charioteers	89	(25.4%)
Remanni-Adad, Assurbanipal's Charioteer	55	
Šumma-ilani, Chariot Driver of the Royal Corps	23	
Aplaya, 'Third Man' of Arda-Mullissi, Crown Prince	9	
Nabû-šumu-iškun, Sennacherib's Charioteer	2	
Village Managers	36	(12.9%)
Bahianu, Village Manager of the Stewardess	21	
Mušallim-Issar, Village Manager of the Chief Eunuch	9	
Se'-madi, Village Manager of the Crown Prince	4	
Idu'a, Village Manager of The Queen Mother	2	
Harem Governesses and Other Royal Women	29	(8.3%)
Other Prominent Officials	52	(15.0%)
Mannu-ki-Arbail, Cohort Commander (of the Royal Guard?)	20	
Silim-Aššur (title unknown, later Vizier, eponym 659)	18	
Inurta-ila'i (title unknown)	6	
Dannaya (title unknown)	8	
Total	204	(61.6%)
Other identifiable members of the ruling class	20	(5.7%)
Total	224	(67.3%)

For this reason, we suggest, their business transactions were kept under royal control and the relevant documents, or copies of them, had to be stored in the royal archives.[22]

The rest of the corpus *not* assignable to the central persons listed in Table III consists of isolated transactions by a variety of individuals. Some of these can be identified as members of the ruling class and include persons such as Šadditu, sister of Esarhaddon, and Abi-rami, sister of the Queen Mother (nos. 251f, both surely residents of the harem); royal eunuchs (nos. 23, 283 and 287); further bodyguards, charioteers and military officers (nos. 19, 116, 127, 139, 140 and 295), as well as a doctor of Esarhaddon (no. 126).[23] It is extremely likely that many more persons figuring in these texts also belonged to the ruling class, but their identity largely remains to be established.

The Nature of the Transactions

By their content, the texts in the present volume fall into two major types, *purchase documents* mostly recording the acquisition of landed property and slaves by the central persons, and *loan documents* mostly recording issues of money, corn, animals and wine by the same persons. Other types of documents are extremely sparsely represented in the corpus and include a few court decisions (nos. 35, 133, 238, 264 and 265) largely relating to economic affairs[24] and a building contract (no. 21). A bird's-eye view of the types of documents and the quantities in which they are represented in the volume is presented in Table IV.

TABLE IV. *Types of Document*

Purchases		223	(63.7%)
Slaves	109		
Land	90		
Land and People	10		
Other	14		
Loans		105	(30.0%)
Money		55	
Silver	45		
Copper	8		
Corn		17	
Barley	16		
Wheat	1		
Animals		10	
Land		5	
Wine		4	
Oil		1	
Men		1	
Varia or fragmentary		11	
Total (Purchases and Loans)		328	(93.7%)
Court decisions		5	
Building contracts		1	
Varia		2	
Fragmentary and unclassifiable		16	
Grand Total		350	

A mere typological survey, however, can only give a superficial idea of the nature of the Nineveh court transactions. To obtain a more satisfactory picture, it is necessary to take into consideration other matters too, like the quantities of money and property involved in the transactions.

The money value of the transactions was mostly expressed in terms of silver minas divided into 60 shekels, more rarely in terms of copper minas and talents.[25] While a passage in the inscriptions of Sennacherib makes it likely that coined money already existed,[26] the value of a silver mina almost certainly depended on its weight. Two principal varieties of the silver mina, probably related to different weight systems, occur in the texts. The "royal mina," or the "mina of the country," exemplified by a series of inscribed lion-weights from Nimrud dating from the reigns of Shalmaneser V through Sennacherib (Figs. 3 and 4), was an almost exact equivant of the modern kilo. The weight of the "Carchemish mina," the other common standard, is unknown, but it cannot have differed much from that of the royal mina.[27] The exchange rate between silver and copper appears to have been 1 : 60, so that a talent of copper (or sixty copper minas) corresponded to one silver mina.[28]

To establish exact correspondencies between ancient and modern currencies is of course impossible, but roughly, an Assyrian silver shekel may be said to have equalled about 5 US dollars at its current value and much more in its real purchasing power.[29] A silver mina would have been worth sixty times more, i.e., about $300.

Now transactions involving modest sums of money (a few shekels of silver only) and small properties (a few decares of land) are extremely poorly represented in the Nineveh corpus.[30] Most of the prices mentioned are defined in minas, not shekels, and in some texts truly large quantities of money (up to 60 minas of silver, something like $18,000)[31] and property (entire villages and hundreds of hectares of land)[32] change hands. Clearly, the texts record transactions by very affluent people, and it is interesting to note, in the light of what was said above, that the most affluent of all were the royal charioteers and bodyguards, who easily surpass everybody else in the corpus by the volume of their investments and spending.[33]

These nouveaux riches appear to have spent their money mainly in amassing land and slaves all around Assyria.[34] Some of them evince a bent for *la dolce vita* by their obvious zeal to acquire vineyards;[35] many of them were active as moneylenders.[36] It is interesting to note, however, that not all the loans given by them were meant to bring profit. Other members of the ruling elite could borrow considerable sums of money and other commodities for no interest,[37] and the interest rates prescribed in loans of this type in the event of nonpayment could be ridiculously low compared with the rates applying in normal loans of the period.[38]

Three loans of wine included in the volume (nos. 181/182, 232 and 233) fall into this category. In each of them the debtor receives a large amount (up to 1,000 litres) of wine, which he is to give back a few months later. No interest is prescribed. Only in the event that the wine is not returned, a penalty will apply: the debtor is to repay the wine in silver according to the market price of Nineveh. This shows that the documents are to be taken as true loans and not, e.g., as retail or wholesale contracts. For if the owner of the wine was interested in simply converting the wine into money, why would the other party not have been required to sell it in Nineveh in the first place, where it obviously would have fetched a better price?

One possible explanation for this type of loan could be that the recipient was a member of the ruling class urgently needing the wine for a particular purpose, e.g. a party for a large number of guests. Buying the wine at a local store in Nineveh would have cost fortunes and was, in fact, unnecessary since the colleague, by virtue of his office, was in control of large quantities of palace wine from which the need could be supplied without any difficulty. By the repayment deadline the debtor would have had time to acquire the

FIG. 3a. *Part of a group of sixteen bronze lion-weights mostly inscribed in Assyrian and/or Aramaic with a weight (the light or heavy mina usually corresponding to about 500 g or 1 kg respectively) and a royal name. From the palace at Nimrud, about 730-720 BC.*
BM 91220-35.

FIG. 3b-c. *Bronze lion-weights (14.934 and 5.043 kg), inscribed in Aramaic with their weights, 15 and 5 royal minas, and marked with a corresponding number of strokes on their flanks. From Nimrud.*
BM 91220-1.

FIG. 4a. *Bronze lion-weights from Nimrud.*
BM 91220-91222 AND 91232.

FIG. 4b-c. *Bronze lion-weights (2.865 and 1.931 kg), 3 and 2 royal minas, from Nimrud.*
BM 91226 AND 91223.

quantity of loaned wine cheaply from elsewhere. Should this prove impossible, he would still have lost nothing: the prescribed "penalty" was simply the amount of money he would have had to pay anyway, had he not been able to avail himself of the cheap loan.[39]

The Ninevite Legal Texts as Historical Documents

As a sizeable collection of dated documents replete with prosopographical information, the present corpus is a source of prime historical importance. With the help of the dates, or, in their absence, the prosopographical evidence of the tablets, every little detail found on them can be fitted in its proper place in a chronological framework than in its turn can be used as a firm frame of reference in analysing other, undated texts from the period. And once properly placed in this chronological grid, even previously insignificant or seemingly meaningless details can turn out to shed unexpected light on contemporary history.

It is not possible, nor indeed within the scope of this introduction to review at length the information content of the corpus. We will limit ourselves to just one practical example encountered during the preparation of the volume, which illustrates the sort of surprises the corpus still (after 100 years of study) holds and is likely to present, once its data are subjected to a systematic and comprehensive chronological evaluation.

Prince or Crown Prince?

Forty-one texts in the present volume contain references to individuals identified as relatives, servants, or officials (scribes, charioteers, 'third men,' eunuchs, village managers etc.) of persons entitled *mār šarri*, literally translated, "the king's son"; in two additional texts (nos. 238 and 264), the title refers to "the king's son" himself. The princes mentioned are as a rule never identified by name. The only exception is constituted by no. 103 with the famous reference to "Arda-Mullissi, the king's son," the notorious murderer of Sennacherib.[40] Fourteen of the texts date from the reign of Sennacherib, 12 from that of Esarhaddon, and 17 from Assurbanipal's reign.[41]

For the present volume, the title *mār šarri* presents a problem of translation, since besides its literal meaning "king's son," i.e. prince in general, it also means "the crown prince." In fact, the latter is the *standard* meaning of the title in contemporary letters, reports and administrative texts, where plain *mār šarri* always refers to the crown prince, while other sons and children of the king were regularly referred to by their names only.[42] It is unclear, however, how far this usage also applies to the legal texts. It has never been systematically investigated whether the title in these texts means broadly "prince," or narrowly "crown prince", or both indiscriminately. Should the latter turn out to be the case, how is one to know in individual cases which translation to choose? Finding a solution to this problem is of considerable importance, since the translations chosen may drastically affect the interpretation of the relevant documents.

The problem is complicated, and it is necessary to review the evidence case by case. In the following discussion, the meaning "crown prince" attested for *mār šarri* in contemporary letters, reports and administrative texts will be referred to as the *normal usage*, whereas occurrences of the literal meaning "king's son" will be labeled as *exceptional*.

Starting from the most straightforward cases, the meaning "crown prince" is certain in no. 287, dated 670-II-1, recording a purchase by a eunuch of "the crown prince (*mār šarri*) of Babylon,"[43] as well as in at least five other documents from the end of Esarhaddon's reign (nos. 283, 288, 297-299), all dated between 672 and 669 B.C.[44] This was the time of the "double crown-princehood" of Assurbanipal and Šamaš-šumu-ukin, and the terminology of the legal documents is entirely consistant with that of the other contemporary texts.

On the other hand, the translation "crown prince" seems definitely excluded in the 17 texts from the beginning of the reign of Assurbanipal, which date from the years 667-660. Assurbanipal himself having been still a youth at the time of his accession, there is no possibility that even his eldest son, probably born in early 670,[45] could have been old enough for promotion to the status of the crown prince in these early years of his reign.

A closer study of the Assurbanipal texts reveals, however, that while the prince *officially* may not yet have been proclaimed heir to the throne, his *public status* nevertheless was very close to one. He was in possession of two full cohorts of his own bodyguard (cf. no. 325 r.19f), a palace superintendent (no. 328 r.7), a secretary (ibid. r.6), and several charioteers and 'third men' just like his royal father, then crown prince, a few years earlier. In fact, he shared with the latter at least three officials, the cohort commander Nabû-šarru-uṣur[46] and the charioteers Šamaš-šarru-uṣur[47] and Zarutî.[48] It would seem that he, as the king's eldest and possibly (as yet) only son, was commonly looked upon as the future king and provided with the pertinent pomp and protection when appearing in public. The most appropriate rendering of *mār šarri* in this case would thus be "*the* prince (par excellence)," with connotations very close to those of "the crown prince."

With these preliminary results, we may now turn to a scrutiny of the remaining evidence, first that from the reign of Esarhaddon. Apart from the evidence from the years 672-669, already treated, there are six further texts from this reign referring to *mār šarri*. One of these (no. 238) is undated, but the context (association with the king) leaves no doubt that the correct rendering in this case is "crown prince,"[49] and a date late in Esarhaddon's reign appears likely.[50] Three of the texts (nos. 201, 257, and 264) date from the year 680, two from the year 676 (nos. 210 and 239, both dated late in the first month). Thus, in addition to several references from 672-669 all conforming to the normal usage and to be translated "crown prince," the title *mār šarri* in Esarhaddon's reign is encountered only in three documents from the very beginning of the reign and in two texts from the year 676.

At first sight the translation "crown prince" seems excluded in these texts, particularly in nos. 257 and 201 dated 680-I-10 and 680-II-28 respectively.

Surely Esarhaddon would not have (and in practice, could not have) rushed to appoint a successor to the throne *barely two weeks after his own accession!*[51] However, closer scrutiny of the texts shows that the rendering "crown prince" actually works here too.

No. 257:3 refers to servants of the "lady of the house" of the *mār šarri*. Keeping in mind that the text was drawn up almost immediately after Esarhaddon's accession, it is clear that this cannot refer to a son of the new king: first of all, he would probably have been too young, and secondly there is no way he could have built up a "house" in the short while his father had been in power, less still in the preceding year(s) when the latter was in exile. Thus the text must refer to a prince of the earlier generation, i.e. a son of Sennacherib.

Is it conceivable that a brother of Esarhaddon would have been called "son of the king" after the latter's accession, rather than "the king's brother"? That seems theoretically possible, but considering the political situation (Esarhaddon having just emerged from a bitter civil war against his brothers) extremely unlikely. It appears much likelier that the prince referred to was Esarhaddon himself, who in fact had, until very recently, been the legitimate crown prince.[52] The scribe drawing up the document may have been uncertain about the current status of the "lady of the house" as well as that of the purchaser, called "a servant of the crown prince,"[53] and therefore preferred to use their old titles.[54] This would explain the concluding statement of the deed, "Purchased in the reign of Esarhaddon, king of Assyria," which would have been added to dispel any potential doubts about the time of the transaction occasioned by the use of the obsolete titles. No. 201, with a similar concluding statement, can be interpreted correspondingly. For no. 264, dated 680-XI-27, see the relevant note in the critical apparatus.

The normal meaning of *mār šarri*, "crown prince," thus works in the early Esarhaddon texts as well. As for the two texts from year 676 (nos. 210 and 239), we maintain that the translation "crown prince" holds in these too and suggest that the prince referred to in them was Esarhaddon's son Sin-nadin-apli, whose promotion to the status of the crown prince is the subject of the oracle query AGS 107 = SAA 4 149.[55] This prince seems to have died soon after his promotion, for excepting the said query nothing is known about him. The individual mentioned in nos. 210 and 230 appears to have been old enough for the promotion, for he was in possession of a merchant (210 r.14), and the dates of the documents (676-I-24 and 676-I-25 respectively) would tally well with a career abruptly broken off soon after the appointment, likely to have taken place in Nisan (cf. below, p. XXXIV and n. 44).

The Promotion of Esarhaddon

Since the normal meaning of *mār šarri*, or its functional equivalent, "the prince par excellence," fits all the references hitherto analyzed, the likelihood is great that this is the case even in the Sennacherib texts not yet analyzed. Chronologically, the 14 documents from this reign with references to *mār šarri* fall into two distinct groups. Six of them date from the years 696-692,[56]

FIG. 5a. *Stone duck-weight (9.82 kg), marked on the flank with nine deep strokes and a tenth shallower one. From Nimrud.*
ND 7888. Photograph: British School of Archaeology in Iraq.

FIG. 5b. *Stone duck-weight (969.7 g), probably from Nineveh.*
BM 91435.

FIG. 6a. *Stone duck-weight (509 g) from Nimrud.*
ND 2507.

FIG. 6b-c. *Stone duck-weights (189.3 and 127.8 g), marked one sixth and one eighth, and with a lion and six and eight strokes on their flanks, from Nimrud. Natural size.*
BM 91438 AND 91442.

two from the very end of Sennacherib's reign (years 683-681).[57] The dates of the remaining six texts are destroyed.

Sennacherib installed his eldest son Aššur-nadin-šumi as king in Babylon in 699. Since this was clearly meant as a permanent arrangement (the rule of Aššur-nadin-šumi lasted for six years until his deportation to Elam in 694-VII/VIII), the need of settling the succession at home must have become pressing in Assyria soon after 699. The earlier group of texts dating from 696-692 can thus very plausibly be assumed to refer to a heir designate chosen at this time, while the later texts would refer to Esarhaddon as the crown prince.

A closer look at the texts confirms these assumptions. It was already pointed out above that one of the texts belonging to the earlier group, no. 103, dated 694-VII-12, is atypical in that it is the only text in the whole corpus mentioning a prince (Arda-Mullissi) by name. This text has been of pivotal importance to the identification of Sennacherib's murderer, but it has remained unclear whether the title *mār šarri* accorded to Arda-Mullissi in the text actually means that he was crown prince at the time concerned (which would of course provide a good motive for the murder).[58] We believe now to be in a position to show that this indeed was the case.

No. 103 is not an isolated document but belongs to a larger whole, the archive of a 'third man' (i.e., the shield-bearer on a chariot) named Aplaya, covering a period of 16 years from 698-III-10 to 683-I-23. This archive consist of purchases (of large tracts) of land and slaves, as well as of debt-notes attesting to a flourishing money-lending business of this archive holder. Structurally, it closely resembles the archives of the royal charioteers Šumma-ilani, Nabû-šumu-iškun and Remanni-Adad elsewhere in this volume. In no. 103, Aplaya is defined as "the 'third man' of Arda-Mullissi, *mār šarri*," just as Nabû-šumu-iškun is called "the [chariot driv]er of Sennacherib, [king of Assyria]" in no. 57, or Remanni-Adad "the chief chariot driver of Assurbanipal, king of Assyria" (passim). Such parallels, certainly meant to bolster the high status of these officials, imply that Arda-Mullissi must have been a crown prince. The same is implied by Aplaya's obvious wealth and the size of his archive, which in this volume is matched only by the above three royal charioteers and a few other highly placed court officials.

For their affluence and power people like Aplaya depended on their royal employers; they would not have been able to carry out their luxurious life without the money their lords poured upon them in order to secure their loyalty. In this light the chronological coverage of Aplaya's archive assumes considerable significance, for it must be related to the time of his employment with Arda-Mullissi. Since the earliest document in the archive, from year 698 B.C., already concerns a major real estate purchase, it appears likely that Arda-Mullissi was already crown prince at that time. This accords well with the implications of Aššur-nadin-šumi's installation as monarch in Babylon in 699, discussed above.

Two further occurrences of the title *mār šarri* in the early Sennacherib group (in no. 85, dated 692-X-6, and no. 130, dated 696) may likewise be taken to refer to Arda-Mullissi. However, in three texts of the group (nos. 37, 39 and 40), referring to a certain Sama', "horse raiser of the *mār šarri*," this is not possible, as in one of the texts from the very same period the word

FIG. 7. *Part of silver ingot (402.9 g) with inscription of Bar-rakib king of Sam'al, about 730 BC, probably representing one light mina of roughly 500 g.*
BM 134918.

mār šarri is replaced by the name Nergal-šumu-[...] in the title of Sama':

39 r.16 (694-I) [Witne]ss Sama', horse raiser of the *mār šarri*
37 r. 7 (694-VII-1) [Witness S]ama', horse raiser of the *mār šarri*
40 r. 4 (693-I) [Witne]ss Sama', horse raiser of the *mār šarri*
41 r. 5 (693-I) Witness Sama', horse raiser of Nergal-šumu-[...]

It should be noted that no. 37 is practically contemporary with no. 103 694-VII-12 referring to Arda-Mullissi, the crown prince.

If *mār šarri* has its normal meaning in these texts too, then one will have to accept the existence of two crown princes in Assyria in the year 694. In view of the later parallel of Assurbanipal and Šamaš-šumu-ukin, it seems possible that the other prince, Nergal-šumu-[...], had been appointed as a successor to Aššur-nadin-šumi on the throne of Babylon; this would explain why he is no longer called *mār šarri* after the latter's deportation (in 694-VII/VIII).[59]

The two *mār šarri* texts from the end of Sennacherib's reign (nos. 109 and 110), on the other hand, belong to the archive of a certain Se'-madi, entitled "the village manager of the crown prince" in both texts.[60] No. 109 is dated 683-[?]-7, the other text 681-XII-16, just 12 (or two) days before Esarhaddon's accession. The latest text in the archive, no. 111, is from the first year of Esarhaddon (680-VII). In this text, the qualification "of the crown prince" is, however, dropped from Se'-madi's title. As pointed out in the critical apparatus to the text, this can only mean that the crown prince concerned was Esarhaddon and that he had been promoted to this status by the year 683 at the latest.

This is a most important piece of information, for the exact year in which Esarhaddon became crown prince has so far remained unknown. The evidence previously available suggested that the promotion had taken place either in Nisan 683 or 682.[61] The latter alternative can now be ruled out and Nisan 683 be taken as the most likely time of the appointment.

We thus have two legal archives from the reign of Sennacherib attributable to officials of two different crown princes: the archive of Aplaya, servant of Arda-Mullissi, covering the time from 698-III-10 to 683-I-23, and the archive of Se'-madi, a servant of Esarhaddon, covering the period 683-[?]-7 to 680-VII. The fact that the last document in the former dates from Nisan 683, the very month in which Esarhaddon would have been appointed, while the latter starts in the same year seems more than a coincidence.

In summary, the title *mār šarri* can be shown to mean "crown prince" in all the texts included in the present volume, with the possible exception of the early Assurbanipal texts where it most likely means "the prince par excellence, (prospective) crown prince." This usage is in accordance with the normal meaning of the title in other contemporary texts and has important historical consequences. We may tabulate the implications of the foregoing analysis to contemporary history as follows:

699 Aššur-nadin-šumi installed as king in Babylon
698 Arda-Mullissi appointed crown prince of Assyria
694 Nergal-šumu-[*ibni*] attested as crown prince [of Babylon?]
693-I Esarhaddon appointed crown prince of Assyria
676-I Sin-nadin-apli appointed crown prince of Assyria
667-660 Assurbanipal's eldest son accepted as heir to the throne (at the age of 4 to 10)

FIG. 8. *Weighing Syrian tribute on a pair of scales (reign of Assurnasirpal).* BM 118800 (detail).

On the Present Edition

The objective of the present edition is to make the corpus of Nineveh legal texts available in an up-to-date critical edition that can be profitably used both by the specialist and the more general reader. Every effort has been expended to make it as complete and reliable as possible, by identification of previously unpublished fragments, repeated collation of the originals, careful comparison of the transliterations to previously published editions, and scrutiny of the manuscript by several experts in Neo-Assyrian. We fully realise, of course, that despite our best efforts, we have not been able to provide a "perfect" edition.

Because of the considerable size of the Nineveh legal corpus it will be edited in two parts. The present volume contains the early part of the corpus through the reign of Esarhaddon, while Pt. II will contain texts from the reigns of Assurbanipal and his successors as well as the undatable texts of the corpus. A major group of texts from the reign of Assurbanipal (the dossier of Remanni-Adad) has exceptionally been included in Pt. I, partly because the early part of this dossier belongs to the reign of Esarhaddon, partly because including it here helps keep the size of Pt. II within reasonable limits.

The Order of Texts in this Edition

In its basic organization, the edition follows the norms established in the Editorial Manual of the Neo-Assyrian Text Corpus Project and exemplified by the previous volumes of the series. The order in which the texts are presented is basically chronological, in that texts from different reigns are presented as separate chapters, and within these chapters texts not assignable to major dossiers or archives are presented in strictly chronological order under the heading 'Varia.' In order to make the archival structure of the corpus stand out as clearly as possible, major dossiers are presented under each reign as separate groups before the 'Varia' sections. The order of the dossiers from the same reign is chronological, and within each dossier texts are presented in chronological order, insofar as possible. Texts with lost eponym dates follow after dated texts.

We are aware that this is not in every respect an ideal arrangement, since virtually contemporary texts may now be widely separated from each other in different dossiers. However, the disadvantages of an all-out chronological arrangement, obscuring the archival structure of the corpus, would have been much greater. We trust that the reader will be able to quickly locate chronologically related texts dispersed through the volume with the help of Table II and the indices.

Texts Included and Excluded

As indicated by its title, the present volume is supposed to contain all legal texts from Nineveh down to the beginning of the reign of Assurbanipal. In order to make sure that all pertinent texts are included, the unpublished material described in the catalogues of Bezold, King, Lambert + Millard and Leichty as possibly belonging to the genre, as well as the uncatalogued Kuyunjik pieces currently being catalogued by Lambert and Finkel, have been sifted through as carefully as possible by the editors and other people involved in the production of the book, particularly J. N. Postgate. Since the provenance of many Kuyunjik tablets cannot be determined with certainty, it is theoretically possible that a few texts from other sites are included in this edition. Conversely, it is also possible that texts of unknown provenance excluded from the volume actually are Nineveh texts.

One of the texts included in the volume (no. 31) is certainly not from Nineveh; it was found in French excavations of Dur-Šarruken behind Sargon's main throne-room suite. The reason for its inclusion is that it fits well with the other texts from the reign of Sargon and is simply too important to be omitted from the volume.

The curious 'bird' text published as no. 288 was likewise included in the volume because of its importance, despite the fact that it is of uncertain date and could accordingly as well have been included in Pt. II.

Transliterations

The transliterations, addressed to the specialist, render the text of the originals in roman characters according to standard Assyriological conventions and the principles outlined in the Editorial Manual. Every effort has been taken to make them as accurate as humanly possible. All the texts edited have been recently collated either by the editor or a competent colleague.

Results of collation are indicated with exclamation marks. Single exclamation marks indicate corrections to published copies, double exclamation marks, scribal errors. Question marks indicate uncertain or questionable readings. Broken portions of text and all restorations are enclosed within square brackets. Parentheses enclose items omitted by ancient scribes.

Translations

The translations seek to render the meaning and tenor of the texts as accurately as possible in readable, contemporary English. In the interest of clarity, the line structure of the originals has not been retained in the translation but the text has been rearranged into logically coherent paragraphs.

Uncertain or conjectural translations are indicated by italics. Interpretative additions to the translation are enclosed within parentheses. All restorations are enclosed within square brackets. Untranslatable passages are indicated by dots.

Month names are rendered by their Hebrew equivalents, followed by a Roman numeral (in parentheses) indicating the place of the month within the lunar year. Personal, divine and geographical names are rendered by English or Biblical equivalents if a well-established equivalent exists (e.g., Esarhaddon, Nineveh); otherwise, they are given in transcription with length marks deleted. The normalization of West Semitic names generally follows the conventions of Zadok West Semites. West Semitic phonemes not expressed by the writing system (/o/ etc.) have generally not been restituted in the normalizations, and the sibilant system follows the NA orthography.

The rendering of professions is a compromise between the use of accurate but impractical Assyrian terms and inaccurate but practical modern or classical equivalents.

Critical Apparatus

The primary purpose of the critical apparatus is to support the readings and translations established in the edition, and it consists largely of references to collations of questionable passages, scribal mistakes corrected in the transliteration, and alternative interpretations or restorations of ambiguous passages. Restorations based on easily verifiable evidence (e.g., parallel passages found in the text itself) are generally not explained in the apparatus; conjectural restorations only if their conjectural nature is not apparent from italics in the translation.

Collations given in copy at the end of the volume are referred to briefly as "see coll."

The critical apparatus does contain some additional information relevant to the interpretation of the texts, but it is not a commentary. Comments are kept to a minimum, and are mainly devoted to problems in the text and elucidation of lexical items or Akkadian expressions necessarily left untranslated. The historical information contained in the texts is generally not commented upon.

Glossary and Indices

The glossary and indices, electronically generated, generally follow the pattern of the previous volumes. The glossary contains all lexically identifiable words occurring in the texts with the exception of suffixless numbers 1-99. The references to professions attached to the index of personal names have been provided by a computer programme written specifically for the volume by Parpola; it is hoped that these will be helpful in the prosopographical analysis of the texts, but it should be noted that the programme omits certain deficiently written professions and the references are accordingly not absolutely complete.

NOTES

[1] Vol. I of ADD, containing the copies of 716 texts (not all of them legal), appeared in 1898; vols. II and III, with more cuneiform copies, an introduction and an edition of four major groups of texts (money loans, legal decisions, deeds of sale and slave sales), in 1901; vol. IV, with edition and discussion of further groups of texts (sales of houses and landed property, leases, votive offerings etc.) and a glossary, appeared posthumously in 1923. Further legal texts from Nineveh not included in ADD I-II were also copied by Johns and published after his death as ADD 1152-1281 in the journal AJSL (vol. 42 [1925/6], pp. 170ff and 228ff).

[2] See in general S. Parpola, *Assur* 2/1 (1979), p. 1f.

[3] The personal names of the texts published by Johns were analyzed by K. Tallqvist in his *Assyrian Personal Names* (Helsinki 1914), the eponym dates by Ungnad in RlA 2 (1938), 440ff. Both studies are badly out of date today.

[4] While ADD does contain a glossary, this is extremely selective and wrought with innumerable mistakes. The name index included in AR likewise contains numerous 'ghost names' and does not differentiate between different persons bearing the same name. There is also no way of telling from the references listed in the index at what time a particular individual lived.

[5] NALK p. xvii. Cf. below, p. XXf.

[6] Another major drawback in this otherwise carefully prepared edition is the total lack of indices and the fact that the witness lists and dates are left untranslated throughout. Since most of the names are written logographically, these essentially important parts of the texts (and the many new readings contained in them vis-à-vis ADD and AR) are unfortunately bound to remain beyond the reach of most users of the book.

[7] For a bibliography of NA legal texts see K. Deller, Or. 34 (1965) 278f listing documents from Assur, Calah, Carchemish, Du-Šarruken, Gezer, Guzana, Huzirina, Imgur-Illil, Kannuʾ, Nineveh, Šibaniba and Tarsus. Further documents have since become available from Maʾallanat (see Garelli, CRRAI 30 [1986], 241ff), Nabula/Nabur (see Donbaz, SAAB 2 [1988], 3ff), Tell Rimah (Postgate, Iraq 32 [1970], 31ff), a site in Syria (Aynard and Nougayrol, RA 65 [1971] 85ff) and Sippar, as well as various sites already represented in Deller's list.

[8] See also idem, "Middle Assyrian tablets: the instruments of bureaucracy," AoF 13 (1986), 10ff.

[9] See above all Kwasman, "Neo-Assyrian legal archives in the Kouyunjik Collection," CRRAI 30 (1986), p. 237ff and NALK p. xviii ff.

[10] Cf. J. Reade, "Archeology and the Kuyunjik Archives," CRRAI 30 (1986), p. 212ff and Parpola, "The Royal Archives of Nineveh," ibid. 223ff.

[11] See G. Smith, *Assyrian Discoveries* (London 1875), p. 417.

[12] See A. H. Layard, *Discoveries in Nineveh and Babylon* (New York 1853), p. 345f (with copy of the tablet on p. 346).

[13] See W. G. Lambert and A. R. Millard, *Catalogue of the Cuneiform Tablets in the Kouyunjik Collection, Second Supplement* (London 1968), pp. 93 and xi.

[14] G. Smith, op. cit. p. 424.

[15] "Many [of the tablets found in the chambers] are sealed with seals, and may prove to be legal contracts or conveyances of land. Others bear rolled impressions of ... engraved cylinders" (Layard, op. cit. p. 346).

[16] Cf. the harem archive discovered in the Review Palace of Nimrud (CTN 3, nos. 33-40), with documents recording transactions by several royal women (including the queen and the harem governess), all found in the same room (S 10).

[17] Bahianu is defined as the "village manager of the stewardess," and thus in all probability was affiliated with the royal harem just discussed.

[18] See Parpola, CRRAI 30 (1986), p. 231ff.

[19] See ibid. for tablets retrieved from the neighbouring mound of Nebi Yunus (the site of the "Review Palace" of Nineveh) and the near-by town of Tarbiṣu.

[20] For details see the two articles referred to in n. 10.

[21] Note the time coverage of the dossier of Mušallim-Issar (742 to 713 B.C.).

[22] Later on, at the retirement of these officials (if they had remained loyal), their possessions could be exempted from taxes, whereby a document listing the exempted property was prepared in the palace on the basis of the original documents which would have been subsequently destroyed. Cf. the grants nos. 9-12 in NARGD, and notice that the text ADD 741+ edited as no. 23 in Fales Censimenti is very likely to represent an appendix to NARGD 10 (dated 657 B.C.). This would explain why no documents relating to business conducted by Assurbanipal's chief eunuch Nabû-šarru-uṣur (the beneficiary of the grant) are extant in the Nineveh legal corpus. Lines 32ff of Fales Censimenti 23, separated with a dividing line from the preceding section listing Nabû-šarru-uṣur's property, could represent a similar appendix to another grant, possibly to Remanni-Adad (cf. l. 34 with nos. 329-331 of this volume). If so, the question remains why Nabû-šarru-uṣur's original documents would have been destroyed while Remanni-Adad's were not.

[23] This text is interesting because it is dated 697-VI, when Esarhaddon would have been only about 15 years old (see LAS 2 p. 231, n. 390, and cf. the discussion ibid. p. 230ff).

[24] See especially no. 35 concerning burglary into the house of a "central person" and possibly referring to the impalement of the thieves on the site in accordance with Codex Hammurabi. It is possible, though, that the verb *zaqāpu* in this text does not have the meaning "impale," in which case the crucial sentence would have to be rendered "the thieves who *attacked* the house of PN" in accordance with the normal NA meaning of the verb.

[25] Copper appears as a means of payment quite frequently in the early texts of the volume (see nos. 2, 3, 6, 7, 15, 19, 21, 22, 29, 32) and is still often encountered in texts from the reign of Sennacherib (17 examples). In later texts, however, it occurs very rarely (only in nos. 214, 264f and 289f).

[26] "I executed with superior artistry cast bronzework (for the figures of various large animals), and upon an inspiration from the god, built clay molds, poured bronze into each, and made the figures of each of them as perfect as minted half-shekel pieces (*pitiq* 1/2 GÍN.TA.ÀM)," Luckenbill Senn. 109 ii 16, also ibid. 123:9.

[27] There is no noticeable difference in prices of real estate and humans stated in terms of royal and Carchemish minas; cf., e.g., no. 138 vs. nos. 34, 45, 257, 305f, 343f and 346f, for slaves costing 1 royal and 1 Carchemish mina respectively, and nos. 85 and 130 vs. nos. 57 and 111 for slaves costing half a royal or Carchemish mina respectively. In this light, one would feel tempted to regard the duck-weights found in various Assyrian sites (see Figs. 5-6 and 23)

as specimens of the Carchemish standard, but various considerations (not least the lion-figure and inscription in Fig. 6b) make this improbable.

28 See, e.g., no. 152 recording the purchase of a woman for a talent of copper, or nos. 56 and 61 referring to men sold or released from bondage for 30 minas of copper, and cf. the previous footnote.

29 The 'rate' is based on recent world market prices of silver, which of course fluctuate considerably depending on the strength of the currency but appear to have remained relatively stable *in real terms* over the past few years (1985-1990) at least. The matter requires furher study, but the suggested 'value' appears in any case to fit the NA evidence tolerably well, cf., e.g., ND 2312 (Iraq 23 pl. 10) referring to garments and coats costing 4 1/2 and 2 1/3 shekels, and no. 241 of the present volume stating 3 minas of silver as the price of a camel.

30 See nos. 115, 161 (purchases of land for 5 and 4 shekels of silver respectively) and 189 (loan of 5 shekels of silver).

31 See no. 253, recording the purchase of 60 hectares of land by Issar-duri, scribe of the queen mother.

32 Cf. nos. 336 (580 hectares), 287 (village of Bahaya, 500 ha) and 245 (200 ha).

33 The 'top spenders' in the volume are Šumma-ilani, chariot driver of the royal corps (cf. nos. 34, 39, 42, 50f), Remanni-Adad, Assurbanipal's charioteer (cf. nos. 311, 318, 323f, 326, 329, 335, and 343f), Nabû-šumu-iškun, Sennacherib's charioteer (cf. no. 57), Mannu-ki-Arbail, cohort commander (cf. nos. 202, also 269?), Zazî, royal eunuch (no. 26), Atar-il, eunuch of the crown prince of Babylon (no. 287), Aplaya, 'third man' of Arda-Mullissi (no. 107), and the unidentified Dannaya (no. 248), Silim-Aššur (no. 234) and Balṭaya (no. 130), all with investments and purchases ranging between 30 and 3 royal and Carchemish minas. It is likely that the name of the central person in no. 196, recording a purchase price as high as 30 Carchemish minas, is to be restored as [Šumma-ila]ni.

34 For purchases of landed property, see especially nos. 10-15 (Inurta-ila'i), 37, 42 and 51f (Šumma-ilani), 101f and 105 (Aplaya), 201, 202, 204, 207, 209-211, 213 and 217 (Mannu-ki-Arbail) and 304, 311, 314-316, 320-322, 325f, 328-340 (Remanni-Adad); for purchases of slaves, note especially nos. 1-9 (Mušallim-Issar), 34, 38-41, 45, 48f and 52-56 (Šumma-ilani), 57f (Nabû-šumu-iškun), 82, 85-89, 92 and 94 (harem governesses), 103 and 106 (Aplaya), 109-112 (Se'-madi, Village Manager of the Crown Prince), 227-229 (Silim-Aššur), 239, 244 and 246 (Dannaya), as well as 297f, 300f, 305f, 309f, 312f, 319, and 341-348 (Remanni-Adad).

35 Particularly Šumma-ilani (see nos. 37 and 50), Mannu-ki-Arbail (nos. 201f) and Remanni-Adad (nos. 314, 326, 329-332, 334 and 336).

36 E.g., Zazî, Šumma-ilani, Addati, Aplaya, Mannu-ki-Arbail, Silim-Aššur, Dannaya, Remanni-Adad (money) and Bahianu (money and corn).

37 For loans with no interest in the present volume see, e.g., nos. 97, 143, 167, 180, 273, 318 and 234. In no. 318, the deputy governor of Arrapha receives from Remanni-Adad as much as 10 minas of Carchemish for no interest.

38 25% in nos. 167 and 318; for the normal interest and penalty rates see the evidence tabulated in S. Ponchia, "Neo-Assyrian corn loans: Preliminary notes," SAAB 4 (1990), 38ff.

39 This interpretation is of course largely speculation but supported by a consideration of the other loans with no interest in the present volume. Unfortunately it is not possible to pursue the matter in more depth in this context.

40 See S. Parpola, "The murderer of Sennacherib," CRRAI 26 (1980), p. 171ff, and cf. S. Zawadzki, "Oriental and Greek traditions about the death of Sennacherib," SAAB 4 (1990), 69ff.

41 Sennacherib: nos. 37, 39, 40, 52, 57, 85, 86, 103, 109, 110, 112, 130, 199, and 200; Esarhaddon: nos. 201, 210, 238, 239, 257, 264, 283, 287, 288, and 297-299; Assurbanipal: nos. 309, 312, 317, 320, 321, 323-325, 328-330, 334, 335, 339, 340, 347, and 348.

42 See the discussion in LAS 2, p. 166f.

43 This was the official title of Šamaš-šumu-ukin after his promotion as crown prince in early 672. The plain *mār šarri* in the witness list of this document may have referred to Assurbanipal but it can also, by way of an abbreviation, have referred to Šamaš-šumu-ukin as well.

44 Note that no. 283, dated 672-II-1, precedes by two weeks the dates recorded on the extant copies of Esarhaddon's succession treaty (672-II-16/18, see SAA 2 p. 58; cf. also ibid. p. XXIX for the date 672-II-12 given for the treaty ceremonies in Assurbanipal's inscriptions). This is consistent with the evidence of the letters suggesting that the promotion of Assurbanipal and Šamaš-šumu-ukin to the status of crown prince had already been made public earlier, perhaps in the course of the royal New Year's reception in Nisan (see discussion in LAS 2, p. 3ff).

45 Assurbanipal seems to have married immediately after his promotion (cf. LAS 2 p. 119, note on 129 r.24 and ABL 308); a series of letters from court physicians datable to Spring 670 refer to a royal suckling identifible as a child of the crown prince, see discussion in LAS 2 p. 109f.

46 No. 325 r.20 (663 B.C.), cf. 299 r.5 (datable to c. 670 on the basis of the reference to the crown prince of Babylon in the witness list).

47 Nos. 317 r.8 (666 B.C.) and 347 r.6, cf. 297 r.12, 298 r.7 (both 671 B.C.) and 299 r.1.

48 No. 309 r.6 (667 B.C.) and passim, cf. 283 r.16 (672 B.C.).

49 "Whoever breaks the agreement, the king and the crown prince shall be his prosecutors," no. 238:9.

50 The archive of Silim-Aššur, to which the document belongs, covers the years 680-670.

51 The date of Esarhaddon's accession is given as 18th or (more likely) 28th of Adar 681 in Grayson Chronicles p. 82:38.

52 Cf. no. 110, dated 681-XII-16, i.e. less than a month before no. 257, where the title *mār šarri* certainly means "crown prince" and refers to Esarhaddon (see p. XXIX).

53 Having been a servant of the crown prince by no means implied that the position was automatically continued after the prince had become king; cf., e.g., ABL 1216 and 1285, the latter recently edited in Festschrift Reiner (1987), p. 257ff.

54 Note that in contemporary letters the title "crown prince" could be applied to Esarhaddon, already king, whenever reference was made to events before his accession (see, e.g., ABL 740 = LAS 258:15ff and ABL 1216, passim).

55 It should be noted that AGS 107 is written in Babylonian script, like all queries predating 672, and shares orthographical features with queries assigned to c. 676-674 on the basis of their subject matter (e.g., the relatively rare spelling *an-nam* for /anna/, which recurs in the Phrygian query no. 1 and the Kaštaritu queries 41, 43 and 49). The outcome of the extispicy was favourable, and therefore the appointment considered was almost certainly brought into effect, even though no concrete evidence of this is otherwise available.

[56] Nos. 37, 39, 40, 85, 103 and 130.
[57] Nos. 109 and 110. The title *mār šarri* is restored in no. 109.
[58] Cf. CRRAI 26 (1980), p. 178 n. 31.
[59] Since Nergal-šumu-[...], judging from his "non-royal" name, presumably also was a senior son of Sennacherib (born before his father had become crown prince), he would qualify well for the second-eldest son referred to in later texts as an accomplice of Arda-Mullissi in Sennacherib's assassination. In the Bible, the name of this son is given as Šar-eṣer, which coupled with the fact that Nergal-šumu-uṣur was a very common name, would make the restoration of the last (broken) name element as [*uṣur*] quite tempting. However, even assuming that the first name element was dropped in the Bible, harmonizing the biblical name form with the hypothetical *Šumu-uṣur would present serious difficulties. It is more likely that the name of the prince is to be restored as Nergal-šumu-ibni on the basis of no. 186:7 dated 683-[?]-7.
[60] Title partially restored in no. 109.
[61] See JCS 39 (1987), 164f.

Abbreviations and Symbols

Bibliographical Abbreviations

AAA	Annals of Archaeology and Anthropology
ABC	J. H. Stevenson, *Assyrian and Babylonian Contracts with Aramaic Reference Notes* (New York 1902)
ABL	R. F. Harper, *Assyrian and Babylonian Letters* (London and Chicago 1892-1914)
ADD	C. H. W. Johns, *Assyrian Deeds and Documents* (Cambridge 1898-1923)
AGS	J. A. Knudtzon, *Assyrische Gebete an den Sonnengott* (Leipzig 1893)
AJSL	American Journal of Semitic Languages and Literatures
AnSt	Anatolian Studies
AoF	Altorientalische Forschungen
AR	J. Kohler - A. Ungnad, *Assyrische Rechtsurkunden* (Leipzig 1913)
BM	tablets in the collections of the British Museum
Bu	tablets in the collections of the British Museum
Budge Deluge	E. A. W. Budge, *The Babylonian Story of the Deluge and the Epic of Gilgamesh* (London 1920)
CAD	The Assyrian Dictionary of the Oriental Institute of the University of Chicago
Cat.	C. Bezold, *Catalogue of the Cuneiform Tablets in the Kouyunjik Collection* I-V (London 1889-1899)
Cat. Suppl.	L. W. King, *Catalogue of the Cuneiform Tablets in the Kouyunjik Collection, Supplement* (London 1914)
CIS	Corpus Inscriptionum Semiticarum
CRRAI	Rencontre assyriologique internationale, comptes rendus
CT	Cuneiform Texts from Babylonian Tablets in the British Museum
CTN	Cuneiform Texts from Nimrud
DT	tablets in the collections of the British Museum
Ep. Ar.	L. Delaporte, *Épigraphes araméens* (Paris 1912)
Fales Censimenti	F. M. Fales, *Censimenti e catasti di epoca neo-assira* (Rome 1973)
Fales Epigraphs	F. M. Fales, *Aramaic Epigraphs on Clay Tablets of the Neo-Assyrian Period* (Rome 1986)
Festschrift Porada	M. Kelly-Buccellati (ed.), *Insight Through Images. Studies in Honor of Edith Porada* (Bibliotheca Mesopotamica 21, Malibu 1986)

Festschrift Reiner	F. Rochberg-Halton (ed.), *Language, Literature, and History: Philological and Historical Studies Presented to Erica Reiner* (American Oriental Series 67, New Haven 1987)
FNALD	J. N. Postgate, *Fifty Neo-Assyrian Legal Documents* (Warminster 1976)
GPA	J. N. Postgate, *The Governor's Palace Archive* (Cuneiform Texts from Nimrud 2, London 1973)
Grayson Chronicles	A. K. Grayson, *Assyrian and Babylonian Chronicles* (Texts from Cuneiform Sources 5, Glückstadt 1975)
Hh	lexical series HAR.ra = *hubullu*
JCS	Journal of Cuneiform Studies
K	tablets in the collections of the British Museum
KAV	O. Schroeder, *Keilschrifttexte aus Assur verschiedenen Inhalts* (Leipzig 1920)
KB	Keilinschriftliche Bibliothek
Ki	tablets in the collections of the British Museum
LAS	S. Parpola, *Letters from Assyrian Scholars to the Kings Esarhaddon and Assurbanipal* I, II (Alter Orient und Altes Testament 5/1-2, Neukirchen-Vluyn 1970, 1983)
Luckenbill Senn.	D. D. Luckenbill, *The Annals of Sennacherib* (Oriental Institute Publications 2, Chicago 1924)
MSL	Materialien zum sumerischen Lexikon; Materials for the Sumerian Lexicon
N.	tablets in the collections of the Musée du Louvre
NALK	T. Kwasman, *Neo-Assyrian Legal Documents in the Kouyunjik Collection of the British Museum* (Studia Pohl, Series Maior 14, Rome 1988)
NARGD	J.N. Postgate, *Neo-Assyrian Royal Grants and Decrees* (Studia Pohl, Series Maior 1, Rome 1969)
ND	field numbers of tablets excavated at Nimrud
Or.	Orientalia, Nova Series
Place Ninive	V. Place, *Ninive et l'Assyrie* I-III (Paris 1867-1870)
R	H. C. Rawlinson, *The Cuneiform Inscriptions of Western Asia* (London 1861-1884)
RlA	Reallexikon der Assyriologie
Rm	tablets in the collections of the British Museum
SAA	State Archives of Assyria
SAAB	State Archives of Assyria Bulletin
Sm	tablets in the collections of the British Museum
TCAE	J. N. Postgate, *Taxation and Conscription in the Assyrian Empire* (Studia Pohl, Series Maior 3, Rome 1974)
TCL	Textes cunéiformes du Louvre
Th	tablets in the collections of the British Museum
WZKM	Wiener Zeitschrift für die Kunde des Morgenlandes
Zadok West Semites	R. Zadok, *On West Semites in Babylonian during the Chaldean and Achaemenid Periods. An Onomastic Study* (Jerusalem 1977)

Other Abbreviations and Symbols

NA	Neo-Assyrian
DN	divine name
GN	geographical name
PN	personal name
RN	royal name
Syr.	Syriac
e.	edge
obv.	obverse
r., rev.	reverse
rs.	right side
s.	(left) side
coll.	collated, collation
mng.	meaning
unpub.	unpublished
var.	variant
!	collation
!!	emendation
?	uncertain reading
: :. ::	cuneiform division marks
*	graphic variants (see LAS I p. XX)
0	uninscribed space or nonexistent sign
x	broken or undeciphered sign
( )	supplied word or sign
(( ))	sign erroneously added by scribe
[[ ]]	erasure
[...]	minor break (one or two missing words)
[......]	major break
...	untranslatable word
......	untranslatable passage
→	see also
+	joined to

TRANSLITERATIONS AND TRANSLATIONS

Texts from the Reigns of Sargon II and Earlier Kings

1. Mušallim-Issar, Village Manager of the Chief Eunuch (742-713)

FIG. 9. *Servants carrying tray with baskets of grapes and pomegranates (reign of Sennacherib).* BM 124799.

1. Mušallim-Issar Purchases Slaves (742-XI-26)

K 422

1 [*ku-um* NA$_4$.KIŠIB-*šú*] *ṣu-bar-šú* [*iš-kun*]
2 [*ṣu-bar* ^{m}*x-x*]-*i* [EN LÚ SUM$^{!}$]

---

3 [*x x x x x x x*]*x r*[*a*$^{!}$ *x x x*]
4 [*x x x x x x x x x x x*] *a a* [*x x*]
5 [*x x x x x x x*] ⸢*x x*⸣ [*x x*] *di*$^{!}$
6 [*x x x x x x x x*] ⸢*x*⸣ *ha* ⸢*x*⸣
7 [*x x x x x x x x x x* LÚ.*t*]*ur-ta-ni*
8 [*x x x x x x x x x x x x*]-*ir*—PAB
9 [*x x x x x x x x x x x x*]—15
10 [*x x x x x x x x x x x x x*]—SAG$^{!}$
11 [*x x x x x x x x x x x x*]—⸢*ú*⸣-*kín*
12 [*x x x x x x x x x x x x*]—SUM-*in-šú*
13 [*x x x x x x x x x x x x x x x*]
14 [*x x x x x x x x x x x x x x x*]-*šú*
15 [*x x x x x x x x x x x x x x x x x x h*]*u*
Rev. lines 1 to 4 entirely broken away
5 *i*-[*x x x x x x x*]-*ni*
6 *nu*-[*x x x x x x x x x x*]-*ni*
7 *la ú-ṣa man-nu ša* [*x* M]A.NA KUG.UD
8 *a-na* ^{m}*mu-šal-lim*—$^{d+}$INNIN$^{!}$ SUM-*nu-ni*
9 LÚ *a-di* UN.MEŠ-*šú ú-še-ṣa*

---

10 IGI ^{m}*si-pa-ra-nu* LÚ.*ṣa-rip*—*tuh-ši-e*
11 [IGI] ⸢^{m}ŠÀ⸣—URU-*a-a* IGI ^{m}*aš-šur*—DI$^{!}$—PAB.MEŠ
12 [LÚ*.*mu*]-*kil*—KUŠ.PA.MEŠ IGI ^{md}30—AŠ LÚ.3.U$_5^{!}$
13 [IGI ^{m}]*na*$^{!}$-*ṣi-i* IGI ^{m}*bi-hi-i*
14 [IGI ^{m}*i*]*m-ma-ni*—*aš-šur*$^{!}$ IGI ^{m}*ia-a-a*
15 [PAB 8 IGI].MEŠ URU.DU$_6^{!}$—^{d}MAŠ-*a-a*
16 [IGI ^{m}*aš*]-*šur*—AŠ—PAB.MEŠ *ša* URU.LÚ. SAG.MEŠ
17 [PAB 9] IGI.MEŠ LÚ.ARAD.MEŠ *ša* LÚ.[GAL]—SA[G$^{!}$]
18 [IGI ^{m}]*na-di-i* LÚ.A.BA *ṣa-bi*[*t* IM]

ADD 75

1 [Instead of his seal he impressed] his fingernail.

2 [Fingernail of ...]î, [owner of the man being sold].

(fingernail impressions)

(Break)

r.6 [If he does not pa]y, he shall not come out. Whoever pays [x m]inas of silver to Mušallim-Issar, shall redeem the man together with his people.

---

10 Witness Sipranu, tanner of coloured leather.

11 [Witness] Libbalayu. Witness Aššur-šallim-ahhe, [ch]ariot driver.

12 Witness Sin-iddina, 'third man.'

13 [Witness] Naṣî. Witness Bihî.

14 [Witness I]mmani-Aššur. Witness Yaya.

15 [A total of 8 witnesses] from Til-Inurta.

16 [Witness Aš]šur-nadin-ahhe, from Eunuch Town.

17 [In all 9] witnesses, servants of the [chief] eunuch.

18 [Witness] Nadî, scribe, keep[er of the contract].

1 Previous editions: AR 652, NALK 184. Collations: Assur 2/5. r.15 DU$_6$ confirmed. r.17 LÚ in LÚ.ARAD.MEŠ was inadvertently omitted in NALK.

19 [ITI.Z]ÍZ UD-26-KAM$^{!}$ *lim-m*[*u*]
20 [^{md}P]A$^{!}$—⸢KALAG⸣-*in-an-ni* LÚ.*tur-*[*ta-nu*]
21e ⸢*ina tar-ṣi*⸣ ^{m}*tukul-ti*—A—⸢É⸣.[ŠÁR.RA]
22e [LUGAL KUR—*aš-šur*.KI]

[19] [Month She]bat (XI), 26th day, epo[nym] year of [Na]bû-da''inanni, commander-in-[chief], in the reign of Tiglath-Pile[ser (III), king of Assyria].

2. Mušallim-Issar Purchases 5 Slaves (737-II-9)

Sm 649 + 1407

1 [*ṣu-pur* ^{m}*x x* ^{m}*u*]*r*$^{!}$*-du* ^{m}*a*[*m*$^{!}$*-x x x x*]
2 [*x x x x*]*-a-a* ^{m}*na-a*ʾ-[*di*—*x x x*]

---

3 ^{m}URU$^{!}$—*tuk-la*$^{!}$*-a-tú-u-a* ^{m}*mu-mar*—DINGIR
4 ^{md}UTU—ZU MÍ.15—*di-*ʾ*i-ni-ni*
5 MÍ.*mu-ki-na-at*—$^{d+}$INNIN PAB 5 LÚ.ZI.MEŠ

6 *ú-piš-ma* ^{m}*mu-šal-lim*—$^{d+}$INNIN
e.7 *ina* ŠÀ 74$^{!}$ MA.NA URUDU.MEŠ *i*[*l*]-⸢*qi*⸣
8 *kas-pu ga-mur* SUM-*ni* DI.KUD$^{!}$ DUG$_{4}$. [DU]G$_{4}$ *la-a-šú*

---

r.1 IGI ^{m}*qur-di*—^{d}U.GUR ^{m}*ṭa-bu-su*
2 IGI ^{m}*ur-di-i* DUMU ^{m}*su-su-ú*
3 IGI ^{m}*aš-šur*—A—AŠ IGI ^{m}SUHUŠ-*i*
4 LÚ*.Ì.ŠUR
5 [I]GI ^{m}*ni-nu-a-a* L[Ú*.*x x x*]
6 [IG]I ^{m}*qur-di*—^{d}[*x x x*]
blank line
7 ITI.GUD UD-9-K[ÁM *lim-mu*]
8e [^{m}]EN—IGI.LAL-[*an-ni x x x*]

ADD 320

[1] [Fingernail of NN, U]rdu, A[m..., ...]a-ya, and Na'[di-...].

(fingernail impressions)

---

[3] Al-tuklatua, Mumar-ili, Šamaš-le'i, Issar-da''ininni, and Mukinnat-Issar, a total of five persons —

[6] Mušallim-Issar has contracted and bought them for 74 minas of copper.

[8] The money is paid completely. Lawsuit or litig[ati]on is void.

[r.1] Witness Qurdi-Nergal, Ṭabussu.

[2] Witness Urdî, son of Susû.

[3] Witness Aššur-aplu-iddina. Witness Ubrî, oil-presser.

[5] Witness Ninuayu, [...].

[6] Witness Qurdi-[...].

[7] Month Iyyar (II), 9th day, [eponym year of] Bel-emur[anni...].

3. Mušallim-Issar Buys a Slave

Sm 1035

beginning broken away
1′ [*x x x x x*] *nu* [*x*] ⸢*x*⸣ [*x x x x*]
2′ [*x x*]-⸢*li*⸣ *ša* URU.*arba-ì*[*l x x x x*]
3′ [*ú-piš*]*-ma* ^{m}*mu-šal-lim*—$^{d+}$INNIN LÚ. [GAL—URU.MEŠ]
4′ [*ina* ŠÀ] 80$^{!}$ MA.NA URUDU.MEŠ 2$^{!}$ ANŠE ŠE$^{!}$. PAD$^{!}$.MEŠ *a-ki pa-ša*$^{!}$-[*ri*]
5′ [*i-z*]*i*$^{!}$*-rip i-si-qi kas-pu ga-mur ta-di-ni*
6′ [LÚ *š*]*u-a-tú za-rip la-a-qí a-pil za-a-ku*
7′ [*tu-a-r*]*u* DI.KUD DUG$_{4}$.DUG$_{4}$ *la-a-šú*

ADD 492

(Beginning destroyed)

[2] [...] of Arbela [...] —

[3] Mušallim-Issar, [village manager, has contracted, purcha]sed, and bought (him) [for] 2 homers of barley (equalling) 80 minas of copper at its current value.

[5] The money is paid completely. That [man] is purchased, acquired, paid off, and cleared. [Any revoca]tion, lawsuit or litigation is void.

2 Previous editions: AR 529, NALK 186. Collations: Assur 2/5. [3] Cf. ^{m}*al—tuk-la*—UN.MEŠ 2R 64 (= ADD App. 1) x 42. Reading *Se* for the first element of the name (NALK) is excluded because /Seʾ/ occurs only in West Semitic names.
3 Previous editions: AR 432, NALK 190. Collations: Assur 2/5. [4] *pašāru* "to solve" occurs here in the technical

8′ [*man-nu ša a*]-⸢*na*⸣ *ur-kiš a-na* UD-*me a-ṣa-ti*
9′ [*lu* ^{m}*x x*]*x-ba-nu lu* DUMU.MEŠ-*šú*
10′ [*lu* DUMU—DUMU].MEŠ-*šú lu* EN—*il-ki-šú*
11′ [*de-nu* D]UG$_4$.DUG$_4$ TA* ^{m}*mu-šal-lim*—$^{d+}$INNIN
12′ [*ub-ta*]-ʾ*u*$^{!}$-*u-ni* 5 MA.NA KUG.UD 1 MA.NA KUG.GI
13′ [*a-na* ^{d}15 *ša*] URU$^{!}$.*arba-ìl* SUM-*an*
14′ [*kas-pu a*]-*na* 10.MEŠ-*te a-na* EN.MEŠ-*šú* GUR-*ár*
15′ [*ina* D]I.KUD$^{!}$-*šú* ⸢DUG$_4$⸣.DUG$_4$ *la-a i-la-qi*
Edge uninscribed
Rev. destroyed

8 [Whoever in the] future, in far-off days, [whether ...]banu or his sons, [grandsons] or labour-duty superior, seeks [a lawsuit or lit]igation against Mušallim-Issar,

12 shall pay 5 minas of silver (and) one mina of gold [to Ištar of] Arbela, and shall return [the money] tenfold to its owners. He shall contest [in] his lawsuit and not succeed.

(Rest destroyed)

4. Mušallim-Issar Buys Slaves

Rm 2,499

beginning broken away
1′ [*x x x*.M]EŠ-*šú gab*$^{!}$-*b*[*i*$^{!}$ *x x x x*]
2′ [*x x x*] *ša* URU.*arba*-[*ìl*.KI *ú-piš-ma*]
3′ [^{m}*mu-š*]*al-lim*—$^{d+}$INNIN LÚ.GAL—URU. MEŠ$^{!}$-[*ni*]
4′ [*x x x in*]*a* ŠÀ-*bi* 16 MA.NA K[UG.UD]
5′ [*il-qí ka*]*s-pu ga-mur t*[*a-din*]
6′ [UN.MEŠ *šú-a-tú zar-pu*] *laq-qi*-⸢*ú*⸣ [*tu-a-ru de-nu*]
rest broken away

ADD 497

(Beginning destroyed)

1 all his [......, ...] of Arbe[la] —

3 [Muša]llim-Issar, village manager, [has contracted and bought them fo]r 16 minas of sil[ver].

5 [The mon]ey is pa[id] completely. [Those *people* are purchased] and acquired.

(Rest destroyed)

5. Mušallim-Issar Buys a Servant (729-III-3)

Rm 187

1 *ṣu-pur* ^{m}30—I EN LÚ

2 ^{m}PAB—*ú-qur* ⸢LÚ*⸣.ARAD-*šú*
3 ⸢*ú*⸣-*piš-ma* ^{m}*mu*-DI—1[5]
rest broken away
Rev. beginning broken away
1′ IGI ^{md}PA—[*x x x*]
2′ ITI.SIG$_4$ UD-3-[KÁM]
3′ *lim-me* ^{m}*lip-hur*—DINGIR
4′ LÚ*.GAR.KUR KUR.*hab-ru-ri*

ADD 195

1 Fingernail of Sin-na'id, owner of the man.

(fingernail impressions)

2 Ahu-uqur, his servant —

3 Mušallim-Is[sar] has contracted and [bought him]

(Break)

r.1 Witness Nabû-[...].

2 Month Sivan (III), 3rd day, eponym year of Liphur-ilu, governor of Habruri.

sense "to convert into cash, liquidate" (cf. AHw. 842a, mng. 3); the phrase *akī pašāri* itself seems to be the functional equivalent of (*a*)*kī mahīri* "according to the market price (of GN)" (no. 158:6, 181 e.1, 232:6 etc.). 8 UD-*me a-ṣa-ti* is a scribal error for UD-*me ṣa-a-ti*.

4 Previous editions: AR 616, NALK 191. 1 See coll.

5 Previous editions: AR 485, NALK 181; → KB 4 (1896) 106f. 2 See coll. 3 The reading of the name is somewhat unsure. r.1 Contrary to NALK, there is no blank space between this line and r.2.

6. Mušallim-Issar Buys 7 Slaves (713-III-3)

Rm 189

beginning broken away

1′ ^{md}*šá-maš—im-me* MÍ-*šú* DUMU-*šú*
2′ 4 DUMU.MÍ.MEŠ-*šú* PAB 7 ZI.MEŠ
3′ LÚ*.ARAD.MEŠ *ša* ^{m}*gab-ri*
4′ *ú-piš-ma* ^{m}*mu-šal-lim*—^{d}15
5′ *ina* ŠÀ 1-*me*-80 MA.NA U[RUD]U.MEŠ
6′ TA* IGI ^{m}*gab-ri*
7′ *il-q*[*i ka*]*s-pu ga-mur*
8′ *ta-din* U[N.ME]Š *šu-a-tú*
9′ *za-ar-pu* ⸢*la*!⸣-[*q*]*i*-⸢*ú*⸣
10′ *tu-a-ru de*-⸢*e*⸣-[*nu*]
11′ *da-ba-bu la-áš-š*[*u*]
12′ *man-nu ša ina ur-kiš*
13′ *ina ma-ti-ma* GIL-*u-ni*
r.1 10 MA.NA KUG.UD *a-na* ^{d}MAŠ
2 *a-šib* URU.*kal-hi* SUM-*an*
3 1 GÚ.UN AN.NA *a-na* LÚ*.E[N.NA]M URU!-*šú*
4 ⸢SUM⸣-*an kas-pu a-na* 10.M[EŠ-*te*]
5 *a-na* EN-*šú*! ⸢*ú*⸣-*t*[*a-ra*]
6 *ina de-ni-š*[*ú* $DUG_4.DUG_4$ *la* TI]
7 *be*-⸢*en-nu*⸣ [*ṣib*!]-⸢*tú*!⸣ *a-na* 1-*me* UD-*me*
8 *sa-ar*!-*tú a-na kàl* UD.MEŠ-*te*

---

9 IGI ^{m}*iz-bu*—SI.SÁ LÚ*.GÍR.LÁ
10 IGI ^{m}DINGIR-*ma—lid-g*[*u*]*l*! LÚ*.GÍR.LÁ
11 IGI ^{m}*sa-gi-i*[*l*]—*bi-i*ʾ-*di*
12 LÚ*.ARAD *ša* LÚ*.SUKKAL
13 IGI ^{m}*aš-šur*!—AŠ! DUMU! ⸢URU!⸣.[NI]NA!
14 IGI ^{m}*si-lim*—^{d}15! LÚ*.Ì.DU_8
15 LÚ*.ARAD ⸢*ša*⸣ LÚ*.EN.NAM *ša* [URU.*k*]*al-hi*
16 [IGI *x x x* L]Ú!.*ma-k*[*i*!-*su*]
17 [*x x x x x x x x x*] ⸢*x*⸣
rest broken away
s.1 ITI.SIG_4 UD-3-KÁM *lim-mu* ^{m}*aš-šur—b*[*a-ni*]
2 LÚ*.GAR.KUR URU.*kal*-[*hi*]
3 4 MA.NA URUDU.MEŠ *ša ṣu-pur*-[*šú*]

ADD 248

(Beginning destroyed)

(fingernail impression)

---

1 Šamaš-immi, his wife, son, and 4 daughters, a total of 7 persons, servants of Gabbaru —

4 Mušallim-Issar has contracted and bought them for 180 minas of copper from Gabbaru.

7 [The mon]ey is paid completely. Those pe[opl]e are purchased and acquired. Any revocation, lawsuit, or litigation is vo[id].

12 Whoever in the future, at any time, breaks the contract, shall pay 10 minas of silver to Ninurta residing in Calah. He shall pay [one] talent of tin to the go[vern]or of his city, and shall re[turn] the money ten[fold] to its owner. [He shall contest] in his lawsuit [and not succeed].

r.7 (Guaranteed against) epileptic [sei]zures for 100 days (and against) fraud forever.

---

9 Witness Izbu-lešir, butcher.

10 Witness Ilumma-lidgul, butcher.

11 Witness Saggil-bi’di, servant of the vizier.

13 Witness Aššur-iddina, a Ninevite.

14 Witness Silim-Issar, porter, servant of the governor of [Ca]lah.

16 [Witness NN], tax col[lector].

(Break)

s.1 Month Sivan (III), 3rd day, eponym year of Aššur-b[ani], governor of Cal[ah].

3 4 minas of copper for [his] fingernail.

6 Previous editions: AR 455, NALK 185; → GPA 91. Collations: Assur 2/5.

7. Mušallim-Issar Buys a Slave

Sm 199 + 447 + 553

1 [*ku-u*]*m* ⸢NA$_4$.KIŠIB-*šú*⸣ [*ṣ*]*u*-⸢*bar*$^{!}$⸣-*šú* GAR-*un*

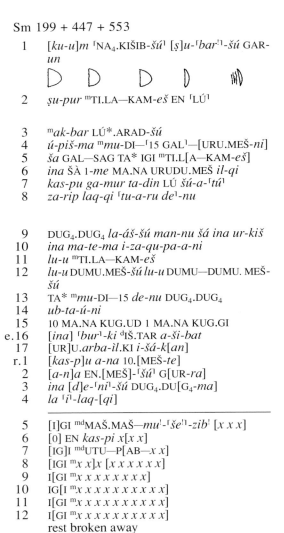

2 *ṣu-pur* ^{m}TI.LA—KAM-*eš* EN ⸢LÚ⸣

3 ^{m}*ak-bar* LÚ*.ARAD-*šú*
4 *ú-piš-ma* ^{m}*mu*-DI—⸢15 GAL⸣—[URU.MEŠ-*ni*]
5 *ša* GAL—SAG TA* IGI ^{m}TI.L[A—KAM-*eš*]
6 *ina* ŠÀ 1-*me* MA.NA URUDU.MEŠ *il-qi*
7 *kas-pu ga-mur ta-din* LÚ *šú-a*-⸢*tú*⸣
8 *za-rip laq-qi* ⸢*tu-a-ru de*⸣-*nu*

9 DUG$_4$.DUG$_4$ *la-áš-šú man-nu šá ina ur-kiš*
10 *ina ma-te-ma i-za-qu-pa-a-ni*
11 *lu-u* ^{m}TI.LA—KAM-*eš*
12 *lu-u* DUMU.MEŠ-*šú lu-u* DUMU—DUMU. MEŠ-*šú*
13 TA* ^{m}*mu*-DI—15 *de-nu* DUG$_4$.DUG$_4$
14 *ub-ta-ú-ni*
15 10 MA.NA KUG.UD 1 MA.NA KUG.GI
e.16 [*ina*] ⸢*bur*⸣-*ki* ^{d}IŠ.TAR *a-ši-bat*
17 [UR]U.*arba-ìl*.KI *i-šá-k*[*an*]
r.1 [*kas-p*]*u a-na* 10.[MEŠ-*te*]
2 [*a-n*]*a* EN.[MEŠ]-⸢*šú*⸣ G[UR-*ra*]
3 *ina* [*d*]*e*-⸢*ni*⸣-*šú* DUG$_4$.DU[G$_4$-*ma*]
4 *la* ⸢*i*⸣-*laq*-[*qi*]

---

5 [I]GI ^{md}MAŠ.MAŠ—*mu*$^{!}$-⸢*še*⸣-*zib*$^{!}$ [*x x x*]
6 [0] EN *kas-pi x*[*x x*]
7 [IG]I ^{md}UTU—P[AB—*x x*]
8 [IGI ^{m}*x x*]*x* [*x x x x x x*]
9 I[GI ^{m}*x x x x x x x x*]
10 IG[I ^{m}*x x x x x x x x x x*]
11 I[GI ^{m}*x x x x x x x x x x*]
12 I[GI ^{m}*x x x x x x x x x x*]
rest broken away

ADD 180

[1] [Inst]ead of his seal he impressed his fingernail.
(fingernail impressions)

[2] Fingernail of Balaṭu-ereš, owner of the man.

[3] Akbar, his servant —

[4] Mušallim-Issar, [village] manager of the chief eunuch, has contracted and bought him from Bala[ṭu-ereš] for 100 minas of copper.

[7] The money is paid completely. That man is purchased and acquired. Any revocation, lawsuit, or litigation is void.

[9] Whoever in the future, at any time, lodges a complaint, whether Balaṭu-ereš or his sons or his grandsons, and seeks a lawsuit or litigation against Mušallim-Issar,

[15] shall pla[ce] 10 minas of silver (and) one mina of gold [in] the lap of Ištar residing in Arbela, [and shall return the mon]ey tenfold to its owners. He shall cont[est] in his lawsuit and not succeed.

[r.5] [Wit]ness Nergal-mušezib [...], owner of the money [...].

[7] [Wit]ness Šamaš-ah[u-...].

(Rest destroyed)

8. Mušallim-Issar Buys Slaves

K 1495

beginning broken away
1′ [*kas-pu g*]*a*-⸢*mur*⸣ [*ta-din*]
2′ [UN.MEŠ] *šu-a-tú za*-⸢*ar*⸣-[*pu la-qi-u*]
3′ [*tu*]-⸢*a*⸣-*ru de-nu* DUG$_4$.DU[G$_4$ *la-áš-šu*]

4′ *m*[*an-n*]*u ša ina ur-kiš a-n*[*a ma-te-ma*]

ADD 480

(Beginning destroyed)

[1] [The money is paid com]pletely. Those [people] are purch[ased and acquired. Any rev]ocation lawsuit or litiga[tion is void].

[4] Who[ev]er in the future, a[t any time],

7 Previous editions: AR 495, NALK 189. [1] See coll. [2, 11] The final element of the name is written KAM-*eš*, as copied by Johns, not APIN-*eš* (NALK). See coll.
8 Previous editions: AR 622, NALK 187. [2, r.4] See coll.

5′ *l*[*u-u*] ^{m}TI.LA—APIN-*eš l*[*u-u* DUMU.MEŠ-*šú*]
6′ *lu-*⸢*u*⸣ *ša de-nu* D[UG$_4$.DUG$_4$]
7′ TA* ^{m}*mu*-DI—1[5 *ub-ta-u-ni*]
8′ *kas-pi a-*⸢*na*⸣ 10.[MEŠ-*te*]
e.9′ ⸢*a*⸣*-na* EN.MEŠ-*šú ú-*[*ta-ra*]
r.1 *a-na de-en-šú i*-DU[G$_4$.DUG$_4$-*ma*]
2 *la i-la-q*[*i*]

---

3 IGI $^{md+}$INNIN—A—AŠ :. A ^{m}[*x x*]
4 IGI ^{m}*e-bi-si-ni*[*š*! *x x*]
5 LÚ.*mu-k*[*il*—KUŠ.PA.MEŠ]
6 IG[I ^{m}*x x x x*]
rest broken away

whe[ther] Balaṭu-ereš o[r his sons], or (whosoever), [seeks] a lawsuit or li[tigation] against Mušallim-Issar, shall [return] the money ten[fold] to its owners. He shall [contest] in his lawsuit and not succ[eed].

---

r.3 Witness Issar-aplu-iddina, son of [NN].
4 Witness Ebisini[š...], cha[riot driver].
6 Wi[tness NN].
(Rest destroyed)

9. Mušallim-Issar Buys Slaves

K 9195

beginning broken away
1′ [UN.MEŠ *šu-a-tú zar-pu*] *laq-*⸢*qi-ú*⸣
2′ [*tu*]*-*⸢*a*⸣*-ru de-nu* DUG$_4$.DUG$_4$ *la-áš-šú*

3′ [*man-nu*] *ša ina ur-kiš ina ma-te-ma*
4′ [*i-z*]*a-qu-pa-a-ni lu-u* ^{m}ERIM!.MEŠ—SIG
5′ [*lu*]*-u* DUMU.MEŠ-*šú* TA* ^{m}*mu*-DI—15
6′ [*de-e*]*-nu* DUG$_4$.DUG$_4$ *ub-ta-ú-n*[*i*!]
7′ [*kas*]*-pu a-na* 10.MEŠ-*te a-na* [EN-*šú*]
8′ [GUR-*r*]*a*! *a-na de-ni-šú*! [DUG$_4$.DUG$_4$-*ma*]
e.9′ [*la*] ⸢*i*⸣*-l*[*aq-qi*]

Rev. broken away

ADD 486

(Beginning destroyed)

1 [Those people are purchased and] acquired. [Any] revocation, lawsuit, or litigation is void.

3 [Whoever] in the future, at any time, [lodges] a complaint, whether Ṣabu-damqu [o]r his sons, (and) seeks [a law]suit or litigation against Mušallim-Issar, [shall ret]urn [the mon]ey tenfold to [its owner. He shall contest] in his lawsuit [and not] suc[ceed].

(Rest destroyed)

9 Previous editions: AR 198, NALK 188. Collations: Assur 2/5.

2. Inurta-ila'i (717-715)

FIG. 10. *Reign of Sennacherib landscape.*
ORIGINAL DRAWING IV, 43.

10. Inurta-ila'i Buys Land (717-XI-16)

K 352 + 83-1-18,291

1 *ku-*⸢*um*⸣ [NA$_4$.KIŠIB-*šú ṣu*]*-pur-šú iš-*⸢*kun*⸣
2 *ṣu-pur* ^{m}*še-*⸢*er-ri*$^{!?}$⸣*—id-ri* EN A.ŠÀ ⸢SUM⸣*-ni*

---

3 É 3 ⸢ANŠE⸣ A.ŠÀ *qa-ni ma-šá-qí-te*
4 SUHUR KAS[KAL *šá* U]RU.⸢*kàl*⸣*-ha* SUHUR ^{m}*za-bi-ni*
5 SUHUR AMA *šá* [URU.ŠE—^{m}]*ar-ma-a-a*
6 É 7BÁN A.ŠÀ SUHUR ^{m}KUR$^{!}$.URI*-a-a*
7 [SUH]UR KASKAL *šá* URU.*kàl-ha* SUHUR ^{m}*za-bi-ni*
8 [SUHU]R ^{m}EN—TI.LA É 3 ANŠE A.ŠÀ
9 [SUH]UR ^{m}HÉ.NUN*-a-a* SUHUR ^{m}*za-bi-ni*
10 [SUHU]R ^{m}EN—TI.LA SUHUR ⸢AMA⸣ *šá* URU.ŠE—[^{m}*zi-zi-i*]
11 [SUHUR] URU.LÚ.BAHÁR.MEŠ É 4 ANŠE [A.ŠÀ]
12 [SUH]UR ^{m}*za-bi-ni* SUHUR ^{m}EN—⸢TI.LA⸣
13 [SUHUR A]MA *šá* URU.ŠE—^{m}*zi-*⸢*zi*⸣*-*[*i*]
14 [*x x x*] ⸢*x* É 1 ANŠE⸣ A.[ŠÀ SUHUR *x x*]
15 ⸢SUHUR⸣ ^{m}*qi-*⸢*bit*⸣*-*[*né*]*-*⸢*e*⸣ [SUHUR KASKAL *ša* URU.*kal-ha*]
16 ⸢É⸣ 4BÁN GIŠ.GU.ZA ⸢*x*⸣[*x x x x x*]

17 [0$^{!}$ É] 1 ANŠE 1BÁN A.ŠÀ *ina* URU.LÚ.[BAHÁR.MEŠ]
18 [*x x x*] *šá* É *ú-piš-ma* [^{md}MAŠ—DINGIR*-a-a*]
19 [TA$^{*!}$ I]GI ^{m}*še-er—id-ri in*[*a* ŠÀ *x* MA.NA]

20 [KUG.UD *i*]*l-qí kas-pu gam-*[*mur ta-din*]
e.21 [A.ŠÀ *šú-a-tú za-rip la*]*q-qí tu-*[*a-ru*]
22 [*de-nu* DUG$_4$].⸢DUG$_4$ *la*⸣*-*[*áš-šú x x x x*]
two lines destroyed

ADD 391

1 Instead of [his seal] he impressed his [fin]gernail.

2 Fingernail of Šer-idri, owner of the land being sold.

(space for fingernail impressions)

---

3 An estate of 3 hectares of land on the edge of an irrigation outlet, adjoining the road [to] Calah, (the field of) Zabinu, and the *side road* to [the village] of the Aramean;

6 an estate of 7 decares of land adjoining (the field of) *Urarṭayu*, the road to Calah, and (the fields of) Zabinu and Bel-(lu)-balaṭ;

8 an estate of 3 hectares of land [adjoin]ing (the fields of) Nuhšaya, Zabinu and Bel-(lu)-balaṭ, the *side road* to the village of [Zizî] and Potter Town;

11 an estate of 4 hectares [of land adjoin]-ing (the fields of) Zabinu and Bel-(lu)-balaṭ, the [sid]e road to the village of Zizî, and [...];

14 an estate of 1 hectare [of land] adjoining [...], (the field of) Qibit[n]ê [and the road to Calah];

16 an estate of 4 decares of throne land ... [......];

17 [an estate] of 1 hectare and 1 decare of land in [Potter Town, ...] of a house —

18 [Inurta-ila'i] has contracted and bought (this property) [from] Šer-idri f[or x minas of silver].

20 The money [is paid] compl[etely. That land is purchased and acqui]red. Any rev[ocation, lawsuit, or liti]gation is vo[id].

(Break)

10 Previous editions: AR 394, NALK 224; → KB 4 (1896) 108f; 3R 48,6 (copy). Collations: Assur 2/5. → no. 13. 5 See coll. For AMA/*um-me* "*side road*," cf. Hebrew *ʾemm hadderek*, "crossroads, parting road," and see the discussion in SAAB 4 (1990), 134-35. 6 *Urarṭayu*: or Akkadayu. The former reading has been tentatively adopted here since the name is elsewhere too (cf. r.13 and nos. 11:1′, 13:5 and 16 r.5) consistently spelled without the determinative KI, as usual in spellings of Urarṭu, while the normal logographic spelling for Akkad was URI.KI (see AOAT 6 pp. 9ff and 370ff). However, logographic spellings of Akkad without KI do occur, albeit very rarely, so the reading Akkadayu is not excluded. 8, 10f See coll. 16 Plots described as "throne (or chair) (GIŠ.GU.ZA) land" were small, possibly

r.1 *lu-u* ŠEŠ.MEŠ-*šú lu-u* DUMU—ŠEŠ.MEŠ-[*šú šá*]
2 TA* ^{md}MAŠ!—DINGIR-*a-a de-e-n*[*u*]
3 DUG$_4$.DUG$_4$ *ub-ta-ʾu-u-n*[*i*]
4 *kas-pu a-na* 10.MEŠ-*te a-na* EN-[*šú* GUR]
5 *ina de-ni-šú* DUG$_4$.DUG$_4$-*ma la i-la*[*q-qí*]

r.1 [whether Šer-idri or his sons, grandsons], brothers or nephews, (whoever) seeks a lawsu[it] or litigation against Inurta-ila'i, [shall return] the money tenfold to i[ts] owner. He shall contest in his lawsuit and not succ[eed].

---

6 ⸢IGI⸣ ^{m}*x*[*x x x x x*] LÚ.[*x x x x*]
7 [IGI ^{m}*x x*]—EN—[*x x x x*]
8 [IGI ^{m}]^{d}IM—[*x x x x*]
9 [IGI ^{m}]^{d}U.GUR—D[Ù LÚ.*x x x*]
10 [IGI ^{m}]*mat-a-a* ⸢LÚ⸣.[*x x x x*]
11 [IGI ^{m}]*aš-šur—nat-kil* LÚ.GA[L!—*x x x*]
12 [IG]I ^{m}*mu-né-piš*—DINGIR LÚ.*ha-z*[*a*]-*a*[*n*!-*nu*]
13 [IG]I ^{m}URI-*a-a*
14 [IG]I ^{m}*qí-bit-né-e*
15 [IG]I ^{m}PAB—DÙG.GA IGI ^{m}TE-*a-a*
16 [IG]I ^{m}*za-bi-ni* PAB 5 DUMU URU-*šú*
space of one line
17 ITI.ZÍZ UD-16-KÁM *lim-mu* ^{m}DÙG—IM—*aš-šur*
18 LÚ.IGI.DUB GAL-*u* IGI ^{md}PA-*u-a* LÚ.A.BA
19 *ṣa-bit dan-ni-te* IGI ^{m}DÙG.GA-*i*
20 IGI ^{m}*a-a-né-e* IGI ^{m}*man-nu—ki-i*—ERIM

6 Witness [......].
7 Witness [...]-Bel-[...].
8 Witness Adad-[...].
9 Witness Nergal-ib[ni, ...].
10 Witness Madayu, [...].
11 Witness Aššur-natkil, chief [...]
12 Witness Muneppiš-ilu, may[or].
13 Witness *Urarṭayu*.
14 Witness Qibitnê.
15 Witness Ahi-ṭaba. Witness Sukkaya.
16 Witness Zabinu. A total of 5 residents of his city.
17 Month Shebat (XI), 16th day, eponym year of Ṭab-šar-Aššur, the chief treasurer.
18 Witness Nabû'a, scribe, keeper of the contract.
19 Witness Ṭabî. Witness Ainê. Witness Mannu-ki-ṣabi.

11. Duplicate of the Preceding Text

83-1-18,688

ADD 394

beginning broken away
1′ [*x x x x x*]*x* A!.Š[À! SUHUR ^{m}K]UR.URI-⸢*a*⸣-[*a* SUHUR]
2′ [KASKAL *šá* URU.*kàl-ha*!] SUHUR [^{m}*za-b*]*i-ni* SUHUR ^{m}⸢EN⸣—T[I!]
3′ [É 3 ANŠE A.Š]À SUHUR ^{m}[HÉ].NUN-*a-a* SUHUR ^{m}EN—T[I!]
4′ [^{m}*za-bi-ni*] SUHUR AMA! ⸢*šá*⸣ URU.ŠE—^{m}*zi-z*[*i*!-*i*]
5′ [SUHUR URU.LÚ.BAHÁ]R!.MEŠ É ⸢4⸣ ANŠE A.ŠÀ SU[HUR]
6′ [^{m}*za-bi-ni* SUHUR ^{m}E]N!—TI! SUHUR AMA *šá* URU.ŠE—^{m}[*zi-zi-i*]
7′ [*x x x x* É 1] ⸢ANŠE⸣ A.ŠÀ SUHUR ^{m}*qi*-[*bit-né-e*]

(Beginning destroyed)
1 [an estate of x *decar*]*es* of lan[d adjoining (the field of) *Ura*]*rṭa*[*yu*, the road to Calah], and (the fields of) [Zab]inu and Bel-(lu)-bal[aṭ];
3 [an estate of 3 hectares of lan]d adjoining (the fields of) [Nuh]šaya, Bel-(lu)-bal[aṭ and Zabinu], the *side road* to the village of Ziz[î and Pott]er [Town];
5 an estate of 4 hectares of land adjoin[ing (the fields of) Zabinu and Be]l-(lu)-balaṭ, the *side road* to the village of [Zizî, and ...];
7 [an estate of 1] hectare of land adjoining Qi[bitnê, ..., and] the road to Calah;

military, holdings varying between 1 and 4 decares in size; see Postgate, CTN 3 (1984) p. 127. The qualification *kussû* "throne, chair" may refer to the shape of the field. r.2, 5 See coll. r.18 While it is likely that the scribes described as "keepers" (*ṣābitu*) of legal documents actually drew up the texts, we do not concur with the position of Postgate who argues (AoF 13 [1986] 18ff) that the phrase *ṭuppu ṣabātu* actually meant "to execute a tablet" rather than "to seize, take a tablet into safekeeping."

11 Previous editions: AR 169, NALK 225. Collations: Assur 2/5. → nos. 10, 13.

8′ [*x x x* (*x*) SUHU]R KASKAL *šá* URU.*kàl*!-*ha* É! 4BÁN [GIŠ.GU.ZA]
9′ [*x x* É 1 AN]ŠE 1BÁN A.ŠÀ *šá* MAN? *šá*! *ina*! *x*[*x x x x*]
10′ [*x x x x*]⸢*x*⸣ *ina ma*-⸢*al*⸣-[*g*]*u-te* [*x x x x x*]
11′ [*x x x x*] É! [*x* ANŠ]E! A.ŠÀ [*x x x x x x*]
12′ [*x x x x* SUH]UR A.ŠÀ [*x x x x*]
13′ [*x x x x x x*] AMA! *ša*! UR[U.ŠE *x x x*]
14′ [*x x x x x x x x x*] ⸢SUHUR⸣ [*x x x x*]
rest broken away
Rev. beginning broken away
1′ [*x x x x x x x x*] ⸢*x*⸣ [*x x x x x x x*]
2′ [*x x x x x x* {md}MA]Š?-*i*! *u*! DUMU.MEŠ-[*šú*]
3′ [DUMU—DUMU.MEŠ-*šú de-e-nu* DUG$_4$. DUG$_4$] ⸢*ub*⸣-*ta*-ʾ*u-u*-[*ni*]
4′ [*x* MA.NA KUG.UD LUH-*u x* MA.N]A KUG.GI *sak-ru* ⸢*ina*!⸣ [*bur-ki*]
5′ [{d}MAŠ *a-šib* URU.*kàl*]-*hi* GAR-*an* 2 ANŠE.KUR.MEŠ BAB[BAR.MEŠ *ina* GÌR.2]
6′ [{d}*aš-šur i-rak-kas* 4? AN]ŠE.*har-bak-kan-ni ina* KI.TA ⸢{d}⸣[MAŠ.MAŠ]
7′ [*ú-še-rab* 1 G]Ú.UN AN.NA *a-na* LÚ.E[N.NAM URU-*šú*]
8′ [SUM-*an kas-pu ana* 10].MEŠ-*te ana* EN.MEŠ-*šú* GUR-*ra* [0]
9′ [*ina de-ni-šu* D]UG$_4$.DUG$_4$-*ma la* TI-*qí*

10′ [IGI {m}*x x*]—AŠ! LÚ.*lah-hi-nu šá*! É—*kad-mu-ri*
11′ [IGI {m}*x x x*]—⸢AŠ⸣ DUMU {m}SUHUŠ—{d}PA
12′ [IGI {m}*x x x*]-*ni* LÚ.SANGA *šá* {d}PA *šá* URU.NI[NA.KI]
13′ [IGI {m}*x*—E]N!—GIN LÚ.GAL—*še-lap-pa-a*-[*a*]
14′ [IGI {m}*x*]*x*—A—PAB DUMU {m}*aš-šur*—*rém-an*-⸢*ni*⸣
15′ [IGI {m}*s*]*e*!-*e*ʾ—[*x x*] LÚ.*šá*—⸢*qur*!⸣-[*bu-ti*]
16′ [IGI {m}*x x x x x x*] ⸢*x x*⸣ [*x x x*]
rest broken away

8 an estate of 4 decares of [*throne* land ...];
9 an estate of 1 hec]tare 1 decare of land [......] in ... [......];

11 an estate of [x hecta]res of land [...... adj]oining the field [of ......], the *side road* to the villa[ge of ......] and [...]
(Break)

r.1 [whoever seeks a lawsuit or litigation against *Nu*]*rtî*, [his] sons [and grandsons], shall place [x minas of refined silver (and) x minas] of pure gold in the [lap of Ninurta residing in Cal]ah.

5 [He shall tie] 2 white horses [to the feet of Aššur, and shall bring 4] *harbakannu* horses to the feet of [Nergal. He shall pay one tal]ent of tin to the gover[nor of his city], and shall return [the money ten]fold to its owner. He shall contest [in his lawsuit] and not succeed.

---

10 [Witness ...]-iddina, steward of the Kadmuri temple.
11 [Witness ...]-iddina, son of Ubru-Nabû.
12 [Witness ...]ni, priest of Nabû of Ninev[eh].
13 [Witness ...-be]lu-ka'in, chief architect.
14 [Witness ...]-aplu-uṣur, son of Aššur-remanni.
15 [Witness S]e'-[...], royal body[guard].
(Rest destroyed)

12. Inurta-ila'i Buys More Land (715)

K 335

1 [*k*]*u*-⸢*um*⸣ NA$_4$.KIŠIB-*šú ṣu-pur-šú* ⸢*iš-kun*⸣
2 [*ṣu*]-⸢*pur*⸣ {md}UTU—*tab-ni*—PAB A LÚ.AZU
3 [EN] A.ŠÀ SUM-⸢*ni*⸣

ADD 382

1 [Inst]ead of his seal he impress[ed] his fingernail.
2 [Fing]ernail of Šamaš-tabni-uṣur, haruspex, [owner] of the land being sold.

(space for seal impressions)

---

10 *malgūtu* is also attested in no. 12:4 and occurs only in the documents of Inurta-ilaʾi.

12 Previous editions: AR 395, NALK 226; → KB 4 (1896) 110f. Collations: Assur 2/5. 2 Despite NALK, the final sign is not ŠÁM but AZU, as copied by Johns; see coll. Šamaš-tabni-uṣur is a good haruspex name, and a haruspex (*mār bārê*) makes a much more plausible landowner than a "son of a bought man."

4 É 1 ANŠE A.ŠÀ *i-na ma-al-gu-te*
5 SUHUR A.ŠÀ *šá* LÚ.SUKKAL SUHUR A.ŠÀ *šá* ^{m}A-*i*

6 É 8BÁN! A.ŠÀ *i-na* KASKAL *qa-at-ni*
7 SUHUR A.ŠÀ *šá* ^{m}PAB—DÙG.GA SUHUR A.ŠÀ ^{m}ARAD—AN.GAL

8 É 1 ANŠE A.ŠÀ *ina* UGU AMA *šá* LÚ.*kal-da-a*
9 SUHUR A.ŠÀ *šá* ^{md}PA—PAB.MEŠ—SU SUHUR A.ŠÀ

10 *šá* ^{md}ŠÚ—EN—PAB É 8BÁN A.ŠÀ SUHUR A. ŠÀ
11 ⌜*šá*⌝ $^{m⌜d}$PA—PAB.MEŠ—SU SUHUR⌝ A.ŠÀ *šá* ^{m}AD—DÙG.GA
12 [*x x x x x x*]-*ra-a-te*
13 [*x x x x*] ⌜É 2 ANŠE⌝ 5BÁN A.ŠÀ
14 [*x x x x x x x x*]-*a-a*
rest broken away
Rev. beginning broken away
1′ ⌜IGI⌝ ^{m}*suk-ka-a-a ina*! IGI! IGI.MEŠ! ⌜DUMU!—NINA!⌝
2′ IGI ^{m}GÌR.2—^{d}15 IGI ^{m}PAB-*u-a-a*
3′ IGI ^{m}SUHUŠ—^{d}15 LÚ.⌜KAŠ.LUL⌝ *šá* LÚ. SUKKAL
4′ IGI ^{md}AMAR.UTU—AŠ LÚ.A.BA
5′ *ṣa-bit dan-ni-te*
blank space of about four lines
6′ *lim-mu* ^{m}*tàk-lak—a-na*—[^{d}]EN
7′ LÚ.GAR.KUR URU.*na-ṣi*-⌜*bi*⌝-[*na*]
8′ 3 MA.NA URUDU.MEŠ *ša ṣ*[*u*]-*p*[*ur*]-[*š*]*ú*!

[4] An estate of 1 hectare of land in the ... adjoining the field of the vizier and the field of Aplî;

[6] an estate of 8 decares of land on the narrow road adjoining the field of Ahi-ṭaba and the land of Urda-Issaran;

[8] an estate of 1 hectare of land upon the *side road* of the Chaldeans, adjoining the field of Nabû-ahhe-riba and the field of Marduk-belu-uṣur;

[10] an estate of 8 decares of land adjoining the field of Nabû-ahhe-riba and the field of Abi-ṭaba;

[12] [*an estate* ......]... [...];

[13] an estate of 2 hectares and 5 decares of land [......]ayu

(Break)

[r.1] Witness Sukkaya; in the presence of Ninevite witnesses.

[2] Witness Šep-Issar. Witness Ahu'aya.

[3] Witness Ubru-Issar, cupbearer of the vizier.

[4] Witness Marduk-iddina, scribe, keeper of the contract.

[6] Eponym year of Taklak-ana-Bel, governor of Naṣibi[na].

[8] 3 minas of copper for [hi]s fi[ngernail].

13. Inurta-ila'i Sells the Land he Bought 7 Years Before (710)

82-3-23,143

1 [*k*]*u-um* NA$_4$.KIŠIB-*šú ṣu-pur-šú iš-kun*
2 [*ṣ*]*u-pur* ^{md}MAŠ—DINGIR-*a-a* EN A.ŠÀ SUM-*ni*

---

3 ⌜É⌝ 3! ANŠE A.ŠÀ *ina qa-an-ni maš-qí-te* SUHUR KASKAL!

4 [*š*]*á*! URU.*kàl-hi* SUHUR ^{m}*za-bi-ni* É 7BÁN A.ŠÀ
5 [SUHU]R ^{m}URI-*a-a* SUHUR KASKAL.2 *šá* URU!.*kàl-hi* SUHUR ^{m}*za-bi-ni*

ADD 392

[1] [Ins]tead of his seal he impressed his fingernail.

[2] [Fing]ernail of Inurta-ila'i, owner of the land being sold.

(blank seal space)

---

[3] [An estate] of 3 hectares of land on the edge of an irrigation outlet, adjoining the road [o]f the city of Calah and (the field of) Zabinu;

[4] an estate of 7 decares of land [adjoin]ing (the field of) *Urarṭayu*, the road of Calah, and (the fields of) Zabinu and Bel-lu-balaṭ;

r.1 See coll.; possibly ⌜PAB! 4! IGI.MEŠ⌝ "a total(!) of 4 (Ninevite) witnesses" (suggestion J.N. Postgate).
13 Previous editions: AR 31, NALK 227.

6 [SUH]UR ^{m}EN—*lu*-TI.LA É 3 ANŠE A.ŠÀ.GA
7 [SUHUR] ^{m}HÉ.N[UN-*a-a* SUH]UR ^{m}EN—*lu*-TI.LA
8 [SUHUR AMA *šá* URU.ŠE—^{m}*z*]*i-zi-i*
rest broken away
r.1′ ⸢IGI ^{m}SUHUŠ$^{?}$⸣—^{d}1[5$^{!}$] LÚ.[KAŠ.LUL]
2′ IGI ^{m}*suk-ka-a-a* LÚ.UŠ.B[AR]
3′ IGI ^{m}*qí-bi-*⸢*ni*⸣*-i* LÚ.⸢UŠBAR$_{5}$⸣ IGI ^{m}*iš-me*—DINGIR
4′ IGI ^{md}*šér—nu-ri* DUMU [^{m}DING]IR—*šúm-ki*
5′ ⸢IGI⸣ ^{m}PAB-*u-a*—SU ⸢IGI⸣ ^{md}*šá-m*[*aš*]—*nam-mir* LÚ.DAM.QAR
6′ [IGI ^{m}*x x x x x* LÚ.A.BA *ṣa-b*]*it* IM
7′ [ITI.*x* UD-*x*]-⸢KÁM *lim-mu*⸣ [^{md}]UTU—EN—PAB
8′ [LÚ.GAR.KUR] URU.*ár-z*[*u-hi*]-*na*

6 an estate of 3 hectares of land [adjoining] Nuh[šaya], Bel-lu-balaṭ, [and the *side road* of the village of Z]izî.
(Break)
r.1 Witness Ubru-Is[sar, cupbearer].
2 Witness Sukkaya, weaver.
3 Witness Qibinnî, weaver. Witness Išme-ilu.
4 Witness Šer-nuri, son of [I]l-šumki.
5 Witness Ahu'a-eriba. Witness Šam[aš]-nammir, merchant.
6 [Witness NN, scribe, kee]per of the tablet.
7 [Month ..., ...]th [day], eponym year of Šamaš-belu-uṣur, [governor] of Arz[uhi]na.

14. Inurta-ila'i Buys Land from Remanni-ilu

83-1-18,379

beginning broken away
1′ ⸢SUHUR⸣ ^{m}[*x x x x x x x x x*]
2′ ⸢SUHUR⸣ ^{m}EN—KASKAL$^{!}$-⸢*x*⸣-[*x x x x*]
3′ ⸢SUHUR⸣ ^{m}A-*i* É [*x x x x x x x x*]
4′ ⸢SUHUR⸣ ^{m}*za-bi-ni* SUHUR ⸢*x*⸣ [*x x x x*]
5′ *ku-tal* DU$_{6}^{!}$ PAB 11 ANŠ[E A.ŠÀ *x x x x*]
6′ [É *x*] ANŠE 8BÁN A.ŠÀ [*x x x x x x*]
7′ ⸢SUHUR⸣ A.ŠÀ *ša* ^{m}A-*i* [*x x x x*]
8′ ⸢SUHUR⸣ A.ŠÀ *ša* ^{m}PAB—*im-*[*me* (*x x x*)]
rest broken away
r.1′ *ina* ŠÀ 2 M[A.NA KUG.UD *x x x x*]
2′ *il-qi* [*kas-pu gam-mur ta-din* A.ŠÀ]
3′ *šu-a-tu za-a*[*r-pi la-qi tu-a-ru de-nu*]
4′ DUG$_{4}$.DUG$_{4}$ *la-áš-šú* [*man-nu ša ina ur-kiš* GIL-*u-ni*]
5′ *lu-u* ^{m}⸢*rém*⸣*-a-*⸢*ni*⸣—DINGIR *l*[*u-u x x x x x x*]
6′ ⸢*lu-u*⸣ *mám-ma-nu-šú* TA* [^{md}MAŠ—DINGIR-*a-a*]
7′ [*de*]*-e-nu* DUG$_{4}$.DU[G$_{4}$ *ub-ta-ʾu-u-ni*]
8′ 1 MA.NA KUG.UD [LUH-*u x* MA.NA KUG.GI *sak-ru*]
9′ ⸢*a-na*⸣ [^{d}*x a-šib* URU.*x x x* SUM-*an*]
rest broken away
s.1 [*x x x x x* 3]-*su* KUG.UD *ša ṣu-pur-šú*

ADD 393

(Beginning destroyed)
1 adjoining (the fields of) [NN], Bel-Harran-[...] and Aplî;
3 an estate of [x hectares of land] adjoining Zabinu and [...], at the back of the mound, a total of 11 hecta[res of land ...];
6 [an estate of x] hectares 8 decares of land [...] adjoining the fields of Aplî [...] and Ahi-im[mi ...]
(Break)
r.1 [Inurta-ila'i has contracted and] bought (said property) for 2 min[as of silver ......].
2 [The money is paid completely]. That [land] is pur[chased and acquired. Any revocation, lawsuit] or litigation is void.
4 [Whoever in the future breaks the contract], whether Remanni-ilu o[r his ...] or any relative of his, and [seeks] a lawsuit or litigat[ion] against [Inurta-ila'i, shall pay] one mina of [refined] silver [and x minas of pure gold] to [the god ... residing in ...]
(Break)
s.1 [...... a thir]d (of a mina) of silver for his fingernail.

14 Previous editions: AR 424, NALK 229. 5 See coll.

15. Inurta-ila'i Buys Land from Uquwa and Ahu'a-eriba

80-7-19,138

beginning broken away

1′ [*ina* ŠÀ *x* MA].⸢NA URUDU⸣.MEŠ TI-*q*[*í kas-pu*]

2′ [*gam-mur ta*]*-ad-din* A.ŠÀ *šu-a-tú* [0]

3′ [*za-rip l*]*aq-qí tu-a-ru de-e-n*[*u*]

4′ [DUG$_4$.DU]G$_4$ *la-áš-šú man-nu šá ina ur-ki*[*š*]

5′ [*ina m*]*a-te-ma i-zaq-qup-an-ni lu-*⸢*u*⸣

6′ [^{m}]*ú-qu-u-a lu-u* ^{m}PAB-*u-a*—S[U]

7′ [*l*]*u-u* DUMU.MEŠ-*šú-nu lu-u* DUMU—DUMU.MEŠ-*šú-*⸢*nu*⸣

8′ *lu-u* PAB.MEŠ-*šú-nu lu-u* DUMU—PAB.MEŠ-*šú-nu*

r.1 [*l*]*u-u mám-ma-nu-šú-nu lu-u* LÚ.GAR-*nu-šú-nu*

2 [*š*]*a* TA* ^{md}MAŠ—DINGIR-*a-a* PAB.MEŠ-[*šú*]

3 [DUMU]—PAB.MEŠ-*šú de-e-nu* DUG$_4$.D[UG$_4$]

4 [*ub-t*]*a-ʾu-u-ni kas-pu a-n*[*a* 10.MEŠ]

5 [*a-na* E]N.MEŠ-*šú* GUR-*ra ina d*[*e-ni-šú*]

6 [DUG$_4$.DU]G$_4$-*ma la i-laq-*[*qí*]

---

7 [IGI ^{m}*mu-n*]*é-piš*—DINGIR LÚ.[*ha-za-nu*]

8 [IGI ^{m}KUR.URI-*a*]*-a* LÚ.[*x x x x*]

9 [IGI ^{m}*x x x x*]-⸢*a*⸣ LÚ.[*x x x x*]

rest broken away

ADD 405

(Beginning destroyed)

1 [Inurta-ila'i has contracted and] bought it [for x min]as of copper.

2 [The money is] paid [completely]. That land [is purchased and ac]quired. Any revocation, lawsu[it, or litigat]ion is void.

4 Whoever in the future, [at a]ny time, lodges a complaint, whether Uquwa or Ahu'a-eri[ba, o]r their sons, grandsons, brothers or nephews, or any relative of theirs, or their prefect, and seeks a lawsuit or litig[ation] against Inurta-ila'i, [his] brothers and [neph]ews, shall return the money ten[fold to] its [own]ers. [He shall contest] in [his lawsuit] and not succe[ed].

---

7 [Witness Mun]eppiš-ilu, [mayor].

8 [Witness *Urarṭay*]*u*, [...].

9 [Witness ...]a, [...].

(Rest destroyed)

16. Fragment of a Purchase Document of Inurta-ila'i

K 13185

beginning broken away

1′ [SUHUR$^{!}$] A.ŠÀ *šá* ^{m}*x*[*x x x x x x*]

2′ [*i-n*]*a*$^{!}$ UGU [*x x x x x x*]

3′ SUHUR A.ŠÀ [*x x x x x x x x*]

rest broken away

Rev. beginning broken away

1′ [*a-š*]*ib*$^{!}$ URU.[*x i-šá-kan kas-pu a-na* 10.MEŠ]

2′ [*a*$^{!}$]-*na* EN.MEŠ-[*šú* GUR-*ra ina de-ni-šú*]

3′ 0$^{!}$ DUG$_4$.DUG$_4$-*ma* [*la i-laq-qí*]

4′ [IGI ^{m}]*mu-né-pi-*[*iš*$^{!}$—DINGIR LÚ.*ha-za-nu*]

5′ [IGI ^{m}]URI-*a-a* [*x x x x x*]

6′ [IGI ^{m}]⸢*x*⸣[*x x x x x x x*]

rest broken away

ADD 518

(Beginning destroyed)

1 adjoining the field of [NN]

2 upon [......]

3 adjoining the field [of ......]

(Break)

r.1 [He shall place ... in the lap of DN res]iding in [..., and shall return the money tenfold t]o [its] owners. He shall contest [in his lawsuit] and [not succeed].

---

4 [Witness] Muneppi[š-ilu, mayor].

5 [Witness] *Urarṭayu*, [...].

(Rest destroyed)

15 Previous editions: AR 418, NALK 228.
16 Previous edition: AR 409.

3. Varia (747-706)

FIG. 11. *Aššur and Mullissu of Nineveh (Maltai rock sculptures). Cf. the penalty formulae of nos. 31, 53, 85, 95, 138, 188, and passim.*
ORIGINAL DRAWING II, 28.

17. Aššur-šallim-ahhe Buys a Threshing Floor (747-II-4)

K 326

1 ⸢*ṣu-pur*⸣ ^{m}*ṣa-bu*—SIG$_5$
2 *ṣu-pur* ^{m}*ab-zi-i*
3 *ṣu-pur* ^{m}SU—*aš-šur*
4 *ṣu-pur* ^{md}UTU—*šal-lim*
5 *ṣu-pur* ^{m}*par-ši-du*

6 PAB 5 LÚ.MEŠ EN *ad-ri*
7 É 9 *qa ad-ru ina* URU.*du-ʾu-ú-a*

8 SUHUR ^{md}IM—*rém-a-ni*
9 SUHUR LÚ.*ša*—UGU—É

10 *ú-piš-ma* ^{m}*aš-šur*—⸢*šal-lim*⸣—PAB.MEŠ
11 *ad-ru* ⸢TA*!⸣ IGI! L[Ú!.MEŠ-*e*]
12 *šu*!-*nu-ti ina* Š[À *x* MA.NA KUG.UD]
e.13 *ina* 1 MA.NA *ša* U[RU.*gar-ga-mis*]
14 *il-qi kas-pu* [*gam-mur*]
15 ⸢*ta-din*⸣ *ad-ru šu-*⸢*a*⸣-[*tú*]
r.1 *za-ar-pat la-*⸢*qi*⸣-[*at*]
2 *tu-a-ru* DUG$_4$.DUG$_4$ [*la-áš-šú*]
3 *man-nu ša ur-*⸢*kiš*⸣ [*ina ma-te-ma*]
4 *ša* TA* ^{m}*aš-šur*—⸢*šal*⸣-*l*[*im*—PAB.MEŠ]
5 *de-nu* DUG$_4$.DUG$_4$ *ub-*[*ta-u-ni*]
6 1 MA.NA KUG.UD ⸢SUM-*an*⸣
7 IGI ^{m}*aš-šur*—*šal-lim*—PAB.MEŠ [LÚ*.*ha-za-nu*]
8 ⸢*ša*⸣ URU.*du-ʾu-*[*ú-a*]
9 IGI ^{m}*šá*—^{d}[*x*—*a-ni*]-*ni*
10 IGI ^{m}*tàk-la*[*k*]—⸢*a*⸣-*na*—EN-*ia*
11 LÚ.*ša*—UGU—É *ša* ^{m}*šúm-ma*—DINGIR-*a-a*
12 IGI ^{m}*su-hi-ru*
13 IGI ^{m}*arba-ìl-a-a*
14 IGI ^{m}*mu-*⸢*šal-lim*⸣—^{d}MAŠ
15e IGI ^{m}*ša-ú-la-a-nu*
16e LÚ*.A.BA *ṣa-bit ṭup-pi*

17e ITI.GUD UD-4-KÁM
s.1 *lim-mu* ^{md}30—*šal-*(*lim*)-*a-ni*
2 LÚ*.GAR.KUR KUR.*ra-ṣa-pi*

ADD 412

1 Fingernail of Ṣabu-damqu,
2 fingernail of Abzî,
3 fingernail of Riba-Aššur,
4 fingernail of Šamaš-šallim,
5 fingernail of Paršidu,
6 a total of 5 men, owners of the threshing floor.

(fingernail impressions)

7 A property of 90 square metres, a threshing floor in Du'ua, adjoining (the estates of) Adad-remanni and the overseer of the household —

10 Aššur-šallim-ahhe has contracted and bought (said) threshing floor from these m[en] for [x minas of silver] by the mina of [Carchemish].

r.2 The money is paid [completely]. That threshing floor is purchased and acqui[red]. Any revocation or litigation [is void].

3 Whoever in the future, [at any time], see[ks] a lawsuit or litigation against Aššur-šall[im-ahhe], shall pay one mina of silver.

7 Witness Aššur-šallim-ahhe, [mayor of] Du'[ua].

9 Witness Ša-[*Aššur*-ani]ni.

10 Witness Taklak-ana-beliya, overseer of the household of Šumma-ila'i.

12 Witness Suhiru.

13 Witness Arbailayu.

14 Witness Mušallim-Inurta.

15 Witness Šaulanu, scribe, keeper of the tablet.

17 Month Iyyar (II), 4th day, eponym year of Sin-šallimani, governor of Raṣappa.

17 Previous editions: AR 334, NALK 44; → KB 4 (1896) 100f; 3R 48,1 (copy). 9 The "household overseer" is Taklak-ana-beliya appearing as a witness in r.10. 11 See coll.

18. ——- (739-XII-19)

Th 1905-4-9,353

1 *ku-um* NA$_4$.KIŠIB-*šú-nu ṣu-pur-šú-nu iš-*[*kun*]
2 *ṣu-pur* ^{m}⸢*sa*$^{!}$-*gab*$^{!}$⸣ *ṣ*[*u-pu*]*r*$^{!}$ ^{m}*šam*$^{!}$-*šá-a-*⸢*ni*$^{!}$⸣—[DI]NGIR$^{!}$
3 [*ṣ*]*u-*[*pur x x x x x x*]-*ba*$^{!}$-*a*$^{!}$-*a*$^{!}$
4 [*x x x x x x x x x*]*x*
5 [*x x x x x x x x*]*x*
rest broken away
Rev. beginning broken away
1′ [I]GI ^{m}[*x x x x*]-MAŠ
2′ IGI ^{m}⸢*šu*⸣-[*x x x-i*]*a*
3′ IGI ^{m}*par-*[*ši-d*]*u*
blank space of one line
4′ IGI ^{md}PA—*ú-*⸢*bal*⸣-*liṭ*
5′ LÚ.A.BA *ṣa-bit ṭup-pi*
6′ ITI.ŠE UD-19-KÁM *lim-mu*
7′ ^{m}30—*tak-lak* LÚ.IGI.UM

ADD 1251

1 Instead of their seals they impr[essed] their fingernails.

2 Fingernail of Sagab, fingernail of Šamšani-ilu, [fi]nger[nail of ...] from [...]ba
(Break)

r.2 Witness *Šu*[*...y*]*a*.

3 Witness Par[šid]u.

4 Witness Nabû-uballiṭ, scribe, keeper of the tablet.

6 Month Adar (XII), 19th day, eponym year of Sin-taklak, treasurer.

19. Šumu-lešir, Recruitment Officer, Buys an Estate (734-IX-26)

Rm 2,19

1 *ku-um* NA$_4$.KIŠIB.MEŠ-*šú-nu ṣu-pur-šú-nu iš-kun-nu*

---

2 *ṣu-pur* ^{md}PA—MAŠ *ṣu-pur* ^{m}*mu*-DI—*aš-šur*
3 *ṣu-pur* ^{m}*aš-šur*—KUR—LAL-*in ṣu-pur* ^{md}PA—⸢I⸣
4 PAB 4 DUMU ^{m}KUR.*i-tú-ʾa-a-a* EN A.ŠÀ. MEŠ
5 É 14 ANŠE A.ŠÀ *ina ma-az-za-ru-t*[*i*]
6 ⸢É⸣ *ad-ru* GIŠ.SAR *ina* ŠÀ URU.SIMUG.KUG.G[I]
7 [*ú*]-*piš-ma* ^{m}MU—⸢GIŠ⸣ LÚ*.*mu-*⸢*šar*⸣-*ki-s*[*u*]
8 [*ina* Š]À ⸢20$^{!}$⸣ [MA.N]A URUDU.MEŠ TA* IGI LÚ.MEŠ-[*e*] 0$^{!}$
9 [*an-nu-ti* EN A].ŠÀ.MEŠ *il-qi kás*$^{!}$-*pu gam-mu*[*r*]
10 [*ta-din* A.ŠÀ *šú*]-*a-tu za-rip la-*⸢*a*⸣-[*qi*]
11 [*tu-a-ru de-nu*] DUG$_4$.DUG$_4$ *la-á*[*š-šú*]
12 [*man-nu ša ina ur-ki*]*š ina ma-ti-*[*ma*]
13 [*lu-u* LÚ.MEŠ-*e an-nu*]-*ti lu-u*$^{!}$ DUM[U. MEŠ-*šú-nu*]

ADD 415

1 Instead of their seals they impressed their fingernails.

(fingernail impressions)

---

2 Fingernail of Nabû-ašared, fingernail of Mušallim-Aššur,

3 fingernail of Aššur-matu-taqqin, fingernail of Nabû-na'id, a total of 4 sons of Itu'ayu, owners of the land.

5 An estate of 14 hectares of land in cultivation, a house, a threshing floor and an orchard in Goldsmith Town –

7 Šumu-lešir, recruitment off[icer, has con]tracted and bought it [fo]r 20 [min]as of copper from [these] gentlemen, [the owners of the la]nd.

9 The money [is paid] comple[tely. Th]at [land] is purchased and acqu[ired. Any revocation, lawsuit], or litigation is vo[id].

12 [Whoever] in the futu[re], at any time, [whether the]se [gentlemen] or [their] son[s ...]

18 2f, r.2 See coll.

19 Previous editions: AR 437, NALK 379; → TCAE 140, KB 4 (1896) 104ff. Collations: Assur 2/5. No. 20 does not physically join this tablet but contains the missing lines of the obverse and beginning of the reverse.

rest broken away

Rev. beginning broken away

1′ [IGI *x x x x x x*] LÚ*.*qu*[*r*$^{!}$-*bu-ti*]

2′ [IGI ^{m}*x x*]-*u-a* DUMU ^{m}*ša—aš*$^{!}$-*šur*$^{!}$—⸢*a*$^{!}$⸣-[*ni-ni*]

3′ [IGI ^{m}*x x*]*x-a* DUMU ^{m}EN—U[RU$^{!}$]

4′ [IGI ^{m}*x x x*]*x-i* DUMU ^{m}*ha-nu-bu*

5′ [IGI] ^{m}*gi*-⸢*ia*⸣-*a* DUMU ^{m}EN—U[RU$^{!}$]

6′ [IG]I ^{md}MAŠ-⸢*i*$^{!}$⸣ DUMU ^{m}KÁ.DINGIR-⸢*a*⸣-[*a*]

7′ IGI ^{m}*su-si*-⸢*ia*⸣ [LÚ*].SIMUG.KUG.GI ⸢*ša* É⸣ LÚ*.[SUKKA]L$^{!}$

8′ IGI ^{m}DINGIR-*ma*—ZU [DUMU] ^{m}*su-si-ia* KI.M[IN]

9′ IGI ^{m}SU—PAB.MEŠ URU.SIMUG.KUG.GI.MEŠ

10′ IGI ^{m}*ur-du* IGI ^{m}*la—tú-ba-šá-ni*—DINGIR

11′ LÚ*.UŠ.BAR *šá* É LÚ*.SUKKAL

12′ ITI.GAN UD-26-KÁM *lim-mu* ^{m}EN—KALAG-*an*

13′ LÚ*.GAR.KUR URU.*kal-hi ina* 2-*e pu-ri-šú*

14e IGI ^{m}SUHUŠ—^{d}PA *ṣa-bit dan-ni-ti*

(Break)

r.1 [Witness NN], royal body[guard].

2 [Witness ...]u'a, son of Ša-Aššur-an[inu].

3 [Witness ...]a, son of Bel-a[li].

4 [Witness ...]i, son of Hannubu.

5 [Witness] Giyâ, son of Bel-a[li].

6 [Witn]ess Nurtî, son of Babilayu.

7 Witness Susiya, goldsmith of the [vizie]r's household.

8 Witness Ilumma-le'i, [son of] Susiya, ditto.

9 Witness Riba-ahhe from Goldsmith Town.

10 Witness Urdu. Witness La-tubašanni-ilu, weaver of the vizier's household.

12 Month Kislev (IX), 26th day, eponym year of Bel-dan, governor of Calah, during his second term.

14 Witness Ubru-Nabû, keeper of the contract.

20. Fragment of a Legal Document of Šumu-lešir

K 7439 + K 16823

beginning broken away

1′ [*man-nu ša*] ⸢*ur*$^{!}$⸣-[*kiš ina ma-ti-ma i*-GIL-*u-ni*]

2′ ⸢TA*⸣ ^{m}MU—GIŠ$^{!}$ [*de-nu* DUG$_4$.DUG$_4$ *ub-ta-u-ni*]

3′ 1 MA.NA SÍG.*qe*[*r-du* KÚ *mar* DUG.*a-ga-ni kur-ru* NAG]

4′ 1 MA.NA ⸢KUG.UD⸣ LU[H-*u* 1 MA.NA KUG.GI *sak-ru*]

5′ [*ina bur-ki* ^{d}*x x x x x x x i-šá-kan*]

r.1 2 ANŠE.KUR.RA ⸢BABBAR.MEŠ⸣ *ina* GÌR.2 ^{d}[*aš-šur i-rak-kas*]

2 4 ANŠE *har-bak-kan-ni ina* GÌR.2 ^{d}MAŠ.MAŠ [*ú-še-rab*]

3 *bi-lat* AN.NA ⸢*a-na*$^{!}$ EN.NAM$^{!}$ URU⸣-[*šú* SUM-*an*]

4 *kás-pu a-na* [10.MEŠ-*te a-na* EN.MEŠ-*šú* GUR]

5 [*x*] ⸢*x x*⸣ [*x x x x x x x x x*]

rest broken away

ADD 303+

(Beginning destroyed)

1 [Whoever in the] fut[ure, at any time, breaks the contract and seeks a lawsuit or litigation] against Šumu-lešir, [shall eat] one mina of plucked wo[ol and shall drink a full *agannu* vessel of tanner's paste. He shall place] one mina of refi[ned] silv[er and one mina of pure gold in the lap of ......].

r.1 [He shall tie] two white horses to the feet of [Aššur, and shall bring] four *harbakannu* horses to the feet of Nergal. [He shall pay] a talent of tin to the governor of [his] city, [and shall return] the money [tenfold to its owners].

(Rest destroyed)

r.3, 5 See coll.

20 Previous editions: AR 607, NALK 380. This fragment does not join no. 19. 1, r.4 See coll.

21. A Building Contract (734)

K 378

1 ^{md}UTU—DÙ—A *x*[*x x x*]
2 ^{m}*la—tú-ba-šá-ni*—[DINGIR ^{m}*x x*]
3 ^{m}GIN—AD-*ia* ^{m}ŠEŠ—DI[NGIR-*a-a*]
4 PAB 6 LÚ.ERIM.MEŠ

---

5 2 GÚ.UN URUDU.MEŠ
6 3 ANŠE 6BÁN NINDA.MEŠ KAŠ$^{!}$.MEŠ$^{!}$
7 *ša*$^{!}$ ITI *dul-lu* DÙ-*uš*$^{!}$
8 *tal-pi-tú gab-bu*
9 GIŠ.ÙR$^{!}$.MEŠ$^{!}$ *ú-ṣa-bat*
e.10 *ú-ri i-si-ár*
11 GIŠ$^{!}$.*pi-sa*$^{!}$-*nu*
12 GAR-*an*
r.1 *šúm-mu li-bi-*˹*tú*$^{!}$˺
2 *ta-ma-ṭí*
3 EGIR$^{!}$ ITI *dul-la-šú*$^{!}$-*nu*$^{!}$
4 DÙ-*uš*$^{!}$ *ú-ga-mur*

---

5 IGI ^{m}AD—*ul*—ZU
6 IGI ^{m}*qur-bu*—DINGIR
7 IGI ^{m}10—PAB—PAB
8 IGI ^{md}MAŠ—U$^{!}$—PAB
9 IGI ^{m}GIŠ.MI$^{!}$—[*x x x*]
10 [IGI] ^{md}PA$^{!}$—[*x x x*]
11 [IGI ^{md}]IM—[*x x x*]
12 [ITI.*x* UD]-6-KA[M]
13e *lim-mu* ^{m}EN—KALAG-*an*
14e *ina* 2-*e pu-ri-šú*

ADD 90

1 Šamaš-bani-apli, [NN], La-tubašanni-[ilu, NN], Ken-abuya, Ahu-i[la'i], a total of six men.

---

5 (Their wage is) 2 talents of copper and 3 homers 6 seahs (c. 700 litres) of bread and beer.

7 They shall work for a month. One shall install beams on the entire *barn*, plaster the roof, and put in the drain pipe.

r.1 If the bricks are in short supply, they shall do their work and finish it in the following month.

---

5 Witness Abi-ul-idi.
6 Witness Qurbu-ilu.
7 Witness Adad-ahu-uṣur.
8 Witness Inurta-belu-u[ṣur].
9 [Witness] Ṣil-[...].
s.1 [Witness] Nabû-[...].
2 [Witness] Adad-[...].
3 [Month ...], 6th day, eponym year of Bel-dan, during his second term.

22. Muaddî Buys 12 Hectares of Land (729-X)

Ki 1904-10-9,147+150+230+236+240+388+391 + Ki 1904-10-9,395 (ADD 1236)

1 *ṣu-*˹*pur*˺ ^{m}*bar-*˹*ru*$^{!}$˺-*qu* EN A.ŠÀ 0$^{!}$

---

2 É [1]3$^{!}$ ANŠE A.ŠÀ *ina* U[RU].*al-li-i*
3 *ša* É LÚ*.*tur-t*[*a-ni*]
4 *gab-di* MÍ.AN.ŠÁR$^{!}$—[*x x x x*]
5 *gab-di* ^{m}*mi-nu—a*[*h-ṭí—ana*—DINGIR]
6 *gab-di* A.ŠÀ *ša* ^{m}[*x x x*]—DINGIR$^{!}$
7 *gab-di* A.ŠÀ *ša* ^{m}*da-gan*—NAM LÚ*.GAL—GI[Š$^{!}$.SA]R$^{!}$
8 A.ŠÀ KASKAL GIŠ.APIN.MEŠ-*te*
9 *ú-*˹*piš*˺*-ma* ^{m}*m*[*u*$^{?}$*-a*]*d*$^{!}$*-di-i*
10 [*ina*] ŠÀ-*bi* 30$^{!}$ MA.[NA] URUDU.MEŠ *il-qi*

ADD 1176+

1 Fingernail of Barruqu, owner of the land.

(fingernail impressions)

---

2 An estate of 13 hectares of land in the city of Allî of the domain of the commander-in-chief, adjoining the woman Aššur-[...], Minu-a[hṭi-ana-ili], and the fields of [...]-ilu and Dagan-*šimti*, manager of the g[arde]n, field, road and the plows —

9 *M*[*ua*]ddî has contracted and bought (said property) [for] 30 mi[nas] of copper.

21 Previous editions: AR 128; → Postgate FNALD 39. 8 *pi* is certain (collated).
22 Previous edition: NALK 354. 1ff, 7, 9 See coll. r.3 Sic; see coll. r.4, 7 See coll.

11 [*kas-p*]*u g*[*a-mur ta*]*-din* A.ŠÀ *za-rip la-qi*
12 [*tu-a-ru de-nu* DUG$_4$.DUG$_4$ *la*]-⸢*áš*!⸣-*šú* [*man*]-*nu šá ina ur-kiš*
rest broken away
Rev. beginning broken away
1′ IG[I ^{m}*x x x x x x x*]
2′ IGI ^{m}KÁ.DINGIR-[*a-a* LÚ.*x x x*]
3′ IGI ^{m}*mi-nu—ah-ṭi—*[*ana*—DINGIR] BE! ÀM!
4′ IGI ^{m}*man-nu—ki-i*—PAB.M[EŠ!] LÚ.SAG
5′ IGI ^{m}*zi-ba*!*-a-te* LÚ.*ha-za-a-nu*
6′ IGI ^{m}*rém-a-ni*—DINGIR IGI ^{md}30—I
7′ IGI ^{m}PAB—*i-tab-ši* IGI ^{m}[*da*]*m*?-*qi*!-⸢*i*!⸣
8′ IGI ^{m}*ki-nu-ú-a* IGI ^{m}*mu-lu-bu*!
9′ IGI ^{m}*ku-ku-lu* IGI ^{m}*k*[*u*]-*lu*!-*lu*!
10′ IGI ^{m}EN—MU—AŠ! LÚ.A.BA
11′ ITI.AB UD-17!-KÁM
12′ *lim-mu* ^{m}*líp-hur*—DINGIR

11 [The mon]ey [is p]aid co[mpletely]. The land is purchased and acquired. [Any revocation, lawsuit, or litigation is] void.
12 Whoever in the future [...]
(Break)
r.1 Witn[ess ......].
2 Witness Babil[ayu, ...].
3 Witness Minu-ahṭi-[ana-ili], ...
4 Witness Mannu-ki-ahi, eunuch.
5 Witness Zibate, mayor.
6 Witness Remanni-ilu. Witness Sin-na'id.
7 Witness Ahu-ittabši. Witness [*Da*]*mqî*.
8 Witness Kenua. Witness Mulubu.
9 Witness Kukulu. Witness K[u]llulu.
10 Witness Bel-šumu-iddina, scribe.
11 Month Tebet, 17th day, eponym year of Liphur-ilu.

23. A Eunuch Buys Land in Mezê (727-X-7)

Ki 1904-10-9,43

1 *ṣu-pur* ^{m}*se—da-l*[*a*!*-a*]
2 *ṣu-pur* ^{m}30—I PAB!-[*šú*]
3 EN A.ŠÀ *ta-da-ni*

---

4 É 2 ANŠE *ša* [^{m}]*se—dàl-a ša* ^{m}30—I
5 *ina*! URU.^{m}*me-ze-e up-piš-ma* 0!
6 LÚ*.SAG *ina* ŠÀ 5! GÍN KUG.UD TI
7 *kas-pu ga-mur ta-din*
8 A.ŠÀ *za-rip* TI
9 *tu-a-ru de-e-nu*
10 *de-e-nu* DUG$_4$.DUG$_4$ *la-šú*
11 *man-nu* GAR-*nu šá* GIL-*u-ni*
12 10 MA.NA KUG.UD LUH-*u*
13 1 MA.NA KUG.GI *sak-r*[*u*]
e.14 SUM-*an*
r.1 *kas-pu a-na* 10.MEŠ-*t*[*e*]
2 *a-na* EN.MEŠ-*šú* GUR-*ra*
3 *ina de-ni-šú*! DUG$_4$.DUG$_4$ *la* TI

---

4 IGI ^{m}*se—ma-ti-i*ʾ
5 IGI ^{m}*za-bu-du*
6 IGI ^{m}*qu-li-i*
7 IGI ^{m}SUHUŠ!—30! *ša* URU.*ṣi-ri-na*
8 IGI ^{m}10—*im-me* DUMU ^{m}ZALÁG—*se-e*
blank space of 2 lines

ADD 1156

1 Fingernail of Se'-da[lâ], fingernail of Sin-na'id, [his] brother, owners of the land being sold.

(fingernail impressions)

---

4 An estate of 2 hectares belonging to Se'-dalâ and Sin-na'id in the town of Mezê —
6 the eunuch has contracted and bought it for 5 shekels of silver.
7 The money is paid completely. The land is purchased and acquired. Any revocation, lawsuit, or litigation is void.
11 Any prefect who breaks the contract shall pay 10 minas of refined silver (and) one mina of pure gold, and shall return the money tenfold to its owners. He shall contest in his lawsuit and not succeed.

---

4 Witness Se'-mati'.
5 Witness Zabudu.
6 Witness Qulî.
7 Witness Ubru-Sin of Ṣirina.
8 Witness Adad-immi son of Nur-Se'.

23 Previous edition: NALK 423. Photo Cat. Suppl. Pl. 2. 1f, 4 See coll. 5 Nothing missing at the end of the line.

r.9 *ina* ITI.AB UD-6$^{!}$-KAM
10 *lim-me* ^{m}EN—KASKAL—U$^{!}$—PAB

11 IGI ^{md}PA—MU—PAB
12 *ṣa-bit* DUB.IM

[9] Month Tebet (X), 6th day, eponym year of Bel-Harran-belu-uṣur.

[11] Witness Nabû-šumu-uṣur, keeper of the tablet.

24. A Fragmentary Sale of Land (723)

K 407

1 *ku-um* NA_4.⸢KIŠIB⸣-[*šú-nu ṣu-pur-šú-nu iš-ku-nu*]
2 *ṣu-pur* ^{m}AD—*x*[*x x x*]
3 *ṣu-pur* ^{m}AD—⸢SU$^{!}$⸣ [EN A.ŠÀ SUM-*ni*]

4 [É] 3 ANŠE A.ŠÀ.GA *ina* URU.[*x x x x*]
5 [SU]HUR *um-me ša* URU.*tu*$^{!}$-*x*[*x x*]
6 [SU]HUR A.ŠÀ *šá* ^{m}ARAD—^{d}[*x x x*]
7 [SUH]UR A.ŠÀ *ša* ^{m}GÌR$^{!}$.2$^{!}$—[*x x x*]
8 [*x x x x*] ⸢LÚ*$^{!}$⸣.*tur-*[*tan x x x x*]
rest broken away
Rev. beginning broken away
1′ [IGI ^{m}*x x x*]-*šú* IGI [^{m}*x x x x x*]
2′ [IGI ^{md}P]A$^{!}$—MU—PAB [*x x x*]
blank space of two lines
3′ [ITI.*x*] UD-22-KAM *lim-m*[*u*]
4′ [^{m}]DI-*ma-nu*—MAŠ MAN [KUR—*aš-šur*.KI]

ADD 395

[1] Instead of [their] seals [they impressed their fingernails].

[2] Fingernail of Abu-[...], fingernail of Abu-eriba, [owners of the land being sold].

(fingernail impressions)

[4] [An estate of] 3 hectares of land in the town of [..., adjoin]ing the *side road* of Tu-[...], the field of Urda-[...], (and) the field of Šep-[..., *the ... of*] the commander-[in-chief]
(Break)

[r.1] [Witness ...]šu. Witness [NN].

[2] [Witness Na]bû-šumu-uṣur, [...].

[3] [Month ...], 22nd day, epo[nym] year of Shalmaneser (V), king of [Assyria].

25. The Governor of Parsua Borrows 50 Cavalrymen (717-I)

K 280

1 50 LÚ*.*ša*—BAD-[HAL.MEŠ *x x*]
2 DUMU.MEŠ-*šú-nu* [*x x x x*]
3 *ina* ŠÀ-*bi* U[RU.*x x x*]
4 *šú-nu a-du* [*x x x x*(*x*)]
5 *a-du* GUD.NI[TÁ.MEŠ-*šú-nu x*(*x*)]
6 ⸢*ša*⸣ DUMU$^{!}$-*šú-u-ni* ⸢*ša*⸣ [*x x x x*]
e.7 [*x x-n*]*i*$^{!}$ *ina pa-an* ^{m}[*x x x*]
8 [LÚ*.EN].NAM URU.*par-s*[*u*$^{!}$-*a šú-nu*]
r.1 *a-du* ŠÀ-*bi* ITI.DUL *ú-š*[*al-lam*]
2 [*i*]*d-dan-šú-nu* [0]
3 *ki-ma gab-bi ú-sa-lim i*[*t-ti-din*]
4 ^{m}*sa-ah-hi-i ina pa-ni-*[*šú*]
5 *ú-ram-mu-ú* [0]
6 ITI.BARAG *lim-mu* ^{m}DÙG.GA—IM—[*aš-šur*]

ADD 695

[1] 50 cavalry[men ...] (and) their sons [...] in the ci[ty ...] —

[4] they along with [...] and along with their oxen [...], which ...[...], at the disposal of [NN], governor of Pars[ua].

[r.1] He shall give them back in [full] by the month Tishri (VII).

[3] As soon as he has gi[ven] them all back in full, they shall release Sahhî [to him].

[6] Month Nisan (I), eponym year of Ṭab-šar-[Aššur].

24 Previous edition: AR 393; → KB 4 (1896) 108f. Collations: Assur 2/5.
25 This tablet has the horizontally oblong *u'iltu* format. 6ff See coll.

26. Zazî Loans 20 Minas of Silver (711-I-21)

K 287

1 20 MA.NA KUG.UD *ina* 1 MA.NA *ša*$^{!}$ KUR.*gar-ga-mis*

2 *ša* ^{m}*za-zi-i* [[*ina*$^{!}$ IGI$^{!}$ $^{md!}$IM$^{!}$—BA$^{!}$]]

3 *ina* IGI ^{m}DI-*mu*—MAN

4 *ina* IGI ^{m}PAB-*bu-u*

5 *ina* IGI ^{m}*aš-šur—mu-tak-kil*—MAN

6 *ina* IGI ^{m}*ka-ak-ki-ia*

7 *ina pu-u-hi i-ta-ṣu*

e.8 *a-na* 3-*su-šú i-rab-bi*

9 IGI ^{m}⸢*lip*$^{!}$⸣-[*hu*]*r*$^{!}$—DINGIR EN—ŠU.2.MEŠ

r.1 IGI ^{m}*arba-ìl-a-a* LÚ*.3-*šú*

2 IGI ^{m}*kur-ri-la-a-a* LÚ*.3-*šú*

3 IGI ^{md}MAŠ—PAB—AŠ LÚ*.2-*u* É.GAL SUMUN$^{!}$

4 IGI ^{m}*se-e*ʾ—*ṭu-ri* LÚ$^{!}$.SIMUG

5 IGI ^{m}*ma-an*—*ki-i* LÚ.:.—UD.KA.BAR

6 ITI.BARAG UD-21-KAM

7 *li-mu* ^{md}MAŠ—DU—IGI

8e LÚ.GAR.KUR URU.*si-me-e*

9e IGI ^{md}PA—NUMUN—GIN—GIŠ LÚ*.A.BA

ADD 5

1 20 minas of silver by the mina of Carchemish, belonging to Zazî, [[at the disposal of Adad-iqiša]], at the disposal of Šulmu-šarri, Ahabû, Aššur-mutakkil-šarri and Kakkiya.

7 They have taken it as a loan. It shall increase by a third.

9 Witness Lip[hu]r-ilu, guarantor.

r.1 Witness Arbailayu, 'third man.'

2 Witness Kur-ila'i, 'third man.'

3 Witness Inurta-ahu-iddina, deputy of the old palace.

4 Witness Se'-ṭuri, smith.

5 Witness Man-kî, ditto of bronze.

6 Month Nisan (I), 21st day, eponym year of Inurta-alik-pani, governor of Si'immê.

9 Witness Nabû-zer-ketti-lešir, scribe.

27. Zazî Buys 23 Hectares of Land

Sm 1342

beginning broken away

1′ [É] 1 ⸢ANŠE SUHUR⸣ [*x x x x x x x x x*]

2′ SUHUR KASKAL URU.*ṣal-li—ib*$^{!}$*-ši* ⸢SUHUR⸣ $^{m!}$⸢*x*⸣[*x x x x*]

3′ É 2 ANŠE SUHUR KASKAL—MAN *ša* URU.É$^{!}$—⸢*x*⸣[*x x*(*x*)]

4′ SUHUR ^{m}ARAD—U.GUR SUHUR URU.É—⸢*ku*⸣-*ti*-⸢*i*$^{!}$⸣ [*x*(*x x*)]

5′ SUHUR LÚ*.ARAD—É.GAL É 1 AN[ŠE *x x x*] SUHUR

6′ KASKAL URU.É—*ku-ti-i* [SUHUR ^{md}*x—b*]*a*$^{!}$-⸢*ni*$^{!}$⸣

7′ SUHUR KÁ—^{d}*sa-gi-*[*il x x x*]-⸢*ṣa*⸣

8′ É 1 ANŠE 2BÁN SUHUR ^{m}DINGIR-*x*[*x x* SUHUR ^{m}]*ha-na-si*

9′ [SUH]UR ^{m}ARAD—U.GUR É 3 ANŠE SU[HUR ^{m}*x x*] *x*-⸢*ba*$^{!}$⸣-*ni*

10′ [SUHUR] ^{md}⸢UTU⸣—*iq-bi* SUHUR AMA URU.DUL—LÚ*.KUR.GAR.RA

ADD 434

(Beginning destroyed)

1 [An estate] of 1 hectare (of land) adjoining [......], the road to Ṣalli-ibši and (the estate of) ...[......];

3 An estate of 2 hectares adjoining the royal road to Bit-[...], (the estate of) Urda-Nergal, the town of Bit-Kutî [...], and (the estate of) the palace personnel;

5 An estate of 1 he[ctare ...] adjoining the road of Bit-Kutî, (the estate of) [...-ba]ni, and the gate of Saggi[l ...];

8 An estate of 1 hectare 2 decares adjoining (the estates of) [NN], Hanasi and Urda-Nergal;

9 An estate of 3 hectares adj[oining ...]-bani, Šamaš-iqbi, the *side road* of Til-Kurgarri, and [...-b]ani;

26 Previous editions: AR 635, NALK 403; → KB 4 (1896) 110f; 3R 47,10 (copy). Collations: Assur 2/5.

27 Previous editions: AR 54, NALK 421. Collations: Assur 2/5. 4 Or: Bit-Tukultî. The reading Kutî is,

e.11′ [SUHUR ^{md}*x—b*]*a-ni* É 1! ANŠE! 6BÁN A.ŠÀ
12′ [*x x x x x x*]*x*-⸢*ku*!⸣ SUHUR *um-me*
13′ [*x x x x x x*]-⸢*ni*⸣-*ri* SUHUR ^{md}UTU—*iq-bi*
r.1 [*x x x x x x x* PA]B! 23! ANŠE A.ŠÀ
2 [*x x x x x x x*] É *ep-šú* 2 GIŠ.IG.MEŠ
3 [*x x x x x x*] *ina* URU.*ha-nu-ri*

4 [*ú-piš-ma* ^{m}*za*?-*z*]*i-i* LÚ*.SAG LUGAL
5 [TA* IGI ^{m}KAR]-⸢*ir*⸣—^{d}KU! *ina* ŠÀ 6 MA.NA 4!-*tú*! LÁ!
6 [KUG.UD *ina* 1 MA.N]A! *ša* LÚ*.DAM.QAR *il*-⸢*qi*!⸣
7 [*kas-pu gam*]-*mur ta-din* A.ŠÀ É *kaq-qi*-⸢*ri*⸣
8 [*pu-ṣe-e* 0! *t*]*a-din tu-a-ru de-en-nu* DU[G_4.DU]G_4! [*l*]*a-šú*
9 [*man-nu*] ⸢*ša*!⸣ *ina ur-kiš ina ma-ti-ma lu-u*! ^{m}KAR-⸢*ir*⸣—[^{d}KU]
10 [*lu-u* DUMU.MEŠ]-⸢*šú*!⸣ *lu-u* DUMU-(DUMU).MEŠ-*šú ša de-en-n*[*u* DUG_4!. DUG_4!]
11 [TA* ^{m}*za*?-*zi*]-⸢*i*!⸣ *ub-ta-u-ni kas-*[*pu ana* 10.MEŠ-*te ana* EN-*šú* GUR]
rest broken away

[11] An estate of 1 hectare 6 decares of land [adjoining ...]ku, the *side road* [of ...], (and the fields of) [...]-niri, Šamaš-iqbi, and [...];

[r.1] [in] all 23 hectares of land [......], a built house, two doors [......] in the town of Hanuru —

[4] [Zaz]î, eunuch of the king, [has contracted and] bought it [from Eṭ]ir-Marduk for 5 3/4 minas of silver [by the min]a of the merchant.

[7] [The money] is paid [comp]letely. The field, house, and building [plot are so]ld. Any revocation, lawsuit, or liti[gat]ion [is vo]id.

[9] [Whoev]er in the future, at any time, whether Eṭir-[Marduk, or] his [sons] or grandsons, seeks a lawsu[it or litigation against Zaz]î, [shall return] the mon[ey tenfold to its owner].

(Rest destroyed)

28. Purchase of Land (710-I-28)

Ki 1904-10-9,98

1 [*ku-um* N]A_4!.KIŠIB-*šú ṣu-pur-šú iš-kun*
2 ⸢*ṣu*!-*pur*⸣ ^{m}*ṣal-mu*—PAB.MEŠ EN A.ŠÀ SUM-*ni*

---

3 É 3 ANŠE A.ŠÀ SUHUR LÚ.*sa*!-⸢*ak*?⸣-*lu*!-*te*
4 [SUHUR] ⸢É⸣ *zi-ib-li* SUHUR ^{md}KU!—KAM-*eš*
5 [*x x x x x x*] ^{m}*da-a-di-i*
6 [*x x x x x x x*] A.ŠÀ *ina* URU.*ku-lu-na*!
7 [*x x x x x x x x*]*x* URU!.*kàl*!-*hi*!
8 [*x x x x x x x x x x*]*x*.MEŠ
rest broken away
Rev. beginning broken away

1′ [IGI ^{m} *x x x x x*LÚ].⸢*ha*!-*za*!⸣-[*nu*]
2′ [IGI ^{m}*x x x*] LÚ.*qur-bu-te*
3′ [IGI ^{m}*x x x*] (blank) PAB-*šú*
4′ ⸢IGI! $^{m!d!}$⸣[PA]-⸢*u*!⸣-*a* LÚ.ARAD *ša* LÚ.GAL—KAŠ.LUL

5′ IGI! $^{m!}$PAB—*la-maš-ši* LÚ.ENGAR—KUR IGI ^{md}PA—PAB-*ir*

ADD 1164

[1] Instead of his seal he impressed his fingernail.

[2] Fingernail of Ṣalmu-ahhe, owner of the field being sold.

(fingernail impressions)

---

[3] An estate of 3 hectares of land adjoining the simpletons, the *manure* house, and (the estates of) Marduk-ereš, [NN and] Dadî;

[6] [An estate of x hectares] of land in Kuluna

[7] [......] Calah

(Rest destroyed)

(Beginning destroyed)

[r.1] [Witness NN], may[or].

[2] [Witness NN], royal bodyguard.

[3] [Witness NN], his brother.

[4] Witness N[ab]û'a, servant of the chief cupbearer.

[5] Witness Ahu-lâmašši, palace farmer. Witness Nabû-naṣir, also a palace farmer.

however, more probable in view of the sequence *ša* ^{m}*ku-ti-i ša* ^{m}*tu-ti-i* in CT 53 46:9 (also ibid. 2).

28 [2ff, 6ff, r.1, 4f] See coll. [4] For ^{d}KU = *Marduk* (not *Kakku*) see note on no. 119 r.12. [r.5ff] Compare no. 115 r.2f.

6′ LÚ.ENGAR—KUR-*ma* IGI ^{m}PAB—*la-maš-ši*
7′ LÚ.ENGAR—KUR *ša* URU.*me-ra*
8′ ITI.BARAG UD-28-KÁM *lim-mu* ^{md}UTU—EN—PAB
9′ LÚ.GAR.KUR URU.*ár-zu-hi-na*
10e [IG]I ^{md}PA—*rém-a-ni* LÚ$^{!}$.A.BA

6 Witness Ahu-lâmašši, palace farmer from the town of Mera.
8 Month Nisan (I), 28th day, eponym year of Šamaš-belu-uṣur, governor of Arzuhina.
10 Witness Nabû-remanni, scribe.

29. 5 Men Borrow Money against Land from Madayu (710-X-17)

Th 1905-4-9,49

1 4-*tú* KUG.UD 47 MA.NA URUDU.MEŠ
2 SAG.DU ^{m}SUHUŠ—^{d}IM
3 ^{m}*ba-la-si-i* ^{m}10—*mu-še-ṣi*
4 ^{m}*iz-bu* ^{m}DINGIR—*iq-bi*
5 ^{m}*ṣe-ra-a-nu*
e.6 TA IGI ^{m}*mad-a-a*
7 *ina* ŠÀ A.ŠÀ.GA
r.1 *it-ta-ṣu šúm-mu* A.ŠÀ.GA
2 *ina* ŠÀ *ú-šal-li* É *ú-kal-lim-šu-u-ni*
3 *la-šu* KUG$^{!!}$.UD URUDU.MEŠ *a-na mit-har*
4 *i-rab-be-u* IGI ^{m}30—I
5 LÚ*.*ṣa-rip—tuh-ši-e* IGI ^{md}PA—NUMUN—GIŠ
6 LÚ*.A.BA IGI ^{m}Ì.GÁL—DINGIR-*a-a*
7e LÚ*.ARAD *ša* LÚ*.*tur-tan* ITI.AB
8e UD-17-KAM *lim-mu* ^{md}UTU—EN—PAB
9e *ša* KUR.*ur-zu-*⌈*hi*⌉*-na*

ADD 1246

1 A quarter (mina) of silver and 47 minas of copper, capital —
2 Ubru-Adad, Balasî, Adad-mušeṣi, Izbu, Ilu-iqbi, and Ṣeranu took it from Madayu (as a loan) against a field.

r.1 If the field is not in the meadow where he indicated it (to be), the silver and copper shall increase by the same amount.
4 Witness Sin-na'id, tanner of coloured leather.
5 Witness Nabû-zeru-lešir, scribe.
6 Witness Ibašši-ila'i, servant of the commander-in-chief.
7 Month Tebet (X), 17th day, eponym year of Šamaš-belu-uṣur of Arzuhina.

30. Paršidu Sells an Estate (710-XII-15)

K 358

1 *k*[*u-u*]*m* NA$_{4}$.KIŠIB-*šú ṣu-pur-šú iš-kun*
2 *ṣu-pur* ^{m}*par-ši-di*
3 EN$^{!!}$ A.ŠÀ SUM-*ni*

---

4 É 4 ANŠE A.ŠÀ.GA *ina ma-za-ru-ti*
5 É : *ad-ru me-šil*$^{!}$ GIŠ.SAR
6 *ina* URU.ŠE—^{m}*la—qé-pu*
7 SUHUR KASKAL *ša* URU.ŠE—GAL.MEŠ
8 [SUHUR] KASKAL$^{!}$ [*ša*] ⌈URU$^{!}$.ŠE$^{!}$⌉—[*x x*]
rest broken away

ADD 416

1 [Instead] of his [s]eal he impressed his fingernail.
2 Fingernail of Paršidu, owner of the land being sold.

(fingernail impressions)

---

4 An estate of 4 hectares of land in cultivation;
5 an estate of ditto, a threshing floor, a half of a garden in the village of La-qep[u], adjoining the road of Kapar-rabuti and the road [of] the village of [...]

29 Previous edition: NALK 148; → Postgate FNALD 27. r.3 Tablet U.UD, scribal error; see coll. r.4 *i-rab-be-u* sic.
30 Previous edition: AR 438; → KB 4 (1896) 112f. Collations: Assur 2/5. 3 Tablet É A.ŠÀ; scribal error. 7 Compare URU.ŠE—*ra-bu* in no. 109:15.

Rev. beginning broken away

1′ ⸢*x x*⸣[*x x x x x x x x*]

2′ IGI ^{md}U.GUR—MAN—P[AB L]Ú$^{!}$.SAG *ša* LÚ*$^{!}$.GAL$^{!}$—*x*[*x*]

3′ IGI ^{m}*hal-di*—PAB IGI ^{m}*hal-di*—[D]Ù

4′ IGI ^{m}*ke-e-a-a* IGI ^{m}*rém-ut*—DINGIR

5′ IGI ^{m}*ia-da*—DINGIR LÚ*$^{!}$.*i-tú-ʾa-a-a*

6′ PAB 6 IGI.MEŠ *ša* URU.ŠE—^{m}*la*—*qé-pi*

7′ IGI ^{m}TA*$^{!}$—^{d}IM—PAB-*u-tú* ARAD *ša* LÚ*$^{!}$.SUKKAL

8′ IGI ^{m}ITI.KIN-*a-a* ARAD *ša* LÚ.GAL—KAŠ. LUL

9′ PAB 2 IGI.MEŠ *ša* URU.ŠE—*da-na-ia*

10′ IGI ^{m}*gír-sa-aʾ* IGI ^{m}EN—*tak-lak*

11′ IGI ^{m}GÌR.2—10 PAB 3 : URU.*ni-hu-ut-a-a*

12e IGI ^{md}PA—PAB.MEŠ—DI *ṣa-bit ṭup-pi*

13e ITI.ŠE UD-15-KAM

14e [*lim*]-*me* ^{md}UTU—U—PAB

(Break)

---

r.2 Witness Nergal-šarru-uṣur, eunuch of the chief [...].

3 Witness Haldi-iṣṣur. Witness Haldi-ibni.

4 Witness Kê-Aya. Witness Remut-ili.

5 Witness Yada'-il, an Itu'ean.

6 A total of 6 witnesses from the village of La-qepu.

7 Witness Issi-Adad-ahhutu, servant of the vizier.

8 Witness Ululayu, servant of the chief cupbearer.

9 A total of 2 witnesses from the village of Dannaya.

10 Witness Girsa'. Witness Bel-taklak.

11 Witness Šep-Adad. A total of 3 ditto from the town Nihut.

12 Witness Nabû-ahhe-šallim, keeper of the tablet.

13 Month Adar (XII), 15th day, [epo]nym year of Šamaš-belu-uṣur.

31. Nabû-kabti-ahhešu, Scribe of Sargon, Buys Land (709-VIII-13)

N III 3157 (ADD 1141)

1 [*ku-um* NA_4.KIŠIB-*šú-nu ṣu-pur-šú*]-⸢*nu iš-ku*⸣-*nu*

2 [*ṣu-pur* ^{m}*x x x ṣu-pu*]*r*$^{!}$ ⸢^{m}*ke*$^{!}$-*e*—*lam*⸣-*ši*

3 [*ṣu-pur* ^{m}*x x x ṣu-pur*] ^{m}*man-nu*—*lu*—PAB-*u-a*

4 [PAB 4 LÚ.MEŠ-*e* URU.*bu-ru-qa*]-*a-a* EN A.ŠÀ *ta-da-ni*

---

5 [É 3] ⸢ANŠE$^{!}$ A$^{!}$.ŠÀ$^{!}$ *ša*$^{!}$⸣ [^{m}]⸢*x x*⸣ *ina* KÁ$^{!}$-*at* URU

6 [*x*] ⸢*x x* SUHUR$^{!}$ A$^{!}$⸣.[Š]À$^{!}$ [*š*]*a*$^{!}$ ⸢^{m}*man*$^{!}$-*nu*$^{!}$—*lu*$^{!}$⸣—PAB-*u*-⸢*a* SUHUR$^{!}$ *ad*$^{!}$⸣-*ri*

7 ⸢*ša*⸣ [^{m}]*kur-ba*-⸢*ni a-di*⸣ UGU$^{!}$ *na-ah-li*$^{!}$ ⸢URU$^{!}$.*na*$^{!}$⸣-*pi-hi*

8 ⸢SUHUR$^{!}$ A$^{!}$⸣.ŠÀ$^{!}$ *ša*$^{!}$ ^{m}*kur*$^{!}$-*ba-ni*$^{!}$ SUHUR A.⸢ŠÀ$^{!}$ *ša*$^{!}$ ^{m}*ke*$^{!}$-*e*$^{!}$—*lam*$^{!}$⸣-*ši*

TCL 9 58

1 [Instead of their seals] they impressed the[ir fingernails].

2 [Fingernail of NN, fingern]ail of Kê-lamši,

3 [fingernail of NN, fingernail of] Mannu-lu-ahu'a,

4 [a total of 4 gentlemen] from [Buruqu], owners of the land being sold.

(fingernail impressions)

---

5 [An estate of *3*] hectares of land *belonging to* [*NN*] in the *neighbourhood* of the town [*of Kê-lamši*], *adjoining* the field of Mannu-lu-ahu'a, the threshing-floor of Kurbanu as far as the wadi of Napihu, and the fields of Kurbanu and Kê-lamši;

31 Previous editions: AR 113, FNALD 78. Photo: Pls. I-II; → Place, *Ninive et l'Assyrie* III Pl. 78,3.

9 ⌈É! 1! ANŠE!⌉ 5BÁN *ina* KÁ! URU! *ša*! ^{m}*ke*!-*e—lam*!-⌈*ši*! SUHUR!⌉ KASKAL URU.*kal-hi*

10 [SUHUR ^{m}*i*]*g*-⌈*li*!⌉-*i*! SUHUR ^{m}DINGIR—APIN-*eš a*!-*di*! UGU! [*na-ah-li*] ⌈*ša*! URU!⌉.[*na-pi-hi*]

11 ⌈É⌉ [1 ANŠE] ⌈5BÁN!⌉ *ina* KÁ URU *ša* ^{m}DINGIR—APIN-*eš* ⌈SUHUR! KASKAL!⌉ [UR]U!.⌈*kal*!⌉-*hi*

12 SUHUR ^{m}⌈EN!⌉—P[AB?-*š*]*ú*? ARAD ⌈*ša*!⌉ LÚ*!.SUKKAL 2-*i* SUHUR! ^{m}ITI.[KI]N!-*a-a*

13 *a-di* UGU *n*[*a*]-*ah-li ša* URU.*na-pi*!-*hi*

14 É 1 ANŠE *qa-an-ni* URU *ša* ^{m}*ke-e*—⌈*lam*!⌉-*ši*! SUHUR! ⌈KASKAL! URU!.*kal*!⌉-*hi*

15 SUHUR ^{m}DINGIR—APIN-*eš* SUHUR! ^{m}*man-nu—lu*—PAB-*u-a* ⌈*a*!-*di*! UGU! *x* GIŠ.APIN?⌉. MEŠ

16 PAB É 7 ANŠE A.ŠÀ *qa-an-ni* URU É ⌈2 ANŠE 2BÁN! A!.ŠÀ!⌉ *ša* [^{m}]IT[I!.K]IN!-*a*!-*a*

17 *ša* ^{m}DINGIR—APIN-*eš* ⌈É? *x*⌉ TA*? *ir*?-*ti*? ⌈*na*?-*ah*?-*lu*? *x*⌉ *e q*[*u*? *x*]

18 SUHUR A.ŠÀ *ša* ^{m}⌈*ke*!—*lam*!⌉-*ši* É ⌈2 ANŠE! 8BÁN?⌉ [*š*]*a*! ^{m}*man-nu—lu*—P[AB-*u-a*]

19 TA*! ŠÀ! *ki-šub*!-*bé*-⌈*e*!⌉ BAD!-*ti a-di* UGU! ⌈*na*!-*ah*!-*li*!⌉ [URU.*na-pi-hi*]

20 SUHUR A.ŠÀ *ša* ^{m}[*ke*]-*e*—[*la*]*m-ši* SUHUR ^{m}PAB-*u-a—a-mur*

21 PAB É ⌈5⌉ AN[ŠE A].ŠÀ *ina* UGU ⌈*na*?⌉-[*ah-l*]*i*! URU.*n*[*a-pi-hi*]

22 É ⌈2⌉ ANŠE [xBÁN] *ša* ^{m}DINGIR—APIN-*eš* SUHUR ^{m}DINGIR—APIN-*eš* SUHUR ^{m}⌈*ke*?-*e*?⌉—[*lam-ši*]

23 SUHUR ^{m}ITI.KI[N-*a-a*] É! 2 ANŠE! 5BÁN ⌈*ša*! ^{m}*ke-e—lam-ši*⌉ [*x x x*]

24 SUHUR ^{md}PA—⌈MU?⌉—PAB SUHUR ^{m}DUMU.UŠ-*i* SUHUR ^{m}[*x x x x*]

25 [É *x* AN]ŠE 2BÁN *ša*! ^{m}*man-nu—lu*—PAB-*u-a* É 1 ANŠE 3⌈BÁN⌉ [*x x x x*]

e.26 [É] 2 [AN]ŠE 7BÁN SUHUR ^{m}*k*[*e*]—⌈*lam*!⌉-*ši* SUHUR ^{m}PAB-*u*!-[*a—a-mur*]

27 [SUHUR] *um*!-*mi ša* LÚ*.SIPA.MEŠ [PAB?] É 6 ANŠE [*x x*]

28 [*ina* UG]U? *um-mi ša* ⌈*x*⌉ LÚ*.SIPA.[MEŠ]

29 [PAB-*ma*] 80 ANŠE A.ŠÀ.GA *in*[*a*! *m*]*a-az-ru-ti ina* G[IŠ.BÁN]

30 [*ša*] 9! *qa* URUDU 26 KÙŠ LUGAL [GÍ]D.DA 24 KÙ[Š DAGAL]

31 [*ša kaq*]-*qí-ri pu-ṣe-e ša in*[*a*? *x*]

r.1 ⌈*x*⌉ KÙŠ GÍD 40 KÙŠ DAGAL *ša ad-ri* SUHUR ^{m}DINGIR—APIN-*eš* ^{m}*k*[*e*!—*lam-ši*]

2 28 KÙŠ GÍD 20 KÙŠ DAGAL *ša* GIŠ.SAR SUHUR ^{m}DINGIR—APIN-*eš* ^{m}*ke*—⌈*lam*!⌉-[*ši*]

3 *ki-qi-lu-tu ina* IGI KÁ *ša* LÚ.MEŠ-*e an-nu-ti*

9 [an estate of] 1 hectare 5 decares in the *neigbourhood* of the town of Kê-lamši, adjoining the road to Calah, [I]glî, and Ilu-ereš, as far as [the wadi] of [Napihu];

11 an estate of [*1* hectare] 5 decares in the *neigbourhood* of the town of Ilu-ereš, adjoining the road to Calah, Bel-*uṣuršu*, servant of the deputy vizier, and Ululayu, as far as the wadi of Napihu;

14 an estate of 1 hectare outside the town of Kê-lamši, adjoining the road to Calah, Ilu-ereš and Mannu-lu-ahu'a, as far as the [...] *ploughs*; in all, a property of 7 hectares of land outside the town.

16 an estate of *2* hectares 2 decares of land belonging to Ululayu and Ilu-ereš, ... *from the edge of the wadi* [...], adjoining the field of Kê-lamši;

18 an estate of 2 hectares 5 decares belonging to Mannu-lu-ah[u'a], from 'open' waste ground as far as the wadi of [Napihu], adjoining the field of Kê-lamši and Ahu'a-amur,

21 in all, a property of 5 hectares of land on the wadi of Napihu.

22 An estate of 2 hectares [x] decares belonging to Ilu-ereš, adjoining Ilu-ereš, *Kê-*[*lamši*], and Ul[ulayu];

23 an estate of 2 hectares 5 decares belonging to Kê-lamši [...], adjoining Nabû-*šumu*-uṣur, Aplî, and [NN];

25 [an estate of x hec]tares 2 decares belonging to Mannu-lu-ahu'a; an estate of 1 hectare 3 decares [......];

26 [an estate of] 2 [hect]ares 7 decares adjoining Kê-lamši, Ahu'a-amur, [and] the *side road* of the shepherds; [*in all*], a property of 6 hectares [... o]n the *side road* of the shepherd[s];

29 in all 80 hectares of land in cultivation by the copper s[eah of] 9 'litres.'

30 26 royal cubits (is) the length, 24 cubi[ts the width of] a vacant lot *i*[*n* ...];

r.1 [x] cubits (is) the length, 40 cubits the width of a threshing-floor adjoining Ilu-ereš and K[ê-lamši];

2 28 cubits (is) the length, 20 cubits the width of a garden adjoining Ilu-ereš and Kê-[lamši];

3 a refuse dump in front of the gate, be-

ina URU.*bu-ru-qi up-piš-ma*
4 ^{md}PA—IDIM—PAB.MEŠ-*šú* LÚ.A.BA É.GAL *ša* ^{m}LUGAL—GI.NA LUGAL KUR—*aš-šur*. K[I]
5 TA* IGI LÚ.MEŠ-*e an-nu-ti ina* ŠÀ 6 MA.NA KUG.UD *il-qí*
6 *kas-pu gam-mur ta-din tu-a-ru* DUG_4. DUG_4 *la-áš-šú ina ur-kiš ma-ti-ma*
7 *lu* LÚ.MEŠ *an-nu-ti lu* DUMU.MEŠ-*šú-nu lu* DUMU—DUMU.MEŠ-*šú-nu lu* PAB.MEŠ-*šú-nu*
8 *lu* LÚ.GAR-*nu-šú-nu lu mam-ma-nu-šú-nu ša i-za-qu-pan-ni de-e-nu*
9 DUG_4.DUG_4 TA ^{md}PA—IDIM—PAB.MEŠ-*šú* PAB.MEŠ-*šú ub-ta-ʾu-u-ni* 1 MA.NA KUG.GI
10 *sak-ru ina bur-ki* ^{d}15 *ša* URU.NINA GAR-*an ina de-ni-šú* DUG_4.DUG_4-*ma là* TI
11 *kás-pu a-na* 10.MEŠ-*te a-na* EN.MEŠ-*šú* GUR-*ra*

---

12 IGI ^{m}*kab-ti-i* LÚ.A.BA *ša* LÚ.EN.NAM *ša* URU.*kal-hi*
13 IGI ^{m}*ti-ku-su* LÚ.*šá*—UGU—URU ^{m}DUMU—^{d}15 LÚ.*ha-za-nu ša* URU.*kal-hi*
14 IGI ^{m}*aš-šur—re-ṣu-u-a* LÚ.SAG LÚ.DUB. SAR *ša* MÍ—É.GAL
15 IGI ^{md}PA—BÀD—PAB LÚ.SAG LÚ.MU *ša* É.GAL
16 IGI ^{md}PA—KAR—ZI.MEŠ LÚ.A.BA *ša* LÚ.GAL—SAG
17 IGI ^{m}*ku-ku-la-a-nu* DUMU ^{m}ARAD—^{d}AG
18 IGI ^{m}*ig-li-i* LÚ.ARAD *ša* ^{m}*kur-ba-ni*
19 IGI ^{m}*na-ad-ba-nu* LÚ.ARAD *ša* LÚ.SUKKAL 2-*i*
20 IGI ^{m}PAB—*la—a-maš-ši* LÚ.ARAD *ša* ^{m}*kur-ba-ni*
21 [PA]B 3 DUMU.MEŠ URU-*šú-nu*
22 [IGI ^{m}]GÌR.2—^{d}15 LÚ.ARAD *ša* LÚ.EN.NAM *ša* URU.HAL.ṢU
23 [IGI ^{m}]⸢*gíd*⸣-*gi*!-*da-a-nu* LÚ.*ka-ṣir* IGI ^{m}*su-si-i* LÚ.*ka-ṣir*
24 PAB 2 ARAD.MEŠ *ša* LÚ.2-*e ša* LÚ.EN.NAM *ša* URU.*kal-hi*
25 IGI ^{m}SUHUŠ—15 LÚ.AŠGAB ARAD *ša* LÚ.EN.NAM *ša* URU.*kal-hi*
26 IGI ^{m}*qur-di*—^{d}IM LÚ.A.BA *ša* É.GAL—*ma-šar-te ša* URU.*kal-hi*
27 *ṣa-bit dan-ni-ti* ITI.APIN UD-13-KÁM *li-mu*
28 ^{m}*man-nu—ki—aš-šur*—ZU LÚ.GAR.KUR URU.*til-e*
29 MU-12-KÁM ^{m}LUGAL—GI.NA LUGAL KUR—*aš-šur*
30 A.MEŠ *ina* PÚ TA URU-*šú i-šat-ti il-ku* TA

longing to these gentlemen, in Buruqu —

4 Nabû-kabti-ahhešu, palace scribe of Sargon, king of Assyria, has contracted and bought (said property) from these gentlemen for six minas of silver. The money is paid completely. Any revocation or litigation is void.

6 In the future, at any time, whether these gentlemen, or their sons, grandsons, or brothers, or their prefect, or any relative of theirs, whoever lodges a complaint and seeks a lawsuit or litigation against Nabû-kabti-ahhešu and his brothers, shall place one mina of pure gold in the lap of Ištar of Nineveh.

10 He shall contest in his lawsuit and not succeed. He shall return the money tenfold to its owners.

---

12 Witness Kabtî, scribe of the governor of Calah.

13 Witness Tikusu, city overseer. (Witness) Mar-Issar, mayor of Calah.

14 Witness Aššur-reṣuwa, eunuch, scribe of the queen.

15 Witness Nabû-duru-uṣur, eunuch, cook of the palace.

16 Witness Nabû-eṭir-napšati, scribe of the chief eunuch.

17 Witness Kukkullanu, son of Urda-Nabû.

18 Witness Iglî, servant of Kurbanu.

19 Witness Nadbanu, servant of the deputy vizier.

20 Witness Ahu-la-amašši, servant of Kurbanu.

21 a total of 3 inhabitants of their town.

22 Witness Šep-Issar, servant of the governor of Birtu.

23 Witness Gidgidanu, tailor. Witness Susî, tailor; a total of 2 servants of the deputy governor of Calah.

25 Witness Ubru-Issar, tanner, servant of governor of Calah.

26 Witness Qurdi-Adad, scribe of the Review Palace of Calah, keeper of the contract.

27 Month Marchesvan (VIII), 13th day, eponym year of Mannu-ki-Aššur-le'i, governor of Tillê; year 12 of Sargon (II), king of Assyria.

30 He can draw water from the well with his town. He does not have to perform labour

URU-*šú la il-lak*
31e 10 MA.NA URUDU.MEŠ *ša ṣu-up-[ri-šú-nu]*

duty with his town.
31 10 minas of copper for [their fin]gernails.

32. Gazilu Buys a Building Plot (707-VI-15)

83-1-18,335

1 [*ṣ*]*u-pur* [^{m}SUHUŠ—*a-la-a-a*]
2 EN [*kaq-qi-ri pu-ṣe-e* SUM-*ni*]

3 *kaq-qi-ri pu-*[*ṣe-e* SUHUR$^{?}$ ^{m}M]AŠ$^{!}$-*i*
4 GIŠ.SAR É 1 ANŠE 6BÁN A.ŠÀ *ina* URU.É—*da-*[*gan*]
5 SUHUR GIŠ.SAR *ša* ^{m}URU.*arba-ìl-a-a*
6 SUHUR ^{m}*qur-di*—15 SUHUR *hi-ri-te*
7 *ša* URU.*a-di-an* SUHUR ^{m}EN—*tàk-lak*
8 *ú-piš-ma* ^{m}*ga-zi-lu*
9 *ina* ŠÀ-*bi* 80 MA.NA URUDU.MEŠ *i-zi-rip*
10 *i-si-qi kas-pu ga-mur ta-din*
11 A.ŠÀ.GA *šu-a-tú za-rip la-qi*
12 *tu-a-*⌜*ru*⌝ *de-nu* DUG$_4$.DUG$_4$ *la-šú*
13 *man-nu šá ur-kiš ina ma-te-ma i-za-qu-*⌜*pa*⌝*-ni*
14 *lu-u* ^{m}SUHUŠ—*a-la-a-a lu-u* DUMU.MEŠ-*šú*
15 *lu-u* ŠEŠ$^{!}$-*šú lu-u mám-ma-nu-šú*
16 ⌜TA$^{!}$⌝ ^{m}*ga-zi-lu* ⌜*ù* DUMU.MEŠ-*šú*⌝
e.17 ⌜*de*⌝-*nu*$^{!}$ DUG$_4$.DUG$_4$ *ub-ta-ʾu-*[*ni*]
r.1 10 MA.NA KUG.UD 5 MA.NA K[UG.GI]
2 *a-na* ^{d}MAŠ *a-šib* URU.*kal-*[*hi* SUM-*an*]
3 2 ANŠE.KUR.RA BABBAR.MEŠ *ina* GÌ[R.2 ^{d}*aš-šur*]
4 *i-ra-kas* 4 ANŠE.*har-b*[*a*$^{!}$*-kan-ni*]
5 *ina* GÌR.2 ^{d}MAŠ.MAŠ *ú-še-*[*rab bi-lat*]
6 AN.NA *a-na* LÚ*.*šak-*⌜*nu*⌝ [URU-*šú* SUM-*an*]
7 *kas-pu a-na* 1-*me-*⌜*ni*$^{!}$ *a*⌝-[*na* EN-*šú*]
8 *ú-tar ina de-ni-šú* D[UG$_4$.DUG$_4$-*ma la* TI]

9 IGI ^{m}I—DINGIR ⌜LÚ*$^{!}$⌝.[*x x x* IGI ^{m}*x x x*]—MAŠ$^{!}$
10 IGI ^{m}ARAD—PAB.MEŠ-*šú* [IGI ^{m}*x x x*]*x*
11 PAB 4 IGI.MEŠ UR[U.*maš-ka-r*]*i*$^{!}$-⌜*ta*$^{!}$⌝-*a-a*

12 IGI ^{md}⌜U.GUR—DÙ⌝ 0$^{!}$ ^{m}⌜^{d}IM—MU—PAB⌝

13 IGI ^{m}⌜*pu-u*⌝-[*lu* IGI ^{m}]⌜$^{d!}$⌝*šá-maš*—⌜*x*⌝-*da-a*

ADD 350

1 [Fin]gernail [of Ubru-Allaya], owner [of the vacant lot being sold].

(fingernail impressions)

3 A vacant l[ot *adjoining Nu*]*rtî*, a garden, an estate of 1 hectare 6 decares of land in the town of Bit-Da[gan], adjoining the garden of Arbailayu, (the estate of) Qurdi-Issar, the canal of Adian, and (the estate) of Bel-taklak —

8 Gazilu has contracted, purchased and acquired it for 80 minas of copper.

10 The money is paid completely. That land is purchased and acquired. Any revocation, lawsuit, or litigation is void.

13 Whoever in the future, at any time, lodges a complaint, whether Ubru-Allaya or his sons or brothers or any relative of his, and seeks a lawsuit or litigation against Gazilu and his sons, [shall pay] 10 minas of silver (and) 5 minas of go[ld] to Ninurta residing in Cal[ah].

r.3 He shall tie 2 white horses to the f[eet of Aššur], and shall bri[ng] 4 *harb*[*akannu*] horses to the feet of Nergal. [He shall pay 1 talent] of tin to the prefect [of his city], and shall return the money a hundredfold t[o its owner]. He shall con[test] in his lawsuit [and not succeed].

r.9 Witness Na'di-ilu, [.... Witness ...]-ašared.

10 Witness Urda-ahhešu. [Witness NN].

11 A total of 4 witnesses from [Maškar]it.

12 Witness Nergal-ibni. Witness Adad-šumu-uṣur.

13 Witness Pu[lu]. Witness Šamaš-[...]dâ.

32 Previous editions: AR 165, NALK 103. Collations: Assur 2/5.

14 IGI ^{md}EN—KASKAL—[*x x x*]
15 IGI ^{m}⸢SANGA$^{!}$⸣—^{d}15 LÚ*.A.⸢BA⸣
16 ITI.⸢KIN⸣ UD-15-K[ÁM]
17 *lim-mu* ^{m}*šá—aš-šur—*[*du-bu*]

s.1 4 MA.NA URUDU.MEŠ *ša ṣu-pur-šú i-ti-ši*

14 Witness Bel-Harran-[...].
15 Witness Sangû-Issar, scribe.
16 Month Elul (VI), 15th day, eponym year of Ša-Aššur-[dubbu].
s.1 He has collected 4 minas of copper for his fingernail.

33. Purchase of Land (706-X)

K 4288

beginning broken away
1′ *gab-d*[*i x x x x x x x x*]
2′ ^{m}10—EN—LAL LÚ.[*x x x x x x x*]
3′ TA* IGI ^{m}*ta-ab-*[*x x x x x x x*]
4′ *kas-pi gam-mur ta-*[*din x x x x*]

5′ *za-rip laq-qi* [*tu-a-ru*]
6′ *de-e-ni* [DUG$_4$.DUG$_4$ *la-áš-šú*]
7′ [*man-nu*] ⸢*ša*⸣ [*x x x x x x x x*]
rest broken away
Rev. beginning broken away

1′ IGI ^{m}[*x x x x x x x x*]
2′ IGI ^{m}[*x x x x x x x x*]
3′ PAB ⸢2$^{?}$⸣ [*x x x x x x x x*]
4′ IGI ^{m}[*x x x x x x x x*]
5′ IGI ^{m}[*x x x x x x x*]
6′ PAB 3 AR[AD$^{?}$.MEŠ *x x x x*]
one line blank
7′ IGI ^{m}DINGIR—*tap-*[*pu-ti x x x x x*]

8′ ITI.AB UD-1$^{?}$-[KÁM]
9′ [*lim-mu* ^{m}*m*]*u-ta*[*k-kil—aš-šur x x x x x*]

ADD 484

(Beginning destroyed)
1 [......], adjoin[ing ...] —

3 Adad-belu-taqqin the [... has contracted and bought it for x minas of silver] from Tab[...].
5 The money is p[aid] completely. [That ...] is purchased and acquired. [Any revocation], lawsuit, or [litigation is void].
7 [Whoe]ver [in the future, at any time]
(Break)
r.1 Witness [NN, ...].
2 Witness [NN, ...].
3 A total of *2* [......].
4 Witness [......].
5 Witness [......]
6 A total of 3 ser[vants of ...].
7 Witness Ilu-tap[puti ...].
8 Month Tebet (X), *1*st day, [eponym year of M]utak[kil-Aššur ...].

33 Previous edition: AR 450. r.3, 7f See coll.

Texts from the Reign of Sennacherib

4. Royal Charioteers

FIG. 12. *Sennacherib's charioteer ready for duty on a campaign.*
ORIGINAL DRAWING I, 62.

34. Šumma-ilani, Chariot Driver, Buys Three Slaves (709-V-20)

K 383

1 ⸢NA$_4$⸣.KIŠIB ^{m}*d*[*a-gan—mil-ki*]
2 EN UN.MEŠ *t*[*a-da-ni*]

3 ^{m}*i-man-nu-u* MÍ.*ú-n*[*u*!*-x x*]-⸢*ni*?⸣
4 ^{m}*mil-ki—ú-ri* PAB 3 ⸢ZI.MEŠ⸣
5 *ú-piš-ma* ^{m}BE-*ma*—DINGIR.MEŠ
6 LÚ.*mu-kil*—KUŠ.PA.MEŠ
7 *ša* ^{m}KA.KÉŠ—LUGAL TA* IGI
8 ^{m}*da-gan—mil-ki ina* ŠÀ 3 MA.NA ⸢KUG.UD⸣
9 *ina* 1 MA.NA-*e šá* URU.*gar-ga-mis* TI-*qí*
10 *kas-pu gam-mur ta-ad-din*
11 UN.MEŠ *šu-a-tú* ⸢*zar*⸣-*pu laq-qí-u*
12 *tu-a-ru de-e-nu* DUG$_4$.⸢DUG$_4$⸣
13 *la-áš-šú man-nu šá ina ur-kiš*
14 *ina ma-te-ma* ⸢*i*⸣-*zaq-qup-an-ni*
15 GIL-*u-ni lu-u*! ^{m}*da-gan—mil*-⸢*ki*⸣
16 *lu-u*! PAB.MEŠ-*šú lu-u* DUMU—PAB.MEŠ-*šú*
17 *lu-u mám-ma-nu-šú lu-u dan-nu*
18 *ša* TA* ^{m}BE-*ma*—DINGIR.MEŠ DUMU.MEŠ-*šú*
19 DUMU—DUMU.MEŠ-*šú de-e-nu* DUG$_4$.DUG$_4$
20 [*u*]*b-ta-ʾu-u-ni*
r.1 [*x* MA.N]A KUG.UD 1 MA.NA KUG.GI
2 [*a*]-*na* ^{d}15 *šá arba-ìl*.KI SUM!-*an*
3 *kas-pu a-na* 10.MEŠ-*te a-na* EN.MEŠ-*šú*
4 GUR-*ra ina de-ni-šú* DUG$_4$.DUG$_4$-*ma*
5 *la i-laq-qí*

---

6 IGI ^{m}*ad-da-a* LÚ.A.BA
7 IGI ^{m}PAB-*i—ra-me* LÚ.:
8 IGI ^{m}*pa-qa-ha* LÚ.GAL—URU.MEŠ
9 IGI ^{m}*na-ad-bi—ia-a-ú* LÚ.DIB—KUŠ.PA. MEŠ
10 IGI ^{m}EN—IGI.LAL-*an-ni*
11 IGI ^{m}*bi-in—di-ki-ri*
12 IGI ^{m}DÙG—IM—^{d}15 IGI ^{m}*tab-ni-i*

13 LÚ.A.BA *ṣa-bit* IM *ina* ITI.NE
14 UD-20-KÁM *lim-mu* ^{m}*man-nu—ki-i—aš-šur*—⸢ZU⸣

ADD 234

1 Seal of D[agan-milki], owner of the people being [sold].

(blank seal space)

3 Immannû, the woman Un[u...]ni, and Milki-uri, a total of 3 persons —

5 Šumma-ilani, chariot driver of *the royal corps*, has contracted and bought them from Dagan-milki for 3 minas of silver by the mina of Carchemish.

10 The money is paid completely. Those people are purchased and acquired. Any revocation, lawsuit, or litigation is void.

13 Whoever in the future, at any time, lodges a complaint or breaks the contract, whether Dagan-milki or his brothers or nephews, or any relative of his or anyone influential,

18 and seeks a lawsuit or litigation against Šumma-ilani, his sons and grandsons, shall pay [x min]as of silver and one mina of gold to Ištar of Arbela, and shall return the money tenfold to its owners. He shall contest in his lawsuit and not succeed.

---

r.6 Witness Addâ, scribe.

7 Witness Ahi-ram, ditto.

8 Witness Paqaha, village manager.

9 Witness Nadbi-Ya'u, chariot driver.

10 Witness Bel-emuranni.

11 Witness Bin-dikiri.

12 Witness Ṭab-šar-Issar. Witness Tabnî, scribe, keeper of the tablet.

13 Month Ab (V), 20th day, eponym year of Mannu-ki-Aššur-le'i.

34 Previous editions: AR 523, NALK 355; → KB 4 (1896) 112ff; 3R 49,1 (copy). 7 *Kiṣir-šarri* "royal corps" is otherwise not attested as a personal name; the determinative m may accordingly be due to a scribal error. As pointed out in NALK, the sign LUGAL looks like IN (coll. I.L. Finkel). 11 The tablet has *šu-a-tú*, as copied by Johns, not *šú-a-tú* (NALK; coll. I.L. Finkel).

35. Restitution of Damages to Šumma-ilani (700)

82-5-22,47

1 [LÚ*.LU]L$^{!}$.MEŠ$^{!}$ ⸢*ša*$^{!}$⸣ *ina*$^{!}$ UGU É
2 ^{m}*šúm-ma*—DINGIR.MEŠ : *iz*$^{!}$*-qa-pu*$^{!}$*-u*$^{!}$*-*⸢*ni*$^{!}$⸣
3 13 MA.NA KUG.UD ^{m}*ki-din*—DINGIR
4 TA*$^{!}$ IGI LÚ*$^{!}$.LUL.MEŠ : *it-ta-ṣa*
5 *a-na* ^{m}*šúm-ma*—DINGIR.MEŠ *it-ti-din*
6 ⸢*šal*$^{!}$⸣*-lu*$^{!}$*-mu*$^{!}$ SUM-*ni*
e.7 IGI ^{m}*ab-da-a*
r.1 IGI ^{md}PA—*ka-šir*
2 LÚ*.*šá*—UGU—*qa*$^{!}$*-(na)-a*$^{!}$*-te*
3 IGI ^{m}*arba-ìl-a-a* KI.MIN
4 IGI ^{m}*se-*ʾ*i-lu*$^{!}$ KI.MIN
5 [IGI ^{md}*š*]*á*$^{!}$*-maš*$^{!}$—ÁG—ZI
6 [IGI ^{m}*x-x*]—SU LÚ*.MU HAL$^{!}$ ANŠE$^{?}$
7 [IGI ^{m}*a-n*]*a*$^{!}$—*aš-šur*—*tak-lak*
8e [ITI.*x*] UD-30-KAM
s.1 *lim-me* ^{m}*me-*⸢*tú*⸣*-*[*nu*]

ADD 112

1 [The thie]ves who were impaled on the house of Šumma-ilani —

3 Kidin-ili took 13 minas of silver from the thieves (and) gave it to Šumma-ilani. It has been paid in full.

7 Witness Abdâ.

r.1 Witness Nabû-kašir, overseer of reeds.

3 Witness Arbailayu, ditto.

4 Witness Se'ilu, ditto.

5 [Witness Š]amaš-ra'im-ketti.

6 [Witness ...]-eriba, cook ...

7 [Witness An]a-Aššur-taklak.

8 [Month ...], 30th day, eponym year of Metu[nu].

36. Šumma-ilani Loans Silver for 50 Percent Interest (695-I-12)

81-2-4,156

1 30 GÍN.MEŠ KUG.UD SAG.DU
2 *ša* ^{m}*šum-ma*—DINGIR.MEŠ-*ni*
3 *ina* IGI ^{m}*aš-šur*—KI-*ia*
4 KUG.UD.MEŠ *a-na* 1/2 GÍN-*šú i-rab-bi*

5 IGI ^{m}*za-ru-ti-i*
6 LÚ*.*mu-kil*—PA.MEŠ *ša* LÚ*.GAL—MU$^{!}$
7 IGI ^{m}URU.*arba-ìl-a-a* LÚ*$^{!}$.3$^{!!}$-*šú*$^{!}$
e.8 IGI ^{m}*ha-šá-na*
9 LÚ*.*mu-tir*—*ṭè-me*
r.1 *ša* LÚ*.GAR
2 IGI ^{m}*pi-ša-ar-mu*
3 LÚ*.*mu-šar-kis* :.$^{!}$
4 IGI ^{m}DINGIR—*qa-tar* LÚ*.⸢*qur*⸣*-bu-tú*$^{!}$
space of 2 lines
5 ITI.BARAG UD-12$^{!}$-KÁM
6e *lim-mu* ^{m}*aš-šur*—EN—PAB

ADD 34

1 30 shekels of silver, capital, belonging to Šumma-ilani, at the disposal of Aššur-isse'a.

4 The silver shall increase by 50 percent per shekel.

5 Witness Zarutî, chariot driver of the chief cook.

7 Witness Arbailayu, 'third man.'

8 Witness Hašanu, intelligence officer of the governor.

r.2 Witness Pišarmu, recruitment officer of ditto.

4 Witness Il-qatar, royal bodyguard.

4 Month Nisan (I), 12th day, eponym year of Aššur-belu-uṣur.

35 Previous editions: AR 235, NALK 356. Collations: Assur 2/5. 2 For *zaqāpu* in the sense "to impale," cf. KAV 1 vii 96 (MA Code) and the other examples cited in CAD Z 53, *zaqāpu* mng. 1d; the normal NA expression for "impaling" was *ana zaqīpi šakānu*, cf. e.g., SAA 1 22:11ff. Impaling thieves at the spot where they broke into a house is prescribed in the Code of Hammurapi (§ 21) (suggestion R.M. Whiting). r.2 Cf. LÚ.*šá*—UGU—*qa-na-a-te* MSL 12 240 v 18 and LÚ.*šá*—UGU—*qa-na-te* ADD 618 r.9. A profession **ša muhhi qāti* is not attested elsewhere. r.6 See coll. Assur 2/5; possibly to be emended to *mutīr ṭēmi* (NALK).

36 Previous editions: AR 264, NALK 357. 6 See coll. 7 Tablet LÚ*.2-*šú*, scribal error (see coll.). r.4 See coll.

37. Šumma-ilani Buys a Vineyard from Il-amar (694-VII-1)

K 346

1 [_ku_]-⸢_um_⸣ NA$_4$.KIŠIB-_šú ṣu-pur-šú_ GAR-_un_
2 [_ṣu_]-_pur_ ^{m}DINGIR—_a-mar_ LÚ*.GAL—_kar-ma-ni_
3 [0] _ša_ URU._ma-ga-nu-ba_
4 EN GIŠ.SAR A.ŠÀ UN.MEŠ SUM-_an_

5 2 GIŠ.SAR.MEŠ _ša til-lit_ É 3 ANŠE A.ŠÀ
6 _ina_ URU.UŠ—_hi-ri-ti_
7 ^{m}_qa-ú-su_ ^{m}_aš-šur_—EN—LAL-_in_
8 LÚ*.NU.GIŠ.SAR ^{m}PAB-_me-e_ LÚ*.⸢ENGAR⸣ MAN$^{!}$
9 3 M[Í.MEŠ] ⸢1⸣ DUMU PAB ⸢7⸣ ZI.MEŠ
10 ⸢_ú_⸣-_piš-m_[_a_ ^{m}_šúm-ma_—DINGIR.ME]Š-_ni_
11 [_ina_] ⸢ŠÀ⸣-_bi_ 25 M[A.NA _x_ KUG.UD]
12 ⸢TA*⸣ IGI ^{m}⸢DINGIR⸣—_a-ma_$^{!}$-[_ra il-qí_]
13 [_ka_]_s-pu_ ⸢_gam_⸣-_mur ta-din_ GI[Š.SAR]. ⸢MEŠ⸣
14 A.ŠÀ UN.MEŠ _šu-a-te za_-⸢_rip_⸣
15 _la-qi-ú tu-a-ru de-e-nu_
16 ⸢DUG$_4$⸣.DUG$_4$ _la-áš-šú man-nu ša ina ur-kiš_
17 _ina ma-te-e_$^{!}$-_me i-zaq-qu-pa_-⸢_ni_⸣
18 ⸢_lu-u_ ^{m}⸣DINGIR—_a-mar lu-u_ ŠEŠ.MEŠ-⸢_šú_⸣
r.1 _lu-u_ ⸢DUMU⸣—PAB.MEŠ-_šú lu-u mám-ma-ni-šú_
2 _ša_ TA*$^{!}$ ^{m}_šúm-ma_—DINGIR.MEŠ-_ni_
3 TA*$^{!}$ DUMU.MEŠ-_šú_ DUMU—DUMU.MEŠ-_šú_
4 ⸢_de_⸣-_e-nu_ DUG$_4$.DUG$_4$ _ub-ta-ʾu-u-ni_
5 [_x_ M]A.NA KUG.UD SUM-_an_ GIŠ.SAR.MEŠ A.ŠÀ
6 [UN.ME]Š _ú-še-eṣ-ṣi_

---

7 [IGI ^{m}_s_]_a-ma-aʾ_ ⸢LÚ*._mu-rib_$^{!}$⸣-[_ba-n_]_u_ [_ša_$^{!}$] ⸢DUMU$^{!}$⸣—MAN$^{!}$
8 [IGI ^{m}EN]—⸢KASKAL⸣—MAN—PAB LÚ*.GUR$^{!}$—UM[UŠ$^{!}$]
9 [IGI ^{m}_x_—NUM]UN—DÙ LÚ*.GAL—⸢_ki-ṣir_⸣
10 ⸢_ša_ GIŠ$^{!}$⸣._ut-tar_.MEŠ
11 IGI ^{m}_mu-še-zib_—DINGIR
12 IGI ^{md}UTU—DINGIR-_a-a_ LÚ*._mu-kil_—⸢PA. MEŠ _ša_$^{!}$ É$^{!}$.GAL$^{!}$⸣
13 IGI ^{m}_ṭu-du-te_ LÚ*.A—SIG
14 _ša_ ^{md}U.GUR—MAŠ
15 IGI ^{md}PA—PAB—AŠ LÚ*.A.BA

16 ITI.DU$_6$$^{!}$ UD-1-KÁM _lim-me_ ^{m}DINGIR—KI-_ia_
17 LÚ*.GAR.KUR URU._dim-maš-qa_

ADD 427

1 [Inst]ead of his seal he impressed his fingernail.

2 [Finger]nail of Il-amar, chief of granaries of Maganuba, owner of the garden, land, and people being sold.

(fingernail impressions)

5 Two vineyards; an estate of 3 hectares of land in the city of Šiddi-hiriti;

7 Qausu; Aššur-belu-taqqin, gardener; Ahi-immê, palace farmer; 3 w[omen]; 1 son; a total of 7 persons —

10 [Šumma-ilan]i has contracted and [bought them fo]r 25 mi[nas of silver] from Il-ama[r].

13 [The mon]ey is paid completely. Those ga[rden]s, land, and people are purchased and acquired. Any revocation, lawsuit, or litigation is void.

16 Whoever in the future, at any time, lodges a complaint, [whether] Il-amar or his brothers, nephews or relatives, and seeks a lawsuit or litigation against Šumma-ilani, his sons or grandsons, shall pay [x mi]nas of silver, and shall redeem the gardens, the land, and the [peopl]e.

---

7 [Witness S]ama', (horse) raiser of the crown prince.

8 [Witness Bel]-Harran-šarru-uṣur, intelligence officer.

9 [Witness ...-zer]u-ibni, cohort commander of large-wheeled chariotry.

11 Witness Mušezib-ili.

12 Witness Šamaš-ila'i, palace chariot driver.

13 Witness Ṭudute, chariot fighter of Nergal-ašared.

15 Witness Nabû-ahu-iddina, scribe.

16 Month Tishri (VII), 1st day, eponym year of Ilu-isse'a, governor of Damascus.

37 Previous editions: AR 186, NALK 358; → KB 4 (1896) 114ff.; 3R 48,4 (copy). Collations: Assur 2/5. 2 The paragogic vowel attached to the name of the seller in no. 38:1 and r.2 implies that the final syllable was stressed and points to West Semitic _Il-āmár_ "God has spoken" (see Zadok West Semites p.82) rather than Akkadian *_Ilu-ammar_ (NALK).

38. Šumma-ilani Buys People from Il-amar (694?)

Bu 91-5-9,84

beginning broken away

1′ [ARAD.M]EŠ$^{!}$-*ni*$^{!}$ *š*[*a*$^{?}$ ^{m}]DINGIR—*a-mar-ra*
2′ [LÚ*.GA]L—*kar-*⸢*ma*⸣-*ni*
3′ [*ú-piš-m*]*a* ^{m}*šum-ma*—⸢DINGIR⸣.MEŠ-*ni*
4′ [*ina* ŠÀ] 1/2$^{!}$ MA.NA KUG.[UD *ina*] *ma-né-*⸢*e*⸣ *ša* MAN
5′ [*il-q*]*i*$^{!}$ *kas-pu* [*g*]*a-mur* SUM-*ni*
6′ [UN.MEŠ] *šú-a-tú z*[*ar-p*]*u la-qi-u*
7′ [*tu*]-⸢*a*⸣-*ru d*[*e*]-⸢*e*⸣-*nu* DUG$_{4}$.D[UG$_{4}$] *la-áš-šú*
r.1 [*man-nu š*]*a ina ur-*[*k*]*iš ina ma-te-ma*
2 [*i-z*]*a*$^{!}$-*qu-pa-ni lu-u* ^{m}DINGIR—*a-ma*[*r*$^{!}$]-*ra*
3 [*lu-u* D]UMU.MEŠ-*šú lu-u* DUMU—DUMU.MEŠ-*šú lu-u* PAB.MEŠ-*šú*
4 [*lu-u* DUMU—PA]B.MEŠ-*šú lu-u* EN—*il-ki-šú*
5 [*ša de-e-n*]*u* DUG$_{4}$.DUG$_{4}$ TA* ^{m}*šum-ma*—DINGIR.MEŠ-[*n*]*i*
6 [*ù* DUMU.M]EŠ-*šú ù* DUMU—DUMU.MEŠ-*šú*
7 [*ù* PAB.MEŠ-*šú*] ⸢*ù*⸣ DUMU—PAB.MEŠ-*šú ub-ta-u-ni*
8 [*x* MA.NA KUG.UD *x* MA].NA ⸢KUG⸣.GI *sak-r*[*u*]

rest broken away

ADD 508

(Beginning destroyed)

1 [servan]ts of Il-amara, [ch]ief of granaries —

3 Šumma-ilani [has contracted and boug]ht [them for] 1/2 mina of sil[ver by] the mina of the king.

5 The money is paid [co]mpletely. Those [people] are p[urch]ased and acquired. [Any] revocation, la[ws]uit, or litigat[ion] is void.

r.1 [Whoever] in the future, at any time, [lodges] a complaint, whether Il-amara or his sons, grandsons, brothers or [neph]ews, or his labour-duty superior,

5 [and] seeks [a lawsui]t or litigation against Šumma-ilani, his [sons], grandsons, [brothers] and nephews, [shall pay x minas of refined silver and x mi]nas of pure gold.

(Rest destroyed)

39. Šumma-ilani Buys Numerous Slaves from Bel-Harran-isse'a (694-I)

83-1-18,343

beginning broken away

1′ PAB [*x* ZI.MEŠ ARAD.MEŠ *šá* ^{m}EN—KASKAL—KI-*ia*]
2′ *ú-pi*[*š-ma* ^{m}BE-*ma*—DINGIR.MEŠ]
3′ *ina* ŠÀ 18 MA.⸢NA⸣ [KUG.UD *ina* 1 MA.NA]
4′ *ša* URU.*gar-ga-*⸢*mis*⸣ [TA* IGI ^{m}EN—KASKAL—KI-*ia*]
5′ TI-[*qí*] *kas-pu gam-mur ta-ad-*[*din* UN. MEŠ *šu-a-te*]
6′ *zar-pu laq-*⸢*qí*⸣-*u tu-*[*a-ru de-e-nu*]
7′ DUG$_{4}$.DUG$_{4}$ *la-áš-šú m*[*an*]-⸢*nu*⸣ *šá ina u*[*r-kiš*]
8′ *ina ma-te-ma i-zaq-qup-an-n*[*i lu-u* ^{m}EN—KASKAL—KI-*ia*]
9′ *lu-u* DUMU.MEŠ-*šú lu-u* DUMU—DU[MU. MEŠ-*šú*]
10′ *lu-u* PAB.MEŠ-*šú lu-u mám-ma-nu-šú* [*ša de-e-nu*]
11′ DUG$_{4}$.DUG$_{4}$ TA* ^{m}BE-*ma*—DINGIR.MEŠ DU[MU. MEŠ-*šú*]

ADD 239

(Beginning destroyed)

1 a total [of x persons belonging to Bel-Harran-isse'a] —

2 [Šumma-ilani] has cont[racted and] bou[ght them from Bel-Harran-isse'a] for 18 minas of [silver by the mina] of Carchemish.

5 The money is pa[id] completely. [Those people] are purchased and acquired. Any rev[ocation, lawsuit], or litigation is void.

7 Whoever in the f[uture], at any time, lodges a complai[nt, whether Bel-Harran-isse'a] or his sons, grand[sons], brothers or relatives, and se[eks a lawsuit] or litigation against Šumma-ilani, [his] so[ns] and grandsons, shall pay 20 minas of silver, and shall return the money [tenfold] to its owners. He

38 Previous editions: AR 610, NALK 359. 1, 4f, r.2 See coll.
39 Previous editions: AR 554, NALK 362. → no. 40.

12′ DUMU—DUMU.MEŠ-*šú ub-ta-ʾu-[u-ni]*
13′ ⸢20⸣ MA.NA KUG.UD SUM-*an kas-pu a-[na* 10.MEŠ-*te]*
14′ *a-na* EN.MEŠ-*šú* GUR-*ra ina de-e-n[i-šú]*
15′ [D]UG$_4$.DUG$_4$-*ma la i-laq-⸢qí⸣*

shall contest in [his] laws[uit] and not succeed.

16′ [IG]I ^{m}*sa-ma-aʾ* LÚ.*mu-ra-ba-nu šá* A—MAN
17′ [IG]I $^{m⸢d}$PA—*hu-us*⸣-*sa-an-ni* LÚ.*mu*-DIB!—PA.MEŠ
18′ [I]G[I] ^{m}[*x x x x*] LÚ.A.BA
19′ [IGI ^{m}*x x x x* L]Ú.A.BA
20′ [IGI ^{m}*x x x x*] LÚ.A.BA
21′ [IGI ^{m}*x x x x* LÚ.A].BA
r.1 IGI ^{m}[*x x x x x*]
2 IGI ^{m}*a-[ti-in-ni* LÚ.A.B]A
3 IGI ^{m}DU[MU!—*x x* LÚ.A].BA
4 IGI ^{m}[*x x x x x x x*]
5 IGI ^{m}[EN—PAB.MEŠ-*šú*] ⸢LÚ⸣.[*mu*-DIB—PA.MEŠ]
6 *ša* ⸢LÚ⸣.GA[L]—KA.⸢KÉŠ⸣
7 IGI ^{m}EN—ZU LÚ.ARAD [*x x x x*]
8 IGI ^{m}*za-a-zi-i* LÚ.[*mu*-DIB—PA.MEŠ]
9 *ša* LÚ.[KAŠ.LUL]
space of 4 lines
10 ITI.BARAG *lim-[mu* ^{m}DINGIR—KI-*ia* LÚ.GAR.KUR]
11 KUR.*d[im*!*-maš-qa]*

16 [Witne]ss Sama', (horse) raiser of the crown prince.
17 [Witne]ss Nabû-hussanni, chariot driver.
18 [Witness NN], scribe.
19 [Witness NN, s]cribe.
20 [Witness NN], scribe.
21 [Witness NN, sc]ribe.
r.1 Witness [NN, ...]
2 Witness A[tinni, scrib]e.
3 Witness M[ar-..., sc]ribe.
4 Witness [NN, ...].
5 Witness [Bel-ahhešu, chariot driver] of the cohort [commander].
7 Witness Bel-le'i, servant of [...].
8 Witness Zazî, [chariot driver] of the [cupbearer].
10 Month Nisan (I), epo[nym year of Ilu-isse'a, governor of] D[amascus].

40. Šumma-ilani Buys 15 Slaves from Bel-Harran-isse'a (693-I)

82-3-23,134

1 [*ku-um* NA$_4$.KIŠIB-*š]ú ṣu-pur-šú iš-kun*
2 [*ṣu-pur* ^{m}EN—KASKAL—K]I-*ia* EN UN.MEŠ SUM-*ni*

---

3 [^{md}*x—ú-ṣa]l-la* 5 ZI.MEŠ
4 [^{m}*x x x]x-mu* 6 ZI.MEŠ
5 [^{m}*x x x x*] 4 ZI.MEŠ
6 PAB ⸢15!⸣ [ZI.MEŠ AR]AD.MEŠ *ša* ^{m}EN—KAS[KAL—K]I-[*i*]*a*
7 *ú-pi[š-ma]* ^{m}*šum-ma*—DI[NGIR].ME[Š!]
8 LÚ*.*mu-kil*—⸢PA⸣.[M]EŠ! [*ina* ŠÀ *x* MA.NA KUG.UD]
9 *ina* MA.NA *ša*! URU.[*gar-ga-mis*]
10 TA* IGI ^{m}EN—KASKAL—KI-*i[a il-qi]*

ADD 238

1 [Instead of his seal] he impressed his fingernail.
2 [Fingernail of Bel-Harran-is]se'a, owner of the people being sold.

(fingernail impressions)

---

3 [...-uṣa]lla — 5 persons;
4 [......]mu — 6 persons;
5 [......] — 4 persons;
6 in all 15 [persons], servants of Bel-Ha[rran-isse']a —
7 Šumma-il[ani], chariot driver, has con[tracted and bought them from Bel-Harran-isse'[a for x minas of silver] by the mina of [Carchemish].

18ff These lines seem to be largely restorable from no. 40 r.6ff. It should be noted, however, that the two texts are not duplicates, and that the witness lists of nos. 40 and 41, written in the same month and year, differ considerably. Note further that no. 40 provides no restoration for r.1, and that the name in r.3 cannot be restored as Abdaʾ, as comparison with no. 40 would suggest. r.3 See coll. r.11 See coll. The second, broken sign is emphatically not *ṣ[i*.
40 Previous editions: AR 201, NALK 361. Collations: Assur 2/5. → no. 39.

11 *kas-pu ga-am-mur ta-*[*ad-din*]
12 UN.MEŠ *za-ar-pu la-*[*qi-u*]
13 *tu-a-ru de-e-nu* DUG$_4$.DUG$_4$ *la-áš-šú*
14 *man-nu ša ina ur-kiš ina mat-e-ma*
15 *i-za-qu-pa-an-ni*
16 *lu-u* ^{m}EN—KASKAL—KI-*ia lu-u* DUMU. MEŠ-*šú*
17 *lu-u* DUMU—DUMU.MEŠ-*šú lu-u* ŠEŠ.MEŠ-*šú*
18 *lu-u mám-ma-nu-šu*
19 *ša de-e-nu* DUG$_4$.DUG$_4$ TA* ^{m}*šum-ma*—DINGIR.MEŠ
20e 0$^{!}$ DUMU.MEŠ-*šú ù* DUMU—DUMU$^{!}$.MEŠ-*šú*
21e *ub-ta-ʾu-u-*[*ni*]
r.1 [*x* MA].⌈NA⌉ KUG.UD *i-dan*
2 [*kas-pu*] ⌈*a*⌉*-na* 10.MEŠ *a-na* EN.MEŠ-*šú ú-ta-ra*
3 [*ina l*]*a de-ni-šú* DUG$_4$.DUG$_4$-*ma la i-laq-qi*

---

4 [IG]I ^{m}*sa-ma-aʾ* LÚ*.*mu-ra-ba-nu ša* DUMU—MAN
5 IGI ^{md}PA—*hu-sa-an-ni* LÚ*.*mu*-DIB—PA. MEŠ
6 IGI ^{m}*hal-ú-a* LÚ*.A.BA
7 IGI ^{m}PAB—ZALÁG LÚ*.A.BA
8 IGI ^{m}*ṣu-ṣa-a* LÚ*.A.BA
9 IGI ^{m}*da*$^{!}$*-lu*$^{!}$*-u-a* LÚ*.A.ZU$^{!}$
10 IGI ^{m}*a-ti-in-ni* LÚ*.A.BA
11 IGI ^{m}*ab-da-aʾ* LÚ*.A.BA
12 IGI ^{m}*pa-qa-*[*ha*] LÚ*.GAL—URU.MEŠ
13 IGI ^{m}EN—PAB.[MEŠ-*šú*] LÚ*.*mu*-D[IB—P]A.M[EŠ]
14 [*š*]*a*$^{!}$ LÚ*$^{!}$.G[AL$^{!}$]—K[A$^{!}$].KÉŠ
15 IGI ^{m}⌈*za*⌉*-a*$^{!}$*-zi-i* [LÚ*.*m*]*u*-DIB—P[A.MEŠ]
16 *ša* LÚ*.KA[Š.LUL]
17 IGI ^{m}EN—ZU LÚ*.ARAD [*x x x x x*]

18 ITI.BARAG *lim-mu* ^{m}SUM—PAB.MEŠ LÚ*.G[AR$^{!}$.KUR URU.BÀD—MAN—GIN]
19 IGI ^{m}DÙG—IM—^{d}AG LÚ*.A.BA *ṣa-bit* [IM]

[11] The money is pa[id] completely. The people are purchased and acq[uired]. Any revocation, lawsuit, or litigation [is void].

[14] Whoever in the future, at any time, lodges a complaint, whether Bel-Harran-isse'a or his sons, grandsons, brothers or relatives, and se[eks] a lawsuit or litigation against Šumma-ilani, his sons and grandsons, shall pay [x mi]nas of silver, and shall return [the money] tenfold to its owners. He shall contest [in] his non-lawsuit and not succeed.

[r.4] [Witne]ss Sama', (horse) raiser of the crown prince.

[5] [Witne]ss Nabû-hussanni, chariot driver.

[6] [Witne]ss Halua, scribe.

[7] [Witness] Ahi-nuri, scribe.

[8] [Witne]ss Ṣuṣâ, scribe.

[9] [Witne]ss Daluwa, physician.

[10] [Witne]ss Atinni, scribe.

[11] [Witne]ss Abda', scribe.

[12] Witness Paqa[ha], village manager.

[13] Witness Bel-ahhe[šu], chariot driver of the coh[ort com]mander.

[15] [Witness Z]azî, [ch]ariot driver [of] the cup[bearer].

[17] Witness Bel-le'i, servant of [...].

[18] Month Nisan (I), eponym year of Iddin-ahhe, governor of [Dur-Šarruken].

[19] [Witn]ess Ṭab-šar-Nabû, scribe, keeper of the [tablet].

41. Šumma-ilani Buys 7 Slaves from Bel-Harran-isse'a (693-I)

81-7-27,27

1 *ku-um* NA$_4$.KIŠI[B-*šú ṣu-pur-šú iš-kun*]
2 *ṣu-pur* ^{m}EN—K[ASKAL—KI-*ia* EN UN.MEŠ]
3 *ta-ad-*[*da-ni*]

ADD 240

[1] Instead of [his] se[al he impressed his fingernail].

[2] Fingernail of Bel-[Harran-isse'a, owner of the people] being so[ld].

(fingernail impressions)

---

41 Previous editions: AR 59, NALK 360. Collations: Assur 2/5.

4 ^{m}DINGIR—*na-tan* [*x x x x x*]
5 ^{m}*a-du-ni—ṭu-*[*ri x x x x x*]
6 3 DUMU.MEŠ-*šú* [*x x x x x*]
7 PAB 7 ZI.MEŠ [ARAD.MEŠ *ša* ^{m}EN—KASKAL—KI-*ia*]
8 *ú-piš-ma* [^{m}*šum-ma*—DINGIR.MEŠ]
9 LÚ*.*mu-kil*—KUŠ.PA.MEŠ [*ina* ŠÀ *x* MA.NA KUG.UD]
10 ⸢*ina*⸣⸣ MA.NA *ša* UR[U.*gar-ga-mis*]
11 TA* IGI ^{m}EN—[KASKAL—KI-*ia*]
12 *il-qi ka*[*s-pu gam-mur*]
13 *ta-ad-din* [UN.MEŠ *za-ar-pu*]
14 *la-*⸢*qi*⸣*-*[*u*]
e.15 *tu-a-ru* [*de-e-nu* DUG$_4$.DUG$_4$ *la-áš-šú*!]
r.1 [*man-n*]*u*! *š*[*a*! *i-za-qu-pa-an-ni*]
2 [*x* MA].NA! K[UG!.UD *i-dan*]
3 *k*[*as-pu*] *a-na* 10.MEŠ ⸢*a-na*⸣ EN-*šú* [*ú-ta-ra*]
4 *ina* [*de-n*]*i-šú* DUG$_4$.DUG$_4$-*ma* [*la i-laq-qi*]

---

5 IGI ^{m}*s*[*a-m*]*a-a*ʾ LÚ*.*mu-r*[*a-ba-nu*]
6 *ša* ^{md}U.GUR—MU!—[*x*]
7 IGI ^{m}*za-zi-i* LÚ*.*mu-k*[*il*—KUŠ.PA.MEŠ]
8 *ša* LÚ*.KAŠ.LU[L]
9 IGI ^{md}UTU—*še-zib* LÚ*.⸢3⸣.[U$_5$ *x x x x*]
10 IGI ^{m}EN—PAB.MEŠ-*šú* L[Ú.*mu-kil*—KUŠ.PA.MEŠ]
11 *ša* LÚ*.GAL—[*ki-ṣir*]
12 IGI ^{m}*man-nu—ki-*[*x x x*]
13 IGI ^{m}*pa-*[*q*]*a*!-⸢*ha*⸣⸣ [LÚ.GAL—URU.MEŠ]
14 IGI ^{m}[*x x*] ⸢*x x*⸣ [*x x x x*]
15 IGI ^{m}[*x x x x*] ⸢*x*⸣ [*x*]

16 ITI.BARAG [UD-*x*-KAM]
17 *lim-mu* ^{m}SUM-[*na*—PAB.MEŠ]
18 LÚ*.GAR.KUR K[UR!.BÀD—MAN—GIN]
19e IGI ^{m}DÙG—IM—^{d}⸢AG⸣
20e LÚ*.A.BA *ṣa-bit* ⸢IM⸣

4 Il-natan [......], Aduni-ṭu[ri ......], his 3 sons, [......], a total of 7 persons, [servants of Bel-Harran-isse'a] —

8 [Šumma-ilani], chariot driver, has contracted and bought them from Bel-[Harran-isse'a for x minas of silver] by the mina of [Carchemish].

12 The mo[ney] is paid [completely. The people are purchased] and acquired. Any revocation, [lawsuit, or litigation is void].

r.1 [Whoev]er [lodges a complaint shall pay x min]as of [silver. He shall return] the mo[ney] tenfold to its owner. He shall contest in his law[suit and not succeed].

---

5 Witness Sama', (horse) raiser of Nergal-šumu-[...].

7 Witness Zazî, char[iot driver] of the cup-bearer.

9 Witness Šamaš-šezib, 'third [man' of ...].

10 Witness Bel-ahhešu, [chariot driver] of the cohort [commander].

12 Witness Mannu-ki-[...].

13 Witness Paqaha, [village manager].

14 Witness [NN].

15 Witness [NN].

16 Month Nisan (I), [...th day], eponym year of Iddin-[ahhe], governor of [Dur-Šarruken].

19 Witness Ṭab-šar-Nabû, scribe, keeper of the tablet.

42. Šumma-ilani Buys a House (692-II-10)

Rm 156

1 ⸢*ku*⸣*-um* NA$_4$.KIŠIB-*šú ṣu-pur-šú* GAR-*un*
2 ⸢*ṣu-pur*⸣ ^{m}*du-si-i* EN É SUM-*ni*

---

3 É *ep-šú a-di* GIŠ.ÙR.MEŠ-*šú*
4 *a-di* GIŠ.IG.MEŠ-*šú* É—NÁ TÙR-*šú*

ADD 326

1 Instead of his seal he impressed his fingernail.

2 Fingernail of Dusî, owner of the house being sold.

(space for seal impressions)

---

3 A built house with its beams and doors, a sleeping room, its yard, its bathroom, ser-

42 Previous editions: AR 173, NALK 373; → Postgate FNALD 5. 5 *Pace* NALK, the sign before *šá* is certainly 2/3, not PÚ (see coll.) r.3 See coll. r.13 LÚ.S[IP]A appears more likely than LÚ.GI[Š.GIGI]R (NALK); see coll. r.21 There is a clear space between the signs GAR and KUR, see coll.

5 É—TU$_5$-*šú* É—2-*e* 2/3$^{!}$ *šá* É *dan-ni*
6 É NIM É.*a-bu-sa-te* É—ŠU
7 KI.MAH *ina* ŠÀ-*bi ú-piš-ma*
8 ^{m}BE-*ma*—DINGIR.MEŠ-*ni* LÚ.*mu-kil*—KUŠ.PA.MEŠ
9 *ša* LÚ.*šá*—UGU—É-*a-ni*
10 *ina* ŠÀ 3 MA.NA KUG.UD *ina šá* LUGAL TI-*qí*$^{!}$
11 *kas-pu gam-mur ta-ad-din*
12 É *šu-a-tú za-rip laq-qí*
13 *tu-a-ru de-e-nu* DUG$_4$.DUG$_4$
14 [*l*]*a-áš-šú man-nu šá ina ur-kiš*
15 ⸢*ù*⸣ *ma-te-e*$^{!}$-*ma i-zaq-qup-an-ni*
16 [G]IL-*ú-ni lu-u* ^{m}*du-si-i*$^{!}$
17 [*l*]*u-u* DUMU.MEŠ-*šú lu-u* PAB.MEŠ-*šú*
18 *lu-u mám-ma-nu-šú ša* TA* ^{m}*šum-ma*—DINGIR.M[EŠ]-*ni*
19 DUMU.MEŠ-⸢*šú*⸣ *de-e-nu* DUG$_4$.DUG$_4$
20 *ub-*[*ta*]-⸢ʾ*u*⸣-*u-ni* MA.NA 5 MA.NA KUG.UD
21 LUH-[*u x* MA.NA KUG.G]I *sak-ru*
22 *ina bur-*[*ki* ^{d}*x x x x x*] ⸢GAR⸣-*an*
r.1 ⸢2⸣ ANŠE.KUR.RA.MEŠ BABBAR.MEŠ [*ina* GÌR.2 ^{d}*aš-šur*]
2 *i-rak-kas* 4 ANŠE.*har-bak-k*[*an-ni*]
3 *ina* GÌR.2 ^{d}MAŠ.MAŠ *ú-šer*$^{!}$-*ra*[*b*]
4 ⸢1⸣ GÚ.UN AN.NA *a-na* LÚ.NAM UR[U-*šú*]
5 [*i*]*d-dan kas-pu a-na* 10.MEŠ-*te*
6 *a-na* EN.MEŠ-*šú* GUR-*ra*
7 ⸢*ina de*⸣-*ni-šú* DUG$_4$.DUG$_4$-*ma la i*$^{!}$-*laq-qí*$^{!}$

vants' quarters, two thirds of the main building, an upper floor, a storehouse, and a wing with a tomb in it —

8 Šumma-ilani, chariot driver of the chamberlain, has contracted and bought it for 3 minas of silver by the (mina) of the king.

11 The money is paid completely. That house is purchased and acquired. Any revocation, lawsuit, or litigation is void.

14 Whoever, at any time and in the future, lodges a complaint or [bre]aks the contract, whether Dusî [o]r his sons, brothers or relatives, who s[ee]ks a lawsuit or litigation against Šumma-ilani and his sons,

20 shall place a mina and 5 minas of refin[ed] silver [and x minas of] pure [gol]d in the la[p of the god ... residing in ...], and shall tie two white horses [to the feet of Aššur] and bring four *harbakannu* horses to the feet of Nergal. He shall pay one talent of tin to the governor of [his] ci[ty], and shall return the money tenfold to its owners. He shall contest in his lawsuit and not succeed.

---

8 IGI ^{m}ARAD-*a-a* LÚ.UŠ.BAR—GÙN
9 IGI ^{m}DINGIR—DÙ ŠEŠ-*šú šá* LÚ.*ha-za-an-nu*
10 IGI ^{m}GIN-*u-a* URU.ŠÀ—URU-*a-a*
11 IGI ^{m}EN—DÙ ARAD *šá* [L]Ú.*šá*—U[G]U—É-*a-ni*
12 IGI ^{m}*šúm-ma*—DINGIR LÚ.DAM.QAR
13 IGI ^{m}*bi-bi-e* LÚ.S[IP]A$^{?}$ GAL
14 IGI ^{m}⸢SIG$_5$⸣—INIM.MEŠ—^{d}15 LÚ.:.
15 [IGI] ⸢^{m}⸣*qa-lu-un-zu* LÚ.:.
16 I[G]I ^{m}*aš-šur*—*še-zib-an-ni* LÚ.DIB—KUŠ.PA.MEŠ
17 IGI ^{md}PA—EN—MU.MEŠ-*te* LÚ.A.BA
18 IGI ^{m}*kit-ti*—DINGIR.MEŠ-*ni* LÚ.3-*šú*
19 IGI ^{m}URU.*arba-ìl-a-*⸢*a*⸣ LÚ.DIB—KUŠ.PA.MEŠ
space of one line

20 ITI.GUD UD-10-KÁM *lim-*⸢*mu*⸣ [^{m}*za-za-a-a*]
21 LÚ.GAR.KUR URU.*ár-p*[*ad-da*]

r.8 Witness Urdaya, weaver of multicoloured trim.

9 Witness Ilu-ibni, brother of the mayor.

10 Witness Kenu'a, from the Inner City.

11 Witness Bel-ibni, servant of the chamberlain.

12 Witness Šumma-ili, merchant.

13 Witness Bibê, chief *shepherd*.

14 Witness Danqu-dibbi-Issar, ditto.

15 Witness Qalunzu, ditto.

16 Witness Aššur-šezibanni, chariot driver.

17 Witness Nabû-bel-šumati, scribe.

18 Witness Ketti-ilani, 'third man.'

19 Witness Arbailayu, chariot driver.

20 Month Iyyar (II), 10th day, eponym year of [Zazaya], governor of Arp[ad].

43. Šumma-ilani Loans Three Minas of Silver (684-I-10)

K 337

1 3$^{!}$ MA.NA 10 GÍN KUG.U[D]
2 *ša* ^{m}*šum-mu*$^{!}$—DINGIR.MEŠ-*ni*
3 *ina* IGI ^{m}EN—SAG.KAL
4 *a-na* 4-*tú-šú i-rab-b*[*i*]
5 IGI ^{md}30—NUMUN—DÙ 3-*šú*
6 IGI ^{md}PA—PAB—PAB LÚ*.*qur-bu-ti*
7 IGI ^{m}*me-i-su* LÚ*.A.BA
8 IGI ^{m}*mil-ka-a-a*
9 IGI ^{md}PA—ZU-*a-ni* 3-*šú*

10 ITI.BARAG UD-10-KÁM
11 *lim-me* ^{m}*man-za-ár-né-e*

ADD 19

1 3 minas and 10 shekels of sil[ver] belonging to Šumma-ilani, at the disposal of Bel-ašared.
4 It shall increase by a fourth.
5 Witness Sin-zeru-ibni, 'third man.'
6 Witness Nabû-ahu-uṣur, royal bodyguard.
7 Witness Misu, scribe.
8 Witness Milkaya.
9 Witness Nabû-le'ani, 'third man.'
10 Month Nisan (I), 10th day, eponym year of Manzarnê.

44. Envelope of the Preceding Text (684)

K 1429

1 [NA$_4$].KIŠIB ^{m}EN—SAG.KAL 3 MA.NA 10 GÍN 0$^{!}$ KUG.UD SAG.DU
2 [*š*]*a* ^{m}*šum-mu*$^{!}$—DINGIR.MEŠ-*ni*

---

3 *ina* IGI ^{m}EN—MAŠ$^{!}$ *a-na pu-u-hi it-ti-ši a-na* 4-[*t*]*ú-šú*
4 *i-rab-bi* IGI ^{md}30—NUMUN—DÙ LÚ.3.U$_5$
5 IGI ^{md}PA—PAB—PAB LÚ.*qur*-ZAG IGI ^{m}*me-i-su* LÚ.A.BA
6 IGI ^{m}*mil-ka-a-a* IGI ^{md}PA—ZU-*a-ni*
7 IGI ^{m}*ia-a*ʾ-*la-a*
Rev. about 8 lines uninscribed

1 [ITI.BARAG UD-10-KÁ]M *lim-me*
2 [^{m}*man-za-ár*]-*né-e*

ADD 20

1 [Se]al of Bel-ašared. 3 minas and 10 shekels of silver, capital,

---

(blank seal space)

---

3 [bel]onging to Šummu-ilani, at the disposal of Bel-ašared. He has taken it as a loan. It shall increase by a fourth.
4 Witness Sin-zeru-ibni, 'third man.'
5 Witness Nabû-ahu-uṣur, royal bodyguard. Witness Misu, scribe.
6 Witness Milkaya. Witness Nabû-le'ani.
7 Witness Ya'ilâ.
r.1 [Month Nisan (I), 10th day], eponym year of [Manzar]nê.

---

45. Šumma-ilani Buys a Maid (682)

83-1-18,344

1 [NA$_4$.KIŠI]B ⌜^{m}EN—DÙ$^{!}$⌝
2 EN MÍ SUM-[*ni*]

ADD 222

1 [Sea]l of Bel-[ibni], owner of the woman being sol[d].

(stamp seal impressions)

43 Tablet. Previous editions: AR 250, NALK 365; → KB 4 (1896) 118f; 3R 47,7 (copy).
44 Envelope. Previous editions: AR 282, NALK 366; → KB 4 (1896) 118ff. Collations: Assur 2/5.
45 Previous editions: AR 500, NALK 367. 1, r.1 See coll. r.5 See coll. The month name is entirely gone.

3 MÍ.*ú-qu-pu-tú* GEMÉ-⸢*šú*⸣
4 *ša* ^{m}EN—DÙ$^{!}$ *ú-piš-ma*
5 ^{m}*šum-*⸢*ma*⸣—DINGIR.MEŠ-*ni*
6 *ina* ŠÀ 1 MA.NA KUG.UD *ša gar-*⸢*gar*⸣*-mis*
7 *il-qi kas-pu gam-mur*
8 [*ta-din* M]Í *šu-a-t*[*e*]
rest broken away

r.1 IGI ⸢^{m}*ha*$^{!}$⸣*-x*[*x x x*]
2 IGI ^{m}*tak-ku-*[*lu*]
3 IGI ^{md}PA—KÀD-*an-*⸢*ni*$^{!}$⸣
4 IGI ^{md}PA—⸢BÀD⸣—PAB

5 LÚ$^{!}$.A$^{!}$.BA$^{!}$ ⸢ITI⸣.[*x*] UD-25-KAM$^{?}$
6 *lim-mu* ^{m}⸢^{d}PA⸣—MAN—PAB
7 GAR.KUR URU.*mar-ha*$^{!}$*-si*

[3] Uquputu, maid of Bel-ibni —
[5] Šumma-ilani has contracted and bought her for one mina of silver (by the mina) of Carchemish.
[7] The money [is paid] completely. That [wom]an [is purchased and acquired].
(Break)
[r.1] Witness Ha[...].
[2] Witness Takku[lu].
[3] Witness Nabû-kuṣuranni.
[4] Witness Nabû-duru-uṣur, scribe.
[5] Month [...], 25th day, eponym year of Nabû-šarru-uṣur, governor of Marqasa.

46. Note of 1,200 Litres of Oil Owed to Šumma-ilani (681-V-21)

K 288

1 NA$_{4}$.KIŠIB ^{m}*aš-šur*—EN—PAB LÚ.GAL—É
2 *ša* URU.*gar-ga-mis* 6 ANŠE Ì.MEŠ *hal-ṣu*
3 *ina* GIŠ.BÁN *šá* 10 *qa* 1 *qa* URUDU.MEŠ *šá*
4 ^{m}*šum-ma*—DINGIR.MEŠ-*ni ina* IGI-*šú*

5 *ina* ITI.ZÍZ Ì.MEŠ SUM-*an šum-ma la* SUM-*ni*
6 *a-na mit-har i-rab-bi*
7 ITI.NE UD-21-KÁM *lim-me* ^{md}PA—PAB. MEŠ—APIN-*eš*
8 *ša* URU.*sa-ma-al-la*

blank space of 2 lines
r.1 IGI ^{md}EN—MAN—DÙ LÚ.3-*šú* É.GAL
2 IGI ^{md}EN—PAB—PAB LÚ.GAL—*ki-ṣir*
3 0! IGI ^{m}PAB—ZALÁG LÚ.:.
4 IGI ^{m}NUMUN—ZI—GIŠ
5 IGI ^{md}*kù*$^{!}$-KÁ—*sa-pi*

blank space of 3 lines

ADD 127

[1] Seal of Aššur-belu-uṣur, the major-domo of Carchemish.
[2] Six homers (c. 1,200 litres) of pressed oil by the copper seah of 10 'litres,' belonging to Šumma-ilani, at his disposal.
[5] He shall give the oil in the month of Shebat (XI). If he does not, it shall increase by an equal amount.
[7] Month Ab (V), 21st day, eponym year of Nabû-ahu-ereš of Sam'al.

[r.1] Witness Bel-šarru-ibni, 'third man' of the palace.
[2] Witness Bel-ahu-uṣur, cohort commander.
[3] Witness Ahi-nuri, ditto.
[4] Witness Zer-ketti-lešir.
[5] Witness Kubabu-sapi.

47. Note of Silver Owed to Šumma-ilani (681-VII-4)

83-1-18,365

1 [*x x x x x x x x x x*]
2 *ša* ^{m}⸢*šúm-mu*—DINGIR.MEŠ-*ni*⸣
3 *ina* IGI ^{m}URU.NINA-*a-*⸢*a*⸣

ADD 30

[1] [......] belonging to Šum[ma]-ilani, at the disposal of Ninuayu.

46 Previous editions: AR 314, NALK 368. [3] GIŠ.BÁN *šá* 10 *qa* 1 *qa* URUDU.MEŠ sic (collated). One Assyrian 'litre' (*qû*) measured about two liters, in contrast to the Babylonian *qû* of about 0.9 litre. [r.3] See ADD III p. 210.
47 Previous editions: AR 254, NALK 377. Collations: Assur 2/5. [4] See ADD III p.58.

4 2 GÍN KUG.UD *ša* ITI 0! *ru-⸢bé⸣-e*

5 ITI.DUL UD-4-KAM
e.6 *lim-⸢mu⸣* ^{md}PA—PAB—APIN-*eš*
7 IGI ^{m}*ha-ni-na-ia*
r.1 IGI ^{m}*il-lu-uk-nu*
2 IGI ^{m}*hu-⸢ha!⸣-ba!-šu*
3 IGI ^{m}*mah-si—ia-a-u*
4 IGI ^{m}⸢*am*⸣-*ma-a*

4 The interest is 2 shekels of silver per month.

5 Month Tishri (VII), 4th day, eponym year of Nabû-ahu-ereš.

7 Witness Haninaya.

r.1 Witness Illuknu.

2 Witness Huhabašu.

3 Witness Mahsi-Ia'u.

4 Witness Ammâ.

48. Šumma-ilani Buys a Maid (680)

Sm 1678 — ADD 212

1 [NA$_4$.KIŠI]B ^{md}PA—NUMU[N!—AŠ]
2 [EN M]Í *ta-da-⸢a!⸣-[ni]*

1 [Sea]l of Nabû-ze[ru-iddina, owner of the wom]an being sol[d].

(stamp seal impressions)

---

3 MÍ.AN-*e—ta-⸢ba⸣-ni* GEM[É-*šú*]
4 *ša* ^{md}PA—[NUM]UN—AŠ
5 *ú-piš-m[a* ^{m}*šúm-m]a*—DINGIR.ME[Š]
6 [*ina* ŠÀ *x* MA.NA KUG.UD]

7 [*i*]*l!-qi* [*kas-pu gam-mur ta-din*]
8 MÍ *šu-a-te za-r*[*i!-ip*]
9 *laq-qi! tu-a-⸢ru⸣ d*[*e-e-nu*]
10 DUG$_4$.DUG$_4$ *la-áš-*[*šu*]
11 [*man*]*-nu ša ina ur-k*[*iš*]
12 [*ina*] *ma-te-ma i-za-q*[*u*]*-pa-a-*[*ni*]
13 [*d*]*e-e-nu* DUG$_4$.⸢DUG$_4$⸣
14 [T]A! ^{m}*šum-ma*—DINGIR.MEŠ
15 [T]A! DUMU.⸢MEŠ⸣-*šú* TA*! DUMU—DU[MU.MEŠ-*šú*]
16 [TA* PA]B.MEŠ-*šú* TA*! DUMU!—P[AB!.MEŠ-*šú*]
r.1 [*ša d*]*e-e-nu* DUG$_4$.DUG$_4$
2 [*ub*]*-ta-ʾu-ni*
3 [*kas*]*-pu ina* 10.MEŠ *ina* EN.MEŠ-*š*[*ú*]
4 ⸢*ú!*⸣-GUR *ina de-e-ni-šú*
5 [D]UG$_4$.DUG$_4$-*ma la* (*i*)*-laq-qi*
6 [*ṣib*]*-tú be-en-n*[*u!*] ⸢*ina!*⸣ 1-*me* UD-*me*
7 [*s*]*a!-ar-⸢tú⸣* [*ina!*] *kal* UD-*m*[*e*]

3 Šamê-tabani, maid of Nabû-[ze]ru-iddina —

5 [Šumma]-ilani, has contracted and bought her [for x minas of silver].

7 [The money is paid completely]. That woman is purc[hased] and acquired. Any revocation, law[suit], or litigation is vo[id].

11 [Who]ever in the fut[ure, at] any time, lodges a compla[int] and seeks a lawsuit or litigation [aga]inst Šumma-ilani, his sons, grand[sons, broth]ers and neph[ews,

r.1 (whoever) seeks [a law]suit or litigation, shall return [the mon]ey tenfold to its owners. He shall contest in his lawsuit and not succeed.

r.6 [(Guaranteed against) seizur]es of epilepsy for 100 da[ys (and against) f]raud forever.

---

8 [IGI ^{m}]^{d}*za-b*[*a$_4$*]*-⸢ba$_4$⸣*—[P]AB—P[A]B
9 [IGI ^{m}*x x x x x x x x x*]
10 IGI ^{m}[*x*]—DINGIR! ⸢LÚ*!.NINDA! LÚ*!.*x*⸣ *x*[*x*]
11 IGI ^{m}*ha-ni-na-a-a*

8 [Witness] Zab[ab]a-ahu-uṣur.

9 [Witness NN, ...].

10 Witness [...]-ilu, baker of the [...].

11 Witness Haninaya.

48 Previous editions: AR 459, NALK 363. Collations: Assur 2/5.

12 IGI ^{m}*da-ga-na—mil-ki*
13 [IGI ^{m}*man*]-⸢*nu*⸣—GIM—ERIM.MEŠ
14 [IGI ^{m}*la*—TÉŠ]-⸢*a*⸣-*na*—DINGIR LÚ*.TIN
15 [IGI ^{m}*x x*]*x-še*?*-a-bu*
16 [IGI ^{m}*x x x*] ⸢*še x*⸣ [*x x x*]
rest broken away

s.1 [*x x x x x* MU]-2⸢4⸣-[KÁM] ⸢$^{m!1d}$30—PAB.M[EŠ—SU]
2 [MAN KUR]—*aš-šur*.K[I]

12 Witness Dagan-milki.
13 [Witness Man]nu-ki-ṣabi.
14 [Witness La-tubaš]anni-ilu, master builder.
15 [Witness ...]abu, [...].
16 [Witness NN]...[...].
(Break)
s.1 [......] 24[th year] of Sennach[erib, king] of Assyria.

49. Duplicate of the Preceding Text

Bu 91-5-9,40

beginning broken away

1′ ⸢MÍ⸣.AN-⸢*e*⸣—*ta-b*[*a-ni* GEMÉ-*šú*]
2′ [*ša*] ^{md}PA—NUMUN—AŠ *ú-*[*piš-ma*]
3′ ^{m}*šúm-ma*—DINGIR.MEŠ *ina* Š[À *x* MA.NA]
4′ KUG.UD TI-*qí kas-*[*pu gam-mur*]
5′ [*t*]*a-din* MÍ *šú-a-t*[*e za-ar-pat*]
6′ [*l*]*a-qi-at* ⸢*tú*⸣-[*a-ru de-e-nu*]
7′ [DU]G_4.DUG_4 *l*[*a-áš-šú man-nu ša*]
8′ [*ina u*]*r-kiš ina* [*ma-te-ma*]
9′ [*lu*]-⸢*u*⸣ [^{md}PA—NUMUN—AŠ *lu-u*]
remainder broken away

ADD 226

(Beginning destroyed)

1 Šamê-tab[ani, maid] of Nabû-zeru-iddina —
3 Šumma-ilani has con[tracted and] bought her fo[r x minas] of silver.
4 The mon[ey is] paid [completely]. Tha[t] woman [is purchased and ac]quired. Any rev[ocation, lawsuit, or lit]igation is v[oid].
7 [Whoever in the f]uture, at [any time, whether Nabû-zeru-iddina or]
(Rest destroyed)

50. Šumma-ilani Buys 50 Hectares of Land and 9 People

K 447

1 [*ṣu*]*-pur* ^{m}*bar*—[*ha-te-e*]
2 ⸢EN A⸣.ŠÀ É UN.⸢MEŠ⸣ S[UM!-*ni*]

3 [É] ⸢50!⸣ ANŠE A.ŠÀ 10-*lim* GIŠ.⸢*til-lit*⸣
4 [É *e*]*p-šú* ^{m}*ha-šá-na*! 4 DUMU.MEŠ-*šú*
5 ⸢MÍ⸣-*šú* ⸢MÍ⸣.*da-an-qi-i* DUMU-*šá*
6 DUM[U.MÍ-*sa* PA]B ⸢9!⸣ ZI.MEŠ ⸢ARAD.MEŠ⸣
7 *š*[*a* ^{m}*bar—ha*]*-te-e ina* URU.*ti-*⸢ʾ*i*⸣*-i*
8 ⸢*ú*⸣-[*piš-ma*] ^{m}*šúm-mu*—DINGIR.MEŠ-*ni*
9 ⸢TA*⸣ [IGI ^{m}*b*]*ar—ha-te-*⸢*e*!⸣ *ina* ŠÀ⸣-*bi*
10 6 MA.⸢NA KUG⸣.UD *ina* ⸢MA⸣.[NA-*e ša* MAN *il-qí*]

ADD 422

1 [Se]al of Bar-[hatê], owner of the land, house, and people being [sold].

(fingernail impressions)

3 [An estate] of 50 hectares of land, 10,000 vines, and [a bui]lt [house];
4 Hašana, his 4 sons and his wife; the woman Danqî, her son and [her] daugh[ter; a tot]al of 9 persons, servants o[f Bar-ha]tê in the town of Ti'i —
8 Šumma-ilani has co[ntracted and bought them] fr[om B]ar-hatê for 6 minas of silver by the mi[na of the king].

49 Previous editions: AR 501, NALK 364.
50 Previous editions: AR 103, NALK 370. Collations: Assur 2/5.

11 *kas-pu ga-a*[*m-mur ta-ad-din*]
12 A.ŠÀ É [UN.MEŠ GIŠ.SAR *šu-a-tú*]
13 *za-a*[*r-pu laq-qí-u*]
r.1 *tu-a-ru de-e-nu* ⸢*da*!⸣*-b*[*a*!*-bu la-áš-šú*]
2 *man-nu ša ina ur-kiš* ⸢GIL⸣-[*u-ni*]
3 *lu* ^{m}*bar—ha-te* ⸢*lu*!⸣ DUMU.MEŠ-⸢*šú*⸣
4 *lu qur-ub-šú* ⸢*lu mám-ma-nu-šú*⸣
5 *ša* TA* ^{m}*šúm-mu*—⸢DINGIR.MEŠ⸣-*ni* ⸢DUMU⸣.MEŠ-*šú*
6 ⸢*de*⸣*-e-nu da-ba-bu* ⸢*ub*⸣*-t*[*a-ʾu*]-⸢*ni*!⸣
7 [10 MA.N]A ⸢KUG.UD⸣ 1 ⸢MA⸣.NA ⸢KUG⸣.GI *s*[*ak*!]-⸢*ru*!⸣
8 [*ina bur-k*]*i*! ^{d}IŠ.TAR *a-ši-bat* ⸢URU⸣.[NINA] ⸢GAR!-*an*!⸣
9 [*kas-pu*] ⸢*a*!⸣*-na* 10.MEŠ *a-*[*na*] EN-*šú* ⸢GUR⸣ [0]
10 [*ina de-n*]*i-šú* DUG$_4$.DUG$_4$-*ma* ⸢*la*⸣ TI
11 [IGI ^{m}DU]MU!—ZALÁG LÚ.2-*u* URU.*m*[*a-g*]*a-nu-ba*
12 [IGI ^{m}*x x*]—⸢^{d}⸣PA LÚ*!.⸢*x-bar*!⸣-*ru*! :.!
13 [IGI ^{m}*x x*]—*qa*!*-mu*0! ⸢LÚ*.*mu-kil*]—PA.MEŠ ⸢:.⸣
14 [IGI ^{m}*x*]—⸢*mu*!⸣*-za-x*[*x* IGI] ^{m}*ra-*⸢*pa-ia*⸣
15e [*x x x*] ⸢*qa*⸣ *qa* [*x x x x x*]
rest broken away

11 The money [is paid] com[pletely]. That land, house, [people, and garden] are purch[ased and acquired]. Any revocation, lawsuit, or litig[ation is void].

r.2 Whoever, at any time, breaks the con[tract], whether Bar-hatê, his sons, or a neighbour or relative of his, and s[eek]s a lawsuit or litigation against Šumma-ilani and his sons, [shall pla]ce [ten min]as of silver (and) one mina of p[ur]e gold [in the la]p of Ištar residing in [Nineveh], and shall return [the money] tenfold to its owner. He shall contest [in] his [lawsu]it and not succeed.

11 [Witness Ma]r-nuri, deputy of Maganuba.
12 [Witness ...]-Nabû, ... of ditto.
13 [Witness ...]-qam, chariot driver of ditto.
14 [Witness ...].... [Witness] Rapaya.
(Rest destroyed)

51. Duplicate of the Preceding Text

K 10474

beginning broken away
1′ ⸢ARAD!.MEŠ ^{m}*bar*!⸣—*h*[*a*!*-te-e*]
2′ *ina* URU.*ti-ʾi-*[*i*]
3′ *ú-piš-ma* ^{m}⸢*šum*⸣-[*mu*—DINGIR.MEŠ-*ni*]
4′ TA* IGI ^{m}*bar*—(*ha*)*-te-*[*e*]
5′ *ina* ŠÀ 6 MA.NA KUG.UD *ina* [MA.NA *ša* MAN]
6′ *il-qí kas-pu gam-mu*[*r*]
7′ *ta-ad-*⸢*din*⸣ A.ŠÀ É
8′ UN.MEŠ GIŠ.SAR *šu-a-*[*tú*]
9′ *za-ár-pu laq-*[*qí-u*]
10′ *tu-a-ru de-*[*e-nu*]
11′ ⸢DUG$_4$.DUG$_4$⸣ *l*[*a-áš-šú*]
e.12′ ⸢*man-nu*⸣ *šá ina ur-*[*kiš* GIL-*u-ni*]
13′ *lu-u* ^{m}*bar—ha-a*[*t*!*-e*]
14′ *lu-u* DUMU.MEŠ-*šú* [0]
15′ *lu-u qur-*⸢*ub*!⸣-[*šú* 0]
r.1 *lu-u mám-ma-n*[*u-šú*]
2 *šá* TA* ^{m}*šúm-m*[*u*—DINGIR.MEŠ-*ni*]
3 *de-e-nu* DUG$_4$.DU[G$_4$]
4 *ub-ta-ʾu-*[*ni*]
5 10 MA.NA KUG.UD 1 MA.[NA KUG.GI]
6 *ina bur-ki* ^{d}IŠ.[TAR *a-ši-bat*]
7 NINA.KI GAR-*an kas-*[*pu a-na* 10.MEŠ]
8 *a-na* EN.MEŠ-*šú* GU[R-*ra*]
9 ⸢*ina de-ni-šú* DUG$_4$!⸣.[DUG$_4$-*ma*]
rest broken away

ADD 423

(Beginning destroyed)
1 servants of Bar-h[atê] in the town of Ti'i —
3 Šum[ma-ilani] has contracted and bought them from Bar-hatê for 6 minas of silver by [the mina of the king].
6 The money is paid completely. That field, house, people, and garden are purchased and acqui[red]. Any revocation, law[suit], or litigation is [void].

12 Whoever, at any ti[me, breaks the contract], whether Bar-ha[tê], his sons, or a neighbour or relative of his, and se[eks] a lawsuit or litigation against Summ[a-ilani and his sons],
r.5 shall place 10 minas of silver and one mi[na of gold] in the lap of Iš[tar residing] in Nineveh, and shall ret[urn] the mon[ey tenfold] to its owners. He shall con[test] in his lawsuit [and not succeed].
(Rest destroyed)

51 Previous editions: AR 104, NALK 371. Collations: Assur 2/5.

FIG. 13. *Hunting birds (reign of Sargon); cf. no. 52.* BM 118829.

52. Šumma-ilani Buys 13 People

83-1-18,339

1 [NA$_4$.KIŠIB ^{m}*x x x x x x x x*]
2 [NA$_4$.KIŠIB ^{m}*x x x x x*] ⌜LÚ*⌝.3-*šú*
3 [NA$_4$.KIŠIB] ^{m}*a*-⌜*ta-a*$^{!}$—*qa*$^{?}$⌝-*mu-ia* LÚ*.GAL—*ki-ṣir*
4 [PA]B$^{!}$ A ^{m}EN—KASKAL—*tak-lak*
5 LÚ.MEŠ EN UN.MEŠ SUM-*an*

ADD 246

1 [Seal of ......], 2 [seal of ...], 'third man,' 3 [seal] of Atâ-*qa*muya, cohort commander, 4 [a]ll sons of Bel-Harran-taklak, gentlemen, owners of the people being sold.

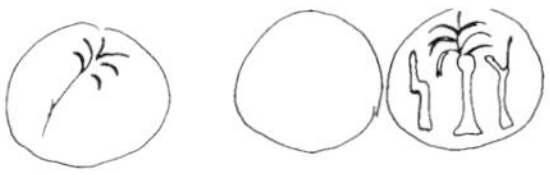

(stamp seal impressions)

6 ^{m}ŠEŠ—*nu-ri* ⌜DAM$^{!}$⌝-*šú* DUMU.MÍ-*šú* PAB 3
7 ^{m}*man-nu*—*ki*—NINA.KI MÍ-*šú* ⌜3$^{!}$⌝ DUMU.MEŠ-*šú*$^{!}$ PAB 5
8 ^{md}PA—KAR MÍ-*šú* ^{md}PA—MU MÍ-*šú*
9 ^{m}*nu-ra-a-a* PAB 13 ZI.MEŠ
10 *ú*-⌜*piš*⌝-*ma* ^{m}*šúm-mu*$^{!}$—DINGIR.MEŠ
11 *ina* ⌜ŠÀ⌝-*bi* ⌜6 1/2⌝ MA.NA KUG.UD *il-qi*

6 Ahi-nuri, his wife and daughter, a total of 3; Mannu-ki-Ninua, his wife and 3 sons, a total of 5; Nabû-eṭir and his wife; Nabû-iddina and his wife; Nuraya; in all 13 persons —

10 Šumma-ilani has contracted, bought, purchased and acquired them for 6 1/2 minas of silver.

52 Previous editions: AR 82, NALK 376. Collations: Assur 2/5.

12 *i-za-rip i-si-qi* ⸢UN$^{!}$⸣.MEŠ *šú-a-te*
13 *za-ár-pu la-qi-ú kas-pu ga-mur*
14 SUM-*ni tu-a-ru de-ni* DUG_4.DUG_4
r.1 *la-a-ši*$^{!}$ *man-nu ša ina ur-kiš*
2 *ina ma-te-me lu-u* ^{m}*ṣil—aš-šur* LÚ*$^{!}$.EN.NAM
3 *lu-u* LÚ*$^{!}$.MEŠ ŠU.2-*šú lu-u* DUMU.MEŠ-*šú-nu*
4 *lu-u me-me-ni-šú-nu* TA* ^{m}*šúm-mu*—DINGIR.MEŠ
5 *i*-GIL-*ú*$^{!}$-*ni kas-pu a-na* 10.⸢MEŠ-*te*$^{!}$⸣
6 *a-na* EN-*šú* SUM-*an* 1 MA.NA ⸢KUG.GI$^{!}$⸣
7 *a-na bur-ki* ^{d}15 *šá* NINA.KI GAR-*an*

---

8 IGI ^{md}PA-*u-a* LÚ*$^{!}$.2-*i ša* UŠ$^{!}$—*kib*$^{!}$-*šú*
9 IGI ^{m}*i-la-a ša*—LÚ*$^{!}$.ŠÁM$^{!}$
10 IGI ^{m}*qa-a* : IGI ^{m}*ha-an-ṭu-šú*

11 IGI ^{m}*rém-a-ni—aš-šur*
12 [I]GI ^{md}PA—MAN—PAB.MEŠ-*šú*
13 [IG]I ^{m}AD-*i—qa-mu*$^{!}$
14 [IG]I ^{m}30—*za-qi*$^{!}$-*pi*
15 [LÚ*].MUŠEN$^{!}$.DÙ
16 [IGI ^{m}]DI-*mu*—ŠEŠ.MEŠ *ša—hu-ṭa-ru*$^{!}$
17 [IGI ^{m}*x x x*].*x* LÚ$^{!}$.ARAD *ša* DUMU—MAN
18 [IGI ^{m}*x x x x x*] ⸢LÚ*⸣.A.BA
rest broken away

[12] Those people are purchased and acquired. The money is paid completely. Any revocation, lawsuit, or litigation is void.

[r.1] Whoever in the future, at any time, whether Ṣil-Aššur, the governor, or the men in his charge, or their sons or relatives, breaks the contract with Šumma-ilani, shall pay the money tenfold to its owner, and shall place one mina of gol[d] in the lap of Ištar of Nineveh.

---

[8] Witness Nabû'a, deputy of the tracker.
[9] Witness Ilâ, bought man.
[10] Witness Qâ, ditto. Witness Hanṭušu.
[11] Witness Remanni-Aššur.
[12] [Wi]tness Nabû-šar-ahhešu.
[13] [Witn]ess Abi-qam.
[14] [Witn]ess Sin-zaqip, fowler.
[16] [Witness] Šulmu-ahhe, staff-bearer.
[17] [Witness NN], servant of the crown prince.
[18] [Witness NN], scribe.
(Rest destroyed)

53. Šumma-ilani Buys Two Slaves

K 444

1 *ṣu-pur* ^{m}*ki-qi-la*$^{!}$-*ni* L[Ú.*x x*]
2 [E]N UN.MEŠ *ta-d*[*a-ni*]

---

3 [^{m}*x x*]—⸢LUGAL$^{?}$⸣—PAB ⸢MÍ⸣.AMA-*šú*
4 [PAB 2 LÚ*].ARAD.MEŠ *ša* ^{m}*ki-qi*-⸢*la*⸣-*ni*
5 [*ú-piš-m*]*a* ^{m}*šum-mu*—DINGIR.MEŠ-*ni*
6 *ina* ŠÀ-*bi* 1 MA.NA KUG.UD.MEŠ
7 *ina* 1 MA.NA-*e ša* URU.*gar-ga-mis*
8 TA* IGI ^{m}*ki-qi-la*$^{!}$-*ni il-qí*
9 *kas-pu ga-mur ta-din*
10 [UN.MEŠ] *za-ar-pu laq-qí-u*
11 [*tu-a*]-*ru* DUG_4.DUG_4 *la-áš-šú*
12 [*man-nu š*]*a* GIL-*ú-ni*
13 [*x* MA].NA KUG.UD 1 MA.NA KUG.⸢GI⸣
14 [*ina*] *bur-ki* ^{d}NIN.[LÍL]
e.15 ⸢*a*⸣-*ši-bat* URU.*ni-nu-a* ⸢GAR⸣-[*an*]
r.1 *kas-pu a-na* 10.MEŠ-*te*
2 *a-na* EN.MEŠ-*šú* GUR-*ra*

ADD 236

[1] Fingernail of Kiqillanu, [..., own]er of the people being so[ld].

(fingernail impressions)

---

[3] [...]-*šarru*-uṣur and his mother, [a total of 2] servants of Kiqillanu —

[5] Šumma-ilani [has contract]ed and bought them from Kiqillanu for one mina of silver by the mina of Carchemish.

[9] The money is paid completely. [The people] are purchased and acquired. [Any rev]ocation or litigation is void.

[12] [Whoeve]r breaks the contract shall pla[ce x mi]nas of silver and one mina of gold [in] the lap of Mul[lissu] residing in Nineveh, and shall return the money tenfold to its owners. He shall contest in his lawsuit and

53 Previous editions: AR 80, NALK 369. Collations: Assur 2/5. [r.6] For the reading of the personal name note the spelling [^{md}P]A—SAG—*iš-ši* in ADD 472 r.15 (collated).

3 *ina de-ni-šú* DUG$_4$.DUG$_4$-*ma là* TI

---

4 IGI ^{m}*za-zi-i* LÚ*.*mu-kil*—KUŠ.PA.MEŠ
5 ⸢IGI⸣ ^{md}UTU—*še-zib* LÚ*.3.U$_5$
6 IGI ^{md}PA—SAG—*i-ši* LÚ*.*mu-kil*—KUŠ.PA.MEŠ
7 IGI ^{md}30—I LÚ.GAL—*ki-ṣir*
8 IGI ^{md}MES—MU—AŠ LÚ.GIŠ.GIGIR—GÌR.2
blank space of about five lines
9 [IT]I.ŠU UD-2-KÁM [*lim-mu* ^{m}*x x x x x*]
10 [IGI ^{m}]^{d}PA!—TI.L[A!-*su*—E]
11 [LÚ*].A.BA *ṣ*[*a-bit dan-ni-te*]

not succeed.

---

r.4 Witness Zazî, chariot driver. 5 Witness Šamaš-šezib, 'third man.' 6 Witness Nabû-reši-išši, chariot driver. 7 Witness Sin-na'id, cohort commander. 8 Witness Marduk-šumu-iddina, horse trainer of the royal guard.

9 [Mon]th Tammuz (IV), 2nd day, [eponym year of ...].

10 [Witness] Nabû-bal[assu-iqbi], scribe, kee[per of the document].

54. Šumma-ilani Buys 5 Slaves

K 13187

beginning broken away
1′ [^{m}]⸢URU!.*arba*!-*ìl*!⸣.K[I!-*a-a x x x*]
2′ DUMU MÍ.*da-hi-x*[*x x x x x*]
3′ MÍ.^{d}15—*nap-šir*-[*x x x x x*]
4′ PAB 5 ZI.MEŠ ARAD.[MEŠ *ša* ^{m}*x x x*]
5′ *ú-piš-ma* ^{m}BE-*m*[*a*—DINGIR.MEŠ-*ni*]
6′ LÚ.*mu-kil*—KUŠ.PA.M[EŠ *ina* ŠÀ-*bi*]
7′ [*x* MA.NA KUG.UD] *ina*! *ša* U[RU!.*gar-ga-mis*]
rest broken away
Rev. beginning broken away
1 [*x x x*] *ia* ⸢*ṣa*!⸣ [*x x x x x*]
2 [*x x x*] *ṣa* (blank) [*x x x x x x*]
blank space
rest broken away

ADD 725

(Beginning destroyed)

1 [A]rbail[ayu ...], son of the woman Dahi[...], Issar-napšir[...], a total of 5 persons, servants [of NN] —

5 Šumm[a-ilani], chariot driver, has contracted and [bought them for x minas of silver] by the (mina) of C[archemish]

(Rest destroyed)

55. Šumma-ilani Buys a Donkey Driver

80-7-19,150

beginning broken away

1′ ^{md}15—*ta*-SU LÚ.UŠ—⸢ANŠE⸣.[MEŠ]
2′ ARAD *ša* ^{md}EN—DÙ *šá*! ^{m}*ki-ṣ*[*ir*!—*x x*]
3′ *ú-piš-ma* ^{m}*šum-ma*—DINGIR.MEŠ *ina* Š[À-*bi*]
4′ 1 1/2 MA.NA KUG.UD *ina ša* LUGAL *in*[*a*! *x x*]
5′ TA* IGI ^{md}EN—DÙ TA* IGI ^{m}[*ki-ṣir*—*x x*]
6′ *il-qí kas-pu gam*-[*mur*] *ta*-[*din*]
7′ LÚ *šu-a*-⸢*tú*⸣ *za-rip laq-q*[*í tu-a-ru*]

ADD 196

(Beginning destroyed)

(blank seal space)

---

1 Issar-tariba, donkey-driver, servant of Bel-ibni and Kiṣ[ir-...] —

3 Šumma-ilani has contracted and bought him from Bel-ibni and [Kiṣir-...] for 1 1/2 minas of silver by the (mina) of the king [...].

6 The money is p[aid] comple[tely]. That man is purchased and acqui[red. Any revoca-

54 Previous editions: AR 541, NALK 372. 1f, 6f See coll.
55 Previous editions: AR 494, NALK 374. 1 The *ta* in the name is written normally (see coll.), and is not *ta** (NALK). 5 See coll. 16 → no. 46:12.

8′ *de-e-nu* DUG$_4$.DUG$_4$ *la-áš-*[*šú*]
9′ *man-nu šá ina* ⸢*ur*⸣*-kiš ina* ⸢*ma-te-e*⸣*-*[*ma*]
10′ *lu-u* ^{md}EN—DÙ ⸢*lu*⸣*-*[*u* ^{m}*ki-ṣir—x x*]
11′ *lu-u* PAB.MEŠ-⸢*šú*⸣*-nu l*[*u-u x x x x x x*]
rest broken away
Rev. beginning broken away
1′ I[GI ^{m}*x x x x x x x x x x*]
2′ IGI ^{m}⸢*ú*⸣-[*x x x x x x x x*]
3′ *ša* ⸢LÚ⸣.[*x x x x*]
one line blank
4′ IGI ^{m}NUMUN—*kit-ti*—GIŠ$^{!}$ [LÚ.*x x x*]
5′ IGI ^{m}HÉ.NUN-*a-a* LÚ.[*x x x*]
space of 2 lines
6′ ⸢IGI⸣ [^{m}*x x x x x x*]*x* ⸢LÚ⸣.[A.BA]
rest broken away

tion], lawsuit, or litigation is vo[id].
9 Whoever in the future, at any ti[me], whether Bel-ibni o[r Kiṣir-...], or their brothers o[r ......]
(Break)
r.1 Wi[tness ......].
2 Witness [NN, ...] of [...].

4 Witness Zer-ketti-lešir, [...].
5 Witness Nuhšaya, [...].
6 Witness [NN, scribe].
(Rest destroyed)

56. Šumma-ilani Buys a Boy

83-1-18,163

beginning broken away

1′ [^{m}*x x x x x* AR]AD-*šú-nu*
2′ [*ša* ^{m}*x x x x x x x x*]—DINGIR-*šu*$^{!}$

ADD 319

(Beginning destroyed)
(seal impression)

1 [NN, ser]vant [of NN and ...]-ilišu —

56 Previous editions: AR 492, NALK 375. 2 The last sign is *šu*, as copied by Johns, not *šú* (NALK), see coll. 3 The number is 50, as copied by Johns, not 30 (NALK), see coll. 7, s.1 See coll.

FIG. 14. *Loaded donkeys (reign of Assurbanipal); cf. no. 55.*
ORIGINAL DRAWING VI, 53.

3′ [*ú-piš-ma* ^{m}*š*]*um-ma*—DINGIR.MEŠ-*ni*
4′ [*ina* ŠÀ] 30$^{!}$ MA.⌈NA⌉ URUDU.MEŠ
5′ [TA*] IGI LÚ.MEŠ-*e an-nu-te*
6′ *il-qi kas-pu gam-mur*
7′ *ta-din* TUR *šu-u-a-te*
8′ *za-rip la-qi tu-u-a-ru*
e.9′ *de-nu* DUG$_4$.DUG$_4$ *la-áš-šú*
10′ *man-nu ša ina ur-kiš* [*ina*] *ma-te-ma*
11′ *i-za-qup-an-ni lu-u*
r.1 LÚ.MEŠ-*e an-nu-te*
2 *lu-u* DUMU.[MEŠ-*šú-nu* DUMU]—DUMU.MEŠ-*šú-nu*
3 [*de-e-nu* DUG$_4$].DUG$_4$
4 [TA* ^{m}*šum-ma*]—DINGIR.MEŠ-*ni*
5 [DUMU.MEŠ-*šú*] DUMU—DUMU.MEŠ-*šú*
6 [*ub-ta-u-ni*] 2 MA.NA [KUG.UD]
7 [*a-na* ^{d}*x a-šib* URU.*x x*].KI
8 [SUM *x x x x x x x*]⌈*x*⌉
rest broken away
s.1 IGI ^{m}*mu*$^{!}$-[*x x x x x x*]
2 IGI ^{m}[*x x x x x x*]*x*

3 [Š]umma-ilani [has contracted and] bought him [from] these men [for] 30 minas of copper.

6 The money is paid completely. That boy is purchased and acquired. Any revocation, lawsuit, or litigation is void.

10 Whoever, in the future [at] any time, lodges a complaint, whether these men or [their] sons [or grand]sons, and [seek]s [a lawsuit or litiga]tion [against Šumma]-ilani, [his sons] and grandsons, [shall pay] two minas of [silver to the god ... residing in ...].

(Break)

s.1 Witness Mu[...],
2 Witness [NN].

57. Nabû-šumu-iškun, Sennacherib's Chariot Driver, Buys 20 Slaves

83-1-18,359

beginning broken away

1′ [^{m}*x x x*] LÚ$^{!}$.DIB *šá* ⌈IGI$^{!}$⌉-*šú* 1$^{!}$ DUMU G[A$^{!}$]
2′ [*x x x* M]Í-*šú* ⌈2 ARAD⌉.MEŠ-*šú* PAB 10 ZI.[MEŠ]
3′ [^{m}*x x x*]*x* 2 MÍ.⌈MEŠ⌉-*šú* 3 DUMU.MEŠ-*šú*
4′ [*x x x*] ARAD.MEŠ-*šú* PAB 10 ZI.MEŠ
5′ [PAB-*ma* 20 U]N.MEŠ *šá* ^{m}SUHUŠ—^{d}PA Š[A]$^{?}$

6′ [*x x*]*x ú-piš-ma* ^{md}PA—MU—GAR-*un*
7′ [LÚ.DIB—KUŠ].PA.MEŠ *šá* ^{md}30—PAB.MEŠ—SU
8′ [MAN KUR—*aš-šur*] *ina* ŠÀ 10 MA.NA KUG.UD *ina* 1 MA.NA

9′ [*šá* URU.*gar-g*]*a*-⌈*mis*⌉ TI-*qí kas-pu*
10′ [*gam-mur ta-din* U]N.MEŠ *šú-a-tú*
11′ [*zar-pu laq-qi-u tu-a-r*]*u de*-⌈*e-nu*⌉
12′ [DUG$_4$.DUG$_4$ *la-áš-šú man-nu*] ⌈*šá*$^{!}$⌉ [*ina ur-kiš*]
rest broken away
Rev. beginning broken away
1′ [IGI ^{m}*x x x x* LÚ].⌈A$^{!}$.BA$^{!}$ *šá*⌉ DUMU—MAN

2′ [IGI ^{m}*x x x x* L]Ú.GAL—*kal*$^{!}$-*lap*$^{!}$
3′ [IGI ^{m}*x x x x* ^{m}]AN.ŠÁR—EN—PAB LÚ.GAR.KUR

ADD 253

(Beginning destroyed)

(space for stamp seal impressions)

---

1 [NN], a prisoner in his custody, 1 suckling child, [......], his wi[fe], 2 servants of his, a total of 10 persons;

3 [NN], his 2 wives, his 3 sons, [x ..., x] servants of his, a total of 10 persons, [in all 20 peo]ple of Ubru-*Nabû* [...] –

6 Nabû-šumu-iškun, [chariot driv]er of Sennacherib, [king of Assyria], has contracted and bought them for 10 minas of silver by the mina [of Carch]emish.

9 The money [is paid completely]. Those [pe]ople [are purchased and acquired. Any revocat]ion, lawsuit, or [litigation is void. Whoe]ver, [at any time in the future]

(Break)

r.1 [Witness NN], scribe of the crown prince.

2 [Witness NN], commander of *outriders*.

3 [Witness NN, ... *of*] Aššur-belu-uṣur, governor.

57 Previous editions: AR 85, NALK 210. Collations: Assur 2/5. 1 See coll.

4′ [IGI ^{m}x x x x ^{m}]⸢^{d}⸣PA—⸢PAB⸣—[SUM]-*na*
5′ [0] LÚ.*mu-tar*—UMUŠ.MEŠ!
6′ [IGI ^{m}x x(x)-BÀ]D—PAB LÚ.: IGI ^{md}PA-*u-a*
7′ [0] LÚ.A.BA

8′ [IGI ^{m}x x x].x-*a* LÚ.3-*šú šá* LÚ.2-*u*
9′ [IGI ^{m}z]*i*!-*zi-i* LÚ.*mu-tar*—UMUŠ.[M]EŠ!
10′ [x x x x].x.MEŠ *la mah-ru-u*!-*t*[*i*!]
11′ [x x x x x] ⸢x⸣ [x] IGI ^{m}⸢I⸣-[x x x x]
rest broken away

4 [Witness ... and] Nabû-ahu-iddina, intelligence officers.
6 [Witness ...-du]ru-uṣur, ditto. Witness Nabû'a, scribe.
8 [Witness NN], 'third man' of the deputy (governor).
9 [Witness Z]izî, intelligence officer.
10 [...] not receiv[ed ......].
11 [...]. Witness [NN].
(Rest destroyed)

58. Nabû-šumu-iškun Buys More Slaves

82-5-22,151

beginning broken away
1′ [*ina* ŠÀ] ⸢13?⸣ MA.N[A! KUG.UD]

2′ ⸢*i*⸣-[*z*]*i-rip i*[*s-si-qi kas-pu*]
3′ [*gam-m*]*ur ta-din* [x x x x]
4′ [*za-á*]*r-pu laq-*[*qi-u tu-a-ru*]
5′ [*de*]-⸢*e*!⸣-[*nu* DUG_4.DUG_4]
rest broken away
Rev. beginning broken away
1′ [TA* ^{m}]$^{d!}$PA!—MU—GAR-*un* TA* DU[MU.MEŠ-*šú*]
2′ [TA*] DUMU—DUMU.MEŠ-*šú ub-ta-*[*u-ni*]
3′ [x M]A.NA KUG.UD 5 MA.NA K[UG.GI]
4′ ⸢*i*⸣-*na bur-ki* ^{d}IM *a-šib* URU.[x x x]

5′ [G]AR-*an kas-pu a-na* 10.MEŠ-*te a-n*[*a* EN-*šú*]
6′ [G]UR-*ra ina de-ni-šú* DUG_4.D[UG_4-*ma*]
7′ [*l*]*a*! TI! *de*!-*en-šú* ⸢DI!⸣.[KUD *la i-šá-mu*]

8′ [IGI ^{m}PAB]-⸢*bu-u*?⸣ [x x x x]
rest broken away

ADD 501

(Beginning destroyed)
1 [Nabû-šumu-iškun] has purchased and b[ought them for] 13 mina[s of silver.]
2 [The money] is paid [compl]etely. [Those people are pu]rchased and acq[uired. Any revocation, law]su[it, or litigation is void].
(Break)

r.1 [whoever] se[eks (a lawsuit or litigation) against] Nabû-šumu-iškun (or) against [his] so[ns shall pl]ace [x mi]nas of silver (and) 5 minas of go[ld] in the lap of Adad residing in [...].
5 [He shall re]turn the money tenfold to [its owner]. He shall con[test] in his lawsuit [and n]ot succeed. The jud[ge shall not heed] his [ca]se.

---

8 [Witness Aha]bû [...]
(Rest destroyed)

59. Marduk-[...], Sennacherib's [...], Buys Slaves (684-XIIa-14)

83-1-18,334

1 NA_4.KIŠIB ^{m}EN—AD—PAB E[N UN.MEŠ SUM-*ni*]

ADD 255

1 Seal of Bel-abu-uṣur, own[er of the people being sold].

(cylinder seal impression)

58 Previous editions: AR 197, NALK 209. 1, r.7 See coll.
59 Previous editions: AR 50, NALK 171; → ABC 19. Captions: CIS II 32, Ep. Ar. 28, Fales Epigraphs 2.

2 ^{m}*ba-ra-a-hu a-di* UN.M[EŠ-*šú*]
3 ⸢^{m}⸣*ṭa-bu-ni a-di* U[N.MEŠ-*šú*]
4 [^{m}*s*]*i-ti-ir-ka-a-nu a*-[*di* UN.MEŠ-*šú*]
5 [*g*]*ab-bu a-na gi-mi*[*r-ti-šú-nu*]

6 *ú-piš-ma* ^{md}MES—[*x x x x x x*]
7 *ša* ^{md}30—PAB.ME[Š—SU MAN KUR—*aš-šur*.KI]
8 *i-na* ŠÀ *bi*-⸢*lat*⸣ [URUDU.MEŠ]
9 [TA* I]GI ^{m}EN—A[D—PAB *il-qi*]
10 [*kas-pu*] *ga*-[*mur ta-din*]
11 [*x x x*] *xx* [*x x x x*]
rest broken away

Rev. beginning broken away
1′ IGI ^{md}PA—KAR-*ir*-⸢*a*⸣-[*ni* LÚ*.*x x x x*]
2′ IGI ^{md}PA—*mu*-SIG$_5$ L[Ú.*x x x x*]
3′ IGI ^{m}KÁ—*ti*$^{!}$-*nu-ra-a-a* LÚ*.*láh-hi*-[*nu x x*]
4′ IGI ^{md}*šá-maš*—MU—PAB LÚ*.SANGA *šá*$^{!}$ ⸢^{d}⸣[*x x*]
5′ IGI ^{m}PAB—*la-mur* LÚ*.SANGA *šá*$^{!}$ ⸢^{d}⸣*x*[*x x*]

6′ IGI ^{m}*na-bu-u-a* LÚ*.SANGA *šá*$^{!}$ ⸢^{d}⸣[*x x*]
7′ IGI ^{m}*un-zar*$_4$-*hu* LÚ*.SANGA *šá*$^{!}$ ^{d}LÁL
8′ IGI ^{m}*mar-di-i* LÚ*.SANGA *šá*$^{!}$ ^{d}GAŠAN$^{!}$—KUR-*ha*
9′ IGI ^{md}ME.ME—NUMUN—DÙ LÚ*.SANGA *ša* ^{d}ME.ME
10′ IGI ^{m}*aš-šur*—ZU-*a-ni* LÚ*.Ì.DU$_8$ *šá* É.GAL
11′ IGI ^{m}*zi-zi-ia* LÚ*.Ì.DU$_8$ *šá* É.GAL

12′ IGI ^{m}DINGIR—KAM-*eš* LÚ*.Ì.DU$_8$ *šá* É.GAL
13′ IGI ^{m}*mu-qa-lil*—IDIM LÚ.:
14′ IGI ^{m}*ba-na-a-a* LÚ.:
15′ IGI ^{m}*ga-lul* LÚ.:
16′ IGI ^{m}NUNUZ-*a-a* A$^{!}$.[BA *ṣa-bit* IM]

17e ITI.DIRI$^{!}$.ŠE UD-14-KAM *lim-mu* ^{m}[*man-za-ár-né-e*]
18e LÚ*.GAR.KUR URU.*ku*$^{!}$-*l*[*a-ni-a*]

19e *š*(*t*)*rkn ṭ*[*bn br*ʾ*ḥ*]

2 Barahu including [his] people, Ṭabuni including [his] pe[ople, and S]itirkanu inclu[ding his people, a]ll (of them) in [their] enti[rety] —

6 Marduk-[..., the ...] of Senna[cherib, king of Assyria], has contracted [and bought them fro]m Bel-ab[u-uṣur] for a talent of [copper].

10 [The money is paid] comple[tely].
(Break)

r.1 Witness Nabû-eṭira[nni, ...].
2 Witness Nabû-mudammiq, [...].
3 Witness Bab-Tinurayu, temple stewa[rd ...].
4 Witness Šamaš-šumu-uṣur, priest of [...].
5 Witness Ahu-lamur, priest of [...].
6 Witness Nabû'a, priest of [...].
7 Witness Unzarhu, priest of Tašmetu.
8 Witness Mardî, priest of Šarrat-nipha.
9 Witness Gula-zeru-ibni, priest of Gula.
10 Witness Aššur-le'ani, porter of the palace.
11 Witness Zizî, porter of the palace.
12 Witness Ilu-ereš, porter of the palace.
13 Witness Muqallil-kabti, ditto.
14 Witness Banaya, ditto.
15 Witness Gallulu, ditto.
16 Witness Pir'aya, scr[ibe, keeper of the tablet].
17 Month Intercalary Adar (XII/2), 14th day, eponym year of [Manzarnê], governor of Kull[ania].
s.1 (Aramaic caption:) Sitirkanu, Ṭ[abuni, Barahu].

5. Bahianu, Village Manager of the Stewardess (704-682)

FIG. 15. *Oil-jars in the magazine room of the Ninurta Temple of Calah. Similar big storage jars for cereals were found in the guard room of the NW Palace of Nimrud.*
MALLOWAN, *Nimrud and Its Remains* I, 92.

60. Bahianu Loans Three Homers of Barley (704-I)

K 325

1 3 ANŠE ŠE.PAD.MEŠ SAG.D[U]
2 ^{md}UTU—PAB—PAB
3 TA* IGI ^{m}*ba-hi-a-ni*
4 *ina pu-u-hi it-ti-ši*

r.1 ITI.BARAG UD-⸢1$^{?}$⸣-KÁM

2 *lim-me* ^{md}PA—*de-e-nu*—DÙ-*uš*

ADD 141

[1] 3 homers of barley, capital —
[2] Šamaš-ahu-uṣur has taken it as a loan from Bahianu.

(fingernail impressions)

[r.1] Month Nisan (I), *1st* day,

(fingernail impressions)

[2] eponym year of Nabû-denu-epuš.

61. Bahianu Redeems a Bondman (700-V-5)

K 304 + K 7490 (ADD 323) + K 9804

1 ⸢*ku*⸣-[*um* NA$_4$.KIŠIB-*šu-nu*] ⸢*ṣu*⸣-*pur-šú-nu* GAR-⸢*nu*⸣
2 *ṣu-p*[*ur* ^{m}*za*]-*ku*$^!$-*ri* *ṣu*-[*pur*] ^{m}*du-kur*—DINGIR
3 EN LÚ *ta*-⸢*da*⸣-*ni*

---

4 ^{m}*man-nu—ki*—URU.*arba-ìl* DUMU-*šú* *ša*$^!$ ^{m}PAB-*ia-u*
5 *ú-piš-ma* ^{m}*ba-hi-a-nu*
6 [TA*] ⸢*pa*⸣-*an* ^{m}*za-ku-ri* TA* IGI ^{m}*du-kur*—DINGIR
7 [*ina* ŠÀ-*b*]*i*$^!$ 30 MA.NA URUDU.MEŠ *ip-ta*-⸢*ṭar*⸣
8 [*kas-pu*] *ga-mur ta-din* LÚ *šú-a*-[*tú*]
9 [*za-ri*]*p*$^!$ *laq*$^!$-*qi*$^!$ *tu-a-ru de*-⸢*e*⸣-[*nu*$^!$]
10 [DUG$_4$].DUG$_4$$^!$ *la*$^!$-*áš*$^!$-*šú man-nu ša ina u*[*r-kiš*]
11 [*ina ma*]-*te*$^!$-*ma*$^!$ *i-za-qu-pa*-⸢*a*$^!$⸣-[*ni*]
12 [10 MA].NA$^!$ KUG$^!$.UD$^!$ SUM$^!$-*an*$^!$ LÚ ⸢*ú*$^!$⸣-[*še-ṣa*]
13 [*ṣib-tú*] *be*$^!$-*en*$^!$-*nu*$^!$ *ana*$^!$ 1-*me* UD-*me*
14 [*s*]*a*$^!$-*ar*$^!$-*tú*$^!$ *ina*$^!$ *kàl* UD.MEŠ

ADD 176+

[1] Inst[ead of their seal]s they impressed their fingernails.
[2] Fingern[ail of Zakku]r, fingernail of Dukur-il, owners of the man being sold.

(fingernail impressions)

---

[4] Mannu-ki-Arbail son of Ahi-Yau —
[5] Bahianu has contracted and released him [fr]om Zakkur and Dukur-il [for] 30 minas of copper.

[8] [The money] is paid completely. That man [is purchased] and acquired. Any revocation, lawsu[it, or litig]ation is void.
[10] Whoever in the fu]ture, at any [time], lodges a complaint shall pay [10 mi]nas of silver to [redeem] the man.
[13] [(Guaranteed against) seizures] of epilepsy for 100 days (and against) fraud forever.

---

60 Previous editions: AR 309, NALK 49.
61 Previous editions: AR 469 and 630, NALK 50. Collations: Assur 2/5.

15 [I]GI$^{!}$ [^{m}]EN$^{!}$—BÀD$^{!}$ LÚ*$^{!}$.GAL—URU.MEŠ-*ni*
16 [IGI] $^{m!}$⸢*du*$^{?}$⸣-*su*$^{!}$-*su*$^{!}$
Edge uninscribed
r.1 IGI$^{!}$ $^{m!}$*m*[*i*]*l*$^{!}$-*ku*—DINGIR IGI ^{m}EN—IGI-*a-ni*
2 IGI$^{!}$ $^{m!d!}$UTU—*še-zib*
3 [IGI$^{!}$] $^{m!}$*a*$^{!}$-*ta-ra*
4 [IGI$^{!}$] $^{m!d!}$M[AŠ$^{?}$]—*mu-še-zib*
5 [ITI.N]E$^{!}$ ⸢UD⸣-5-KÁM
6 [*x x*]-*bu-u*
7 *lim-mu* ^{m}*mi*-⸢*tu*⸣-*nu*
8 LÚ*$^{!}$.GAR.KUR U[RU].⸢*i*⸣-*sa-na*
9 [IGI ^{m}]⸢^{d}⸣[A]G$^{!}$—SUM—PAB.MEŠ
10 [LÚ*.A.BA] DIB *dan-ni-ti*
11 ⸢2$^{!}$ MA.NA⸣ URUDU.MEŠ *ša ṣu-pur-šú*$^{!}$-*nu*

15 [Witness Be]l-duri, village manager.
16 [Witness] Dususu.

r.1 Witness M[i]lku-il. Witness Bel-emuranni.
2 Witness Šamaš-šezib.
3 [Witness] Atara.
4 [Witness] *I*[*nurta*]-mušezib.
5 [Month A]b (V), 5th day [...]..., eponym year of Metunu, governor of Isana.
9 [Witness Na]bû-nadin-ahhe, [scribe, keep]er of the contract.
11 Two minas of copper for their fingernails.

62. Bahianu Loans 4 Homers of Barley (696-V-18)

Ki 1904-10-9,56

1 4 ANŠE ⸢ŠE⸣.PAD.MEŠ
2 ⸢^{m}⸣*ga-ru-ṣu*
3 TA* IGI ^{m}*ba-hi-a-ni*

4 *ina pu-u-hi* ÍL-*ši*
r.1 ITI.NE UD-18$^{!}$-KÁM
2 *lim-mu* ^{m}DI-*mu*—EN

ADD 1159

1 4 homers of barley —
2 Garruṣu has taken it as a loan from Bahianu.
(stamp seal impressions)

r.1 Month Ab (V), 18th day, eponym year of Šulmu-beli.

63. Note of 10 Minas of Copper Owed to Bahianu (695-IX-3)

K 290

1 NA$_{4}$.KIŠIB ^{m}EN—GIŠ
2 10 MA.NA URUDU SAG.DU
3 *ša* ^{m}*ba-hi-a-nu ina* IGI-*šú*

4 *ina* ⸢ITI⸣.AD$^{!}$ UD-21-KÁM SUM-*an*
5 *šum-ma la i-dan*
e.6 *a-na mit-har* GAL-*bi-u*
7 ITI.AD$^{!}$ UD-3-KÁM
r.1 *lim-mu* ^{m}*aš-šur*—U—PAB
2 IGI ^{md}PA—PAB—PAB
3 IGI ^{m}*man-nu*—*ki*—^{d}PA

ADD 31

1 Seal of Bel-lešir.
2 10 minas of copper, capital, belonging to Bahianu, at his disposal.
(stamp seal impressions)
4 He shall pay in the month of *Ab* (*V*), on the 21st day.
5 If he does not pay, it shall increase by the same amount.
7 Month *Ab* (*V*), 3rd day, eponym year of Aššur-belu-uṣur.
r.2 Witness Nabû-ahu-uṣur.
3 Witness Mannu-ki-Nabû.
(stamp seal impression)

62 Previous edition: NALK 51.
63 Previous editions: AR 280, NALK 52. 4, 7 ITI.AD (clearly written twice, see coll.) is presumably an idiosyncratic pseudo-logograpic writing of the month *ābu* (suggestion R.M. Whiting).

4 IGI ^{m}U.GUR—DÙ-*ni* A.BA
5 IGI ^{m}DÙG—EN *šá*—UGU—É

4 Witness Nergal-ibni, scribe.
5 Witness Ṭab-Bel, overseer of the household.
(stamp seal impression on edge)

64. Note of 7 Minas of Copper Owed to Bahianu (693)

K 3501

1 7 MA.NA URUDU.MEŠ
2 *ša* ^{m}*ba-hi-a-nu*
3 *ina* IGI ^{m}*kab-ti*—DINGIR.MEŠ-*ni*
4 *a-na* 1/2 MA.NA-*šú-nu* GAL-*u*
5 IGI ^{m}*a-a*—*ni-iʾ-ri*
e.6 IGI ^{md}PA—NUMUN—⌜BA$^{!}$-*ša*$^{!}$⌝
Rev. 2 line space
1 *lim-me* ^{m}AŠ—[PAB.MEŠ]
2 A.BA ^{md}ŠÚ$^{!}$—MAN—PAB

ADD 29

1 7 minas of copper belonging to Bahianu, at the disposal of Kabti-ilani.

4 It shall increase 50 percent per mina.
5 Witness Aya-niri.
6 Witness Nabû-zeru-iqiša.
r.1 Eponym year of Iddin-ahhe.
2 Scribe: Marduk-šarru-uṣur.

65. Bahianu Buys Land and People (692)

Sm 240

1 [NA_4.KIŠI]B$^{!}$ ^{m}*lu-ki-ma-ma*
2 [NA_4.KIŠ]IB$^{!}$ ^{m}NUMUN—SI.SÁ

3 [EN A.ŠÀ.M]EŠ UN.MEŠ SUM-*nu*

---

4 [É *x* ANŠE] A.ŠÀ.GA.MEŠ
5 [SUHUR *x x*]-*lu*$^{!}$-*ub-la* 0$^{!}$
6 [*x x x x x x-a*]*n*$^{!}$-*ni-ia*$^{!}$
7 [*x x x x x x*]*x* A.QAR.MEŠ
8 [*x x x x x x* L]Ú.ENGAR

9 [*x x x ú-piš-ma* ^{m}*b*]*a-hi-a-nu*
10 [*ina* ŠÀ *x* MA.NA KUG.UD] *ina*$^{!}$ *ša* M[AN$^{!}$]
11 [*x x x x x x x x x x x x x*]*x*[*x*]
rest broken away
Rev. beginning broken away
1′ [*x x x x x x x* A.ŠÀ.M]EŠ$^{!}$ U[N$^{!}$.MEŠ]
2′ [*x x x a-na* MU.AN.N]A$^{!}$.MEŠ
3′ [KÚ UD-*mu ša* KUG.UD SUM-*nu*]-*ni*
4′ [A.ŠÀ.MEŠ UN.MEŠ] *ú-še-ṣu-u*

5′ [ITI.*x* UD]-23-KAM
6′ [*lim-mu* ^{m}*za-z*]*a-a-a*

ADD 440

1 [Se]al of Lukimama, [seal of] Zeru-lešir,

(cylinder seal impression)

3 [owners of the field]s and people being sold.

---

4 [An estate of x hectare]s of land
5 [adjoining ...l]ubla
6 [......a]nniya
7 [......] irrigated fields
8 [NN], farmer, [...] —
9 [B]ahianu [has contracted and acquired (said property) for x minas of silver] by the (mina) of the ki[ng].
(Break)
r.1 [He shall enjoy the fiel]ds and the pe[ople for yea]rs [...]. [On the day that they pa]y [the silver], they shall redeem [the fields and the people].
5 Month [...], 23rd [day], eponym year of Zazaya.

---

64 Previous editions: AR 279, NALK 53. r.2 The tablet has ^{d}ŠÚ, as copied by Johns, not MAŠ.[MA]Š (NALK).
65 Previous edition: AR 151. Collations: Assur 2/5.

7′ [IGI ^{md}*x*]—PAB—PAB LÚ*.*láh-hi-nu*
8′ [IGI ^{m}*qur-d*]*i*—^{d}IM GAL—*ú-rat*
9′ [IGI ^{m}*x x*]*x-ši-i*
10′ [IGI ^{m}]⸢DINGIR$^{!}$—*pa*$^{!}$⸣-*a*$^{!}$-*di*
11′ [IGI ^{md}P]A-*u-a* SIMUG.KUG.GI
12′ [IGI ^{m}*s*]*u*$^{!}$-*ra-ra-a-te*
13′ [IGI ^{m}SAN]GA—15 LÚ*.A.BA
14′ [IGI ^{m}]^{d}PA—*rém-a-ni*

7 [Witness ...]-ahu-uṣur, temple steward.
8 [Witness Qurd]i-Adad, team commander.
9 [Witness ...]šî.
10 [Witness] Ili-pada.
11 [Witness Na]bû'a, goldsmith.
12 [Witness S]urarate.
13 [Witness San]gû-Issar, scribe.
14 [Witness] Nabû-remanni.

66. Bahianu, Village Manager of the Stewardess, Releases a Woman (688-I)

Sm 461

1 NA$_4$.KIŠIB ^{m}*ba-hi-a-ni*
2 LÚ.GAL—URU.MEŠ *ša* MÍ.*láh-hi-ni-te*

3 MÍ$^{!}$.⸢*ú*$^{!}$⸣-*hi*$^{!}$-*ma-a*
4 [MÍ-*šú ša* ^{md}E]N$^{?}$—DÙ$^{!}$-⸢*uš*$^{!}$⸣
5 [*x x x x x*]*x lu*$^{!}$ [*x x*]
6 [*x x x x*] *sa*$^{!}$ *x*[*x x x*]
rest broken away
Rev. beginning broken away
1′ [*x x x x*] GÌR$^{!}$.2$^{!}$ *x*[*x x x*]
2′ [*x x x x*] GIBÍL$^{!}$ *x*[*x x x*]
3′ [*mám-ma* TA*] *mám-ma*
4′ [*la i*]-⸢*da*⸣-*bu-ub*
5′ [TA* *pa-a*]*n*$^{!}$ *a-ha-iš*
6′ [*uṭ*]-*ṭu*$^{!}$-*ru* DUG$_4$.DUG$_4$ *la-áš-šú*
7′ IGI ^{m}*su-ra-*[*ra*]-*a*$^{!}$-*te*
8′ IGI ^{m}*man-nu*—GIM—URU.*arba-ìl*
9′ IGI ^{md}PA—⸢*hu*⸣-*sa-a-ni*
10′ IGI ^{m}*rém-ni*—DINGIR

11′ ITI.BARAG 0$^{!}$ *lim-mu* ^{m}SUM—PAB.MEŠ
12′ *ša* URU.*ṣi-me-ra*

ADD 491

1 Seal of Bahianu, village manager of the temple stewardess.

(cylinder seal impression)

3 Uhimâ, [the wife of Be]l-epuš
(Break)

r.3 [Neither shall] litigate [against] the other. [They are mutua]lly paid off, there is no complaint.

7 Witness Sura[ra]te.
8 Witness Mannu-ki-Arbail.
9 Witness Nabû-hussanni.
10 Witness Remanni-ilu.
11 Month Nisan (I), eponym year of Iddin-ahhe of Ṣimirra.

67. Note of 23 Homers of Barley Owed to Bahianu (688-IV-23)

83-1-18,407

1 23 ANŠE ŠE.PAD.MEŠ
2 *ša* ^{m}*ba-hi-a-ni*
3 [*ina* I]GI ^{md}PA-*ú-u-a*

ADD 133

1 23 homers of barley belonging to Bahianu [are at the dis]posal of Nabûwa.

66 Previous edition: AR 58. Collations: Assur 2/5.
67 Previous editions: AR 307, NALK 54. Collations: Assur 2/5. Photo Budge Deluge 10. The cylinder seal on this tablet is identical with that on no. 68.

(cylinder seal impression)

4 *ina ad-ri a-na* SAG.DU-*šá*
5 *šum-ma la* SUM-*ni*
6 *a-na* ANŠE 5BÁN-*šá*
r.1 ITI.ŠU 23!
2 *lim-me* ^{m}SUM-*na*—PAB.MEŠ
3 LÚ*.GAR.KUR URU.*ṣi-me-ra*

4 (He shall pay) its capital at the threshing floor. If he does not pay, (it shall increase) 5 seahs per homer.

r.1 Month Tammuz (IV), 23rd day, eponym year of Iddin-ahhe, governor of Ṣimirra.

68. Duplicate of the Previous Text (688-IV-23)

83-1-18,408

Obv. totally broken away
Edge uninscribed
r.1 [*x x x*] ITI.ŠU UD-23
2 [*lim*]-*me* ^{m}SUM-*na*—PAB.MEŠ LÚ*.GAR.KUR
3 URU.*ṣi-me-er*

ADD 145

(Beginning destroyed)

r.1 Month Tammuz (IV), 23rd (day), eponym year of Iddin-ahhe, governor of Ṣimirra.

(cylinder seal impression)

69. Bahianu Loans 10 Homers of Barley (688-X-6)

Ki 1904-10-9,292+310+314+316

1 20! ANŠE ŠE.PAD.[MEŠ]
2 ⌈*ša*⌉ ^{m}*ba-*[*hi-a-ni*]
3 *ina* IGI ^{m}PAB-[*u-a*]-⌈*a*!⌉
blank space
4 *ina pu-u-hi* [Í]L-*ši*
5 IGI ^{m}*na*!-*n*[*a*!-*a*]-⌈*a*!⌉
6 IGI ^{md}PA-⌈*u-a*⌉
7 LÚ*.A—SIG
r.1 ⌈*a*!⌉-[*n*]*a*! 1! :.! 2BAN!-*a-a*
2 [*i-rab-b*]*i*!
blank space of two lines
3 [ITI.*x* UD]-6-KÁM
4 [*lim*]-*mu* ^{m}AŠ—PAB.MEŠ
5 LÚ*.GAR.KUR URU.*ṣi-me-*⌈*er*⌉

ADD 1213+

1 20 homers of barley belonging to Bah[ianu, at the dis]posal of Ahu'[ay]a.

4 He has taken it as a loan.
(fingernail impressions)
5 Witness Nan[ay]a.
6 Witness Nabû'a, chariot fighter.
r.1 [It shall increa]se two seahs per homer.

3 [Month ...], 6th [day, epony]m year of Iddin-ahhe, governor of Ṣimirra.

70. Bahianu Loans 4 Homers of Barley (686-VI-29)

83-1-18,406

1 2 ANŠE ŠE.PAD.MEŠ
2 ^{md}PA—ZALÁG—*nam-mir*

ADD 134

1 Two homers of barley — Nabû-nurunammir;

68 Previous editions: AR 331. The fragment has been included here because the seal impression and date are identical with no. 67.
69 Previous edition: NALK 56. 5, r.1 See coll.
70 Previous editions: AR 308, NALK 57. Photo Budge Deluge 10. → no. 72 (which is the repayment).

3 1 :. ^{m}*la*—TÉŠ-*a-ni*—DINGIR
4 1 :. ^{m}*ṣab-ta-a-nu*
5 *ša* ^{m}*ba-hi-a-ni*
6 *ina pa-ni-šú-nu*
7 *ina pu-u-hi it-ta-ṣu*

r.1 ITI.KIN UD-29-KÁM

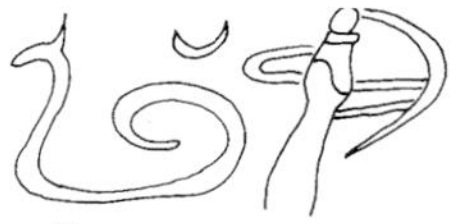

2 *lim-mu* ^{m}EN—IGI-*a-ni*
3 LÚ*.*tur-tan-nu*

3 one ditto — La-tubašanni-ilu;
4 one ditto — Ṣabutanu;
5 (barley) belonging to Bahianu, at their disposal.
7 They have taken it as a loan.
r.1 Month Elul (VI), 29th day,

(cylinder seal impression)

2 eponym year of Bel-emuranni, commander-in-chief.

71. Bahianu Loans Two Homers of Barley (685-I-27)

K 340

1 2 ANŠE ŠE.PAD.MEŠ
2 *ša* ^{m}*ba-hi-a-ni*
3 *ina* IGI ^{m}*as-ta-qu-um-me*

4 *ina pu-u-hi it-ti-ši*
5 *a-na* 1 :. 3BÁN-*a-a*
6 *ta-rab-bi*

r.1 ITI.BARAG UD-27-KÁM
2 *lim-me* ^{m}*aš-šur*—KALAG-*in*-MAN

ADD 131

1 Two homers of barley belonging to Bahianu, at the disposal of Astaqumme.

(stamp seal impression)

4 He took it as a loan. It shall increase by 3 seahs per homer.

(stamp seal impression)

r.1 Month Nisan (I), 27th day, eponym year of Aššur-da''inanni.

72. A Barley Loan Paid Back to Bahianu (685-VII)

K 135

1 1 ANŠE ^{m}*ṣa-bu-ta-a-nu*
2 1 : ^{m}*la*—*tu-ba-šá-a-ni*—DING[IR]
3 PAB 2 : ŠE.PAD.MEŠ
4 *a-na* ^{m}*ba-hi-a-ni*
e.5 *ú-sa-li-mu*
r.1 ^{md}PA—ZALÁG—*nam-mir*
2 *la ú-šal-lim*
3 ITI.DU$_{6}$! 0!
4 *lim-mu* ^{m}*aš-šur*—KALAG-*in-a-ni*

ADD 135

1 One homer — Ṣabutanu,
2 one ditto — La-tubašanni-i[lu],
3 a total of two ditto of barley;
4 they have paid it in full to Bahianu.
r.1 Nabû-nuru-nammir has not paid.

3 Month Tishri (VII), eponym year of Aššur-da''inanni.

71 Previous editions: AR 323, NALK 59. r.2 MAN sic (coll.), scribal error since the name can only be Aššur-da''inanni.
72 Previous editions: AR 236, NALK 58. Collations: Assur 2/5. → no. 70 (which is the initial loan).

73. Bahianu Loans 10 Homers of Barley (684-III-21)

83-1-18,405

1 10 ANŠE ŠE.PAD.MEŠ
2 *ša* ^{m}*ba-hi-a-ni*

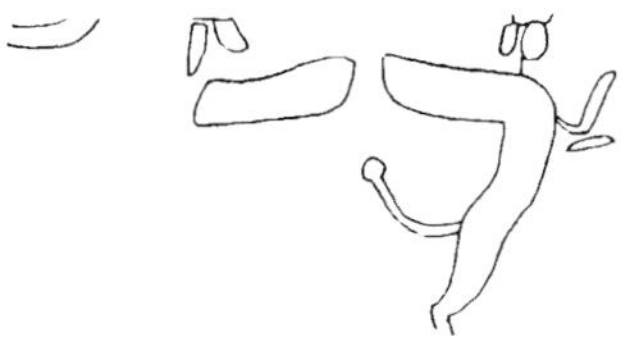

rest broken away
r.1 ITI.SIG$_4$ UD-21-KÁM
2 *lim-mu* ^{m}*ma-za-ar-né-e*
3 IGI ^{m}30—PAB—AŠ
4 IGI ^{m}*na*$^{!}$*-na*$^{!}$*-a-a*
s.1 [I]GI ^{m}*da-an-d*[*a-ru*]
2 A.BA

ADD 142

1 10 homers of barley belonging to Bahianu

(cylinder seal impression)

(Break)

(cylinder seal impression)

r.1 Month Sivan (III), 21st day, eponym year of Manzarnê.

3 Witness Sin-ahu-iddina.

4 Witness Nanaya.

s.1 Witness Dand[aru], scribe.

74. Bahianu Loans 4 Homers of Wheat (684-IX)

Rm 176

1 4 ANŠE ŠE.GIG.MEŠ
2 *ša* ^{m}*ba-hi-a-ni*
3 *ina* IGI ^{m}*la—a-maš-ši*—EN
4 *ina pu-u-hi it-ti-ši*

5 *a-na* 1 :. 5BÁN-*a-a*
6 ⸢*i-rab-bi*⸣
r.1 ITI.GAN UD-[*x*-KÁM]
space of 3 lines
2 *lim-mu* ^{m}*ma-an-za-né-e*

ADD 149

1 4 homers of wheat belonging to Bahianu, at the disposal of La-amašši-Bel.

4 He has taken it as a loan.

(cylinder seal impression)

5 It shall increase by 5 seahs per homer.

r.1 Month Kislev (IX), [...th] day, eponym year of Manzarnê.

75. Bahianu Loans 4 Homers of Barley (682-I-21)

K 373

1 4 ANŠE ŠE.PAD.MEŠ
2 *ša* ^{m}*ba-hi-a-ni*

ADD 132

1 4 homers of barley belonging to Bahianu, at the disposal of Gabbî. He has taken it as a loan.

(stamp seal impression)

73 Previous editions: AR 310, NALK 60. r.4 See coll.
74 Previous editions: AR 309, NALK 61.
75 Previous editions: AR 311, NALK 62; → KB 4 (1896) 150f.

3 *ina* IGI ^{m}*ga-bi-i*
4 *ina pu-u-hi it-ti-ši*
r.1 *a-na* 1 :. 5BÁN-*a-a*
2 *ta-rab-bi*

3 4 LÚ*!.*e-ṣi-di*
4 ITI.BARAG UD-21-KÁM
5 *lim-mu* ^{md}PA—MAN—(PAB)

r.1 It shall increase by 5 seahs per homer.

(stamp seal impression)

3 4 harvesters.

4 Month Nisan (I), 21st day, eponym year of Nabû-šarru-(uṣur).

76. Bahianu Loans Barley (682-II-10)

K 1858

beginning broken away
1′ [*x* ^{m}]A.10—*dàl*!-[*a*]
2′ *ša* ^{m}*ba-hi-*⸢*a-ni*⸣
3′ *ina* IGI-*šú-nu*
4′ *ina pu-u-hi it-ta-ṣu*
r.1 ITI.GUD UD-⸢10!⸣-KÁM

2 ⸢*lim*⸣*-mu* ^{md}PA—MAN—PAB

ADD 143

(Beginning destroyed)

1 [......] — Apladad-dalâ;

2 (barley) belonging to Bahianu, at their disposal. They have taken it as a loan.

r.1 Month Iyyar (II), 10th day,

(two stamp seal impressions)

2 eponym year of Nabû-šarru-uṣur.

77. Bahianu Loans Three Homers of Barley (682-I-25)

K 338

1 1 ANŠE 2BÁN ŠE.PAD.MEŠ
2 ^{md}30—MAN—PAB
3 7BÁN ^{m}U.GUR—MAŠ
4 7BÁN ^{m}*re-mut-ti*—DINGIR
5 7BÁN ^{m}DI.KUD—*kur-ba-ìl*

6 *ša* ^{m}*ba-hi-a-ni*
7 *ina pa-ni-šú-nu*
8 *ina pu-u-hi it-ta-ṣu*
9 ITI.GUD UD-25!-[KÁM!]
10 *lim-mu* ^{md}PA—MAN—P[AB]

ADD 136

1 One homer and two seahs of barley — Sin-šarru-uṣur,

3 7 seahs — Nergal-ašared,

4 7 seahs — Remutti-ili,

5 7 seahs — Dayyan-Kurbail

(fingernail impressions)

6 belonging to Bahianu, at their disposal. They have taken it as a loan.

9 Month Iyyar (II), 25th day, eponym year of Nabû-šarru-u[ṣur].

76 Previous editions: AR 332, NALK 63.
77 Previous editions: AR 312, NALK 64. 9 The day is 25, as given in ADD (coll. I.L. Finkel).

78. 12 Persons Borrow Barley from Bahianu

83-1-18,323

beginning broken away
1′ 1 [: ^{m}*x x x x x*]
2′ 1 : [^{m}*x x x x x*]
3′ 1 : ^{m}*š*⸢*e*!⸣-*x*[*x x x*]
4′ 1 : ^{m}ARAD!—*x*[*x x x*]
5′ 1 : ^{m}*ga-lu*[*l*]
6′ 5BÁN ^{m}SUHUŠ—PAB.ME[Š]
7′ 5BÁN ^{md}UTU—PAB-*ir*
8′ 1 : ^{m}SU!—DINGIR.MEŠ-*ni*
9′ 1 : ^{m}PAB-*u-ni-i*

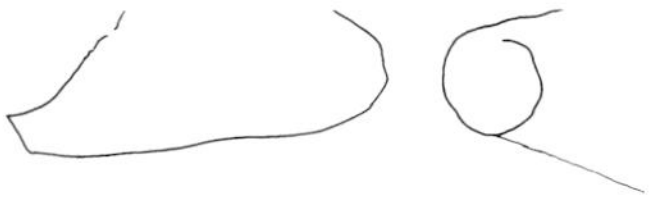

r.1 5BÁN ^{m}*qur-di*—15
2 5BÁN ^{m}*kù*-KÁ—PAB—AŠ
3 1 : ^{m}*kù*-KÁ—DINGIR-*a-a*
4 *ša* ^{m}*ba-hi-a-n*[*i ina pa-ni-šú-nu*]
5 *ina pu-u-hi it*-[*ta-ṣu*]

6 [ITI.BAR]AG UD-10-[*x*-KÁM]
rest broken away
s.1 [*x x x x x x n*]*a-as-ha-at*

ADD 138

(Beginning destroyed)
1 One [ditto — ......],
2 one ditto — [......],
3 one ditto — Še[...],
4 one ditto — Urda-[...],
5 one ditto — Gallu[lu],
6 5 seahs — Ubru-ahhe,
7 5 seahs — Šamaš-naṣir,
8 one ditto — Riba-ilani,
9 one ditto — Ahunî,

(stamp seal impression)

r.1 5 seahs — Qurdi-Issar,
2 5 seahs — Kubabu-ahu-iddina,
3 one ditto — Kubabu-ila'i;
4 (barley) belonging to Bahia[nu, at their disposal].
5 [They have ta]ken it as a loan.
6 [Month Ni]san (I), *1*[*0*th] day.
(Break)
s.1 [...] withdrawn.

79. Bahianu Loans 12 Homers of Barley

K 9591

1 [2 AN]ŠE ŠE.[P]AD.M[EŠ ^{m}*x x x x*]
2 ⸢2⸣ :. ^{m}*a-a*—⸢*x*⸣[*x x*]
3 ⸢2⸣ :. ^{m}DI-*mu*—*l*[*a-mur*]
4 ⸢2⸣ :. ^{m}*mar*—*bi-i'-di*
5 ⸢2⸣ :. ^{m}*dàl-a*—DINGIR
6 ⸢2⸣ :. ^{m}10—EN—PAB

7 [P]AB 12 :. ŠE.PAD.MEŠ
8 ⸢*ša*⸣ ^{m}*ba-hi-a-ni*
9 [*ina p*]*a-ni-šú-nu*
rest broken away

ADD 720

1 [2 ho]mers of barl[ey — NN],
2 2 ditto — Aya-[...],
3 2 ditto — Šulmu-l[amur],
4 2 ditto — Mar-bi'di,
5 2 ditto — Dalâ-il,
6 2 ditto — Adad-belu-uṣur;
7 a total of 12 ditto of barley belonging to Bahianu, [at] their disposal.
(Rest destroyed)

78 Previous editions: AR 328, NALK 68. Collations: Assur 2/5.
79 Previous editions: AR 329, NALK 66.

80. Bahianu Loans 6 Shekels of Silver

K 14288

1 6$^{!}$ GÍN KUG.UD ^{m}*ba-hi-a-*[*nu*]
2 [*a*]-*na* ^{m}*ha-le-e-ṣi* [*ina pu-hi*]
3 [*i*]*t-ti-din* ^{m}TA*—^{d}IM—⸢PAB⸣-[*ú-tú*]
illegible traces
5 LÚ*.A.BA [^{m}*x x x*]

ADD 792

1 Bahia[nu] has [loa]ned 6 shekels of silver to Haleṣi.
3 Issi-Adad-ahh[utu] ......
5 Scr[ibe: NN].

80 Previous editions: AR 238, NALK 67.

6. Harem Governesses and Other Royal Women (694-681)

FIG. 16. *Queen in mural crown with an attendant (ninth-century tile fragment from Nineveh).*
AAA 18, pl. XXXI.

81. Addati, Harem Governess, Lends Two Minas of Silver (694-VIII-1)

80-7-19,48

1 2 MA.NA [KUG.U]D$^{!}$ SAG.DU
2 *ina* 1 MA.[NA] *ša*$^{!}$ URU.*gar-ga-mis*
3 *ša* MÍ.[*ad-da*]-*ti* MÍ.*šá-kín-te*
4 *ina* IGI ^{m}[*bi-b*]*i*$^{!}$-*ia* LÚ*.2-*i* LÚ.GAL—URU.MEŠ
5 *ku-um* 2 ⸢MA.NA⸣ KUG.UD É 12 ANŠE
6 A.ŠÀ.GA *ina* UGU EDIN$^{!}$ URU.*aš-šur*
7 ^{m}*qur-di*—^{d}IM MÍ-*šú* 3 DUMU.MEŠ-*šú*
8 ^{m}*kan-dàl-a-nu* MÍ-*šú*
9 PAB 7 ZI.MEŠ 12 ANŠE *a-na šá-par-ti*
e.10 *ina* IGI MÍ.*ad-da-ti šak-nu*

11 *ina* ŠÀ UD-*me*$^{!}$ *ša* KUG.UD SUM-*u-ni*
r.1 UN.MEŠ A.ŠÀ.GA *ú-še-ṣa*

---

2 IGI ^{md}PA—NUMUN$^{!}$—GIŠ LÚ*.A.BA DUMU—URU.NINA
3 IGI ^{md}*šu-ri-ha*—DINGIR-*a-a*
4 IGI ^{md}UTU—PAB—AŠ LÚ*.A.ZU
5 IGI ^{m}*dà-ri*—EN IGI ^{m}*ṭa-bi-i* LÚ*.NINDA
6 IGI ^{m}*za-bi-nu* LÚ*.*ka-ṣir* IGI ^{m}*an-da-ra-nu*
7 IGI ^{md}UTU—PAB—PAB LÚ*.SIPA—MUŠEN.MEŠ
8 IGI ^{m}*sa-gíb-i* LÚ*.Ì.DU$_{8}$

9e IGI ^{md}PA—*šal-lim* ITI.APIN UD-1-KAM
10e *lim-mu* ^{m}DINGIR—KI-*ia* LÚ*.GAR.KUR URU.*di-maš-qa*

ADD 58

1 Two minas [of silve]r, capital, by the mi[na] of Carchemish, belonging to [Adda]ti, governess, at the disposal of [Bib]iya, deputy village manager.

5 In lieu of two minas of silver, an estate of 12 hectares of land outside the city of Aššur, (plus) Qurdi-Adad, his wife, his 3 sons, (and) Kandalanu and his wife — a total of 7 persons (and) 12 hectares (of land) are placed as a pledge at the disposal of Addati.

11 On the day he pays the silver, he shall redeem the people (and) the field.

---

r.2 Witness Nabû-šumu-lešir, Ninevite scribe.

3 Witness Šuriha-ila'i.

4 Witness Šamaš-ahu-iddina, physician.

5 Witness Dari-Bel. Witness Ṭabî, baker.

6 Witness Zabinu, tailor. Witness Andaranu.

7 Witness Šamaš-ahu-uṣur, gooseherd.

8 Witness Sagibî, porter.

9 Witness Nabû-šallim.

9 Month Marchesvan (VIII), 1st day, eponym year of Ilu-isse'a, governor of Damascus.

82. Addati, Governess, Purchases a Woman

Rm 2,165

beginning broken away
1′ *ina* [ŠÀ *x* MA.NA KUG.UD *ta-al-qi*]

2′ *kas-pu* [*gam-mur ta-din*]
3′ MÍ *šu-a-tú* ⸢*zar*⸣-*p*[*at la-qi-at*]

ADD 223

(Beginning destroyed)

1 [Addati, governess, has contracted and bought her] for [x minas of silver].

2 The money [is paid completely]. That woman is purch[ased and acquired]. Any

81 Previous editions: AR 150, NALK 7. 6 See coll. 11, r.2 See coll.
82 Previous editions: AR 515, NALK 8. 4f There is no room for restoring [*man-nu šá*] and [GIL-*u-ni*] at the end of these lines.

4′ *tu-a-ru de-e-nu* DUG$_4$.DUG$_4$ [*la-áš-šú*]
5′ *ina ur-kiš ina im—ma-te-m*[*a*]
6′ *lu-u* ^{m}AD—*sa-lam lu-u* DUMU.M[EŠ-*šú*]
7′ *lu-u* ŠEŠ.MEŠ-*šú lu-u* DUMU.ME[Š—ŠEŠ.MEŠ]-*šú*
8′ *lu-u* LÚ.*šak-an-šú lu-*⌜*u*⌝ [*x x x x*]
9′ *lu-u qur-ub-šu ša* ⌜*de*⌝-[*e-nu* DUG$_4$.DUG$_4$]
10′ TA*$^{!}$ MÍ.*ad-*⌜*da*⌝-[*ti x x x*]
11′ ⌜*ù*⌝ EGIR-*šú* [*x x x x*]
12′ ⌜*x*⌝ [*x x x x x x x x x x x*]
rest broken away

revocation, lawsuit or litigation [is void].

5 [Whoever], at any time in the futu[re], whether Abi-salam or [his] son[s], brothers or neph[ews], or his prefect, [...], or neighbour, seeks a lawsu[it or litigation] against Adda[ti, ...], and his (sic) *successor*

(Rest destroyed)

83. The Governess Gets a Fine (694-XII-10)

K 370

1 40 MA.NA URUDU.MEŠ SAG.⌜DU⌝
2 *sa-ár-tú ša* LÚ*$^{!}$.SUKKAL
3 ⌜*e*⌝*-me-du-u-ni*
4 [*ina* IG]I MÍ.*šá-ki-in-te*
5 IGI ^{m}DINGIR—*im-me*
6 [IG]I ^{m}DINGIR—*ú*-KALAG-*ni*
e.7 IGI ^{md}PA—PAB—PAB
r.1 IGI ^{m}*la*—TÉŠ-*ni*—DINGIR
space of 3 lines
2 ITI.ŠE UD-10-KÁM
3 *lim-me* ^{m}DINGIR—KI-*e-a*

ADD 162

1 40 minas of copper, capital, fine imposed by the vizier, [at the dispos]al of the governess.

5 Witness Il-immi.
6 Witness Ilu-uda''inanni.
7 Witness Nabû-ahu-uṣur,
8 Witness La-tubašanni-ilu.
r.1 Month Adar (XII), 10th day, eponym year of Ilu-isse'a.

84. The Governess Loans Sheep (694-XII-10)

83-1-18,330

1 11$^{!}$ UDU.U$_8$.MEŠ
2 ⌜*a*⌝-*di* (blank) UDU.NITÁ.MEŠ-*ši-na*
3 *ša* MÍ.*šá-ki-in-tú*
4 *ina* IGI ^{md}PA—AŠ—PAB
5 IGI ^{m}DINGIR—*ú*$^{!}$-KALAG-*an-ni*
e.6 IGI ^{md}PA—PAB—PAB
7 IGI ^{m}*man-nu*—*ki*-0$^{!}$—15
r.1 IGI ^{m}*la*—TÉŠ-*ni*—DINGIR LÚ*.A.B[A]
space of 2 lines
2 ITI.ŠE UD-10-KÁM
3 *lim-me* ^{m}DINGIR—KI-*e-a*

ADD 120

1 11 ewes plus their rams, belonging to the governess, at the disposal of Nabû-nadin-ahi.

5 Witness Ilu-uda''inanni,
6 Witness Nabû-ahu-uṣur,
7 Witness Mannu-ki-Issar,
r.1 Witness La-tubašanni-ilu, scri[be].

2 Month Adar (XII), 10th day, eponym year of Ilu-isse'a.

85. The Governess of the Central City Harem Buys Two Slaves (692-X-6)

K 437

1 [NA$_4$.KIŠIB] ^{m}[*x x x x x*]

ADD 242

1 [Seal of NN, s]eal of Kiqil[lanu], owners

83 Previous editions: AR 643, NALK 418; → KB 4 (1896) 116f; no. 84; 3R 47,8 (copy).
84 Previous editions: AR 306, NALK 419. 1, 5, 7 See coll.
85 Previous editions: AR 457, NALK 411. Collations: Assur 2/5.

2 [N]A$_4$.KIŠIB ^{m}*ki-qil-*⸢*la*$^{!}$⸣*-*[*nu*]
3 EN UN.MEŠ SUM-⸢*ni*⸣

4 ^{md}PA—I MÍ.*ak-ba-ra-a*
5 PAB 2 ZI.MEŠ ARAD.MEŠ-*ni*
6 *šá* LÚ.MEŠ-*e an-nu-u-te*
7 *ú-piš-ma* MÍ.GAR-*tú šá* MURUB$_4$—URU
8 *ina* ŠÀ 1 MA.NA KUG.UD *ina* 1 MA$^{!}$-*e šá* MAN
9 TA* IGI LÚ.MEŠ-*e an-nu-ti*
10 *il-qi kas-pu gam-mur ta-ad-din*
11 UN.MEŠ *šu-a-tú za-ár-pu*
12 *la-qi*$^{!}$*-ú tu-a-ru*
13 *de-*⸢*e*⸣*-nu* DUG$_4$.DUG$_4$ *la-áš-šú*
14 [*man-n*]*u šá ina ur-kiš ina ma-te-ma*
15 [*i-za-qu-pa-n*]*i* ⸢4$^{!}$⸣ MA.NA KUG.UD
16 [LUH-*u x* MA.NA KUG.G]I *sak-ru*
r.1 *ina bur-ki* ^{d}15 *šá* URU.NINA GAR-*an*
2 *kas-p*[*u a-na* 10].MEŠ-*te a-na* EN-*šú*
3 GUR-⸢*ra*⸣ [*ina de*]*-ni-šú* DUG$_4$.DUG$_4$-*ma*
4 *la i-laq-qí ṣib-ti be-en*
5 *a-na* 1-*me* UD-*me*$^{!}$ *sa-ár-tu*
6 *a-na kal* UD.MEŠ

7 IGI ^{m}*e-ni*—DINGIR ARAD *šá* A—MAN
8 IGI ^{m}*šá*—^{d}15—*du-bu*
9 IGI ^{m}PAB—*na-ad-bi*
10 IGI ^{md}UTU—SUM-*na*
11 IGI ^{md}⸢PA$^{!}$⸣—MAŠ
blank space of two lines
12 ITI.AB UD-9$^{!}$-⸢KÁM⸣
13 *lim-mu* ^{m}*za-*[*zi*]*-*⸢*i*⸣

of the people being sold.

(space for stamp seal impressions)

4 Nabû-na'id and the woman Akbarâ, a total of two persons, servants of these men —

7 the governess of the central city (harem) has contracted and bought them from these men for one mina of silver by the king's mina.

10 The money is paid completely. Those people are purchased and acquired. Any revocation, lawsuit, or litigation is void.

14 [Whoev]er in the future, at any time, [lodges a compla]int, shall place 4 minas of [refined] silver (and) [x minas] of pure [gol]d in the lap of Ištar of Nineveh. He shall return the mone[y tenfol]d to its owner. He shall contest [in] his law[suit] and not succeed.

r.4 (Guaranteed against) seizures of epilepsy for 100 days (and against) fraud forever.

7 Witness Eni-il, servant of the crown prince.

8 Witness Ša-Issar-dubbu.

9 Witness Ahi-nadbi.

10 Witness Šamaš-iddina.

11 Witness Nabû-ašared.

12 Month Tebet (X), 9th day, eponym year of Zazî.

86. The Governess of the Central City Harem Buys Twenty Slaves

K 8754

beginning broken away
1′ MÍ.*su-u-*[*x x x*] ⸢*x x*⸣ [*x x x x x x x*]
2′ 2 DUMU.MEŠ-*šú* DUMU.MÍ-*su* ⸢*x*⸣ [*x x x x x x x x x*]
3′ 2 DUMU.MEŠ-*šú* PAB 4 ^{m}*mad*$^{!}$*-a-a* [*x x x x x x x x x x*(*x x*)]
4′ ^{m}*ú-ra-a-a* MÍ-*šú* ^{m}*si-t*[*i*$^{!}$*-ir-x x x x x x x x x*]
5′ ^{md}U.GUR—SUM-*na* PAB 20 LÚ*$^{!}$.Z[I.MEŠ ARAD.MEŠ]-*ni*$^{!}$
6′ *ša* ^{m}URU.*arba-il-a-a tu*$^{!}$*-*[*piš-ma* MÍ.*x x x x x*]
7′ [MÍ].⸢*šá*⸣-GIM$^{!}$-*tú ša* [MURUB$_4$]—⸢URU$^{!}$⸣ [*x x x x x x x x x*]

ADD 261

(Beginning destroyed)

1 the woman Su[..., *his wife*], his two sons, his daughter, [*a total of* 5; NN, *his wife*], his two sons, a total of 4;

3 Madayu, [......, *a total of x*]; Urayu and his wife; Sit[ir......, *a total of x*]; Nergal-iddina; in all 20 per[sons, servants] of Arbailayu —

7 [NN], governess of the [central] city (harem), has con[tracted and bought them] for 8 minas of [silver].

86 Previous editions: AR 87, NALK 414. → TCAE 140f. Collations: Assur 2/5.

8′ *ina* ŠÀ ⸢8! MA.NA⸣ [KUG.UD TI *x x x x x x x*]
4 obliterated, virtually illegible lines
13′ [*x x x x*] ⸢*de*⸣-*e*-[*nu*] ⸢DUG$_4$!⸣.[DUG$_4$ *x x x x x x x x*]
14′ [*x x x x* 2 AN]ŠE!.KUR.RA.[MEŠ *x x x x x x x x*]
3 illegible lines
e.18′ [*x x x*] ⸢*x nu*?⸣ *a*! ⸢*x x*⸣ *ub*! [*x kas-pu a-na* 10.MEŠ-*te*]
r.1 [*ana* EN.MEŠ-*šú*] *ú-ta-ra* [*ina de-ni-šú*]
2 [DUG$_4$.DUG$_4$-*m*]*a la* ⸢*i*⸣-[*laq-qi*]

(Break)

13 [whoever seeks] a lawsu[it] or liti[gation *against the governess shall tie two white hor*]ses [*to the feet of Aššur*].

(Break)

r.1 He shall return [the money tenfold to its owners. He shall contest in his lawsuit] and not suc[ceed].

---

3 [IGI ^{md}]AMAR.UTU—APIN-*eš* LÚ*.*mu*-[*ša*]*r*-*k*[*is*]
4 [IGI] ^{m}*hal*-⸢*ma*⸣-*nu* LÚ*.*mu-šar-kis*
5 IGI ^{md}PA—EN—PAB LÚ*.*h*[*a-za*]-*nu ša* URU.*ni-nu-a*
6 IGI ^{md}PA—AM—DINGIR.MEŠ LÚ*.*ha-za*-⸢*nu*⸣ *ša* URU-*ni-nu*-[*a*]
7 IGI ^{md}PA—MAN-*a*-[*ni* LÚ*].⸢*šá*!—UGU!⸣—URU *ša* URU.*ni-nu*-[*a*]
8 IGI ^{m}⸢*na-ni*⸣-*i* LÚ*.⸢A!.BA!⸣ *ša* DUMU—⸢LUGAL⸣
9 IGI ^{m}*na-din*!-*ia* LÚ*.⸢DAM.QAR⸣ ANŠE. KUR.R[A.MEŠ!]
10 IGI ^{md}*hal-di—rém-a-ni* LÚ*.DAM.QAR
11 IGI ^{m}⸢d!PA!⸣—[SIG$_5$]-*iq* ⸢LÚ*⸣.2-*u ša* LÚ*.A.BA—É.GAL
12 IGI ^{m}[*x x x x x*]-⸢*da-ku*?⸣ *ša* URU.*ni-nu-a*
13 IGI ^{m}[*x*]-*a-ni*-⸢*a*!⸣ [LÚ*.*šá*—UG]U!—É—DINGIR.MEŠ *ša* URU.ŠÀ—URU
14 [IGI ^{m}*x x x x x*] *ša* MÍ—É.GAL
15 [IGI ^{m}*x x*]—PAB—PAB LÚ*!.3-[*šú*!] *ša* ^{md}30—LUGAL—DINGIR.MEŠ
16 [IGI ^{m}*x x x*]—$^{d!}$[*x*] LÚ*!.[3-*šú*] *ša* LÚ*.*tur-ta-ni*
17 [IGI ^{m}*x x x x*] ⸢*x x x*⸣ [*x*] DUMU URU.*ni-nu-a*
rest broken away

3 Witness Marduk-ereš, recruitment officer.
4 Witness Halmanu, recruitment officer.
5 Witness Nabû-belu-uṣur, mayor of Nineveh.
6 Witness Nabû-rim-ilani, mayor of Nineveh.
7 Witness Nabû-šarrani, city overseer of Nineveh.
8 Witness Nanî, scribe of the crown prince.
9 Witness Nadin-Ea, horse merchant.
10 Witness Haldi-remanni, merchant.
11 Witness Nabû-dammiq, deputy of the palace scribe.
12 Witness [NN], ... of Nineveh.
13 Witness [...]ania, overseer of the temples of the Inner City.
14 Witness [NN, ...] of the queen.
15 Witness [...]-ahu-uṣur, 'third man' of Sin-šar-ilani.
16 Witness [NN, '*third man*'] of the commander-in-chief.
17 Witness [NN], citizen of Nineveh.
(Rest destroyed)

87. The Governess of the Central City Harem Buys Slaves

Bu 89-4-26,122

beginning broken away
1′ ⸢*x x*⸣ [*x x x x*(*x*) MÍ.*šá*]-⸢*kin*!-*tú*! *ša*⸣ MU[RUB$_4$!—URU]
2′ *ina* ŠÀ 10 MA.[NA KUG.UD *i*]*l-qi*
3′ *kas-pu gam-mur ta-din* UN.MEŠ *šu-a-tu*
4′ *za-ar-pu laq-qi*!-*ú tu-a-ru de-e-nu*
5′ DUG$_4$.DUG$_4$ *la-áš-šú man-nu ša ina ur-kiš*
6′ *ina ma-te-e-ma i-zaq-qu-pan-ni*
7′ *lu-u* ^{m}*se-e*ʾ—*gab-ba-ri lu-u* DUMU.MEŠ-*šú*

ADD 263

(Beginning destroyed)

1 [the gov]erness of the cen[tral city] (harem) has contracted [and bou]ght them for 10 mi[nas of silver].

3 The money is paid completely. Those people are purchased and acquired. Any revocation, lawsuit, or litigation is void.

5 Whoever in the future, at any time,

87 Previous editions: AR 175, NALK 415. Collations: Assur 2/5.

8′ *lu-u* ⌈DUMU⌉—DUMU.MEŠ-*šú lu-u* ŠEŠ. MEŠ-*šú lu-u* DUMU.MEŠ—ŠEŠ.MEŠ-*šú*
9′ *ša* TA*$^{!}$ MÍ.*šá-kín-tú* DUMU.MEŠ-*šú* DUMU—DUMU.MEŠ-*šú*
10′ *de-*⌈*e*⌉*-nu* DUG$_4$.DUG$_4$ *ub-ta-ʾu-u-ni*
r.1 10 ⌈MA⌉.NA KUG.UD LUH-*u* 1 MA.NA KUG. GI *sak-ru*
2 *ina bur-ki* ^{d}IŠ.TAR *a-ši-bat* URU.NINA *i-šak-kan*
3 2 ANŠE.KUR.RA.MEŠ BABBAR.MEŠ *ina*$^{!}$ GÌR.2 *aš-šur i-rak-kas*
4 4 ANŠE.*har-ba-kan-ni ina* KI.TA ^{d}ŠEŠ.GAL *ú-še-rab*
5 *kas-pu a-na* 10.MEŠ-*te a-na* EN.MEŠ-*šú* GUR-*ra*
6 *ina de-ni-šú* DUG$_4$.DUG$_4$-*ma la i-laq-qi*
7 IGI ^{md}PA—EN—PAB LÚ*.*ha-za-nu*
8 IGI ^{md}PA—AM—DINGIR.ME[Š]
9 [I]GI ^{m}IM—⌈*aš*$^{!}$*-šur*$^{!}$⌉
10 [IGI] ^{md}PA—MU—[*x x*]
11 [IGI] ^{m}⌈EN$^{!}$⌉—[*x x x*]
rest broken away

lodges a complaint, whether Se'-gabbari or his sons, grandsons, brothers or nephews, and seeks a lawsuit or litigation against the governess, his (sic) sons and grandsons,

r.1 shall place 10 minas of refined silver and one mina of pure gold in the lap of Ištar residing in Nineveh, shall tie two white horses to the feet of Aššur, shall bring four *harbakannu* horses to the feet of Nergal, and shall return the money tenfold to its owners. He shall contest in his lawsuit and not succeed.

7 Witness Nabû-belu-uṣur, mayor.
8 Witness Nabû-rim-ilani.
9 Witness Šar-Aššur.
10 Witness Nabû-šumu-[...].
11 Witness Bel-[...].
(Rest destroyed)

88. Ahi-ṭalli, Harem Woman, Buys a Girl (687-XI-12)

DT 12

1 NA$_4$.KIŠIB MÍ.*da-li-ia-a*
2 EN MÍ.TUR SUM-*ni*

---

3 [M]Í$^{!}$.*a-na*—AD—*da-la-ti*
4 [DU]MU.MÍ-*sa* 5 *ru-ṭu*
5 ⌈*ú*⌉*-piš-ma* MÍ.PAB—*ṭal-li*
6 MÍ.ERIM—É.GAL TA* IGI
7 MÍ.*da-li-ia-a ina* ŠÀ
8 1/2 MA.NA KUG.UD *il-qí*
9 *kas-pu gam-mur ta-ad-din*
10 MÍ.TUR *šu-a-tú*
11 *zar-pat laq-qí-at*
12 *tu-a-ru de-e-nu* DUG$_4$.DUG$_4$
13 *la-áš-šú* [*man*]-⌈*nu*⌉ *šá*$^{!}$ *ina ur-kiš*
Edge uninscribed
r.1′ [*ina ma-te-ma i-za-qup-an-ni*]
2′ G[IL$^{?}$*-u-ni x x x x*]

ADD 317

1 Seal of the woman Daliya, owner of the girl being sold.

(blank seal space)

---

3 Ana-abi-dalati, her daughter of 5 spans —
5 Ahi-ṭalli, harem woman, has contracted and bought her from Daliya for 1/2 mina of silver.

9 The money is paid completely. That girl is purchased and acquired. Any revocation, lawsuit, or litigation is void.

13 [Whoever] at any time [in the future lodges a complaint ...]
(Break)

88 Previous editions: AR 39, NALK 12. 3f See coll. 6 Despite NALK p.16, the evidence cited CAD S 216 sub 2a-b s.v. firmly establishes that MÍ.ERIM—É.GAL was the Neo-Assyrian word for "harem woman" and has to be read *sekretu*, at least in royal inscriptions (in letters the reading may have been different, possibly *erimtu*). Taking MÍ.ERIM—É.GAL as a logogram for *šakintu* "(harem) governess" is out of the question for the simple reason that there was only one *šakintu* per palace (see discussion CAD Š/1 p.166), while MÍ.ERIM.(MEŠ)—É.GAL.(MEŠ) are attested in great numbers in individual (harem) palaces. Since no. 88 is the earliest of the Ahi-ṭalli documents and the only one in which she is called MÍ.ERIM—É.GAL in contrast to the documents dated 686-683 in which she appears as *šakintu*, the logical conclusion is that she started as a harem woman under the governess Addati and was promoted to the head of the harem in 686. The unidentified MÍ.ERIM—É.GAL in no. 91:11 (681 B.C.) may have been Ahi-ṭalli's successor. 13, r.2ff See coll.

3′ *x*[*x x x x x x x*]
4′ *l*[*a*$^{!}$ *x x x x x x x*]
5′ *x*[*x x x x x x x*]
break of three lines
9′ [IG]I$^{!}$ $^{m⌈}$*x*$^{⌉}$[*x x x x x*]
10′ [IGI] ^{md}PA—PAB$^{!}$-[*x x x x*]
two line space
11′ [ITI]-ZÍZ UD-22-KÁM
12′ [*lim*]-*mu* ^{md}30—PAB.MEŠ—SU MAN KUR—*aš-šur*

r.9 [Witne]ss [...].
10 [Witness] Nabû-ahu-[...].

11 [Month] Shebat (XI), 22nd day, [epo]nym year of Sennacherib, king of Assyria.

89. Ahi-ṭalli, Governess, Buys Three Slaves (686-XII-18)

81-2-4,149

1 NA$_{4}$.KIŠIB ^{m}MAN-*a-ni*
2 EN UN.MEŠ SUM-*an*

3 ^{m}IM.4-*i* ARAD-[*šú* ^{m}*x*]*x*—IM—AN.ŠÁR
4 MÍ.^{d}*ur-kit*—DINGIR-*a-a* [*x x x x*]
5 É PAB 3$^{!}$ ZI.MEŠ ⌈É$^{?}$⌉ [*x*] ⌈*x*⌉

6 *tu-piš-ma* MÍ.PAB—*ṭa-li*
7 MÍ.*šá-kín-ti ša* URU.MURUB$_{4}$—⌈URU⌉
8 *ina* ⌈ŠÀ⌉-*bi* 4 MA.NA KUG.UD *ta-*⌈*al*⌉*-qi*
9 *kas-pu ga-mur ta-din*
10 UN.MEŠ *šu-a-te za-ar-pu*
11 *la-qi-u tu-a-ru*
12 *de-ni* DUG$_{4}$.DUG$_{4}$ *la-šú*
r.1 *man-nu šá* TA* MÍ.*šá-kín-*⌈*ti*⌉
2 *de-ni* DUG$_{4}$.DUG$_{4}$ *ub-ta-ʾu-u-ni*
3 15 MA.NA KUG.UD SUM-*an*

4 *ṣib-ti a-na* 1-*me* UD-*mu sa-ar-ti*
5 *a-na kal* UD.MEŠ

6 IGI ^{m}PAB—DU LÚ*$^{!}$.*qur*-ZAG
7 IGI ^{m}*na-bu-u-a* :
8 IGI ^{m}10$^{!}$—KI-*ia* :
9 IGI ^{m}*šá-ma-aʾ* LÚ*$^{!}$.A.BA
10 IGI ^{m}MAN—SIPA$^{!!}$-*u-a*$^{!}$ LÚ*$^{!}$.*qur*-ZAG
11 IGI ^{m}*kù*$^{!}$-KÁ—SU LÚ*$^{!}$.Ì.DU$_{8}$
12 IGI ^{md}MAŠ—*kib-si*—PAB :
13 IGI ^{m}*e-zi*—*pa*-⌈*šar*$^{!}$⌉
14 IGI ^{m}BA-*šá-a*

15 ITI.ŠE UD-18$^{!}$-KAM
16 *lim-mu* ^{m}EN—IGI.LAL-*a-ni* LÚ*.*tur-tan*

ADD 232

1 Seal of Šarranu, owner of the people being sold.

(cylinder seal impression)

3 Amurrî, [his] servant; [...]-šar-Aššur; Urkit-ila'i; [...]; a household of all together 3 persons [...] —

6 Ahi-ṭalli, governess of the central city (harem), has contracted and bought them for 4 minas of silver.

9 The money is paid completely. Those people are purchased and acquired. Any revocation, lawsuit or litigation is void.

r.1 Whoever seeks a lawsuit or litigation against the governess shall pay 15 minas of silver.

4 (Guaranteed against) seizures for 100 days (and against) fraud forever.

6 Witness Ahu-illika, royal bodyguard.
7 Witness Nabû'a, ditto.
8 Witness Adad-isse'a, ditto.
9 Witness Šama', scribe.
10 Witness Šarru-re'û'a, royal bodyguard.
11 Witness Kubabu-eriba, porter.
12 Witness Inurta-kibsi-uṣur, ditto.
13 Witness Ezi-pašar.
14 Witness Iqišâ.

15 Month Adar (XII), 16th day, eponym year of Bel-emuranni, commander-in-chief.

89 Previous editions: AR 458, NALK 13. Collations: Assur 2/5. r.10 Tablet ^{m}MAN—ŠAB-*u-a* (scribal error).

90. Ahi-ṭalli, Governess, Buys 17 Persons With an Orchard (683-II-1)

82-5-22,34

1 NA$_4$.KIŠIB ^{m}*mar-tú-u*$^{ʾ!}$ LÚ.GAL—URU.MEŠ *ša* MÍ—(KUR)
2 NA$_4$.KIŠIB ^{m}*mar-di-i*
3 PAB 2 LÚ.MEŠ ARAD.MEŠ *šá* LÚ.EN.NAM
4 *ša* KUR.*bar-hal-za* EN UN.MEŠ SUM-*ni*

---

5 ^{m}*rém-ut*—DINGIR.MEŠ AMA-*šú* 3 PAB.MEŠ-*šú* PAB 5 ZI
6 ^{md}UTU—TI DUMU-*šú* ^{m}*sa-si-i* 2 DUMU.MEŠ-*šú*
7 MÍ-*šú* ^{md}PA-*u-a* 3 PAB.MEŠ-*šú* NIN-*šú* PAB 5 ZI
8 ^{m}*za-bi-nu* LÚ.NU.GIŠ.SAR MÍ-*šú* GIŠ.SAR
9 *šá za-mar* PAB 17 ZI.MEŠ GIŠ.SAR *ina* URU.*na-bu-ur*$^{!}$
10 LÚ.ARAD.MEŠ *šá* ^{m}[*mar-t*]*ú-u*$^{ʾ!}$ *šá* ^{m}*mar-di-i*$^{!}$
11 *ú-piš-m*[*a* MÍ.PAB—*ṭ*]*al-li*
12 MÍ.*šá-*[*kín-tú*] *šá* URU.NINA.KI
13 T[A* IGI LÚ.MEŠ *an*]-*nu-tu*
14 [*ina* ŠÀ *x* MA.NA KUG.UD *šá* UR]U.*gar-ga-m*[*is*]
15 [*il-qí kas-pu ga*]*m-mur* 0$^{!}$
16 [*ta-din*$^{!}$ UN.MEŠ GIŠ.S]AR.MEŠ 0$^{!}$
17 [*za-rip la-q*]*í*$^{!}$ *tu-a-ru di-i-*[*nu*]
r.1 [DUG$_4$.DUG$_4$ *la-áš-šú man-nu šá ur-kiš*]
2 [*ina ma-te-e*]-*ma*$^{!}$ [*i-za-qup-an-ni*]
3 [*i*-GIL-*u-n*]*i*$^{!}$ *di-i-n*[*u*$^{!}$] 0$^{!}$
4 ⌜DUG$_4$.DUG$_4$ TA*⌝ MÍ.*šá-kín-te*
5 *ub-ta-ʾu-u-ni kas-pu a-na* 10.MEŠ
6 *a-na* EN.MEŠ-*šú* GUR *ina de-ni-šú* DUG$_4$.DUG$_4$-*ma*
7 *la i-laq-qí*

---

8 IGI ^{md}PA—MU—AŠ LÚ.A.BA
9 IGI ^{m}*la-hi-ra-a-a*
10 IGI ^{m}NUMUN—15 LÚ.GAL—UŠ.BAR.ME
11 IGI ^{m}*na-*⌜*bu-ti-i*⌝ LÚ.UŠ.BAR
12 IGI ^{md}ŠÚ—AŠ LÚ.A—SIG
13 IGI ^{m}MAN—IGI.LAL-*an-ni*
14 IGI ^{md}PA—PAB-*ir* IGI ^{m}*ma-zu-gu*
15 IGI ^{m}*ba-ni-i* LÚ.A.BA

16 ITI.GUD UD-1-KÁM MU-23 ^{md}30—PAB.MEŠ—SU
17 MAN KUR—*aš-šur*.KI *lim-me* ^{m}*man-nu—ki*—10—MAN$^{!}$
18 [*š*]*á* URU.*ṣu-pi-te*

ADD 447

1 Seal of Martu', village manager of the *queen*; seal of Mardî; a total of two men, servants of the governor of Barhalza, owners of the people being sold.

(space for seal impressions)

---

5 Remut-ilani, his mother and his 3 brothers, a total of 5 persons; Šamaš-uballiṭ and his son; Sasî, his two sons and his wife; Nabû'a, his 3 brothers and his sister, a total of 5 persons; Zabinu, gardener, his wife, and a fruit orchard; in all 17 persons and an orchard in the city of Nabur, servants of Martu' and Mardî —

11 [Ahi-ṭa]lli, gov[erness] of Nineveh, has contracted and [bought them] fr[om these men for x minas of silver by the mina of] Carche[mish].

15 [The money is paid compl]etely. [Those people and the orcha]rd [are purchased and acquired]. Any revocation, laws[uit or litigation is void].

r.2 [Whoever in the future, at any time], lodges a complaint, breaks the contra]ct, and seeks a lawsuit or litigation against the governess, shall return the money tenfold to its owners. He shall contest in his lawsuit and not succeed.

---

8 Witness Nabû-šumu-iddina, scribe.
9 Witness Lahirayu.
10 Witness Zar-Issar, chief weaver.
11 Witness Nabutî, weaver.
12 Witness Marduk-iddina, chariot fighter.
13 Witness Šarru-emuranni.
14 Witness Nabû-naṣir. Witness Mazzugu.
15 Witness Banî, scribe.

16 Month Iyyar (II), 1st day, year 23 of Sennacherib, king of Assyria, eponym year of Mannu-ki-Adad-milki [o]f Ṣupat.

90 Previous editions: AR 61, NALK 14; → KB 4 (1896) 11. 9 The last sign is *ur*, as copied by Johns, not *lu* (NALK). 10, 17, r.17 See coll.

91. A Harem Woman Buys 27 Persons With their Property (681-VI-27)

K 333

1 NA$_{4}$.KIŠIB ^{m}*mil-ki-ia* LÚ.EN.NAM
2 *šá* URU.*tal-mu-si* EN A.ŠÀ.MEŠ É.MEŠ
3 GIŠ.SAR.MEŠ UN.MEŠ *ta-da-ni*

---

4 ^{m}*e-hi—ia-a* MÍ-*šú* 3 DUMU.MEŠ-*šú* 2 DUMU.MÍ.MEŠ-*šú*
5 ^{m}GIŠ.BAL-*a* MÍ-*šú* 2 DUMU.MEŠ-*šú* ^{m}DÙG.GA—*ru-hi-ti* MÍ-*šú*
6 DUMU-*šú* ^{m}*nab-te-e* MÍ-*šú* AMA-*šú* PAB-*šú* ^{m}*dul*$^{!}$*-la-a-a-qa-nun*
7 MÍ-*šú* AMA-*šú* DUMU-*šú* PAB-*šú* ^{m}*ú-ri—ia-a* MÍ-*šú* AMA-*šú*
8 PAB-*šú* PAB 27 ZI.MEŠ *a-di* A.ŠÀ.MEŠ-*šú-nu* *a-di* É.MEŠ-*šú-nu*
9 *a-di* GIŠ.SAR.MEŠ-*šú-nu* *a-di* GUD.MEŠ-*šú-nu* *a-di* UDU.MEŠ-*šú-nu*
10 *a-di qin-ni-šú-nu ina* URU.*da*$^{!}$*-di-ú-al-la*
11 *ina* EN.NAM URU.*tal-mu-si tu-piš-ma* MÍ.ERIM—É.GAL
12 *ku-um* 20 MA.NA KUG.UD *ina* 1 MA.NA-*e šá* URU.*gar-ga-mis*
13 *a-na šá-par-te šá-kin man-nu šá u*[*r-ki*]*š u*$^{!}$ *ma-te-ma*
14 *lu-u* ^{m}*mil-ki-iá*$^{!}$ EN.NAM *lu-u* LÚ.2-*e-šú*
15 *lu-u* LÚ.GAL—URU.MEŠ-*šú lu-u* LÚ.*ha-za-nu* URU-*šú*
16 [*lu-u*] DUMU-*šú lu-u* DUMU—DUMU-*šú šá i-za-qu-*[*pa-an-ni*]
17 [GIL-*u-ni x* MA.N]A KUG.UD *ina* ⌈*bur*⌉*-k*[*i* ^{d}*x x x x*]
rest (about 5 lines) broken away

Rev. beginning (about 10 lines) broken away
1′ IGI ^{m}⌈*ú*$^{!}$⌉*-x*[*x x x x x x x x x x*]
2′ IGI ^{m}*am—ra-mu* LÚ.TÚG.KA.KÉŠ *šá* É.GAL
3′ IGI ^{m}*na-bu-ti-i* GAL—*ki-ṣir šá* UŠ.BAR.MEŠ
4′ IGI ^{md}PA—*rém-a-ni* LÚ.A.BA *ṣa-bit dan*$^{!}$*-ni-te*

5′ ITI.KIN UD-27-KÁM *lim-mu* ^{md}PA—PAB—KAM-*eš*
6′ LÚ.GAR.KUR URU.*sa-am-al-la*

ADD 59

1 Seal of Milkiya, governor of Talmusu, owner of the field, houses, gardens and people being sold.

(blank seal space)

---

4 Ehi-yâ, his wife, three sons and two daughters; Pilaqqâ, his wife and two sons; Ṭab-ruhiti, his wife and son; Nabtê, his wife, mother and brother; Dullaya-qanun, his wife, mother, son and brother; Uriah, his wife, his mother and his brother; in all 27 persons plus their fields, houses, gardens, cattle, sheep and kinsmen in the town of Dadi-ualla in the province of Talmusu —

11 the palace concubine has contracted them; they are placed as a pledge in lieu of 20 minas of silver by the mina of Carchemish.

13 Whoever in the future, at any time, lodges a compl[aint or breaks the contract], whether Milkiya, governor, or his deputy or village manager, or the mayor of his city [or] his sons or grandsons, [shall place x min]as of silver in the la[p of ...].

(Break)

r.1 Witness [......].

2 Witness Am-ram, tailor of the palace.

3 Witness Nabutî, cohort commander of the weavers.

4 Witness Nabû-remanni the scribe, keeper of the contract.

5 Month Elul (VI), 27th day, eponym year of Nabû-ahu-ereš, governor of Sam'al.

91 Previous editions: AR 123, NALK 15. Collations: Assur 2/5. 6 The tablet unequivocally has *nab* (see coll.) but it is possible that this is a scribal error for *ia*.

92. Ahi-ṭalli, Harem Governess of Nineveh, Buys People

K 1503

beginning broken away

1′ [x x x x x x x x x]-⌜ku$^{?}$⌝-ni
2′ [x x x x tu-piš-ma M]Í$^{!}$.PAB$^{!}$—ṭar-li
3′ [MÍ.šá-kín-tú ša UR]U$^{!}$.⌜NINA⌝ 0$^{!}$
4′ [TA IGI ^{m}x x x]x-ni
5′ [x x x x x x x x x]x-šú$^{!}$
6′ [TI man-nu ša ur-kiš] ina ma$^{!!}$-ti-ma
7′ [lu-u ^{m}x x x-ni] lu-u DUMU.MEŠ
8′ [DUMU—DUMU.MEŠ-šú lu-u x]x URU.MEŠ-šú
9′ [x x x x x x x]-šú
10′ [x x x x x x š]a$^{!}$ DI.KUD

two lines destroyed

r.1 [x x x x x x x x x] kas-pu
2 [a-na 10.MEŠ-te a]-na EN.MEŠ-šú GUR-ra
3 [x MA.NA KUG.UD x MA].NA KUG.GI
4 [ina bur-ki ^{d}x a-šib URU].hal-i-na i-šá-kan
5 [x ANŠE.KUR.RA.MEŠ BABBAR.MEŠ ina GÌR.2] ^{d}15 i-ra-ka-sa
6 [x ANŠE.har-ba]-kan-ni ina GÌR.2
7 [^{d}x x x x x ú-še]-ra$^{!}$-ba$^{!!}$
8 [ina de-ni-šú DUG$_4$.DUG$_4$-ma N]U$^{!}$ BA$^{!}$.TI

---

9 [IGI ^{m}x x x x LÚ].SAG ša ^{m}EN—GIŠ
10 [IGI ^{m}x x x x x] URU.sa-su$^{!}$-ka$^{!}$
11 [IGI ^{m}x x x x KUR.g]il$^{!}$-za-a-nu
12 [IGI ^{m}x x x x URU$^{?}$].ad-a-ri
13 [x x x x x x x x x]x URU-šú

rest broken away

ADD 570

(Beginning destroyed)

2 Ahi-ṭalli, [governess of] Nineveh, [has contracted and bought *them* from ...]ni [for ......].

6 [Whoever in the future], *at any time*, whether ...] or (his) sons [or grandsons, or the ....] of his city,

9 [seeks] a lawsuit [or litigation against Ahi-ṭalli]

(Break)

r.1 He shall return the money [tenfold] to its owners, and shall place [x minas of silver and x mi]nas of gold [in the lap of the god ... residing in] *Hal*ina.

r.5 He shall tie [x white horses to the feet of] Ištar, [and shall br]ing [x *harba*]*kannu* horses to the feet of [.... He shall litigate in his lawsuit and] not succeed.

---

9 [Witness NN], eunuch of Bel-lešir.
10 [Witness NN, from] Sasuka.
11 [Witness NN, from G]ilzanu.
12 [Witness NN, *from*] Adari.
13 [......] of his city

(Rest destroyed)

93. Ahi-ṭalli, Governess of the Central City Harem, Buys an Estate

Bu 91-5-9,197

beginning broken away

1′ [É x ANŠE A.ŠÀ x x x]x-ri [0]
2′ [x x x x x SUHUR KASKAL ša] a-na URU.ba-na-[x]
3′ [il-la-ku-ni SUHUR KASKAL š]a$^{!}$ ina ŠÀ-bi—URU il-l[a-ku-ni]
4′ [x x x x x U]RU.ŠE ša ^{m}hu-ni-[i]

ADD 643

(Beginning destroyed)

(cylinder seal impression)

---

1 [An estate of x hectares of land ...... adjoining the road which leads] to Bana[... and the road which] lea[ds] to the Inner City,

4 [... *adjoining* the vil]lage of Hunnî,

92 Previous edition: AR 176. 1ff See coll. 6 Tablet MAN-ti-ma (scribal error). r.4, 7f, 11f See coll.

93 Previous editions: AR 448, NALK 17. 1 See coll.; restoring a]d-ri-[MEŠ] is excluded. 6, 8f See coll. 11 The reading KAS[KAL is uncertain. r.1, 3 See coll. 10 See coll.; contra NALK, the sign nu is on the tablet.

5′ [SUHUR *mu*$^{?}$]-⸢*ṣu*$^{!}$⸣-*u*ʾ *ša* ^{md}IM—PAB-[*ir*]
6′ [SUHUR ^{md}U].GUR—PAB—PAB ⸢SUHUR⸣ $^{m⸢d⸣}$30—APIN-[*eš*]
7′ [*x x x x*].MEŠ SUHUR [^{m}*x x*]*x-hu* [*x x*]
e.8′ [SUHUR *x*] *ša* ^{m}PAB—*la*-[*maš*$^{?}$]-*ši* [*x x*]
9′ [*x x x*] LUGAL *ia-a-x*[*x x x*] ⸢LÚ*⸣.[*x x x*]

10′ [*x x a*]*d-ri*.MEŠ É 3BÁN [*x x x x x*]
11′ [*x* SUHUR] KASKAL—MAN SUHUR KAS[KAL$^{!}$ *x x x x*]

r.1 [PAB] 80$^{!}$ A.ŠÀ 3 É.MEŠ 3 ⸢*ad*$^{!}$⸣-[*ri*.MEŠ GIŠ.SAR PÚ *tab-ri-u*]
2 [*š*]*a* LÚ.MEŠ-*e an*-[*nu-te*]

3 *ú-piš-ma* MÍ.*a-hi—ṭar-li* MÍ.GAR-⸢*tú*$^{!}$ *ša*⸣ MUR[UB$_4$—URU]
4 *ša* URU.*ni-n*[*u-a*]
5 *ina ba-la-ṭi ša* LUGAL *ina* ŠÀ-*bi* 6 MA.NA KUG.UD ⸢*il*⸣-[*qi*]
6 *kas-pu ga-mur ta-din* A.ŠÀ.MEŠ É.MEŠ *ad-ri*.MEŠ
7 GIŠ.SAR PÚ *tab-ri-ʾu šu-a-tú za-rip-pu la-qi-ʾu*
8 *tu-a-ru de-e-nu* DUG$_4$.DUG$_4$ *la-áš-šú*
9 *man-nu ša ina ur-kiš-ši ina ma-te-ma lu-u* LÚ.MEŠ *an-nu-te*
10 *lu-u* DUMU.MEŠ-*šú*-⸢*nu*$^{!}$⸣ *lu-u* DUMU—DUMU.[MEŠ-*šú-nu šá*] *de*$^{!}$-[*e-nu*] DUG$_4$. DUG$_4$
11 TA* MÍ.GAR-*te ub-ta*-[ʾ*u-u*]-*ni*
12 [*kas-p*]*u a-na* 10.MEŠ *a-n*[*a* EN.MEŠ-*šú* GUR-*ra*]
rest broken away

5 [*adjoining the e*]*xit* of Adad-naṣ[ir and (the estates of) Ner]gal-ahu-uṣur and Sin-er[eš]
7 [......] adjoining ... [...]
8 [......] of Ahu-lâ[maš]ši [...]
9 [......] the king ...[...] ... [...]
10 [... threshing flo]ors; an estate of 3 decares [... adjoining] the king's road and adjoining the ro[ad to ...].

r.1 [In a]ll 80 hectares of land, 3 houses, 3 thres[hing floors, a garden, a well and a *grazing land* be]longing to the[se] men —

3 Ahi-ṭalli, governess of the cen[tral city] (harem) of Nin[eveh], has contracted and bou[ght] (said property) for 6 minas of silver for the king's 'life.'

6 The money is paid completely. That land, houses, threshing floors, garden, well and *grazing land* are purchased and acquired. Any revocation, lawsuit, or litigation is void.

9 Whoever in the future, at any time, whether these men or th[eir] sons or grand[sons], seeks a lawsuit or litigation against the governess, [shall return the mon]ey tenfold [to its owners].
(Rest destroyed)

94. The Governess of the Central City Harem [releases] 31 People

Ki 1904-10-9,62

1 MÍ$^{!}$.GAŠAN$^{!}$—PAB MÍ$^{!}$.[*x x x x x x x*]
2 ^{md}PA—*de-ni*—[DÙ-*uš* ^{m}*x x x x*]
3 ^{m}PAB—*im-me*-⸢*e*⸣ [^{m}*x x x x x x*]
4 ^{m}*tam-lu*$^{!}$-*u-t*[*i*$^{!}$ ^{m}*x x x x x x*]
5 ^{md}15—*ta*-SU [^{m}*x x x x x x x*]
6 ^{md}PA—GÁL-*ši* [^{m}*x x x x x x x*]
7 ^{m}TU—DINGIR.MEŠ LÚ*.[*x x x x x x*]
8 ^{md}PA—GI ^{m}*mar-tú*-[*x* ^{m}*x x x x x*]
9 ^{m}*sa-la-ma*—^{d}IM [^{m}*x x x x x x*]
e.10 ^{m}*ha*-⸢*an*$^{!}$⸣-*ni*-⸢*i*$^{!}$⸣ *ša*$^{!}$ [*x x x x x*]

11 É 40 A.ŠÀ.GA *ina* ŠÀ U[RU$^{!}$.*x x x x x*]

---

r.1 PAB 31 [U]N$^{!}$.MEŠ ŠE.BAR [*x x x x x x*]

ADD 1163

1 The woman Beltu-uṣur, [NN, NN],
2 Nabû-deni-[epuš, NN, NN],
3 Ahi-immê, [NN, NN],
4 Tamlut[i, NN, NN],
5 Issar-tariba, [NN, NN],
6 Nabû-ušabši, [NN, NN],
7 *Erba*-ilani, [NN, NN],
8 Nabû-ušallim, Mart[u', NN],
9 Salam-Adad, [NN, NN],
10 Hannî, [......];
11 an estate of 40 (hectares of) land in the city [...];

---

r.1 in all 31 people, *barley* [......], an estate

94 This tablet has the horizontally oblong *uʾiltu* format and accordingly cannot be a purchase document. The lack of seal impressions furthermore indicates that a debt-note cannot be in question. 1, 4, 10f, r.1f See coll.

2 É 40 A.ŠÀ.GA *ina* ŠÀ UR[U.*x x* ^{m}*x x x x*]
3 *ina* ŠÀ-*bi* 17 1/2 MA.NA KU[G.UD TA* IGI MÍ.*x x x*]
4 MÍ.*šá-kín-te ša* MURU[B_4—URU *ú-se-ṣi*$^{?}$]
rest uninscribed

of 40 (hectares of) land in the cit[y ...] —
[3] [NN has *released*] (said property) [*from* NN], governess of the cent[ral city] (harem), for 17 and a half minas of si[lver].

95. The Governess Forfeits a Pledged Field

K 1337

e.1 A.ŠÀ *šá* MÍ.*šá-kín-te*
2 A.ŠÀ *šá* ^{m}*i*$^{!}$-*ni*$^{!}$-*bi—aš-šur a-na šá-par-ti*
3 KÚ-*u-ni* LÚ*$^{!}$.A—KIN *ša* É—EN.MEŠ-*šú*
4 *it-ta-lak* A.ŠÀ É—EN.MEŠ-*šú*
5 *ur-ta-me še-e*[*b*]-*šú* ŠE$^{!}$.*nu-sa-hi ku-*⸢*um*⸣
6 KUG.UD-*šú ú-sa-ni-lum* A.ŠÀ É—EN.MEŠ-*šú*
7 [*x x x x x x x x* ^{m}]^{d}PA—*sa-lim*
e.8 [*x x x x x x x x*]-*hi ur*$^{!}$-*ta-*⸢*me*$^{!}$⸣
9 [*x x x x x x x x*] $^{m!}$PAB—SU
r.1 [*x x x x x*] *x* ⸢*ku*$^{!}$-*um*$^{!}$⸣ ŠE.*nu-sa-hi*
2 *šá x*[*x x*]*x ú-sa-ni-lum* A.ŠÀ É—EN.MEŠ-*šú*
3 *man-nu šá* GIL-*u-ni* 2 KUR.MEŠ BABBAR.MEŠ *ina aš-š*[*ur*]
4 SUM-*an* 1 MA.NA KUG.GI *ina* ^{d}NIN.LÍL SU[M-*an*]
5 *a-de-e ša* (LUGAL) ŠU.2-*šú ú-ba-ʾu*
6 IGI ^{m}*kab*$^{!}$-*lu*$^{!}$—15 GAL—GAG.MEŠ IGI ^{m}⸢*x x*⸣
7 IGI ^{m}*sa-na*—DINGIR LÚ*.A—KIN *ša* GAL—É
8 IGI ^{md}PA—*rém-a-ni* A.BA

ADD 62

[1] A field belonging to the governess, a field which Inbi-Aššur has been enjoying as a pledge —
[3] the messenger of its owner's household has gone and forfeited the field of his lord's household.
[5] In lieu of the silver due to him, they have *suspended* the corn and straw taxes. A field of the owner's household
[7] [......] Nabû-šallim
[8] [......] forfeited
[9] [......] Ahu-eriba
[r.1] In lieu of the straw tax which [...] *suspended*, a field of the owner's household (*shall be taxed*).
[3] Whoever breaks the contract shall give two white horses to Aššur, and shall pay one mina of gold to Mullissu. The treaty of (the king) shall call him to account.
[6] Witness Kablu-Issar, *rab sikkāti*. Witness ....
[7] Witness Sana-il, messenger of the major-domo.
[8] Witness Nabû-remanni, scribe.

96. The Lady Barsipitu Buys 4 Slaves

80-7-19,49

1 [*ku-um* N]A_4.KIŠIB-*šú ṣu-pur-šú iš-kun*
2 [*ṣu*]-⸢*pur*⸣ ^{m}KÁ.DINGIR-*a-a* EN UN.MEŠ SUM-*ni*

ADD 244

[1] [Instead of] his seal he impressed his fingernail.
[2] [Fing]ernail of Babilayu, owner of the people being sold.

(fingernail impressions)

95 Previous editions: AR 131, TCAE 303, NALK 16. Collations: Assur 2/5. [6] *ú-sa-ni-lum* is here interpreted as /*ussanīlū*/ (Š pret. of *niālu*), lit. "they have buried, laid in the grave" (cf. CAD N/1 p.206). The earlier interpretations proposed in the NALK (*šlm* Dtn) and TCAE (*šlm* Dtt) involve various phonological and grammatical difficulties and must be rejected.
96 Previous editions: AR 159, NALK 72. Collations: Assur 2/5.

3 ^{m}*ta-ri-bi*—^{d}15 ŠEŠ-*šú* MÍ-*šú* DUMU.MÍ-*sa* PAB 4 Z[I.MEŠ]
4 LÚ*.ARAD.MEŠ-*ni ša* ^{m}KÁ.DINGIR-*a-a*

5 *tu-piš-ma* MÍ.BÁR.SIPA.KI-*i-tú*
6 TA* IGI ^{m}KÁ.DINGIR-*a-a ina* ŠÀ-*bi* 3 MA.NA KUG.⸢UD⸣
7 *ina* 1 MA.NA-*e ša* LÚ*.DAM.QAR *ta-al-qi*
8 *kas-pu ga-mur ta-din* UN.MEŠ *šu-a-tú*
9 *za-ar-pu la-qi-ú tu-a-ru de-e-nu*

10 DUG$_4$.DUG$_4$ *la-a-šú man-n[u] ša ina ur-kiš*
11 *ina ma-te-ma i*-GIL-*u-ni lu-u* ^{m}KÁ.DINGIR-*a-a*
12 *lu-u* DUMU.MEŠ-*šú lu-u* DUMU—DUMU.MEŠ-*šú lu-u* ŠEŠ.MEŠ-*šú*
13 *lu-u* DUMU—ŠEŠ.MEŠ-*šú lu-u* LÚ*.GAR-*nu-šú lu-u qur-ub-šú*
14 *lu-u mám-ma-nu-šú ša de-ni* DUG$_4$.DUG$_4$
15 TA* MÍ.BÁR.SIPA.KI-*i-tú ù* EGIR-*šú*
16 *ub-ta-ʾu-u-ni* 1 MA.NA 0! SÍG.*qer-du* KÚ
17 *mar* DUG.*a-ga-nu kur-ru* NAG 1 MA.NA ⸢KUG⸣.U[D LUH-*u*]
18 1 MA.NA KUG.GI *sak-ru ina bur-ki* ^{d}I[M!]
19 *a-šib* URU.*ú-rak-ka* GAR-[*an*!]
20 *kas-pu a-na* 10.MEŠ-*te a-na* EN.M[EŠ-*šú* GUR]
21 *ina de-ni-šú* DUG$_4$.DUG$_4$-*ma*! *la* [*i-laq-qi*]

r.1 I[GI ^{m}*x x x x x x x x x x x*]
2 IG[I ^{m}*x x x x x x x x x x x*]
3 IGI [^{m}*x x x x x x x x x x x*]
4 IGI ^{m}*x*[*x* (*x*) *x*]*x*—DINGIR LÚ*.[SAG]
5 PAB 6 IGI.MEŠ LÚ*.SAG.MEŠ
1 line blank
6 IGI ^{m}URU.NINA-*a-a* LÚ*.*ha-za-nu*
7 IGI ^{m}ARAD—^{d}30 ARAD *šá* ⸢LÚ*⸣.SUKKAL
8 IGI ^{m}*ha-am-bi-i* LÚ*.GAL—SIMUG.KUG.GI.MEŠ
9 IGI ^{m}*rém-a-ni*—10 LÚ*.NAGAR!
10 IGI ^{m}DINGIR—PAB ARAD *ša* LÚ*.*tur-ta-nu*

11 IGI ^{m}*aš-šur*—PAB—AŠ LÚ*.Ì.ŠUR
12 IGI ^{m}PAB—DU—*ka* ARAD *ša* ^{md}30—⸢SU⸣
13 IGI ^{m}GIN—PAB ARAD *ša* LÚ*.IGI.DUB

14 IGI ^{m}*hal-di*—KAR-*ir* LÚ*.UŠ.BAR
15 IGI ^{md}PA—*šal-lim* LÚ*.A.BA
16 IGI ⸢^{m}⸣*sa-gi-bi-i* LÚ*.Ì.DU$_8$ *ša* É.[GAL]
17 IGI ^{m}[D]INGIR—*ib-ni* ⸢LÚ*⸣.A.B[A!] ⸢*ṣa-bit*⸣ [*ṭup-pi*]
2 lines blank
18 ⸢ITI⸣.APIN! [UD-*x*-KÁM]
19 [*lim-mu*] ⸢^{m}⸣*aš-šur*—[EN—PAB LÚ*.GAR.KUR]
20 0! U[RU!.*šá-hu-up-pa*]

3 Taribi-Issar, his brother, wife, and daughter, a total of 4 per[sons], servants of Babilayu —

5 Barsipitu has contracted and bought them from Babilayu for 3 minas of silver by the mina of the merchant.

8 The money is paid completely. Those people are purchased and acquired. Any revocation, lawsuit, or litigation is void.

10 Whoever in the future, at any time, breaks the contract, whether Babilayu, or his sons, grandsons, brothers, or nephews, or his prefect, or a neighbour or relative of his who seeks a lawsuit or litigation against Barsipitu and his (sic) successor,

16 shall eat one mina of plucked wool, shall drink a full *agannu* vessel of tanner's paste, shall pla[ce] one mina of [refined] sil[ver] (and) one mina of pure gold in the lap of A[dad] residing in the city of Urakka, [and shall return] the money tenfold to its own[er]. He shall contest in his lawsuit and not [succeed].

r.1 Wi[tness ......].

2 Witn[ess ......].

3 Witness [......].

4 Witness [...]-ilu, [eunuch].

5 A total of 6 eunuch witnesses.

6 Witness Ninuayu, mayor.

7 Witness Urda-Sin, servant of the vizier.

8 Witness Hambî, chief goldsmith.

9 Witness Remanni-Adad, carpenter.

10 Witness Ilu-iṣṣur, servant of the commander-in-chief.

11 Witness Aššur-ahu-iddina, oil-presser.

12 Witness Ahu-illika, servant of Sin-eriba.

13 Witness Kenu-uṣur, servant of the treasurer.

14 Witness Haldi-eṭir, weaver.

15 Witness Nabû-šallim, scribe.

16 Witness Sagibî, porter of the palace.

17 Witness Ilu-ibni, scribe, keeper of the [tablet].

18 Month Marchesvan (VIII), [...th day, eponym year of] Aššur-[belu-uṣur, governor of Šahuppa].

97. The Lady Indibî Loans 17 Minas of Silver (693-V-9)

K 414

1 17 MA.NA KUG.UD *ina ma-né-e ša* LÚ*$^{?}$. ⌈DAM$^{?}$⌉.Q[AR$^{?}$]
2 *ša* MÍ.*in-di-bi-i*
3 *ina* IGI ^{m}*ar-ba-a-a*
4 ITI.DU$_{6}^{!}$ KUG.UD *ina* SAG.DU-*šú* SUM-*an*
5 *šum-ma la* SUM-*ni*
6 2 GÍN *a-na ma-né-e ša* ITI-*šú*
7 GIŠ.SAR *ša* GIŠ$^{!}$.*til-lit*$^{!}$ [0] *zaq-pu*
e.8 *ina* URU.ŠE—^{m}EN—PAB.MEŠ SUHUR GIŠ.SAR *šá*
9 ^{m}*ha-ba-su* SUHUR ^{m}*se-e*ʾ—*ba*$^{!}$-*rak*$^{!}$-⌈*ki*$^{!}$⌉
r.1 SUHUR GIŠ.SAR LÚ.GAL—A.BA
2 ^{m}*dà-ri*—EN MÍ-*šú* 3 DUMU.MEŠ-*šú*

ADD 66

1 17 minas of silver by the mina of *the merchant*, belonging to Indibî, at the disposal of Arbayu.

4 He shall pay the silver in its original amount in Tishri (VII). If he does not pay, (it shall increase) two shekels per mina per month.

7 A vineyard in the village of Bel-ahhe, adjoining the vineyards of Habasu, Se'-barakki and the chief scribe, (and) Dari-Bel, his wife, 3 sons and 2 daughters, together with his property, (everything, down to the) chaff

97 Previous editions: AR 124, NALK 112; → Postgate FNALD 24. Collated by I.L. Finkel. 1, 4, 7, 9 See coll. r.4 ^{m}*hu-ul-li* sic. r.9ff See coll.

FIG. 17. *Working on the king's bow (reign of Assurbanipal). Cf. no. 115.* BM 124884.

3 2$^{!}$ DUMU.MÍ.MEŠ-*šú a-di qi-ni-ti-šú*
4 *ha-am-šu hu-ṣa-bu* ^{m}*hu*$^{!}$*-ul*$^{!}$*-li*$^{!}$ DUMU.MÍ-*šú*
5 *a-na šá-par-ti šá-kín me-tu hal-qu*
6 *ina* UGU EN-*šú-nu ina* UD-*me ša* KUG.UD *a-*˹*di*˺
7 *ru-bé-e-šú ú-še-rab-a-ni*

8 GIŠ.SAR UN.MEŠ *ú-še-ṣa* ITI.NE UD-9-˹KÁM˺
9 *lim-mu* ^{m}SUM-*ni*—PAB.MEŠ (IGI) ^{m}*man-nu—ki-i*—˹$^{d!}$*x x*˺
10e [IG]I ^{m}˹^{d}ŠÚ˺—NUMUN$^{!}$—DÙ IGI ^{m}PAB-*u-a-nu*
11e [IG]I ^{m}*ma-ka-me-*˹*e*˺ LÚ*.˹ZADIM BAN˺. ME!
12e IGI ^{m}*rém-a-ni*—DINGIR
13e IGI ^{md}UTU—PAB—PAB
14e *ša* LÚ.˹*qur-ub*˺*-te*

and twig, and Hulli and his daughter, are placed as a pledge.

5 (If) they die or flee, the responsibility is upon their owner. On the day he brings the silver plus its interest, he shall redeem the orchard and the people.

8 Month Ab (V), 9th day, eponym year of Iddin-ahhe.

9 (Witness) Mannu-ki-[...].

10 Witness Marduk-zeru-ibni. Witness Ahu-anu.

11 Witness Makkamê, bow-maker.

12 Witness Remanni-ilu.

13 Witness Šamaš-ahu-uṣur, of the (king's) stand-by.

98. A Woman Purchases a Maid (682-XI-7)

80-7-19,353

1 [N]A$_4$.KIŠIB ^{m}*se-e'—za-ba-di*
2 [EN] MÍ SUM-*ni*

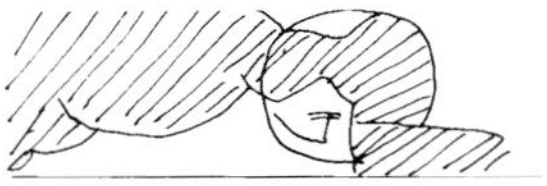

3 [M]Í.AD—*ha-a'-li* [GEMÉ-*šú*$^!$]
4 *ša* ^{m}*se-e'—za-ba-[di]*
5 *ú-piš-ma* MÍ.⸢*la*⸣—*te-gi*$^!$—⸢*a*$^!$⸣-*[na—x x]*
6 TA*$^!$ *pa-an* ^{m}*se-e'—za-b[a]-di*
7 *ina* ŠÀ-*bi* 9 GÍN.MEŠ KUG.UD *il-qí*
8 *kas-pu gam-mur [ta]*-⸢*ad*⸣-*din*
9 MÍ *šu-a*-⸢*tu*⸣ *zar-[pa]t* ⸢*laq*$^!$-*qi*$^!$⸣-*at*
10 *tu-a-ru de-e-nu* DUG$_4$.DUG$_4$ *la-áš-šú*

11 *man-nu ša ina ur-kiš u*$^!$ *ma-[te]*-⸢*me*$^!$⸣
12 *i-za-qu-p[a-ni]*
13 ⸢GIL⸣.MEŠ-*u-[ni]*
r.1 ⸢2$^?$⸣ [M]A.NA KUG.UD 2 ⸢MA⸣.[NA KUG.GI]
2 *ina bur-ki* ^{d}NIN.GAL GAR-*an*
3 4 ANŠE.KUR.RA BABBAR.MEŠ *ina* KI.TA
4 ^{d}30 *a-šib* URU.KASKAL *i-rak-kas*
5 *kas-pu ana* 10.MEŠ-*te ana* EN-*šú* GUR-*ra*
6 *ina de-ni-šú* DUG$_4$.DUG$_4$-*ma la* ⸢TI-*qi*⸣

7 IGI ^{m}*ha-an-di-i* LÚ.⸢*na*$^!$⸣-*ši-i*
8 IGI ^{m}ZALÁG-*a-nu* LÚ.NIGÍR
9 ⸢IGI⸣ ^{m}*[h]a*$^!$-⸢*su*$^!$⸣-*si-i* DUMU ^{m}*zib-di-i*
10 [IGI ^{m}*x*]—*dàl*$^!$-*a* LÚ.⸢NIGÍR$^!$⸣
11 [IGI ^{m}*g*]*ir*$^?$—*ṣap*$^!$-⸢*hu*⸣-*n[i*$^!$]
12 ⸢ITI⸣.ZÍZ UD-7-KÁM
13 *lim-mu* ^{md}AG—MAN—PAB
14 LÚ.GAR.KUR URU.*mar-qa-si*

ADD 215

1 [Se]al of Se'-zabadi, [owner] of the woman being sold.

(stamp seal impressions)

3 Abi-ha'li, [the maid] of Se'-zaba[di] —

5 the woman La-teggi-a[na-...] has contracted and bought her from Se'-zabadi for 9 shekels of silver.

8 The money is [p]aid completely. That woman is purchased and acquired. Any revocation, lawsuit, or litigation is void.

11 Whoever in the fu[tur]e and at any time lodges a co[mplaint] and breaks the con[tract] shall place *two* minas of silver and two mi[nas of gold] in the lap of Nikkal, shall tie 4 white horses to the feet of Sin residing in Harran, and shall return the money tenfold to its owner. He shall contest in his lawsuit and not succeed.

r.7 Witness Handî, carrier.

8 Witness Nuranu, herald.

9 Witness Hasusî son of Zabdî.

10 [Witness ...]-dalâ, herald.

11 [Witness *G*]*ir*-ṣaphuni.

12 Month Shebat (XI), *7*th day, eponym year of Nabû-šarru-uṣur, governor of Marqasa.

99. A Royal Concubine Purchases Real Estate

Sm 1677

beginning broken away
1′ [*x x x x x x x x x*]⸢*x*⸣[*x x x*]
2′ [*x x x x x x x x x*] 5$^!$ GIŠ.I[G$^!$.MEŠ]
3′ [(*x*) *x x x x x x x x*] ^{m}*lib-luṭ*
4′ [(*x*) *x x x x x x x x*]*x-a-a*
5′ [(*x*) *x x x x x x*]*x-di* SUHUR ⸢*su*$^!$⸣-*qa-qi*
6′ [(*x*) *x x x x x t*]*u-piš-ma*
7′ [MÍ.*x x x* MÍ.ERIM]—⸢É⸣.GAL *ša* U$^!$.U$^!$

ADD 519

(Beginning destroyed)

2 [......], 5 do[ors],

3 [......] Liblut̩,

4 [......]aya,

5 [......], adjoining a street [...] —

7 [NN, *con*]*cubine* of *the king*, has [con]-

98 Previous editions: AR 166, NALK 144. Collations: Assur 2/5. 5 See coll.
99 Previous edition: AR 369.

8′ [TA* IGI ^{md}P]A$^!$—*šal-lim ina* ŠÀ-*bi*
9′ [*x* MA.NA KUG.U]D$^!$ *ša* URU.*gar-ga-mis*

10′ [*tal-qi kas*]-*pu gam-mur ta-din*
11′ [*x x x x šú*]-⸢*a*$^!$⸣-*te za-rip la-qi*
12′ [*tu-a-ru*] *de-e-nu* DUG$_4$.DUG$_4$ *la-áš-šú*
13′ [*man-nu ša ur-ki-i*]*š*$^!$ *ina ma-te-ma*
e.14′ [*i-za-qu-pa*]-*an-ni lu-u*
15′ [^{md}PA—*šal-lim lu-u*] DUMU.MEŠ-*šú* DUMU—DUMU.MEŠ-[*šú*]
16′ [*ša de-e*]-*nu* DUG$_4$.DUG$_4$
r.1 [TA* MÍ.*x x x ub-ta*$^!$]-ʾ*u-u-ni* 10 MA.NA [KUG.UD]
2 [*x* MA.NA KUG.G]I$^!$ *ina bur-ki* ^{d}IŠ.TAR
3 [*a-ši-bat* URU].*ni*$^!$-*na*$^!$-*a*$^!$ *i-šak-*[*kan*]
4 [*kas-pu a-na* 10].MEŠ-*te a-na* EN.MEŠ-*šú*
5 [GUR-*ra ina*] *de-ni-šú*
6 [DUG$_4$.DUG$_4$]-*ma la i-la-qi*

---

7 [IGI ^{m}*ha-a*]*n-ṭu*
8 [IGI ^{m}*x x*—A]PIN-*eš*
9 [IGI ^{m}*x x*]-⸢*ú*⸣-*tú*
10 [IGI ^{m}*ma-mì*]-⸢*i*$^!$⸣
11 [IGI ^{m}HÉ.NU]N$^!$-*a-a*
12 [IGI ^{m}*ar-z*]*e-zu*$^!$
13 [IGI ^{m}*x x x*]-⸢LAL$^!$⸣
rest broken away

tracted and [bought it from Na]bû-šallim for [x minas of sil]ver by the (mina) of Carchemish.

10 [The mon]ey is paid completely. [Th]at [...] is purchased and acquired. [Any revocation], lawsuit or litigation is void.

13 [Whoever in the futu]re, at any time, [lodges a compl]aint, whether [Nabû-šallim or] his sons (or) grands[ons, and] seeks a [laws]uit or litigation [against ...],

r.1 shall pla[ce] 10 minas [of silver (and) x minas of go]ld in the lap of Ištar [residing in] Nineveh, [and shall return the money ten]fold to its owners. [He shall contest in] his lawsuit and not succeed.

---

7 [Witness Ha]nṭu.
8 [Witness ...]-ereš.
9 [Witness ...]utu.
10 [Witness Mam]î.
11 [Witness Nuh]šaya.
12 [Witness Arz]ezu.
13 [Witness ...]-taqqin.
(Rest destroyed)

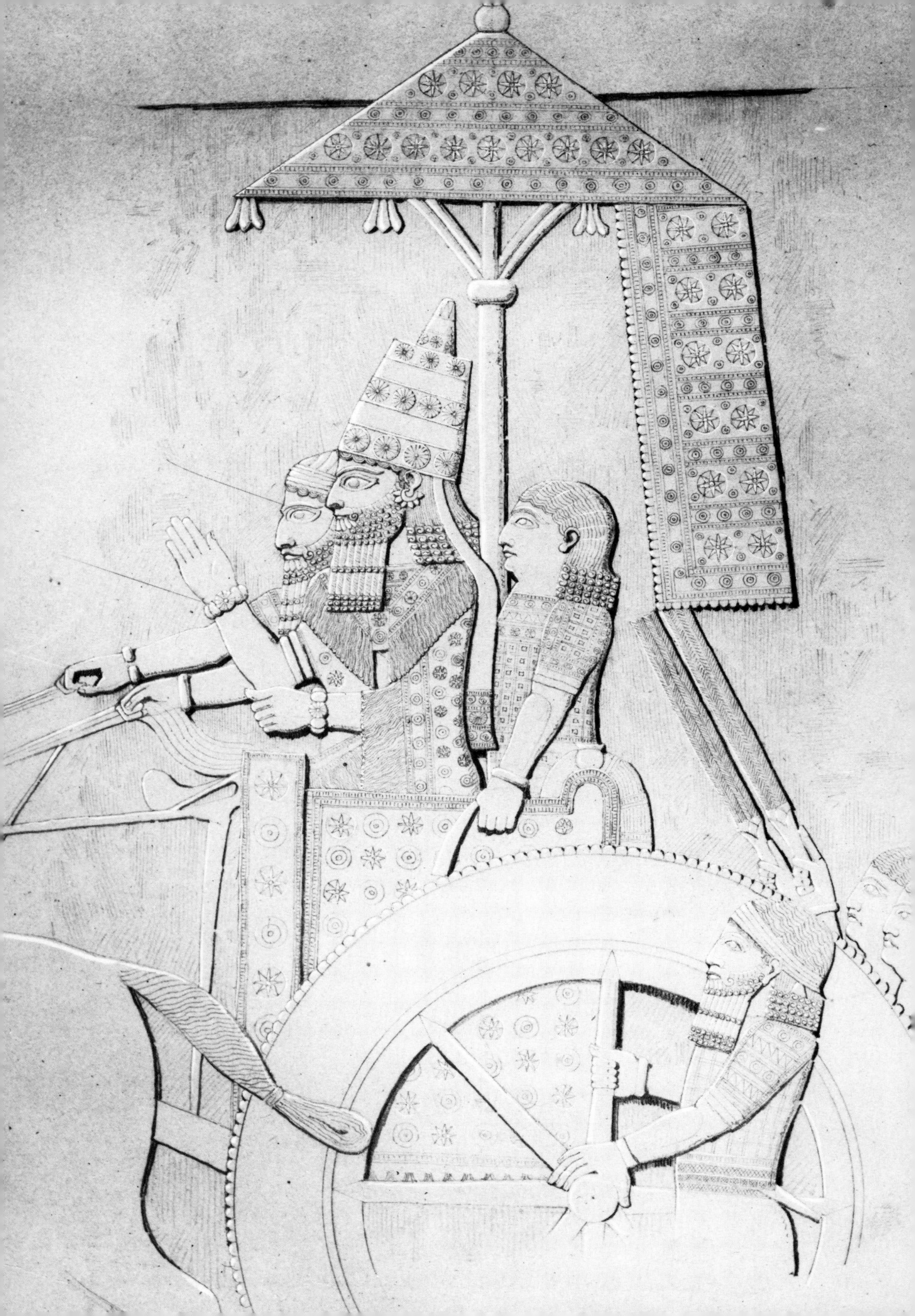

7. Aplaya, 'Third Man' of Arda-Mullissi, Crown Prince (698-683)

FIG. 18. *Assurbanipal with his charioteer and 'third man.'*
ORIGINAL DRAWING VII, 21.

100. Aplaya Buys a Tower and 10 Hectares of Land (698-III-10)

83-1-18,331

1 *ku-um* NA$_4$.KIŠIB-*šú-nu* ^{m}*ha-ru-ra-*[*a-nu*!]
2 ^{m}*sa-li-la-a-nu ṣu-bar-šú-nu iš-k*[*u*]*n*!

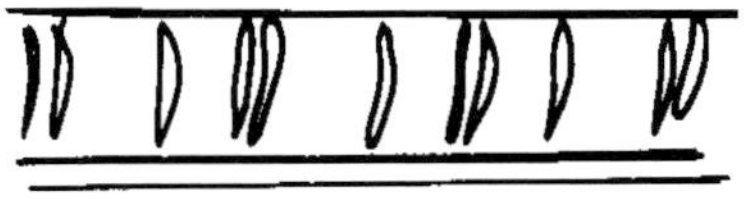

3 URU.*i-si-tú bé-et* 10 AN[ŠE A.ŠÀ.GA]
4 *ina* ŠÀ-*bi ú-šal-li ina* URU.[*x x x*]
5 ^{m}*ab-di—ku-bu-bi* MÍ-[*šú* 2 DUMU.MEŠ-*šú*]
6 PAB 4 LÚ*!.ZI.MEŠ *ša* ^{m}*h*[*a-ru-ra-a-nu*] 0!
7 ⸢*ù*!⸣ [^{m}*sa-li-la-a-nu ú-piš*]-*ma* ^{m}[DUMU.UŠ-*a-a*]
8 [TA* ŠU.2-*šú-nu ina* ŠÀ *x* MA.NA KUG.UD *il-qí*]
9 [URU.*i-si-tú a-du* A].⸢ŠÀ⸣.G[A.MEŠ]
10 [^{m}*ab-di—ku-bu*]-⸢*bi*⸣ *a-du* U[N!.MEŠ-*šú*]
11 [*ap-lu zar-pu* T]I!-*qi-ú* 0!
12 [*tu-a-ru de-e-nu*] DUG$_4$.DUG$_4$ 0!
13 [*la-áš-šú man-nu*] ⸢*ša*⸣ *ina ár-kat*! UD-*me* 0!
14 [*ša e-la-a*]*n*!-*ni* : *lu-u* ^{m}*ha-ru-*[*ra-a-nu*]
15 [*lu-u* ^{m}*sa-l*]*i-la-a-nu*
16 [*lu-u* DUMU.ME]Š!-*šú-nu lu-u* DUMU—DUMU.MEŠ-*š*[*ú-nu*]
17 [*lu-u* PAB].MEŠ!-*šú-nu lu-u* DUMU.MEŠ!—ŠE[Š!.MEŠ-*šú-nu*]
18 [*lu-u* LÚ*.*h*]*a-za-na-šú-nu lu-u* L[Ú.GAR-*nu*?-*šú-nu*]
19 [*lu-u* I]M!.RI.A KI.MIN KI.MIN [*x x x*]
20 [*lu-u mám*]-*ma-šú-nu e-la-an-*[*ni*]
21 [TA* ^{m}]DUMU.UŠ-*a-a* [*ù* DUMU.MEŠ-*šú*]
e.22 [*de-nu*] ⸢DUG$_4$.DUG$_4$ *i*⸣-[*gar-ru-ni*]
r.1 [*i-qab-bu-u-ni ma-a kas-pu*]
2 [*la gam-mur la ta-ad-din i-si-tú*]
3 [*a-di* A.ŠÀ.GA.MEŠ ^{m}*ab-di*]—*ku*!-*b*[*u*!-*bi*]
4 [*a-di* UN].MEŠ! *la laq-qi-*[*u*! *la ap-lu*]
5 [*x x x x*]-*mur*! *ú-ma-a ka*[*s*!-*pu ih-hur*]
6 [*a-na* 12.TA-*a*]-⸢*a*!⸣ *a-na* EN-*šú* [GUR-*ra*]
7 [*ina de-ni-šú*] DUG$_4$.DUG$_4$-*ma* ⸢*la*⸣ [*i-laq-qi*!]

---

8 [IGI ^{m}U.GUR—*š*]*al*!-*lim-an-ni* LÚ*.GAL—[*x x x*]
9 [IGI ^{m}*x x x*] ⸢LÚ*!⸣.GAL—⸢*sa*!⸣-*x*[*x x x*]

ADD 473

1 Instead of their seals Harura[nu] and Salilanu impressed their fingernails.

(fingernail impressions)

---

3 A tower (and) an estate of 10 hec[tares of land] in the midst of a meadow in the town of [...]; Abdi-Kububi, [his] wife and [two sons], a total of 4 persons belonging to H[aruranu] and [Salilanu] —

7 [Aplaya has contracted and bought (said property) from them for x minas of silver].

8 [That tower together with the fie]lds [and Abdi-Kubu]bi together with [his] peo[ple are paid for, purchased and] acquired. [Any revocation, lawsuit] or litigation [is void].

13 [Whoever] in the future [comes forwa]rd, whether Haru[ranu or Sali]lanu [or] their [sons], grandsons, [brothers] or nephews, [or] their mayor or [*prefect*, or] their kinsman, [...], or relative, (who) comes forward and in[stitutes a lawsuit or] litigation against Aplaya [and his sons, saying]:

r.1 "[The money has not been paid completely; the tower together with the fields and Abdi]-Kub[ubi together with his people are not purch]ased and [paid for ...]...,"

5 shall [return the money he received twelvef]old to its owner. He shall contest [in his lawsuit] and not [succeed].

---

r.8 [Witness Nergal]-šallimanni, chief [...].

9 [Witness NN], chief [...].

100 Previous editions: AR 96, NALK 27. Collations: Assur 2/5. r.3 Tablet ^{m}*man-nu—ki—*16—SU; scribal error. r.5 Cf. no. 164:15f, *kas-pi*! *im-hur-nu a-na* 10-*a-a a-na* EN-*šú* GUR.

10 [IGI ^{m}AN.GAL—me]-si$^{!}$ LÚ*$^{!}$.⸢rak$^{!}$⸣-su$^{!}$ [x x x]
11 [IGI ^{md}IM—k]a-šir [LÚ*.x x x]
12 ⸢IGI$^{!}$⸣ [^{m}]⸢^{d}AMAR$^{!}$⸣.[UTU—MU—AŠ LÚ*.x x x]
13 ⸢IGI ^{m}⸣[x x x x x]⸢x⸣[x x x x]
14 IGI ^{m}⸢x⸣[x x x x x x x x]
15 DUMU URU.N[INA.KI]
16 IGI ^{m}ba-qu-[x x x x x]
17 IGI ^{md}IM—tak-lak L[Ú$^{!}$.x x x]
18 IGI ^{m}DINGIR—PAB : IGI ^{m}bal-t[i$^{!}$—x x]
19 IGI ^{md}BA.Ú—PAB.MEŠ—A[Š]
20 IGI ^{md}PA—PAB.MEŠ—SU LÚ*.⸢A⸣.[BA]

21 ṣa-bit ṭup-pi ITI.SIG$_4$ UD-10-[KÁM]
22 lim-me ^{m}DI-mu—LUGAL
s.1 [x x x x x x x x x]x i-ta-ṣu

10 [Witness Issaran-me]si, *conscript* [...].
11 [Witness Adad-k]ašir, [...].
12 Witness Mar[duk-šumu-iddina, ...].
13 Witness [NN, ...].
14 Witness [NN], resident of Ni[neveh].
16 Witness Baqu[......].
17 Witness Adad-taklak, [...].
18 Witness Ilu-naṣir, ditto. Witness Balt[i-...].
19 Witness Babu-ahhe-iddina.
20 Witness Nabû-ahhe-riba, sc[ribe], keeper of the tablet.
21 Month Sivan (III), 10th day, eponym year of Šulmu-šarri.
s.1 They collected [...... *for their fingernails*].

101. Partial Duplicate of the Previous Text

K 439 + K 17997

beginning broken away
1′ [ina URU.x x x x ^{m}ab-di—ku-b]u-[bi]
2′ [MÍ-šú 2 DUMU.MEŠ-šú PAB 4 LÚ*.Z]I. ME[Š]
3′ [ša ^{m}ha-ru-ra-a-nu ù ^{m}sa-l]i-la-a-[nu]
4′ [ú-piš-ma ^{m}DUMU.UŠ-a]-⸢a⸣ TA* ŠU.2-šú-n[u]
5′ [ina ŠÀ x MA.NA KUG.UD i]l-qí kas-pu ga[m-mur]
6′ [ta-din URU].⸢i$^{!}$⸣-si$^{!}$-tú a-di A.Š[À.GA.MEŠ]
7′ [^{m}ab-di]—ku$^{!}$-bu-bi a-di UN.[MEŠ-šú]
8′ [ap]-⸢lu$^{!}$⸣ [zar-pu laq-q]í tu-a-ru ⸢DUG$_4$$^{!}$⸣.DUG$_4$ [la-áš-šú]
9′ [man-nu] šá ina mat$^{!}$-e$^{!!}$-ma$^{!}$ ina$^{!}$ ⸢EGIR$^{!}$⸣ [UD-me]
10′ ⸢šá$^{!}$⸣ e-la-an-ni lu-u ^{m}ha-ru-ra-a-⸢nu$^{!}$⸣
11′ lu-u ^{m}sa-li-la-a-nu lu-u šú-nu
12′ lu-u DUMU.MEŠ-šú-nu lu-u DUMU—DUMU.MEŠ-šú-nu
13′ lu-u PAB.MEŠ-šú-nu lu-u DUMU—ŠEŠ-šú-nu
14′ lu-u LÚ.GAR-nu lu-u LÚ.šá-pi-ru
15′ lu-u mám-ma EN—il-ki-šú-nu
16′ šá e-la-a-ni de-e-nu DUG$_4$.DUG$_4$
17′ TA*$^{!}$ ⸢^{m}DUMU.UŠ-a-a⸣ ù DUMU.MEŠ-šú
18′ i-gar-ru-u-ni i-qab-bu-u-ni
19′ ma-⸢a kas⸣-pu la gam-mur ⸢la⸣ ta-ad-d[in]
20′ i-si-tú a-di ⸢A⸣.[ŠÀ.GA.MEŠ ^{m}ab-di—ku-bu-bi]
r.1 a-di UN.MEŠ-[šú la ap-lu la zar-pu]
2 la laq-qí-u l[a x x x x x x]

ADD 474+

(Beginning destroyed)

1 [in the town ...; Abdi-Ku]bu[bi, his wife and two sons, a total of 4 per]sons [belonging to Haruranu and Sal]ila[nu] —

4 [Aplaya has contracted and bou]ght (said property) from them [for x minas of silver].

5 The money [is paid] comple[tely]. The tower together with the fie[lds and Abdi]-Kububi together with [his] people [are paid for, purchased and acquired]. Any revocation or litigation [is void].

9 [Whoever] at any time in the [future] comes forward, whether Haruranu or Salilanu, whether they or their sons, grandsons, brothers or nephews, or a prefect, commissioner or any labour-duty superior of theirs, who comes forward and institutes a lawsuit or litigation against Aplaya and his sons, saying:

19 "The money is not completely paid. [The] tower together with the fi[elds and Abdi-Kububi] together with [his] people [are not paid for, purchased], acquired [...],"

101 Previous editions: AR 96a, NALK 28; → TCAE 67. Collations: Assur 2/5. Restorations from nos. 100 and 102. 9 Tablet *mat*-NIM-*ma*; scribal error.

3 1 MA.NA KUŠ.TAB.BA ⸢KÚ⸣ [*am—mar*]
4 DUG.*a-gan-ni kur-ru* ⸢NAG! DUMU!⸣.[UŠ-*šú a-na* ^{d}30]
5 GIBÍL DUMU.⸢MÍ-*su*⸣ GAL-*tú* TA*! 3BÁN! MÚD!—⸢ERIN⸣
6 *a-na be-lit—*^{d}EDIN *i-šar-rap*
7 *kas-pu ih-hur a-na* 12-A.TA.AN
8 *a-na* EN.MEŠ-*šú* GUR-*ra ina de-ni-šú*
9 DUG$_4$.DUG$_4$-*ma la i-laq-qí*

r.3 shall eat one mina of oxhide, (and) drink [a full] *agannu* vessel of tanner's paste. He shall burn his first-bo[rn son before Sin], and shall burn his eldest daughter with 3 seahs of cedar resin before Belet-ṣeri. He shall return the money he received twelvefold to its owners. He shall contest in his lawsuit and not succeed.

---

10 IGI ^{md}U.GUR—*šal-lim-a-ni* LÚ.⸢*x x*⸣
11 IGI ^{m}AN.GAL—*me-si* LÚ.*rak!-s*[*u!*]
12 [IGI] ^{md}IM—*ka-šir* LÚ.[*x x x*]
13 [IGI] ^{md}AMAR.UTU—MU—AŠ LÚ.[*x x x*]
14 [*x x x x x*] *ka bu* [*x x x x x x*]
rest broken away

r.10 Witness Nergal-šallimanni, [chief ...].
11 Witness Issaran-mesi, *conscript*.
12 Witness Adad-kašir, [...].
13 Witness Marduk-šumu-iddina, [...].
(Rest destroyed)

102. Aplaya Buys an Estate (698?)

K 1488

beginning broken away
1′ [^{m}*man-nu*]—*ki!-i—aš!*-[*šur* ^{m}*li-iʾ-ti-ru-u*]

2′ [^{m}*x x x*]-*ri ú-p*[*iš!-ma* ^{m}A-*a-a*]
3′ [TA* *pa-ni*]-*šú-nu ina* ŠÀ 2 MA.N[A KUG. UD TI-*qi*]
4′ [*kas-pu g*]*a-mur ta-ad-din* ⸢A.ŠÀ⸣ [É GIŠ. SAR]
5′ [*šu-a-tú*] ⸢*za*⸣-*rip laq*-⸢*qi*⸣ [*t*]*ú*-⸢*a-ru*⸣
6′ [*de-e*]-*nu* DUG$_4$.⸢DUG$_4$ *la*⸣-*áš-šú*

7′ [*man-nu šá ina m*]*a-te-e!-ma ina* EGIR-*kàt!*
8′ [UD-*me šá e*]-*la-an-ni lu-u* ^{md}PA—BÀD—PAB
9′ [*lu-u* ^{m}*man-nu!*]—*ki-i*—⸢*aš-šur*⸣ *lu-u* ^{m}*li-iʾ-ti-ru-u*
10′ [*lu-u* ^{m}*x x*]-*ru*-⸢*ku*⸣-[*x x*] *lu-u* DUMU.MEŠ-*šú*-⸢*nu*⸣
11′ [*lu-u* DUMU—DUMU].MEŠ-*šú*-⸢*nu*⸣ [*lu-u* PAB].MEŠ-*šú-nu*
12′ *l*[*u!-u* DUMU—PAB].MEŠ-*šú-nu l*[*u!-u mam*]-*ma!*
13′ L[Ú.EN]—⸢*il*⸣-*ki-šú-nu šá e-la*-⸢*an-ni*⸣
r.1 ⸢*de*⸣-*e-nu* DUG$_4$.DUG$_4$ TA* ^{m}A-*a-a*
2 *u* ⸢DUMU⸣.MEŠ-*š*[*ú*] *i-gar-ru-ú-ni*
3 ⸢*i-qab*⸣-*bu-u-ni ma-a kas-pu la! gam-mur*
4 *l*[*a*] *ta-din* A.ŠÀ É GIŠ.SAR *la a-pil*

5 ⸢*la*⸣ *za-rip la laq-qi* 1 MA.NA KUŠ.TAB.BA
6 ⸢KÚ⸣ *am—mar* DUG.*a-gan-ni* NAG
7 DUMU.UŠ-*šú a-na* ^{d}30 GIBÍL DUMU.MÍ-*su*
8 GAL-*te!* TA* 2BÁN MÚD—ERIN *a-na be-lit—*

ADD 436

(Beginning destroyed)

1 [of Nabû-duru-uṣur, Mannu]-ki-Aš[šur, Li'tirû and NN] —

2 [Aplaya has co]ntracted [and bought (said property) from] them for 2 minas [of silver].

4 [The money is] paid completely. That field, [house, and orchard] are purchased and acquired. Any revocation, [law]suit, or litigation is void.

7 [Whoever at] any time in the fut[ure co]mes forward, whether Nabû-duru-uṣur, [Mannu]-ki-Aššur, Li'tirû, [or ...]ruku[...], or their sons, [grandso]ns, [brother]s, o[r nephe]ws, or [an]y labour-duty [superior] of theirs, who comes forward and institutes a lawsuit or litigation against Aplaya and his sons, saying:

r.3 "The money is not completely paid. The field, house and orchard are not paid for, cleared and bought,"

5 shall eat one mina of oxhide (and) drink a full *agannu* vessel of tanner's paste. He shall burn his first-born son before Sin, and

102 Previous editions: AR 163, NALK 35. Collations: Assur 2/5. The orthography and formulary of the tablet imply that it was written by the scribe Nabû-ahhe-riba, cf. no. 100 (698 B.C.).

$^{d!}$EDIN
9 *i-šar-rap kas-pu* ⸢*ih*⸣*-hur a-*⸢*na*⸣ 1[2$^{!}$-T]A$^{!}$*-a-a*
10 *a-na* ⸢EN⸣.MEŠ*-šú* GUR*-ra ina d*[*e*$^{!}$*-ni-šú*]
11 DUG$_4$.DUG$_4$*-ma la* T[I$^{!}$*-qi*]

shall burn his eldest daughter with 2 seahs of cedar balsam before Belet-ṣeri. He shall return the money he received twelvefold to its owners. He shall contest in [his lawsuit] and not suc[ceed].

---

12 IGI ^{m}ITI.KIN*-a-*[*a x x x x x*]
13 IGI ^{m}[*n*]*a*$^{!}$*-ha*[*r-a-ú x x x x x*]
14 IGI ^{m}⸢^{d}⸣[*x x x x x x x*]
15 IGI $^{m!}$[*x x x x x x x x x*]
16 IGI [^{m}*x x x x x x x x x x*]
rest broken away

12 Witness Ulula[yu ...].
13 Witness Naha[rau ...].
14 Witness [......].
15 Witness [......].
16 Witness [......].
(Rest destroyed)

103. Aplaya, 'Third Man' of the Crown Prince, Buys a Slave (694-VII-12)

Bu 89-4-26,120

ADD 201

1 NA$_4$.KIŠIB ^{m}*zu-un-bu*
2 EN DUMU*-šú* SUM*-ni*

---

3 ^{md}U.GUR—KAR*-ir* DUMU*-šú*
4 *ú-piš-ma* ^{m}A*-iá* LÚ.3*-šú*
5 *šá* ^{m}ARAD—^{d}NIN.LÍL DUMU—MAN
6 TA* IGI ^{m}*zu-un-b*[*i*]
7 *ina* ŠÀ 2 MA.NA KUG.UD *ina* 1 M[A.NA]
8 *šá* URU.*gar-ga-mis i-*[*zi-rip*]
9 *i-si*$^{!}$*-qi kas-pu* [*gam-mur*]
10 *ta-din* DUMU*-šú za-*[*rip laq-qi*]
11 [*t*]*u*$^{!}$*-a*$^{!}$*-ru de-nu* [DUG$_4$.DUG$_4$ *la-áš-šú*]

12 ⸢*x x*⸣ 1*-me* UD*-me*$^{!}$ [*x x x x x*]
rest broken away

r.1 [IGI ^{m}*x x*]*-ba*$^{!}$*-*⸢*a*$^{!}$⸣ [*x x x*]
2 [IGI ^{m}*x x*]*-nu* [*x x x*]
3 [IGI ^{m}*x x*] ⸢*x*⸣ [*x x x*]
4 [IGI ^{m}*x x x*] ⸢*x*⸣ [*x x x*]
5 [IGI ^{m}*x x x*—A]Š$^{!}$ [*x x x*]
6 [IGI ^{m}*x x x*] ⸢*x*⸣ [*x x*]
7 [IGI ^{m}*x x x*]*-*⸢*i*⸣*-ni* [*x x*]
8 [IGI] $^{m!d!}$IŠ$^{!}$.TAR$^{!}$—BA$^{!}$*-*[*šá*]
blank space of about 3 lines
9 ITI.DUL UD-12-KÁM
10 *lim-mu* ^{m}DINGIR—KI*-ia*

1 Seal of Zunbu, the owner selling his son.

(blank seal space)

---

3 Nergal-eṭir, his son —
4 Aplaya, 'third man' of Arda-Mullissi, the crown prince, has contracted and boug[ht] him from Zunbu for 2 minas of silver by the m[ina] of Carchemish.
9 The money [is] paid [completely]. His son is pur[chased and acquired. Any re]vocation lawsu[it or litigation is void].
12 [(Guaranteed against) seizures of epilepsy for] 100 days (and against) [fraud forever].
(Break)
r.1 [Witness ...]bâ, [...].
(Six broken lines with names of witnesses)

8 [Witness] Issar-iqi[ša].

9 Month Tishri (VII), 12th day, eponym year of Ilu-isse'a.

103 Previous editions: AR 38, NALK 29. Collations: Assur 2/5. 5 → S. Parpola, CRRAI 26 176 n. 7 and 177 n. 21. 9, 11f See coll.

104. Aplaya Loans Silver (690-VII)

K 911

vitrified
1 [*x x x x x x x x*]
2 [*ina* 1 MA.NA-*e*] ⸢*šá*! URU⸣.*gar-ga-mis*
3 [*ša*] ⸢^{m}⸣A-[*a-a*] *ina* IGI 0!
4 [^{m}]EN—A—S[UM!-*na x x x*]*x*
5 *ina* ⸢IGI⸣ ^{m}[*x x x*]
6 2 ⸢GÍN.MEŠ⸣ *ina* [MA].NA *š*[*a* IT]I-*šú*
e.7 *i-r*[*a-a*]*b-bi*
8 ITI.DUL U[D-*x*]-KÁM
r.1 *lim-*[*mu* ^{m}]^{d}PA—GIN—PAB
2 IG[I ^{m}DIN]GIR!—*ha-na*!-*ni*
3 IGI ^{m}PAB—APIN-*eš*
4 IGI ^{m}APIN-*eš*—[1]5
5 [IGI] ^{m}⸢*x*—*sa*⸣-*gab*

ADD 55

1 [x shekels of silver by the mina] of Carchemish, [belonging to] Apl[aya], at the disposal of Bel-apla-id[dina ...] and [NN].

6 It shall increase 2 shekels per mina per month.

8 Month Tishri (VII), [...]th day, epon[ym year] of Nabû-kenu-uṣur.

r.2 Wit[ness I]l-hanani.
3 Witness Ahu-ereš.
4 Witness Ereš-Issar.
5 [Witness ...]-sagab.

105. Aplaya Buys an Estate of 30 Hectares (690-XII-9)

Ki 1904-10-9,13

1 *ku-um* NA$_4$.KIŠIB-*šú-nu ṣu-*⸢*pur-šú*⸣-*nu*
2 *iš-kun*

3 *ṣu-pur* ^{md}*šá-maš—ia-da-a'*
4 *ṣu-pur* ^{m}*da-nu-ni-*⸢*i*⸣ 0!
5 EN A.ŠÀ *ta-dan-a-ni*
6 É 30 ANŠE A.ŠÀ É *a-na gi-mir-ti-šú*
7 [*n*]*a*!-⸢*hal*! PÚ É TÙR⸣ GIŠ!.SAR!.MEŠ
8 [*x x x x x x x x x x x x x*]
9 [*x x x x x x x x x x x x* ^{m}]⸢^{d}⸣PA—ZALÁG-*ir*
rest broken away
r.1′ IGI ^{md}⸢*x*⸣[*x x*]*x* ⸢*x*⸣ *x*[*x x*]
2′ IGI ^{m}*ia-hu-u-*⸢*ṭu*⸣ IGI ^{m}AD—ÚR!-*x*[*x*]
3′ IGI ^{m}*man-nu—ki—me-ti-i-na* IGI ^{m}PAB—⸢AŠ!⸣
4′ IGI ^{m}*ši-ma-a-nu* IGI ^{m}*ha-bíl*!—GIN
5′ IGI ^{m}*lu-u*—Á!-*i* PAB 9 LÚ*.IGI.MEŠ-*e*!
6′ IGI ^{m}AN.GAL—*me-si* IGI ^{md}IM—*ka-šir*
7′ IGI ^{m}GÌR.2-*a-a* IGI ^{m}*i-di-i*
8′ IGI ^{m}*i-qi-su* IGI ^{md}UTU—MU—AŠ ŠEŠ-*šú*

ADD 1152

1 Instead of their seals they impressed their fingernails.

(fingernail impressions)

3 Fingernail of Šamaš-yada', fingernail of Danunî, owners of the land being sold.

6 An estate of 30 hectares of land, a house in its entirety, [a wa]di, a well, a house, a courtyard, orchards, [......]
9 [......] Nabû-nammir
(Break)
r.1 Witness [......].
2 Witness Yahuṭu. Witness Abi-sun[...].
3 Witness Mannu-ki-metina. Witness Ahu-iddina.
4 Witness Šimanu. Witness Habil-ken.
5 Witness Lu-ahi. A total of 9 witnesses.
6 Witness Issaran-mesi. Witness Adad-kašir.
7 Witness Šep-Ea. Witness Iddî.
8 Witness Iqisu. Witness Šamaš-šumu-iddina, his brother.

104 Previous editions: AR 247, NALK 31. Collations: Assur 2/5.
105 Previous edition: NALK 32. $^{r.2ff, s.2}$ See coll.

9′ IGI ^{m}*ha-a-ri*—PAB.MEŠ IGI ^{m}*ki-di-ni—mar-duk*
10′ IGI ^{m}*hu*$^{!}$—*ma-ma-a-ti* LÚ*.A.BA

11e *ṣa-bit ṭup-pi ina* ITI.ŠE UD-8$^{!}$-KÁM
12e *lim-me* ^{md}PA—GIN—PAB
s.1 [IGI ^{m}*x x x* IGI] ^{m}*a-du-ú-ri*
2 [IGI ^{m}*x x x* IGI ^{m}*n*]*a*$^{!}$*-bu-za-aʾ* LÚ*.DAM.QAR
3 [*x x x x x ša ṣu-p*]*ur-šu-nu i-tah-ru*

9 Witness Hari-ahhe. Witness Kidinni-Marduk.
10 Witness Humamati, scribe, keeper of the tablet.
11 Month of Adar (XII), 8th day, eponym year of Nabû-kenu-uṣur.
s.1 [Witness .... Witness] Aduru.
2 [Witness .... Witness N]abuza', merchant.
3 They have received [... for] their fin[ger-nails].

106. Aplaya Buys Slaves (688)

Bu 91-5-9,59

beginning broken away
1′ [*de*]-⸢*e*$^{!}$⸣-*nu*$^{!}$ DUG$_4$.⸢DUG$_4$⸣ [*la-áš-šú*]
2′ [*man*]-*nu šá ina ur*-⸢*kiš*⸣ *ina ma-te-e-me*$^{!}$
3′ ⸢*i*⸣-*qa-bu-u-ni ma-a* UN.MEŠ
4′ *la-a* ⸢*ad*$^{!}$⸣-*din lu-u* ^{m}*i-qi-si*
5′ *lu-u* DUMU.MEŠ-*šu lu-u* DUMU—DUMU.MEŠ-*šú*
6′ *lu-u* PAB.MEŠ-*šú šá i-qab-bu-ni ma-a*
7′ ⸢UN⸣.MEŠ *la-a ad-din* KUG.UD.MEŠ
8′ *a-na* 10-*a-te a-na* EN.MEŠ-*šú*
9′ *ú-ta-ra*
10′ IGI ^{md}UTU—DIL—SI.[SÁ]
11′ IGI ^{m}EN—B[ÀD]

ADD 264

(Beginning destroyed)
1 [Any revocation, lawsu]it, or litigation [is void].
2 [Whoe]ver in the future, at any time, says: "I did not sell the people," whether Iqisu or his sons, grandsons or brothers, who says: "I did not sell the people," shall return the silver tenfold to its owners.

10 Witness Šamaš-edu-lešir.
11 Witness Bel-d[uri].

106 Previous editions: AR 527, NALK 30. Collations: Assur 2/5.

FIG. 19. *Reign of Sennacherib landscape.*
ORIGINAL DRAWING I, 43.

12′ IGI [^{m}]*bar-ruq-q*[*u*]
13′ IGI ^{md}PA—*še*-[*zib*]
r.1 [IGI] ^{md}UTU—MU$^{!}$—SUM-*na*
2 IGI ^{md}PA—BA-*šá-an-ni*
3 IGI ^{m}PAB—*ma-ma-a-*⸢*te*⸣
4 IGI ^{md}EN—[*x*]
5 IGI ^{md}IM—*ka*-[*šir*]
6 ⸢IGI⸣ ^{m}AN.⸢GAL⸣—*me*-[*si*]
blank space of about 8 lines
7 [ITI.*x* UD-*x*-KAM *li*]*m-mu* ^{m}AŠ—PAB.MEŠ
8 [LÚ.GAR.KUR URU.BÀD—LUGA]L$^{!}$—⸢*ú*$^{!}$⸣-*k*[*in*$^{!}$]
rest broken away

12 Witness Barruqu.
13 Witness Nabû-še[zib].
r.1 [Witness] Šamaš-šumu-iddina.
2 Witness Nabû-iqišanni.
3 Witness Humamati.
4 Witness Bel-[...].
5 Witness Adad-ka[šir].
6 Witness Issaran-me[si].
7 [Month ..., ...th day, epon]ym year of Iddin-ahhe, [governor of Dur-Šarr]uk[en].
(Rest destroyed)

107. Aplaya Loans Three Minas of Silver (686-V-2)

K 343

1 3 MA.NA KUG.UD *ina ša* URU.*gar-gar-mis*
2 *ša* ^{m}DUMU.UŠ-*ia*
3 *ina* IGI ^{m}*su-ka-a-a*
4 6 GÍN.MEŠ *ša* ITI-*šú*
5 GAL-*bi* ITI.NE UD-2-KÁ[M]
e.6 *lim-mu* ^{m}EN—IGI.LAL-*a-ni*
7 LÚ*.*tur-tan*
r.1 IGI ^{md}PA—*še-zib*
2 IGI ^{m}*ab-da-*⸢*li*⸣
3 IGI ^{md}15—BÀD
4 IGI ^{m}A.10—*hu-ut-ni*
5 IGI ^{m}ARAD—^{d}15

ADD 28

1 Three minas of silver by the (mina) of Carchemish, belonging to Aplaya, at the disposal of Sukkaya.
4 It will increase by 6 shekels per month.
5 Month Ab (V), 2nd day, eponym year of Bel-emuranni, commander-in-chief.
r.1 Witness Nabû-šezib.
2 Witness Abd-eli.
3 Witness Issar-duri.
4 Witness Apladad-hutni.
5 Witness Urda-Issar.

108. Aplaya Loans 1/2 Mina of Silver (683-I-25)

83-1-18,370

1 [N]A$_4$.KIŠIB ^{md}GAŠAN—APIN-*eš ki-ṣ*[*ir-ti*]
2 1/2 MA.NA KUG.UD SAG.DU *ina* 1 MA.NA-*e*$^{!}$ *gar*-[*ga-mis*]

---

3 *ša* ^{m}DUMU.UŠ-*a-a ina* IGI ^{md}GAŠAN—APIN$^{!}$-*eš*
4 4 GÍN KUG.UD *ša* ITI-*šú i-rab-bi*
5 IGI ^{md}MAŠ—*rém-a-ni* IGI ^{md}PA—GÁL-*ši*

ADD 51

1 [S]eal of Belet-ereš. An enve[lope (copy) concerning] 1/2 mina of silver, capital, by the mina of Car[chemish],

---

(blank seal space)

---

3 belonging to Aplaya, at the disposal of Belet-ereš.
4 It will increase 4 shekels of silver per month.
5 Witness Inurta-remanni. Witness Nabû-ušabši.

107 Previous editions: AR 248, NALK 33.
108 Previous editions: AR 252, NALK 34. Collations: Assur 2/5.

6 IGI ^{m}*kan-da-la-ni*
r.1 IGI ^{m}*sa-me-e*ʾ IGI ^{md}PA—PAB—⌜PAB⌝
2 ITI.BARAG UD-25-KÁM *lim-mu* ^{m}*man-nu*—⌜*ki*⌝—^{d}IM
3 *ša* URU.*ṣu-pi-te* IGI ^{m}URU$^{!}$—ZALÁG$^{!}$-⌜*i*$^{!}$⌝

6 Witness Kandalanu.
r.1 Witness Same'. Witness Nabû-ahu-uṣur.
2 Month Nisan (I), 25th day, eponym year of Mannu-ki-Adad of Şupat.
3 Witness El-nurî.

8. Se'-madi, Village Manager of the Crown Prince (683-680)

FIG. 20. *An Assyrian crown-prince. Courtesy Metropolitan Museum of Art (32.143.13). Gift of John D. Rockefeller, Jr., 1932.*

109. Se'-madi, Village Manager of the Crown Prince, Buys Three Slaves (683)

K 1856

1 [NA$_4$.KIŠIB ^{m}AR]AD—^{d}15
2 [EN UN.MEŠ] SUM-ni

3 ^{m}mar—ia-te-eʾ ^{m}se-eʾ—im-⌜me⌝
4 [^{m}]mu-ra-a PAB 3 ZI.MEŠ ARAD.MEŠ
5 [ša ^{m}]⌜ARAD⌝—$^{d!}$15 ú-piš-⌜ma⌝
6 [^{m}se-eʾ$^{!}$—ma]-⌜ʾa$^{!}$⌝-di LÚ*.GAL—⌜URU⌝.MEŠ
7 [ša DUMU—MAN ina] ⌜ŠÀ⌝-bi 50 GÍN.MEŠ ⌜KUG.UD⌝
8 [TA* ^{m}ARAD—^{d}1]5$^{!}$ il-qi
9 [kas-pu gam-mur ta-di]n$^{!}$-ni$^{!}$
rest broken away
Rev. beginning broken away
1′ [x x x x x x x x x] ⌜x⌝
2′ [x x x x x x x x x]
3′ [IGI ^{m}x x x x x]-⌜x⌝.MEŠ
4′ [IGI ^{m}x x x x x] LÚ*$^{!}$.A.BA
5′ [IGI ^{m}x x x x x] LÚ*$^{!}$.ENGAR
6′ [x x x x x] URU.ŠE—ra-bu
7′ [IGI ^{m}PAB$^{?}$—ia]-ba-ba LÚ*$^{!}$.ENGAR

8′ [ITI.x UD]-⌜7$^{?}$⌝-KAM lim-me
9′ [^{m}man-nu—ki—10 GAR.KUR URU].ṣu-ba-te
10′ [IGI ^{md}x]—⌜PAB⌝—AŠ LÚ*.A.BA

ADD 278

1 [Seal of U]rda-Issar, [owner of the people] being sold.

(cylinder seal impression)

3 Mar-yate', Se'-immi and Murâ, a total of 3 persons, servants [of] Urda-Issar —

6 [Se'-m]adi, village manager [of the crown prince], has contracted and bought them [from Urda-Is]sar for 50 shekels of silver.

9 [The money] is pai[d completely].

(Break)

r.3 [Witness NN]....

4 [Witness NN], scribe.

5 [Witness NN], farmer.

6 [...... from] Kaprabu.

7 [Witness *Ahi*-ya]baba, farmer.

8 [Month...], 7th day, eponym year of [Mannu-ki-Adad, governor of] Ṣupat.

10 [Witness ...]-ahu-iddina, scribe.

110. Se'-madi, Village Manager, Buys 7 Slaves (681-XII-16)

81-2-4,150

1 NA$_4$.KIŠIB ^{m}ARAD—^{d}15
2 EN UN.MEŠ ta-da-ni

ADD 231

1 Seal of Urda-Issar, owner of the people being sold.

(two stamp seal impressions)

109 Previous editions: AR 531, NALK 300. 9, r.8 See coll.
110 Previous editions: AR 202, NALK 301. Collations: Assur 2/5. 7f Note that in this text, written two (or 12)

3 ^{m}*ha-am-nu-nu* MÍ-*šú* MÍ.AMA-*šú*
4 ^{m}*ad-da-a* ^{m}DINGIR—*su*$^{!}$*-ri* 0$^{!}$ ŠEŠ.MEŠ-*šú*
5 2 NIN.MEŠ-*šú* PAB 7 ZI.MEŠ
6 ARAD.MEŠ *ša* ^{m}ARAD—^{d}15
7 *ú-piš-ma* ^{m}*se-e'—ma-*⌜*a'*⌝*-du*
8 LÚ*.GAL—URU.MEŠ *ša* DUMU—MAN
9 *ina* ŠÀ 2 MA.NA KUG.UD *ina ša* 0$^{!}$ *gar-ga-mis*

^{3} Hamnunu, his wife and mother, Addâ and Il-suri, his brothers, and his two sisters, a total of 7 persons, servants of Urda-Issar —

^{7} Se'-madi, village manager of the crown prince, has contracted and bought them for two minas of silver by the (mina) of Carchemish.

10 *il-qi kás-pu ga-mur ta-din*
11 UN.MEŠ *šu-a-tú zar*$_{4}$*-pu la-qi-u*
12 *tu-a-ru de-nu* DUG$_{4}$.DUG$_{4}$
13 *la-áš-šú man-nu šá ina ur-kiš*
14 *ina ma-te-ma i-za-qu-pa-ni*
e.15 *de-nu* DUG$_{4}$.DUG$_{4}$ *ub-ta-u-*[*ni*]
r.1 10 MA.NA KUG.UD 1 MA.NA KUG.GI
2 *ina bur-ki* ^{d}IŠ.TAR *a-ši-bat*
3 URU.NINA GAR-*an kas-pu a-na* 10.MEŠ-*te*
4 *a-na* EN.MEŠ-*šú ú-ta-ra*
5 *ina la de-*⌜*ni-šú*⌝ DUG$_{4}$.DUG$_{4}$*-ma*
6 *la i-la*$^{!}$*-qi*

^{10} The money is paid completely. Those people are purchased and acquired. Any revocation, lawsuit, or litigation is void.

^{13} Whoever in the future, at any time, lodges a complaint and se[eks] a lawsuit or litigation shall place 10 minas of silver (and) one mina of gold in the lap of Ištar residing in Nineveh. He shall return the money tenfold to its owners. He shall contest in his lawsuit and not succeed.

7 IGI ^{m}10—*ta-ka-a*
8 IGI ^{m}DI-*mu*—EN LÚ*$^{!}$.GAL—URU.MEŠ
9 IGI ^{m}10—*sa-na-ni* LÚ*$^{!}$.3-*šú*
10 IGI ^{m}*se-e'—hu-ut-ni* LÚ*$^{!}$.GIŠ$^{!}$.GIGIR$^{!}$
11 IGI ^{md}PA—I
12 IGI ^{m}0$^{!}$
blank space of 3 lines
13 ITI.ŠE UD-*mu*-16-KÁM
14 *lim-mu* ^{md}PA—PAB—APIN-*eš*

$^{r.7}$ Witness Adda-takâ.
^{8} Witness Šulmu-beli, village manager.
^{9} Witness Adda-sanani, 'third man.'
^{10} Witness Se'-hutni, horse trainer.
^{11} Witness Nabû-na'id.
^{12} Witness (blank)
^{13} Month Adar (XII), 16th day, eponym year of Nabû-ahu-ereš.

111. Se'-madi, Village Manager, Buys 7 More Slaves (680-VII)

K 76 — ADD 229

1 NA$_{4}$.KIŠIB ^{m}ARAD—^{d}15
2 EN UN.MEŠ SUM-*ni*

^{1} Seal of Urda-Issar, owner of the people being sold.

(stamp seal impressions)

3 ^{m}*ú-si-a'* 2 MÍ.MEŠ-*šú*
4 MÍ.*me-e'-sa-a* MÍ.*ba-di-a*
5 ^{m}*se—gab-a* ^{m}EN—KASKAL—*tàk-lak*
6 2 DUMU.MÍ.MEŠ *pir-su*

^{3} Hosea and his two wives, Me'sâ and Badia; Se'-gabbâ and Bel-Harran-taklak; two weaned daughters; a total of 7 persons, ser-

days before the accession of Esarhaddon, Se'-madi is entitled "village manager the crown prince," as in no. 109, written two years earlier. The qualification "of the crown prince" is, however, dropped in no. 111, dated in Esarhaddon's first year. This implies 1) that the crown prince referred to was Esarhaddon and 2) that he had been promoted to this status by 683 at the latest. See also the note on no. 264:4.

111 Previous editions: AR 64, NALK 302; → KB 4 (1896) 124f, ABC 4, CIS II 17, Fales Epigraphs no. 5. Collations: Assur 2/5.

7 PAB 7 ZI.MEŠ LÚ*.ARAD.MEŠ
8 *ša* ^{m}ARAD—^{d}15
9 *ú-piš-ma* ^{m}*se—ma-a-di*
e.10 *ina* ŠÀ-*bi* 3 MA.NA KUG.UD
11 *il-qi kas-pu*
r.1 *ga-mur ta-ad-din*
2 *tu-a-ru de-e-nu*
3 DUG$_4$.DUG$_4$ *la-a-šú*

---

4 IGI ^{m}EN—ZALÁG LÚ*.*tam*-QAR
5 IGI ^{m}*am—ia-te-e'-ú*
6 IGI ^{m}*sa-an-gi-i*
7 IGI ^{m}*ku*$^{!}$*-i-sa-a*
8 IGI ^{m}*se*—BÀD
9 IGI ^{m}(blank)

10 ITI.DUL *lim-mu* ^{m}*da-na-nu*

11e *dnt . hwšʿ w*
12e 6 *g . 'nš* 7 *. zy 'rd'*[*šr*]

vants of Urda-Issar —

9 Se'-madi has contracted and bought them for 3 minas of silver.

11 The money is paid completely. Any revocation, lawsuit, or litigation is void.

---

r.4 Witness Bel-nuri, merchant.
5 Witness Am-yate'.
6 Witness Sangî.
7 Witness Kuisâ.
8 Witness Se'-duri.
9 Witness (blank)
10 Month Tishri (VII), eponym year of Dananu.
11 Aramaic caption: Deed of Hosea and 6 *others*, 7 people of Urda-Is[sar].

112. Se'-madi, Village Manager, Buys 6 Persons and an Estate

Bu 89-4-26,128

beginning broken away
possibly space for seals
1′ [*x x x x x x x*]⸢*x x*⸣[*x x x*]
2′ [*x x x x x x x*] DUMU-*šú x*[*x x x*]
3′ [*x x x* DUMU] ⸢GA$^{!}$⸣ PAB ⸢6⸣ ZI.[MEŠ ARAD.MEŠ]
4′ [*ša*? ^{m}]*bi*—⸢*da*$^{!}$⸣-[*di* É *x* ANŠE A.ŠÀ]
5′ [*x*]-*lim*-6$^{!}$-*me*$^{!}$ GIŠ$^{!}$.*t*[*il*$^{!}$-*lit x x x*]
6′ [P]Ú *ina* ŠÀ-*bi* URU$^{!}$.[*x x x x x*]
7′ *ú-piš-ma* ^{m}*s*[*e-e'—ma-a-di*]
8′ LÚ*.GAL—URU.MEŠ [*ša* DUMU—MAN]
rest broken away

r.1 [*a-n*]*a*$^{!}$ [10].MEŠ$^{!}$-⸢*te*$^{!}$⸣ [*a-na* EN.MEŠ-*šú* GUR]
2 [*ina de*]-*ni-šú* DUG$_4$.D[UG$_4$-*ma la i-laq-qi*]

---

3 [IGI ^{m}]*mu-na*$^{!}$*-se-e*$^{!}$ [LÚ*.*x x x x*]
4 [IGI ^{m}]*sa-ni-i* LÚ*.GAL—[*x x x*]
5 URU.*zi*-[*x x x*]
6 [IGI ^{m}]*se-e*—ZALÁG [*x x x*]
7 IGI ^{m}EN—⸢*mu*$^{!}$⸣-[*x*(*x*) L]Ú$^{!}$.GIŠ.GIGIR *qur*$^{!}$*-bu*$^{!}$-[*ti*]

8 [IGI ^{m}]⸢^{d}⸣[*x*]*x*[*x x*]
9 [IGI ^{m}*x*]-*ri*-[*x*]—KUR—LAL

ADD 455

(Beginning destroyed)

2 [......] his son [...],

3 [..., a] suckling [child], a total of 6 persons, servants of] Bi-D[adi];

4 [an estate of x hectares of land, x] thousand 600 vines [...], a well, in the town [...] —

7 S[e'-madi], village manager [of the crown prince] has contracted

(Break)

1 [He shall return the money] tenfold t[o its owners]. He shall contest [in] his lawsuit [and not succeed].

---

3 Witness Manasseh, [...].
4 Witness Sanî, chief [...] of the town of Zi[...].
6 Witness Se'-nuri, [...].
7 Witness Bel-mu[...], horse trainer of *the royal bo*[*dyguard*].
8 Witness [...].
9 Witness [...]-matu-taqqin.

112 Previous edition: AR 381.

10 [IGI ^{m}*x*]-*ri*-*i*-U$^{!}$ 0$^{!}$
11 [IGI ^{m}*x*]*x*-*la*$^{!}$ URU.*a*-*mu*$^{!}$-*x*[*x x*]
traces of 3 more lines, probably witnesses

10 Witness [...]...
11 Witness [...]la [from] the town Amu[...].
(Rest destroyed)

9. Varia (702-681)

FIG. 21. *Procession through garden (reign of Assurbanipal).*
BM 118915.

113. Purchase of a Vegetable Garden (702-V-25)

Rm 174

1 *ku-um* NA$_4$.KIŠIB-*šú ṣu-pur-šú iš-kun*
2 *ṣu-pur* ^{m}*ba-tu-ʾa-a*
3 EN GIŠ.SAR SUM-*ni*

4 [GI]Š.SAR *ša* Ú.SAR URU.*kal-gu-rig*$^{!}$
5 [*ša*] ^{m}*ba-tú-ʾa-a ú-piš-ma*
6 [^{m}*x x*]*x-ši ina* ŠÀ-*bi* 5 GÍN.MEŠ KUG.UD
7 [*x x*(*x*) *il-qi kas-pu gam*]-*mur* 0$^{!}$
rest broken away
Rev. beginning broken away

1′ [*kas-pu ana*] 10.MEŠ-*te* ⌜*a*$^{!}$-*na*⌝ [EN-*šú* GUR]
2′ [*ina de-ni*]-*šú* DUG$_4$.DUG$_4$-*ma là* TI

3′ IGI ^{m}*šu-ma-a-a*
4′ IGI ^{m}*ki*$^{!}$-*ni-ih-ma-a*
5′ IGI ^{m}*ha-ti-a-nu*
6′ *ina* ITI.NE UD-25-KAM
7′ *lim-mu* ^{md}PA—ZU

ADD 365

1 Instead of his seal [he imp]ressed his fingernail.

2 Fingernail of Batu'a, owner of the garden being sold.

(fingernail impressions)

4 A vegetable garden (in) Kalgurig, [belonging to] Batu'a —

6 [...]ši has contracted and [bought it] for 5 shekels of silver.

7 [The money is paid complet]ely.

(Break)

r.1 [He shall return the money] tenfold to [its owner]. He shall contest [in] his [lawsuit] and not succeed.

3 Witness Šumaya.

4 Witness Kinihmâ.

5 Witness Hatianu.

6 Month Ab (V), 25th day, eponym year of Nabû-le'i.

114. Fragment of a Sales Document (702)

BM 134582

1 [*ku-um* NA$_4$.KIŠIB-*šú ṣu-pur-šú iš-kun*]
2 [*ṣu-pur* ^{m}*x x x* EN *x* SUM]-⌜*ni*⌝

3 [*x x x x x x x x*] ⌜SAG$^{?}$.ME$^{?}$⌝
4 [*x x x x x x x x*]*x-a-a*
5 [*x x x x x x x x*]*x*

Iraq 32 12

1 [Instead of his seal he impressed his fingernail].

1 [Fingernail of NN, owner of the ... being so]ld.

(fingernail impressions)

(Break)

113 Previous edition: AR 370. Collations: Assur 2/5. 6 Judging from the traces and the width of the break, the name of the buyer probably was either [...-ša]bši or [Ahu-lu]rši.
114 Copy: Iraq 32 (1970), Pl. XXV.

6 [*x x x x x x x x*].*x*
rest broken away
Rev. beginning broken away

1′ [ITI.*x*] UD-27-KÁM
2′ [*lim-me* ^{m}]⌈^{d}⌉PA—ZU LÚ*.GAR.KUR URU.*ár-ba-ìl*
3′ [IGI ^{md}PA$^{?}$—NU]MUN—BA-*šá ṣa-bit* IM

(fingernail impressions)

r.1 [Month ...], 27th day, [eponym year] of Nabû-le'i, governor of Arbela.

3 [Witness *Nabû*-ze]ru-iqiša, keeper of the tablet.

115. Purchase of Land (702)

Ki 1904-10-9,162

1 [NA$_4$.KIŠIB ^{m}*x x x*]-⌈*ni*$^{!}$⌉
2 [EN A.ŠÀ.G]A *ta-dan-ni*

3 [É] 4 ANŠE A.ŠÀ.GA *ina* URU.*du-ni*
4 [*x x*].*x mi-šil bu-ri* 5$^{!}$-*su*$^{!}$ *ša bu-ri*

5 [*ú-pi*]*š-ma* ^{m}*aš-šur*—A—PAB *ina* ŠÀ-*bi*
6 [*x* MA.N]A$^{!}$ K[UG$^{!}$.UD] *ša*$^{!}$ ⌈LUGAL$^{!}$ TI$^{!}$-*qí*$^{!}$⌉
rest broken away
Rev. beginning broken away

1′ [IGI ^{md}*x*].*x*—SUM$^{!}$-⌈*na*$^{!}$ ^{m}⌉ARAD—PAB.MEŠ-*šú*
2′ [IGI ^{m}]⌈^{d}⌉AG$^{!}$—I$^{!}$ $^{m!d}$PA—PAB-*ir* LÚ*.ENGAR—KUR
3′ [IGI ^{m}*x x x*].*x-ši*$^{!}$ URU.*me-ra-a-a*
one line blank
4′ [ITI.*x* UD-*x*-K]AM
5′ [*lim-mu* ^{md}PA—ZU] GAR.KUR URU.*arba-ìl*
6′ [IGI ^{m}*x x x x* LÚ*].⌈A$^{!}$⌉.BA$^{!}$⌉

ADD 1180

1 [Seal of ......]ni, [owner of the lan]d being sold.

(fingernail impressions)

3 [An estate of] 4 hectares of land in the town of Dunnu; [...] 1/2 of a well; 1/5 of a well —

5 Aššur-aplu-uṣur has contracted and [bought it] for [x min]as of s[ilver] (by the mina) of the king.

(Break)

r.1 [Witness *Šama*]*š*-iddina. Urda-ahhešu.

2 [Witness] Nabû-na'id. (Witness) Nabû-naṣir, palace farmer.

3 [Witness NN], from the town of Mera.

4 [Month ..., ...]th [day, eponym year of Nabû-le'i], governor of Arbela.

6 [Witness NN], scribe.

116. A Bodyguard Buys Three Women (700-VI-20)

Rm 160

1 [NA$_4$.KIŠIB ^{m}*x x x x x x x x*]
2 EN [MÍ.MEŠ *ta-da-ni*]

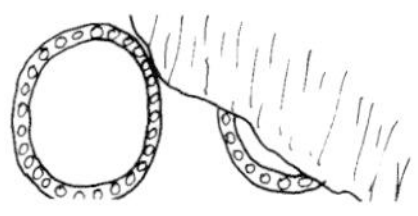

ADD 294

1 [Seal of ......], owner [of the women being sold].

(stamp seal impressions)

115 Previous edition: NALK 36. 4 See coll. For the rendering *bu-ri* "well" (not *pu-ri* "parcel of land") cf. the parallel 6-*su ša* PÚ, no. 119:16. 6, r.1ff. See coll. r.2f Cf. no. 28 r.5ff. r.5f See coll.
116 Previous editions: AR 49, NALK 109. Collations: Assur 2/5.

3 MÍ.DIL$^{!}$-*qi*-⸢*di*$^{!}$⸣-*ra* MÍ.[*x x x x x*]
4 MÍ.*ba-ba-a-a* DUMU.[MÍ-*sa*]
5 PAB 3 ZI.MEŠ ARAD.ME[Š-*šú*]

6 *ú-piš-ma* ^{m}*ri*$^{!}$-*sa*-[*a-a*]
7 [LÚ].⸢*qur*$^{!}$-*bu*$^{!}$⸣-*ti ša*$^{!}$ [*x x x*]
8 [*ina* ŠÀ *x* M]A.NA$^{!}$ KUG$^{!}$.[UD *x x*]
rest broken away
Rev. beginning broken away
1′ [IGI ^{m}*x*]⸢*x x*⸣[*x x x x x x*]
2′ [IGI ^{m}]*a-a*—PAB.MEŠ LÚ*.EN[GAR$^{!}$ *x x x*]
3′ [IGI] ^{m}EN—ZU LÚ*.ENGA[R *x x x*]
4′ [IGI] ^{m}*dà-ri*—EN LÚ*.ENGA[R *x x x*]
5′ [IGI] ^{m}*na-bi*—*ra-mu* LÚ*.ENGA[R *x x x*]
6′ [IGI] ^{m}*ba-la*—*im-me* AR[AD *x x x x*]
7′ IGI ^{m}*za-ba-a-a* KUR.*bar*-[*hal-zi-a-a*]
8′ IGI ^{m}*šá*$^{!}$-*a-da* URU.[*x x x*]
9′ IGI ^{m}*a-me-qi* URU.[*x x x*]

10′ [I]TI.KIN UD-2[*x*-KAM]
11′ [*li*]*m-mu* ^{m}*mi-t*[*ú-nu*]
12e [IGI] ^{md}⸢MAŠ$^{!}$⸣—[*x x x*]

3 *Edu*-qidira, the woman [...], and [her] daughter Babaya, a total of 3 persons, [his ser]vants —

6 Risa[ya], bodyguard of [...], has contracted [and bought them for x min]as of sil[ver].

(Break)

r.1 [Witness NN]... [...].
2 [Witness] Aya-ahhe, far[mer ...].
3 [Witness] Bel-le'i, far[mer ...].
4 [Witness] Dari-bel, far[mer ...].
5 [Witness] Nabi-ram, farm[er ...].
6 [Witness] Ba'al-immi, ser[vant of ...].
7 [Witne]ss Zabayu, from Bar[halzi].
8 [Witne]ss Šada, from [...].
9 [Witne]ss Ameqi, from [...].

10 [Mo]nth Elul (VI), *2*[*0th* day], eponym year of Met[unu].

12 [Witness] Inurta-[...].

117. Tarhundapî Loans Barley (700)

K 12976

1 [*x*] ANŠE ŠE.PAD.MEŠ
2 [*šá* ^{m}*ta*]*r*$^{!}$-*hu-da-pi-i*
rest broken away
Rev. beginning broken away
blank space of two lines
1′ [*lim-mu* ^{m}]*mi-tu-nu*

ADD 144

1 [x] homers of barley [belonging to Ta]rhundapî [...]

(Break)

r.1 [Eponym year of] Metunu.

118. Tarhundapî Buys a Slave (698-XII-30)

82-5-22,36

1 NA$_4$.KIŠIB ^{m}*a-si-i*
2 EN LÚ SUM-*ni*

---

3 ^{m}*a-tar*—*ha-mu* ARAD-*šú*
4 *ša*$^{!}$ ^{m}*a-si-i*
5 *ú-piš-ma* ^{m}*tar-hu-un-da-pi*-⸢*i*⸣
6 *ina* ŠÀ 32 GÍN KUG.UD *il-q*[*í*]$^{!}$
7 *kas-pu gam-mur ta-ad*-⸢*din*⸣
8 LÚ *šú-a-tú za-rip laq-qí*
9 *tu-a-ru de-e-nu*
10 DUG$_4$.DUG$_4$ *la-áš-šú*

ADD 198

1 Seal of Asî, owner of the man being sold.

(blank seal space)

---

3 Atar-hamu, servant of Asî —

5 Tarhundapî has contracted and boug[ht him] for 32 shekels of silver.

7 The money is paid completely. That man is purchased and acquired. Any revocation, lawsuit, or litigation is void.

117 Previous edition: AR 305. 2 See coll.
118 Previous editions: AR 472, NALK 385. Collations: Assur 2/5.

11 *man-n*[*u ša*] *ina u*[*r*]-*kiš*
12 ⸢*ina ma*⸣-*te-e*!-*ma* GIL-*u-ni*
13 [*lu-u*] ^{m}*a-si-i*
14 [*lu-u* DU]MU.MEŠ-*šú lu*!-[*u*!]
15 [DUMU!]—DUMU!.MEŠ-⸢*šú*!⸣
16 [*ša de-e-nu*] ⸢DUG$_4$.DUG$_4$⸣ 0!
17 [TA* ^{m}*tar-hu-un-da-pi-i ub*]-⸢*ta*⸣-*u-ni*
rest broken away
Rev. beginning broken away
1′ [*ina*] ⸢*bur-ki*⸣ [^{d}15 *a-ši-bat*]
2′ 0! NINA.KI GAR-[*an*]
3′ ⸢*kas-pu* 0! *a-na*⸣ [10.MEŠ-*t*]*e*!
4′ ⸢*a-na* EN⸣.[M]EŠ-*šú*! GUR-*ra*

5′ IGI ^{m}*a*-[*x*]-⸢ʾ*u*!⸣-*ú*
6′ IGI ^{m}[*x x x*]-⸢*i*!⸣
7′ IGI ^{m}⸢*na*!⸣-*zi*-[*x x*]
8′ IGI ^{m}*nu-nu-a* [*x x*]
9′ IGI ^{m}*na*-⸢*ni-i*⸣
10′ IGI ^{md}PA—MU—A[Š! L]Ú.A.BA
space of one line
11′ ITI.ŠE UD-30-KÁM
12′ *lim-me* ^{m}DI-*mu*—MAN

11 Whoev[er] in the future, at any time, breaks the contract, [whether] Asî [or] his [so]ns or [grand]sons, [and s]eeks [a lawsuit] or litigation [against Tarhundapî]
(Break)

r.1 shall pla[ce ...... in] the lap of [Ištar residing in] Nineveh, and shall return the money [tenfo]ld to its owners.

---

5 Witness A[...]'u.
6 Witness [...]î.
7 Witness Nazi[...].
8 Witness Nunua, [...].
9 Witness Nanî.
10 Witness Nabû-šumu-[iddina], scribe.
11 Month Adar (XII), 30th day, eponym year of Šulmu-šarri.

119. Nabû-šarru-uṣur Buys 5 Hectares of Land (699-V-10)

Ki 1904-10-9,133 — ADD 1167

1 [*ku-um*] NA$_4$.KIŠ[IB-*šú*] *ṣu-pur-šú iš-kun*
2 *ṣu*-[*pur*] ^{md}⸢IM!⸣-*i* EN A.ŠÀ ⸢SUM⸣-*ni*

1 [Instead of his] sea[l] he impressed his fingernail.
2 Finger[nail] of Addî, owner of the land being sold.

(fingernail impressions)

---

3 8BÁN A.ŠÀ *ina* [URU.ŠE]—É—*bala*-[*ṭ*]*i*
4 SUHUR A.ŠÀ *š*[*a*] ^{m}*ga-gi-i*
5 SUHUR A.ŠÀ [*ša*] ^{md}UTU—BA-*šá*

6 6BÁN A.ŠÀ [SUHUR KAS]KAL URU.*kar*—^{d}15
7 SUHUR A.ŠÀ [*ša*] ^{md}IM-*i*
8 SUHUR [A.ŠÀ *š*]*a* ^{md}UTU—BA-*šá*

9 3BÁN A.ŠÀ GIŠ.GU.ZA *ina ú-šal*!-*li*
10 SUHUR $^{m!}$*ga-gi-i* SUHUR ^{md}UTU—BA-*šá*
11 1 ANŠE *ina ú-šal*!-*li* SUHUR A.ŠÀ
12 *ša* [^{md}]IM-*i* SUHUR ^{md}UTU—BA-*šá*

13 3 ANŠE A.ŠÀ *ina mu*-⸢*le-e*⸣
14 SUHUR $^{m⸢d⸣}$IM-*i* SUHUR ^{md}UTU—BA-[*šá*]
15 PAB 5! ANŠE 2BÁN A.ŠÀ É *ad-ri* GIŠ.SAR

3 Eight decares of land in [the village of] Bit-bala[ṭ]i, adjoining the fields of Gagî and Šamaš-iqiša;
6 6 decares of land [adjoining the ro]ad to Kar-Issar and the fields [of] Addî and Šamaš-iqiša;
9 3 decares of *throne* land in a meadow adjoining Gagî and Šamaš-iqiša;
11 1 hectare in a meadow adjoining the fields of Addî and Šamaš-iqiša;
13 3 hectares of land on high ground adjoining Addî and Šamaš-iqi[ša];
15 a total of 5 hectares and 2 decares of

119 Previous edition: NALK 204. 2, 16, r.3 See coll. r.12 The reading *Kakku* proposed in CTN 3 p.272 for

16 ⸢6!⸣-su! ša PÚ ina URU.ŠE—ki-luh!-te!

17 [ú]-piš-ma ^{md}PA—MAN—PAB
18 [TA* IGI] $^{m!d!}$IM!-i! ina ŠÀ 1 MA.NA [KUG].UD
19 [ina ma-né]-⸢e!⸣ ša URU.gar-ga-mis [il-q]i

r.1 [kas-p]u! ga-am-[mur 0] ⸢ta⸣-din
2 A.ŠÀ É ad-ru GIŠ.[SA]R! PÚ! šú-a-tú
3 za-ar-pu l[aq!-qi]-u! tu-a-ru
4 de-e-nu da-⸢ba⸣-bu la-áš-šú

5 man-nu [ša ina] ur-kiš ma-te-e-ma
6 lu ^{md}I[M!-i lu DUMU].MEŠ-šú mám-ma-nu-šú
7 ša! (TA*) ^{md}PA—MA[N!—PAB] de-e-[nu]
8 da-ba-bu ub-t[a-u-ni i-gar-ru-u-ni]
9 kas-pu a-na 10.MEŠ a!-[na EN-šú GUR-ra]
10 ina de-ni-šú DUG_4.[DUG_4-ma la T]I!
11 IGI ^{m}ur-du [LÚ.GIŠ].GIGIR—GÌR.2

12 IGI $^{m!}$ki-ṣ[ir—^{d}x] A! [^{m}]^{d}KU!—APIN!-eš!

13 IGI ^{md}[x x]-sa A! ^{m}mar-da-ni
14 [IGI ^{m}ga-g]i-i IGI ^{md}UTU—BA-šá
15 IGI ^{md}PA—PAB!-ir! A ^{m}EN—lu—TI

16 IGI ^{m}kal-bu A ^{m}AD!—šam-ši
17 IGI ^{m}e-⸢da!⸣-a!-a IGI! ^{m}i[p!-par-š]i!-du!
18 IGI ^{md}PA—BA-šá-ni URU!.⸢ki!-ṣir!⸣-[t]a!-⸢a-a⸣

19 IGI ^{m}SU[HUŠ!]—$^{d!}$⸢7!⸣.BI ina ITI.NE UD-10-KÁM
20 [lim]-⸢mu⸣ ^{m}EN—MAN-a-ni ^{md}PA—dan-na-ka—IGI
21e LÚ*.A.BA

land, a house, a threshing floor, an orchard, and 1/6 of a well in the village of Kiluhte —

17 Nabû-šarru-uṣur [ha]s contracted and [bou]ght (said land) [from] Addî for one mina of [sil]ver [by the mi]na of Carchemish.

r.1 [The mone]y is paid [comple]tely. That land, house, threshing floor, orchard, and well are purchased and ac[quired]. Any revocation, lawsuit, or litigation is void.

5 Whoever, [in] the future, at any time, whether A[ddî, or] his [sons] (or) relatives, s[eeks and starts] a laws[uit] or litigation (against) Nabû-ša[rru-uṣur, shall return] the money tenfold t[o its owner]. He shall cont[est] in his lawsuit [and not succ]eed.

11 Witness Urdu, [gro]om of the *ša šepi* guard.

12 Witness Kiṣ[ir-...]. Witness Marduk-ereš.

13 Witness [...]sa, son of Mardanu.

14 Witness [Gag]î. Witness Šamaš-iqiša.

15 Witness Nabû-naṣir, son of Bel-lu-balaṭ.

16 Witness Kalbu, son of Abu-šamši.

17 Witness Edayu. Witness I[pparš]idu.

18 Witness Nabû-iqišanni from Kiṣirtu. Witness U[bru]-Sebetti.

19 Month Ab (V), 10th day, [eponym] year of Bel-šarrani.

20 Nabû-dannaka-lamur, scribe.

120. Purchase of a Vineyard (699-VII-22)

K 450

1 ⸢ṣu-pur⸣ ^{m}PAB—DINGIR-⸢a!-a⸣ [x x x x]
2 EN GIŠ.SAR [GIŠ.til-lit-te SUM-n]i!

3 [GIŠ.SAR x]-⸢lim! GIŠ!.til⸣-lit!-te ina! URU!.me!-du!-⸢un⸣
4 [x x x x x] ^{m}pi-⸢qa⸣-qi
5 [x x x x x x]x-⸢te⸣-e
6 [x x x x x x x x]-di

ADD 371

1 Fingernail of Ahu-ila'i, [...], owner of the [vine]yard [being so]ld.

(fingernail impressions)

3 [A vineyard] of [x] thousand vines in the town Medun [adjoining the land of] Piqaqu (Break)

^{d}KU must be rejected, since the reading ^{d}KU = *Marduk* is unequivocally attested in a spelling of Marduk-šumu-uṣur, the name of the well-known chief haruspex of Esarhaddon (^{md}KU—MU—PAB, AGS 89 = SAA 4 227 s.2). The divine name *Kakku* (Aššur's deified weapon) was consistently spelled ^{d}GIŠ.TUKUL. r.15ff See coll.

120 Previous edition: AR 387. Collations: Assur 2/5. r.2 Or URU.sa-ri.

rest broken away
Rev. beginning broken away
1′ [*x x x x x* ^{m}]⸢*se*!?⸣—AD! U[RU.*x x*]
2′ [*x x x x x x x*] ⸢*x*⸣ *ša*! URU!.*ir*?-*ri*!
3′ [IGI] ^{m}SAG!.DU!-*a*!-*nu* LÚ*.SAG
4′ IGI ^{m}⸢*qur*⸣-*di*—10 URU!.⸢*li*!-*x*⸣-*gam*!-*a-a*
5′ [IG]I! $^{m!}$*ana-ku* 0!
6e [ITI].DUL UD-22?-⸢KAM⸣ [*lim-mu* ^{m}EN—MAN-*a-ni*]
7e LÚ*.GAR.KUR URU.*kur-ba-ìl*

r.1 [Witness ...] *Se-abi* from [...].
2 [Witness ...] of *Ir*ri.
3 Witness Kaqqadanu, eunuch.
4 Witness Qurdi-Adad from [...].
5 Witness Anaku.
6 Month Tishri (VII), *22*nd day, ep[onym year of Bel-šarrani], governor of Kurbail.

121. Purchase of [...] (698-II-2)

K 393 + K 1470 (ADD 510)

1 [*ku-um* NA_4].KIŠIB-*šú ṣu-pur*-[*šú*]
2 [*iš-ku*]*n*! *ṣu-pur* ^{m}DINGIR—SU!

3 [EN *x x x x*] *ta-da-a-ni*
4 [*x x x x x x*].*x* ^{m}*man-nu*—GIM—PAB.MEŠ
5 [*x x x x x x x*] *di*
6 [*x x x x x x x x*] ⸢1⸣ MA.NA KUG.UD
rest broken away
Rev. beginning broken away
1′ [*x x x x x x x x*] ^{md}30!—*x*[*x x x*]
2′ [*x x x x x x*] LÚ*.TUR *ša* ^{md}AMAR.UTU—MAN!—P[AB]

3′ [IGI ^{m}*x-m*]*u*!-*u-a* DUMU URU.NINA-*a* 0!
4′ [IGI ^{m}*x x*]-*i*
5′ [IGI ^{m}]ITI.KIN-*a-a* EN URUDU!.MEŠ
6′ [IGI] $^{m!}$UTU-*ši*—E
7′ [IG]I ^{md}PA—MU—*iš-kun*
8′ [L]Ú.A.BA *ṣa-bit ṭup-pi*

9′ [IT]I.GUD 2-KÁM *lim-mu* ^{m}DI-*mu*—MAN

10′ [IGI ^{m}*b*]*i*?-*u-a-si-i* 0! *ša*—GÌR.2
11′ [IGI ^{m}*x x-r*]*a-ni-i* LÚ*.AR[AD *x x x*]
e.12′ [*x x x x x* LU]GAL!
13′ [IGI ^{m}*x x x*]—EN-*iá* LÚ*!.[*x x x*]
14′ [IGI ^{m}*x x x*]⸢*x*⸣—MU—*iš*-[*kun x x*]
15′ [IGI ^{m}*x x x*]⸢*x*⸣[*x x x*] *a ti* [*x x*]

ADD 475+

1 [Instead of] his seal he im[pressed his] fingernail.
2 Fingernail of Ilu-eriba,

(fingernail impressions)

3 [owner of the ...] being sold.
4 [......] Mannu-ki-ahhe
5 [......] ...
6 [...... for] one mina of silver
(Break)
r.1 [......] Sin-[...]
2 [Witness NN], manservant of Marduk-šarru-uṣur.
3 Witness [...]mua, from Nineveh.
4 Witness [...]î.
5 Witness Ululayu, owner of the copper.
6 Witness Šamši-iqbi.
7 Witness Nabû-šumu-iškun, scribe, keeper of the tablet.
9 Month Iyyar (II), 2nd (day), eponym year of Šulmu-šarri.
10 [Witness B]iwasî, *ša šēpi* guard.
11 [Witness ...]ranî, servant of [NN], royal [...].
13 [Witness ...]-beliya, [...].
14 [Witness ...]-šumu-iš[kun, ...].
15 [Witness ....].

121 Previous edition: AR 525.

122. Purchase of a Slave (698-VII-18)

Bu 91-5-9,121

1 *ṣu-pur* ^{m}*aš-šur*—I A ^{m}*mar-da-*[*ni*$^{?}$]
2 EN LÚ SUM-*ni*

3 [*x x x x x x x x*]*x*
rest broken away
Rev. beginning broken away
1′ [*x x x x*]*x* MÁ.DU.DU.MEŠ
2′ [IGI ^{m}*ra*]-*hi-me*—DINGIR *šá* URU.*ha-at-pi-*⌈*na*$^{!}$-*x*⌉
3′ [IGI ^{md}P]A—MU—GIŠ LÚ.A.BA
4′ [I]TI.DUL UD-18-KÁM
5′ [*l*]*im-me* ^{m}DI-⌈*mu*⌉—LUGAL

ADD 191

1 Fingernail of Aššur-na'di, son of Marda[nu], owner of the man being sold.

(seal space)

(Break)

r.1 [...] boatmen.
2 [Witness Ra]him-il, from the town Hatpina[...].
3 [Witness Na]bû-šumu-lešir, scribe.
4 Month Tishri (VII), 18th day, eponym year of Šulmu-šarri.

123. Sale of Orchards for the Maintenance of Captives (698-IX-15)

K 1604

1 NA$_4$.KIŠIB ^{m}⌈PAB⌉—*ia-*⌈*qar*⌉ LÚ*.2-*ú ša* ⌈URU.*arrap*$^{!}$-*ha*$^{!}$⌉ [0$^{!}$]

2 [1 GIŠ.SAR *x*] 10 ⌈*x*⌉-*a-ni*$^{!}$ 1 GIŠ.SAR ⌈2$^{!}$⌉ [*x x x*]
3 [1 GIŠ.SAR *x x*]⌈*x x*⌉ PAB 3 GIŠ.SAR.MEŠ
4 [*e-nu ša* A.ME]Š$^{!}$ ⌈É$^{!}$⌉ LÚ*$^{!}$.NU.GIŠ.SAR
5 [*ina* ŠÀ-*bi*] *ú-piš-ma* ^{m}PAB—*ia-*⌈*ba*⌉-*ba*
6 [*ina* ŠÀ *x*]-⌈ME$^{!}$⌉ URUDU.MEŠ 0$^{!}$ *a*$^{!}$-*na*$^{!}$ *ša-az-bu*$^{!}$-*si*
7 *š*[*a*$^{!}$ LÚ*].⌈*hu*$^{!}$⌉-*ub-te*$^{!}$ *ša* LÚ*.⌈SUKKAL$^{!}$⌉ *ina* UGU
8 GIŠ.MÁ GUB-*u-ni ina* UGU LÚ*.2-*ú* SUM-*ni*
9 *kas-pu gam-mur ta-din* GIŠ.SAR.MEŠ
10 *e-nu ša* A.MEŠ É LÚ*.NU.GIŠ.SAR
11 *za-ar-pu la-qi-ú tu-a-ru*
12 [*d*]*e*$^{!}$-*nu* DUG$_4$.DUG$_4$-*bu la-áš-šú*
13 [*man-nu*] *ša ina* EGIR ⌈UD-*mu*⌉ *i-za-qu-*[*pa-ni*]
e.14 [*lu-u*] ⌈^{m}PAB⌉—*ia-ba-ba* ⌈:⌉ DUMU.MEŠ-[*šú*]
r.1 [DUMU—DUMU.MEŠ-*šú*] *lu-u* [PAB.MEŠ-*šú*]
2 [*šá ina de*]-⌈*ni*$^{!}$-*šú*$^{!}$ DUG$_4$⌉.DU[G$_4$$^{!}$-*u-ni*]
3 [*x x x x*]*x lu*$^{!}$ *qu x*[*x x x x*]
4 [*kas-pu a-na* 10.ME]Š ⌈*a-na*⌉ [E]N.MEŠ-*šú* G[UR-*ra*]

ADD 468

1 Seal of Ahiqar, deputy (governor) of Arrapha.

(cylinder seal impression)

2 [1 garden ...]...; 1 garden (with) 2 [...]; [1 garden ...]; a total of 3 gardens [including a spri]ng, a house, and a gardener —
5 Ahi-yababa has contracted and sold them *on behalf of* the deputy [for x] hundred (minas of) copper for the maintenance o[f the ca]ptives whom the vizier boarded on a ship.

9 The money is paid completely. The gardens, the spring, the house and the gardener are purchased and acquired. Any revocation, lawsuit, or litigation is void.
13 [Whoever] in the future [lodges] a complaint, [whether] Ahi-yababa or [his] sons, [grandsons, or brothers], and conte[sts in his law]suit, [shall ...] ... [...]. He shall return [the money tenfol]d to its owners.

122 Previous edition: AR 471. r.1f See coll.
123 Previous editions: AR 439, NALK 19. Collations: Assur 2/5.

5 [IGI ^{m}*x x x-d*]*a*!-*a* LÚ*!.*m*[*u-x x x*]
6 [IGI ^{m}*x x*]-⸢*ku*⸣ LÚ*!.*šá*!-[*x x x x*]
7 [IGI ^{m}*x x x x*]-⸢*a*!⸣ IGI ^{m}⸢*e*!-*ni*!—DINGIR!⸣
8 [IGI ^{m}*x x x*]—⸢APIN⸣-*e*[*š*] IGI ^{md}UTU!—⸢*x*⸣
9 [IGI ^{m}*x x x*]-⸢*i*! LÚ*!.HAL!⸣
10 [IGI ^{m}*x x*]⸢*x x*⸣ LÚ*!.A!.BA! *ša*! ⸢*x x*⸣
11 [IGI ^{m}*x x*] ⸢*x x x*⸣ LÚ*.A.⸢BA⸣ [*š*]*a* [UR]U.*arrap-ha*
12 [IGI ^{m}*x x x*]-⸢*x*⸣ GAL

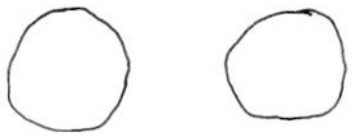

13 *ina* ITI.GAN UD-15-KÁM
14 *lim*-⸢*mu*⸣ ^{m}DI-*mu*—LUGAL
15 LÚ*.GAR.KUR [UR]U.*hal*!-*zi*!—[AD.BAR]

r.5 [Witness ...]dâ, [...].
6 [Witness ...]ku, [...].
7 [Witness ...]â. Witness Eni-il.
8 [Witness ...]-ereš. Witness Šamaš-[...].
9 [Witness ...]î, haruspex.
10 [Witness NN], scribe of [...]
11 [Witness NN], (city) scribe of Arrapha.
12 [Witness NN]....

(stamp seal impressions)

13 Month Kislev (IX), 15th day, eponym year of Šulmu-šarri, governor of Halzi[atbar].

124. Riba-ilani the Merchant Buys a House (698-XII-21)

K 316

1 *ṣu-pur* ^{m}*man-nu—ki*—PAB.MEŠ *ṣu-pur* ^{m}TA*—^{d}⸢IM!—PAB!⸣-*tú*
2 *be-lí* É SUM-*ni mu-ṣu-ú a-di* ⸢TÙR⸣

3 É *ep-šú a-di* GIŠ.ÙR.MEŠ-*šú* 2 GIŠ.⸢IG⸣.MEŠ
4 *ina* ŠÀ-*bi* SUHUR É ^{md}PA—BÀD—⸢PAB⸣
5 SUHUR É ^{md}UTU—MU—PAB SUHUR É ^{m}⸢ITI.KIN⸣-*a-a*
6 SUHUR É ^{md}PA—PAB-*ir* SUHUR ^{md}UTU—⸢*ú*!-*bal*!-*liṭ*!⸣
7 *ú-piš-ma* ^{m}SU—DINGIR.MEŠ-*ni* LÚ*.⸢DAM⸣.QAR
8 ⸢TA*⸣ *pa-an* ^{m}*man-nu—ki-i*!—PAB.⸢MEŠ⸣
9 [*ina*] ŠÀ 3 2/3 MA.NA KUG.UD ⸢*il*⸣-[*qi*]
10 *kas-pu gam-mur ta-din* [É *šu-a-tú*]
11 *za-rip la-qi tu*-⸢*a*⸣-[*ru de-e-nu*]

12 DUG$_4$.DUG$_4$ *la-áš*-[*šú man-nu šá ina ur-kiš*]
13 *ina ma-te-ma lu*-[*u* LÚ.MEŠ-*e an-nu-te*]
14 *lu-u* DUMU.MEŠ-*š*[*ú-nu lu-u* DUMU—DUMU.MEŠ-*šú-nu*]
15 *ša* TA* ^{m}S[U—DINGIR.MEŠ-*ni x x x x x*]
rest (2 lines and edge) broken away
r.1 ⸢*kas*⸣-*pu* [*a-na* 10.MEŠ *a-na* EN.MEŠ-*šú* GUR]
2 *ina de-ni-šú* ⸢DUG$_4$⸣.[DUG$_4$-*ma x x x*]

3 IGI ^{m}*du-gul*—IGI—DIN[GIR] L[Ú!.*x x*]

ADD 328

1 Fingernail of Mannu-ki-ahhe; fingernail of Issi-Adad-ahhutu, owners of the house being sold. The exit together with the courtyard,

(fingernail impressions)

3 a built house with its beams and two doors, adjoining the houses of Nabû-duru-uṣur, Šamaš-šumu-uṣur, [Ulul]ayu, Nabû-naṣir, and Šamaš-uballiṭ —

7 Riba-ilani the merchant has contracted and bou[ght] it from Mannu-ki-ahhe [fo]r 3 2/3 minas of silver.

10 The money is paid completely. [That house] is purchased and acquired. Any revoc[ation, lawsuit], or litigation is voi[d].

12 [Whoever in the future], at any time, wheth[er these men] or th[eir] sons [or grandsons, seeks a lawsuit or litigation] against Ri[ba-ilani ......]

(Break)

r.1 [He shall return] the money [tenfold to its owner]. He shall cont[est] in his lawsuit and [not succeed].

3 Witness Dugul-pan-i[li, ...].

124 Previous editions: AR 357, NALK 99; → KB 4 (1896) 114-115. Collations: Assur 2/5. 1 See coll.

4 IGI ^{md}PA—PAB *ša—gi-né-šú š[a! x x]*
5 IGI ^{m}ARAD—^{d}15 DUMU MÍ.*hi?-[x x x]*
6 IGI ^{md}U.GUR—PAB—PAB LÚ*.GAL—50 *ša* ⸢*x x x*⸣
7 IGI ^{m}*za-ha-ṭu-ṭu* LÚ*.*ka-ṣir*
8 IGI ^{m}SU—^{d}15 LÚ*.*ka-ṣir*
9 IGI ^{m}*ba-ba-a-nu* LÚ*.NAGAR—GIŠ.UMBI[N].⸢MEŠ!⸣
10 IGI ^{md}PA—PAB—PAB LÚ*.GAL—*kal-li-*⸢*e*⸣
11 IGI ^{m}*za-ru-*⸢*ti*⸣*-i* LÚ*.A.BA
12 IGI ^{m}ITI.⸢KIN⸣-*a-a*
blank space of about 4 lines
13 IGI ^{m}*ba-ni-i* LÚ*.A.BA *ṣa-bit dan-ni-ti*
14 ITI.ŠE UD-21-KÁM *lim!-mu* $^{md+}$EN—MAN-*a-ni*
15 LÚ*.GAR.KUR URU.*kur-ba-ìl*
s.1 4 MA.NA URUDU.MEŠ *ša ṣu-pur-šú*

4 Witness Nabû-iṣṣur, official in charge of the regular offering o[f ...].
5 Witness Urda-Issar, son of the woman [...].
6 Witness Nergal-ahu-uṣur, commander-of-50 of [...].
7 Witness Zahaṭuṭu, tailor.
8 Witness Riba-Issar, tailor.
9 Witness Babanu, wheelwright.
10 Witness Nabû-ahu-uṣur, postmaster.
11 Witness Zarutî, scribe.
12 Witness Ululayu.
13 Witness Banî, scribe, keeper of the contract.
14 Month Adar (XII), 21st day, eponym year of Bel-šarrani, governor of Kurbail.
s.1 4 minas of copper for his fingernail.

125. Purchase of Two Estates (698)

Ki 1904-10-9,161 + Ki 1904-10-9,386 (ADD 1233)

ADD 1179+

1 *[ku-u]m* NA$_4$.KIŠIB-*šú ṣu-pur-šú*
2 *[i]š-kun ṣu-pur* ^{md}PA—HAL-*ni*
3 EN A.ŠÀ SUM-*na*

1 [Inste]ad of his seal he impressed his fingernail.
2 Fingernail of Nabû-šimanni, owner of the field being sold.

(fingernail impressions)

4 É 3 ANŠE 8BÁN A.ŠÀ
5 SUHUR ^{md}AMAR.UTU—APIN-*eš ši-di* PA.BARA[G?.G]A!
6 SUHUR ^{m}*gír—ṣa-pu-nu* SUHUR ^{m}*x[x x]*
7 [É *x*] ANŠE SUHUR KASKAL GIŠ.A.(TU).GAB.[LIŠ!]
8 [*x x x*] SUHUR ^{md}PA—*še!-zib!-[an-ni]*
9 [*ú-piš-ma* ^{md}]P[A?—*x*—A]Š?
10 [*ina* ŠÀ *x* GÚ].UN! 7! [M]A!.NA URUDU.MEŠ
11 [*il*]*-qí! kas!-pu! ga-am-ru*
12 [*ta-din*] A!.ŠÀ *šu-a-tu*
13 [*za-ri*]*p! laq-qí!*
r.1 [*man-nu š*]*a de-e-ni* DUG$_4$.DUG$_4$
2 [*ub-ta-u-ni š*]*a! ina ur-kiš*
3 [*ina ma-te-ma i*-GI]L!*-ú-ni*
4 [*i-qab-bu-u-ni m*]*a!-a!* A.ŠÀ
5 [*la za-rip la laq-qí*] (blank!)
6 [IGI ^{m}*man-n*]*u!—ki*—PAB.MEŠ

4 An estate of 3 hectares 8 decares of land adjoining Marduk-ereš, alongside *the canal of the shrine*, and adjoining Gir-Ṣapunu and [...];
7 [an estate of x] hectares adjoining the road of *the popl[ar]* (*grove*), [...] and Nabû-šezib[anni] —
9 [*Na*]*bû-*[*...-idd*]*ina* [has contracted and bou]ght (said property) [for x tale]nts and 7 minas of copper.
11 The money [is paid] completely. That land [is acqui]red and purchased.
r.1 [Whoe]ver [seeks] a lawsuit or litigation and in the future, [at any time, br]eaks the contract [and says]:
4 "The field [is not acquired and bought]" (...).
6 [Witness Mann]u-ki-ahhe.

125 5f, 8f See coll. 10-12 The new readings in these lines come from a small unnumbered fragment joined to the numbered tablet. r.3f See coll. r.5 Penalty clauses omitted by the scribe. r.13 See coll.

7 ⸢IGI$^{!}$⸣ $^{m!}$APIN-*eš*—^{d}15
8 IGI ^{m}AD—SU
9 IGI ^{md}U.GUR—PAB-*ir*
10 4 LÚ*.*mu-šar-kis*.MEŠ-*ni*

11 [I]GI$^{!}$ ^{m}SU—PAB.MEŠ LÚ*.GAL—KÀD-*ri*
12 IGI$^{!}$ $^{m!}$EN—MAN—PAB LÚ*.ENGAR—É.GAL
13 ⸢IGI ^{m}⸣*e-ṣi-di-a-a* :.$^{!}$
14 [IGI ^{md}]⸢PA$^{!}$⸣—PAB$^{!}$-*ir* :.

15 [ITI.*x*] UD-27-KAM
16e [*lim*]-*mu* ^{m}DI-*mu*—LUGAL
17e [LÚ*].GAR.KUR URU.*hal-zi*—AD.BAR
s.1 IGI$^{!}$ $^{m!⸢d⸣}$[*x*]—ZALÁG$^{!}$-*i*[*r*$^{!}$]
2 LÚ*$^{!}$.A$^{!}$.⸢BA$^{!}$⸣

7 Witness Ereš-Issar.
8 Witness Abu-eriba.
9 Witness Nergal-naṣir; 4 recruitment officers.
11 Witness Riba-ahhe, cohort commander.
12 Witness Bel-šarru-uṣur, palace farmer.
13 Witness Eṣidayu, ditto.
14 [Witness] Nabû-naṣir, ditto.
15 [Month ...], 27th day, eponym year of Šulmu-šarri, governor of Halziatbar.

s.1 Witness [...]-nammir, scribe.

126. Esarhaddon's Doctor Buys an Estate (697-VI)

K 4674

ADD 381

1 [NA$_4$.KI]ŠIB ^{m}*na-*[*x x x x*]
2 [N]A$_4$.KIŠIB ^{m}*k*[*i-x x x x*]
3 [E]N A.ŠÀ *ta-d*[*a-ni*]
4 ⸢É$^{?}$⸣ 10 A.ŠÀ URU.[*x x x*]

---

5 [SUHUR ^{m}]⸢*da*$^{!}$⸣-*a-a-*⸢*ni*⸣ [*x x x*]
6 [*x x* SUH]UR$^{!}$ $^{m!}$*ra-an-*⸢*qi*$^{!}$⸣-*ra-*[*x*]
7 [SUHUR ^{m}*x*]-⸢*ma*$^{!}$⸣-*nu*$^{!}$-*ru*$^{!}$—⸢E$^{!}$⸣ [0]
8 [*ú-pi*]*š-ma* ^{m}⸢*še*$^{!}$⸣-*ma-*⸢*hu*$^{!}$⸣ [0]
9 [L]Ú.A$^{!}$.ZU$^{!}$ ^{m}⸢*aš-šur*$^{!}$⸣—PAB—SUM-*n*[*a*]
10 [*ina* ŠÀ] 1/2 MA.NA KUG.UD *il-*[*qi*]
e.11 [0$^{!}$ *gam-m*]*ur* ⸢*ta*⸣-*di-ni*
12 [A.ŠÀ] *šú-a-*⸢*tú za*$^{!}$-*rip*$^{!}$⸣ [0]
r.1′ [*laq-qi*] *tu*$^{!}$-⸢*a*$^{!}$⸣-[*ru*]
2′ [*de-e-nu*] DUG$_4$.D[UG$_4$ *la-áš-šú*]

3′ [*ša* GIL-*u*]-*ni* 2 ⸢MA⸣.[NA KUG.UD]
4′ [*ina bur-ki*] ^{d}10$^{!}$ *i*$^{!}$-*š*[*ak*$^{!}$-*kan*]
5′ [*kas-pu ana* 10.MEŠ *a*]-*na* EN-*šu ú-*[GUR]
6′ [*ina de-e*]-*ni* DUG$_4$.DUG$_4$-*m*[*a là* TI]

7′ [IGI ^{m}*x*]-*ri-ma* L[Ú.*x x x*]
8′ [IGI ^{m}*x*]-⸢*na*$^{?}$⸣-*na* L[Ú.*x x x*]
9′ [IGI ^{m}*x*]-⸢*bu*$^{!}$-*ri*$^{!}$⸣ [*x x x*]
10′ [IGI ^{m}*x x*]-*šu*$^{!}$ *x*[*x x x x*]
11′ [IGI ^{m}*x x*]-⸢*šu*$^{!}$ *x*⸣[*x x x*]

1 [Sea]l of N[a..., se]al of K[i..., ow]ners of the field bein[g sold].
4 An estate of 10 (hectares of) land in the ci[ty ...]

(stamp seal impressions)

---

5 [adjoining] (the fields of) Dayyanu [...], Ranqira[... and *Šul*]*manu-...-iqbi* –
8 Šemahu, the doctor of Esarhaddon, [has co]ntracted and bou[ght it for] 1/2 mina of silver.
e.11 It is paid [complet]ely. That [field] is purchased [and acquired].
r.1 Any revocat[ion, lawsuit], or lit[igation is void].
3 [Whoever brea]ks the contract shall pl[ace] 2 mi[nas of silver in the lap] of Adad, [and shall return the money tenfold t]o its owner. He shall contest [in] his lawsuit a[nd not succeed].

---

7 [Witness ...]rima [...].
8 [Witness]...[...].
9 [Witness ...]buri[...].
10 [Witness] ...[...]
11 [Witness] ...[...].

126 Previous edition: AR 427. 4, 6ff See coll. 7 There is a clear space between the last two signs, so the last name element is possibly to be read E = *iqbi*. The beginning of the name is possibly to be restored [*Šul*]*manu*. 11 No room for *kas-pu* in this line. r.4 See coll.

12′ [*x x x*] $^{m!}$⸢ARAD$^{!}$⸣—[^{d}*x x*]
13′ [ITI.KI]N$^{?}$ UD$^{!}$-*me*$^{!}$-10$^{!}$-[KAM]
14e [*lim-mu*] ^{md}⸢PA⸣—BÀ[D—PAB]

12 [...] Urda-[...].
13 [Month *El*]*ul* (VI), 10th day, [eponym year of] Nabû-dur[u-uṣur].

127. Atuehu, 'Third Man,' Buys a Slave (697-X-7)

K 300

1 *ku-um* NA$_4$.KIŠIB-*šú ṣu-*⸢*pur*⸣-[*šú*]
2 *iš-kun : ṣu-pur*
3 ^{m}*ha-ak-ku-bu* EN LÚ* SUM-*an*

4 ^{md}UTU—SU LÚ*.ARAD-*šú ša* ^{m}*ha-ak-ku-bu*
5 *ú-piš-ma* ^{m}*a-tu-e-hu*
6 LÚ*.3.U$_5$ TA* IGI ^{m}*ha-ak-ku-bu*
7 *ina* ŠÀ 30 GÍN KUG.UD.MEŠ *il-qi*

8 *kas-pu ga-mur ta-ad-din*
9 LÚ* *šu-a-ti za-rip laq-qi*
10 [*tu-a*]-⸢*ru*⸣ *de-e-ni da-ba-bu*

11 [*la-áš-šú man*]-*nu ša ina ur-kiš*
12 [*i-za-qu-pa-ni* GIL-*u*]-*ni*
rest broken away
Rev. beginning broken away
1′ [*x x x x x x x x*] ⸢*x*⸣
2′ [IGI ^{m}*x x x* LÚ*].DAM.QAR
3′ IGI ^{m}⸢*a-ba*$^{?}$⸣-*gu-ú* LÚ*.A.BA
4′ KUR.LÚ*.*ar-ma-a-a*
5′ IGI ^{m}*ab-du*—^{d}*a-gu-u-ni*
6′ LÚ*.3.U$_5$ 2-*i*
7′ *lim-mu* ^{md}PA—BÀD—PAB
8′ ITI.AB UD-7-KAM
9′ LÚ*.A.BA ^{m}EN—AŠ
10′ 1 MA.NA URUDU.MEŠ *ša ṣu-pur-šú*
11′ IGI ^{m}*at-ta-*ʾ*a-*⸢*ni*⸣

ADD 179

1 Instead of his seal he impressed [his] fingernail.
2 Fingernail of Hakkubu, owner of the man being sold.

(fingernail impressions)

4 Šamaš-eriba, servant of Hakkubu —
5 Atuehu, 'third man,' has contracted and bought him from Hakkubu for 30 shekels of silver.
8 The money is paid completely. That man is purchased and acquired. [Any revoc]ation, lawsuit, or litigation [is void].
11 [Who]ever in the future [lodges a complaint and breaks the contr]act
(Break)

r.2 [Witness NN], merchant.
3 Witness Abagû, Aramean palace scribe.
5 Witness Abdu-Aguni, deputy 'third man.'

7 Eponym year of Nabû-duru-uṣur; month Tebet (X), 7th day.
9 Scribe: Bel-iddina.
10 One mina of copper for his fingernail.
11 Witness Atta'ani.

128. Purchase of Slaves (696-V-5)

83-1-18,372

1 [NA$_4$.KIŠIB ^{m}*x x x x x x*]
2 [EN *x x x x x x x ta-da*]-*ni*

ADD 614

(Beginning destroyed)
1 [Seal of NN, owner of the ...... be]ing sold.

(seal space)

127 Previous editions: AR 473, NALK 47. Collations: Assur 2/5.
128 Previous edition: AR 72. [3] See coll.

2′ [x x x x x x x x]-*ni*! MÍ-*šú*
3′ ^{m}[x x x x x x x x] DUMU.MÍ-*su*
4′ MÍ.[x x x x x x x x x x] ⌈x⌉
5′ ^{m}[x x x x x x x x x x]-*a*
rest broken away
Rev. beginning broken away
1′ ⌈IGI!⌉ [^{m}x x x x x x x]
blank space of two lines
2′ IGI ^{md}PA-⌈*ú*⌉-*u-a* LÚ*.A.B[A]
one line blank
3′ ITI.NE UD-5-KÁM
4′ *lim-m*[*u*] ^{m}DI-*m*[*u*]—EN
5′ [GAR.KUR] URU.*tal-mu-si*

2 [...]ni, his wife, [*NN his son*], his daughter,
4 the woman [......]
(Break)

r.1 Witness [......].

2 Witness Nabû'a, scribe.

3 Month Ab (V), 5th day, eponym year of Šulmu-beli, [governor] of Talmusa.

129. Purchase of a House, Garden and People (696)

Ki 1904-10-9,198

1 [NA$_4$.KIŠIB ^{m}x]—^{d}AMAR.UTU
2 [EN É GIŠ].SAR! UN!.MEŠ SUM-*an*

rest broken away
Rev. beginning broken away
1′ [IGI ^{m}x x x]—DINGIR.ME
2′ [IGI ^{m}x x x]x-*ba*!-*ri*
3e [ITI.x UD-x]-KÁM
4e [*lim-mu* ^{m}DI-*mu*]—*be*!-*lí*!

ADD 1200

1 [Seal of ...]-Marduk, [owner of the house, gar]den and people being sold.

(stamp seal impressions)

(Break)

r.1 [Witness ...]-ilani.
2 [Witness ...]-bari.
3 Month [..., ...]th day, [eponym year of Šulmu]-beli.

130. Balṭaya Buys 17 Persons (696)

K 1513

1 [NA$_4$.KIŠIB ^{m}]I—DINGIR LÚ*.2-*e*!
2 [EN UN].MEŠ SUM-*ni*

3 [^{m}x x x x]x-⌈*šú*!⌉ 2 DUMU.MEŠ-*šú* DUMU.⌈MÍ!⌉-[*su*]
4 [PAB 4 ^{md}]⌈PA!⌉—[x x x MÍ-*šú* 2] DUMU.MEŠ-⌈*šú*⌉ DUMU.MÍ 2 [GE]M[É.MEŠ!]
5 PAB 7! ^{m}GIŠ.MI—E[N x x] ⌈x x⌉-*šú*! [x x x]

ADD 241

1 [Seal of] Na'di-ilu, deputy (governor), [owner of the people] being sold.

(cylinder seal impression)

3 [NN], his two sons and [his] daughter, [a total of 4];
4 Nabû-[..., his wife, two] sons, daughter, and two maids, a total of 7;
5 Ṣilli-B[el], his [... and ...], a total of 3;

129 1f, r.2, 4 See coll.
130 Previous editions: AR 73, NALK 84. Collations: Assur 2/5.

6 PAB 3 ^{m}*aš-šur*—EN—PAB MÍ-*šú* PAB-[*šú* PAB 3$^{!}$]
7 PAB 17 LÚ*.ZI.[M]EŠ ARAD.MEŠ *ša* ⸢^{m}⸣[I—DINGIR]
8 *ú-piš-ma* ^{m}*b*[*a*]*l*$^{!}$*-ṭa-ia* TA* IGI
9 ^{m}I—DINGIR *ina* Š[À] ⸢8⸣ 1/2 MA.NA KUG.UD
10 *ina* MA.NA-*e š*[*a* MA]N *il-qí*
11 *kas-pu ga-m*[*ur ta*]*-din* UN.MEŠ
12 ⸢UR$_5$⸣*-tú za-a*[*r-p*]*u* TI-⸢*ú*⸣
13 *tu-a-ru de-*[*e-nu*] DUG$_4$.DU[G$_4$ *la-áš-šú*]

14 *man-nu ša in*[*a ur-ki*]*š ina ma-*[*te-ma*]
15 *i*-GIL-[*ú*$^{!}$]*-ni*
16 *kas-*[*pu ana* 10].⸢MEŠ-*te*⸣ [*ana* EN.MEŠ-*šú*]
e.17 GU[R *ina de-n*]*i-šú* DU[G$_4$.DUG$_4$-*ma*]
18 *l*[*a*] ⸢*i*$^{!}$⸣*-laq-*[*qí*]
r.1 IGI ^{m}⸢*ga-x*⸣-[*x x x*]
2 IGI ^{m}*ta-r*[*i-ba—x x*] LÚ*$^{!}$.[*x x*]
3 IGI ^{md}P[A]—⸢*ka*$^{!}$⸣*-in*—MAN$^{!}$ LÚ*$^{!}$.⸢GAL$^{!}$⸣—[*xxx*]

4 IGI ^{m}*hal-*⸢*la*$^{!}$⸣*-pa*$^{!}$*-a-a* LÚ*$^{!}$.:
5 IGI ^{m}⸢*ba*$^{!}$*-du*$_8$$^{!}$⸣*-du*$_8$$^{!}$ LÚ*$^{!}$.:
6 IGI ^{m}⸢ITI.AB$^{!}$⸣*-a-a* LÚ*$^{!}$.*mu-*⸢*kil*⸣—*ap*.MEŠ
7 IGI ^{m}*hal-*[*d*]*i*$^{!}$—⸢ŠEŠ$^{!}$⸣—PAB LÚ*$^{!}$.*mu*$^{!}$-GUR$^{!}$—UMUŠ

8 IGI ^{m}*arba-*⸢*ìl*$^{!}$⸣*-a-a* LÚ*$^{!}$.GAL—Ì.DU$_8$
9 IGI ^{m}SUHU[Š$^{!}$—*x x*] LÚ*$^{!}$.Ì.DU$_8$
10 IGI ^{m}SU[HUŠ—*x x x* LÚ*].⸢*ha-za*⸣*-nu* ⸢*ša*$^{!}$⸣ URU.*qu-da*$^{!}$*-ru*$^{!}$
11 IGI ^{m}*da-*[*x x* LÚ*.*x š*]*a*$^{!}$ ⸢DUMU⸣—MAN
12 ⸢IGI ^{md}⸣3[0$^{!}$—TI-*s*]*u*—⸢E LÚ*⸣.[A]—SIG$_5$
blank space of about 7 lines

13 [ITI.*x* UD]-18-⸢KÁM⸣
14 [*lim-mu* ^{m}DI-*mu*]—EN

[6] Aššur-belu-uṣur, his wife and brother, [a total of 3]; in all 17 persons, servants of [Na'di-ilu] —

[8] Balṭaya has contracted and bought them from Na'di-ilu f[or] 8 1/2 minas of silver by the mina o[f the ki]ng.

[11] The money is [pa]id complete[ly]. Those men are pur[chased] and acquired. Any revocation, law[suit], or litiga[tion is void].

[14] Whoever in the fu[ture], at [any ti]me, breaks the contract, shall ret[urn the] mon[ey ten]fold [to its owners]. He shall cont[est in] his [lawsuit and not] succeed.

[r.1] Witness Ga[...].
[2] Witness Tar[iba-...].
[3] Witness Nabû-ka''in-šarru, commander of [...].
[4] Witness Hallapayu, ditto.
[5] Witness Baddudu, ditto.
[6] Witness Kanunayu, chariot driver.
[7] Witness Haldi-ahu-uṣur, intelligence officer.
[8] Witness Arbailayu, head porter.
[9] Witness Ubru-[...], porter.
[10] Witness Ub[ru-...], the mayor of Qudaru.
[11] Witness Da[..., ...] of the crown prince.
[12] Witness Sin-balassu-iqbi, chariot fighter.
[13] Month [...], 18th day, eponym year of [Šulmu]-beli.

131. A Fragmentary Purchase Document (695-XI)

K 1478

Obv. broken away
Rev. beginning broken away
1′ [*x* MA.NA] KUG.UD 1 MA.NA KUG.G[I]
2′ [*a-na* ^{d}]MAŠ *a-šib* URU.*kàl-hi* S[UM-*an*]
3′ *kas-pu a-na* 10.MEŠ-*te a-na* E[N.MEŠ-*šú*]
4′ [GUR] *ina de-ni-šú* DUG$_4$.DUG$_4$-[*ma*]
5′ *la i-laq-*[*qi*]

6′ IGI ^{m}*hi-ma-ri-i* LÚ*.[*x x*]
7′ IGI ^{m}ARAD—DINGIR.MEŠ-*ni* [LÚ*.*x x*]
8′ IGI ^{md}MAŠ—*kib-su*—PA[B LÚ*.*x x*]
9′ *ša* LÚ*.EN.NAM

ADD 569

(Beginning destroyed)

[r.1] [He shall] p[ay x minas] of silver (and) one mina of gol[d to] Ninurta residing in Calah, [and shall return] the money tenfold to its [owners]. He shall cont[est] in his lawsuit [and] not succeed.

---

[6] Witness Himarî, [...].
[7] Witness Urda-ilani, [...].
[8] Witness Inurta-kibsi-uṣu[r, ...] of the governor.

131 Previous edition: AR 567. Collated by I.L. Finkel. r.14 See coll.

10′ IGI ^{m}*tab-li-[x x]*
11′ ITI.ZÍZ UD-[*x*-KAM]
12′ *lim-me* ^{m}*aš-šur*—E[N—PAB]
13′ LÚ*.GAR.KUR [URU.*šá-hup-pa*]

14′ IGI ^{md}PA.TÚG—DI[NGIR$^{!}$-*a-a*]

10 Witness Tabli[...].

11 Month Shebat (XI), [...]th day, eponym year of Aššur-be[lu-uṣur], governor of [Šahuppa].

14 Witness Nušku-il[a'i ...].

132. Sale of a Slave (695)

K 917

1 ^{m}EN—KASKAL—⸢KI$^{?}$-*ia*$^{?}$ LÚ*.*x*⸣ [*x x*]
2 ^{m}*man-nu—ki*—[*x* LÚ*].BAD-HAL :
3 ^{m}*ki*-⸢*ṣir*$^{?}$⸣—[*aš-šur x x x*]
4 PAB 3 EN.MEŠ LÚ* SUM-*ni*

5 ^{m}*ma-ku*-[*x x x x* ARAD-*su-nu*]
6 *ša* $^{md+}$EN—KASKAL—⸢KI$^{?}$⸣-[*ia ša* ^{m}*man-nu—ki—x*]
7 *ša* ^{m}*ki*-⸢*ṣir*$^{?}$⸣—*aš-šur* [*ú-tap-pi-šu*]
8 *a-na* ^{m}*si-lim*—[*aš-šur*$^{?}$ *i-tan-nu*]
9 *man-nu ša* 4 1/2 MA.NA KUG.UD SUM-*an*-[*u-ni*]
10 ARAD-⸢*šu*$^{?}$⸣ *ú-še-ṣa*
11 IGI ^{m}*aš-šur*—PAB—AŠ
12 LÚ*.GAL—*ki-ṣir*
e.13 IGI ^{m}I—*aš-šur* LÚ*.*še*-[*lap-pa-a-a*]
r.1 IGI ^{md}IM$^{!}$—⸢*x*⸣[*x x*].*x* PAB
2 *ša* ^{md}[*x x x x x x x*]
3 IGI ^{m}*x*[*x x x x x x x*]
4 IGI ^{m}[*x x x x x x x*]
5 [IGI ^{m}*x x x*] ⸢*x x*⸣ [*x x*]
6 [IGI] ^{m}[*x x x x x x x*]
7 I[GI ^{m}*x x x x x x x*]
s.1 ITI.[*x* UD]-15-KÁM
2 *lim-mu* ^{m}*aš-šur*—U—PAB

ADD 616

1 Bel-Harran-*issiya*, [...]; Mannu-ki-[...], cavalryman ditto; Kiṣir-[Aššur, ...]; a total of 3 owners of the man being so[ld].

(fingernail impressions)

5 Maku[..., servant] of Bel-Harran-*issi*[*ya*, Mannu-ki-...] and Kiṣir-Aššur —

8 [they have contracted and sold] him to Silim-[*Aššur*]. Whoever pays 4 1/2 minas of silv[er], shall redeem his servant.

11 Witness Aššur-ahu-iddina, cohort commander.

13 Witness Na'id-Aššur, *ar*[*chitect*].

r.1 Witness Adad-[...], brother of [NN].

(Break)

s.1 [Month ...], 15th [day, eponym year of] Aššur-belu-uṣur.

133. Court Decision Concerning a Theft (694-I-24)

BM 123360

1 ^{m}*kan-ni* ^{m}*kas-ka-a-a* ^{m}*ba-bi-ri* [0]
2 ^{m}*ta-ka-li* ^{m}*na-an-na* PAB 5 LÚ.ERIM.MEŠ
3 *sa-ar-tú ina* É ^{m}*ta-a e-tap-šú*
4 *a-nu-tú ša* 14 MA.NA 30 GÍN KUG.UD *qa—ṣi-bit-te*

5 *ina* ŠU.2-*šú-nu i-ṣab-tu ina* IGI ^{m}AN.GAL—NUMUN—DÙ *qur*-ZAG
6 *ina* IGI ^{md}15—I LÚ*.*qur*-ZAG *ina* IGI ^{m}*gír-te* 2-*e*

Iraq 32 2

1 Kannu, Kaskayu, Babiri, Takali and Nanna, a total of five men, committed a theft in the house of Tâ. They were caught red-handed with goods worth 14 minas 30 shekels of silver.

5 They came forward for judgment before Issaran-zeru-ibni, a royal bodyguard, Issarna'id, a royal bodyguard, and Girittu, the

132 The tablet is very effaced and the readings are uncertain.
133 Previous edition: Postgate, Iraq 32 (1970) 133. 10 Lit., "We are thieves."

7 *a-na de-e-ni iq-ṭar-bu iq-ṭí-bu-ni-šú-nu*
8 [*m*]*a-a ina* NINA.KI *ina* IGI LÚ*.SUKKAL LÚ*.*sar-tin-ni*
9 *a-na de-e-ni li-kal-ka la i-ma-gúr*
e.10 [*m*]*a-a* LÚ*.LUL.MEŠ *a-ni-nu* 44 MA.NA 10 GÍN [K]UG.UD
11 [*s*]*a-ar-tú in-du* 14 MA.NA KUG.UD *x*
r.1 [S]AG.DU *sa-ar-te a-na* ^{m}[*ta*]*-a*
2 *ú-s*[*a-li-mu x x x x x x x x x*]*x*
3 *sa-a*[*r*?-*x x x x x x x x x x x*]
4 TA* [*x x x x x x x x x* G]IL-*u-ni*
5 *x*[*x x x x x x x x x x x x*]-*ma*
6 *x*[*x x x x x x x x x x*] *qur*-ZAG
7 IGI ^{m}[*x x x x x x*—G]IG? *qur*-ZAG
8 IGI ^{m}[*x x x x x*]*x da-gíl*—MUŠEN.MEŠ
9 IGI ^{md}[*x x x x* IGI ^{m}*x*]⌜*x x*⌝—IGI.LAL :
10 [IGI] ^{m}SUHU[Š—*x* IGI ^{md}*x*]—*ka-ši*[*r*] :
11e [IG]I ^{m}*ta-u-a-ri* : IGI ^{md}*šá-maš-u-a* Ì.[DU$_8$?]
12e [I]GI ^{m}*ka-ka-a-nu* IGI ^{m}*ma-u-a-u* DAM.QA[R].M[EŠ]
s.1 [IGI] ^{m}PAB—DINGIR-*a-a* LÚ*.*ta-x*[*x*(*x*)]
2 IGI ^{m}*sa-am-si* IGI ^{m}*kak-ku-u*
3 ITI.BARAG UD-24-KÁM
4 [*l*]*im-me* ^{m}DINGIR—KI-*ia*

deputy (governor), who told them: "Go off to Nineveh for judgment before the vizier and the *sartinnu*."

9 They did not consent to this but said: "We are guilty."

10 44 minas 10 shekels of silver were imposed as the fine, and they have restituted to Tâ 14 minas of silver, the capital value of the theft.

r.3 The fi[ne ......]

4 [...... Whoever br]eaks the agreement [......].

6 Wit[ness ....], royal bodyguard.

7 Wit[ness ...]..., royal bodyguard.

8 Witness [......], augur.

9 Witness [.... Witness ...]-lamur, ditto.

10 [Witness] Ubru-[.... Witness ...]-kaši[r], ditto.

11 [Witne]ss Tawari, ditto. Witness Šamašua, po[rter].

12 Witness Kakkanu, witness Mawau, merchants.

s.1 Witness Ahi-ila'i, [...].

2 Witness Samsi. Witness Kakkû.

3 Month Nisan (I), 24th day, eponym year of Ilu-isse'a.

134. Fragment of a Slave Sale (694-V-15)

K 389

Obv. broken away
Rev. beginning broken away
1′ [*a-na* 10.MEŠ *a-na* EN.MEŠ]-*šú*!
2′ [GUR *ina de-ni-šú* DU]G$_4$.DUG$_4$-*ma*
3′ *l*[*a i-laq-qi ṣib-t*]*i be-en-nu*
4′ *a-na* 1-*me* UD.MEŠ *sa-ar-ti*
5′ *a-na* EGIR UD.MEŠ

6′ IGI ^{m}*ab-da-a* LÚ*.HAL?
7′ IGI ^{m}PAB—*a-bu-u*
8′ IGI ^{m}*pu-ú-lu* LÚ*.AŠGAB
9′ IGI ^{m}*ha-da-sa-a* LÚ*.DAM.QAR
10′ IGI ^{m}*bir*—^{d}*šá*-⌜*maš*⌝ LÚ*.DAM.QAR
11′ IGI ^{md}15—BÀD
12′ IGI ^{md}MAŠ—DINGIR-*a-a*

ADD 281

(Beginning destroyed)

r.1 [He shall return the money tenfold to] its [owners. He shall con]test [in his lawsuit] and n[ot succeed].

3 (Guaranteed against) [seizur]es of epilepsy for 100 days and (against) fraud forever.

---

6 Witness Abdâ, *haruspex*.

7 Witness Ahabû.

8 Witness Pulu, tanner.

9 Witness Hadasâ, merchant.

10 Witness Bir-Ša[maš], merchant.

11 Witness Issar-duri.

12 Witness Inurta-ila'i.

134 Previous edition: AR 456. Collated by I.L. Finkel. r.5 See coll.

13′ IGI ^{md}PA—DI-*im* LÚ*.A.BA
14′ ITI.NE UD-15-KÁM
15′ *lim-me* ^{m}DINGIR—KI-*ia*
16e LÚ*.GAR.KUR URU.*di-maš-qa*

13 Witness Nabû-ušallim, scribe.
13 Month Ab (V), 15th day, eponym year of Ilu-isse'a, governor of Damascus.

135. Purchase of Slaves (694-V-29)

81-2-4,157

1 *ṣu-pur* ^{m}*ši*-[*x x x x x x*]
2 NA$_4$.KIŠIB ^{m}*bur-x*[*x x x x x x*]
3 EN UN.MEŠ S[UM-*ni*]

---

4 [*x x x x x x x x x*]*x*
5 [*x x x x x x x x x*]*x*
rest broken away
Rev. beginning broken away
1′ [*x x x x x*] *x x* [*x x x x*]
2′ [IGI ^{m}]⸢*x x*⸣[*x*] IGI$^{!}$ ^{m}⸢DI$^{!}$⸣-*m*[*u*$^{!}$—*x x x*]
3′ [0$^{!}$] (blank) *ša* MÍ—É.GAL
4′ IGI ^{m}DINGIR—*lip*$^{!}$-*hur*
5′ IGI ^{m}URU.ŠÀ—URU-*a-a* ⸢*ṣa*⸣-*bit ṭup-pi*

6′ ITI.NE UD-29-KÁM *lim-me* ^{m}DINGIR—KI-*ia*
7′ LÚ.GAR.KUR URU.*di-maš-qa*

ADD 272

1 Fingernail of Ši[...],
2 seal of Bur-[...],
3 owners of the people be[ing sold].

(space for seals and nailmarks)
(Break)

r.2 [Witness NN]. Witness Šulm[u-..., ...] of the queen.
4 [Witne]ss Ilu-liphur.
5 Witness Libbalayu, keeper of the tablet.
6 Month Ab (V), 29th day, eponym year of Ilu-isse'a, the governor of Damascus.

136. Aššur-ibni Loans Barley (694)

K 1867

1 1 ANŠE ŠE.PAD.MEŠ SA[G.DU *šá*]
2 ^{m}*aš-šur—ib-n*[*i x x*]

rest broken away
Rev. beginning broken away

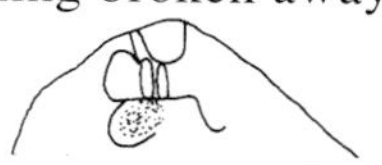

1′ *lim-mu* ^{m}DINGIR—KI-*i*[*a*]

ADD 140

1 1 homer of barley, cap[ital belonging to] Aššur-ibn[i ...].
(cylinder seal impression)

(Break)

(cylinder seal impression)

r.1 eponym year of Ilu-isse'a.

137. A Copper Loan with a Pledge of Land (693)

Ki 1904-10-9,148

1 [*x* MA].NA URUDU.MEŠ *ša* ^{m}*ur-da-a*

ADD 1177

1 [x mi]nas of copper belonging to Urdâ,

135 Previous edition: AR 526. Collations: Assur 2/5.
136 Previous editions: AR 317, NALK 39.
137 Previous edition: NALK 397. 2, 4 See coll. 4 *ku-ri-bat* is perhaps to be linked with Aramaic **krb* "to

2 [*ina* IGI ^{m}]*man-nu—ki-i—*^{d}15 É 1 ANŠE ⌜5BÁN?⌝
3 ⌜É!⌝ 1 ANŠE 5BÁN *ina* SAG! *ka-pi* É *x*[*x*]
4 ⌜É!⌝ 1 ANŠE *ku-ri-bat*! *ina* UGU *na-*[*hal-li*]

a[t the disposal] of Mannu-ki-Issar.

2 An estate of 1 hectare *5* decares (of land), an estate of 1 hectare 5 decares on top of the (river) bank, an estate of x[...], and an estate of 1 hectare of *plowed* (*field*) on the wadi

---

(space for seal impressions)

---

rest broken away
Rev. beginning broken away

(Break)

1′ [IGI ^{m}*x*]*x*—PAB IGI [^{m}*x x x x x x*]
2′ [IGI ^{m}]*šum-mu*—DINGIR-*a-a* I[G]I $^{m!}$NUMUN-[*x x x*]
3′ [IGI ^{m}*x*]*—ma*!*-di*! IGI ^{m}*ur*!*-du*! (IGI!) ^{m}*di*!*-di*!
4′ [IGI ^{m}*x*]*-qu-ra-a* IGI ^{m}*ti*!*-ka-la*
5′ [IGI ^{m}A]D!—SU IGI ^{md}PA—MU—GIŠ LÚ.A.[BA]
6′ [ITI.*x* UD-*x*]*x lim-me* ^{m}SUM-*na*—PAB.M[EŠ!]

r.1 [Witness ...]-naṣir. Witness [NN].
2 [Witness] Šumma-ila'i. Wit[ne]ss Zeru[...].
3 [Witness *Il*]-madi. Witness Urdû. (Witness) Didi.
4 [Witness ...]qurâ. Witness Tikala.
5 [Witness Ab]u-eriba. Witness Nabû-šumu-lešir, sc[ribe].
6 [Month ..., ...th day], eponym year of Iddin-ahhe.

138. Purchase of Three Slaves (693)

Rm 2,18 — ADD 243

1 NA$_4$.KIŠIB ^{m}DI-*mu*—EN
2 EN UN.MEŠ *ta-*⌜*da*⌝*-ni*

1 Seal of Šulmu-beli, owner of the people being sold.

(cylinder seal impression)

---

3 ^{m}PAB-*bu-ú* L[Ú.*x x* ^{m}*x x*]
4 LÚ.UŠ—ANŠE.AB.[BA.MEŠ]
5 MÍ.*ri-mu-t*[*ú*(*x*) MÍ-*šú*]
6 PAB 3 Z[I.MEŠ ARAD.MEŠ]
7 *ša* ^{m}DI-*m*[*u*—EN]
8 *ú-piš-ma* ^{m}*x*[*x x x*]⌜*x x*⌝
9 TA* IGI ^{m}DI-*mu*—EN
10 *ina* ŠÀ-*bi* 3 MA.NA KUG.UD *ina* 1 MA.NA-*e ša* MAN
11 *il-qi*! *kas-pu ga-mur*
12 *ta-din* UN.MEŠ *šu-a-tú*
13 *zar*$_4$*-pu laq-qi-ú*
14 ⌜*tu*⌝*-a-ru de-e-nu* DUG$_4$.DUG$_4$
e.15 *la-áš-šú*! *man-nu*! *ša*! *ur-kiš*!
r.1 [*ina ma-te-ma i-za-q*]*u-pa-ni*
2 [*lu-u* ^{m}DI-*mu*—EN *lu-u* DUMU].MEŠ-*šú*
3 [*lu-u* DUMU—DUMU.MEŠ-*šú lu-u mám-*

3 Ahabû, [...; NN], ca[mel] driver, (and) [*his wife*] Rimutt[u]; a total of 3 persons, [servants] of Šul[mu-beli] —

8 [...] has contracted and bought them from Šulmu-beli for three minas of silver by the mina of the king.

11 The money is paid completely. Those people are purchased and acquired. Any revocation, lawsuit, or litigation [is] void.

15 Whoever in the futu[re, at any time, lodges a com]plaint, [whether Šulmu-beli or] his [so]ns, [grandsons or relat]ives, [and

plow" cf. Syr. *krōbō* "furrow; fallow ground." r.5f See coll.
138 Previous edition: AR 207. Collations: Assur 2/5.

m]*a*$^{!}$*-ni-šú*
4 [*ša* TA ^{m}*x x x x x* DUMU].MEŠ-*šú*
5 [*de-e-nu* DUG$_4$].DUG$_4$
6 [*ub-ta-u-ni x* MA.NA KUG].UD LUH-*u*
7 [*x* MA.NA KUG.GI *sak-ru ina bur-ki*] ^{d}NIN.LÍL
8 [GAR-*an kas-pu*] *a-na* 10.MEŠ
9 [*ana* EN-*šú* GUR-*ra ina*] *de-ni-šú*
10 [DUG$_4$.DUG$_4$-*ma*] *la* TI
11 [IGI ^{m}DI]-*mu*—LUGAL
12 [IGI ^{m}]SU—^{d}15 LÚ.MU
13 [IGI ^{m}]ARAD—PAB.MEŠ-*šú*
14 IGI ^{m}DINGIR—KA—PAB
15 IGI ^{m}KI.TA-*a-a*
16 IGI ^{m}*la—tu-ba-šá-a-ni*—^{d}15
17 IGI ^{m}*la—tu-ba-šá-a-ni*—DINGIR
18 [IGI ^{m}*x x x x x* A.B]A

19e [ITI.*x*] UD-⸢20⸣-[KAM]
20e *lim-mu* ^{m}*id-di*[*n*]—⸢*a*$^{!}$⸣-[*hi*$^{?}$]

seeks a lawsuit or liti]gation [against ... and his so]ns,

r.6 [shall place x minas of] refined [silve]r [and x minas of pure gold in the lap] of Mullissu, [and shall return the money] tenfold [to its owner. He shall contest in] his lawsuit [and] not succeed.
11 [Witness Šul]mu-šarri.
12 [Witness] Riba-Issar, cook.
13 [Witness] Urda-ahhešu.
14 [Witn]ess Ilu-piya-uṣur.
15 Witness Šaplaya.
16 Witness La-tubašanni-Issar.
17 Witness La-tubašanni-ilu.
18 Witness [NN, s]cribe.
19 Month ..., 20th day, eponym year of Iddin-a[hhe].

139. Sin-šarru-uṣur, Prefect, Loans 4 Minas of Silver (693)

79-7-8,287

1 2 MA.NA KUG.UD SAG.DU
2 *ša* ^{m}30—MAN—PAB LÚ*.GAR-*nu*
3 *ina* IGI ^{m}PAB-*u*—SU

4 4 GÍN.MEŠ KUG.UD *a-na* 1 MA.NA
5 *ša* ITI-*šú* GAL-*bi*
6 [*m*]*a*$^{!}$-⸢*a*⸣ 1 MA.NA *šá-ni-u la* GAL-*bi*

7 IT[I.*x* UD]-12-KÁM
8 *lim-*[*mu* ^{m}]AŠ—PAB.MEŠ

r.1 IGI ^{m}E[N$^{!}$—IG]I$^{!}$.LAL$^{!}$-*a-ni*
2 IGI ^{m}*qu*[*r*$^{!}$*-d*]*i*$^{?}$—URU.KASKAL
3 IGI ^{m}BE$^{!}$-[*ma*—P]AB$^{!}$.MEŠ
4 IGI ^{m}*aš-šur*—[*a-l*]*ik*$^{!}$—IGI LÚ*.GAR-⸢*nu*⸣
5 IGI ^{m}NU[MUN]-*u*-⸢*tú*⸣ IGI ^{md}PA—PAB—AŠ

ADD 32

1 2 minas of silver, capital, belonging to Sin-sarru-uṣur, prefect, at the disposal of Ahu'a-eriba.
4 It shall bear interest by 4 shekels of silver per mina per month.
6 [He sa]id the other mina shall not bear interest.
7 Month [...], 12th [day], eponym year of Iddin-ahhe.
r.1 Witness B[el-em]uranni.
2 Witness Qu[rd]i-Harran.
3 Witness Šum[ma]-ahhe.
4 Witness Aššur-[al]ik-pani, prefect.
5 Witness Z[ar]utu. Witness Nabû-ahu-iddina.

140. Sin-šarru-uṣur Purchases Slaves

Rm 168

beginning broken away
1′ [*x*] ⸢*x x x*⸣ *ú-*[*p*]*iš-ma* ^{m}3[0$^{!}$—LUGAL—PAB]
2′ *ina* ŠÀ-*bi* 1 1/2 MA.NA 5 GÍN.MEŠ KUG.U[D

ADD 262

(Beginning destroyed)
1 S[in-šarru-uṣur] has contracted and

139 Previous editions: AR 245, NALK 327. Collations: Assur 2/5. This document was found at Nebi Yunus. 3 PAB$^{!}$ not PA$^{!}$ (NALK) is on the tablet.
140 Previous editions: AR 553, NALK 328 r.9f The italicized name elements, taken from Johns' copy, are no

il-qi]

3′ *kas-pu gam-mur ta-din* UN.MEŠ *za-*[*ar-pu*]
4′ TI-*ú de-ni* DUG$_4$.DUG$_4$ *la-áš-*[*šú*]

5′ *man-nu ša ina ur-kiš ina ma-ti-ma* GI[L-*u-ni*]
6′ *lu-u* ^{m}30—SUM—PAB *lu-u* DUMU.MEŠ-*šú lu-*[*u mám-m*]*a*$^{!}$*-n*[*u*$^{!}$*-šú*]
7′ *de-ni* DUG$_4$.DUG$_4$ TA* ^{m}30—[LUG]AL$^{!}$-⌈PAB$^{!}$⌉
8′ TA* DUMU.MEŠ-*šú ub-ta-u-*[*ni*]
9′ 10 MA.NA KUG.UD 5 MA.NA KUG.GI 4 [ANŠE.KUR.RA.MEŠ]
10′ BABBAR.MEŠ *a-na* ^{d}30 *a-šib* URU.[KASKAL]
11′ ⌈*i*⌉*-dan* KUG.UD *a-na* 10.MEŠ-⌈*te*⌉
12′ [*a-n*]*a* EN.MEŠ-*šú* GUR *a-na d*[*e-ni-šú*]
13′ [DU]G$_4$.DUG$_4$*-ma la i-laq-*[*qi*]

---

r.1 [IGI ^{m}]*x x-*[*x x x x*]
2 IGI ^{m}⌈*man*$^{?}$*-nu*$^{?}$⌉-[*x x x*]
3 IGI ^{m}⌈*x x x x*⌉ [*x x x*]
4 IGI ^{m}⌈*x x x x*⌉ [*x x x*]
5 IGI ^{m}⌈*x x x x*⌉ [*x x x*]

6 IGI ^{m}⌈*rém*$^{?}$*-a*$^{?}$*-ni*$^{?}$⌉—[*x x x*]
7 IGI ^{m}10$^{?}$-[*x x x x*]
8 LÚ*.⌈ARAD$^{!}$⌉ [*x x x*]
9 IGI ^{m}[*ha-an-du*] LÚ*.[*x x x x*]
10 IGI ^{m}[EN]—*la-mur* LÚ*.[A.BA]
11 [IGI ^{m}*x x x*]-⌈*i*⌉ LÚ*.DAM.[QAR]
12 [*ša*] É$^{!}$ MÍ—É.GAL
rest broken away

[bought them] for 1 1/2 minas and 5 shekels of sil[ver].

3 The money is paid completely. The people ar[e purchased] and acquired. Any lawsuit or litigation is vo[id].

5 Whoever in the future, at any time, breaks [the contract], whether Sin-nadin-ahi or his sons or [rel]atives, and seeks a lawsuit or litigation against Sin-[šar]ru-uṣur and his sons, shall pay 10 minas of silver, 5 minas of gold, and four white [horses] to Sin residing in [Harran], and shall return the silver tenfold [t]o its owners. [He shall] contest in [his lawsui]t and not succ[eed].

---

r.1 Witness [......].
2 Witness *Mannu*-[...].
3 Witness [......].
4 Witness [......].
5 Witness [......].
6 Witness *Remanni*-[...].
7 Witness Adad-[...], servant of [...].
9 Witness [*Handu*, ...].
10 Witness [*Bel*]-lamur, scribe.
11 Witness [NN], merchant of the queen's house.

141. A Fragmentary Sale Document (692-I)

K 7343

1 [NA$_4$.KIŠIB ^{m}*x x x x*]
2 E[N *x x x x x*]

---

traces of a stamp seal impression
rest broken away

r.1′ *a-n*[*a* EN-*šú* GUR-*ra*]
2′ *ina de-*[*ni-šú* DUG$_4$.DUG$_4$*-ma*]
3′ *la* [*i-la-qí*]

4′ IGI ^{m}*x*[*x x x*]
5′ IGI ^{m}15—[*x x x*]
6′ IGI ^{m}EN—[*x x x*]
7′ IGI ^{m}*ba*$^{!}$-[*x x x*]

ADD 158

1 [Seal of ...], owner [of the ... being sold].

(stamp seal impression)
(Break)

r.1 [He shall return the money tenfold] t[o its owner].

2 [He shall contest in his] law[suit and] not [succeed].

---

4 Witness [...].
5 Witness Issar-[...].
6 Witness Bel-[...].
7 Witness Ba[...].

longer extant on the tablet.

141 Previous edition: AR 557. r.4, 7f, r.1 See coll.

8′ IGI ^{m}*ta*[*b*$^{?}$-*x x x*]
9e IGI ^{m}[*x x x x*]
s.1 [^{m}*x x x*] LÚ*.A.BA ITI.BARAG 0$^{!}$
2 [UD-*x*-KAM *lim-m*]*u* ^{m}*za-ze-e*

8 Witness Ta[b...].
8 Witness [NN].
s.1 [NN], scribe.
2 Month Nisan (I), [...th day, epony]m year of Zazê.

142. An Egyptian Scribe Buys a House in Nineveh (692-III-16)

K 294

1 *ṣu-pur* ^{m}LUGAL—*lu—dà-ri*
2 *ṣu-pur* ^{m}*a-tar—su-ru*
3 *ṣu-pur* MÍ.*a-mat—*^{d}*su-u*ʾ*-la*
4 MÍ-*šú ša* ^{m}EN—BÀD LÚ*$^{!}$.3-*šú ša a-rit*
5 EN É SUM-*an*

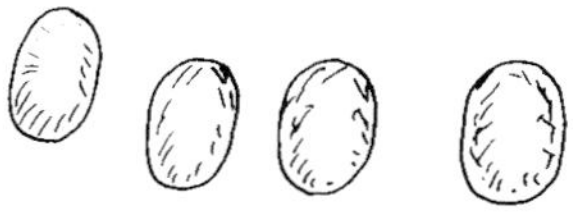

6 É *ep-šú a-di* GIŠ.ÙR.MEŠ-*šú*
7 *a-di* GIŠ.IG.MEŠ-⌈*šú*⌉ TÙR
8 *ina* URU.*ni-nu-u*$^{!}$*-a* SUHUR É ^{m}*man-nu—ki—*PAB.MEŠ
9 SUHUR É (^{m})DINGIR—KI-*ia*
10 SUHUR *su-qa-qi ú-piš-ma*
11 ^{m}GIŠ.MI—*aš-šur* LÚ*.A.BA
e.12 LÚ*.*mu-ṣu-ra-a-a*
13 *ina* ŠÀ 1 MA.NA KUG.UD *ša* LUGAL
r.1 TA* IGI ^{m}LUGAL—*lu—dà-ri*
2 TA* IGI MÍ.*a-tar—su-ru*
3 TA* IGI MÍ.*a-mat—su-u*ʾ*-la* MÍ-*šú ša* ^{m}EN—BAD$^{!}$
4 *il-qi kas*$^{!}$*-pu*$^{!}$ *gam-mur ta-*⌈*din*⌉
5 É *šú-a-tú za-rip* TI
6 *tu-a-ru de-e-ni u* DUG$_{4}$.DUG$_{4}$
7 *la-áš-šu*$^{!}$ *man-nu ša ina ur-kiš*
8 *ina ma-te-ma lu* LÚ.MEŠ-*e an-nu-ti*$^{!}$
9 *ša de-ni u* DUG$_{4}$.DUG$_{4}$
10 TA* ^{m}*ṣil—aš-šur ub-ta-*ʾ*u-u-ni*
11 10 MA.NA KUG.UD SUM-*an*

12 IGI ^{m}*šu-sa-an-qu ha-at-na* MAN
13 IGI ^{m}*har-ma-ṣa* LÚ*.3-*šú*

14 IGI ^{m}*ra-su-u*ʾ LÚ*.GAL$^{!}$—MÁ.DU.DU
15 IGI ^{md}PA—BÀD—PAB LÚ*.*mu-ri-ba-nu*
16e IGI ^{m}*har-ma-ṣa* LÚ*.GAL—MÁ.DU.DU
17e IGI ^{md}30—MAN—PAB IGI ^{m}*zi-it-t*[*i*$^{!}$]

ADD 324

1 Fingernail of Šarru-lu-dari,
2 fingernail of Atar-suru,
3 fingernail of Amat-Su'la, wife of Bel-duri, shield-bearing 'third man,'
5 owners of the house being sold.

(stamp seal impressions)

6 A built house with its beams, doors and a yard in Nineveh, adjoining the house of Mannu-ki-ahhe, the house of Ilu-issiya, and the street —

11 Ṣilli-Aššur, Egyptian scribe, has contracted and bought it for one mina of silver (by the mina) of the king from Šarru-lu-dari, Atar-suru and Amat-Su'la, the wife of Bel-duri.

r.4 The money is paid completely. That house is purchased and acquired. Any revocation, lawsuit, or litigation is void.

7 Whoever in the future, at any time, whether these men (or anyone else), seeks a lawsuit and litigation against Ṣilli-Aššur, shall pay 10 minas of silver.

12 Witness Šusanqu, the king's brother-in-law.
13 Witness Harmaṣa, 'third man.'
14 Witness Rasu', chief boatman.
15 Witness Nabû-duru-uṣur, (horse) raiser.
16 Witness Harmaṣa, chief boatman.
17 Witness Sin-šarru-uṣur. Witness Zitt[i].

142 Previous editions: AR 36, NALK 333; → KB 4 (1896) 116-117. Collations: Assur 2/5. r.3 Note BAD for BÀD; the scribe did not have enough room to write out the sign.

s.1 ITI.SIG$_4$ UD-16-KAM *lim-me* ^{m}*za-za-a*
2 LÚ*$^{!}$.GAR.KUR URU.*ár-pad-da* IGI ^{md}UTU—GIN—PAB
3 IGI ^{m}*mi-tu-ru* IGI ^{md}PA—MU—AŠ$^{!}$

s.1 Month Sivan (III), 16th day, eponym year of Zazaya, governor of Arpad.
2 Witness Šamaš-kenu-uṣur.
3 Witness Mituru. Witness Nabû-šumu-iddina.

143. Debt-note for *iškaru* Silver (692-VI-29)

80-7-19,47

1 1 MA.NA KUG.UD *ina ša* MAN
2 *iš*-QAR *ša* MÍ.AMA—MAN
3 *ša* ^{md}PA—*tàk-lak*
4 *ina* IGI ^{md}U.GUR—DINGIR-*a-a*
5 *ina* ITI.DUL *ina* SAG.DU-*šú*
6 SUM-*an šum-ma la i-din*
e.7 KUG.UD *ina* 1/2 MA.NA-⸢*e*$^{!}$⸣
8 GAL-*bi*
r.1 ITI.KIN UD-2⸢9$^{!}$⸣-KÁM
2 *lim-me* ^{m}*za-za-a-a*
3 IGI ^{md}⸢*a-a*⸣—SI.⸢SÁ⸣
4 IGI ^{m}*mi*$^{!}$-*ti*$^{?}$-*mu*
5 IGI ^{m}*si-i-ri*
6e IGI ^{md}PA—KAR-*ir*
7e LÚ*.A.BA
s.1 IGI ^{m}*šá—la—maš*$^{!}$
2 [IG]I ^{m}*ka-pa-ru*

ADD 33

1 One mina of silver (by the mina) of the king, *iškāru* money of the queen mother belonging to Nabû-taklak, at the disposal of Nergal-ila'i.
5 He shall pay its capital sum in Tishri (VII). If he does not pay, the silver shall increase by 1/2 mina.
r.1 Month Elul (VI), 29th day, eponym year of Zazaya.
3 Witness Ea-lešir.
4 Witness *Mitimu*.
5 Witness Siri.
6 Witness Nabû-eṭir, scribe.
s.1 Witness Ša-la-mašê.
2 [Wit]ness Kaparu.

144. Fragment of a Slave Sale (692-IX-4)

Sm 917

beginning (about 6 lines) broken away
1′ [*x x x x*] *an*$^{!}$ [*x x x*]
2′ [*ú-piš-ma* ^{m}*aš*]-*šur*$^{!}$—[*x x x*]
3′ [LÚ.*x x* U]RU$^{!}$.BÀD$^{!}$—[MAN—GIN]
4′ [*ina* ŠÀ *x*] GÍN KUG.UD
5′ [TA* IGI ^{m}K]Á$^{!}$.DINGIR$^{!}$.K[I$^{!}$-*a-a*]
6′ [*il-qi*] *kas-pu gam-mur* [0]
7′ [*ta-ad-din*] LÚ *šu-a-tú* [0]
8′ [*za-rip laq*]-*qi tu-a-ru* [0]
9′ [*de-e-nu*] DUG$_4$.DUG$_4$ *la-áš*-[*šú*]
10′ [*man-nu šá*] GIL-*u-ni* [0]
11′ [*x* MA.NA KUG].UD 10 [MA.NA KUG.GI]
rest broken away
Rev. beginning broken away
1′ [IGI ^{m}*x x x x*]-*šá*$^{!}$
2′ [IGI ^{m}]^{d}1[5$^{?}$]—⸢GAL$^{!}$⸣

ADD 189

(Beginning destroyed)

2 [Aš]šur-[..., ... of] Dur-[Šarruken, has contracted and bought him from B]abil[ayu for x] shekels of silver.

6 [The mon]ey is [paid] completely. That man [is purchased and acqu]ired. Any revocation, [lawsuit] or litigation is void.

10 [Whoever] breaks the contract [shall place x minas of silve]r and 10 [minas of gold]

(Break)

r.1 [Witness ...]ša.
2 Witness *Is*[*sar*]-rabi.

143 Previous editions: AR 291, NALK 211. → TCAE 96. 6 Tablet has *šum-ma* as copied by Johns (see coll.), not BE-*ma* (NALK). r.1, 3f, s.1 See coll.
144 Previous edition: AR 474. 2, 5, r.1f See coll.

3′ [ITI].GAN UD-4-KÁM
4′ [*li*]*m-me* ^{m}*za-za-ia*

^{3} Month Kislev (IX), 4th day, eponym year of Zazaya.

145. Purchase of Slaves (692-XI-1)

K 360

1 *ku-um* NA$_4$.KIŠIB-[*šú-nu ṣu-pur-šú-nu iš-ku-nu*]
2 *ṣu-pur* ^{m}*su-r*[*a-a-a*]
3 ^{m}KUR.*gar-ga-meš*$^{!}$*-a-*[*a*]
4 ^{md}PA—ZALÁG-*ir* PAB 3 LÚ.[MEŠ]
5 *be-lí* LÚ*.UN.MEŠ *ta-*[*da-ni*]
rest broken away
Rev. beginning broken away
1′ [IGI ^{m}*x x x x x* IGI ^{m}]⸢*im*$^{?}$*-ma*$^{!}$*-ni*⸣—DINGIR
2′ [IGI ^{m}*x x x x*]*x*—SU LÚ.A.BA
3′ ITI.ZÍZ UD-1-KÁM *lim-me*
4′ ^{m}*za-za-ku*

ADD 286

^{1} Instead of [their] sea[ls they impressed their fingernails].
^{2} Fingernails of Sura[yu], Gargameša[yu], and Nabû-nammir, a total of three gentlemen, owners of the people being so[ld].
(Break)

$^{r.1}$ [Witness] *Immani*-il.
^{2} [Witness ...]-*riba*, scribe.
^{3} Month Shebat (XI), 1st day, eponym year of Zazaku.

146. Tariba-Issar Takes Land as Security for a Debt (692)

80-7-19,42

1 [NA$_4$.KIŠIB ^{md}MAŠ]—KAM-*eš*

2 [*x* MA.NA KUG.UD *š*]*a* ^{m}*ta*-SU—15
3 [*ina* IGI ^{md}MA]Š$^{!}$—KAM-*eš*
4 [*x* ANŠE A.ŠÀ] *ina* URU.*šú-ra*
5 [SUHUR KASKAL *š*]*á*$^{!}$ URU.*dan-na-a-ni*
6 [SUHUR A.Š]À *šá* ^{m}*a-a—me-tu-nu*
7 [*a-na šá*]-*par-ti šá-kín*
e.8 [3 *ka*]*r-ap-hi* 3 *me-re-še*
9 [A].ŠÀ KÚ KUG.UD
r.1 [*in*]*a*$^{!}$ UGU ŠE.*ta-ra-me* SUM-*an*
2 [A].ŠÀ *ú-še-ṣa*

---

3 [IG]I$^{!}$ ^{m}*si-ip-ra-a-nu*
4 [IGI] ^{md}A.10—DINGIR-*a-a*
5 [IGI ^{m}]SUHUŠ—^{d}15
6 [IGI ^{m}]$^{d!}$30—MAN—PAB
7 [IGI ^{m}]⸢^{d}⸣UTU—*ú-pa-hír*
blank space of two lines

ADD 69

^{1} [Seal of Inurta]-ereš.

(stamp seal impression)

^{2} [x minas of silver belong]ing to Tariba-Issar, [at the disposal of Inur]ta-ereš.
^{4} [x hectares of field] in the town of Šura, [adjoining the road t]o Dannanu [and the fi]eld of Aya-metunu, are placed [as a pl]edge.
^{8} He shall have the usufruct of the field [for three fal]low years and three crop years.
^{9} One shall place the silver upon the corn heap, and one shall redeem the field.

$^{r.3}$ [Wit]ness Sipranu.
^{4} [Witness] Apladad-ila'i.
^{5} [Witness] Ubru-Issar.
^{6} [Witn]ess Sin-šarru-uṣur.
^{7} [Witness] Šamaš-upahhir.

145 Previous edition: AR 528, → KB 4 (1896); 3R 47,11 (copy). Collated by I.L. Finkel. ^{3} KUR.*gar-ga-meš* sic; see coll. $^{r.1}$ See coll. ⸢*im*?⸣ could be ⸢I⸣. $^{r.2}$ *x*]*x* could be ⸢PAB⸣.
146 Previous editions: AR 134, NALK 387. Collations: Assur 2/5.

8 [ITI.*x* UD-*x*]-KÁM *lim-mu*
9 [^{m}*za-za*]-⸢*a*⸣-*a*

8 [Month ..., ...]th [day], eponym year of [Zaz]aya.

147. —— (690-I-14)

BM 121054

beginning broken away

1′ [*x x x x x x x x x x x x x*]*x*
2′ [*x x x x x x x x x x x x* ^{d}A]G
3′ [*x x x x x x x x x x x x*]-*šú*
4′ [*x x x x x x x x x x x x*]-⸢*ti*⸣
rest broken away
Rev. beginning broken away
1′ [IGI ^{m}*x-x*]—⸢^{d}IM⸣ [*x x x x x*]
2′ [IGI ^{m}]*ik-ka-ru* IGI ^{md}AG—⸢*da*⸣-[*la-a*]
3′ [IGI] ^{md}AG—*šal-lim* IGI ^{m}*qa-ri-bu*
4′ [IGI] ^{m}*du-un-qi—la—te-ep-pa-áš* IGI ^{md}AG—AŠ—PAB
5′ [IGI] ^{m}TA*—^{d}IM—ŠEŠ-*u-tú* IGI ^{m}*zer-ma-hu*
6′ IGI ^{m}*ha-an-ṭu* IGI ^{m}GIŠ.MI—*ba-ni*
blank space of one line
7′ ITI.BARAG UD-14-KÁM *lim-mu* ^{md}AG—GIN—PAB
8′ ⸢LÚ*⸣.[GAR.KU]R URU.*sa-mir-i-na*
9′ [IGI ^{m}*x x x*] LÚ.A.BA *ṣa-bit dan-ni-te*
10′ [*x x x x x x ša ṣ*]*u-up-ri-šú-n*[*u*]
rest broken away
s.1 *x*]*x-u-ni* [

Iraq 32 13

(Beginning destroyed)

(fingernail impressions)

1 [.....]
2 [......-Na]bû
3 [......] his
(Break)

r.1 [Witness ...]-Adad, [...].
2 [Witness] Ikkaru. Witness Nabû-da[lâ].
3 [Witness] Nabû-šallim. Witness Qaribu.
4 [Witness] Dunqi-la-teppaš. Witness Nabû-nadin-ahi.
5 [Witness] Issi-Adad-ahhutu. Witness Zermahu.
6 Witness Hanṭu. Witness Ṣillu-bani.
7 Month Nisan (I), 14th day, eponym year of Nabû-kenu-uṣur, governor of Samaria.
9 [Witness NN], scribe, keeper of the contract.
10 [x shekels of silver for] the[ir fin]gernails.
(Rest destroyed)

148. Fragment of a Slave Sale (690-III-2)

BM 121104

1 NA$_{4}$.KIŠIB ^{m}DUG$_{4}$.DUG$_{4}$—TÉŠ [0]
2 [N]A$_{4}$.KIŠIB ^{m}PAB—ZALÁG
3 [PAB] ⸢2 LÚ⸣ EN LÚ SUM-*ni*
rest broken away
Rev. beginning broken away
1′ [IGI ^{m}*k*]*e-ni-*[*i x x x*]
2′ ⸢IGI⸣ ^{m}*si-in—ka-*⸢*šir*? A.BA⸣
3′ ITI.SIG$_{4}$ UD-2-KÁM
4′ *lim-me* ^{md}PA—GIN—PAB
5′ [LÚ*].GAR.KUR URU.*sa-mir-*[*n*]*a*

Iraq 32 14

1 Seal of Lidbubu-lipušu, seal of Ahi-nuri, [a total of] 2 men, owners of the man being sold.
(Break)
r.1 [Witness K]en[î, ...].
2 Witness Sin-ka*šir*, scribe.
3 Month Sivan (III), 2nd day, eponym year of Nabû-kenu-uṣur, governor of Samaria.

147 Previous edition: Iraq 32 13. See Iraq 32 13.
148 Previous edition: Iraq 32 14.

149. A Broken Real Estate Sale (689)

Bu 89-4-26,33

1 [*x x x x x x*]*x* EN A.ŠÀ.MEŠ GIŠ.SAR.MEŠ UN$^{!}$.MEŠ$^{!}$ SUM-*ni*

---

2 [*x x x x x x x x x a-na g*]*i-mir-ti-šú*
3 [*x x x x x ina m*]*a-za-ru-te* ÍD A.MEŠ *ka-a-a-ma*$^{!}$*-nu*$^{!}$
4 [*x x x x x x x za*$^{?}$]*-ka*$^{!}$*-šá iz-zak-ru*

5 [*x x x x x x x x*]*-la*$^{!}$*-a* LÚ.GIŠ.APIN
6 [*x x x x x x x x x x*]*x* ZI.MEŠ
7 [*x x x x x x x x*]*x*—SU$^{!}$ PAB 5$^{!}$ ZI.MEŠ
rest broken away
Rev. beginning broken away
1′ [IGI ^{m}*x x x x x x x x x x x*] :
2′ [IGI ^{m}*x x x x x x x x x x*] : :
3′ [IGI ^{m}*x x x x x x x x* URU].*ni-nu-a*
4′ [IGI ^{m}*x x x x x x*] :
5′ [IGI ^{m}*x x x x x*] (blank) :
6′ [IGI ^{m}*x x x x x*] :
7′ [*x x x x x x x x* M]EŠ
8′ [ITI.*x* UD-*x*-KAM *lim-mu* ^{m}*gi-hi-lu*] LÚ.GAR.KUR
9′ [0 URU.*ha-ta-r*]*ik*$^{!}$*-ka*

ADD 432

1 [Seal of ...], owner of the fields, gardens, and people being sold.

(space for stamp seal impressions)

---

2 [...... in its ent]irety
3 [...... fields] in cultivation, a canal with permanent water-flow.
4 [......] its [*free*]*dom from encumbrances has been declared*
5 [......]lâ, plowman,
6 [......, a total of x] persons,
7 [......]-*eriba*, a total of 5 persons,
(Break)
r.1 [Witness ......], ditto.
2 [Witness NN, ...] ditto ditto.
3 [Witness NN, ...] of Nineveh.
4 [Witness NN, ...] ditto.
5 [Witness NN, ...] ditto.
6 [Witness NN, ...] ditto.
8 [Month ..., ...th day, eponym year of Gihilu], governor [of Hatar]ikka.

150. Dummuqâ is Owed 5 1/2 Minas of Silver by 6 Men (688-XII-25)

Bu 91-5-9,4

1 5 MA.NA 1/2 MA.NA KUG.UD *šá* ^{m}*du-mu-qa-a*
2 *ina* IGI ^{m}*ba-la-su* LÚ.*qe-e-pi*
3 *ina* IGI ^{m}*ṣi-la-a ina* IGI ^{m}AD—GI.NA$^{!}$
4 *ina* IGI ^{md}PA—*še-zib ina* IGI $^{m⌜}$*a*$^{!⌝}$*-di*—DINGIR
5 *ina* IGI ^{m}*ia-a-ke-e ina* ITI.⌜GUD$^{!}$ *id*⌝*-du-nu*
6 *šum-ma la id-din-nu-ni* 1 M[A.N]A 5 GÍN.MEŠ
7 *ša* ITI-*šu i-ra-ab-bi*

---

8 IGI ^{m}*bar-ruq-qu*
9 IGI ^{m}PAB—SI.⌜SÁ⌝
r.1 IGI ^{m}DI-*mu*—LUGAL
2 IGI ^{m}*ad-di*—*id-ri*
3 IGI ^{m}*man-nu*—*ki-i*—*arba-ìl*.KI

4 ITI.ŠE UD-25-KÁM *lim-mu* ^{m}SUM-*na*—⌜PAB⌝.MEŠ

ADD 17

1 5 1/2 minas of silver belonging to Dummuqâ, at the disposal of Balassu the (royal) delegate, Ṣillaya, Abi-ken, Nabû-šezib, Adi-il, and Yakê.

5 They shall pay in Iyyar (II). If they do not pay, it shall increase by one m[ina] 5 shekels per month.

---

8 Witness Barruqu.
9 Witness Ahu-lešir.
r.1 Witness Šulmu-šarri.
2 Witness Addi-idri.
3 Witness Mannu-ki-Arbail.
4 Month Adar (XII), 25th day, eponym year of Iddin-ahhe.

149 Previous edition: AR 432. Collations: Assur 2/5.
150 Previous editions: AR 246, NALK 94. 3ff See coll.

151. Purchase of a Woman (687-III)

Rm 161

1 NA$_4$.KIŠIB ^{md}[*x x x*]
2 EN MÍ-⸢*šú*$^!$⸣ [SUM-*ni*]

rest broken away
Rev. beginning broken away
1′ 1 MA.⸢NA⸣ [KUG.UD *x* MA.NA KUG.GI]
2′ *ina bur*^{ur}*-ki* ⸢^{d}⸣[*x x x x x*]
3′ *i-šak-kan kas-pu a*-⸢*na*⸣ [10.MEŠ-*te*]
4′ *ina* EN.MEŠ-⸢*šú*$^!$⸣ *ú*-GUR-*r*[*a*]
5′ *ina de-ni-šú i*-DUG$_4$.DUG$_4$ *la* [*x x*]

6′ IGI ^{m}*du-du-u-a* LÚ*.A—SI[G]
7′ *ša* LÚ*.EN.NAM *ša* URU.*kal*-[*ha*]
8′ IGI ^{m}ARAD—^{d}15 IGI ^{m}*qa-q*[*a*$^!$*-a*$^?$]
9′ IGI ^{m}*mu-qu-ru* IGI ^{m}⸢I$^?$⸣—[*x x x*]

10′ ITI.SIG$_4$ ⸢UD⸣-[*x*-KAM]
11e *lim-mu* ^{m}⸢^{d}⸣[30—PAB.MEŠ—SU]
12e MAN KUR—[*aš-šur*.KI]
s.1 [IGI] ^{md}PA—MU—AŠ LÚ*.A.BA

ADD 225

1 Seal of [NN], the owner [selling] his wife.

(cylinder seal impression)

(Break)

r.1 He shall place one mina [of silver and x minas of gold] in the lap of [...], and shall retu[rn the money tenfold] to its owners. He shall contest in his lawsuit and not [succeed].

6 Witness Duduwa, chariot fighter of the governor of Cal[ah].

8 Witness Urda-Issar. Witness Qaq[â].

9 Witness Muqquru. Witness *Na'd*[*i*-...].

10 Month Sivan (III), [...th] day, eponym year of [Sennacherib], king of [Assyria].

13 [Witness] Nabû-šumu-iddina, scribe.

152. Purchase of a Woman (687-IV-15)

K 419

beginning broken away
1′ *ina* ŠÀ-*bi bi-lat* URUDU.[MEŠ]
2′ *il-qi kas-pu ga-mu*[*r ta-din*]
3′ *tu-a-ru* DUG$_4$.DUG$_4$ *la-a*-[*šu*]

4′ *man-nu ša ina ur-kiš lu-u ina*$^!$ ⸢*ma*$^!$*-ti*$^!$*-ma*$^!$⸣
5′ *i-za-qu-ba*$^!$*-ni*
6′ *ma-a* MÍ *a-paṭ-ṭar*
7′ 1 MA.NA KUG.UD SUM-*an i*$^!$*-paṭ*$^!$*-ṭar*$^!$

8′ 0$^!$ ITI.ŠU UD-15-KÁM
e.9′ *lim-mu* ^{m}30—PAB.MEŠ—SU
10′ MAN KUR—*aš-šur*.KI
r.1 IGI ^{m}*man-nu*—GIM—10 GAL—[*x x*]
2 IGI ^{m}*ru-ra-di-di*
3 LÚ*.SAG *šá* MÍ.*šá-kín-te*
4 IGI ^{m}*ga-lu-lu* Ì.DU$_8$
5 IGI ^{m}*zi-zi-ia* :

ADD 218

(Beginning destroyed)

1 has bought (her) for one talent copper.

2 The money is paid completely. Any revocation or litigation is void.

4 Whoever in the future or at any time lodges a complaint, saying: "I will release the woman," shall pay one mina of silver to release her.

8 Month Tammuz (IV), 15th day, eponym year of Sennacherib, king of Assyria.

r.1 Witness Mannu-ki-Adad, chief [...].

2 Witness Ruradidi, eunuch of the (harem) governess.

4 Witness Gallulu, porter.

5 Witness Ziziya, ditto.

151 Previous edition: AR 499. r.4, 8f See coll.
152 Previous editions: AR 188, NALK 170. Collations: Assur 2/5.

6 IGI ^{m}*mu-qa-lil*—IDIM-*tú* :
7 IGI ^{md}PA—BÀD—PAB LÚ.SAG
8 IGI ^{m}[*du*]-*un*$^{!}$-*qí*—15 [0$^{?}$]
9 [IGI ^{m}*x x x*]-*a-a*
rest broken away

6 Witness Muqallil-kabti, ditto.
7 Witness Nabû-duru-uṣur, eunuch.
8 Witness [D]unqi-Issar.
9 [Witness ...]aya
(Rest destroyed)

153. Purchase of a House and People (687-IV)

K 1440

1 NA$_{4}$.KIŠIB ^{m}DI-*mu*—PAB.MEŠ
2 EN É UN.MEŠ SUM-*ni*

3 ⸢É⸣ *ep-*[*šú x x x x*]
rest broken away
Rev. beginning broken away
1′ ⸢IGI$^{!}$ ^{m}*hal*$^{!}$-*di*$^{!}$⸣—[*x x*]
2′ IGI ^{md}PA—NUMU[N$^{!}$—*x x*]
3′ ITI.ŠU UD-[*x*-KAM]
4′ *lim-mu* ^{md}[30—PAB.MEŠ-SU]
5′ MAN KUR—*a*[*š-šur*.KI]

ADD 454

1 Seal of Šulmu-ahhe, owner of the house and people being sold.
(Blank seal space)
3 A built hou[se ...]
(Break)
r.1 Witness *Haldi*-[...].
2 Witness Nabû-zer[u-...].
3 Month Tammuz (IV), [...th] day, eponym year of [Sennacherib], king of Assyria.

154. Purchase of Three Storehouses in Central Nineveh (687-V-22)

K 405

1 [NA$_{4}$.KIŠIB ^{m}DI.KUD—*kur-ba-ìl*]
2 ⸢EN É SUM⸣-*ni*

3 3 É ⸢ŠU.2.MEŠ$^{!}$ TÙR⸣ [0]
4 1 GIŠ.IG *ina* ŠÀ-*bi*
5 *ina* URU.NINA.KI
6 *gab-di* ^{m}*na-ha-ra-ú*
7 *gab-di* $^{md+}$PA-*u-a*
e.8 *gab-di* ^{m}*ku-ma-*⸢*a*⸣*-a*
9 *ú-piš-ma* ^{m}*di-li*[*l*$^{!}$—^{d}15]
r.1 TA* IGI ^{m}DI.KUD—*kur-ba-*⸢*il*$^{!}$⸣
2 *ina* ŠÀ 30 ⸢GÍN⸣.MEŠ KUG.UD
3 *il-qi kas-pu gam-mur*
4 *ta-*SUM*-ni* É *šu-a-te*
5 ⸢*za*⸣*-ar-pi la-*⸢*qi*⸣
6 ⸢*tú*⸣*-a-ru* ⸢*de-e*⸣*-*[*nu*]
7 DUG$_{4}$.DUG$_{4}$ *la-*⸢*áš*⸣*-*[*šú*]
8 *man-nu šá i-*GIL*-u-ni*
9 10 MA.NA KUG.UD *i-*⸢*dan*⸣

ADD 335

1 [Seal of Dayyan-Kurbail], owner of the house being sold.

(stamp seal impression)

3 Three storehouses including a courtyard and a door, in Nineveh, adjoining (the houses of) Naharau, Nabû'a and Kummayu —

e.9 Dili[l-Issar] has contracted and bought them from Dayyan-Kurbail for 30 shekels of silver.
r.3 The money is paid completely. That house is purchased and acquired. Any revocation, lawsu[it], or litigation is voi[d].

8 Whoever breaks the contract shall pay 10 minas of silver.

153 Previous edition: AR 368. Collated by I.L. Finkel. r.1f See coll.
154 Previous editions: AR 337, NALK 93; → CIS II 16; ABC 1; KB 4 (1896) 118f; 3R 46,10 (copy); Fales Epigraphs 1. Collations: Assur 2/5. r.10 Or (less likely): LÚ*.*sar*]-*tin-ni*.

10 IGI ^{m}ARAD—$^{⌈d!⌉}$[*x* LÚ*.*qa*]-*tin*$^{!}$-*ni*
11 [IG]I ^{m}DÙG—I[M—*x x x x*]
rest broken away

s.1 IGI ^{m}*lu—šá-kín* IGI ^{md}UTU—⌈*x*⌉[*x x x*]
2 IGI ^{md}PA—PAB—AŠ IGI $^{m⌈}$BE$^{!⌉}$-*ma*—DINGIR.MEŠ ITI.N[E]

3 UD-22 *lim-mu* ^{md}30—PAB.MEŠ—SU LUG[AL KUR—*aš-šur*]
rs.1 *dynkrbʾ*[*l*]

10 Witness Urda-[..., *ti*]*ller*.
11 Witness Ṭab-š[ar-...].
(Break)
s.1 Witness Lu-šakin. Witness Šamaš-[...].
2 Witness Nabû-ahu-iddina. Witness Šumma-ilani.
3 Month Ab (V), 22nd day, eponym year of Sennacherib, ki[ng of Assyria].
rs.1 (Aramaic caption:) Dayyan-Kurbaʾi[l].

155. A Fragmentary Real Estate Sale (687-VII-15)

82-5-22,32

beginning broken away
1′ *x*[*x x x x x x x x x x*]
2′ D[U$^{?}$-*u-ni x x x x x x x x x*]
3′ TA [*x x x x x x x x x*]

4′ É [*x x x x x x x x x*]
5′ SUHUR UR[U.ŠE—*x x x x x*]
6′ SUHUR URU.Š[E$^{?}$—*x x x x x*]

7′ ^{md}BA.Ú—[*x x x x x x x x x*]
8′ 3$^{?}$ DUMU.MÍ.MEŠ-[*šú x x* PAB *x* ZI.MEŠ]

9′ *ú-piš*-[*ma* ^{m}*x x x x x x*]
10′ *ina* ŠÀ 1-*me* [*x* MA.NA URUDU.MEŠ]
11′ T[A* IG]I ^{m}[*x x x x x*]
rest broken away
Rev. beginning broken away
1′ IGI [^{m}*x x x x x x x x*]
2′ IGI ^{m}*mar*-[*x x x x x*]
3′ IGI ^{m}*rém-an-ni*—[*x x* LÚ.*x x*]
4′ IGI ^{m}*it-ta*-[*x x x* LÚ.*x x*]
5′ IGI ^{m}GIG—*a*-[*da-lal* LÚ.*x x x*]
6′ IGI ^{m}SUHUŠ—^{d}[*x* LÚ.*x x x*]
7′ IGI ^{m}SUHUŠ—^{d}PA LÚ.[*x x x*]

8′ ITI.DUL UD-15-KÁM [*lim-mu* ^{md}30—PAB.MEŠ—SU]
9′ LUGAL KUR—[*aš-šur*.KI]

ADD 456

(Beginning destroyed)
1 [...... *adjoining the road that*]
2 *le*[*ads from ... to ....*]
3 from [......];
4 an estate [of x hectares of land ......]
5 adjoining the vil[lage of ......]
6 adjoining the *villa*[*ge* of ......]
7 Babu-[......],
8 [his] *3* daughters [and ..., a total of x persons] —
9 [...] has contracted [and bought] (said property) for *100* [minas of copper] from [...]
(Break)

r.1 Witness [......]
2 Witness Mar-[......]
3 Witness Remanni-[......]
4 Witness Itta[......]
5 Witness Marṣiš-a[dallal, ...]
6 Witness Ubru-[......].
7 Witness Ubru-Nabû, [...].
8 Month Tishri (VII), 15th day, [eponym year of Sennacherib], king of [Assyria].

156. Pre-payment for a Slave (687-VII-18)

83-1-18,364

1 1 MA.NA KUG.UD 30$^{!}$ GÍN.MEŠ
2 *ša* ^{m}*man-nu—ki—arba-ìl*
3 *ina* IGI ^{m}ARAD—*ia-ar-da*$^{!}$-*a*

ADD 100

1 One mina 30 shekels of silver belonging to Mannu-ki-Arbail, at the disposal of Urda-Yardâ.

155 Previous edition: AR 451.
156 Previous editions: AR 636, NALK 150. Collations: Assur 2/5. r.6 See coll.

4 ^{m}*mu-na-bi-du*
5 *a-du* 5$^{!}$ UD.MEŠ *ú-ba-la*
6 *šum-ma la id-din*
7 ^{m}ARAD—*ia-ar-da*$^{!}$*-a*
e.8 *ú-šal-la-ma*
r.1 ^{m}SU—^{d}IM EN—ŠU.2.MEŠ
2 IGI ^{m}I—DINGIR
3 IGI ^{m}*bi-iʾ-šu*
4 IGI ^{m}*la—tú-*TÉŠ*-ana—*DINGIR
5 IGI ^{m}AD—*ul*—ZU

6 ITI.DUL UD-18$^{!!}$-KAM
7 *lim-mu* ^{m}30—PAB.MEŠ—SU
8 MAN KUR—*aš-šur*
s.1 IGI ^{m}*si-par-a-nu*

4 He shall bring Munnabidu within 5 days. If he does not give (him), Urda-Yardâ shall pay it back in full.

r.1 Riba-Adad is the guarantor.
2 Witness Na'di-ilu.
3 Witness Bi'šu.
4 Witness La-tubašanni-ilu.
5 Witness Abi-ul-idi.
6 Month Tishri (VII), 18th day, eponym year of Sennacherib, king of Assyria.
s.1 Witness Sipranu.

157. Mannu-ki-Arbail Loans Copper (687-VII-20)

K 413

1 ⌜3⌝1 MA.NA URUDU.MEŠ SAG.DU
2 *šá* ^{d}15 *šá* URU.*arba-ìl*
3 ^{m}GÌR.2—^{d}IM
4 TA* IGI ^{m}*man-nu—ki*—URU.[*arba-ìl*]
5 *ina pu-u*$^{!}$*-hi i-*⌜*ti*⌝*-*[*ši*]
6 *ina* UD-1-KÁM *šá*$^{!}$ IT[I.*x*]
e.7 *i-da-*[*an*]
8 *šúm-mu l*[*a* SUM]*-ni*
r.1 *a-na* 3-*s*[*i*$^{!}$*-šú*]
2 *i-rab-b*[*i*]
3 IGI ^{m}DÙG.GA—IM—[*x x*]
4 IGI ^{m}AD—*la-rim*
5 IGI ^{m}*ia—da-du*
6 [IG]I ^{m}*bal-ṭa-a-a*
7 [IGI] ^{m}*qu-u-ia* IGI ^{m}*za*$^{!}$-[*x x*]
8e IGI ^{md}PA—PAB.MEŠ—SU

9e ITI.DU$_{6}$ UD-20-KÁM
10e *lim-me* ^{m}30—PAB.MEŠ—[SU]

ADD 43

1 *31* minas of copper, capital, belonging to Ištar of Arbela —
3 Šep-Adad has tak[en] it as a loan from Mannu-ki-[Arbail].
6 He shall pay on the 1st of [...]. If he does n[ot pay], it will increase by a thi[rd].

r.3 Witness Ṭab-šar-[...].
4 Witness Abi-larim.
5 Witness Ya-dadu.
6 Witness Balṭayu.
7 Witness Quya. Witness Za[...].
8 Witness Nabû-ahhe-riba.
9 Month Tishri (VII), 20th day, eponym year of Sennache[rib].

158. A Futures Contract in Wine (687-IX-3)

K 423

1 [*x x x*].MEŠ *ša* KUR.*gar-ga-mis*
2 $^{\ulcorner m!\urcorner}$*q*[*ur*$^{?}$*-b*]*u*$^{!}$—AD-*u-a*
3 *a-na* ^{m}EN—PAB.MEŠ *ina* ŠÀ-*bi*
4 9 ANŠE GEŠTIN.MEŠ *ina* (GIŠ).BÁN *ša* 9 *qa*
5 *ina* KUR.É—*za-ma-a-ni* SUM-*na*
6 [*šum*]-*ma la* SUM-*ni a-ki ma-hi-ri*
7 [*šá* U]RU.NINA SUM-⌜*an*$^{!}$⌝
r.1 IGI ^{m}*ri-ba-a-a*

ADD 125

1 *Q*[*urb*]*u*-abu'a shall repay [x *shekels of silver*] of Carchemish to Bel-ahhe with 9 homers of wine, by the seah of 9 'litres,' in Bit-Zamani.
6 [I]f he does not, he shall pay according to the market price [of] Nineveh.
r.1 Witness Ribaya.

157 Previous editions: AR 281, NALK 151. r.17 DUL$^{!}$.
158 Previous edition: AR 218. Collated by I.L. Finkel. 2 See coll.

2 IGI ^{m}*ba-ti-i-ti*
3 LÚ.*še-la-pa-a-a* IGI ^{m}GÌR.2—*aš-šur*
4 IGI ^{m}*ú-bu-ku*
5 IGI ^{m}*man-nu—ki*—URU.NINA
6 IGI ^{md}PA—EN—DINGIR.MEŠ

7 ITI.GAN UD-3-KÁM
8 [*lim-me*] ^{md}30—PAB.MEŠ—SU

2 Witness Batiti, *architect*.
3 Witness Šep-Aššur.
4 Witness Ubbuku.
5 Witness Mannu-ki-Ninua.
6 Witness Nabû-bel-ilani.
7 Month Kislev (IX), 3rd day, [eponym year of] Sennacherib.

159. Sale of a Building Plot Near Arbela (687)

Rm 185

1 ⸢*ku*⸣-[*u*]*m* NA_4.KIŠIB-*šú* ⸢*ṣu*⸣-*p*[*ur-šú iš-kun*]

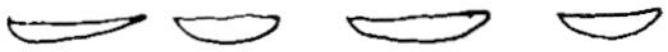

2 *ṣu-pur* ^{md}AG—*še-zib-a-ni* [*x x!*]
3 *kaq-qi-ri pu-ṣe-*⸢*e*⸣
4 *ina ku-tal-li ša* URU.*arba-ì*[*l*]
5 SUHUR A.ŠÀ *ša* ^{m}*ṭu-ki-*⸢*i*⸣$^{!}$ [0]
6 [SUHUR A.Š]À ^{md}⸢AG⸣$^{!}$—[*x x x*]
rest broken away
Rev. beginning broken away
1′ ⸢IGI⸣$^{!}$ [*x x x x x x*]
blank space of three lines
2′ IGI ^{md}30—AD—PAB L[Ú].A.[BA]
3′ *ṣa-bit* IM ITI.[*x* UD-*x*-KAM]
4′ *lim-mu* ^{md}3[0$^{!}$—PAB.MEŠ—SU]

ADD 353

1 Instead of his seal [he impressed his] fingern[ail].

(fingernail impressions)

2 Fingernail of Nabû-šezibanni, [...].
3 A vacant lot behind the city of Arbela, adjoining the field of Ṭukî and [the fiel]d of Nabû-[...]
(Break)

r.1 Witness [......].
2 Witness Sin-abu-uṣur, scri[be], keeper of the tablet.
3 Month [..., ...th] day, eponym year of Se[nnacherib].

160. Ribate Buys an Estate of Three Hectares (687-X-7)

83-1-18,342

1 NA_4.⸢KIŠIB ^{m}*man-nu—lu*$^{!}$*-sa*⸣$^{!}$*-me*$^{!}$
2 NA_4.KIŠIB ^{md}IM—PAB-⸢*ir*⸣$^{!}$
3 NA_4.KIŠIB ^{m}*ṭa-bu-su*
4 EN A.ŠÀ SUM-[*ni*]

5 É 3 ANŠE *bu-u-ru dan-nu*
6 É 4BÁN$^{!}$ *e-nu bir-ti*$^{!}$ *hi-ri-a*$^{!}$*-te*
7 SUHUR *hi-ri-te* SUHUR ^{m}PAB—SIG
8 SUHUR A.ŠÀ *šá* ^{m}ITI.AB-*a-a*
9 SUHUR ^{m}DINGIR—*ka-bar* SUHUR *hi-ri-te*
10 SUHUR A.ŠÀ *šá* ^{m}PAB—*ú-qur*
11 SUHUR A.ŠÀ *šá* ^{m}*sa-a-si-i*

ADD 624

1 Seal of Mannu-lus[a]me,
2 seal of Adad-naṣir,
3 seal of Ṭabussu,
4 owners of the land being sold.

(blank seal space)

5 An estate of 3 hectares, (with) a big well;
6 an estate of 4 decares with a spring between the ditches, adjoining a ditch, (the field of) Ahu-damqu, the field of Kanunayu, Ilu-kabar, a ditch, and the fields of Ahu-uqur and Sasî —

159 Previous edition: AR 335. Collations: Assur 2/5.
160 Previous editions: AR 135, NALK 292. → no. 161. 1f, 6, 13, r.15 See coll.

12 ⌜*ú*⌝-*piš-ma* ^{m}*ri-ba-te*
13 *ina* ŠÀ 25$^{!}$ ⌜GÍN⌝.MEŠ KUG.UD A.Š[À]
14 *a-na* M[U$^{!}$.AN.NA].MEŠ A.ŠÀ ⌜*e*⌝-[*kal*]
15 ⌜*e*$^{!}$⌝-*r*[*a-áš e-ṣi-id*] ⌜*x x*⌝ [*x x*]
16 ⌜*x x x x*⌝ [*x x x x*]

r.1 *e-da-nu šá-kí*[*n*$^{!}$ *x x* KUG.UD]
2 *ina* UGU *ta-ra-m*[*e i-ša-ku-nu*]
3 0$^{!}$ *ú-še-ṣu-*[*u*]

---

4 IGI ^{m}*šúm-ma*—[DINGIR LÚ.SANGA]
5 IGI ^{md}ME.ME—MU—[GIŠ]
6 IGI ^{m}ŠÚ—DÙ IGI ^{m}PAB—*la*-⌜*maš*⌝-[*ši*]

7 IGI ^{m}MA.MÚ—*iq*-⌜*bi*⌝
8 IGI ^{m}KÁ.DINGIR.KI-*a-a* ^{m}PAB—AŠ
9 IGI ^{m}ITI.AB-*a-a* ^{m}⌜SUHUŠ⌝—^{d}15
10 IGI ^{m}*mu-qa-li-i*
11 IGI ^{m}HÉ.NUN-*a-a* ^{m}*iz-bu*
12 IGI ^{md}PA—*šá-kín*—DI-*mu*
13 IGI ^{m}*di-na-nu*
14 IGI ^{md}PA—DÙ—A LÚ*.A.BA

15 ITI.AB UD-7$^{!}$-KÁM ⌜*lim-mu*⌝ ^{m}30—PAB.MEŠ—SU
16 ⌜LUGAL⌝ KUR—*aš-šur*.K[I]

12 Ribate has contracted and shall enjoy the land for y[ears] for 25 shekels of silver.

15 He shall cultiv[ate and reap it *for x fallow and x crop years*].

r.1 The term is fixe[d. They shall place the silver] upon the corn heap, and shall redeem (their land).

---

4 Witness Šumma-[ilu, priest].
5 Witness Gula-šumu-[lešir].
6 Witness Marduk-ibni. Witness Ahu-lâmašši.
7 Witness Mamu-iqbi.
8 Witness Babilayu. Ahu-iddina.
9 Witness Kanunayu. Ubru-Issar.
10 Witness Muqallî.
11 Witness Nuhšaya. Izbu.
12 Witness Nabû-šakin-šulmi.
13 Witness Dinanu.
14 Witness Nabû-bani-apli, scribe.
15 Month Tebet (X), 7day, eponym year of Sennacherib, king of Assyria.

161. Ribate Adds to his Land (686-X-7)

Bu 91-5-9,209

1 NA$_4$.KIŠIB ^{m}*man-nu—li-s*[*a-me*]
2 NA$_4$.KIŠIB ^{md}IM—PAB-*ir*$^{!}$
3 NA$_4$.KIŠIB ^{m}*ṭa-bu-su*
4 NA$_4$.KIŠIB ^{md}IM—*iq-bi* EN A.ŠÀ SU[M-*ni*]

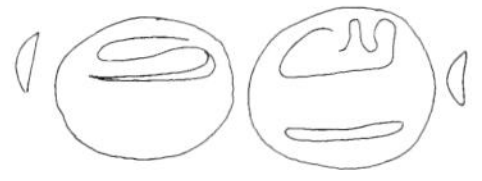

---

5 É 1 ANŠE 3BÁN A.ŠÀ *bir-ti hi*-⌜*ri*⌝-*a-te*
6 SUHUR A.ŠÀ *ša*$^{!}$ ^{m}ITI.AB-*a-a* [0]
7 SUHUR A.ŠÀ *ša* ^{m}*mu-qa*-⌜*li-i*⌝
8 SUHUR A.ŠÀ *ša* ^{m}HÉ.NUN-*a-a* [0]
9 SUHUR A.ŠÀ *ša* ^{m}*mu-še-zib*—^{d}[*x x*]
10 *ú-piš-ma* ^{m}*ri-ba-a-*[*te*]
11 *ina* ŠÀ-*bi* 4 GÍN.MEŠ KUG.[UD]
12 TA* IGI LÚ.MEŠ *an-nu-*[*te*]
13 A.ŠÀ *i-zi-rip i-s*[*i-qi*]
e.14 *kas-pu ga-mur ta-*[*din*]
15 A.ŠÀ *šu-a-tú za-rip l*[*a-qi*]
16 *tu-a-ru de-e-nu* DUG$_4$.[DUG$_4$]

ADD 374

1 Seal of Mannu-lis[ame],
2 seal of Adad-naṣir,
3 seal of Ṭabussu,
4 seal of Adad-iqbi, owners of the land being s[old].

(fingernail and stamp seal impressions)

---

5 An estate of 1 hectare 3 decares of land between ditches, adjoining the fields of Kanunayu, Muqallî, Nuhšaya, and Mušezib-[...] —

10 Ribate has contracted, purchased, and b[ought] the field from the[se] men for 4 shekels of sil[ver].

e.14 The money is pa[id] completely. That field is purchased and acq[uired]. Any revo-

161 Previous editions: AR 397, NALK 293. 1 See coll.

17 *la-a-šú*
r.1 *man-nu ša ur-kiš ina ma-a-*⸢*te*⸣*-m*[*a*]
2 *ša i-za-qup-an-ni lu-u* LÚ*$^{!}$.[MEŠ *an-nu-te*]
3 *lu* DUMU.MEŠ-*šú-nu lu* PAB.MEŠ-*šú-n*[*u*]
4 *lu mám-ma-nu-šú-nu* TA* ^{m}SU.MEŠ-*t*[*e*]
5 *ù* DUMU.MEŠ-*šú* DUMU—DUMU.MEŠ-*šú*
6 *de-e-nu* DUG$_4$.DUG$_4$ *ub-ta-ʾu-u-ni*
7 *kas-pu a-na* 10-*a-te a-na* EN.MEŠ-*šú*$^{!}$
8 GUR-*ra ina de-ni-šú* DUG$_4$.DUG$_4$-*ub*
9 *là* TI

---

10 IGI ^{md}ŠÚ—DÙ ^{m}⸢PAB⸣—AŠ
11 IGI ^{m}*šúm-ma*—DINGIR LÚ*.⸢SANGA⸣
12 IGI ^{m}PAB—*la-maš-ši* ^{m}⸢U.GUR⸣—MAŠ
13 IGI ^{m}MA.MÚ—*iq-bi*

14 IGI ^{m}ITI.AB-*a-a* ^{m}DINGIR—*ka-bar*
15 IGI ^{md}UTU—*rém-a-ni* ^{m}SUHUŠ—15
16 IGI ^{m}*mu-qa-li-i* ^{m}HÉ.NUN-*a-a*
17 IGI ^{md}PA—DÙ—A LÚ*.A.BA

18e ITI.AB UD-7-KÁM *lim-mu*
19e ^{m}EN-IGI.LAL-*a-ni* LÚ*.⸢*tur-ta*⸣-[*nu*]

cation, lawsuit or li[tigation] is void.

r.1 Whoever in the future, at any time, lodges a complaint, whether [these] men or their sons, brothers or relatives, and seeks a lawsuit or litigation against Ribat[e], his sons and grandsons, shall return the money tenfold to its owners. He shall contest in his lawsuit and not succeed.

---

10 Witness Marduk-ibni. Ahu-iddina.
11 Witness Šumma-ilu, priest.
12 Witness Ahu-lâmašši. Nergal-ašared.
13 Witness Mamu-iqbi.
14 Witness Kanunayu. Ilu-kabar.
15 Witness Šamaš-remanni. Ubru-Issar.
16 Witness Muqallî. Nuhšaya.
17 Witness Nabû-bani-apli, scribe.
18 Month Tebet (X), 7th day, eponym year of Bel-emuranni, commander-in-chief.

162. —— (686-I)

83-1-18,900

1 ⸢NA$_4$⸣.KIŠIB ^{m}*x*[*x x x x x*]
2 LÚ.[*x x x x x x x x*]
3 N[A$_4$.KIŠIB ^{m}*x x x x x*]
4 N[A$_4$$^{!}$.KIŠIB ^{m}*x x x x x*]
5 N[A$_4$$^{!}$.KIŠIB ^{m}*x x x x x*]
rest broken away
Rev. beginning broken away
1′ ⸢IGI⸣ [^{m}*x x x x x x x*]
2′ IGI ^{m}[*x x x x x x x*]
3′ IGI ^{m}[*x x x x x x x*]
one line blank
4′ IGI ^{md}PA—[*x x x* LÚ.A.BA]
5′ ITI.BARAG [UD-*x*-KAM *lim-me* ^{m}EN—IGI.LAL-*ni*]
6′ [M]U.AN.NA ⸢20⸣-[KAM ^{md}30—PAB.MEŠ—SU]

ADD 535

1 Seal of [NN], ...[...],
3 [seal of NN],
4 [seal of NN],
5 [seal of NN],
(Break)

r.1 Witness [......].
2 Witness [......].
3 Witness [......].
4 Witness Nabû-[..., scribe].
5 Month Nisan (I), [...th day, eponym year of Bel-emuranni], 20th year [of Sennacherib].

163. Purchase of an Estate in Šibaniba (686-II-15)

81-7-27,25

1 [NA$_4$.KIŠIB ^{m}P]AB—BÀD
2 [EN A.ŠÀ] É UN.MEŠ SUM-*ni*

ADD 453

1 [Seal of A]hu-duri, [owner of the land], house, and people being sold.

162 Previous edition: AR 629. [1] See coll.
163 Previous edition: AR 187. Collations: Assur 2/5.

(stamp seal impressions)

3 [É *x* ANŠE A].ŠÀ É *ad-ru*
4 [*x x* É *ši*]-*qi ina* URU.*ši-ba-ni-ba*

5 [*x x x x*] ^{m}*mil-ki—su*$^{!}$-[*ri*]
6 [*x x x x x*]-⸢*a*⸣$^{!}$ MÍ-*šú* [0]
7 [*x x x x* ^{m}*ba*]*l-ṭa-a-a*
8 [*x x x* MÍ.UR]U$^{!}$.NINA$^{!}$.KI$^{!}$-⸢*i*⸣$^{!}$-[*tú*]
9 [*x x x x*]*x* ^{md}IM—S[U]
10 [*x x x x x*]-*šá*—⸢NIGÍN⸣$^{!}$-*hur* M[Í$^{!}$-*šú*]
11 [*x x x x x x*]-*tú*
rest broken away
Rev. beginning broken away
1′ [*tu-a-ru de-nu* DUG$_4$].DUG$_4$ *la-áš-šú*

2′ [*man-nu šá ina ur-kiš ina*] *ma-ti-ma*
3′ [GIL-*u-ni x* MA].NA KUG.UD 4$^{!}$ MA.[NA KUG.GI]
4′ [*a-na* ^{d}15 *a-ši-bat* U]RU$^{!}$.NINA SUM-*an*
5′ [A.ŠÀ UN.MEŠ] ⸢É⸣$^{!}$ *ú-še-ṣa*

6′ [IGI ^{m}*x x x x x*] LÚ*.*mu-kil*—KU[Š.PA.MEŠ]
7′ [IGI ^{m}*x x x*]—PAB LÚ*.A.BA
8′ [IGI ^{m}*x x x x x*]*x* A ^{m}EN—KI-*ia*
9′ [IGI ^{m}DI-*mu*]—EN—*la-áš-me* LÚ*.*mu-*[*kil*—KUŠ.PA.MEŠ]

10′ [IGI ^{md}]⸢PA⸣—*rém-a-ni* LÚ*.SIMUG.KUG.GI *šá* [*x x x*]
11′ [IGI ^{md}]PA-*u-a* LÚ*.GAL—Ì.DU$_8$
12′ [IGI ^{m}]*ú-si-i* LÚ*.GAL—*ki-ṣir*
13′ [IGI ^{m}]^{d}PA—SU LÚ*.A.BA

14′ [IGI ^{m}]URU.*arba-ìl-a-a* LÚ*.GAL—UŠ.BAR.MEŠ
15′ [IG]I ^{md}PA—GIN—A A.BA
16′ [IT]I.GUD UD-15-KAM
17′ [*lim*]-*me* ^{m}EN—IGI.LAL-*a-ni*
18′ LÚ*.*tur-ta-nu*

3 [An estate of x hectares of la]nd, a house, a threshing floor, [..., irri]gated [land] in Šibaniba;

5 [...] Milki-su[ri], his wife [NN, ...];

7 [B]alṭaya [..., his wife] Ninui[tu, ...];

9 Adad-er[iba, his] wi[fe ...]ša-*lishur*, [...]
(Break)

r.1 [Any revocation, lawsuit, or litigat]ion is void.

2 [Whoever in the future, at any t]ime, breaks the contract, shall pay [x min]as of silver and 4 min[as of gold to Ištar residing in] Nineveh, (and) shall redeem [*the field, the people and the ho*]*use*.

---

6 [Witness NN], chariot dr[iver].

7 [Witness ...]-uṣur, scribe.

8 [Witness ...] son of Bel-isse'a.

9 [Witness Šulmu]-beli-lašme, cha[riot driver].

10 [Witness Na]bû-remanni, goldsmith of [...].

11 [Witness] Nabû'a, head porter.

12 [Witness] Usi', cohort commander.

13 [Witness] Nabû-eriba, scribe.

14 [Witness] Arbailayu, chief weaver.

15 [Wit]ness Nabû-ka''in-aplu, scribe.

16 Month Iyyar (II), 15th day, eponym year of Bel-emuranni, commander-in-chief.

164. ——- (686-III-9)

K 1576 + Rm 163

1 [NA$_4$.KIŠIB ^{m}mar$^{?}$-d]u$^{!}$-⸢ú⸣ LÚ*.GAL—URU.MEŠ

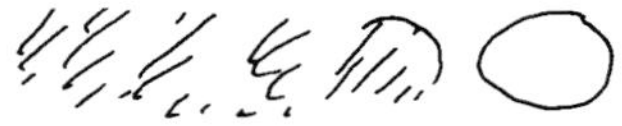

about 7 lines broken away

9 ⸢i⸣$^{!}$-[x x x x x x x]

10 ⸢šu⸣$^{!}$-[a-tu za-rip u]p$^{!}$-pu

11 la$^{!}$-[qi tu-a-ru]

12 de$^{!}$-[n]i$^{!}$ [DUG$_4$.DUG$_4$ la-áš]-šú

13 man-nu ⸢ša⸣$^{!}$ [ina EGIR-at UD-me]

e.14 e-la-a[n-ni x x x x]

15 kas-pi$^{!}$ im-hur-nu

r.1 a-na 10-a-a [[a-a$^{!}$]]

2 a-na EN-šú GUR

3 IGI ^{m}man-nu—ki—15$^{!!}$—ZU$^{!!}$

4 LÚ*.GAL—ki-ṣir ša MÍ—É.GAL

5 IGI ^{m}ba-nu-nu LÚ*.GAL—ki-ṣir KI.MIN

6 IGI ^{m}ITI.KIN-a-a LÚ*.qur-bu-tú

7 [IGI] ^{md}MAŠ-i LÚ*.GAL—da-a-a-[li]

8 [ša U]RU.kal-ha

9 [IGI ^{m}]ARAD—15 LÚ*.SIMUG.KUG.[GI]

10 [IGI ^{m}]^{d}MAŠ—ra$^{!}$-ši IGI ^{m}[x x x]

11 IGI ^{md}PA—MAN—PAB LÚ*.3-šú

12 ša MÍ—É.GAL

13 IGI ^{m}na-bu-u-a-a

14 LÚ*.GIŠ.GIGIR ša—GÌR.2

15 IGI ^{m}na-bu-u-a-a

16 IGI ^{m}ku-si-si-i

17 lim-me ^{m}EN—IGI.LAL-a-ni LÚ*.tur-ta-[nu]

18 ITI.SIG$_4$ UD-9-KAM

19e IGI ^{md}PA—NUMUN—AŠ

20e ṣa-bit [ṭup-pi]

ADD 612

1 [Seal of *Mar*d]û, village manager.

(Seal impressions)

(Break)

10 That [... is acquired, *p*]*aid* and tak[en over. Any revocation], lawsu[it or litigation is vo]id.

13 Whoever [in the future] comes forwa[rd and breaks the contract], shall return the money he has received tenfold to its owner.

r.3 Witness Mannu-ki-Issar-le'i, cohort commander of the queen.

5 Witness Banunu, cohort commander ditto.

6 Witness Ululayu, royal bodyguard.

7 [Witness] Nurtî, chief scout of Calah.

9 [Witness] Urda-Issar, goldsmith.

10 [Witness] Inurta-raši. Witness [NN].

11 Witness Nabû-šarru-uṣur, 'third man' of the queen.

13 Witness Nabû'aya, horse trainer of the *ša-šēpi* guard.

15 Witness Nabû'aya.

16 Witness Kusisî.

17 Eponym year of Bel-emuranni, commander-in-chief. Month Sivan (III), 9th day.

19 Witness Nabû-zeru-iddina, keeper of [the tablet].

165. ——-

83-1-18,391

beginning broken away

1′ [x x x x x x x x x x]x

2′ [x x x x x x x x x x]-mis

3′ [x x x x x x x x x x] ša

ADD 594

(Beginning destroyed)

164 Previous edition: AR 558. 1, 10, 15 See coll. r.3 Tablet ^{m}man-nu—ki—16—SU (see coll.); scribal error. r.10 See coll.

165 Previous edition: AR 581. This tablet is datable to about 686 B.C. on the basis of the witness list (cf. no. 164, Mannu-ki-Issar-le'i, Banunu).

4′ [*x x x x x x x x x*] LUH
5′ [*x x x x x x x x x*]-*u-ni*
6′ [*x* MA.NA KUG.UD] 2? MA.NA KUG.GI
r.1 [*ina bur-ki* ^{d}IŠ].TAR *ša* URU.NINA
2 [*i-šak*]-*kan*
3 [*kas-pu a-na* 10].MEŠ-*te*
4 [*a-na* EN.MEŠ]-*šú* GUR
5 [*ina de-ni-šú* DU]G$_4$.DUG$_4$-*ma là* TI

6 [He shall pl]ace [x minas of silver and] *two* minas of gold [in the lap of Iš]tar of Nineveh, and shall return [the money ten]fold [to] its [owners. He shall co]ntest [in his lawsuit] and not succeed.

---

6 [IGI ^{m}*x x x x*] GAL—*ki-ṣir ša* MÍ.KUR

7 [IGI ^{md}P]A—I :.
8 [IGI ^{m}*ba*]-*nu-nu* [:.]
9 [IGI ^{m}*man-n*]*u—ki*—^{d}15—ZU
rest broken away

6 [Witness NN], cohort commander of the queen.
7 [Witness Na]bû-na'id, ditto.
8 [Witness Ba]nunu, [ditto].
9 [Witness Mann]u-ki-Issar-le'i.
(Rest destroyed)

166. Fragmentary Sale of Slaves (686-IV-1)

K 308

1 NA$_4$.KIŠIB ^{m}*sar-ú-ar-ri*
2 EN UN.MEŠ SUM-*ni*

---

3 NA$_4$.KIŠIB ^{m}*mar—sam-si* LÚ.2-*u*
4 NA$_4$.KIŠIB ^{m}*se-e*—⌜NU?⌝ LÚ.GAL—É
5 NA$_4$.KIŠIB ^{m}*se-e—ha*-⌜*ti*!⌝ LÚ.*šá*—UGU—URU
6 NA$_4$.KIŠIB ^{m}*na*!-*hi*-⌜*ra*!⌝-[*x* LÚ.*m*]*u-kil*—KUŠ.PA.MEŠ
rest broken away
Rev. beginning broken away
1′ [*x x x x x x x x x*] *la laq-qi*

2′ IGI ^{m}*zi-zi-i* LÚ.DAM.QAR
3′ IGI ^{m}*pa-ru-ṭu*
4′ IGI ^{m}*iq-bi*—DINGIR IGI ^{md}30—PAB-*ir*
5′ IGI ^{m}*ab-di—a*-⌜*zu*!⌝-*zi* IGI ^{m}*ka-ku-si*
6′ IGI ^{m}ARAD—^{d}UTU [IGI ^{md}]UTU—SU

7′ IGI ^{m}I—DINGIR I[GI ^{md}]ŠÚ—SU
8′ IGI ^{md}30—PAB-*ir* LÚ.NIGÍR

9′ ITI.ŠU UD-1-KÁM *lim-mu* ^{md}EN—IGI.LAL-*an-ni*
10′ LÚ.*tur-tan-nu*

ADD 285

1 Seal of Sar-uarri, owner of the people being sold.

(blank seal space)

---

3 seal of Mar-samsi, deputy,
4 seal of Se'-..., major-domo,
5 seal of Se'-hati, city overseer,
6 seal of Nahira[*nu*, chari]ot driver,
(Break)

r.1 [He shall contest in his lawsuit and] not succeed.

---

2 Witness Zizî, merchant.
3 Witness Paruṭṭu.
4 Witness Iqbi-ilu. Witness Sin-naṣir.
5 Witness Abdi-Azuzi. Witness Kakkussu.
6 Witness Urda-Šamaš. Witness Šamaš-eriba.
7 Witness Na'di-ilu. Wi[tness] Marduk-eriba.
8 Witness Sin-naṣir, herald.
9 Month Tammuz (IV), 1st day, eponym year of Bel-emuranni, commander-in-chief.

166 Previous edition: AR 550. Collated by I.L. Finkel. 4, 6, r.5 See coll.

167. Note of Silver Owed to Bel-lamur (686-VIII-20)

79-7-8,189

1 1 1/2 MA.NA KUG.UD *ina* 1 *ma-né-e šá* MAN
2 *ša* ^{m}EN—*la-mur*
3 *ina pa-an* ^{m}*suk-ku-a-a*
4 *ina* ITI.AB KUG.UD *i-dan*
5 *šúm-ma la i-din a-na* 4-*tú-šú*
6 KUG.UD *i-rab-bi*
e.7 IGI ^{m}*a-zi-i*
8 IGI ^{m}EN—KASKAL—BÀD
r.1 IGI ^{m}U.GUR—DÙ
2 IGI ^{m}DI-*mu*—EN—*la-áš-me*
3 IGI ^{md}PA.TÚG—DINGIR-*a-a*
4 IGI ^{md}PA—SU
5 IGI ^{md}PA—EN—MU.MEŠ LÚ*.Ì.DU$_8$
1 line space
6 ITI.APIN UD-20-KÁM
7 *lim-mu* ^{m}EN—IGI-*a-ni*

ADD 9

1 1 1/2 minas of silver by the mina of the king belonging to Bel-lamur, at the disposal of Sukkaya.

4 He shall pay in Tebet (X). If he does not, the silver shall increase by a fourth.

7 Witness Azî.

8 Witness Bel-Harran-duri.

r.1 Witness Nergal-ibni.

2 Witness Šulmu-beli-lašme.

3 Witness Nušku-ila'i.

4 Witness Nabû-eriba.

5 Witness Nabû-bel-šumati, porter.

6 Month Marchesvan (VIII), 20th day, eponym year of Bel-emuranni.

168. —— (686)

K 1864

1 [NA$_4$.KIŠIB ^{m}]⸢*a*!⸣-*da*!—*na-a*-⸢*gi*!⸣
2 [EN *x x x*] *ta-da-ni*

rest broken away
Rev. beginning broken away
1′ [IGI ^{m}*x x x x*] ⸢*hi*? *x*⸣
2′ [IGI ^{m}*x x x x*]-*e*
3′ [IGI ^{m}*x x x x*]-*u-a*
4′ [ITI.*x* UD-*x*-KÁM]
5e [*lim-mu* ^{m}EN—IGI].LAL-*an-ni*
6e [LÚ.*tur-t*]*a-a-nu*

ADD 482

1 [Seal of] Adda-nagi, [owner of the ...] being sold.

(stamp seal impressions)

(Break)

r.4 Month [..., xth day, eponym year of Bel-em]uranni, [commander]-in-chief.

169. Purchase of 30 Hectares of Land, People, and Fowl (686)

Bu 91-5-9,95

1 NA$_4$.KIŠIB ^{m}*ga-di*—DINGIR
2 EN A.ŠÀ UN.MEŠ MUŠEN.MEŠ SUM-*an*

ADD 443

1 Seal of Gadi-il, owner of the land, people, and fowl being sold.

167 Previous editions: AR 249, NALK 80. Copy: Cat. 1715.
168 Previous edition: AR 559.
169 Previous editions: AR 97, NALK 386. Collations: Assur 2/5.

(space for stamp seal impressions)

3 ⸢É⸣ 30 ANŠE A.ŠÀ SUHUR KASKAL—LUGAL
4 [*šá* TA* U]RU.*ma-li-ia-ti*
5 [*a-na* UR]U.*kan-nu-u*ʾ DU-*ku-u-ni*
6 [SUHUR *na-hal*]-*li šá* TA* URU.*a-di-an*
7 [*a*]-*na* URU.Š[E]—^{m}[*x*]-⸢*x*⸣-*ha*! DU-*ku-u-ni*
8 SUHUR KASKAL *šá* TA* URU.ŠE—DINGIR
9 *a-na* URU.*kan-nu-u*ʾ DU-⸢*ku*⸣-[*u*]-*ni*
10 ⸢*a*⸣-*di* UGU ÍD *ina* Š[À *x x x*]
11 [*ka*]*q-qi-*[*ri p*]*u-ṣe-e ina* URU.[*x x x*]
12 ⸢^{m}*tar*⸣-*hu-*⸢*un*⸣-*dáp*!-*pi-i* LÚ.*x*[*x x x*]
13 [*x x x x x*]*x-šu* DUMU-[*šu* 0]
14 [*x x x x x x x x*] MÍ-[*šu*]
rest broken away

Rev. beginning broken away
1′ [*kas-pu ga-m*]*ur* ⸢*ta-din*⸣ [A.ŠÀ]
2′ [U]N.MEŠ MUŠEN.MEŠ *šu-a-t*[*e zar-pu* TI-*u*]
3′ [*tu*]-⸢*a*⸣-*ru de-e-nu* DUG_4.[DUG_4 *la-áš-šú*]

4′ [*man-nu šá ina ur*]-*kiš ina mat-e-ma* G[IL-*u-ni*]
5′ [*kas-pu a*]-*na* 10.MEŠ-*te a-na* E[N.MEŠ-*šú* GUR]
6′ [*ina de*]-*ni-šu* DUG_4.DUG_4-*m*[*a la* TI]

7′ [IGI ^{m}*x x*]-⸢*i*!⸣ DUMU ^{m}[*x x x x*]
4 lines destroyed
13′ [IGI ^{m}*x x x x*] ⸢*x x*⸣ [*x*]
14′ [IGI ^{m}*x x x*]—*aṣ-bat*! LÚ.Ì.⸢DU_8⸣
15′ [ITI.*x*] UD-12-KÁM
16′ [*lim-mu* ^{m}EN—I]GI.LAL-*an-ni* LÚ*.*tur-tan*

3 An estate of 30 hectares of land adjoining the king's road leading [from] Maliyati [to] Kannu', [the *w*]*adi* running from Adi*an* to the vill[age] of [...]ha, and the road leading from the village of the god to Kannu', all the way to the river, i[n ...];

11 [a vac]an[t l]ot in the city [of ...];

12 Tarhundapî [..., his] son [NN, his] wife [...]

(Break)

r.1 [The money] is paid [comp]letely. Th[at land, peo]ple, and fowl [are purchased and acquired. Any revo]cation, [law]suit or liti[gation is void].

4 [Whoever in the fu]ture, at any time, bre[aks the contract, shall return the money] tenfold to [its] own[ers]. He shall contest [in] his [law]suit and [not succeed].

7 [Witness ...]î, son of [...].
(Break)
13 [Witness ...]-aṣbat, porter.
14 [Month ...], 12th day, [eponym year of Bel-e]muranni, commander-in-chief.

170. Note of Copper Owed to Kur-ila'i (685-II-16)

Ki 1904-10-9,182

1 40! MA.NA URUDU.MEŠ
2 *ša* ^{m}*kur*—DINGIR-*a-a*
3 *ina* IGI ^{m}*qí-bit*—15
4 *a-na* 3-*si-šú-nu* GAL-*u*
5 ITI.GUD UD-16-KÁM
6 *lim-me* ^{m}*aš-šur*—KALAG-*in-an-ni*
r.1 IGI ^{m}AD—*ul*—ZU
2 IGI ^{m}U.U!—*bu-nu*
3 IGI ^{m}*si-na-a*
4 IGI ^{m}*ta-bal-a-a*

ADD 1190

1 40 minas of copper belonging to Kur-ila'i, at the disposal of Qibit-Issar.

4 It will increase by a third.

5 Month Iyyar (II), 16th day, eponym year of Aššur-da''inanni.

r.1 Witness Abi-ul-idi.
2 Witness Dadi-bunu.
3 Witness Sinâ.
4 Witness Tabalayu.

6 Or (since the formula is otherwise attested only with roads): [SUHUR *hu*]-*li* "(adjoining) the ro]ad ...".
170 Tablet. Previous edition: NALK 143b. 1, r.2 See coll.

171. Envelope of the Preceding Text (685-II-16)

Ki 1904-10-9,183

beginning broken away
1′ [*a-na* 3-*s*]*i*-⸢*šú*⸣-*nu* GAL-[*u*]
2′ ITI.GUD UD-16-KÁM
3e [*li*]*m-me* ^{m}*aš-šur*—KALAG-*in-an-ni*
r.1′ [I]GI ^{m}AD—*ul*—ZU
2′ [I]GI ^{m}U.U$^{!}$—*bu-nu*

3′ [IG]I ^{m}*si-na-a*
4′ [IGI] ^{m}*ta-bal-a-*[*a*]
5′ [IGI ^{m}]^{d}PA—*rém-a-ni*

ADD 1191

(Beginning destroyed)
1 will increase by a third.
2 Month Iyyar (II), 16th day, eponym year of Aššur-da''inanni.
r.1 Witness Abi-ul-idi.
2 Witness Dadi-bunu.

(cylinder seal impression)

3 [Witne]ss Sinâ.
4 [Witness] Tabalayu.
5 [Witness] Nabû-remanni.

172. Purchase of Slaves (685-VII-26)

80-7-19,53

1 NA$_{4}$.KIŠIB ^{m}*ti-ri-i* LÚ*.GAR-*nu*
2 URU.KASKAL-*a*$^{!}$-*a*$^{!}$ EN UN.MEŠ SUM-*ni*

3 [*x x x x x*] ⸢*x x*⸣—[^{d}]⸢*na-na-a*$^{!}$⸣ MÍ-*šú*
4 [*x x x x x x x x* PAB] 6 ZI.MEŠ
rest broken away
Rev. beginning broken away
1′ [*x x x x*]*x* ⸢*x*⸣ [*x x x*]
2′ [IGI ^{m}*x x x x*]—A$^{!}$ LÚ*.A.[BA]
3′ ITI.DUL UD-25$^{!}$-KÁM
4′ *lim-mu* ^{m}*aš*$^{!}$-*šur*$^{!}$—KALAG-*in-a-ni*
5′ *ša* KUR.*qu-e*
6e 1 GÍN KUG.UD *ša ṣu-pur-šú*

ADD 274

1 Seal of Tirî, prefect of the Harranians, owner of the people being sold.

(cylinder and stamp seal impressions)

3 [NN], his wife [...]-Nanaya, [......, a total of] 6 people
(Break)

r.2 [Witness ...]-*apli*, scribe.
3 Month Tishri (VII), 25th day, eponym year of Aššur-da''inanni of Que.
6 1 shekel of silver for his fingernail.

173. Purchase of an Estate (685-VIII)

K 1430

1 NA$_{4}$.KIŠIB ^{md}PA—KAR-*ir*—ZI.MEŠ
2 DUMU ^{m}*ib-ni-ia* LÚ.A.BA

ADD 430

1 Seal of Nabû-eṭir-napšati, son of Ibniya, scribe, owner of the field and people being

171 Envelope. Previous edition: NALK 143a. r.2 See coll.
172 Previous edition: AR 69. Collations: Assur 2/5. 1f For the rendering "prefect of the Harranians" (rather than "Harranite prefect") cf. PN LÚ.GAR-*nu* LÚ.*hal-ta-a-a* ADD 860 r. ii 1, PN LÚ.GAR-*nu* NIM.MA-*a-a* ADD 857 i 33, and PN LÚ.GAR-*nu gu*[*r-r*]*i* ibid. ii 20. Harranians are attested as a group in ADD 1046 i 6.
173 Previous edition: AR 32. Collations: Assur 2/5. → no. 208.

3 EN A.ŠÀ UN.MEŠ SUM-*ni*

sold.

(space for seal impressions)

4 É 20 ANŠE A.ŠÀ *ú*$^{!}$-*gar*$^{!}$-*ru*
5 GIŠ.SAR *ša* Ú.SAR ⸢*ša*⸣ ^{m}NUMUN-*i*
6 *bur*$^{!}$ ^{md}PA—SIG$_5$ MÍ-*su-šú*$^{!}$
7 1 DUMU.MÍ *x*[*x x*]*x* [*x x x x x*]
rest broken away
Rev. beginning broken away
1′ IGI ^{m}⸢*a*?⸣-[*x x x*]
2′ IGI ^{m}⸢^{d}PA⸣—[*x x x*]
3′ IGI ^{m}⸢*la*?⸣-[*x x x*]
blank space of two lines
4′ ITI.AP[IN UD-*x*-KÁM *lim-m*]*u*
5′ ^{m}*aš-šur*—KAL[AG-*in-an*]-*ni*
6′ IGI ^{md}PA—[KA]R-*ir*—ZI.MEŠ
7′ LÚ.A.BA *ṣa-bit ṭup-pi*

4 An estate of 20 hectares of land, an irrigated field, a vegetable garden belonging to Zarî son of Nabû-dammiq, his wife, 1 daughter [......]
(Break)
r.1 Witness A[...].
2 Witness Nabû-[...].
3 Witness La[...],
4 Month Mar[chesvan (VIII), ...th day, epony]m year of Aššur-da''i[nan]ni.
6 Witness Nabû-[eṭ]ir-napšati, scribe, keeper of the tablet.

174. Purchase of a Slave (685-XII-20)

Ki 1904-10-9,139+238+401 + Ki 1904-10-9, 393+404 (ABL 1235)

1 NA$_4$.KIŠIB ^{m}*mu*-LAL—DINGIR EN LÚ 0$^{!}$

2 ^{m}*ša*$^{!}$—15—*du*$^{!}$-[*b*]*u*$^{!}$ ⸢ARAD$^{!}$-*šú*⸣ 0$^{!}$
3 *ú-tap-piš* ^{m}SUHUŠ—[*x x x*]
4 TA* IGI ^{m}*mu*-LAL—DINGIR [0]
5 *ina* ŠÀ-*bi* 20 GÍN.MEŠ KUG.UD
6 *i-zi-rip i-si-qi*
7 *kas-pu ga-mur ta-din*
r.1 LÚ *šu-a-tú za-rip la-qi*
2 *tu-a-ru de-nu* DUG$_4$.DUG$_4$ *la*$^{!}$-*šú*
3 *ṣib-tú ina* 1-*me* UD-*me*
4 *sa-ár-tú ina kàl* UD-*me*
5 ⸢*man-nu*⸣ *ša*$^{!}$ *ib*$^{!}$-*bal-kát-u-n*[*i*]
6 *kas*$^{!}$-*p*[*u*$^{!}$] ⸢*a*⸣-*na* 10.MEŠ *ina* EN.MEŠ-*šú* [GUR-*ra*]
7 ⸢*ina*⸣ *de-ni*-⸢*šú*⸣ DUG$_4$.DUG$_4$ ⸢*la*?⸣ [TI-*q*]*i*$^{!}$

8 [IGI ^{m}*x*]-*bi-si-i* 0$^{!}$
9 [IGI] ^{m}HÉ.NUN$^{!}$-*a*$^{!}$-*a*$^{!}$ LÚ*.GAL—*ki-ṣir ša* LÚ*.GA[L$^{!}$—S]AG$^{!}$
10 [IGI ^{m}]^{d}30—AD—PAB LÚ*.Ì.DU$_8$
11 [IGI] ^{m}*ku-lu-u*ʾ—15

ADD 1170+

1 Seal of Mutaqqin-ilu, owner of the man.

(cylinder seal impression)

2 Ša-Issar-dubbu, his servant —
3 Ubru-[...] has contracted, purchased, and bought him from Mutaqqin-ilu for 20 shekels of silver.
7 The money is paid completely. That man is purchased and acquired. Any revocation, lawsuit, or litigation is void.
r.3 (Guaranteed against) seizures for 100 days (and against) fraud forever.
5 Whoever transgresses [shall return] the money tenfold to its owners. He shall litigate in his lawsuit and not suc[ceed].

8 [Witness ...]bisî.
9 [Witness] Nuhšaya, cohort commander of the chi[ef eu]nuch.
10 [Witness] Sin-abu-uṣur, porter.

174 Previous edition: NALK 393. 2, r.6f See coll. r.8 Nothing missing at the end of the line. r.9, s.1f See coll.

12 ⸢IGI⸣ ^{m}*tar-di-ia*$^{!}$*-a*
13 ⸢IGI⸣ ^{md}15—MU—GIŠ
14 [IGI] ^{md}PA—TI.LA
15e I[GI ^{m}]^{d}PA—SU LÚ*.A.BA

16e *ina* MU.AN.NA 21 ^{m}30—PAB.MEŠ—SU
17e MAN KUR—*aš-šur*.KI
s.1 ITI.ŠE$^{!}$ UD-20$^{!}$-KÁM$^{!}$ *l*[*im-mu* ^{m}*aš-šur*—KALA]G$^{!}$-*ni*$^{!}$*-a-ni*
2 *x*[*x x x*] *x* [*x x x*] *x*
3 ⸢3$^{!}$⸣ MA.NA [URUDU.MEŠ *šá ṣu-p*]*ur-šú*

11 Witness Kulu'-Issar.
12 Witness Tardiya.
13 Witness Issar-šumu-lešir.
14 [Witness] Nabû-uballiṭ.
15 Wi[tness] Nabû-eriba, scribe.
16 In the 21st year of Sennacherib, king of Assyria.
s.1 Month Adar (XII), 20th day, ep[onym year of Aššur-da''i]nanni, [governor of Que].
3 3 minas [of copper for] his [finger]nail.

175. Mušallim-ilu Loans Silver (685)

K 395

1 [NA$_4$.KIŠIB] 0$^{!}$ ^{m}*ia-a-di*—DINGIR 4 MA.NA
2 [KUG.UD SA]G$^{!}$.DU *ša* ^{m}*mu-šal-lim*—DINGIR

---

rest broken away
Rev. beginning broken away
1′ [ITI.*x* UD]-8-KÁM *lim-mu* ^{m}*aš-šur*—KALAG-*a-ni*

ADD 36

1 [Seal of] Yadi-il. Four minas of [silver, capi]tal belonging to Mušallim-ilu.

(space for stamp seal impressions)

(Rest destroyed)
(Beginning destroyed)
r.1 Month [...], 8th [day], eponym year of Aššur-da''inanni.

176. Mušallim-ilu Buys Two Estates

82-5-22,31

beginning broken away

1′ É 5 ANŠE A.Š[À.GA *x x x*]⸢*x a*$^{!}$⸣
2′ SUHUR *ha-*⸢*x*⸣[*x x*] ⸢*kam*$^{!}$⸣ [*x x x*]*-mar*$^{!}$
3′ SUHUR ⸢*na*⸣*-hal-li* ⸢*dan*⸣-[*ni x x x*]
4′ SUHUR KASKAL *ša* [*a-na*] URU.⸢*x-hu*$^{?}$*-ú*$^{!}$⸣*-te*$^{!}$
5′ DU-*u-ni* [*x*]⸢*x x x*⸣ *x*[*x*]*x* A.ŠÀ.GA
6′ SUHUR ⸢É⸣ ^{m}*za*$^{!}$-⸢*ba*$^{!}$*-a*$^{!}$⸣*-a*
7′ SUHUR É ^{m}⸢*qi*$^{!}$⸣*-di-ni*
8′ *an-nu-u-te* SUHUR.MEŠ$^{!}$ *ša*$^{!}$ É$^{!}$
9′ *ú-piš-ma* ^{m}*mu-*⸢*šal*⸣*-lim*—DINGIR
10′ [*ina* ŠÀ]-*bi* 20 MA.NA URUDU.MEŠ
11′ [*ina*] MA.NA-*e ša* KUR$^{!}$-*e* 0$^{!}$
Edge uninscribed
r.1 *kas-pu ga-mur ta-din*
2 É A.ŠÀ.GA ⸢*šu*⸣*-a-te za-*⸢*ri*$^{!}$⸣*-i*[*p*$^{!}$]
3 *la-qi man-nu ša* 0$^{!}$ *ur-kiš*
4 *ina ma-a-te-ma i-bal-kàt-u-ni*

ADD 376

(Beginning destroyed)
(blank seal space)

---

1 An estate of 5 hectares of lan[d ...], adjoining [......], the big wadi [...], and the road leading [to] the town [...]hute;
5 [an estate of x ...] of land adjoining the houses of Zabayu and Qidinu; these are the adjoining (houses) of the house —

9 Mušallim-ilu has contracted and (bought said property) [fo]r 20 minas of copper [by] the mina of the *mountain*.
r.1 The money is paid completely. That house (and) land are purchased and acquired. Whoever in the future, at any time, trans-

175 Previous editions: AR 242, NALK 182. Collations: Assur 2/5.
176 Previous editions: AR 430, NALK 183; → TCAE 178f. Collations: Assur 2/5. 11 KUR-*e* is possibly a mistake for KUR "(mina of) the land".

5 *lu-u* ^{m}*za-ba-a-a-u lu-u* DUMU.MEŠ-*šú*
6 1 MA.NA KUG.UD 2 ⸢MA$^{!}$.NA$^{!}$⸣ KUG.GI
7 *ina bu-ur-ki* ⸢^{d}⸣[IŠ.T]AR$^{!}$ *a-ši-pat*
8 URU.*arba-ìl*.KI *i*$^{!}$-*š*[*ak*$^{!}$-*kan*$^{!}$] *kas-pu ina* 10.MEŠ 0$^{!}$
9 *ina* ⸢EN⸣.MEŠ-*šú* [GUR-*ra*] *ina de-*⸢*ni*⸣-*šú*
10 *i-*⸢*da-bu*⸣-[*bu*] *la i-laq-*⸢*qi*⸣
11 ⸢*de*⸣-[*en-šú* DI.KUD *la i-š*]*á*$^{!}$-*m*[*u*$^{!}$]-*u*
12 [IGI ^{m}*x x x x x x*] ⸢*x*⸣
13 [IGI ^{m}*x x x x x x x x*] ⸢*x x*⸣
14 [IGI ^{m}*x x x x x x x g*]*a*
rest broken away
s.1 10-*tú*$^{!}$ *nu-sa-hi*$^{!}$ *ù* [4-*tú ši-ib-ši*]

gresses, whether Zabayu or his sons, shall [place] one mina of silver and two minas of gold in the lap of [Išta]r residing in Arbela, and shall return the money tenfold to its owners.

9 He shall conte[st] in his lawsuit and not succeed. [The judge shall not h]eed his ca[se].

(Break)

s.1 The corn tax is 1/10 and [the straw tax 1/4].

177. Purchase of Slaves (684-II-8)

Rm 167

1 NA$_4$.KIŠIB ^{md}AG—SU
2 EN UN.MEŠ SUM-*ni*

3 ^{m}*kan-da-la-nu* ⸢3⸣ DUMU.MEŠ-*šú*
4 MÍ-*šú* 2 DUMU.MÍ.⸢MEŠ⸣-*šú* ŠEŠ-*šú* 2 DUMU.MEŠ-*šú*
5 *ú-piš-ma* ^{m}ITI.⸢KIN⸣-*a-a*
6 TA*$^{!}$ IGI ^{md}AG$^{!}$—SU *ina* ŠÀ-*bi*
7 6$^{!}$ MA.NA KUG.UD *ina* 1 MA.NA-*e*
8 *ša* URU.*gar-ga-mis il-qi*
9 *kas-pu gam-mur ta-din* UN.MEŠ
10 *šu-a-te zar*$_4$-*pu laq-qi-u*
11 *man-nu šá ina ur-kiš ina ma-te-ma* GIL-*u-ni*
12 *lu-u* ^{md}PA—SU *lu-u* LÚ.EN.NAM *lu-u* LÚ.2-*u*
13 *ša de-e-nu* DUG$_4$.(DUG$_4$) *ub-ta-u-ni*
e.14 12 MA.NA KUG.UD SUM-*an*

r.1 IGI ^{md}AG—ZU-*a-ni*
2 LÚ.3.U$_5$
3 IGI ^{m}DI$^{!}$-*mu*$^{!}$—EN$^{!}$—*la*$^{!}$-*mur*$^{!}$ KI.MIN
4 IGI ^{m}ZALÁG-*a-nu* LÚ.GAL—*ki-ṣir*
5 IGI ^{m}*man*$^{!}$-*nu*$^{!}$—*ki*$^{!}$—$^{d!}$15$^{!}$—ZU$^{!}$ LÚ$^{!}$.KI.MIN
6 IGI ^{m}HÉ.NUN-*a-a* LÚ.Ì.DU$_8$
7 IGI ^{m}U$^{!}$.U$^{!}$—DÙ LÚ.3.U$_5$
8 IGI ^{m}A—*še-zib-an-ni* LÚ.A—SIG
9 IGI ^{m}*ku*$^{!}$-*si-si-i* IGI ^{md}MAŠ$^{!}$-*i*

ADD 230

1 Seal of Nabû-eriba, owner of the people being sold.

(cylinder seal impression)

3 Kandalanu, his 3 sons, wife and two daughters, his brother and his two sons —

5 Ululayu has contracted and bought them from Nabû-eriba for 6 minas of silver by the mina of Carchemish.

9 The money is paid completely. Those people are purchased and acquired.

11 Whoever in the future, at any time, breaks the contract, whether Nabû-eriba or the governor or the deputy (governor), and seeks a lawsuit or litig[ation], shall pay 12 minas of silver.

r.1 Witness Nabû-le'ani, 'third man.'
3 Witness Šulmu-beli-lamur, ditto.
4 Witness Nuranu, cohort commander.
5 Witness Mannu-ki-Issar-le'i, ditto.
6 Witness Nuhšaya, porter.
7 Witness Dadi-ibni, 'third man.'
8 Witness Aplu-šezibanni, chariot fighter.
9 Witness Kusisî. Witness Nurtî.

177 Previous editions: AR 60, NALK 394; → KB 4 (1896) 120f. Collations: Assur 2/5.

10 IGI ^{m}*ri-sa-a-a*
11 IGI ^{m}*ta-ti-i*
12 LÚ.A.BA *ṣa-bit e-gír-te*!
13 IGI ^{m}U.GUR—DINGIR IGI ^{m}*hu—ma-ma-*⸢*te*⸣
14 IGI ^{md}PA—MAŠ LÚ.A.BA
15 IGI ^{m}*aš-šur*—AD—PAB LÚ.A.BA

16 ITI.GUD UD-8-KAM *li-mu*
17 ^{m}*man-za-ar-né-e* LÚ.EN.NAM
18 KUR.*kul-la-ni-a*
19 MU-22-KÁM ^{md}30—PAB.MEŠ—SU
20 LUGAL KUR—*aš-šur*.KI

[10] Witness Risaya.
[11] Witness Tatî, scribe, keeper of the tablet.
[13] Witness Nergal-ili. Witness Humamati.
[14] Witness Nabû-ašared, scribe.
[15] Witness Aššur-abu-uṣur, scribe.
[16] Month Iyyar (II), 8th day, eponym year of Manzarnê, governor of Kullania, year 22 of Sennacherib, king of Assyria.

178. Sailu Pays Off His Debts to Šamaš-ila'i (683-III-7)

Sm 475

1 4 MA.NA KUG.UD *ha-bu-li*
2 *ša* ^{md}UTU—DINGIR-*a-a*
3 *ša ina* UGU ^{m}*sa-i-li*
4 ^{m}*sa-i-lu a-na* ^{md}UTU—DINGIR-*a-a*
5 *ú-sa-lim it-ti-din*
6 *ú-ṭu-ru* TA* IGI *a-he-iš*
r.1 *mám-ma* TA* *mám-ma la i-da-bu-bu*
2 ITI.SIG$_{4}$ UD-7-KÁM
3 *lim-mu* ^{m}*man-nu—ki*—10
4 IGI ^{m}*sa-e-ru*
5 IGI ^{m}U.U!-*i*
6e IGI ^{m}*rém-ut*—^{d}BA.⸢Ú⸣

ADD 155

[1] 4 minas of silver, debts (owed) to Šamaš-ila'i by Sa'ilu — Sa'ilu has paid them in full to Šamaš-ila'i.

[6] They are mutually paid off. Neither shall litigate against the other.

[r.2] Month Sivan (III), 7th day, eponym year of Mannu-ki-Adad.
[4] Witness Sa'eru.
[5] Witness Dadî.
[6] Witness Remut-Babu.

179. Purchase of Slaves (683?-IV)

81-7-27,141

1 NA$_{4}$.KIŠIB [^{m}*x x x x x*]
2 EN UN.MEŠ [*ta-da-ni*]

rest broken away
Rev. beginning broken away
1′ [GAR-*a*]*n kas*!-*p*[*u*! *a-na* 10.MEŠ *a-na* EN.MEŠ-*šú* GUR]
2′ [*ina de-n*]*i*!-⸢*šú*!⸣ DU[G$_{4}$.DUG$_{4}$-*ma x x x x*]

ADD 300

[1] Seal of [NN], owner of the people [being sold].

(stamp seal impressions)

(Break)

[r.1] [shall pla]ce [...... in the lap of ...... and shall return] the mone[y tenfold to its owners]. He shall con[test in] his [lawsu]it [and not succeed].

178 Previous editions: AR 237, NALK 340; → KB 4 (1896) 120f. [r.5] See coll.
179 Previous edition: AR 545.

3′ [IG]I ^{m}*si-lim—x*[*x x x x*]
4′ [IGI] ^{m}*ha-an-di-*[*i x x x*]
5′ [IGI] ^{m}*se*$^{!}$*—na*$^{!}$*-x*[*x x x x*]
6′ [IG]I ^{m}*hu-x*[*x x x*]
7′ [IGI] ^{m}*ia*—P[AB$^{!}$.MEŠ]
8′ [IGI] ^{md}PA—PAB—[PAB$^{?}$ *x x*]
9′ [IGI] ^{m}*mil-ki—r*[*a-mu*]
blank space of one line
10′ ITI.ŠU [UD-*x*-KÁM]
11′ *lim-mu* ^{m}*man-nu—*[*ki*—^{d}IM$^{?}$]

3 [Witne]ss Silim-[...].
4 [Witness] Hand[î, ...].
5 [Witness] Se'-na[...].
6 [Witne]ss Hu[...].
7 [Witness] Ya-ah[he].
8 [Witness] Nabû-ahu-[*iddina*, ...].
9 [Witness] Milki-r[amu].
10 Month Tammuz (IV), [...th day], eponym year of Mannu-[ki-*Adad*].

180. Note of Silver Owed by Mannu-ki-Ninua (683-VI-25)

83-1-18,393

1 1/2 MA.NA KUG.UD *ina ša* LUGAL
2 *ša* ^{md}UTU*—da-ru*
3 *ina* IGI ^{m}*man-nu—*⌜*a*$^{?}$⌝*-ki—*⌜NINA$^{!}$.KI$^{!}$⌝
4 É-[*su ina šá-par-ti*]
5 ⌜*šá*$^{?}$⌝-[*kín x x x x x x*]*-šú la-áš-šú*
two lines broken away
8 [*šum*]*-ma* KUG.UD *l*[*a* SUM*-ni x x x x x*]
e.9 [*ina* Š]À*-bi* UD*-me ša* KUG.UD *ú*$^{!!}$*-šal*$^{!!}$*-l*[*am-u-ni*]
10 SUM*-an-u-ni a-na* É*-šú e-ra-a*[*b*]
r.1 ITI.KIN UD-25-KAM MU-22-KAM
2 ^{md}30—PAB.MEŠ—SU MAN ŠÚ
3 IGI ^{md}15*—ta-ri-bi*
4 IGI ^{m}ARAD—^{d}15 IGI ^{m}*il-lu-u*
5 IGI ^{m}*ṣil*—$^{d+}$EN$^{!}$
6e IGI ^{m}*si-lim—se* IGI ^{m}*mu-šal-lim—*^{d}ŠÚ
7e LÚ.A.BA

ADD 89

1 1/2 mina of silver by the (mina) of the king belonging to Šamaš-daru, at the disposal of Mannu-*a*ki-Ninua.
4 [His] house *is pl*[*aced as a pledge*]. There is no [...].
(Break)
8 [I]f he does n[ot pay] the silver, [......].
9 The day that he pays back the silver *in full*, he shall enter his house.
r.1 Month Elul (VI), 25th day, year 22 of Sennacherib, king of the world.
3 Witness Issar-tariba.
4 Witness Urda-Issar. Witness Illû.
5 Witness Ṣil-Bel.
6 Witness Silim-Se'. Witness Mušallim-Marduk, scribe.

181. A Wine Loan (683-X-25)

K 361B

1 NA$_{4}$.KIŠIB ^{m}*par-t*[*a-a-ma*]
2 2 ANŠE 5BÁN GIŠ.GE[ŠTIN.MEŠ]
3 *ša* ^{m}*man-nu—ki—*N[INA.KI]

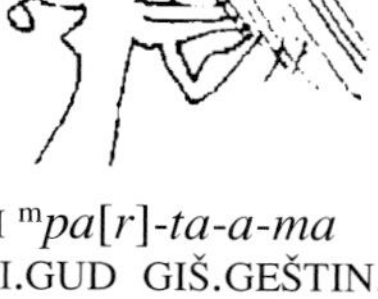

4 *ina* IGI ^{m}*pa*[*r*]*-ta-a-ma*
5 *ina* ITI.GUD GIŠ.GEŠTIN.MEŠ *ina* NINA.KI SUM*-an*

ADD 123

1 Seal of Part[ama].
2 Two homers 5 seahs of wi[ne] belonging to Mannu-ki-N[inua],

(cylinder seal impression)

4 at the disposal of Partama.
5 He shall give the wine back in Iyyar (II)

180 Previous editions: AR 136, NALK 339. Collated by I.L. Finkel. 3, r.9f See coll. r.9 The signs *ú* and *šal* are carelessly written; *ú* looks like GUR-TAB. See coll. r.10 See coll.
181 Envelope. Previous editions: AR 219, NALK 164a; → Postgate FNALD 36A. Photo Festschrift Porada Pl. 47:2.

6 *šúm-mu la i-di-ni*
e.1 *ki ma-hi-ri ša* URU.*ni-nu-a*
r.1 ⸢KUG.UD⸣ SUM-*an*
2 ⸢ITI.AB⸣ UD-25 *lim-me* ^{m}*man-nu—ki—*^{d}IM
3 IGI ^{m}*sa-na-nu* IGI ^{md}UTU—PAB-*ir*
4 IGI ^{md}PA—*tak-*⸢*lak*⸣ IGI ^{md}PA—*n*[*a-as-hir*]
5 IGI ^{m}DIL—*šal-lim* [IGI ^{m}]*rém-u*[*t*—DINGIR]
6 IGI ^{m}[^{d}]UTU—[*tak-lak* IGI ^{m}NUMUN—15]

in Nineveh.

6 If he does not, he shall pay (in) silver according to the market price of Nineveh.

r.2 Month Tebet (X), 25th day, eponym year of Mannu-ki-Adad.

3 Witness Sananu. Witness Šamaš-naṣir.

4 Witness Nabû-taklak. Witness Nabû-n[ashir].

5 Witness Edu-šallim. [Witness] Remu[t-ili].

6 Witness Šamaš-[taklak. Witness Zar-Issar].

182. Inner Tablet of the Preceding Text (683-X-25)

K 361A

1 2 ANŠE 5BÁN GIŠ.GEŠTIN.MEŠ
2 *ša* ^{m}*man-nu—ki—*NINA.KI
3 *ina* IGI ^{m}*par-ta-a-ma*
4 [*ina*] ITI.GUD GIŠ.GEŠTIN.MEŠ
5 [*ina* U]RU.*ni-nu-a* SUM-*an*
6 [*šúm-mu*] ⸢*là i*⸣-[*d*]*i-ni*
e.7 [*ki ma-h*]*i-ri ša* NINA.KI
8 [KUG.UD] SUM-*an*
r.1 [ITI.AB UD]-⸢25⸣-KÁM
2 [*lim-me* ^{m}*man*]*-nu—ki—*^{d}IM
3 [IGI ^{m}]*sa-na-a-nu*
4 IGI ^{md}UTU—PAB-*ir* IGI ^{md}PA—*na-sa-*⸢*hir*!⸣
5 IGI ^{m}*rém-ut—*DINGIR IGI ^{m}DIL—*šal-lim*
6 IGI ^{md}UTU—*tak-lak* IGI ^{m}NUMUN—15
7e IGI ^{md}PA—*tak-lak*

ADD 122

1 Two homers 5 seahs of wine belonging to Mannu-ki-Ninua (are) at the disposal of Partama.

4 He shall give the wine back [in] Iyyar (II) [in] Nineveh.

6 [If] he does not, he shall pay (in) [silver according to the mark]et price of Nineveh.

r.1 [Month Tebet] (X), 25th [day, eponym year of Man]nu-ki-Adad.

3 [Witness] Sananu.

4 Witness Šamaš-naṣir. Witness Nabû-nashir.

5 Witness Remut-ili. Witness Edu-šallim.

6 Witness Šamaš-taklak. Witness Zar-Issar.

7 Witness Nabû-taklak.

183. Sin-remanni Loans Two Minas of Silver (683)

K 394

1 2 MA.NA KUG.UD
2 *ina* 1 MA.NA *ša* 0! *gar-ga-mis*
3 *ša* ^{md}30—*rém-ni*
4 *ina* IGI ^{m}*man-nu—ki—*AN.GAL
5 ⸢GAL!—É!⸣ *ša* SUKKAL.MEŠ
6 [*x x x*] MA.NA ⸢*x x x*⸣
rest broken away
Rev. beginning broken away
1′ [ITI.*x* UD-*x*-K]AM!

ADD 47

1 Two minas of silver by the mina of Carchemish, belonging to Sin-remanni, at the disposal of Mannu-ki-Issaran, [ma]jor-domo of the viziers.

6 [...] minas [...]

(Break)

r.1 [Month ..., ...]th [day], eponym year of

182 Tablet. Previous editions: AR 220, NALK 164b; → Postgate FNALD 36B.
183 Previous editions: AR 251, NALK 326. Collations: Assur 2/5.

2′ ⸢*lim-mu*⸣ ^{m}*man-nu—ki*—10
3′ IGI! $^{m!}$MAN LÚ*.NAR

Mannu-ki-Adad.
3 Witness *Šarru*, singer.

184. Note of Copper Owed to Sin-remanni

80-7-19,314

1 *bi-lat* 3 MA.N[A URUDU.MEŠ]
2 SAG.MEŠ *šá* ^{d}[15 *šá* URU.*arba—ìl*]
3 *ša* ^{md}30—[*re-man-ni*]
4 *ina* IGI ^{m}*gab-*[*x x x*]
5 IGI ^{m}EN—KASKAL—[*x x x*]
6 IGI ^{m}*ba-ni-*[*i x x*]
7 IGI ^{md}U[TU?—*x x x*]
r.1 IGI ^{m}*bi-si*!-*x*[*x x x x x*]
2 IGI ^{m}GÌR.2—[*x x x*]
blank space of 1 line
3 ⸢ITI⸣ [[ ]] [*x x x*]
4 IGI ^{md}AMA[R.UTU—*x x x*]

ADD 108

1 One talent and 3 min[as of copper], first fruits of [Ištar of Arbela], belonging to Sin-[remanni], at the disposal of Gab[...].
5 Witness Bel-Harran-[...].
6 Witness Ban[î ...].
7 Witness Ša[maš-...].
r.1 Witness Bisi[...].
2 Witness Šep-[...],
3 Month [..., ...th day, eponym year of NN].
4 Witness Marduk-[..., *scribe*].

185. Sin-remanni Buys Slaves

Bu 89-4-26,131

beginning broken away
1′ [*x x x x x x x x x x t*]*ú*!
2′ [*x x kas-pu gam-mur ta*]-*din*!
3′ [UN?.MEŠ *šu-a-tu zar-pu la-q*]*í*!-*ʾu*!-*u*!
4′ [*tu-a-ru de-e-nu* DU]G$_4$.DUG$_4$!
5′ [*la-áš-šú man-nu ša*] ⸢*ur-kiš*!⸣
6′ [*ina* EGIR UD.MEŠ *e-l*]*a*!-*an-ni*
e.7′ [*lu-u* ^{m}*x x x x*] LÚ*.2-⸢*e*⸣ 0!
8′ [*lu-u* DUMU-*šú lu-u*] DUMU—DUMU-*šú*
9′ [*lu-u* L]Ú!.EN.NAM *ša* URU.⸢*arrap-ha*⸣
r.1 [*šá e*]-*la-an-ni* TA* ^{md}30—*re-man-ni*
2 [DUMU.MEŠ-*šú* DUMU]—DUMU.MEŠ-*šú de-e-nu*
3 [DUG$_4$.DU]G$_4$ *i-gar-ru-u-ni ma-a*
4 [*kas-pu*] *la* 0! *ga-mur la-a ta*!-*din*!
5 [*ma-a x*] *šu*!-*a-ti*! *la ta-din*
6 [*x*] MA.NA KUG.UD *ina bur-ki* ^{d}15
7 [*ša*!] URU.*ni-nu-a i-šá-kan*
8 ⸢2?⸣ MA.NA KUG.GI *sak-ru ina bur-ki*
9 ^{d}MAŠ *i-šá-kan*

---

10 [IGI] ^{m}LUGAL—IGI.(LAL)-*a-ni* LÚ*!.*qur*-ZAG
11 [IGI ^{m}D]I-*mu*—EN—*la-áš*-(*me*) LÚ*!.3.[U$_5$]
12 [IGI ^{m}*x x x x*]-⸢*ni*!⸣ [*x x x x*]
rest broken away

ADD 506

(Beginning destroyed)
2 [The money is pa]id [completely. Those *people* are purchased and acqu]ired. [Any revocation, lawsuit, or liti]gation is [void.
5 [Whoever] in the future, [in distant days, com]es forward, [whether PN] the deputy, [or his sons or] his grandsons [or t]he governor of Arrapha,

r.1 [whoever c]omes forward and institutes a lawsuit [or litigation] against Sin-remanni, [his sons (or) grand]sons, saying: "[The money] is not paid completely, that [*property*] is not sold,"
6 shall place [x] minas of silver in the lap of Ištar [of] Nineveh, and shall place *2* minas of pure gold in the lap of Ninurta.

---

10 Witness Šarru-emuranni, royal bodyguard.
11 Witness Šulmu-beli-lašme, 'third man'.
(Rest destroyed)

184 Previous editions: AR 303, NALK 329. Collations: Assur 2/5. 6, r.1 See coll.
185 Previous editions: AR 612, NALK 325. Collations: Assur 2/5.

186. An Officer of the Crown Prince Acquires a Vineyard (683)

81-7-27,26

beginning broken away

1′ [*x x x* GIŠ.S]AR *til-li-te*
2′ [*x x x*]*x* ⸢*x x*⸣ [*x x x*].KI
two lines destroyed
5′ SU[HUR *x x x x x x-q*]*i*!
6′ SUHUR [*x x*] ⸢*x x x x x*⸣
7′ *ú-piš-ma* ^{m}*gi-r*[*u-x x*]
8′ LÚ*.*mu*-⸢*tir*!⸣—*ṭè-me*
e.9′ [*š*]*a* $^{md⸢}$U.GUR—MU!⸣—DÙ
r.1 [*ina* Š]À-*bi* GÚ.U[N URUDU.MEŠ]
2 [*il-qi x x*]*x* 8 ANŠE GEŠ[TIN.MEŠ]
3 [*x x a-na šá*]-*par-ti*! K[Ú!]
4 [*man-nu ša ina* EGIR U]D!.MEŠ DU-⸢*u*!⸣-[*ni*]
5 [URUDU.MEŠ SUM-*u-n*]*i*! GIŠ.SAR
6 [*til-li-te ú-še*]-*ṣa*

7 [IGI ^{m}*x x x*] URU.ŠE—^{m}*mil*-⸢*ki*!⸣-*x*[*x*]

8 [IGI ^{m}*šá—la*]—*ma-ši-i*
9 [IGI ^{m}*x x*]⸢*x*⸣-KUR-*a-a*
10 [IGI ^{m}*x x*]*x-a-a ša* GÚ.UN
11 [URUDU.MEŠ?] *i-di-nu-ni*
12 [IGI ^{m}*di*]-⸢*lil*⸣—^{d}15

13 [ITI.*x* U]D-7-KAM
14 [*lim-mu* ^{m}*man-nu—ki*]—10
last line broken away
s.1 [IGI ^{md}]PA!—[*x x x x x*]
2 [IGI] ^{md}I[M—*x x x x x x x*]

ADD 463

(Beginning destroyed)

(stamp seal impressions)

1 [...] a vineyard [in ......] adjoi[ning ...] and [...] —

7 Giru[...], information officer [o]f Nergal-šumu-ibni, has contracted and [acquired] it [f]or a tale[nt of copper].

r.2 He shall enjoy as a pledge 8 homers of wi[ne ...].

4 [*Whoever in the fu*]*ture comes* [*and pays the copper* shall red]eem the [vine]yard.

7 [Witness NN, from] the village of Milki-[...].

8 [Witness Ša-la]-mašê.

9 [Witness NN]...ayu.

10 [Witness ...]ayu, who paid the talent [of copper].

12 [Witness Di]lil-Issar.

13 [Month ...], 7th day, eponym year of [Mannu-ki]-Adad.

s.1 [Witness] Nabû-[...].

2 [Witness] Ad[ad-...].

187. Purchase of a House and Gardens (682-II-24)

81-2-4,162

1 [NA$_{4}$].KIŠIB ^{m}*ha-a-bi*
2 [EN] ⸢É!⸣ A.ŠÀ GIŠ.SA[R]
3 [GIŠ.SA]R *ša* Ú.SAR [SUM-*n*]*i*!

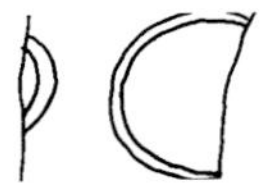

ADD 437

1 [Se]al of Habi, [owner of] the house, field, orch[ard and] [veget]able gard[en being sold].

(stamp seal impressions)

186 Previous editions: AR 193, NALK 106. Collations: Assur 2/5.
187 Previous edition: AR 440. Collations: Assur 2/5.

4 [É *ep*]-*šú a-di* [*x x x x*]
rest broken away
Rev. beginning broken away
1′ [*ina de-ni-šú*] ⌜DUG$_4$⌝!.[DUG$_4$-*ma x x x*]

2′ [IGI ^{m}*x x x*]-*la* IGI ^{m}[*x x x x x*]
3′ [IGI ^{m}*x x*]*x-a-a* IGI ^{m}*ma*[*r*!-*x*]*x*
4′ [IGI ^{m}*x x x*—M]AŠ? IGI ^{m}UD-*ia*?
5′ [IGI ^{m}*xxxxx*]—⌜DÙ⌝ IGI ^{m}[DINGIR—*m*]*a*!-*a-di*

6e [ITI].GUD UD-24-[KÁM]
7e [*lim-m*]*u* ^{md}PA—MAN—P[AB]

[4] [A bu]ilt house with [*its doors*]
(Break)
[r.1] He shall con[test in his lawsuit and not succeed].

---

[2] [Witness ...]la. Witness [NN].
[3] [Witness ...]ayu. Witness Ma[r...].
[4] [Witness ...-*aš*]*ared*. Witness *Šamšiya*.
[5] [Witness ...]-ibni. Witness [Il-m]adi.
[6] [Month] Iyyar (II), 24th day, [eponym ye]ar of Nabû-šarru-u[ṣur].

188. Purchase of a Vineyard (682-II-25)

Rm 180

1 NA$_4$.KIŠIB ^{m}*qu-u-a-a*! DUMU [^{m}]*k*[*ù*!-KÁ—*x x*]
2 URU.*tar-qa-na-a-a* EN GIŠ.[SAR SUM-*ni*]

ADD 363

[1] Seal of Quwayu son of *K*[*ubabu-...*] from Tarqana, owner of the vine[yard being sold].

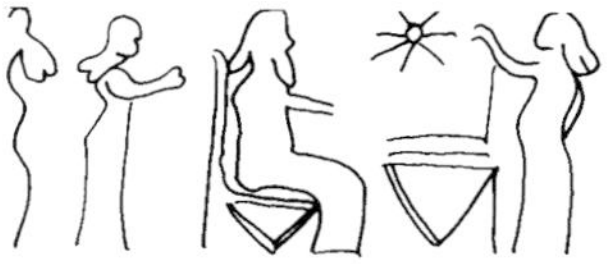

(cylinder seal impression)

---

3 [GI]Š.SAR *ša til-lit-te*! [*x x*]
4 [*ina*! ŠÀ! UR]U.*tu-ur-s*[*a-na x x*]
5 [SUHUR GI]Š.SAR *ša* ^{m}[*x x x*]
6 [SUHUR GIŠ.SA]R *ša* ^{m}[*x x x*]
rest broken away
Rev. beginning broken away
1′ IG[I *x x x x* IGI] ^{m}*tar-di-tú*—⌜PAB⌝!.M[EŠ!]
2′ IGI ^{m}[*x x x* LÚ.*m*]*u-kil*—PA.MEŠ IGI ^{m}*aš-šur*—MAN—P[AB]
3′ IGI $^{m⌜d⌝}$[*x x*]—SU IGI ^{m}*ul-lu* LÚ*.Ì.DU$_8$ [0]
4′ IGI ^{m}*qí-bit—aš-šur* IGI ^{m}DINGIR—*mu*-LAL

5′ ITI.GUD UD-25-KÁM *lim-mu* ^{md}PA—MAN—PAB *ša* URU.*mar-qa-si*
6′ GIŠ.SAR *ša gi-né-e ša aš-šur* ^{d}NIN.LÍL

7′ *šu-u* IGI ^{m}SU—PAB.MEŠ LÚ*.*qe-pu* URU.*kar*—^{d}UTU
8′ IGI ^{m}DUMU.UŠ-*a-a* A ^{m}*mu*-DI—*aš-šur* :

9′ IGI ^{m}*man-nu—ka*—PAB.MEŠ LÚ*.*ha-za-nu*
10e *ša* URU.*tu-ur-sa-na*
s.1 A.MEŠ *qa-n*[*i*! *x x x x x x x x*]

[3] [A vine]yard [... in the cit]y of Turs[ana ..., adjoining the viney]ards of [NN] and [NN]
(Break)

[r.1] Wi[tness .... Witness] Tarditu-ah[he].
[2] Witness [NN, cha]riot driver. Witness Aššur-šarru-u[ṣur].
[3] Witness [...]-eriba. Witness Ullu, porter.
[4] Witness Qibit-Aššur. Witness Ilu-mutaqqin.
[5] Month Iyyar (II), 25th day, eponym year of Nabû-šarru-uṣur of Marqasa.
[6] It is a vineyard providing regular offerings to Aššur and Mullissu.
[7] Witness Riba-ahhe, legate of Kar-Šamaš.
[8] Witness Aplaya son of Mušallim-Aššur, ditto.
[9] Witness Mannu-ka-ahhe, mayor of Tursana.
[s.1] The water outsi[de *the wineyard* ......].

188 Previous edition: AR 371. Collations: Assur 2/5.

[s.1] Or: The water outsi[de *the town*.

189. Nabû-remanni Loans 5 Shekels of Silver (682-VII-5)

K 339

1 5 GÍN KUG.[UD]
2 *ša* ^{md}PA—*rém-a-*⌜*ni*⌝
3 *ina* IGI ^{m}*na-di-ni*
4 *ina* 4-*ut-ti-šú* GAL
5 [[*ina*$^{!}$ ⌜ITI$^{!}$.GAN$^{!}$⌝ [S]UM-*an*]]
e.6 ITI.DUL UD-5
r.1 *lim-mu* ^{md}PA—MAN—PAB
2 IGI ^{md}PA—LAL-*a-ni*
3 IGI ^{m}*qi-ti*—BE$^{!}$
4 IGI ^{m}ITI.AB-*a-a*
5 IGI ^{m}*har-ma-ki*

ADD 21

1 Five shekels of sil[ver] belonging to Nabû-remanni, at the disposal of Nadinu.

4 It will increase by a fourth; he shall pay in Kislev (IX).

6 Month Tishri (VII), 5th day, eponym year of Nabû-šarru-uṣur.

r.2 Witness Nabû-taqqinanni.

3 Witness Qiti-Illil.

4 Witness Kanunayu.

5 Witness Harmaku.

190. Cloth for the King's Napkin (682-V-7)

K 379

1 *ur-su-tu ša* 4 [TÚG.*x x*]
2 4 TÚG.*nik-si du*[*l*$^{!}$*-lu*]
3 *qa-at-nu ša* ^{d}*x*[*x x x*]
4 *ina pa-an* ^{m}*ur-da-*⌜*a*$^{!}$⌝ [0]
5 LÚ.GAL—UŠ.BAR.M[EŠ]
6 1-*me*-25 MA.NA URUDU.MEŠ
7 *ár*$^{!}$*-hiš ep-pa-pa-a*[*l*$^{!}$]
8 IGI ^{md}PA-*ú-a* LÚ.[*x x*]
9 IGI ^{m}*an-di-a-a* [0]
r.1 IGI ^{md}*aš-šur*—MU—PAB
2 IGI ^{m}*ba-hi-a-*[*nu*]
3 IGI ^{md}PA—PAB—[*x*]
4 IGI ^{m}*tak*$^{?}$*-li-*[*x x*]

5 ITI.NE UD-7-[KÁM]
6 *li*$^{!}$*-mu* ^{md}PA—MAN—[PAB]
7 LÚ.GAR.KUR URU.*mar-qa-*[*si*]
s.1 TÚG.*sa-su-pu*
2 *ša* UGU MAŠ.QA

ADD 679

1 A *parcel* of 4 [...] and 4 pieces of *cut cloth*, fine wor[k], belonging to the god [...], at the disposal of Urdâ, chief weav[er].

6 He shall quickly pay 125 minas of copper.

8 Witness Nabû'a, [...].

9 Witness Andiayu.

r.1 Witness Aššur-šumu-uṣur.

2 Witness Bahian[u].

3 Witness Nabû-ahu-[...].

4 Witness *Tak*li[...].

5 Month Ab (V), 7th day, eponym year of Nabû-šarru-[uṣur], governor of Marqa[si].

s.1 A napkin (to be placed) over the (king's) shoulders.

191. Sale of a Garden (682)

K 445

1 ⌜NA$_4$.KIŠIB⌝ ^{m}*qur-*⌜*di*⌝—15—*la-mur*
2 NA$_4$.KIŠIB ^{m}I—*aš-šur*
3 [PA]B 2 LÚ.MEŠ-*e* EN GIŠ.SAR SUM-*ni*

ADD 370

1 Seal of Qurdi-Issar-lamur,

2 seal of Na'id-Aššur,

3 [in a]ll 2 men, owners of the garden being sold.

---

189 Previous editions: AR 253, NALK 201. Collations: Assur 2/5.

190 Previous edition: AR 292. Collations: Assur 2/5. s.1 For the rendering, cf. TÚG.*sa-su-up-pu ina* UGU MAŠ.QA LUGAL *i-kar-ru-ru* Or. 21 135:10, and parallel passages in other NA cultic rituals.

rest broken away
Rev. beginning broken away
1′ [*x x x x x x*] LÚ*.ARAD *ša* ⸢LÚ*$^{!}$.EN$^{!}$⸣.[NAM]
2′ [ITI.*x*] UD-11-KAM
3′ [*lim-mu* ^{md}PA—MA]N—PAB LÚ*.GAR.KUR URU.*mar-qa-si*
one line blank
4′ [*šá*] GIŠ.SAR *šú-a-tú* ŠE.*nu-sa-hi-šú*
5′ [*l*]*a i-na-su-hu il-ku*$^{!}$
6′ TA* URU$^{!}$-*šú*$^{!}$ *la*$^{!}$ *il-lak*

(cylinder seal impression)

(Break)

r.1 [Witness NN], servant of the *gove*[*rnor*].

2 [Month ...], 11th day, [eponym year of Adad-šar]ru-uṣur, governor of Marqasi.

4 The corn taxes [of] that garden shall not be exacted, he shall not do the labour service with his town.

192. A Broken Slave Sale (682)

Rm 147

1 NA$_4$.KIŠIB ^{m}*si-ip-*[*ra-a-nu*]
2 EN UN.MEŠ SU[M]

3 ^{m}PAB-*u-a x*[*x x x x x x*]
rest broken away
Rev. beginning broken away
1′ [IGI ^{m}*x x*—^{d}]⸢15$^{?}$⸣ LÚ*.*mu-kil*—KUŠ.⸢PA$^{!}$⸣.[MEŠ]
2′ IGI ^{m}[AN.ŠÁR—DINGIR]-⸢*a*⸣-*a* LÚ*.3-*šú*
3′ IGI ^{m}EN—KI-⸢*ia*⸣ LÚ*.*mu-tir—ṭè-me*
4′ IGI ^{md}30—EN—PAB LÚ*.GAL—*ki-ṣir*
5′ IGI ^{m}*hi-nu-mu ki-ṣir*—MAN
6′ IGI ^{m}*šu-ma-a ki-ṣir*—MAN
7′ IGI ^{m}*rém-ut ki-ṣir*—MAN
8′ IGI ^{m}*a-hu-ni-i*$^{!}$ *ki-ṣir*—MAN
9′ IGI ^{m}*pal-hu—še-zib*
10e LÚ.DAM.QAR
s.1 [*x x x x x x lim*]-*me* ^{md}PA—MAN—PAB
2 [LÚ.GAR.KUR U]RU.*mar-qa-sa*

ADD 276

1 Seal of Sip[ranu], owner of the people [being sold].

(two circular stamp seals)

3 Ahu'a [......]
(Break)

r.1 [Witness ...]-*Issar*, chariot driver.
2 [Witness Aššur-il]a'i, 'third man.'
3 Witness Bel-isse'a, intelligence officer.
4 Witness Sin-belu-uṣur, cohort commander.
5 Witness Hinnumu, (of the) royal corps.
6 Witness Šumaya, royal corps.
7 Witness Remuttu, royal corps.
8 Witness Ahunî, royal corps.
9 Witness Palhu-šezib, merchant.
s.1 [Month ..., ...th day], eponym year of Nabû-šarru-uṣur, [governor] of Marqasa.

191 Previous edition: AR 114; → TCAE 64. Collations: Assur 2/5. [1] *ni* (ADD, AR) is not on the tablet.

193. Purchase of Slaves (681-II-12)

K 354

1 NA$_4$.KIŠIB $^{m⸢d⸣}$⸢AG$^{!}$⸣—SU ⸢LÚ$^{!}$⸣.[*x x x*]
2 ⸢ARAD$^{!}$⸣ LÚ$^{!}$.⸢EN$^{!}$⸣.[NAM] EN UN.MEŠ SU[M$^{!}$-*ni*]

3 [^{m}*x x x*]—NUMUN MÍ-*šú* PAB ⸢2⸣ [0]
4 [^{m}*x x x x*] MÍ-*šú* PAB ⸢2⸣ [0]
5 [^{m}*x x x x*] ⸢2⸣ DUMU.MEŠ-*šú* ⸢*x*⸣[*x x x*]

6 [MÍ.*x x x x*] DUMU-*šá* PAB$^{!}$ [2]
7 [*x x x x x*] ⸢URU⸣.*hi*$^{?}$-*x*[*x x x x*]
rest (about half of the obverse) broken away
Rev. beginning broken away
1′ [*x x x x x*] *ni* [*x x x x x!*]
2′ [*x x x x* EN.M]EŠ$^{!}$-*šú ú*-[*ta-ra*$^{!}$]

3′ [IGI ^{m}]⸢U$^{!}$.GUR$^{!}$⸣—DÙ LÚ$^{!}$.3$^{!}$-[*šú*]
4′ [IGI ^{m}]*man-nu—ki*—PAB.MEŠ L[Ú$^{!}$.*x x x x*]
5′ [IGI ^{m}]DÙG.GA-*i* LÚ$^{!}$.*rak*-[*su*$^{?}$]
6′ [IGI ^{m}]EN—PAB—AŠ LÚ$^{!}$.GIŠ.GIGIR—*na*-[*kam-ti*]

8′ IGI ^{m}ARAD—^{d}*gu-la* LÚ$^{!}$.2-*ú*
9′ *ša* LÚ$^{!}$.GAL—A.ZU
10′ [IGI] ^{md}PA—⸢MU$^{!}$⸣—[*x*] LÚ$^{!}$.A.BA *ṣ*[*a-bit dan-ni-te*]

11′ [ITI.GU]D UD-12-KÁM
12e [*lim-m*]*u* ^{md}PA—PAB.MEŠ—[KAM-*eš*]
13e [LÚ$^{!}$.GAR].KUR *ša sa-ma*$^{!}$-[*al-la*]
s.1 [*x x x x x x x x*]*x-a ša*$^{!}$ KUR.[*x x*]

ADD 277

1 Seal of Nabû-eriba, [...], servant of the gover[nor], owner of the people being so[ld].

(stamp seal impressions)

3 [NN], his wife, a total of 2;
4 [NN], his wife, a total of 2;
5 [NN], his 2 sons [...];
6 [NN], her son, a total of [2];
7 [......] the city of [...]
(Break)

r.1 [......] shall re[turn the money tenfold to] its [owne]rs.

3 [Witness] Nergal-ibni, 'third [man].'
4 [Witness] Mannu-ki-ahhe, [...].
5 [Witness] Ṭabî, *cons*[*cript*].
6 [Witness] Bel-ahu-iddina, trainer of re[serve] horses.
8 Witness Urda-Gula, deputy of the chief physician.
10 [Witness] Nabû-šumu-[...], scribe, kee[per of the document].
11 [Month Iyy]ar (II), 12th day, eponym year of Nabû-ahhe-[ereš, gover]nor of Sam'[al].
s.1 [......]... of the land of [...].

194. Purchase of Land (681-II-13)

BM 128026 + BM 128146

1 [NA$_4$.KIŠIB ^{m}*x x x*]

2 ⸢LÚ⸣.[*x x x x x*]
3 *ša* ^{md}[*x x x* EN A.ŠÀ]

Iraq 32 6

1 [Seal of NN],

(stamp seal impressions)

2 [...] of [NN, owner of the land being sold].

192 Previous edition: AR 532.
193 Previous edition: AR 62. Collations: Assur 2/5.

4 É 8 A[NŠE A.ŠÀ]
5 *ina* ⸢GIŠ.BÁN *ša* 8⸣ *q*[*a*]
6 *ina ma-za-ru-u-te*
7 SUHUR ^{m}*gu-da-a-*⸢ʾ*u*⸣
8 [SU]HUR ^{m}*da-*⸢*na-ti*⸣—DINGIR
9 [SUHUR] ^{m}*qa-ra-ha-a*
10 [SUHUR *x*]*x* ^{md}UTU—DÙ-*u-a*
11 [*x x x*]*x*[*x x x x*]
rest broken away
Rev. beginning broken away
1′ [*x* MA.N]A [KUG].⸢GI⸣ *s*[*ak*]-⸢*ru*⸣
2′ [SUM-*a*]*n kas-pu* ⸢3?⸣*-a-te*
3′ ⸢*a-na*⸣ EN.MEŠ-*šú*
4′ *ú-ta-a-ra*

5′ IGI ^{m}ZALÁG—^{d}IM
6′ IGI ^{m}*gu-da-a-*ʾ*u*
7′ IGI ^{m}*da-na-ia-ti*—⸢DINGIR⸣
8′ IGI ^{m}*mu-še-zib*—^{d}*x*[*x*]
9′ IGI ^{m}*x*[*x x x x x*]
10′ IGI ^{m}[*x x x x x*]
11′ IGI ^{m}*hu*[*m-x x x x*]
12′ IGI ^{m}*x*[*x x x x x*]
13′ IGI ^{m}*x*[*x x x x x*]
14e IGI ^{m}[*x x x x x*]
15e IGI [^{m}*x x x x x*]
s.1 [IGI ^{m}]^{d}PA—⸢ÁG!⸣—Z[I LÚ.A.BA]

2 ITI.GUD UD-13-KÁM *lim-me* [^{md}PA—PAB—KAM-*eš*]
3 *ša* URU.*sa-am-a-al-l*[*a* 0]
4 UR[U? D]U$_{6}$? *an* ⸢*za*⸣*-ku-u x*[*x x x x*]

4 An estate of 8 he[ctares of land], by the seah of 8 'litres,' in cultivation, [ad]joining (the estates of) Guda'u, Daniati-il, Qarahâ, (and) the [... of] Šamaš-banû'a
(Break)

r.1 [He shall pa]y [*3* min]as of p[ur]e [go]ld, and shall return the money *three*fold to its owners.

---

5 Witness Nur-Adad.
6 Witness Guda'u.
7 Witness Daniati-il.
8 Witness Mušezib-[...].
9 Witness [NN].
10 Witness [NN].
11 Witness Hu[m...].
12 Witness [NN].
13 Witness [NN].
14 Witness [NN].
15 Witness [NN].
s.1 [Witness] Nabû-ra'im-ketti, [scribe].
2 Month Iyyar (II), 13th day, eponym year of [Nabû-ahu-ereš] of Sam'al.
4 The *town and the tell are exempt* [...].

195. Šamaš-ila'i, Chief [...], Buys 6 Slaves (681-V-25)

Sm 218

1 NA$_{4}$.KIŠIB ^{m}*lu-u—bal-aṭ*
2 EN LÚ.UN.MEŠ SUM-*ni*

---

3 ^{md}PA—*še-zib* MÍ-*šu* 4 DUMU.M[EŠ!-*š*]*ú*!
4 [PAB] 6 ZI.MEŠ LÚ.ARAD.ME[Š-*ni*]
5 [*ša*] ^{m}*lu-u—bal-aṭ ú-pi*[*š-m*]*a*!
6 [^{md}UT]U—⸢DINGIR⸣*-a-a* LÚ.GAL—[*x x x*] ⸢*x x*⸣
7 [TA* IGI ^{m}*lu-u*]—*bal-*[*aṭ x x x*]
rest broken away
Rev. beginning broken away
1′ [*x x x x x* L]Ú.*še-*[*l*]*ap-pa-*⸢*a*⸣-[*a*]
2′ [IGI ^{m}*x x x*]-*an-ni*
3′ [IGI ^{m}*x x x*]-⸢*ib*!⸣ LÚ.*na-sik-ku*

ADD 269

1 Seal of Lu-balaṭ, owner of the people being sold.

(space for seal impressions)

---

3 Nabû-šezib, his wife, [hi]s 4 son[s, a total] of 6 people, servants [of] Lu-balaṭ —
6 [Šama]š-ila'i, chi[ef ......], has contr[acted and bought them from Lu]-balaṭ
(Break)
r.1 [Witness NN], archit[ect].
2 [Witness ...]anni.
3 [Witness ...]ib, sheikh.

194 Copy: Iraq 32 (1970), Pl. XXI.

4′ [IGI ^{m}*m*]*ar*$^{!}$-*da*$^{!}$-*a-na* IGI ^{m}*na-tan*
5′ [IGI ^{m}]*ba-la-su* IGI ^{m}*bar—za-qe-e*
6′ IGI ^{m}DINGIR—ZU LÚ.A.BA *ṣa-bit*

7′ *dan-ni-te* ITI.NE UD-25-KÁM
8′ *lim-mu* ^{md}PA—PAB—KAM-*eš*
9′ IGI ^{md}*ra-man—dàl-a* URU.*šá—za-bi-na-a-a*
10′ IGI ^{m}PAB—IGI.LAL A ^{m}*aš-šur*—AD—PAB

4 [Wit]ness Mardanu. Witness Natan.
5 [Witness] Balassu. Witness Bar-zaqê.
6 [Wit]ness Ilu-le'i, scribe, keeper of the document.
7 Month Ab (V), 25th day, eponym year of Nabû-ahu-ereš.
9 Witness Ramman-dalâ, from Šazabinâ.
10 Witness Ahu-lamur, son of Aššur-abu-uṣur.

196. Purchase of Slaves (681-VIII-14)

83-1-18,345

ADD 279

1 NA_4.KIŠIB ^{m}EN—KASKAL—*k*[*u-ṣur*]-⸢*a*$^{!}$⸣-*ni*$^{!}$
2 EN UN.MEŠ SUM-⸢*ni*⸣

1 Seal of Bel-Harran-k[uṣur]ani, owner of the people being sold.

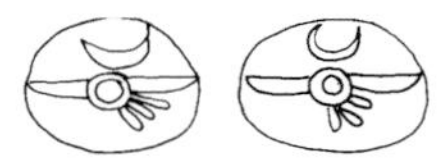

(two stamp seal impressions)

3 [^{m}*a*]-⸢*tar*$^{!}$—*šúm*$^{!}$-*ki*$^{!}$⸣ ARAD-*šú*
4 [*x x x x x x x x x*]
5 [*ú-piš-ma* ^{m}*x x x x*]-⸢*ni*⸣
6 [TA* IGI ^{m}E]N—⸢KASKAL⸣—[*ku*]-*ṣur-a-ni*
7 [*ina* ŠÀ] ⸢*x*⸣ 30$^{!}$ [GÍN KUG.UD]
8 [*ina ša* URU.*gar-ga-mi*]*s*$^{!}$ TI-[*qí*]
rest broken away
r.1′ [*ina*$^{!}$] *de-ni-šú* DUG_4.DUG_4-*ma là* ⸢TI⸣

3 [At]ar-šumki, his servant, [......] —
5 [...]ni [has contracted] and bought them [from Be]l-Harran-[ku]ṣurani [fo]r 30 [minas of silver, by the mina of Carchemi]sh.
(Break)
r.1 He shall contest [in his law]suit and not succeed.

2′ IGI ^{m}*kan-dàl-a-nu*
3′ IGI ^{m}*ra-di-mu*
4′ IGI ^{m}*ha-ru-ṣa-a*
5′ IGI ^{m}EN—KASKAL—BÀD LÚ*$^{!}$.NAR
6′ IGI ^{m}DINGIR—*gab-e*
7′ IGI ^{md}PA—PAB—PAB

8′ ITI.APIN UD-14-KÁM
9′ *lim-mu* ^{md}PA—PAB—KAM-*eš*
10′ LÚ*$^{!}$.GAR.KUR URU.*sam-al-li*

s.1 ⸢*d*⸣*nt* ^{c}*tr*$^{!}$*s*$^{!}$[*mk*]

2 [Witness] Kandalanu.
3 Witness Radimu.
4 Witness Haruṣâ.
5 Witness Bel-Harran-duri, singer.
6 Witness Il-gabbê.
7 Witness Nabû-ahu-uṣur.
8 Month Marchesvan (VIII), 14th day, [epon]ym year of Nabû-ahu-ereš, governor of Sam'al.
s.1 (Aramaic caption:) Deed of Atar-š[umki].

195 Previous edition: AR 63. Collations: Assur 2/5.
196 Previous edition: AR 533; → ABC 3. Caption: Ep. Ar. 13, ABC 3, Fales Epigraphs 4. Collations: Assur 2/5.

197. Tabni-Issar Buys a Maid (681-II-5)

Sm 701

1 NA$_4$.KIŠIB ^{m}*dà-ri*—AD-*u-a*
2 EN MÍ SUM-*ni*

---

3 MÍ.^{d}*na-na*—TUK-*ši*!! GEMÉ-*šú*
4 *ša* ^{m}*dà-ri*—AD-*u-a ú-piš-ma*
5 ^{m}*tab-ni*—^{d}15 *ina* ŠÀ 1 1/2 MA.[NA]
6 [KUG.UD *x x x x*] TI-*qí ka*[*s-pu*]
7 [*gam-m*]*ur ta-din* MÍ *šú*-[*a-te zar-pat*]

8 [*la*]-⌈*qi*⌉-*at man-nu š*[*a i-za-qu-pa-ni*]
9 [*lu-u* ^{m}*dà-r*]*i*—AD-[*u-a lu-u* DUMU.MEŠ-*šú*]
10 [*lu-u* DUMU—DUMU.MEŠ-*šú l*]*u*!-*u* [ŠEŠ.MEŠ-*šú*]
11 *l*[*u-u* DUMU—PAB.MEŠ-*šú ša* TA*!]
12 ^{m}*tab-ni*—^{d}15 DUM[U.MEŠ-*šú* DUMU—DUMU-*šú*]
13 *de-e-nu ub-ta-u-ni*
14 2 MA.NA KUG.UD SUM-*an*!
r.1 MÍ *ú-še-ṣa*
2 IGI ^{m}*bar-r*[*uq*]
3 IGI ^{m}*ag-*[*ru*]
4 IGI ^{m}PA!—[*za-qip*—SIG]
5 IGI ^{m}*x*[*x x x x x*]
6 IGI ^{m}*ki-ma-*[*ma-a-a*]
7 IGI ^{m}*ri-ha-*[*te*]
blank space of 5 lines
8 ITI.GUD UD-5-KÁM *lim-*[*mu ša*]

9 *á*[*r*]-*kàt* ^{md}PA—MAN—PAB
10 LÚ.GAR.KUR *mar-qa-sa*

ADD 213

1 Seal of Dari-abu'a, owner of the woman being sold.

(space for stamp seal impressions)

---

3 Nanâ-lurši, maid of Dari-abu'a —

5 Tabni-Issar has contracted and [bou]ght her for 1 1/2 mi[nas of silver ...].

6 The mo[ney] is paid [comp]letely. Th[at] woman [is purchased and acq]uired.

8 Whoever [lodges a complaint whether Dar]i-ab[u'a or his sons or his grandsons o]r [his brothers] o[r his nephews, and] seeks a lawsuit [against] Tabni-Issar, [his] son[s or grandsons], shall pay two minas of silver to redeem the woman.

r.2 Witness Barr[uqu].

3 Witness Ag[ru].

4 Witness Nabû-[zaqip-enši].

5 Witness [NN].

6 Witness Kima[maya].

7 Witness Riha[ti].

8 Month Iyyar (II), 5th day, the year after the eponym year of Nabû-šarru-uṣur, governor of Marqasa.

198. Purchase of a Maid

K 1608A

beginning broken away
1′ [*tu-a-ru de-nu* DUG$_4$].⌈DUG$_4$⌉

2′ [*la-áš-šú man-nu ša* GI]L-*u*!-*ni*
3′ [*x* MA.NA KUG.UD *x* MA].NA KUG.GI
4′ *ina bur-ki* ^{d}IM *a-šib* URU.*ana-na*! GAR
5′ *kas-pu a-na* 10.MEŠ-*te*
6′ *a-na* EN.MEŠ-*šú* GUR
r.1 ^{m}*ku-ru-ku* EN—ŠU.2.MEŠ *ša*! MÍ
2 IGI ^{m}*iš-ta*—^{d}*šér*

ADD 228

(Beginning destroyed)

1 [Any revocation, lawsuit, or litig]ation [is void].

2 [Whoever breaks the] contract shall place [x minas of silver (and) x mi]nas of gold in the lap of Adad residing in Anah. He shall return the money tenfold to its owners.

r.1 Kuruku is the guarantor of the woman.

2 Witness Išta-Šer.

197 Previous editions: AR 189, NALK 381. Collations: Assur 2/5. 3 See coll.
198 Previous editions: AR 641, NALK 382. Collations: Assur 2/5.

3 IGI ^{m}*ag-ru*
4 ⸢IGI⸣ ^{m}*bar-ruq*
5 [IGI ^{m}]*ri-ha-te*
6 [IGI ^{m}]$^{⸢d!⸣}$PA—[*za*$^{!}$]-*qip*—SIG
7 [IGI ^{m}*ki-ma-ma*]-*a-a*
rest broken away

3 Witness Agru.
4 Witness Barruqu.
5 [Witness] Rihati.
6 [Witness] Nabû-zaqip-enši.
7 Witness [Kimam]aya.
(Rest destroyed)

199. Purchase of Slaves

K 371

1 NA$_4$.KIŠ[IB] ^{m}*r*[*ém*$^{?}$-*x x x*]
2 [EN U]N.MEŠ
rest broken away
Rev. beginning broken away
1′ [*x x la*] ⸢*i-laq-qi*⸣

2′ IGI ^{m}*a-bi-lu* LÚ.GAL—*ki-ṣir*
3′ IGI ^{m}*sa-e-ru* LÚ.3.[U$_5$]
4′ IGI ^{m}EN—NUMUN—AŠ [*x x x*]
5′ IGI ^{md}PA—I LÚ.*su-sa-n*[*u*$^{?}$ *x x*]
6′ IGI ^{m}KAM—DINGIR LÚ.3.U$_5$ *ša* A-[MAN]

7′ IGI ^{md}PA—*nam-mir* L[Ú.*x x x*]
8′ IGI ^{md}PA-*u-a* LÚ.ARAD [*x x x x*]
9′ IGI ^{md}30—LAL-*in* LÚ.*mu*-[*x x x*]
10′ IGI ^{m}*se-e*ʾ—*pa-rak-ka* [*x x*]
11′ IGI ^{m}DINGIR—*im-me* LÚ.[*x x x x*]
12′ IGI ^{m}⸢*ha*⸣-*an-di-i* [*x x x*]
13e [IGI] ^{m}*man-nu*—*ki*—^{d}IM [*x x x*]
rest broken away

ADD 273

1 Seal of *R*[*emanni-*...], owner of the people [being sold].
(Break)
r.1 [He shall contest in his lawsuit and not] succeed.

---

2 Witness Abilu, cohort commander.
3 Witness Sa'iru, 'thir[d man].'
4 Witness Bel-zeru-iddina, [...].
5 Witness Nabû-na'id, horse trai[ner ...].
6 Witness Ereš-ilu, 'third man' of the cro[wn prince].
7 Witness Nabû-nammir, [...].
8 Witness Nabû'a, servant of [...].
9 Witness Sin-mutaqqin, [...].
10 Witness Se'-barakka, [...].
11 Witness Il-immi, [...].
12 Witness Handî, [...].
13 Witness Mannu-ki-Adad, [...]
(Rest destroyed)

200. Purchase of a House

K 1603

1 NA$_4$.KIŠIB ^{md}UTU—AD-*u-a*
2 DUMU ^{m}*ka-a-ki ša* URU.*ma-ga-ni*-⸢*ib*$^{!}$⸣
3 EN É *ta*-SUM-*ni*

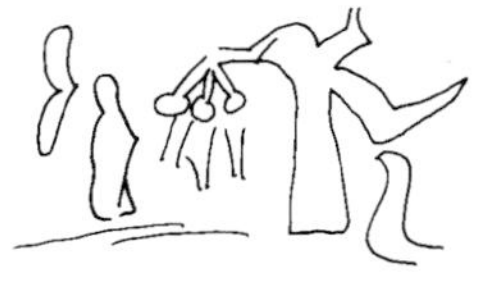

ADD 337

1 Seal of Šamaš-abu'a son of Kaki from Maganuba, owner of the house being sold.

(cylinder seal impression)

199 Previous edition: ADD 550. Dating this document to the reign of Sennacherib is made likely by the names of the witnesses, most of whom are well attested in texts dating between 693-681 (Il-immi 693, Seʾ-barakka 693, Nabû-nammir 692, 690, 686, and 685, Nabû-naid 681, Handî 682, 683, Saeru 683).
200 Previous editions: AR 178. The dating of this document to the reign of Sennacherib is tentative only (cf. Bahianu and Daniyati-ilu, Iraq 32 6 [681 B.C]).

4 ⌜*x x*⌝ É *tal-pi-te*
5 [*x x x*]*x* 1 A$^{!}$.MEŠ *bi il*$^{?}$ *kan na ki-qí*$^{!}$*-il-te*
6 [SUHUR É] ^{m}*ba-hi-a-ni*
7 [SUHUR É] ^{m}*da-ni-ia-ti*—DINGIR

8 [*kaq-qi-ri p*]*u*$^{!}$*-ṣe-e* 30 GÍD$^{!}$.D[A]$^{!}$
9 [*x x x x ina*] URU.*ma-g*[*a-ni-ib*]
10 [*x x x x x x x x*] *di* [*x x x*]
rest broken away
Rev. beginning broken away
1′ [2 MA.NA KUG].UD 1 MA.NA KUG.GI
2′ [*ina bur-ki* ^{d}NI]N$^{!}$.LÍL GAR-*an*
3′ [2 ANŠE.KUR.RA.MEŠ] BABBAR.MEŠ *ina* GÌR.2$^{!}$ *aš-šur*
4′ [*a-šib* É.ŠÁR.RA] KÉŠ$^{!}$
5′ [*ina de-ni-šú i-da*]*-bu-bu-ma*
6′ [*la i-laq*]*-qi*

7′ [IGI ^{m}*x x x x x*] A—SIG *šá* ⌜GAŠAN$^{!}$⌝—É$^{!}$ *šá* DUMU—MAN
8′ [IGI ^{m}*x x x x* DUMU ^{m}*x*]-⌜*x*⌝*-u-ni*
9′ [IGI ^{m}*x x x x* DUMU ^{m}]*ma-ri-i*ʾ
10′ [IGI ^{m}*x x x x*] DUMU ^{m}PAB-*u-a*—SU
11′ [IGI ^{m}*x x x x x x*] *ša* URU.*ha-ta-ia-te*
12′ [IGI ^{m}*x x x x x x*]*x*
rest vitrified

4 [...] house, a *barn*
5 [...] water ... *dung heap*
6 adjoining the house of Bahianu and the house of Daniati-ilu,
8 a vacant lot 30 (cubits) long [...] in the town Mag[anuba]
(Break)

r.1 shall place [two minas of sil]ver and one mina of gold [in the lap of Mul]lissu, and shall tie [two] white [horses] to the feet of Aššur [residing in Ešarra]. [He shall con]test [in his lawsuit] and [not suc]ceed.

---

7 [Witness NN], chariot fighter of the lady of the house of the crown prince.
8 [Witness NN], son of [...]unu.
9 [Witness NN], son of Mari'.
10 [Witness NN, son of Ahu'a-eriba.
11 [Witness NN, ...] of Hatayate.
(Rest destroyed)

Texts from the Reign of Esarhaddon

10. Mannu-ki-Arbail, Cohort Commander (680-673)

FIG. 22. *An Assyrian village, perhaps Balatu, with domed roofs (about 700 BC).*
ORIGINAL DRAWING IV, 51.

201. Mannu-ki-Arbail Buys a Vineyard (680-II-28)

83-1-18,460 | ADD 360

1 [NA$_4$.KIŠIB ^{m}]*id-ri-iá* EN GIŠ.SAR SUM-*ni*

---

2 GIŠ.SAR *zaq-pu šá* GIŠ.*til-lit*
3 *ina* URU.*ur-ul-li* SUHUR *ad-ri*
4 SUHUR *qab-li* SUHUR KASKAL *šá ina* URU.*kip-šu-u-ni*
5 DU-*u-ni* SUHUR *šá a-na mu-še-bi-rit* DU-*ni*
6 SUHUR GIŠ.SAR *šá* ^{md}IM—DÙ-*ni*
7 *ú-piš-ma* ^{m}*man-nu—ki-i*—URU.*arba-ìl*
8 LÚ.GAL—*ki-ṣir* TA* IGI
9 ^{m}*ad-ra-iá ina* ŠÀ 31 GÍN.MEŠ KUG.UD
10 TI-*qí kas-pu gam*$^{!}$-*mur ta-ad-din*
11 GIŠ.SAR *šu-a-tú za-rip laq-qí*
12 *tú-a-ru* ⌜*de*⌝-*e-nu* DUG$_4$.DUG$_4$
13 *la-áš-šú man-nu šá ina ur-kiš a-na ma-te-ma*
14 *i-zaq-qup-an-ni lu-u* ^{m}*ad-ri-iá*
15 *lu-u* DUMU.⌜MEŠ⌝-*šú lu-u* DUMU—DUMU.MEŠ-*šú*
16 *lu-u* PAB.MEŠ-*šú lu-u* DUMU—PAB.MEŠ-*šú*
17 *šá de-e-nu* DUG$_4$.DUG$_4$
18 TA* ^{m}*man-nu—ki-i*—URU.*arba-ìl*
19 DUMU.MEŠ-*šú u* DUMU—DUMU.MEŠ-*šú*
20 [*u*]*b-ta-'u-u-ni* 10 MA.NA KUG.UD LUH-*u*
21 [5$^{?}$ M]A.NA KUG.GI *sak-ru*
r.1 *ina bur-ki* ^{d}IŠ.TAR *a-ši-bat*
2 URU.NINA GAR-*an kas-pu a-na* 10.MEŠ-*te*
3 *a-na* EN.MEŠ-*šú* GUR-*ra ina de-ni-šú*
4 DUG$_4$.DUG$_4$-*ma la* TI-*qí*

---

5 IGI ^{md}PA—PAB—AŠ LÚ.SANGA
6 IGI ^{m}A-*i* IGI ^{m}*du-sa-a*
7 IGI ^{md}*šér*—⌜*ú*⌝-*a-ri* LÚ.GAL—*šad*$^{!}$-*dan-ni*
8 IGI ^{m}UD-7-KÁM—DINGIR-*a-a* ARAD *ša* A—MAN
9 IGI ^{m}*hal-di*—DINGIR-*a-a* LÚ.NU.GIŠ.SAR
10 IGI ^{m}*aš-šur*—MU—GIŠ
11 IGI ^{m}*ia-da-nu*

---

1 [Seal of] Edriya, owner of the garden being sold.

(space for stamp seal impressions)

---

2 A planted vineyard in the town of Urulli, adjoining a threshing floor, a grove, the road which goes to Kipšuna, one which leads to the ferry, and the garden of Adad-ibni —

7 Mannu-ki-Arbail, the cohort commander, has contracted and bought it from Adraya for 31 shekels of silver.

10 The money is paid completely. That vineyard is purchased and acquired. Any revocation, lawsuit, or litigation is void.

13 Whoever in the future, at any time, lodges a complaint, whether Adriya or his sons, grandsons, brothers or nephews, and seeks a lawsuit or litigation against Mannu-ki-Arbail, his sons and his grandsons, shall place 10 minas of refined silver (and) [5 mi]nas of pure gold in the lap of Ištar residing in Nineveh. He shall return the money tenfold to its owners. He shall contest in his lawsuit and not succeed.

---

r.5 Witness Nabû-ahu-iddina, priest.

6 Witness Aplî. Witness Dusâ.

7 Witness Šer-uari, coffer-master.

8 Witness Sebetti-ila'i, servant of the crown prince.

9 Witness Haldi-ila'i, gardener.

10 Witness Aššur-šumu-lešir.

11 Witness Yadanu.

201 Previous editions: AR 373, NALK 152; → Postgate FNALD 4. 1, 10, 14, r.7 See coll. r.8 For the reading of the PN, cf. UD-7-KAM = *seb-ti* (for *sebetti*, between *šeššetti* and *samanti*) Hh I 184, and the spelling UD-7-KAM for *sebet ūmī* in ABL 370:10 (see LAS 2 p. 198). Note also the PN 7.BI—DINGIR—KUR, CTN 3 145 iii 14.

12 IGI [md]PA—LAL-*in-a-ni* LÚ.A.BA
blank space of 5 lines
13 ITI.GUD UD-28-KÁM *lim-mu* [m]*da-na-nu*
14 *ina tar-ṣi* [m]*aš-šur*—PAB—AŠ MAN KUR—*aš-šur*.KI
15 2 UD-*mu*.MEŠ 2 MI.MEŠ
16 A.MEŠ *ut-ru-te* NAG

12 Witness Nabû-taqqinanni, scribe.

13 Month Iyyar (II), 28th day, eponym year of Dananu, in the reign of Esarhaddon, king of Assyria.

15 He can draw extra water for two days and two nights.

202. Mannu-ki-Arbail Buys a Vineyard in Kipšuna (680-IV-18)

K 332

1 ⸢NA_4.KIŠIB [m]*bal*⸣-*ṭa-a-a*
2 LÚ*.A.⸢BA![?]⸣ EN GIŠ.SAR
3 *ša* GIŠ.*til-lit-*[*ti*!] SUM-*ni*

---

4 GIŠ.SAR *ša* GIŠ.*til-lit-ti*!
5 *ina* URU.*kip-šu-na*
6 SUHUR GIŠ.SAR *ša* [m]PAB—⸢DU⸣-*ka*
7 SUHUR ÍD :. *ša* [m]*ur*-⸢*ba-a-a*⸣
8 SUHUR ⸢SUHUŠ[?]⸣ *bur-ti*!
9 [*ú*]-⸢*piš*⸣-*ma* [m]*man-nu*—⸢*ki-i*—*arba*⸣-*ìl*
10 [T]A IGI [m]*bal-ṭa-a-a*
11 [*ina*] ŠÀ 4 ⸢MA⸣.NA KUG.UD
12 [*š*]*a* URU.*gar-ga-mis*
13 [*i*]*l-qi kas-pu gam-mur*
14 [SU]M!-*ni* GIŠ.⸢SAR⸣ *šu-a*-⸢*tú*⸣
e.15 [*za-ri*]*p laq*-⸢*qi*⸣ *tú-a*-⸢*ru*⸣
16 [*de-nu*!] DUG_4.⸢DUG_4⸣ *la-áš-šú*
r.1 [*man-nu šá*] *in*[*a ur*]-*kiš*
2 [*ina ma-t*]*e-ma* ⸢*i-za*⸣-*qu-pa-ni*
3 [GI]L-*u-ni* 12 MA.NA KUG.UD
4 [*x* MA.N]A KUG.GI *a-na* [d]15
5 [*a-ši-bat*] ⸢URU.*ni-nu*⸣-*a* SUM-*an*
6 [*kas-pu*] ⸢*a-na* 10.MEŠ⸣-[*te*] ⸢*a*⸣-*na* EN.MEŠ-*šú* GUR
7 [*ina de-ni*]-*šú* DUG_4.DUG_4-*ma là* TI

---

8 ITI.ŠU UD-18-KÁM
9 *lim-me* [m]*da*-⸢*na*⸣-*nu*
10 *ša* URU.*man*-⸢*ṣu-a*⸣-*te*
11 IGI [md]*aš-šur*—DINGIR-*a*-⸢*a*⸣
12 ⸢IGI⸣ [md]PA—KAR-*ir-an-ni*
13 IGI [m]*sa-me-e*ʾ
14 ⸢IGI⸣ [m]*ú-su-na-a*
15 ⸢IGI⸣ [m]*la-ap-sa-re-e*
16 ⸢IGI⸣ [m]*da-ia*!-*a* 0!
17e IGI [m]⸢*a*⸣-*si-nu-u*

s.1 [*ina tar-ṣi* [m]*aš-šur*]—PAB—AŠ MAN KUR—*aš-šur* GIŠ.SAR ⸢*laq-qi*⸣

ADD 359

1 Seal of Balṭaya, scribe, owner of the vineyard being sold.

(space for stamp seal impressions)

---

4 A vineyard in the city of Kipšuna adjoining the garden of Ahu-illika, the canal of ditto of Urbayu, and the *foundation* of a well —

9 Mannu-ki-Arbail has contracted and bought it from Balṭaya [for] 4 minas of silver (by the mina) of Carchemish.

13 The money [is pa]id completely. That vineyard [is purch]ased and acquired. Any revocation, [lawsuit], or litigation is void.

r.1 [Whoever] in [the fut]ure, [at any t]ime, lodges a complaint [and breaks] the contract, shall pay 12 minas of silver [and x min]as of gold to Ištar [residing in] Nineveh, and shall return [the money] tenfold to its owners. He shall contest [in] his [lawsuit] and not succeed.

---

8 Month Tammuz (IV), 18th day, eponym year of Dananu of Manṣuati.

11 Witness Aššur-ila'i.

12 Witness Nabû-eṭiranni.

13 Witness Same'.

14 Witness Usunâ.

15 Witness Lapsarê.

16 Witness Dayâ.

17 Witness Asinû.

s.1 The vineyard was purchased [in the reign of Esar]haddon, king of Assyria.

202 Previous editions: AR 372, NALK 153. Collations: Assur 2/5.

203. Fragment of a Purchase of Slaves (680-II)

K 7507

1 NA$_4$.KIŠIB ^{m}*ina-*[*x x x x*]
2 NA$_4$.KIŠIB ^{m}SUHUŠ—[*x x x*]
3 NA$_4$.KIŠIB ^{m}*ha-an-*[*x x x*]
4 NA$_4$.KIŠIB ^{m}SIG$_5$—IN[IM$^?$.MEŠ—LUGAL]
5 [LÚ].MEŠ EN UN.MEŠ [SUM-*ni*]

rest broken away
Rev. beginning broken away
1′ [IG]I ^{m}*sa-me-*[*e*ʾ *x x x*]
2′ ITI.GUD *lim-m*[*u* ^{m}*da-na-nu*$^?$]
3′ *ti-ri-ṣi* ^{m}*aš-š*[*ur*—PAB—AŠ]
4e MAN KUR—[*aš-šur*.KI]

ADD 299

1 Seal of [......],
2 Seal of Ubru-[...],
3 Seal of Han[...],
4 Seal of Danqu-*d*[*ibbi-šarri*],
5 [gentlem]en, owners of the people [being sold].
(seal impressions)
(Break)

r.1 Witness Sam[e', ...].
2 Month Iyyar (II), eponym ye[ar of *Dananu*], in the reign of Es[arhaddon], king of As[syria].

204. Mannu-ki-Arbail Buys a Garden in Nineveh (679-VII-13)

K 341

1 NA$_4$.KIŠIB ^{m}*bi-bi-i* EN—GIŠ.GIGIR
2 EN GIŠ.SAR SUM-*ni*

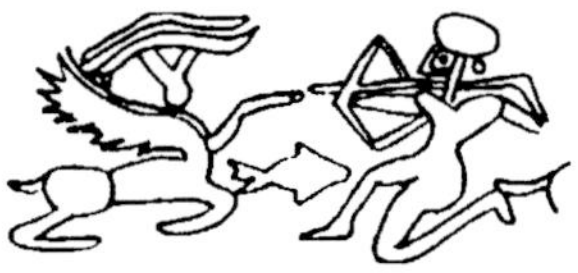

3 GIŠ.SAR *ša* Ú.SAR *ina* URU.*ni-nu-a*
4 *ina* IGI *ti-tu-ri* SUMUN
5 SUHUR GIŠ.SAR *ša* ^{md}PA—GIN—*du-gul* LÚ*.A—S[IG]
6 SUHUR GIŠ.SAR *ša* ^{d}MAŠ.MAŠ
7 SUHUR KASKAL—MAN SUHUR ÍD
8 *ú-piš-ma* ^{m}*man-nu—ki—arba-*[*ìl*]
9 [*ina* ŠÀ *x* MA.N]A K[UG.UD] ⸢*il*⸣-[*qi*]
rest broken away
Rev. beginning broken away
1′ *ina d*[*e-ni-šú* DUG$_4$.DUG$_4$-*ma la i-laq-qi*]

2′ IGI ^{md}PA—[*x x x x x x*]
3′ IGI ^{m}*aš-šur*—MU—G[IN$^?$ *x x x x*]
4′ IGI ^{m}*qur-di*—^{d}⸢15$^{!}$⸣ [LÚ.GAL—*ki-ṣir*]
5′ IGI ^{m}*gi-ni-ia* L[Ú.*x x x*]
6′ IGI ^{m}*da-ni-i* L[Ú.*x x x*]

ADD 364

1 Seal of Bibî, chariot fighter, owner of the garden being sold.

(cylinder seal impression)

3 A vegetable garden in Nineveh facing the old bridge, and adjoining the garden of Nabû-kenu-dugul the chariot fighter, the garden of Nergal, the king's road, and the river —

8 Mannu-ki-Arbail has contracted and bou[ght it for x mi]nas of sil[ver]
(Break)
r.1 [He shall contest] in [his lawsuit and not succeed].

2 Witness Nabû-[......].
3 Witness Aššur-šumu-ka[''in, ...].
4 Witness Qurdi-Issar, [cohort commander].
5 Witness Ginniya, [...].
6 Witness Danî, [...].

203 Previous edition: AR 546.
204 Previous editions: AR 374, NALK 154. Collated by I.L. Finkel. r.3f See coll.

7′ IGI ^{md}IM—SUM—MU LÚ.⸢GAL—*ki-ṣir*⸣
8′ IGI ^{m}SUHUŠ—KASKAL LÚ.: *gi-mir-a-a*
9′ IGI ^{m}PAB—DINGIR-*a-a ša*—GÌR.2
10′ IGI ^{m}DI-*mu*—EN—*la-áš-me* LÚ*.MU
11′ IGI ^{m}*rém-a-ni*—BE LÚ.SUM.NINDA
12′ IGI ^{m}SUHUŠ—^{d}7.BI LÚ.DAM.QAR
13e [ITI].DUL UD-13-KÁM *lim-mu* ^{m}TA*—^{d}IM—*a-ni-*⸢*nu*⸣

[7] Witness Adad-nadin-šumi, cohort commander.
[8] Witness Ubru-Harran, Cimmerian ditto.
[9] Witness Ahi-ila'i, *ša šepi* guard.
[10] Witness Šulmu-beli-lašme, cook.
[11] Witness Remanni-Illil, confectioner.
[12] Witness Ubru-Sebetti, merchant.
[13] Month Tishri (VII), 13th day, eponym year of Issi-Adad-aninu.

205. ——

81-2-4,457

beginning broken away
1′ [*x x x x x x x x x x*] *x*
2′ [*x x x x x x x x x x*] *la* TI
rest broken away
Rev. beginning broken away
1′ [IGI ^{m}*x x*]-*di-a* LÚ.*šá*—GÌR.2
4′ [IGI ^{m}*x x*]*x-ta-a*ʾ LÚ.3-*šú*
3′ [IGI ^{m}DI-*mu*—EN]—*la-áš-me* LÚ.MU
4′ [IGI ^{m}*x x x x x*] LÚ.2-*u*
5′ [IGI ^{m}*rém-a-ni*—BE LÚ].SUM.NINDA
rest broken away

ADD 588

(Beginning destroyed)
[2] [He shall contest in his lawsuit and] not succeed.
(Break)
[r.1] [Witness ...]dia, *ša šēpi* guard.
[4] [Witness ...]ta', 'third man.'
[3] [Witness Šulmu-beli]-lašme, cook.
[4] [Witness NN], deputy.
[5] [Witness Remanni-Illil], confectioner.
(Rest destroyed)

206. Note of a Mule Owed to Mannu-ki-Arbail (679-XI-15)

Bu 91-5-9,10

1 0$^{!}$ ANŠE.GÌR$^{!}$.NUN.NA SIG
2 *ša* ^{m}*man-nu*—GIM—URU.*arba-ìl*
3 *ina* IGI ^{m}GIŠ.BAL—*li-pi-re*$^{!}$-*e*
4 ^{m}*ur-da-a* EN—ŠU.2.MEŠ
5 *ina* ITI.GUD SUM-*an*
6 [*šum-ma l*]*a* SUM-*an*
7 ⸢30$^{?}$⸣ MA.NA KUG.UD
r.1 *a-na* LUGAL SUM-*an*
2 ITI.ZÍZ UD-15-⸢KÁM⸣
3 *lim-mu* ^{m}TA—^{d}IM—*a-ni-nu*
4 IGI ^{m}*ar-ze-zu* LÚ*.GAL$^{!}$—*ki*$^{!}$-*ṣir*$^{!}$
5 IGI ^{m}*ma-mì-i* LÚ*.:
6 [IGI ^{m}]*ha*—*ba-sa-tú* LÚ*.GAL—Ì.DU$_{8}$.MEŠ
7 [IGI ^{m}*k*]*ù*$^{!}$-*ba-bu*—DINGIR-*a-a*
8e [IGI] ^{m}*a*-⸢*bi*⸣-*lu-re-e*
9e IGI ^{m}*aš-šur*—DINGIR-*a-a*

ADD 150

[1] A good mule belonging to Mannu-ki-Arbail, at the disposal of Pilaqqi-lipirê.
[4] Urdâ is the guarantor.
[5] He shall give it back in Iyyar (III). [If he does n]ot, he shall pay *30* minas of silver to the king.
[r.2] Month Shebat (XI), 15th day, eponym year of Issi-Adad-aninu.
[4] Witness Arzezu, cohort commander.
[5] Witness Mamî, ditto.
[6] [Witness] Habasti, head porter.
[7] [Witness K]ubabu-ila'i.
[8] [Witness] Abilurê.
[9] Witness Aššur-ila'i.

205 No previous edition.
206 Previous editions: AR 222, NALK 155. [1] See coll.; nothing missing before ANŠE. [3] See coll. The reading and interpretation of the name is uncertain. If Akkadian, it could mean "May the (or my) spindle [an emblem of Ištar] sprout forth," i.e. "May my devotion to Ištar bring me progeny"; cf. ^{m}GIŠ.BAL-*a*, no. 90:5. If foreign, it could be read ^{m}*is-pal-li-pi-re-e*, cf. the toponyms Išpilipria and Ispallurê (AOAT 6 p. 177f). [7, r.3, 7] See coll.

207. Mannu-ki-Arbail Purchases Land (678-II-21)

Th 1905-4-9,43

beginning broken away
1′ [*x x x*] ⸢*x*⸣ [*x x x x*]
2′ [TA IGI ^{m}]⸢*x x*⸣-*l*[*u il-qi*]

3′ [*kas*]-*pu*! *ga-mur*! *t*[*a*!-*din*]
4′ [A].ŠÀ *šu-a-te za-r*[*ip*]
5′ [*la-q*]*i*! *tu-a-ru d*[*e-nu*]
6′ [DU]G$_4$.DUG$_4$ *la-áš*-[*šú*]
e.7′ [*m*]*an-nu šá ina u*[*r*]-⸢*kiš*⸣ [0]
8′ *lu-u* $^{m!}$*si-i-lu*! [0]
9′ ⸢*lu*⸣-*u* DUMU.MEŠ-*šú* [0]
r.1 ⸢*ša*!⸣ *de-e-nu* DU[G$_4$.DUG$_4$]
2 TA* ^{m}*man-nu—ki—a*[*rba*!-*ìl*]
3 *ub-ta-u*-[*ni*]
4 10 MA.NA KUG.U[D LUH-*u*]
5 *ina bur-ki* ⸢^{d}⸣[*x x* GAR]
6 *ina de-ni-šú* D[UG$_4$.DUG$_4$-*ma là* TI]

---

7 IGI ^{m}*si*-⸢*x*⸣ [*x x x x*]
8 [IGI] ⸢^{m}⸣[*x x x x x x*]
rest broken away

s.1 ITI.GUD UD-21-K[ÁM! *lim-mu* ^{m}U.GUR—MAN—PAB]
2 [0] LÚ*.GA[L—KAŠ.LUL]

ADD 1240

(Beginning destroyed)

1 [Mannu-ki-Arbail has purchased and acquired it from *S*]*il*[*u*] for [......].

3 [The mo]ney is p[aid] completely. That [fi]eld is purch[ased and acq]uired. Any revocation, la[wsuit, or liti]gation is voi[d].

7 [Who]ever in the fu[tu]re, whether Silu or his sons, seeks a lawsuit or li[tigation] against Mannu-ki-A[rbail, shall place] 10 minas of [pure] sil[ver] in the lap of [DN]. He shall lit[igate] in his lawsuit [and not succeed].

---

7 Witness Si[...].
8 Witness [NN].
(Break)

s.1 Month Iyyar (II), 21st day, eponym year of [Nergal-šarru-uṣur], chief [cupbearer].

208. Note of Silver Owed to Mannu-ki-Arbail (678-VI-3)

Rm 173

1 12 1/2 MA.NA 5 GÍN KUG.[UD *x x*]
2 *ša* ^{m}*man-nu—ki-i*—[*arba-ìl*]
3 *ina* IGI ^{m}*ṣil*—EN [*x x x*]

---

4 [IT]I.DUL KUG.UD SUM-*a*[*n*]
5 [*šum*]-*ma la i*-[*din*]
6 ⸢KUG⸣.UD *i-ra*-[*bi*]

e.7 ITI.KIN UD-3!-KÁM *lim-mu* ^{m}U.G[UR—MAN—PAB]
r.1 IGI ^{m}MAŠ!—EN—[*x x x*]
2 IGI ^{m}*man-nu—ki-i*—[PAB.MEŠ]
3 IGI ^{m}*man-nu—ki-i*—[AD]
4 IGI ^{md}PA—PAB.MEŠ—[*x x*]
5 IGI ^{md}PA—KAR—ZI.MEŠ
6 LÚ*.A.BA

ADD 18

1 12 1/2 minas 5 shekels of sil[ver] belonging to Mannu-ki-[Arbail], (are) at the disposal of Ṣilli-Bel [...].

(blank seal space)

---

4 He shall pay the silver in Tishri (VII). [I]f he does not p[ay], the silver shall bear interest.

7 Month Elul (VI), 3rd day, eponym year of Ne[rgal-šarru-uṣur].

r.1 Witness Inurta-belu-[...].
2 Witness Mannu-ki-[ahhe].
3 Witness Mannu-ki-[abi].
4 Witness Nabû-ahhe-[...].
5 Witness Nabû-eṭir-napšati, scribe.

207 Previous edition: NALK 168. 1ff, r.2 See coll.
208 Previous edition: AR 269, NALK 166. 3 See coll. r.1 See coll. r.2f There is no room for LÚ*.*rak-su* at the end of these lines.

209. Sale of a House, Field and Threshing-Floor

K 3487

beginning broken away

1′ [NA$_4$.KIŠIB ^{m}*x x* A ^{m}]ITI.NE-*a-a*

2′ [NA$_4$.KIŠIB MÍ.*x*]-*da-ta* DUMU.MÍ-*su*

3′ [PAB 2 LÚ].MEŠ-*e* LÚ*.NINDA.MEŠ *ša* LÚ*.IGI.DUB GAL-*e*

4′ [EN É A.ŠÀ *ad*]-*ri ta-da-ni*

rest broken away

Rev. beginning broken away

1′ [IGI ^{m}*x x x x* LÚ*.*mu-kil*]—KUŠ.PA.MEŠ

2′ [IGI ^{m}*x x x x* LÚ*].*mu-kil*—KUŠ.PA.MEŠ

3′ [IGI ^{md}PA—NU]MUN—AŠ LÚ*.A.BA

4′ [IGI ^{md}PA]—KAR-*ir*—ZI.MEŠ LÚ*.A.BA

5′ [IGI ^{m}*x x*]-*nu* LÚ*.A.BA

6′ [*ša* LÚ*].IGI.DUB GAL-*e*

7′ [IGI ^{md}*x*]—*še-zib* LÚ*.*ha-za-nu*

8e [*x x x x*] URU.*arba-ìl*

ADD 617

(Beginning destroyed)

1 Seal of [NN], son of Abaya,

2 Seal of [...]data, his daughter,

3 [a total of 2 person]s, bakers of the grand treasurer, [owners of the house, field and thre]shing-floor being sold.

(Break)

r.1 [Witness NN, chariot] driver.

2 [Witness NN], chariot driver.

3 [Witness Nabû-ze]ru-iddina, scribe.

4 [Witness Nabû]-eṭir-napšati, scribe.

5 [Witness ...]nu, scribe of the grand treasurer.

7 [Witness ...]-šezib, mayor [*of*] Arbela.

210. Mannu-ki-Arbail Buys a House (676-I-24)

83-1-18,337

1 NA$_4$.KIŠIB ^{m}*še-li-pi*

2 EN É *ta-da-ni*

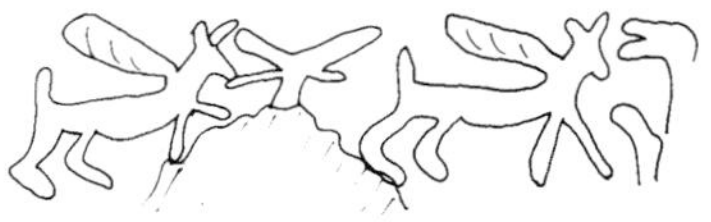

3 É *ep-*[*šú a-di* GIŠ.ÙR].MEŠ-*šú a-*⸢*di*⸣ [GIŠ].⸢IG⸣.MEŠ-*šú*

4 *me-šil a*[*d-ri x x x x*] A.QAR URU.⸢*zi*?⸣-*da-da*

5 *tak*!-*pi-*[*x x x ina g*]*i-mir-*⸢*ti*⸣-*šá*

6 SUHUR É [^{m}U?].U!—*iq-bi*

7 SUHUR [É ^{m}*x x*]-*mu*—*e-ri*

8 *ú-*[*piš-ma* ^{m}*man-n*]*u*—*ki*—URU.*arba-ìl*

9 [TA* IGI ^{m}*še*]-*li-pi*

10 [*ina* ŠÀ *x* MA.NA] KUG.UD

11 [*ša* URU.*gar-ga-mis i*]*l*!-*qi kas-pu*

12 [*gam-mur ta-din*] É *za-rip*

13 [*laq-qi tu-a-ru d*]*e-nu* DUG$_4$.⸢DUG$_4$⸣

14 [*la-áš-šú man-nu ša ina*] ⸢*ur*⸣-[*kiš*]

break of 2 lines

e.17 [TA*] ^{m}*man-nu*—*k*[*i*—URU.*arba-ìl*]

18 ⸢*ù*!⸣ DUMU.MEŠ-*šú ub-t*[*a-u-ni*]

19 2! MA.NA KUG.UD 2 MA.[NA KUG.GI]

r.1 *ina* ^{d}IŠ.TAR *a-ši-pat*! URU.*arba-ìl* S[UM!-*an*]

ADD 330

1 Seal of Šelepu, owner of the house being sold.

(cylinder seal impression)

3 A bui[lt] house [with] its [beams] and doors, a half of a thr[eshing floor ... in] the irrigated land (of) the town of Zidada, a ...[... in] its entirety, adjoining the house [of *Da*]*di*-iqbi and [the house of ...]mu-eri —

8 [Mann]u-ki-Arbail has [contracted and boug]ht it [from Še]lepu [for x minas] of silver (by the mina) [of Carchemish].

11 The money [is paid completely]. The house is purchased [and acquired. Any revocation, law]suit, or litigation is void.

14 [Whoever in] the fut[ure, *at any time, lodges a complaint, whether Šelepu or his sons*], and se[eks *a lawsuit or litigation* against] Mannu-k[i-Arbail] and his sons, shall [pay] two minas of silver (and) two

209 Previous edition: AR 577.

210 Previous editions: AR 195, NALK 156. Collations: Assur 2/5. 4 See coll. r.3 The tablet has *i-la-qi*, as

2 *kas-pu ina* 10.MEŠ-*te ina* EN.MEŠ-*šú ú*-[GUR]
3 *ina de-ni-šú* DUG$_4$.DUG$_4$ *la i-la-qi*
4 *de-e-šú*! DI.KUD *la i-šá-mu-u*

---

5 IGI ^{m}GÌR.2—15 LÚ*.A.BA
6 IGI ^{md}PA—MU—AŠ LÚ*.A.BA
7 IGI ^{m}*ki-ṣir*—15 LÚ*.3.U$_5$
8 *ša* LÚ*.GAL—KAŠ.LUL
9 IGI ^{m}NUMUN—^{d}15
10 IGI ^{m}*man-nu—ki*—PAB.MEŠ LÚ*.*ra-ka-su*
11 IGI ^{m}EN—BÀD
12 IGI ^{m}*aš-šur*—MAN—PAB LÚ*.A.BA
13 IGI ^{md}ŠÚ—SU
14 IGI ^{m}*su-hu-ra-mu-u* LÚ*.DAM.QAR *ša*! ⸢DUMU—MAN⸣
15 IGI ^{m}*man-nu—k*[*i*]—AD LÚ*.*ra-ka-su ša* LÚ*.GAL—⸢SAG⸣
16 ITI.BARAG UD-24-KAM
17 *lim-mu* ^{m}*ba-an-ba-a* LÚ*.SUKKAL 2-*u*
18 *ina tar-ṣi* ^{m}*aš-šur*—PAB—AŠ MAN KUR—*aš-šur*

min[as of gold] to Ištar residing in Arbela, and shall [return] the silver tenfold to its owners.

r.4 He shall contest in his lawsuit and not succeed. The judge shall not heed his case.

---

r.5 Witness Šep-Issar, scribe.

6 Witness Nabû-šumu-iddina, scribe.

7 Witness Kiṣir-Issar, 'third man' of the chief cupbearer.

9 Witness Zar-Issar.

10 Witness Mannu-ki-ahhe, *conscript*.

11 Witness Bel-duri.

12 Witness Aššur-šarru-uṣur, scribe.

13 Witness Marduk-eriba.

14 Witness Suhuramû, merchant of the crown prince.

15 Witness Mannu-ki-abi, *conscript* of the chief eunuch.

16 Month Nisan (I), 24th day, eponym year of Banbâ, the second vizier, in the reign of Esarhaddon, king of Assyria.

211. Mannu-ki-Arbail Buys an Estate (676?)

83-1-18,770

beginning broken away
1′ [É *x* ANŠ]E! ⸢A!⸣.[ŠÀ *ina* UR]U!.⸢*ka*!⸣-*a*[*n*!-*nu-u*']
2′ [SU]HUR *um-me š*[*a*!] URU.*ka-an-nu*!-[*u*']
3′ SUHUR KASKAL *ša a-na* URU.*nu*-⸢*hu*!⸣-*bi* D[U-*u-ni*]
4′ GIŠ.SAR *ina* ŠÀ-*bi* [*x x*]-⸢*ú*⸣-*ri*
5′ SUHUR GIŠ.SAR *ša* [*x*(*x*) *x*]*x-a-ši-di*
6′ PAB!-*ma*! 40! A.ŠÀ *x*[*x x*]*x* ⸢*x x x*⸣
7′ [*x x x x x x x x*]*x x*[*x*]
rest broken away
Rev. beginning broken away
1′ 10 MA.NA KUG.UD [*x* MA].⸢NA!⸣ [KUG.GI *sak-ru*]
2′ *ina* ^{d}IŠ.TAR *a-ši-pat*! URU.*ni-nu-a* S[UM-*an*]
3′ *kas-pu ina* 10.MEŠ-*te ina* EN.MEŠ-*šú ú*!-GU[R]
4′ *ina de-ni-šú* DUG$_4$.DUG$_4$-*ma la i-la-qi*
5′ *de-e-šú*! DI.KUD *la i-šá-mu-u*

6′ [IG]I ^{m}*a*[*r*!-*z*]*e*!-*zu* LÚ*!.GAL—*ki-ṣ*[*ir*]
7′ [IGI ^{m}*ha—ba-sa-tú*] ⸢GAL⸣—LÚ*.Ì.DU$_8$.M[EŠ]

ADD 460

(Beginning destroyed)

1 [An estate of x hec]tares of fie[ld in] Kannu', adjoining the *side road* of Kannu' and the road that leads to Nuhub;

4 including a garden [...] adjoining the garden of [...]ašidi,

6 a total of 40 (hectares of) land [......]

(Break)

r.1 He shall g[ive] 10 minas of silver [and x mi]nas [of pure gold] to Ištar residing in Nineveh, and shall return the money tenfold to its owners.

4 He shall contest in his lawsuit and not succeed. The judge shall not listen to his case.

---

6 [Witness] A[rze]zu, cohort commander.

7 [Witness Habasti], head porter.

copied by Johns, not *i-laq-qi* (NALK), see coll.
211 Previous edition: AR 199.

8′ [IGI ^{m}*ki-ṣir*—^{d}15 LÚ*].⸢GAL—*ki*⸣-*ṣ*[*ir*]
rest broken away

^{8} [Witness Kiṣir-Issar], cohort commander.
(Rest destroyed)

212. A Broken Purchase Document of Mannu-ki-Arbail (676-I-25)

83-1-18,269

beginning broken away
1′ [*x x*] ⸢*man-nu šá*⸣ *ina*$^{!}$ *u*[*r*$^{!}$-*kiš ina ma-te-ma*]
2′ [*e-la*]-*an-ni lu-u* ^{m}*ki-ṣ*[*ir*—^{d}15]
3′ [*lu-u* DUMU].MEŠ-*šú lu-u mám-ma-nu-šu* [0]
4′ [*šá i-za-qu*]*p*$^{!}$-*an-ni* TA* ^{m}*man-nu*—*ki*—*ar*[*ba-ìl*]
5′ [*u* DUMU.M]EŠ$^{!}$-*šú*$^{!}$ *de-e-nu* DUG$_4$.DU[G$_4$]
6′ [*ub-ta-ʾ*]*u-u-ni kas-pu* 10-TA.ÀM
7′ [*a-na* EN.MEŠ-*šú* GU]R$^{!}$-[*r*]*a ina de-ni-šú*
8′ [DUG$_4$.DUG$_4$-*ma l*]*a i-laq-qí*
edge and first line of reverse obliterated
r.2 [IGI ^{m}*man-nu*]—*ki-i*—PAB.MEŠ ⸢LÚ⸣.*r*[*ak*$^{!}$-*su*]
3 [IGI ^{m}*man*]-*nu*—*ki-i*—AD LÚ.*ra*[*k-s*]*u*
4 [IGI ^{m}]NUMUN—^{d}15
5 [IGI ^{md}]PA—MU—AŠ *ṣa-bit* IM

6 [ITI.BAR]AG UD-25-KÁM 5-KÁM$^{!}$ MU.AN.[NA]
7 [^{m}*aš-šur*—P]AB—SUM-*na* MAN KUR—AN.ŠÁ[R.KI]
8 [*lim-mu*] ^{m}*ban-b*[*a-a* LÚ.SUKKAL 2-*u*]
rest broken away

ADD 502

(Beginning destroyed)

^{1} Whoever i[n the future, at any time, comes forward], whether Kiṣ[ir-Issar or] his [so]ns or relatives, [whoever lodges a comp]laint and seeks a lawsuit or litigation against Mannu-ki-Ar[bail and] his [son]s, [shall ret]ur[n] the money tenfold [to its owners. He shall contest] in his lawsuit [and no]t succeed.

$^{r.2}$ [Witness Mannu]-ki-ahhe, *conscri*[*pt*].

^{3} [Witness Man]nu-ki-abi, *conscript*.

^{4} [Witness] Zar-Issar.

^{5} [Witness] Nabû-šumu-iddina, keeper of the tablet.

^{6} [Month Ni]san (I), 25th day, year 5 [of Esarh]addon, king of Assyria, eponym year of Banb[â, the second vizier].

(Rest destroyed)

213. Mannu-ki-Arbail Buys a Garden (676?)

K 13072

beginning broken away
1′ [^{m}*man-nu*—*ki*—*arba-ìl* TA* IGI ^{m}*ki-ṣi*]*r*$^{!}$—[^{d}15]
2′ [*ina* ŠÀ-*bi x* MA.N]A$^{!}$ KUG.UD *il*-[*qí*]

3′ [*kas-pu g*]*a-mur ta-din*
4′ [GIŠ.SA]R$^{!}$ *šu-a-te za-ár-pi*$^{!}$ *la-qi*
5′ *tu-a-ru de-nu* DUG$_4$.DUG$_4$ *la-áš-šú*
Edge traces of an Aramaic epigraph
r.1 [*man*]-*nu* ⸢*ša*⸣ *ina ur-kiš ina ma-te-e-ma*
2 [*e-l*]*a-an-ni lu-u* ^{m}*ki-ṣir*—15
3 [*lu-u* DU]MU-*šú lu-u mám-mu-nu-šú*
4 [*ša* GIL-*u-ni i-za-qu*]*p*$^{!}$-⸢*an*⸣-*ni*
5 [TA* ^{m}*man-nu*—*ki-i*—UR]U.*arba-ìl*
6 [*de-nu* DUG$_4$.DUG$_4$ *ub-ta-u-ni x* M]A$^{!}$.NA$^{!}$
rest broken away

ADD 489

(Beginning destroyed)

^{1} [Mannu-ki-Arbail has contracted and] bou[ght it from Kiṣi]r-[Issar for x min]as of silver.

^{2} [The money] is paid [com]pletely. That [gar]den is purchased and acquired. Any revocation, lawsuit, or litigation is void.

$^{r.1}$ [Who]ever in the future, at any time, [comes f]orward, whether Kiṣir-Issar [or] his [s]on or relative, [and seeks a lawsuit or litigation against Mannu-ki]-Arbail, [shall pay x mi]nas [of silver]

(Rest destroyed)

212 Previous editions: AR 562, NALK 157. $^{1, 4ff, r.2f, 6f}$ See coll.
213 Previous edition: AR 382. → Fales Epigraphs 40.

214. Mannu-ki-Arbail Loans Copper (676-III-11)

K 350

1 2 GÚ.UN URUDU.MEŠ SAG.MEŠ
2 *ša* ^{d}15 *ša* URU.*arba-ìl*
3 *ša* ^{m}*man-nu—ki—arba-ìl*
4 *ina* IGI ^{md}UTU—PAB.MEŠ-*e*—DI
5 *ina* ITI.NE *id-dan*^{an}
6 *šum-ma la-a id-di-ni*
e.7 *a-na* 3-*su-šú-nu*
r.1 *i-rab-bi-u*
2 *ina* ITI.SIG$_4$ UD-11-KAM
3 *lim-mu* ^{m}*ban-ba-a*

4 IGI ^{m}*kù*-KÁ—KAM-*eš*
5 IGI ^{m}*qu-u-a* ^{m}MAN—*iq-bi*
6 IGI ^{m}SIG$_5$—INIM.MEŠ—LUGAL
7e IGI ^{md}PA-*u-a*

ADD 40

1 Two talents of copper, first fruits of Ištar of Arbela, belonging to Mannu-ki-Arbail, at the disposal of Šamaš-ahhe-šallim.

5 He shall pay in Ab (V). If he does not pay, it will increase by a third.

r.2 Month Sivan (III), 11th day, eponym year of Banbâ.

4 Witness Kubabu-ereš.

5 Witness Quwa. Šarru-iqbi.

6 Witness Danqu-dibbi-šarri.

7 Witness Nabû'a.

215. Pledging Gabbu-Adad to Mannu-ki-Arbail (676-XI-10)

83-1-18,366

1 BE-*ma ina* SAG.DU! ITI
2 ^{m}EN—KAR-*ir* ^{m}*gab-bu*—^{d}IM
3 *la-a na-ṣa a-na* ^{m}*man-nu—ki—arba-ìl*
4 *la-a i-din*! *sa-ar-ti*
5 ⸢*ša*! É!⸣-*šú ú-šal*-⸢*lam*⸣
6 ITI.ZÍZ UD-10-KAM
7 *lim-mu* ^{m}*ban-ba-a*

e.8 IGI ^{md}PA—KAR-*ir-a-ni*
9 IGI ^{m}PAB—*a-bu*
r.1 IGI ^{m}*a-bu-nu*
2 IGI ^{m}⸢NINA!⸣.KI-*a-a*
3 IGI ^{m}*mu-sa-la-me*
4 IGI ^{m}*na-mu-u*
5 IGI ^{m}*ka-bar*—DINGIR

ADD 167

1 If at the beginning of the month Bel-eṭir does not bring Gabbu-Adad and give him to Mannu-ki-Arbail, he shall pay in full the fine on his house.

6 Month Shebat (XI), 10th day, eponym year of Banbâ.

8 Witness Nabû-eṭiranni.

9 Witness Ahabu.

r.1 Witness Abunu.

2 Witness Ninuayu.

3 Witness Musallamu.

4 Witness Namû.

5 Witness Kabar-il.

216. Mannu-ki-Arbail Loans Silver to Ahuni (673-II-1)

83-1-18,333

1 ⸢NA$_4$!⸣.KIŠIB ^{m}*a-hu*-⸢*ni*⸣
2 *ša* URU.*kar*—^{d}NIN.LÍL 20 GÍN.MEŠ KUG.UD
3 *ša* ^{m}*man-nu—ki-i*—URU.*arba-ìl*
4 *ina* IGI ^{m}*a-hu-ni*
5 *ina* ITI.GUD *ina* ŠÀ-*bi* ITI.GUD KUG.UD *ina* SA[G].⸢DU⸣-*šú*
6 SUM-*an* BE-*ma* (*la*) SUM-*ni*! *ina* 4-*tú-šú* GAL-*bi*

ADD 8

1 [Se]al of Ahuni of Kar-Mullissu.

2 20 shekels of silver belonging to Mannu-ki-Arbail, at the disposal of Ahuni.

5 He shall pay the silver in its principal amount in Iyyar, within the month of Iyyar (II). If he does not pay, it will increase by a

214 Previous editions: AR 293, NALK 158; → KB 4 (1896) 126-12; 3R 47,5 (copy).
215 Previous editions: AR 223, NALK 159. Collations: Assur 2/5. Photo Budge Deluge 10 2.
216 Previous editions: AR 257, NALK 160. 1 See coll.

7 *ina* ITI.GUD UD-1-KÁM *lim-mu* ^{m}*a-tar*—DINGIR
8 LÚ.EN.NAM KUR.*la-hi-ra*
9 IGI ^{m}*me-le-za-za*
e.10 IGI ^{md}PA—KA[R-*ir-a*]*n*-[*ni*]
Rev. broken away

fourth.
[7] Iyyar (II), 1st day, eponym year of Atar-il, governor of Lahiru.
[9] Witness Melezaza.
[10] Witness Nabû-eṭiranni.
(Rest destroyed)

217. Mannu-ki-Arbail Buys 32 Hectares of Land

Sm 921

1 *ku-um* [NA_4.KIŠIB-*šú ṣu-pur-šú iš-kun*]

---

2 *ṣu-pur* ^{m}⸢DINGIR⸣—[*ma-la-ku*]
3 EN A.ŠÀ [SUM-*ni*]
4 É 30 ANŠE A.Š[À *x x x*]
5 *ša* A.MEŠ É 2 AN[ŠE *x x x*]
6 *ša* ŠE.GIŠ.Ì : *ina x*[*x x x*]
7 *i-na-ra-šu*-[*x*(*x*)]
8 *ina* URU.*ha-me*-[*e*]
9 SUHUR ÍD SUHUR [*x x*]
10 SUHUR *sa-ha*-⸢*ru*⸣ [*x x*]
11 *ú-piš-ma* ^{m}*man*-⸢*nu*⸣—*k*[*i*—URU.*arba-ìl*]
12 TA* IGI ^{m}DINGIR—*ma-la*$^{!}$-*k*[*u*$^{!}$]
13 *ina* ŠÀ-*bi* 11 GÍN.MEŠ ⸢KUG.UD⸣ [TI]

14 *kas-pu* ⸢*ga*⸣-*mur* ⸢*ta-din*⸣
15 ⸢A.ŠÀ⸣ [*šu-a-tú za-rip laq-qi*]
two lines destroyed

e.18 *l*[*u*$^{!}$-*u x x x x x*]
19 *lu-u* [*x x x*] ⸢*x x*⸣ [*x x x x*]
20 *lu-u qur-u*[*b-šú* 0]
21 *lu-u* [*mám-ma-nu-šú*]
r.1 *ša de-n*[*u* DUG_4.DUG_4]
2 TA* ^{m}*m*[*an-nu*—*ki*—URU.*arba-ìl*]
3 *ù* DUM[U.MEŠ-*šú ub-ta-u-ni*]
4 6$^{!}$ MA.NA K[UG.UD LUH-*u*]
5 1 MA.NA KUG.[GI *sak-ru*]
6 *ina bur-ki* ⸢^{d}⸣[*x* GAR-*an*]
7 *ina de-ni-šú* [DUG_4.DUG_4-*ma*]
8 *la i-la*[*q-qi*]

---

9 IGI ^{m}*a*-[*bu-nu x x x*]
10 IGI ^{m}*man*-[*nu*—*ki-i*—PAB.MEŠ]
11 IGI ^{m}*tu*$^{!}$-[*x x x*]
12 IGI ^{m}*man*-[*nu*—*ki-i*—AD$^{?}$]
13 A ^{m}[*x x x x*]
14 IGI ⸢^{m}⸣[*x x x x x*]
15 IGI [^{m}*x x x x x*]

ADD 378

[1] Instead of [his seal he impressed his fingernail].

(fingernail impressions)

---

[2] Fingernail of Il-[malak], owner of the land [being sold].
[4] An estate of 30 hectares of la[nd, ...] of water; an estate of 2 hect[ares ...] of sesame in ...[...], ...[...]
[8] in the city of Hamê adjoining the river, [...], and a *tower* [...] —

[11] Mannu-ki-[Arbail] has contracted and [bought] (said property) from Il-malak for 11 shekels of silver.
[14] The money is paid completely. [That] land [is purchased and acquired].
(Break)
[18] or [his prefect], neig[hbour or relative], (whoever) [seeks] a laws[uit or litigation] against Ma[nnu-ki-Arbail] and [his] son[s, shall place] 6 minas of [refined] si[lver] and one mina of [pure] go[ld] in the lap of [DN. He shall contest in h]is lawsuit and not suc[ceed].

---

[9] Witness A[bunu ...].
[10] Witness Man[nu-ki-ahhe].
[11] Witness Tu[...].
[12] Witness Man[nu-ki-*abi*], son of [...].
[14] Witness [NN].
[15] Witness [NN].

217 Previous editions: AR 429, NALK 165; → Fales Epigraphs 23.

16 ITI.ŠE! [UD-*x*-KÁM *lim-mu* {m}*x x x*]

s.1 *dnt . ʾlmlk . zy . ʾrq . ḥm*ᶜ

16 Month Adar (XII), [...th day, eponym year of ...].

s.1 (Aramaic caption:) Deed of Il-malak of the land of Hamê.

218. Mannu-ki-Arbail Buys 20 Hectares of Land

Rm 2,20

1 [*ku*]-*um* NA$_4$.KIŠIB-⌈*šú*⌉ [*ṣu-pur-šú* GAR-*un*]

2 *ṣu-pur* {m}*ha-sa-b*[*u* LÚ*.*x x x*]
3 EN A.ŠÀ [SUM-*ni*]

4 ⌈É 20? ANŠE A.ŠÀ⌉ *ina* URU.*n*[*i*?-*x x x*]
5 [SUHU]R A.ŠÀ *ša* {m}[*x x x x x*]
6 SUHUR A.ŠÀ *ša* {m}[*x x x x x*]
7 *ú-piš-ma* {m}*man-nu—ki*—[URU.*arba-ìl*]
8 TA* IGI {m}*ha-sa-*⌈*bu*⌉ [*ina* ŠÀ *x x x x x*]
9 *il-qi kas-pu gam-*[*mur ta-din* A.ŠÀ *šú-a-tú*]
10 ⌈*za-rip*⌉ *la-qi tu-a-r*[*u de-e-nu* DUG$_4$.DUG$_4$ *la-áš-šú*]

11 [*man-nu ša ina u*]*r-kiš* [*ina ma-te-ma*]
12 [*i-za-qu-pa-ni*] *lu-u* [{m}*ha-sa-bu*]
13 [*lu-u* DUMU.MEŠ-*šú*] *lu-u* [*x x x x*]
rest broken away

r.1 ⌈IGI {m}⌉D[I!-*mu*—EN—*la-áš-me*?]
2 IGI {m}*a-b*[*u*?-*nu*]
3 IGI {m}*ha*—[*ba-as-tú*]
4 IGI {m}*na*!-[*mu-u*]
5 IGI {m}ZALÁG—DINGIR-[*a-a*]
space of 3 lines
6 IGI {md}⌈PA—KAR⌉-*ir* [LÚ*.A.BA]
7 ITI.GU[D UD-*x*-KAM]
8 *lim-mu* [{m}*x x x x x*]
9 LÚ*.GAR.[KUR *x x x x*]

ADD 375

1 [In pl]ace of his seal [he impressed his fingernail].

2 Fingernail of Hasab[u ...], owner of the land [being sold].

(fingernail impressions)

4 An estate of 20 hectares of land in *N*[*ineveh*, adjoini]ng the field of [NN] and the field of [NN] —

7 Mannu-ki-[Arbail] has contracted and bought it from Hasabu [for ......].

9 The money [is paid] compl[etely. That land] is purchased and acquired. Any revocati[on, lawsuit, or litigation [is void.

11 Whoever in the future, [at any time, lodges a complaint], whether [Hasabu, his sons] or [...]

(Break)

r.1 Witness Š[ulmu-*beli-lašme*].
2 Witness *Ab*[*unu*].
3 Witness Ha[basti].
4 Witness Na[mû].
5 Witness Nur-ila['i].
6 Witness Nabû-eṭir, [scribe].
7 Month Iyyar (II), [...th day], eponym year of [...], governor of [...].

219. Mannu-ki-Arbail Buys a Servant

Ki 1904-10-9,44

beginning broken away

1′ [{m}PA]B!—*li-ti* ⌈ARAD⌉-*šú*
2′ *ú*!-⌈*piš*!⌉-*ma*! {m}*man-nu*—⌈*ki*⌉—URU.*arba-ìl*
3′ T[A! IGI] {m}NUMUN!-*i*!

ADD 1157

(Beginning destroyed)

1 [Ah]i-le'iti, his servant —

2 Mannu-ki-Arbail has contracted, purchased, and acquired him fr[om] Zarî for 1

218 Previous editions: AR 426, NALK 167. 4 See coll.
219 Previous edition: NALK 162. 9 See coll. 11 EN appears to have here the phonetic value *be* (secondarily)

4′ *a-na* 1 1/2 MA.NA KUG.UD.MEŠ
5′ *a-na* 1 *ma-né*$^{!}$-*e*$^{!}$ *ša* KUR.*gar*$^{!}$-*ga*$^{!}$-⸢*mis*$^{!}$⸣
6′ *i-zi-rip i-si-qi*
7′ *kas-pu gam-mur ta-din-ni*
8′ [L]Ú *šu-a-tum za-ar-pi*
9′ *laq-qi tu-a-ru de-nu*$^{!}$
10′ [D]UG$_4$.DUG$_4$ *la-áš-šú*
11′ [*ṣib-t*]*ú*$^{!}$ EN$^{!}$-*e-nu a-na* 1-*me* UD-*me*
12′ [*sa-a*]*r-tú ina kal* MU.AN.NA.MEŠ
r.1 *man-nu ša ina ur-kiš ina ma-ti-mu*
2 *lu-u* ^{m}NUMUN-*i lu-u* DUMU.MEŠ-*šú*
3 *lu-u* DUMU—DUMU.MEŠ-*šú lu-u* ŠEŠ.MEŠ-*šú*
4 *lu-u* EN—*il-ki-šú ša de-nu*
5 DUG$_4$.DUG$_4$ TA* ^{m}*man-*⸢*nu*⸣—*ki*—⸢URU⸣.*arba-ìl*
6 *ù* DUMU.MEŠ-*šú ù* DUMU—DUMU.MEŠ-*šú*
7 *ub-ta-ʾu-u-ni* GÚ.UN MA.NA KUG.UD
8 1 MA.NA KUG.GI *ina bur-ki* ^{d}IŠ.TAR
9 *a-ši-bat* URU.*arba-*⸢*ìl*⸣ *i-šak-kan kas*$^{!}$-[*p*]*u*$^{!}$
10 *a-na* 10.MEŠ-*te ina* EN.MEŠ-*šú* ⸢GUR⸣-*ra*
11 *a-na de-ni-šú* DUG$_4$.DUG$_4$-*ma la i-laq-qi*
12 *de-in-šú* ^{d}DI$^{!}$.⸢KUD$^{!}$⸣ *la i-šá-mu*

---

13 ⸢IGI⸣ ^{m}[*x x x x x x x x x*]
rest broken away
s.1 IGI ^{d}NU—LU[G]AL$^{!}$ (blank) [*x x x x x*]

1/2 minas of silver by the mina of Carchemish.

7 The money is paid completely. That man is purchased and acquired. Any revocation, lawsuit, [or li]tigation is void.

11 (Guaranteed against) epilepsy for 100 days (and against) [fr]aud forever.

r.1 Whoever in the future, at any time, whether Zarî or his sons, grandsons or brothers, or his labour-duty superior, seeks a lawsuit or litigation against Mannu-ki-Arbail, his sons and grandsons,

7 shall place a talent of silver and one mina of gold in the lap of Ištar residing in Arbela, and shall return the money tenfold to its owners. He shall contest in his lawsuit and not succeed. The divine judge shall not heed his case.

---

13 Witness [NN].

(Break)

s.1 Witness: the king's statue.

220. A Fragmentary Purchase Document of Mannu-ki-Arbail

Rm 470

beginning broken away
r.1′ *lu-*[*u* ^{m}*x x x lu-u* DUMU.MEŠ-*šú*]
2′ *lu-u* DUMU—DUMU.MEŠ-⸢*šú*⸣ *lu-u* [*x x x x x*]
3′ *ša* TA* ^{m}*man-nu—ki—arba-ìl* [*ù* DUMU.MEŠ-*šú*]
4′ *de-nu*$^{!}$ DUG$_4$.DUG$_4$ *ub-ta-u-*⸢*ni*⸣
5′ 2 MA.NA KUG.UD 1 MA.NA KUG.GI
6′ *ina bur-ki* ^{d}MAŠ *a-šib* URU.*kàl-hi* GAR-*an*
7′ *kas-pu a-na* 10.MEŠ *a-na* EN.MEŠ-*šú* GUR
8′ *ina*$^{!}$ *de-ni-šú* DUG$_4$.DUG$_4$ *la i-laq-qi*

9′ IGI ^{m}*qur-di*—^{d}15 IGI ^{m}*gi-in-na-a-a*
10′ [IG]I ^{m}*ha—ba-as-ti*
11′ [IGI] ^{m}*ma-le-e-za-zi*
12′ [IGI] ^{md}PA—*tàk-lak* IGI ^{md}PA—⸢NUMUN⸣—[GIN]
13′ [IGI] ^{md}PA—EN—GIN IGI ^{m}[*x x x x x*]
14′ [IGI ^{m}GÌ]R$^{!}$.2$^{!}$—*aš-šur*$^{!}$ [*x x x x*]
rest broken away

ADD 493

(Beginning destroyed)

r.1 [Whoever ... breaks the contract], whet[her NN or his sons], grandsons or [...], and seeks a lawsuit or litigation against Mannu-ki-Arbail [and his sons],

5 shall place two minas of silver and one mina of gold in the lap of Ninurta residing in Calah. He shall return the money tenfold to its owners. He shall contest in his lawsuit and not succeed.

---

9 Witness Qurdi-Issar. Witness Ginnaya.

10 [Wit]ness Habasti.

11 [Witness] Malezazi.

12 [Witness] Nabû-taklak. Witness Nabû-zeru-[ka''in].

13 [Witness] Nabû-belu-ka''in. Witness [NN].

14 [Witness Še]p-Aššur. [...].

derived from spellings like EN-*lí* = *bēlī*. See coll.
r.9, 12, s.1 See coll.

220 Previous editions: AR 619, NALK 161.
r.8, 14 See coll.

11. Silim-Aššur (680-670)

FIG. 23. *Stone duck-weight (268.8 g) from Assyrian or post-Assyrian settlement at Khirbet Qasrij (KQ1).* IRAQ MUSEUM, Baghdad.

221. Note of Silver and Barley Owed to Silim-Aššur (680-III)

83-1-18,201

1 ⌈10⌉ MA$^{!}$.NA KUG$^{!}$.UD 1-*me*-20 ANŠE ŠE.PAD.[MEŠ]
2 ⌈*a*⌉-*du ru-bé-šú ša* ^{m}*si-lim—aš-šur*
3 [*i*]*na*$^{!}$ IGI ^{m}*ha-an-da-sa-ni*
4 [*i*]*na*$^{!}$ IGI ^{md}MES—MU—PAB
5 ⌈*a*$^{!}$⌉-*na*$^{!}$ ITI.KIN *i-du-nu*
6 [*šúm*]-*mu la i-din-nu*
e.7 [KUG.UD$^{!}$ *ina*] ⌈1/2⌉ MA.NA-*šú i-rab-bi*

8 [^{m}EN—AP]IN EN—ŠU.2.MEŠ
r.1 [IGI] ⌈$^{m!d}$⌉PA—*la—tú-šar-a-ni*
2 IGI ^{m}*mil-ka-ia* : ^{m}*nu-ra-a-ni*
3 IGI ^{m}*man-nu—a-ki—arba-ìl*
4 IGI ^{m}*sa-la-ma-me* LÚ*.*qur-bu-tú*
5 IGI ^{m}*nu-uš-ku*—DINGIR-*a-a*

6 ITI.SIG$_{4}$ [*x*]
7 [*lim*]-*mu* ^{m}*da-na-a-nu*
s.1 [EGI]R$^{!}$ *du*$^{!}$-*r*[*a-ri x*]*x*

ADD 113

1 10 minas of silver and 120 homers of barley plus its interest, belonging to Silim-Aššur, at the disposal of Handasani and Marduk-šumu-uṣur.

5 They shall pay in Elul (VI). If they do not, the silver shall increase 50 percent per mina.

8 [Bel-er]eš is the guarantor.

r.1 [Witness] Nabû-la-tuššaranni.

2 Witness Milkaya. Ditto Nurani.

3 Witness Mannu-aki-Arbail.

4 Witness Salamame, royal bodyguard.

5 Witness Nušku-ila'i.

6 Month Sivan (III), [...th] (day), eponym year of Dananu.

s.1 [Aft]er the remission of de[bts ...].

222. Note of Sheep Owed to Silim-Aššur (680-III)

Bu 89-4-26,32

1 72 UDU.MEŠ *ša* ^{m}*si*$^{!}$-*lim*$^{!}$—*aš*$^{!}$-⌈*šur*$^{!}$⌉
2 *sam-mah-u*-⌈*te*$^{!}$⌉
3 *ina* IGI ^{m}*ha-an-da-sa-ni*
4 *ina* IGI ^{m}*mar-duk*
1 line blank
5 [*ina* IT]I.NE SUM-*nu*
e.6 [*šum-ma l*]*a i*$^{!}$-*din-nu*
7 [*a-na mi*]*t-har* ⌈*x*⌉ *x x*
r.1 [^{m}E]N—APIN EN—ŠU.MEŠ
2 IGI ^{md}PA—PAB.MEŠ—AŠ
3 IGI ^{m}DÙ—APIN-*eš*
4 IGI ^{m}*bi*-⌈*li*$^{!}$⌉-*i*
5 ITI.SIG$_{4}$
6 *lim-me* ^{m}*da-na-ni*
s.1 [IGI ^{m}]A—PAB

ADD 119

1 72 miscellaneous sheep belonging to Silim-Aššur, at the disposal of Handasanu and Marduk.

5 They shall give them back [in] Ab (V). [If] they do not, they shall ... an equal amount.

r.1 [B]el-ereš is the guarantor.

2 Witness Nabû-ahhe-iddina.

3 Witness Gabbu-ereš.

4 Witness Bilî.

5 Month Sivan (III), eponym year of Dananu.

s.1 [Witness] Aplu-uṣur.

221 Previous editions: AR 637, NALK 303. Collations: Assur 2/5.
222 Previous editions: AR 221, NALK 304. Collations: Assur 2/5 4 Marduk here seems to be an abbreviation for Marduk-šumu-uṣur (no. 221:4). 7 See coll.

223. Note of Silver Owed to Silim-Aššur (679-III-12)

K 400

1 1 MA.NA KUG.UD *ša* URU.*gar-ga-mis*
2 *ša* ^{m}*si-lim—aš-šur*
3 *ina* IGI ^{m}ARAD—^{d}15
4 ⸢*ku-um ru-bé-e ša* KUG.UD⸣
5 É 6 ANŠE A.ŠÀ *ina* URU.*ha-ta-a*
6 *ina* GIŠ.BÁN *ša* 10 *qa* É ^{m}*si-lim—aš-šur*
7 IGI.2.MEŠ *i-šak-kan-u-ni i-na-áš-ši*
8 *a-na* MU.AN.NA.MEŠ KÚ
9 4 *me-re-še* 4 *kar-ap-hi*
r.1 KÚ *me-re-še-šu ú-sal-lim*
2 SAG.DU KUG.UD *ina* UGU ŠE.*ta-ra-me*
3 *i-šak-kan* A.ŠÀ-*šú ú-še-ṣa* 4 ANŠE *me*!!-*re*!!-*še*!!
4 2 ANŠE *kar-ap-hi* PAB 6 ANŠE A.ŠÀ *za-ku-te*
5 IGI ^{m}PAB—BÀD IGI ^{m}*se-e'—nu-ri*
6 IGI ^{md}*šér*—DINGIR-*a-a* IGI ^{m}A—PAB
7 IGI ^{m}*man-nu—ki—arba*!-*ìl* LÚ.A—SIG IGI ^{m}*gur-di-i*
8 IGI ^{m}*bi-ta-ti-i* IGI ^{m}U.GUR—MAŠ
9 ITI.SIG$_4$ UD-12-KAM *lim-mu* ^{m}TA*!—10—*ni-nu*

ADD 83

1 One mina of silver (by the mina) of Carchemish belonging to Silim-Aššur, at the disposal of Urda-Issar.

4 In lieu of the interest on the silver, Silim-Aššur shall take an estate of 6 hectares of land of his choice in the town of Hatâ, according to the seah of 10 'litres,' and shall have the usufruct of it for years. He shall enjoy it for 4 crop years and 4 fallow years.

r.1 (After) he has completed his cultivation, he (i.e., Urda-Issar) shall place the capital sum of the silver on the corn heap and redeem his land.

3 Four hectares of cultivated (and) 2 hectares of fallow (land), a total of 6 hectares of exempt land.

5 Witness Ahi-duri. Witness Se'-nuri.

6 Witness Šer-ila'i. Witness Aplu-uṣur.

7 Witness Mannu-ki-Arbail, chariot fighter. Witness Gurdî.

8 Witness Bitatî. Witness Nergal-ašared.

9 Month Sivan (III), 12th day, eponym year of Issi-Adad-aninu.

224. Duplicate of the Previous Text (679)

K 3496

1 [*x x x x* 1 MA].NA KUG.UD *šá* URU.*gar-ga-mis*
2 [*ša* ^{m}*si-lim—aš-šur ina* I]GI ^{m}ARAD—^{d}15
3 [*ina pu-u-h*]*i*! *it-t*[*i-š*]*i*
4 [4 ANŠE *me-re-š*]*e* 2 ANŠE A.ŠÀ *ka-rap-hi*
blank seal space
5 [PAB 6 ANŠE A].ŠÀ *za-ku-te ina* URU.*ha-ta-a*
6 [*ina* GIŠ.BÁN *šá* 10] *qa* A.ŠÀ É ^{m}*si-lim—aš-šur*
7 [IGI.2.MEŠ *i-šak-kan*]-*u-ni i-na-áš-ši*
e.8 [*a-na* MU.AN.NA.MEŠ KÚ] ⸢4⸣ *me-re-*⸢*še*⸣
broken away
Rev. beginning (about 5 lines) broken away

ADD 84

1 [One] mina of silver (by the mina) of Carchemish [belonging to Silim-Aššur, at the dispos]al of Urda-Issar. He has ta[ken it as a lo]an.

4 Silim-Aššur shall take [4 hectares of cultivat]ed and 2 hectares of fallow land, [a total of 6 hectares of] exempt land of his choice in the town of Hatâ, [according to the seah of 10] 'litres,'

8 [and he shall have the usufruct of it for years. He shall enjoy it for] 4 crop years [and 4 fallow years].

(Break)

223 Previous editions: AR 140, NALK 305; → Postgate FNALD 23; KB 4 (1896) 126f; 3R 50,2 (copy). r.3 *me-re-še* (*me*!! sup. ras.) is carelessly written and looks like *pa-an-zi* (coll. FNALD, confirmed by I.L. Finkel).

224 Previous editions: AR 139, NALK 306. 1 The line is cramped and difficult to read, but the sign *ina* (coll. NALK, omitted by Johns and the duplicate no. 223) seems possible. 8 See coll.

1′ [*lim-mu* ^{m}TA*—10]—*a-ni-nu* ⸢IGI ^{m}PAB—BÀD⸣

2′ [IGI ^{m}*se-e*ʾ—*nu-ri* IGI ^{m}]^{d}*šér*—DINGIR-*a-a*
3′ [IGI ^{m}A—PAB IGI ^{m}*man-nu*—*ki*]—*arba-ìl*
4′ [LÚ*.A—SIG IGI ^{m}*gur-di*]-*i*
5′ [IGI ^{m}*bi-ta-ti-i* IGI ^{m}U.GUR]—MAŠ

r.1 [eponym year of Issi-Adad]-aninu. Witness Ahi-duri.
2 [Witness Se'-nuri. Witness] Šer-ila'i.
3 [Witness Aplu-uṣur. Witness Mannu-ki]-Arbail, [chariot fighter].
4 [Witness Gurd]î.
5 [Witness Bitatî. Witness Nergal]-ašared.

225. —— (677-XII-6)

K 4283

Obv. entirely broken away; ends of 3 lines on edge
1′ [*x x x x x x x x*] LUGAL
2′ [*x x x x x x x x*]
3′ [*x x x x x x x x*] *i-na*
two lines destroyed
6′ [*x x x x x x x x*]*x*
rest broken away
Rev. beginning broken away
1′ [*ana* 10.MEŠ *ana* E]N$^{!}$.MEŠ-⸢*šú ú*$^{!}$⸣-[*tar*]
2′ [*ina d*]*e-ni-šú* DUG_4.DUG_4-*ma*
3′ [*la*] *i-laq-qi*

4′ [IGI ^{m}]^{d}PA—*tak-lak*
5′ [IGI ^{m}]^{d}PA.TÚG—DINGIR-*a-a*
6′ [IGI ^{m}PA]B—BÀD
7′ [IGI ^{m}]⸢A$^{!}$⸣—PAB
8′ [IGI ^{m}U].U—*la*$^{!}$-*rim*
9′ [IGI ^{m}*n*]*àr-gi-i*
10′ [IGI ^{m}]*sa*$^{!}$-*ru*—*ki-na*
11′ [IGI ^{m}]^{d}ŠÚ$^{!}$-*ia*
12′ [IGI ^{m}]^{d}EN—PAB-*ir*

13′ [ITI.Š]E UD-6-KÁM
14′ [*lim*]-*mu* ^{m}AD—*ra-m*[*u*]

ADD 576

(Beginning destroyed)

r.1 He shall ret[urn the money tenfold to] its [own]ers. He shall contest [in] his [law]suit and [not] succeed.

---

4 [Witness] Nabû-taklak.
5 [Witness] Nušku-ila'i.
6 [Witness Ah]i-duri.
7 [Witness] Aplu-uṣur.
8 [Witness Da]di-larim.
9 [Witness] Nargî.
10 [Witness] Sarru-kena.
11 [Witness] Mardukaya.
12 [Witness] Bel-naṣir.
13 [Month Ad]ar (XII), 6th day, [epo]nym year of Abi-ram.

226. Silim-Aššur Rents an Estate (676-X-12)

K 438

1 ⸢NA_4⸣.KIŠIB ^{m}*ha-na-*⸢*nu*⸣
2 EN A.ŠÀ SUM-*ni*

---

3 É 3 ANŠE A.ŠÀ *ma-az-ru-*⸢*te*⸣

ADD 629

1 Seal of Hanan, owner of the land being sold.

(blank seal space)

---

3 An estate of 3 hectares of cultivated land

225 Previous edition: AR 561. r.7ff See coll.
226 Previous editions: AR 146, NALK 315; → TCAE 177. Collated by I.L. Finkel. 6f, r. 5, 8f See coll.

4 *ina* GIŠ.BÁN *šá* 10 *qa* A.ŠÀ *za-ku-te*
5 *i-na* URU.*ha-ta-a*
6 SUHUR AMA *šá* URU.*šu-r*[*i*$^{!}$ *x x*]
7 SUHUR KASKAL *šá* URU.*šu-r*[*i*$^{!}$ *x x*]
8 SUHUR A.ŠÀ *šá* ^{m}*pu-ṭi*-[*x x*]
9 LÚ.GAL—50 A.ŠÀ *ina* ⸢*ma*⸣-[*az-ru-te*]
10 *la* ŠE.*nu-sa-hi ú*-[*piš-ma*]
11 ^{m}*si-lim—aš-šur* LÚ.*šá*—[*x x x*]
12 *ina* ŠÀ 1/2 MA.NA 4 GÍN.[MEŠ KUG.UD]

according to the seah of 10 'litres,' exempt land in the town of Hatâ, adjoining the *side road* to Šur[i ...], the road to Šur[i ...], and the field of Puṭ[i...], the commander-of-fifty — cul[tivated] land with no corn taxes —

[11] Silim-Aššur, the [...], has [contracted and] bought it for 1/2 mina 4 shekels [of silver].

13 TI-*qí a-na* MU.AN.N[A.MEŠ]
14 KÚ 4 *me-re-še* 4 *ka*-[*rap-hi* KÚ]

[13] He shall have the usufruct of it for years. [He shall enjoy it for] 4 crop years and 4 fallow years.

15 *me-re-še-šu ú-š*[*al-lam*]
16 SAG.DU KUG.UD *ina* U[GU ŠE.SU$_7$]
r.1 *i-šak-kan* A.[ŠÀ-*šú ú-še-ṣa*]

[15] (When) he comp[letes] his cultivation, he (i.e. Hanan) shall place the capital sum of silver on the corn [heap, and shall redeem his] land.

2 ⸢ITI.AB⸣ UD-12-KÁM [*lim-mu* ^{m}*ban-ba-a*]

[r.2] Month Tebet (X), 12th day, [eponym year of Banbâ].

---

3 IGI ^{m}A—PAB [IGI ^{m}*x x x x*]
4 IGI ^{md}[*x x x x x x x*]
5 IGI ^{md}P[A$^{!}$—*x x x x x x*]
6 IGI ^{m}*su*-[*x x x x x x x x*]
7 IGI ^{m}*m*[*an-nu—ki-i—arba-ìl*]
8 IGI ^{md}E[N$^{!}$—*x x x x x x*]
9 IGI ^{m}*pu-ṭ*[*u*$^{!}$-*x x x x x*]
10 IGI ^{m}*ha-me*-[*x x x x x x*]

[3] Witness Aplu-uṣur. [Witness NN].
[4] Witness [......].
[5] Witness Na[bû-...].
[6] Witness Su[......].
[7] Witness M[annu-ki-Arbail].
[8] Witness Be[l-...].
[9] Witness Puṭ[u...].
[10] Witness Hame[...].

11 ITI.AB UD-12-[KÁM *lim-mu* ^{m}*ban-ba-a*]
12 LÚ.SUKKAL ^{md}⸢*x x*⸣ [*x x x*]
13 *šum-ma du-ra-ru šá-kín* ^{m}*s*[*i-lim—aš-šur*]
14 KUG.UD-*šú i-da-gal*

[11] Month Tebet (X), 12th day, [eponym year of Banbâ], the vizier. [NN, *scribe*].

[13] If a remission of debts takes place, S[ilim-Aššur] shall retrieve his silver.

227. Silim-Aššur Buys a Boy (675-XII-1)

Bu 91-5-9,94

ADD 186

1 NA$_4$.KIŠIB ^{m}DINGIR—KAM-*eš* EN
2 TUR *ta-da-a-ni*

[1] Seal of Ilu-ereš, owner of the boy being sold.

(blank seal space)

---

3 ^{m}*a-a*—⸢*ṭu*⸣-*ri* ARAD-*šu ša*
4 ^{m}DINGIR—KAM-*eš ú-piš-ma*
5 ^{m}*si-lim—aš-šur ina* ŠÀ 30 GÍN.MEŠ
6 KUG.UD TI-*qí kas-pu gam-mur*
7 *ta-ad-din* TUR *šu-a-tú za-rip*
8 TI-*qí tú-a-ru de-e-nu*
9 DUG$_4$.DUG$_4$ *la-áš-šú man-nu šá ina ur*-[*kiš*]

[3] Aya-ṭuri, servant of Ilu-ereš —

[5] Silim-Aššur has contracted and bought him for 30 shekels of silver.

[6] The money is paid completely. That boy is purchased and acquired. Any revocation, lawsuit, or litigation is void.

227 Previous editions: AR 476, NALK 308. [2, 7] Tablet has TUR, as copied by Johns, not LÚ* (see coll.)

10 *[ina]* ⌈*ma*⌉*-[te-m]a [i-z]a*$^{!}$*-q[u*$^{!}$*-pa-an-ni]*
rest broken away
Rev. beginning broken away
1′ IGI $^{m⌈d}$30—DINGIR-*a-a*⌉
2′ IGI ^{m}SU—^{d}[IM]
3′ IGI ^{m}*ab-di-i* [0]
4′ IGI ^{m}*a-tan-ha*—$^{d⌈}$UTU⌉
5′ IGI ^{m}10—*na-gi*
6′ IGI ^{m}*na-tú-nu*
7′ IGI ^{m}*ra-hi-mì-i*
8′ IGI ^{md}15—I
9′ IGI ^{md}ŠÚ—MU—PAB LÚ.A.BA
10′ ITI.ŠE UD-1-KÁM *lim-mu*
11′ ^{md}PA—PAB.MEŠ—AŠ LÚ.IGI.DUB
12′ [[*bu x x*]] GAL-*u*

9 Whoever in the fut[ure], at any t[ime, lodges a com]pl[aint]
(Break)
r.1 Witness Sin-ila'i.
2 Witness Eriba-[Adad].
3 Witness Abdî.
4 Witness Atanha-šamaš.
5 Witness Adda-nagi.
6 Witness Natunu.
7 Witness Rahimî.
8 Witness Issar-na'id.
9 Witness Marduk-šumu-uṣur, scribe.
10 Month Adar (XII), 1st day, eponym year of Nabû-ahhe-iddina, chief treasurer.

228. Silim-Aššur Buys a Maid

Bu 89-4-26,22

1 [NA$_4$.KI]ŠIB ^{md}PA—⌈BÀD⌉—*ku-ṣur*
2 [LÚ*].SAG EN MÍ SUM-*ni*

3 [MÍ].^{d}NIN.LÍL—BÀD—PAB$^{!}$ GEMÉ
4 *šá* ^{md}PA—BÀD—*ku-ṣur ú-piš-ma*
5 ^{m}*si-lim—aš-šur* TA* IGI ^{md}PA—BÀD—*ku-ṣur*
6 *ina* ŠÀ-*bi* 1/2$^{!}$ MA.NA KUG.UD ⌈*il-qí*⌉
7 *kas-pu gam-mur ta-din* MÍ *šu-a-tú*
8 *zar-pat la-qi-at tú*$^{!}$*-a-ru*
9 *de-nu*$^{!}$ DUG$_4$.DUG$_4$ *la-áš-šu*
10 *man-nu ša [ina ur]-kiš ina ma-*⌈*te*⌉*-ma*
11 [GIL-*u-ni lu-u*] ^{md}PA—BÀD—*ku-ṣur*
12 [*lu-u* PAB.MEŠ-*šú lu-u* DUMU]—⌈PAB$^{!}$⌉.MEŠ-*šú*
13 [*ša de-nu* DUG$_4$.DUG$_4$ *ub-ta*]-⌈*u*⌉*-n[i]*
rest broken away

ADD 227

1 [Sea]l of Nabû-duru-kuṣur, eunuch, owner of the woman being sold.

(blank seal space)

3 Mullissu-duru-uṣur, the maid of Nabû-duru-kuṣur —
5 Silim-Aššur has contracted and bought her from Nabû-duru-kuṣur for 1/2 mina of silver.
7 The money is paid completely. That woman is purchased and acquired. Any revocation, lawsuit, or litigation is void.
10 Whoever i[n the] future, at any time, [breaks the contract, whether] Nabû-duru-kuṣur [or his brothers or] neph[ews, and se]ek[s a lawsuit or litigation]
(Rest destroyed)

229. Silim-Aššur Buys Three Servants (675)

Ki 1904-10-9,46

1 [NA$_4$.KIŠIB] ^{m}*šum-ma—i-b[a-ši*—Z]I$^{!}$
2 [EN AR]AD.MEŠ SUM-*in*

ADD 1158

1 [Seal] of Šumma-ib[ašši-ket]tu, [owner of the serva]nts being sold.

228 Previous editions: AR 514, NALK 318. Collated by I.L. Finkel. 6 ⌈*il-qí*⌉ is partly erased. 12 See coll. For restoration cf. ND 496:12 and 17 (Iraq 13 pl. XVI), another deed with a eunuch seller.
229 Previous edition: NALK 307. Photo Cat. Suppl. Pl. 2. 1, 6, r.2 See coll.

3 ^{m}*da-an-du-si* DUMU.MÍ-*šú*
4 ^{m}*la—qe-pu* DUMU-*šú*
5 PAB 3 ZI.MEŠ ARAD.MEŠ-*šú*
6 *ša* ^{m}*šum-ma—i-ba-ši—*ZI$^{!}$
7 *ú-piš-ma* ^{m}*si-lim—aš-šur*
8 *ina* ŠÀ 30 GÍN.MEŠ KUG.UD TI
9 *kas-pu gam-mur ta-din*
10 [UN.MEŠ] *šu-a-tú za-ar-pu*
11 [*la-qi-u*] *tu-a-ru*
e.12 [*de-nu* DUG$_4$.DUG$_4$ *la-áš-š*]*ú*$^{!}$
13 [*x* MA].⌈NA$^{!}$⌉ K[UG$^{!}$.UD *x* MA.NA] K[UG$^{!}$.GI]
r.1 [*ina bu*]*r-ki* ^{d}IŠ.TAR *a-ši-*⌈*bat*⌉
2 [UR]U$^{!}$.NINA$^{!}$ GAR-*an kas-pu ina* 11$^{!}$.MEŠ
3 [*ina*] EN$^{!}$.MEŠ-*šú* GUR-*ra ina* ⌈*de-ni*⌉-*šú*
4 DUG$_4$.DUG$_4$-*ma la i-laq-*⌈*qi*⌉

(stamp seal impressions)

3 Dandusi, his daughter, and La-qepu, his son, a total of 3 persons, servants of Šumma-ibašši-kettu —

7 Silim-Aššur has contracted and bought them for 30 shekels of silver.

9 The money is paid completely. Those [people] are purchased and [acquired]. Any revocation, [lawsuit, or litigation is voi]d.

13 He shall place [x mi]nas of si[lver and x minas of] go[ld in the l]ap of Ištar residing in Nineveh, and shall return the money elevenfold [to] its owners. He shall contest in his lawsuit and not succeed.

---

5 IGI ^{md}PA.TÚG—DINGIR-*a-a*
6 IGI ^{m}A—PAB
7 IGI ^{md}PA—MAN—PAB
8 IGI ^{m}DÙG.GA—IM—^{d}IM
9 IGI ^{md}PA—*tak-lak*
10 IGI ^{md}PA—*ba-ni*
11 IGI ^{m}PAB—BÀD
12 IGI ^{m}*hu-ra-a-a*
blank space of 2 lines

s.1 [ITI.*x*] UD-1-KÁM
2 [*lim-mu*] ^{md}PA—PAB.MEŠ—AŠ

r.5 Witness Nušku-ila'i.
6 Witness Aplu-uṣur.
7 Witness Nabû-šarru-uṣur.
8 Witness Ṭab-šar-Adad.
9 Witness Nabû-taklak.
10 Witness Nabû-bani.
11 Witness Ahu-duri.
12 Witness Hurayu.
s.1 [Month ...], 1st day, [eponym year of] Nabû-ahhe-iddina.

230. —— (675)

K 1570

Obv. destroyed
Rev. beginning broken away
1′ [IGI] ^{md}PA.TÚG—⌈DINGIR⌉-[*a-a*]
2′ [IGI] ^{m}A—[PAB]
3′ [IGI] ^{md}PA—MAN—[PAB]
4′ [IGI] ^{m}DÙG—IM—^{d}[IM]
5′ [IGI] ^{md}PA—*tak-la*[*k*]
6′ [IGI] ^{md}PA—*ba-ni*
7′ [IGI ^{m}]PAB—BÀ[D$^{!}$]
rest broken away

ADD 601

(Beginning destroyed)
r.1 [Witness] Nušku-il[a'i].
2 [Witness] Aplu-[uṣur].
3 [Witness] Nabû-šarru-[uṣur].
4 [Witness] Ṭab-šar-[Adad].
5 [Witness] Nabû-taklak.
6 [Witness] Nabû-bani.
7 [Witness] Ahu-du[ri].
(Rest destroyed)

230 Previous editions: AR 674, NALK 316.

231. ——-

K 14295

beginning broken away

1′ [IGI ^{m}*x x*] LÚ*.[*x x x*]

2′ [IGI ^{m}*x*]-*li*-[*x x x*]

3′ [IGI ^{m}*sa-la*$^{?}$-[*ma*$^{?}$*-me*]

4′ [IG]I ^{md}PA.TÚG—DINGIR-[*a-a*]

5′ IGI ^{m}A—PAB LÚ*.[*x x*]

rest broken away

ADD 798

(Beginning destroyed)

1 Witness [NN], [...].

2 Witness [...]li[...].

3 Witness Sa*l*[*amame*].

4 Witness Nušku-ila'i.

5 Witness Aplu-uṣur [...].

(Rest destroyed)

232. Note of 5 Homers of Wine Owed to Silim-Aššur (675-XII-5)

81-2-4,151

1 5 ANŠE GEŠTIN.MEŠ

2 *ina* 1 *qa ša* MAN *ša* ^{m}*si-lim—aš-šur*

3 *ina* IGI ^{m}SUHUŠ—URU.KASKAL

4 *ina* UD-1-KAM *šá* ITI.BARAG

5 *i-dan* BE-*ma la i-din*

e.6 GEŠTIN.MEŠ *a-ki ma-hi-ri*

7 *ša* URU.NINA.KI SUM-*an*

r.1 IGI ^{md}PA.TÚG—DINGIR-*a-a*

2 IGI ^{m}*gur-ra-a-a*

3 IGI ^{md}PA—MAN—PAB

4 IGI ^{m}PAB—BÀD

5 IGI ^{m}*ú-bu-*⌜*ru*⌝*-u-te*

6 ITI.ŠE UD-5-KAM

7e *lim-mu* ^{md}PA—PAB.MEŠ—AŠ

ADD 124

1 5 homers of wine according to the royal 'litre,' belonging to Silim-Aššur, at the disposal of Ubru-Harran.

4 He shall *give* it back on the first day of Nisan (I). If he does not, he shall pay the wine (in silver) according to the market price of Nineveh.

r.1 Witness Nušku-ila'i.

2 Witness Gurrayu.

3 Witness Nabû-šarru-uṣur.

4 Witness Ahu-duri.

5 Witness Uburutu.

6 Month Adar (XII), 5th day, eponym year of Nabû-ahhe-iddina.

233. Another Wine Transaction of Silim-Aššur (674-II)

Bu 89-4-26,10

1 NA_4.KI[ŠIB ^{m}*s*]*i-me*$^{!}$-[*s*]*i-me*

2 LÚ.GAL—URU.MEŠ *šá* ⌜MÍ$^{?}$.*a*⌝*-hu-si-te*

3 5 ANŠE 2BÁN$^{!}$ GEŠTIN.MEŠ

4 [*ina*] 1 ⌜*qa*$^{!}$ *šá*$^{!}$ MAN$^{?}$⌝ *šá* ^{m}⌜*si*⌝*-lim—aš-šur*

5 *ina* IGI ^{m}*si-me*$^{!}$*-s*[*i*$^{!}$*-i*]*-me*

6 *ina* ITI.NE SUM-⌜*an*⌝

7 ^{m}*me-eh-sa-a* ⌜EN⌝—Š[U.2].MEŠ$^{!}$

8 *ša* GEŠTIN.MEŠ IGI ^{md}PA.TÚG—DINGIR-*a-a*

9 IGI ^{m}A—PAB

r.1 IGI ^{m}PAB—⌜BÀD⌝

2 ITI.GUD *lim-mu* ^{m}⌜LUGAL—ZALÁG⌝

ADD 126

1 Se[al of S]imesime, village manager of the lady Ahusitu.

3 5 homers 2 seahs of wine [by] the 'litre' of *the* [*ki*]*ng* belonging to Silim-Aššur, at the disposal of Simes[i]me.

6 He shall pay in Ab (V). Mehsâ is the guarantor of the wine.

8 Witness Nušku-ila'i.

9 Witness Aplu-uṣur.

r.1 Witness Ahu-duri.

2 Month Iyyar (II), eponym year of Šarru-nuri.

232 Previous editions: AR 224, NALK 309. → Or 33 261 n.1. 5 Or: "pay."

233 Previous editions: AR 638, NALK 310. Collations: Assur 2/5.

234. Note of Silver Owed to Silim-Aššur (672-III-29)

K 284

1 3 MA.NA 30 GÍN.MEŠ KUG.UD 0$^{!}$
2 *ina* 1 MA.NA *ša* URU.*gar-ga-mis*
3 *ša* ^{m}*si-lim—aš-šur*
4 *pa-an* ^{md}ŠÚ—SU
5 ITI.NE UD-1-KÁM KUG.UD *i-dan*
6 *šúm-ma la id-din*
7 *a-na* 1/2 GÍN-*šú* GAL-*bi*
r.1 IGI ^{m}*ka-da-mu*
2 IGI ^{md}PA—NUMUN—DÙ
3 IGI ^{m}EN—AŠ
4 IGI ^{m}DUMU.UŠ—PAB
5 IGI ^{m}*tab*-URU-*a-a*
blank space of 2 lines
6e *ina*$^{!}$ ITI.SIG$_{4}$ UD-29-KÁM
7e *lim-me* ^{md}PA—EN—PAB

ADD 15

1 3 minas 30 shekels of silver by the mina of Carchemish, belonging to Silim-Aššur, at the disposal of Marduk-eriba.

5 He shall pay the silver back on the 1st of Ab (V). If he does not, it shall increase 50 percent per shekel.

r.1 Witness Kadammu.

2 Witness Nabû-zeru-ibni.

3 Witness Bel-iddina.

4 Witness Aplu-uṣur.

5 Witness Tabalayu.

6 Month of Sivan (III), 29th day, eponym year of Nabû-belu-uṣur.

235. Note of Silver Owed to Silim-Aššur (671-VIII-29)

Rm 175

1 NA$_{4}$.KIŠIB ^{m}*za-bi-na-a*
2 1 MA.NA KUG.UD *ina* 1 MA.NA *šá* KUR.*gar-gá*$^{!}$*-mis*
3 SAG.MEŠ *šá* ^{d}15 *šá* URU.*arba-ìl*
4 *ša* ^{m}*si-lim—aš-šur ina* IGI.MEŠ-*šú*

5 *ina* ITI.ŠE 1 1/2 MA.NA KUG.UD *i-dan*

6 BE-*ma la* SUM-*ni* 2 GÍN.MEŠ
7 *a-na* 1 MA.NA *šá* ITI-*šú i-rab-bi*
8 ITI.APIN UD-29$^{!}$-KÁM *lim-mu* ^{m}ITI.AB-*a-a*
e.9 IGI ^{md}30—MAN—PAB LÚ.DIB—KUŠ.PA.MEŠ
r.1 IGI ^{m}*ab-du-nu* LÚ.GIŠ.GIGIR LUGAL
blank space of 5 lines
2 IGI ^{m}PAB—SU LÚ.:.$^{!}$
3 IGI ^{m}*aš-šur*—I
4 IGI ^{md}15—MU—AŠ LÚ.A.BA

ADD 41

1 Seal of Zabinâ.

2 One mina of silver by the mina of Carchemish, first fruits of Ištar of Arbela belonging to Silim-Aššur, at his disposal.

(blank seal space)

5 He shall pay 1 1/2 minas of silver in Adar (XII).

6 If he does not, it will increase by 2 shekels per mina each month.

8 Month Marchesvan (VIII), 29th day, eponym year of Kanunayu.

9 Witness Sin-šarru-uṣur, chariot driver.

r.1 Witness Abdunu, horse trainer of the king.

2 Witness Ahu-eriba, ditto.

3 Witness Aššur-na'di.

4 Witness Issar-šumu-iddina, scribe.

236. Silim-Aššur Loans 10 Shekels of Silver (670-II-10)

83-1-18,373

1 N[A$_{4}$.KIŠIB ^{m}]*mi-i-nu—*[*ah-ṭi*]*—a-na—*DINGIR

ADD 99

1 Se[al] of Minu-[ahṭi]-ana-ili.

234 Previous editions: AR 260, NALK 311.
235 Previous editions: AR 294, NALK 312.
236 Previous editions: AR 240, NALK 313. 3 Tablet *šúm-mu* (scribal error). The translation assumes that

2 10 ⸢GÍN⸣.[MEŠ KUG].UD$^{!}$ *šá* [^{m}*si-lim*—AN.ŠÁR]

---

3 *ina* IGI-*šú ku*$^{!!}$-*mu* ^{m}*pu-du-pi-ia-ti*
4 ^{m}*mi-i-nu—ah-ṭi—*⸢*a*⸣-*na*—DINGIR KUG.UD
5 *a-na* ^{m}*si-lim*—AN.ŠÁR$^{!}$ ⸢SUM⸣-*an*
6 BE-*ma* ^{m}*pu-du-pi-ia-ti*
e.7 ⸢KUG⸣.UD *la-a i-da-na* [*x x*]

r.1 ITI.GUD UD-10-KÁM *lim-mu* ^{m}DI-*mu*—E[N]—⸢*la*⸣-*áš-me*

---

2 IGI ^{m}*man-nu—ki*—ERIM.MEŠ
3 IGI ^{m}SU—^{d}10$^{!}$ IGI ^{m}DI-*mu*—PAB.MEŠ
4 IGI ^{m}*a-i—su*$^{!}$-*ú-ri*

5 *a-na* UD-20-KÁM KUG.UD SUM-*an*

2 10 shekels [of sil]ver belonging to [Silim-Aššur]

(blank seal space)

---

3 at his disposal, in lieu of Pudupiyati.

4 Minu-ahṭi-ana-ili shall pay the silver to Silim-Aššur.

6 If Pudupiyati does not pay the silver, [...].

r.1 Month Iyyar (II), 10th day, eponym year of Šulmu-beli-lašme.

(blank seal space)

---

2 Witness Mannu-ki-ṣabi.

3 Witness Eriba-Adad. Witness Šulmu-ahhe.

4 Witness Ai-suri.

5 He shall pay the silver on the 20th day.

237. Note of 12 Minas of Silver Owed to Silim-Aššur (670-VII)

83-1-18,374

1 12 MA.NA KUG.UD
2 SAG.MEŠ *ša* 15 *ša arba-ìl*
3 *ša* NINDA$^{!}$.MEŠ É—DINGIR
4 *ša* ^{m}*si-lim—aš-šur*
5 *ina* IGI ^{m}*za-ru-ti-i*
e.6 DUMU ^{m}*gu-gi-i*
7 *a-na* 4-*ut-ti-šú* GAL-⸢*bi*⸣
r.1 IGI ^{m}*si-lim*—⸢DINGIR$^{?}$⸣
2 IGI ^{md}[*x*]—*šal*$^{!}$-*lim*$^{!}$
3 IGI $^{md!}$*šá*$^{!}$-*maš*$^{!}$—⸢*nap*$^{!}$-*lis*$^{!}$⸣
4 IGI ^{m}*ú-bu-q*[*u*]
5 IGI ^{m}*a-hu-nu*
6e IGI ^{m}*ha*$^{!}$-*nu-nu*$^{!}$
7e IGI$^{!}$ $^{m!}$⸢*x*⸣[*x x x*]

8e ITI.D[UL UD-*x*-KÁM]
9e *lim-mu* ^{m}DI-*mu*—EN—H[AL]

ADD 44

1 12 minas of silver, first fruits of Ištar of Arbela, of the bread of the temple, belonging to Silim-Aššur, at the disposal of Zarutî son of Gugî.

7 It will increase by a fourth.

r.1 Witness Silim-*ili*.

2 Witness [...]-šallim.

3 Witness Šamaš-naplis.

4 Witness Ubbuqu.

5 Witness Ahunu.

6 Witness Hanunu.

7 Witness [NN].

8 Month Tis[hri (VII), ...th day], eponym year of Šulmu-beli-lašme.

Minu-ahṭi-ili had borrowed the money *for* Pudupiyati. The loan was apparently granted only on the condition that M. agreed to repay the loan personally; the clause in l.7 seems to have been added to make sure that M. would actually retrieve the money from Pudupiyati. r.3f See coll.

237 Previous editions: AR 295, NALK 314. Collations: Assur 2/5. r.1 The last sign could also be read ⸢*aš-šur*⸣.

238. A Court Decision Regarding an Estate of Silim-Aššur

83-1-18,367

1 [*de-e-nu ša*] SUKKAL$^{!}$ *sar-tin*
2 [*a-na* ^{m}*x x x*]-MAŠ
3 [*x x x x x x*] ⸢*e*⸣-*me-du-u-ni*
4 [*x x hur-sa-an*] ⸢*i*⸣-*tu-ra*
5 [*x x x* ANŠ]E A.ŠÀ *ú-ta-me*
6 ⸢*ša*⸣ [^{m}*s*]*i-lim—aš-šur ša* ^{m}⸢PAB⸣-*u-a-a*
7 *ina* URU.1-*tú* URU$^{!}$.ŠE$^{!}$—$^{m!}$*a*$^{!}$-*hu*$^{!}$-*u-ni*

8 DI-*mu ina bir-ti-šú-nu mám-ma mám-ma*

9 *la* DUG$_4$.DUG$_4$ *man-nu ša i*-GIL-*u-ni*
10 ⸢LUGAL$^{!}$⸣ *u*$^{!}$ DUMU—LUGAL *lu-u* EN *de-ni-šú*
e.11 [*x* MA.NA KU]G$^{!}$.UD$^{!}$ SUM-*an*
12 [*kas-pu a-na* 10.MEŠ] ⸢*a*⸣-*na* EN-*šú* [GUR-*ra*]
r.1 [IGI ^{m}*x x x* IGI ^{m}*x x*]-*an-ni* :
2 [IGI ^{m}*x x x* IGI ^{m}*x x x x*] :
3 [IGI ^{m}*x x x* IGI ^{m}*x*]—⸢15$^{!}$⸣ :

4 [IGI ^{m}*na-b*]*u*$^{!}$-*u-a* LÚ*.*qur-bu-tú*$^{!}$
5 IGI ⸢^{m}*nu*$^{!}$-*uš*$^{!}$-*ku*$^{!}$⸣—DINGIR-*a-a* :
6 IGI ^{m}PAB—BÀD IGI ^{m}ZALÁG—^{d}*šá-maš*
7 IGI ^{md}*šá-maš*—KAM-*eš*
8 IGI ^{m}*e-di*—⸢DINGIR⸣
9 IGI ^{m}ITI.⸢KIN⸣-[*a*]-*a*
10 [IGI ^{m}*a*]-*bu-nu*
s.1 [IGI] ^{m}MAN—PAB

ADD 168

1 [The judgement which] the vizier and the *sartinnu* imposed [upon ...]... [......].

4 [...] refused [*the ordeal and*] *forfeited* [*two estates* of x hect]ares of land, those of [S]ilim-Aššur and Ahuaya in *Issete* and the village of Ahunu.

8 Peace is between them. Neither shall litigate against the other.

9 Whoever breaks the agreement, the king and the crown prince shall be his prosecutors. He shall pay [x minas of] silver and shall [return the money tenfold] to its owner.

r.1 [Witness NN. Witness ...]anni, ditto.
2 [Witness NN, ditto. Witness NN], ditto.
3 [Witness NN, ditto. Witness ...]-Issar, ditto.
4 [Witness Nab]û'a, royal bodyguard.
5 Witness Nušku-ila'i, ditto.
6 Witness Ahu-duri. Witness Nur-Šamaš.
7 Witness Šamaš-ereš.
8 Witness Edi-il.
9 Witness Ululayu.
10 [Witness A]bunu.
s.1 [Witness] Šarru-uṣur.

238 Previous editions: AR 651, NALK 317. Collations: Assur 2/5. [3] There are several possibilities to read the last name element (-Inurta, -Šamaš, -ašared). [4] See AR 232:7f, NALK 317 and Postgate FNALD p.154, note on 41:9. [5] Instead of "forfeited" (*ur-ta-me*) the text actually has "adjured" (*ú-ta-me*).

12. Dannaya (676-672)

FIG. 24. *Two-humped camels (about 825 BC). Cf. no. 214.*
BM 118885 (detail).

239. Dannaya Buys Three Maids (676-I-25)

K 410

1 NA$_4$.KIŠIB ^{md}30—PAB—SUM-*na*
2 NA$_4$.KIŠIB ^{m}*tu-u-i*
3 PAB 2 LÚ.MEŠ-*e* EN MÍ.MEŠ SUM-*ni*

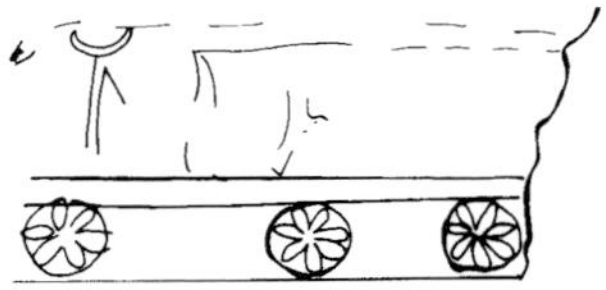

4 MÍ.*ha-za-la-a* MÍ.*hu-d*[*a-x x x*]
5 MÍ.NIN—*im-ma-a* [PAB 3 MÍ].MEŠ
6 [GE]MÉ.MEŠ *ša* LÚ.MEŠ [*an-nu-t*]*e*

7 [*ú-pi*]*š-ma* ^{m}[*da-n*]*a*$^{!}$*-a-a*
8 [*ina* ŠÀ *x* GÍ]N.MEŠ KUG.UD
9 [*ina* 1 MA].NA-*e ša* URU.*gar-ga-mis*
10 [TA IGI LÚ].MEŠ-*e an-nu-u-te*
11 [*x x il-q*]*i kas-pu* [0$^{!}$]
12 [*gam*$^{!}$*-mur*$^{!}$ *ta-din*] MÍ.MEŠ *šú-*[*a-te*]
rest broken away

Rev. beginning broken away
1′ [*kas-pu a-na* 10.MEŠ]-*te a-na* E[N.MEŠ-*šú*]
2′ [GUR *ina de-ni-šú*] DUG$_4$.DUG$_4$-*ma là* [TI]

3′ [IGI ^{m}*ib-n*]*a-a-a* DUMU ^{m}EN—MAN—DÙ
4′ [IGI ^{m}*x x x*]—*iq-bi* LÚ*.Ì.DU$_8$
5′ [IGI ^{m}*x x x*]-*a*$^{?!}$ LÚ*$^{!}$.DAM.QAR
6′ IGI ^{m}U.GUR—[MAN]—PAB LÚ*.GIGIR ⌜*ša*$^{!}$⌝ *u*$^{!!}$*-rat*

7′ IGI ^{md}PA—NU[MUN$^{?}$—*x x x x x šá*] ⌜A—MAN⌝
8′ IGI ^{m}*ha-làh-*[*a-a x x*]
blank space of one line
9′ IGI ^{m}*mar-du-u-a* L[Ú.A.BA]
blank space of two lines
10′ ITI.BARAG UD-25-[KAM]
11′ *lim-me* ^{m}*ban-ba-a*
12′ LÚ*.SUKKAL LÚ*.2-*u*

ADD 256

1 Seal of Sin-ahu-iddina, seal of Tuwi, a total of 2 men, owners of the women being so[ld].

(cylinder seal impression)

4 Hazalâ, Hud[a...], Ahati-immâ, [a total of 3 women, [female s]ervants of [these] gentleme[n] —

7 [Dann]aya [has contr]acted and [boug]ht them [from] these [gentleme]n [for x shek]els of silver [by the min]a of Carchemish.

11 The money is [paid completely]. T[hose] women [are purchased and acquired]
(Break)

r.1 [He shall return the money ten]fold to [its] own[ers]. He shall contest [in] his [lawsuit] and not [succeed].

3 [Witness Ibn]aya, son of Bel-šarru-ibni.
4 [Witness ...]-iqbi, porter.
5 [Witness ...]a', merchant.
6 [Witness] Nergal-[šarru]-uṣur, horse trainer of teams.
7 Witness Nabû-*ze*[*ru*-..., ...] of the crown prince.
8 Witness Halah[hayu, ...].
9 Witness Mardua, *s*[*cribe*].
10 Month Nisan (I), 25th day, eponym year of Banbâ, second vizier.

239 Previous edition: AR 536. Collations: Assur 2/5. r.6 Tablet *nu-rat* (scribal error).

240. Note of Silver Owed to Dannaya (676-III-4)

K 1397

1 ⸢3⸣8 GÍN KUG.UD
2 [*ša*] ^{m}*dan-na-a-a*
3 ⸢*ina* IGI⸣ ^{m}*la—qe-pi*
4 *ina* UD-20-KÁM *ša* ITI.ŠU
5 SUM-*an šúm-ma*
e.6 *la—din a-na* 4-*tú-šú*
7 GAL-*bi*
r.1 IGI 0${}^{!}$ ^{d}UTU IGI${}^{!}$ ^{d}U.GUR${}^{!}$
2 IGI ^{m}*man-nu—iq-bi*
3 IGI ^{m}*mi-i-su*
4 ⸢IGI⸣ ^{m}*mar-duk*
5 [IGI ^{m}]^{d}PA—*nat-kil* LÚ*.*qur-bu-*(*te*)
6 [IGI ^{md}]MAŠ.MAŠ—KAR-*ir*

7 [ITI.SI]$G_4$${}^{!}$ UD-4-KÁM
8e [*lim-mu* ^{m}]*ban-ba-a*

ADD 11

[1] 38 shekels of silver [belonging to] Dannaya, at the disposal of La-qepu.

[4] He shall pay back on the 20th of Tammuz (IV). If he does not, it will increase by a fourth.

[r.1] Witness Šamaš. Witness Nergal.
[2] Witness Mannu-iqbi.
[3] Witness Misu.
[4] Witness Marduk.
[5] [Witness] Nabû-natkil, royal bodyguard.
[6] [Witness] Nergal-eṭir.
[7] [Month Siv]an (III), 4th day, [eponym year of] Banbâ.

241. Note of Two Camels Owed to Dannaya (674-VII-14)

K 377

1 2 ANŠE.A.((A)).AB.BA
2 *ša* 2-*a-a kar-ru-u-ni*
3 *ša* ^{m}*dan-na-ia*
4 *ina* IGI ^{m}*ia-hu-ṭu*
5 *ina* IGI ^{m}DINGIR—GIN—[PAB]
e.6 *ina* IGI ^{m}10—A—[AŠ]
7 *ina* UD-1-KAM *š*[*a* ITI.APIN]
r.1 *gam-mal id-du-*[*nu*]

2 *šúm-mu la id-din-nu* 6 MA.NA

3 KUG.UD *id-du-nu* ITI.DU_6 UD-14-KAM
4 *lim-mu* ^{m}MAN—*nu-ri*
5 IGI ^{m}*si-qi*—^{d}15${}^{!}$ IGI ^{m}DI—MAN
6 IGI ^{m}10—KALAG-*an*

s.1 [*šú*]*m-mu* KUG.UD *là* SUM
2 [0] 2 GÍN *a-na* 1 MA.NA
3 *i*-GAL${}^{!}$-*bi*

ADD 117

[1] Two double-humped camels belonging to Dannaya, at the disposal of Yahuṭu, Ilu-kenu-[uṣur], and Adad-aplu-[iddina].

[7] They shall give the camels back on the 1st of [Marchesvan] (VIII).

[r.2] If they do not give them, they shall pay 6 minas of silver.

[3] Month Tishri (VII), 14th day, eponym year of Šarru-nuri.

[5] Witness Siqi-Issar. Witness Šulmu-šarri.
[6] Witness Adad-dan.

[s.1] [I]f they do not pay the silver, it will increase by *2* shekels per mina.

240 Previous editions: AR 256, NALK 86. [4] Contra ITU.ŠU. [8] This line is written in a smaller script. [r.1] If the readings here (coll. Kwasman) are correct, this is the only NA legal document so far known confirmed before divine witnesses. Cf., however, no. 219 s.1.
241 Previous editions: AR 225, NALK 87b; → Postgate FNALD 38.

242. Duplicate of the Previous Text (674-VII-14)

K 14313 (83-1-18)

beginning broken away
1′ [*in*]*a* ⸢IGI ^{m}*ia-hu-ṭu*⸣
2′ *ina* IGI ^{m}DINGIR—GIN—PAB A *x*[*x x x*]
3′ *ina* IGI ^{m}10—A—AŠ LÚ*.3.⸢U$_5$⸣

4′ *ina* UD-1-KAM *ša* ITI.APIN
5′ [*ina*] KUR.*ru-ṣa-pa id-du-nu*
6′ [*šúm-m*]*u* ⸢*la*⸣ [*id-din-nu*]
rest broken away

ADD 800

(Beginning destroyed)

1 [at the] disposal of Yahuṭu, Ilu-kenu-uṣur son of [...], and Adad-aplu-iddina, 'third man.'

4 They shall give them back on the 1st of Marchesvan (VIII) [in] Raṣappa.

6 [I]f [they] do not [give]

(Rest destroyed)

243. Note of Sheep Owed to Dannaya (673-II-7)

K 376

1 NA$_4$.KIŠIB ^{m}*ia-hu-ṭi* LÚ.2-*u* KUR.*ra-ṣ*[*ap-pa*]

2 2-*me* UDU.U$_8$.MEŠ 1-*me*-50 UDU.ÙZ.MEŠ
3 2-*me*-30 DUMU MU.AN.NA PAB 5-*me*-80!! UDU.MEŠ
blank space of 3 lines
4 *ša* ^{m}*dan-na-a-a* LÚ.[*x x x x x*]
5 *ina* IGI ^{m}*ia-hu-ṭi* [LÚ.2-*u* KUR.*ra-ṣap-pa*]
6 *ina* IGI ^{m}DINGIR—GIN—P[AB A ^{m}*x x x x*]
7 *ina* IGI [^{m}10—A—AŠ LÚ.3.U$_5$]

8 *ina* ITI.[*x* UD-*x*-KÁM *id-du-nu šúm-mu*]
e.9 *la* [*id-din-nu x* MA.NA KUG.UD *id-du-nu*]

10 IGI [^{m}*x x x x x x x x x x x x*]
r.1 IGI ^{m}*ba-ṭu-ṭa-*[*nu*] LÚ.A.[BA!]
2 IGI ^{m}10—PAB-*ir* LÚ.[*x x*]
3 IGI ^{m}PAB—ZALÁG IGI ^{m}DUMU.UŠ-⸢*a*⸣-*a*
4 LÚ.A.BA
blank space of about 3 lines
5 ITI.GUD UD-7-KÁM
6 *lim-mu* ^{m}*a-tar*—DINGIR.MEŠ
7 IGI ^{md}30—SUM-*na*—PAB.MEŠ
8 IGI ^{m}*aš-šur*—DINGIR-*a-a*

ADD 118

1 Seal of Yahuṭu, deputy (governor) of Raṣ[appa].

2 200 ewes, 150 she-goats, 230 yearlings, a total of 580 she[ep] belonging to Dannaya, the [...],

5 at the disposal of Yahuṭu, [deputy of Raṣappa], Ilu-kenu-u[ṣur, son of ...], and [Adad-aplu-iddina, 'third man].'

8 [They shall give them back] on [the ...th of .... If they] do not, [they shall pay x minas of silver].

10 Witness [NN, ...].

r.1 Witness Baṭuṭa[nu], scr[ibe].

2 Witness Adad-naṣir, [...].

3 Witness Ahi-nuri. Witness Aplaya, scribe.

5 Month Iyyar (II), 7th day, eponym year of Atar-ili.

7 Witness Sin-nadin-ahhe.

8 Witness Aššur-ila'i.

242 Previous editions: AR 225, NALK 87a.
243 Previous editions: AR 315, NALK 88; → KB 4 (1896) 128f. Collations: Assur 2/5. 3 Tablet 5-*me*-50 (scribal error).

244. Dannaya Buys a Slave (672-VI-5)

K 334

1 NA$_4$.KIŠIB ^{m}*ha-ta-a-a*
2 EN LÚ SUM-*a-ni*

---

3 ^{m}*lu*—PAB.MEŠ ARAD-*šú*
4 *ú-⌈piš⌉-ma* (^{m})*dan-na-a-a*
5 TA* IGI ^{m}*ha-ta-a-a*
6 *ina* ŠÀ 20 GÍN KUG.UD *il-qi*
7 *kas-pu ga-mur ta-din*
8 LÚ *šu-a-te za-rip laq-qi*
9 *tu-a-ru de-e-nu* DUG$_4$.DUG$_4$ *la-áš-šú*
10 *⌈man⌉-nu ša i*-GIL-*u-ni*
11 [*x* MA].NA KUG.[UD *x* MA.NA KUG.G]I!
rest broken away
Rev. beginning broken away
1′ [*ina d*]*e*!-*n*[*i*!-*šú* DUG$_4$.DUG$_4$-*ma la i-laq-qi*]

2′ IGI ^{md}⌈*šá-maš*⌉—[DINGIR]-⌈*a-a*⌉ [LÚ.*x x*]
3′ ⌈IGI⌉ ^{m}*hi-ma-ri-i* :
4′ IGI ^{m}*za-ab-da-a* LÚ*.*mu-kil*—PA.MEŠ 0!
5′ IGI ^{m}*ha-ra*—U.U! :
6′ IGI ^{m}*man-nu-*(*ki*)—PAB.MEŠ
7′ LÚ*.*ša—hu-ṭa-ri*
8′ IGI ^{m}ARAD—^{d}MAŠ LÚ*.NAGAR
9′ ITI.KIN UD-5-KAM
10′ *lim-me* ^{md}PA—EN—PAB!!
11′ IGI ^{m}ARAD—^{d}MAŠ LÚ*.A.BA

ADD 178

1 Seal of Hattayu, owner of the man being sold.

(blank seal space)

---

3 Lu-ahhe, his servant —

4 Dannaya has contracted and bought him from Hattayu for 20 shekels of silver.

6 The money is paid completely. That man is purchased and acquired. Any revocation, lawsuit, or litigation is void.

10 Whoever breaks the contract [shall pay x min]as of sil[ver and x minas of go]ld.

(Break)

r.1 [He shall contest in his l]awsu[it and not succeed].

---

r.2 Witness Šamaš-[il]a'i, [...].
3 Witness Himarî, ditto.
4 Witness Zabdâ, chariot driver.
5 Witness Hara-Dadi, ditto.
6 Witness Mannu-ki-ahhe, staff bearer.
8 Witness Urda-Inurta, carpenter.
9 Month Elul (VI), 5th day, eponym year of Nabû-belu-uṣur.
11 Witness Urda-Inurta, scribe.

245. Dannaya Takes 210 Hectares of Land for a Silver Debt (672-XII-4)

K 349

1 [NA$_4$.KIŠIB ^{m}*x-x*]*x*—⌈DÙG!.GA!⌉ LÚ*.2-⌈*i*?⌉
2 [*š*]*a* URU.*ra-ṣa-pa*

---

3 [EN] UN.MEŠ A.ŠÀ.GA *ta-⌈da⌉-an*

4 ⌈É!⌉ 2-*me* A.ŠÀ.GA
5 *ina* ⌈URU⌉.*qu-ba-a-te*
6 [SUH]UR URU.*til—ra-ha-ia-te*

ADD 64

1 [Seal of ...]-ṭaba, deputy (governor) [o]f Raṣappa,

(three stamp seals)

---

3 [owner] of the people and land being sold.

4 An estate of 200 (hectares of) land [in] the town of Qubate, [adjoin]ing the towns of

244 Previous editions: AR 486, NALK 89; → KB 4 (1896) 128-131; 3R 49,5 (copy). r.4 There is no *šá* MAN (NALK) at the end of the line. r.10 Tablet ^{md}PA—EN—AŠ, scribal error.
245 Previous editions: AR 152, NALK 90. Collations: Assur 2/5.

7 [S]UHUR URU.É—^{d}*ra-man-nu*
8 SUHUR URU.É—LÚ*.*šá*—UGU-*hi*—URU
9 ⸢SUHUR⸣ URU.BÀD—^{d}*na-na-a*
10 ^{m}DÙG.GA—*ri-gi-ma-tú*—^{d}IM
11 MÍ-*šú* 2 MÍ.TUR.MEŠ-*šú*
12 ^{md}PA—MAN—DINGIR.MEŠ MÍ-*šú*
13 2 GUD.NITÁ 10 ANŠE ŠE.NUMUN.MEŠ *a-ar-šú*
e.14 *ina ku-*⸢*mu*⸣ 15 MA.NA ⸢KUG.UD⸣
15 *ina* 1 MA.[NA-*e*] ⸢*ša* URU⸣.*gar-ga-*[*mis*]
r.1 *ina* IGI ^{m}⸢*dan*$^{!}$⸣^{an}*-na*$^{!}$*-a*
2 *a-na ši*$^{!}$*-par*$^{!}$*-ti*
3 *šá*$^{!}$*-ki*$^{!}$*-an*$^{!}$ *man-nu*$^{!}$
4 *š*[*a*$^{!}$ KUG.UD.ME]Š *ú-še-ra-ba-an-ni*
5 [UN.MEŠ A.Š]À.GA
6 ⸢*ú-še*⸣*-ṣi*
7 [IG]I ^{md}PA—*še-zib*
8 [IG]I ^{m}*da-ru-ra-a*
9 [IG]I ^{m}*ha-ra*—MAN$^{!}$
10 [IG]I ^{m}*man-nu*—*ki*—PAB.MEŠ
11 IGI ^{m}*ha-ba-a-si-te-ma*$^{!}$
12 ⸢IGI⸣ ^{m}*za-*⸢*ib*$^{!}$*-da-a*⸣*-ni*
13 ITI.ŠE UD-4-KÁM

14 *lim-*(*me*) ^{md}PA—U—PAB
15 *ki-ṣir* ^{md}*aš*$^{!}$*-šur*—PAB.MEŠ—AŠ
16 [MAN] ⸢KUR⸣—*aš-šur*

Til-rahayate, Bit-Ramannu, Bit-ša-muhhi-ali, and Dur-Nanâ; Ṭaba-rigimatu-Adad, his wife and two girls of his; Nabû-šar-ilani and his wife; 2 oxen; (and) 10 hectares of sown field,

14 are placed as a pledge at the disposal of Dannaya in lieu of 15 minas of silver by the mi[na o]f Carche[mish].

r.3 Whoeve[r] brings the [silver] shall redeem the [people and the lan]d.

7 [Wit]ness Nabû-šezib.
8 [Wit]ness Darurâ.
9 [Wit]ness Hara-Dadi.
10 [Wit]ness Mannu-ki-ahhe.
11 Witness Habasitema.
12 Witness Zabdanu.
13 Month Adar (XII), 4th day, eponym year of Nabû-belu-uṣur, *staff* of Esarhaddon, king of Assyria.

246. Dannaya Buys a Slave

81-2-4,158

beginning broken away

1′ ^{m}*ak-ba-ru x*[*x x x x*]
2′ ^{m}*man-nu*—*ki-i*—PAB.MEŠ [ARAD-*šú*]
3′ *šá* ^{md}PA—PAB—[AŠ]
4′ *ú-piš-ma* ^{m}*dan-*⸢*na*⸣-[*a*]
5′ *ina* ŠÀ 1/2 MA.NA KUG.UD *i*[*l-qi*]
6′ *kas-pu gam-mur ta-din* [LÚ *šu-a-tú*]
7′ *za-rip laq-qi tú-a-*⸢*ru de*⸣-[*e-nu*]

8′ DUG$_{4}$.DUG$_{4}$ *la-áš-šú man-nu šá ina* ⸢*ur-kiš*⸣
9′ *ina ma-te-ma i-zaq-qup-an-*⸢*ni*⸣
10′ *lu-u* ^{m}⸢^{d}PA—PAB—AŠ⸣ *lu-u* ⸢DUMU⸣.MEŠ-*šú*
11′ *lu-u* DU[MU—DUMU.MEŠ-*šú* T]A ^{m}*dan-na-a*
12′ *u* DU[MU.MEŠ-*šú de-e-nu*] ⸢DUG$_{4}$.DUG$_{4}$⸣
13′ *u*[*b-ta-ʾu-u*]*-ni*
14′ [*kas-pu a-na* 10.MEŠ-*te a-na* E]N.MEŠ-*šú*
15′ [GUR *ina de-ni-šú* DUG$_{4}$.DUG$_{4}$*-ma la i-laq-q*]*i*

ADD 251

(Beginning destroyed)
(seal space)

1 Akbaru, [*son* of] Mannu-ki-ahhe, [a servant] of Nabû-ahu-[iddina] —

4 Danna[ya] has contracted and bo[ught] him for 1/2 mina of silver.

6 The money is paid completely. [That man] is purchased and acquired. Any revocation, law[suit] or litigation is void.

8 Whoever in the future, at any time, lodges a complaint, whether Nabû-ahu-iddina or his sons or gran[dsons], and s[eeks a lawsuit] or litigation [agai]nst Dannaya and [his] so[ns, shall return the money tenfold to] its [own]ers. [He shall contest in his lawsuit and not succe]ed.

246 Previous editions: AR 490, NALK 91. Collated by I.L. Finkel. 1 The restoration of this line should indicate that Akbaru is related to Mannu-ki-ahhe. One suggestion is to read D[UMU] although the trace shows a sign that looks like the beginning of *su*. 4, r.5 See coll.

rest broken away
Rev. beginning broken away
1′ ⸢IGI ᵐPAB!⸣-*i—qa-m*[*u* LÚ].⸢DAM.QAR!⸣
2′ [0] *ki-ṣir* MAN
3′ IGI ᵐPAB—*ia-qar* ⸢LÚ⸣.[*x x x*]
4′ IGI ᵐDÙ!-⸢*iá*!⸣ L[Ú!.*x x*]⸢*x*⸣
5′ IGI ᵐᵈP[A!—*x x x* LÚ.A.B]A
rest broken away

(Break)

r.1 Witness Ahi-qam, merchant (from the) king's staff.

3 Witness Ahiqar, [...].

4 Witness Banay[a, ...].

5 Witness Nab[û-...], scribe.

(Rest destroyed)

13. Harem Governesses and Other Royal Women

FIG. 25. *The queen of Assyria (about 645 BC).*
BM 124920 (detail).

247. Note of a Mule Owed to the Governess of the Kilizi Harem (679-VIII)

Ki 1904-10-9,180

1 NA$_4$.KIŠIB [^{m}*x x x x*] ⸢*x*⸣ ^{md}PA$^{!}$—KALAG-*in-an-ni*
2 NA$_4$.K[IŠIB *x x x x x x x x x*]-*a*$^{!}$
3 ANŠE.*k*[*u*$^{!}$-*du-nu x x x x x x x*] ⸢*x*⸣
4 URU.ŠE—⸢*x*⸣[*x x x x x x x x-r*]*i*$^{!}$

5 *šá* MÍ.*šá-kín-te*$^{!}$ *šá* URU.*kàl-zi ina* IGI.MEŠ-*šú-nu*
6 ITI.APIN *lim-mu* ^{m}*šá*—^{d}IM—*a-ni-nu*

7 IGI ^{m}*man-nu—ki-i*—URU.*arba-ìl*
e.8 IGI ^{md}PA—MU—*iš-kun* LÚ.A.BA
9 IGI ^{m}*ina*—IM—*aš-šur*—DU-*ak* LÚ.GAL—*mug*$^{!}$-*gi*
r.1 IGI ^{md}PA—*de*-⸢*ni*⸣—*a-mur* LÚ.2-*ú*
2 IGI ^{m}*ma-mì-i*
blank space of three lines
3 IGI ^{m}*qur-di*—^{d}15 LÚ.GAL—KA.KÉŠ
4 IGI ^{m}*ha—ba-áš-ti-i*
5 IGI ^{m}*ár-ze-e-zu*
6 IGI ^{md}PA-*u*$_8$-*a* LÚ.GAL—KA.KÉŠ
7 IGI ^{m}HÉ.NUN-*a-a* LÚ.Ì.DU$_8$

ADD 1188

1 Seal of [NN, seal of] Nabû-da'inanni,
2 se[al of NN ......].
3 A m[ule, ...], the village [of ......],

(space for seal impressions)

5 belonging to the governess of (the harem of) Kilizi, at their disposal.
6 Month Marchesvan (VIII), eponym year of Ša-Adad-aninu.
7 Witness Mannu-ki-Arbail.
8 Witness Nabû-šumu-iškun, scribe.
9 Witness Ina-šar-Aššur-allak, *rab mūgi*.
r.1 Witness Nabû-deni-amur, deputy.
2 Witness Mamî.
3 Witness Qurdi-Issar, cohort commander.
4 Witness Habasti.
5 Witness Arzezu.
6 Witness Nabû'a, cohort commander.
7 Witness Nuhšaya, porter.

248. Fragment of a Silver Loan

K 918

1 *ki*-[*ṣir*]-⸢*te*⸣ 10 MA.NA KUG$^{!}$.UD$^{!}$ SAG.DU
2 [*ina* 1 MA.NA-*e*] ⸢*šá*⸣ U[RU.*g*]*ar-ga-mis*
3 [*x x x x x x x x x x*]-*ni*
break of 4 lines
8 *šum-ma ina* ITI.A[B *x x x la* SUM-*ni*]
9 KUG.UD *a-na* 4-*tú-šú* [*i-rab-bi*]
10 ITI.AB UD-10$^{!}$-KÁM *lim-mu* [^{m}*x x x*]

e.11 IGI ^{m}*a-hi—ba-as-tú* LÚ.[GAL—Ì.DU$_8$.MEŠ]
r.1 IGI ^{md}UTU—A[Š]

ADD 52

1 Envelope of 10 minas of silver, capital,
2 by the mina of Carchemish
(Break)
8 If [he does not pay ...] in Kanun (X), the silver [shall increase] by a fourth.
10 Month Kanun (X), 10th day, eponym year of [NN].
11 Witness Ahi-bastu, [head porter].
r.1 Witness Šamaš-idd[ina].

247 Previous edition: NALK 409. [3] See coll.
248 Previous edition: AR 276. An early Esarhaddon date for this document is suggested by the name of the scribe, attested for the years 698, 687, 683 and 676, and by the witnesses Nuhšaya and Habasti attested with the title "porter" and "chief porter" respectively from 685 on (cf. e.g. no. 247, dated 679, where the two appear together).

(seal space)

2 IGI ^{m}HÉ.NUN-*a-a*
3 IGI ^{m}PA—MU—AŠ LÚ.A.B[A]

2 Witness Nuhšaya.
3 Witness Nabû-šumu-iddina, scribe.

249. ——-

Sm 1476

Obv. broken away
Rev. beginning broken away
1′ IGI ^{m}*man-nu—ki—ar*[*ba-il x x x x*]
2′ IGI ^{m}DINGIR—*lu*-[*x x x x x x x*]
3′ IGI ^{m}HÉ.NUN-[*a-a* LÚ.Ì.DU$_8$]
4′ IGI ^{md}15—[*x x x x x x x*]

5′ IGI ^{md}PA-*u*-[*a* LÚ.GAL—KA.KÉŠ]
6′ IGI ^{m}*qur-di*—^{d}15 LÚ.[GAL—KA.KÉŠ]
7′ IGI ^{m}*ma-mì-i* LÚ.GAL—KA.K[ÉŠ]
8′ IGI ^{md}PA—MU—GAR-*un* [LÚ.A.BA]
rest broken away

ADD 602

(Beginning destroyed)

r.1 Witness Mannu-ki-Arbail, [...].
2 Witness Ilu-[..., ...].
3 Witness Nuhš[aya, porter].
4 Witness Issar-[..., ...]
5 Witness Nabû'a, [cohort commander].
6 Witness Qurdi-Issar, [cohort commander].
7 Witness Mamî, cohort commander.
8 Witness Nabû-šumu-iškun, [scribe].
(Rest destroyed)

250. Abi-rahî, Sister of the Governess, Buys Three Slaves

81-2-4,152

1 [N]A$_4$.KIŠIB ^{m}*mi*-[*na-hi-mi*]
2 E[N] M[Í].MEŠ$^{!!}$ S[UM]-*ni*

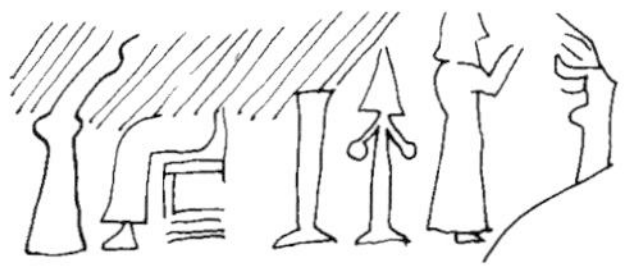

3 MÍ.*ia-qar*—PAB.MEŠ DUMU.⌈MÍ-*sa*⌉
4 MÍ.*a-bi—ia-ah-ia*
5 PAB 3 ZI.MEŠ
6 *ša* ^{m}*mi-na-hi-mi*
7 *ú-piš-ma* MÍ.AD—*ra-hi-i*
8 NIN-*sa ša* MÍ.*šá-kín-te*
9 *ina* ŠÀ 2 MA.NA KUG.UD
10 *ina* 1 MA.NA *ša* URU.*gar-ga-mis*
e.11 *il-qí kas-pu gam-mur*
12 *ta-din* UN.MEŠ *šu-a-tú*
13 *zar-pu laq-qi-u*
14 *tu-a-ru*
r.1 *de-e-nu da-ba-bu*

ADD 245

1 Seal of Me[nahem], owner of the *wo*[*me*]*n* being sold.

(cylinder seal impression)

3 Yaqar-ahhe, her daughter, (and) the woman Abi-yahya, a total of 3 persons belonging to Menahem —

7 Abi-rahî, sister of the governess, has contracted and bought them for two minas of silver by the mina of Carchemish.

11 The money is completely paid. The people in question are acquired and purchased. Any revocation, lawsuit or litigation is void.

249 Previous editions: AR 675, NALK 410.
250 Previous editions: AR 81, NALK 2; → ABC 20; CIS 33; Fales Epigraphs 6. Collations: Assur 2/5. 2 See coll. 7 For this name (not to be emended into Abi-ram on the basis of no. 252:13!) see Zadok West Semites p.104. r.3 The scribe has inadvertently omitted KUG.UD in this line.

2 *la-a-šú man-nu šá* GIL-*u-ni*
3 10 MA.NA 1 MA.NA KUG.GI
4 *ina bur-ki* ^{d}15 *a-šib*$^{!}$ NINA.KI GAR-*an*
5 *kas-pu ana* 10.MEŠ *ana* EN-*šú* GUR
6 *ina de-ni-šú* DUG$_{4}$.DUG$_{4}$-*ma là* TI

---

7 IGI ^{m}*si-lim*—DINGIR LÚ*.⸢SANGA⸣
8 IGI ^{m}*di-di-*⸢*i*⸣ [0]
9 IGI ^{m}*mil-ki—la*$^{!}$-[*rim*]
10 IGI ^{m}URU$^{!}$—*ú*-[*x x*]
11 [IGI ^{m}*x*]—PAB-*x*[*x x x*]
a break of about two lines
14e [GAR.K]UR KUR.*x*[*x x x x*]

s.1 *l mnḥm*

r.2 Whoever breaks the contract, shall place 10 minas (of silver) and one mina of gold in the lap of Ištar residing in Nineveh, and shall return the money tenfold to its owner. He shall contest in his lawsuit and not succeed.

---

7 Witness Silim-ili, priest.
8 Witness Dadî.
9 Witness Milki-la[rim].
10 Witness *El*-u[...].
11 Witness [...]-*ahu*-[...].
12 [Month of ..., ...th day, eponym year of NN], governor of [...].
s.1 (Aramaic caption:) *Concerning* Menahem.

251. Šadditu, Sister of Esarhaddon, Buys Land

K 3146 + K 7379 (ADD 441) + K 7400 (ADD 740) + K 13192

beginning (about 15 lines) broken away
1′ [*x x x x x x*] ŠÀ ⸢*lu*$^{!}$⸣ [*x x x x*]
2′ [*x x x x x* SUH]UR ÍD SUH[UR *x x x x x*]
3′ [*x x x x x*] É$^{!}$ ^{m}PAB—SIG$_{5}$ ^{md}⸢U.GUR⸣—*ú-ba*[*l-liṭ*]
4′ [*x x x x*]⸢*x*⸣ MÍ-*šú ú-piš-ma* ⸢MÍ⸣.KUR-*i-t*[*ú*]
5′ [DUMU].MÍ [^{md}]30—PAB.MEŠ—SU MAN KUR—*aš-šur* NIN-*su*
6′ *ša* ^{m}*aš*-[*šur*—PA]B—AŠ MAN KUR—*aš-šur-ma ina* ŠÀ-*bi* 8 MA.NA ⸢KUG.UD⸣
7′ *ina ma-né*-[*e*] *ša* URU.*gar-ga-mis il-qi*
8′ *kas-pu gam*-⸢*mur*⸣ *ta-din* GIŠ.SAR É A.ŠÀ UN.MEŠ *šu-a*-[*te zar-pu*]
9′ *laq-qi-ʾu* ⸢*tu*⸣*-a-ru de*-[*e*]*-nu* DUG$_{4}$.DUG$_{4}$ *la-áš*-[*šú*]
10′ *man-nu šá ina ur-kiš im—ma*-[*te-m*]*a i-za-qu-pa-ni* GIL-*u-ni*
11′ *lu-u* LÚ.MEŠ-*e* ⸢*an*⸣*-nu-ti* [*lu-u* DU]MU.MEŠ-*šú-nu*
12′ *lu-u* DUMU—DUMU.MEŠ-*šú-nu lu-u* ŠEŠ.[MEŠ-*šú-nu*] ⸢*lu*⸣*-u* DUMU—PAB-*šú*-(*nu*)
13′ *lu-u šak-nu-šú-nu ša* T[A MÍ.KU]R-⸢*i*⸣*-ti*$^{!}$ *ù* DUMU.MEŠ-*šá*
14′ *ù* DUMU—DUMU.MEŠ-*šá d*[*e-e-nu* DUG$_{4}$.DUG$_{4}$ *ub*]-⸢*ta*⸣*-ʾu*-[*u-ni*]
15′ 10 MA.NA KUG.UD LUH-*u* [*x* MA.NA KUG.GI *sak-ru*]
16′ *ina bur*-⸢*ki*⸣ ^{d}IŠ.TAR *a*-[*ši-bat* URU.NINA.KI

ADD 804

(Beginning destroyed)

1 [......] in ...[...]
2 [... adjoin]ing the river, [....... and] the house of Ahu-damqu;
3 Nergal-ubal[liṭ ...] and his wife —
4 Šaddit[u, daug]hter [of] Sennacherib, king of Assyria, and sister of Es[arh]addon, king of Assyria, has contracted and bought (said property) for 8 minas of silver by the mina of Carchemish.
8 The money is paid completely. That garden, house, land and people [are purchased] and acquired. Any revocation, law[su]it, or litigation is voi[d].
10 Whoever in the future, at any t[ime], lodges a complaint and breaks the con[tract], whether these gentlemen [or] their [so]ns, grandsons, brother[s] or nephews, or their prefect, and seeks a law[suit or litigation] aga[inst Šadd]itu and her sons and grandsons,
15 shall place 10 minas of refined silver (and) [x minas of pure gold] in the lap of Ištar

251 Previous editions: AR 102, NALK 405. Collations: Assur 2/5. 1, 4 See coll. 5 No room for [*su*] between DUMU.MÍ and [^{md}]30; see coll. 17f See coll.; there is no MEŠ between AMBAR and *ša*.

GAR-*an*]
e.17′ 7$^{!}$ GI AMBAR *ša*$^{!}$ [*la ki-ṣir ina* KÁ ^{d}*aš-šur*]
18′ *i-zaq-qa*[*p* 2 ANŠE.KUR.RA.MEŠ BABBAR.MEŠ]
r.1 *ina* GÌR.2 [^{d}*aš-šur i-rak-kas* 4 ANŠE *har-ba-kan-ni*]
2 *ina* KI.[TA ^{d}MAŠ.MAŠ *ú-še-rab*]
3 *ina l*[*a d*]*e-ni-šú* [DUG$_4$.DUG$_4$-*ma*]
4 *l*[*a*] *i-*[*laq-qi*]

re[siding in Nineveh], and shall set up 7 marsh reeds which are [without nodes at the gate of Aššur].

18 [He shall tie two white horses] to the feet of [Aššur, and shall bring four *harbakannu* horses] to the fe[et of Nergal. He shall contest] in his no[n-law]suit and n[ot] suc[ceed].

---

5 [IGI] ^{m}*sa-si-*[*i x x x x x*]
6 [IG]I ^{m}SUHUŠ—⸢*x*⸣[*x x x x x x x*]
7 [IG]I ^{m}⸢EN⸣—⸢*lu*⸣-[*x x x x x x x x*]
8 [IG]I ^{m}*ṣil-*[*x x x x x x x x*]
9 [IG]I ^{md}[*x x x x x x x x*]
10 [IG]I ^{m}[*x x x x x x x x*]
rest broken away

5 [Witness] Sasî, [...].
6 [Witne]ss Ubru-[..., ...].
7 [Witne]ss Bel-lu-[*balaṭ*, ...].
8 [Witne]ss Ṣil-[..., ...].
9 [Witne]ss [......]
(Rest destroyed)

252. Abi-rami, Sister of the Queen Mother, Leases Land (674-III-11)

80-7-19,51

1 [NA$_4$.KIŠIB ^{m}*x x*] *ina*$^{!}$ KUR.*ha-zi*$^{!}$*-te*
2 [DUMU ^{m}*a-mu*]*r*—⸢DINGIR⸣
3 [EN$^{!}$] ⸢A$^{!}$⸣.Š[À] SUM-*ni*

ADD 70

1 [Seal of NN] of Gaza, [son of Amu]r-ilu, [own]er of the lan[d] being given over.

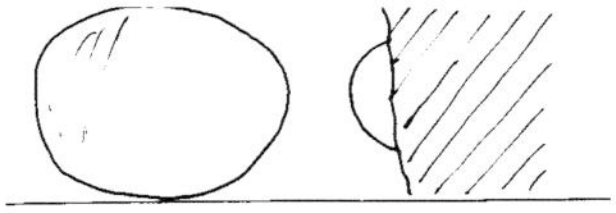

(stamp seal impressions)

---

4 É 3$^{!}$ ANŠE$^{!}$ 4BÁN$^{?}$ ⸢A⸣.[ŠÀ$^{!}$ *x x*]
5 SUHUR ^{m}PAB—*ia-*[*x x x*]
6 SUHUR ^{m}DINGIR—*i*[*a-x x*]
7 [SUHUR ^{m}DING]IR$^{!}$-⸢*a*$^{!}$⸣-[*a—x x x*]
rest broken away
Rev. beginning broken away
1′ [U]RU$^{!}$.*ši-*[*x*] ⸢*x x*⸣ [*x x*]
2′ *ina mu*$^{!}$*-le-*⸢*e*$^{!}$⸣ [0]
3′ PAB É 8 ANŠE 3BÁN$^{!}$ ⸢A⸣.[ŠÀ]
4′ *za-ku-te la* ŠE.*ši-ib-še l*[*a*$^{!}$ ŠE.*nu-sa-hi*]
5′ *ina* URU.*bar-ú-*⸢*ri*$^{!}$⸣ [0]
6′ *ú-piš-ma* MÍ.AD—*ra-mi*
7′ NIN-*sa ša* AMA—LUGAL
8′ *ku-um* 1/2 MA.NA KUG.UD *a-na šá-par*$^{!}$-[*ti*]
9′ 3 *kar-ap-hi* 3 *mi*$^{!}$*-re-še*
10e ⸢KÚ KUG.UD⸣ *ina* UGU
11e ŠE.*ta-ra-mi* GAR-*an* A.ŠÀ *ú-še-ṣa*

4 An estate of 3 hectares 4 *decares* of lan[d ...], adjoining (the estates of) Ahi-ya[*qar*], Il-ya[...] and Ila['i-...]
(Break)

r.1 the city of Ši[...], on a hill — a total of 8 hectares 3 decares of exempt land, void of straw and [corn] taxes, in the town of Baruri —

6 Abi-rami, the sister of the queen mother, has contracted it and will enjoy it as a pledge for three fallow years (and) three cultivated years in lieu of 1/2 mina of silver.

10 (If) he places the silver upon the corn-heap, he shall redeem the land.

12e IGI ^{m}*si-lim*—DINGIR$^{!}$ IGI$^{!}$ ^{m}*di*$^{!}$-⸢*di*$^{!}$⸣-*a*$^{!}$
13e [IGI ^{m}*pal-h*]*u*$^{!}$—*ú*$^{!}$*-še-zib*$^{!}$
s.1 [IGI ^{m}*x x* IG]I ^{m}PAB—KAM$^{!}$-*eš* IGI ^{md}PA—MAN-*a-ni*

12 Witness Silim-Aššur. Witness Didiya.
13 [Witness Palh]u-ušezib.
s.1 [Witness NN]. [Witn]ess Ahu-ereš. Witness Nabû-šarrani.

252 Previous editions: AR 115, NALK 3; → TCAE 176. Collations: Assur 2/5.

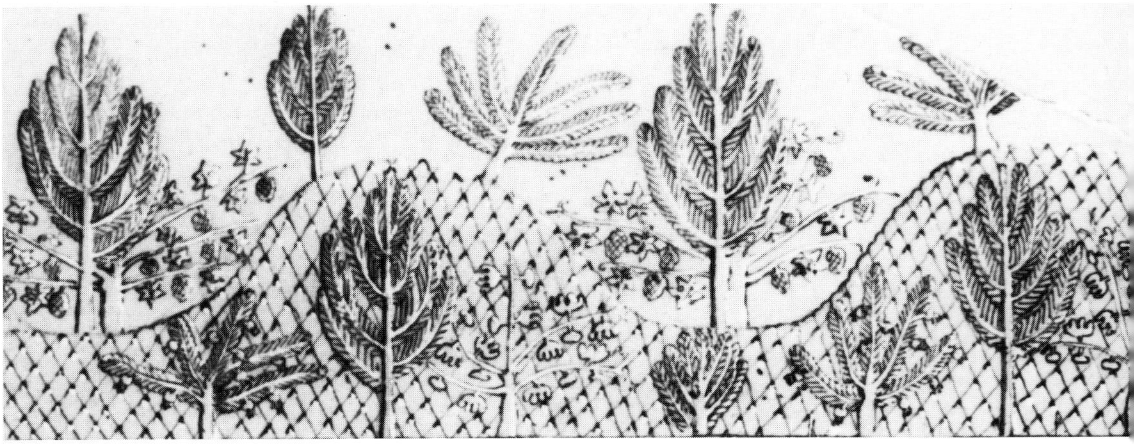

FIG. 26. *Landscape near Nineveh, with grapes, figs and pomegranates growing.*
ORIGINAL DRAWING I, 57.

2 [IGI ^{m}*x*]—SU PAB 3 ⸢URU⸣.*bar-ú-*⸢*ri*$^{!}$⸣

3 [IGI ^{md}*x*]—AŠ$^{!}$ A.BA$^{!}$ ⸢ITI⸣.SIG$_4$ UD-11-KÁM
4 [*lim-mu* ^{m}L]UGAL—*nu-ri* LÚ*.GAR.KUR KUR.*bar-hal-*⸢*zi*$^{!}$⸣

2 [Witness ...]-eriba; a total of three (from) Baruri.
3 [Witness ...]-iddina, scribe.
3 Month Sivan (III), 11th day, [eponym year of Šar]ru-nuri, governor of Barhalzi.

253. Issar-duri, the Queen Mother's Scribe, Buys a Large Estate

K 453

beginning broken away
1 ⸢*x x x*⸣ [*x x x x x x x x x x*]
2 ^{m}*šum-ma*—^{d}I[M *x x x x x x x x x*]
3 ^{m}*gab-bu—a-mur* [LÚ].⸢ENGAR⸣ [*x x x x x x x*]
4 ^{md}PA—AŠ—PAB.ME[Š 1] DUMU 4 LA[L$^{!}$ *x x x x*]
5 1 MÍ 1 DUMU 3 LAL É 60 ANŠE A.ŠÀ.GA
6 31 ZI.MEŠ GIŠ.SAR *ša til-lit up*$^{!}$*-*⸢*piš*⸣*-ma*

7 $^{md!}$15$^{!}$—BÀD LÚ.A.BA *ša* MÍ.AMA—LUGAL
8 *ina* ŠÀ 1 1/2 MA.NA LÁ *ina* 1 GÚ.UN KUG.UD ⸢TA*⸣ IGI

9 ^{m}*pa-ru-ṭi* ⸢*il*⸣*-qí* KUG.⸢UD⸣ *gam-mur ta-*⸢*din*⸣
10 ⸢A.ŠÀ⸣ GIŠ.SAR [U]N.MEŠ ⸢*šu*⸣*-a-tú zar*$_4$*-pu*
11 *laq-qí-ʾu tu-a-ru* DUG$_4$.DUG$_4$ *la-áš-šú*

12 *man-nu šá ina ur-kiš ù mat-*⸢*e*⸣*-ma*
r.1 [*lu*]*-u* ^{m}⸢*pa*⸣*-ru-ṭu lu-u* DUMU.MEŠ-*šú* DUMU—DUMU.⸢MEŠ⸣-*šú*
2 [*lu*]-⸢*u*⸣ ŠEŠ.MEŠ-*šú* DUMU—PAB.MEŠ-*šú i-zaq-qup-an-ni*
3 [T]A $^{md!}$15$^{!}$—BÀD ⸢DUMU⸣.MEŠ-*šú de-e-nu*$^{!}$

ADD 428

(Beginning destroyed)
2 Šumma-Ad[ad, ...];
3 Gabbu-amur, farmer, [......];
4 Nabû-nadin-ahhe, 1 boy of 4 span[s ...];
5 [NN], 1 woman, 1 boy of 3 spans; an estate of 60 hectares of land, 31 persons and a vineyard —
7 Issar-duri, scribe of the queen mother, has contracted and bought (said property) for 1 1/2 minas less than one talent of silver from Paruṭṭu.
9 The silver is paid completely. That land, garden, and [peo]ple are purchased and acquired. Any revocation or litigation is void.
12 Whoever in the future or at any time lodges a complaint, [whe]ther Paruṭṭu or his sons, grandsons, brothers or nephews, and seeks a lawsuit or litigation [again]st Issar-duri and his sons, shall place [x tale]nts of

253 Previous editions: AR 106, NALK 114. Collated by I.L. Finkel. r.5 See coll.

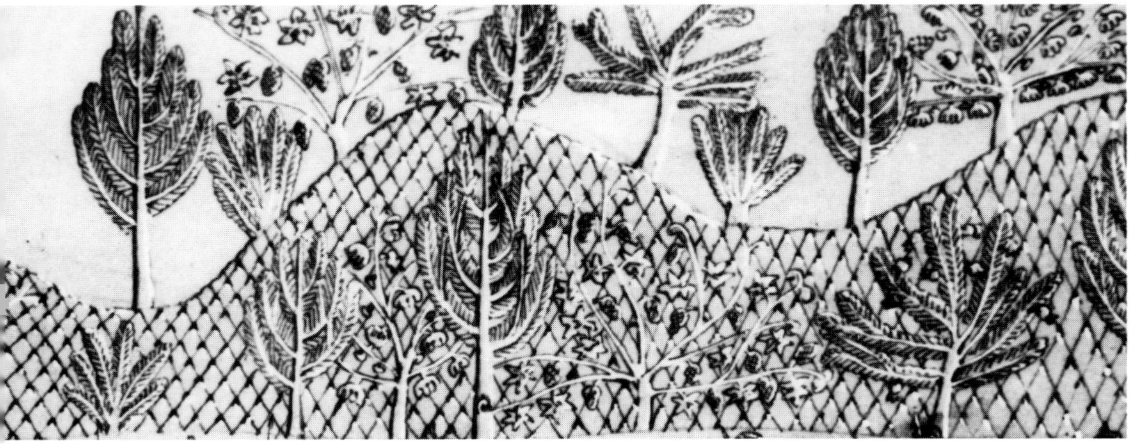

4 DUG$_4$.DUG$_4$ *ub-ta-ʾu-u-ni*
5 [*x* GÚ.U]N! KUG.UD 10 MA.NA KUG.GI *ina bur-ki* d15
6 [*a-ši-bat* URU].NINA GAR-*an* KUG.UD *ina* 10-A.TA.AN
7 [*a-na*] EN.MEŠ-*šú* GUR *ina de-ni-šú* DUG$_4$.DUG$_4$-⌜*ma*⌝ *là* TI

---

8 IGI m[*x x x x x*] LÚ.3.U$_5$ AMA—MAN
9 [IGI m*x x x x x*] ⌜LÚ⌝.GAL—*ki-ṣir* :
10 [IGI m*x x x x*]⌜*x*⌝ LÚ.A.BA :
11 [IGI m*x x x x x* LÚ].⌜*qur*⌝-*bu-ti*
12 [IGI m*x x x x x x*] ⌜GÌR⌝.2
rest broken away

silver and 10 minas of gold in the lap of Ištar [of] Nineveh, and shall return the silver tenfold [to] its owners. He shall contest in his lawsuit and not succeed.

---

8 [Witness NN], 'third man' of the queen mother.
9 [Witness NN], cohort commander of ditto.
10 [Witness NN], scribe of ditto.
11 [Witness NN], royal bodyguard.
12 [Witness NN], *ša šēpi* guard.
(Rest destroyed)

254. Fragmentary Purchase Document of Issar-duri

Bu 91-5-9,123

beginning broken away
1′ [*tu-a*]-⌜*ru*!⌝ *de*-[*e-nu* DUG$_4$.DUG$_4$]
2′ *la-áš-šú man-nu* ⌜*šá*⌝ *ina* ⌜*ur*⌝-[*kiš*]
3′ *ù ma-te-ma i-zaq-qup*-[*an-ni*]
4′ *lu-u* m*mar-di-i lu-u* DUMU.[MEŠ-*šú*]
5′ *lu-u* DUMU—DUMU.MEŠ-*šú* TA! md15—⌜BÀD⌝
6′ *ù* DUMU.MEŠ-*šú ù* DUMU—DUMU.MEŠ-*šú*
7′ *de-e-nu* DUG$_4$.DUG$_4$
8′ *ub-ta-ʾu-u-ni*
9′ 10 MA.NA KUG.UD 2 MA.NA KUG.GI
10′ *a*-[*n*]*a* d15 *šá* URU.NINA SUM-*an*
r.1 *kas-pu a-na* 10.MEŠ-*te a-na* EN.MEŠ-⌜*šú* GUR⌝

---

2 IGI mdEN—URU.KASKAL—MAN—PAB LÚ.GAL—

ADD 507

(Beginning destroyed)
1 [Any revoc]ation, lawsu[it or litigation] is void.
2 Whoever in the fut[ure], or at any time, lodges a complaint, whether Mardî or [his] sons or grandsons, and seeks a lawsuit or litigation against Issar-duri and his sons and grandsons, shall pay 10 minas of silver and two minas of go[ld] to Ištar of Nineveh, and shall return the money tenfold to its owners.

---

r.2 Witness Bel-Harran-šarru-uṣur, major-

254 Previous editions: AR 611, NALK 115. 1, 5, r.2f, 7f See coll.

⸢É!⸣ [^{md}P]A$^{?}$—SAG$^{!}$.KAL$^{!}$
3 IGI ^{m}*mil-ki—id-ri* LÚ.G[AL$^{?}$—*x x x*]
4 IGI ^{md}U.GUR—PAB—PAB IG[I] ⸢^{m}⸣[*x x x x*]
5 IGI ^{md}PA—NUMUN—DÙ IG[I ^{m}*x x x x*]
6 IGI ^{md}15—A[Š—A *x x x x x x*]
7 IGI ^{m}ARAD—^{d}[*x x x x x x*]
8 [IGI ^{m}]⸢*ki*!⸣*-ma-*[*ma-a-a x x x*]
rest broken away

domo of [*Na*]*bû*-ašared.
3 Witness Milki-idri, chief [...].
4 Witness Nergal-ahu-uṣur. Witness [NN].
5 Witness Nabû-zeru-ibni. Witn[ess ...].
6 Witness Issar-nad[in-apli ......].
7 Witness Urda-[......].
8 [Witness] Kima[maya ...].
(Rest destroyed)

255. Idu'a, Town Manager of the Queen Mother, Sells People (678)

K 1617

1 [NA$_4$.KIŠ]IB ^{m}⸢*i*!⸣*-du*$^{!}$*-u-a* LÚ*.GAL—U[RU].(MEŠ)
2 [*ša* UR]U.*la-hi-ra ša* É AMA—MAN
3 [EN] UN.MEŠ *ta-da-ni*

4 [^{m}*x x x x*]-⸢*a*!⸣ LÚ*.ENGAR
5 [^{m}*x x x x x*] ⸢LÚ*!⸣.ENGAR$^{!}$
rest broken away
Rev. beginning broken away
1′ [IGI ^{m}*x x x*]—10 LÚ*.A.BA
blank space of one line
2′ [IGI ^{m}ARAD]—^{d}*na-na-a* LÚ*.A.BA
3′ [ITI.*x x x*] UD-7-KAM
4′ [*lim-mu* ^{m}U].GUR—MAN—PAB LÚ*.GAL—KAŠ.LUL

ADD 301

1 [Se]al of Idu'a, town manager [of] Lahiru of the domain of the queen mother, [owner] of the people being sold.

(cylinder seal impression)

4 [...], farmer;
5 [...], farmer;
(Break)
r.1 [Witness ...]-*Adad*, scribe.
2 [Witness Urda]-Nanaya, scribe.
3 [Month ...], 7th day, [eponym year of Ne]rgal-šarru-uṣur, chief cupbearer.

256. Fragmentary Purchase Document of Idu'a, Town Manager

Rm 166

1 NA$_4$.KIŠIB ^{m}*i-du-*[*u-a*]
2 LÚ.GAL—[URU].MEŠ EN [UN.MEŠ SUM-*ni*]

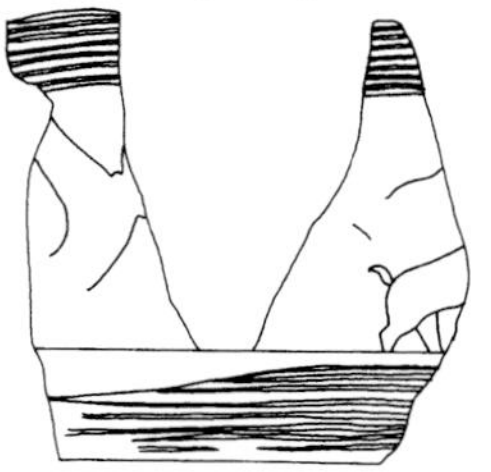

3 [^{m}*x x x*]—EN 2 M[Í.MEŠ *x x x*]
rest broken away

ADD 306

1 Seal of Idu['a, town] manager, owner [of the people being sold.]

(cylinder seal impression)

3 [...]-Bel, 2 wo[men ...]
(Break)

255 Previous edition: AR 535. Collations: Assur 5/2. r.4 The sign MAN is spaced out.
256 Previous edition: AR 544.

Rev. beginning broken away
1′ ITI.KIN U[D-*x lim-mu* ᵐ*x x x*]
2′ LÚ.*tur-t*[*a-nu*]

r.1 Month Elul, [...th day, eponym year of PN], comma[nder-in-chief].

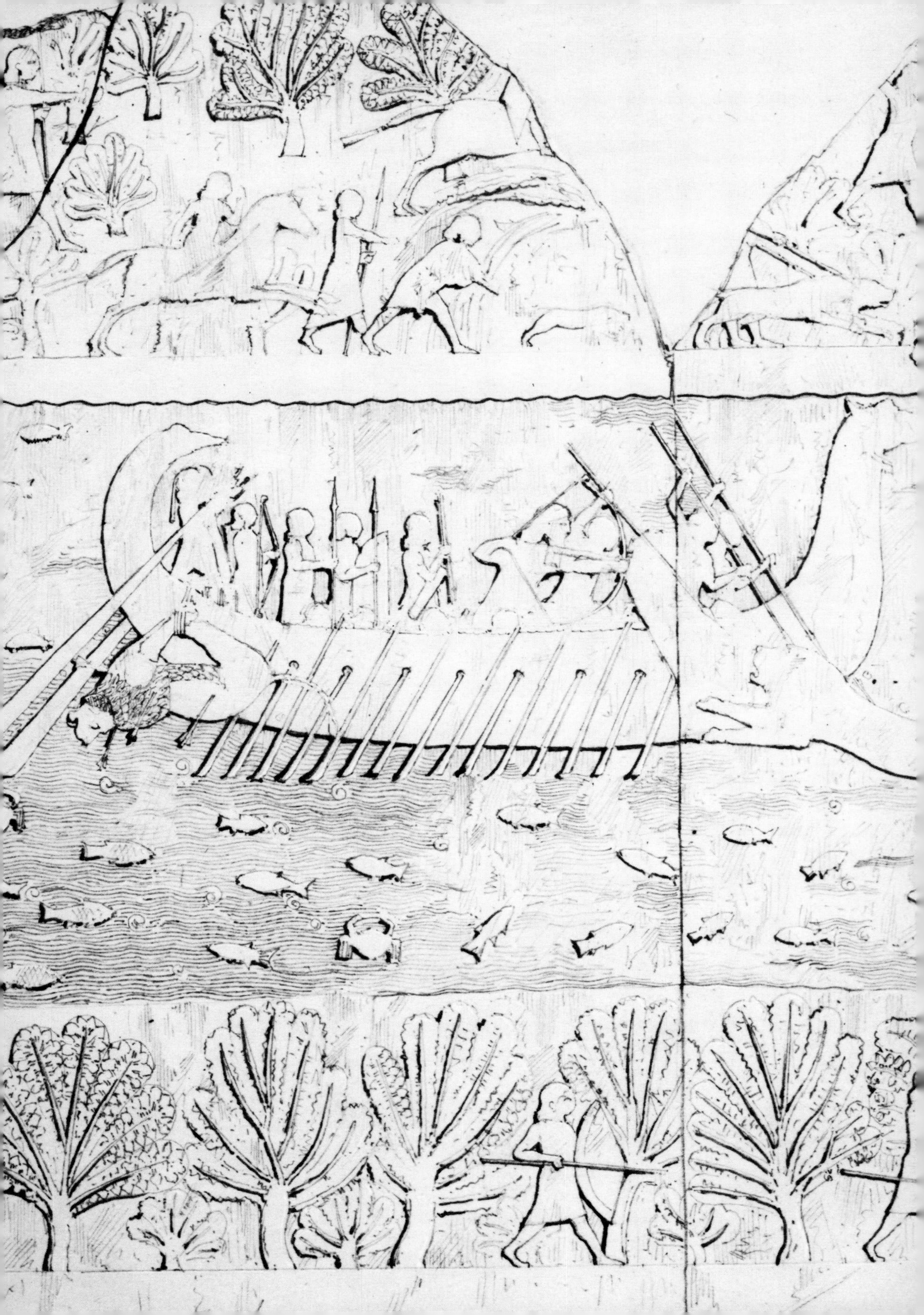

14. Varia (680-669)

FIG. 27. *River scene, probably near Nineveh (reign of Assurbanipal).*
ORIGINAL DRAWING V, 22.

257. A Servant of a Prince Buys a Slave (680-I-10)

Ki 1904-10-9,189 | ADD 1194

1 ⸢NA$_4$.KIŠIB⸣ ^{md}PA—*ṣal-li* ŠEŠ-*šú ša* ^{m}*ha-za*—DINGIR
2 NA$_4$.KIŠIB MÍ.*ri-šá*-0$^{!}$—AD-*šá* MÍ.NU.KÚŠ.Ù
3 *ša* ^{m}*ha-za*—DINGIR PAB 2 LÚ.MEŠ-*e* ARAD.MEŠ-*ni*
4 *ša* GAŠAN—É *ša* DUMU—MAN EN LÚ SUM-*ni*

1 Seal of Nabû-ṣalli, brother of Hazail, 2 seal of Riša-abiša, widow of Hazail, 3 a total of 2 gentlemen, servants of the lady of the house of the crown prince, owners of the man being sold.

(stamp seal impressions)

5 ^{m}*mar—su-ri* ARAD-*šú-nu*
6 *ša* LÚ.MEŠ-*e an-nu-te ú-piš-ma*
7 ^{m}DINGIR—PAB ARAD *ša* DUMU—LUGAL URU.*il*$^{!}$-*lat*$^{!}$-*a-a*
8 TA* *pa-an* LÚ.MEŠ-*e an-nu-te*
9 *ina* ŠÀ 1 MA.NA KUG.UD *ina ma-né-e*
10 *ša* URU.*gar-ga-mis il-qí*
11 *kas-pu* ⸢*gam*⸣-*mur ta-din* LÚ *šu-a-tú*
12 *za-rip la-qí tu-a-ru de-e-nu*

13 DUG$_4$.DUG$_4$ *la-áš-šú man-nu ša ina ur-kiš*
14 *ina ma-ti-ma i-za-qu-pa-a-*⸢*ni*$^{!}$⸣
15 *lu-u* ^{md}PA—*ṣal-li lu-u* MÍ.*r*[*i-šá*—A]D-*šá*
16 *lu-u* 0$^{!}$ DUMU.⸢MEŠ⸣-*šú-nu lu-u* P[AB.MEŠ-*šú-nu*]
17 *lu-u* LÚ.GAR-*nu-šú-nu lu-*[*u x x x x x x*]
e.18 *lu-u* EN—*il-ki-*⸢*šú*⸣-*nu l*[*u-u x x x x x x*]
r.1 ⸢*ša*⸣ TA* ^{m}DINGIR—PAB ⸢*ù*⸣ [D]U[MU.MEŠ-*šú*]
2 *de-nu* DUG$_4$.DUG$_4$ *ub-*⸢*ta*⸣-[*u-ni*]
3 2 MA.NA KUG.UD *e-ṣip* SUM-⸢*an*⸣
4 LÚ *ú-še-aṣ ina de-ni-šú*
5 DUG$_4$.DUG$_4$-*ma la* TI-*qí*

5 Mar-suri, servant of these gentlemen — 7 Ilu-iṣṣur, servant of the crown prince, from the town of Illat, has contracted and bought him from these gentlemen for one mina of silver by the mina of Carchemish.

11 The money is paid completely. That man is purchased and acquired. Any revocation, lawsuit, or litigation is void.

13 Whoever in the future, at any time, lodges a complaint, whether Nabû-ṣalli or R[iša-a]biša, or their sons or br[others], or their prefect, [...], labour-duty superior o[r ...],

r.1 and se[eks] a lawsuit or litigation against Ilu-iṣṣur and [his s]o[ns], shall pay the double amount of two minas of silver to redeem the man. He shall contest in his lawsuit and not succeed.

6 IGI ^{m}ARAD—^{d}PA LÚ.MUŠEN.DÙ
7 IGI ^{m}AD—PAB LÚ.:
8 IGI ^{m}*ṣal-mu*—PAB.MEŠ LÚ.GIŠ.GIGIR
9 IGI ^{m}DI.KUD—*kur-ba-ìl*
10 LÚ.*kal-la-bu*
11 IGI ^{m}*qu-qu-u-*⸢*a*⸣ LÚ.*kal-la-bu*
12 IGI ^{m}*da-ú-li-i* LÚ.:
13 IGI ^{m}*mi-nu*—DÙ—DINGIR LÚ.GIŠ.GIGIR
blank space of one line$^{!}$
14 IGI ^{m}*di-lil*—^{d}15 LÚ.A.BA

r.6 Witness Urda-Nabû, fowler.
7 Witness Abu-uṣur, ditto.
8 Witness Ṣalmu-ahhe, horse trainer.
9 Witness Dayyan-Kurbail, *outrider*.
11 Witness Ququ'a, *outrider*.
12 Witness Daulî, ditto.
13 Witness Minu-epuš-ili, horse trainer.
14 Witness Dilil-Issar, scribe, keeper of

257 Previous edition: NALK 111; → Postgate FNALD 10. Photo Cat. Suppl. Pl. 2. 3 See note on no. 264:4. 7 See coll. r.22 *ú-še-aṣ* sic.

15 DIB IM
16 ITI.BARAG UD-10-KÁM
17 *lim-mu* ^{m}*da-na-nu* LÚ.GAR.KUR URU.*man-ṣu*.MEŠ
18 *ina tar-iṣ* ^{m}*aš-šur*—PAB—SUM-*na* LUGAL KUR—*aš-šur*.KI
19e *la-qí*

the tablet.

16 Month Nisan (I), 10th day, eponym year of Dananu, governor of Manṣuati.

18 Purchased in the reign of Esarhaddon, king of Assyria.

258. Sale of Land (680-I-28)

K 322

1 NA$_4$.KIŠIB ^{md}30—MAN—DINGIR.MEŠ EN A.ŠÀ
2 GIŠ.SAR *ta-da-ni*

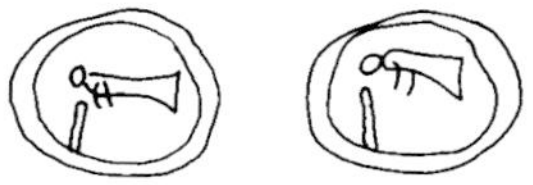

3 É [A.ŠÀ GIŠ.S]AR *x*[*x x x x*]
rest broken away
Rev. beginning broken away
1′ IGI ^{md}AG—*tak-lak* [*x x x*]
2′ IGI ^{m}A—MU LÚ.*ma-hi-ṣu*
3′ IGI ^{m}DI-*mu*—PAB.MEŠ KI$^{!}$.MIN
4′ IGI ^{md}MAŠ.MAŠ—MAN—PAB DUMU ^{m}DI.KUD—10
5′ IGI ^{m}URU.*kal-ha-a-a* LÚ.*mu-kil*—KUŠ.PA.MEŠ

6′ ITI.BARAG UD-28-KÁM
7′ *lim-mu* ^{m}*dan-na-nu*
8′ *šá* URU.*mar-qa-sa*
s.1 ŠE.NUMUN *ar-šú is-se*$^{!}$-*n*[*iš*$^{!}$ *x x x x x*]

ADD 631

1 Seal of Sin-šar-ilani, owner of the field and garden being sold.

(stamp seal impressions)

3 A house, [a field, and a gar]den [...]
(Break)

r.1 Witness Nabû-taklak, [...].
2 Witness Aplu-iddina, archer.
3 Witness Šulmu-ahhe, ditto.
4 Witness Nergal-šarru-uṣur, son of Dayyan-Adad.
5 Witness Kalhayu, chariot driver.
6 Month Nisan (I), 28th day, eponym year of Dananu of Marqasa.
s.1 The sown seed [is] als[o ....].

259. Edu-šallim Borrows Silver (680-II-16)

K 3789B

1 ⌜5⌝ ANŠE A.ŠÀ *ša* ^{m}*e-du*—*šal-lim*
2 [*ina* UR]U.*kar*—A.10 ^{m}*mu-še-zib*
3 [5/6] ⌜MA.NA⌝ KUG.UD *a-na* ^{m}*e*-⌜*du*—*šal*⌝-*lim*

4 ⌜*i*⌝-*ti-din* 5/6 MA.NA *ša* A.ŠÀ ^{m}*mu-še-zib*
5 TA* ^{m}*e-du*—*šal-lim kal-e*

ADD 74

1 5 hectares of land belonging to Edu-šallim [in the ci]ty of Kar-Apladad.

2 Mušezib has paid [5/6] minas of silver to Edu-šallim.

(cylinder seal impression)

4 Mušezib shall enjoy with Edu-šallim 5/6 minas (worth of the produce) of the land.

258 Previous edition: AR 441. 3, s.1 See coll.
259 Envelope. Previous editions: AR 138, NALK 95a. Collations: Assur 5/2. 5 *kal-e* is a scribal error for *e-kal* (thus no. 260:6).

e.6 *ina* UD-*me ša* 5/6 MA.NA KUG.UD
7 ^{m}*e-du—šal-lim a-na* ^{m}*mu-še-zib*
r.1 SUM-*nu-u-ni* A.ŠÀ-*šú u-še-ṣa*

2 IGI ^{m}*il-tap-pa* IGI ^{md}PA—SIG$^{!}$—DINGIR.MEŠ

3 IGI ^{m}*a-bi-da-nu* IGI ^{m}EN—APIN-*eš*
4 IGI ^{md}UTU—*tak-lak*
5 IGI ^{m}NUMUN—15 IGI ^{m}*kù*-KÁ—APIN-*eš*
6 IGI ^{m}*lu-u—ba-laṭ* IGI ^{m}*la—tú*-TÉŠ-*ni*—DINGIR

7 ITI.GUD UD-16-KÁM
8e *lim-mu* ^{m}*da-na-a-nu*
9e *ša* KUR.*man-ṣu-a-te*
s.1 EGIR *da*$^{!}$-⌜*ra*$^{!}$-*ri*$^{!}$⌝
2 U[D$^{!}$ *x x*]
3 ⌜*a*$^{?}$⌝-[*x x*]

6 On the day that Edu-šallim pays 1 1/2 minas of silver to Mušezib, he shall redeem his land.

r.2 Witness Iltappa. Witness Nabû-damqi-ilani.

3 Witness Abidanu. Witness Bel-ereš.

4 Witness Šamaš-taklak.

5 Witness Zar-Issar. Witness Kubabu-ereš.

6 Witness Lu-balaṭ. Witness La-tubašanni-ilu.

7 Month Iyyar (II), 16th day, eponym year of Dananu of Manṣuati.

s.1 After the remission of debts [......].

260. Inner Tablet of the Preceding Text (680-IV-6)

K 3789A

1 5 ANŠE A.ŠÀ *ša* ^{m}*e-du—š*[*al-lim*]
2 *ina* URU.*kar*—A.10
3 ^{m}*mu-še-zi-bu* 5/6 (MA).NA KUG.UD
4 *a-na* ^{m}*e-du—šal-lim i-ti-din*

5 5/6 MA.NA *ša* A.ŠÀ ^{m}*mu-še-zib*
6 *i-si-šú e-kal*
e.7 *ina* UD-*me ša* KUG.UD SUM-*u*-[*ni*]
r.1 A.ŠÀ-*šú u-še-ṣa*

2 IGI ^{md}PA—SIG$_{5}$—DINGIR.MEŠ
3 IGI ^{m}*il-tap-pa*
4 IGI ^{m}*a-bi-da-a-nu*
5 IGI ^{m}EN—KAM-*eš*

6 IGI ^{m}*lu-u—ba-laṭ* IGI ^{m}*la*$^{!}$—*tú*$^{!}$-⌜*ba*$^{!}$⌝-0$^{!}$
7e IGI ^{m}*kù*$^{!}$-*bab*—[KA]M-*eš*
8e IGI ^{m}NUMUN—15

s.1 *ša* EGIR
2 ⌜ŠU$^{!}$⌝ UD-6-KÁM

ADD 73

1 Five hectares of land belonging to Edu-š[allim] in the city of Kar-Apladad.

3 Mušezibu has paid 5/6 [mi]nas of silver to Edu-šallim.

5 Mušezibu shall enjoy with him 5/6 minas (worth of the produce) of the land.

7 On the day that [he] pays the silver, he shall redeem his land.

r.2 Witness Nabû-damqi-ilani.

3 Witness Iltappa.

4 Witness Abidanu.

5 Witness Bel-[er]eš.

6 Witness Lu-balaṭ. Witness La-tuba(šanni-ilu).

7 Witness Kubabu-[er]eš.

8 Witness Zar-Issar.

s.1 The (year) following (the remission of debts).

2 6th of Tammuz (IV).

261. A Fragmentary Slave Sale (680-III-22)

DT 167

1 [NA$_{4}$].KIŠIB ^{md}*ra-man*—⌜*dal*$^{!}$-*a*$^{!}$⌝

ADD 298

1 [Se]al of Ramman-dalâ, [own]er of the

260 Inner tablet. Previous editions: AR 137, NALK 95b. Collations: Assur 2/5.
261 Previous edition: AR 534. Collations: Assur 2/5.

2 [E]N UN.MEŠ SUM-*a-ni*

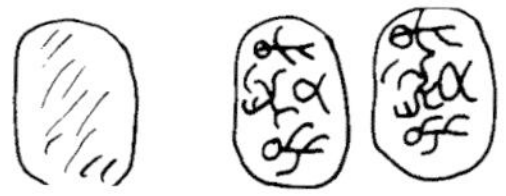

rest broken away

Rev. beginning broken away

1′ [IGI ^{m}*x x*]-*u-ni*

2′ [IGI ^{m}P]AB$^{!}$—BÀD

3′ [IGI ^{m}*x*]*x-zi-iz*$^{!}$

blank space of two lines

4′ [I]TI.SIG$_4$ UD-22-KÁM

5′ [*l*]*im-mu* ^{m}*da-na-nu*

people being sold.

(stamp seal impressions)

(Break)

r.1 [Witness ...]uni.

2 [Witness Ah]i-duri.

3 [Witness ...]ziz.

4 [Mon]th Sivan (III), 22nd day, [epon]ym year of Dananu.

262. Sangû-Issar Loans Silver (680-VII-21)

83-1-18,371

1 NA$_4$.KIŠIB ^{m}*a-du-na—i-zi*

2 1 MA.NA KUG.UD *ina ša* URU.*gar-ga-mis*

3 *ša* ^{m}SANGA—^{d}15

4 *ina* IGI ^{m}*a-du-na—iz* LÚ*.*šá—mut-qi-ti-šú*

5 *a-na* 4-*ut-ti-šú i*-GAL-*bi*

6 ITI.DUL UD-21-KÁM

7 *lim-me* ^{m}*da-na-nu*

r.1 IGI ^{m}URU.*arba-ìl-a-a*

2 IGI ^{md}PA—DÙ—PAB.MEŠ

3 IGI ^{m}*su-ra-ra-te*

4 IGI ^{m}PAB—*a-bi*

5 IGI ^{m}*sa-gab*

6 IGI ^{m}SUHUŠ—^{d}PA

ADD 26

1 Seal of Aduna-izzi.

2 One mina of silver by the (mina) of Carchemish, belonging to Sangû-Issar, at the disposal of Aduna-izzi, candy peddler.

5 It will increase by a fourth.

6 Month Tishri (VII), 21st day, eponym year of Dananu.

r.1 Witness Arbailayu.

2 Witness Nabû-bani-ahhe.

3 Witness Surarate.

4 Witness Ahabu.

5 Witness Sagab.

6 Witness Ubru-Nabû.

263. Duplicate of the Previous Text (680-VII-21)

82-5-22,41

1 1 MA.NA KUG.UD *ina ša gar-ga-*[*mis*]

2 *ša* ^{m}SANGA—15

3 *ina* IGI ^{m}*a-du-na—iz*

4 *ina pu-u-hi i-ti-ši*

5 *a-na* 4-*ut-ti-šú* GAL

6 [IT]I.DUL UD-21

e.7 *lim-me* ^{m}*da-na-nu*

r.1 IGI ^{m}URU.*arba-ìl-a-a*

ADD 3

1 One mina of silver by the (mina) of Carche[mish], belonging to Sangû-Issar, at the disposal of Aduna-izzi.

4 He has taken it as a loan. It will increase by a fourth.

6 [Mon]th Tishri (VII), 21st day, eponym year of Dananu.

r.1 Witness Arbailayu.

262 Previous editions: AR 255, NALK 345. → no. 263. The tablet is not an envelope. r.4-6 The names are spaced out.

263 Previous editions: AR 283, NALK 346.

2 IGI ^{md}PA—DÙ—PAB.MEŠ
3 IGI ^{m}*a-a*—PAB.MEŠ
4 IGI ^{m}SUHUŠ—^{d}PA

2 Witness Nabû-bani-ahhe.
3 Witness Aya-ahhe.
4 Witness Ubru-Nabû.

264. A Court Decision Concerning Property of a Prince (680-XI-27)

82-5-22,38

1 *de-e-nu ša* LÚ.*sar-tin-nu*
2 *a-na* ^{m}*ha-ni-i e-me-du-u-ni*
3 3-*me* UDU.MEŠ *a-di sa-ár-ti-ši-na*
4 *ša* DUMU—MAN *ina* IGI ^{m}*ha-ni-i*
5 MÚD.MEŠ *ša* LÚ.SIPA 1-*en* LÚ 2 GÚ.UN URUDU.MEŠ
6 *sa-ár-tu-šú* ^{m}*ha-ni-i*
7 *a-di* UN.MEŠ-*šú a-di* A.ŠÀ.MEŠ-*šú*
8 *ku-um* 3-*me* UDU.MEŠ *a-di sa-ár-ti-ši-na*
9 *ku-(um)* MÚD.MEŠ *ša* LÚ.SIPA.MEŠ
e.10 *na-ši-na* (blank)
11 *man-nu ša ú-ba-ʾu-šú-u-ni*
r.1 *lu-u* LÚ.GAR-*nu-šú lu-u* LÚ.GAL—*ki-ṣir*-⸢*šú*⸣
2 *lu-u mám-ma-nu-šú u-ba-ʾu-u-šú-ni*
3 3-*me* UDU.MEŠ *a-di sa-ár-ti-ši-na*
4 MÚD.MEŠ-*šú ša* LÚ.SIPA 1 LÚ 2 GÚ.UN URUDU.MEŠ
5 *ša sar*!!-*ti i-da-nu-u-ni* ^{m}*ha-ni-i*
6 *ú-še-ṣa hur-sa-an i-tu*!-*ra*
7 IGI ^{m}*tab-ni-i* LÚ.A.BA
8 IGI ^{m}*ṣal-mu*—MAN—*iq-bi*
9 IGI ^{md}UTU—ZI—AŠ
10 IGI ^{m}*am-si-i*
s.1 ITI.ZÍZ UD-27-KÁM!
2 *lim-mu* ^{m}*da-na-nu*

ADD 164

1 A judgment which the *sartinnu* imposed upon Hanî.

3 Hanî owes the crown prince 300 sheep plus their fine.

5 The blood (money) of the shepherd is one man, and his fine is two talents of copper. Hanî with his people and fields are taken in lieu of the 300 sheep plus their fine and the blood (money) of the shepherd.

11 Whoever seeks him out, whether his prefect or his cohort commander or any relative of his (who) seeks him out and pays the 300 sheep along with their fine and the blood (money) for the shepherd, one man plus the two talents of copper of the fine, shall redeem Hanî.

r.6 He refused the river ordeal.

7 Witness Tabnî, scribe.

8 Witness Ṣalam-šarri-iqbi.

9 Witness Šamaš-kettu-iddina.

10 Witness Amsî.

s.1 Month Shebat (XI), 27th day, eponym year of Dananu.

265. A Court Decision on Behalf of Sangû-Issar (679-XII-10)

Rm 165

1 NA_4.KIŠIB ^{md}PA—LAL-*iṣ*
2 ARAD *ša* ^{m}*ṣa-pa-nu*

3 4 ZI.MEŠ ARAD.MEŠ *šá* ^{m}SANGA—^{d}15
4 *is-si-riq ina* IGI LÚ.SUKKAL *uq-ṭar-ri-ib-šú*

ADD 161

1 Seal of Nabû-tariṣ, servant of Ṣapanu.

(blank seal space)

3 He stole 4 persons, servants of Sangû-Issar. The latter took him before the vizier,

264 Previous editions: AR 658, NALK 108; → Postgate FNALD 44; M. Roth, Festschrift Reiner (1987), p. 357. 4 Cf. note on no. 110. The formulation of the present passage may imply that the crime had taken place while Esarhaddon was still crown prince, i.e. 11 months earlier. Cf. no. 257, written 12 or 22 days after Esarhaddon's accession and referring to the "the lady of the house of the *crown* prince." 10 See coll. r.5 Text LÚ-*ti*; scribal error (cf. obv. 6). r.6 See coll.

265 Previous editions: AR 51, NALK 347; → Postgate FNALD 46. Collations: Assur 5/2. 6 TA* SI: possibly to

5 2-*me*-10 MA.NA URUDU.MEŠ *e-te-mì-is-su*
6 *ku-um sa-ar-ti-šú* URUDU.MEŠ TA*$^{!}$ SI$^{!}$
7 *it-ti-din man-nu* 2-*me*-10 MA.NA URUDU.MEŠ
8 *a-na* ^{m}SANGA—^{d}15 *id-dan-u-ni*
9 ARAD-*šú ú-še-ṣa man-nu šá ib-bal-lak-kàt-u-ni*
10 *aš-šur ù* ^{d}UTU EN *de-né-e-šú*
11 10 MA.NA KUG.UD 10 MA.NA KUG.GI
12 *ina bur-ki* ^{d}NIN.LÍL GAR-*an*

---

13 IGI ^{md}PA—KAR-*ir* LÚ.A.BA *šá* [SU]KKAL
14 IGI ^{m}GÁL-*ši*—DINGIR LÚ.*šá*$^{!}$—IGI—DI.KUD.MEŠ
15 *ša* URU.*kàl*-⸢*ha*⸣

r.1 [IG]I ^{m}(blank)
2 IGI ^{m}*me-i-su* LÚ.A.BA
3 IGI ^{m}DINGIR—*pa-da* LÚ.:.
4 IGI ^{m}*a-zi*—DINGIR LÚ.:.
5 IGI ^{md}PA—*kil-la-an-ni*
6 IGI ^{m}*ṣa-a-a-di* LÚ.GAL—NAGAR
7 IGI (^{m})DUGUD-*i* LÚ.A$^{!}$.BA$^{!}$ DIB IM

8 ITI.ŠE UD-10-KÁM *lim-mu* ^{m}TA—^{d}10—*an-ni*

9 IGI ^{m}GÌR.2—*aš-šur* LÚ.*qur*-ZAG
10 IGI ^{m}DÙ-*a-a* DUMU ^{md}EN—MAN—DÙ
11 IGI ^{m}DÙ-*a-a* DUMU ^{md}PA—A—AŠ LÚ.A.BA

who imposed upon him 210 minas of copper (as a fine).

6 In lieu of his fine, the copper, he has given ....

7 Whoever pays 210 minas of copper to Sangû-Issar shall redeem his servant.

9 Whoever violates the agreement, Aššur and Šamaš shall be his prosecutors. He shall place 10 minas of silver and 10 minas of gold in the lap of Mullissu.

---

13 Witness Nabû-eṭir, scribe of the [vi]zier.

14 Witness Ibašši-ilu, president of the court of Calah.

r.1 [Wit]ness (blank).

2 [Wit]ness Misu, scribe.

3 Witness Il-pada, ditto.

4 Witness Azi-il, ditto.

5 Witness Nabû-killanni.

6 Witness Ṣaiadu, chief carpenter.

7 Witness Kabtî, scribe, keeper of the tablet.

8 Month Adar (XII), 10th day, eponym year of Issi-Adad-aninu.

9 Witness Šep-Aššur, royal bodyguard.

10 Witness Banaya, son of Bel-šarru-ibni.

11 Witness Banaya, son of Nabû-aplu-iddina, scribe.

266. Purchase of Slaves

K 1498

beginning broken away

1′ ^{md}*šá-maš*—*a-a-li* LÚ.*šá*—[*x x*]
2′ ^{m}*ia*-⸢*nu*⸣-*qu* DUMU-*šú* ⸢MÍ⸣.[*x x x x x*]
3′ ^{m}*da*-⸢*lu*$^{!}$⸣-*ú*$^{!}$-*a*$^{!}$ DUMU-*šú* MÍ.*x*[*x x x*]
4′ MÍ.*ba-ú-ia-a* [*x x x x x*]
5′ MÍ.*d*[*i*]-*im-ba*$^{!}$-⸢*a*$^{?}$⸣ [*x x x x*]

6′ ^{m}*da*-⸢*di*$^{!}$-*i*$^{!}$⸣ [*x x x x*]
7′ MÍ.*sa-an-x*[*x x x x x*]
8′ PAB [*x* ZI.MEŠ ARAD.MEŠ]
9′ *ša* [^{m}*x x x x ú-piš-ma*]

ADD 288

(Beginning destroyed)

(blank seal space)

1 Šamaš-ayali, [...],

2 Yanuqu, his son, [...]

3 Daluwa, his son, [...]

4 the woman Bauyâ [...]

5 the woman Dimbâ [...]

6 Dadî, [...]

7 the woman San[...]

8 in all [x persons, servants of NN] —

9 [...] has contracted

be read *issi qanni* and rendered "a substitute" (lit., "an 'instead'"); cf. the parallels cited CAD Q 82 sub *qannu* 3a-3.
r.1 The line was not completed by the scribe.
266 Previous edition: AR 77. An early Esarhaddon date (679?) for this document is suggested by the witnessess Azi-il (attested 679, 673) and Misu (attested 679, 676), appearing together in no. 265 (679); note also the witness Ṭab-bit-Issar (676 BC).

10′ $^{m!}$[*x x x x x x x*]
rest broken away
Rev. beginning broken away
1′ [*ina de-ni*]-⌜*šú*! DUG$_4$⌝.DUG$_4$-[*ma là* TI]
2′ *ṣib-tu be-en-nu a-na* [1-*me* UD-*me*]
3′ [*s*]*a-ar-tu kàl* M[U.AN.NA.MEŠ]

4′ IGI ^{m}*a-tar-a-a* [*x x x x*]
5′ IGI $^{md!}$30—*ṣa*-⌜*la*!-*a*!⌝ [*x x*]
6′ IGI ^{m}DÙG—IM—^{d}1[5 *x x*]!
7′ IGI ^{md}PA—PAB—AŠ [*x x x*]!
8′ IGI ^{m}DÙG.GA—É!—^{d}15 [*x x*]

9′ IGI ^{m}DINGIR—KA-*ia*-⌜*a*⌝—[*x x x*]
10′ IGI ^{m}*a-zi*—DINGIR LÚ.[A.BA]
11′ IGI ^{m}*mi-i-su* [LÚ.A.BA]
12′ [IGI] ^{m}*hal-li-ṣi*! [*x x x x x*]
rest broken away

s.1 [*ina tar-ṣi* ^{m}*aš-šur*—PAB—AŠ] MAN KUR—*aš-šur*.KI *šúm-mu* [*x x x*]!
2 [*x x x x x*]*x la i-din* 10 MA.NA KUG.UD [*x x x*]

(Break)

r.1 he shall contest in his lawsuit and not succeed.

2 (Guaranteed against) seizures of epilepsy for 100 days (and against) fraud forever.

---

4 Witness Ataraya, [...].
5 Witness Sin-ṣalâ, [...].
6 Witness Ṭab-šar-Iss[ar, ...].
7 Witness Nabû-ahu-iddina, [...].
8 Witness Ṭab-bet-Issar, [...].
9 Witness Ilu-pia-[..., ...].
10 Witness Azi-il, [scribe].
11 Witness Misu, [scribe].
12 Witness Halleṣi, [...].
(Rest destroyed)

s.1 In the reign of Esarhaddon, king of Assyria. If [.....] does not pay, [he shall ...] 10 minas of silver.

267. Purchase of a Slave (677-X-1)

83-1-18,328

1 NA$_4$.KIŠIB ^{m}*se-e—sa-ka-a*
2 ⌜LÚ*⌝.GAL—É EN LÚ SUM-*nu*

ADD 194

1 Seal of Se'-sakâ, major-domo, owner of the man being sold.

(three stamp seals)

---

3 $^{m!}$[*x x*]-*ri-i* : ARAD-*šú*
4 [*ša* ^{m}*se-e—sa*]-*ka-a* LÚ.GAL—É
5 [*ú-piš-ma* ^{m}*šér*]—⌜*ú*⌝-*a-ri*
rest broken away
Rev. beginning broken away
1′ IGI [^{m}3]0—⌜EN!⌝—[P]AB
2′ IGI ^{m}30—NUMUN!—SUM-*na*
3′ IGI ^{m}*se-e—šúm-ki*
4′ IGI ^{m}*sal-sa-li* LÚ*.A.BA

5′ ITI.AB UD-1-KAM
6′ *lim-mu* ^{m}AD—*ra-mi*!

3 [...]rî, servant [of Se'-sak]â, major-domo —
5 [Šer]-uari [has contracted and bought him]
(Break)
r.1 Witness [Si]n-belu-uṣur.
2 Witness Sin-zeru-iddina.
3 Witness Se'-šumki.
4 Witness Salsali, scribe.
5 Month Tebet (X), 1st day, eponym year of Abi-ram.

267 Previous edition: AR 475. r.1f, 6 See coll.

268. Pledge of a Field (679-X-1)

Ki 1904-10-9,29

1 [NA$_4$.KIŠIB ^{m}]⸢*sa*$^{!?}$⸣-*la*$^{!}$-*me* É ANŠE 5BÁN A.ŠÀ
2 [*x x x x*] URU.*hat-ta-a*
3 [*x x x x a*]-*na* MU.MEŠ KÚ
three lines blank

4 SUHUR ^{m}*me-si-me-s*[*i*]
5 SUHUR ^{m}*ab-di—a-a*$^{!}$ [0]
6 SUHUR *šá pi-li-is*$^{!}$-*ta*$^{!}$-[*a-a*]
7 *ku-um* 15$^{!}$ GÍN.MEŠ KUG.UD *a-na* [*šá-par-ti* GAR]
e.8 3 *me-re-še* 3 *ka-rap-hi*

r.1 IGI ^{m}*man-nu—ki-i*—URU.*arba*-[*ìl*]
2 IGI ^{m}PAB-*bu-u*$^{!}$ LÚ.GAL—[A.BA]
3 IGI ^{m}*ab-di—a*-⸢*a*$^{!}$⸣
4 IGI ^{m}*me-si-me-si*
blank space of two lines
7 IGI ^{m}DÙ-*i* IGI ^{m}ARAD—^{d}15
8 IGI ^{m}PAB-*ú-nu*
9 IGI ^{m}ARAD—^{d}15 IGI ^{md}PA—*re-eh-ti*—PAB

10 [ITI].AB UD-1-KÁM *lim-mu* ^{m}TA*—^{d}IM—*a-ni-nu*
11 [IGI ^{m}]*a-a-bu*—PAB

ADD 1154

1 [Seal of] Salamu. An estate of a hectare 5 decares of land [... *in*] the town Hattâ —
3 [NN] shall have the usufruct of it for years.
4 Adjoining Mesimesi, Abdi-Aya and the (estate) of the Philist[ines].

7 [It is placed] as [a pledge] in lieu of 15 shekels of silver.
8 3 crop years, 3 fallow years.
r.1 Witness Mannu-ki-Arbail.
2 Witness Ahabû, chief [scribe].
3 Witness Abdi-Aya.
4 Witness Mesimesi.
7 Witness Banî. Witness Urda-Issar.
8 Witness Ahuni.
9 Witness Urda-Issar. Witness Nabû-rehtu-uṣur.
10 Month Tebet (X), 1st day, eponym year of Issi-Adad-aninu.
11 Witness Ayabu-*ahi*.

269. Purchase of Land and People (679)

Bu 91-5-9,173

beginning broken away
1′ ^{m}*x*[*x x x x x x x x x x x*]
2′ 4 MÍ.GUR[UŠ.TUR$^{!}$.MEŠ *x x x x x x*]
3′ ^{md}UTU—KI-*i*[*a x x x x x x x x*]
4′ 2 MÍ.TUR.MEŠ [*x x x x x x x x*]
5′ 3 GIŠ.SAR.[MEŠ *x x x x x x x x*]
6′ *ti-din-tú* [*x x x x x x x x x*]
7′ *a-na* ^{m}*ka*[*b*$^{!}$-*x x x x x x x x x*]

8′ *ú-piš*-[*ma* ^{m}*x x x x x x* TA IGI]
9′ ^{m}*hal-di—x*[*x x x x x x x x x*]
10′ *ina* ŠÀ-*bi* 10 [MA.NA KUG.UD *šá* URU.*gar-ga-mis*]
11′ [*i*]*l*$^{!}$-⸢*qi*$^{!}$⸣ [*kas-pu gam-mur ta-ad-din*]
rest broken away
Rev. beginning broken away
1′ GUR-*r*[*a x x x x x x x x x x*]
2′ *ša* GIŠ.SA[R.MEŠ *x x ina de-ni-šú* DUG$_4$.DUG$_4$-*ma*]
3′ *la i-l*[*a*$^{!}$-*qi*]

ADD 462

(Beginning destroyed)

2 4 nubile gi[rls ......]
3 Šamaš-isse'[a ......]
4 2 girls [......]
5 3 garden[s ......]
6 a gift [......]
7 to Ka[b......] —
8 [NN] has contracted and bought (said property) [from] Haldi-[...] for 10 [minas of silver by the mina of Carchemish].

11 [The money is paid completely].
(Break)
r.1 •He shall return [the money tenfold to its owner, and shall ......] of the orchard[s ...].
2 [He shall contest in his lawsuit and] not succeed.

268 1, 5ff See coll.
269 Previous edition: AR 375.

4′ IGI ^{md}PA—[*x x x x x x*]
5′ IGI ^{m}EN—*l*[*u-x x x x x x*]
6′ IGI ^{m}*ha—ba-*[*as-tu x x x*]
7′ IGI ^{m}*e-z*[*i*$^{!}$*—x x x x x x*]
8′ IGI ^{m}*rém-ut-*[*x x x x x x*]

9′ IGI ^{md}PA—[*x x x x x x*]
10′ IGI ^{md}PA—[*x x x x x*]
11′ IGI ^{m}[*x x x x x x x x*]
12′ IGI ^{m}[*x x x x x x x x*]
13′ [IG]I ^{m}[*x x x x x x x*]
rest broken away

s.1 [IGI ^{m}*x x x* L]Ú$^{!}$.A.BA IGI ^{m}*kil-lam-ši* IGI ^{md}UTU—PAB-*ir*
2 [ITI.*x*] UD-17-KÁM *lim-mu* ^{m}TA*—10—*a-ni-nu*
3 [IGI ^{m}*x x x*]*x* IGI ^{m}*hal-mu-su* L[Ú.*x x x x*]

4 Witness Nabû-[......].
5 Witness Bel-l[u-......].
6 Witness Haba[sti, ...].
7 Witness Ez[i-......].
8 Witness Remut-[......].
9 Witness Nabû-[......].
10 Witness Nabû-[......].
11 Witness [......].
12 Witness [......].
13 [Witne]ss [......].
(Break)

s.1 [Witness NN], scribe. Witness Kê-lamši. Witness Šamaš-naṣir.
2 Month [...], 17th day, eponym year of Issi-Adad-aninu.
3 [Witness NN]. Witness Halmusu, [...].

270. Fragment of a Legal Document (679)

83-1-18,362

1 [NA$_4$.KIŠ]IB ^{m}U.GUR—MAN—PAB L[Ú$^{!}$.*x x*]

rest broken away
Rev. beginning broken away
1′ IGI ^{md}PA—EN—GIN ⌜LÚ*$^{!}$.GAL$^{!}$—*ki*$^{!}$-*ṣir*$^{!}$⌝
2′ *šá* É—2-*e*
3′ IGI ^{m}IM—^{d}PA—*a-la-ka*

s.1 [ITI.*x* UD-*x*-KAM *lim-mu* ^{m}T]A—^{d}IM—⌜*a*⌝-[*ni-nu*]

ADD 534

1 [Sea]l of Nergal-šarru-uṣur, [...].

(cylinder seal impression)

(Break)

r.1 Witness Nabû-belu-ka''in, cohort commander of the domestics.
3 Witness Šar-Nabû-allaka.
s.1 [Month ..., ...th day, eponym year of Is]si-Adad-a[ninu].

271. Pledge of More than 24 Hectares of Land (678)

K 449

1 [NA$_4$.KIŠIB ^{m}*x x x x x x x x*]
2 E[N *x x x x x x x x*]

3 ⌜É⌝ 10 ANŠE É *zi-ib-li* SUHUR
4 [*na-hal*$^{?}$ SUH]UR ^{md}PA-*u-a* SUHUR KASKAL.2 *šá a-na* URU.*ib-li* DU-*u-ni*

ADD 630

1 [Seal of ......], own[er of the ... being sold].
(blank seal space)
3 An estate of 10 hectares (with) a *manure* house, adjoining [*the wadi*], (the estate of)

270 Previous edition: AR 560. 1, r.1 See coll.
271 Previous edition: AR 145. Collated by I.L. Finkel. 6, 14, 21f, r.6, 9 See coll.

5 [SUH]UR KASKAL *šá a-na* URU.*su-mur-u-nu* DU-*u-ni*

6 [*x*] MAN *i-kar-ri-ka* É 8 ANŠE
7 [*x*] *bu-ra-a-ni* ⸢SUHUR⸣ *na-hal*
8 [SUH]UR *um-me šá* URU.*ia-ra-nu*
9 [SUH]UR A.ŠÀ *za-ku-ti šá* A.ŠÀ
10 [*šá* ^{m}]NUMUN-*ut-ti-i* É 6 ANŠE
11 [*x bu*]*-ra-ni* ⸢SUHUR⸣ KASKAL.2 *šá a-na*
12 [URU.ŠE—*t*]*e-ma-na-a-a* DU-*u-ni*
13 [SUHUR AMA$^{?}$] *šá* URU.ŠE—*te-ma-na-a-a*

14 [É *x* ANŠE SUHUR] ⸢A⸣.ŠÀ *šá* ^{m}*ak-pa-lu*$^{!}$
15 [SUHUR KASKAL *šá a-na*] URU.ŠE—^{d}UTU DU-*u-ni*
16 [SUHUR KASKAL *šá a-na*] URU.*ib-ʾa-la*

17 [DU-*u-ni* É *x* ANŠE *x x*] GIŠ.SAR *šá* Ú.SAR
18 [SUHUR *x x x x x* SUHUR ^{m}]^{d}PA-*u-a*
e.19 [*x x x x x* A.ŠÀ] *šá* ^{md}PA—NUMUN—DÙ

20 [É *x* ANŠE *x x x x x* ^{m}]*di-lil*—10
21 [*x x x x x x x x x* S]UHUR$^{!}$ ^{md}PA-*u-a*
22 [*x x x x x x x x x* ^{m}K]Á$^{!}$.DINGIR$^{?}$.KI$^{?}$-*a-a*
23 [*x x x x x x x x x x x*] ANŠE
r.1 [*x x x x x x x x x x x x x*]*-ru*
2 [*x x x x x x x x x x x*] *ú-piš-ma*
3 [^{m}*x x x x x ina* ŠÀ *x*] MA.NA KUG.UD

4 [*il-qi a-na* MU.AN.NA].MEŠ KÚ
5 [3 *me-re-še* 3 *ka*]*r-ap-hi*

6 [UD-*mu ša* KUG.UD *i-dan-u-ni* A.ŠÀ-*š*]*ú*$^{!}$ *ú-*(*še*)*-ṣa*

---

7 [IGI ^{m}*x x x x x x x x x*]*-a*
8 [IGI ^{m}*x x x x x x x*]*-a-a*
9 [IGI ^{m}*x x x x x x*]—⸢d⸣10$^{!}$
10 [IGI ^{m}*x x x x x*] LÚ.UŠ.BAR

11 [IGI ^{m}*x x x x x*] LÚ.:.
12 [IGI ^{m}*x x x x x*]*x-an*
13 [IGI ^{m}*x x x x x*] LÚ.DIB—KUŠ.PA.MEŠ
14 [*x x x x x x x x x*]*-e*
15 [IGI ^{m}]NUMUN-*ti-i* LÚ.A.ZU

16 [ITI.*x* UD]-3-KÁM *lim-me*
17 [^{md}U.GUR]—MAN—PAB LÚ.GAL—KAŠ.LUL
18 [IGI ^{m}]^{d}PA—MU—PAB L[Ú.A.B]A

Nabû'a, the road leading to Ibla, and the road leading to Sumurunu, ...;

6 an estate of 8 hectares (with) [x] wells, adjoining the wadi, the *side road* to Yaranu, and the exempt field of the land of Zarutî;

10 an estate of 6 hectares (with) [x] wells, adjoining the road leading to [the village of Te]manayu [and the *side road*] of the village of Temanayu;

14 [an estate of x hectares, adjoining] the field of Akpalu, [the road] leading [to the vill]age of Šamaš, [and the road leading to] Ibla;

17 [an estate of x hectares x decares (with) a vege]table garden, [adjoining ......] Nabû'a, [...... the field] of Nabû-zeru-ibni;

20 [an estate of x hectares ....adjoining] Dilil-Adad, [....... ad]joining Nabû'a [....... *B*]*abil*ayu;

23 [in all .... hec]tares [........] —

r.2 [NN] has contracted and [acquired it for x] minas of silver.

4 He shall have the usufruct of it [for yea]rs; [*3* crop years, *3*] fallow years.

6 [On the day he pays the silver], he shall redeem hi[s land].

---

7 [Witness NN]....

8 [Witness ...]aya.

9 [Witness ...]-Adad.

10 [Witness NN], weaver.

11 [Witness NN], ditto.

12 [Witness ......].

13 [Witness NN], chariot driver.

14 [Witness ......].

15 [Witness] Zarutî, physician.

16 [Month ...], 3rd [day], eponym year of [Nergal]-šarru-uṣur, chief cupbearer.

18 [Witness] Nabû-šumu-uṣur, sc[ri]be.

272. Pledge of a Woman (677-XII-7)

Bu 91-5-9,138

1 [NA$_4$.KIŠIB ^{m}*x-x*—K]AM-*eš*

---

2 [*x* GÍN$^{?}$ KUG.UD *ša* ^{md}]PA.⸢TÚG⸣—PAB
3 [SAG.MEŠ$^{?}$ *ša* ^{d}15 *š*]*a arba-ìl*.KI
4 [*ina* IGI ^{m}*x x x* LÚ.LU]NGA

5 [MÍ.*la—a-maš*]-*ši a-na šap-ri*
6 [*kam-m*]*u-sat a-di* 10 UD-*me*
7 0$^{!}$ [S]UM-*an* BE-*ma la* SUM-*an*
8 [MÍ] *zar-pat na-ši-at*

9 [IGI] ^{m}URU.*arba-ìl-a-a* IGI ^{m}*sa-gi-bi-i*
10 [IGI ^{m}*b*]*ar-ruq-qu* LÚ.A.BA
11 [ITI].ŠE UD-7-KÁM *lim-mu* ^{m}AD—*ra-mu*
12 [LÚ*$^{!}$].SUKKAL [GAL]-*ú*
Rev. beginning (3 lines) broken away

1′ *ina* IGI ^{m}[*x x x* LÚ.LUNGA]
2′ MÍ.*la—a-maš-ši* [*a-na šap-ri*]

3′ *kam-mu-sat a-di* 10 UD-*me*
4′ KUG.UD SUM-*an* BE-*ma la* SUM-⸢*an*⸣
5′ [MÍ] *zar-pat na-ši-at*

6′ [IGI ^{m}URU].*arba-ìl-a-a* IGI ^{m}*sa-gi-bi-i*
7′ [IGI ^{m}*bar*]-*ruq-qu* LÚ.A.BA
8′ [ITI.ŠE] UD-7-KÁM *lim-mu* ^{m}AD—*ra-mu*
9′ [LÚ*.SUKKAL] GAL-*ú*
4 lines blank

ADD 72

1 Seal of [...]-ereš.

(space for stamp seal impressions)

---

2 [x *shekels* of silver belonging to] Nušku-naṣir, [*first fruits* of Ištar o]f Arbela, a[t the disposal of NN the br]ewer.

5 [The woman La-amaš]ši is placed [as a pledge].

6 He shall pay within 10 days. If he does not pay, [the woman] is acquired and taken.

9 [Witness] Arbailayu. Witness Sagibî.

10 [Witness] Barruqu, scribe.

11 [Month] Adar (XII), 7th day, eponym year of Abi-ram, [grand] vizier.

(Break)

r.1 at the disposal of [NN the brewer].

2 The woman La-amašši is placed [as a pledge].

3 He shall pay the silver within 10 days. If he does not pay, [the woman] is acquired and taken.

---

6 [Witness] Arbailayu. Witness Sagibî.

7 [Witness Bar]ruqu, scribe.

8 [Month Adar] (XII), 7th day, eponym year of Abi-ram, grand [vizier].

273. A Silver Loan (676-VII-1)

K 356

1 ⸢5$^{!}$⸣ MA.NA 6 GÍN LÁ *šá*$^{!}$ *gar*$^{!}$-[*g*]*a*$^{!}$-*mis*$^{!}$
2 *šá* ^{m}DÙG$^{!}$—É—15
3 *ina* IGI ^{m}GÌR.2—*aš-šur*

4 ITI.DU$_6^{!}$ UD-1-KÁM
5 *lim-mu* ^{m}*ba-an-ba-a*
6 IGI ^{m}U.GUR—AD—PAB
7 IGI ^{md}MES—*iq-bi*
e.8 IGI ^{m}*qí-bit—aš-šur*
r.1 IGI ^{m}*du*-⸢*gul*⸣—15
2 IGI ^{m}*qí-bit*—⸢DINGIR⸣
3 IGI ^{m}U.G[UR]—I

ADD 37

1 Five minas (of silver) minus 6 shekels (by the mina) of Carchemish belonging to Ṭab-bit-Issar, at the disposal of Šep-Aššur.

4 Month Tishri (VII), 1st day, eponym year of Banbâ.

6 Witness Nergal-abu-uṣur.

7 Witness Marduk-iqbi.

8 Witness Qibit-Aššur.

r.1 Witness Dugul-Issar.

2 Witness Qibit-ili.

3 Witness Ner[gal]-na'id.

272 Previous edition: AR 129. → ADD 61.
273 Previous editions: AR 243, NALK 389. Collations: Assur 2/5.

274. Ahi-milki Buys a Slave (676-VIII-17)

83-1-18,340

1 NA$_4$.KIŠIB ^{m}*sa-a*-AD
2 EN LÚ* SUM-*an-ni*

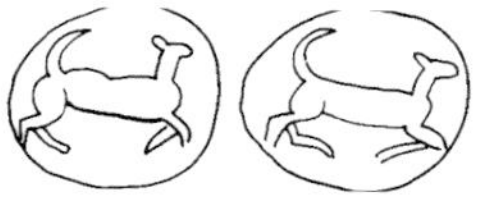

3 ^{m}*la-du-qi-i* ARAD-*šú*
4 *ša* ^{m}*sa-a*-AD *ú-piš-ma*
5 ^{m}PAB—*mil-ki ina* ŠÀ-*bi* 2 MA.NA KUG.UD
6 *ina* 1 MA.NA-*e šá* URU.*gar-ga-mis*

7 *il-qi kas-pu ga-mur ta-ad-din*
8 ⸢LÚ*⸣ UR$_5$.MEŠ *zar*$^{!}$*-pu la-*⸢*qi*⸣
9 *t*[*u*]-⸢*a*⸣*-ri de-e-*⸢*nu*$^{!}$⸣ [DU]G$_4^{!}$.D[UG$_4$ *la-áš-šú*]
10 *man-nu ša ina ur-*[*kiš ina ma-te-ma*]
11 *i-za-qa-p*[*a*$^{!}$*-ni x x x x*]
12 ⸢*x*⸣ [*x x x x x x x*]
rest broken away
Rev. beginning broken away
1′ ⸢*šá*$^{!}$⸣ T[A ^{m}PAB—*mil-ki* DUMU.MEŠ-*šú*]
2′ ⸢DUMU—DUMU.MEŠ⸣-[*šú de-ni* DUG$_4$.DUG$_4$ *ub-ta-u-ni*]
3′ 20 MA.NA KUG.UD [*x* MA.NA KUG.GI]
4′ *ina bur-ki* ^{d}15 ⸢*a*⸣-[*ši-bat* URU.*x*]
5′ GAR-*an* KUG.UD *a-na* 10.MEŠ-[*šú a-na* EN-*šú* GUR]
6′ *ina la de-ni-*(*šú*) DUG$_4$.DUG$_4$ ⸢*la* TI⸣

7′ IGI ^{m}⸢*qi*$^{!}$⸣*-ti*—DINGIR.MEŠ
8′ ⸢IGI ^{m}⸣*šá*—*la*—*ma-šá-e* LÚ*.*ha-za-nu*
9′ IGI ^{m}*mu-du-bi-ra-a-a*
10′ IGI ^{m}*ṣa-du-ru*$^{!}$ IGI ^{md}UTU—*še-zib*
11′ PAB 4 IGI.MEŠ DUMU URU-*šú*

12′ IGI ^{m}*li*—*qi-pu*
13′ IGI ^{m}*bu-bu-u-tú*
14′ IGI ^{m}SUHUŠ$^{?}$*-su-nu* LÚ*.NINDA
15′ IGI ^{md}PA—PAB.MEŠ—AŠ LÚ*.NINDA
16′ IGI ^{m}EN—*lu*—*dà-ri*

17e ⸢ITI⸣.APIN UD-17-KAM
18e *lim-mu* ^{m}*ban-ba-a*
19e LÚ*.SUKKAL LÚ*.2-⸢*ú*$^{!}$⸣

ADD 175

1 Seal of Sa'abu, owner of the man being sold.

(two stamp seals)

3 Laduqqî, a servant of Sa'abu —

5 Ahi-milki has contracted and bought him for two minas of silver by the mina of Carchemish.

7 The money is paid completely. That man is purchased and acquired. Any revocation, lawsu[it, or lit]igat[ion is void].

10 Whoever in the fut[ure, at any time], lodges a compl[aint]
(Break)

r.1 and seeks a [lawsuit or litigation] aga[inst Ahi-milki, his sons and] grandsons, shall place 20 minas of silver (and) [x minas of gold] in the lap of Ištar resid[ing in ..., and shall return] the money tenfold [to its owners]. He shall contest in (his) non-lawsuit and not succeed.

r.7 Witness Qiti-ilani.
8 Witness Ša-la-mašê, mayor.
9 Witness Mudabirayu.
10 Witness Ṣadduru. Witness Šamaš-šezib.
11 A total of 4 witnesses, natives of his city.
12 Witness La-qepu.
13 Witness Bubutu.
14 Witness Ubrussunu, baker.
15 Witness Nabû-ahhe-iddina, baker.
16 Witness Bel-lu-dari.
17 Month Marchesvan (VIII), 17th day, eponym year of Banbâ, second vizier.

274 Previous editions: AR 203, NALK 22. Collations: Assur 2/5.

275. Aššur-iddina Buys Several Estates (675-III-1)

Ki 1904-10-9,192+299

1 ⌈NA$_4$⌉.K[IŠIB] ^{m}⌈KUR$^{?}$.*ha*$^{?}$-*sa*⌉-*a*-⌈*a*⌉
2 ⌈NA$_4$.KIŠIB⌉ ^{m}PAB-[*u*]-⌈*a*⌉—⌈*x x*⌉

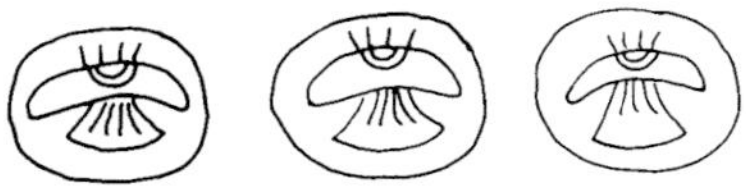

3 EN *tab-ri*-[*u*] ⌈*ta*$^{!}$-*da*$^{!}$⌉-*a*-[*ni*]
4 *ina* URU.*mu*$^{!}$-*lu*$^{!}$-*x*[*x*] *in*[*a x x x*]
5 ⌈É$^{!}$ 12$^{!}$⌉ ANŠE$^{!}$ ⌈A$^{!}$⌉.[ŠÀ] [0]
6 [É] ⌈2$^{?}$⌉ ANŠE A.ŠÀ SUHUR [*n*]*a-hal*$^{!}$-⌈*li*⌉
7 ⌈*ša* ^{m}*ha-sa*$^{?}$⌉-*a-a* 0$^{!}$ SUHU[R ^{m}]⌈DÙG.GA⌉—IM—⌈*sag*$^{!}$⌉-*gi-ìl*$^{!}$
8 ⌈É⌉ 1 ANŠE SUHUR ^{m}DÙG.GA—IM—⌈*sa*$^{!}$⌉-*gi*$^{!}$-[*ìl*]
9 ⌈É⌉ 1 ANŠE SUHUR ^{m}⌈^{d}IM⌉—*rém-a-ni*
10 ⌈É⌉ 1 ANŠE SUHUR KASKAL ⌈*ša na*⌉-*hal* URU.1-*te*
11 SUHUR KASKAL *ša* 0$^{!}$ *a*-⌈*da*⌉-*ri*
12 É 3BÁN SUHUR ^{m}AŠ—PAB.[MEŠ]
13 SUHUR KASKAL MAN$^{!}$ É 4BÁN *ina* ⌈*x*⌉ [*x x*]*x*
14 SUHUR ^{m}SU—^{d}IM [0]
15 É 3 ANŠE SUHUR *na-hal-li*
16 [É] 11$^{!}$ ANŠE SUHUR ^{md}ŠÚ—APIN-*eš*
17 É 1 ANŠE 5BÁN SUHUR ^{m}DÙG.GA—IM—*sag-gi*$^{!}$-[*ìl*]
18 [*x x x x*]*x* É.MEŠ
e.19 [SUHUR ^{m}DÙG].⌈GA⌉—IM—*sag-gi*$^{!}$-⌈*ìl*$^{!}$⌉
20 É 1 [AN]ŠE$^{!}$ 2BÁN SUHUR :. :. :.-*ma*
21 SUHUR ^{md}ŠÚ—APIN-*eš*
22 0$^{!}$ É 6BÁN$^{!}$ *bi*$^{!}$ *du*$^{!}$ *hi pi*
23 É [*x x x x x x*]-*da*$^{!}$-*ti*$^{!}$
r.1 É 4BÁN ⌈SUHUR$^{?}$⌉ :. :. :.-*ma*
2 É 4BÁN ⌈*x x x*⌉ [*x*]-*bi-bi-na*$^{!}$
3 É 5BÁN A.ŠÀ URU.ŠE—*ṭu-ba*
4 É 4BÁN A.ŠÀ KASKAL *ša a-da-ri*
5 É 6BÁN-*ma* KASKAL *ša* ⌈URU⌉.*a-me-di*
6 É 8BÁN *qu*$^{!}$-*ta*$^{!}$-*nu*$^{!}$
7 ⌈SUHUR⌉ ^{m}SU—^{d}IM SUHUR ^{md}ŠÚ—APIN-*eš*

ADD 1196

1 S[eal] of *Ha*sayu, seal of Ahu'a-[...],

(stamp seal impressions)

3 owners of the *tabriu* being sold in the town Mulu[...] (and) *in* [...].

5 An estate of 12 hectares of la[nd];

6 an estate of 2 hectares of land, adjoining the wadi of Ha*sa*yu (and) Ṭab-šar-Saggil;

8 an estate of 1 hectare adjoining Ṭab-šar-Sagg[il];

9 an estate of 1 hectare adjoining Adad-remanni;

10 an estate of 1 hectare adjoining the road of the wadi of *Issete* and the road to Adari;

12 an estate of 3 decares adjoining Iddin-ah[he] and the king's road;

13 an estate of 4 decares in [...], adjoining Riba-Adad;

15 an estate of 3 hectares adjoining the wadi;

16 [an estate] of 11 hectares adjoining Marduk-ereš;

17 [an estate] of 1 hectare 5 decares adjoining Ṭab-šar-Sagg[il];

18 [...] houses [adjoining Ṭa]b-šar-Saggil.

20 an estate of 1 hectares 2 decares adjoining ditto and Marduk-ereš;

22 an estate of 6 decares ......;

23 an estate [of ... adjoining ...]dati;

r.1 an estate of 4 decares *adjoining* ditto;

2 an estate of 4 decares [...]...;

3 an estate of 5 decares of field (in) the village of Ṭuba;

4 an estate of 4 decares of field (along) the road to Adari;

5 an estate of 6 decares (along) the road to Amidi;

6 an estate of 8 decares, *qutānu* plot, adjoining Riba-Adad and Marduk-ereš;

275 1, 22, r.1, 10, s.1ff See coll.

8 ⌈É⌉ 5BÁN SUHUR KA! *na!-hal!*

9 ⌈SUHUR⌉ *ku-su!* É 3BÁN *tab-ri-u*
10 ⌈SUHUR!⌉ *pa!-gi!* SUHUR ^{m}*ur-šu!-me!* ⌈*x x*⌉
11 [SUHU]R! *a!-da!-ri! ša* ^{m}*mar-*⌈*da*!⌉-[*a*?]

12 ⌈*ú*⌉*-piš-ma* ^{m}*aš-šur*—AŠ
13 [TA IG]I LÚ.MEŠ *a-nu-u-ti*
14 *ina* ŠÀ-*bi* 3 MA.NA 1/2! MA! KUG.UD
15 *ina* [*ma*]-*né-e ša* URU.*gar-ga-mis il!-qi!*

16 *kas-*[*pu*] *ga-mur* ⌈*ta*!⌉*-di-ni* A.ŠÀ *šu-nu-tú!*
17 *kaq-*[*qí-r*]*i pu-ṣe-e za-r*[*ip*] *la-qi-u*
18 *t*[*u-a*]*-ru de-nu* DUG$_4$.DUG$_4$ *la-*[*šú*]

19 *man-nu* [*š*]*a* GIL-*ni! lu-u* LÚ.MEŠ *an-nu-te*
20 TA* ^{m}*aš-šur*—AŠ DUMU.[MEŠ]-*šú de-*⌈*nu*!⌉ DUG$_4$.[DU]G$_4$ [*ub-ta-u-ni*]
21 10 MA.NA KUG.UD ⌈*i*⌉-[*dan*] A.ŠÀ-*šú ú-še-ṣi*

22 IGI ^{md}PA—AD—⌈PAB⌉ LÚ*!.[*x x x*]
23 IGI ^{m}⌈DÙG.GA⌉—IM—⌈*sa*!⌉-[*gi-il x x x*]-*ki*
24e [IGI] ^{m}⌈*x x x x*⌉ [*x x x x*]
25e [IGI ^{m}]⌈*x x x x*⌉ [*x x x x x*]
26e [IGI ^{m}*x x x*] A! [*x x x x x*]
27e IGI [^{m}*x x x x x x x x x*]

s.1 [IGI ^{m}*šá—la*]—⌈*ma*!⌉-*še!-e* [L]Ú!.*x*[*x x*] IGI ^{m}*a-da-lal*
2 [IGI ^{m}]⌈*x*⌉-[*p*]*a!-áš!*—*tu!-a!-*⌈*ri*!⌉ ITI.SIG$_4$ UD-1-KÁM
3 IGI ^{m}*a-a—mì!-il!-*⌈*ki*!⌉ *lim-mu* ^{md}PA—PAB.MEŠ—AŠ
4 LÚ*.⌈*ma*!⌉-*se!-nu*

8 an estate of 5 decares adjoining the mouth of the wadi and the ...;

9 an estate of 3 decares, *tabriu*, adjoining the ..., Uršume [...] and the *threshing-floor* of Mard[â] —

12 Aššur-iddina has contracted and purchased (said property) from these gentlemen for 3 1/2 minas of silver by the [mi]na of Carchemish.

16 The mon[ey] is paid completely. The said fields and vacant l[ot] are acquired and purchased. Any re[voca]tion, lawsuit or litigation is vo[id].

19 Whoever breaks the contract, whether these gentlemen (or anyone), and [seeks] a lawsuit or litigation with Aššur-iddina and his sons, shall pay 10 minas of silver to redeem his field.

22 Witness Nabû-abu-uṣur, [...].
23 Witness Ṭab-šar-Sag[gil, ...].
24 [Witness] ... [...].
25 [Witness] ... [...].
26 [Witness NN], son of [NN].
27 Witness [......].

s.1 [Witness Ša-la]-mašê, [...]. Witness Adallal.

2 Witness [..]paš-tuari. Month Sivan (III), 1st day.

3 Witness Aya-milki. Eponym year of Nabû-ahhe-iddina, treasurer.

276. A Fragmentary Loan Document (675)

K 1575

1 [*x x x x x*]*x-e*
2 [*x x x x* ^{m}*l*]*u!*—TI!
3 [*x x x x x x*]-⌈*bi*⌉ *ina qa!* URUDU.MEŠ

---

4 [*x x x x* URU].⌈*ú*!⌉*-pe-e*
5 [*x x x x x*]-*ti*
6 [*x x x x x x x x*]*x*
7 [*x x šum-ma la id*]-*di-nu*

Edge broken away

r.1 [IGI ^{m}*x x x x*]-⌈*i*!⌉

ADD 95

1 [......]
2 [...... *belonging to* L]u-balaṭ,
3 [......] by a copper litre

(space for stamp seal impressions)

---

4 [......] Upî
5 [......]
6 [......]
7 [... *If*] *they* [*do not p*]*ay*, [.......].

r.1 [Witness ...]î.

276 Previous edition: AR 661.

2 [IGI ^{m}*x x*—DINGIR.M]EŠ$^{!}$-*ni*
3 [IGI ^{m}*x-x*]-⸢*a*$^{!}$⸣-*a*
4 [IGI ^{m}*x-x*]-⸢*a*$^{!}$⸣-*nu*
5 [ITI.*x* UD-*x*-KAM$^{!}$ *lim*]-*mu* ^{md}PA—PAB.MEŠ—AŠ

2 [Witness ...-il]ani.
3 [Witness ...]ayu.
4 [Witness ...]anu.
5 [Month ..., ...th day, epon]ym year of Nabû-ahhe-iddina.

277. A Fragmentary Estate Sale (674-VII)

83-1-18,360

1 NA$_{4}$.KIŠIB ^{md}PA-*u-a* [0]
2 *ša* URU.*til*—*ha-ú-a*[*r*]
3 EN É A.ŠÀ *ad-ru tab-ri-*[*u*]
4 PÚ *ina tar-ba-ṣu* SUM-*ni*$^{!}$

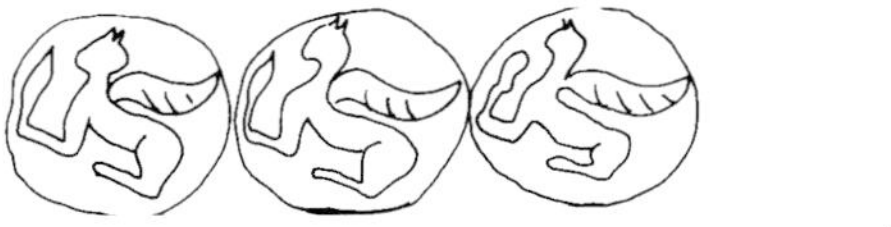

5 [É *x*] ⸢ANŠE⸣ A.ŠÀ SUHUR ⸢A.ŠÀ⸣ [*x x*]
rest broken away
Rev. beginning broken away
1′ IGI ^{m}EN—KASKAL—⸢BÀD LÚ*$^{!}$⸣.*x*[*x x x x*]
2′ IGI ^{m}*qur-di-i* IGI ^{m}*ia*-[*x x x*]
3′ IGI ^{m}*na-hi-ri-i* : ^{m}*dan*-[*x x x*]
4′ IGI ^{m}*ú*$^{!}$-*ta-a* : ^{m}*lu*-[*x x x*]
5′ IGI ^{m}KIN-*a-a* : ^{m}AD—*ia*-⸢*qar*⸣
6′ IGI ^{m}ZALÁG-*a-nu* : ^{m}*da-na-ia* : ^{m}*dim*$^{!}$-*x*[*x x*]
7′ IGI ^{m}AN.GAL—EN—PAB : ^{md}PA—PAB-*ir*
8′ IGI ^{m}*ia-di-i*ʾ PAB 2 *ša* URU.2—LÚ*$^{!}$.SAG$^{!}$.MEŠ
9′ IGI ^{m}NIGIN-*ár*—DINGIR : ^{m}*hi-ri*—PAB$^{!}$
10e PAB 2 *ša* URU.2—*ṣa-a-ṣi*
11e ITI.DUL *lim-mu*
12e ^{m}MAN—ZALÁG GAR.KUR *bar-hal-za*
s.1 ŠE.*nu-sa*-[*hi x x x x x x x x*]
2 *ina* URU.*til*—*ha-ú-ar* [*x x x x x*]

ADD 404

1 [Se]al of Nabû'a of Til-hawar, owner of the house, field, threshing-floor, *tabriu* and well in the courtyard being sold.

(stamp seal impressions)

5 [An estate of x] hectares of land adjoining the fi[eld of ...]
(Break)
r.1 Witness Bel-Harran-duri, [...].
2 Witness Qurdî. Witness Ya[...].
3 Witness Nahirî. Ditto Dan[...].
4 Witness Utâ. Ditto Lu[...].
5 Witness Ululayu. Ditto Abi-yaqar.
6 Witness Nuranu. Ditto Dannaya. Ditto Dim[...].
7 Witness Issaran-belu-uṣur. Ditto Nabû-naṣir.
8 Witness Yadi'. A total of two (witnesses) from Eunuch *Town*.
9 Witness Sahar-ili. Ditto Hiri-ahi.
10 A total of two from the *town* of Ṣaṣu.
11 Month Tishri (VII), eponym year of Šarru-nuri, governor of Barhalzi.
s.1 The corn ta[xes *of that land shall not be exacted*].
2 In Til-hawar [...].

278. Šamaš-šallim Buys 35 Hectares of Land (674-X-25)

K 285

1 NA$_{4}$.KIŠIB ^{md}PA—ZU

ADD 383

1 Seal of Nabû-le'i, owner of the land

277 Previous edition: AR 442; → TCAE 178. r.1, 4ff, 8f, 11 See coll.
278 Previous editions: AR 33, NALK 343; → KB 4 (1896) 126-127; 3R 50,4 (copy). 5, r.13 Or *Saṣiṣu*; see coll.

2 EN A.ŠÀ SUM-*a-ni*

3 É 35 ANŠE A.ŠÀ *ina ma-za-ru-te*
4 *ina* GIŠ.BÁN *ša* 9 *qa*
5 *ina* URU.*sa-i-ri* SUHUR ^{m}*ir-ṣi-ṣi*
6 SUHUR A.ŠÀ *šá* ^{md}UTU—MAN—PAB
7 SUHUR A.ŠÀ *šá* ^{md}UTU—*šal-lim*
8 SUHUR *mu-sa-kil-a-te*
9 *ú-piš-ma* ^{md}UTU—*šal-lim*
10 *ina* ŠÀ 5 MA.NA KUG.UD TI
11 *kas-pu gam-mur ta-din*
12 A.ŠÀ *za-rip la-qi tú-a-ru*
13 *de-e-nu* DUG$_4$.DUG$_4$ *la-áš-šú*
14 *man-nu ša ina ur-kiš ina ma-te-ma*
e.15 GIL-*u-ni lu* ^{md}PA—ZU
16 *lu-u* DUMU.MEŠ-*šú lu-u* PAB.MEŠ-*šú*
17 TA ^{md}UTU—*šal-lim*
r.1 DUMU.MEŠ-*šú* DUMU—DUMU.MEŠ-*šú*
2 *de-e-nu ub-ta-u-ni*
3 10 MA.NA KUG.UD 1 MA.NA KUG.GI
4 *ina bur-ki* ^{d}IŠ.TAR *a-ši-bat*
5 NINA.KI GAR-*an kas-pu ana* 10.MEŠ
6 *a-na* EN.MEŠ-*šú* GUR-*ra ina de-ni-šú*
7 *i-*DUG$_4$.DUG$_4$-*ma la i-laq-qi*

8 IGI ^{m}*mar-di-i* IGI ^{m}10—MU—AŠ
9 IGI ^{md}PA—MU$^{!}$—PAB
10 IGI ^{m}*mu-še-zib*—DINGIR
11 IGI ^{m}*ha—ba-as-te*
12 IGI ^{m}⸢EN⸣—KASKAL—BÀD
13 IGI ^{m}*ir-ṣi-ṣi*
14 IGI ^{m}HÉ.NUN-*a-a*
15 IGI ^{m}*ba-hi-i*
16 IGI ^{md}PA—*šá-gim*$^{!!}$
17 LÚ*.A.BA
18 ITI.AB UD-25$^{!}$-KÁM
19e *lim-me* ^{m}MAN—ZALÁG

being sold.

(stamp seal impressions)

3 An estate of 35 hectares of land in cultivation by the seah of 9 'litres' in the city of Sairu, adjoining *Irṣiṣu*, the field of Šamaš-šarru-uṣur, the field of Šamaš-šallim, and the *fatteners* —

9 Šamaš-šallim has contracted and bought (said property) for five minas of silver.

11 The money is paid completely. The land is purchased and acquired. Any revocation, lawsuit, or litigation is void.

14 Whoever in the future, at any time, breaks the contract, whether Nabû-le'i or his sons or brothers, and seeks a lawsuit against Šamaš-šallim, his sons and grandsons,

r.3 shall place 10 minas of silver and one mina of gold in the lap of Ištar residing in Nineveh, and shall return the money tenfold to its owners. He shall contest in his lawsuit and not succeed.

r.8 Witness Mardî. Witness Adad-šumu-iddina.
9 Witness Nabû-šumu-uṣur.
10 Witness Mušezib-ilu.
11 Witness Habasti.
12 Witness Bel-Harran-duri.
13 Witness *Irṣiṣu*.
14 Witness Nuhšaya.
15 Witness Bahî.
16 Witness Nabû-šagim, scribe.
18 Month Tebet (X), 25th day, eponym year of Šarru-nuri.

279. Fragment of a Sale Document (674-XI)

83-1-18,390

1 NA$_4$.KIŠIB ^{m}IGI—^{d}⸢PA$^{!}$⸣—*ṭ*[*è-mì*]
2 NA$_4$.KIŠIB ^{m}ITI.AB-*a-*⸢*a*⸣ [*x x x*]

ADD 504

1 Seal of Pan-Nabû-ṭ[emi],
2 Seal of Kanunayu [...],

10 See coll. r.16 Tablet ^{md}PA—*šá*-BAN (scribal error); see coll.

279 Previous edition: AR 569. For the restoration of the eponym date note no. 245 (672 BC), dated *limmu* PN *kiṣir* RN *šar māt Aššūr*.

3 NA$_4$.KIŠIB ^{md}PA$^{!}$—*še-zib-*⸢*a*$^{!}$⸣*-*[*ni*$^{!}$]
4 NA$_4$.KIŠIB ^{m}DI-*mu—x*[*x x x*]
5 NA$_4$.KIŠIB ^{md}UTU—*ku*$^{!}$*-x*[*x*]
6 PAB 5 LÚ.MEŠ EN [*x x x x*]

3 Seal of Nabû-šeziba[nni],
4 Seal of Šulmu-[...],
5 Seal of Šamaš-ku[...],
6 a total of 5 gentlemen, owners of the [......].

(stamp seal impressions)

rest broken away
Rev. beginning broken away
1′ ⸢IGI⸣ [^{m}*x x x x x x x*]
2′ IGI ^{m}*x*[*x x x x x*]
3′ IGI ^{m}*šúm-ma—*[*x x x x*]
4′ IGI ^{m}10-[*x x x x x*]
5′ IGI ^{m}*x*[*x x x x x x x*]
6′ IGI ^{m}[*x x x x x x*]
blank space of one line
7′ ITI.ZÍZ [UD-*x*-KAM]
8′ [*lim*]*-mu* ^{m}L[UGAL$^{!}$—*nu-ri*]
9e [*ki*]*-iṣ*$^{!}$*-ri x*[*x x x x*]
10e MAN [KUR—*aš-šur*.KI]

(Break)

r.1 Witness [NN].
2 Witness [NN].
3 Witness Šumma-[...].
4 Witness Adad-[...].
5 Witness [NN].
6 Witness [NN].
7 Month Shebat (XI), [...th day, eponym] year of Ša[rru-nuri], *corps* [of ...], king [of Assyria].

280. A Fragmentary Estate Sale (673-I)

83-1-18,698

1 NA$_4$.[KIŠIB ^{m}*x x x*]—PAB.MEŠ DUMU ^{md}A-MAR.UTU—APIN-*eš*
2 EN [A.ŠÀ.MEŠ] ⸢É$^{!}$⸣.MEŠ GIŠ.SAR.MEŠ UN.MEŠ *ta-da-ni*

ADD 431

1 Seal of [...]-ahhe son of Marduk-ereš,
2 owner of [the fields], houses, gardens, and people being sold.

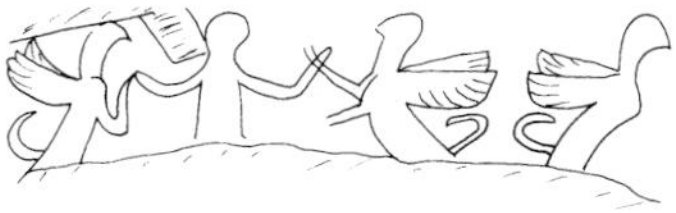

(cylinder seal impression)

3 ⸢É⸣ [*x x x x x x x x x x x x x*]
rest broken away
Rev. beginning broken away
1′ [I]G[I ^{m}*x x x x x x x x x x x x x*]
2′ IGI ^{m}[*x x x x x x x x x x x x x x*]
3′ IGI ^{m}⸢$^{d!}$⸣[*x x x x x x x x x x x*]
4′ IGI ^{m}*x*[*x x x x x x x x x x x x x x*]
5′ IGI ^{m}*x*[*x x x x x x x x x x x x x*]
6′ IGI ^{m}*s*[*i*$^{!}$*-x x x x x x x x x x x x*]
7′ PAB *x*[*x x x x x x x x x x x x x x*]

8′ IGI ^{md}P[A-*x x x x x x x x*]
9′ IGI ^{m}PA—*tak-*[*lak x x x x x x x*]
10′ IGI ^{m}*ha-am-*[*x x x x x x x x x x*] MAN$^{!}$

3 An estate [......]
(Break)

r.1 [Wi]tne[ss ......].
2 Witness [......].
3 Witness [......].
4 Witness [......].
5 Witness [......].
6 Witness S[i......].
7 A total of [......].
8 Witness Nab[û-......].
9 Witness Nabû-tak[lak, ...].
10 Witness Ham[..., ...] of the king.

280 Previous edition: AR 98. Collations: Assur 2/5. See coll.

11′ IGI ^{m}*aš-šur*—MAN—[PAB *x x x x x x x*]
12′ IGI ^{md}PA—KA[R$^{!}$-*x x x x x x*]
13′ IGI ^{md}PA—*še-zib* [*x x x x x* URU.*a*]*rrap*$^{!}$-*ha*$^{!}$
14′ IGI ^{m}*a-zi*—DIN[GIR *x x x x x*]
15′ ITI.BA[RAG$^{!}$ UD-*x*-K]AM *lim-*[*mu* ^{m}*i*]*t*$^{!}$*-ri*—DINGIR
16′ L[Ú.GAR.K]UR URU.*la-h*[*i-ri*]

11 Witness Aššur-šarru-[uṣur, ...].
12 Witness Nabû-e[ṭir-......].
13 Witness Nabû-šezib, [... of] Arrapha.
14 Witness Azi-i[l, ...].
15 Month N[isan (I), ...]th day, epon[ym year of A]tar-il, [gover]nor of Lah[iru].

281. Fragment of a Debt-Note (673-XIIa-21)

Bu 91-5-9,27

beginning broken away
1′ *ù du* ⸢*du*⸣ *x*[*x x x x x x x x*]
2′ *ina* IGI ^{m}*di-di-*⸢*i*⸣ [*x x x x x x*]
3′ *ina* SAG.DU DINGIR GIBIL ⸢*šá*⸣ IT[I$^{!}$.*x id-dan*]
4′ *šum-ma la id-din e-ṣi-ip*
5′ ITI.DIRI.ŠE UD-21-KÁM *lim-mu* ^{m}*at-ri*—DINGIR
6′ IGI ^{m}PAB—BÀD IGI ^{md}PA—LUGAL—PAB
7′ IGI ^{m}BE-*ma*—^{d}IM IGI ^{m}PAB—DU-*ka*$^{!}$

ADD 53

(Beginning destroyed)
1 and [......], at the disposal of Diddî, [...].
3 [He shall pay] on the new moon of the month [...]. If he does not pay (then), he shall pay double.
5 Month Adar Sheni (XII/2), 21st day, eponym year of Atar-il.
6 Witness Ahu-duri. Witness Nabû-šarru-uṣur.
7 Witness Šumma-Adad. Witness Ahu-il-lika.

282. Fragment of a Debt-Note (672-I-26)

K 13015

beginning broken away
1′ [*šum-ma*] ⸢*la i*$^{!}$*-din*⸣
2′ *a-na* 4-*tú-šú* GAL-*bi*
3′ ⸢ITI.BARAG⸣ UD-26-KÁM
e.4′ *lim-*⸢*mu*⸣ ^{md}PA—EN—PAB
5′ LÚ*.⸢GAR⸣.KUR 0$^{!}$ BÀD—MAN—GIN
r.1 IGI ^{m}*ta-qis* LÚ*.LUNGA$^{!}$
2 [IG]I ^{md}UTU—DINGIR-*a-a* LÚ*.A.BA
rest broken away

ADD 14

(Beginning destroyed)
1 [If] he does not pay, it shall increase by a fourth.
3 Month Nisan (I), 26th day, eponym year of Nabû-belu-uṣur, governor of Dur-šarruken.
r.1 Witness Taqisu, brewer.
2 [Witne]ss Šamaš-ila'i, scribe.
(Rest destroyed)

283. Ilu-iṣbatanni, King's Eunuch, Buys 40 Hectares of Land (672-II-1)

K 1601 + 83-1-18,484

beginning broken away

ADD 425

(Beginning destroyed)
(space for seal impressions)

281 Previous edition: AR 258. Collations: Assur 2/5. The tablet is horizontal.
282 Previous edition: AR 259. 5f See coll.
283 Previous editions: AR 413, NALK 37. Collations: Assur 2/5. The date of this text can hardly be restored as

1′ É 2 ANŠE [A.ŠÀ] ⸢SUHUR!⸣ ^{m}*man-nu—ki-*⸢*i—*
arba-ìl⸣.K[I]
2′ LÚ.GIŠ.⸢GIGIR⸣ [SUHUR 0!] ÍD 1 ANŠE 4BÁN
3′ SUHUR ^{m}PAB—*q*[*a-mu*] ⸢É!⸣ 8BÁN SUHUR
^{m}*man-*⸢*nu*⸣*—ki—*PAB.M[EŠ]
4′ SUHUR ⸢É!⸣ [^{m}*x x*]*-ma-ti-te*! É 2BÁN
5′ SU[HUR *x x* SUHUR *n*]*a-hal* É 3BÁN SUHUR
6′ ^{m}[*x x x x x x x x x x x x x*] ⸢*x*⸣
7′ [É *x*] ANŠE A.ŠÀ [*x x x x x x*]
8′ [É] 1 ANŠE 5BÁN :! ^{m}PAB—*qa-*⸢*mu*!⸣ [*x x x x x*]
9′ ⸢É⸣ 1 ANŠE 5BÁN A.ŠÀ *šá* MÍ.*sa-*⸢*ma*!⸣-[*x x x*]
10′ É 2 ANŠE *ina* MURUB$_4$—URU SUHUR ^{m}*ha-*
a[*n-x*]-⸢*ti*⸣
11′ É 7! ANŠE A.ŠÀ URU.^{md}EN.ZU!—KAR!-*ir*!
12′ É 2 ANŠE A.ŠÀ *na-hal dan-nu* ^{m}PAB*—qa-mu*!!
13′ É 5 ANŠE A.ŠÀ *šá* ^{m}*a-ba—*DINGIR *u* ^{m}*a-gi-nu*
14′ É 3BÁN SUHUR ^{m}*lu-ba-áš-a-na—*DINGIR
15′ É 2BÁN SUHUR ^{m}*ab-di—hi-mu-nu u* ^{m}PAB—
qa-mu
16′ ^{m}*man-ni-i* É 3 ANŠE 5BÁN : ^{m}*ka-*⸢*ki*⸣*-i*
17′ LÚ.SIMUG.KUG.GI É 3 ANŠE 5BÁN A.ŠÀ
18′ ^{m}PAB*—qa-mu* ^{m}*ma-ad-*⸢*ki*⸣*-ri* É 5 [ANŠE] 0!
19′ A.ŠÀ ^{m}PAB—*qa-mu* ^{m}*a-du-ru* É [*x* ANŠE]
e.20′ A.ŠÀ *un-zar*$_4$*-hi* ^{m}*na-ni-i* L[Ú.*x x x* É *x* ANŠE]
21′ A.ŠÀ *un-zar*$_4$*-hi* URU.ŠE*—kal-du*! [*x x x x*]
22′ PAB É 34 ANŠE A.ŠÀ *mu-l*[*e*!*-e*]
r.1 PAB É 40! A.ŠÀ ⸢É *x x x x x x*⸣ [*x x*]
2 ⸢*a-di* UN.MEŠ⸣ [*x x x x x*]*-nu* ⸢*x*⸣ [*x x x*]
3 *ina* URU.[*x x x x x x x x*] ⸢*ú*⸣*-pi*[*š-ma*]
4 ^{m}DINGIR!—⸢DIB!⸣*-an-ni* ⸢LÚ!.SAG MAN⸣ *ina*
Š[À*-bi*]
5 10 MA.NA KUG.UD TI*-qí kas-pu gam-*⸢*mur*
ta⸣*-*[*din*]
6 A.ŠÀ É *šu-a-tú* TI*-qí tu-a-ru*

1 An estate of 2 hectares [of land] adjoining (the estate of) Mannu-ki-Arbail the horse trainer and the river;
2 1 hectare 4 decares, adjoining Ahi-qamu;
3 an estate of 8 decares adjoining Mannu-ki-ahhe and the house of [...]matite;
4 an estate of 2 decares adjoin[ing ... and a wa]di;
5 an estate of 3 decares adjoining [......];
7 [an estate of x] hectares of land [......];
8 [an estate of] 1 hectare 5 decares adjoining Ahi-qamu [......];
9 an estate of 1 hectare 5 decares of land belonging to the woman Sa[...];
10 an estate of 2 hectares in the centre of the city, adjoining Ha[n...]ti;
11 an estate of 7 hectares of land (in) the town of Sin-eṭir;
12 an estate of 2 hectares of land (adjoining) the big wadi and Ahi-qamu;
13 an estate of 5 hectares of land belonging to Aba-il and Aginu;
14 an estate of 3 decares adjoining Lubašanni-ilu;
15 an estate of 2 decares adjoining Abdi-Hi-munu, Ahi-qamu and Mannî;
16 an estate of 3 hectares 5 decares adjoining Kakkî the goldsmith;
17 an estate of 3 hectares 5 decares of land [adjoining] Ahi-qamu and Madkiri;
18 an estate of 5 [hectares] of land (adjoining) Ahi-qamu and Aduru;
19 an estate of [x *hectares*], (adjoining) the field of the domestics *of* Nanî [...];
20 [an estate of x hectares], (adjoining) the field of the domestics of the Chaldean village [...];
21 a total area of 34 hectares of hil[l land], a total area of 40 hectares of land [......], including the people [......], in the city [of ...] —
r.4 Ilu-iṣbatanni, eunuch of the king, has contracted and bought it f[or] 10 minas of silver.
5 The money is pa[id] completely. That land and house is purchased. Any revocation,

664, since the eponym of that year (Šarru-lu-dari) was the governor of Dur-Šarruken, not of Dur-Šarrukku. 12 Tablet ^{m}PAB*—qa-bi* (scribal error).

FIG. 28. *Hill near Nineveh (reign of Assurbanipal).*

7 *de-e-nu* DUG$_4$.DUG$_4$ 0$^{!}$ *man-nu šá ina ur-kiš*
8 *ina ma-te-ma* GIL-*ú*$^{!}$-*ni* 1 GÚ.UN KUG.UD
9 10 MA.NA KUG.GI *a*-⸢*na*⸣ *aš-šur a-šib* É.ŠÁR.RA
10 ⸢SUM-*an*⸣ *kas-pu a-na* 10.MEŠ-*te a-na*
11 [EN-*š*]*ú* GUR-*ra ina de-ni-šú* DUG$_4$.DUG$_4$-*ma*
12 *la* TI-*qí*

lawsuit, or litigation (is void).

7 Whoever in the future, at any time, breaks the contract, shall pay one talent of silver and 10 minas of gold to Aššur residing in Ešarra, and shall return the money tenfold to it[s owner]. He shall contest in his lawsuit and not succeed.

---

13 [IG]I ^{m}BE-*ma*—DINGIR ⸢LÚ.GAL⸣—*ki*-⸢*ṣir*⸣ 0$^{?}$
14 IGI ^{m}*ha—ba-áš-t*[*i* LÚ.G]AL—Ì.⸢DU$_8$⸣.[MEŠ]
15 IGI ^{m}*man-nu—ka—da* LÚ.3-*šú šá* A—[MAN]
16 IGI ^{m}NUMUN-*ut-i* LÚ.DIB—KUŠ.⸢PA⸣.[MEŠ *šá* A—MAN]
17 IGI ^{m}*ni-ih-ra-mu* LÚ.3$^{!}$-[*šú šá* A—MAN]
18 IGI ^{m}*tab*-URU-*a-a* LÚ.: IGI ^{m}[*x x x x x*]
19 IGI ^{md}PA—BA-*šá* LÚ.⸢*ša*$^{!}$—IGI$^{!}$⸣—[É.GAL$^{?}$]
20 IGI ^{m}*man-nu—ki-i*—AD LÚ.*ha-za-*[*nu šá* URU.*x x x*]
21 IGI ^{m}*lu-ba-áš-a-na*—DINGIR IGI ^{m}PAB$^{!}$—*q*[*a*$^{!}$-*mu*]
22 IGI ^{m}*la—qé-pu* IGI ^{m}SANGA—^{d}1[5]
23 LÚ.A.BA ITI.GUD UD-1-KÁM *lim-mu* [^{md}PA—EN—PAB]
24 LÚ.GAR.KUR URU.BÀD—^{m}MAN-⸢*uk*⸣-[*ku*]

13 Witness Šumma-ilu, cohort commander.
14 Witness Habast[i, hea]d porter.
15 Witness Mannu-ka-Adda, 'third man' of the crown prince.
16 Witness Zarutî, chariot driver [of the crown prince].
17 Witness Nihramu, 'thir[d man' of the crown prince].
18 Witness Tabalayu, ditto. Witness [NN].
19 Witness Nabû-iqiša, [*palace*] superintendent.
20 Witness Mannu-ki-abi, may[or of ...].
21 Witness Lubašanni-ilu. Witness Ahiqa[mu].
22 Witness La-qepu. Witness Sangû-Issar, scribe.
23 Month Iyyar (II), 1st day, eponym year of [Nabû-belu-uṣur], governor of Dur-Šarruk[ku].

284. Nabû'a Purchases Two Servants (671-XII-26)

83-1-18,338

1 [NA$_4$].KIŠIB$^{!}$ [^{md}P]A—[EN—PAB]

---

2 MÍ.⸢*mar-qi*⸣-*hi-t*[*a*$^{!}$]-⸢*a*$^{!}$ GEMÉ⸣-[*šú* DUMU-*šá*]
3 PAB 2 ⸢ZI.MEŠ ARAD.MEŠ *ša*⸣ ^{m}[^{d}PA—EN—PAB]
4 *ú-*[*p*]*iš*-⸢*ma*⸣ ^{m}[^{d}PA]-*u-*[*a*]
5 TA* *pa-an* ^{m}[^{d}PA]—EN—[PAB]
6 *ina* ŠÀ 2 MA.NA KUG.U[D] *ina*$^{!}$ 1$^{!}$ M[A.NA]
7 *ša* URU.*gar-ga-mis* [*i-zi-rip*]
8 *i-si*-⸢*qí*⸣ *kas-pu* ⸢*ga*⸣-[*mur*] *ta-din*$^{!}$
9 ⸢UN$^{!}$⸣.M[EŠ$^{!}$ *šu*]-⸢*a*⸣-*t*[*ú*] *za-ar-p*[*u*$^{!}$ *la-qí-u*$^{!}$]
10 [*tu-a-ru de*]-⸢*e*⸣-*nu* DUG$_4$.D[UG$_4$ *la-áš-šú*]
11 [*man-nu šá ina ur-kiš*] *ina ma-t*[*i-ma*]

ADD 257

1 [Se]al of [Na]bû-[belu-uṣur].

(blank seal space)

2 Marqihitâ, his ma[id, and her son], a total of two persons, servants of [Nabû-belu-uṣur] —
4 [Nab]û'a has contracted, [purchased], and bought them from [Nabû]-belu-[uṣur] for two minas of sil[ver] by the mi[na] of Carchemish.
8 The money is [paid] comp[letely. Th]ose [people] are purcha[sed and acquired]. [Any revocation, law]suit or litig[ation is void].
11 [Whoever in the future], at any ti[me,

284 Previous editions: AR 66, NALK 194; → ABC 5; Ep. Ar. 15; Fales Epigraphs 14. Collations: Assur 2/5.

12 [*i-za-qu-p*]*a*$^!$-*a*$^!$-[*ni*]
three lines destroyed
e.16 [*x x x*] *br*⌈*h*⌉ [*x x x x x*]
17 [*x x x*]*d nb*$^!$*w*$^!$[*blṣr x x*]

r.1 [*ša*$^!$ TA*] ^{md}PA-*u-a* [DUMU.MEŠ-*šú*]
2 [DUMU—DUMU.MEŠ$^!$]-*šú de-e-nu* DU[G$_4$.DUG$_4$]
3 [*ub-t*]*a*-0$^!$-*u-ni* 5$^!$ MA.NA K[UG.UD LUH-*u*]
4 ⌈2⌉ MA.NA KUG.GI *sak-ru ina b*[*ur-ki* ^{d}MAŠ]
5 *a-šib* URU.*kàl-hi* GAR-⌈*an*⌉

6 *ṣib-tú be-en-nu a-na* 1-*me* UD.[MEŠ]
7 *sa-ar-tú a-na* DÙ.A$^!$ *x*[*x x x*]
8 *kas-pu a-na* 10.MEŠ *a-na* EN.ME[Š-*šú* GUR]
9 *ina de-ni-šú* DUG$_4$.⌈DUG$_4$⌉-*m*[*a l*]*a* [TI]

10 [[*kas-pu*]]
11 [[*ina*]] [*d*]*nt . mrqḥt*’

---

12 IGI ^{m}MU-*a-a* DUMU ^{md}U[TU—*x x x*]
13 IGI ^{m}ZALÁG$^!$-*a-a* DUMU ^{m}*hu*-[*x x x*]
14 IGI ^{m}SANGA—^{d}15 ARAD *ša* L[Ú$^!$.*x x x*]
15 ⌈IGI⌉ ^{m}*man-nu—li-im-me* DUMU ^{m}[*x x x x*]

16 [IGI ^{m}]⌈$^{d!}$⌉PA$^!$—ZU$^!$ DUMU $^{md!}$PA$^!$—[*x x*]
17 [IGI ^{m}]⌈ARAD$^!$⌉—^{d}15 DUMU ^{m}⌈TA*$^?$⌉—*x*[*x x*]
18 [IGI ^{m}]⌈GÌR.2$^!$⌉-[*a*]-*a*$^!$ DUMU ^{m}*qi*$^!$-[*x x x*]
19 [IGI ^{m}*x x*]-⌈*la*$^!$-*a*⌉-[*a*]
20e [DU]MU$^!$ ^{m}SUHU[Š—*x x x x*]
21e [IT]I.ŠE UD-26-K[ÁM]
22e [*lim*]-*mu* ^{m}I[T]I.AB-⌈*a*⌉-[*a*]
s.1 [IGI ^{m}]NUMUN—^{d}15 DIB *dan-ni-t*[*e*$^!$]

2 [*x* G]ÍN$^!$ KUG.UD *ša* UMBIN-⌈*šú*⌉

lodges] a comp[laint]
(Break)
e.16 (Aramaic caption:) [*Marqihitâ and*] her son [...], [...] Nabû-[belu-uṣur].
r.1 [and s]eeks a lawsuit or liti[gation against] Nabû'a, [his sons and grandsons], shall place 5 minas of [refined] si[lver] and two minas of pure gold in the l[ap of Ninurta] residing in Calah.
6 (Guaranteed against) seizures of epilepsy for 100 days (and against) fraud for[ever].
8 [He shall return] the money tenfold to [its] owners. He shall contest in his lawsuit a[nd n]ot [succeed].
10 [[The money]]
12 (Aramaic caption:) [De]ed of Marqihitâ.

---

12 Witness Šumaya, son of Ša[maš-...].
13 Witness Nuraya, son of Hu[...].
14 Witness Sangû-Issar, servant of t[he ...].
15 Witness Mannu-Limmi, son of [...].
16 [Witness] Nabû-le'i, son of Nabû-[...].
17 [Witness] Urda-Issar, son of *Issi*-[...].
18 [Witness] Šepaya, son of Qi[...].
19 [Witness NN]..., [so]n of Ubr[u-...].
21 [Mon]th Adar (XII), 26th day, eponym year of Kanunayu.
s.1 [Witness] Zar-Issar, keeper of the contract.
2 [x] shekels of silver for his fingernail.

285. Fragment of a Legal Document of the Chief of Accounts

80-7-19,135

beginning broken away
1′ [*x x x x x x x x x*]⌈*x*⌉-*mu*$^!$
2′ [*x x x x x x x x x*] *bu*$^!$ TAB$^!$
3′ [*x x x x x x x ina*] ⌈MU⌉.AN.NA
4′ [*ša ina* 1 GÍN KUG.UD 6BÁ]N$^!$ ⌈ŠE$^!$.PAD$^!$⌉.MEŠ ⌈*tal*$^!$⌉-*lik*$^!$-*u-ni*
5′ [*ú-piš-ma* TA IGI$^?$ ^{m}]⌈^{d}AG$^!$⌉—BA-*šá*
6′ [^{m}*x x x x x* L]Ú.GAL—NÍG.ŠID
7′ [*ina* ŠÀ *x* MA.NA KUG].⌈UD$^!$⌉ *ina*$^!$ *ma*$^!$-⌈*né*$^!$⌉-[*e*]
rest broken away
Rev. beginning broken away
1′ [*x x x x x* DUMU.UŠ-*šú*] ⌈GAL$^!$⌉-*ú*$^!$ [0]

ADD 632

(Beginning destroyed)
3 [...... in] the year [when one shekel of silver] bought si[x seahs] of barley —

5 [NN], chief of accounts, [has contracted and bought it *from*] Nabû-iqiša [for x minas of sil]ver by the mina [of ...]
(Break)
r.1 He shall burn [his first-born son in the

285 Previous edition: AR 160. 1f, 4f See coll. 5 The word order assumed in the restoration (*uppišma* followed by *issu pān*, and not by the name of the purchaser) is very unusual and otherwise attested in GPA 30:8 only. Taking Nabû-iqiša as the purchaser is difficult because there is room for about six signs in the break before the name. Should he nevertheless be the purchaser, a profession must be restored in l.6 ("Nabû-iqiša, [the ... of] the chief of accounts

2′ [*ina ha-am-ri ša*] ^{d}IM GIBÍL
3′ [*ina de-ni-šú* DUG$_4$].DUG$_4$ *la* TI

sacred precinct of] Adad. [He shall cont]est [in his lawsuit] (and) not succeed.

4′ [IGI ^{m}*x x x x*] LÚ*.A.BA
5′ [IGI ^{m}*x x x x*]—LAL$^{!}$ LÚ*.DAM.QAR
6′ [IGI ^{m}*x x x x* L]Ú*.EN—GIŠ.MÁ$^{!}$
7′ [IGI ^{m}*x x x x*] LÚ*.EN—GIŠ.MÁ$^{!}$
8′ [IGI ^{m}*x x x* L]Ú*$^{!}$.3-*šú*$^{!}$ *šá a*$^{!}$-*pa*$^{!}$.MEŠ
9′ [IGI ^{m}*x x x x* L]Ú.3-*šú ša*$^{!}$:$^{!}$
10′ [IGI ^{m}*x x x x*] LÚ*.3-*š*[*ú x x*]
rest broken away

[4] [Witness NN], scribe.
[5] [Witness ...]-taqqin, merchant.
[6] [Witness NN], boat owner.
[7] [Witness NN], boat owner.
[8] [Witness NN], 'third man,' (holder) of reins.
[9] [Witness NN], 'third man,' ditto.
[10] [Witness NN], 'third man' [...].
(Rest destroyed)

286. Adad-Kapara Purchases a Maid (670-I)

K 14294 (ADD 796) + 80-7-19,301 ADD 499+

1 NA$_4$.KIŠIB ^{m}SUHUŠ—^{d}[*x x x*]
2 EN—URU URU.*šá-di-kan-ni* EN [MÍ SUM-*ni*]

[1] Seal of Ubru-[...], city lord of Šadikanni, owner [of the woman being sold].

(cylinder seal impression)

---

3 MÍ.*ra-ma-a*—[*ia-a* GEMÉ-*šú*]
4 *šá* ^{m}SUHUŠ—[^{d}*x x x x x*]
5 *ú-piš-m*[*a* ^{m}10—*ka-pa-ra*]
6 *ina* ŠÀ-*bi* ⸢50⸣$^{!}$ [GÍN.MEŠ KUG.UD TI]
7 *kas-pu ga-*[*mur ta-din*]
8 ⸢GEMÉ⸣ *šu-a-*[*te za-ár-pat*]
9 [*x x x*] *x* [*x x x x x x*]
rest broken away
Rev. beginning broken away
1′ ⸢IGI$^{!}$ $^{m!}$*li*⸣$^{!}$-*p*[*u*$^{!}$-*šu*$^{?}$ *x x x x*]
2′ IGI ^{md}PA—[*x x x x x*]
3′ IGI ^{m}SUHUŠ—[*x x x x x*]
4′ IGI [^{m}*x x*] ⸢*x*⸣ [*x x x*]
5′ IGI ^{m}*ia-bur*$^{!}$-*x*[*x x x x x*]
6′ ⸢IGI ^{m}⸣^{d}PA—GIŠ$^{!}$ [LÚ*.*x x x x x*]
7′ IGI ^{m}*gi-mil-*[*lu*$^{?}$ *x x x x*]
8′ IGI ^{m}ARAD—^{d}AG ⸢LÚ*⸣.[*x x x*]
9′ IGI ^{m}*ha-na-na* [*x x x*]
10′ IGI ^{md}PA—MU—AŠ DUMU ^{m}⸢*im*⸣-[*x x x*]
11′ ITI.BARAG *lim-mu ša* EGIR ^{m}ITI.AB-⸢*a*⸣-[*a x x*]
s.1 [*šá*$^{?}$ MÍ.*ra-ma-a*]—⸢*ia*⸣-*a ša a-na* ^{m}10—*ka-pa-ra* SUM-*u-ni*

[3] Ramâ-[Yâ, the maid] of Ubru-[...] —
[5] [Adad-kapara] has contracted and [bought her] for 50 [shekels of silver].
[7] The money is [paid] comple[tely]. That maid [is purchased and acquired].
(Break)

[r.1] Witness Lip[ušu, ...].
[2] Witness Nabû-[......].
[3] Witness Ubru-[......].
[4] Witness [......].
[5] Witness Yabur[..., ...].
[6] Witness Nabû-lešir, [...].
[7] Witness Gimil[*lu*, ...].
[8] Witness Urda-Nabû, [...].
[9] Witness Hanan, [...].
[10] Witness Nabû-šumu-iddina, son of Im[...].
[11] Month Nisan (I), eponym year of (the official) after Kanunayu.
[s.1] [*Concerning* Ramâ]-Yâ, who was sold to Adad-kapara.

[has contracted ..."). r.1, 5, 8f See coll.
286 Previous editions: AR 511 and 563; NALK 4. 6, r.1, 5 See coll.

287. The Eunuch of the Crown Prince of Babylon Buys a Village (670-II-1)

Sm 3

1 NA_4.KIŠIB ^{md}U.GUR—DINGIR-*a-a* LÚ*.EN.NAM
2 *ša* KUR.*la-hi-ri*
3 NA_4.KIŠIB ^{md}30—MAN—PAB LÚ*.2-*ú* :.
4 :. ^{m}*mu-ra-su-ú* LÚ*.3-*šú* :.
5 :. ^{m}*za-bi-nu* LÚ*.*mu-kil*—PA.MEŠ :.
6 PAB 4 LÚ.MEŠ-*e* EN URU *ta-da-a-ni*

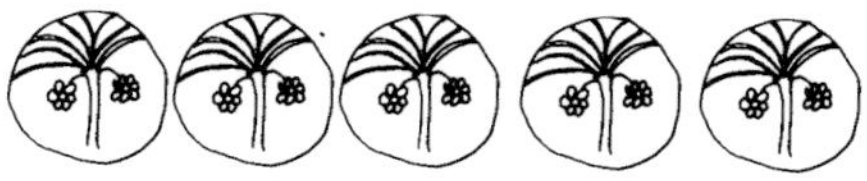

7 URU.ŠE—^{m}*ba-ha-a-a a-di gi-mir-ti-šú*
8 É 5-*me* A.ŠÀ *a-di*[!!] ŠE.NUMUN-*šú ar-ši*
9 SUHUR URU[!].ŠE[!]—^{m}*tap-ha—a-ri-*[[*x*]]
10 SUHUR A.ŠÀ *ša* URU.ŠE—^{m}*ṣil*—EN LÚ*.SIPA *sa-kul-lat*
11 SUHUR A.ŠÀ *ša* URU.*pa-qu-tú ša* URU.⌜BÀD[!]⌝—MAN—GIN[!]-*a-a*
12 SUHUR A.ŠÀ *ša* URU.ŠE—^{m}PAB—*ia-qar u* URU.ŠE—^{m}*ṣil*—EN
13 *ú-piš-ma* ^{m}*a-tar*—DINGIR LÚ*.SAG
14 *ša* DUMU—LUGAL URU.KÁ.DINGIR
15 TA* *pa-an* LÚ.MEŠ-*e an-nu-ti*
16 [*a*[!]-*n*]*a* ŠÀ-*bi* 14 MA.NA KUG.UD
17 [*ina*] ⌜1[!]⌝ [MA.NA]-*e ša* LUGAL
18 [*il-qí ina* MU.A]N.NA KÚ
Edge uninscribed
r.1 [1 MU.AN.NA[?]] ŠE.NUMUN
2 [1 MU.AN.N]A[!] *kar-ap-hi*

3 [EGIR[?] 2[?]] MU.AN.NA KUG.UD *ina* UGU
4 [*ta-r*]*a-me i-šá-kan* A.ŠÀ-*šú*
5 *ú-še-ṣa* A.ŠÀ *šú-a-tú* ŠE.*nu-sa-hi-šú*
6 *la i-na-su-hu* ŠE.IN.NU-*šú*
7 *la i-šá-ba-áš*

---

8 IGI ^{m}30—EN—PAB LÚ*.GAL—*ki-ṣir ša* KUR
9 IGI ^{m}*ra*[!]-*pi-i*' LÚ*.3-*šú*
10 *ša* É.GAL
11 IGI ^{m}EN—I LÚ*.IGI.DUB *ša* DUMU—⌜MAN⌝

12 IGI ^{m}*man-nu—ki*—ŠÀ—URU LÚ*.A.BA
13 IGI ^{md}AMAR.UTU—MAN-*a-ni* LÚ*.GAL[!]—Ì[!].ME[!]
14 IGI ^{m}*gi-na-a-a* KUR.NIM.MA-*a-a*

ADD 625

(stamp seal impressions)

1 Seal of Nergal-ila'i, governor of Lahiru,
3 seal of Sin-šarru-uṣur, deputy of ditto,
4 ditto of Murasû, 'third man' of ditto.
5 ditto of Zabinu, chariot driver of ditto.
6 a total of 4 men, owners of the town being sold.

(stamp seal impressions)

---

7 The village of Bahaya in its entirety, an estate of 500 (hectares of) land with its sown fields, adjoining the village of Tapha-ari[...], and the land of the village of Ṣilli-Bel the herdsman, the land of the towns of Paqutu and Dur-Šarrukkayu, and the land of the villages of Ahiqar and Ṣilli-Bel —

13 Atar-il, eunuch of the crown prince of Babylon, has contracted [and acquired] it from these gentlemen [for] 14 minas of silver by the [mi]na of the king.

18 He shall have the usufruct of it [for a y]ear.

r.1 [One year of] seeding, [one yea]r of fallowing.

3 [*After the second*] year one shall place the silver upon [the cor]n heaps, and one shall redeem one's land.

5 Corn or straw taxes shall not be exacted from that land.

---

8 Witness Sin-belu-uṣur, cohort commander of the palace.

9 Witness Rapi', 'third man' of the palace.

11 Witness Bel-na'id, treasurer of the crown prince.

12 Witness Mannu-ki-Libbali, scribe.

13 Witness Marduk-šarrani, oil master.

14 Witness Ginnaya, an Elamite.

287 Previous editions: AR 116, NALK 46; → TCAE 176. 7 The purchaser, Atar-il, sells the village bought here in ADD 627. That document, previously dated to 671 BC (the eponymy of Kanunayu the sartinnu), actually dates from the year 666 (the eponymy of Kanunayu of the New Palace) and has accordingly been excluded from the present volume. 8f, 11 See coll. 16 There is no room for [*i-n*]*a* at the beginning of the line. r.2, 13 See coll.

15 IGI ^{md}PA—MU—GAR LÚ*.A.BA
space of 3 lines
16 ITI.GUD UD-1-KÁM
17 *lim-mu* ^{m}DI-*mu*—EN—*la-áš-me*
18 GAR.KUR *de-ri*
s.1 (blank) SUHUR A.ŠÀ *ša* URU.Š[E—*x x x x x*]
2 (blank) *ša la* [*x x x x x*]

15 Witness Nabû-šumu-iškun, scribe.

16 Month Iyyar (II), 1st day, eponym year of Šulmu-beli-lašme, governor of Der.
s.1 Adjoining the field of the vill[age of ...].
2 Without [......].

288. A 'Genie' Buys Land at the 'Gate of Hell'

K 8398

1 [*ṣu-pur x x x x x x x*] ^{m}*ur-bu-ru*
2 [DUMU ^{m}*li-pu-ú-gu* LÚ.^{d}]⸢ALAD$^{!}$⸣ *šá* URU.*kar*—^{d}U.GUR
3 [*x x x x x x x x* K]UR.*ga-su-pi*

---

4 [É *x* ANŠE A.ŠÀ *ina*] *ú-šal-li šá* ⸢*ka*⸣ [*x x*]-*tar*$^{!}$
5 [SUHUR *x x x* SUHUR ^{m}]⸢*a*⸣-*ki-su* SUHUR ^{m}*ha-am*$^{!}$-*x*[*x x-r*]*u*$^{!}$
6 [*x x x x x*]*x*.MEŠ ⸢*x*⸣ DI-*mu x*[*x x x x x x x*]
7 [*x x x x x*] ⸢É$^{!}$⸣.GAL$^{!}$ 2$^{!}$-*u*$^{!}$ [*x x x x x x x x*]
9 [*x x x x*]*x* É$^{!}$ [*x x x x x x x x x x*]
10 [*x x x*]⸢*x*⸣ SUHUR ^{m}*ma*-[*x x x x x x x x*]
11 [*x x*]-*ra-a-te ina kit*$^{!}$-[*x x x x x x x x*(*x x*)]
12 ⸢SUHUR$^{!}$ *qa*$^{?}$-*bu*$^{!}$⸣-*ri ša*$^{!}$ ⸢A$^{!}$⸣.[MEŠ *ina* ŠÀ-*bi la-áš-šú-u-ni*]
13 *šá* ŠE.BAR *ina*$^{!}$ ⸢ŠÀ$^{!}$-*bi*$^{!}$⸣ *la*$^{!}$ *ú-še*-[*ṣu-ú-n*]*i*$^{!}$ ⸢É$^{!}$ 2$^{!}$⸣ A[NŠE$^{!}$ A.ŠÀ]
14 *ina* EDIN *x x*[*x*(*x*) *x*]*x-te*$^{!}$ É *d*[*a*$^{!}$ *k*]*iš* É *ta-ba*-[*x x x*]
15 A.ŠÀ *e-ru-šú* ⸢*la*$^{!}$⸣ *né-mu*$^{!}$-*lu*$^{!}$ ŠE.NUMUN$^{!}$ ⸢*ub*⸣-*bu-lu la i*-[*na-ši-u*$^{?}$]
16 SUHUR ÍD.*ú-la-ia šá* KÁ—*ir-kal-li* PAB URU$^{!}$.[*x x x*]
17 A.ŠÀ *la ke-e-te ina* URU.*za-ku-u-te šá* KÁ—*ir-k*[*al*$^{!}$-*li*]
18 *ú-piš-ma* ^{m}*har-ha-an-da-a* LÚ.$^{d!}$ALAD$^{!}$ *šá* É D[UMU$^{!}$—LUGAL]
19 TA* IGI ^{m}*ur-bu-ru* DUMU ^{m}*li-pu-ú-gu ina* Š[À 7$^{?}$ MA.NA$^{?}$]
20 *ku-pa-a-te ina* 5 MA.NA UD.DA MÍ.*ar-na*$^{!}$—*ši*-[*x x x*]

ADD 469

1 [*Fingernail of* ......] Urburu,
2 [son of Lipugu], a genie of Kar-Nergal,
3 [......] land of Gasupi.

(space for fingernail impressions)

---

4 [An estate of *x hectares of land* in] the meadow of [...], [*adjoining* ..., adjoining] Akisu, adjoining Ham[...]ru,
6 [...] ... [...]
7 [...] *another palace* [...]
9 [...] house [......]
10 [...] adjoining Ma[......],
11 [...]s in [......]
12 adjoining the grave(yard), *where* [*there is no*] *wa*[*ter*] (and) where no barley is brought forth;
13 an estate of two hectares [of land] in the steppe (of) the town [...]te, an estate of [...], an estate of [...] — they cultivate the field (with) no profit, they [produce] no dry seed —
16 adjoining the River Ulaya of the Gate of Hell, all (in) the city [...];
17 an irreal field in the town Zakuti of the Gate of Hell —
18 Harhandâ, genie of the house of the cr[own prince] has contracted and purchased (said property) from Urburu, son of Lipugu, for [*7 minas*] of bird fodder and 5 minas of *daylight* (*granted by*) Arna-ši[...], the

288 Previous edition: AR 407. Collations: Assur 2/5. 1 LÚ.^{d}ALAD (cf. obv. 18; LÚ omitted in obv. 21 and r. 6) is assumed here to refer to votaries or oblates of the god Nergal (cf. obv. 2) impersonating winged and beaked genii; the 'birds' appearing as witnesses would have been other devotees associated with the cult of this netherworld god (cf. the 'feathered dead' in Babylonian netherworld descriptions). Despite the weird content of the text, one should be wary of taking it as a parody; note that beside 'bird names' and 'netherworld toponyms' (which can all be explained in terms of the cultic setting), the text also contains some perfectly normal personal names (r. 6ff) and toponyms (e.g., Kar-Nergal, a well-attested 'real' town near Cutha, the center of Nergal's cult). 18 If the restoration is correct, this would be a reference to Šamaš-šumu-ukin as the crown prince of Babylon and date the text to the end of the reign of Esarhaddon (c. 670-669; see LAS 2 p. 271).

21	MÍ.AMA ^{d}ALAD.MEŠ *il-qi kas-pu kám-[mur ta-din]*	'mother' of the genies. ^{21} The money is completely [paid]; he has bought the field for no profit. Any revocation [or litigation is void].
22	*la né-mu-lum* A.ŠÀ *i-si-qi t[u$^{!}$-a-ru* DUG$_4$.DUG$_4$ *la-áš-šú]*	
23	*man-nu šá ina ur-kiš ina ma-te-ma* ⸢*i*⸣-[GIL-*u-ni]*	^{23} Whoever in the future, at any time, [lodges a complaint], whether Urburu or his sons [or grandsons], and seeks a lawsuit or litigation against Harhandâ and his sons, [shall pay] 10 talents of [...].
24	*lu-u* ^{m}*ur-bu-ru lu-u* DUMU.MEŠ-*šú* [DUMU—DUMU.MEŠ-*šú*]	
r.1	*ša* TA* ^{m}*har-ha-an-da-a ù* DUMU.MEŠ-*šú* [*de-e-nu*]	
2	DUG$_4$.DUG$_4$ *ub-ta-ʾu-u-ni* 10 GÚ.UN [*x x x x*]	
3	4 ITI ⸢*ša*⸣ ITI.NE ITI.KIN *ina i-ga-[ri x x x x(x)]*	^{3} [He shall *spend*] four months of Ab (V) and Elul (VI) at the wall [...], shall provide four foundation stones, and shall pay five minas of *daylight* and 7 minas of [*bird fodder*]. He shall contest in his lawsuit and ... [...].
4	4$^{!}$ *pu*-⸢*la*$^{!}$-*a*$^{!}$-*ni*$^{!}$⸣ SUM-*an* 5 MA.NA UD.DA 7 MA.[NA *ku-pa-a-te*]	
5	SUM-*an* ⸢*ina de-ni*⸣-*šú* DUG$_4$.DUG$_4$-*ma zi-ki-[x x x x]*	

6	IGI ^{m}*sa-[a—ṣi]-id-qi* ^{d}ALAD *ša* T[A$^{!}$ *x x x*]	^{6} Witness S[â-ṣ]idqi, a genie *from* [...].
7	IGI ^{m}*sa-s[a]*-⸢*lu*$^{!}$-*u* LÚ*$^{!}$.2$^{!}$-*u*$^{!}$⸣ *ša* ⸢LÚ*$^{!}$⸣.A$^{!}$-*x*[*x x x*]	^{7} Witness Sasallû, deputy of [...].
8	IGI ^{m}DÙG.GA—*sa*-⸢*la*⸣-*me* LÚ*.⸢*x x šá*$^{?}$ É$^{?}$⸣ [*x x x*]	^{8} Witness Ṭab-salame, [...] *of the house* [of ...].
9	IGI ^{m}*ú-a-ú-a* :$^{!}$ ⸢*ak*$^{!}$⸣-[*k*]*u-u*$^{!}$ ⸢*šá*$^{!}$⸣ URU$^{!}$.[*x x x*]	^{9} Witness Woewoe, ditto, the 'owl' of the city of [...].
10	IGI ^{m}*qu-a-qu-a* :$^{!}$ *qa-ri-bu šá*$^{!}$ *b*[*i*]*r-ti* [*x x x*]	^{10} Witness Cawcaw, ditto, the 'crow' between [...].
11	IGI ^{m}*hal-li—ar-ra-ka-a-te* ⸢:$^{!}$⸣ KUR$^{!}$.GI.MUŠEN *šá* KUR$^{!}$.*x*[*x x*]	^{11} Witness Longlegs, ditto, the 'goose' of [...]
12	IGI ^{m}MURUB$_4$$^{!}$—*hur-da-a-te*$^{!}$:$^{!}$ *a*$^{!}$-*dam-mu-mu al-*[*x x x*]	^{12} Witness Middle-of-*Vulvas*, ditto, the 'wasp' [...] whose wife [...] over the ... of Mount Kašiye[ri].
13	*ša* DAM-*sà ina* UGU *ṣu*$^{?}$-*ha-ta-a-te*$^{!}$ *šá*$^{!}$ KUR$^{!}$.*kaš-ie*-[*e-ri*]	
14	IGI ^{m}*di-ib-ba-a* ⸢*x bi*$^{?}$ *tu*$^{!}$ *ga x*⸣ *x*[*x x x*]	^{14} Witness Dibbâ ... [...].
15	[IGI ^{m}*x x x x*]*x* 1 *qa*$^{!}$ [*x*] ⸢LÚ*$^{!}$⸣.[*x x x x x*]	^{15} [Witness ...] ...[...].
16	[*x x x x x*]-*a-a* ⸢*i i ša*⸣ *qa* ⸢*la*⸣ [*x x*]	^{16} [Witness ...]ayu ... [...].
17	[*x x x x x*(*x*)] GÌR$^{!}$.NUN.NA ⸢*šá*$^{!}$⸣ *ka-li*-⸢*e*$^{!}$⸣ [*x x*]	^{17} [Witness NN], the 'express mule' [...].
18	[*x x x x x x*(*x*)]*x qa* ⸢*x x su*⸣ *uh si* ^{d}15 [0]	^{18} [Witness ...] .... *of* Ištar.
19	[*x x x x x x x*] LÚ*.GAR.KUR 0$^{!}$ EDIN	^{19} [Witness NN], governor of the steppe.

20	[*x x x x x x x x*]⸢*x*⸣ DINGIR$^{!}$.MEŠ	^{20} [......] gods
21	[*x x x x x x x* UD]-⸢30$^{?}$-KÁM⸣	^{21} [*Month* ...], *30th* [*day*],
22	[*x x x x x x x x x*]*x* ⸢^{m}*na*$^{?}$⸣-*bu*$^{!}$-⸢*a*⸣-*a*$^{!}$	^{22} [......] *Nabû'aya*.

23e	[*x x x x x x x x x x x x x*]*x-a-ti*	^{23} [......]...

289. Šamaš-abu-uṣur Buys a Slave (670)

83-1-18,560 | ADD 181

1 [*ku-um* NA$_4$.KIŠ]IB-*šú ṣu-bar-šú* ⸢*iš-kun*⸣

---

2 [*ṣu-bar*] ^{m}*aš-šur*—PAB-*ir* EN LÚ

3 ^{m}PAB—*le-ʾi-ti* : ARAD-*šú*
4 *ú-tap-piš* ^{md}UTU—AD—PAB
5 TA* IGI ^{m}*aš-šur*—PAB-*ir*
6 *ina* ŠÀ-*bi* 50 MA.NA URUDU.ME!

7 *i-si-qi*!! *kas-pu gam-(mur) ta-din-ni*
8 LÚ *šu-a-tú za-rip la-qi*!!
9 GUR *de-nu* DUG$_4$.DUG$_4$ *la-šú*

10 *man-nu šá ina ur-kiš ina ma-te-ma*
11 *lu* ^{m}*aš-šur*—PAB-*ir lu* DUMU.MEŠ-*šú*
12 *lu* ŠEŠ.MEŠ-*šú lu* LÚ*.EN.NAM-*su*
13 *man-n*[*u š*]*a de-nu* DUG$_4$.DUG$_4$
14 [TA* ^{md}]UTU—AD—PAB
15 [DUMU.MEŠ-*šú*] *ú-ub-*⸢*ta-ʾu*⸣*-u-ni*
16 [*x* MA.NA KUG.U]D 1 MA.NA KUG.GI
r.1 [*ina bur-ki*] ^{d}IM EN URU.*kàl-zi* ⸢GAR⸣-*an*
2 [*kas-pu ana* 10.MEŠ-*te*] ⸢*ina*⸣ EN-*šú u*-GUR
3 [*ina de-ni-šú* D]UG$_4$.DUG$_4$ *la* TI-*qí*

4 [*man-nu šá i-ba*]*l*!-*ka*!-⸢*tú*!⸣-*ni*
5 [*x x x x x*]*x* SUM-*an*
6 [*x x x x ṣib-tú*] *be*!-*nu*
7 [*a-na* 1-*me* UD.MEŠ *sa-ar-tú ana*] *kal* UD.MEŠ
8 [IGI ^{m}*x x x x*] SANGA *šá* ^{d}IGI.DU
9 [IGI ^{m}*x x x-n*]*a*?-*a-a* GAL—⸢50?⸣
10 [IGI ^{m}*x x x x x*] ARAD *šá* ^{m}⸢*x x*⸣*-nu-*[*x*]
11 ⸢IGI⸣ ^{m}[*x x x x*]-*a*!-*ni* ⸢LÚ*!.ENGAR!⸣
12 [IGI ^{m}*x x x x*]-*a* GAL—*ki-ṣir*
1 line space
13 ITI!.⸢*x x*⸣ UD-⸢3⸣-KÁM
14 *lim-mu* ^{m}DI-*mu*—EN—*la-*[*áš-me*]
15 LÚ*.GAR.KUR URU.*d*[*e-e-r*]*i*
16 [IG]I ^{m}DÙG.GA—IM—^{d}PA LÚ*.A.BA
17 [*x* MA.N]A URUDU.MEŠ ⸢*šá*⸣ *ṣu-pur-šú*

1 [Instead of] his [sea]l he impressed his fingernail.

(blank seal space)

---

2 [Fingernail] of Aššur-naṣir, owner of the man.

3 Ahu-le'iti, his slave —

4 Šamaš-abu-uṣur has contracted and bought him from Aššur-naṣir for 50 minas of copper.

7 The money is paid comple[tely]. That man is purchased and acquired. Any revocation, lawsuit or litigation is void.

10 Whoever in the future, at any time, whether Aššur-naṣir or his sons or brothers or his governor, whoever seeks a lawsuit or litigation [against] Šamaš-abu-uṣur [or his sons], shall place [x minas of silv]er and one mina of gold [in the lap] of Adad, the lord of Kilizi, and shall return [the money tenfold] to its owner. He shall contest [in his lawsuit] and not succeed.

r.4 [Whoever trans]gresses, shall pay [......].

6 [(Guaranteed against) seizures of epil]epsy [for 100 days (and against) fraud for]ever.

8 [Witness NN], priest of Palil.

9 [Witness ...n]ayu, commander-of-*fifty*.

10 [Witness ...] servant of [NN].

11 Witness [...]ani, farmer.

12 Witness [...]a, cohort commander.

13 Month [...], 3rd day, eponym year of Šulmu-beli-l[ašme], governor of Der.

16 [Wit]ness Ṭab-šar-Nabû, scribe.

17 [x min]as of copper for his fingernail.

289 Previous editions: AR 460, NALK 338. Coll. by I.L. Finkel. 7f *qi* is written like *iq* (*i-si-iq*, *la-iq*), as occasionally in other NA texts too; see coll. r.4, 10f, 13 See coll.

290. Duplicate of the Preceding Text (670)

83-1-18,357

1 *ku-um* NA$_4$.KIŠIB-*šú ṣu-*⌈*pur*⌉*-šú* GAR-*u*[*n*]

---

2 *ṣu-pur* ^{m}*aš-šur*—PAB-*ir* EN LÚ ^{m}PAB—*le-*⌈*ʾi-ti*⌉
3 ARAD-*šú ú-piš-ma* ^{md}UTU—AD—PAB
4 TA* IGI ^{m}*aš-šur*—PAB-*ir ina* ŠÀ 50 MA.NA
5 URUDU.MEŠ *is-si-qí kas-pu gam-mur*
6 *ta-ad-din* LÚ *šu-a-tú za-rip* ⌈TI⌉*-qí*
7 ⌈GUR⌉ *de-e-nu* DUG$_4$.DUG$_4$ *la-áš-šú*
8 [*man-nu šá ina u*]*r-kiš ina ma-te-ma*
9 [*lu-u* ^{m}*aš-šur*—PAB]-*ir lu-u* DUMU.MEŠ-*šú*
10 [*lu-u* ŠEŠ.MEŠ-*šú l*]*u-u* LÚ.EN.NAM-*su*
11 [*ša de-e-nu* DUG$_4$.DUG$_4$ TA* ^{m}]^{d}UTU—AD—PAB
12 [DUMU.MEŠ-*šú* DUMU—DUMU.MEŠ-*šú ub-ta-ʾu*]-⌈*u*⌉-*ni*
13 [*x* MA.NA KUG.UD LUH-*u* 1 MA.NA KUG].⌈GI⌉
rest broken away
Rev. beginning broken away
1′ [LÚ*.GAR.KUR UR]U$^{!}$.*de*$^{!}$-[*e-ri*]
2′ [*x* MA.NA URU]DU *šá ṣu-pur-*[*šú*]

ADD 199

1 Instead of his seal he impressed his fingernail.

(blank seal space)

---

2 Fingernail of Aššur-naṣir, owner of the man. Ahu-le'iti, his servant —

3 Šamaš-abu-uṣur has contracted and bought him from Aššur-naṣir for 50 minas of copper.

5 The money is paid completely. That man is purchased and acquired. Any revocation, lawsuit or litigation is void.

8 [Whoever in the] future, at any time, [whether Aššur-naṣ]ir or his sons [or brothers o]r his governor, s[eeks a lawsuit or litigation against] Šamaš-abu-uṣur, [his sons and grandsons, shall place x minas of refined silver and one mina of pure g]old

(Break)

r.1 [eponym year of Šulmu-beli-lašme, governor of] De[r].

2 [x minas of cop]per for [his] fingernail.

291. Note of Silver Owed to Eriba-Adad (670)

K 977

1 1/2 MA.NA KUG.UD SAG.DU
2 *ša* ^{d}15 *ša* URU.*arba-ìl*
3 *ša* ^{m}SU—^{d}IM
4 *ina* IGI ^{m}[*x x*]—⌈DINGIR$^{!}$⌉
5 *a-na* 4-[*ut-ti-šú i-ra*]*b*$^{!}$*-bi*
6 ITI.[*x* UD]-1-KÁM
7 *lim-*[*mu* ^{m}DI-*m*]*u*—EN—*la-áš-me*
e.9 IGI ^{m}TE-*a-a*
10 IGI ^{m}ARAD—^{d}15
r.1 IGI ^{m}*ta-qi-su*
2 IGI ^{m}*a-ka-ku-a*$^{?}$
3 IGI ^{m}U.GUR—DÙ
4 IGI ^{m}*aš-šur*—DI—*a-mur*
5 IGI ^{md}PA—*kib-si*—(PAB)

ADD 42

1 One half mina of silver, capital of Ištar of Arbela belonging to Eriba-Adad, at the disposal of [...]-*ilu*.

5 [It shall inc]rease by a fourth.

6 Month [...], 1st [day], epon[ym year of Šulm]u-beli-lašme.

9 Witness Sukkaya.

10 Witness Urda-Issar.

r.1 Witness Taqisu.

2 Witness Akaku*a*.

3 Witness Nergal-ibni.

4 Witness Aššur-šulmu-amur.

5 Witness Nabû-kibsi-(uṣur).

290 Previous editions: AR 478, NALK 337.
291 Previous editions: AR 296, NALK 97; → KB 4 (1896) 130-131. Collated by I.L. Finkel. 4, r.2 See coll.

292. Edu-šallim Loans Silver (669-VII-23)

K 363B

1 10$^{!}$ [GÍN KUG.UD SAG.DU]
2 ⸢*ša*$^{!}$⸣ [^{m}DIL—*šal-lim*]
3 *in*[*a*$^{!}$ IGI ^{m}SU—^{d}IM]

4 *š*[*a* URU.*su-pu-ri—e-de-te*]
rest broken away
Rev. beginning broken away
1′ IGI [^{m}*x x x x x x x x x*]
2′ IGI [^{m}*x x x x x x x x x*]
3′ IGI [^{m}*x x x x x x x x x*]
4′ I[GI *x x xx x x x*]
5′ IG[I ^{m}*x x x x x x x x*]
s.1 [IT]I.DUL UD-23-K[ÁM]
2 [*li*]*m-mu* ^{md}UTU—KUR—*a-a-bi*
3 [IG]I ^{md}AMAR.UTU—AD—PAB

ADD 104

1 Ten [shekels of silver, capital] belonging [to Edu-šallim], a[t the disposal of Eriba-Adad]

(cylinder seal impression)

4 f[rom Supuri-eddete].
(Break)
r.1 Witn[ess ......].
2 Witn[ess ......].

s.1 [Mon]th Tishri (VII), 23rd day, [epo]-nym year of Šamaš-kašid-ayabi.
3 [Wit]ness Marduk-abu-uṣur.

293. Inner Tablet of the Preceding Text (669-VII-23)

K 363A

1 10 GÍN KUG.UD SAG.DU
2 [*š*]*a* ^{m}DIL—⸢*šal*⸣-*lim*
3 ⸢*ina*⸣ IGI ^{m}SU—^{d}IM
4 *ša* URU.⸢*su*⸣-*pu-ri—e-de-te*
5 [M]Í.NIN$^{!}$-[*s*]*u-nu* GE[MÉ$^{?}$]-*su*
e.6 *ina* ITI.SIG_4 [*ina kas-pi*] ⸢*i-dan*⸣
7 [*šú*]*m*$^{!}$-*mu* ⸢MÍ$^{!}$⸣.T[U]R$^{!}$-*su*
r.1 *la i-di-na*
2 KUG.UD *a-na* 1/2 GÍN-*šú*
3 *ú-ra-ba i-dan*^{an}
4 [*šú*]*m-mu i-ti-din*
5 [*x x x*] ⸢*gab*$^{!}$⸣-*bu-ma* ⸢*x x*⸣
6e I[TI.DUL UD]-23-KÁM
7e [*lim-m*]*e*$^{!}$ ^{md}UTU—KUR—*a-a-bi*
8e IGI ^{m}*man-nu—ki*—ŠÀ—URU
s.1 [IGI ^{m}*x-s*]*u-nu*

ADD 103

1 10 shekels of silver, capital [be]longing to Edu-šallim, are at the disposal of Eriba-Adad from Supuri-eddete.
5 He shall give Ahassunu, his *ma*[*id*, for the money] in Sivan (III).
7 [I]f he does not give his gi[r]l, he shall increase the silver by 1/2 shekel (and) pay it.
4 If he pays it, the whole [...] ...

6 Mo[nth Tishri] (VII), 23rd [day, eponym year of] Šamaš-kašid-ayabi.
8 Witness Mannu-ki-Libbali.
s.1 [Witness ...s]unu.

292 Envelope. Previous editions: AR 241, NALK 96a.
293 Tablet. Previous editions: AR 241, NALK 96b; → KB 4 (1896) 132-133. Collations: Assur 2/5. 5 Despite line 7, reading MÍ.[TUR] here seems excluded since there is not enough room for TUR in the break. r.8 URU written over an erasure.

294. Purchase of Slaves

Rm 2,193

beginning broken away
1′ ^{m}*sa-gi-bi-i* LÚ.UŠ.BAR MÍ-*šú*
2′ ^{m}*se-e*ʾ—*nu-ri* MÍ-*šú* 2 DUMU.MÍ$^{?}$.MEŠ-[*šú*]
3′ PAB 6 Z[I.MEŠ ARAD.MEŠ]
4′ *ša* ^{md}[*x x x x*]
rest broken away
Rev. beginning broken away
1′ [IGI ^{m}PA]B—BÀD DUMU ^{m}*pa*-[*x x x*]
2′ IGI ^{m}*ha-am-na-nu* LÚ.*mu-kil*—KUŠ.[PA.MEŠ]
3′ IGI ^{m}10—*ra-hi-mu* LÚ.3.U$_{5}$
4′ IGI ^{m}*za-an-za-nu* LÚ.GAL—*ki-ṣir*
5′ IGI ^{m}*gab-ri-i* LÚ.KI.MIN
6′ IGI ^{m}*man-nu*—*ki*—URU.ŠÀ—URU
7′ *ṣa-bit ṭup-pi*

8′ ITI.NE UD-22-KÁM
rest broken away

ADD 268

(Beginning destroyed)
1 Sagibî, weaver, and his wife;
2 Se'-nuri, his wife and two daughters;
3 a total of 6 per[sons, servants of NN]
(Break)

r.1 [Witness Ah]u-duri, son of Pa[...].
2 Witness Hamnanu, chariot driver.
3 Witness Adad-rahim, 'third man.'
4 Witness Zanzanu, cohort commander.
5 Witness Gabrî, ditto.
6 Witness Mannu-ki-Libbali, keeper of the tablet.
8 Month Ab (V), 22nd day,
(Rest destroyed)

295. Marduk-belu-uṣur, 'Third Man' of Ša-Nabû-šû, Acquires a Field

K 1420

beginning broken away
1′ [*x x x x x x x x x*] ⌜*x*⌝ [*x x x*]
2′ [*x x x x x x x x x*] ⌜*x*⌝ *u*! ⌜*x*⌝
3′ [*x x x*] ⌜*i*⌝-*sa-he-i*[*š*! *x x x*]
4′ [*ú-pi*]*š-ma* ^{md}AMAR.UTU—EN—⌜PAB⌝
5′ [LÚ.3].U$_{5}$ *ša* ^{m}*šá*—^{d}PA—*su-u*
6′ [TA* IG]I ^{m}*man-nu*—*ki*—^{d}IM
7′ [*ku-um*] 50 GÍN.MEŠ KUG.UD
e.8′ [*a-na*] *šá-par-ti* 0!
9′ [*a-na*] MU.AN.NA.MEŠ (KÚ)
r.1 [DUMU]-*šú* 3 MU.AN.NA.MEŠ
2 [*ina* IGI ^{md}AMAR.UTU—EN—PAB] *ú-šab*
3 [*i-pa-làh-šú* UD-*mu ša* MU].AN.NA.MEŠ-*šú*
4 [*ú-šal-lam-u-ni* K]UG.UD *ú-še-rab*
5 [DUMU-*šú* A.ŠÀ-*šú ú-še*]-*ṣa*

---

6 [IGI ^{m}*x x x x x x x x x x*] É!
remainder broken away

ADD 71

(Beginning destroyed)
3 [...] together [...] —

4 Marduk-belu-uṣur, [the 'third] man' of Ša-Nabû-šû, [has c]ontracted and (shall enjoy) it [as a] pledge [fro]m Mannu-ki-Adad [in lieu] of 50 shekels of silver [for] years.

r.1 His [son] shall stay for three years [with Marduk-belu-uṣur and serve him. On the day he completes] his years, he shall bring the silver, and red[eem his son and field].

---

6 [Witness NN, ...] of the house.
(Rest destroyed)

294 Previous edition: AR 88. This document is dated to the end of Esarhaddon's reign by the scribe Mannu-ki-Libbali, who is known from no. 287 (670) and 293 (669 BC). Cf. also ABL 211, referring to incidents following the conquest of Egypt (671 BC).
295 Previous editions: AR 147, NALK 169. Collated by I.L. Finkel. → no. 97, and ADD 67 and ADD 1193. 3 See coll.

15. Remanni-Adad, Chariot Driver of the King (671-660)

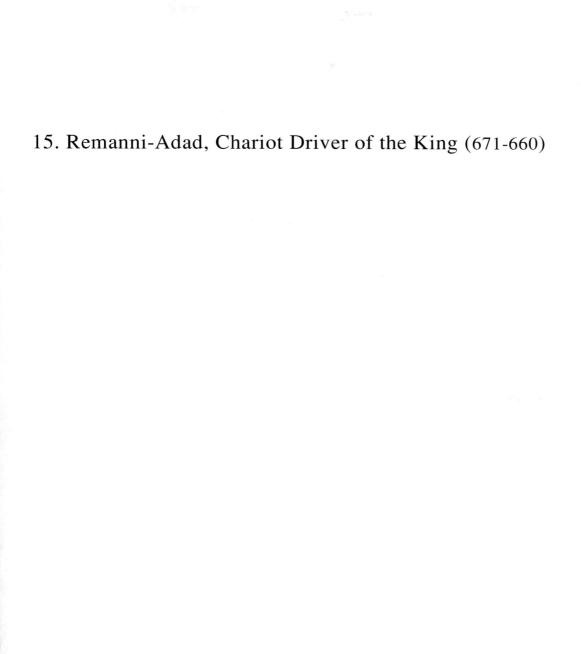

FIG. 29. *Assurbanipal's charioteer at work.*
BM 124850-1 (detail).

296. Note of Rams, Oxen, etc. owed to Remanni-Adad (671-I-1)

K 6107

1 5-*me* UDU.NITÁ.MEŠ
2 26 GUD ⌜50⌝ ANŠE.NI[TÁ$^{!}$.MEŠ]
3 [*š*]*a* ^{m}[*ré*]*m-a-ni*—⌜10⌝
4 [*ina* IG]I ^{m}*arba-ìl-a-a* [L]Ú.2-*u*
5 [*ina*] IGI ^{m}SUHUŠ—^{d}PA L[Ú.*x x*]
6 *ina* IGI ^{md}[I]M—DINGIR-*a-a*

e.7 *ina* ITI.BARAG SUM-[*nu*]
8 *šum-ma la* SU[M-*nu*]
r.1 [UDU.NITÁ.MEŠ G]UD$^{!}$.MEŠ$^{!}$ ANŠ[E$^{!}$.NITÁ.MEŠ]
2 [*x x a-na*] *mit-har* ⌜*i*$^{!}$⌝-[GAL-*u*]
3 ITI.B[ARAG U]D-1 *li-mu*
4 ^{m}ITI.AB-*a-a* LÚ*.[*sar-tin*]
5 IGI ^{m}*sa-si-*[*i*]
6 IGI ^{m}*i-sa-na-*[*a-a*]
7e IGI ^{m}*ba-la-*[*si-i*]
8e IGI ^{m}*di-di-*[*i*]

ADD 121

1 500 rams, 26 oxen and 50 donkey sta[llions] belonging to Remanni-Adad,

4 [at the dispos]al of Arbailayu, deputy (governor),
5 [at] the disposal of Ubru-Nabû, [...],
6 (and) at the disposal of [Ad]ad-ila'i.
7 [They] shall give them back in Nisan (I). If [they do] not, [the rams, ox]en, and don[keys shall bear interest] by an equal amount.
r.3 Month Ni[san] (I), 1st day, eponym year of Kanunayu, the [*sartinnu*].
5 Witness Sasî.
6 Witness Isan[ayu].
7 Witness Bala[sî].
8 Witness Did[î].

297. Remanni-Adad, Chariot Driver, Buys 5 Servants (671-XII-1)

K 416

1 [N]A_4.KIŠIB ^{m}*i—da-a-te—*EN—*a-la-ka*
2 [N]A_4.KIŠIB ^{md}IM—LUGAL—PAB
3 [N]A_4.KIŠIB ^{m}LUGAL—MU—*ki-in*
4 PAB 3 LÚ.MEŠ-*e* DUMU ^{m}*aš-šur—šal-lim—*[PAB.MEŠ]
5 EN UN.MEŠ SUM-*ni*

6 ^{m}DINGIR—GIN—PAB ^{m}*ṣil—aš-šur* [^{m}*x x x*]
7 2 MÍ.TUR.MEŠ PAB 5 Z[I.MEŠ]
8 ⌜LÚ⌝.ARAD.MEŠ *šá* LÚ.[MEŠ-*e an-nu-ti*]
9 [*ú*]-⌜*piš-ma*⌝ ^{m}*rém-an-n*[*i—*^{d}IM]
10 [LÚ.DIB—KUŠ].PA.[MEŠ *x x x*]
rest broken away
Rev. beginning broken away
1′ [IG]I ^{md}PA—KAR-[*ir*] LÚ.[DIB—KUŠ.PA.MEŠ]
2′ IGI ^{md}PA—NUMUN—AŠ LÚ.[:. *šá* A—MAN]

ADD 266

1 [S]eal of Iddate-Bel-allaka, [s]eal of Adad-šarru-uṣur, [s]eal of Šarru-šumu-ukin, a total of 3 men, sons of Aššur-šallim-[ahhe], owners of the people being sold.

(seal space)

6 Ilu-kenu-uṣur, Ṣil-Aššur, [NN], 2 girls, a total of 5 per[sons], servants of [these] men —

9 Remann[i-Adad, chariot dri]ver, [has] contracted [...]
(Break)
r.1 Witness Nabû-eṭir, [chariot driver].
2 Witness Nabû-zeru-iddina, [ditto of the crown prince].

296 Previous editions: AR 226, NALK 234. Collations: Assur 2/5.
297 Previous editions: AR 538 NALK 235; → KB 4 (1896) 130-131; 3R 49,4 (copy).

3′ IGI ^{md}PA—MAN—PAB LÚ.[GAL—*ki-ṣir* :.]

4′ IGI ^{m}*na-ha-ra-a-ú* LÚ.[*x x x x*]
5′ IGI ^{md}EN—URU.KASKAL—MAN—PAB LÚ.[*x x*]
6′ IGI ^{m}*gal-*⸢*lul*⸣ LÚ.GAL—*ki-ṣ*[*ir*]
7′ [IG]I ^{m}DÙG—IM—[*x x x*] ⸢:.⸣
8′ [IG]I ^{m}*ha—ba-*[*as*]*-ti* LÚ.GAL—Ì.[DU$_8$]
9′ [IG]I ^{m}*ba-su-u-a* IGI ^{m}URU.*kàl-ha-*⸢*a*⸣*-*[*a*]
10′ [IG]I ^{md}PA—KAR-*ir* IGI ^{m}*ši-ma-nu* LÚ*.DAM.[QAR]

11′ ITI.ŠE UD-1-KÁM *lim-mu* ^{m}ITI.AB-*a-a*
12′ LÚ.*sar-tin-nu* IGI ^{md}*šá-maš*—MAN—PAB
12 LÚ.⸢DIB⸣—[K]UŠ.PA.MEŠ
13′ *šá* A—M[AN] IGI ^{md}IM—*bé-*⸢*sun*⸣

3 Witness Nabû-šarru-uṣur, [cohort commander of ditto].
4 Witness Naharau, [...].
5 Witness Bel-Harran-šarru-uṣur, [...].
6 Witness Gallulu, cohort comman[der].
7 [Witne]ss Ṭab-šar-[...], ditto.
8 [Witne]ss Habasti, head por[ter].
9 [Witne]ss Basu'a. Witness Kalhayu.
10 [Witne]ss Nabû-eṭir. Witness Šimanu, merch[ant].
11 Month Adar (XII), 1st day, eponym year of Kanunayu, the *sartinnu*.
12 Witness Šamaš-šarru-uṣur, chariot driver of the crown pri[nce].
13 Witness Adad-bessunu.

298. Partial Duplicate of the Previous Text (671)

83-1-18,353

beginning broken away
1′ [*za-á*]*r*$^{!}$*-p*[*u*$^{!}$ *la-qi-u tu-a-ru*]
2′ *de-e-nu* DUG$_4$.DUG$_4$ *l*[*a-áš-šú*]

3′ *man-nu ša ur-kiš a-na ma-t*[*e-ma*]
4′ *i-za-qu-*⸢*pa*⸣*-a-ni de-*[*e-nu*]
5′ DUG$_4$.DUG$_4$ *ub-ta-ú-*[*ni*]
6′ *lu-u* ^{m}*de-ti*—EN—DU$^{!}$-*k*[*a*$^{!}$]
7′ *lu-u* DUMU-(*šú*) *lu-u* DUMU—DUMU-*š*[*ú*]
8′ *lu-u* ŠEŠ.MEŠ-*šú lu-u* ⸢DUMU⸣—ŠEŠ.[MEŠ-*šú*]
9′ *ša* TA*! ^{m}*rém-a-ni*—^{d}IM
10′ DUMU-*šú* DUMU—DUMU-*šú de-e-nu*
11′ DUG$_4$.DUG$_4$ *ub-ta-ú-ni*
e.12′ [*x*] MA.NA KUG.UD ⸢LUH-*ú*⸣ 5 MA.NA
13′ [K]UG.GI *sa-*⸢*ak-ru*⸣ *ina bur-ki*
r.1 [^{d}]MAŠ *a-ši-*[*b*]*i* URU.⸢*kàl*⸣*-hi*
2 *i-šá-ka-an kas-pi*$^{!}$ *ina* 10.MEŠ
3 *ina* EN.MEŠ-⸢*e*⸣*-šú ú-ta-ra*
4 *a-na de-e-ni-šú i-da-bu-bu*
5 *la i-la-qi* ⸢LUGAL$^{?}$⸣ EN *de-e-nu-*⸢*i*$^{!}$*-šú*$^{!}$⸣

---

6 IGI ^{m}*ki-ṣir—aš-šur* LÚ*.*mu*$^{!}$*-ki*[*l*$^{!}$—KUŠ.PA.MEŠ]
7 IGI ^{md}*šá-maš*—MAN—PAB [LÚ*.:. DUMU—MAN]

8 IGI ^{md}PA—⸢NUMUN$^{!}$⸣—AŠ [LÚ*.:. DUMU—MAN]

9 IGI ^{md}PA—MAN—PAB [LÚ*.GAL—*ki-ṣir* :.]
rest broken away

ADD 503

(Beginning destroyed)

1 [Those ... are purchased and acquired. Any revocation], lawsuit, or litigation is v[oid].

3 Whoever in the future, at any ti[me], lodges a complaint or se[eks] a law[suit] or litigation, whether Deti-Bel-allaka or his son, grandson, brothers, or nephews,

9 whoever seeks a lawsuit or litigation against Remanni-Adad, his son and grandson, shall place [x] minas of refined silver and 5 minas of pure gold in the lap of Ninurta residing in Calah, and shall return the money tenfold to its owners. He shall contest in his lawsuit and not succeed. *The king* shall be his prosecutor.

---

6 Witness Kiṣir-Aššur, cha[riot driver].
7 Witness Šamaš-šarru-uṣur, [ditto of the crown prince].
8 Witness Nabû-zeru-iddina, [ditto of the crown prince].
9 Witness Nabû-šarru-uṣur, [cohort commander of ditto].
(Rest destroyed)

298 Previous editions: AR 614, NALK 280. Collations: Assur 2/5.

299. A Purchase Document of Remanni-Adad (c. 671-669)

K 448

beginning broken away

1′ *ina*! Š[À! *x* MA.NA KUG.UD *šá* URU.*gar-ga-mis*]

2′ TI-⸢*qí*⸣ *ka*[*s-p*]*u gam-mur* [*ta-din x x x x*]

3′ *šu-*⸢*a-tú*⸣ [*zar-p*]*u* TI-*ú* [*tu-a-ru*]

4′ *de-*⸢*e*⸣*-nu* DUG$_4$.DUG$_4$ *la-áš-šú man-n*[*u šá ur-kiš*]

5′ *ina* ⸢*ma*⸣*-te-ma* ⸢*i*⸣*-zaq-qup-an-ni* GIL-*u*-[*ni*]

6′ *lu-u* ^{md}⸢UTU⸣—PAB—PAB *lu-u* DUMU.MEŠ-*šu*!

7′ *lu-u* ⸢DUMU—DUMU⸣.MEŠ-*šú lu-u* PAB.MEŠ-*šú lu-u* DUMU—PAB.MEŠ-*šú*

8′ *lu-u mám-ma-nu-šú lu-u* LÚ*.GAR-*nu-šú* ⸢*lu*⸣*-u*

9′ EN—⸢*i*⸣*l-ki-šú šá* TA* ^{m}⸢*rém-an*⸣-[*ni*]—^{d}10

10′ *ù* DUMU.MEŠ-*šú ù* ⸢DUMU—DUMU⸣.MEŠ-*šu*!

11′ *de-e-nu* DUG$_4$.DUG$_4$ *ub-ta-*ʾ*u-u-*⸢*ni*⸣

12′ 5 MA.NA KUG.UD LUH-*ú* 2 MA.NA KUG.[GI]

13′ *sak-ru ina bur-ki* ^{d}MAŠ *a-šib* URU.*kàl-hi* GAR-*an*

14′ *kas-pu a-na* 10.MEŠ *a-na* EN-*šú* GUR-*ra ina d*[*e-ni-šú*]

15′ DUG$_4$.DUG$_4$-*ma la* ⸢*i*⸣-[*laq-qi*]

r.1 IGI ^{md}UTU—MAN—PAB LÚ.DIB—⸢KUŠ⸣.PA.MEŠ *šá* A—MAN

2 IGI ^{md}*za-ba*$_4$-⸢*ba*$_4$⸣—SU LÚ.⸢:⸣ *šá* A—⸢MAN⸣

3 IGI ^{md}PA—NUMUN—AŠ LÚ.: *šá* ⸢A⸣—[MAN]

4 IGI ^{md}PA—*šal-lim* LÚ.:. *šá* :. ⸢KÁ.DINGIR⸣.[KI]

5 IGI ^{md}PA—MAN—PAB LÚ.GAL—⸢*ki*⸣*-ṣir* [*šá* A—MAN]

6 IGI ^{md}IM—*bé-sún* IGI ^{m}*šum-ma*—[DINGIR.MEŠ-*ni*]

7 IGI ^{m}*man-nu—ki-i—*[*arba-ìl*] IGI ^{m}NUMUN-[*u-t*]*i-i*

8 LÚ.⸢Ì!.DU$_8$! A!—MAN!⸣

blank space of 3 lines

9 ⸢*x*⸣ [*x x x x x*] ⸢*x*⸣ [*x x x*] ⸢*x*⸣

rest broken away

ADD 477

(Beginning destroyed)

[1] [Remanni-Adad has contracted and] bought (said property) fo[r x minas of silver (by the mina) of Carchemish].

[2] The mo[ne]y [is paid] completely. Those [...... are purch]ased and acquired. [Any revocation], lawsuit, or litigation is void.

[4] Who[ever in the future], at any time lodges a complaint and breaks the contract, whether Šamaš-ahu-uṣur or his sons, grandsons, brothers, or nephews, or his relative, or his prefect or labour-duty superior, and seeks a lawsuit or litigation against Reman[ni]-Adad and his sons and grandsons,

[12] shall place 5 minas of refined silver and two minas of pure go[ld] in the lap of Ninurta residing in Calah, and shall return the money tenfold to its owner. He shall contest in [his] la[wsuit] and not su[cceed].

[r.1] Witness Šamaš-šarru-uṣur, chariot driver of the crown prince.

[2] Witness Zababa-eriba, ditto of the crown prince.

[3] Witness Nabû-zeru-iddina, ditto of the crown [prince].

[4] Witness Nabû-šallim, ditto of the ditto of Babylon.

[5] Witness Nabû-šarru-uṣur, cohort commander [of the crown prince].

[6] Witness Adad-bessunu. Witness Šumma-[ilani].

[7] Witness Mannu-ki-[Arbail]. Witness Zar[ut]î, porter of the crown prince.

(Rest destroyed)

299 Previous editions: AR 625, NALK 261.

300. Remanni-Adad Acquires a Camel Driver (670-I-28)

83-1-18,341

1 ⌜NA$_4$.KIŠIB⌝ ^{m}*sa-*⌜*ʾu*⌝*-ú-ti*
2 ⌜NA$_4$.KIŠIB⌝ ^{md}EN—MAN—PAB
3 ⌜NA$_4$.KIŠIB⌝ ^{m}*ak-bu-ru*
4 [PAB 3 L]Ú!.MEŠ! EN! LÚ SUM-*ni*

---

5 [^{m}*x x x x* LÚ.UŠ—*g*]*am-mal*.MEŠ LÚ.ARAD-*šú-nu*
6 [*šá* LÚ.MEŠ *an-nu-te*] *up-piš-ma*
7 [^{m}*rém-a-ni*—^{d}IM LÚ.*m*]*u*!*-ki*[*l*!—KUŠ.PA.MEŠ]
rest broken away
Rev. beginning broken away
1′ [*la*] *i-l*[*aq-qi*]

2′ [IGI ^{md}*z*]*a-ba$_4$-ba$_4$*—SU LÚ.[DIB—KUŠ.PA.MEŠ]
3′ [IGI ^{md}P]A!—*še-zib* LÚ.[:.]
4′ [IGI ^{m}*man-nu*]—⌜*ki*⌝—*aš-šur* LÚ.[:.]
5′ [IGI ^{m}*man-nu*]—⌜*ki*⌝—MAN LÚ.[:.]
6′ [IGI ^{m}]*dan-*⌜*na*⌝*-a-a* LÚ.[:.]
7′ [IGI ^{md}PA]—NUMUN—AŠ LÚ.[:.]
8′ [IG]I ^{md}PA—MAN—PAB LÚ.[GAL—*ki-ṣir*]
space of 6 lines
9′ ITI.BARAG UD-28-KAM
10′ *lim-mu* ^{m}DI-*mu*—EN—*la-áš-me*

ADD 202

[1] Seal of Sa'uti, seal of Bel-šarru-uṣur, seal of Akburu,

[4] [a total of 3 gentl]emen, owners of the man being sold.

(stamp seal impressions)

---

[5] [NN], camel [driver], servant [of these gentlemen] —

[7] [Remanni-Adad, chariot] dri[ver] has contracted

(Break)

[r.1] [He shall contest in his lawsuit and not] suc[ceed].

---

[2] [Witness Z]ababa-eriba, [chariot driver].
[3] [Witness N]abû-šezib, [ditto].
[4] [Witness Mannu]-ki-Aššur, [ditto].
[5] [Witness Mannu]-ki-šarri, [ditto].
[6] [Witness] Dannaya, [ditto].
[7] [Witness Nabû]-zeru-iddina, [ditto].
[8] [Wit]ness Nabû-šarru-uṣur, [cohort commander].
[9] Month Nisan (I), 28th day, eponym year of Šulmu-beli-lašme.

301. Remanni-Adad Purchases a Weaver (670-VI-20)

K 327

1 NA$_4$.KIŠIB ^{m}*mu-še-zib—mar-duk*
2 LÚ.GAR-*nu šá* ANŠE.KUR.MEŠ *šá* É
3 GIBIL EN LÚ SUM-*ni*

---

4 ^{m}PAB-*ši-na* LÚ.UŠBAR$_5$—TÚG.*ṣip-rat*
5 ARAD-*šu ša* ^{m}*mu-še-zib—mar-duk*
6 *ú-piš-ma* ^{m}*rém-an-ni*—^{d}IM
7 LÚ.DIB—KUŠ.PA.MEŠ *šá* MAN TA* IGI
8 ^{m}*mu-še-zib—mar-duk ina* ŠÀ 1 1/2 MA.NA

ADD 172

[1] Seal of Mušezib-Marduk, prefect of the horses of the New Palace,

[3] owner of the man being sold.

(blank seal space)

---

[4] Ahušina, weaver of *ṣipratu*-garments, servant of Mušezib-Marduk —

[6] Remanni-Adad, chariot driver of the king, has contracted and bought him from

300 Previous editions: AR 477, NALK 237. [4] See coll. [r.1] The line is spaced and there is no room for more than one sign in the break before *i*. [r.3] See coll.
301 Previous editions: AR 461, NALK 238; → ADD III 296ff. Collations: Assur 2/5. [2f] → Postgate, AnSt 30 (1980) 70.

9 *ina ša* MAN *il-qí kas-pu gam-mur*
10 *ta-ad-*⸢*din*⸣ LÚ *šu-a-tú za-rip*
11 *la-qí* [*tu-a-r*]*u*$^{!}$ *de-e-nu* DUG$_4$.DUG$_4$
12 *la-áš-š*[*ú man-nu ša ina ur-kiš*] ⸢*ina*$^{!}$⸣ *ma*$^{!}$-⸢*te*$^{!}$⸣-[*m*]*a*$^{!}$
13 *i-zaq-qup-*⸢*an*⸣-[*ni* GIL-*u-ni*]
14 *lu-u* ^{m}*mu-še-zib—mar-duk* [*lu-u* DUMU.MEŠ-*šú*$^{!}$]
15 *lu-u* PAB.MEŠ-*šu lu-u* DUMU—D[UMU$^{!}$.MEŠ-*šú*]
16 *ša de-e-nu* DUG$_4$.DU[G$_4$ TA*]
17 ^{m}*rém-an-ni—*^{d}IM DUM[U.MEŠ-*šú*]
18 *ù* DUMU—DUMU.MEŠ-*šú ub-t*[*a-u-ni*]
19 5$^{!}$ MA.NA KUG.UD LUH-[*u x* MA.NA]
r.1 KUG.GI *sak-*[*ru ina bur-ki* ^{d}15]
2 *a-šib* URU.N[INA.KI GAR-*an*]
3 *ina de-ni-šu* [DUG$_4$.DUG$_4$-*ma la* TI-*qí*]
4 *kas-pu a-na* 10.[MEŠ-*te a-na* EN-*šú*]
5 GUR-*ár ṣib-tú* [*be-nu ana* 1-*me* UD-*me sa-ár-tú a-na*]
6 *kàl* UD.[MEŠ-*te* 0]

---

7 IGI ^{md}30—*rém-*[*an-ni*]
8 IGI ^{md}*za-ba*$_4$*-ba*$_4$—[SU]
9 IGI ^{md}IM—[*x x x*]
10 IGI ^{md}PA—SU LÚ.2-*u*
11 IGI ^{m}PAB-*ú*$^{!}$*-a*—SU
12 IGI ^{md}IM—*bé-sún*
13 DUMU ^{m}*iš-man-ni—*^{d}10
14 IGI ^{m}*šum-ma—ta-še-zib* LÚ.ARAD
15 *ša* ^{d}15
16 IGI ^{md}PA—MU—PAB.MEŠ LÚ.A.BA
17 A ^{md}PA—*šal-lim-šu-nu šá* URU.*im-gúr—*^{d}BE
18 ITI.KIN UD-20-KÁM *lim-me* ^{m}DI-*mu*—EN—HAL
19 LÚ.GAR.KUR BÀD.DINGIR.KI

Mušezib-Marduk for 1 1/2 minas (of silver) by the (mina) of the king.

9 The money is paid completely. That man is purchased and acquired. [Any revoc]ation, lawsuit, or litigation is voi[d].

12 [Whoever in the future], at any t]ime, lodges a compla[int or breaks the contract], whether Mušezib-Marduk or his [sons], brothers or grand[sons], and se[eks] a lawsuit or litig[ation against] Remanni-Adad, [his] so[ns] and grandsons, [shall place] 5 minas of refined silver and [x minas] of pu[re] gold [in the lap of Ištar] residing in Ni[neveh].

r.3 [He shall contest] in his lawsuit [and not succeed]. He shall return the money [tenfold to its owner].

r.5 (Guaranteed against) seizures of [epilepsy for 100 days and against fraud] forever.

---

7 Witness Sin-rem[anni].
8 Witness Zababa-[eriba].
9 Witness Adad-[...].
10 Witness Nabû-eriba, deputy.
11 Witness Ahu'a-eriba.
12 Witness Adad-bessunu, son of Išmanni-Adad.
14 Witness Šumma-tašezib, servant of Ištar.
16 Witness Nabû-nadin-ahhe, scribe, son of Nabû-šallimšunu of Imgur-Illil.
18 Month Elul (VI), 20th day, eponym year of Šulmu-beli-lašme, governor of Der.

302. Purchase of a House (670?)

82-5-22,33

1 [*ku*]*-um* NA$_4$.KIŠIB-*šú* [*ṣu-pur-šú iš-kun*]

---

2 [*ṣ*]*u-pur* ^{m}GÌR.2—^{d}⸢15$^{!}$⸣ [EN É *ta-da-ni*]
3 [É] *ep-šú a-di* GIŠ.[ÙR.MEŠ-*šú*]

ADD 332

1 [In]stead of his seal [he impressed his fingernail].

(fingernail impressions)

---

2 Fingernail of Šep-Issar, [owner of the house being sold].

3 A built [house] with [its] be[ams] and

302 Previous edition: AR 360.

4 [*a-di* G]IŠ.IG.MEŠ-*šú maš-x*[*x x x x*]
5 [*x x*(*x*)] *ku-tal-li* [*x x x x*]
6 [*x x*] ⌈É⌉—KI.NÁ [*x x x x x*]
7 [SUHUR] ^{md}[*x x x x*]
8 [SUHUR] ^{m}*s*[*i*!-*x x x x x*]
9 [*x x x*] ANŠE [*x x x x x*]
10 [*x x x x*]*x* [*x x x x x*]
11 [TA IGI] ^{m}GÌR.2—[^{d}15 *x x*]
rest broken away
Rev. beginning broken away

1′ [4 ANŠE.*har-b*]*a*!-*kan*!-⌈*ni*⌉? [*ina* KI.TA ^{d}MAŠ.MAŠ? *ú-še-rab*]
2′ [*x* MA.NA KUG].UD! *a-na bu*[*r-ki* ^{d}*x x x x i-šak-kan*]
3′ [*kas-pu*] *a-na* 10.MEŠ-[*te a-na* EN.MEŠ-*šú* GUR-*ra*]
4′ [*ina*] *de-ni-šú* DU[G$_4$.DUG$_4$-*ma la i-laq-qi*]

5′ [IG]I ^{md}PA—NUMUN—[*x x x x*]
6′ [IG]I ^{m}*man-nu—ki-i*—[*x x x x*]
7′ [IG]I ^{m}*aš-šur*—AD—PAB [*x x x x*]
8′ [IGI] ^{md}NU—MAN—*iq-*[*bi x x x*]
9′ [IGI] ^{m}SUHUŠ—^{d}U!.G[UR! *x x x*]
10′ [IGI] ^{m}*sa-ka-a*[ʾ *x x x*]!
11′ [IGI] ^{m}SUHUŠ—^{d}[*x x x*]
12′ [DUMU?] URU.NINA.[KI]
blank space of three lines
13′ IGI ^{m}*tab-ni*—^{d}[*x x* LÚ.A.BA]!

14′ [*ṣa*]!-*bit ṭup-pi* I[TI!.*x* UD-*x*-KAM]
15′ [*li*]*m*!-*mu* ^{m}DI-[*x x x x x*]!
16′ [L]Ú.GAR.KUR UR[U.*x x x*]

doors, ...[...]
5 [...] the rear [...]
6 [...] bedroom [...]
7 adjoining [......]
8 adjoining Si[......]
9 [...] hectares [...] —
10 [NN has contracted and bought (said property) from] Šep-[Issar]
(Break)
r.1 [He shall bring four *harb*]*akannu* [horses to the feet of Nergal]. [He shall place x minas of sil]ver to the l[ap of ......, and shall return the money] tenfold [to its owners].
4 He shall co[ntest] in his lawsuit [and not succeed].

---

5 Witness Nabû-zeru-[......].
6 Witness Mannu-ki-[......].
7 Witness Aššur-abu-uṣur [...].
8 Witness Ṣalam-šarri-iq[bi ...].
9 Witness Ubru-Ner[gal ...].
10 Witness Saka[' ...].
11 Witness Ubru-[...], a Ninev[ite].
13 Witness Tabni-[..., scribe, ke]eper of the tablet.
14 Mon[th ..., ...]th day, eponym year of *Šul*[*mu-beli-lašme*], governor of [*Der*].

303. —— (670?-VIII-1)

K 1477

Obv. destroyed
Rev. beginning broken away
1′ [IGI] ^{m}*si-x*[*x x x x x x*]
2′ PAB 2 IGI.MEŠ [*x x x x x*]
3′ IGI ^{m}*si-lim*—DINGIR L[Ú.*x x x x*]
4′ IGI ^{md}PA—PAB.MEŠ—SU [*x x x x*]
5′ [IT]I.APIN UD-1-KÁM *lim-m*[*u* ^{m}*x x x x x*]
6′ [LÚ].⌈GAR⌉!.[KUR] URU.BÀD.[DINGIR.KI]

ADD 637

(Beginning destroyed)
r.1 Witness Si[......],
2 a total of 2 witnesses [from ...].
3 Witness Silim-ili, [...].
4 Witness Nabû-ahhe-riba, [*scribe*].
5 Month Marchesvan (VIII), 1st day, eponym ye[ar of *Šulmu-beli-lašme*], governor of *De*[*r*].

303 Previous edition: AR 683.

304. Remanni-Adad Purchases Gardens (669-I)

K 388

1 NA$_4$.KIŠIB ^{m}*ze-e-*[*x x x*]
2 LÚ.NU.GIŠ.SAR ARAD L[Ú$^{!}$.*x x x*]
3 EN GIŠ.SAR.MEŠ [SUM-*ni*]

rest broken away
Rev. beginning broken away
1′ IGI ^{m}[*x x x x x*]
2′ IGI ^{m}*mu-šal-*[*lim—x x*]
3′ IGI ^{m}I—DINGIR L[Ú.*x x*]
4′ IGI ^{m}NUMUN-*ti-*⸢*i*⸣ [LÚ.GAL—*ki-ṣir*]
5′ IGI ^{md}PA—⸢KUR$^{!}$⸣-*u-a* LÚ.[*x x x x*]

6′ ITI.BARAG UD-20$^{?}$-[KÁM]
7e *lim-me* ^{md}UTU—KUR—[*a-a-bi*]
8e *ša* URU.⸢*x*⸣[*x x x x*]
9e IGI ^{m}ITI.KI[N-*a-a* LÚ.A.BA]

ADD 366

1 Seal of Ze[...], gardener, servant of [NN], owner of the gardens [being sold].

(stamp seal impressions)

(Break)
r.1 Witness [......].
2 Witness Mušal[lim-...].
3 Witness Na'id-ilu, [...].
4 Witness Zarutî, [cohort commander].
5 Witness Nabû-šadû'a, [...].
6 Month Nisan (I), *20*[th] day, eponym year of Šamaš-kašid-[ayabi] of [...].
9 Witness Ulu[layu, scribe].

305. Remanni-Adad Buys a Baker (669)

Bu 91-5-9,166 + 83-1-18,352 (ADD 188)

1 [NA$_4$.KIŠI]B ^{m}*mu-ki-nu—aš-šur*
2 [LÚ*.ARAD]-⸢*šú*$^{!}$⸣ *ša*$^{!}$ LÚ*$^{!}$.*šá*$^{!}$—IGI$^{!}$—É.GAL
3 [EN L]Ú SUM-*ni*

4 ^{md}PA—EN—PAB L[Ú*].NINDA$^{!}$ ARAD-*šú*
5 *ša* ^{m}*mu-*GI.NA—[*aš-šur*]
6 *ú-piš-ma* ^{m}*rém-a-ni*—[10]
7 LÚ*.*mu-kil*—PA.MEŠ *dan-nu ina* [ŠÀ]
8 1 MA.NA KUG.UD *ina* URU *šá* ⸢*gar*$^{!}$⸣-[*ga-mis*]

9 *i-zi-rip i-si-qi kas-*[*pu*]
10 *gam-mur ta-din* ARAD *šú-a-te* [*za-rip*]
11 *laq-qi tú-a-ru de-nu* DUG$_4$.DU[G$_4$]
12 *la-áš-šú man-nu ša ina ur-kiš*
13 *ina ma-te-ma lu-u* ^{m}*mu-*GI.NA—*aš-š*[*ur*]
14 *lu-u* DUMU.MEŠ-*šú lu* 0$^{!}$ ŠEŠ.MEŠ-*šú*
15 [*ša*$^{!}$] TA*$^{!}$ ^{m}*rém-a-ni*—10
r.1 [*ù*] DUMU.MEŠ-*š*[*ú de-n*]*u*$^{!}$ DUG$_4$.DUG$_4$
2 *ub-ta-u-ni* 10 MA.NA KUG.UD

ADD 183+

1 [Sea]l of Mukin-Aššur, [servant] of the palace superintendent, [owner of the ma]n being sold.

(cylinder seal impression)

4 Nabû-belu-uṣur, baker, servant of Mukin-[Aššur] —
6 Remanni-[Adad], chief chariot driver, has contracted, purchased, and acquired him for one mina silver by the (mina) of Car[chemish].
9 The mon[ey] is paid completely. That servant [is purchased] and acquired. Any revocation, lawsuit, or litig[ation] is void.
12 Whoever in the future, at any time, whether Mukin-Aš[šur] or his sons or brothers, seeks [a lawsu]it or litigation against Remanni-Adad [and] his sons, shall pay 10 minas of silver. He shall contest in his lawsuit

304 Previous editions: AR 52, NALK 239. Collations: Assur 2/5.
305 Previous editions: AR 466 and 479, NALK 241. Collations: Assur 2/5. → no. 306.

3 SUM-*an ina de-ni-šú* DUG$_4$.DUG$_4$-[*ma*]
4 *la* TI *ṣib-tú bé*$^{!}$*-nu ina* [1-*me* UD.MEŠ]
5 *sa*-⸢*ar*⸣-*tú ina kàl* [UD.MEŠ]

---

6 I[GI ^{md}MAŠ.MA]Š$^{!}$—M[AN$^{!}$—PAB LÚ*.3-*šú*]
7 [IGI ^{m}*ú-ar-bi-si* LÚ*.:]
8 [IGI ^{md}*šá-maš*—MAN—PAB LÚ*.DI]B$^{!}$—K[UŠ. PA.MEŠ]
9 [IGI ^{md}PA—*še-z*]*ib*$^{!}$ [LÚ*.:]
10 [IGI ^{m}NUMUN-*u-ti-i*] LÚ*$^{!}$.GAL$^{!}$—*ki*$^{!}$-[*ṣir*]
11 [IGI ^{md}*x*]—⸢*ú*⸣$^{!}$*-pa-hír*$^{!}$
4 lines blank
12 [ITI.*x* UD]-21$^{!}$-KÁM$^{!}$
13 [*lim-mu* ^{md}UTU—K]UR—*a-a-bi*
14 [IGI ^{m}*a*]*-hi*$^{!}$*—ṭa-ba*
15 [IGI ^{md}PA]—SUM—PAB.MEŠ LÚ*.A.BA

[and] not succeed.

r.4 (Guaranteed against) seizures of epilepsy for [100 days] and against fraud for[ever].

---

6 W[itness Ner]gal-šar[ru-uṣur, 'third man].'

7 [Witness Uarbisi, ditto].

8 [Witness Šamaš-šarru-uṣur, chari]ot dr[iver].

9 [Witness Nabû-šez]ib, [ditto].

10 [Witness Zarutî], cohort commander.

11 [Witness ...]-upahhir.

12 [Month ...], 21st [day, eponym year of Šamaš-ka]šid-ayabi,

14 [Witness A]hi-ṭaba.

15 [Witness Nabû]-nadin-ahhe, scribe.

306. Duplicate of the Previous Text (669)

K 1140

beginning broken away
1 [^{md}PA—EN—PAB LÚ*.NINDA ARAD]-*šú*
2 [*šá* ^{m}*mu*-GI.NA—*aš*]*-šur*

3 [*ú-piš-ma* ^{m}*rém-a*]-⸢*ni*⸣—^{d}10
4 [LÚ.DIB]—⸢KUŠ.PA.MEŠ *dan*⸣-*nu ina* ŠÀ
5 [1 MA].⸢NA⸣ KUG.UD *ina* URU *šá*$^{!}$ *gar-ga-mis*

6 *i-zi-rip i-si-qi kas-pu gam-mur*
7 *ta-ad-din* ARAD *šú-a-tú za-rip*
8 *laq-qi tú-a-ru de-e-nu* DUG$_4$.DUG$_4$

9 *la*-⸢*áš*⸣*-šú man-nu šá ina ur-kiš ina ma-te-ma*
10 *lu-u* ^{m}*mu*-GI.NA—^{d}*aš-šur*
11 *lu-u* DUMU.MEŠ-*šú lu-u* PAB.MEŠ-*šú*
12 TA* ^{m}*rém-a-ni*—^{d}10
13 TA* DUMU.MEŠ-*šú*$^{!}$ *de-e-nu* DUG$_4$.DUG$_4$
14 *ub-ta-ʾu-u-ni*
r.1 [10 MA.NA KUG.UD SUM-*an*] *ina de-ni-šú*
2 [DUG$_4$.DUG$_4$-*ma la*] ⸢TI⸣-*qí*
3 [*ṣib-tú be-nu a-na* 1]-⸢*me*⸣ UD-*me*
4 [*sa-ar-tú ana kàl*] UD.MEŠ

---

5 [IGI ^{md}MAŠ.MAŠ—MAN—PAB L]Ú.3-*šú*
6 [IGI ^{m}*ú-ar-bi*]*-si* LÚ.:
7 [IGI ^{md}*šá-maš*—MAN—PAB LÚ.DIB]—KUŠ. PA.MEŠ
8 [IGI ^{md}PA—*še-zib* LÚ].:
9 [IGI ^{m}NUMUN-*u-ti-i* LÚ.GAL—*ki-ṣi*]*r*
10 [IGI ^{md}*x*—*ú-pa-hí*]*r*
rest broken away

ADD 187

(Beginning destroyed)

1 [Nabû-belu-uṣur, baker, servant] o[f Mukin-Aš]šur —

3 [Rema]nni-Adad, chief [chariot] driver, [has contracted], purchased, and acquired him for [one mi]na of silver by the (mina) of Carchemish.

6 The money is paid completely. That servant is purchased and acquired. Any revocation, lawsuit, or litigation is void.

9 Whoever in the future, at any time, whether Mukin-Aššur or his sons or brothers, seeks a lawsuit or litigation against Remanni-Adad and his sons, [shall pay 10 minas of silver. He shall contest] in his lawsuit [and not] succeed.

r.3 (Guaranteed against) [seizures of epilepsy for 1]00 days [and against fraud fo]rever.

---

5 [Witness Nergal-šarru-uṣur], 'third man.'

6 [Witness Uarbi]si, ditto.

7 [Witness Šamaš-šarru-uṣur, char]iot driver.

8 [Witness Nabû-šezib], ditto.

9 [Witness Zarutî, cohort command]er.

10 [Witness ...-upahhi]r.

(Rest destroyed)

306 Previous editions: AR 465, NALK 240; → ABL 609 (copy). 5 The exceptional spelling URU *šá gar-ga-mis* (the signs URU *šá* transposed for *šá* URU) also appears on the duplicate, no. 305:8. The two texts were apparently not written by the same scribe, however (Coll. T. Kwasman). 10 GI.NA is spaced out.

307. Remanni-Adad Loans Silver (668-II-10)

K 387

1 3 MA.NA KUG.UD.M[EŠ$^{!}$]
2 [*ina* 1 MA.N]A *ša* URU.⌈*gar-ga-mis*⌉
3 [*ša* ^{m}*ré*]*m-a-ni*—^{d}IM LÚ*.[DIB—PA.MEŠ]

4 [*ina* IGI ^{m}*ba-ni*]-*i* LÚ*.2-*u*
5 ⌈*ina* IGI ^{m}⌉*ṭu-si-i* LÚ*.*x*[*x x x*]
6 ^{m}*di-*[*d*]*i-i* LÚ*.*x*[*x x* MÍ-*šú*]
7 *a-na šá-bar-te* GA[R-*nu*]

8 KUG.UD.MEŠ *la i-*[*rab-bi*]
e.9 UD-*mu ša* KUG.UD [SUM-*nu-ni*]
10 UN.MEŠ *ú-*[*še-ṣu-u*]

r.1 IGI ^{m}MAN—DING[IR-*a-a* LÚ*.*x x*]
2 IGI ^{m}*x*[*x x x x x*]
3 IGI ^{m}*ha—ba-a*[*s*$^{!}$*-te* LÚ*.GAL—Ì.DU$_8$]
4 IGI ^{m}*aš-šur*—KAR-*i*[*r*]
5 IGI ^{md}[PA—MU]—PAB$^{!}$ [LÚ*.GAL—Ì.DU$_8$]
6 IGI ^{m}*šúm-mu*—DINGIR LÚ*$^{!}$.[GAL—*ki-ṣir*]

7 ITI.GUD UD-10$^{!}$-K[ÁM$^{!}$]
8e *lim-mu* ^{m}*mar—la-ar-*[*me*]

ADD 65

1 3 minas of silver [by the] mina of Carchemish [belonging to Re]manni-Adad the [chariot driver],

4 [at the disposal of Ban]î, deputy,

5 (and) at the disposal of Ṭusî, [...].

6 Di[d]î, [..., and his wife] are pla[ced] as a pledge.

8 The silver shall not bear in[terest]. On the day that [they pay] the silver, they shall [redeem] the people.

r.1 Witness Šarru-i[la'i].

2 Witness [NN, ...].

3 Witness Haba[sti, head porter].

4 Witness Aššur-eṭ[ir, ...].

5 Witness [Nabû-šumu]-uṣur, [head porter].

6 Witness Šummu-ilu, [cohort commander].

7 Month Iyyar (II), 10th day, eponym year of Mar-lar[im].

308. Remanni-Adad Buys [...] (668?)

Ki 1904-10-9,31

beginning broken away
1′ [*x x x x x*]*x x*[*x x x x x x x*]
2′ [TA* IGI ^{m}*da*$^{?}$]-⌈*di*$^{?}$⌉*-i* [*ina* ŠÀ *x x x x*]
3′ [*il-qi*] *kas-pu g*[*a*$^{!}$*-mur ta-din tu-a-ru*]
4′ [*de-nu*] DUG$_4$.DUG$_4$ *la-*[*áš-šú*]

5′ [*man-nu šá*] *ina ur-kiš ina* [*ma-te-ma*]
6′ [*lu-u* ^{m}U.U$^{?}$]-*i lu-u* DUMU.[MEŠ-*šú*]
7′ [*l*]*u-u* ŠEŠ.MEŠ$^{!}$-*šú lu* LÚ.[*x x x*]
8′ [*l*]*u-u* [*m*]*ám*$^{!}$*-ma*$^{!}$*-nu-šú ša x*[*x x x*]
e.9′ [*man-nu*] *ša* TA* ^{m}*rém-a-ni*—^{d}IM
10′ [DUMU.MEŠ-*šú* DUMU]—DUMU.MEŠ-*šú*
11′ [*de-nu* DUG$_4$.DUG$_4$ *ub-t*]*a-u*$^{!}$*-ni*
12′ [*x* MA.NA KUG.UD] 1 MA.NA KUG.GI
r.1 *ina bur-ki* ^{d}⌈NIN⌉.LÍL *i-šá-kan*
2 2 ANŠE.KUR.RA BABBAR.MEŠ *ina* GÌR.2 *aš-šur i-rak-kas*
3 *kas-pu a-na* 10.MEŠ *a-na* EN.MEŠ-*šú ú*-GUR
4 *ina de-ni-šú* DUG$_4$.DUG$_4$*-ma la i-*⌈*laq*⌉*-qí*

---

5 IGI ^{m}*si-lim—aš-šur* LÚ.SUKKAL GAL-[*ú*]

ADD 1155

(Beginning destroyed)

1 [Remanni-Adad, chief chariot driver, has contracted and bought it from *Da*]*dî* [for ......].

3 The money [is paid] com[pletely. Any revocation, lawsuit], or litigation is v[oid].

5 [Whoever] in the future, at an[y time, whe]ther [*Dad*]î or [his] sons [o]r brothers, or [his ...] or any relative of his, [whoever lodges a complaint and seeks a] law[suit or litigation] against Remanni-Adad, [his sons and grand]sons,

12 shall place [x minas of silver] and one mina of gold in the lap of Mullissu, shall tie two white horses to the feet of Aššur, and shall return the money tenfold to its owners. He shall contest in his lawsuit and not succeed.

---

r.5 Witness Silim-Aššur, grand vizier.

307 Previous editions: AR 141, NALK 242. Collated by I.L. Finkel. 6, r.7 See coll.
308 Previous edition: NALK 284.

6 IGI ^{m}*šúm-mu*—DINGIR LÚ.GAL—*ki-ṣir*
7 IGI ^{m}*hab-as-ti* LÚ.GAL—Ì.DU$_{8}$.M[EŠ]
8 IGI ^{md}PA—MU—PAB LÚ.GAL—Ì.DU$_{8}$.[MEŠ]
9 IGI ^{md}PA—SU LÚ.2-*u ša* GAL—[*ú-rat*]
10 IGI ^{m}NU—MAN—*iq-bi* [*x x x x*]
11 [*x x x x*] ⸢*x x*⸣ [*x x x x*]

6 Witness Šummu-ilu, cohort commander.
7 Witness Habasti, head por[ter].
8 Witness Nabû-šumu-uṣur, head porter.
9 Witness Nabû-eriba, deputy of the te[am-commander].
10 Witness Ṣalam-šarri-iqbi, [...].
(Rest destroyed)

309. Remanni-Adad Buys a Eunuch (667-I)

Bu 91-5-9,179

1 NA$_{4}$.KIŠIB ^{md}UTU—[AD-*u-a*]
2 EN LÚ [SUM-*ni*]

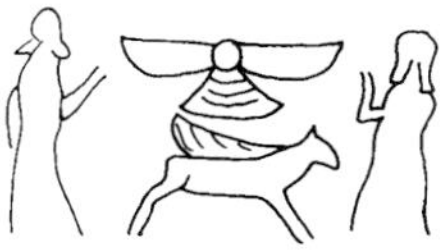

3 ^{m}PAB—*la-mur* LÚ*.⸢SAG⸣
4 LÚ*.ARAD-*šú ša* ^{md}UTU—AD-*u-a*
5 *ú-piš-ma* ^{m}⸢*rém*⸣-*a-na*—^{d}IM
6 LÚ*.*mu-kil*—KUŠ.PA.MEŠ *dan-*⸢*nu*⸣
7 ⸢*ša*⸣ ^{m}*aš-šur*—DÙ—A MAN KUR—*aš-šur*
8 [*ina* ŠÀ *x* M]A!.NA! ⸢KUG⸣.UD *il-qí*
9 [*kas-pu gam-mur*] ⸢*ta*!⸣-*din* L[Ú! *š*]*u*!-*a*!-*tú*
10 [*za-rip laq-qi tu*]-⸢*a*⸣-*ru* [*de-e-nu*]
rest broken away

r.1 [*x* MA.NA KUG.UD *x* MA.NA KUG].⸢GI!⸣
2 [*ina bur-ki* ^{d}]⸢IŠ⸣.TAR
3 ⸢*a-ši-bat* URU.NINA.KI⸣ GAR-*an*
4 *kas-pu ana* 10.MEŠ *a-na* EN.MEŠ-*šú* GUR
5 *ina de-ni-šú* DUG$_{4}$.DUG$_{4}$ *là* TI

6 IGI ^{m}NUMUN-*u-ti-i* LÚ*.DIB—PA.MEŠ *šá* A—MAN
7 IGI ^{md}⸢*šá-maš*⸣—[*šal*!]-⸢*lim*⸣ LÚ*.[:] *šá* É.GAL

8 IGI ^{m}⸢*ba*!⸣-*n*[*i*!-*i*] LÚ*.A.ZU
9 IGI ^{m}⸢*ṣil*!⸣-*la-a-a* LÚ*.DAM.QAR
10 [IG]I ^{md}PA—SU LÚ*.2-*u ša* 0! GAL—*u-rat*.MEŠ

11 IGI ^{m}PAB-*u*—*a-mur* LÚ*.GIŠ.GIGIR
12 IGI ^{m}*šam-šá-ni*—DINGIR LÚ*.GIŠ.GIGIR
13 IGI ^{md}PA—NUMUN!—AŠ ⸢LÚ*.GIŠ.GIGIR⸣

ADD 200

1 Seal of Šamaš-[abu'a], owner of the man [being sold].

(cylinder seal impression)

3 Ahu-lamur, eunuch, servant of Šamaš-abu'a —
5 Remanni-Adad, chief chariot driver of Assurbanipal, king of Assyria, has contracted and bought him [for x mi]nas of silver.
9 [The money] is paid [completely]. That ma[n is purchased and acquired. Any rev]ocation, [lawsuit or litigation is void].
(Break)
r.1 [...] shall place [x minas of silver (and) x minas of go]ld [in the lap of] Ištar residing in Nineveh, and shall return the money tenfold to its owners. He shall contest in his lawsuit and not succeed.

6 Witness Zarutî, chariot driver of the prince.
7 Witness Šamaš-šallim, ditto of the palace.
8 Witness Ban[î], physician.
9 Witness Ṣillayu, merchant.
10 [Wit]ness Nabû-eriba, deputy of the team-commander.
11 Witness Ahû-amur, horse trainer.
12 Witness Šamšanni-ilu, horse trainer.
13 Witness Nabû-zeru-iddina, horse trainer.

309 Previous editions: AR 482, NALK 243. Collations: Assur 2/5.

14 IGI ^{m}NU—MAN—*iq-b[i x x x x]*
15e IGI ^{m}*ia-*⸢*da*⸣*-[x x x x]*
16e ITI.BARAG UD-[*x*-KÁM]
s.1 [*l*]*im-mu* ^{m}*gab-ba-ru*
2 [IGI ^{md}]*gu-la*—NUMUN—KAM-*eš* LÚ*.A.BA

14 Witness Ṣalam-šarri-iqb[i, ...].
15 Witness Yada['-*il*, ...].
16 Month Nisan (I), [...th day], [e]ponym year of Gabbaru.
2 [Witness] Gula-zeru-ereš, scribe.

310. Remanni-Adad Buys a Slave (667-XII-16)

K 372

1 ⸢NA$_4$⸣.KIŠIB ^{md}UTU—DINGIR-*a-a* [LÚ.*x x*]
2 *ša* URU.BÀD—MAN—GIN EN LÚ [SUM-*ni*]

rest broken away

r.1 [*x* MA.NA KUG.G]I$^{!}$ ⸢*ina*$^{!}$ *bur*$^{!}$-*ki*$^{!}$ $^{d!}$15$^{!}$⸣ N[INA$^{!}$.KI]
2 [*i-šak-k*]*an*$^{!}$ *kas-pu ana* 10.MEŠ-*te ana* EN-*šú*
3 [*ú-ta*$^{!}$]-*ra*

4 [IGI ^{m}]⸢*ú*⸣-*a-ar-bi-is* ⸢LÚ.3.U$_5$$^{!}$⸣
5 [IGI] ^{md}UTU—MAN—PAB LÚ.*mu*-DIB—PA.MEŠ
6 IGI ^{m}*sa-kan* LÚ.*mu*-DIB—PA.MEŠ
7 IGI ⸢^{md}⸣PA—*še-zib* LÚ.:
8 IGI ^{m}[^{d}P]A—SU LÚ.2-*u ša* LÚ.GAL—*ú*-⸢*rat*⸣
9 IGI ^{m}*man-nu—ki*—URU.KASKAL LÚ.GIŠ.GIGIR—DU$_8$
10 IGI ^{m}DINGIR$^{!}$—*mu-še-zib* LÚ.:
11 IGI ^{m}⸢*dà*⸣-*ri*—MAN LÚ.:
12 IGI ^{m}AD—NU—ZU LÚ.A.B[A]
13 *ṣa-bit dan-nat šu-*⸢*a*⸣*-[te*$^{!}$]
14 IGI ^{md}15—BÀD LÚ.A.B[A 0$^{?}$]
15 IGI ^{m}*sa-i-*⸢*ru*⸣ LÚ.⸢3⸣.U$_5$-*šú*
16 IGI ^{m}*se-e*$^{\prime!}$—*da-la-a* LÚ.GIŠ$^{!}$.GIGIR$^{!}$—DU$_8$.MEŠ
17 ITI.ŠE UD-16-⸢KÁM⸣
18 *lim-mu* ^{m}*gab-*⸢*ba-ru*⸣
19e [IGI] ^{md}AG—A—AŠ A.BA *ša* MÍ—É.GAL

ADD 185

1 Seal of Šamaš-ila'i, [...] of Dur-Šarruken, owner of the man [being sold].

(cylinder seal impression)

(Break)

r.1 [He shall plac]e [x minas of silver and x minas of gol]d in the lap of Ištar of N[ineveh, and shall ret]urn the money tenfold to its owner.

4 [Witness] Uarbis, 'third man.'
5 [Witness] Šamaš-šarru-uṣur, chariot driver.
6 Witness Sakkannu, chariot driver.
7 Witness Nabû-šezib, ditto.
8 Witness [Na]bû-eriba, deputy of the team-commander.
9 Witness Mannu-ki-Harran, horse trainer of the open chariotry.
10 Witness Ilu-mušezib, ditto.
11 Witness Dari-šarru, ditto.
12 Witness Abi-ul-idi, scribe, keeper of this contract.
14 Witness Issar-duri, scribe.
15 Witness Sa'iru, 'third man.'
16 Witness Se'-dalâ, horse trainer of the open chariotry.
17 Month Adar (XII), 16th day, eponym year of Gabbaru.
19 [Witness] Nabû-aplu-iddina, scribe of the queen.

310 Previous editions: AR 483, NALK 244. Collations: Assur 2/5.

311. Remanni-Adad Buys a House (666-XI-1)

83-1-18,461B

1 [NA$_4$].KIŠIB ^{md}15—BÀD NA$_4$.KIŠIB ^{m}*lu—šá-kin*
2 [D]UMU ^{m}⸢*ab*$^{!}$⸣-*ši-e-šu* LÚ.*mu-ṣur-a-a*
3 EN É SUM-*ni*

---

4 É *ep-šu*$^{!}$ *a-di* GIŠ.ÙR.MEŠ-*šú a-di*
5 GIŠ.IG.MEŠ-*šú ina* URU.É—^{m}SU—DINGIR
6 *qa-an-ni šá* URU.ERIM.MEŠ—^{d}IM
7 *ú-piš-ma* ^{m}*rém-an-ni*—^{d}IM LÚ.DIB—⸢KUŠ.PA⸣.MEŠ
8 *dan-nu ša* ^{m}*aš-šur*—DÙ—A LUGAL KUR—*aš-šur*.KI
9 TA* *pa-an* ^{md}15—BÀD TA* IGI ^{m}*lu—šá-kin*
10 *ina* ŠÀ 4 MA.NA KUG.UD *ina* 1 MA.NA-⸢*e*⸣ *šá* URU.*gar-ga-mis*
11 TI-*qí kas-pu gam-mur ta-ad-din*
12 ⸢É⸣ *za-rip laq-qí tu-a-ru de-e-nu*

13 [DU]G$_4$.DUG$_4$ *la-áš-šú man-nu šá ina ur-kiš*
14 [*ina ma-t*]*e*$^{!}$-*e-ma i-zaq-qup-an-ni*
15 [LÚ.M]EŠ-*e*$^{!}$ ⸢*an-nu*⸣-*te lu-u* ⸢DUMU⸣.M[EŠ$^{!}$-*šú-nu*]
rest broken away
r.1 [IGI ^{m}*p*]*a*$^{!}$-*x*[*x x x*] LÚ.[*x x*]
2 [IGI ^{m}]AD$^{!}$—[*x x*] LÚ.[*x x*]
3 [IGI ^{m}*se-e*]$^{'!}$—DINGIR-*a-a* LÚ.:.
4 [IGI ^{m}*b*]*a*$^{!}$-*hi*$^{!}$-*a-nu*$^{!}$ LÚ.:.

5 IGI ⸢^{md}⸣ŠÚ—*rém-a-ni* ⸢LÚ⸣.:.
6 ⸢PAB⸣ 6 IGI.MEŠ URU.É—^{m}SU—DINGIR-*a-a*
7 IGI ^{md}15—SUM—A LÚ.A.BA *ṣa-bit dan-*⸢*ni*⸣*-te*

8 ITI.ZÍZ UD-1-KÁM *lim-mu* ^{m}⸢ITI.AB⸣-*a-a*
9 LÚ.NAM É—GIBIL

ADD 331

1 Seal of Issar-duri, seal of Lu-šakin, [s]on of Abšiešu the Egyptian, owners of the house being sold.

(blank seal space)

---

4 A built house with its beams and doors in the town Bet-Riba-ilu (on) the outskirts of the city of Ṣab-Adad —

7 Remanni-Adad, chief chariot driver of Assurbanipal, king of Assyria, has contracted and bought it from Issar-duri and Lu-šakin for 4 minas of silver by the mina of Carchemish.

11 The money is paid completely. The house is purchased and acquired. Any revocation, lawsuit, or [liti]gation is void.

13 Whoever in the future, [at any ti]me, lodges a complaint, [whether] these [gentlemen] or [their] so[ns]

(Break)

r.1 [Witness P]a[..., ...].
2 [Witness] Abi-[..., ...].
3 [Witness Se]'-ila'i, ditto.
4 [Witness B]ahianu, ditto.
5 Witness Marduk-remanni, ditto.
6 A total of 6 witnesses from Bet-Riba-ilu.
7 Witness Issar-nadin-apli, scribe, keeper of the contract.
8 Month Shebat (XI), 1st day, eponym year of Kanunayu, governor of the New Palace.

312. Remanni-Adad Buys 5 Servants (666-IV-20)

K 399 (ADD 192) + K 7357 + K 10448 (ADD 529) + K 13056

1 NA$_4$.KIŠIB ^{m}[^{d}EN]—⸢A—AŠ⸣
2 LÚ*.GAL—*z*[*a-ma*]-*ri šá* URU.*tar-bu-si-*⸢*ba*⸣
3 EN LÚ*.UN.[ME]Š *ta-da-a-ni*

ADD 801

1 Seal of [Bel]-aplu-iddina, chief s[ing]er of Til-Barsip, owner of the people being sold.

---

311 Previous editions: AR 356, NALK 245. 2, 4 See coll. 10 The word MA.NA-*e* is preceded by the sign I, as copied by Johns, see coll. 15 No room for [*lu-u*] at the beginning of the line, see coll. r.1ff See coll.
312 Previous editions: AR 65a and 537, NALK 246.

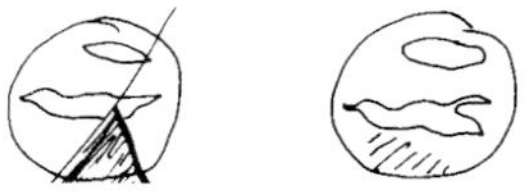

(two stamp seal impressions)

---

4 $^{m!}$[*gab*$^{?}$*-e* LÚ**.ka-ṣir* MÍ*-šú*]
break of about seven lines
12 ⸢*ina* ŠÀ⸣ [3 MA.NA KUG.UD *šá* URU.*gar-g*]*a-mis*

13 *il-*⸢*qi*⸣ [*kas-pu gam-mur ta-ad-din*$^{!}$]
14 LÚ*.⸢UN⸣.[MEŠ *šu-a-tú za-ár-p*]*u*
15 *la-qi-*[*ú tu-a-ru de-e-nu*]

16 DUG$_4$.DUG$_4$ [*la-áš-šú man-nu šá ina ur-ki*]*š*$^{!}$
17 ⸢*ina*⸣ *ma-*⸢*te*⸣*-*[*ma i-za-qu-pa-a-ni*]
e.18 *i-*GIL*-u-ni lu-u* ^{m}⸢EN⸣—A—AŠ
19 ⸢*lu*⸣*-u* DUMU.MEŠ*-šú* :$^{!}$ DUMU—DUMU.MEŠ-⸢*šú*⸣
20 ⸢*lu*⸣*-u* [PAB.MEŠ*-šú* :$^{!}$ DUM]U$^{!}$—PAB.MEŠ*-e-šú*
21 [*l*]*u-u* [*x x x x x x x x x x x x x x*]
r.1 [*lu*]*-u* [*mám-ma-nu-šú ša* TA* ^{m}*rém-a-ni*—^{d}IM]
blank space of two lines
2 [*lu-u* DUMU.MEŠ*-šú* : DUMU—DUMU.MEŠ]-*šú*
3 [*de-e-nu* DUG$_4$.DUG$_4$ *ub-ta-ʾu*]*-u-ni*
4 [*kas-pu a-na* 10.MEŠ*-te a-na* EN].MEŠ*-šú*
two lines broken away

4 [*Gabbê*, tailor; his wife]
(Break)
12 [Remanni-Adad has contracted and] bought them for [3 minas of silver (by the mina) of Carch]emish.
13 [The money is paid completely. Those] people [are purchas]ed and acquir[ed. Any revocation, lawsuit], or litigation [is void.
16 Whoever in the fut]ure, at any ti[me, lodges a complaint] and breaks the contract, whether Bel-aplu-iddina or his sons, grandsons, [brothers or nep]hews, [o]r [..., o]r [any relative of his],

r.1 and [se]eks a lawsuit or litigation [against Remanni-Adad, his sons and grandsons, shall return the money tenfold to] its [own]ers.
(Break)

---

7 [IGI ^{m}*si-lim*—^{d}*aš-šur* LÚ*.SUKKAL *dan*]*-nu*
8 [IGI ^{m}NUMUN*-u-ti-i* LÚ**.mu-kil*—KU]Š.PA.MEŠ *šá* DUMU—[MAN]
9 [IGI ^{m}NUMUN*-u-ti-i* LÚ*.GAL—*ki-ṣi*]*r*$^{!}$ *šá* (DUMU)—MAN

10 [IGI ^{md}*šá-maš*]—MAN—⸢PAB⸣ LÚ**.mu-kil*—PA.⸢MEŠ⸣
11 [IGI ^{m}*sa-ka*]*n*$^{!}$*-nu* LÚ**.mu-k*[*il*—PA.MEŠ]
12 [IGI ^{md}P]A—SU LÚ*.⸢2⸣-[*u*]
13 ⸢*ša*⸣ LÚ*.⸢GAL⸣—*ú-ra*[*t*]
14 IGI ^{m}*aš-šur*—DINGIR*-a-a* DUMU$^{!}$ [^{m}]MAN—DÙ$^{!}$
15 IGI $^{md!}$U.GUR—MAN—PAB
16 ⸢*ša*$^{!}$⸣ LÚ*$^{!}$.MAH$^{!}$ URU [*šá* UR]U.*tar-bu-si-ba*
17 ITI.ŠU UD-20-⸢KÁM⸣
18 *lim-mu* ^{m}ITI.AB*-a-*⸢*a*⸣
19 ⸢*ša*⸣ É—G[IBI]L

r.7 [Witness Silim-Aššur, gr]and [vizier].
8 [Witness Zarutî, chariot] driver of the [prince].
9 [Witness Zarutî , cohort comman]der of the prince.
10 [Witness Šamaš]-šarru-uṣur, chariot driver.
11 [Witness Sakkan]nu, chariot dri[ver].
12 [Witness Na]bû-eriba, deputy of the team-com[mander].
14 Witness Aššur-ila'i, son of Šarru-ibni.
15 Witness Nergal-šarru-uṣur, (son) of the city emissary of Til-Barsip.
17 Month Tammuz (IV), 20th day, eponym year of Kanunayu of the N[ew] Palace.

313. Duplicate of the Previous Text (666-IV-20)

K 347

1 [NA$_4$.KIŠIB ^{md}EN]—A—AŠ LÚ.GAL
2 [LÚ.*za-ma-r*]*i*$^{!}$ ⸢*šá*⸣ URU.*tar-bu-si-e*
3 [EN U]N.MEŠ *ta-da-a-ni*

ADD 258

1 [Seal of Bel]-aplu-iddina, chief [singe]r of Til-Barsip, [owner of the pe]ople being sold.

313 Previous editions: AR 65b, NALK 247; → KB 4 (1896) 134-135. Collations: Assur 2/5. → no. 312.

---

4 [^{m}*gab*$^{?}$]-*e* LÚ.*ka-ṣir* MÍ-*šú*
5 [AMA]-⸢*šu*$^{!}$⸣ 2 DUMU.MEŠ-*šu* PAB 5 ZI.MEŠ
6 [ARAD.M]EŠ *šá* ^{md}EN—A—SUM-*na*
7 [*ú-pi*]*š-ma* ^{m}*rém-a-ni*—^{d}IM
8 [LÚ.*mu-kil*]—KUŠ.PA.MEŠ *šá* MAN TA* IGI
9 [^{md}EN]—A—AŠ *i-na* ŠÀ 3 MA.NA
10 [KUG.UD *šá* URU.*g*]*ar-ga-*⸢*mis*⸣ TI-*qí*

11 [*kas-pu gam-m*]*ur* ⸢*ta-ad-din*⸣
12 [UN.MEŠ *š*]*u-a-*⸢*tú*⸣ *za-á*[*r*$^{!}$*-p*]*u*
13 [*la-qí-u tu-a*]-*ru*$^{!}$ *de*$^{!}$-⸢*e*$^{!}$⸣-[*nu*]

14 [DUG$_4$.DUG$_4$ *la-áš-šú*] ⸢*man*$^{!}$⸣-*nu* [*šá ina ur-kiš*]
rest broken away
Rev. beginning broken away
1′ [LÚ.2-*u šá*] ⸢LÚ⸣.G[AL—*u-rat*]
2′ [IGI ^{m}*aš*]-⸢*šur*⸣—DINGIR-*a-a* DUMU [^{m}MAN]—D[Ù$^{!}$]
3′ [IGI ^{m}]^{d}U.GUR—MAN—PAB ⸢A⸣ LÚ.MAH

4′ [*š*]*á* URU.*tar-bu-si-e*$^{!}$ ITI.ŠU
5′ [UD-2]0-KÁM *lim-mu* ^{m}ITI.AB-*a-a*
6′ *šá* É—GIBIL

(space for stamp seal impressions)

---

4 [*Gabb*]*ê*, tailor, his wife, [mother], and two sons, a total of 5 persons, [servan]ts of Bel-aplu-iddina —

7 Remanni-Adad, [chariot] driver of the king, [has contr]acted and bought them from [Bel]-aplu-iddina for 3 minas of [silver] (by the mina) of Carchemish.

11 [The money] is paid [complete]ly. Those [people] are purch[ased and acquired. Any rev]ocation, lawsu[it, or litigation is void].

14 [Who]ever [in the future]
(Break)

r.1 [deputy of] the tea[m-commander].

2 [Witness Aš]šur-ila'i, son of [Šarru]-ib[ni].

3 [Witness] Nergal-šarru-uṣur, son of the emissary [o]f Til-Barsip.

4 Month Tammuz (IV), [2]0th [day], eponym year of Kanunayu of the New Palace.

314. Remanni-Adad Buys an Estate in Ispallurê (666-XI-10)

K 1499

1 [NA$_4$].KIŠIB ^{m}*ba-ri-ki* LÚ.GA[L—*x x*]
2 NA$_4$.KIŠIB ^{m}*a-ba—il* 0$^{!}$ [*x x*$^{!}$]
3 EN UN.MEŠ GIŠ.SAR.MEŠ É.MEŠ [SUM-*ni*]

---

4 1 GIŠ.SAR 1-*lim* GIŠ$^{!}$.*til*$^{!}$-*lit*$^{!}$ [*ina* KUR.*i-za-li*]
5 SUHUR GIŠ.SAR *šá* ^{m}⸢*x*⸣[*x x x x*]
6 2-*u* GIŠ.SAR ⸢2$^{!}$⸣-[*l*]*i*[*m*$^{!}$ GIŠ.*til-lit x x*]
7 [*x x x x x x x x x x*]

8 [PAB 2] GIŠ.SAR [0] 3$^{!}$-*l*[*im* GIŠ.*til-lit*]
9 [0 ^{m}*b*]*a*$^{!}$-*al*$^{!}$-*su*$^{!}$-*ri* L[Ú$^{!}$.NU.GIŠ.SAR]
10 [MÍ]-⸢*šú*$^{!}$⸣ DUMU-*šú*$^{!}$ DUMU.MÍ-*su* ^{m}*x*[*x x x*]

11 ⸢PAB⸣ 7 ZI.MEŠ 2 É.MEŠ 2 GIŠ.S[AR.MEŠ]
12 GIŠ.*til-lit*.MEŠ 4 NA$_4$.*i*$^{!}$-*ga-*[*ra-te*]
13 *ina*$^{!}$ KUR$^{!}$.*i-za-li š*[*á*$^{!}$] ^{m}*ba-ri-k*[*i ù* ^{m}*a-ba—il*]
14 *ina* URU.*is-pal-lu-r*[*e*$^{!}$-*e x x x x*]

ADD 448

1 [Se]al of Bariki, chie[f ...], seal of Abail,

3 owners of the people, vineyards and houses [being sold].

(space for stamp seal impressions)

---

4 A vineyard of 1,000 vines [in Izalla], adjoining the vineyard of [NN];

6 A second vineyard of 2,00[0 vines *in ..., adjoining the vineyard of NN*];

8 [a total of two] vineyards (with) 3,0[00 vines];

9 [B]a'al-suri, g[ardener], his [wife], son, and daughter; [NN, his *wife* and ...];

11 in all 7 persons, two houses, two vineyards and 4 stone wal[ls] in Izalla [belonging to] Barik[i and Abail], in the town Ispallur[ê ...] —

314 Previous editions: AR 443, NALK 265. Collations: Assur 2/5.

15 *ú-piš-ma* ^{m}*rém-an-ni*—$^{⸢d⸣}$[IM LÚ.DIB—KUŠ.PA.MEŠ]
16 *dan-nu šá* ^{m}*aš-šur*—DÙ—A MAN KUR—*aš-šur*.[KI]
17 TA* IGI ^{m}*ba-ri-ki* TA* [IGI ^{m}*a-ba—il*]
18 TI-*qí kas-pu gam-mur ta*-[*din* UN.MEŠ GIŠ.SAR.MEŠ]
19 É.MEŠ NA$_4$.*i*$^{!}$-*ga-r*[*a*$^{!}$-*te šú-a-tú zar-pu*]
20 *laq-qi-u tú-a-ru d*[*e-nu* DUG$_4$.DUG$_4$ *la-áš-šú*]
21 *man-nu šá ina ur-kiš ina ma*-[*te-e-ma i-zaq-qup-an-ni*]
22 *lu-u* ^{m}*ba-ri-ki l*[*u-u* ^{m}*a-ba—il*]
e.23 *lu-u* DUMU.MEŠ-*šú*-⸢*nu*⸣ [*lu-u* DUMU—DUMU.MEŠ-*šú-nu*]
24 *lu-u* PAB.MEŠ-*šú-nu lu-u* DU[MU—PAB.MEŠ-*šú-nu*]
r.1 *lu-u* LÚ.EN.NA[M$^{!}$-*su-nu x x x x*]
2 *lu-u mám-ma-nu-šú-nu* ⸢*šá*$^{!}$⸣ [TA* ^{m}*rém-an-ni*—^{d}IM]
3 DUMU.MEŠ-*šú* DUMU—DUMU.MEŠ-*šú de*$^{!}$-[*nu* DUG$_4$.DUG$_4$]
4 *ub-ta-u-ni* 1 GÚ.UN KUG.[UD LUH-*u* 1 MA.NA KUG.GI]
5 *sak-ru ina bur-ki* ^{d}IŠ.T[AR$^{!}$ *a-ši-bat*]
6 URU.NINA GAR-*an kas-pu a-na* ⸢10⸣.[MEŠ *a-na* EN-*šú* GUR-*ra*]
7 *ina de-ni-šú* DUG$_4$.DUG$_4$-*ma* [*la i-laq-qi*]

---

8 ⸢IGI ^{m}*šum-ma*⸣—^{d}*aš-šur* LÚ.EN.NAM [*x x x*]
9 IGI ^{md}MAŠ.MAŠ—MAN—PAB LÚ.3-*šú* [*dan-nu*]
10 IGI ^{m}*sa-si-i* LÚ.*ha-za-nu* UR[U$^{!}$.*x x*]
11 IGI ^{md}15—MU—KAM-*eš* LÚ.GAL—⸢A$^{!}$⸣.[BA]
12 [IGI ^{m}]^{d}IM—MU—PAB LÚ.GAL—[MAŠ.MAŠ$^{?}$]
13 [IGI ^{m}M]U$^{!}$-*a-a* DUMU $^{m⸢d!⸣}$[PA—NUMUN—GIŠ]
14 [IGI ^{md}PA—SU]M$^{!}$—MU LÚ.[*x x x*]
15 [IGI ^{m}*x x x x x x x x x x*]
16 ⸢IGI $^{m⸣d}$*šá-ma*[*š*—MAN—PAB LÚ.DIB—KUŠ.PA.MEŠ]
17 IGI ^{md}PA—*še-zib* ⸢LÚ⸣.[DIB—KUŠ.PA.MEŠ]
18 IGI ^{md}PA—SU LÚ.⸢2$^{!}$⸣-[*u šá* LÚ.GAL—*ú-rat*]
19 IGI ^{md}15—MU—AŠ LÚ.[*x x x x*]
20 IGI ^{m}PAB—*la-mur* IGI ^{m}[*x x x x x*]
21 IGI ^{m}*a-qa-ba* IGI ^{m}*ba*-[*x x x*]
22 IGI ^{m}*bar-zi-ku-tú* ^{m}*b*[*u-x x x x*]
23 IGI ^{m}PAB—BÀD PAB 7 IGI.ME[Š URU.*is-pal-lu-ra-a-a*]
24 IGI ^{md}15—MU—A LÚ.[A.BA *ṣa-bit dan-ni-te*]
25 ITI.ZÍZ UD-10-KÁM *lim*$^{!}$-*mu*$^{!}$ [^{m}ITI.AB-*a-a* É—

15 Remanni-[Adad], chief [chariot driver] of Assurbanipal, king of Assyria, has contracted and bought (said property) from Bariki and [Abail].

18 The money is p[aid] completely. [Those people, vineyards], houses, and stone wal[ls are purchased] and acquired. Any revocation, law[suit, or litigation is void].

21 Whoever in the future, at any ti[me, lodges a complaint], whether Bariki [or Abail] or their sons, [grandsons], brothers or nep[hews], or [their] governor, [...] or relative, and seeks a law[suit or litigation against Remanni-Adad] and his sons and grandsons,

r.4 shall place one talent of [refined] sil[ver and one mina of] pure [gold] in the lap of Iš[tar residing] in Nineveh, and [shall return] the money ten[fold to its owner]. He shall contest in his lawsuit and [not succeed].

---

8 Witness Šumma-Aššur, governor of [...].

9 Witness Nergal-šarru-uṣur, [chief] 'third man.'

10 Witness Sasî, mayor of [...].

11 Witness Issar-šumu-ereš, chief scr[ibe].

12 [Witness] Adad-šumu-uṣur, chief [*exorcist*].

13 [Witness Šu]maya son of [Nabû-zeru-lešir].

14 [Witness Nabû-nad]in-šumi, [... exorcist].

15 [Witness ......].

16 Witness Šama[š-šarru-uṣur, chariot driver].

17 Witness Nabû-šezib, [chariot driver].

18 Witness Nabû-eriba, depu[ty of the team-commander].

19 Witness Issar-šumu-iddina, [...].

20 Witness Ahu-lamur. Witness [NN].

21 Witness Aqaba. Witness Ba[...].

22 Witness Barzikutu. B[u...].

23 Witness Ahu-duri, a total of 7 witnesses [from Ispallurê].

24 Witness Issar-nadin-apli, [scribe, keeper of the contract].

25 Month Shebat (XI), 10th day, eponym

GIBIL]
26e [IGI ^{m}*x x*—^{d}]IM L[Ú.*x x x x*]
27e [IGI ^{md}PA—*r*]*e-eh-tú*—PAB [0$^{?}$]
28e [IGI ^{m}]*aš-šur*—KI-*iá* IGI ^{m}[*x x x*]
s.1 LÚ.3-*šú* IGI ^{m}PAB—[*x*]⸢*x x*⸣ [LÚ.A.BA] *ár-ma-a-a*

year of [Kanunayu of the New Palace].
26 [Witness ...]-Adad, [...].
27 [Witness Nabû-r]ehtu-uṣur.
28 [Witness] Aššur-isse'a. Witness [NN], 'third man.'
s.1 Witness Ahu-[...], Aramean [scribe].

315. Remanni-Adad Buys Land and Personnel (666-XII-1)

K 306

beginning broken away
space for seal impressions
1′ É ⸢60 ANŠE⸣ [A.ŠÀ *ina* GIŠ.BÁN *ša* 10 *qa*]
2′ É *tal-pi-tú a-*⸢*na gi*⸣-[*mir-ti-šá*]
3′ É 2BÁN *ad-ru i-na* URU.DUL—*na-h*[*i-ri*]

4′ ^{m}*qar-ha-a* LÚ.ENGAR ^{m}*e*$^{!}$-*ni*—D[INGIR$^{!}$]
5′ 1 DUMU *pir-su* ^{m}*ab-šá-a* ŠEŠ-*š*[*ú*$^{!}$]
6′ MÍ.*pa-pa*$^{!}$-*a* AMA-*šú*$^{!}$-*nu* PAB 5 ZI.[MEŠ]
7′ É 60 ANŠE A.ŠÀ É *tal-pi-t*[*ú*$^{!}$]
8′ *a-na gi-mir-ti-šá ú-piš-m*[*a*]
9′ ^{m}*rém-a-ni*—^{d}IM LÚ.DIB—KUŠ.[PA.MEŠ]
10′ [*ša*] $^{m!}$*aš-šur*—DÙ—A LUGAL KUR—*aš-šur*. K[I$^{!}$]
11′ [TA* IG]I ^{md}*nu-uš-hu*—*sa-l*[*ìh*$^{?}$-*an-ni*]
12′ [*ina* ŠÀ *x* M]A.NA KUG.UD *ina* 1 MA.NA-*e*
13′ [*ša*] ⸢URU⸣.*gar-ga-mis* TI-*qí*
14′ [*kas*]-⸢*pu*⸣ *gam-mur ta-ad-*[*di*]*n*$^{!}$
15′ [A.ŠÀ.MEŠ] ⸢É⸣ UN.MEŠ *šu-*⸢*a*⸣-[*tu*]
16′ [*za-a*]*r*$^{!}$-*pu* ⸢*la*$^{!}$⸣-*q*[*í*$^{!}$-*u*]
rest broken away
Rev. beginning broken away
1′ [IGI ^{m}]PAB—*la-maš-ši* L[Ú$^{!}$.3.U_5]
2′ [IGI] ^{m}*se-e*ʾ—*ha-ri* LÚ.[:]
3′ IGI ^{md}PA—SU LÚ.2-*u* LÚ.GAL—[*ú-rat*]

4′ IGI ^{m}*man-nu*—*ki*-⸢*i*—URU⸣.KASKAL LÚ*$^{!}$.GIŠ.G[IGIR—DU_8.MEŠ]
5′ IGI ^{m}*se-e*ʾ—*dàl-a*$_4$:$^{!}$
6′ IGI ^{m}I—^{d}10 ⸢:$^{!}$⸣ [0]
7′ IGI ^{md}15—SUM$^{!}$—A LÚ$^{!}$.A.⸢BA⸣ [*ṣa-bit dan-ni-te*]

8′ ITI.ŠE UD-1-KÁM *lim-mu* ^{m}ITI.AB-[*a-a*]
9′ É—GIBIL

ADD 420

(Beginning destroyed)
(blank seal space)
1 An estate of 60 hectares [of land by the seah of 10 'litres'], a *barnyard* in [its] enti[rety], (and) a plot of 2 decares, a threshing floor, in Til-Nahiri;
4 Qarhâ , farmer, Eni-i[l], a weaned boy, Abšâ, h[is] brother, and Papâ, their mother;
6 in all 5 pers[ons], an estate of 60 hectares of land and a *barnyard* in its entirety —
9 Remanni-Adad, chariot dri[ver of A]ssurbanipal, king of Assyria, has contracted and bought (said property) [fro]m Nušhu-sall[ihanni for x min]as of silver by the mina [of] Carchemish.
14 [The mon]ey is paid completely. Those [fields], buildings, and people [are purchas]ed and acqu[ired].
(Break)
r.1 [Witness] Ahu-lâmašši, ['third man'].
2 [Witness] Se'-hari, [ditto].
3 Witness Nabû-eriba, deputy team-c[ommander].
4 Witness Mannu-ki-Harran, horse tr[ainer of open chariotry].
5 Witness Se'-dalâ, ditto.
6 Witness Na'di-Adad, ditto.
7 Witness Issar-nadin-apli, scribe, [keeper of the contract].
8 Month Adar (XII), 1st day, eponym year of Kanun[ayu] of the New Palace.

315 Previous editions: AR 100, NALK 248; → KB 4 (1896) 134-137. Collations: Assur 2/5. r.7 Issar-nadin-apli is the scribe of the duplicate. However, the tablets were (according to Kwasman) apparently written by two different persons.

316. Duplicate of the Previous Contract (666-XII-1)

81-7-27,28

1 [NA$_4$.KIŠIB] ^{md}*nu-uš-hu—sa-lìh*$^!$*-an-[ni]*
2 [LÚ.G]IŠ.GIGIR—DU$_8$.MEŠ EN A.ŠÀ UN.MEŠ ⌈SUM-*ni*⌉

---

3 [É 60 ANŠE] A.ŠÀ *ina* GIŠ.BÁN *ša* 10 *qa*.MEŠ
4 [É *tal-pi-tú*] *a-na gi-mir-ti-šú*
5 [É 2BÁN *ad-r*]*u ina* URU.DUL—*na-hi-*⌈*ri*⌉

6 [^{m}*qar-ha-a* LÚ.ENGAR ^{m}]⌈*e*$^!$⌉*-n*[*i*$^!$—DINGIR DUMU *pir-su*]
7 [^{m}*ab-šá-a* Š]EŠ-⌈*šú* MÍ⌉.*p*[*a-pa-a* AMA-*šú-nu*]
8 [PAB 5 ZI.M]EŠ É 60 [ANŠE A.ŠÀ]
9 [É *ta*]*l*$^!$-⌈*pi*⌉*-tu* [*a-na gi-mir-ti-šú*]
10 [*ú-piš-m*]*a* [^{m}*rém-a-ni*—^{d}IM]
rest broken away
r.1 [*ina de-ni*]-⌈*šú*$^!$⌉ D[UG$_4$$^!$.DUG$_4$*-ma la* TI]

---

2 [IG]I ^{m}*si-lim—aš-šur* [LÚ.SUKKAL *dan-nu*]
3 [IGI ^{m}]^d*šá-maš*—MAN—PAB LÚ.DIB—KUŠ.⌈PA.MEŠ⌉
4 [IGI] ^{md}PA—*še-zib* :.
5 [IGI] ^{m}*šum-ma*—DINGIR.MEŠ*-ni* :.
6 [IG]I ⌈^{m}⌉*bar-ru-qu* :.
7 [IGI] ⌈^{m}⌉*sa-ak-kan* :.
8 [IGI] ⌈^{m}⌉PAB—*la-maš-ši* LÚ.3.U$_5$
9 [IGI ^{m}]*se-e*ʾ—*ha-ri* :.
10 [IGI ^{m}]⌈^{d}⌉PA—SU LÚ.2-*u* LÚ.GAL—*ú-rat*

11 [IGI ^{m}*man*]-⌈*nu—ki*⌉—URU.KASKAL LÚ*.GIŠ.GIGIR—DU$_8$.MEŠ
12 [IGI ^{m}*se*]-⌈*e*ʾ⌉—*dàl-a*$_4$ ⌈:.⌉
13 [IGI ^{m}I]—⌈^{d}⌉IM :
14 [IGI ^{md}15—SU]M$^!$—A LÚ*.A.BA *ṣa-bit dan-ni-*⌈*te*⌉

15e [ITI.ŠE U]D-1-KAM *li-mu*
16e [^{m}IT]I.AB*-a-a* É—⌈GIBIL⌉

ADD 421

1 [Seal] of Nušhu-sallihan[ni, hor]se trainer of the open chariotry, owner of the land and people being sold.

(stamp seal impressions)

---

3 [An estate of 60 hectares] of land by the seah of 10 'litres,' [a *barnyard*] in its entirety, [and a plot of 2 decares, a thres]hing floor, in Til-Nahiri;

6 [Qarhâ, farmer], En[i-il, a weaned boy, Absâ] his brother, and P[apâ, their mother;

8 in all 5 person]s, an estate of 60 [hectares of land, and a *barn*]*yard* [in its entirety] —

10 [Remanni-Adad ... has contracted a]nd

(Break)

r.1 He shall [contest in] his [lawsuit and not succeed].

---

2 [Witne]ss Silim-Aššur, [grand vizier].

3 [Witness] Šamaš-šarru-uṣur, chariot driver.

4 [Witness] Nabû-šezib, ditto.

5 [Witness] Šumma-ilani, ditto

6 [Witne]ss Barruqu, ditto.

7 [Witness] Sakkannu, ditto.

8 [Witness] Ahu-lâmašši, 'third man.'

9 [Witness] Se'-hari, ditto.

10 [Witness] Nabû-eriba, deputy team-commander.

11 [Witness Man]nu-ki-Harran, horse trainer of the open chariotry.

12 [Witness Se]'-dalâ, ditto.

13 [Witness Na'di]-Adad, ditto.

14 [Witness Issar-nad]in-apli, scribe, keeper of the contract.

15 [Month Ab] (V), 1st [d]ay, eponym year of [Ka]nunayu of the New Palace.

316 Previous editions: AR 100a, NALK 249. Collations: Assur 2/5.

317. Remanni-Adad Loans Silver against Pledge (666)

Bu 89-4-26,7	ADD 60
1 [NA$_4$.KIŠIB ^{md}]NU—LUGAL—*iq-bi* L[Ú.*x x*] 2 [NA$_4$.KIŠIB ^{m}]⸢I$^{!}$⸣—^{d}MAŠ LÚ.*da-gíl—a*$^{!}$-[*x x*] 3 [LÚ.ARAD.MEŠ]-*ni šá* ^{md}NU—LUG[AL—*iq-bi u* ^{m}I—^{d}MAŠ] 4 [*ku-um* 1 1/2 MA].⸢NA⸣ KUG.UD *a-na šá-pa*[*r-ti ina* IGI ^{m}*rém-a-ni*—^{d}IM]	1 [Seal of] Ṣalam-šarri-iqbi, [..., seal of] Na'di-Inurta, *aug*[*ur*]. 3 [The serv]ants of Ṣalam-šar[ri-iqbi and Na'di-Inurta are placed] as a pled[ge in lieu of 1 1/2 mi]nas of silver [at the disposal of Remanni-Adad],
	(space for stamp seal impressions)
5 LÚ.DIB—KUŠ.PA.MEŠ *dan-nu šá* LUGA[L$^{!}$ *šak-nu*] 6 ⸢*man*⸣-*nu šá* 1 1/2 MA.NA KUG.UD.MEŠ *a-na* ^{m}*rém-*[*a-ni*—^{d}IM] 7 [*i*]*d-dan-u-ni* LÚ.ARAD.MEŠ-*šú* ⸢*ú*⸣-[*še-ṣa*] 8 [IG]I ^{md}UTU—MAN—PAB LÚ.DIB—KUŠ.P[A.MEŠ *šá* DUMU-MAN] 9 [IG]I ^{m}BE-*ma*—DINGIR.MEŠ-*ni* LÚ.: [:.] 10 [IG]I ^{m}*bar-ruq-qu* LÚ.: [:.] e.11 [IG]I ^{m}*sa-*⸢*ak*⸣-*kan* LÚ.:. :.$^{!}$ 12 IGI ^{md}PA—NUMUN$^{!}$—AŠ LÚ.:. :. r.1 IGI ^{md}30—MAŠ LÚ.3-*šú dan-nu šá* DUMU—MAN 2 IGI ^{m}PAB—*la-maš-ši* LÚ.3-*šú šá* MAN 3 IGI ^{md}PA—SU$^{!}$ LÚ.2-*u šá* LÚ*.GAL—⸢*ú*⸣-[*rat*]	5 chief chariot driver of the ki[ng]. 6 Whoever pays the 1 1/2 minas of silver to Rem[anni-Adad], shall [redeem] his servants. 8 [Wit]ness Šamaš-šarru-uṣur, chariot dr[iver of the prince]. 9 [Wit]ness Šumma-ilani, ditto [ditto]. 10 [Wit]ness Barruqu, ditto [ditto]. 11 [Wit]ness Sakkannu, ditto ditto. 12 Witness Nabû-zeru-iddina, ditto ditto. r.1 Witness Sin-ašared, chief 'third man' of the prince. 2 Witness Ahu-lâmašši, 'third man' of the prince. 3 Witness Nabû-eriba, deputy of the te[am]-commander.
! !	(space for stamp seal impressions)
4 [IG]I ^{md}PA—NUMUN—AŠ LÚ.GIŠ.GIGIR—DU$_8$.MEŠ 5 [IG]I ^{m}⸢I⸣—^{d}IM LÚ.⸢:.⸣ 6 [IGI ^{m}*x x*—A]Š$^{!}$ LÚ.⸢:.$^{!}$⸣ 7 [IGI ^{m}*ba*]-*ni-i ṣa-bit e-gír-*[*ti*] 8 [ITI.*x* UD-*x*]4$^{!}$-KÁM *lim-me* ^{m}ITI.AB-*a-*[*a*] 9 [*šá* É—GIBI]L IGI ^{m}*na-di-nu* LÚ.A.BA *šá* LU[GAL]	4 [Wit]ness Nabû-zeru-iddina, horse trainer of the open chariotry. 5 [Wit]ness Na'di-Adad, ditto. 6 [Witness ...-id]dina, ditto. 7 [Witness Ba]nî, keeper of the document. 8 [Month ....]th day, eponym year of Kanuna[yu of the New Pala]ce. 9 Witness Nadinu, scribe of the ki[ng].

317 Previous editions: AR 153, NALK 236. Collations: Assur 2/5. 3 Since *dāgil iṣṣūri* "augur" is the only NA profession beginning with *dāgil*, the end of the line is possibly to be restored *a-*[*ṣu-ri*], an otherwise unattested syllabic spelling of *iṣṣūru* rendering spoken /*eṣṣūri*/.

318. Remanni-Adad Loans 10 Minas of Silver (665-X-22)

K 365

1 [N]A$_4$.KIŠIB ^{m}*man-nu—ki-i*—PAB LÚ.2-*u arrap*$^{!}$-*ha*$^{!}$
2 [N]A$_4$.KIŠIB ^{md}PA—MAŠ 10 MA.NA KUG.UD
3 [S]AG.DU *ina* 1 MA.NA-*e šá* URU.*gar-ga-mis*
4 *ša* ^{m}*rém-an*$^{!}$-*ni*—^{d}IM LÚ.DIB—KUŠ.PA.MEŠ *dan-nu*

5 ⌜*ina* IGI-*šú-nu ina* ITI⌝.BARAG SAG.DU KUG.UD SUM-*nu*
6 [BE-*ma la* SU]M-*nu* KUG.UD *a-na* 4-*ti-šú i-rab-bi*
7 [IGI ^{m}*bar-ru*]-*qu* LÚ.DIB—KUŠ.PA.MEŠ
e.8 [IGI ^{m}*sa-k*]*an* LÚ.:
9 [IGI ^{md}PA—NUMUN—SU]M-*na* LÚ.:
r.1 [IGI ^{m}*x x x* L]Ú.SAG
1 line blank
2 IGI ^{md}PA—ŠU.2—*ṣa-bat* LÚ.SAG
3 IGI ^{m}SUHUŠ—*aš-šur* LÚ.*rak-su*
4 ITI.AB UD-22-KÁM *lim-mu* ^{m}*man-nu—ki*—MAN

ADD 35

1 [S]eal of Mannu-ki-ahi, deputy (governor) of Arrapha; [s]eal of Nabû-ašared.

2 10 minas of silver, [ca]pital, by the mina of Carchemish, belonging to Remanni-Adad, chief chariot driver,

(blank seal space)

5 at their disposal. They shall pay back the capital of the silver in Nisan (I). [If they do not pa]y, the silver shall increase by a fourth.

7 [Witness Barru]qu, chariot driver.

8 [Witness Sakk]annu, ditto.

9 [Witness Nabû-zeru-idd]ina, ditto.

r.1 [Witness NN], eunuch.

2 Witness Nabû-qati-ṣabat, eunuch.

3 Witness Ubru-Aššur, *conscript.*

4 Month Tebet (X), 22nd day, eponym year of Mannu-ki-šarri.

319. Remanni-Adad Buys Two Slaves (665-XI-10)

82-5-22,29

1 NA$_4$.KIŠIB ^{m}*se—na-tan*
2 EN UN.MEŠ SUM-*ni*

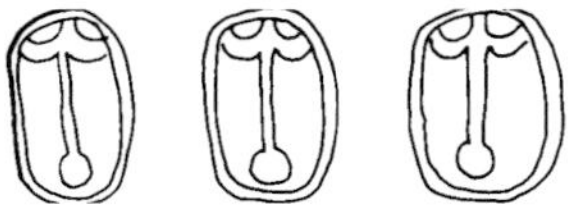

3 ^{m}*di-na-na* MÍ.*ga-bi-a* MÍ-*šú*
4 PAB 2 ZI LÚ.ARAD.MEŠ$^{!}$ *ša* ^{m}*se—na-tan*
5 *ú-piš-ma* ^{m}*rém-an-ni*—^{d}IM LÚ.*mu*$^{!}$-*kil*$^{!}$—KUŠ.PA.MEŠ

6 *ina* ŠÀ-*bi* 1 MA.NA KUG.UD *il-qi kas-pu ga-mur*
7 *ta-din*$^{!}$ UN.MEŠ *za-ár-pu la-qí-u*
8 *tu-a-ru de-e-ni* DUG$_4$.DUG$_4$ *la-áš-šú*
9 *man-nu ša ina ur-kiš ma-te-me*
10 *lu-u* ^{m}*se—na-tan lu-u mám-ma-nu-š*[*ú*]
11 *ša i-zaq-qu-*⌜*pa*⌝-*ni*
12 GIL-*u-ni de-e-ni* DUG$_4$.DU[G$_4$]
13 TA* ^{m}*rém-an-ni*—^{d}IM ⌜*ù*$^{!}$⌝ [DUMU.MEŠ-*šú*]

ADD 237

1 Seal of Se'-natan, owner of the people being sold.

(stamp seal impressions)

3 Dinana and Gabiya, his wife, a total of 2 persons, servants of Se'-natan —

5 Remanni-Adad, chariot driver, has contracted and bought them for one mina of silver.

6 The money is paid completely. The people are purchased and acquired. Any revocation, lawsuit, or litigation is void.

9 Whoever in the future, at any time, whether Se'-natan or his relative, lodges a complaint and breaks the contract and seeks a lawsuit or litiga[tion] against Remanni-

318 Previous editions: AR 262, NALK 250. Collated by I.L. Finkel. 1 See coll.
319 Previous editions: AR 71, NALK 251. Collations: Assur 2/5.

14 *ub-ta-ʾu-u-*[*ni*]
r.1 1 MA.NA KUG.UD 1 [MA.NA KUG.GI]
2 *ina bur-ki* ^{d}⸢GAŠAN$^{!}$—NINA$^{!}$⸣.[KI GAR-*an*]
3 *kas-pi a-na* 10.MEŠ-*te a-n*[*a*$^{!}$ EN-*šú* GUR-*ra*]
4 *ina de-ni-šú* DUG$_4$.DUG$_4$ *la* TI

Adad and [his sons], [r.1] [shall place] one mina of silver (and) one [mina of gold] in the lap of the Lady of Nineveh, [and shall return] the money tenfold t[o its owner]. He shall contest in his lawsuit and not [succeed].

---

5 IGI ^{m}EN—DUMU.UŠ—SUM-*na* LÚ.EN.N[AM$^{!}$ *x x*]
6 IGI ^{md}30—AD—PAB LÚ.[*x x*]
7 IGI ^{md}U$^{!}$.GUR$^{!}$—LUGAL—PAB LÚ.*šá*—UGU—URU
8 IGI ^{m}*ki-ṣir—aš-šur*$^{!}$ LÚ$^{!}$.*ha*$^{!}$*-za*$^{!}$*-nu*$^{!}$
9 IGI ^{m}*al*$^{!}$—DINGIR—*mil-ki* DUMU ^{m}EN—ZALÁG
10 IGI ^{m}EN—*tak-lak*

11 IGI ^{m}*ri-hi-me*—MAN$^{!}$ LÚ.DAM.QAR
12 IGI ^{m}DINGIR—*de-ni*—IGI.LAL DUMU $^{md!+}$[E]N—⸢A⸣—SUM-*na*

13 IGI ^{md}IM—*š*[*al-l*]*im* DUMU ^{m}*a-*⸢*tar*$^{!}$⸣*-a*
14 IGI ^{m}*ni-nu-a-a* IGI ^{m}*ba*$^{!}$*-ri-ki*$^{!}$
15 [IG]I ^{m}PAB—DINGIR-*a-a* IGI ^{md}PA—*še-zib-an-ni*
16 [I]GI ^{m}GIN-*i* LÚ.A.BA

17 ITI.ZÍZ UD-10-KÁM
18e *lim-mu* ^{m}*man-nu—ki-i*—LUGAL

[5] Witness Bel-aplu-iddina, go[vernor ...].
[6] Witness Sin-abu-uṣur, [...].
[7] Witness Nergal-šarru-uṣur, city overseer.
[8] Witness Kiṣir-Aššur, mayor.
[9] Witness El-il-milki, son of Bel-nuri.
[10] Witness Bel-taklak.
[11] Witness Rahim-Dadi, merchant.
[12] Witness Ilu-deni-lamur, son of [Be]l-aplu-iddina.
[13] Witness Adad-ša[lli]m, son of Atarâ.
[14] Witness Ninuayu. Witness Bariku.
[15] [Wit]ness Ahi-ila'i. Witness Nabû-šezibanni.
[16] [Wit]ness Kenî, scribe.
[17] Month Shebat (XI), 10th day, eponym year of Mannu-ki-šarri.

320. Remanni-Adad Purchases Land (664-X-17)

80-7-19,83

beginning broken away
1′ ⸢EN$^{!}$ É$^{!}$⸣ [A.ŠÀ UN.MEŠ SU]M-*ni*

ADD 377

(Beginning destroyed)
[1] owner of the house, [land, and people being sol]d.

(space for stamp seal impression)

2′ É 15 ANŠE A.ŠÀ SUHUR KASKAL *šá*$^{!}$ URU.ŠE—^{m}[*dan-na-a*]
3′ 0$^{!}$ *a-*[*n*]*a* URU.ŠE—^{m}*il-di-ši* DU-⸢*ú*⸣-[*ni*]
4′ [*x* GIŠ.SA]R$^{!}$.MEŠ SUHUR A.ŠÀ *šá* ^{m}*lu*$^{!}$-[*x x x*]

5′ [SUHUR A.ŠÀ *šá*] ⸢^{m}SUM$^{!}$⸣*-na-a* É 4 ANŠE [A.ŠÀ]
6′ [SUHUR KASKAL *šá* TA* UR]U.ŠE—^{m}*dan-na-a a-na* U[RU$^{?}$.ŠE]
7′ [^{m}*x x x* DU]-⸢*u*$^{!}$⸣*-ni* PAB 5 SUHUR ^{m}HAL-*a-*[*ni*—^{d}*x*]
rest broken away
r.1 [IGI] $^{md!}$30—MAŠ LÚ.3-*šú šá*$^{!}$ D[UMU$^{!}$—MAN]

[2] An estate of 15 hectares of land adjoining the road which lea[ds] (from) the village of [*Dannaya*] to the village of Ildiši;
[4] [x gar]dens adjoining the field of Lu[... and the field of] Iddinaya;
[5] an estate of 4 hectares of [land adjoining the road which [lea]ds [from the vill]age of Dannaya to the vil[lage of ...], a total of 5 (hectares) adjoining the field of Išma[nni-...]
(Break)

[r.1] Witness Sin-ašared, 'third man' of the pr[ince].

320 Previous editions: AR 399, NALK 252. Collations: Assur 2/5. → no. 321. [1] See coll.

2 IGI ^{m}NUMUN-*ut-ti-i* LÚ.GAL—*ki-ṣir* [:]
3 IGI ^{md}PA—SU LÚ.2-*u šá* LÚ.GAL—[*ú-rat*]
4 IGI ^{md}U.GUR—MAN—PAB LÚ.3$^{!}$-*š*[*ú*]
5 IGI ^{m}DÙ-*i* LÚ.2-*u šá* LÚ.GAL—[A.ZU]
6 IGI ^{md}*za-ba$_4$-ba$_4$*—SU LÚ.⸢3⸣-[*šú*]
7 IGI ^{m}*aš-šur*—ZU LÚ.⸢3⸣-[*šú*]
8 IGI ^{m}*man-nu*—*ki*—ERIM.MEŠ PAB-*šú šá* ^{m}GIN-*a-n*[*i*—^{d}15]
9 [IT]I.AB UD-17-KÁM *lim-mu* ^{m}MAN—*lu*—*dà-r*[*i*]
10 [LÚ$^{!}$.GA]R.KUR URU.BÀD—^{m}MAN—GI[N]

2 Witness Zarutî, cohort commander [of ditto].
3 Witness Nabû-eriba, deputy of the team-[commander].
4 Witness Nergal-šarru-uṣur, 'third m[an].'
5 Witness Banî, deputy of the chief [physician].
6 Witness Zababa-eriba, 'third [man].'
7 Witness Aššur-le'i, 'third [man].'
8 Witness Mannu-ki-ṣabe, brother of Kinanni-[Issar].
9 [Mon]th Tebet (X), 17th day, eponym year of Šarru-lu-dari, [gov]ernor of Dur-Šarruk[en].

321. Duplicate of the Previous Text

K 1602

1 [NA$_4$.KIŠIB ^{m}]GIN$^{!}$-⸢*a*⸣-*ni*—^{d}15 LÚ*.[*x x x*]
2 [UR]U$^{!}$.*qat$^{!}$-ta-na-a-a* EN A.ŠÀ.GA U[N.MEŠ]
3 [*t*]*a-da-*[*ni*]

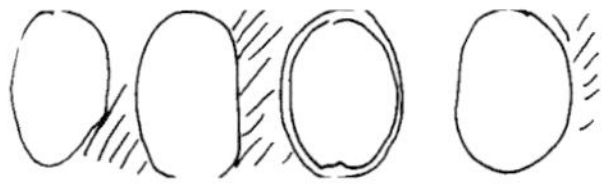

4 [É 15 ANŠE A].ŠÀ.G[A S]UHUR ⸢KASKAL *ša*⸣ URU.ŠE—^{m}[*dan-na-a*]
5 *a$^{!}$*-⸢*na*$^{!}$⸣ [URU.ŠE—^{m}*il-di-ši il*]*-lak-u-ni* SUHUR [*x x x x*]
6 [*x* GIŠ.SAR.MEŠ SUHUR A$^{!}$.ŠÀ$^{!}$ *šá* ^{m}*lu-x x x*] SUHUR A.ŠÀ *ša* ^{m}SUM-*ni$^{!}$*-[*ia*]
7 [É 4 ANŠE A.ŠÀ SUHUR KASKAL *šá* TA* UR]U.ŠE—^{m}*dan-na-a* [0]
8 [*a-na* URU.ŠE—^{m}*x x x il-lak*]-*u*-[*ni*]
9 [PAB 5 SUHUR ^{m}HAL-*a-ni*—^{d}*x x* SUHUR] KASKAL$^{!}$ *ša$^{!}$* ⸢*a$^{!}$-na*$^{!}$⸣ [URU.ŠE]
10 [^{m}*x x x il-lak-u-ni x x x*] *bu* [*x x x x*]
rest broken away
Rev. beginning broken away
1′ IGI $^{m⸢d⸣}$[*šá-maš*—MAN—PAB$^{?}$ LÚ*.*mu-kil*—KUŠ.PA.MEŠ]
2′ IGI ^{md}A[MAR.UTU—MAN—PAB] A [^{m}*gab-bi-i*]
3′ IGI ^{m}NUMUN-*u-t*[*i-i* L]Ú.*mu*-[*kil*—KUŠ.PA.MEŠ]
4′ ⸢IGI⸣ ^{md}30—[MAŠ L]Ú.3$^{!}$-[*š*]*ú$^{!}$* [*ša* DUMU-MAN]
5′ [IGI ^{m}NUMUN-*u*]-*ti-i* LÚ*.GA[L—*ki-ṣir ša*

ADD 439

1 [Seal of] Kinanni-Issar, Qatnean [...], owner of the land and peo[ple being] sol[d].

(stamp seal impressions)

4 [An estate of 15 hectares of l]and [adjoin]ing the road [which l]eads (from) the village of [*Dannaya*] to [the village of Ildiši] and adjoining [...];
6 [x gardens adjoining the field of Lu... and] the field of Iddini[ya];
7 [an estate of 4 hectares of land adjoining the road [lea]ding [from the vil]lage of Dannay[a to the village of ...];
9 [a total of 5 (hectares) adjoining Išmanni-... and] the road [lead]ing to [the village of ...]

(Break)

r.1 Witness [*Šamaš-šarru-uṣur, chariot driver*].
2 Witness Ma[rduk-šarru-ušur], son of [Gabbî].
3 Witness Zarut[î], chariot driver.
4 Witness Sin-[ašared], 'third [m]an' [of the prince].
5 [Witness Zaru]tî, co[hort commander of

321 Previous editions: AR 110, NALK 253. Collations: Assur 2/5. → no. 320.

DUMU—MAN]
6′ [IGI ^{m}]^{d}PA—SU LÚ*.2-*u* *š*[*a* LÚ*.GAL—*ú-rat*]
7′ [IGI ^{m}*d*] ^{m}U.GUR—MAN—PAB LÚ*.[3-*šú ša* DUMU—MAN]
8′ [IGI] ^{m}*ba-ni-i* LÚ*.⸢2$^{!}$⸣-[*u ša* LÚ*.GAL—A.ZU]
9′ [IGI ^{m}]$^{d!}$*za*$^{!}$-⸢*ba*$_{4}$$^{!}$⸣-[*ba*$_{4}$—SU LÚ*.3-*šú*]
rest broken away

the prince].
6 [Witness] Nabû-eriba, deputy [team-commander].
7 [Witness] Nergal-šarru-uṣur, ['third man'].
8 [Witness] Banî, deputy [chief physician].
9 [Witness] Zababa-eri[ba, 'third man'].
(Rest destroyed)

322. Remanni-Adad Buys Land and [...]

K 16094

beginning broken away
1′ [T]A IGI ⸢^{m}GIN$^{!}$-*a*⸣$^{!}$-[*ni*—^{d}15 *il-qi kas-pu gam-mur*]
2′ *ta-din-ni* A.Š[À *x x x šu-a-tú*]
3′ *za-ár-pu laq*-[*qi-u tu-a-ru de-e-nu*]
4′ DUG$_{4}$.DUG$_{4}$ *la-áš*-[*šú ina ur-kiš ina ma-te-ma*]
5′ [*man-nu*] *ša i-za-q*[*up-an-ni i*-GIL-*u-ni*]
6′ [*e-l*]*a-a-ni* [*x x x x x x x*]
7′ [*de*]-⸢*e*⸣-*nu* D[UG$_{4}$.DUG$_{4}$ *x x x x*]
8′ TA* ^{m}*rém-a*-[*ni*—^{d}IM *x x x x x*]
9′ *x*[*x x x x x x x x x x x x x*]
rest broken away

K 16094

(Beginning destroyed)
1 [bought them] from Kina[nni-Issar for ......].
2 [The money] is paid [completely]. The field [and ...] are purchased and acqu[ired. Any revocation, lawsuit], or litigation is void.
5 [Whoe]ver [in the future, at any time], lodges a complaint, [breaks the contract, or com]es forward [... and seeks a law]suit [or litigation] against Rema[nni-Adad ...]
(Rest destroyed)

323. Remanni-Adad Loans Silver, 75 Rams, and a Heifer (664-X-25)

K 404

1 10 MA.NA KUG.UD *ina ša* URU.*gar-ga-mis*
2 75 UDU.NITÁ.MEŠ 1 GUD.ÁB.⸢NIGIN⸣
3 *ša* ^{m}*rém-a-ni*—^{d}IM LÚ*.DIB—*a-pa-te*
4 *ina* IGI ^{m}URU.*arba-ìl-a-a* LÚ*.2-*u* KUR.*bar-hal-zi*
5 *ina* IGI ^{md}PA—SU—PAB.MEŠ LÚ*.A.BA
6 *ina* IGI ^{m}*maš-qa-ru* LÚ*.3-*si-šú*
7 *ina* IGI ^{m}DINGIR—*dàl-a* LÚ*.:.
8 *ina pu-u-hi i-ta-ṣu*
9 ⸢*a-na*⸣ 3-*si-šú i-ra-bi*
e.10 UDU.MEŠ GUD.ÁB.NIGIN *ina* ITI.ŠE SUM-*an*
11 *šum-ma la* SUM-*ni* UDU.MEŠ *ú-lu-du*

r.1 [IT]I.AB 25-KÁM ⸢*lim*⸣-*mu* ^{m}MAN—*lu*—*dà-ri*

2 [IG]I ^{md}MAŠ.MAŠ—MAN—PAB LÚ*.3-*si-šú*
3 IGI ^{m}*ú-a-ár-me-ri* LÚ*.:.
4 IGI ^{md}*šá-maš*—MAN—P[AB LÚ*].DIB—*a-pa-te*
5 IGI ^{md}PA—*še-zi*[*b*] LÚ*.:. IGI ^{m}*bar-ruq*

ADD 115

1 10 minas of silver by the (mina) of Carchemish, 75 rams, and one heifer belonging to Remanni-Adad, chariot driver,
4 at the disposal of Arbailayu, deputy (governor) of Barhalza, Nabû-riba-ahhe the scribe, Mašqaru the 'third man,' and Il-dalâ ditto.
8 They have taken it as a loan. It shall increase by a third.
10 One shall give back the sheep and the heifer in Adar (XII). If not, the sheep will give birth.
r.1 [Mon]th Tebet (X), 25th day, eponym year of Šarru-lu-dari.
2 [Wit]ness Nergal-šarru-uṣur, 'third man.'
3 Witness Uarmeri, ditto.
4 Witness Šamaš-šarru-u[ṣur], chariot driver.
5 Witness Nabû-šezib, ditto. Witness Barruqu.

322 This fragment belongs together with nos. 320 and 321 but does not make a physical join.
323 Previous editions: AR 321, NALK 254; → Postgate FNALD 31; 3R 47,1 (copy). s.1 3$^{!!}$ written 2; scribal error.

6 IGI ^{m}*šum-ma*—DINGIR.MEŠ LÚ*.:. IGI ^{m}*sa-kan-nu* ⸢:.⸣
7 IGI ^{m}*aš-šur*—DINGIR-*a-a* LÚ*.GAL—*ki-ṣir qur*-ZAG
8 IGI ^{m}NUMUN-*u-ti-i* LÚ*.DIB—*a-pa-te* A—MAN
9 IGI ^{m}⸢NUMUN⸣-*u-ti-i* LÚ*.GAL—*ki-ṣir* A—MAN
10 IGI ^{m}PAB—*ba-áš-te* LÚ*.GAL—Ì.DU$_8$
s.1 [IGI] ^{m}U.GUR—MAN—PAB 3$^{!!}$-*si-šú*
2 [IGI ^{md}ŠÚ]—MAN—PAB
3 A ^{m}*gab-bi-i*

[6] Witness Šumma-ilani, ditto. Witness Sakkannu, ditto.
[7] Witness Aššur-ila'i, cohort commander of the royal bodyguard.
[8] Witness Zarutî, chariot driver of the prince.
[9] Witness Zarutî, cohort commander of the prince.
[10] Witness Habasti, head porter.
[s.1] [Witness] Nergal-šarru-uṣur, 'third man.'
[2] [Witness Marduk]-šarru-uṣur, son of Gabbî.

324. Duplicate of the Previous Text

83-1-18,382

1 [NA$_4$.KIŠIB ^{m}URU.*arba-ìl-a-a* LÚ].⸢2-*u*⸣ URU.*bar-hal-za*
2 [NA$_4$.KIŠIB ^{md}PA—SU—PAB.MEŠ] LÚ.A.BA
3 [NA$_4$.KIŠIB ^{m}*maš-qa-ru*] LÚ.3.U$_5$
4 [NA$_4$.KIŠIB ^{m}DINGIR—*dàl-a*] LÚ.:.
5 [10 MA.NA KUG.UD *in*]*a* ⸢1⸣ MA.NA-*e*
6 [*ša* URU.*gar-ga*]-*mis*
blank space of one line
7 [75 UDU.NITÁ.MEŠ 1 GU]D.ÁB.NIGIN SIG$_5$-*tú*
8 [*ša* ^{m}*rém-a-ni*—^{d}IM LÚ].DIB—KUŠ.PA.MEŠ
9 [*ša* ^{m}*aš-šur*—DÙ—A MAN] KUR—*aš-šur*.KI
10 [*ina* IGI ^{m}URU.*arba-ìl-a-a* LÚ.2-*u*] KUR.*bar-hal-za*
11 [*ina* IGI ^{md}PA—SU—PAB.MEŠ L]Ú.A.BA
e.12 [*ina* IGI ^{m}*maš-qa-ru*] LÚ.3-*šú*
13 [*ina* IGI ^{m}DINGIR—*dàl-a*] LÚ.:.
r.1 [*ina pu-u-hi i-ta-ṣ*]*u a-na* 3-*si-šú*
2 [*i-ra-bi* UDU.MEŠ GUD.Á]B.NIGIN
3 [*ina* ITI.ŠE SUM-*an šum*]-*ma la id-din*
4 [UDU.MEŠ *ú-lu-du* IGI ^{md}]MAŠ.MAŠ—MAN—PAB LÚ.3-*šú*
5 [IGI ^{md}*šá-maš*—MAN—PAB L]Ú.DIB—KUŠ.PA.MEŠ
6 [IGI ^{m}*bar-ruq* LÚ.:. IG]I ^{md}PA—*še-zib* LÚ.:.
7 [IGI ^{m}*šum-ma*—DINGIR.MEŠ LÚ.:. IGI] ⸢^{m}⸣*sak-kan* LÚ.:.
8 [IGI ^{m}*aš-šur*—DINGIR-*a-a* LÚ.GAL]—⸢KA⸣.KÉŠ LÚ*.*qur*-ZAG
9 [IGI ^{m}NUMUN-*u-ti-i* LÚ.GAL]—KA.KÉŠ *šá* DUMU—LUGAL
10 [IGI ^{m}PAB—*ba-áš-te* LÚ.GA]L—Ì.DU$_8$
11e [IGI ^{m}U.GUR—MAN—PAB 3-*šú* IGI] ⸢^{md}⸣ŠÚ—MAN—PAB A ^{m}*gab-e*

ADD 116

[1] [Seal of Arbailayu], deputy (governor) of Barhalza,
[2] [seal of Nabû-riba-ahhe], scribe,
[3] [seal of Mašqaru], 'third man,'
[4] [seal of Il-dalâ] ditto.
[5] [10 minas of silver b]y the mina [of Carche]mish, [75 rams, and one] good heifer [belonging to Remanni-Adad], chariot driver [of Assurbanipal, king] of Assyria,
[10] [at the disposal of Arbailayu, deputy] of Barhalza, [Nabû-riba-ahhe t]he scribe, [Mašqaru] the 'third man,' [and Il-dalâ] ditto.
[r.1] [They have t]aken it [as a loan]. It shall [increase] by a third. [One shall give back the sheep and the] hei[fe]r [in Adar (XII). I]f not, [the sheep will give birth].
[4] [Wit]ness Nergal-šarru-uṣur, 'third man.'
[5] [Witness Šamaš-šarru-uṣur], chariot driver.
[6] [Witness Barruqu, ditto. Witn]ess Nabû-šezib, ditto.
[7] [Witness Šumma-ilani, ditto. Witness] Sakkannu, ditto.
[8] [Witness Aššur-ila'i], cohort commander of the royal bodyguard.
[9] [Witness Zarutî, cohort] commander of the prince.
[10] [Witness Habasti, he]ad porter.
[11] [Witness Nergal-šarru-uṣur, 'third man.' Witness] Marduk-šarru-uṣur, son of Gabbê.

324 Previous editions: AR 320, NALK 255. The principal difference between this text and no. 323 is the absence of a date after r.4 here.

325. Remanni-Adad Buys an Entire Village (663-X-25)

K 324

1 NA$_4$.KIŠIB ^{md}MAŠ-DINGIR$^{!}$—*a-a* LÚ*.2-*u ša* ⌜URU.*da-na-a-a*⌝
2 NA$_4$.KIŠIB ^{m}*as-qu$^{!}$-di* LÚ*.A.BA ⌜*ša* AMA$^{!}$⌝—[MAN]
3 NA$_4$.KIŠIB ^{m}*hi-ri*—PAB.MEŠ LÚ*.*mu-kil*—KUŠ.PA.⌜MEŠ$^{!}$⌝
4 NA$_4$.KIŠIB ^{md}IM—TI.LA LÚ*.3.U$_5$
5 NA$_4$.KIŠIB ^{md}PA—*rém-a-ni* LÚ.GAL—*ki-ṣ*[*ir*]
6 NA$_4$.KIŠIB ^{m}15—DINGIR-*a-a* LÚ*.:.
7 NA$_4$.KIŠIB ^{m}*mil-ki—id-ri* [LÚ*.:.]
8 NA$_4$.KIŠIB ^{m}*man-nu—ki*—URU.*arba-ìl* LÚ*.⌜A$^{!}$⌝—[SIG]
9 NA$_4$.KIŠIB ^{m}NUMUN—GIN ⌜LÚ.:.⌝
10 NA$_4$.KIŠIB ^{m}U.U—DÙ LÚ.:.
11 PAB 10 LÚ.MEŠ-*e* URU.*da*-⌜*na*⌝-*a-a*
12 EN URU *a*-⌜*na*⌝ *gi-mir-t*[*e*]-*šú* SUM-*ni*

rest broken away

Rev. beginning broken away
1′ TA* ^{m}*rém-a-ni*—^{d}⌜IM⌝ *ù* DUMU.MEŠ-*šu*
2′ DUMU—⌜DUMU⌝.MEŠ-*šú de-nu* DUG$_4$.DUG$_4$ *ub-ta-ʾu-u-ni*
3′ 2 GÚ.UN ⌜KUG.UD⌝ LUH-*u* 1 GÚ.UN KUG.GI *sak-ru*
4′ *ina bur-ki* ^{d}IŠ.TAR ⌜*a-šib*⌝ URU.NINA.KI GAR-*an*
5′ 2 ANŠE.KUR.RA BABBAR.MEŠ *ina* GÌR.2 *aš-šur i-rak-kas*
6′ *kas-pu a-na* 10.MEŠ *a-na* EN.MEŠ-*šú* GUR-⌜*ra*⌝
7′ *ina de-ni-šú* DUG$_4$.DUG$_4$-*ma la i-laq*-⌜*qi*⌝

8′ IGI ^{m}ITI.AB-*a-a* LÚ*.*sar-tin-nu*
9′ IGI ^{m}*si-lim—aš-šur* ⌜LÚ*⌝.SUKKAL *dan-nu*
10′ IGI ^{md}MAŠ.MAŠ—⌜MAN—PAB⌝ LÚ*.3.U$_5$
11′ IGI ^{m}*ú-bar*-⌜*bi*$^{!}$-*si*$^{!}$⌝ LÚ*.:.
12′ IGI ^{md}*šá-maš*—MAN—PAB ⌜LÚ*⌝.*mu-kil*—KUŠ.PA.ME[Š]
13′ IGI ^{md}PA—*še-zib* ⌜LÚ*⌝.:.
14′ IGI ^{m}*bar-ruq* :. IGI ^{m}⌜*sa*⌝-*kan-nu* :.
15′ IGI ^{md}*za-ba$_4$-ba$_4$*—SU LÚ*.3-*šú* [IGI] ^{m}⌜PAB⌝—*la-maš-ši* :.
16′ IGI ^{m}U.GUR—MAN—PAB :. IGI ^{m}*ha—ba-as*-⌜*te*⌝ LÚ*.GAL—Ì.DU$_8$.MEŠ

ADD 470

1 Seal of Inurta-ila'i, deputy of the town of Dannaya;
2 seal of Asqudu, scribe of [the queen] mother;
3 seal of Hiri-ahhe, chariot driver;
4 seal of Adad-uballiṭ, 'third man';
5 seal of Nabû-remanni, cohort commander;
6 seal of Issar-ila'i, ditto;
7 seal of Milki-idri, [ditto];
8 seal of Mannu-ki-Arbail, cha[riot fighter];
9 seal of Zeru-ukin, ditto;
10 seal of Dadi-ibni, ditto; a total of 10 gentlemen from Dannaya, owners of the town being sold in its entirety.

(stamp seal impressions)

(Break)

r.1 [whoever] seeks a lawsuit or litigation against Remanni-Adad and his sons (and) grandsons, shall place two talents of refined silver and one talent of pure gold in the lap of Ištar residing in Nineveh, shall tie two white horses to the feet of Aššur, and shall return the money tenfold to its owners.

7 He shall contest in his lawsuit and not succeed.

8 Witness Kanunayu, *sartinnu*.
9 Witness Silim-Aššur, grand vizier.
10 Witness Nergal-šarru-uṣur, 'third man.'
11 Witness Ubarbisi, ditto.
12 Witness Šamaš-šarru-uṣur, chariot driver.
13 Witness Nabû-šezib, ditto.
14 Witness Barruqu, ditto. Witness Sakkannu, ditto.
15 Witness Zababa-eriba, 'third man.' Witness Ahu-lâmašši, ditto.
16 Witness Nergal-šarru-uṣur, ditto. Witness Habasti, head porter.

325 Previous editions: AR 168, NALK 256. 2, 8, 10, r.20, 22f See coll.

17′ IGI ^{md}PA—SU LÚ*.2-*u ša* LÚ*.⸢GAL⸣—*ú-rat*

18′ IGI ^{m}*ba-ni-i* LÚ*.2-*u ša* LÚ*.GAL—A.ZU

19′ IGI ^{m}NUMUN-*u-te-i* LÚ*.GAL—⸢*ki*⸣-*ṣir ša* LÚ*.*qur*-ZAG *š*[*a* A—MAN]

20′ IGI ^{md}PA—MAN—PAB :. *ša*—GÌR.2 *ša* A—MAN

21′ IGI ^{md}30—MAŠ LÚ.3.U_5 *ša* A—MAN

22′ IGI ^{m}PAB-*u*!—*a*!-*mur* LÚ*.GIŠ.GIGIR—DU_8 IGI ^{m}*man-nu—ki*—KASKAL ⸢:.⸣

23′ ITI.AB UD-25-KAM *lim-me* ^{m}EN—*na-a*ʾ-*di*! [L]Ú.*tur-ta-*[*nu*]

17 Witness Nabû-eriba, deputy of the team-commander.

18 Witness Banî, deputy of the chief physician.

19 Witness Zarutî, cohort commander of the bodyguard o[f the prince].

20 Witness Nabû-šarru-uṣur, ditto of the *ša-šēpi* guard of the prince.

21 Witness Sin-ašared, 'third man' of the prince.

22 Witness Ahû-amur, horse trainer of the open chariotry. Witness Mannu-ki-Harran, ditto.

23 Month Tebet (X), 25th day, eponym year of Bel-na'id, commander-in-c[hief].

326. Remanni-Adad Buys a Town near Nerab

K 446

beginning broken away

1′ URU.*mu-si-*⸢*na*—A⸣—[AŠ *a-na gi-mir-ti-šú x x x*]

2′ *a-di* A.ŠÀ.GA.MEŠ-*š*[*ú* UN.MEŠ-*šú* É *x* ANŠE A.ŠÀ]

3′ *ina* GIŠ.BÁN *šá* 9 *qa* URUDU.MEŠ *za-*[*ku-te la* ŠE.*ši-ib-še*]

4′ *la* ŠE.*nu-sa-hi* SUHUR *ta-*⸢*hu*⸣-[*me šá* URU.*x x x x*]

5′ ⸢SUHUR⸣ *ta-hu-me šá* URU.DÙG.GA—⸢GIŠ.MI!⸣—[*x x x x x*]

6′ SUHUR URU.*né-ri-bi šá* LÚ.EN.NAM ⸢URU!⸣.[*ar-pad-da*]

7′ 1 GIŠ.SAR *šá* GIŠ.*til-lit* 1-*lim*-5-*me* GIŠ.*til-*[*lit ina* ŠÀ]

8′ 1 GIŠ.SAR Ú.SAR ^{m}DI-*mu*—EN LÚ.EN[GAR 0!]

9′ ^{m}*ia*—PAB.MEŠ DUMU-*šú ṣu-hur-tú* MÍ.*ú-a-r*[*i-x x*]

10′ MÍ-*šú* PAB 3 ^{m}*ka-ma-su* LÚ.ENGAR ^{m}*hu-ru-bi-sa-*[*x*]

11′ DUMU-*šú ṣu-hur-tú* MÍ.*lu—bal-ṭa-at* MÍ-*šú* PAB ⸢3 ZI.MEŠ⸣

12′ PAB 6 Z[I].MEŠ URU.*mu-si-na*—A—AŠ *a-na gi-mir-ti-šú*

13′ *ina na-gi-e šá* KUR.*ar-pad-da ina* ŠU.2 URU.*né-ri-bi*

14′ *ša*! LÚ.NAM KUR.*ar-pad-da ú-piš-*[*ma*]

15′ ^{m}*rém-an-ni*—^{d}IM LÚ.*mu-kil*—KUŠ.PA.MEŠ *d*[*an-nu*]

ADD 471

(Beginning destroyed)
(space for stamp seal impressions)

---

1 The town of Musina-aplu-[iddina in its entirety ...], with its fields [and people];

2 [an estate of x hectares of land] by the copper seah of 9 'litres,' ex[empt land with no straw] and corn taxes, adjoining the bor[der of the town ...], adjoining the border of the town of Ṭab-ṣil-[...], and adjoining the city Nerab of the governor of [Arpad];

7 one vineyard with 1,500 vines [in it] and one vegetable garden;

8 Šulmu-Bel, far[mer], Ya-ahhe, his adolescent son, his wife Uar[i...], a total of 3;

10 Kamasu, farmer, Hurubisa[...], his adolescent son, his wife Lu-balṭat, a total of 3 persons;

12 in all 6 pers[on]s (and) the town of Musina-aplu-iddina in its entirety in the district of Arpad next to the city Nerab of the governor of Arpad —

15 Remanni-Adad, c[hief] chariot driver of

326 Previous editions: AR 167, NALK 260; → TCAE 178. Collations: Assur 2/5. 13 Note that *ina* ŠU.2 here means "next to, near," possibly under Aramaic influence (reading ŠU as *idi*). It occurs again in no. 335:10. Postgate would prefer "within admininistrative (area) of".

16′ *šá* ^{m}*aš-šur*—DÙ—A MAN KUR—*aš-šur*.KI *ina* ŠÀ 17 1/2 MA.N[A KUG.UD]
17′ *ina* 1 MA.NA-*e šá* URU.*gar-ga-mis* TA* I[GI]
18′ ^{m}*man-nu—ki-i*—URU.NINA TA* IGI ^{md}30—MU—[*x*]
19′ TA* IGI ^{m}*i-ka-ri* TI-*qí*! *kas-pu gam-m*[*ur*]
20′ *ta-din* URU A.ŠÀ GIŠ.SAR GIŠ.*til-lit* GIŠ.SA[R Ú.SAR]
21′ ⸢UN⸣.MEŠ *šú-a-tú za-ár-pu laq-qí*!-*u tú-a-*[*ru*]
22′ ⸢*de*⸣-*e-nu* DUG$_4$.DUG$_4$ *la-áš-šú man-nu šá ina ur-kiš*
23′ ⸢*ù*⸣ *ma-te-ma man-nu šá i-zaq-qup-an-*[*ni*]
e.24′ *lu-u* ^{m}*man-nu—ki*—URU.NINA *lu-u* ^{md}3[0—MU—*x*]
25′ [*lu*]-*u* ^{m}*i-ka-ru lu-u* DUMU.MEŠ-[*šú-nu*]
26′ [*lu-u* DUMU—D]UMU.MEŠ-*šú-nu lu-u* PAB.ME[Š-*šú-nu*]
r.1 [*lu-u* DUMU—PAB].MEŠ-[*šú-nu*] *lu-u* LÚ.GAR-*n*[*u-šú-nu*]
2 [*lu-u* LÚ.*h*]*a-za-na-šú-nu lu-u* LÚ.NAM-[*šú-nu*]
3 [*lu*]-*u mám-ma-nu-šú-nu qur-bu man-*⸢*nu*⸣ *šá e-la-*[*an-ni*]
4 [*šá*] TA* ^{m}*rém-an-ni*—^{d}IM LÚ.DIB—KUŠ.PA.ME[Š]
5 *dan-nu šá* ^{m}*aš-šur*—DÙ—A MAN KUR—*aš-šur*.KI TA* DUMU.MEŠ-*šú*
6 DUMU—DUMU.MEŠ-*šú de-nu* DUG$_4$.DUG$_4$ *ub-ta-u-ni*
7 2 ANŠE.KUR.RA.MEŠ BABBAR.MEŠ *ina* GÌR.2 *aš-šur i-rak-kas*
8 4 ANŠE.*har-ba-kan-ni ina* GÌR.2 ^{d}MAŠ.MAŠ *ú-še-rab*
9 2 GÚ.UN KUG.UD LUH-*u* 1 ⸢GÚ.UN KUG⸣.GI *sak-ru*
10 *ina bur-ki* ^{d}IŠ.T[AR *a-ši-bat* URU.NIN]A GAR-*an*
11 *kas-pu a-na* 10.MEŠ-[*te a-na* EN.MEŠ-*šú* GU]R-*ra*
12 *ina de-ni-šú* DU[G$_4$.DUG$_4$-*ma la i-laq-q*]*i*
13 *de-en-šú* D[I.KUD *la i-šá-mu*]

---

14 IGI ^{md}MAŠ.MAŠ—MAN—P[AB LÚ.3.U$_5$]
15 IGI ^{m}*ú-ar-*⸢*bi-is*⸣ [LÚ.:.]
16 IGI ^{md}*šá-maš*—MAN—PAB L[Ú.*mu-kil*—KUŠ.PA.MEŠ]
17 IGI ^{m}NUMUN-*ut-ti-i* ⸢LÚ⸣.[GAL—*ki-ṣir*]
18 ⸢IGI⸣ ^{m}*aš-šur*—DINGIR-*a-a* ⸢LÚ⸣.[GAL—*ki-ṣir*]

19 [IGI] ^{m}*bar-ruq* ⸢LÚ⸣.[DIB—KUŠ.PA.MEŠ]
20 IGI ^{m}PAB—*la-m*[*aš-ši* LÚ.3.U$_5$]
21 IGI ^{md}*za-*[*ba$_4$-ba$_4$*—SU LÚ.3.U$_5$]
22 IGI ^{m}*aš-šur*—[*x x x x x x x*]
23 IGI ^{m}⸢*x*⸣[*x x x x x x x x x*]
rest broken away

Assurbanipal, king of Assyria, has contracted [and] bought (said property) for 17 1/2 min[as of silver] by the mina of Carchemish from Mannu-ki-Ninua, Sin-šumu-[...] and Ikkaru.

19 The money is paid compl[etely]. That town, field, vineyard, [vegetable] garden and people are purchased and acquired. Any revoca[tion], lawsuit, or litigation is void.

22 Whoever in the future, and at any time, lodges a compl[aint], whether Mannu-ki-Ninua, S[in-šumu-...] or Ikkaru, or [their] sons, [gran]dsons, brothers [or nephews], or [their] prefect, mayor, governor, or relative,

r.3 whoever comes forw[ard] and seeks a lawsuit or litigation against Remanni-Adad, chief chariot driver of Assurbanipal, king of Assyria, and his sons and grandsons,

7 shall tie two white horses to the feet of Aššur, shall bring four *harbakannu* horses to the feet of Nergal, shall place two talents of refined silver and one talent of pure gold in the lap of Iš[tar residing in Nine]veh, and [shall ret]urn the money tenfo[ld to its owners].

12 He shall con[test] in his lawsuit [and not succee]d. Th[e judge shall not heed] his case.

---

14 Witness Nergal-šarru-u[ṣur, 'third man'].
15 Witness Uarbis, [ditto].
16 Witness Šamaš-šarru-uṣur, [chariot driver].
17 Witness Zarutî, [cohort commander].
18 Witness Aššur-ila'i, [cohort commander].
19 [Witness] Barruqu, [chariot driver].
20 Witness Ahu-lâ[mašši, 'third man'].
21 Witness Za[baba-eriba, 'third man'].
22 Witness Aššur-[......].
23 Witness [.......].
(Rest destroyed)

327. Fragment of a Remanni-Adad Witness List (663-X-28)

83-1-18,723

Obv. destroyed
Rev. beginning broken away
1′ [IGI ^{m}*bar-r*]*uq-q*[*u* LÚ.DIB—KUŠ.PA.MEŠ]
2′ [IGI ^{m}*aš-šur*—DING]IR-*a-a* [LÚ*.GAL—*ki-ṣir qur*-ZAG]
3′ [IGI ^{m}*sa-a*]*k-kan* L[Ú.DIB—KUŠ.PA.MEŠ]
4′ [IGI ^{md}ŠÚ—MA]N—PAB A ^{m}[*gab-bé-e*]

5′ [IGI ^{md}U.GUR]—MAN—PAB LÚ*.3-[*šú*]
6′ [IGI ^{m}]⌈^{d}⌉*za-ba$_4$-ba$_4$*—SU [LÚ*.3-*šú*]
7′ [IGI] ⌈^{m}⌉ITI.AB-*a-a* IGI ^{m}[*x x x x x*]
8′ [I]TI.AB UD-28-KÁM *lim-*[*mu* ^{m}EN—*na-a*ʾ*-di*]
9′ [L]Ú.GAR.KUR URU.*k*[*u*$^{?}$*-mu-hi*]

ADD 611

(Beginning destroyed)

r.1 [Witness Barr]uq[u, chariot driver].

2 [Witness Aššur-il]a'i, [cohort commander of the royal bodyguard].

3 [Witness Sa]kkannu, [chariot driver].

4 [Witness Marduk-šar]ru-uṣur, son of [Gabbê].

5 [Witness Nergal]-šarru-uṣur, 'third [man].'

6 [Witness] Zababa-eriba, ['third man].'

7 [Witness] Kanunayu. Witness [NN].

8 [Mon]th Tebet (X), 28th day, epo[nym year of *Bel-na'id*], governor of *C*[*ommagene*].

328. Remanni-Adad Buys a House in Nemed-Ištar (663?)

Ki 1904-10-9,21

beginning broken away
1′ PAB$^{!}$ [2 DUMU.MEŠ *x x x*]—^{d}IM
2′ EN.[MEŠ] ⌈É$^{!}$⌉ SUM-*ni*

3′ É *ep-šu ina gi-mir*$^{!}$*-ti-šu*
4′ *a-di* GIŠ.ÙR.MEŠ-*šú a-di* GIŠ.IG.[MEŠ-*šú*]
5′ *ina* URU.*né-med*—^{d}15 SUHUR KASKAL—[LUGAL]
6′ SUHUR É ^{m}DÙG.GA-*i* SUHUR ^{m}*ka-x*[*x x*]
7′ SUHUR É ^{m}DI-*mu*—EN—*la-mur*
8′ SUHUR É $^{m!}$A$^{!}$-*ia* SUHUR SILA
9′ *ú-piš-ma* ^{m}*rém-a-ni*—^{d}IM
10′ LÚ*.*mu-kil*—PA-*a-te ša* ^{m}*aš-šur*—DÙ—A MAN KUR—*aš-šur*
11′ *ina* ŠÀ-*bi* 5$^{!}$ MA.NA KUG.UD *il-qi*
12′ [*ka*]*s-pu ga-mur ta-din* É *za-rip*
13′ [TI *tú-a*]-⌈*ru*$^{!}$⌉ *de-nu* DUG$_4$.DUG$_4$ *la-áš-šú*

e.14′ [*man-nu ša in*]*a*$^{!}$ *ur-kiš u ma-te-ma*
15′ [*lu-u* ^{md}]PA—*ma-li*$^{!}$*-ik u* ^{m}*šum-ma*—DINGIR
16′ [*lu-u*] DUMU.MEŠ-*šú-nu u* DUMU—DUMU.MEŠ-*šú-nu u* 0$^{!}$

ADD 1153

(Beginning destroyed)

1 a total of [2 *sons* of ...]-Adad, owner[s of] the house being sold.

(cylinder seal impression)

3 A built house in its entirety with its beams and door[s] in the city of Nemed-Issar, adjoining [the king's] road, adjoining the house of Ṭabî, Ka[...], the houses of Šulmu-beli-lamur and Aplaya, and adjoining the street —

9 Remanni-Adad, chariot driver of Assurbanipal, king of Assyria, has contracted and bought it for 5 minas of silver.

12 [The mon]ey is paid completely. The house is purchased [and acquired. Any revo]cation, lawsuit, or litigation is void.

14 [Whoever i]n the future, and at any time, [whether] Nabû-malik and Šumma-ilu, [or] their sons, grandsons and [brothers, o]r

327 Previous editions: AR 682, NALK 282. r.8 The epomym Bel-naʾdi is otherwise attested with the title *turtānu* only, but cf. ADD 472 r.23 where Mar-larim, otherwise referred to as *turtānu*, is entitled *tu*]*rtān* URU.*ku-mu-hi*. The closest parallels to the witness list occur in nos. 323 (664), 320 (664) and 325 (663 B.C.). r.9 See coll.

328 Previous edition: NALK 283. Photo Cat. Suppl. Pl. 2. 6, 8 See coll. 15 Tablet *–ma-li-ik* not *–ma-lik* (NALK); see coll. r.1, 7ff, 14 See coll.

17′ [_lu_]-_u_ LÚ*.GAR-_in-šú-nu u_ LÚ*._ha-za-nu_ ⸢URU⸣-_šú_-(_nu_)
r.1 [TA ^{m}_rém-a-ni_—^{d}I]M$^{!}$ _u_ DUMU.MEŠ-_šú_
2 [_u_ DUMU—DUMU.MEŠ-_šú de-nu_] DUG$_4$.DUG$_4$
3 [_ub-ta-ʾu-u-ni x_ MA.NA KUG.U]D 1 MA.NA KUG.GI
4 [_ina bur-ki_ ^{d}15 _a-ši_]-_bat_ NINA GAR-_an_
5 [_kas-pu a-na_ 10.MEŠ-_te a-n_]_a_ EN-_šú_ GUR

---

6 [IGI ^{m}_x x x x_ LÚ*].A.BA _ša_ DUMU—MAN
7 [IGI ^{m}_x x x_ LÚ*._šá_]—IGI—É.GAL A$^{!}$—⸢MAN$^{?}$⸣
8 [IGI ^{m}_ha—ba-as_]-⸢_te_⸣ LÚ*.GAL—Ì.[DU$_8$]
9 [IGI ^{m}_ba-ni-i_ LÚ*].⸢2⸣-_u ša_ LÚ*.⸢GAL⸣—[A.ZU]
10 [IGI ^{md}_x x_]_x_—BA-_šá_ L[Ú._x x x x_]
11 [IGI ^{m}_x x x_] ⸢LÚ*⸣._mu_$^{!}$-_kil_$^{!}$—[PA.MEŠ _x x_]
12 IGI ^{m}⸢_aš-šur_$^{!}$—MAN$^{!}$—PAB$^{!}$ LÚ*._mu_⸣-[_kil_—PA.MEŠ _x x_]
13 IGI ^{md}PA—SU$^{!}$ LÚ*.[2-_u_ LÚ*.GAL—_ú-rat_]
14 IGI ^{m}_sa_$^{!}$-⸢_kan_$^{!}$⸣-[_nu_ LÚ*._mu_$^{!}$-_kil_$^{!}$—PA.MEŠ]
15 IGI ^{m}[_x x x x x x x x x x_]
16 IT[I._x_ UD-_x_-KAM _lim-mu_ ^{m}_x x x x_]
rest broken away

their prefect and the mayor of their city,

r.1 [seeks a lawsuit] or litigation [against Remanni-Ad]ad, his sons [and grandsons], shall place [x minas of sil]ver and one mina of gold [in the lap of Ištar res]iding in Nineveh, and shall return [the money tenfold t]o its owner.

---

r.6 [Witness NN], scribe of the prince.

7 [Witness NN], palace superintendent of the prince.

8 [Witness Habas]ti, head por[ter].

9 [Witness Banî], deputy of the chief [physician].

10 [Witness ...]-iqiša, [...].

11 [Witness NN], chari[ot driver ...].

12 Witness Aššur-šarru-ušur, char[iot driver ...].

13 Witness Nabû-eriba, [deputy team commander].

14 Witness Sakkan[nu, chariot driver].

15 Witness [NN, ...].

16 Month [..., ...th day, eponym year of ...].
(Rest destroyed)

329. Remanni-Adad Buys Vineyards in Singara (660-IV-26)

K 317

1 NA$_4$.KIŠIB ^{md}IM—PAB-_ir_

---

2 LÚ.A.BA _šá_ É ^{m}AN.ŠÁR—ZU
3 EN GIŠ.SAR LÚ _ta-da-a-ni_ GIŠ.SAR
4 _ina_ KUR._si-in-ga-ra ina_ É ^{d}15
5 1-_lim_ GIŠ._til-lit ina_ ŠÀ-_bi_ É 2 ANŠE
6 A.ŠÀ _qab-lu šá_ GIŠ._al-la-an_ É
7 6 ANŠE A.ŠÀ _ú-šal-lu_ É ŠE.NUMUN.MEŠ
8 É _ina_ ŠÀ-_bi_ GIŠ.SAR _ia-ar-hu_
9 SUHUR GIŠ.SAR _šá_ LÚ.SUKKAL SUHUR GIŠ.SAR
10 _šá_ ^{m}EN—_mu-šal-lim_ SUHUR GIŠ.SAR
11 _šá_ ^{m}DUMU.UŠ-_a-a_ SUHUR GIŠ.SAR _šá_ ^{m}PAB—APIN-EŠ
12 ^{m}_lu-su_$^{?}$-_mu_ LÚ.NU.GIŠ.SAR _ú_-⸢_piš-ma_⸣
13 ^{m}_rém-an-ni_—^{d}IM LÚ.DIB—KU[Š.PA.MEŠ]
14 _ina_ ŠÀ 4 MA.NA ⸢KUG.UD⸣ _ina_ 1 [MA.NA-_e_]

ADD 444

1 Seal of Adad-naṣir,

(blank seal space)

---

2 scribe of the house of Aššur-le'i, owner of the vineyard and the man being sold.

4 A vineyard in Singara, in the house of Ištar, 1,000 vines within it; an estate of two hectares of land; a grove of oak trees; an estate of 6 hectares of land, including a meadow, a seed-corn house and a house; a garden and a pool adjoining the gardens of the vizier, Bel-mušallim, Aplaya, and Ahu-ereš; Lusumu, gardener —

13 Remanni-Adad the chariot [driver] has contracted and [bought it] for 4 minas of silver by the [mina] of Carchemish.

329 Previous editions: AR 445, NALK 257; → KB 4 (1896) 136-139. → no. 330. 9, r.19 Tablet has _šá_, as copied by Johns, not _ša_ (NALK); see coll. 11 See coll.

15 *šá* URU.*gar-ga-*⌜*mis*⌝ *il-*[*qí kas-pu gam-mu*]*r*
16 *ta-ad-din* GIŠ.SAR ⌜*qab-lu šú-a-tú*⌝ *zar-pu*
17 *laq-qí*?-*ú tu-a-ru de-e-nu*

18 DUG$_4$.⌜DUG$_4$⌝ *la-áš-šú man-nu šá* ⌜*ina*⌝ *ur-kiš ina* [*ma-te-ma*]
19 *i-zaq-qup-an-ni* GIL-*u-ni lu-*[*u*]
20 ^{md}IM—PAB-*ir lu-u* DUMU.MEŠ-*šú l*[*u*!-*u*]
21 DUMU—DUMU.MEŠ-⌜*šú*⌝ *šá* TA* [^{m}*rém-an-ni*—^{d}IM]
r.1 DUMU.MEŠ-*šú* DUMU—DU[MU.MEŠ-*šú de-e-nu*]
2 DUG$_4$.DUG$_4$ *ub-t*[*a-ʾu-ni x* MA.NA]
3 KUG.UD LUH-*ú* ⌜1⌝ [MA.NA KUG.GI *sak-ru*]
4 *ina bur-ki* ^{d}IŠ.[TAR *a-ši-bat* URU.NINA.KI]
5 GAR-*an kas-pu a-n*[*a* 10.MEŠ-*te a-na*]
6 EN.MEŠ-*šú* GUR-*ra ina d*[*e-ni-šú* DUG$_4$.DUG$_4$-*ma*]
7 *la i-*[*laq-qí*]

---

8 IGI ^{m}*si-lim—aš-šur* L[Ú.SUKKAL *dan-nu*]
9 IGI ^{m}LUGAL—DINGIR-*a-a* L[Ú.GAL—*ki-ṣ*]*ir*
10 *šá* ⌜LÚ.*qur*⌝-ZAG
11 IGI ^{md}15—⌜MU⌝—KAM-*eš* LÚ.GAL—A.BA
12 IGI ^{md}ŠÚ—GAR—MU LÚ.GAL—MAŠ.MAŠ

13 IGI ^{md}AMAR.UTU—MAN—PAB LÚ.DIB—KUŠ.PA.MEŠ
14 *ša* MÍ—É.GAL
15 IGI ^{m}*man-nu—ki-i—aš-šur* LÚ.:.! *šá* DUMU—MAN
16 IGI ^{m}*tar-di-tú—aš-šur* LÚ.3-*šú šá* DUMU—MAN
17 IGI ^{md}PA—NUMUN—AŠ LÚ.DIB—KUŠ.PA.MEŠ
18 IGI ^{m}NUMUN—GIN LÚ.DIB—KUŠ.PA.MEŠ
19 IGI ^{md}PA—SU LÚ.2-*u šá* LÚ.GAL—*u-rat*

20 IGI ^{md}ŠÚ—NUMUN—DÙ LÚ.A.BA
21 ITI.ŠU UD-26-KÁM *lim-mu* ^{m}*gír—ṣa-pu-nu*

15 [The money] is paid [complete]ly. That vineyard and grove are purchased and acquired. Any revocation, lawsuit, or litigation is void.

18 Whoever in the future, a[t any time], lodges a complaint or breaks the contract, wheth[er] Adad-naṣir or his sons o[r] grandsons, whoever se[eks a lawsuit] or litigation against [Remanni-Adad], his sons and grand[sons],

r.2 shall place [x minas] of refined silver and one [mina of pure gold] in the lap of Išt[ar residing in Nineveh], and shall return the money [tenfold to] its owners. [He shall contest] in [his] la[wsuit and] not suc[ceed].

---

8 Witness Silim-Aššur, [grand vizier].

9 Witness Šarru-ila'i, [cohort com]mander of the royal bodyguard.

11 Witness Issar-šumu-ereš, chief scribe.

12 Witness Marduk-šakin-šumi, chief exorcist.

13 Witness Marduk-šarru-uṣur, chariot driver of the queen.

15 Witness Mannu-ki-Aššur, ditto of the prince.

16 Witness Tarditu-Aššur, 'third man' of the prince.

17 Witness Nabû-zeru-iddina, chariot driver.

18 Witness Zeru-ukin, chariot driver.

19 Witness Nabû-eriba, deputy of the team-commander.

20 Witness Marduk-zeru-ibni, scribe.

21 Month Tammuz (IV), 26th day, eponym year of Gir-Ṣapunu.

330. Duplicate of the Preceding Text (660-IV-26)

Bu 91-5-9,162

ADD 445

1 NA$_4$.[KIŠIB ^{md}IM—PAB-*ir*]

1 Se[al of Adad-naṣir],

(cylinder seal impression)

---

2 [LÚ.A.BA] *ša*! [É ^{m}AN.ŠÁR—ZU]

2 [scribe] of [the house of Aššur-le'i,

330 Previous editions: AR 446, NALK 258. → no. 329.
2 See coll. The right half of the tablet is broken away

3 [EN GIŠ.S]AR ⸢LÚ⸣ [*ta-da-ni*]

4 [GIŠ.SAR *ina*] KUR.*si-i*[*n-ga-ra ina* É—^{d}15]
5 [1-*lim* GI]Š.*til-lit* [*ina* ŠÀ-*bi*]
6 [É] ⸢2⸣ ANŠE A.ŠÀ [*qab-lu šá* GIŠ.*al-la-an*]
7 [É] ⸢6⸣ ANŠE A.ŠÀ ⸢*ú*⸣-[*šal-lu*]
8 [É ŠE.NUMUN.ME]Š ⸢É⸣ [*ina* ŠÀ-*bi*]
rest broken away
Rev. beginning broken away

1′ [KUG.GI *sak-ru ina bur-ki* ^{d}15] ⸢*a*!-*ši*!-*bat*!⸣ N[INA!.KI GAR]
2′ *kas-pu* ⸢*a*⸣-[*na* 10.MEŠ-*te a-na* EN.MEŠ-*šú* GUR-*ra*]
3′ *ina de-ni-šú* ⸢DUG$_4$⸣.[DUG$_4$-*ma la i-laq-qí*]

4′ IGI ^{m}*si-lim—aš-*[*šur* LÚ.SUKKAL *dan-nu*]
5′ IGI ^{m}LUGAL—DINGIR-*a*-[*a* LÚ.GAL—*ki-ṣir šá qur*-ZAG]
6′ IGI ^{m}15—MU—KAM-*e*[*š* LÚ.GAL—A.BA]
7′ IGI ^{md}AMAR.UTU—GAR—M[U LÚ.GAL—MAŠ.MAŠ]

8′ IGI ^{md}AMAR.UTU—MAN—PAB [LÚ.DIB—KUŠ.PA.MEŠ *šá* MÍ—É.GAL]
9′ IGI ^{m}*man-nu—ki—aš-šur* L[Ú.: *šá* DUMU—MAN]
10′ IGI ^{m}*tar-di-it—aš-šur* L[Ú.3-*šú šá* DUMU—MAN]

11′ IGI ^{md}PA—NUMUN—AŠ L[Ú!.DIB—KUŠ.PA.MEŠ]
12′ IGI ^{m}NUMUN—GIN [LÚ.DIB—KUŠ.PA.MEŠ]
13′ IGI ^{md}PA—SU [LÚ.2-*u šá* LÚ.GAL—*u-rat*]
space of 2 lines
14′ IGI ^{md}AMAR.UTU—NUMUN—DÙ [LÚ.A.BA]
15′ ITI.ŠU UD-26-KAM [*lim-mu* ^{m}*gír—ṣa-pu-nu*]

owner of the gar]den and the man [being sold].

4 [A vineyard in] Si[ngara, in the house of Ištar, 1,000 vi]nes [within it; an estate] of two hectares of land; [a grove of oak trees; an estate] of 6 hectares of land, [including] a m[eadow], [a seed-cor]n house and a house;
(Break)

r.1 [He shall place x minas of refined silver and one mina of pure gold in the lap of Ištar] residing in Ni[neveh, and shall return] the money te[nfold to its owner]. He shall con[test] in his lawsuit [and not succeed].

---

4 Witness Silim-Aš[šur, grand vizier].
5 Witness Šarru-ila'[i, cohort commander of the royal bodyguard].
6 Witness Issar-šumu-er[eš, chief scribe].
7 Witness Marduk-šakin-šu[mi, chief exorcist].
8 Witness Marduk-šarru-uṣur, [chariot driver of the queen].
9 Witness Mannu-ki-Aššur, [ditto of the prince].
10 Witness Tarditu-Aššur, ['third man' of the prince].
11 Witness Nabû-zeru-iddina, [chariot driver].
12 Witness Zeru-ukin, [chariot driver].
13 Witness Nabû-eriba, [deputy of the team-commander].
14 Witness Marduk-zeru-ibni, [scribe].
15 Month Tammuz (IV), 26th day, [eponym year of Gir-Ṣapunu].

331. Remanni-Adad Buys Vineyards in Singara (660-V-3)

Rm 183

1 NA$_4$.KIŠIB ^{m}10—PAB-*ir* LÚ.⸢A⸣.[BA]
2 A ^{md}PA—PAB-*ir* LÚ.A.BA *ša* É [^{m}AN.ŠÁR—ZU]
3 EN GIŠ.SAR *ta-da-a-n*[*i*]

ADD 362

1 Seal of Adad-naṣir, sc[ribe], son of Nabû-naṣir, scribe of the house [of Aššur-le'i], owner of the vineyard being sold.

(cylinder seal impression)

---

and there is absolutely no trace at the end of the line of the sign ZU shown in Johns' copy. r.1 See coll.
331 Previous editions: AR 378, NALK 259.

4 GIŠ.⌈SAR!⌉ *ina* KUR.*si-in-ga-*⌈*ra*⌉ *ina*! ⌈É⌉—[^{d}15]
5 2-*lim* 6!-*me* [[x]] GIŠ.*til-l*[*it ina* ŠÀ-*bi*]
6 É *a-na gi-mir-*⌈*ti*⌉-[*šú*]
7 ⌈SUHUR⌉ GIŠ.SAR.MEŠ *šá* ^{m}[*x x x x*]
8 [SUHUR] GIŠ.SAR *ša*! ^{m}[*x x x x x*]
rest broken away
Rev. beginning broken away
1′ I[GI ^{m}*x x x x x x*]
2′ IGI ^{m}[*x x x*] ⌈*x x*⌉ [*x x x*]
3′ IGI [^{m}*dà*]-*ri*—MAN LÚ.[GIŠ.GIGIR—DU$_8$]

4′ IGI ^{md}UTU—*šal-lim* L[Ú.DIB—PA.MEŠ]
5′ IGI ^{m}DINGIR—*mu-še-zib* L[Ú.GIŠ.GIGIR—DU$_8$]
6′ IGI ^{md}AMAR.UTU—NUMUN—DÙ L[Ú.A.BA]

7′ ITI.NE UD-3-KAM [0]
8′ *lim-mu* ^{m}*gír—ṣa-pu-*[*nu*]

4 A vineyard in Singara, in the house [of Ištar], 2,600 vin[es within it];
6 an estate in [its] entirety adjoining the gardens of [NN] and the garden of [NN]
(Break)

r.1 Wit[ness ...].
2 Wi[tness ...] ... [...].
3 Witness [Da]ri-šarru, [horse trainer of the open chariotry].
4 Witness Šamaš-šallim, [chariot driver].
5 Witness Ilu-mušezib, [horse trainer of the open chariotry].
6 Witness Marduk-zeru-ibni, [scribe].
7 Month Ab (V), 3rd day, eponym year of Gir-Ṣap[unu].

332. Remanni-Adad Buys Land, People and Vineyards

K 461 + K 1510 (ADD 599)
beginning broken away
1′ ⌈EN⌉ UN.MEŠ A.⌈ŠÀ⌉ GIŠ.S[AR.MEŠ *ta-da-ni*]

2′ É 10 ANŠE A.ŠÀ *ina* GIŠ.BÁN *ša* 9 *q*[*a*]

3′ 1 GIŠ.SAR *til-lit* SUHUR ÍD.*i-lab-b*[*i-a-šú*]
4′ SUHUR GIŠ.SAR *ša* ^{m}MAN—*lu—dà-ri* SUHUR Í[D!.*x x*]
5′ 1 GIŠ.SAR *til-lit* SUHUR GIŠ.SAR *ša x*[*x x x x x*]
6′ S[UHUR! ÍD].⌈*i*⌉-*lab-bi-a-šú* SUHUR [*x x x x x*]

7′ [É *tal-pi-tú a-n*]*a gi-mir-t*[*i-šú* SUHUR *x x x x*]
8′ [SUHUR GIŠ.SAR *š*]*a* ^{m}*a-a*—⌈*x*⌉[*x x x x x*]
rest broken away
Rev. beginning broken away
1′ [*kas-pu a-na* 10.ME]Š!-⌈*te*! *a*⌉-*n*[*a* EN-*šú* GUR]
2′ [*ina de-ni-šú*] DUG$_4$.DUG$_4$-*ma* [*là* TI-*qí*]

3′ [IGI ^{md}MAŠ].MAŠ—MAN—PAB LÚ*.[3-*šú dan-nu*]

ADD 433+
(Beginning destroyed)
1 owner of the people, land, and vineyar[ds being sold].

(cylinder seal impression)

2 An estate of 10 hectares of land by the seah of 9 ‘litres’;
3 one vineyard adjoining the river Ilab-b[iašu], the *vineyard* of Šarru-lu-dari, and the riv[er ...];
5 one vineyard adjoining the *vineyard* of [...], the Ilabbiašu [river], and [...];
7 [*a barnyard* in its] entirety [adjoining ......, the garden o]f Aya[......]
(Break)
r.1 [He shall return the money ten]fold to [its owners]. He shall contest [in his lawsuit] and [not succeed].

3 [Witness Ner]gal-šarru-uṣur, [chief ‘third man’].

332 Previous editions: AR 108+672, NALK 262. Collations: Assur 2/5.

4′ [IGI ^{md}*š*]*á-maš*—MAN—PAB LÚ*.[*mu-kil*—PA.MEŠ]
5′ [IGI] ⸢^{m}⸣^{d}MES—MAN—PAB L[Ú.*mu-kil*—PA.MEŠ *šá* MÍ—É.GAL]

6′ IGI ^{m}*si-lim*—*aš-šur* LÚ*.SUKKAL *dan*-⸢*nu*⸣ IGI ^{md}PA—*še*-[*zib*]
7′ IGI ^{m}*sa-ka-nu* LÚ*.*mu-kil*—PA.MEŠ
8′ IGI ^{m}PAB—*la-maš-ši* A ^{md}MAŠ.MAŠ—MAN—PAB LÚ*.3-*šú*

9′ IGI ^{m}*ha*—*ba-as-ti* LÚ*.GAL—Ì.DU$_{8}$.MEŠ
10′ IGI ^{md}PA—SU LÚ*.2-*u ša* LÚ*.GAL—*ú-ra*[*t*]
11′ IGI ^{md}UTU—AD-*u-a* LÚ*.*ha-za*-[*nu š*]*a* URU.NI[NA.KI]
12′ IGI ^{m}PAB-*u*—*a-mur* IGI ^{md}UTU—*šal*-[*lim* IG]I ^{md}P[A$^{!}$—MAN—PAB]
13′ IGI ^{m}⸢*man*⸣-*nu*—*ki*—URU.KASKAL IGI ^{m}[*x x x x x*]
14′ IGI ^{m}[*x x x x x x x x x x x x*]
rest broken away

^{4} [Witness Š]amaš-šarru-uṣur, [chariot driver].
^{5} [Witness] Marduk-šarru-uṣur, [chariot driver of the queen].
^{6} Witness Silim-Aššur, grand vizier. Witness Nabû-še[zib].
^{7} Witness Sakkannu, chariot driver.
^{8} Witness Ahu-lâmašši son of Nergal-šarru-uṣur, 'third man.'
^{9} Witness Habasti, head porter.
^{10} Witness Nabû-eriba, deputy of the team-commander.
^{11} Witness Šamaš-abu'a, may[or o]f Ni[neveh].
^{12} Witness Ahû-amur. Witness Šamaš-šal[lim. Witn]ess Na[bû-šarru-uṣur].
^{13} Witness Mannu-ki-Harran. Witness [NN].
^{14} Witness [......].
(Rest destroyed)

333. Remanni-Adad Buys Land in the Province of Harran

K 1511

beginning broken away
1′ [*x x* PAB] ⸢8$^{!}$⸣ ZI.MEŠ ⸢É⸣ [*x* ANŠE A.ŠÀ$^{?}$]
2′ [GIŠ.SAR *x-l*]*im* GIŠ.*til-lit* É *ad*-[*ru*]
e.3′ [GI]Š$^{!}$.MURUB$_{4}$$^{!}$ *ina* KUR.*na-gi*-⸢*i*⸣ [0]
4′ [*š*]*á* URU.KASKAL *ú-piš-ma*

5′ [^{m}*r*]*ém-a-ni*—^{d}IM
6′ [LÚ.*mu*]-⸢*kil*⸣—PA.MEŠ
r.1 [*ina* ŠÀ *x* MA.N]A KUG.UD *š*[*a*]
2 [URU.*gar-ga-mis x x*]⸢*x x*⸣[*x*]
rest broken away

ADD 451

(Beginning destroyed)
^{1} [... In all] 8 persons, an estate [*of x hectares of land*, a vineyard of x] thousand vines, a house, a threshing [floor] and a grove in the district of Harran —
^{5} [R]emanni-Adad, [char]iot driver, has contracted and [bought] (said property) [for x min]as of silver (by the mina) o[f Carchemish]
(Rest destroyed)

334. Remanni-Adad Buys Land in the Rab Šaqê Province

80-7-19,348 (+) 83-1-18,350 (+) 83-1-18,387

1 [N]A$_{4}$.KIŠ[IB ^{m}*x x x* NA$_{4}$.KIŠIB] ^{m}GIN—AD$^{!}$-*u-a* A-*šú*
2 [PA]B$^{!}$ 2$^{!}$ L[Ú.*x x x x x*]-*a-a* EN A.ŠÀ.GA
3 É *ši*$^{!}$-*q*[*i*$^{!}$ UN.MEŠ GIŠ.SA]R *ta-da-a-ni*

ADD 429

^{1} [S]ea[l of NN, seal of] Ken-abua, his son,
^{2} [in] all 2 m[en from ...], owners of the field under irrigation, [people, and vineya]rd being sold.

333 Previous editions: AR 109, NALK 268. $^{1, 3, r.2}$ See coll.
334 Previous editions: AR 105, NALK 274, 275, 276; → ABC 18; CIS II 1; Fales Epigraphs 16. Collations: Assur 2/5. The three tablets do not physically join.

(stamp seal impressions)

4 [É *x* ANŠE A.ŠÀ.GA *x x*] ⸢SUHUR⸣ A.ŠÀ *ša* ^{m}GÌR!.2!—15
5 [*x x x x x x x x x x x x x*]-*ra-a-nu*
6 [*x x x x x x x x* SUHUR A.ŠÀ] ⸢*ša*⸣ ^{m}*ga-lul*
7 [*x x x x x x x x x x x x x x* É] 6! ANŠE
8 [A.ŠÀ SUHUR KASKAL *ša a-na* URU.*x x x* DU-*u*]-⸢*ni*⸣
3 lines broken away
12 [*x x x x x x x x x*]*x qi*! [*x x x x*]
13 [*x x x x x x x x x*]*x ṣi nu ú x*[*x x*]
14 [*x x x x x x x x x x x x x*]-*a-nu* ⸢*x*⸣
15 [SUHUR KASKAL *ša a-na* URU.*x x x* DU]-*u-ni* : ^{m}*ku-sa-ni*!
16 [*x x x x x x x x x x x x x*]*x-ak-pu*
17 [É *x* ANŠE A.ŠÀ.GA *x x x x x*] SUHUR ⸢GIŠ⸣.SAR
18 [*ša* ^{m}*x x* SUHUR KASKAL *ša a-na* URU.*x*]*x-hi-li* DU-*u-ni*
19 [SUHUR *x x x* SUHUR A.ŠÀ *ša* ^{m}*bi*]-⸢*su*!⸣-*u-a* LÚ*.A.BA
20 [SUHUR *x x x* SUHUR A.ŠÀ *ša* ^{m}]^{d}UTU—*rém-a-ni* SUHUR A.ŠÀ
21 [*ša* ^{m}*x x x x x x x*] ⸢É!⸣ 22! ANŠE A.ŠÀ.GA
22 [*x x x x x ina ma-za*]-*ru-ti ina* GIŠ.BÁN *ša* 10 *qa*
23 [*x x x x x x x x x* SUH]UR É ^{m}ARAD—PAB.MEŠ-*šú* : ^{m}TE-*a-a*
24 [*x x x x x* GIŠ.SAR] *ša* GIŠ.*til-lit* SUHUR GIŠ.SAR
25 [*ša* ^{m}*x x x x x*] SUHUR : *ša* ^{md}IM—KALAG-*an*
26 [*x x x x x x x x*] : ^{m}*bé-e*!-*lu*!—*ha-lu-ṣu*
27 [*x x x x x x x*] ^{md}PA—PAB—PAB LÚ*.ENGAR ^{m}PAB—*pa-da*
28 [DUMU-*šú* PAB 2 ZI.MEŠ] ^{m}*si-lim*—U.U! 4 DUMU.MEŠ-*šú*
29 [1 DUMU.MÍ-*su* PAB] ⸢6⸣ ZI ^{m}*ab-du-u-ni* LÚ*.ENGAR
30 [*x x x x x x*]*x-šú* PAB 2 ZI PAB-*ma* 8 ZI.MEŠ
31 [*x x x x x t*]*al-pi-ta-a-te* 1 GIŠ.SAR *til-lit*
Edge uninscribed
r.1 [*x x x x x x x x x x i*]*na ma-*[*az-za-ru-ti*]
2 [*ú-piš-ma* ^{m}*rém-an-ni*—^{d}IM LÚ*.*m*]*u*!-*kil*—[KUŠ.PA.MEŠ]
3 [*dan-nu šá* ^{m}*aš-šur*—DÙ—A MAN KUR]—*aš*!-*šur*! [*ina* ŠÀ-*bi*]
4 [*x* MA.NA KUG.UD *ina* 1 MA.N]A *ša*! URU!.[*gar-ga-mis*!]
5 [TA* IGI ^{m}*x x x* ^{m}GIN]—AD!-*u-a* [*il-qi*]
6 [*kas-pu ga-mur ta-din*]-*ni* A.ŠÀ.GA ⸢GIŠ⸣.[SAR]
7 [É *ši-qi* UN.MEŠ *šú*]-*a-tú za-ár-p*[*u*] [0]
8 [*laq-qi-u tu-a-ru de-nu* DU]G$_{4}$.DUG$_{4}$ *la-áš-šú*

4 [An estate of x hectares of land ...] adjoining the field of Šep-Issar, [......]ranu, [...... adjoining the field] of Gallulu, [......];

7 [an estate of] 6 hectares [of land adjoining the road which lead]s [to ...]

(Break)

15 [adjoining the road which le]ads [to ...], adjoining Kusanu, [......]...;

17 [an estate of x hectares of land ...] adjoining the garden [of NN, the road which] leads [to the town ...]hili, [...... the field of Bi]suwa the scribe, [...... the field of] Šamaš-remanni, and the field [of ...];

21 an estate of 22 hectares of land [... in culti]vation, by the seah of 10 'litres,' [...... adjo]ining the estates of Urda-ahhešu, Sukkaya, [and ...];

24 [a vine]yard adjoining the *vineyards* of [...], Adad-dan, [......] and Belu-haluṣu;

27 [......] Nabû-ahu-uṣur, farmer, Ahi-pada, [his son, a total of 2 persons];

28 Silim-Dadi, his 4 sons [*and one daughter*, a total of] 6 persons;

29 Abdunu, farmer, his [...], a total of 2 persons;

30 in all 8 persons, [......, x *barn*]*yards*, 1 vineyard, [*x hectares of field*] in cu[ltivation] —

2 [Remanni-Adad, chief ch]ariot [driver of Assurbanipal, king of] Assyria, has contracted and bou[ght (said property) from NN and Ken]-abua [for x minas of silver by to the mi]na of [Carchemish].

6 [The money is pa]id [complet]ely. [Th]at land, vine[yard], [*barnyard*s, and people] are purch[ased and acquired. Any revocation, lawsuit, or liti]gation is void.

9 [*man-nu ša ina ur-kiš ina ma-te-me*] ⌜*i*⌝-*za-qu-pa-a-ni*
10 [GIL-*u-ni lu* ^{m}*x x lu* ^{m}GIN—A]D$^{!}$-*u-a* DUMU.MEŠ-*šú-nu*
11 [DUMU—DUMU.MEŠ-*šú-nu* ŠEŠ.MEŠ-*šú-nu* DUMU—Š]EŠ.MEŠ-*šú-nu* LÚ*.GAR-*nu-šú-*[*nu*]
12 [*x x x x x x* L]Ú.*qur-bu-šú-nu*
13 [TA* ^{m}*rém-a-ni*—^{d}IM DUMU.MEŠ-*šú*] DUMU—DUMU.MEŠ-*šú de-e-nu*
14 [DUG$_4$.DUG$_4$ *ub-ta-u-ni* 2 ANŠE.KUR.RA BABB]AR$^{!}$ *ina* GÌR.2 *aš-šur i-rak-kas*
15 [4 ANŠE *har-ba-kan-ni ina* GÌR.2 ^{d}30 *šá* URU.K]ASKAL *ú-še-rab*
16 [*x* MA.NA KUG.UD *x* MA.NA KUG.GI *ina b*]*ur-ki* ^{d}IŠ.TAR
17 [*a-ši-bat* URU.*x x i-šak-kan x x*] ⌜*x*⌝ *bé-ni a-na* 1-*me* UD.MEŠ
18 [*sa-ar-tú a-na kàl* UD.MEŠ *kas-pu*] *ana* 10.MEŠ-*te* ⌜*ana*⌝ EN.MEŠ-*šú*
19 [GUR *ina de-ni šú* DUG$_4$.DUG$_4$-*ma l*]*a i*-⌜*laq*⌝-*qi*

---

20 [IGI ^{md}U.GUR—MAN—PAB LÚ*.3]-*šú dan-nu*
21 [IGI ^{md}*šá-maš*—MAN—PAB LÚ*].DIB—KUŠ.PA.MEŠ
22 [IGI ^{md}UTU$^{?}$]—⌜*šal*⌝$^{!}$-*lim* LÚ*.[*x x x*]
two lines destroyed
25 [IGI] ⌜^{m}⌝[*x x x x x x* LÚ*].GAL$^{!}$—⌜SAG$^{!}$⌝
26 [IG]I ^{m}PAB—*l*[*a-maš-ši* LÚ*.3-*šú*] LÚ*.:
27 IGI ^{md}ŠÚ—*la*$^{!}$-[*x x x x x*] 0$^{!}$
28 IGI ^{m}*am-me-n*[*i*$^{!}$—*x x x x*] LÚ*.:
29 [I]GI ^{m}*bi-bi*$^{!}$-[*x x x x x*] LÚ*.:
30 IGI ^{m}*ha-di-*[*x x x x x x*] LÚ*.:
31 [IG]I ^{m}*gúr-d*[*i-i* LÚ.GIŠ.GIGIR—DU$_8$.ME]Š$^{?}$-*te*
32 [IGI] ^{md}P[A$^{!}$—*x x x x x x*]-IM : :
33 [IGI ^{m}]^{d}[*x x x x x x x x*] *ša* A—MAN
34 [IGI ^{m}*x x x x x x x* LÚ*.A.B]A$^{!}$—KUR
35 [IGI ^{m}*x x x x x x x* LÚ*.GIŠ.GI]GIR
broken away

rs.1 *d*[*nt by*]*t w ḥ*[*q*]*ly ḥ k*$^{!}$*nb*$^{!}$ *zy*
2 *n*[*xxx*]*d b mt rbšqn*

[9] [Whoever in the future, at any time], lodges a complaint [or breaks the contract, whether NN or Ken]-abua, or their sons, [grandsons, brothers or nep]hews, or their prefect [......] or their neighbour, and seeks a lawsuit or [litigation] against Remanni-Adad, [his sons] and grandsons,

[14] shall tie [2 white hors]es to the feet of Aššur, shall bring [4 *harbakannu* horses to the feet of Sin of Ha]rran, and [shall place x minas of silver and x minas of gold in the l]ap of Ištar [residing in Nineveh].

[17] (Guaranteed against) [seizures of] epilepsy for 100 days [(and against) fraud forever].

[18] [He shall return the money] tenfold to its owners. [He shall con]test [in his lawsuit] and not succeed.

---

[20] [Witness Nergal-šarru-uṣur], chief ['third] man.'

[21] [Witness Šamaš-šarru-ušur, chariot] driver.

[22] [Witness *Šamaš*]-šallim, [...].

(Break)

[25] [Witness NN], chief eunuch.

[26] [Wit]ness Ahu-l[âmašši, 'third man'] of ditto.

[27] Witness Marduk-la[...], ditto.

[28] Witness Ammi[ni-...], ditto.

[29] [Wit]ness Bibi[ya ...] ditto.

[30] Witness Hadi[...], ditto.

[31] [Witne]ss Gurd[î, *horse trainer of the op*]*en* [*chariotry*].

[32] [Witness] Na[bû-......] ditto ditto.

[33] [Witness NN, ...] of the prince.

[34] [Witness ....], palace [scri]be.

[35] [Witness ...... horse tra]iner.

(Rest destroyed)

[s.1] (Aramaic caption:) De[ed concerning the hou]se and f[ie]lds of *H* (and) Ken-abua [...] in the Land of the Chief Cupbearer.

335. Remanni-Adad Purchases Land near Qatna

K 1447

beginning broken away

1′ [É] 2 ANŠ[E A.ŠÀ *ša* LÚ*.*x x x x*]-⸢*a*⸣-*a*
2′ *ina* URU.*q*[*a*$^{!}$-*di-né-e* SUHUR *x x x x*]
3′ SUHUR ÍD.*h*[*a*$^{!}$]-⸢*bur*$^{!}$⸣ [SUHUR ^{m}*x x x*]—SI.SÁ
4′ SUHUR *ma-ú*$^{!}$-*te ša* [^{m}*x x x x x-n*]*i*$^{!}$

5′ É 10 ANŠE A.⸢ŠÀ *ša*$^{!}$ LÚ*$^{!}$.*x x x x*⸣-*a-a*
6′ *ina* URU.*qa-di-né-e* SUHUR URU.ŠE—^{m}*ki-i-ni*
7′ SUHUR KÁ.GAL *ša* URU.*qa-di-né-e* SUHUR KASKAL—MAN
8′ *ša* URU.BÀD—*a-du-ku*—1-*lim* PAB 50 ANŠE A.ŠÀ
9′ É *ši-qi* É *ad-ru* 2 GIŠ.SAR.MEŠ Ú.SAR.MEŠ
10′ *ina* URU.*bur-ri-im* UM$^{!}$ URU.*qa-di-né-e*

11′ *ú-piš-ma* ^{m}*rém-a-ni*—^{d}IM LÚ*.*mu-kil*—KUŠ.*a-pa-te*
12′ *dan-nu ša* ^{m}*aš-šur*—DÙ—A MAN KUR—*aš-šur*.KI
e.13′ *ina* ŠÀ-*bi* 10 MA.NA KUG.UD *ina ša* URU.*gar-ga-mis*
14′ TA*$^{!}$ IGI ^{m}EN—MAN—PAB TA*$^{!}$ IGI ^{md}PA-*u-a*
15′ TA*$^{!}$ IGI ^{m}*aš-šur*—*ši-i il-qi kas-pu*
16′ *ga-mur ta-din*$^{!}$-*ni* A.ŠÀ É *ad-ru* GIŠ.SAR
r.1 *šú-a-tú za-ar-pu laq-qi-ú tu-a-*⸢*ru*⸣
2 *de-e-nu* DUG$_4$.DUG$_4$ *la-áš-šú ina ur-kiš-ši*

3 *ina ma-te-ma man-nu ša i-za-qu-pa-a-ni*
4 *lu-u* LÚ.MEŠ-*e an-nu-te* DUMU.MEŠ-*šú-nu* DUMU—DUMU.MEŠ-*šú-nu*
5 ŠEŠ.MEŠ-*šú-nu* DUMU—ŠEŠ.MEŠ-*šú-*(*nu*) LÚ*.GAR-*nu-šú-nu* LÚ.*ha-za-na-šú-nu*

6 LÚ*.*mu-mu-nu-šú-nu qur-bu man-nu ša e-la-a-ni*
7 TA*$^{!}$ ^{m}*rém-a-ni*—^{d}IM LÚ*.*mu-kil*—KUŠ.*a-pa*.MEŠ *dan-nu*
8 TA*$^{!}$ DUMU.MEŠ-*šú* DUMU—DUMU.MEŠ-*šú de-e-nu* DUG$_4$.DUG$_4$
9 [*ub-t*]*a-u-ni* 1 GÚ.UN MA.NA KUG.UD LUH-*u* 10 MA.NA KUG.GI
10 *sak-ru ina bur-ki* ^{d}IŠ.TAR *a-ši-bat* URU.NINA.KI
11 *i-šak-kan kas-pu a-na* 10.MEŠ-*te ana* EN.MEŠ-*šú ú-*⸢*ta*⸣$^{!}$-*r*[*a*$^{!}$]
12 *ina la de-ni-šu* ⸢DUG$_4$.DUG$_4$⸣-*ma la* ⸢*i-laq*⸣-*qi*

---

13 [IGI ^{m}*si-lim*—*aš-šu*]*r* LÚ*.SUKKAL *dan-nu*
14 [IGI ^{m}*x x x x x* L]Ú.SUKKAL 2-*u* IGI ^{m}*ú-bar-bi-si* 3-*si-šú* [*dan*]-*nu*

ADD 418

(Beginning destroyed)

1 [An estate] of two hec[tares of land of the ...]eans, in Q[atna, adjoining ......], the Ha[bur] River, (the field of) [...]-lešir, and the maintenance field of [...];

5 an estate of 10 hectares of land of the [...]eans, in Qatna, adjoining the village of Kini, the city gate of Qatna, and the royal road of Dur-Katlimmu;

8 a total of 50 hectares of land under irrigation, a house, a threshing floor, and two vegetable gardens in the town of Burrim next to the city of Qatna —

11 Remanni-Adad, chief chariot driver of Assurbanipal, king of Assyria, has contracted and bought it for 10 minas of silver by the (mina) of Carchemish from Bel-šarru-uṣur, Nabû'a and Aššur-ši'i.

15 The money is paid completely. That field, house, threshing floor and gardens are purchased and acquired. Any revocation, lawsuit, or litigation is void.

r.3 In the future, at any time, whoever lodges a complaint, whether these men, their sons, grandsons, brothers or nephews, or their prefect or mayor, or any close relative of theirs,

6 whoever comes forward and seeks a lawsuit or litigation against Remanni-Adad, chief chariot driver, and his sons and grandsons, shall place one talent of refined silver and 10 minas of pure gold in the lap of Ištar residing in Nineveh, and shall return the money tenfold to its owners. He shall contest in his non-lawsuit and not succeed.

---

13 [Witness Silim-Aššu]r, grand vizier.

14 [Witness NN], second vizier. Witness Uarbisi, [chi]ef 'third man.'

335 Previous editions: AR 211, NALK 263. Collations: Assur 2/5. 10 The tablet does read UM here, but perhaps this is a scribal error for ŠU.2, see note on no. 326:13. r.9 Tablet "one talent mina"; scribal error.

15 [IGI ^{md}ŠÚ—MA]N—PAB A ^{m}*gab-bé-e*

16 [IGI ^{m}*x x x x*] 3-*si-šú* IGI ^{m}*aš-šur*—GIN—PAB 3-*si-šú*
17 [IGI ^{m}*x x x x* 3-*s*]*i-šú* IGI ^{m}*man-nu—ki—aš-šur*
18 [LÚ*.DIB—*a-pa-te š*]*a* DUMU—LUGAL
19 [IGI ^{md}*šá-maš*—MAN—PAB DIB—*a-pa*]-*te* IGI ^{m}*bar-ruq* KI.MIN
20 [IGI ^{md}PA—*še-zib* KI.MIN IGI ^{m}]NUMUN—GIN KI.MIN
21 [IGI ^{md}PA—SU LÚ*.2-*u ša* GAL]—*ú-rat*.MEŠ

22 [IGI ^{m}*x x x x x x x x x x*]⸢*x*⸣
23 [IGI ^{m}*man-nu—ki*—URU.KASKAL LÚ*.GIŠ.GIG]IR$^!$—DU$_8$.MEŠ [IGI ^{m}*x x x x x x x x x x x x*]⸢*x*⸣
rest broken away

15 [Witness Marduk-šar]ru-uṣur, son of Gabbê.
16 [Witness NN], 'third man.' Witness Aššur-kenu-uṣur, 'third man.'
17 [Witness ... 'third] man.' Witness Mannu-ki-Aššur, [chariot driver o]f the prince.
19 [Witness Šamaš-šarru-uṣur, chariot] driver. Witness Barruqu, ditto.
20 [Witness Nabû-šezib, ditto. Witness] Zeru-ukin, ditto.
21 [Witness Nabû-eriba, deputy of the team]-commander.
22 [Witness ....].
23 [Witness Mannu-ki-Harran], horse trainer of the open chariotry.
24 [Witness ....].
(Rest destroyed)

336. Remanni-Adad Buys an Estate in the Province of Arrapha

K 9747

beginning broken away
1′ [É *ši*]-*qi*$^!$ G[IŠ.SAR GIŠ.*til-lit x x x x x x x x x* É]
2′ 10 ANŠE A.ŠÀ ⸢1$^!$⸣ GIŠ.SAR ⸢GIŠ$^!$⸣.[*til-lit x x x x x x x x*]
3′ [*x x x x x*] URU.ŠE—*dan*$^!$-*a*-⸢*a*⸣ [*x x x x x x x x x*]⸢*x x*⸣
4′ [*x x x x* URU.Š]E$^!$—$^{m!}$*zu*$^!$-*um*$^!$-*bi* ⸢*x*⸣[*x x x x x*]⸢*x*⸣ *tal-pi-tú*
5′ [*x x x x*] *ina* URU.^{d}UTU—*ri-qa* PAB-*ma* ⸢5⸣-*me*-80 ANŠE A.ŠÀ.MEŠ 10 GIŠ.SAR.MEŠ
6′ ⸢GIŠ$^!$.*til*$^!$-*lit*$^!$⸣ 6 GIŠ.SAR.MEŠ ⸢*ši*$^!$⸣-*qi* A.MEŠ É$^!$.MEŠ$^!$ *ina na-gi-i* KUR.*arrap-ha*
7′ [*š*]*a* ^{md}⸢AMAR.UTU—SU *ša*⸣ ^{m}SU—PAB.MEŠ *ša*$^!$ ^{m}GIN$^!$-*i*$^!$ *ina* URU.⸢^{d}⸣UTU—*r*[*i-qa*]
8′ ⸢*ú-piš-ma* ^{m}*rém-a-ni*⸣—^{d}IM LÚ*.*mu-kil*$^!$—KUŠ.[PA.MEŠ *dan-nu*]
9′ [*š*]*a* ^{m}⸢*aš-šur*⸣—DÙ—⸢DUMU.UŠ⸣ LUGAL KUR—*aš-šur*.KI *ina* Š[À *x x x x x x x x x*]
10′ [*x x x š*]*a e-gír-ra*.MEŠ-*te* ⸢TA*$^!$⸣ [IGI LÚ.MEŠ *an-nu-te*]
11′ [0 ^{m}*rém*]-*a-ni*—^{d}IM LÚ*.*m*[*u-kil*—KUŠ—PA.MEŠ *dan-nu*]
r.1 [*i*]*l*-⸢*qi*⸣ *kas-pu ga-mur ta-din-ni* A.ŠÀ.MEŠ ⸢É$^!$⸣.[MEŠ GIŠ.SAR.MEŠ *ši-qi*]
2 ⸢*ad*⸣-*ri*.MEŠ ÍD.IGI.2.MEŠ *šu-a-tu za-ar-pa laq*-[*qi-a*]

3 *tu-a-ru de-e-nu* DUG$_4$.DUG$_4$ *la-áš-šú ina ur-kiš-ši i*[*na*$^!$ *ma-te-ma*]

ADD 419

(Beginning destroyed)
1 [under irr]igation, *a vi*[*neyard* ......];
2 10 hectares of land, one vine[yard ......]
3 [...] village of Dannaya [......]
4 [... vill]age of Zumbi [......], a *barnyard*

5 [...] in the town of Šamaš-riqa; in all 580 hectares of land, 10 vineyards, 6 irrigated gardens, and houses in the district of Arrapha, [bel]onging to Marduk-eriba, Riba-ahhe and Kenî, in Šamaš-r[iqa] —
8 Remanni-Adad, [chief] chariot dri[ver o]f Assurbanipal, king of Assyria, has contracted and bo[ught] (said property) from [these gentlemen] fo[r ......] documents.

r.1 The money is paid completely. Those lands, houses, [irrigated gardens], threshing floors and springs are purchased and acqu[ired]. Any revocation lawsuit, or litigation is void.
3 (Whoever) in the future, [at any time],

336 Previous editions: AR 444, NALK 271. Collations: Assur 2/5.

4 *lu-u* ^{md}AMAR.UTU—SU *lu-u* ^{m}SU—PAB.MEŠ *lu-u* ^{m}GIN-*i* DUMU ^{m}S[U$^{!}$—PAB—MEŠ]
5 *lu-u* DUMU.MEŠ-*šú-nu lu-u* DUMU—DUMU.MEŠ-*šú-nu lu-u* ŠEŠ.MEŠ-*šú-nu* DUMU—ŠEŠ.MEŠ-*šú*-[*nu*]
6 ⌈*lu*⌉-*u* LÚ.GAR-*nu-šú-nu lu-u mám-ma-šú-nu qur-bu ša e-la-a-ni*
7 T[A$^{!}$ ^{m}*ré*]*m-a-ni*—^{d}IM DUMU.MEŠ-*šú ù* DUMU—DUMU.MEŠ-*šú de-e-nu*
8 [DUG$_4$.DUG$_4$ *ub-ta-u-ni i*]-⌈*gar*⌉-*ru-u-ni ma-a kas-pu la ga-mur*
9 [*la ta-din-ni* A.ŠÀ.MEŠ GIŠ.SAR.MEŠ *ši-qi*] A.MEŠ *ad-ri*.MEŠ
10 [ÍD.IGI.2.MEŠ *šu-a-tu la za-ar-pa la laq-qi-a x* G]Ú.⌈UN KUG⌉.UD LUH-*u*
rest broken away

whether Marduk-eriba or Riba-ahhe or Kenî son of Riba-[ahhe], or their sons, grandsons, brothers or nephews, or their prefect, or any relative of theirs, comes forward [and seeks] or institutes a lawsuit or [litigation] [against Re]manni-Adad, his sons and grandsons, saying:

r.8 "The money is has not been paid completely. Those lands, irrigated gardens, threshing floors [and springs are not purchased and acquired],"

10 [shall pay x] talents of refined silver
(Rest destroyed)

FIG. 30. *Assyrian palace garden, with trees, buildings, an aqueduct, and irrigation channels.* BM 124939 (detail).

337. Remanni-Adad Buys Land

K 6275

beginning broken away

1′ [É *x* AN]ŠE A.ŠÀ.GA
2′ [*x x x*] URU.ŠE—^{m}*an-da-ra-ni*
3′ [*x x x*].MEŠ É *a-na* URU.*da-ri-g*[*i*$^{!}$]
4′ [*x x x*]*x* É 3 ANŠE É *ši-*[*qi*$^{!}$ *x x*]

5′ [*ú-piš-ma*] ^{m}*rém-an-ni*—[^{d}IM]
6′ [LÚ*.DIB—KUŠ.PA].MEŠ [*dan-nu*]
rest broken away

ADD 515

(Beginning destroyed)
(seal space)

1 [An estate of x hec]tares of land
2 [...] the village of Andaranu
3 [...] a house in the town of Darigu
4 [...] an estate of 3 hectares under irrig[ation ...] —
5 Remanni-[Adad, chief chariot driv]er, [has contracted and bought]
(Rest destroyed)

338. Remanni-Adad Buys an Estate

Ki 1904-10-9,181

beginning (three lines) broken away
1′ [NA$_4$.KIŠIB ^{m}*x x x x x x*]—15$^{!}$
2′ [NA$_4$.KIŠIB ^{m}*x x x x x x*]—15$^{!}$
3′ [NA$_4$.KIŠIB ^{m}*x x x x x x*] ⸢*x*⸣
4′ [EN *x x x x x x x x x x*] SU[M-*ni*]

5′ ⸢É⸣ 10 ANŠE A.ŠÀ KÁ *ia-ar-h*[*a* 0]
6′ [SUHUR] KASKAL$^{!}$.2$^{!}$ *š*[*a*$^{!}$ T]A$^{!}$ É—^{m}SU—DINGIR [0]
7′ [*a-na x x x x i*]*l-lak-u-n*[*i*]
8′ [*x x x x x š*]*a* É *sa-*⸢*a*$^{!}$⸣-[*x*(*x*)]
9′ [*x x x x x x x*] ⸢*x x x*⸣ [*x x x*]
rest broken away
Rev. beginning broken away
1′ *m*[*an-nu ša ina ur-kiš ina m*]*a-te-ma*
2′ *i-*[*za-qup-an-ni* GIL-*u-ni l*]*u-u* LÚ.[MEŠ-*e*]
3′ *an-n*[*u-te lu-u* DUMU].MEŠ-*šú-nu* [*ša de-e-nu*]
4′ DUG$_4$.D[UG$_4$ TA* ^{m}*ré*]*m*$^{!}$*-a-ni*—[^{d}IM]
5′ [DU]MU.MEŠ-⸢*šú*⸣ [DUMU-DUM]U.MEŠ-*šú ub-*[*ta-u-ni*]
6′ [*k*]*as*$^{!}$*-pu a-na* ⸢10.MEŠ⸣-*te a-na* [EN.MEŠ-*šú*]
7′ [GUR]-*ra* IGI ^{m}ITI.AB-*a-a* LÚ.*sa*[*r*$^{!}$*-tin-nu*]
8′ [IGI] ^{m}*si-lim—aš-šur* LÚ.SUKKAL IGI ^{m}[*x x x x*]*x*
9′ [LÚ].*mu-kil*—KUŠ.PA.MEŠ *ša* L[Ú$^{!}$*tur-ta*]*n*$^{?}$
10′ [IGI ^{m}]*sa*$^{!}$*-si-i*ʾ LÚ.*ha-za-a*[*n*$^{!}$]-*nu*

ADD 1189

(Beginning destroyed)
1 [Seal of NN, *son of* ...]-Issar;
2 [Seal of NN, *son of* ...]-Issar;
3 [Seal of ......],
4 [owners of the land ...] being sold.

(blank seal space)

5 An estate of 10 hectares of land, a gate, a po[ol, adjoining] the road which leads from Bet-Riba-ilu [to ..., *adjoining* the ... o]f the ... house [....]
(Break)

r.1 Wh[oever in the future, at any] time, lodges [a complaint an breaks the contract, wh]ether the[se] men [or] their [sons, and seeks a lawsuit] or litiga[tion against Re]manni-[Adad], his [so]ns and [grands]ons, [shall re]turn [the mon]ey tenfold to [its owner].
7 Witness Kanunayu, *sa*[*rtinnu*].
8 [Witness] Silim-Aššur, vizier.
8 Witness [NN], chariot driver of the [*commander-in-chi*]*ef*.
10 [Witness] Sasî, mayor.

337 Previous editions: AR 408, NALK 270. Collations: Assur 2/5.
338 Previous edition: NALK 285. 6, 8, r.6, 9f, 12 See coll.

11′ [IGI ^{m}]^{d}*šá-maš*—LUGAL—PAB LÚ.DIB—KUŠ-(PA).MEŠ
12′ [IGI] ^{m}*bar-ruq* :.! IGI ^{md}PA—KAR IGI ^{md}30—*rém-a*!-*ni*!
13′ [IGI ^{m}*s*]*a-ak*!-*kan*! LÚ.: IGI ^{md}PA—NUMUN—PAB
14′ [IGI ^{m}*i*]*n-na-an-ni* LÚ.*šá*—UGU—NINA.KI
15′ [IGI ^{md}PA—SU L]Ú.2-*u* GAL—*u-rat*
16′ [IGI ^{m}PAB-*u*—*a-mur* L]Ú.GIŠ.GIGIR—DU$_{8}$.MEŠ
17′ [IGI ^{m}*man-nu*—*ki*—KASKAL] LÚ.:.!
rest (three lines) broken away

11 [Witness] Šamaš-šarru-uṣur, chariot driver.
12 [Witness] Barruqu, ditto. Witness Nabû-eṭir. Witness Sin-remanni.
13 [Witness S]akkannu, ditto. Witness Nabû-zeru-uṣur.
14 [Witness I]nnanni, superintendent of Nineveh.
15 [Witness Nabû-eriba], deputy team-commander.
16 [Witness Ahû-amur], horse trainer of the open chariotry.
17 [Witness Mannu-ki-Harran], ditto.
(Rest destroyed)

339. Remanni-Adad Buys Land

Bu 91-5-9,41

beginning broken away
1′ [*x x x x x x x x x x x x*] PAB
2′ [*x x x x x x x x x x x x*] MAN
3′ [*ú-piš-ma* ^{m}*rém-an-ni*—^{d}IM LÚ.DIB—PA].MEŠ! *dan*!-*nu*
4′ [*ša* ^{m}*aš-šu*]*r*!—DÙ!—[A LUGAL KUR—*aš-šur*].KI
5′ *ina* ŠÀ-*bi* 1/2 MA.NA [KUG.UD *i*]*l-qi*
6′ *gas-pu ga-m*[*ur ta-a*]*d-din*
7′ A.ŠÀ *za-ar-pi* [*laq-qi*! *man-nu*] *ša ina ur*!-*k*[*iš*!]
8′ *ina ma-te-ma i*-GIL-*u*-[*ni lu-u* LÚ].MEŠ *an-nu-t*[*i*]
9′ *lu-u* DUMU.MEŠ-*šú*-[*n*]*u ša*! T[A ^{m}*rém-an-ni*—^{d}IM]
10′ DUMU.MEŠ-*šú* DU[MU]—DUMU.MEŠ-*šú d*[*e-nu* DUG$_{4}$.DUG$_{4}$]
e.11′ *ub-ta-ʾu-u-ni ka*[*s*!-*pu a-na* 10.MEŠ-*te*]
12′ [*a-na* E]N!.[MEŠ]-*šú*! [GUR]-*ra*
r.1 [*ina de-ni-šú* DUG$_{4}$].⸢DUG$_{4}$⸣-*ma la* ⸢*i*⸣-*laq-qi*

---

2 [IGI ^{md}U.GUR—MAN]—PAB LÚ.3-*šú dan-nu*
3 [IGI ^{m}*ú-ar*]-⸢*bi*⸣-*is* LÚ.3.U$_{5}$
4 [IGI ^{md}*šá-maš*—MAN]—PAB LÚ.DIB—PA.MEŠ
5 [IGI ^{md}PA—*še*]-*zib* LÚ.:
6 [IGI ^{m}*x x x*]*x* : IGI ^{m}*bar-ruq* :
7 [IGI ^{md}AMAR.UTU—M]U!—PAB LÚ.GAL—HAL

ADD 408

(Beginning destroyed)
3 [Remanni-Adad], chief [chariot driver of Assu]rbani[pal, king of Assyr]ia, [has contracted and bo]ught it for 1/2 mi[na of silver].
6 The money [is pa]id compl[etely]. The land is purchased [and acquired].
7 [Whoever] in the future, at any time, breaks the contr[act, whether] the[se men] or their sons, and seeks a law[suit or litigation] agai[nst Remanni-Adad], his sons and grandsons, [shall ret]urn the mon[ey tenfol]d [to] its [owne]rs. [He shall con]test [in his lawsuit] and not succeed.

---

r.2 [Witness Nergal-šarru]-uṣur, chief ‘third man.’
3 [Witness Uarb]is, ‘third man.’
4 [Witness Šamaš-šarru]-uṣur, chariot driver.
5 [Witness Nabû-še]zib, ditto.
6 [Witness ...], ditto. Witness Barruqu, ditto.
7 [Witness Marduk-šu]mu-uṣur, chief haruspex.

339 Previous editions: AR 415, NALK 286. Collations: Assur 2/5.

8 [IGI ^{m}*ba-ni-i*] LÚ$^{!}$.2-*u* LÚ.GAL—A.ZU
9 [IGI ^{m}*x x x*]-*a* LÚ.DIB—PA.MEŠ *ša* É GAŠAN$^{!}$—[É$^{!}$]
10 [IGI ^{md}PA—SU] LÚ.2-*u* LÚ.GAL—*ú-rat*
11 [IGI ^{m}*x x x x*]*x* IGI ^{m}*bu-di*$^{!}$—[*b*]*a*$^{!}$-*al*$^{!}$
12 [IGI ^{m}*x x x*]-*di* PAB 3 IGI.MEŠ [*x x x*]
13 [IGI ^{m}*x x x x x*] LÚ*$^{!}$.[*x x x x*]
rest broken away

[8] [Witness Banî], deputy of the chief physician.

[9] [Witness NN], chariot driver of the house of the lady [of the palace].

[10] [Witness Nabû-eriba], deputy team-commander o[f the prince].

[11] [Witness NN]. Witness Budi-Ba'al.

[12] [Witness ...]di, a total of 3 witnesses [from ...].

(Rest destroyed)

340. Remanni-Adad Buys Land, Gardens and People

82-5-22,139

beginning broken away
1′ [A.ŠÀ.MEŠ GIŠ.SAR.MEŠ UN].MEŠ *za-*⌈*ár-pu*⌉ [0]
2′ [*la-qi-u tu-a-ru d*]*e-nu*$^{!}$ DUG$_4$.DUG$_4$ *la-áš-šú*

3′ [*man-nu šá ina ur-kiš*] *ina ma-te-ma*
4′ [*lu-u* ^{m}*x x x x lu*]-*u* DUMU.MEŠ-*šú*
5′ [*lu-u* DUMU—DUMU.MEŠ-*šú*] *lu-u* PAB.MEŠ-*šú*
6′ [*lu-u* DUMU—PAB.MEŠ-*šú ša e*]-*la-an-ni*
7′ [TA* ^{m}*rém-an-ni*—^{d}]IM DUMU.MEŠ-*šú*
8′ [DUMU—DUMU.MEŠ-*šú de*]-*nu* DUG$_4$.DUG$_4$
9′ [*ub-ta-u-ni ma-a*] *kas-pu la gam-mur*
10′ [*la ta-ad-din* A.ŠÀ.ME]Š$^{!}$ GIŠ.SA[R.ME]Š$^{!}$
11′ [UN.MEŠ *la za-ar-pu*] *la* [*la-qi-u*$^{!}$]
rest broken away
Rev. beginning broken away
1′ [*x x* KUG.UD *ina* 10]-⌈A$^{!}$.TA$^{!}$⌉.[AN]
2′ [*a-na* EN-*šú* GUR *i*]*na*$^{!}$ *la de-ni-*[*šú*]
3′ [DUG$_4$.DUG$_4$-*ma la* T]I-*qí*

4′ [IGI ^{m}MAN—*lu*—*dà-ri*] LÚ.EN.NAM URU.BÀD—^{m}MAN—GIN
5′ [IGI ^{m}*x x x x x*] LÚ.: *šá* URU.*a-me-di*
6′ [IGI ^{m}*x x x x x*] LÚ.: *šá* URU.*tú-uš-hi*
7′ [IGI ^{m}*x x x x x*] LÚ.3-*šú dan-nu*
8′ [IGI ^{m}*x x x x x* LÚ].DIB—KUŠ.PA.MEŠ
9′ [IGI ^{m}*x x x x x* LÚ].GAL—*ki-ṣir*
10′ [IGI ^{m}*x x x x x*] LÚ.3-*šú*
11′ [IGI ^{m}*ha—ba-as-te*] LÚ.GAL—Ì.DU$_8$.MEŠ
12′ [IGI *x x x x x x x x x x šá* DUMU]—MAN
13′ [*x x x x x x x x x x x x x*]*x*
rest broken away

ADD 372

(Beginning destroyed)

[1] [the fields, gardens and peop]le are acquired [and purchased. Any revocation, lawsuit] or litigation is void.

[3] [Whoever in the future], at any time, [whether NN], or his sons grandsons, brothers or [nephews] comes forward [and seeks a law]suit or litigation [against Remanni-A]dad, and his sons [and grandsons, saying]:

[9] "The money is not completely [paid, the field]s, gar[de]ns and [people are] not [acquired and purchased],"

(Break)

[r.1] [shall return the money ten]fold [to its owner. He shall contest] in [his] non-lawsuit [and not] succeed.

---

[4] [Witness *Šarru-lu-dari*], governor of Dur-Šarruken.

[5] [Witness NN], ditto of Amidi.

[6] [Witness NN], ditto of Tušhan.

[7] [Witness NN], chief 'third man.'

[8] [Witness NN], chariot driver.

[9] [Witness NN], cohort commander.

[10] [Witness NN], 'third man.'

[11] [Witness Habasti], head porter.

[12] [Witness NN, ... of the pri]nce.

(Rest destroyed)

340 r.1 The atypical spelling 10-A.TA.AN also occurs in no. 253 r.6, a deed of Issar-duri.

341. Remanni-Adad Buys 30 Slaves

83-1-18,348

beginning broken away
1′ 1 [*x x x x x x x x x x x x x*]
2′ 2$^{!}$ Z[I.MEŠ *x x x x x x x x x x*]
3′ ^{m}ZALÁG—[*x x x x x x x x x x x*]
4′ ^{m}⸢*šá*$^{!}$—$^{d!}$⸣[*x x x x x x x x*]
5′ ^{m}⸢^{d}⸣[*x x x x x x x x x x*]
6′ ^{m}*ba-n*[*i*$^{!}$*-i x x x x x x x*]
7′ ^{m}APIN$^{!}$-*ka-x*[*x x x x x x x x*]
8′ PAB 12 ZI.[MEŠ ^{m}*x x x x x x*]
9′ MÍ-*šú* DUMU.MÍ-⸢*su*⸣ ^{m}I—[*x x x x x*]
10′ PAB 5 ZI.MEŠ 0$^{!}$
r.1 PAB 30 ZI.MEŠ LÚ*.ARAD.MEŠ *ša* É-*šú ú-piš-ma*
2 ^{m}*rém-a-ni*—10 LÚ*.*mu-kil*—KUŠ.PA.MEŠ *ša* MAN KUR—*aš-šur*
3 *ina* ŠÀ 30$^{!}$ MA.NA KUG.UD TA* IGI ^{m}*arba-ìl-a-a*
4 A.ŠÀ.MEŠ É.MEŠ UN.MEŠ *il*$^{!}$*-qi*$^{!}$ *kas*$^{!}$*-pu*
5 *gam-*[*mur ta-din* A.ŠÀ.MEŠ É.MEŠ UN].MEŠ
6 [*šu-a-tú zar-pu la-qi-u tu*]*-a-ru*$^{!}$

7 [*de-nu* DUG$_4$.DUG$_4$ *la-áš-šú man*]*-nu*
8 [*ša ur-kiš ina ma-te-ma i-za-qu*]*-ban*$^{!}$*-ni*$^{!}$
9 [TA* ^{m}*rém-a-ni*—10 DUMU.MEŠ-*šú* DUMU—DUMU.MEŠ]-*šú*$^{!}$
10 [*de-e-nu* DUG$_4$.DUG$_4$ *ub-ta-ʾu*]*-ni*$^{!}$
11 [*x* MA.NA KUG.UD LUH *x* MA.NA KUG.GI *sak*]-⸢*ru*$^{!}$⸣
rest broken away
s.1 [*x x x x x*]*x*[*x x x x*]
2 [*x x x x x*] ⸢*su*⸣ [*x x x x*]
3 [IGI ^{m}ARAD—^{d}*n*]*a-na*$^{!}$*-a* ⸢LÚ*⸣.[*x x x x*]
4 [*x x x*] IGI ^{m}*x*[*x x x x*]

ADD 424

(Beginning destroyed)
2 2 per[sons ....]
3 Nur-[......]
4 Ša-[......]
5 [.......]
6 Ban[î, ...],
7 Ereš-[..., NN]; a total of 12 persons.
8 [NN], his wife and daughter; Na'di-[... and NN]; a total of 5 persons,
r.1 in all 30 persons, servants of his house —
2 Remanni-Adad, chariot driver of the king of Assyria, has contracted and bought (said) fields, houses and people for 30 minas of silver from Arbailayu.
4 The money [is paid] comple[tely. Those fields, houses and peop]le [are purchased and acquired. Any rev]ocation, [lawsuit, or litigation is void].
7 [Who]ever i[n the future, at any time, lodges a com]plaint [and see]ks [a lawsuit or litigation with Remanni-Adad], his [sons and grandsons, shall place x minas of refined silver and x minas of pu]re [gold]
(Break)

r.3 [Witness Urda-N]anaya, [...].
4 [...]. Witness [NN].

342. Remanni-Adad Buys 10 Slaves

K 1563

beginning broken away

1′ ^{m}*si-in*—DU—IGI [LÚ.*x x x* DUMU-*šú*]
2′ MÍ-*šú* DUMU.MÍ-*su pir-su* [^{m}*x x x* DUMU-*šú*]
3′ MÍ-*šú* DUMU.MÍ-*su* ^{m}*ú-ṣa-*[*x x x x x*]
4′ LÚ.*šá*—U.SAG.MEŠ-*šú* MÍ-*šú* PAB 10 [ZI.MEŠ]
5′ *ú-piš-ma* ^{m}*rém-an-ni*—^{d}IM L[Ú.*mu-kil*—KUŠ.PA.MEŠ]

ADD 247

(Beginning destroyed)
(blank seal space)

---

1 Sin-alik-pani, [..., his son], wife and weaned daughter; [NN, his son], wife and daughter; Uṣa[...], hatter, and his wife, a total of 10 [persons] —
5 Remanni-Adad, [chariot driver], has

341 Previous editions: AR 90, NALK 279. Collations: Assur 2/5.
342 Previous editions: AR 83, NALK 269. 2 At the end of the line restore possibly ^{m}*ú-ṣa-*[*mir—ak-šu-du*] (cf. GPA 224 r.2; no other name beginning with *Uz/ṣa-* is attested in the NA onomasticon).

6′ TA* IGI LÚ.MEŠ-*e an-nu-t*[*e ina* ŠÀ-*bi*]

7′ ⸢*x* MA.NA KUG.UD *ša* URU⸣.*gar-ga-mis* TI-*q*[*í*! *kas-pu*]
8′ [*gam-mur ta*]-⸢*din*⸣ UN.MEŠ *šú-a-tú za-a*[*r-pu la-qí-u*]
9′ [*tu-a-ru d*]*e-e-nu* DUG$_4$.DUG$_4$ *la-áš*-[*šú*]
10′ [*ṣib-tú be-en*]-*nu a-na* 1-*me* UD.MEŠ *sa-ar*-[*tú*]
11′ [*a-na kàl* MU.A]N.NA.MEŠ *man-nu šá ina ur-ki*[*š*]
12′ [*ina ma-te-ma* G]IL-*u-ni lu-u* LÚ.MEŠ-*e* ⸢*an*⸣-[*nu-te*]
13′ [*lu-u* DUMU.MEŠ]-*šú*!-*nu lu-u* DUMU—DUMU.MEŠ-*šu*!-[*nu*]
14′ [*lu-u x x x x*]⸢*x*⸣.MEŠ EN—*il-ki-šú-nu de*-⸢*e*⸣-[*nu*]
15′ [DUG$_4$.DU]G$_4$ TA* ^{m}*rém-an-ni*—^{d}IM *ù* DU[MU.MEŠ-*šú*]
16′ [*ub-t*]*a-ʾu-u-ni* 1 GÚ.UN KUG.UD 10 MA.NA [KUG.GI]
17′ [*a-n*]*a* ⸢^{d}⸣15 *ša*! NINA.KI SUM-*an kas-p*[*u a-na*]
r.1 [10.MEŠ-*te a-n*]*a* ⸢EN⸣.MEŠ-*šú* G[UR-*ra*]
2 [*ina de-ni-šú*] DUG$_4$.DUG$_4$-*ma la* [*i-laq-qí*]

---

3 [IGI ^{md}MAŠ].MAŠ—MAN—PAB LÚ.3.⸢U$_5$⸣ [*dan-nu*]
4 [IGI ^{m}*x-x*—KA]M-*eš* LÚ.3.[U$_5$]
5 [IGI ^{m}*ú-a*]*r-bi-is* LÚ.3.[U$_5$]
6 [IGI ^{m}NUMUN-*ú-t*]*i-i* LÚ.*mu-kil*—KUŠ.[PA.MEŠ]
7 [IGI ^{md}*šá-maš*]—LUGAL—PAB LÚ.[:.]
8 [IGI ^{md}PA—*še*]-*zib* LÚ.[:.]
9 [IGI ^{m}*x x x x x*] LÚ.[*x x*]
10 [IGI] ^{m}⸢*x x x*⸣-[*g*]*i*!-*me* LÚ.[*x x*]
11 ⸢IGI⸣ ^{m}EN—IGI.LAL LÚ.[*x x*]
12 IGI ^{m}LUGAL—GIN—PAB IGI ^{m}*suk-ka*-⸢*a*⸣-[*a* LÚ.ARAD]
13 *ša* LÚ.KAŠ.LUL IGI ^{md}IM—PAB.MEŠ—[AŠ? LÚ.*x x*]
14 IGI ^{md}PA—SU LÚ.2-*e ša* L[Ú.GAL—*ú-rat*]
15 IGI ^{md}UTU—*šal-lim* LÚ.[*mu-kil*—KUŠ.PA.MEŠ]
1 line space
16 ⸢ITI.BARAG!⸣ UD-21-KÁM [*lim-mu* ^{m}*x x x x x*]
17 [IGI] ⸢^{m}⸣^{d}3[0—*x x x x x x x x x*]

contracted and bought (said people) from these gentlemen [for] x minas of silver (by the mina) of Carchemish.

7 [The money is pa]id completely. Those people are purch[ased and acquired. Any revocation, law]suit, or litigation is voi[d].

10 (Guaranteed against) [seizures of epile]psy for 100 days (and against) frau[d fore]ver.

11 Whoever in the future, [at any time, br]eaks the contract, whether th[ese] men [or] their [sons] or grandsons, [or ...] their labour-duty superior, and seeks a lawsu[it or liti]gation against Remanni-Adad and [his] s]ons,

16 shall pay one talent of silver and 10 minas of [gold t]o Ištar of Nineveh, and shall re[turn] the mon[ey tenfold t]o its owners. He shall contest [in his lawsuit] and not [succeed].

---

r.3 [Witness Ner]gal-šarru-uṣur, 'third man.'
4 [Witness ...-e]reš, 'third [man].'
5 [Witness Ua]rbis, 'third [man].'
6 [Witness Zaru]tî, chariot dr[iver].
7 [Witness Šamaš]-šarru-uṣur, [ditto].
8 [Witness Nabû-še]zib, [ditto].
9 [Witness NN, ...].
10 [Witness ...g]ime, [...].
11 Witness Bel-lamur, [...].
12 Witness Šarruken-uṣur. Witness Sukka[ya, servant] of the cupbearer.
13 Witness Adad-ahhe-[*iddina*, ...].
14 Witness Nabû-eriba, deputy of th[e team-commander].
15 Witness Šamaš-šallim, [...].

16 Month Nisan (I), 21st day, [eponym year of ...].
17 [Witness] Si[n-......].

343. Remanni-Adad Buys 5 Slaves for 5 Minas of Silver

83-1-18,689

1 [NA$_4$.KIŠIB ^{m}KALAG-a]-⸢ni⸣—U.GUR NA$_4$.KIŠIB ^{m}zi!-l[i-i]
2 [NA$_4$.KIŠIB ^{m}kur-la]-a-a NA$_4$.KIŠIB ^{m}aš-šur—šal-lim—PAB.MEŠ
3 [DUMU.MEŠ] ^{m}gab-bu—DINGIR.MEŠ—APIN-eš
4 [PAB 4 LÚ].ME EN UN.MEŠ SUM-ni

---

5 [x x x] ⸢MÍ⸣-šu PAB 2 ^{m}[GIG]—⸢a-da-la⸣-l[i]
6 [x x x x PAB] 2 ⸢LÚ⸣.ṣu-hur-te
7 [MÍ.man-nu—x-x-x] ⸢AMA⸣-šu-nu PAB 5 ZI.MEŠ
8 [ARAD.MEŠ ša L]Ú.MEŠ-e an-nu-te
9 [ú-piš-ma ^{m}rém]-⸢a⸣-ni—^{d}IM LÚ.DIB—KUŠ.PA.[MEŠ 0!]
10 [ša ^{m}aš-šur—DÙ]—⸢A⸣ MAN KUR—aš-šur.KI
11 [ina ŠÀ 5 MA.NA KUG.UD ina šá U]RU.gar-ga-mis
12 [TA* IGI ^{m}KALAG-a-ni—U.GUR T]A IGI [^{m}zi-li-i]
rest broken away
Rev. entirely broken away

ADD 270

1 [Seal of Da''ina]nni-Nergal, seal of Zil[î, seal of Kur-il]a'i, seal of Aššur-šallim-ahhe, [sons of] Gabbu-ilani-ereš,

4 [a total of 4 me]n, owners of the people being sold.

(blank seal space)

---

5 [...] and his wife, a total of 2; [Marṣiš]-adallal, [..., a total of] 2 youths; [Mannu-...], their mother; in all 5 persons, [servants of] these [gentlem]en —

9 [Rem]anni-Adad, chariot driver [of Assurban]ipal, king of Assyria, [has contracted and bought them] for 5 minas of silver by (the mina) of] Carchemish [from Da''inanni-Nergal, Zilî]

(Rest destroyed)

344. Duplicate of the Previous Document

80-7-19,140

beginning broken away
1′ [x x]⸢x x x x⸣[x x x x x x]
2′ [^{m}GI]G—a-da-la-li ^{m}⸢ba!⸣-[x x x]
3′ [PAB 2] ⸢LÚ⸣.ṣu-hur-te MÍ.man-nu—[x x]
4′ [AM]A-šú-nu PAB 5 ZI.MEŠ LÚ*.[ARAD.MEŠ]
5′ ša LÚ.MEŠ-e an-[nu-te]
6′ ú-piš-ma ^{m}rém-a-ni—^{d}IM LÚ*.DI[B—KUŠ.PA.MEŠ]
7′ dan-nu ša ^{m}aš-šur—DÙ—A MAN KUR—[aš-šur.KI]
8′ ⸢ina ŠÀ⸣-bi 5 MA.NA KUG.⸢UD⸣ ina! ša ⸢URU⸣.[gar-ga-mis]
9′ TA* IGI ^{m}KALAG-a-ni—U.GUR TA* IGI ^{m}zi!-[li-i]
10′ TA* IGI ^{m}kur-la-a-a TA* IGI ^{m}⸢aš-šur—šal-lim⸣—[PAB.MEŠ]
11′ il-qi kas!-⸢pu! ga⸣-mur ta-din-ni [0]
12′ [UN.MEŠ šú-a]-tú [za]-ár-pu laq-qi-⸢u⸣

ADD 271

(Beginning destroyed)

2 [Mar]ṣiš-adallal, Ba[...],

3 [a total of 2] youths; Mannu-[...], their mother;

4 in all 5 persons, [servants] of the[se] gentlemen —

6 Remanni-Adad, chief ch[ariot driver] of Assurbanipal, king of Ass[yria], has contracted and bought them for 5 minas of silver by the (mina) of [Carchemish] from Da''inanni-Nergal, Zi[lî], Kur-ila'i, and Aššur-šallim-[ahhe].

11 The money is paid completely. [Th]ose [people are pu]rchased and acquired. [Any

343 Previous editions: AR 67, NALK 273. → no. 344. 1 See coll. 7 The sign PAB, omitted in NALK, is on the tablet (see coll.)
344 Previous editions: AR 68, NALK 272. 1ff, 8, 14, r.3 See coll.

13′ [*tu-a-ru d*]*e-e-nu* DUG$_4$.DUG$_4$ *la-áš-š*[*ú*]
14′ [*ina ur-kiš ina*] ⸢*ma*⸣-*te-ma* ⸢*man*⸣-*nu ša* ⸢*e*$^!$⸣-[*la-ni*]
15′ [*i-za*]-*qu*-⸢*pa*⸣-[*ni i*-GIL-*u-ni*]

r.1 [*lu-u* ^{m}KALAG-*a-n*]*i*—⸢U.GUR *lu-u*⸣ [^{m}*zi-li-i*]
2 [*lu-u* ^{m}*kur-la-a*]-*a lu-u* ^{m}*aš*-[*šur—šal-lim*—PAB.MEŠ]
3 [*lu-u*] DUMU.MEŠ-[*šú*]-*nu* DUMU—DUMU.M[EŠ-*šú-nu* ŠEŠ.MEŠ-*šú-nu*]
4 [*lu-u*] ⸢DUMU⸣—ŠEŠ.(MEŠ)-*šú-nu lu-u* LÚ*.GAR-*nu*-[*šú-nu*]
5 [*lu-u h*]*a-za-nu-šú-nu lu-u mu*-⸢*mu-nu-šú*⸣-[*nu*]
6 [*ša*] TA* ^{m}*rém-a-ni*—^{d}⸢IM⸣ [LÚ*.DIB—KUŠ.PA.MEŠ]
7 [TA*] DUMU.MEŠ-*šú* DUMU—DUMU.[MEŠ-*šú d*]*e*-[*e-nu*]
8 [DUG$_4$].DUG$_4$ [*u*]*b-ta*-⸢*u*⸣-[*ni x x x x x x x*]
rest broken away

revocation, la]wsuit, or litigation is voi[d].

[14] [In] the future, at any [time], whoever [comes forward, lodges] a complaint, [and breaks the c]ontract,

[r.1] whether Da''inan]ni-Nergal, [Zilî, Kur-ila']i or Aš[šur-šallim-ahhe, or] their sons, grandsons, [brothers or] nephews, or [their] prefect [or] mayor, or any relative of th[eirs],

[6] and seeks a lawsu[it or liti]gation against Remanni-Adad, [chariot driver], and his sons and grandsons [...]

(Rest destroyed)

345. Remanni-Adad Buys Three Slaves

K 1505

1 [NA$_4$.KIŠIB ^{md}PA—A—SUM-*na*]
2 [EN] ⸢UN⸣.[ME]Š [SUM-*ni*]

3 [^{m}*x x*]-*a*$^!$—DÙG$^!$.G[A$^!$] ARAD-*šú*
4 [MÍ.*x x x*]—⸢DINGIR$^!$⸣-*a-a* MÍ-*šú*
5 [MÍ.*x x*]-*a*$^!$-*tú* DUMU.MÍ-*su*
6 [PAB 3 Z]I.MEŠ *ú-piš-ma*
7 [^{m}*rém-a-ni*]—^{d}⸢IM⸣ LÚ.*mu-kil*—⸢KUŠ⸣.PA.MEŠ
8 [*dan-nu šá* ^{m}*aš-šur*]—DÙ$^!$—A LUGAL 0$^!$
9 [TA* IGI ^{m}]^{d}PA—A—SUM-*na*
10 [*ina* ŠÀ *x*] GÍN.MEŠ KUG.UD
11 [*il-qí* UN.MEŠ *šú-a*]-⸢*tu*$^?$⸣ *zar*$^!$-[*pu la-qí-ú*]
rest broken away
Rev. beginning broken away

1′ [*kas-pu a-na* 10].MEŠ$^!$ ⸢*a*⸣-[*na* EN-*šú* GUR]
2′ [*ina de-ni-šú*] ⸢*i*⸣-*da*-⸢*bu*⸣-*u*[*b*$^!$-*ma la i-laq*]-⸢*qí*⸣
3′ [*de-en-šú*] *da-a-a-ni l*[*a*$^!$ *i-š*]*e*$^!$-[*m*]*e*$^!$

4′ [IGI ^{m}*sa-*ʾ]*i*$^!$-*ru* LÚ.3.U$_5$
5′ [IGI ^{md}P]A$^!$—IGI.LAL$^?$-*an* LÚ.3.U$_5$
6′ [IGI ^{md}]EN$^!$—*ú*$^!$-[[*sat*$^?$]] LÚ.*ha-za-nu*

ADD 322

[1] [Seal of Nabû-aplu-iddina, owner] of the people [being sold].

(cylinder seal impression)

[3] [...]a-ṭa[b], his servant, [...]-ila'i, his wife, [...]atu, his daughter, [a total of 3 per]sons —

[7] [Remanni]-Adad, [chief] chariot driver [of] king [Assur]banipal, has contracted and [bought them from Na]bû-aplu-iddina [for x] shekels of silver.

[11] [Tho]se [people] are purch[ased and acquired].

(Break)

[r.1] [He shall return the money ten]fold to [its owner]. He shall conte[st in his lawsuit and not suc]ceed. The judge shall not [he]ed [his case].

[4] [Witness Sa]'iru, 'third man.'

[5] [Witness Na]bû-*emuranni*, 'third man.'

[6] [Witness] Bel-*usat*, mayor.

345 Previous editions: AR 200, NALK 266. Collations: Assur 2/5.

7′ [IGI] $^{m⸢d!⸣}$U$^{!}$.GUR$^{!}$—DINGIR-⸢*a*$^{!}$-*a*$^{!}$⸣ LÚ$^{!}$.A$^{!}$.BA$^{!}$
8′ [IGI ^{m}*h*]*u—ba-šá-a-te* LÚ.GAR.U.U
9′ [IGI ^{m}]⸢*a*$^{!}$⸣-*kul-la-a-nu*
10′ [IGI ^{m}E]N$^{?}$—*la-mur* LÚ.GAL—URU.MEŠ-*ni*
rest broken away

7 [Witness] Nergal-ila'i, scribe.
8 [Witness H]ubašati, driller.
9 [Witness] Akkullanu.
10 [Witness *Be*]*l*-lamur, village manager.
(Rest destroyed)

346. Remanni-Adad Purchases a Slave

K 1485

beginning broken away
1′ [LÚ.*m*]*u-kil*—⸢KUŠ⸣.PA.MEŠ *d*[*an-nu*]
2′ [*ša*] ^{m}*aš-šur*—DÙ—A MAN KUR—*aš-š*[*ur*.KI]
3′ ⸢*ina*⸣ ŠÀ-*bi* 1 MA.NA KUG.UD *ina* 1 MA.N[A-*e ša*]
4′ ⸢URU⸣.*gar-ga-mis il*-⸢*qi*⸣
5′ ⸢*kas*⸣-*pu gam-mur ta-ad-din*
6′ LÚ *šú-a-tu za-rip laq-qi*
7′ ⸢*tu-a*⸣-*ru de-e-nu* ⸢DUG$_4$⸣.DUG$_4$
8′ ⸢*la*⸣-*áš-šú man-nu ša ina ur-kiš ina ma-te*-⸢*ma*⸣
9′ *i-za-qu-pa-an-ni*
r.1 *lu-u* ^{md}PA—PAB *lu-u* DUMU.MEŠ-*šú*
2 *lu-u* DUMU—DUMU.MEŠ-*šú ša de-e-nu*
3 DUG$_4$.DUG$_4$ TA* ^{m}*rém-a-ni*—^{d}IM
4 DUMU.MEŠ-*šú* DUMU—DUMU.MEŠ-*šú ub-ta-u-ni*
5 10 MA.NA KUG.UD 1 MA.NA KUG.GI
6 *ina bur-ki* ^{d}15 *šá* NINA GAR-*an*
7 ⸢*kas*⸣-[*pu*] *a-na* 10.MEŠ-*te* [*a*]-⸢*na*⸣ EN.MEŠ-*šú*
8 [GUR *ina de-ni-šú* DUG$_4$.DUG$_4$-*ma la i-laq*]-⸢*qi*⸣
rest broken away

ADD 203

(Beginning destroyed)

1 [Remanni-Adad], ch[ief chari]ot driver [of] Assurbanipal, king of Assy[ria, has contracted and] bought him for one mina of silver by the mina [of] Carchemish.

5 The money is paid completely. That man is purchased and acquired. Any revocation, lawsuit, or litigation is void.

8 Whoever in the future, at any time, lodges a complaint, whether Nabû-naṣir or his sons or grandsons, and seeks a lawsuit or litigation against Remanni-Adad and his sons and grandsons,

r.5 shall place 10 minas of silver and one mina of gold in the lap of Ištar of Nineveh, [and shall return] the mon[ey] tenfold to its owners. [He shall contest in his lawsuit and not suc]ceed.

(Rest destroyed)

347. Remanni-Adad Buys a Slave

81-2-4,153

1 [N]A$_4$.KIŠIB $^{m⸢d⸣}$ŠÚ—MAN—PAB$^{!}$
2 NA$_4$.KIŠIB ^{m}MAN—*lu—dà-ri*
3 EN LÚ *ta-da-ni*

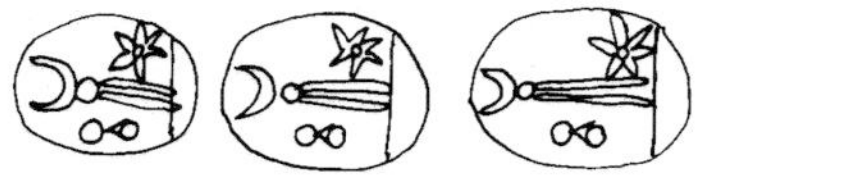

4 [^{m}]^{d}PA—*ia-a-li* ARAD-*šú-n*[*u*$^{!}$]

ADD 174

1 [S]eal of Marduk-šarru-uṣur,
2 seal of Šarru-lu-dari,
3 owners of the man being sold.

(stamp seal impressions)

4 Nabû-iyyali, servant of Marduk-šarru-

346 Previous editions: AR 484, NALK 264.
347 Previous editions: AR 497, NALK 277.

5 [*š*]*a* ^{md}ŠÚ—MAN—PAB ⸢*ša*⸣ ^{m}MAN—[*lu—dà-ri*]
6 *ú-piš-ma* ^{m}*rém-*⸢*a*⸣*-ni—*⸢^{d}⸣[IM]
7 LÚ.*mu-kil—*⸢KUŠ.PA⸣.MEŠ [0]
8 *ina* ŠÀ-*bi* 1 MA.NA KUG.UD [0]
9 [*in*]*a* 1 MA.NA-⸢*e*⸣ *ša* URU.*gar-g*[*a-mis*]
10 [*i*]*l-qí kas-pu* ⸢*ga*⸣*-mur* [*ta-din*]
11 [LÚ *šu*]*-a-te za-rip* [*la-qí*]
12 [*tu-a-r*]*u de-*⸢*e*⸣*-*[*nu*]
r.1 ⸢DUG$_4$⸣.DUG$_4$ *la-áš-*[*šú*]
2 [*man*]*-nu ša* ⸢*ina*⸣ *ur-kiš u*! *ina*! *m*[*a*!*-te-ma*]
3 *i-za-*⸢*qu*⸣*-pa-a-ni* [0]
4 *man-nu* GIL-*u-ni* [0]
5 ⸢5!⸣ MA.NA KUG.[U]D SUM-*an* [0]

---

6 [I]G[I] ⸢^{m}⸣^{d}*šá-maš*—MAN—PAB ⸢LÚ⸣.[*m*]*u-k*[*il*—PA.MEŠ]
7 [*ša*] DUMU—[MAN]
8 [IGI ^{m}]^{d}PA—*še-*⸢*zib* LÚ⸣.[:]
9 [IGI] ^{m}*šum-ma—*[DINGIR.MEŠ-*ni* LÚ.:]
10 [IG]I ^{m}*sa-*[*a*]*k-k*[*an-n*]*u* [LÚ.:]
11 [IG]I ^{m}*bar-*[*r*]*uq-qu* [0]
12 [IGI] ^{m}⸢^{d}⸣[PA—SU] LÚ.2-⸢*ú*⸣ [0]
13 [IGI] ^{m}[PAB—*la-m*]*ur* LÚ.GIŠ.[GIGIR]
14 [IGI ^{m}*man-nu—ki*]—KASKAL LÚ*.GIŠ.⸢GIGIR⸣
rest of reverse and upper edge uninscribed
Side destroyed

uṣur and Šarr[u-lu-dari] —

[6] Remanni-[Adad], chariot driver, has contracted and [bou]ght him [fo]r one mina of silver by the mina of Carch[emish].

[10] The money [is paid] completely. [Th]at [man] is purchased and ac[quired]. [Any revocati]on, lawsu[it], or litigation is voi[d].

[r.2] [Who]ever in the future, a[t any time], lodges a complaint, whoever breaks the contract, shall pay 5 minas of sil[ve]r.

---

[6] [Wi]tn[ess] Šamaš-šarru-uṣur, char[iot driver of] the pri[nce].
[8] [Witness] Nabû-šezib, [ditto].
[9] [Witness] Šumma-[ilani, ditto].
[10] [Wit]ness Sakk[an]nu, [ditto].
[11] [Wit]ness Barruqu.
[12] [Witness Nabû-eriba], deputy.
[13] [Witness Ahu-lam]ur, horse [trainer].
[14] [Witness Mannu-ki]-Harran, horse trainer.
(Rest uninscribed)

348. Remanni-Adad Buys Slaves

83-1-18,259

beginning broken away
1′ [TA* IGI ^{m}]⸢DINGIR—*ta*⸣-[*ka*?*-a* LÚ*.*x x x*]
2′ [*ša*] ⸢É!⸣.SAG.Í[L! *ina* ŠÀ *x* MA.NA KUG.UD]
3′ [*il*]*-qi kas-p*[*u gam-mur*]
4′ [*t*]*a-din* UN.M[EŠ *šu-a-tu*]
5′ [*za*]*-ar-pu l*[*a-qi-u tu-a-ru*]
6′ [*d*]*e-e-nu* DUG$_4$.[DUG$_4$ *la-áš-šú*]
7′ [*man*]*-nu ša ina* ⸢*ur*⸣-[*kiš* GIL-*u-ni*]
8′ *lu-u* ^{m}DINGIR—*ta-k*[*a*?*-a lu-u* DUMU.MEŠ-*šú*]
9′ *lu-u* DUMU—DUMU.MEŠ-*šú ša* [TA* ^{m}*rém-an-ni*—^{d}IM]
10′ [*de*]-⸢*e*⸣*-nu* DUG$_4$.[DUG$_4$ *ub-ta-u-ni*]
11′ [*kas-p*]*u a-n*[*a* 10.MEŠ*-te a-na* EN-*šú*]
r.1 GUR-*ra ina de-*[*ni-šú* DUG$_4$.DUG$_4$*-ma*]
2 *la i-*[*laq-qi*]
3 IGI ^{m}NUMUN-*ti-i* [LÚ*.DIB—KUŠ.PA.MEŠ]
4 *ša* DUMU—[MAN]
5 IGI ^{m}*ha—ba-*[*as-te* LÚ*.GAL—Ì.DU$_8$]
6 IGI ^{md}30—I [*x x x x*]
7 IGI ^{m}*ṣil-*[*la-a-a* LÚ*.DAM.QAR]

ADD 297

(Beginning destroyed)

[1] [Remanni-Adad has contracted and bou]ght them [from] Il-ta[*kâ*, the ... of] Esaggil [for x *minas* of silver].

[3] The mone[y is pa]id [completely]. [Those] people [are pur]chased and ac[quired. Any revocation, la]wsuit, or litiga[tion is void].

[7] [Who]ever in the fut[ure breaks the contract], whether Il-ta*k*[*â* or his sons] or grandsons, [and seeks a law]suit or liti[gation] against Remanni-Adad, shall return [the mon]ey ten[fold to its owner. He shall contest] in [his] law[suit] and not suc[ceed].

[r.3] Witness Zarutî, [chariot driver] of the pri[nce].
[5] Witness Haba[sti, chief porter].
[6] Witness Sin-na'di, [...].
[7] Witness Ṣil[laya, merchant].

348 Previous editions: AR 547, NALK 278. [2] See coll.

8 IGI ^{md}IM—[*x x x x x*]
9 [IGI ^{m}]⸢*x*⸣[*x x x x x x*]
rest broken away

^{8} Witness Adad-[......].
(Rest destroyed)

349. A Fragmentary Purchase Document of Remanni-Adad

83-1-18,579

beginning broken away
1′ [LÚ.DIB—KUŠ.PA.MEŠ *š*]*a*$^!$ M[AN$^!$ KUR—*aš-šur*]
2′ [*ina* ŠÀ *x* MA.NA KUG.UD T]A$^!$ IGI$^!$ [LÚ.MEŠ-*e*]

3′ [*an-nu-te il-qi*] ⸢*kas*$^!$⸣-*pu*$^!$ [*gam-mur ta-din*]
two lines destroyed
r.1 [DUMU—DUMU.MEŠ-*šú-nu l*]*u-u* PAB.MEŠ-*šú-nu ša de*-[*nu*]
2 [DUG$_4$.DUG$_4$ TA* ^{m}*rém-a-n*]*i*$^!$—^{d}IM *ù* DUMU.MEŠ-⸢*šú*⸣
3 [DUMU—DUMU.MEŠ-*š*]*ú ub-ta-ʾu-u-ni*
4 [*x* MA.NA KUG.UD *x* MA.N]A KUG.GI *a-na* ^{d}IŠ.TAR
5 [*a-ši-bat* URU.NINA.KI S]UM-*an kas-pu* [*a*]-⸢*na*⸣ 10.MEŠ
6 [*a-na* EN.MEŠ-*šú ú*]-*tar-ra ina de-ni-šú* DUG$_4$.DU[G$_4$-*ma là* T]I$^!$-⸢*qí*⸣

---

7 [IGI ^{md}MAŠ].MAŠ—MAN—PAB LÚ.⸢DIB⸣—[KUŠ.PA.MEŠ]
8 [IGI ^{m}*x x—r*]*ém-a-ni* LÚ$^!$.[*x x x x*]
9 [IGI ^{m}*sa-kan*]-*nu* LÚ$^!$.[DIB—KUŠ.PA.MEŠ]
rest broken away

ADD 596

(Beginning destroyed)

^{1} [Remanni-Adad, chariot driver o]f the ki[ng of Assyria, has contracted and bought (said property) fro]m [these gentlemen for x minas of silver].

^{3} The money [is paid completely].

(Break)

$^{r.1}$ [whether ..., their sons, grandsons o]r brothers, (who) seeks a law[suit] or litigation [against Remanni]-Adad and his sons [and grandsons, sh]all pay [x minas of silver and x mi]nas of gold to Ištar [residing in Nineveh, and sh]all return the money tenfold [to its owners]. He shall contest in his lawsuit [and not succeed].

---

^{7} [Witness Ner]gal-šarru-uṣur, chariot [driver].

^{8} [Witness ...-r]emanni, [*chariot driver*].

^{9} [Witness Sakkan]nu, [chariot driver].

(Rest destroyed)

350. A Fragmentary Purchase Document of Remanni-Adad

K 1507

Obv. broken away
Rev. beginning broken away
1′ [*ina de-ni*]-*šú*$^!$ ⸢*i*$^!$⸣-DU[G$_4^!$.DUG$_4$ *la* TI]

2′ [IGI ^{m}]^{d}MAŠ.MAŠ—MAN—PAB [LÚ*.3.U$_5$]
3′ [IGI] ^{m}*ú-ar-bi-i*[*s* LÚ*.3.U$_5$]
4′ [IG]I ^{md}*šá-maš*—MAN—PAB L[Ú.DIB—PA.MEŠ]

5′ [I]GI ^{m}*sa-kan*-[*nu* LÚ*.:. :.]
6′ [IG]I ^{m}*bar-ruq* L[Ú.:. :.]

ADD 571

(Beginning destroyed)

$^{r.1}$ He shall conte[st in] his [lawsuit and not succeed].

---

^{2} [Witness] Nergal-šarru-uṣur, ['third man'].

^{3} [Witness] Uarbi[s, 'third man'].

^{4} [Witne]ss Šamaš-šarru-uṣur, [chariot driver].

^{5} [Wit]ness Sakkan[nu, ditto].

^{6} [Wit]ness Barruqu, [ditto].

349 Previous editions: AR 579, NALK 281. $^{1, r.3, 6, 8f}$ See coll.
350 Previous editions: AR 590, NALK 267. ^{1} See coll.

7′ [I]GI ^{md}UTU—ZI—[*x x x x x*]
8′ [I]GI ^{m}*ha—ba-as-*[*te* LÚ*.GAL—Ì.DU$_8$]
9′ IGI ^{m}*ki-ṣi*[*r—aš-šur* LÚ*.DIB—PA.MEŠ]
10′ IGI ^{md}PA—NUMU[N—AŠ LÚ*.:. :.]
11′ [IG]I ^{m}*da-ha-*[*x x x x*]
rest broken away

7 [Wit]ness Šamaš-kettu-[..., ...].
8 [Wit]ness Habasti, [head porter].
9 Witness Kiṣ[ir-Aššur, chariot driver].
10 Witness Nabû-ze[ru-iddina, ditto].
11 [Wit]ness Daha[...].
(Rest destroyed)

GLOSSARY AND INDICES

Logograms and Their Readings

A → *mar'u;* A.BA → *ṭupšarru;* A—MAN → *mār šarri;* A.MEŠ → *mê;* A.QAR → *ugāru;* A—SIG → *mār damqi;* A.ŠÀ → *eqlu;* A.ŠÀ.GA → *eqlu;* AMA → *ummu;* AMA—LUGAL → *ummi šarri;* AMA—MAN → *ummi šarri;* AMBAR → *appāru;* AN.NA → *annuku;* ANŠE.A.A.AB.BA → *gammalu;* ANŠE.GÍR.NUN.NA → *kūdunu;* ANŠE.KUR, ANŠE.KUR.RA → *sissû;* ANŠE.NITÁ → *mūru;* ARAD → *urdu;*

BA.TI → *laqû;* BABBAR → *paṣû;* BAD → *patû;* BÀD.DINGIR.KI → *Dēru;* BÀD—MAN—GIN → *Dūr-Šarrukēn;* BAN → *qassu;* BE → *šumma;*

^{d}AG → *Nabû;* ^{d}ALAD → *šēdu;* ^{d}DI.KUD → *Madānu;* ^{d}GAŠAN—KUR → *Šarrat nipha;* ^{d}GAŠAN—NINA.KI → *Bēlet Nīnua;* ^{d}IGI.DU → *Pālil;* ^{d}IM → *Adad;* ^{d}IŠ.TAR → *Issār;* ^{d}LÁL → *Tašmētu;* ^{d}MAŠ → *Inurta;* ^{d}MAŠ.MAŠ → *Nergal;* ^{d}ME.ME → *Gula;* ^{d}NIN.GAL → *Nikkal;* ^{d}NIN.LÍL → *Mullissu;* ^{d}NU—LUGAL → *ṣalam šarri;* ^{d}PA → *Nabû;* ^{d}ŠEŠ.GAL → *Nergal;* ^{d}UTU → *Šamaš;* ^{d}10 → *Adad;* ^{d}15 → *Issār;* ^{d}30 → *Sīn;*

DAGAL → *rapāšu;* DAM → *aššatu;* DAM.QAR → *tamkāru;* DI → *šulmu;* DI.KUD → *daiānu, dēnu;* DIB → *ṣabātu, mukīl appāti;* DINGIR → *ilu;* DU → *alāku;* DUB.IM → *ṭuppu;* DUG$_4$.DUG$_4$ → *dabābu;* DUMU → *mar'u;* DUMU—DUMU → *mār mar'i;* DUMU—LUGAL, DUMU—MAN → *mār šarri;* DUMU.MÍ → *mar'utu;* DUMU—NINA → *Nīnua;* DUMU—PAB, DUMU—ŠEŠ → *mār ahi;* DUMU—URU.NINA → *Nīnua;* DUMU.UŠ → *aplu;* DÙ → *epāšu;* DÙ.A → *kalu;* DU$_6$ → *tillu;*

EDIN → *ṣēru;* EGIR → *arkatu, urki, urkīu;* EN → *bēl, bēlu, bennu;* EN—GIŠ.GIGIR → *bēl mugirri;* EN.NAM → *pāhutu;* EN—ŠU, EN—ŠU.2 → *bēl qātāti;* EN—URU → *bēl āli;* É → *bēt, bētu;* É—DINGIR → *bēt ili;* É—EN → *bēt bēli;* É.GAL → *ekal, ekallu;* É—GIBIL → *bētu eššu;* É.KI.NÁ, É—NÁ → *bēt maiāli;* É.SAG.ÍL → *Esaggil;* É.ŠÁR.RA → *Ešarra;* É—ŠU → *bēt qāti;* É—TU$_5$ → *bēt ramāki;* É—2-*u* → *bētu šaniu;*

GA → *zizibu;* GAL → *rabû;* GAL—É → *rab bēti;* GAL—GAG → *rab sikkāti;* GAL—LÚ.Ì.DU$_8$ → *rab atê;* GAL—SAG → *rab ša-rēši;* GAL—URU → *rab ālāni;* GAL—50 → *rab hanšê;* GAR → *šakānu;* GAR.KUR → *šaknu;* GAŠAN—É → *bēlat bēti;* GEMÉ → *amtu;* GEŠTIN → *karānu;* GI → *qanû;* GIBIL → *eššu;* GIBÍL → *qalû;* GÍD, GÍD.DA → *arāku;* GIL → *parāku;* GÍN → *šiqlu;* GÌR.NUN.NA → *kūdunu;* GÌR.2 → *šēpu;* GIŠ → *iṣu;* GIŠ.A.TU.GAB.LIŠ → *ṣarbutu;* GIŠ.APIN → *epinnu;* GIŠ.BÁN → *sūtu;* GIŠ.GEŠTIN → *karānu;* GIŠ.GU.ZA → *kussiu;* GIŠ.IG → *dassu;* GIŠ.MÁ → *eleppu;* GIŠ.MURUB$_4$ → *qablu b;* GIŠ.SAR → *kiriu;* GIŠ.ÙR → *gušūru;* GUB → *uzuzzu;* GUD → *alpu;* GUD.ÁB.NIGIN → *sāhirtu;* GUD.NITÁ → *alpu;* GUR → *tuāru;* GÚ.UN → *biltu;*

HAL → *bārû;*

ÍD → *nāru;* ÍD.IGI.2 → *ēnu;* IGI → *pānu, šību;* IGI.2 → *ēnu;* ÍL → *našû;* IM → *ṭuppu;* IM.RI.A → *kimtu;* ITI → *urhu;* ITI.AB → *kanūnu;* ITI.AD → *ābu;* ITI.APIN → *arahsamnu;* ITI.BARAG → *nisannu;* ITI.DIRI.ŠE → *addāru diri;* ITI.DUL → *tašrītu;* ITI.DU$_6$ → *tašrītu;* ITI.GAN → *kislīmu;* ITI.GUD → *aiāru;* ITI.KIN → *elūlu;* ITI.NE → *ābu;* ITI.SIG$_4$ → *simānu;* ITI.ŠE → *addāru;* ITI.ŠU → *tamūzu;* ITI.ZÍZ → *šabāṭu;* Ì → *šamnu;* Ì.DU$_8$ → *atû;*

KA → *pû;* KASKAL, KASKAL.2 → *hūlu;* KASKAL—LUGAL, KASKAL—MAN → *hūl šarri;* KAŠ → *šikāru;* KÁ → *bābu;* KÁ.DINGIR.KI → *Bābili;* KÁ.GAL → *abullu;* KÉŠ → *riksu;* KI.MAH → *kimahhu;* KI.TA → *šapal;* KUG.GI → *hurāṣu;* KUG.UD → *ṣarpu;* KUR → *mātu;* KUR-*e* → *šadû;* KUR—AN.ŠÁR.KI → *māt Aššūr;* KUR.BÀD—MAN—GIN → *Dūr-Šarrukēn;* KUR.GI.MUŠEN → *kurkû;* KUR.NIM.MA → *Elamtu;* KUŠ.TAB.BA → *gildu;* KÙŠ → *ammutu;* KÚ → *akālu;*

LAL → *rūṭu;* LÁ → *maṭû;* LUGAL → *šarru;* LUH → *masû;* LÚ → *amēlu;* LÚ.A.BA → *ṭupšarru;* LÚ.A.BA—É.GAL, LÚ.A.BA—KUR → *ṭupšar ekalli;* LÚ.A—KIN → *mār šipri;* LÚ.A—SIG, LÚ.A—SIG$_5$ → *mār damqi;* LÚ.A.ZU → *asû;* LÚ.ARAD → *urdu;* LÚ.ARAD—É.GAL → *urda ekalli;* LÚ.AŠGAB → *aškāpu;* LÚ.AZU → *bārû;* LÚ.BAD—HAL → *ša-pēthalli;* LÚ.^{d}ALAD → *šēdu;* LÚ.DAM.QAR → *tamkāru;* LÚ.DIB → *ṣabtu, mukīl;* LÚ.DIB—KUŠ.PA, LÚ.DIB—PA → *mukīl appāti;* LÚ.DUB.SAR → *ṭupšarru;* LÚ.EN → *bēl;* LÚ.EN—GIŠ.MÁ → *bēl eleppi;* LÚ.EN.NAM

→ *pāhutu;* LÚ.ENGAR → *ikkāru;* LÚ.ENGAR—É.GAL, LÚ.ENGAR—KUR → *ikkār ekalli;* LÚ.ERIM → *ṣābu;* LÚ.GAL—A.BA → *rab ṭupšarri;* LÚ.GAL—A.ZU → *rab asê;* LÚ.GAL—É → *rab bēti;* LÚ.GAL—GIŠ.SAR → *rab kirie;* LÚ.GAL—HAL → *rab bārê;* LÚ.GAL—Ì → *rab šamni;* LÚ.GAL—Ì.DU$_8$ → *rab atê;* LÚ.GAL—KA.KÉŠ → *rab kiṣri;* LÚ.GAL—KÀD → *rab kiṣri;* LÚ.GAL—KAŠ.LUL → *rab šāqê;* LÚ.GAL—MAŠ.MAŠ → *rab āšipi;* LÚ.GAL—MÁ.DU.DU → *rab mallāhi;* LÚ.GAL—MU → *rab nuhatimmi;* LÚ.GAL—NAGAR → *rab naggāri;* LÚ.GAL—NÍG.ŠID → *rab nikkassi;* LÚ.GAL— SAG → *rab ša-rēši;* LÚ.GAL—SIMUG.KUG.GI → *rab ṣarrāpi;* LÚ.GAL—URU.MEŠ → *rab ālāni;* LÚ.GAL—UŠ.BAR → *rab išpāri;* LÚ.GAR, LÚ.GAR.KUR → *šaknu;* LÚ.GAR.U.U → *pallišu;* LÚ.GIGIR → *susānu;* LÚ.GÍR.LÁ → *ṭābihu;* LÚ.GIŠ.APIN → *ša-epinni;* LÚ.GIŠ.GIGIR → *susānu;* LÚ.GIŠ.GIGIR—DU$_8$ → *susān ša-pattūti;* LÚ.GIŠ. GIGIR—GÌR.2 → *susān ša-šēpi;* LÚ.GUR—UMUŠ → *mutīr ṭēmi;* LÚ.HAL → *bārû;* LÚ.IGI → *šību;* LÚ.IGI.DUB, LÚ.IGI.UM → *masennu;* LÚ.Ì.DU$_8$ → *atû;* LÚ.Ì.ŠUR → *ṣāhitu;* LÚ.KAŠ.LUL → *šāqiu;* LÚ.LUL → *parriṣu;* LÚ.LUNGA → *sirāšû;* LÚ.MAH → *ṣīru;* LÚ.MU → *nuhatimmu;* LÚ.MUŠEN.DÙ → *ušandû;* LÚ.NAGAR → *naggāru;* LÚ.NAGAR—GIŠ.UMBIN → *naggār magarri;* LÚ.NAM → *pāhutu;* LÚ.NAR → *nuāru;* LÚ.NIGÍR → *nāgiru;* LÚ.NINDA → *āpiu;* LÚ.NU.GIŠ.SAR → *nukaribbu;* LÚ.SAG → *ša-rēši;* LÚ.SANGA → *sangû;* LÚ.SIMUG → *nappāhu;* LÚ.SIMUG.KUG.GI → *ṣarrāpu;* LÚ.SIPA → *rāʾiu;* LÚ.SIPA—MUŠEN → *rāʾi iṣṣūri;* LÚ.SUKKAL → *sukkallu;* LÚ.SUM.NINDA → *karkadinnu;* LÚ.TIN → *etinnu;* LÚ.TÚG.KA.KÉŠ → *kāṣiru;* LÚ.TUR → *ṣehru;* LÚ.UŠBAR$_5$ → *išpāru;* LÚ.UŠBAR$_5$—TÚG → *išpār ṣiprāti;* LÚ.UN → *nīšī;* LÚ.UŠ → *rādiu;* LÚ.UŠ—ANŠE → *rādi imāri;* LÚ.UŠ—ANŠE.AB.BA → *rādi gammali;* LÚ.UŠ.BAR → *išpāru;* LÚ.UŠ.BAR—GÙN → *išpār birme;* LÚ.ZADIM → *sasinnu;* LÚ.ZI → *napšutu;* LÚ.3.U$_5$ → *tašlīšu;*

MA, MA.NA → *manû;* MAN → *šarru;* MAŠ.QA → *naglubu;* MÁ.DU.DU → *mallāhu;* MI → *mūšu;* MÍ → *issu;* MÍ.AMA → *ummu;* MÍ.AMA—LUGAL → *ummi šarri;* MÍ.AMA—MAN → *ummi šarri;* MÍ.ERIM—É.GAL → *sekret ekalli;* MÍ—É.GAL → *issi ekalli;* MÍ.GAR → *šakintu;* MÍ.GURUŠ.TUR → *batūssu;* MÍ.KUR → *issi ekalli;* MÍ.NU.KÚŠ.Ù → *almattu;* MÍ.TUR → *ṣehertu;* MU → *šumu, šattu;* MU.AN.NA → *šattu;* MÚD → *dāmu;* MÚD—ERIN → *dām erēni;* MURUB$_4$—URU → *qabsi āli;* MUŠEN → *iṣṣūru;*

NAG → *šatû;* NA$_4$.KIŠIB → *kunukku;* NIM → *elû;* NIN → *ahātu;* NINA, NINA.KI → *Nīnua;* NINDA → *kusāpu;* NU → *la;*

PAB → *ahu, gimru;* PÚ → *būrtu;*

SAG → *rēšēti, rēšu;* SAG.DU → *kaqqudu;* SANGA → *sangû;* SI → *qarnu;* SIG → *damāqu;* SÍG → *qerdu;* SIG$_5$ → *damāqu;* SILA → *sūqu;* SIMUG.KUG.GI → *ṣarrāpu;* SUHUR → *ṭēhi;* SUHUŠ → *išdu;* SUKKAL → *sukkallu;* SUM → *tadānu;* SUMUN → *labīru;*

ŠÀ → *libbu;* ŠE.BAR → *uṭṭutu;* ŠE.GIG → *kibtu;* ŠE.GIŠ.Ì → *šamaššammi;* ŠE.IN.NU → *tibnu;* ŠE.NUMUN → *zarʾu;* ŠE.PAD → *kurummutu;* ŠE.SU$_7$ → *tarammu;* ŠEŠ → *ahu;* ŠU, ŠU.2 → *qātu;* ŠÚ → *kiššatu;*

TA → *issi/u;* TAB → *eṣāpu;* TI → *laqû;* TÚG → *niksu, sasuppu;* TUR → *ṣahāru;* TÙR → *tarbāṣu;*

UD → *ūmu;* UD.DA → *ṣētu;* UDU → *immeru;* UDU.NITÁ → *iābilu;* UDU.ÙZ → *enzu;* UDU.U$_8$ → *agurrutu;* UGU → *muhhu;* UMBIN → *ṣupru;* UN → *nīšī;* URU → *ālu;* URU.BÀD—MAN—GIN → *Dūr-Šarrukēn;* URU.DUL.LÚ.KUR.GAR.RA → *Til-kurgarrê;* URU.HAL.ṢU → *Birtu;* URU.KASKAL → *Harrānu;* URU.KÁ.DINGIR → *Bābili;* URU.LÚ.BAHÁR → *āl pahhāri;* URU.LÚ.SAG → *āl ša-rēšāni;* URU.MURUB$_4$—URU → *qabsi āli;* URU.NINA, URU.NINA.KI → *Nīnua;* URU.SIMUG.KUG.GI → *āl ṣarrāpi;* URU.ŠÀ—URU → *Libbi-āli;* URU.ŠE → *kapru, Kapar;* URU.2.LÚ.SAG → *āl ša-rēšāni;* URUDU → *erû;* UR$_5$ → *šuātu;* UŠ → *rādiu;* UŠ.BAR → *išpāru;* Ú.SAR → *urqu;*

ZI → *napšutu;*

1BÁN, 2BÁN, 3BÁN etc. → *sūtu;* 10 → *ešrāia, ešrāti;* 10.A.TA.AN → *ešrāia;* 11 → *isseššerāti;* 12 → *šinšerāti* 2/3 → *šinip;* 3-*a-ti* → *šalšāti;* 3-*su* → *šalussu;* 3-*šú* → *tašlīšu;* 5/6 → *parasrab;* 5-*su* → *hamussu;* 15 → *imittu;*

Glossary

abarakku see *masennu,*
ābu (Ab, name of the 5th month): ITI.AD 63:4, e. 7, ITI.NE 46:7, 62 r. 1, 97 r. 8, 107:5, 113 r. 6, 119 r. 19, 128 r. 3, 134 r. 14, 135 r. 6, 190 r. 5, 195 r. 7, 214:5, 233:6, 234:5, 288 r. 3, 294 r. 8, 331 r. 7, 34 r. 13, ITI.N[E] 154 s. 2, IT]I.NE 222:5, [ITI.N]E 61 r. 5,
abullu "gate": KÁ.GAL 335:7,
abussu "storehouse": É.*a-bu-sa-te* 42:6,
adammumu "wasp": *a-dam-mu-mu* 288 r. 12,
addāru (Adar, name of the 12th month): ITI.ŠE 18 r. 6, 30 r. 13, 83 r. 2, 84 r. 2, 89 r. 15, 105 r. 11, 110 r. 13, 118 r. 11, 124 r. 14, 150 r. 4, 174 s. 1, 217 r. 16, 227 r. 10, 232 r. 6, 235:5, 245 r. 13, 265 r. 8, 297 r. 11, 310 r. 17, 315 r. 8, 323 e. 10, 324 r. 3, [ITI].ŠE 272:11, [ITI.ŠE 316 r. 15, [ITI.ŠE] 272 r. 8, [ITI.Š]E 225 r. 13, [IT]I.ŠE 284 r. 21,
addāru diri (intercalary Adar, reading uncert.): ITI.DIRI.ŠE 59 r. 17, 281:5,
adê "treaty": *a-de-e* 95 r. 5,
adi "until, plus": *a-di* 1 r. 9, 31:7, 10, 13, 15, 19, 42:3, 4, 59:2, 3, 84:2, 91:8, 9, 10, 97 r. 3, 6, 101:6, 7, 20, r. 1, 124:2, 3, 142:6, 7, 169:10, 187:4, 210:3, 264:3, 7, 8, r. 3, 272:6, r. 3, 283 r. 2, 287:7, 8, 302:3, 311:4, 326:2, 328:4, *a-[di* 59:4, *[a-di* 100 r. 3, 4, 302:4, *a-du* 25:4, 5, r. 1, 100:9, 10, 156:5, 221:2,
adru "threshing floor": *ad-ri* 17:6, 31:6, r. 1, 67:4, 119:15, 201:3, *ad]-ri* 209:4, *a[d-ri* 210:4, *ad-ri*.MEŠ 93 r. 6, 336 r. 2, 9, *ad-[ri*.MEŠ 93 r. 1, *a]d-ri*.MEŠ 93 e. 10, *ad-ru* 17:7, 11, e. 15, 19:6, 30:5, 119 r. 2, 163:3, 277:3, 315:3, 335:9, e. 16, *ad-r]u* 316:5, *ad-[ru]* 333:2, *a-da-ri* 275:11, r. 4, 11,
agannu (a bowl): DUG.*a-gan-ni* 101 r. 4, 102 r. 6, DUG.*a-ga-ni* 20:3, DUG.*a-ga-nu* 96:17,
agurrutu "ewe": UDU.U_8.MEŠ 84:1, 243:2,
ahāiš "each other": *a-ha-iš* 66 r. 5, *a-he-iš* 178:6, *i-sa-he-i[š* 295:3,
ahātu "sister": NIN-*sa* 250:8, 252 r. 7, NIN-*su* 251:5, NIN-*šú* 90:7, NIN.MEŠ-*šú* 110:5,
ahu "brother": PAB-*šú* 28 r. 3, 91:6, 7, 8, 320 r. 8, PAB-[*šú* 130:6, PAB-[*šú*] 23:2, PAB.MEŠ-*šu* 301: 15, PAB.MEŠ-*šú* 31 r. 9, 34:16, 38 r. 3, 39:10, 42:17, 90:5, 7, 106:6, 201:16, 228:12, 278 e. 16, 299:7, 306:11, 340:5, PAB.MEŠ-*šú*] 38 r. 7, PAB.MEŠ-[*šú*] 15 r. 2, PA]B.MEŠ-*šú* 48:16, [PAB.MEŠ-*šú* 312 e. 20, [PAB.MEŠ-*šú*] 123 r. 1, PAB.ME[Š-*šú-nu*] 326 e. 26, PAB.MEŠ-*šú-nu* 15:8, 31 r. 7, 55:11, 101:13, 314 e. 24, 349 r. 1, PAB.MEŠ-*šú-n[u]* 161 r. 3, PAB].MEŠ-*šú-nu* 100:17, 102:11, P[AB.MEŠ-*šú-nu*] 257:16, ŠEŠ-*šú* 32:15, 42 r. 9, 96:3, 105 r. 8, 177:4, 257:1, ŠEŠ-*š[ú]* 315:5, Š]EŠ-*šú* 316:7, [ŠEŠ.MEŠ-*šú*] 197: 10, ŠEŠ.MEŠ-*šú* 10 r. 1, 37:18, 40:17, 82:7, 87:8, 96:12, 110:4, 219 r. 3, 253 r. 2, 289:12, 290:10, 298:8, 305:14, 308:7, ŠEŠ.MEŠ-*šú-nu* 334 r. 11, 335 r. 5, 336 r. 5, ŠEŠ.MEŠ-*šú-nu*] 344 r. 3, ŠEŠ.[MEŠ-*šú-nu*] 251:12,
aiāru (Iyyar, name of the 2nd month): ITI.GUD 2 r. 7, 17 r. 17, 42 r. 20, 76 r. 1, 77:9, 90 r. 16, 150:5, 170:5, 171:2, 177 r. 16, 181:5, 182:4, 188 r. 5, 194 s. 2, 197 r. 8, 201 r. 13, 203 r. 2, 206:5, 207 s. 1, 216:5, 7, 233 r. 2, 236 r. 1, 243 r. 5, 259 r. 7, 283 r. 23, 287 r. 16, 307 r. 7, ITI.GU[D 218 r. 7, [ITI].GUD 187 r. 6, [ITI.GU]D 193 r. 11, [IT]I.GUD 121 r. 9, 163 r. 16,
akālu "to eat": *e-kal* 260:6, *e-[kal]* 160:14, *kal-e* 259:5, KÚ 20:3, 96:16, 101 r. 3, 102 r. 6, 146 e. 9, 223:8, r. 1, 226:14, 252 r. 10, 268:3, 271 r. 4, 287:18, KÚ] 224 e. 8, 226:14, K[Ú] 186 r. 3, [KÚ 65 r. 3, [KÚ] 295 e. 9, KÚ-*u-ni* 95:3,
akī "as": *a-ki* 3:4, 158:6, 232 e. 6,
akkû (a kind of owl): *ak-[k]u-u* 288 r. 9,
alādu see *ulādu,*
alāku "to go, come": *il-lak* 31 r. 30, 191 r. 6, *il-lak-u-ni* 321:10, *il-lak]-u-[ni]* 321:8, *il]-lak-u-ni* 321:5, *i]l-lak-u-n[i]* 338:7, *il-l[a-ku-ni]* 93:3, *[il-la-ku-ni* 93:3, *it-ta-lak* 95:4, *li-kal-ka* 133:9, *tal-lik-u-ni* 285:4, DU-*ku-u-ni* 169:5, 7, DU-*ku-[u]-ni* 169:9, DU-*ni* 201:5, DU-*u-ni* 176:5, 201:5, 271:4, 5, 12, 15, 334:18, DU-*u-[ni]* 186 r. 4, DU-*u]-ni* 334: 8, DU]-*u-ni* 320:7, 334:15, D[U-*u-ni* 155:2, D[U-*u-ni]* 211:3, [DU-*u-ni* 271:17, DU-*ú-[ni]* 320:3,
allānu "oak": GIŠ.*al-la-an* 329:6, GIŠ.*al-la-an]* 330:6,
almattu "widow": MÍ.NU.KÚŠ.Ù 257:2,
alpu "ox": GUD 296:2, G]UD.MEŠ 296 r. 1, GUD. MEŠ-*šú-nu* 91:9, GUD.NITÁ 245:13, GUD.NI[TÁ.MEŠ-*šú-nu* 25:5,
ālu "city, town": URU 31:5, 9, 11, 14, 16, 287:6, 305:8, 306:5, 312 r. 16, 325:12, 326:20, UR[U 194 s. 4, URU-*šú* 6 r. 3, 10 r. 16, 31 r. 30, 91:15, 92 r. 13, 191 r. 6, 274 r. 11, URU-*šú*] 11 r. 7, URU-[*šú* 20 r. 3, UR[U-*šú*] 42 r. 4, [URU-*šú* 32 r. 6, URU-*šú-nu* 31 r. 21, URU-*šú-(nu)* 328 e. 17, URU.MEŠ-*šú* 92:8,
amēlu "man": LÚ 1:2, r. 9, 5:1, 7:2, 7, 55:7, 61:3, 8, 12, 118:2, 8, 122:2, 127:3, 9, 132:4, 144:7, 148:3, 174:1, r. 1, 244:2, 8, 257:4, 11, r. 22, 264:5, r. 4, 267:2, 274:2, 8, 289:2, 8, 290:2, 6, 300:4, 301:3, 10, 309:2, 310:2, 329:3, 330:3, 346:6, 347: 3, L[Ú 309:9, L]Ú 305:3, [LÚ 3:6, 246:6, 347:11, [L]Ú 219:8, LÚ].ME 343:4, LÚ.MEŠ 17:6, 31 r. 7, 52:5, r. 3, 90:3, 13, 93 r. 9, 161:12, 239:6, 275 r. 13, 19, 279:6, 300:6, 336:10, LÚ.[MEŠ 161 r. 2, LÚ. [MEŠ] 145:4, LÚ].MEŠ 339:8, L]Ú.MEŠ 300:4, [LÚ]. MEŠ 203:5, LÚ.MEŠ-*e* 19:13, 31:4, r. 3, 5, 56:5, r. 1,

85:6, 9, 93 r. 2, 124:13, 142 r. 8, 191:3, 239:3, 251:11, 257:3, 6, 8, 287:6, 15, 297:4, 325:11, 335 r. 4, 342:6, 12, 344:5, LÚ.MEŠ-[*e*] 19:8, LÚ.[MEŠ-*e*] 338 r. 2, LÚ].MEŠ-*e* 209:3, 239:10, L[Ú.MEŠ-*e*] 17:11, L]Ú.MEŠ-*e* 343:8, [LÚ.MEŠ-*e*] 349:2, [LÚ.M]EŠ-*e* 311:15, LÚ.[MEŠ-*e* 297:8,

ammar see *mar,*

ammutu "cubit": KÙ[Š 31 e. 30, KÙŠ 31 e. 30, r. 1, 2,

amtu "maid, slave-girl": GEMÉ 228:3, 286:8, GE[MÉ]-*su* 293:5, GEMÉ-*šú* 45:3, 197:3, GEMÉ-*šú*] 49:1, 286:3, GEMÉ-[*šú* 284:2, GEM[É-*šú*] 48:3, [GEMÉ-*šú*] 98:3, [GE]MÉ.MEŠ 239:6, [GE]M[É.MEŠ] 130:4,

ana "to": *ana* 11 r. 8, 27 r. 11, 61:13, 98 r. 5, 126 r. 5, 130:16, 225 r. 1, 250 r. 5, 278 r. 5, 289 r. 2, 301 r. 5, 306 r. 4, 309 r. 4, 310 r. 2, 334 r. 18, 335 r. 11, *ana*] 113 r. 1, 289 r. 7, [*ana* 86 r. 1, 130:16, 138 r. 9, 225 r. 1, *a-na* 1 r. 8, 3:8, 14, 6 r. 1, 3, 4, 5, 7, 8, 7 r. 1, 8:8, e. 9, r. 1, 9:7, 8, 10 r. 4, 11 r. 7, 14 r. 9, 16 r. 1, 20 r. 3, 4, 23 r. 1, 2, 26 e. 8, 29 r. 3, 31 r. 11, 32 r. 2, 6, 7, 34 r. 3, 35:5, 36:4, 39:14, 40 r. 2, 41 r. 3, 42 r. 4, 5, 6, 43:4, 44:3, 46:6, 50 r. 9, 51 r. 7, 8, 52 r. 5, 6, 7, 53 r. 1, 2, 58 r. 5, 59:5, 63 e. 6, 64:4, 65 r. 2, 67:4, 6, 71:5, 72:4, 74:5, 75 r. 1, 81:9, 85 r. 2, 5, 6, 86 e. 18, 87 r. 5, 89 r. 4, 5, 90 r. 5, 6, 91:13, 93:2, r. 12, 95:2, 96:20, 97:6, r. 5, 99 r. 4, 100 r. 6, 101 r. 4, 6, 7, 8, 102 r. 7, 8, 9, 10, 105:6, 106:8, 110 r. 3, 4, 113 r. 1, 118 r. 3, 4, 119 r. 9, 123:6, r. 4, 124 r. 1, 131 r. 3, 132:8, 133:7, 9, r. 1, 134 r. 1, 4, 5, 138 r. 8, 139:4, 140:10, 11, 12, 149:2, 151 r. 3, 157 r. 1, 158:3, 160:14, 161 r. 7, 164 r. 1, 2, 165 r. 3, 167:5, 169:9, r. 5, 170:4, 174 r. 6, 178:4, 179 r. 1, 180 e. 10, 186 r. 3, 194 r. 3, 198:5, 6, 201:5, 13, r. 2, 3, 202 r. 4, 6, 206 r. 1, 211:3, 214 e. 7, 215:3, 219:4, 5, 11, r. 10, 11, 220 r. 7, 221:5, 223:8, 226:13, 234:7, 235:7, 236:5, r. 5, 237 e. 7, 238 e. 12, 239 r. 1, 240 e. 6, 241 s. 2, 245 r. 2, 246:14, 248:9, 252 r. 8, 254 r. 1, 259:3, e. 7, 260:4, 262:5, 263:5, 264:2, 265:8, 266 r. 2, 268:7, 269:7, 271:4, 5, 11, r. 4, 272:5, 274 r. 5, 278 r. 6, 282:2, 283 r. 9, 10, 284 r. 6, 7, 8, 286 s. 1, 291:5, 293 r. 2, 298:3, r. 4, 299:14, 301 r. 4, 302 r. 2, 3, 306 r. 3, 307:7, 308 r. 3, 309 r. 4, 312 r. 4, 314 r. 6, 315:2, 8, 316:4, 317:4, 6, 318:6, 319 r. 3, 320:6, 321:5, 9, 323:9, 324 r. 1, 325:12, r. 6, 326:1, 12, r. 11, 328 r. 5, 330 r. 2, 331:6, 332 r. 1, 334:8, 15, 18, r. 17, 18, 335 r. 11, 337:3, 338 r. 6, 339 e. 11, 342:10, 345 r. 1, 346 r. 7, 348:11, 349 r. 4, *a-na*] 271:15, 16, 296 r. 2, 301 r. 5, 329 r. 5, 342:17, *a-n*[*a* 8:4, 15 r. 4, 58 r. 5, 93 r. 12, 141 r. 1, 319 r. 3, 329 r. 5, 332 r. 1, 348:11, *a-n*]*a* 328 r. 5, 332:7, 342 r. 1, *a-*[*na* 32 r. 7, 39:13, 119 r. 9, 330 r. 2, 345 r. 1, *a-*[*na*] 50 r. 9, *a-*[*n*]*a* 254:10, 320:3, *a*]*-na* 3:8, 14, 92 r. 2, 126 r. 5, 169 r. 5, 268:3, [*a-na* 3:13, 15 r. 5, 56 r. 7, 92 r. 2, 100 r. 6, 112 r. 1, 124 r. 1, 131 r. 2, 134 r. 1, 146:7, 163 r. 4, 165 r. 4, 169:5, 171:1, 212:7, 222 e. 7, 224 e. 8, 238:2, 272 r. 2, 289 r. 7, 316:9, 321:8, 338:7, 339 e. 12, 340 r. 2, 342:11, 349 r. 6, [*a-na*] 176:4, 253 r. 7, 295 e. 8, 9, [*a-n*]*a* 7 r. 2, 112 r. 1, 140:12, 287:16, 342:17, [*a*]*-na* 16 r. 2, 34 r. 2, 80:2, 169:7, 346 r. 7, 349 r. 5,

anīnu "we": *a-ni-nu* 133 e. 10,

anniu "this": *an-nu-te* 56:5, r. 1, 93 r. 9, 257:6, 8, 275 r. 19, 311:15, 335 r. 4, 343:8, *an-nu-te*] 124:13, 161 r. 2, 300:6, 336:10, *an-nu-t*[*e* 342:6, *an-nu-*[*te*] 161:12, *an-n*[*u-te* 338 r. 3, *an-*[*nu-te*] 93 r. 2, 342:12, 344:5, [*an-nu-te* 349:3, [*an-nu-t*]*e* 239:6, *an-nu-ti* 31 r. 3, 5, 7, 85:9, 142 r. 8, 251:11, 287:15, *an-nu-ti*] 297:8, *an-nu-t*[*i*] 339:8, *an-nu*]*-ti* 19:13, [*an-nu-ti* 19:9, *an*]*-nu-tu* 90:13, *an-nu-u-te* 85:6, 176:8, 239:10,

annû see *anniu,*

annuku "lead": AN.NA 6 r. 3, 11 r. 7, 20 r. 3, 32 r. 6, 42 r. 4,

anūtu see *unūtu,*

apālu "to answer, pay": *a-pil* 3:6, 102 r. 4, *ep-pa-pa-a*[*l*] 190:7,

āpiu "baker": LÚ.NINDA 48 r. 10, 81 r. 5, 274 r. 14, 15, 306:1, L[Ú].NINDA 305:4, LÚ.NINDA.MEŠ 209:3,

aplu "heir": *ap-lu* 101 r. 1, *ap-lu*] 100 r. 4, [*ap-lu* 100:11, [*ap*]*-lu* 101:8, DUMU.UŠ-*šú* 102 r. 7, DUMU.UŠ-*šú*] 285 r. 1, DUMU.[UŠ-*šú* 101 r. 4,

appāru "reed": AMBAR 251 e. 17,

appāti "reins": *a-pa*.MEŠ 285 r. 8,

arahsamnu (Marchesvan, name of the 8th month): ITI.APIN 31 r. 27, 81 r. 9, 96 r. 18, 167 r. 6, 196 r. 8, 235:8, 242:4, 247:6, 274 r. 17, ITI.APIN] 241 e. 7, ITI.AP[IN 173 r. 4, [IT]I.APIN 303 r. 5,

arāku "to be long": GÍD 31 r. 1, 2, GÍD.D[A] 200:8, [GÍ]D.DA 31 e. 30,

arāšu "to cultivate": *ar-ši* 287:8, *ar-šú* 258 s. 1, *a-ar-šú* 245:13, *e-r*[*a-áš* 160:15, *e-ru-šú* 288:15,

arhiš "quickly": *ár-hiš* 190:7,

arītu "shield": *a-rit* 142:4,

arkatu "rear part": *ár-kat* 100:13, *á*[*r*]*-kàt* 197 r. 9, EGIR-*kàt* 102:7,

asû "physician": LÚ.A.ZU 40 r. 9, 81 r. 4, 271 r. 15, 309 r. 8, [L]Ú.A.ZU 126:9,

aṣû see *uṣû,*

ašābu see *ušābu,*

aškāpu "tanner": LÚ.AŠGAB 31 r. 25, 134 r. 8,

aššatu "wife": DAM-*sà* 288 r. 13, DAM-*šú* 52:6,

atû "gate-guard": Ì.DU$_8$ 152 r. 4, Ì.[DU$_8$] 133 r. 11, LÚ.Ì.DU$_8$ 6 r. 14, 59 r. 10, 11, 12, 81 r. 8, 89 r. 11, 96 r. 16, 130 r. 9, 167 r. 5, 169 r. 14, 174 r. 10, 177 r. 6, 188 r. 3, 239 r. 4, 247 r. 7, 299 r. 8, LÚ.Ì.DU$_8$] 249 r. 3,

ba''û "to seek": *ub-ta-'u-*[*ni*] 32 e. 17, 51 r. 4, *ub-ta-'u*]*-ni* 341 r. 10, *ub-t*[*a-'u-ni* 329 r. 2, *ub-t*[*a-'u*]*-ni* 50 r. 6, [*ub*]*-ta-'u-ni* 48 r. 2, *ub-ta-'u-u-ni* 31 r. 9, 37 r. 4, 87:10, 89 r. 2, 90 r. 5, 96:16, 142 r. 10, 161 r. 6, 219 r. 7, 253 r. 4, 254:8, 288 r. 2, 299:11, 306:14, 325 r. 2, 339 e. 11, 349 r. 3, *ub-ta-'u-u-ni*] 14 r. 7, *ub-ta-'u-u-n*[*i*] 10 r. 3, *ub-ta-'u-u-*[*ni*] 11 r. 3, 40:21, 319:14, *ub-ta-'u-*[*u-ni*] 39:12, *ub-ta-'u*]*-u-ni* 290:12, 312 r. 3, *ub-ta-*[*'u-u*]*-ni* 93 r. 11, *ub-ta*]*-'u-u-ni* 99 r. 1, *ub-*[*ta*]*-'u-u-ni* 42:20, *ub*]*-ta-'u-*[*u-ni*] 251:14, *u*[*b-ta-'u-u*]*-ni* 246:13, [*ub-ta-'u-u-ni* 328 r. 3, [*ub-ta-'*]*u-u-ni* 212:6, [*ub-ta*]*-'u-u-ni* 3:12, [*ub-t*]*a-'u-u-ni* 15 r. 4, 342:16, [*u*]*b-ta-'u-u-ni* 34:20, 201:20, *ub-ta-u-ni* 27 r. 11, 38 r. 7, 177:13, 197:13, 213 r. 6, 220 r. 4, 278 r. 2, 305 r. 2, 314 r. 4, 326 r. 6, 334 r. 14, 336 r. 8, 346 r. 4, *ub-ta-u-ni*] 8:7, 20:2, 217 r. 3, 274 r. 2, 348:10, *ub-ta-u-*[*ni*] 110 e. 15, 140:8, 207 r. 3, *ub-ta-*[*u-ni*] 58 r. 2, 257 r. 20, *ub-ta*]*-u-n*[*i*] 228:13, *ub-t*[*a-u-ni* 119 r. 8, *ub-t*[*a-u-ni*] 210 e. 18, 301:18, *ub-t*]*a-u-ni* 308 e. 11, *ub-*[*ta-u-ni*] 17 r. 5, 338 r. 5, *ub*]*-ta-u-ni* 118:17, [*ub-ta-u-ni* 125 r. 2, 138 r. 6, 340:9, [*ub-*

ta-u-ni] 56 r. 6, 275 r. 20, [*ub-t*]*a-u-ni* 335 r. 9, [*u*]*b-ta-u-*[*ni* 344 r. 8, *ub-ta-ú-ni* 7:14, 298:11, *ub-ta-ú-n*[*i*] 9:6, *ub-ta-ú-*[*ni*] 298:5, [*ub-t*]*a-*0*-u-ni* 284 r. 3, *u-ba-ʾu-u-šú-ni* 264 r. 2, *ú-ba-ʾu* 95 r. 5, *ú-ba-ʾu-šú-u-ni* 264 e. 11, *ú-ub-ta-ʾu-u-ni* 289:15,

bābtu "neighbourhood, city quarter": KÁ-*at* 31:5,

bābu "gate, doorway": KÁ 31:9, 11, r. 3, 251 e. 17, 338:5,

balāṭu "life; to live": *ba-la-ṭi* 93 r. 5,

bar (Aram. word) "son": *brh* 284 e. 16, *bur* 173:6,

bārû "haruspex": HAL 35 r. 6, LÚ.AZU 12:2, LÚ.HAL 123 r. 9, 134 r. 6,

batūssu "girl": MÍ.GUR[UŠ.TUR.MEŠ 269:2,

bēl āli "city lord": EN—URU 286:2,

bēl eleppi "boat owner": LÚ.EN—GIŠ.MÁ 285 r. 7, L]Ú.EN—GIŠ.MÁ 285 r. 6,

bēl ilki "labour-duty superior": EN—*il-ki-šú* 3:10, 38 r. 4, 219 r. 4, 299:9, EN—*il-ki-šú-nu* 101:15, 257 e. 18, 342:14, L[Ú.EN]—*il-ki-šú-nu* 102:13,

bēl mugirri "chariot owner/fighter": EN—GIŠ.GIGIR 204:1,

bēl qātāti "guarantor": EN—ŠU.MEŠ 222 r. 1, EN—ŠU.2.MEŠ 26 e. 9, 156 r. 1, 198 r. 1, 206:4, 221 e. 8, EN—Š[U.2].MEŠ 233:7,

bēlat bēti "lady of the household": GAŠAN—É 200 r. 7, 257:4, GAŠAN—[É] 339 r. 9,

bēlu "lord": *be-lí* 124:2, 145:5, EN 5:1, 7:2, r. 6, 10:2, 13:2, 17:6, 19:4, 9, 22:1, 23:3, 28:2, 31:4, 32:2, 34:2, 37:4, 40:2, 41:2, 42:2, 45:2, 50:2, 52:5, 61:3, 85:3, 88:2, 89:2, 90:4, 91:2, 96:2, 103:2, 105:5, 110:2, 111:2, 113:3, 114:2, 116:2, 118:2, 119:2, 120:2, 121 r. 5, 122:2, 125:3, 127:3, 135:3, 138:2, 142:5, 148:3, 149:1, 151:2, 153:2, 154:2, 160:4, 161:4, 166:2, 169:2, 172:2, 173:3, 174:1, 177:2, 179:2, 188:2, 191:3, 192:2, 193:2, 194:3, 195:2, 196:2, 197:2, 200:3, 201:1, 202:2, 203:5, 204:2, 210:2, 217:3, 218:3, 226:2, 227:1, 228:2, 238:10, 239:3, 244:2, 256:2, 257:4, 258:1, 265:10, 267:2, 274:2, 275:3, 277:3, 278:2, 279:6, 280:2, 286:2, 287:6, 289:2, r. 1, 290:2, 297:5, 298 r. 5, 300:4, 301:3, 304:3, 309:2, 310:2, 311:3, 312:3, 314:3, 316:2, 319:2, 320:1, 321:2, 325:12, 329:3, 331:3, 332:1, 334:2, 343:4, 347:3, E[N 59:1, 141:2, 271:2, E[N] 250:2, [EN 1:2, 24:3, 48:2, 65:3, 109:2, 115:2, 121:3, 128:2, 129:2, 130:2, 163:2, 168:2, 199:2, 209:4, 229:2, 302:2, 305:3, 313:3, 330:3, 338:4, [EN] 12:3, 98:2, 187:2, 245:3, 252:3, 255:3, 345:2, [E]N 53:2, 126:3, 261:2, EN-*šu* 126 r. 5, EN-*šú* 6 r. 5, 27 r. 11, 41 r. 3, 50 r. 9, 52 r. 6, 85 r. 2, 98 r. 5, 100 r. 6, 119 r. 9, 138 r. 9, 141 r. 1, 164 r. 2, 238 e. 12, 250 r. 5, 274 r. 5, 289 r. 2, 299:14, 310 r. 2, 314 r. 6, 319 r. 3, 328 r. 5, 332 r. 1, 340 r. 2, 345 r. 1, EN-*šú*] 32 r. 7, 58 r. 5, 301 r. 4, 348:11, EN-[*šú* 10 r. 4, [EN-*šú* 113 r. 1, [EN-*šú*] 9:7, [EN-*š*]*ú* 283 r. 11, EN-*šú-nu* 97 r. 6, EN.MEŠ 132:4, EN.[MEŠ] 328:2, EN.MEŠ-*e-šú* 298 r. 3, EN.ME[Š-*šú* 284 r. 8, EN.MEŠ-*šú* 3:14, 8 e. 9, 11 r. 8, 20 r. 4, 23 r. 2, 31 r. 11, 34 r. 3, 39:14, 40 r. 2, 42 r. 6, 51 r. 8, 53 r. 2, 87 r. 5, 90 r. 6, 92 r. 2, 93 r. 12, 99 r. 4, 101 r. 8, 102 r. 10, 106:8, 110 r. 4, 112 r. 1, 124 r. 1, 140:12, 151 r. 4, 161 r. 7, 174 r. 6, 176 r. 9, 179 r. 1, 194 r. 3, 198:6, 201 r. 3, 202 r. 6, 210 r. 2, 211 r. 3, 212:7, 219 r. 10, 220 r. 7, 229 r. 3, 253 r. 7, 254 r. 1, 278 r. 6, 302 r. 3, 308 r. 3, 309 r. 4, 325 r. 6, 326 r. 11, 329 r. 6, 330 r. 2, 334 r. 18, 335 r. 11, 342 r. 1, 346 r. 7, 349 r. 6, EN.MEŠ-*šú*] 86 r. 1, 130:16, EN.MEŠ-*š*[*ú*] 48 r. 3, EN.MEŠ-[*šú* 16 r. 2, EN.MEŠ]-*šú* 134 r. 1, 165 r. 4, EN.M[EŠ-*šú* 96:20, EN.M]EŠ-*šú* 193 r. 2, EN.[MEŠ]-*šú* 7 r. 2, EN.[M]EŠ-*šú* 118 r. 4, EN].MEŠ-*šú* 312 r. 4, E[N.MEŠ-*šú* 169 r. 5, E[N.MEŠ-*šú*] 131 r. 3, 239 r. 1, E]N.MEŠ-*šú* 15 r. 5, 225 r. 1, 246:14, E]N.[MEŠ]-*šú* 339 e. 12, [EN.MEŠ-*šú*] 338 r. 6, [E]N.MEŠ-*šú* 123 r. 4,

bennu "epilepsy": *be-en* 85 r. 4, *be-en-nu* 6 r. 7, 61:13, 134 r. 3, 266 r. 2, 284 r. 6, *be-en-n*[*u*] 48 r. 6, *be-en*]*-nu* 342:10, *be-nu* 289 r. 6, 306 r. 3, [*be-nu* 301 r. 5, *bé-ni* 334 r. 17, *bé-nu* 305 r. 4, EN-*e-nu* 219:11,

bēt bēli "government": É—EN.MEŠ-*šú* 95:3, 4, 6, r. 2,

bēt ili "temple": É—DINGIR 237:3,

bēt maiāli "bedroom": É—KI.NÁ 302:6, É—NÁ 42:4,

bēt qāti "storehouse": É—ŠU 42:6,

bēt ramāki "bathroom": É—TU_5-*šú* 42:5,

bētānu see *ša-bētāni*,

bētu "house, where": *bé-et* 100:3, *by*]*t* 334 s. 1, É 10:3, 6, 8, 11, 14, 16, 18, 11:5, 7, 8, 9, 11, 12:4, 6, 8, 10, 13, 13:3, 4, 6, 14:3, 17:7, 19:5, 6, r. 7, 11, 22:2, 3, 23:4, 27:3, 5, 8, 9, e. 11, r. 2, 7, 28:3, 4, 29 r. 2, 30:3, 4, 5, 31:9, 11, 14, 16, 17, 18, 21, 22, 23, 25, e. 27, 32:4, 35:1, 37:5, 42:2, 3, 5, 6, 12, 50:2, 12, 51:7, 81:5, 89:5, 93 e. 10, 94 e. 11, r. 2, 102 r. 4, 105:6, 7, 112:4, 119:15, r. 2, 123:4, 10, 124:2, 3, 4, 5, 6, 125:4, 126:4, 129:2, 133:3, 137:2, 3, 4, 140 r. 12, 142:5, 6, 8, 9, r. 5, 153:2, 3, 154:2, 3, r. 4, 155:4, 160:5, 6, 161:5, 163:2, 3, 4, r. 5, 169:3, 173:4, 176:1, 6, 7, 8, r. 2, 187:2, 194:4, 200:3, 4, 209:4, 210:2, 3, 6, 12, 217:4, 5, 218:4, 223:5, 6, 224:6, 226:3, 245:4, 251:3, 8, 252:4, r. 3, 253:5, 255:2, 258:3, 268:1, 271:3, 6, 10, 17, 275:5, 8, 9, 10, 12, 13, 15, 17, e. 20, 22, 23, r. 1, 2, 3, 4, 5, 6, 8, 9, 277:3, 278:3, 280:3, 283:1, 3, 4, 5, 9, 10, 11, 12, 13, 14, 15, 16, 17, 18, 19, e. 20, 22, r. 1, 6, 287:8, 288:9, 13, 14, 18, r. 8, 295 r. 6, 301:2, 302:2, 311:3, 4, 12, 315:1, 2, 3, 7, 15, 316:8, 320:1, 2, 5, 326:2, 328:2, 3, 6, 7, 8, 12, 329:2, 4, 5, 6, 7, 8, 330:8, 331:2, 6, 332:2, 333:1, 2, 334:3, 21, 23, 335:5, 9, e. 16, 337:3, 4, 338:5, 8, 339 r. 9, É] 10:17, 200:6, 7, 334:7, 336:1, [É 11:3, 14:6, 31:5, 25, 50:4, 65:4, 93:1, 102:4, 124:10, 125:7, 163:3, 187:4, 210:7, 211:1, 271:14, e. 20, 277:5, 283:7, 288:4, 316:3, 4, 5, 9, 321:4, 7, 330:2, 8, 332:7, 334:4, 17, r. 7, 336:1, 337:1, [É] 24:4, 27:1, 31 e. 26, 50:3, 115:3, 275:6, 16, 283:8, 302:3, 330:6, 7, 335:1, É-[*su* 180:4, É-*šú* 180 e. 10, 215:5, 341 r. 1, É.MEŠ 91:2, 93 r. 1, 6, 275:18, 280:2, 314:3, 11, 19, 336:6, 341 r. 4, 5, É.[MEŠ 336 r. 1, É.MEŠ-*šú-nu* 91:8, see also *ša-bēti-šanie*,

bētu eššu "New Palace": É—GIBIL 311 r. 9, 313 r. 6, 315 r. 9, 316 r. 16, É—GIBIL] 314 r. 25, É—GIBI]L 317 r. 9, É—G[IBI]L 312 r. 19,

bētu šaniu "domestic quarters": É—2-*e* 42:5, 270 r. 2,

biltu "talent": *bi-lat* 20 r. 3, 59:8, 152:1, 184:1, *bi-lat*] 32 r. 5, GÚ.UN 6 r. 3, 21:5, 42 r. 4, 186 r. 10, 214:1, 219 r. 7, 253:8, 264:5, r. 4, 283 r. 8, 288 r. 2, 314 r. 4, 325 r. 3, 326 r. 9, 335 r. 9, 342:16, GÚ.U[N 186 r. 1, GÚ.U]N 253 r. 5, GÚ].UN 125:10, G]Ú.UN 11 r. 7, 336 r. 10,

birti "between": *bir-ti* 160:6, 161:5, *b[i]r-ti* 288 r. 10, *bir-ti-šú-nu* 238:8,
bītu see *bētu,*
bu''û see *ba''û,*
burku "lap": *bur-ki* 7 e. 16, 20:5, 31 r. 10, 51 r. 6, 52 r. 7, 53:14, 58 r. 4, 85 r. 1, 87 r. 2, 92 r. 4, 96:18, 98 r. 2, 99 r. 2, 110 r. 2, 118 r. 1, 165 r. 1, 185 r. 6, 8, 198:4, 200 r. 2, 201 r. 1, 207 r. 5, 217 r. 6, 219 r. 8, 220 r. 6, 250 r. 4, 251:16, 253 r. 5, 265:12, 274 r. 4, 278 r. 4, 298 e. 13, 299:13, 301 r. 1, 308 r. 1, 309 r. 2, 310 r. 1, 314 r. 5, 319 r. 2, 325 r. 4, 326 r. 10, 328 r. 4, 329 r. 4, 330 r. 1, 335 r. 10, 346 r. 6, *bur-ki]* 126 r. 4, 138 r. 7, 289 r. 1, *bur-k[i* 91:17, *bur-k]i* 50 r. 8, *bur-[ki* 42:22, *bu[r-ki* 302 r. 2, *bu]r-ki* 229 r. 1, *b[ur-ki* 284 r. 4, *b]ur-ki* 334 r. 16, *[bur-ki]* 11 r. 4, *bur^{ur}-ki* 151 r. 2, *bu-ur-ki* 176 r. 7,
būrtu "well": *bur-ti* 202:8, PÚ 31 r. 30, 93 r. 1, 7, 105:7, 119:16, r. 2, 277:4, [P]Ú 112:6,
būru "well": *bu-ra-a-ni* 271:7, *bu]-ra-ni* 271:11, *bu-ri* 115:4, *bu-u-ru* 160:5,
dabābu "to contest; litigation": *da-ba-bu* 6:11, 50 r. 6, 119 r. 4, 8, 127:10, 250 r. 1, *da-b[a-bu* 50 r. 1, *i-da-bu-bu* 178 r. 1, 298 r. 4, *i-da-bu-[bu]* 176 r. 10, *i-da]-bu-bu-ma* 200 r. 5, *i]-da-bu-ub* 66 r. 4, *i-da-bu-u[b-ma* 345 r. 2, *i-*DUG$_4$.DUG$_4$ 151 r. 5, *i-*DU[G$_4$.DUG$_4$ 350 r. 1, *i-*DUG$_4$.DUG$_4$*-ma* 278 r. 7, *i-*DU[G$_4$.DUG$_4$*-ma]* 8 r. 1, DUG$_4$.DUG$_4$ 3:7, 15, 6 r. 6, 7:9, 13, 9:2, 6, 10 r. 3, 14 r. 4, 17 r. 2, 5, 19:11, 20:2, 22:12, 23:10, r. 3, 31 r. 6, 9, 32:12, e. 17, 34:12, 19, 37:16, r. 4, 38 r. 5, 39:7, 11, 40:13, 19, 41 e. 15, 42:13, 19, 48:10, 13, r. 1, 51:11, 52:14, 53:11, 55:8, 56 e. 9, 66 r. 6, 82:4, 85:13, 87:5, 10, 88:12, 89:12, r. 2, 90 r. 4, 93 r. 8, 10, 96:10, 14, 98:10, 99:12, e. 16, 100:12, e. 22, 101:8, 16, 102:6, r. 1, 106:1, 110:12, e. 15, 111 r. 3, 118:10, 16, 124:12, 125 r. 1, 138:14, 140:4, 7, 142 r. 6, 9, 144:9, 152:3, 154 r. 7, 161 r. 6, 174 r. 2, 7, 201:12, 17, 202 e. 16, 210:13, r. 3, 213:5, r. 6, 218:10, 219 r. 5, 220 r. 4, 8, 227:9, 228:9, 13, 229 e. 12, 238:9, 244:9, 246:8, 12, 251:9, 14, 253:11, r. 4, 254:7, 257:13, r. 20, 274 r. 2, 6, 275 r. 18, 278:13, 283 r. 7, 288:22, r. 2, 289:9, 13, 290:7, 11, 298:2, 5, 11, 299:4, 11, 301:11, 305 r. 1, 306:8, 13, 308:4, e. 11, 309 r. 5, 312:16, r. 3, 314:20, 319:8, r. 4, 322:4, 325 r. 2, 326:22, r. 6, 328:13, r. 2, 329:18, r. 2, 335 r. 2, 8, 336 r. 3, 340:2, 8, 341 r. 7, 10, 342:9, 344:13, 346:7, r. 3, 347 r. 1, DUG$_4$.DUG$_4$] 11 r. 3, 27 r. 10, 58:5, 82:9, 217 r. 1, 254:1, 314 r. 3, 339:10, DUG$_4$.DU[G$_4$ 8:3, 14 r. 7, 130:13, 301:16, DUG$_4$.DU[G$_4$] 51 r. 3, 212:5, 305:11, 319:12, DUG$_4$.D[UG$_4$ 126 r. 2, 284:10, 338 r. 4, DUG$_4$.D[UG$_4$] 15 r. 3, 38:7, DUG$_4$.(DUG$_4$) 177:13, DUG$_4$.[DUG$_4$ 86:13, 169 r. 3, 348:6, 10, DUG$_4$.[DUG$_4$] 161 e. 16, DUG$_4$.[DU]G$_4$ 2 e. 8, 275 r. 20, DUG$_4$].DUG$_4$ 10 e. 22, 56 r. 3, 138 r. 5, 163 r. 1, 198:1, 285 r. 3, DU[G$_4$.DUG$_4$] 207 r. 1, 284 r. 2, DU[G$_4$.DU]G$_4$ 27 r. 8, DU]G$_4$.DUG$_4$ 185:4, 334 r. 8, D[UG$_4$.DUG$_4$ 322:7, D[UG$_4$.DUG$_4$] 8:6, D]UG$_4$.DUG$_4$ 3:11, 289 r. 3, [DUG$_4$.DUG$_4$ 33:6, 57:12, 90 r. 1, 103:11, 164:12, 313:14, 334 r. 14, 336 r. 8, 349 r. 2, [DUG$_4$.DU]G$_4$ 15:4, 185 r. 3, 342:15, [DUG$_4$].DUG$_4$ 61:10, 344 r. 8, [DU]G$_4$.DUG$_4$ 49:7, 207:6, 311:13, [DU]G$_4$.D[UG$_4$ 274:9, [D]UG$_4$.DUG$_4$ 219:10, DUG$_4$.DUG$_4$*-bu* 123:12, DUG$_4$.DUG$_4$*-ma* 10 r. 5, 16 r. 3, 31 r. 10, 34 r. 4, 40 r. 3, 41 r. 4, 42 r. 7, 50 r. 10, 53 r. 3, 85 r. 3, 87 r. 6, 90 r. 6, 92 r. 8, 96:21, 98 r. 6, 100 r. 7, 101 r. 9, 102 r. 11, 110 r. 5, 113 r. 2, 196 r. 1, 201 r. 4, 202 r. 7, 204 r. 1, 211 r. 4, 219 r. 11, 225 r. 2, 229 r. 4, 239 r. 2, 244 r. 1, 246:15, 250 r. 6, 253 r. 7, 257 r. 23, 283 r. 11, 288 r. 5, 299:15, 308 r. 4, 314 r. 7, 325 r. 7, 332 r. 2, 334 r. 19, 335 r. 12, 342 r. 2, 346 r. 8, DUG$_4$.DUG$_4$*-ma]* 141 r. 2, 269 r. 2, 329 r. 6, 348 r. 1, DUG$_4$.DUG$_4$*-m[a* 126 r. 6, 169 r. 6, 284 r. 9, DUG$_4$.DUG$_4$*-[ma* 266 r. 1, DUG$_4$.DUG$_4$*-[ma]* 131 r. 4, 305 r. 3, DUG$_4$.DU[G$_4$*-ma* 349 r. 6, DUG$_4$.DU[G$_4$*-ma]* 7 r. 3, DUG$_4$.D[UG$_4$*-ma* 112 r. 2, DUG$_4$.D[UG$_4$*-ma]* 58 r. 6, DUG$_4$.[DUG$_4$*-ma* 119 r. 10, 124 r. 2, 187 r. 1, 330 r. 3, DUG$_4$.[DUG$_4$*-ma]* 51 r. 9, DUG$_4$].DUG$_4$*-ma* 339 r. 1, DU[G$_4$.DUG$_4$*-ma* 179 r. 2, 302 r. 4, 326 r. 12, DU[G$_4$.DUG$_4$*-ma]* 130 e. 17, DU]G$_4$.DUG$_4$*-ma* 134 r. 2, 165 r. 5, D[UG$_4$.DUG$_4$*-ma* 32 r. 8, 207 r. 6, 316 r. 1, D]UG$_4$.DUG$_4$*-ma* 11 r. 9, [DUG$_4$.DUG$_4$*-ma* 212:8, 301 r. 3, 306 r. 2, 340 r. 3, [DUG$_4$.DUG$_4$*-ma]* 9:8, 138 r. 10, 217 r. 7, 251 r. 3, [DUG$_4$.DUG$_4$*-m]a* 86 r. 2, [DUG$_4$.DUG$_4$]*-ma* 99 r. 6, [DUG$_4$.DU]G$_4$*-ma* 15 r. 6, [DU]G$_4$.DUG$_4$*-ma* 140:13, [D]UG$_4$.DUG$_4$*-ma* 39:15, 48 r. 5, DUG$_4$.DUG$_4$*-ub* 161 r. 8, DUG$_4$.DU[G$_4$*-u-ni]* 123 r. 2,
dagālu "to look; to retrieve": *i-da-gal* 226 r. 14,
dāgil iṣṣūri "augur": *da-gíl*—MUŠEN.MEŠ 133 r. 8,
daiānu "judge": *da-a-a-ni* 345 r. 3, DI.KUD 2 e. 8, 3:7, 92:10, 176 r. 11, 210 r. 4, 211 r. 5, DI.[KUD 58 r. 7, D[I.KUD 326 r. 13,
dâku see *duāku,*
daltu see *dassu,*
dām erēni "cedar balsam": MÚD—ERIN 101 r. 5, 102 r. 8,
damāqu "to be good, nice": SIG 206:1, SIG$_5$*-tú* 324:7,
dāmu "blood": MÚD.MEŠ 264:5, 9, MÚD.MEŠ*-šú* 264 r. 4,
danānu "to be strong": *dan-nat* 310 r. 13, *dan-ni* 42:5, *dan-[ni* 176:3, *dan-ni-te* 10 r. 19, 12 r. 5, 91 r. 4, 147 r. 9, 195 r. 7, 311 r. 7, 316 r. 14, *dan-ni-te]* 53 r. 11, 193 r. 10, 314 r. 24, 315 r. 7, *dan-ni-t[e]* 284 s. 1, *dan-ni-ti* 19 r. 14, 31 r. 27, 61 r. 10, 124 r. 13, *dan-nu* 34:17, 160:5, 283:12, 305:7, 306:4, 309:6, 311:8, 314:16, 317:5, r. 1, 318:4, 325 r. 9, 326 r. 5, 332 r. 6, 334 r. 20, 335:12, r. 7, 13, 339:3, r. 2, 340 r. 7, 344:7, *dan-nu]* 316 r. 2, 329 r. 8, 330 r. 4, 332 r. 3, 336:8, 11, *dan]-nu* 312 r. 7, *d[an-nu]* 326:15, 346:1, *[dan-nu* 334 r. 3, 345:8, *[dan-nu]* 314 r. 9, 337:6, 342 r. 3, *[dan]-nu* 335 r. 14,
dannutu "document, deed": *dnt* 111 r. 11, 196 s. 1, 217 s. 1, *d[nt* 334 s. 1, *[d]nt* 284 r. 11,
darāru "remission of debts": *da-ra-ri* 259 s. 1, see also *durāru,*
dassu "door": GIŠ.IG 154:4, GIŠ.IG.MEŠ 27 r. 2, 124:3, GIŠ.I[G.MEŠ] 99:2, GIŠ.IG.MEŠ*-šú* 42:4, 142:7, 311:5, GIŠ.IG.[MEŠ*-šú]* 328:4, G]IŠ.IG.MEŠ*-šú* 302:4, [GIŠ].IG.MEŠ*-šú* 210:3,
dēnu "judgment": *de-en-nu* 27 r. 8, *de-en-n[u* 27 r. 10, *de-en-šú* 8 r. 1, 58 r. 7, 326 r. 13, *de-[en-šú* 176 r. 11, *[de-en-šú]* 345 r. 3, *de-e-ni* 33:6, 125 r. 1, 127:10, 133:7, 9, 142 r. 6, 319:8, 12, *de-e]-ni* 126 r. 6, *de-e-ni-šú* 48 r. 4, 298 r. 4, *de-e-n[i-šú]* 39:14, *de-e-nu* 11 r. 3, 15 r. 3, 23:9, 10, 31 r. 8, 34:12, 19, 37:15, r. 4, 40:13, 19, 42:13, 19, 50 r. 1, 6, 51 r. 3, 55:8, 57:11, 82:4, 85:13, 87:4, 10, 88:12, 93 r. 8, 96:9, 98:10, 99:12, 101:16, 102 r. 1, 111 r. 2, 118:9, 119 r. 4, 138:14, 161 e. 16, r. 6, 169 r. 3, 177:13, 185:4, r. 2, 197:13, 201:12, 17, 207 r. 1,

212:5, 218:10, 227:8, 244:9, 250 r. 1, 253 r. 3, 254:7, 257:12, 264:1, 274:9, 278:13, r. 2, 283 r. 7, 284 r. 2, 290:7, 11, 298:2, 10, 299:4, 11, 301:11, 16, 306:8, 13, 311:12, 326:22, 329:17, 334 r. 13, 335 r. 2, 8, 336 r. 3, 7, 346:7, r. 2, *de-e-nu*] 39:6, 10, 49:6, 100:12, 118:16, 124:11, 246:12, 312:15, 322:3, 329 r. 1, 338 r. 3, *de-e-n*[*u*] 10 r. 2, 15:3, *de-e-n*]*u* 38 r. 5, *de-e-*[*nu*] 6:10, 61:9, 86:13, 119 r. 7, 154 r. 6, 313:13, 342:14, 347:12, *de-e*]*-nu* 99 e. 16, *de-*[*e-nu* 82:9, 254:1, *de-*[*e-nu*] 51:10, 93 r. 10, 130:13, 246:7, 298:4, *de-*[*e*]*-nu* 251:9, *de*]*-e-nu* 284:10, *d*[*e-e-nu* 251:14, *d*[*e-e-nu*] 48:9, *d*[*e*]*-e-nu* 38:7, *d*]*e-e-nu* 48 r. 1, 342:9, 344:13, *d*]*e-*[*e-nu*] 344 r. 7, [*de-e-nu* 41 e. 15, 56 r. 3, 138 r. 5, 238:1, 312 r. 3, 341 r. 10, [*de-e-nu*] 126 r. 2, 144:9, 288 r. 1, 309:10, [*de-e*]*-nu* 9:6, 102:6, [*de*]*-e-nu* 14 r. 7, 106:1, 322:7, 348:10, [*de*]*-e-*[*nu* 58:5, [*d*]*e-e-nu* 48:13, 348:6, *de-e-nu-i-šú* 298 r. 5, *de-e-šú* 210 r. 4, 211 r. 5, *de-in-šú* 219 r. 12, *de-né-e-šú* 265:10, *de-ni* 52:14, 89:12, r. 2, 96:14, 140:4, 7, 142 r. 9, 274 r. 2, 334 r. 19, *de-*[*n*]*i* 164:12, *de-ni-šu* 11 r. 9, 301 r. 3, 335 r. 12, *de*]*-ni-šu* 169 r. 6, *de-ni-šú* 9:8, 10 r. 5, 23 r. 3, 31 r. 10, 32 r. 8, 34 r. 4, 40 r. 3, 42 r. 7, 51 r. 9, 53 r. 3, 58 r. 6, 87 r. 6, 90 r. 6, 92 r. 8, 96:21, 98 r. 6, 99 r. 5, 101 r. 8, 110 r. 5, 119 r. 10, 124 r. 2, 131 r. 4, 134 r. 2, 138 r. 9, 151 r. 5, 161 r. 8, 165 r. 5, 174 r. 7, 176 r. 9, 196 r. 1, 200 r. 5, 201 r. 3, 207 r. 6, 210 r. 3, 211 r. 4, 212:7, 217 r. 7, 219 r. 11, 220 r. 8, 229 r. 3, 238:10, 246:15, 250 r. 6, 253 r. 7, 257 r. 22, 269 r. 2, 274 r. 6, 278 r. 6, 283 r. 11, 284 r. 9, 285 r. 3, 288 r. 5, 289 r. 3, 302 r. 4, 305 r. 3, 306 r. 1, 308 r. 4, 309 r. 5, 314 r. 7, 319 r. 4, 325 r. 7, 326 r. 12, 330 r. 3, 339 r. 1, 346 r. 8, 349 r. 6, *de-ni-šú*] 16 r. 2, 86 r. 1, 100 r. 7, 187 r. 1, 239 r. 2, 332 r. 2, 342 r. 2, 345 r. 2, *de-ni-š*[*ú* 6 r. 6, *de-ni-*[*šú*] 340 r. 2, *de-ni*]*-šú* 113 r. 2, 202 r. 7, 266 r. 1, 316 r. 1, 350 r. 1, *de-n*]*i-šú* 50 r. 10, 130 e. 17, 179 r. 2, *de-*[*ni-šú* 141 r. 2, 348 r. 1, *de*]*-ni-šú* 85 r. 3, 112 r. 2, 123 r. 2, *d*[*e-ni-šú* 204 r. 1, 329 r. 6, *d*[*e-ni-šú*] 15 r. 5, 102 r. 10, 140:12, 299:14, *d*]*e-ni-šú* 225 r. 2, 251 r. 3, *d*]*e-n*[*i-šú* 244 r. 1, [*de-n*]*i-šú* 41 r. 4, [*d*]*e-ni-šú* 7 r. 3, *de-nu* 3:11, 7:8, 13, 8:3, 6, 9:2, 17 r. 5, 22:12, 32:12, e. 17, 56 e. 9, 103:11, 110:12, e. 15, 163 r. 1, 174 r. 2, 198:1, 213:5, 219:9, r. 4, 220 r. 4, 228:9, 13, 257 r. 20, 275 r. 18, 20, 289:9, 13, 305:11, 325 r. 2, 326 r. 6, 328:13, 334 r. 8, *de-nu*] 4:6, 14 r. 3, 19:11, 328 r. 2, *de-n*[*u* 217 r. 1, *de-n*]*u* 305 r. 1, *de-*[*nu* 314 r. 3, *de-*[*nu*] 349 r. 1, *de*]*-nu* 340:8, *d*[*e-nu* 314:20, 339:10, *d*[*e-nu*] 207:5, *d*]*e-nu* 210:13, 340:2, [*de-nu* 10 e. 22, 20:2, 213 r. 6, 229 e. 12, 308 e. 11, 341 r. 7, [*de-nu*] 100 e. 22, 202 e. 16, 308:4, [*d*]*e -nu* 123:12, *di-i-n*[*u*] 90 r. 3, *di-i-*[*nu*] 90:17, D]I.KUD-*šú* 3:15, see also *ša-pān-dēnāni,*

dīnu see *dēnu,*

dullu "work": *dul-la-šú-nu* 21 r. 3, *dul-lu* 21:7, *du*[*l-lu*] 190:2,

durāru "debt remission": *du-ra-ru* 226 r. 13, *du-r*[*a-ri* 221 s. 1, see also *darāru,*

edānu "term, deadline": *e-da-nu* 160 r. 1,

egirtu "letter, document": *e-gír-ra*.MEŠ-*te* 336:10, *e-gír-te* 177 r. 12, *e-gír-*[*ti*] 317 r. 7,

ekal māšarti "review palace": É.GAL—*ma-šar-te* 31 r. 26,

ekallu "palace": É.GAL 26 r. 3, 31 r. 4, 15, 37 r. 12, 46 r. 1, 59 r. 10, 11, 12, 91 r. 2, 287 r. 10, 288:7, 309 r. 7, É.[GAL] 96 r. 16, see also *ša-pān-ekalli,*

eleppu "boat": GIŠ.MÁ 123:8, see also *bēl eleppi,*

elû A "to go up; (D) to remove, set aside": *e-la-an-ni* 101:10, 102:13, *e-la-an-*[*ni*] 100:20, *e-la-a*[*n-ni* 164 e. 14, *e-la-a*]*n-ni* 100:14, *e-la-*[*an-ni*] 326 r. 3, *e-l*]*a-an-ni* 185:6, *e*]*-la-an-ni* 102:8, 185 r. 1, 340:6, [*e-la*]*-an-ni* 212:2, [*e-l*]*a-an-ni* 213 r. 2, *e-la-a-ni* 101:16, 335 r. 6, 336 r. 6, [*e-l*]*a-a-ni* 322:6, *e-*[*la-ni*] 344:14,

elû B "upper": NIM 42:6,

elūlu (Elul, name of the 6th month): ITI.KIN 32 r. 16, 70 r. 1, 91 r. 5, 143 r. 1, 180 r. 1, 208 e. 7, 221:5, 244 r. 9, 256 r. 1, 288 r. 3, 301 r. 18, [ITI.KI]N 126 r. 13, [I]TI.KIN 116 r. 10,

emādu "to impose, lean": *e-me-du-u-ni* 83:3, 238:3, 264:2, *e-te-mì-is-su* 265:5, *in-du* 133 e. 11,

emāru see *imāru,*

ēnu "eye, spring": *e-nu* 123:10, 160:6, [*e-nu* 123:4, ÍD.IGI.2.MEŠ 336 r. 2, [ÍD.IGI.2.MEŠ 336 r. 10, IGI.2.MEŠ 223:7, [IGI.2.MEŠ 224:7,

enzu "goat": UDU.ÙZ.MEŠ 243:2,

epāšu "to do, make, perform; (D) to contract": *ep-šu* 311:4, 328:3, *ep-šú* 27 r. 2, 42:3, 124:3, 142:6, 302:3, *ep-*[*šú* 153:3, 210:3, *ep*]*-šú* 187:4, *e*]*p-šú* 50:4, *e-tap-šú* 133:3, *tu-piš-ma* 89:6, 91:11, 92:2, 96:5, *tu-piš-ma*] 94 r. 2, *tu-*[*piš-ma* 86:6, *t*]*u-piš-ma* 99:6, *up-piš-ma* 23:5, 31 r. 3, 253:6, 300:6, *ú-piš-ma* 2:6, 5:3, 6:4, 7:4, 10:18, 17:10, 22:9, 32:8, 34:5, 41:8, 42:7, 45:4, 51:3, 52:10, 54:5, 55:3, 57:6, 59:6, 61:5, 65:9, 85:7, 88:5, 93 r. 3, 98:5, 103:4, 109:5, 110:7, 111:9, 112:7, 113:5, 116:6, 118:5, 123:5, 124:7, 127:5, 130:8, 138:8, 142:10, 154 e. 9, 160:12, 161:10, 176:9, 177:5, 186:7, 197:4, 201:7, 204:8, 217:11, 218:7, 219:2, 227:4, 228:4, 229:7, 244:4, 246:4, 250:7, 251:4, 252 r. 6, 257:6, 271 r. 2, 274:4, 275 r. 12, 278:9, 287:13, 288:18, 290:3, 301:6, 305:6, 309:5, 311:7, 314:15, 319:5, 328:9, 329:12, 333 e. 4, 335:11, 336:8, 341 r. 1, 342:5, 344:6, 345:6, 347:6, *ú-piš-ma*] 4:2, 266:9, *ú-piš-m*[*a* 37:10, 48:5, 90:11, 286:5, *ú-piš-m*[*a*] 315:8, *ú-piš-*[*ma* 155:9, 269:8, *ú-piš-*[*ma*] 326:14, *ú-piš*]*-ma* 100:7, *ú-pi*[*š-ma* 39:2, *ú-pi*[*š-ma*] 40:7, 283 r. 3, *ú-pi*[*š-m*]*a* 195:5, *ú-p*[*iš-ma* 102:2, *ú-*[*piš-ma* 210:8, *ú-*[*piš-ma*] 49:2, 50:8, 226:10, *ú-*[*p*]*iš-ma* 140:1, 284:4, [*ú-piš-ma* 27 r. 4, 56:3, 101:4, 125:9, 144:2, 196:5, 267:5, 285:5, 306:3, 334 r. 2, 339:3, 343:9, [*ú-piš-ma*] 337:5, [*ú-piš-m*]*a* 38:3, 53:5, 316:10, [*ú-piš*]*-ma* 3:3, [*ú-pi*]*š-ma* 115:5, 126:8, 239:7, 295:4, 313:7, [*ú*]*-piš-ma* 19:7, 119:17, 202:9, 297:9, *ú-tap-piš* 174:3, 289:4, [*ú-tap-pi-šu*] 132:7, DÙ-*uš* 21:7, r. 4,

epēšu see *epāšu,*

epinnu "plough": GIŠ.APIN.MEŠ 31:15, GIŠ.APIN.MEŠ-*te* 22:8,

eqlu "field": A.[ŠÀ 10:14, 211:1, 252:4, A.[ŠÀ] 252 r. 3, 275:5, A.[Š]À 31:6, A.ŠÀ 10:2, 3, 6, 8, 17, 11:5, 7, 9, 11, 12, 12:3, 4, 5, 6, 7, 8, 9, 10, 11, 13, 13:2, 3, 4, 14:5, 6, 7, 8, 15:2, 16:1, 3, 19:5, 10, 22:1, 2, 6, 7, 8, 11, 23:3, 8, 24:3, 6, 7, 27 e. 11, r. 1, 7, 28:2, 3, 6, 30:3, 31:4, 5, 8, 16, 18, 20, 32:4, 37:4, 5, 14, r. 5, 50:2, 3, 12, 51:7, 93:1, r. 1, 95:2, 4, 6, e. 1, r. 2, 102:4, r. 4, 105:5, 6, 119:2, 3, 4, 5, 6, 7, 9, 11, 13, 15, r. 2, 125:3, 4, 12, r. 4, 126:3, 4, 159:5, 160:4, 8, 10, 11, 14, 161:4, 5, 6, 7, 8, 9, 13, e. 15, 169:2, 3, 173:3, 4, 187:2, 209:4, 211:6,

217:3, 15, 218:3, 4, 5, 6, 9, 223:5, r. 4, 224:4, 6, 226:2, 3, 4, 8, 9, 238:5, 251:8, 252 r. 11, 253:10, 258:1, 259:1, 4, 260:1, 5, 268:1, 271:9, 14, 275:6, r. 3, 4, 16, 277:3, 5, 278:2, 3, 6, 7, 12, 283:7, 9, 11, 12, 13, 17, 19, e. 20, 21, 22, r. 1, 6, 287:8, 10, 11, 12, r. 5, s. 1, 288:4, 15, 17, 22, 315:7, 316:2, 3, 320:2, 4, 5, 321:6, 7, 326:20, 329:6, 7, 330:6, 7, 332:1, 2, 334:4, 19, 20, 335:1, 5, 8, e. 16, 336:2, 338:5, 339:7, A.ŠÀ] 14 r. 2, 112:4, 146:4, 163:2, 194:3, 4, 271 e. 19, 288:13, 316:8, 326:2, 333:1, 334:6, A.Š[À 11:1, 217:4, 322:2, A.Š[À] 160:13, 252:3, A.Š]À 11:3, 146:6, 159:6, A].ŠÀ 31:21, 163: 3, 224:5, [A.ŠÀ 10 e. 21, 119:8, 163 r. 5, 258:3, 315:1, 320:1, 334:8, [A.ŠÀ] 10:11, 126 e. 12, 169 r. 1, 283:1, 320:5, [A].ŠÀ 146 e. 9, r. 2, 207:4, A.[ŠÀ-*šú* 226 r. 1, A.ŠÀ-*šú* 223 r. 3, 259 r. 1, 260 r. 1, 275 r. 21, 287 r. 4, 295 r. 5, A.ŠÀ-*š*]*ú* 271 r. 6, A.ŠÀ.ME]Š 340:10, A.ŠÀ.MEŠ 19:4, 91:2, 93 r. 6, 149:1, 336:5, r. 1, 9, 341 r. 4, 5, A.ŠÀ.M]EŠ 65:3, r. 1, A].ŠÀ.MEŠ 19:9, [A.ŠÀ.MEŠ 65 r. 4, 340:1, [A.ŠÀ.MEŠ] 280:2, 315:15, A.ŠÀ.MEŠ-*šú* 264:7, A.ŠÀ.MEŠ-*šú-nu* 91:8, A.ŠÀ.GA 13:6, 24:4, 29 e. 7, r. 1, 30:4, 31 e. 29, 32:11, 81:6, r. 1, 94 e. 11, r. 2, 115:3, 176:5, r. 2, 245:3, 4, 253:5, 321:2, 334:2, 4, 17, 21, r. 6, 337:1, A.ŠÀ.GA] 100:3, A.ŠÀ.G]A 115:2, A.Š[À.GA 176:1, A.Š]À.GA 245 r. 5, A].ŠÀ.G[A 321:4, A.[ŠÀ.GA.MEŠ 101:20, A.ŠÀ.GA.MEŠ 65:4, 100 r. 3, A.Š[À.GA.MEŠ] 101:6, A].ŠÀ.G[A.MEŠ] 100:9, A.ŠÀ.GA.MEŠ-*š*[*ú* 326:2, *ḫ*[*q*]*ly* 334 s. 1,

erābu "to enter": *e-ra-a*[*b*] 180 e. 10, *ú-šer-ra*[*b*] 42 r. 3, *ú-še-rab* 87 r. 4, 295 r. 4, 326 r. 8, 334 r. 15, *ú-še-rab*] 251 r. 2, 302 r. 1, *ú-še-*[*rab* 32 r. 5, [*ú-še-rab* 11 r. 7, [*ú-še-rab*] 20 r. 2, *ú-še-rab-a-ni* 97 r. 7, *ú-še*]*-ra-ba* 92 r. 7, *ú-še-ra-ba-an-ni* 245 r. 4,

erēbu see *erābu,*

erēšu see *arāšu,*

erû "copper": URUDU 31 e. 30, 63:2, URU]DU 290 r. 2, URUDU.ME 289:6, URUDU.MEŠ 2 e. 7, 3:4, 6 s. 3, 7:6, 12 r. 8, 15:1, 19:8, 21:5, 22:10, 29:1, r. 3, 31 r. 31, 32:9, s. 1, 46:3, 56:4, 61:7, r. 11, 64:1, 83:1, 121 r. 5, 123:6, 124 s. 1, 125:10, 127 r. 10, 137:1, 157:1, 170:1, 176:10, 190:6, 214:1, 264:5, r. 4, 265:5, 6, 7, 276:3, 289 r. 17, 290:5, 326:3, URUDU.MEŠ] 155:10, 184:1, 186 r. 1, URUDU.[MEŠ] 152:1, U[RUD]U.MEŠ 6:5, [URUDU.MEŠ 174 s. 3, 186 r. 5, [URUDU.MEŠ] 59:8, 186 r. 11,

eṣādu "to reap, harvest": *e-ṣi-id*] 160:15,

eṣāpu "to double": *e-ṣip* 257 r. 21, *e-ṣi-ip* 281:4,

ēṣidu "harvester": LÚ.*e-ṣi-di* 75 r. 3,

ešrāia "tenfold": 10-*a-a* 164 r. 1, 10.A.TA.AN 253 r. 6, 10].A.TA.[AN] 340 r. 1, 10.TA.ÀM 212:6,

ešrāti "tenfold": 10-*a-te* 106:8, 161 r. 7, 10-*tú* 176 s. 1, 10.ME]Š 123 r. 4, 10.MEŠ 40 r. 2, 41 r. 3, 48 r. 3, 50 r. 9, 90 r. 5, 93 r. 12, 119 r. 9, 124 r. 1, 126 r. 5, 134 r. 1, 138 r. 8, 174 r. 6, 176 r. 8, 179 r. 1, 220 r. 7, 225 r. 1, 250 r. 5, 278 r. 5, 284 r. 8, 298 r. 2, 299:14, 308 r. 3, 309 r. 4, 325 r. 6, 349 r. 5, 10.MEŠ] 15 r. 4, 16 r. 1, 51 r. 7, 238 e. 12, 10.[MEŠ 314 r. 6, 10].MEŠ 345 r. 1, 10.MEŠ-[*šú* 274 r. 5, [10.MEŠ-*te* 20 r. 4, 342 r. 1, [10.MEŠ-*te*] 151 r. 3, [10.MEŠ-*t*]*e* 118 r. 3, [10].MEŠ-*te* 112 r. 1, 10.ME]Š-*te* 332 r. 1, 10.MEŠ-*te* 3:14, 9:7, 10 r. 4, 27 r. 11, 31 r. 11, 34 r. 3, 42 r. 5, 52 r. 5, 53 r. 1, 58 r. 5, 87 r. 5, 92 r. 2, 96:20, 98 r. 5, 110 r. 3, 113 r. 1, 131 r. 3, 140:11, 169 r. 5, 198:5, 201 r. 2, 210 r. 2, 211 r. 3, 219 r. 10, 246:14, 254 r. 1, 283 r. 10, 310 r. 2, 312 r. 4, 319 r. 3, 328 r. 5, 329 r. 5, 330 r. 2, 334 r. 18, 335 r. 11, 338 r. 6, 346 r. 7, 348:11, 10.MEŠ-*te*] 39:13, 86 e. 18, 289 r. 2, 339 e. 11, 10.MEŠ-*t*[*e*] 23 r. 1, 10.MEŠ-[*te* 302 r. 3, 326 r. 11, 10.MEŠ-[*te*] 202 r. 6, 10.MEŠ]-*te* 239 r. 1, 10.M[EŠ-*te*] 6 r. 4, 10.[MEŠ-*te* 301 r. 4, 10.[MEŠ-*te*] 7 r. 1, 8:8, 10].MEŠ-*te* 11 r. 8, 85 r. 2, 99 r. 4, 130:16, 165 r. 3,

eššu "new": GIBIL 281:3, 301:3,

etinnu "master builder": LÚ.TIN 48 r. 14,

eṭāru "to save; (D) to pay in full, to pay off a debt": [*uṭ*]*-ṭu-ru* 66 r. 6, *ú-ṭu-ru* 178:6,

eṭēru see *eṭāru,*

gabbu "all": *gab-bi* 25 r. 3, *gab-b*[*i* 4:1, *gab-bu* 21:8, [*g*]*ab-bu* 59:5, *gab-bu-ma* 293 r. 5,

gabdi (reading uncert.) "adjoining to": *gab-di* 22:4, 5, 6, 7, 154:6, 7, e. 8, *gab-d*[*i* 33:1, see also *ṭēhi,*

gamāru "to finish": *gam-mur* 14 r. 2, 31 r. 6, 33:4, 34:10, 37:13, 39:5, 42:11, 45:7, 48:7, 56:6, 85:10, 87:3, 88:9, 98:8, 99:10, 100 r. 2, 101:19, 102 r. 3, 109:9, 118:7, 123:9, 124:10, 140:3, 142 r. 4, 144:6, 154 r. 3, 177:9, 185:2, 201:10, 202:13, 219:7, 227:6, 228:7, 229:9, 246:6, 250 e. 11, 251: 8, 253:9, 257:11, 269:11, 278:11, 283 r. 5, 290:5, 299:2, 301:9, 305:10, 306:6, 311:11, 312:13, 314: 18, 315:14, 340:9, 346:5, *gam-mur*] 41:12, 49:4, 309:9, 322:1, 348:3, *gam-mu*[*r*] 19:9, 51:6, *gam-mu*]*r* 329:15, *gam-m*[*ur*] 326:19, *gam-m*]*ur* 126 e. 11, 313:11, *gam-*(*mur*) 289:7, *gam-*[*mur* 10:20, 218:9, 341 r. 5, *gam-*[*mur*] 55:6, *gam*]*-mur* 27 r. 7, 113:7, *ga*[*m-mur*] 101:5, *ga*]*m-mur* 90:15, [*gam-mur* 15:2, 57:10, 82:2, 210:12, 239:12, 342:8, 349: 3, [*gam-mur*] 17 e. 14, 103:9, [*gam-m*]*ur* 58:3, 197:7, *ga-am-mur* 40:11, *ga-am-*[*mur* 119 r. 1, *ga-a*[*m-mur* 50:11, *ga-am-ru* 125:11, *ga-mur* 2 e. 8, 3:5, 4:5, 6:7, 7:7, 23:7, 32:10, 52:13, 53:9, 61:8, 89:9, 93 r. 6, 96:8, 110:10, 111 r. 1, 127:8, 138:11, 161 e. 14, 174:7, 176 r. 1, 185 r. 4, 207:3, 217:14, 244:7, 274:7, 275 r. 16, 319:6, 328:12, 334 r. 6, 335 e. 16, 336 r. 1, 8, 344:11, 347:10, *ga-mu*[*r* 152:2, *ga-m*[*ur* 130:11, 339:6, *ga-m*]*ur* 169 r. 1, *ga-*[*mur* 59:10, 286:7, *ga-*[*mur*] 284:8, *g*[*a-mur* 22:11, 308:3, *g*]*a-mur* 8:1, 102:4, 213:3, [*g*]*a-mur* 38:5, *kám-*[*mur* 288:21, *ú-ga-mur* 21 r. 4,

gammalu "camel": *gam-mal* 241 r. 1, ANŠE.A.((A)).AB.BA 241:1,

garû "to contest": *i-*[*gar-ru-ni*] 100 e. 22, *i-gar-ru-u-ni* 101:18, 185 r. 3, *i-gar-ru-u-ni*] 119 r. 8, *i*]*-gar-ru-u-ni* 336 r. 8, *i-gar-ru-ú-ni* 102 r. 2,

gildu "oxhide, fur": KUŠ.TAB.BA 101 r. 3, 102 r. 5,

gimirtu "totality, entirety": *gi-mir-t*[*e*]*-šú* 325: 12, *gi-mir-ti-šá* 315:8, *g*]*i-mir-ti-šá* 210:5, *gi-mir-ti-šu* 328:3, *gi-mir-ti-šú* 105:6, 287:7, 316:4, 326: 1, 12, *gi-mir-ti-šú*] 316:9, *gi-mir-ti-*[*šú*] 331:6, *gi-mir-t*[*i-šú* 332:7, *gi-*[*mir-ti-šú*] 315:2, *g*]*i-mir-ti-šú* 149:2, *gi-mi*[*r-ti-šú-nu*] 59:5,

gimru "total": PAB 2:5, 6:2, 10 r. 16, 14:5, 17:6, 19:4, 21:4, 30 r. 6, 9, 11, 31:16, 21, r. 24, 32 r. 11, 33 r. 3, 6, 34:4, 37:9, 39:1, 40:6, 41:7, 52:6, 7, 9, 54:4, 57:2, 4, 72:3, 81:9, 85:5, 86:3, 5, 89:5, 90:3, 5, 7, 9, 91:8, 94 r. 1, 96:3, r. 5, 100:6, 101:2, 105 r. 5, 109:4, 110:5, 111:7, 112:3, 116:5, 119:15, 123:3, 130:5, 6, 7, 132:4, r. 1, 133:2, 138:6, 145:4, 149:7, 155:8, 193:3, 4, 6, 223 r. 4, 229:5, 239:3,

243:3, 250:5, 252 r. 3, s. 2, 257:3, 266:8, 274 r. 11, 277 r. 8, 10, 279:6, 280 r. 7, 283 e. 22, r. 1, 284:3, 287:6, 288:16, 294:3, 297:4, 7, 303 r. 2, 311 r. 6, 313:5, 314:11, r. 23, 315:6, 319:4, 320:7, 325:11, 326:10, 11, 12, 328:1, 334:28, 30, 335:8, 339:1, r. 12, 341:8, 10, r. 1, 342:4, 343:5, 7, 344:4, PAB] 172:4, 333:1, 334:29, 343:6, PA]B 27 r. 1, 50:6, [PAB 1 r. 15, 17, 31:4, 53:4, 130:4, 209:3, 224:5, 239:5, 300:4, 314:8, 316:8, 321:9, 343:4, 344:3, 345:6, [PAB] 31 e. 27, 93 r. 1, 148:3, 195:4, [PA]B 31 r. 21, 52:4, 191:3, 334:2, [P]AB 79:7, PAB-*ma* 211:6, 334:30, 336:5, [PAB-*ma* 57:5, [PAB-*ma*] 31 e. 29,

ginû "regular offering": *gi-né-e* 188 r. 6,

gušūru "roof-beam": GIŠ.ÙR.MEŠ 21:9, GIŠ.ÙR.MEŠ-*šú* 42:3, 124:3, 142:6, 311:4, 328:4, GIŠ.ÙR].MEŠ-*šú* 210:3, GIŠ.[ÙR.MEŠ-*šú*] 302:3,

habullu "debt": *ha-bu-li* 178:1,

halāqu "to disappear": *hal-qu* 97 r. 5,

halāṣu "to press, squeeze": *hal-ṣu* 46:2,

hamru "sacred precinct": *ha-am-ri* 285 r. 2,

hāmu "litter, chaff": *ha-am-šu* 97 r. 4,

hamussu "one fifth": 5-*su* 115:4,

harbakannu (a breed of horses): *har-bak-kan-ni* 20 r. 2, *har-ba-kan-ni* 334 r. 15, *har-ba-kan-ni*] 251 r. 1, AN]ŠE.*har-bak-kan-ni* 11 r. 6, ANŠE.*har-bak-k*[*an-ni*] 42 r. 2, ANŠE.*har-ba-kan-ni* 87 r. 4, 326 r. 8, ANŠE.*har-ba*]-*kan-ni* 92 r. 6, ANŠE.*har-b*[*a-kan-ni*] 32 r. 4, ANŠE.*har-b*]*a-kan-ni* 302 r. 1,

harrānu see *hūlu,*

hatannu "brother-in-law": *ha-at-na* 142 r. 12,

hazannu "mayor": *h*]*a-za-nu-šú-nu* 344 r. 5, LÚ.*ha-za-an-nu* 42 r. 9, LÚ.*ha-za-a*[*n*]-*nu* 338 r. 10, LÚ.*ha-z*[*a*]-*a*[*n-nu*] 10 r. 12, LÚ.*ha-za-a-nu* 22 r. 5, LÚ.*ha-za-na-šú-nu* 335 r. 5, LÚ.*h*]*a-za-na-šú-nu* 100:18, 326 r. 2, LÚ].*ha-za-nu* 130 r. 10, LÚ].*ha-za-*[*nu*] 28 r.1 LÚ.*ha-za-nu* 31 r. 13, 86 r. 6, 87 r. 7, 91:15, 96 r. 6, 188 r. 9, 209 r. 7, 274 r. 8, 314 r. 10, 319 r. 8, 328 e. 17, 345 r. 6, LÚ.*ha-za-nu*] 16 r. 4, LÚ.*ha-za-*[*nu* 283 r. 20, 332 r. 11, LÚ.*h*[*a-za*]-*nu* 86 r. 5, LÚ.[*ha-za-nu*] 15 r. 7, [LÚ.*ha-za-nu*] 17 r. 7,

hirītu "ditch, canal": *hi-ri-a-te* 160:6, 161:5, *hi-ri-te* 32:6, 160:7, 9,

hubtu "captives": LÚ].*hu-ub-te* 123:7,

hūl šarri "king's road, highway": KASKAL—LUGAL 169:3, KASKAL—[LUGAL] 328:5, KASKAL—MAN 27:3, 93 e. 11, 204:7, 335:7,

hūlu "road, way": KASKAL 10:7, 15, 11:8, 12:6, 13:3, 22:8, 27:2, 6, 30:7, 8, 31:9, 11, 14, 93:2, 3, 125:7, 146:5, 169:8, 176:4, 201:4, 211:3, 226:7, 271:5, 15, 16, 275:10, 11, 13, r. 4, 5, 320:2, 6, 321:4, 7, 9, 334:8, 15, 18, KAS[KAL 10:4, 93 e. 11, KAS]KAL 119:6, [KASKAL 11:2, KASKAL.2 13:5, 271:4, 11, 338:6,

hurāṣu "gold": KUG.GI 3:12, 7:15, 11 r. 4, 14 r. 8, 20:4, 23:13, 31 r. 9, 34 r. 1, 38 r. 8, 50 r. 7, 52 r. 6, 53:13, 87 r. 1, 92 r. 3, 95 r. 4, 96:18, 110 r. 1, 138 r. 7, 140:9, 165:6, 176 r. 6, 185 r. 8, 198:3, 200 r. 1, 201:21, 202 r. 4, 219 r. 8, 220 r. 5, 250 r. 3, 251:15, 253 r. 5, 254:9, 265:11, 278 r. 3, 283 r. 9, 284 r. 4, 289:16, 301 r. 1, 308 e. 12, 325 r. 3, 326 r. 9, 328 r. 3, 329 r. 3, 334 r. 16, 335 r. 9, 341 r. 11, 346 r. 5, 349 r. 4, KUG.GI] 51 r. 5, 98 r. 1, 144:11, 151 r. 1, 163 r. 3, 210 e. 19, 274 r. 3, 314 r. 4, 319 r. 1, KUG.G[I] 131 r. 1, KUG.G]I 42:21, 85:16, 99 r. 2, 244:11, 310 r. 1, KUG.[GI 217 r. 5, KUG.[GI] 299:12, KUG].GI 290:13, 309 r. 1, K[UG.GI] 32 r. 1, 58 r. 3, 229 e. 13, [KUG.GI 211 r. 1, 330 r. 1, [KUG.GI] 342:16, [KUG].GI 194 r. 1, [K]UG.GI 298 e. 13,

hursān "ordeal": *hur-sa-an* 264 r. 6, *hur-sa-an*] 238:4,

husinnu see *ša-husinnīšu,*

huṣābu "piece, chip": *hu-ṣa-bu* 97 r. 4,

huṭāru see *ša-huṭāri,*

iābilu "ram": UDU.NITÁ.MEŠ 296:1, 323:2, 324:7, [UDU.NITÁ.MEŠ 296 r. 1, UDU.NITÁ.MEŠ-*ši-na* 84:2,

iarhu "pond": *ia-ar-h*[*a* 338:5, *ia-ar-hu* 329:8,

igāru "wall": *i-ga-*[*ri* 288 r. 3, NA_4.*i-ga-r*[*a-te* 314:19, NA_4.*i-ga-*[*ra-te*] 314:12,

ikkāru "farmer": LÚ.ENGAR 37:8, 109 r. 5, 7, 255:4, 5, 289 r. 11, 315:4, 316:6, 326:10, 334:27, 29, LÚ.ENGA[R 116 r. 3, 4, 5, LÚ.EN[GAR 116 r. 2, 326:8, L]Ú.ENGAR 65:8, [LÚ].ENGAR 253:3,

ikkār ekalli "palace farmer": LÚ.ENGAR—É.GAL 125 r. 12, LÚ.ENGAR—KUR 28 r. 5, 7, 115 r. 2, LÚ.ENGAR—KUR-*ma* 28 r. 6,

ilku "labour duty": *il-ku* 31 r. 30, 191 r. 5, see also *bēl ilki,*

illīdiš see *līdiš,*

ilu "god": DINGIR 281:3, DINGIR.MEŠ 288 r. 20,

imāru "homer; hectare": AN[ŠE 27:5, 31:21, 100:3, 217:5, AN]ŠE 11:9, 31:25, 79:1, 337:1, ANŠE 3:4, 10:3, 8, 11, 14, 17, 11:3, 5, 7, 12:4, 8, 13, 13:3, 6, 14:6, 19:5, 20 r. 2, 21:6, 22:2, 23:4, 24:4, 27:1, 3, 8, 9, e. 11, r. 1, 28:3, 30:4, 31:5, 9, 14, 16, 18, 22, 23, 25, e. 27, 29, 32:4, 35 r. 6, 37:5, 46:2, 50:3, 60:1, 62:1, 67:1, 6, 69:1, 70:1, 71:1, 72:1, 73:1, 74:1, 75:1, 77:1, 81:5, 9, 93:1, 105:6, 112:4, 115:3, 117:1, 119:11, 13, 15, 125:4, 7, 136:1, 137:2, 3, 4, 146:4, 158:4, 160:5, 161:5, 163:3, 169:3, 173:4, 176:1, 181:2, 182:1, 186 r. 2, 217:4, 218:4, 221:1, 223:5, r. 3, 4, 224:4, 5, 226:3, 232:1, 233:3, 245:13, 251 r. 1, 252:4, r. 3, 253:5, 259:1, 260:1, 268:1, 271:3, 6, 10, 14, 17, e. 20, 23, 275:5, 6, 8, 9, 10, 15, 16, 17, 277:5, 278:3, 283:1, 2, 7, 8, 9, 10, 11, 12, 13, 16, 17, e. 22, 288:4, 302:9, 315:1, 7, 320:2, 5, 321:4, 7, 326:2, 329:5, 7, 330:6, 7, 332:2, 333:1, 334:4, 7, 17, 21, r. 15, 335:5, 8, 336:2, 5, 337:4, 338:5, ANŠE] 31:11, 65:4, 283:19, e. 20, 316:3, ANŠ[E 14:5, 335:1, ANŠ]E 11:11, 211:1, 238:5, A[NŠE 194:4, 288:13, [AN]ŠE 31 e. 26, 275 e. 20, [ANŠE 316:8, [ANŠE] 283:18,

imēru see *imāru,*

immatīma "at any time": *im—ma-te-m*[*a*] 82:5, *im—ma-*[*te-m*]*a* 251:10, *mat-e-ma* 40:14, 101:9, 169 r. 4, 253:12, *ma-a-te-ma* 176 r. 4, *ma-a-te-m*[*a*] 161 r. 1, *ma-te-e-ma* 42:15, 87:6, 118:12, 119 r. 5, 213 r. 1, *ma-te-e-*[*ma*] 55:9, *ma-te-e*]-*ma* 90 r. 2, *ma-t*]*e-e-ma* 311:14, *ma-*[*te-e-ma* 314:21, *m*]*a-te-e-ma* 102:7, *ma-te-e-me* 37:17, 106:2, *ma-te-ma* 7:10, 9:3, 32:13, 34:14, 38 r. 1, 39:8, 48:12, 56 e. 10, 85:14, 88 r. 1, 91:13, 93 r. 9, 96:11, 99:13, 110:14, 124:13, 125 r. 3, 138 r. 1, 142 r. 8, 177:11, 201:13, 228:10, 246:9, 254:3, 278:14, 283 r. 8, 288:23, 289:10, 290:8, 299:5, 305:13, 306:9, 326:23, 328 e. 14, 335 r. 3, 339:8, 340:3, 341 r. 8, 342:12, 344:14, 346:8, *ma-te-ma*] 8:4, 17 r. 3, 212:1, 218:11, 274:10, 322:4, 336 r. 3, *ma-te-*[*ma* 312:17, *ma-te-*[*m*]*a* 301:12, *ma-t*[*e-ma*] 298:3, *ma-t*]*e-ma* 202 r. 2, *ma-*[*te-ma*] 130:14, *ma-*[*te-m*]*a*

227:10, *ma]-te-ma* 61:11, *m[a-te-ma]* 347 r. 2, *m]a-te-ma* 15:5, 338 r. 1, *[ma-te-ma]* 49:8, 308:5, 329:18, *ma-te-me* 52 r. 2, 319:9, *ma-te-me]* 334 r. 9, *ma-[te]-me* 98:11, *ma-ti-ma* 6:13, 20:1, 27 r. 9, 31 r. 6, 92:6, 140:5, 152:4, 163 r. 2, 257:14, *ma-ti-[ma]* 19:12, *ma-t[i-ma]* 284:11, *ma-ti-mu* 219 r. 1,

immeru "sheep": UDU.MEŠ 222:1, 243:3, 264:3, 8, r. 3, 323 e. 10, 11, 324 r. 2, [UDU.MEŠ 324 r. 4, UDU.MEŠ-*šú-nu* 91:9,

ina "in": *ina* 1 r. 21, 2 e. 7, 6:5, 12, 13, r. 6, 7:6, 9, 10, r. 3, 8:4, 9:3, 10:17, r. 5, 11:9, 10, r. 4, 5, 6, 12:8, r. 1, 13:3, 14 r. 1, 4, 15:4, r. 5, 16 r. 2, 17:7, 12, e. 13, 19:5, 6, 12, r. 13, 20:1, r. 1, 2, 21 r. 14, 22:2, 12, 23:5, 6, r. 3, 9, 24:4, 25:3, e. 7, r. 4, 26:1, 3, 4, 5, 6, 7, 27 r. 3, 5, 6, 9, 28:6, 29 e. 7, r. 2, 30:4, 6, 31:5, 9, 11, 21, e. 29, r. 3, 5, 6, 10, 30, 32:4, 9, 13, r. 3, 5, 8, 34:8, 9, 13, 14, r. 4, 13, 35:1, 36:3, 37:6, 16, 17, 38 r. 1, 39:3, 7, 8, 14, 40:9, 14, 41:10, r. 4, 42:7, 10, 14, 22, r. 3, 7, 43:3, 44:3, 45:6, 46:3, 4, 5, 47:3, 48:11, r. 3, 4, 6, 49:3, 8, 50:7, 9, 10, r. 2, 51:2, 5, e. 12, r. 6, 9, 52:11, r. 1, 2, 53:6, 7, r. 3, 54:6, 7, 55:3, 4, 9, 56 e. 10, 57:8, 58 r. 6, 60:4, 61:10, 14, 62:4, 63:3, 4, 64:3, 65:10, 67:4, 69:3, 4, 70:6, 7, 71:3, 4, 74:3, 4, 75:3, 4, 76:3, 4, 77:7, 8, 78 r. 4, 5, 81:2, 4, 6, e. 10, 11, 82:1, 5, 84:4, 85:8, 14, r. 1, 86:8, 87:2, 5, 6, r. 2, 3, 4, 6, 88:7, 13, 89:8, 90:9, r. 6, 91:10, 11, 12, 17, 92:6, r. 5, 6, 93:3, r. 5, 9, 94 e. 11, r. 2, 3, 95 r. 3, 4, 96:6, 7, 10, 11, 18, 21, 97:1, 3, 4, e. 8, r. 6, 98:7, 11, r. 2, 3, 6, 99:8, 13, r. 2, 100:4, 8, 13, 101:9, r. 8, 102:3, 7, r. 10, 103:7, 104:3, 5, 6, 105 r. 11, 106:2, 107:1, 3, 108:2, 3, 110:9, 13, 14, r. 2, 5, 111 e. 10, 112:6, 113:6, r. 6, 115:3, 5, 118:6, 11, 12, 119:3, 9, 11, 13, 16, 18, r. 10, 19, 120:3, 123:7, 8, 13, r. 2, 13, 124:4, 12, 13, r. 2, 125 r. 2, 127:7, 11, 130:9, 10, 14, e. 17, 131 r. 4, 133:3, 5, 6, 8, 134 r. 2, 137:3, 4, 138:10, r. 7, 139:3, 140:2, 5, 141 r. 2, 142:8, e. 13, r. 7, 8, 143:1, 4, 5, e. 7, 146:4, 149:3, 150:2, 3, 4, 5, 151 r. 2, 4, 5, 152:1, 4, 154:4, 5, r. 2, 155:10, 156:3, 157:5, 6, 158:3, 4, 5, 159:4, 160:13, r. 2, 161:11, r. 1, 8, 163:4, r. 2, 167:1, 3, 4, 169:10, 11, r. 4, 170:3, 174:5, r. 3, 4, 6, 7, 16, 176 r. 4, 7, 8, 9, 177:6, 7, 11, 178:3, 180:1, 3, 4, 181:4, 5, 182:3, 183:2, 4, 184:4, 185 r. 6, 8, 186 r. 4, 189:3, 4, 190:4, 194:5, 6, 197:5, 198:4, 200 r. 3, 201:3, 4, 9, 13, r. 1, 3, 14, 202:5, 204:3, 4, r. 1, 206:3, 5, 207 e. 7, r. 5, 6, 208:3, 210:5, r. 1, 2, 3, 18, 211:1, 4, r. 2, 3, 4, 212:1, 7, 213 r. 1, 214:4, 5, r. 2, 215:1, 216:4, 5, 6, 7, 217:6, 8, 13, r. 6, 7, 218:4, 11, 219:12, r. 1, 8, 10, 220 r. 6, 8, 222:3, 4, 223:3, 5, 6, r. 2, 224:2, 5, 226:4, 9, 12, 16, 227:5, 9, 228:6, 10, 229:8, r. 2, 3, 232:2, 3, 4, 233:5, 6, 234:2, r. 6, 235:2, 4, 5, 236:3, 237:5, 238:7, 8, 239 r. 2, 240:3, 4, 241:4, 5, e. 6, 7, 242:2, 3, 4, 243:5, 6, 7, 8, 244:6, 245:5, e. 14, 15, r. 1, 246:5, 8, 9, 15, 247:5, 248:8, 250:9, 10, r. 4, 6, 251:6, 7, 10, 16, e. 17, r. 1, 2, 3, 252:1, r. 2, 5, 10, 253:8, 12, r. 5, 6, 7, 254:2, 257:9, 13, 14, r. 22, 36, 259 e. 6, 260:2, e. 7, 262:2, 4, 263:1, 3, 4, 264:4, 265:4, 12, 269:10, r. 2, 271 r. 3, 272 r. 1, 273:3, 274:5, 6, 10, r. 4, 6, 275:4, 13, r. 14, 15, 276:3, 277:4, s. 2, 278:3, 4, 5, 10, 14, r. 4, 6, 281:2, 3, 283:10, r. 3, 4, 7, 8, 11, 284:6, 11, r. 4, 9, 285:4, 7, 286:6, 287:18, r. 3, 288:11, 12, 13, 14, 17, 19, 20, 23, r. 3, 5, 13, 289:6, 10, r. 2, 290:4, 8, 291:4, 292:2, 293:3, e. 6, 296:6, e. 7, 298 e. 13, r. 2, 3, 299:1, 5, 13, 14, 301:8, 9, 12, r. 1, 3, 305:7, 8, 12, 13, r. 3, 4, 5, 306:4, 5, 9, r. 1, 307:5, 308:5, r. 1, 2, 4, 309 r. 5, 310 r. 1, 311:5, 10, 13, 312:12, 16, 17, 313:14, 314:13, 14, 21, r. 5, 7, 315:1, 12, 316:3, 5, 317:4, 318:3, 5, 319:6, 9, r. 2, 4, 322:4, 323:1, 4, 5, 6, 7, 8, e. 10, 325 r. 4, 5, 7, 326:3, 7, 13, 16, 17, 22, r. 7, 8, 10, 12, 328:3, 5, 11, 329:4, 5, 8, 14, 18, r. 4, 6, 330:4, r. 1, 3, 331:4, 5, 332:2, 333 e. 3, 334:22, r. 4, 9, 14, 15, 16, 19, 335:2, 6, 10, e. 13, r. 2, 3, 10, 12, 336:5, 6, 7, 9, r. 3, 338 r. 1, 339:5, 7, 8, 340:3, r. 1, 341 r. 3, 8, 342:6, 11, 343:11, 344:8, 346:3, 8, r. 6, 8, 347:8, r. 2, 348:2, 7, r. 1, 349 r. 6, *ina]* 38:4, 99 r. 5, 109:7, 119 r. 5, 138 r. 9, 163 r. 2, 200:9, 210:14, 221 e. 7, 285:3, 288:4, 330:4, 344:14, *in[a* 10:19, 31 e. 29, 31, 55:4, 130:14, 202 r. 1, 275:4, *in]a* 4:4, 324:5, 328 e. 14, *i[na* 336 r. 3, *i]na* 334 r. 1, 340 r. 2, *[ina* 3:4, 15, 11 r. 9, 15:1, 5, 17 r. 3, 19:8, 20:5, 31 e. 28, 38:4, 40:8, r. 3, 41:9, 42 r. 1, 48:6, 49:8, 50 r. 8, 10, 56:4, 57:12, 58:1, 61:7, 11, 65:10, 67:3, 79:9, 80:2, 83:4, 85 r. 3, 86 r. 1, 88 r. 1, 90:14, r. 2, 92 r. 4, 8, 100 r. 7, 101:1, 5, 104:2, 112 r. 2, 113 r. 2, 116:8, 119:19, 123:5, 6, 125:10, r. 3, 126:10, r. 4, 6, 137:2, 138 r. 1, 144:4, 146:3, 164:13, 165 r. 1, 5, 169 r. 6, 176:10, 179 r. 2, 180 e. 9, 182:5, 185:6, 186 r. 1, 187 r. 1, 188:4, 196:7, 8, 200 r. 2, 5, 202 r. 2, 7, s. 1, 204:9, 210:10, 213:2, 218:8, 11, 222:5, 224:3, 6, 225 r. 2, 228:10, 229 r. 1, 239:8, 9, 244 r. 1, 248:2, 259:2, 266 r. 1, s. 1, 272:4, 285:7, r. 2, 3, 289 r. 1, 3, 293 e. 6, 295 r. 2, 296:4, 302 r. 1, 307:2, 4, 308:2, 309:8, r. 2, 311:14, 314:4, 315:12, 316 r. 1, 324:10, 11, e. 12, 13, r. 1, 3, 328 r. 4, 330:5, 8, 332 r. 2, 333 r. 1, 334 r. 3, 339 r. 1, 342:12, r. 2, 343:11, 344:14, 345:10, r. 2, 349:2, 350 r. 1, *[ina]* 7 e. 16, 22:10, 37:11, 48:12, r. 7, 53:14, 56 e. 10, 118 r. 1, 124:9, 176:11, 182:4, 196 r. 1, 202:11, 227:10, 229 r. 3, 233:4, 242:5, 287:17, 296:5, 302 r. 4, *[in]a* 146 r. 1, 242:1, 347:9, *[i]na* 221:3, 4, *[[ina* 26:2, 189:5, *[[ina]]* 284 r. 11, *i-na* 12:4, 6, 58 r. 4, 59:8, 225:3, 226:5, 313:9, 315:3, *[i-n]a* 16:2,

īnu see *ēnu*,

irtu "breast": *ir-ti* 31:17,

isītu "tower": *i-si-tú* 101:20, *i-si-tú]* 100 r. 2, URU].*i-si-tú* 101:6, URU.*i-si-tú* 100:3, [URU.*i-si-tú* 100:9,

issēn "one": 1-*en* 264:5,

issēniš "also, in addition": *is-se-n[iš* 258 s. 1,

isseššerāti (reading unc.) "elevenfold": 11.MEŠ 229 r. 2,

issi ekalli "queen": MÍ—É.GAL 31 r. 14, 86 r. 14, 135 r. 3, 140 r. 12, 164 r. 4, 12, 310 r. 19, 329 r. 14, MÍ—É.GAL] 330 r. 8, 332 r. 5, MÍ—(KUR) 90:1, MÍ.KUR 165 r. 6,

issi/u "with/from": *i-si-šú* 260:6, TA 3:11, 6:6, 7:5, 13, 8:7, 9:5, 10 r. 2, 14 r. 6, 15 r. 2, 17:11, r. 4, 19:8, 20:2, 29 e. 6, 31:17, 19, r. 5, 9, 30, 32:16, 33:3, 34:7, 18, 35:4, 37:12, r. 2, 3, 38 r. 5, 39:11, 40:10, 19, 41:11, 42:18, 48:15, 16, 50:9, r. 5, 51:4, r. 2, 52 r. 4, 53:8, 55:5, 58 r. 1, 60:3, 61:6, 62:3, 82:10, 85:9, 87:9, 88:6, 89 r. 1, 90 r. 4, 93 r. 11, 96:6, 15, 98:6, 101:4, 17, r. 5, 102 r. 1, 8, 103:6, 124:8, 15, 127:6, 130:8, 133 r. 4, 138:9, r. 4, 140:7, 8, 142 r. 1, 2, 3, 10, 154 r. 1, 155:3, 157:4, 161:12, r. 4, 169:4, 6, 8, 174:4, 177:6, 178:6, r. 1, 185 r. 1, 191 r. 6, 201:8, 18, 207 r. 2, 212:4, 213:1, 217:12, r. 2, 218:8, 219 r. 5, 220 r. 3, 228:5, 244:5, 253:8,

254:5, 257:8, r. 19, 259:5, 265:6, 269:8, 275 r. 20, 278 e. 17, 284:5, 285:5, 287:15, 288:19, r. 1, 289:5, 290:4, 11, 298:9, 299: 9, 301:7, 305:15, 306:12, 13, 308 e. 9, 311:9, 312 r. 1, 313:8, 314:17, 319:13, 320:6, 321:7, 322:8, 325 r. 1, 326:17, 18, 19, r. 4, 5, 329:21, 335 e. 14, 15, r. 7, 8, 336:10, 338 r. 4, 341 r. 3, 342:6, 15, 344:9, 10, r. 6, 346 r. 3, 349 r. 2, TA] 66 r. 3, 197:11, 284 r. 1, 301:16, T[A 90:13, 155:11, 219:3, 251:13, 274 r. 1, 288 r. 6, 336 r. 7, 339:9, T]A 246:11, 338:6, 343:12, 349:2, (TA) 119 r. 7, [TA 10:19, 27 r. 5, 11, 39:4, 48:16, 56 r. 4, 58 r. 1, 59:9, 66 r. 5, 92:4, 99:8, r. 1, 100:8, 21, 102:3, 109:8, 118:17, 119:18, 144:5, 195:7, 196:6, 207:2, 210:9, 213 r. 5, 239:10, 275 r. 13, 289:14, 295:6, 302:11, 308:2, 314 r. 2, 315:11, 328 r. 1, 334 r. 5, 13, 340:7, 341 r. 9, 343:12, 345:9, 348:1, 9, [TA] 56:5, 58 r. 2, 61:6, 210 e. 17, 344 r. 7, [T]A 48:14, 15, 202:10, 253 r. 3, 322:1,

issu "woman, wife": MÍ 45:2, 48:8, 49:5, 82:3, 98:2, 9, 152:6, 197:2, 7, r. 1, 198 r. 1, 228:2, 7, 253:5, M]Í 45:8, 48:2, [MÍ 286:2, [MÍ] 272:8, r. 5, MÍ-*su-šú* 173:6, MÍ-*šu* 195:3, 343:5, MÍ-[*šu*] 169:14, MÍ-*šú* 6:1, 50:5, 52:7, 8, 81:7, 8, 86:4, 90:7, 8, 91:4, 5, 6, 7, 96:3, 97 r. 2, 110:3, 128:2, 130:4, 6, 142:4, r. 3, 151:2, 163:6, 172:3, 177:4, 193:3, 4, 245:11, 12, 251:4, 294:1, 2, 313:4, 319:3, 326:10, 11, 341: 9, 342:2, 3, 4, 345:4, MÍ-*šú*] 138:5, 307:6, 312:4, MÍ-[*šú* 100:5, M[Í-*šú*] 163:10, M]Í-*šú* 57:2, [MÍ-*šú* 66:4, 101:2, [MÍ]-*šú* 314:10, MÍ.MEŠ 239:3, 12, MÍ]. MEŠ 239:5, M[Í.MEŠ 256:3, M[Í.MEŠ] 37:9, M[Í].MEŠ 250:2, [MÍ.MEŠ 116:2, MÍ.MEŠ-*šú* 57:3, 111:3, see also *issi ekalli*,

iṣṣūru "bird": MUŠEN.MEŠ 169:2, r. 2,

išdu "foundation": SUHUŠ 202:8,

iškāru "assigned quota, tax": *iš*-QAR 143:2,

išpār birmi "weaver of multicoloured trim": LÚ. UŠ.BAR—GÙN 42 r. 8,

išpār ṣiprāti "weaver of ṣ. garments": LÚ.UŠBAR$_5$—TÚG.*ṣip-rat* 301:4,

išpāru "weaver": LÚ.UŠBAR$_5$ 13 r. 3, LÚ.UŠ.BAR 19 r. 11, 90 r. 11, 96 r. 14, 271 r. 10, 294:1, LÚ.UŠ.B[AR] 13 r. 2, UŠ.BAR.MEŠ 91 r. 3,

itti see *issi*,

kaiamānu "constantly": *ka-a-a-ma-nu* 149:3,

kallāpu "outrider(?)": LÚ.*kal-la-bu* 257 r. 28, 29,

kalliu "mule express": *ka-li-e* 288 r. 17,

kallumu "to show": *ú-kal-lim-šu-u-ni* 29 r. 2,

kalu "all": *kal* 48 r. 7, 85 r. 6, 89 r. 5, 219:12, 289 r. 7, *kàl* 6 r. 8, 61:14, 174 r. 4, 266 r. 3, 301 r. 6, 305 r. 5, 334 r. 18, 342:11, *kàl*] 306 r. 4, DÙ.A 284 r. 7,

kammusu "to sit, live, stay": *kam-mu-sat* 272 r. 3, [*kam-m*]*u-sat* 272:6,

kanūnu (Kanun, name of the 10th month): ITI.AB 22 r. 11, 23 r. 9, 29 r. 7, 33 r. 8, 85 r. 12, 127 r. 8, 160 r. 15, 161 r. 18, 167:4, 181 r. 2, 226 r. 2, 11, 248:10, 267 r. 5, 278 r. 18, 318 r. 4, 325 r. 23, ITI.A[B 248:8, [ITI].AB 268 r. 10, [ITI.AB 182 r. 1, [IT]I.AB 320 r. 9, 323 r. 1, [I]TI.AB 327 r. 8,

kapru "village": UR[U.ŠE 11:13, U[RU.ŠE] 320:6, U]RU.ŠE 93:4, [URU.ŠE] 321:9,

kāpu "embankment, cliff": *ka-pi* 137:3,

kaqqudu "head": SAG.DU 29:2, 36:1, 44:1, 63:2, 81:1, 83:1, 108:2, 139:1, 157:1, 215:1, 223 r. 2, 226:16, 248:1, 281:3, 291:1, 293:1, 318:5, SAG.DU] 292:1, SAG.D[U] 60:1, SA[G.DU 136:1, SA]G.DU 175: 2, [S]AG.DU 133 r. 1, 318:3, SAG.DU-*šá* 67:4, SAG. DU-*šú* 97:4, 143:5, SA[G].DU-*šú* 216:5,

kaqquru "ground": *kaq-qi-ri* 27 r. 7, 32:3, 159: 3, [*kaq-qi-ri* 32:2, 200:8, [*ka*]*q-qi-*[*ri* 169:11, *kaq-*[*qí-r*]*i* 275 r. 17, *kaq*]-*qí-ri* 31 e. 31,

karāku "to gather": *i-kar-ri-ka* 271:6,

karānu "wine": GEŠTIN.MEŠ 158:4, 232:1, e. 6, 233:3, 8, GEŠ[TIN.MEŠ] 186 r. 2, GIŠ.GE[ŠTIN.MEŠ] 181:2, GIŠ.GEŠTIN.MEŠ 181:5, 182:1, 4,

karaphu "fallow": *kar-ap-hi* 223:9, r. 4, 252 r. 9, 287 r. 2, *ka*]*r-ap-hi* 146 e. 8, 271 r. 5, *ka-rap-hi* 224:4, 268 e. 8, *ka-*[*rap-hi* 226:14,

karāru "to lay, throw": *kar-ru-u-ni* 241:2,

karkadinnu "confectioner": LÚ].SUM.NINDA 205 r. 5, LÚ.SUM.NINDA 204 r. 11,

kaspu "money": *gas-pu* 339:6, *kas-pi* 7 r. 6, 8:8, 33:4, 164 e. 15, 298 r. 2, 319 r. 3, *kas-pi*] 293 e. 6, *kas-pu* 2 e. 8, 3:5, 6 r. 4, 7:7, 10:20, r. 4, 11 r. 8, 15 r. 4, 16 r. 1, 17 e. 14, 23:7, r. 1, 31 r. 6, 32:10, r. 7, 34:10, r. 3, 38:5, 39:5, 13, 40:11, 42:11, r. 5, 45:7, 50:11, 51:6, 52:13, r. 5, 53:9, r. 1, 55:6, 56:6, 57:9, 58 r. 5, 82:2, 85:10, 86 e. 18, 87:3, r. 5, 88:9, 89:9, 90:15, r. 5, 92 r. 1, 93 r. 6, 96:8, 20, 98:8, r. 5, 101:5, 19, r. 7, 102 r. 3, 9, 103:9, 110 r. 3, 111 e. 11, 113:7, 118:7, r. 3, 119 r. 9, 123:9, 124:10, r. 1, 125:11, 127:8, 130:11, 131 r. 3, 138:11, 140:3, 142 r. 4, 144:6, 151 r. 3, 152:2, 154 r. 3, 161 e. 14, r. 7, 174:7, 176 r. 1, 8, 177:9, 185:2, 194 r. 2, 198:5, 201:10, r. 2, 202:13, 210:11, r. 2, 211 r. 3, 212:6, 217:14, 218:9, 219:7, 220 r. 7, 227:6, 228:7, 229:9, r. 2, 239:11, 244:7, 246:6, 250 e. 11, r. 5, 251:8, 254 r. 1, 257:11, 274:7, 278:11, r. 5, 283 r. 5, 10, 284:8, r. 8, 286:7, 288:21, 289:7, 290:5, 299:14, 301:9, r. 4, 306:6, 308:3, r. 3, 309 r. 4, 310 r. 2, 311:11, 314:18, r. 6, 319:6, 322:1, 325 r. 6, 326:19, r. 11, 329:15, r. 5, 330 r. 2, 335 e. 15, r. 11, 336 r. 1, 8, 340:9, 341 r. 4, 344:11, 346:5, 347:10, 349:3, r. 5, *kas-pu*] 15:1, 58:2, 100 r. 1, 138 r. 8, 334 r. 18, 342:7, *kas-p*[*u* 85 r. 2, 179 r. 1, 342:17, 348:3, *kas-p*[*u*] 174 r. 6, *kas-*[*pu* 27 r. 11, 49:4, 51 r. 7, 130:16, *kas-*[*pu*] 275 r. 16, 305:9, 346 r. 7, *kas-*[*p*]*u* 219 r. 9, *kas*]-*pu* 99:10, *ka*[*s-pu* 41:12, 100 r. 5, 339 e. 11, *ka*[*s-pu*] 197:6, *ka*[*s-p*]*u* 299:2, *ka*]*s-pu* 4:5, 6:7, *k*[*as-pu*] 41 r. 3, [*kas-pu* 3:14, 8:1, 14 r. 2, 27 r. 7, 48:7, 99 r. 4, 102:4, 109:9, 113 r. 1, 123 r. 4, 126 r. 5, 165 r. 3, 169 r. 1, 5, 213:3, 238 e. 12, 239 r. 1, 246:14, 269:11, 289 r. 2, 309:9, 312:13, r. 4, 313:11, 328 r. 5, 332 r. 1, 334 r. 6, 345 r. 1, [*kas-pu*] 40 r. 2, 50 r. 9, 59:10, 61:8, 185 r. 4, 202 r. 6, 302 r. 3, [*kas-p*]*u* 7 r. 1, 22:11, 93 r. 12, 119 r. 1, 348:11, [*kas*]-*pu* 9:7, 48 r. 3, 207:3, 315:14, [*ka*]*s-pu* 37: 13, 328:12, [*k*]*as-pu* 338 r. 6, [[*kas-pu*]] 284 r. 10, *kás-pu* 19:9, 20 r. 4, 31 r. 11, 110:10, see also *ṣarpu*,

kāṣiru "tailor": LÚ.*ka-ṣir* 31 r. 23, 81 r. 6, 124 r. 7, 8, 312:4, 313:4, LÚ.TÚG.KA.KÉŠ 91 r. 2,

kettu "truth": *ke-e-te* 288:17,

kî "like": *ki* 181 e. 1, [*ki* 182 e. 7,

kibtu "wheat": ŠE.GIG.MEŠ 74:1,

kīma "as soon as": *ki-ma* 25 r. 3,

kimahhu "tomb": KI.MAH 42:7,

kimtu "kin": I]M.RI.A 100:19,

kiqillutu "dung heap": *ki-qi-lu-tu* 31 r. 3, *ki-qí-il-te* 200:5,

kiriu "garden; orchard, vineyard": GI]Š.SAR 188:5, GIŠ].SAR 129:2, GIŠ.SAR 19:6, 30:5, 31 r. 2, 32:4, 5, 37:4, 50:12, 51:8, 90:8, 9, 93 r. 1, 7, 97:7, e. 8, r. 1, 8, 102 r. 4, 113:3, 119:15, 120:2, 123:2, 3, 173:5, 186 r. 5, 188 r. 6, 191:3, r. 4, 201:1, 2, 6, 11, 202:2, 4, 6, 14, s. 1, 204:2, 3, 5, 6, 211:4, 5, 251:8, 253:6, 10, 258:2, 271:17, 314:4, 5, 6, 8, 326:7, 8, 20, 329:3, 8, 9, 10, 11, 16, 331:3, 4, 8, 332:3, 4, 5, 8, 334:17, 24, 31, 335 e. 16, 336:2, GIŠ.SAR] 102:4, 334:24, GIŠ.SA[R 326:20, GIŠ.SA[R] 187:2, GIŠ.SA]R 188:6, 334:3, GIŠ.S]AR 186:1, 258:3, 330:3, GIŠ.[SAR 188:2, GIŠ.[SAR] 334 r. 6, GIŠ.[SA]R 119 r. 2, G[IŠ.SAR 336:1, [GI]Š.SAR 113:4, 188:3, [GIŠ.SAR 120:3, 330:4, 333:2, [GIŠ.SA]R 187:3, 213:4, GI[Š.SAR].MEŠ 37:13, GIŠ.SAR.MEŠ 37:5, r. 5, 91:3, 105:7, 123:3, 9, 149:1, 280:2, 304:3, 314:3, 321:6, 331:7, 335:9, 336:5, 6, r. 1, 9, 340:1, GIŠ.SAR.MEŠ] 314:18, GIŠ.SAR.[MEŠ 269:5, GIŠ.SA[R.ME]Š 340:10, GIŠ.SA[R.MEŠ 269 r. 2, GIŠ.SA]R.MEŠ 320:4, GIŠ.S[AR.MEŠ 332:1, GIŠ.S[AR.MEŠ] 314:11, GIŠ.S]AR.MEŠ 90:16, GIŠ.SAR.MEŠ-*šú-nu* 91:9,

kislīmu (Kislev, name of the 9th month): ITI.GAN 19 r. 12, 74 r. 1, 123 r. 13, 158 r. 7, 189:5, [ITI].GAN 144 r. 3,

kiṣir šarri "king's staff, royal corps": *ki-ṣir*—MAN 192 r. 5, 6, 7, 8,

kiṣirtu "case, envelope": *ki-[ṣir]-te* 248:1, *ki-ṣ[ir-ti]* 108:1,

kiṣru "cohort": *[ki]-iṣ-ri* 279 r. 9, *ki-ṣir* 245 r. 15, 246 r. 2, 251 e. 17,

kiššatu "world, universe": ŠÚ 180 r. 2,

kišubbû "waste land": *ki-šub-bé-e* 31:19,

kubšu see *ša-kubšīšu,*

kūdunu "mule": ANŠE.*k[u-du-nu* 247:3, ANŠE.GÍR.NUN.NA 206:1, GÌR.NUN.NA 288 r. 17,

kūmu "instead": *ku-mu* 236:3, 245 e. 14, *ku-um* 10:1, 18:1, 19:1, 24:1, 41:1, 42:1, 81:5, 91:12, 95:5, r. 1, 100:1, 105:1, 113:1, 127:1, 145:1, 217:1, 223:4, 252 r. 8, 264:8, 265:6, 268:7, 290:1, *ku-(um)* 264:9, *ku-[um* 61:1, *ku-[u]m* 159:1, *k[u-u]m* 30:1, *[ku-um* 1:1, 28:1, 31:1, 40:1, 96:1, 114:1, 121:1, 289:1, 317:4, *[ku-um]* 119:1, 295:7, *[ku-u]m* 7:1, 125:1, *[ku]-um* 37:1, 218:1, 302:1, *[k]u-um* 12:1, 13:1,

kunukku "seal": NA$_4$.KI[ŠIB 233:1, NA$_4$.KIŠIB 34:1, 46:1, 59:1, 63:1, 66:1, 88:1, 89:1, 90:1, 2, 91:1, 103:1, 110:1, 111:1, 118:1, 123:1, 135:2, 138:1, 148:1, 151:1, 153:1, 160:1, 2, 3, 161:1, 2, 3, 4, 162:1, 166:1, 3, 4, 5, 6, 169:1, 172:1, 173:1, 174:1, 177:1, 179:1, 181:1, 188:1, 191:1, 2, 192:1, 193:1, 195:1, 196:1, 197:1, 200:1, 202:1, 203:1, 2, 3, 4, 204:1, 210:1, 216:1, 226:1, 227:1, 235:1, 239:1, 2, 243:1, 244:1, 247:1, 256:1, 257:1, 2, 258:1, 262:1, 265:1, 267:1, 274:1, 275:2, 277:1, 278:1, 279:1, 2, 3, 4, 5, 286:1, 287:1, 3, 300:1, 2, 3, 301:1, 304:1, 309:1, 310:1, 311:1, 312:1, 314:2, 319:1, 325:1, 2, 3, 4, 5, 6, 7, 8, 9, 10, 329:1, 331:1, 343:1, 2, 347:2, NA$_4$.KIŠIB] 334:1, NA$_4$.KIŠ[IB] 199:1, NA$_4$.K[IŠIB 247:2, NA$_4$.K[IŠIB] 275:1, NA$_4$.[KIŠIB 280:1, 330:1, N[A$_4$.KIŠIB 162:3, 4, 5, 236:1, [NA$_4$].KIŠIB 44:1, 187:1, 261:1, 284:1, 311:1, 314:1, [NA$_4$.KI]ŠIB 126:1, 228:1, [NA$_4$.KIŠIB 52:1, 2, 109:1, 115:1, 116:1, 128:1, 129:1, 130:1, 141:1, 146:1, 154:1, 163:1, 164:1, 168:1, 194:1, 201:1, 209:1, 2, 245:1, 252:1, 268:1, 271:1, 272:1, 313:1, 317:1, 2, 321:1, 324:1, 2, 3, 4, 338:1, 2, 3, 343:1, 2, 345:1, [NA$_4$.KIŠIB] 52:3, 85:1, 175:1, 229:1, 316:1, [NA$_4$.KIŠI]B 45:1, 48:1, 65:1, 305:1, [NA$_4$.KIŠ]IB 65:2, 255:1, 270:1, [N]A$_4$.KIŠIB 85:2, 98:1, 108:1, 126:2, 148:2, 250:1, 297:1, 2, 3, 318:1, 2, 347:1, [N]A$_4$.KIŠ[IB 334:1, NA$_4$.KIŠIB-*šu-nu]* 61:1, NA$_4$].KIŠIB-*šú* 121:1, NA$_4$.KIŠIB-*šú* 7:1, 12:1, 13:1, 30:1, 37:1, 42:1, 113:1, 114:1, 125:1, 127:1, 159:1, 218:1, 290:1, 302:1, NA$_4$.KIŠIB-*šú]* 1:1, NA$_4$.KIŠIB-*š]ú* 40:1, NA$_4$.KIŠI[B-*šú* 41:1, NA$_4$.KIŠ[IB-*šú]* 119:1, NA$_4$.KIŠ]IB-*šú* 289:1, N]A$_4$.KIŠIB-*šú* 28:1, 96:1, [NA$_4$.KIŠIB-*šú* 10:1, 217:1, NA$_4$.KIŠIB-*šú-nu* 18:1, 31:1, 100:1, 105:1, NA$_4$.KIŠIB-*[šú-nu* 24:1, 145:1, NA$_4$.KIŠIB.MEŠ-*šú-nu* 19:1,

kupātu "bird fodder": *ku-pa-a-te* 288:20, *ku-pa-a-te]* 288 r. 4,

kuribtu (a kind of field): *ku-ri-bat* 137:4,

kurkû "goose": KUR.GI.MUŠEN 288 r. 11,

kurru "tanner's paste": *kur-ru* 20:3, 96:17, 101 r. 4,

kurummutu "barley (ration)": ŠE.PAD.MEŠ 3:4, 60:1, 62:1, 67:1, 70:1, 71:1, 72:3, 73:1, 75:1, 77:1, 79:7, 117:1, 136:1, 285:4, ŠE.PAD.[MEŠ] 69:1, 221:1, ŠE.[P]AD.M[EŠ 79:1,

kusāpu "bread": NINDA.MEŠ 21:6, 237:3,

kussiu "throne, chair": GIŠ.GU.ZA 10:16, 119:9, [GIŠ.GU.ZA] 11:8,

kusu (a topographical feature): *ku-su* 275 r. 9,

kutallu "rear": *ku-tal* 14:5, *ku-tal-li* 159:4, 302:5,

lā "not": *(la)* 216:6, *la* 1 r. 7, 6 r. 6, 7 r. 4, 8 r. 2, 10 r. 5, 11 r. 9, 15 r. 6, 23 r. 3, 31 r. 30, 32 r. 8, 34 r. 5, 39:15, 40 r. 3, 42 r. 7, 46:5, 48 r. 5, 50 r. 10, 57 r. 10, 58 r. 7, 63:5, 67:5, 72 r. 2, 85 r. 4, 86 r. 2, 87 r. 6, 90 r. 7, 96:21, 97:5, 98 r. 6, 99 r. 6, 100 r. 2, 4, 7, 101:19, r. 1, 2, 9, 102 r. 3, 4, 5, 11, 110 r. 5, 6, 112 r. 2, 119 r. 10, 125 r. 5, 131 r. 5, 133:9, 138 r. 10, 139:6, 140:13, 141 r. 3, 143:6, 150:6, 151 r. 5, 156:6, 158:6, 166 r. 1, 167:5, 169 r. 6, 174 r. 7, 176 r. 10, 11, 178 r. 1, 181:6, 185 r. 4, 5, 191 r. 6, 201 r. 4, 204 r. 1, 205:2, 208:5, 210 r. 3, 4, 211 r. 4, 5, 217 r. 8, 219 r. 11, 12, 220 r. 8, 221:6, 226:10, 229 r. 4, 232:5, 234:6, 235:6, 238:9, 241 r. 2, 242:6, 243 e. 9, 244 r. 1, 246:15, 248:8, 252 r. 4, 257 r. 23, 266 s. 2, 269 r. 3, 272:7, r. 4, 274 r. 6, 276:7, 278 r. 7, 281:4, 282:1, 283 r. 12, 285 r. 3, 287 r. 6, 7, s. 2, 288:13, 15, 17, 22, r. 16, 289 r. 3, 293 r. 1, 296 e. 8, 298 r. 5, 299:15, 301 r. 3, 302 r. 4, 305 r. 4, 307:8, 308 r. 4, 316 r. 1, 318:6, 319 r. 4, 323 e. 11, 324 r. 3, 325 r. 7, 326:3, 4, r. 12, 13, 329 r. 7, 330 r. 3, 335 r. 12, 336 r. 8, 10, 339 r. 1, 340:9, 11, r. 2, 3, 342 r. 2, 345 r. 2, 346 r. 8, 348 r. 2, 350 r. 1, *la]* 199 r. 1, 306 r. 2, *l[a* 88 r. 4, 101 r. 2, 134 r. 3, 157 e. 8, 180:8, 251 r. 3, 252 r. 4, 345 r. 3, *l[a]* 102 r. 4, 130 e. 18, 251 r. 4, *l]a* 40 r. 3, 206:6, 212:8, 222 e. 6, 284 r. 9, 334 r. 19, *[la* 16 r. 3, 41 r. 4, 66 r. 4, 100 r. 2, 125 r. 5, 200 r. 6, 251 e. 17, 314 r. 7, 336 r. 9, 340:10, *[la]* 9 e. 9, 225 r. 3, 300 r. 1, *[l]a* 58 r. 7, 191 r. 5, *la-a* 3:15, 106:4, 7, 185 r. 4, 214:6, 215:3, 4, 236 e. 7, *là* 31 r. 10, 53 r. 3, 113 r. 2, 126 r. 6, 161 r. 9, 165 r. 5, 182:6, 196 r. 1, 202 r. 7, 207 r. 6, 239 r. 2, 241 s. 1, 250 r. 6, 253 r. 7, 266 r. 1, 309 r. 5, 349 r. 6, *[là* 332 r. 2, N]U 92 r. 8,

labīru "old": SUMUN 26 r. 3, 204:4,

lahhinu "temple steward": LÚ.*lah-hi-nu* 11 r. 10, LÚ.*láh-hi-nu* 65 r. 7, LÚ.*láh-hi-[nu* 59 r. 3,

lahhinutu "temple stewardess": MÍ.*láh-hi-ni-te*

66:2,

laqû "to buy, acquire": *il-qi* 7:6, 14 r. 2, 17 e. 14, 19:9, 22:10, 27 r. 6, 41:12, 45:7, 52:11, 56:6, 85:10, 109:8, 110:10, 111 e. 11, 113:7, 127:7, 138:11, 142 r. 4, 152:2, 154 r. 3, 177:8, 218:9, 244:6, 251:7, 274:7, 275 r. 15, 288:21, 312:13, 319:6, 322:1, 328:11, 335 e. 15, 341 r. 4, 344:11, 346:4, *il-qi]* 40:10, 59:9, 140:2, 207:2, 349:3, *il-q[i* 6:7, *il-q]i* 239:11, *il-[qi]* 93 r. 5, 124:9, 126:10, 204:9, *i[l-qi]* 246:5, *i[l]-qi* 2 e. 7, *i]l-qi* 87:2, 210: 11, 339:5, *[il-qi* 186 r. 2, 271 r. 4, *[il-qi]* 144:6, 308:3, 334 r. 5, *[il-q]i* 38:5, 119:19, *[il]-qi* 348:3, *[i]l-qi* 48:7, 202:13, 269:11, 336 r. 1, *il-qí* 31 r. 5, 51:6, 53:8, 55:6, 88:8, 98:7, 130:10, 228:6, 250 e. 11, 253:9, 257:10, 301:9, 309:8, *il-qí]* 37:12, 50: 10, 100:8, *il-[qí* 329:15, *il-[qí]* 118:6, 213:2, *i]l-qí* 10:20, 101:5, *[il-qí* 4:5, 90:15, 287:18, 345:11, *[il]-qí* 125:11, *[i]l-qí* 347:10, *i[s-si-qi* 58:2, *is-si-qí* 290:5, *i-laq-qi* 40 r. 3, 87 r. 6, 134 r. 3, 176 r. 10, 199 r. 1, 219 r. 11, 220 r. 8, 225 r. 3, 229 r. 4, 278 r. 7, 325 r. 7, 334 r. 19, 335 r. 12, 339 r. 1, *i-laq-qi]* 41 r. 4, 112 r. 2, 204 r. 1, 244 r. 1, 302 r. 4, 314 r. 7, *i-laq-q]i* 246:15, 326 r. 12, *i-laq-[qi]* 7 r. 4, 131 r. 5, 140:13, *i-laq]-qi* 200 r. 6, 346 r. 8, *i-la[q-qi]* 217 r. 8, *i-l[aq-qi]* 9 e. 9, 300 r. 1, *i- [laq-qi]* 86 r. 2, 251 r. 4, 299:15, 348 r. 2, *(i)-laq-qi* 48 r. 5, *[i-laq-qi]* 96:21, 100 r. 7, *i-laq-qí* 34 r. 5, 39:15, 42 r. 7, 85 r. 4, 90 r. 7, 101 r. 9, 212:8, 308 r. 4, *i-laq-qí]* 16 r. 3, 330 r. 3, *i-laq-[qí]* 15 r. 6, 130 e. 18, *i-laq]-qí* 345 r. 2, *i-la[q-qí]* 10 r. 5, *i-[laq-qí]* 329 r. 7, *[i-laq-qí]* 342 r. 2, *i-la-qi* 3:15, 99 r. 6, 110 r. 6, 210 r. 3, 211 r. 4, 298 r. 5, *i-la-q[i]* 8 r. 2, *i-l[a-qi]* 269 r. 3, *[i-la-qí]* 141 r. 3, *i-si-qi* 3:5, 32:10, 52:12, 103:9, 174:6, 219:6, 288:22, 289:7, 305:9, 306:6, *i-s[i-qi]* 161:13, *i-si-qí* 284:8, *laq-qi* 7:8, 33:5, 48:9, 61:9, 102:5, r. 5, 127:9, 166 r. 1, 202 e. 15, s. 1, 219:9, 244:8, 246:7, 305:11, 306:8, 309:10, 346:6, *laq-qi]* 103:10, 217:15, *laq]-qi* 144:8, *[laq-qi* 210:13, 339:7, *[laq-qi]* 126 r. 1, *laq-qi-a* 336 r. 10, *laq-[qi-a]* 336 r. 2, *laq-qi-at* 98:9, *laq-qi-ʾu* 251:9, *laq-qi-u* 57:11, 177:10, 250 e. 13, 314:20, 344:12, *laq-qi-[u* 100 r. 4, *laq-[qi-u* 58:4, 322:3, *l[aq-qi]-u* 119 r. 3, *[laq-qi-u* 334 r. 8, *laq-qi-ú* 4:6, 9:1, 87:4, 138:13, 335 r. 1, *laq-qí* 42:12, 118:8, 125:13, 201:11, 311:12, *laq-qí]* 125 r. 5, *laq-q[í* 55:7, *laq-q]í* 101:8, *la]q-qí* 10 e. 21, *l]aq-qí* 15:3, *laq-qí-at* 88:11, *laq-qí-ʾu* 253:11, *laq-qí-u* 34:11, 39:6, 53:10, 101 r. 2, 326:21, *laq-qí-u]* 50:13, *laq-[qí-u]* 51:9, *laq-qí-ú* 329:17, *la-a-[qi]* 19:10, *la-a-qí* 3:6, *la-qi* 14 r. 3, 22:11, 32:11, 56:8, 99:11, 124:11, 154 r. 5, 174 r. 1, 176 r. 3, 213:4, 218:10, 274:8, 278:12, 289:8, *la-[qi* 164:11, *l[a-qi]* 161 e. 15, *[la-q]i* 207:5, *la-qi-at* 228:8, *la-qi-at]* 82:3, *la-qi-[at]* 17 r. 1, *[la]-qi-at* 197:8, *[l]a-qi-at* 49:6, *la-qi-ʾu* 93 r. 7, *la-qi-u* 38:6, 89:11, 110:11, 275 r. 17, 298:1, 341 r. 6, *la-qi-u]* 8:2, *la-qi-[u]* 41:14, *la-[qi-u]* 40:12, *l[a-qi-u* 348:5, *[la-qi-u* 340:2, *[la-qi-u]* 229:11, 340: 11, *la-qi-ú* 37:15, 52:13, 85:12, 96:9, 123:11, *la-qi-[ú* 312: 15, *la-[q]i-ú* 6:9, *la-qí* 257:12, r. 37, 301:11, *la-q]í* 90:17, *[la-qí]* 347:11, *la-q]í-ʾu-u* 185:3, *la-qí-u* 319:7, *la-qí-u]* 284:9, 342:8, *la-q[í-u]* 315:16, *[la-qí-u* 313:13, *la-qí-ú]* 345:11, *[tal-qi* 99:10, *ta-al-qi* 89:8, 96:7, *ta-al-qi]* 82:1, BA.TI 92 r. 8, TI 23:6, 8, r. 3, 31 r. 10, 50 r. 10, 53 r. 3, 58 r. 7, 86:8, 113 r. 2, 138 r. 10, 142 r. 5, 161 r. 9, 165 r. 5, 196 r. 1, 202 r. 7, 205:2, 229:8, 250 r. 6, 253 r. 7, 274 r. 6, 278:10, 285 r. 3, 305 r. 4, 309 r. 5, 319 r. 4, TI] 6 r. 6, 32 r. 8, 126 r. 6, 169 r. 6, 207 r. 6, 266 r. 1, 286:6, 316 r. 1, 350 r. 1, T]I 119 r. 10, [TI 92:6, 328:13, [TI] 217:13, 239 r. 2, 284 r. 9, TI-*qi* 98 r. 6, TI-*qi]* 102:3, T[I-*qi*] 102 r. 11, T]I-*qi-ú* 100:11, TI-*qí* 11 r. 9, 34:9, 42:10, 49:4, 57:9, 115:6, 197:6, 201:10, r. 4, 226:13, 227:6, 8, 257 r. 23, 283 r. 5, 6, 12, 289 r. 3, 290:6, 299:2, 306 r. 2, 311:11, 313:10, 314:18, 315:13, 326:19, TI-*qí]* 301 r. 3, 332 r. 2, TI-*q[í* 15:1, 342:7, TI-[*qí*] 39:5, 196:8, T]I-*qí* 340 r. 3, 349 r. 6, [TI-*q*]*í* 174 r. 7, TI-*u*] 169 r. 2, TI-*ú* 130:12, 140:4, 299:3,

laššu "is not": *la-áš-šu* 142 r. 7, 228:9, *la-áš-šu]* 8:3, *la-áš-š[u]* 6:11, *la-áš-[šu]* 48:10, *la-áš-šú* 7:9, 9:2, 14 r. 4, 15:4, 31 r. 6, 34:13, 37:16, 38:7, 39:7, 40:13, 53:11, 56 e. 9, 57:12, 61:10, 66 r. 6, 85:13, 87:5, 88:13, 90 r. 1, 93 r. 8, 98:10, 99:12, 102:6, 110:13, 118:10, 119 r. 4, 123:12, 138 e. 15, 163 r. 1, 180:5, 201:13, 202 e. 16, 213:5, 219:10, 227:9, 244:9, 246:8, 253:11, 254:2, 257:13, 278:13, 290: 7, 299:4, 305:12, 306:9, 311:13, 319:8, 326:22, 328:13, 329:18, 334 r. 8, 335 r. 2, 336 r. 3, 340:2, 341 r. 7, 346:8, *la-áš-šú]* 33:6, 41 e. 15, 50 r. 1, 103:11, 126 r. 2, 130:13, 169 r. 3, 218:10, 274:9, 284:10, 288:22, 313:14, 314:20, 348:6, *la-áš-š[ú* 301:12, *la-áš-š[ú]* 344:13, *la-áš-š]ú* 229 e. 12, *la-áš-[šú* 124:12, 322:4, *la-áš-[šú]* 55:8, 140:4, 144: 9, 154 r. 7, 207:6, 251:9, 342:9, 347 r. 1, *la-áš]-šú* 164:12, *la-á[š-šú]* 19:11, *la-[áš-šú* 10 e. 22, *la-[áš-šú]* 308:4, *la]-áš-šú* 22:12, *l[a-áš-šú* 49:7, *l[a-áš-šú]* 51:11, 298:2, *[la-áš-šú* 100:13, 127:11, 185:5, 198:2, 210:14, 312:16, *[la-áš-šú]* 17 r. 2, 82:4, 101:8, 106:1, *[l]a-áš-šú* 42:14, *la-áš-šú-u-ni]* 288: 12, *la-a-ši* 52 r. 1, *la-a-[šu]* 152:3, *la-a-šú* 2 e. 8, 3:7, 96:10, 111 r. 3, 161 e. 17, 250 r. 2, *la-šu* 29 r. 3, *la-šú* 23:10, 32:12, 89:12, 174 r. 2, 289:9, *la-[šú]* 275 r. 18, *[l]a-šú* 27 r. 8,

leqû see *laqû*,

libbu "heart": [ŠÀ 82:1, [ŠÀ] 305:7, ŠÀ 2 e. 7, 6:5, 7:6, 10:19, 14 r. 1, 15:1, 19:6, 23:6, 27 r. 5, 29 e. 7, r. 2, 31:19, r. 5, 34:8, 39:3, 40:8, 41:9, 42:10, 45:6, 48:6, 51:5, 57:8, 59:8, 65:10, 81 e. 11, 85:8, 86:8, 87:2, 88:7, 90:14, 94 e. 11, 100:8, 101:5, 102:3, 103:7, 110:9, 116:8, 118:6, 119:18, 123:6, 124:9, 125:10, 127:7, 142 e. 13, 144:4, 154 r. 2, 155:10, 160:13, 188:4, 197:5, 201:9, 202:11, 204: 9, 210:10, 218:8, 226:12, 227:5, 229:8, 239:8, 244: 6, 246:5, 250:9, 251:1, 253:8, 257:9, 271 r. 3, 278:10, 284:6, 285:7, 290:4, 301:8, 306:4, 308:2, 309:8, 311:10, 312:12, 313:9, 315:12, 326:16, 329:14, 333 r. 1, 341 r. 3, 343:11, 345:10, 348:2, 349:2, ŠÀ] 3:4, 38:4, 56:4, 58:1, 126:10, 196:7, 326:7, Š[À 17:12, 49:3, 169:10, 288:19, 299:1, 336: 9, Š[À] 130:9, Š]À 19:8, ŠÀ-*bi* 4:4, 22:10, 25:3, r. 1, 32:9, 37:11, 42:7, 50:9, 52:11, 53:6, 89:8, 93 r. 5, 94 r. 3, 96:6, 98:7, 99:8, 100:4, 109:7, 111 e. 10, 112:6, 113:6, 115:5, 124:4, 138:10, 140:2, 152:1, 154:4, 158:3, 161:11, 174:5, 177:6, 211:4, 213:2, 216:5, 217:13, 228:6, 251:6, 269:10, 274:5, 275 r. 14, 286:6, 287:16, 288:12, 13, 289:6, 319:6, 328: 11, 329:5, 8, 335 e. 13, 339:5, 344:8, 346:3, 347:8, ŠÀ-*bi*] 54:6, 123:5, 330:5, 8, 331:5, 334 r. 3, 342:6, ŠÀ-*b*]*i* 61:7, ŠÀ-[*bi* 94 r. 2, ŠÀ]-*bi* 176:10, Š[À-*bi*] 55:3, 283 r. 4, Š]À-*bi* 180 e. 9, 186 r. 1,

libittu "brick": *li-bi-tú* 21 r. 1,

limmu "eponym year": *lim-me* 5 r. 3, 23 r. 10, 35 s. 1, 37 r. 16, 43:11, 44 r. 1, 46:7, 60 r. 2, 64 r. 1, 67 r. 2, 71 r. 2, 83 r. 3, 84 r. 3, 90 r. 17, 100 r. 22, 105 r. 12, 109 r. 8, 118 r. 12, 131 r. 12, 134 r. 15, 135 r. 6, 137 r. 6, 142 s. 1, 143 r. 2, 145 r. 3, 148 r. 4, 157 r. 10, 162 r. 5, 164 r. 17, 170:6, 181 r. 2, 194 s. 2, 202 r. 9, 222 r. 6, 234 r. 7, 239 r. 11, 244 r. 10, 262:7, 263 e. 7, 271 r. 16, 278 r. 19, 301 r. 18, 304 r. 7, 317 r. 8, 325 r. 23, *lim-(me)* 245 r. 14, *lim]-me* 192 s. 1, [*lim-me* 114 r. 2, 182 r. 2, [*lim-me*] 158 r. 8, [*lim-m*]*e* 293 r. 7, [*lim*]*-me* 30 r. 14, 68 r. 2, 163 r. 17, [*li*]*m-me* 144 r. 4, 171:3, [*l*]*im-me* 122 r. 5, 133 s. 4, *lim-mu* 6 s. 1, 10 r. 17, 12 r. 6, 13 r. 7, 17 s. 1, 18 r. 6, 19 r. 12, 21 r. 13, 22 r. 12, 25 r. 6, 28 r. 8, 29 r. 8, 32 r. 17, 34 r. 14, 36 r. 6, 40 r. 18, 41 r. 17, 42 r. 20, 45 r. 6, 47 e. 6, 59 r. 17, 61 r. 7, 62 r. 2, 63 r. 1, 66 r. 11, 70 r. 2, 72 r. 4, 73 r. 2, 74 r. 2, 75 r. 5, 76 r. 2, 77:10, 81 r. 10, 85 r. 13, 89 r. 16, 91 r. 5, 97 r. 9, 98 r. 13, 103 r. 10, 107 e. 6, 108 r. 2, 110 r. 14, 111 r. 10, 113 r. 7, 121 r. 9, 123 r. 14, 124 r. 14, 127 r. 7, 132 s. 2, 136 r. 1, 138 r. 20, 146 r. 8, 147 r. 7, 149:8, 150 r. 4, 151 r. 11, 152 e. 9, 153 r. 4, 154 s. 3, 156 r. 7, 159 r. 4, 160 r. 15, 161 r. 18, 166 r. 9, 167 r. 7, 172 r. 4, 175 r. 1, 178 r. 3, 179 r. 11, 183 r. 2, 188 r. 5, 189 r. 1, 195 r. 8, 196 r. 9, 201 r. 13, 204 r. 13, 206 r. 3, 207 s. 1, 208 e. 7, 210 r. 17, 214 r. 3, 215:7, 216:7, 217 r. 16, 218 r. 8, 223 r. 9, 226 r. 11, 227 r. 10, 232 r. 7, 233 r. 2, 235:8, 236 r. 1, 237 r. 9, 241 r. 4, 243 r. 6, 247:6, 248:10, 256 r. 1, 257 r. 35, 258 r. 7, 259 r. 8, 264 s. 2, 265 r. 8, 267 r. 6, 268 r. 10, 269 s. 2, 270 s. 1, 272:11, r. 8, 273:5, 274 r. 18, 275 s. 3, 277 r. 11, 281:5, 282 e. 4, 283 r. 23, 286 r. 11, 287 r. 17, 289 r. 14, 297 r. 11, 300 r. 10, 307 r. 8, 310 r. 18, 311 r. 8, 312 r. 18, 313 r. 5, 314 r. 25, 315 r. 8, 318 r. 4, 319 r. 18, 320 r. 9, 323 r. 1, 328 r. 16, 329 r. 21, 331 r. 8, *lim-mu*] 2 r. 7, *lim-m*[*u* 203 r. 2, 303 r. 5, *lim-m*[*u*] 1 r. 19, 24 r. 3, 128 r. 4, *lim-m*]*u* 141 s. 2, 173 r. 4, *lim-*[*mu* 39 r. 10, 104 r. 1, 139:8, 197 r. 8, 280 r. 15, 291:7, 327 r. 8, *lim*]*-mu* 276 r. 5, *li*]*m-mu* 106 r. 7, *l*[*im-mu* 174 s. 1, [*lim-mu* 33 r. 9, 53 r. 9, 65 r. 6, 115 r. 5, 117 r. 1, 120 r. 6, 129 r. 4, 130 r. 14, 155 r. 8, 168 r. 5, 169 r. 16, 186 r. 14, 191 r. 3, 224 r. 1, 226 r. 2, 240 r. 8, 252 s. 4, 255 r. 4, 305 r. 13, 330 r. 15, 342 r. 16, [*lim-mu*] 96 r. 19, 126:14, 212 r. 8, 229 s. 2, [*lim-m*]*u* 187 r. 7, 193 r. 12, [*lim*]*-mu* 69 r. 4, 88 r. 12, 119 r. 20, 125 r. 16, 221 r. 7, 225 r. 14, 279 r. 8, 284 r. 22, [*li*]*m-mu* 116 r. 11, 292 s. 2, 302 r. 15, [*l*]*im-mu* 261 r. 5, 309 s. 1, *li-mu* 26 r. 7, 31 r. 27, 177 r. 16, 190 r. 6, 296 r. 3, 316 r. 15,

līmu "thousand": [1-*lim* 330:5, 1-*lim* 314:4, 329:5, 1-*lim*-5-*me* 326:7, 2-*lim* 331:5, 2-[*l*]*i*[*m* 314:6, 3-*l*[*im* 314:8, 10-*lim* 50:3,

lū "or": *lu* 3:9, 10, 31 r. 7, 8, 50 r. 3, 4, 66:5, 119 r. 6, 123 r. 3, 142 r. 8, 161 r. 3, 4, 251:1, 278 e. 15, 289:11, 12, 305:14, 308:7, 334 r. 10, [*lu* 3:9, 10, *lu-u* 7:11, 12, 8:6, 9:4, 10 r. 1, 14 r. 5, 6, 15:5, 6, 7, 8, r. 1, 19:13, 27 r. 9, 10, 32:14, 15, 34:15, 16, 17, 37:18, r. 1, 38 r. 2, 3, 4, 39:8, 9, 10, 40:16, 17, 18, 42:16, 17, 18, 51 e. 13, 14, 15, r. 1, 52 r. 2, 3, 4, 55:10, 11, 56 e. 11, r. 2, 82:6, 7, 8, 9, 87:7, 8, 91:14, 15, 16, 92:7, 8, 93 r. 9, 10, 96:11, 12, 13, 14, 99 e. 14, 100:14, 16, 17, 18, 101:10, 11, 12, 13, 14, 15, 102:8, 9, 10, 106:4, 5, 6, 123 r. 1, 124:14, 138 r. 2, 3, 140:6, 152:4, 161 r. 2, 176 r. 5, 177:12, 197:9, 201:14, 15, 16, 207 e. 8, 9, 212:2, 3, 213 r. 2, 3, 217 e. 19, 20, 21, 218:12, 13, 219 r. 2, 3, 4, 220 r. 1, 2, 238:10, 246:10, 11, 251:11, 12, 13, 253 r. 1, 254:4, 5, 257:15, 16, 17, e. 18, 264 r. 1, 2, 275 r. 19, 278 e. 16, 288:24, 290:9, 298:6, 7, 8, 299:6, 7, 8, 301:14, 15, 305:13, 14, 306:10, 11, 308:6, 311:15, 312 e. 18, 19, 20, 314:22, e. 23, 24, r. 1, 2, 319:10, 326 e. 24, 25, 26, r. 1, 2, 329:20, 335 r. 4, 336 r. 4, 5, 6, 338 r. 3, 339:8, 9, 340:5, 342:12, 13, 344 r. 1, 2, 4, 5, 346 r. 1, 2, 348:8, 9, *lu-u*] 49:9, 99 e. 15, 185 e. 8, 228:11, 12, *lu-*[*u* 55:10, 124:13, 140:6, 220 r. 1, 257:17, *lu-*[*u*] 118:14, 329:19, *lu*]*-u* 340:4, *l*[*u-u* 8:5, 14 r. 5, 55:11, 102:12, 197:11, 217 e. 18, 257 e. 18, 314:22, *l*[*u-u*] 8:5, 329:20, *l*]*u-u* 197:10, 290:10, 338 r. 2, 349 r. 1, [*lu-u* 19:13, 27 r. 10, 38 r. 3, 4, 92:7, 100:15, 16, 17, 18, 19, 20, 102:9, 10, 11, 118:14, 138 r. 2, 3, 185 e. 7, 8, 9, 197:9, 10, 212:3, 213 r. 3, 218:13, 228:12, 251:11, 290:9, 10, 301:14, 308:6, 312 r. 2, 314 e. 23, 326 e. 26, r. 1, 2, 328 e. 15, 340:4, 5, 6, 342:13, 14, 344 r. 1, 2, 5, [*lu-u*] 91:16, 118:13, 123 e. 14, 328 e. 16, 344 r. 3, 4, [*lu*]*-u* 9:5, 49:9, 253 r. 1, 2, 312 r. 1, 326 e. 25, r. 3, 328 e. 17, [*l*]*u-u* 15:7, r. 1, 42:17, 308:7, 8, 312 e. 21,

mā "thus": *ma-a* 100 r. 1, 101:19, 102 r. 3, 106:3, 6, 152:6, 185 r. 3, 336 r. 8, *ma-a*] 340:9, *m*]*a-a* 125 r. 4, [*ma-a* 185 r. 5, [*m*]*a-a* 133:8, e. 10, 139:6,

maʾuttu "maintenance": *ma-ú-te* 335:4,

magāru "to agree": *i-ma-gúr* 133:9,

mahāru "to accept, receive": *ih-hur* 101 r. 7, 102 r. 9, *ih-hur*] 100 r. 5, *im-hur-nu* 164 e. 15, *i-tah-ru* 105 s. 3, *mah-ru-u-t*[*i*] 57 r. 10,

mahīru "market price": *ma-hi-ri* 158:6, 181 e. 1, 232 e. 6, *ma-h*]*i-ri* 182 e. 7,

māhiṣu "archer": LÚ.*ma-hi-ṣu* 258 r. 2,

mākisu "toll collector": L]Ú.*ma-k*[*i-su*] 6 r. 16,

malgūtu (mng. unknown): *ma-al-gu-te* 12:4, *ma-al-*[*g*]*u-te* 11:10,

mallāhu "boatman": MÁ.DU.DU.MEŠ 122 r. 1,

mamma "anyone": *mam*]*-ma* 102:12, *mám-ma* 66 r. 3, 101:15, 178 r. 1, 238:8, [*mám-ma* 66 r. 3, *mám-ma-šú-nu* 336 r. 6, *mám*]*-ma-šú-nu* 100:20,

mammannu "relative": *mam-ma-nu-šú-nu* 31 r. 8, *mám-ma-ni-šú* 37 r. 1, *mám-m*]*a-ni-šú* 138 r. 3, *mám-ma-nu-šu* 40:18, 212:3, *mám-ma-nu-šú* 14 r. 6, 32:15, 34:17, 39:10, 42:18, 50 r. 4, 96:14, 119 r. 6, 264 r. 2, 299:8, 308:8, *mám-ma-nu-š*[*ú*] 319:10, *mám-ma-n*[*u-šú*] 51 r. 1, *mám-m*]*a-n*[*u-šú*] 140:6, [*mám-ma-nu-šú* 312 r. 1, [*mám-ma-nu-šú*] 217 e. 21, *mám-ma-nu-šú-nu* 15 r. 1, 161 r. 4, 314 r. 2, 326 r. 3, *mám-mu-nu-šú* 213 r. 3, *me-me-ni-šú-nu* 52 r. 4, *mu-mu-nu-šú-*[*nu*] 344 r. 5, LÚ.*mu-mu-nu-šú-nu* 335 r. 6,

mannu "who?": *man-nu* 1 r. 7, 6:12, 7:9, 15:4, 17 r. 3, 22:12, 23:11, 32:13, 34:13, 37:16, 40:14, 42:14, 49:7, 50 r. 2, 51 e. 12, 52 r. 1, 55:9, 56 e. 10, 61:10, 87:5, 89 r. 1, 90 r. 1, 91:13, 92:6, 93 r. 9, 95 r. 3, 98:11, 110:13, 119 r. 5, 124:12, 130:14, 132:9, 138 e. 15, 140:5, 142 r. 7, 152:4, 154 r. 8, 161 r. 1, 164:13, 174 r. 5, 176 r. 3, 177:11, 185:5, 197:8, 198:2, 201:13, 210:14, 212:1, 219 r. 1, 227:9, 228:10, 238:9, 244:10, 245 r. 3, 246:8, 250 r. 2, 251:10, 253:12, 254:2, 257:13, 264 e. 11, 265:7, 9, 274:10, 275 r. 19, 278:14, 283 r. 7, 288:23, 289:10, 298:3, 301:12, 305:12, 306:9, 311:13, 312:16, 313:14, 314:21, 317:6, 319:9, 326:22, 23,

r. 3, 329:18, 335 r. 3, 6, 342:11, 344: 14, 346:8, 347 r. 4, *man-nu*] 57:12, 100:13, 339:7, *man-n[u* 118:11, 289:13, 299:4, *man-n[u]* 96:10, *man*]-*nu* 127:11, 341 r. 7, *m[an-nu* 338 r. 1, *m[an-n]u* 8:4, *m[an]-nu* 39:7, [*man-nu* 3:8, 14 r. 4, 19:12, 20:1, 38 r. 1, 53:12, 99:13, 102:7, 125 r. 1, 144:10, 163 r. 2, 169 r. 4, 186 r. 4, 202 r. 1, 218:11, 284:11, 289 r. 4, 290:8, 308:5, 328 e. 14, 334 r. 9, 340:3, [*man-nu*] 9:3, 27 r. 9, 33:7, 101:9, 123:13, 308 e. 9, 322:5, [*man-n*]*u* 41 r. 1, 85:14, [*man*]-*nu* 48:11, 88:13, 106:2, 213 r. 1, 347 r. 2, 348:7, [*m*]*an-nu* 207 e. 7,

manû "mina": *ma-né-e* 38:4, 97:1, 6, 167:1, 219:5, 257:9, *ma-né-*[*e*] 251:7, 285:7, *ma-né*]-*e* 119:19, [*ma*]-*né-e* 275 r. 15, MA 275 r. 14, MA-*e* 85:8, MA.NA 2 e. 7, 3:4, 12, 4:4, 6:5, r. 1, s. 3, 7:6, 15, 11 r. 4, 12 r. 8, 14 r. 8, 17:12, e. 13, r. 6, 20:3, 4, 23:12, 13, 26:1, 27 r. 5, 29:1, 31 r. 5, 9, 31, 32:9, r. 1, s. 1, 34:8, r. 1, 35:3, 38:4, r. 8, 39:3, 13, 40:8, 9, 41:9, 10, 42:10, 20, 21, 43:1, 44:1, 45:6, 48:6, 50:10, r. 7, 51:5, r. 5, 52:11, r. 6, 53:6, 13, 54:7, 55:4, 56:4, r. 6, 57:8, 58 r. 3, 61:7, r. 11, 63:2, 64:1, 65:10, 81:1, 5, 82:1, 83:1, 85:8, 15, 16, 86:8, 87 r. 1, 88:8, 89:8, r. 3, 90:14, 91:12, 92 r. 3, 93 r. 5, 94 r. 3, 95 r. 4, 96:6, 16, 17, 18, 97:1, 99:9, r. 1, 2, 100:8, 101:5, r. 3, 102 r. 5, 103:7, 107:1, 108:2, 110:9, r. 1, 111 e. 10, 119:18, 121:6, 124:9, s. 1, 126:10, 127 r. 10, 130:9, 131 r. 1, 132:9, 133:4, e. 10, 11, 138:10, r. 6, 7, 139:1, 4, 6, 140:2, 9, 142 e. 13, r. 11, 143:1, 144:11, 146:2, 150:1, 151 r. 1, 152:7, 154 r. 9, 155:10, 156:1, 157:1, 165:6, 167:1, 170:1, 174 s. 3, 175:1, 176:10, r. 6, 177:7, e. 14, 178:1, 180:1, 183:1, 2, 6, 185 r. 6, 8, 190:6, 197:14, 198:3, 200 r. 1, 201:20, 202:11, r. 3, 206:7, 207 r. 4, 208:1, 210 e. 19, 211 r. 1, 217 r. 4, 5, 219:4, r. 7, 8, 220 r. 5, 221:1, 223:1, 226:12, 228:6, 234:1, 2, 235:2, 5, 7, 237:1, 238 e. 11, 241 r. 2, s. 2, 243 e. 9, 244:11, 245 e. 14, 246:5, 248:1, 250:9, 10, r. 3, 251:6, 15, 252 r. 8, 253:8, r. 5, 254:9, 257:9, r. 21, 259:3, 4, e. 6, 260:5, 262:2, 263:1, 265:5, 7, 11, 266 s. 2, 271 r. 3, 273:1, 274:5, r. 3, 275 r. 14, 21, 278:10, r. 3, 283 r. 5, 9, 284:6, r. 3, 4, 285:7, 287:16, 288:20, r. 4, 289:6, 16, 290:4, 13, r. 2, 291:1, 298 e. 12, 299:1, 12, 301:8, 19, 302 r. 2, 305:8, r. 2, 306 r. 1, 307:1, 308 e. 12, 309 r. 1, 310 r. 1, 311:10, 312:12, 313:9, 314 r. 4, 317:6, 318:2, 319:6, r. 1, 323:1, 324:5, 328:11, r. 3, 329:14, 334 r. 4, 16, 335 e. 13, r. 9, 339:5, 341 r. 3, 11, 342:7, 16, 343:11, 344:8, 346:3, r. 5, 347:8, r. 5, 348:2, 349:2, r. 4, MA.NA] 10:19, 39:3, 49:3, 131 r. 1, 210:10, 229 e. 13, 288:19, 301:19, 329 r. 2, MA.N[A 58:1, 102:3, 184:1, 326:16, MA.N]A 11 r. 4, 27 r. 6, 34 r. 1, 50 r. 7, 91:17, 115:6, 194 r. 1, 202 r. 4, 204:9, 213:2, 289 r. 17, 307:2, MA.[NA-*e*] 245 e. 15, 333 r. 1, 334 r. 4, 349 r. 4, MA.[NA 51 r. 5, 87:2, 98 r. 1, 126 r. 3, 163 r. 3, 210 e. 19, 245 e. 15, 288 r. 4, MA.[NA] 22:10, 81:2, 197:5, MA].NA 15:1, 38 r. 8, 40 r. 1, 41 r. 2, 53:13, 61:12, 92 r. 3, 137:1, 163 r. 3, 198:3, 211 r. 1, 224:1, 229 e. 13, 244:11, 306:5, 317:4, M[A.NA 14 r. 1, 37:11, M[A.NA] 103: 7, 284:6, M[A.N]A 150:6, M]A.NA 1 r. 7, 37 r. 5, 58 r. 3, 116:8, 201:21, 213 r. 6, 309:8, 315:12, (MA). NA 260:3, [MA.NA 51:5, 144:11, 269:10, 319 r. 1, 329 r. 3, [MA.N]A 19:8, [MA].NA 104:6, [M]A.NA 98 r. 1, 125:10, MA.NA-*e* 34:9, 53:7, 91:12, 96:7, 108:2, 130:10, 138:10, 143 e. 7, 176:11, 177:7, 274:6, 311:10, 315:12, 318:3, 324:5, 326:17, 347: 9, MA.NA-*e*] 104:2, 248:2, MA.N[A-*e* 346:3, MA. [NA-*e* 50:10, MA].NA-*e* 239:9, [MA.NA-*e*] 329:14, [MA.NA]-*e* 287:17, MA.NA-*šú* 221 e. 7, MA.NA-*šú-nu* 64:4,

mar "as much/many as": *am—mar* 102 r. 6, [*am—mar*] 101 r. 3, *mar* 20:3, 96:17,

mār ahi "nephew": DUMU.ME[Š—ŠEŠ.MEŠ]-*šú* 82:7, DUMU.MEŠ—ŠEŠ.MEŠ-*šú* 87:8, DUMU.MEŠ—ŠE[Š.MEŠ-*šú-nu*] 100:17, DUMU—PAB-*šú*-(*nu*) 251: 12, DUM]U—PAB.MEŠ-*e-šú* 312 e. 20, DUMU—PAB. MEŠ-*šú* 34:16, 37 r. 1, 38 r. 7, 197:11, 201:16, 253 r. 2, 299:7, 340:6, DUMU—PA]B.MEŠ-*šú* 38 r. 4, DUMU—P[AB.MEŠ-*šú*] 48:16, DUMU]—PAB.MEŠ-*šú* 228:12, [DUMU]—PAB.MEŠ-*šú* 15 r. 3, DUMU—PAB. MEŠ-*šú-nu* 15:8, DUMU—PAB]. MEŠ-*šú-nu* 102:12, DUMU—PAB].MEŠ-[*šú-nu*] 326 r. 1, DU[MU—PAB. MEŠ-*šú-nu*] 314 e. 24, DUMU—ŠEŠ-*šú-nu* 101:13, DUMU—ŠEŠ.MEŠ-*šú* 96:13, DUMU—ŠEŠ.MEŠ-[*šú* 10 r. 1, DUMU—ŠEŠ.[MEŠ-*šú*] 298:8, DUMU—ŠEŠ.MEŠ-*šú*-(*nu*) 335 r. 5, DUMU—ŠEŠ.MEŠ-*šú*-[*nu*] 336 r. 5, DUMU—ŠEŠ.(MEŠ)-*šú-nu* 344 r. 4, DUMU—Š]EŠ.MEŠ-*šú-nu* 334 r. 11,

mār damqi "chariot fighter, nobleman": A—SIG 200 r. 7, LÚ.A—SIG 37 r. 13, 69:7, 90 r. 12, 177 r. 8, 223 r. 7, LÚ.A—SI[G] 151 r. 6, LÚ.A—S[IG] 204:5, LÚ.A—[SIG] 325:8, [LÚ.A—SIG 224 r. 4, LÚ.[A]—SIG$_5$ 130 r. 12,

mār marʾi "grandson": DUMU.(DUMU).MEŠ-*šú* 27 r. 10, [DUMU.DUM]U.MEŠ-*šú* 338 r. 5, DUMU—DUMU-*šú* 91:16, 185 e. 8, 298:10, DUMU—DUMU-*šú*] 197:12, DUMU—DUMU-*š*[*ú*] 298:7, DUMU—DUMU.MEŠ-*šá* 251:14, DUMU—DUMU.MEŠ-*šu* 299: 10, DUMU—DUMU.MEŠ-*šú* 7:12, 34:19, 37 r. 3, 38 r. 3, 6, 39:12, 40:17, 20, 56 r. 5, 58 r. 2, 87:8, 9, 96:12, 106:5, 138 r. 3, 161 r. 5, 197:10, 201:15, 19, 219 r. 3, 6, 220 r. 2, 253 r. 1, 254:5, 6, 278 r. 1, 290:12, 299:7, 301:18, 312 e. 19, 314 r. 3, 325 r. 2, 326 r. 6, 328 r. 2, 329:21, 334 r. 13, 335 r. 8, 336 r. 7, 346 r. 2, 4, 348:9, DUMU—DUMU.MEŠ-*šú*] 340: 5, DUMU—DUMU.MEŠ-[*šú* 274 r. 2, DUMU—DUMU. MEŠ-[*šú*] 99 e. 15, DUMU—DUMU.MEŠ]-*šú* 312 r. 2, 341 r. 9, DUMU—DUMU.[MEŠ-*šú* 344 r. 7, DUMU—DUMU].MEŠ-*šú* 3:10, DUMU—DU[MU.MEŠ-*šú* 329 r. 1, DUMU—DU[MU.MEŠ-*šú*] 39:9, 48:15, DUMU—D[UMU.MEŠ-*šú*] 301:15, DUMU]—DUMU.MEŠ-*šú* 185 r. 2, 308 e. 10, DU[MU—DUMU.MEŠ-*šú* 246:11, DU[MU]—DUMU.MEŠ-*šú* 339:10, [DUMU—DUMU. MEŠ-*šú* 11 r. 3, 92:8, 340:8, [DUMU—DUMU.MEŠ-*šú*] 123 r. 1, 288:24, [DUMU—DUMU.MEŠ-*š*]*ú* 349 r. 3, [DUMU—DUMU.MEŠ]-*šú* 284 r. 2, [DUMU]—DUMU. MEŠ-*šú* 118:15, DUMU—DUMU.MEŠ-*šú-nu* 15:7, 31 r. 7, 101:12, 251:12, 328 e. 16, 335 r. 4, 336 r. 5, DUMU—DUMU.MEŠ-*šú-nu*] 124:14, 314 e. 23, DUMU—DUMU.MEŠ-*š*[*ú-nu*] 100:16, DUMU—DUMU. M[EŠ-*šú-nu* 344 r. 3, DUMU—DUMU.[MEŠ-*šú-nu* 93 r. 10, DUMU—DUMU].MEŠ-*šú-nu* 102:11, DUMU—D]UMU.MEŠ-*šú-nu* 326 e. 26, DUMU]—DUMU.MEŠ-*šú-nu* 56 r. 2, [DUMU—DUMU.MEŠ-*šú-nu* 334 r. 11, 349 r. 1,

mār šarri "crown prince": A.[MAN] 199 r. 6, A—MAN 39:16, 85 r. 7, 201 r. 8, 239 r. 7, 299 r. 1, 2, 8, 309 r. 6, 323 r. 8, 9, 325 r. 20, 21, 328 r. 7, 334 r. 33, A—MAN] 283 r. 16, 17, 297 r. 2, 299 r. 5, 325 r. 19, A—M[AN] 297 r. 13, A—[MAN] 283 r. 15, 299 r. 3, DUMU.MAN] 317:8, 321 r. 4, DUMU—LUGAL

86 r. 8, 238:10, 257:7, 287:14, 324 r. 9, 335 r. 18, D[UMU—LUGAL] 288:18, DUMU—MAN 37 r. 7, 40 r. 4, 52 r. 17, 57 r. 1, 103:5, 109:7, 110:8, 130 r. 11, 200 r. 7, 210 r. 14, 257:4, 264:4, 287 r. 11, 317 r. 1, 328 r. 6, 329 r. 15, 16, DUMU—MAN] 112:8, 298 r. 7, 8, 321 r. 5, 7, 330 r. 9, 10, DUMU—[MAN] 312 r. 8, 347 r. 7, 348 r. 4, DUMU]—MAN 340 r. 12, D[UMU—MAN] 320 r. 1, (DUMU)—MAN 312 r. 9,

mār šipri "messenger": LÚ.A—KIN 95:3, r. 7,

marʾu "son": A-*šú* 334:1, DUMU 2 r. 2, 6 r. 13, 10 r. 16, 11 r. 11, 14, 13 r. 4, 19:4, r. 2, 3, 4, 5, 6, 23 r. 8, 31 r. 17, 37:9, 54:2, 57:1, 86 r. 17, 98 r. 9, 100 r. 15, 121 r. 3, 124 r. 5, 169 r. 7, 173:2, 188:1, 200:2, r. 8, 9, 10, 237 e. 6, 239 r. 3, 243:3, 253:4, 5, 258 r. 4, 265 r. 10, 11, 274 r. 11, 280:1, 284 r. 12, 13, 15, 16, 17, 18, 286 r. 10, 288:19, 294 r. 1, 297:4, 301 r. 13, 312 r. 14, 313 r. 2, 314 r. 13, 315:5, 316:6, 319 r. 9, 12, 13, 336 r. 4, DUMU] 112:3, [DUMU 252:2, 288:2, [DUMU] 19 r. 8, 302 r. 12, [DU]MU 284 r. 20, [D]UMU 311:2, DUMU-*šá* 50:5, 193:6, DUMU-*šá*] 284:2, DUMU-[*šu* 169:13, DUMU-*šú* 6:1, 61:4, 90:6, 91:6, 7, 16, 103: 2, 3, 10, 112:2, 185 e. 8, 229:4, 266:2, 3, 298:10, 314:10, 326:9, 11, DUMU-*šú*] 342:1, 2, DUMU-(*šú*) 298:7, DU]MU-*šú* 213 r. 3, [DUMU-*šú* 295 r. 5, 334: 28, [DUMU]-*šú* 295 r. 1, DUMU-*šú-u-ni* 25:6, DUMU. MEŠ 31 r. 21, 92:7, 328:1, [DUMU.MEŠ] 343:3, DUMU. MEŠ-*šá* 251:13, DUMU.MEŠ-*šu* 106:5, 299:6, 313:5, 325 r. 1, DUMU.MEŠ-*šú* 3:9, 7:12, 9:5, 32:14, 16, 34:18, 37 r. 3, 39:9, 40:16, 20, 41:6, 42:17, 19, 48:15, 50:4, r. 3, 5, 51 e. 14, 52:7, 57:3, 81:7, 86:2, 3, 87:7, 9, 90:6, 91:4, 5, 96:12, 97 r. 2, 99 e. 15, 101:2, 17, 130:3, 4, 140:6, 8, 161 r. 5, 176 r. 5, 177:3, 4, 193:5, 201:15, 19, 207 e. 9, 210 e. 18, 219 r. 2, 6, 246:10, 253 r. 1, 3, 254:6, 278 e. 16, r. 1, 288:24, r. 1, 289:11, 290:9, 299:10, 305:14, 306:11, 13, 312 e. 19, r. 2, 314 r. 3, 326 r. 5, 328 r. 1, 329:20, r. 1, 334:28, 335 r. 8, 336 r. 7, 339:10, 340:4, 7, 341 r. 9, 344 r. 7, 346 r. 1, 4, 349 r. 2, DUMU.MEŠ-*šú*] 8:5, 100:5, 21, 197:9, 218:13, 220 r. 1, 3, 274 r. 1, 301:14, 334 r. 13, 348:8, DUMU. MEŠ-*š*[*ú* 305 r. 1, DUMU.MEŠ-*š*[*ú*] 102 r. 2, DUMU.M EŠ-[*šú*] 11 r. 2, 123 e. 14, DUMU.MEŠ]-*šú* 27 r. 10, DUMU.M[EŠ-*šú*] 82:6, DUMU.M[EŠ-*š*]*ú* 195:3, DUMU.M]EŠ-*šú* 38 r. 6, 212:5, DUMU.[MEŠ-*šú*] 254: 4, 308:6, DUMU.[MEŠ]-*šú* 275 r. 20, DUMU].MEŠ-*šú* 119 r. 6, 138 r. 2, 4, 212:3, DUM[U.MEŠ-*šú* 197:12, 217 r. 3, DUM[U.MEŠ-*šú*] 301:17, DU[MU.MEŠ-*šú* 246:12, DU[MU.MEŠ-*šú*] 39:11, 58 r. 1, 342:15, DU]MU.MEŠ-*šú* 118:14, D]UMU.MEŠ-*šú* 38 r. 3, [DUMU.MEŠ-*šú* 185 r. 2, 290:12, 308 e. 10, [DUMU. MEŠ-*šú*] 56 r. 5, 284 r. 1, 289:15, 319:13, [DU]MU. MEŠ-*šú* 338 r. 5, [D]U[MU.MEŠ-*šú*] 257 r. 19, DUMU. ME]Š-*šú-nu* 100:16, DUMU.MEŠ-*šú-nu* 15:7, 25:2, 31 r. 7, 52 r. 3, 93 r. 10, 101:12, 102:10, 161 r. 3, 257:16, 314 e. 23, 328 e. 16, 334 r. 10, 335 r. 4, 336 r. 5, DUMU.MEŠ-*šú-*[*n*]*u* 339:9, DUMU.MEŠ-*š*[*ú-nu* 124:14, DUMU.MEŠ-[*šú-nu*] 326 e. 25, DUMU. MEŠ-[*šú*]-*nu* 344 r. 3, DUMU.MEŠ]-*šú-nu* 342:13, DUMU.M[EŠ-*šú-nu*] 311:15, DUMU. [MEŠ-*šú-nu* 56 r. 2, DUMU].MEŠ-*šú-nu* 338 r. 3, DUM[U.MEŠ-*šú-nu*] 19:13, DU]MU.MEŠ-*šú-nu* 251: 11, DUMU—DUMU. MEŠ-*šu-*[*nu*] 342:13,

marʾutu "daughter": DUMU.MÍ 130:4, 173:7, [DUMU].MÍ 251:5, DUMU.MÍ-*sa* 96:3, 250:3, DUMU. [MÍ-*sa*] 116:4, DUM[U.MÍ-*sa* 50:6, [DU]MU.MÍ-*sa* 88:4, DUMU.MÍ-*su* 86:2, 101 r. 5, 102 r. 7, 128:3, 209:2, 314:10, 334:29, 341:9, 342:2, 3, 345:5, DUMU.MÍ-[*su*] 130:3, DUMU.MÍ-*šú* 52:6, 97 r. 4, 229:3, DUMU.MÍ.MEŠ 111:6, DUMU.MÍ.MEŠ-*šú* 6:2, 91:4, 97 r. 3, 177:4, DUMU.MÍ.MEŠ-[*šú* 155:8, DUMU.MÍ.MEŠ-[*šú*] 294:2,

mārtu see *marʾutu,*

māru see *marʾu,*

masennu "treasurer": LÚ.*ma-se-nu* 275 s. 4, LÚ]. IGI.DUB 209 r. 6, LÚ.IGI.DUB 10 r. 18, 96 r. 13, 209:3, 227 r. 11, 287 r. 11, LÚ.IGI.UM 18 r. 7,

masû "to wash": LUH 165:4, 341 r. 11, LUH-*u* 11 r. 4, 23:12, 87 r. 1, 138 r. 6, 201:20, 251:15, 290:13, 314 r. 4, 325 r. 3, 326 r. 9, 335 r. 9, 336 r. 10, LUH-*u*] 96:17, 207 r. 4, 217 r. 4, 284 r. 3, LUH-[*u* 42:21, 301:19, LU[H-*u* 20:4, [LUH-*u* 14 r. 8, 85:16, LUH-*ú* 298 e. 12, 299:12, 329 r. 3,

mašennu see *masennu,*

mašqītu "irrigation outlet": *maš-qí-te* 13:3, *ma-šá-qí-te* 10:3,

mati see *immati,*

matīma see *immatīma,*

mātu "land, country": *mt* 334 s. 2, KUR 287 r. 8, KUR.MEŠ 95 r. 3,

maṭû "to be defective, lacking": *ta-ma-ṭí* 21 r. 2, LÁ 27 r. 5, 253:8, 273:1,

mazrūtu "cultivation": *ma-az-ru-te* 226:3, *ma-*[*az-ru-te*] 226:9, *m*]*a-az-ru-ti* 31 e. 29, *ma-az-za-ru-t*[*i*] 19:5, *ma-*[*az-za-ru-ti*] 334 r. 1, *ma-za-ru-te* 278:3, *m*]*a-za-ru-te* 149:3, *ma-za-ru-ti* 30:4, *ma-za*]*-ru-ti* 334:22, *ma-za-ru-u-te* 194:6,

mê "water": A.ME]Š 123:4, A.MEŠ 31 r. 30, 123: 10, 149:3, 188 s. 1, 200:5, 201 r. 16, 217:5, 336:6, r. 9, A.[MEŠ 288:12,

meat "hundred": [1-*me* 266 r. 2, 305 r. 4, 1-*me* 6 r. 7, 7:6, 48 r. 6, 61:13, 85 r. 5, 89 r. 4, 103:12, 134 r. 4, 155:10, 174 r. 3, 219:11, 284 r. 6, 289 r. 7, 301 r. 5, 334 r. 17, 342:10, 1]-*me* 306 r. 3, 1-*me-ni* 32 r. 7, 1-*me*-20 221:1, 1-*me*-25 190:6, 1-*me*-50 243:2, 1-*me*-80 6:5, 2-*me* 243:2, 245:4, 2-*me*-10 265:5, 7, 2-*me*-30 243:3, 3-*me* 264:3, 8, r. 3, 5-*me* 287:8, 296:1, 5-*me*-80 243:3, 336:5, 6-*me* 331:5,

mērēšu "cultivated land, cultivation": *me-re-še* 146 e. 8, 223:9, r. 3, 224 e. 8, 226:14, 268 e. 8, 271 r. 5, *me-re-š*]*e* 224:4, *me-re-še-šu* 223 r. 1, 226:15, *mi-re-še* 252 r. 9,

mišlu "half": *me-šil* 30:5, 210:4, *mi-šil* 115:4, 1:2 36:4, 38:4, 52:11, 55:4, 64:4, 88:8, 94 r. 3, 108:2, 126:10, 130:9, 132:9, 140:2, 143 e. 7, 150: 1, 167:1, 180:1, 197:5, 208:1, 219:4, 221 e. 7, 226:12, 228:6, 234:7, 235:5, 246:5, 252 r. 8, 253:8, 259 e. 6, 260:3, 275 r. 14, 293 r. 2, 301:8, 317:4, 6, 326:16, 339:5, 1:2] 259:3,

mithār "equal amount": *mit-har* 29 r. 3, 46:6, 63 e. 6, 296 r. 2, *mi*]*t-har* 222 e. 7,

muātu "to die": *me-tu* 97 r. 5,

mugirru see *bēl mugirri,*

muhhu "top, on": UGU 12:8, 16:2, 31:7, 10, 13, 15, 19, 21, 35:1, 81:6, 97 r. 6, 123:7, 8, 137:4, 146 r. 1, 160 r. 2, 169:10, 178:3, 190 s. 2, 223 r. 2, 252 r. 10, 287 r. 3, 288 r. 13, UG]U 31 e. 28, U[GU 226:16, see also *ša-muhhi-,*

mukīl appāti "chariot driver": DIB—*a-pa*]*-te* 335 r. 19, LÚ.*mu-kil—ap*.MEŠ 130 r. 6, LÚ.*m*[*u-kil*— KUŠ—PA.MEŠ 336:11, LÚ.*mu-kil*—KUŠ.*a-pa-te* 335: 11, LÚ.*mu-kil*—KUŠ.*a-pa*.MEŠ 335 r. 7, LÚ].*mu-kil*—

KUŠ.PA.MEŠ 209 r. 2, LÚ.*mu-kil*—KU[Š.PA.MEŠ] 163 r. 6, LÚ.*mu-kil*—KU]Š.PA.MEŠ 312 r. 8, LÚ.*mu-kil*—KUŠ.PA.ME[Š] 325 r. 12, LÚ.*mu-kil*—KUŠ.PA.MEŠ 34:6, 41:9, 42:8, 53 r. 4, 6, 258 r. 5, 309:6, 319:5, 325:3, 326:15, 341 r. 2, 345:7, 347:7, LÚ.*mu-kil*—KUŠ.PA.MEŠ] 321 r. 1, LÚ.*mu-kil*—KUŠ.PA.M[EŠ 54:6, LÚ.*mu-kil*—KUŠ.PA.[MEŠ] 192 r. 1, LÚ.*mu-kil*—KUŠ.[PA.MEŠ 336:8, LÚ.*mu-kil*—KUŠ.[PA.MEŠ] 294 r. 2, 342 r. 6, LÚ.*mu-kil*]—KUŠ.PA.MEŠ 209 r. 1, LÚ.*mu-ki*[*l*—KUŠ.PA.MEŠ] 298 r. 6, LÚ.*mu-k*[*il*—KUŠ.PA.MEŠ] 8 r. 5, 41 r. 7, LÚ.*mu-*[*kil*—KUŠ.PA.MEŠ] 163 r. 9, LÚ.*m*]*u-kil*—KUŠ.PA.MEŠ 166:6, LÚ.*m*]*u-kil*—[KUŠ.PA.MEŠ] 334 r. 2, LÚ.*m*]*u-ki*[*l*—KUŠ.PA.MEŠ] 300:7, LÚ.[*mu-kil*—KUŠ.PA.MEŠ] 342 r. 15, L[Ú.*mu-kil*—KUŠ.PA.MEŠ] 41 r. 10, 326 r. 16, 342:5, L]Ú.*mu-*[*kil*—KUŠ.PA.MEŠ] 321 r. 3, [LÚ].*mu-kil*—KUŠ.PA.MEŠ 338 r. 9, [LÚ.*mu-kil*]—KUŠ.PA.MEŠ 313:8, [LÚ.*mu*]*-kil*—KUŠ.PA.MEŠ 1 r. 12, [LÚ.*m*]*u-kil*—KUŠ.PA.MEŠ 346:1, LÚ.*mu-kil*—PA-*a-te* 328:10, LÚ.*mu-kil*—PA.MEŠ 36:6, 37 r. 12, 50 r. 13, 244 r. 4, 287:5, 305:7, 312 r. 10, 332 r. 7, LÚ.*mu-kil*—PA.MEŠ] 328 r. 14, LÚ.*mu-kil*—PA.[M]EŠ 40:8, LÚ.*mu-kil*—[PA.MEŠ 328 r. 11, LÚ.*mu-k*[*il*—PA.MEŠ] 312 r. 11, LÚ.*mu-*[*kil*—PA.MEŠ 328 r. 12, LÚ.*m*]*u-kil*—PA.MEŠ 188 r. 2, LÚ.[*mu-kil*—PA.MEŠ] 332 r. 4, LÚ.[*m*]*u-k*[*il*—PA.MEŠ] 347 r. 6, L[Ú.*mu-kil*—PA.MEŠ 332 r. 5, [LÚ.*mu*]*-kil*—PA.MEŠ 333 e. 6, LÚ.*mu-*DIB—PA.MEŠ 39:17, 40 r. 5, 310 r. 5, 6, LÚ.*mu-*D[IB—P]A.M[EŠ] 40 r. 13, LÚ.[*mu-*DIB—PA.MEŠ] 39 r. 5, 8, [LÚ.*m*]*u-*DIB—P[A.MEŠ] 40 r. 15, LÚ].DIB—*a-pa-te* 323 r. 4, LÚ.DIB—*a-pa-te* 323:3, r. 8, [LÚ.DIB—*a-pa-te* 335 r. 18, LÚ.DIB—KUŠ.(PA).MEŠ 338 r. 11, LÚ].DIB—KUŠ.PA.MEŠ 324:8, 334 r. 21, 340 r. 8, LÚ.DIB—KU[Š.PA.MEŠ] 329:13, LÚ.DIB—KUŠ.PA.ME[Š] 326 r. 4, LÚ.DIB—KUŠ.PA.MEŠ 34 r. 9, 42 r. 16, 19, 235 e. 9, 271 r. 13, 299 r. 1, 301:7, 311:7, 316 r. 3, 317:5, 318:4, 7, 329 r. 13, 17, 18, LÚ.DIB—KUŠ.PA.MEŠ] 314:15, r. 16, 327 r. 1, LÚ.DIB—KUŠ.PA.[MEŠ 283 r. 16, 343:9, LÚ.DIB—KUŠ.P[A.MEŠ 317:8, LÚ.DIB—KUŠ.[PA.MEŠ] 315:9, LÚ.DIB—[KUŠ.PA.MEŠ] 349 r. 7, LÚ.DIB—[K]UŠ.PA.MEŠ 297 r. 12, LÚ.DIB]—KUŠ.PA.MEŠ 306 r. 7, LÚ.DI[B—KUŠ.PA.MEŠ] 344:6, LÚ.DI]B—K[UŠ.PA.MEŠ] 305 r. 8, LÚ.[DIB—KUŠ.PA.MEŠ] 297 r. 1, 300 r. 2, 314 r. 17, 326 r. 19, 349 r. 9, L[Ú.DIB—KUŠ.PA.MEŠ] 327 r. 3, 330 r. 11, L]Ú.DIB—KUŠ.PA.MEŠ 324 r. 5, [LÚ.DIB—KUŠ].PA.MEŠ 57:7, [LÚ.DIB—KUŠ].PA.[MEŠ 297:10, [LÚ.DIB—KUŠ.PA.MEŠ 330 r. 8, 349:1, [LÚ.DIB—KUŠ.PA.MEŠ] 330 r. 12, 344 r. 6, 348 r. 3, [LÚ.DIB—KUŠ.PA].MEŠ 337:6, [LÚ.DIB]—KUŠ.PA.MEŠ 306:4, LÚ.DIB—PA.MEŠ 309 r. 6, 339 r. 4, 9, LÚ.DIB—PA.MEŠ] 350 r. 9, LÚ.DIB—PA].MEŠ 339:3, LÚ.[DIB—PA.MEŠ] 307:3, L[Ú.DIB—PA.MEŠ] 331 r. 4, 350 r. 4,

mūlû "height, hill": *mu-le-e* 119:13, 252 r. 2, *mu-l*[*e-e*] 283 e. 22,

murabbānu "(horse) raiser": LÚ.*mu-ra-ba-nu* 39:16, 40 r. 4, LÚ.*mu-r*[*a-ba-nu*] 41 r. 5, LÚ.*mu-rib-*[*ba-n*]*u* 37 r. 7, LÚ.*mu-ri-ba-nu* 142 r. 15,

mūru "donkey stallion" (reading uncert.): ANŠE.NI[TÁ.MEŠ] 296:2, ANŠ[E.NITÁ.MEŠ] 296 r. 1,

musakkiltu (mng. unkn.): *mu-sa-kil-a-te* 278:8,

mūṣû "exit": *mu*]*-ṣu-u*ʾ 93:5, *mu-ṣu-ú* 124:2,

mušarkisu "recruitment officer": LÚ.*mu-šar-kis* 36 r. 3, 86 r. 4, LÚ.*mu-*[*ša*]*r-k*[*is*] 86 r. 3, LÚ.*mu-šar-kis*.MEŠ*-ni* 125 r. 10, LÚ.*mu-šar-ki-s*[*u*] 19:7,

mušēbirtu "ferry": *mu-še-bi-rit* 201:5,

mūšu "night": MI.MEŠ 201 r. 15,

mutīr ṭēmi "information officer": LÚ.*mu-tar*—UMUŠ.MEŠ 57 r. 5, LÚ.*mu-tar*—UMUŠ.[M]EŠ 57 r. 9, LÚ.*mu-tir*—*ṭè-me* 36 e. 9, 186:8, 192 r. 3, LÚ.*mu-*GUR—UMUŠ 130 r. 7, LÚ.GUR—UM[UŠ] 37 r. 8,

mutqītu see *ša-mutqītišu*,

nabalkutu "to rebel, contravene": *ib-bal-kát-u-n*[*i*] 174 r. 5, *ib-bal-lak-kàt-u-ni* 265:9, *i-bal-kàt-u-ni* 176 r. 4, *i-ba*]*l-ka-tú-ni* 289 r. 4,

nadānu see *tadānu*,

naggār magarri "cartwright, wheelwright": LÚ.NAGAR—GIŠ.UMBI[N].MEŠ 124 r. 9,

naggāru "carpenter": LÚ.NAGAR 96 r. 9, 244 r. 8,

nāgiru "herald": LÚ.NIGÍR 98 r. 8, 10, 166 r. 8,

nagiu "district": *na-gi-e* 326:13, *na-gi-i* 336:6, KUR.*na-gi-i* 333 e. 3,

naglubu "shoulder": MAŠ.QA 190 s. 2,

nahlu "wadi, brook": *na-ah-li* 31:7, 19, *na-*[*ah-l*]*i* 31:21, *n*[*a*]*-ah-li* 31:13, [*na-ah-li*] 31:10, *na-ah-lu* 31:17, *na-hal* 271:7, 275:10, r. 8, 283:12, *n*]*a-hal* 283:5, [*na-hal* 271:4, [*n*]*a-hal* 105:7, *na-hal-li* 176:3, 275:15, *na-hal*]*-li* 169:6, *na-*[*hal-li*] 137:4, [*n*]*a-hal-li* 275:6,

nappāh siparri "bronzesmith": LÚ.:.—UD.KA.BAR 26 r. 5,

nappāhu "smith": LÚ.SIMUG 26 r. 4,

napšutu "life; person": LÚ.ZI.MEŠ 2:5, 100:6, LÚ.ZI. [M]EŠ 130:7, LÚ.Z[I.MEŠ 86:5, LÚ.Z]I.ME[Š] 101:2, ZI 90:5, 7, 319:4, 334:29, 30, ZI.MEŠ 6:2, 34:4, 37:9, 39:1, 40:3, 4, 5, 41:7, 50:6, 52:9, 54:4, 57:4, 81:9, 85:5, 89:5, 90:9, 91:8, 109:4, 110:5, 111:7, 116:5, 149:6, 7, 172:4, 195:4, 229:5, 250:5, 253:6, 265:3, 266:8, 284:3, 313:5, 314:11, 326:11, 333:1, 334:30, 341:10, r. 1, 343:7, 344:4, ZI.MEŠ] 155:8, 334:28, ZI.M]EŠ 316:8, ZI.[MEŠ 112:3, 341:8, ZI. [MEŠ] 57:2, 315:6, Z[I.MEŠ 138:6, 294:3, 341:2, Z[I.MEŠ] 96:3, 297:7, Z[I].MEŠ 326:12, Z]I.MEŠ 345: 6, [ZI.MEŠ 40:6, [ZI.MEŠ] 342:4,

nāru "river": ÍD 149:3, 169:10, 202:7, 204:7, 217:9, 251:2, 283:2,

nâru see *nuāru*,

nasāhu "to pull out, uproot": *i-na-su-hu* 191 r. 5, 287 r. 6, *n*]*a-as-ha-at* 78 s. 1,

nasīku "sheikh": LÚ.*na-sik-ku* 195 r. 3,

nāšiu "carrier, porter": LÚ.*na-ši-i* 98 r. 7,

našû "to lift, carry, take": *it-ta-ṣa* 35:4, *it-ta-ṣu* 29 r. 1, 70:7, 76:4, 77:8, *it-*[*ta-ṣu*] 78 r. 5, *it-ti-ši* 44:3, 60:4, 71:4, 74:4, 75:4, *it-t*[*i-š*]*i* 224:3, *i-na-áš-ši* 223:7, 224:7, *i-*[*na-ši-u*] 288:15, *i-ta-ṣu* 26:7, 100 s. 1, 323:8, *i-ta-ṣ*]*u* 324 r. 1, *i-ti-ši* 32 s. 1, 263:4, *i-ti-*[*ši*] 157:5, *na-ṣa* 215:3, *na-ši-at* 272:8, r. 5, *na-ši-na* 264 e. 10, ÍL*-ši* 62:4, [Í]L*-ši* 69:4,

nēmulu "profit, gain": *né-mu-lu* 288:15, *né-mu-lum* 288:22,

niksu (a cloth): TÚG.*nik-si* 190:2,

nisannu (Nisan, name of the first month): ITI.BARAG 25 r. 6, 26 r. 6, 28 r. 8, 36 r. 5, 39 r. 10, 40 r. 18, 41 r. 16, 43:10, 60 r. 1, 66 r. 11, 71 r. 1, 75 r. 4, 108 r. 2, 133 s. 3, 141 s. 1, 147 r. 7, 162 r. 5, 210 r. 16, 232:4, 239 r. 10, 257 r. 34, 258 r. 6, 282:3, 286 r. 11, 296 e. 7, 300 r. 9, 304 r. 6, 309 r. 16, 318:5, 342 r. 16, ITI.BA[RAG 280 r. 15, ITI.B[ARAG 296 r. 3, [ITI.BARAG 44 r. 1, [ITI.BAR]AG 78 r. 6, 212 r. 6,

nīšī "people": LÚ.UN.MEŠ 145:5, 195:2, LÚ.UN.

[ME]Š 312:3, LÚ.UN.[MEŠ 312:14, UN.MEŠ 34:2, 11, 37:4, 14, 39:5, 40:2, 12, 50:2, 51:8, 52:5, 12, 53:2, 59:1, 65:3, 81 r. 1, 85:3, 11, 87:3, 89:2, 10, 90:4, 16, 91:3, 96:2, 8, 97 r. 8, 106:3, 7, 110:2, 11, 111:2, 129:2, 130:11, 135:3, 138:2, 12, 140:3, 149:1, 153: 2, 163:2, 166:2, 169:2, 172:2, 173:3, 177:2, 9, 179:2, 192:2, 193:2, 196:2, 203:5, 245:3, 250 e. 12, 251:8, 255:3, 261:2, 280:2, 283 r. 2, 297:5, 307 e. 10, 314:3, 18, 315:15, 316:2, 319:2, 7, 320:1, 326:21, 332:1, 334:3, r. 7, 341 r. 4, 342:8, 343:4, 345:11, UN.MEŠ] 41:2, 65 r. 4, 109:2, 163 r. 5, UN.M[EŠ 284:9, 348:4, UN.[ME]Š 345:2, UN].MEŠ 100 r. 4, 130:2, 340:1, 341 r. 5, U[N.ME]Š 6:8, U[N.MEŠ] 65 r. 1, 321:2, U]N.MEŠ 57:5, 10, 199:2, 313:3, [UN.ME]Š 37 r. 6, [UN.MEŠ 4:6, 9:1, 41:13, 50:12, 185:3, 245 r. 5, 256:2, 313:12, 340:11, 344:12, [UN.MEŠ] 8:2, 38:6, 53:10, 229:10, [U]N. MEŠ 94 r. 1, 169 r. 2, 253:10, UN.MEŠ-*šú* 1 r. 9, 264:7, 326:2, UN.MEŠ-*šú*] 59:4, UN.MEŠ-[*šú* 101 r. 1, UN.M[EŠ-*šú*] 59:2, UN.[MEŠ-*šú*] 101:7, U[N.MEŠ-*šú*] 59:3, 100:10,

nuāru "singer, musician": LÚ.NAR 183 r. 3, 196 r. 5,

nuhatimmu "cook": LÚ.MU 31 r. 15, 35 r. 6, 138 r. 12, 204 r. 10, 205 r. 3,

nukaribbu "gardener": LÚ.NU.GIŠ.SAR 37:8, 90: 8, 123:4, 10, 201 r. 9, 329:12, L[Ú.NU.GIŠ.SAR] 314:9, LÚ.NU.GIŠ.SAR 304:2,

nusāhu "corn tax": *nu-sa-hi* 176 s. 1, ŠE.*nu-sa-hi* 95:5, r. 1, 226:10, 326:4, ŠE.*nu-sa-hi*] 252 r. 4, ŠE.*nu-sa-*[*hi* 277 s. 1, ŠE.*nu-sa-hi-šú* 191 r. 4, 287 r. 5,

pāgu (a topographical feature): *pa-gi* 275 r. 10,

pāhutu "governor; province": EN.NAM 20 r. 3, 91:11, 14, LÚ.EN.NAM 6 r. 15, 31 r. 12, 22, 24, 25, 52 r. 2, 90:3, 91:1, 131 r. 9, 151 r. 7, 177:12, r. 17, 216:8, 287:1, 314 r. 8, 326:6, 340 r. 4, LÚ.EN.N[AM 319 r. 5, LÚ.EN.[NAM] 191 r. 1, 193:2, LÚ.E[N.NAM 11 r. 7, LÚ.E[N.NA]M 6 r. 3, L]Ú.EN.NAM 185 e. 9, [LÚ.EN].NAM 25 e. 8, LÚ.EN.NAM-*su* 289:12, 290: 10, LÚ.EN.NA[M-*su-nu* 314 r. 1, LÚ.NAM 42 r. 4, 311 r. 9, 326:14, LÚ.NAM-[*šú-nu*] 326 r. 2,

palāhu "to fear": [*i-pa-làh-šú* 295 r. 3,

pallišu "driller": LÚ.GAR.U.U 345 r. 8,

pānu "face, presence": *pa-an* 25 e. 7, 61:6, 98:6, 124:8, 167:3, 190:4, 234:4, 257:8, 284:5, 287:15, 311:9, *pa-a*]*n* 66 r. 5, *pa-ni-*[*šú*] 25 r. 4, *pa-ni-šú-nu* 70:6, 77:7, *pa-ni-šú-nu*] 78 r. 4, *pa-ni*]*-šú-nu* 102:3, *p*]*a-ni-šú-nu* 79:9, IGI 6:6, 7:5, 12 r. 1, 17:11, 19:8, 26:2, 3, 4, 5, 6, 27 r. 5, 28 r. 5, 29 e. 6, 31 r. 3, 5, 32 r. 9, 33:3, 34:7, 35:4, 36:3, 37:12, 40:10, r. 19, 41:11, 43:3, 44:3, 47:3, 51:4, 53:8, 55:5, 56:5, 60:3, 61:6, 62:3, 64:3, 71:3, 74:3, 75:3, 81:4, e. 10, 84:4, 85:9, 88:6, 90:13, 92:4, 96:6, 97:3, r. 12, 13, 99:8, 103:6, 104:3, 5, 107:3, 108:3, 127:6, 128 r. 1, 130:8, 132:11, e. 13, r. 1, 3, 4, 133:5, 6, 8, 135 r. 2, 137:2, r. 1, 3, 4, 5, 138:9, 139:3, 142 r. 1, 2, 3, 143:4, 144:5, 146:3, 150:2, 3, 4, 5, 154 r. 1, 156:3, 157:4, 161:12, 170:3, 174:4, 177:6, 178:6, 180:3, 181:4, 182:3, 183:4, 184:4, 189:3, 195:7, 196:6, 201:8, 202:10, 204:4, 206:3, 207:2, 208:3, 210:9, 213:1, 214:4, 216:4, 217:12, 218:8, 221:3, 4, 222:3, 4, 223:3, 228:5, 232:3, 233:5, 237:5, 239:10, 240:3, 241:4, 5, e. 6, 242:1, 2, 3, 243:5, 6, 7, 244:5, 245 r. 1, 253:8, 262:4, 263:3, 264:4, 265:4, 272:4, r. 1, 273:3, 281:2, 285:5, 288:19, 289:5, 290:4, 291:4, 293:3, 295 r. 2, 296:5, 6, 301:7, 307:4, 5, 308:2, 311:9, 313:8, 314:17, 317:4, 322:1, 323:4, 5, 6, 7, 324:10, 11, e. 12, 13, 326:18, 19, 334 r. 5, 335 e. 14, 15, 341 r. 3, 342:6, 343:12, 344:9, 10, 345:9, 348:1, 349:2, IGI] 219:3, 269:8, 302:11, IG[I 188 r. 1, IG]I 83:4, 155:11, 252 s. 1, 275 r. 13, 295:6, 296:4, 315:11, I[GI 132 r. 7, 166 r. 7, 292 r. 4, I[GI] 326:17, I[G]I 137 r. 2, I]GI 10:19, 59:9, 67:3, (IGI) 137 r. 3, [IGI 50:9, 53 r. 10, 125 r. 14, 132 r. 5, 137 r. 1, 2, 3, 4, 5, 314:17, 321 r. 7, 336:10, [IGI] 132 r. 6, 207 r. 8, [IG]I 28 r. 10, 88 r. 9, 133 r. 11, [I]GI 133 r. 12, IGI-*šú* 46:4, 57:1, 63:3, 236:3, IGI-*šú-nu* 76:3, 318: 5, IGI.MEŠ-*šú* 235:4, IGI.MEŠ-*šú-nu* 247:5,

parāku "to obstruct, break a contract": *i*-GIL-*u-ni* 96:11, 154 r. 8, 238:9, 244:10, 312 e. 18, *i*-GIL-*u-ni*] 20:1, 322:5, 344:15, *i*-GIL-*u*-[*ni* 339:8, *i*-[GIL-*u-ni*] 288:23, [*i*-GIL-*u-n*]*i* 90 r. 3, *i*-GIL-*ú-ni* 52 r. 5, *i*-GIL-[*ú*]*-ni* 130:15, *i*-GI]L-*ú-ni* 125 r. 3, GIL-*ni* 275 r. 19, GIL-*u-ni* 6:13, 23:11, 34:15, 95 r. 3, 118:12, 144:10, 177:11, 213 r. 4, 250 r. 2, 251:10, 278 e. 15, 319:12, 329:19, 338 r. 2, 347 r. 4, GIL-*u-ni*] 14 r. 4, 51 e. 12, 301:13, 348:7, GIL-*u*-[*ni*] 299:5, GIL-*u*]*-ni* 126 r. 3, 127:12, GIL-[*u-ni*] 50 r. 2, GI[L-*u-ni*] 140:5, GI]L-*u-ni* 198:2, G[IL-*u-ni* 88 r. 2, G[IL-*u-ni*] 169 r. 4, G]IL-*u-ni* 133 r. 4, 342:12, [GIL-*u-ni* 91:17, 163 r. 3, 228:11, 334 r. 10, [GI]L-*u-ni* 202 r. 3, GIL-*ú-ni* 53:12, 283 r. 8, [G]IL-*ú-ni* 42:16, GIL. MEŠ-*u*-[*ni*] 98:13,

parasrab "five sixths": 5/6 259:4, e. 6, 260:3, 5, [5/6] 259:3,

parrișu "criminal, thief": LÚ.LUL.MEŠ 35:4, 133 e. 10, [LÚ.LU]L.MEŠ 35:1,

pașû "to be white": BABB]AR 334 r. 14, BABBAR. MEŠ 20 r. 1, 32 r. 3, 42 r. 1, 87 r. 3, 92 r. 5, 95 r. 3, 98 r. 3, 140:10, 200 r. 3, 308 r. 2, 325 r. 5, 326 r. 7, BABBAR.MEŠ] 251 e. 18, BAB[BAR.MEŠ 11 r. 5,

pašāru "to convert; current value": *pa-ša-*[*ri*] 3:4,

pattūtu see *ša-pattūti,*

patû "to open": BAD-*ti* 31:19, see also *petû,*

pațāru "to release": *a-paț-țar* 152:6, *ip-ta-țar* 61:7, *i-paț-țar* 152:7,

pēthallu see *ša-pēthalli,*

petû see *patû,*

pirsu "weaned child": *pir-su* 111:6, 315:5, 342: 2, *pir-su*] 316:6,

pisannu "gutter": GIŠ.*pi-sa-nu* 21 e. 11,

pû "mouth, utterance": *pi* 275 e. 22, KA 275 r. 8,

pūhu "loan": *pu-hi*] 80:2, *pu-u-hi* 26:7, 44:3, 60:4, 62:4, 69:4, 70:7, 71:4, 74:4, 75:4, 76:4, 77:8, 78 r. 5, 157:5, 263:4, 323:8, 324 r. 1, *pu-u-h*]*i* 224:3,

pūlu "limestone": *pu-la-a-ni* 288 r. 4,

pūru "lot, term": *pu-ri-šú* 19 r. 13, 21 r. 14,

pușû "white colour; blank space": *pu-șe-e* 31 e. 31, 32:2, 159:3, 275 r. 17, *pu-*[*șe-e* 32:3, *p*]*u-șe-e* 169:11, 200:8, [*pu-șe-e* 27 r. 8,

qablu "grove": *qab-li* 201:4, *qab-lu* 329:6, 16, [*qab-lu* 330:6, [GI]Š.MURUB$_4$ 333 e. 3,

qabsi āli "city centre": MURUB$_4$—URU 85:7, 283: 10, MURU[B$_4$—URU 94 r. 4, MUR[UB$_4$—URU] 93 r. 3, MU[RUB$_4$—URU] 87:1, [MURUB$_4$]—URU 86:7, URU. MURUB$_4$—URU 89:7,

qabû "to say": *iq-ți-bu-ni-šú-nu* 133:7, *i-qab-bu-ni* 106:6, *i-qab-bu-u-ni* 101:18, 102 r. 3, [*i-qab-*

bu-u-ni 100 r. 1, 125 r. 4, *i-qa-bu-u-ni* 106:3,

qabūru see *qubūru,*

qalû "to burn": GIBÍL 66 r. 2, 101 r. 5, 102 r. 7, 285 r. 2,

qannu "outside": *qa-an-ni* 13:3, 31:14, 16, 311: 6, *qa-ni* 10:3, *qa-n[i* 188 s. 1,

qanû "reed, cane": GI 251 e. 17, see also *ša-muhhi-qanāti,*

qaqqadu see *kaqqudu,*

qaqqaru see *kaqquru,*

qarābu "to approach, arrive; (stat.) to be present": *iq-ṭar-bu* 133:7, *qur-bu* 326 r. 3, 335 r. 6, 336 r. 6, *qur-bu-[ti]* 112 r. 7, *uq-ṭar-ri-ib-šú* 265:4,

qāribu "raven": *qa-ri-bu* 288 r. 10,

qarnu "horn": SI 265:6,

qassu "bow": BAN.ME 97 r. 11,

qāt ṣibitti "red-handed": *qa—ṣi-bit-te* 133:4,

qatinnu "tiller": LÚ.*qa]-tin-ni* 154 r. 10,

qatnu "thin, fine": *qa-at-ni* 12:6, *qa-at-nu* 190:3,

qātu "hand": ŠU 260 s. 2, ŠU.2 326:13, ŠU.2-*šú* 52 r. 3, 95 r. 5, ŠU.2-*šú-nu* 100:8, 133:5, ŠU.2-*šú-n[u]* 101:4, ŠU.2.MEŠ 154:3,

qēpu "royal delegate": LÚ.*qe-e-pi* 150:2, LÚ.*qe-pu* 188 r. 7,

qerdu "plucked wool": SÍG.*qer-du* 96:16, SÍG. *qe[r-du* 20:3,

qerēbu see *qarābu,*

qinītu "property": *qi-ni-ti-šú* 97 r. 3,

qinnu "family": *qin-ni-šú-nu* 91:10,

qû "litre": *qa* 17:7, 31 e. 30, 46:3, 50 r. 15, 158:4, 223:6, 224:6, 226:4, 232:2, 233:4, 276:3, 278:4, 288 r. 15, 16, 18, 326:3, 334:22, *qa]* 315:1, *q[a]* 194:5, 332:2, *qa*.MEŠ 316:3,

qubūru "grave": *qa-bu-ri* 288:12,

qurbu "neighbour": *qur-ub-šu* 82:9, *qur-ub-šú* 50 r. 4, 96:13, *qur-ub-[šú* 51 e. 15, *qur-u[b-šú* 217 e. 20, L]Ú.*qur-bu-šú-nu* 334 r. 12,

qurbūtu see *ša-qurbūti,*

qurubtu "(king's) stand-by": LÚ.*qur-ub-te* 97 r. 14,

qutānu (a type of field): *qu-ta-nu* 275 r. 6,

rā'i iṣṣūri "gooseherd": LÚ.SIPA—MUŠEN.MEŠ 81 r. 7,

rā'iu "shepherd": LÚ.SIPA 264:5, r. 4, 287:10, LÚ.S[IP]A 42 r. 13, LÚ.SIPA.MEŠ 31 e. 27, 264:9, LÚ.SIPA.[MEŠ] 31 e. 28,

rab ālāni "village manager": GAL—[URU.MEŠ-*ni*] 7:4, LÚ.GAL—URU.MEŠ 34 r. 8, 40 r. 12, 66:2, 81:4, 90:1, 109:6, 110:8, r. 8, 112:8, 164:1, 233:2, LÚ. GAL—U[RU].(MEŠ) 255:1, LÚ.GAL—[URU].MEŠ 256: 2, LÚ.[GAL—URU.MEŠ] 3:3, [LÚ.GAL—URU.MEŠ] 41 r. 13, LÚ.GAL—URU.MEŠ-*ni* 61:15, 345 r. 10, LÚ. GAL—URU.MEŠ-[*ni*] 4:3, LÚ.GAL—URU.MEŠ-*šú* 91: 15,

rab asê "chief physician, chief doctor": LÚ. GAL—A.ZU 193 r. 9, 325 r. 18, 339 r. 8, LÚ.GAL—A.ZU] 321 r. 8, LÚ.GAL—[A.ZU] 320 r. 5, 328 r. 9,

rab āšipi "chief exorcist": LÚ.GAL—MAŠ.MAŠ 329 r. 12, LÚ.GAL—MAŠ.MAŠ] 330 r. 7, LÚ.GAL—[MAŠ.MAŠ] 314 r. 12,

rab atê "head porter": GAL—LÚ.Ì.DU_8.M[EŠ] 211 r. 7, LÚ.GAL—Ì.DU_8 130 r. 8, 163 r. 11, 323 r. 10, LÚ.GAL—Ì.DU_8] 307 r. 3, 348 r. 5, 350 r. 8, LÚ.GAL—Ì.[DU_8] 297 r. 8, 328 r. 8, LÚ.GA]L—Ì.DU_8 324 r. 10, [LÚ.GAL—Ì.DU_8] 307 r. 5, LÚ.GAL—Ì.DU_8.MEŠ 206 r. 6, 325 r. 16, 332 r. 9, 340 r. 11, LÚ.GAL—Ì.DU_8.M[EŠ] 308 r. 7, LÚ.GAL—Ì.DU_8.[MEŠ] 308 r. 8, LÚ.G]AL—Ì.DU_8.[MEŠ] 283 r. 14, LÚ.[GAL—Ì.DU_8.MEŠ] 248 e. 11,

rab bārê "chief haruspex": LÚ.GAL—HAL 339 r. 7,

rab bēti "major-domo": GAL—É 95 r. 7, 183:5, LÚ.GAL—É 46:1, 166:4, 254 r. 2, 267:2, 4,

rab daiāli "chief scout": LÚ.GAL—*da-a-a-[li]* 164 r. 7,

rab hanšê "commander-of-fifty": GAL—50 289 r. 9, LÚ.GAL—50 124 r. 6, 226:9,

rab išpāri "chief weaver": LÚ.GAL—UŠ.BAR.ME 90 r. 10, LÚ.GAL—UŠ.BAR.MEŠ 163 r. 14, LÚ.GAL—UŠ.BAR.M[EŠ] 190:5,

rab kallāpi "commander of outriders(?)": L]Ú. GAL—*kal-lap* 57 r. 2,

rab kallî "postmaster": LÚ.GAL—*kal-li-e* 124 r. 10,

rab karmāni "chief of granaries": LÚ.GAL—*kar-ma-ni* 37:2, [LÚ.GA]L—*kar-ma-ni* 38:2,

rab kirie "garden manager": LÚ.GAL—GI[Š.SA]R 22:7,

rab kiṣri "cohort commander": GAL—*ki-ṣir* 91 r. 3, 165 r. 6, 289 r. 12, LÚ].GAL—*ki-ṣir* 340 r. 9, LÚ].GAL—*ki-ṣ[ir]* 211 r. 8, LÚ.GAL—*ki-ṣir* 37 r. 9, 46 r. 2, 52:3, 53 r. 7, 132:12, 163 r. 12, 164 r. 4, 5, 174 r. 9, 177 r. 4, 192 r. 4, 199 r. 2, 201:8, 204 r. 7, 206 r. 4, 253 r. 9, 270 r. 1, 283 r. 13, 287 r. 8, 294 r. 4, 299 r. 5, 308 r. 6, 320 r. 2, 323 r. 7, 9, 325 r. 19, 330 r. 5, LÚ.GAL—*ki-ṣi]r* 306 r. 9, 312 r. 9, LÚ.GAL—*ki-ṣ[ir]* 211 r. 6, 297 r. 6, 325:5, LÚ.GAL—*ki-[ṣir]* 305 r. 10, LÚ.GAL—[*ki-ṣir*] 41 r. 11, LÚ. GA[L—*ki-ṣir* 321 r. 5, LÚ.[GAL—*ki-ṣir* 297 r. 3, LÚ. [GAL—*ki-ṣir*] 300 r. 8, 307 r. 6, 326 r. 17, 18, L[Ú.GAL—*ki-ṣ*]*ir* 329 r. 9, [LÚ.GAL—*ki-ṣir* 298 r. 9, 327 r. 2, [LÚ.GAL—*ki-ṣir*] 204 r. 4, 304 r. 4, LÚ. GAL—*ki-ṣir-šú* 264 r. 1, LÚ.GAL—KÀD-*ri* 125 r. 11, LÚ.GAL—KA.KÉŠ 247 r. 3, 6, LÚ.GAL—KA.KÉŠ] 249 r. 5, LÚ.GAL—KA.K[ÉŠ] 249 r. 7, LÚ.GAL—K]A.KÉŠ 324 r. 9, LÚ.GAL]—KA.KÉŠ 324 r. 8, LÚ.GA[L]—KA.KÉŠ 39 r. 6, LÚ.G[AL]—K[A].KÉŠ 40 r. 14, LÚ. [GAL—KA.KÉŠ] 249 r. 6,

rab mallāhi "chief boatman": LÚ.GAL—MÁ.DU. DU 142 r. 14, 16,

rab mūgi (a high military official): LÚ.GAL—*mug-gi* 247 e. 9,

rab naggāri "chief carpenter": LÚ.GAL—NAGAR 265 r. 6,

rab nikkassi "chief of accounts": L]Ú.GAL—NÍG. ŠID 285:6,

rab nuhatimmi "chief cook": LÚ.GAL—MU 36:6,

rab sagullāti "overseer of the herds": LÚ.GAL—*sa-x[x* 100 r. 9,

rab sikkāti (a high official): GAL—GAG. MEŠ 95 r. 6,

rab ṣarrāpi "chief goldsmith": LÚ.GAL—SIMUG. KUG.GI.MEŠ 96 r. 8,

rab šaddāni "coffer-master": LÚ.GAL—*šad-dan-ni* 201 r. 7,

rab šamni "oil master": LÚ.GAL—Ì.ME 287 r. 13,

rab šāqê "chief cupbearer": *rbšqn* 334: s. 2, LÚ.GAL—KAŠ.LUL 28 r. 4, 30 r. 8, 210 r. 8, 255 r. 4, 271 r. 17, LÚ.GA[L—KAŠ.LUL] 207 s. 2,

rab ša-rēši "chief eunuch": GAL—SAG 7:5, LÚ]. GAL—SAG 334 r. 25, LÚ.GAL—SAG 31 r. 16, 210 r.

15, LÚ.GA[L—S]AG 174 r. 9, LÚ.[GAL]—SA[G] 1 r. 17,
rab šelappāie "chief architect": LÚ.GAL—*še-lap-pa-a-[a]* 11 r. 13,
rab ṭupšarri "chief scribe": LÚ.GAL—A.BA 97 r. 1, 329 r. 11, LÚ.GAL—A.BA] 330 r. 6, LÚ.GAL—A.[BA] 314 r. 11, LÚ.GAL—[A.BA] 268 r. 2,
rab urāti "team commander": GAL—*u-rat* 338 r. 15, GAL—*u-rat*.MEŠ 309 r. 10, GAL—*ú-rat* 65 r. 8, GAL—[*ú-rat*] 308 r. 9, GAL]—*ú-rat*.MEŠ 335 r. 21, LÚ.GAL—*u-rat* 329 r. 19, LÚ.GAL—*u-rat*] 330 r. 13, LÚ.G[AL—*u-rat*] 313 r. 1, LÚ.GAL—*ú-rat* 310 r. 8, 316 r. 10, 325 r. 17, 339 r. 10, LÚ.GAL—*ú-rat*] 314 r. 18, 321 r. 6, 328 r. 13, LÚ.GAL—*ú-ra*[*t*] 312 r. 13, 332 r. 10, LÚ.GAL—*ú-*[*rat*] 317 r. 3, LÚ.GAL—[*ú-rat*] 315 r. 3, 320 r. 3, L[Ú.GAL—*ú-rat*] 342 r. 14,
rab zammāri "chief singer": LÚ.GAL—*z*[*a-ma*]*-ri* 312:2,
rabû "to be great, grow": *i-rab-be-u* 29 r. 4, *i-rab-bi* 26 e. 8, 36:4, 44:4, 46:6, 74:6, 108:4, 167:6, 221 e. 7, 235:7, 318:6, *i-rab-b*[*i*] 43:4, 157 r. 2, *i-ra*]*b-bi* 291:5, *i-*[*rab-bi*] 307:8, [*i-rab-bi*] 248:9, *i-rab-bi-u* 214 r. 1, *i-ra-ab-bi* 150:7, *i-r*[*a-a*]*b-bi* 104 e. 7, *i-ra-bi* 323:9, *i-ra-*[*bi*] 208:6, [*i-ra-bi* 324 r. 2, *i-*GAL-*bi* 241 s. 3, 262:5, *i-*[GAL-*u*] 296 r. 2, *ta-rab-bi* 71:6, 75 r. 2, *ú-ra-ba* 293 r. 3, GAL 42 r. 13, 123 r. 12, 189:4, 263:5, GAL-*bi* 107:5, 139:5, 6, 143 e. 8, 216:6, 234:7, 237 e. 7, 240 e. 7, 282:2, GAL-*bi-u* 63 e. 6, GAL-*e* 209:3, r. 6, GAL-*te* 102 r. 8, GAL-*tú* 101 r. 5, GAL-*u* 10 r. 18, 64:4, 170:4, 227 r. 12, GAL-[*u*] 171:1, GAL-*ú* 272 r. 9, 285 r. 1, GAL-[*ú*] 308 r. 5, [GAL]-*ú* 272:12,
rabuttu "one fourth": 4-*ti-šú* 318:6, [4-*tú* 176 s. 1, 4-*tú* 27 r. 5, 29:1, 4-*tú-šú* 43:4, 167:5, 216:6, 240 e. 6, 248:9, 282:2, 4-[*t*]*ú-šú* 44:3, 4-*ut-ti-šú* 189:4, 237 e. 7, 262:5, 263:5, 4-[*ut-ti-šú* 291:5,
rādi gammali "camel driver": LÚ.UŠ—*g*]*am-mal*.MEŠ 300:5, LÚ.UŠ—ANŠE.AB.[BA.MEŠ] 138:4,
rādi imāri "donkey driver": LÚ.UŠ—ANŠE.[MEŠ] 55:1,
rādi kibsi "tracker": UŠ—*kib-šú* 52 r. 8,
rakāsu "to bind, attach": *i-rak-kas* 11 r. 6, 42 r. 2, 87 r. 3, 98 r. 4, 251 r. 1, 308 r. 2, 325 r. 5, 326 r. 7, 334 r. 14, *i-rak-kas*] 20 r. 1, *i-ra-kas* 32 r. 4, *i-ra-ka-sa* 92 r. 5, KÉŠ 200 r. 4,
raksu "recruit, mercenary(?)": LÚ.*rak-su* 100 r. 10, 318 r. 3, LÚ.*rak-s*[*u*] 101 r. 11, LÚ.*rak-*[*su*] 193 r. 5, LÚ.*ra*[*k-s*]*u* 212 r. 3, LÚ.*r*[*ak-su*] 212 r. 2, LÚ.*ra-ka-su* 210 r. 10, 15,
rammû "to leave, release": *ur-ta-me* 95:5, e. 8, *ú-ram-mu-ú* 25 r. 5,
rapāšu "to be wide, extensive": DAGAL 31 r. 1, 2, DAGAL] 31 e. 30,
rēʾû see *rāʾiu*,
rēšēti "first fruits": SAG.ME 114:3, SAG.MEŠ 184: 2, 214:1, 235:3, 237:2, [SAG.MEŠ 272:3,
rēšu "head, top, beginning": SAG 137:3,
rubê "interest": *ru-bé-e* 47:4, 223:4, *ru-bé-e-šú* 97 r. 7, *ru-bé-šú* 221:2,
rūṭu "span": *ru-ṭu* 88:4, LAL 253:5, LA[L 253:4,
sagullu "herd": *sa-kul-lat* 287:10,
sahāru "tower (Aram. word)": *sa-ha-ru* 217:10,
sāhirtu "free-roaming cow, heifer": GUD.ÁB.NIGIN 323:2, e. 10, GUD.Á]B.NIGIN 324 r. 2, GU]D.ÁB.NIGIN 324:7,
sakāru "to refine": *sak-ru* 11 r. 4, 31 r. 10, 42:21, 85:16, 87 r. 1, 96:18, 138 r. 7, 185 r. 8, 201:21, 284 r. 4, 299:13, 314 r. 5, 325 r. 3, 326 r. 9, 330 r. 1, 335 r. 10, *sak-ru*] 14 r. 8, 20:4, 211 r. 1, 217 r. 5, 251:15, 329 r. 3, *sak-r*[*u*] 23:13, 38 r. 8, *sak-*[*ru* 301 r. 1, *sak*]*-ru* 341 r. 11, *s*[*ak*]*-ru* 50 r. 7, 194 r. 1, *sa-ak-ru* 298 e. 13,
saklu "simpleton": LÚ.*sa-ak-lu-te* 28:3,
sakullu see *sagullu*,
samāhu "to unite; (D) to mix": *sam-mah-u-te* 222:2,
sangû "priest": LÚ.SANGA 11 r. 12, 59 r. 4, 5, 6, 7, 8, 9, 161 r. 11, 201 r. 5, 250 r. 7, LÚ.SANGA] 160 r. 4, SANGA 289 r. 8,
sartinnu (a high state official): *sar-tin* 238:1, LÚ.[*sar-tin*] 296 r. 4, LÚ.*sar-tin-ni* 133:8, LÚ.*sar-tin-nu* 264:1, 297 r. 12, 325 r. 8, LÚ.*sa*[*r-tin-nu*] 338 r. 7,
sartu "crime; fine": *sar-ti* 264 r. 5, *sa-ar-te* 133 r. 1, *sa-ar-ti* 89 r. 4, 134 r. 4, 215:4, *sa-ar-ti-šú* 265:6, [*s*]*a-ar-tu* 266 r. 3, *sa-ar-tú* 6 r. 8, 133:3, 284 r. 7, 289 r. 7, 305 r. 5, *sa-ar-*[*tú*] 342:10, [*sa-ar-tú* 306 r. 4, 334 r. 18, [*sa-a*]*r-tú* 219:12, [*s*]*a-ar-tú* 48 r. 7, 61:14, 133 e. 11, *sa-ár-ti-ši-na* 264:3, 8, r. 3, *sa-ár-tu* 85 r. 5, *sa-ár-tu-šú* 264:6, *sa-ár-tú* 83:2, 174 r. 4, 301 r. 5,
sasinnu "bow maker": LÚ.ZADIM 97 r. 11,
sasuppu "napkin": TÚG.*sa-su-pu* 190 s. 1,
sēgallu see *issi ekalli*,
sekret ekalli "palace concubine": MÍ.ERIM—É.GAL 88:6, 91:11, MÍ.ERIM]—É.GAL 99:7,
siāru "to plaster": *i-si-ár* 21 e. 10,
sinništu see *issu*,
simānu (Sivan, name of the 3rd month): ITI.SIG$_4$ 5 r. 2, 6 s. 1, 73 r. 1, 100 r. 21, 142 s. 1, 148 r. 3, 151 r. 10, 164 r. 18, 178 r. 2, 214 r. 2, 221 r. 6, 222 r. 5, 223 r. 9, 234 r. 6, 252 s. 3, 275 s. 2, 293 e. 6, [ITI.SI]G$_4$ 240 r. 7, [I]TI.SIG$_4$ 261 r. 4,
sirāšû "brewer": LÚ.LUNGA 282 r. 1, LÚ.LUNGA] 272 r. 1, LÚ.LU]NGA 272:4,
sissû "horse": ANŠE.KUR.MEŠ 11 r. 5, 301:2, ANŠE.KUR.RA 20 r. 1, 32 r. 3, 98 r. 3, 308 r. 2, 325 r. 5, 334 r. 14, AN]ŠE.KUR.RA.[MEŠ 86:14, ANŠE.KUR.RA.MEŠ 42 r. 1, 87 r. 3, 92 r. 5, 251 e. 18, 326 r. 7, ANŠE.KUR.RA.MEŠ] 200 r. 3, ANŠE.KUR.R[A.MEŠ] 86 r. 9, [ANŠE.KUR.RA.MEŠ] 140:9,
sugullu see *sagullu*,
sukkallu "vizier": LÚ.SUKKAL 6 r. 12, 12:5, r. 3, 19 r. 11, 30 r. 7, 31:12, r. 19, 83:2, 96 r. 7, 123:7, 133:8, 210 r. 17, 212 r. 8, 226 r. 12, 239 r. 12, 265:4, 274 r. 19, 308 r. 5, 312 r. 7, 325 r. 9, 329:9, 330 r. 4, 332 r. 6, 335 r. 13, 338 r. 8, LÚ.[SUKKA]L 19 r. 7, L[Ú.SUKKAL 329 r. 8, L]Ú.SUKKAL 335 r. 14, [LÚ].SUKKAL 272:12, [LÚ.SUKKAL 316 r. 2, [LÚ.SUKKAL] 272 r. 9, SUKKAL 238:1, [SU]KKAL 265:13, SUKKAL.MEŠ 183:5,
suqāqu "alley": *su-qa-qi* 99:5, 142:10,
sūqu "street": SILA 328:8,
sūsān nakkamti "trainer of reserve horses": LÚ.GIŠ.GIGIR—*na-*[*kam-ti*] 193 r. 6,
sūsān ša-pattûti "horse trainer of the open chariotry": LÚ.GIŠ.GIGIR—DU$_8$ 310 r. 9, 325 r. 22, LÚ.[GIŠ.GIGIR—DU$_8$] 331 r. 3, L[Ú.GIŠ.GIGIR—DU$_8$] 331 r. 5, LÚ.GIŠ.GIGIR—DU$_8$.MEŠ 310 r. 16, 316 r. 11, 317 r. 4, LÚ.GIŠ.GIG]IR—DU$_8$.MEŠ 335 r. 23, LÚ.GIŠ.G[IGIR—DU$_8$.MEŠ] 315 r. 4, L]Ú.GIŠ.GIGIR—DU$_8$.MEŠ 338 r. 16, [LÚ.G]IŠ.GIGIR—DU$_8$.MEŠ 316:2, LÚ.GIŠ.GIGIR—DU$_8$.ME]Š-*te* 334 r. 31,

sūsān ša-šēpi "horse trainer of the royal guard": LÚ.GIŠ.GIGIR—GÌR.2 53 r. 8, [LÚ.GIŠ].GIGIR—GÌR.2 119 r. 11,

sūsānu "horse trainer, chariot-man": LÚ.*su-sa-n*[*u* 199 r. 5, LÚ.GIGIR 239 r. 6, LÚ.GIŠ.GIGIR 110 r. 10, 164 r. 14, 235 r. 1, 257 r. 26, 31, 283:2, 309 r. 11, 12, 13, 347 r. 14, LÚ.GIŠ.GI]GIR 334 r. 35, LÚ.GIŠ.[GIGIR] 347 r. 13, L]Ú.GIŠ.GIGIR 112 r. 7,

sūtu "seah": GIŠ.BÁN 46:3, 194:5, 223:6, 224:6, 226:4, 278:4, 315:1, 316:3, 326:3, 332:2, 334:22, (GIŠ).BÁN 158:4, G[IŠ.BÁN] 31 e. 29, 1BÁN 10:17, 11:9, 2BÁN 27:8, 31:16, 25, 77:1, 102 r. 8, 119:15, 233:3, 275 e. 20, 283:4, 15, 315:3, 316:5, 3BÁN 31:25, 93 e. 10, 101 r. 5, 119:9, 161:5, 252 r. 3, 275:12, r. 9, 283:5, 14, 3BÁN-*a-a* 71:5, 4BÁN 10:16, 11:8, 160:6, 252:4, 275:13, r. 1, 2, 4, 283:2, 5BÁN 12:13, 31:9, 11, 23, 78:6, 7, r. 1, 2, 137:2, 3, 181:2, 182:1, 268:1, 275:17, r. 3, 8, 283:8, 9, 16, 17, 5BÁN-*a-a* 74:5, 75 r. 1, 5BÁN-*šá* 67:6, 6BÁN 21:6 27 e. 11, 32:4, 119:6, 275 e. 22, 6BÁ]N 285:4, 6BÁN-*ma* 275 r. 5, 7BÁN 10:6, 13:4, 31 e. 26, 77:3, 4, 5, 8BÁN 12:6, 10, 14:6, 31:18, 119:3, 125:4, 275 r. 6, 283:3,

ṣabātu "to seize, capture": *i-ṣab-tu* 133:5, *ṣa-bit* 10 r. 19, 12 r. 5, 17 r. 16, 18 r. 5, 19 r. 14, 23 r. 12, 30 r. 12, 31 r. 27, 34 r. 13, 40 r. 19, 41 r. 20, 59 r. 16, 91 r. 4, 96 r. 17, 100 r. 21, 105 r. 11, 114 r. 3, 121 r. 8, 124 r. 13, 135 r. 5, 147 r. 9, 159 r. 3, 164 r. 20, 173 r. 7, 177 r. 12, 195 r. 6, 212 r. 5, 294 r. 7, 310 r. 13, 311 r. 7, 314 r. 24, 316 r. 14, 317 r. 7, *ṣa-bi*[*t* 1 r. 18, *ṣa-b*]*it* 13 r. 6, *ṣ*[*a-bit* 53 r. 11, 193 r. 10, [*ṣa-bit* 315 r. 7, [*ṣa*]-*bit* 302 r. 14, *ú-ṣa-bat* 21:9, DIB 61 r. 10, 257 r. 33, 265 r. 7, 284 s. 1,

ṣabtu "prisoner": LÚ.DIB 57:1,

ṣābu "men, troops": LÚ.ERIM.MEŠ 21:4, 133:2,

ṣāhitu "oil-presser": LÚ.Ì.ŠUR 2 r. 4, 96 r. 11,

ṣarbutu "poplar": GIŠ.A.(TU).GAB.[LIŠ] 125:7,

ṣārip tuhšî "tanner of colored leather": LÚ.*ṣa-rip—tuh-ši-e* 1 r. 10, 29 r. 5,

ṣarpu "silver": KUG.UD 1 r. 7, 3:12, 6 r. 1, 7:15, 11 r. 4, 14 r. 1, 8, s. 1, 17 r. 6, 20:4, 23:6, 12, 26:1, 29:1, r. 3, 31 r. 5, 32 r. 1, 34:8, r. 1, 35:3, 36:1, 37 r. 5, 38 r. 8, 39:13, 40 r. 1, 42:10, 20, 44:1, 45:6, 47:4, 49:4, 50:10, r. 7, 51:5, r. 5, 52:11, 53:13, 55:4, 57:8, 58 r. 3, 61:12, 65 r. 3, 80:1, 81:5, e. 11, 82:1, 85:8, 15, 87:2, r. 1, 88:8, 89:8, r. 3, 90:14, 91:12, 17, 92 r. 3, 93 r. 5, 96:6, 97:1, 4, r. 6, 98:7, r. 1, 100:8, 101:5, 102:3, 103:7, 107:1, 108:2, 4, 109:7, 110:9, r. 1, 111 e. 10, 113:6, 118:6, 121:6, 124:9, 126:10, 130:9, 131 r. 1, 132:9, 133:4, e. 11, 138:10, 139:1, 4, 140:9, 11, 142 e. 13, r. 11, 143:1, e. 7, 144:4, 146:2, e. 9, 150:1, 152:7, 154 r. 2, 9, 156:1, 160:13, 163 r. 3, 167:1, 4, 6, 172 r. 6, 174:5, 176 r. 6, 177:7, e. 14, 178:1, 180:1, 8, e. 9, 181 r. 1, 183:1, 185 r. 6, 197:14, 198:3, 201:9, 20, 202:11, r. 3, 206:7, 208:4, 6, 210:10, e. 19, 211 r. 1, 213:2, 216:2, 5, 217:13, 219 r. 7, 220 r. 5, 221:1, 223:1, 4, r. 2, 224:1, 226:16, 227:6, 228:6, 229:8, 234:1, 5, 235:2, 5, 236:4, e. 7, r. 5, 237:1, 239:8, 240:1, 241 r. 3, s. 1, 243 e. 9, 244:6, 245 e. 14, 246:5, 248:1, 9, 250:9, 251:6, 15, 252 r. 8, 10, 253:8, 9, r. 5, 6, 254:9, 257:9, r. 21, 259:3, e. 6, 260:3, e. 7, 262:2, 263:1, 265:11, 266 s. 2, 268:7, 269:10, 271 r. 3, 6, 272:2, r. 4, 274:5, r. 3, 5, 275 r. 14, 21, 278:10, r. 3, 283 r. 5, 8, 284 s. 2, 285:4, 286:6, 287:16, r. 3, 290:13, 291:1, 292:1, 293:1, r. 2, 295:7, 298 e. 12, 299:1, 12, 301:19, 305:8, r. 2, 306:5, r. 1, 307 e. 9, 309:8, r. 1, 311:10, 312:12, 315:12, 317:4, 318:2, 5, 6, 319:6, r. 1, 323:1, 324:5, 325 r. 3, 326 r. 9, 328:11, 329:14, r. 3, 333 r. 1, 334 r. 4, 16, 335 e. 13, r. 9, 336 r. 10, 340 r. 1, 341 r. 3, 11, 342:7, 16, 343:11, 344:8, 345:10, 346:3, r. 5, 347:8, 349:2, r. 4, KUG.UD] 17:12, 37:11, 40:8, 41:9, 48:6, 54:7, 58:1, 65:10, 126 r. 3, 160 r. 1, 165:6, 196:7, 226:12, 308 e. 12, 326:16, 348:2, KUG.U[D 96:17, 140:2, 207 r. 4, KUG.U[D] 43:1, 284:6, KUG.U]D 99:9, 289:16, 328 r. 3, KUG.[UD 38:4, 116:8, 208:1, 244:11, 314 r. 4, KUG.[UD] 161:11, 189:1, KUG.[U]D 347 r. 5, KUG]. UD 138 r. 6, 144:11, 200 r. 1, 236:2, 285:7, 302 r. 2, KU[G.UD 94 r. 3, KU]G.UD 238 e. 11, K[UG.UD 41 r. 2, 217 r. 4, 229 e. 13, 284 r. 3, K[UG.UD] 4:4, 115:6, 204:9, K]UG.UD 295 r. 4, [KUG.UD 10:20, 27 r. 6, 39:3, 86:8, 151 r. 1, 175:2, 197:6, 221 e. 7, 313:10, 339:5, [KUG.UD] 56 r. 6, 99 r. 1, 182 e. 8, [KUG.U]D 81:1, [KUG].UD 119:18, [K]UG.UD 133 e. 10, KUG.UD-*šú* 95:6, 226 r. 14, KUG.UD.MEŠ 36:4, 53:6, 106:7, 127:7, 219:4, 307:8, 317:6, KUG.UD. M[EŠ] 307:1, KUG.UD.ME]Š 245 r. 4,

ṣarrāpu "goldsmith": LÚ.SIMUG.KUG.GI 163 r. 10, 283:17, LÚ.SIMUG.KUG.[GI] 164 r. 9, [LÚ]. SIMUG.KUG.GI 19 r. 7, SIMUG.KUG.GI 65 r. 11,

ṣehertu "girl": MÍ.TUR 88:2, 10, MÍ.T[U]R-*su* 293 e. 7, MÍ.TUR.MEŠ 269:4, 297:7, MÍ.TUR.MEŠ-*šú* 245: 11,

ṣehru "boy, manservant": LÚ.TUR 121 r. 2, TUR 56:7, 227:2, 7,

ṣēru "open country, plain": EDIN 81:6, 288:14, r. 19,

ṣētu "daylight": UD.DA 288:20, r. 4,

ṣibittu see *qāt ṣibitti*,

ṣibtu "seizure": *ṣib-ti* 85 r. 4, 89 r. 4, *ṣib-t*]*i* 134 r. 3, *ṣib-tu* 266 r. 2, *ṣib-tú* 174 r. 3, 284 r. 6, 301 r. 5, 305 r. 4, *ṣib-tú*] 289 r. 6, [*ṣib-tú* 306 r. 3, 342:10, [*ṣib-tú*] 61:13, [*ṣib-t*]*ú* 219:11, [*ṣib*]-*tú* 6 r. 7, 48 r. 6,

ṣīru "emissary": LÚ.MAH 312 r. 16, 313 r. 3,

ṣītu "exit; loss": *a-ṣa-ti* 3:8,

ṣuhattu (mng. obscure): *ṣu-ha-ta-a-te* 288 r. 13,

ṣuhurtu "youth, adolescence": *ṣu-hur-tú* 326:9, 11, LÚ.*ṣu-hur-te* 343:6, 344:3,

ṣupru "nail, claw": [*ṣu-bar* 1:2, [*ṣu-bar*] 289:2, *ṣu-bar-šú* 1:1, 289:1, *ṣu-bar-šú-nu* 100:2, [*ṣ*]*u-bar-šú* 7:1, *ṣu-pur* 5:1, 7:2, 10:2, 17:1, 2, 3, 4, 5, 18:2, 19:2, 3, 22:1, 23:1, 2, 24:2, 3, 28:2, 30:2, 41:2, 42:2, 53:1, 105:3, 4, 113:2, 120:1, 121:2, 122:1, 124:1, 125:2, 127:2, 135:1, 142:1, 2, 3, 145:2, 159:2, 217:2, 218:2, 290:2, *ṣu-pur*] 31:3, *ṣu-pu*]*r* 31:2, *ṣu-p*[*ur* 61:2, *ṣu-*[*pur*] 61:2, 119:2, *ṣ*[*u-pu*]*r* 18:2, [*ṣu-pur* 2:1, 31:2, 3, 40:2, 114:2, 288:1, [*ṣu*]-*pur* 12:2, 37:2, 50:1, 96:2, [*ṣ*]*u-pur* 13:2, 32:1, 302:2, [*ṣ*]*u-*[*pur* 18:3, *ṣu-p*]*ur-šu-nu* 105 s. 3, *ṣu-pur-šú* 12:1, 13:1, 14 s. 1, 28:1, 30:1, 32 s. 1, 37:1, 40:1, 41:1, 42:1, 96:1, 113:1, 114:1, 119:1, 124 s. 1, 125:1, 127 r. 10, 172 r. 6, 217:1, 289 r. 17, 290:1, *ṣu-pur-*[*šú*] 6 s. 3, 121:1, 127:1, 290 r. 2, *ṣu-p*[*ur-šú* 159:1, *ṣu-p*]*ur-šú* 174 s. 3, *ṣu*]*-pur-šú* 10:1, *ṣ*[*u*]-*p*[*ur*]-[*š*]*ú* 12 r. 8, [*ṣu-pur-šú* 218:1, 302:1, *ṣu-pur-šú-nu* 18:1, 19:1, 24:1, 61:1, r. 11, 105:1, 145:1, *ṣu-pur-šú*]-*nu* 31:1, *ṣu-up-*[*ri-šú-nu*] 31 r. 31, *ṣ*]*u-up-ri-šú-n*[*u*] 147 r. 10, UMBIN-*šú* 284 s. 2,

ša "that; what; of": *ša* 1 r. 7, 16, 17, 3:2, 8, 4:2, 6:3, 12, r. 12, 15, s. 3, 7:5, 8:4, 6, 9:3, 10:15, 11:13, 12 r. 8, 14:7, 8, r. 4, s. 1, 17 e. 13, r. 3, 4, 8, 11,

19:12, r. 7, 21:7, 22:3, 6, 7, 23:4, r. 7, 24:5, 7, 25:6, 26:1, 2, 27:3, r. 6, 9, 10, 28 r. 4, 7, 29 r. 7, 9, 30:7, r. 2, 6, 7, 8, 9, 31:5, 7, 8, 9, 10, 11, 12, 13, 14, 16, 17, 18, 20, 22, 23, 25, e. 27, 28, 31, r. 1, 2, 3, 4, 8, 10, 12, 13, 14, 15, 16, 18, 19, 20, 22, 24, 25, 26, 31, 32:5, 7, s. 1, 33:7, 34:7, 18, 35:1, 36:2, 6, r. 1, 37:3, 5, 16, r. 2, 10, 12, 14, 38:4, 39:4, r. 6, 9, 40:6, 9, 14, 19, r. 4, 16, 41:7, 10, r. 6, 8, 11, 42:9, 18, 43:2, 45:4, 6, 46:2, 8, 47:2, 4, 48:4, 11, 50:10, r. 2, 5, 51:5, 52 r. 1, 8, 17, 53:4, 7, 54:4, 7, 55:2, 4, r. 3, 56 e. 10, 59:7, r. 9, 61:4, 10, r. 11, 63:3, 64:2, 65:10, r. 3, 66:2, 4, r. 12, 67:2, 69:2, 70:5, 71:2, 73:2, 74:2, 75:2, 76:2, 77:6, 78 r. 4, 79:8, 81:2, 3, e. 11, 82:9, 83:2, 84:3, 86:6, 7, r. 5, 6, 7, 8, 11, 12, 13, 14, 15, 16, 87:1, 5, 9, 89:7, 90:1, 4, 92:3, 6, r. 9, 93:4, 5, e. 8, r. 3, 4, 5, 9, 94 r. 4, 95:3, r. 5, 7, 96:4, 7, 10, 14, r. 10, 12, 13, 16, 97:1, 2, 6, 7, r. 6, 14, 98:4, 11, 99:7, 9, 13, 100:6, 13, 105 s. 3, 107:1, 2, 4, 108:3, 4, r. 3, 110:6, 8, 9, 111:8, 113:4, 115:4, 6, 116:7, 118:4, 119:12, 16, 19, r. 7, 120 r. 2, 121 r. 2, 123:1, 4, 7, 10, 13, r. 10, 124:15, r. 6, s. 1, 127:4, 11, r. 10, 130:7, 14, r. 10, 131 r. 9, 132:6, 7, 9, r. 2, 133:4, 135 r. 3, 137:1, 138:7, 10, e. 15, 139:2, 5, 140:5, 142:4, e. 13, r. 3, 7, 9, 143:1, 2, 3, 147 r. 10, 150:7, 151 r. 7, 152:4, 156:2, 158:1, 4, 159:4, 5, 161:6, 7, 8, 9, r. 1, 2, 164:13, r. 4, 12, 165:3, r. 1, 6, 167:2, 169:8, 170:2, 172 r. 5, 6, 173:5, 174 r. 5, 9, 175:2, 176:4, 8, 11, r. 3, 177:8, 13, 178:2, 3, 180:1, 2, e. 9, 181:3, e. 1, 182:2, e. 7, 183:2, 3, 5, 184:3, 185 e. 9, 186 r. 4, 10, 187:3, 188:3, 5, 6, r. 5, 6, 10, 189:2, 190:1, 3, s. 2, 191 r. 1, 193 r. 9, 13, s. 1, 194:3, 5, s. 3, 196:8, 197:4, 11, 198:2, r. 1, 199 r. 6, 200:2, r. 11, 201 r. 8, 202:3, 4, 6, 7, r. 10, 204:3, 5, 6, 206:2, 207 r. 1, 208:2, 209:3, 210:14, r. 8, 14, 15, 211:3, 5, 213 r. 1, 214:2, 3, 215:5, 216:2, 3, 217:5, 6, r. 1, 218:5, 6, 11, 219:5, r. 1, 4, 220 r. 3, 221:2, 222:1, 223:1, 2, 4, 6, 227:3, 228:10, 229:6, 232:2, e. 7, 233:8, 234:2, 3, 235:4, 237:2, 3, 4, 238:6, 9, 239:6, 9, r. 6, 240:4, 241:2, 3, 242:4, 243:4, 244:10, 245 e. 15, 250:6, 8, 10, 251:6, 7, 13, e. 17, 252 r. 7, 253:6, 7, 255:2, 257:1, 3, 4, 6, 7, 10, 13, r. 19, 259:1, 4, e. 6, r. 9, 260:1, 5, e. 7, s. 1, 262:2, 3, 263:1, 2, 264:1, 4, 5, 9, e. 11, r. 4, 5, 265:2, 15, 266:9, 269 r. 2, 271 r. 6, 272:2, 3, 274:4, 10, 275:7, 10, 11, r. 4, 5, 11, 15, 277:2, r. 8, 10, 278:4, 14, 284:3, 7, r. 14, s. 2, 285 r. 9, 286 r. 11, s. 1, 287:2, 10, 11, 12, 14, 17, r. 8, 10, 11, s. 1, 2, 288:12, r. 1, 3, 6, 7, 13, 16, 291:2, 3, 292:2, 293:4, 294:4, 295:5, r. 3, 298:3, 9, 301:5, 9, 12, 16, r. 15, 304 r. 8, 305:2, 5, 12, 307:2, e. 9, 308:8, e. 9, r. 9, 309:4, 7, r. 10, 310:2, r. 8, 19, 311:8, 312 r. 1, 13, 16, 19, 314 r. 2, 315:1, 316:3, 318:4, 319:4, 9, 11, 321:4, 6, 9, r. 5, 7, 8, 322:5, 323:1, 3, 325:1, 2, r. 17, 18, 19, 20, 21, 326:14, 328:10, e. 14, r. 6, 9, 329 r. 14, 330:2, 331:2, 8, 332:2, 4, 5, r. 10, 334:4, 6, 8, 15, 18, 19, 20, 22, 24, 25, r. 4, 9, 33, 335:1, 4, 5, 7, 8, 12, e. 13, r. 3, 6, 21, 336:7, r. 6, 338 r. 1, 9, 339:7, 9, r. 9, 340:6, 341 r. 1, 2, 342:7, 17, r. 13, 14, 343:8, 344:5, 7, 8, 14, 346:8, r. 2, 347:5, 9, r. 2, 348:7, 9, r. 4, 349 r. 1, *ša*] 3:13, 20:1, 49:7, 93:2, 118:11, 185:5, 197 r. 8, 238:1, 285 r. 2, 346:3, *š*[*a* 38:1, 41 r. 1, 50:7, 104:6, 123:7, 124 r. 4, 130:10, 197:8, 241 e. 7, 245 r. 4, 292:3, 321 r. 6, 325 r. 19, 338:6, *š*[*a*] 119:4, 211:2, 333 r. 1, *š*]*a* 38 r. 1, 53:12, 92:10, 93:3, 119:8, 125 r. 1, 2, 130 r. 11, 146:2, 272:3, 289:13, 332:8, r. 11, 335 r. 18, 336:10, 338:8, 349:1, [*ša* 31 e. 31, 38 r. 5, 39:10, 48 r. 1, 56:2, 99 e. 16, 100:14, 101:3, 109:5, 7, 112:4, 8, 118:16, 119 r. 5, 126 r. 3, 138 r. 4, 164 r. 8, 209 r. 6, 210:11, 213 r. 4, 224:2, 228:13, 255:2, 267:4, 284 r. 1, 285:4, 290:11, 307:3, 321 r. 4, 324:6, 8, 9, 334:18, 21, 25, 338 r. 3, 339:4, 341 r. 8, 343:10, [*ša*] 30:8, 31 e. 30, 37 r. 7, 49:2, 104:3, 113:5, 119:5, 7, 140 r. 12, 185 r. 7, 195:5, 240:2, 296:3, 305:15, 315:10, 13, 344 r. 6, 346:2, 347 r. 7, 348:2, [*š*]*a* 15 r. 2, 31:6, 18, 40 r. 14, 44:2, 93 r. 2, 123 r. 11, 186 e. 9, 202:12, 245:2, 275 r. 19, 293:2, 336:7, 9, 347:5, *šá* 7:9, 10:4, 5, 7, 10, 13, 18, 11:2, 4, 6, 8, 9, r. 10, 12, 12:5, 7, 8, 9, 10, 11, r. 3, 13:5, 8, 15:4, 16:1, 19 r. 11, 22:12, 23:11, 24:6, 32:13, 34:9, 13, r. 2, 39:1, 7, 16, 42:5, 10, 14, r. 9, 11, 46:3, 51 e. 12, r. 2, 52 r. 7, 55:2, 9, 57:1, 5, 7, 12, r. 1, 8, 59 r. 4, 5, 6, 7, 8, 10, 11, 12, 85:6, 7, 8, 14, r. 1, 7, 88:13, 89 r. 1, 90:3, 9, 10, 12, 14, r. 1, 91:2, 12, 13, 16, r. 2, 3, 95:2, e. 1, r. 2, 3, 96 r. 7, 97 e. 8, 101:9, 10, 16, 102:7, 8, 13, 103:5, 8, 104:2, 106:2, 6, 110:13, 122 r. 2, 124:12, 146:6, 150:1, 152 r. 3, 154 r. 8, 157:2, 6, 160:8, 10, 11, 163 r. 2, 10, 167:1, 169:6, r. 4, 174 s. 3, 177:11, 184:2, 200 r. 7, 201:2, 4, 5, 6, 13, 17, 207 e. 7, 212:1, 224:1, 6, 226:4, 6, 7, 8, 227:9, 228:4, 232:4, 233:2, 4, 235: 2, 3, 7, 236:2, 246:3, 8, 247:5, 248:2, 250 r. 2, 251:10, 253:12, 254:2, 10, 258 r. 8, 265:3, 9, 13, 268:6, 269:10, 270 r. 2, 271:4, 5, 8, 9, 11, 13, 14, 15, 16, 17, e. 19, 273:1, 2, 274:6, r. 1, 278:6, 7, 281:3, 283:9, 13, r. 7, 15, 16, 17, 20, 284:11, 285 r. 8, 286:4, 288:2, 4, 13, 16, 17, 18, 23, r. 8, 9, 10, 11, 13, 17, 289:10, r. 4, 8, 10, 17, 290:8, r. 2, 297:8, r. 2, 13, 299:1, 4, 9, r. 1, 2, 3, 4, 301:2, 7, r. 17, 305:8, 306:5, 9, 309 r. 6, 7, 311:6, 10, 13, 312:2, 12, 16, r. 8, 9, 313:2, 6, 8, 10, r. 6, 314:5, 16, 21, r. 18, 317:3, 5, 6, 8, r. 1, 2, 3, 9, 318:3, 320:2, 4, 6, r. 1, 3, 5, 8, 321:6, 7, 324 r. 9, 326:3, 4, 5, 6, 7, 13, 16, 17, 22, 23, r. 3, 5, 329:2, 6, 9, 10, 11, 15, 18, 21, r. 10, 15, 16, 19, 330:6, r. 5, 8, 9, 10, 13, 331:7, 332 r. 5, 334 r. 3, 15, 340:3, r. 5, 6, 12, 342:11, 343:11, 345:8, 346 r. 6, *šá*] 10 r. 1, 93 r. 10, 136:1, 144:10, 202 r. 1, 239 r. 7, 308:5, 313 r. 1, 320:5, *š*[*á*] 314:13, *š*]*á* 146:5, [*šá* 57:9, 117:2, 123 r. 2, 158:7, 169:4, 185 r. 1, 212:4, 271:10, 286 s. 1, 299 r. 5, 300:6, 306:2, 312 r. 16, 313:14, 317 r. 9, [*šá*] 191 r. 4, 326 r. 4, [*š*]*á* 13:4, 90 r. 18, 313 r. 4, 333 e. 4,

šabāšu "to collect": *i-šá-ba-áš* 287 r. 7,

šabāṭu (Shebat, name of the 11th month): [ITI]. ZÍZ 88 r. 11, ITI.ZÍZ 10 r. 17, 46:5, 98 r. 12, 131 r. 11, 145 r. 3, 206 r. 2, 215:6, 264 s. 1, 279 r. 7, 311 r. 8, 314 r. 25, 319 r. 17, [ITI.Z]ÍZ 1 r. 19,

šadû "mountain; east": KUR-*e* 176:11,

šadussu "one sixth": 6-*su* 119:16,

šakānu "to place, set": *iš-kun* 10:1, 12:1, 13:1, 28:1, 30:1, 40:1, 96:1, 105:2, 113:1, 119:1, 127:2, 289:1, *iš-kun*] 41:1, 114:1, 159:1, 217:1, 302:1, *iš-k*[*u*]*n* 100:2, *iš-*[*kun*] 18:1, [*iš-kun*] 1:1, 0 [*iš-ku*]*n* 121:2, [*i*]*š-kun* 125:2, *iš-kun-nu* 19:1, *iš-ku-nu* 31:1, *iš-ku-nu*] 24:1, 145:1, *i-šak-kan* 87 r. 2, 151 r. 3, 219 r. 9, 223 r. 3, 226 r. 1, 334 r. 17, 335 r. 11, *i-šak-kan*] 302 r. 2, *i-šak-*[*kan*] 99 r. 3, *i-š*[*ak-kan*] 126 r. 4, 176 r. 8, [*i-šak-k*]*an* 310 r. 2, [*i-šak*]-*kan* 165 r. 2, *i-šak-kan-u-ni* 223:7, *i-šak-kan*]-*u-ni* 224:7, *i-ša-ku-nu*] 160 r. 2, *i-šá-kan* 16 r. 1, 92 r.

4, 185 r. 7, 9, 287 r. 4, 308 r. 1, *i-šá-kan]* 20:5, *i-šá-k[an]* 7 e. 17, *i-šá-ka-an* 298 r. 2, *šak-nu* 81 e. 10, *šak-nu]* 317:5, *šá-kin* 91:13, *šá-kín* 97 r. 5, 146:7, 226 r. 13, *šá-kí[n* 160 r. 1, *šá-[kín* 180:5, *šá-ki-an* 245 r. 3, GAR 198:4, GAR] 207 r. 5, 268:7, 330 r. 1, GAR-*an* 11 r. 5, 21 e. 12, 31 r. 10, 42:22, 50 r. 8, 51 r. 7, 52 r. 7, 85 r. 1, 98 r. 2, 110 r. 3, 200 r. 2, 201 r. 2, 220 r. 6, 229 r. 2, 250 r. 4, 252 r. 11, 253 r. 6, 265:12, 274 r. 5, 278 r. 5, 284 r. 5, 289 r. 1, 299:13, 309 r. 3, 314 r. 6, 325 r. 4, 326 r. 10, 328 r. 4, 329 r. 5, 346 r. 6, GAR-*an]* 217 r. 6, 251:16, 301 r. 2, 319 r. 2, GAR-*[an]* 53 e. 15, 96:19, 118 r. 2, [GAR-*an* 138 r. 8, [GAR-*a]n* 179 r. 1, [G]AR-*an* 58 r. 5, GAR-*nu* 23:11, 61:1, GA[R-*nu]* 307:7, GAR-*un* 7:1, 37:1, 42:1, GAR-*un]* 218:1, GAR-*u[n]* 290:1,

šakintu "harem governess": MÍ.*šá]-kin-tú* 87:1, MÍ.*šá-kín-te* 81:3, 90 r. 4, 94 r. 4, 95 e. 1, 152 r. 3, 247:5, 250:8, MÍ.*šá-kín-ti* 89:7, r. 1, MÍ.*šá-kín-tú* 87:9, MÍ.*šá-[kín-tú]* 90:12, [MÍ.*šá-kín-tú* 92:3, MÍ.*šá-ki-in-te* 83:4, MÍ.*šá-ki-in-tú* 84:3, [MÍ].*šá*-GIM-*tú* 86:7, MÍ.GAR-*te* 93 r. 11, MÍ.GAR-*tú* 85:7, 93 r. 3,

šaknu "governor, prefect": *šak-nu-šú-nu* 251:13, GAR.KUR 45 r. 7, 109 r. 9, 115 r. 5, 277 r. 12, 287 r. 18, [GAR.KUR] 128 r. 5, [GAR.K]UR 250 r. 14, LÚ.*šak-an-šú* 82:8, LÚ.*šak-nu* 32 r. 6, LÚ.GAR 36 r. 1, LÚ.GAR-*in-šú-nu* 328 e. 17, LÚ.GAR-*nu* 101:14, 139:2, r. 4, 172:1, 301:2, LÚ. GAR-*nu-šú* 96:13, 264 r. 1, 299:8, LÚ.GAR-*nu-šú-nu* 15 r. 1, 31 r. 8, 257:17, 335 r. 5, 336 r. 6, LÚ.GAR-*nu-šú-[nu]* 334 r. 11, LÚ.GAR-*nu-[šú-nu]* 344 r. 4, LÚ.GAR-*n[u-šú-nu]* 326 r. 1, L[Ú.GAR-*nu-šú-nu]* 100:18, LÚ.GAR.KUR 5 r. 4, 6 s. 2, 12 r. 7, 17 s. 2, 19 r. 13, 26 r. 8, 28 r. 9, 31 r. 28, 37 r. 17, 41 r. 18, 42 r. 21, 57 r. 3, 59 r. 18, 61 r. 8, 67 r. 3, 68 r. 2, 69 r. 5, 81 r. 10, 91 r. 6, 98 r. 14, 114 r. 2, 120 r. 7, 123 r. 15, 124 r. 15, 131 r. 13, 134 r. 16, 135 r. 7, 142 s. 2, 149:8, 190 r. 7, 191 r. 3, 196 r. 10, 197 r. 10, 252 s. 4, 257 r. 35, 282 e. 5, 283 r. 24, 288 r. 19, 289 r. 15, 301 r. 19, LÚ.GAR.KUR] 39 r. 10, 96 r. 19, LÚ.GAR.[KUR 218 r. 9, LÚ.G[AR.KUR 40 r. 18, LÚ.[GAR.KU]R 147 r. 8, L[Ú.GAR.K]UR 280 r. 16, [LÚ].GAR.KUR 125 r. 17, 148 r. 5, [LÚ].GAR.[KUR] 303 r. 6, [LÚ.GAR.KUR 106 r. 8, 192 s. 2, 290 r. 1, [LÚ.GAR.KUR] 13 r. 8, [LÚ.GAR].KUR 193 r. 13, [LÚ.GA]R.KUR 320 r. 10, [L]Ú.GAR.KUR 302 r. 16, 327 r. 9,

šalāmu "to be sound, whole; (D) to pay back, restitute": *šal-lu-mu* 35:6, *ú-sal-lim* 223 r. 1, *ú-sa-lim* 25 r. 3, 178:5, *ú-sa-li-mu* 72 e. 5, *ú-s[a-li-mu* 133 r. 2, *ú-sa-ni-lum* 95:6, r. 2, *ú-šal-lam* 215:5, *ú-š[al-lam]* 25 r. 1, 226:15, *ú-šal-l[am-u-ni]* 180 e. 9, *[ú-šal-lam-u-ni* 295 r. 4, *ú-šal-la-ma* 156 e. 8, *ú-šal-lim* 72 r. 2,

šalšāti "threefold": 3-*a-te* 194 r. 2,

šalussu "one third": 3-*s[i-šú]* 157 r. 1, 3-*si-šú-nu* 170:4, 3-*s]i-šú-nu* 171:1, 3]-*su* 14 s. 1, 3-*su-šú* 26 e. 8, 3-*su-šú-nu* 214 e. 7,

šamaššammi "sesame": ŠE.GIŠ.Ì 217:6,

šamnu "oil": Ì.MEŠ 46:2, 5,

šamû "to hear": *i-šá-mu* 219 r. 12, *i-šá-mu]* 58 r. 7, 326 r. 13, *i-šá-mu-u* 210 r. 4, 211 r. 5, *i-š]á-m[u]-u* 176 r. 11, *i-š]e-[m]e* 345 r. 3,

šangû see *sangû,*

šaniu A "deputy": LÚ.2-*e* 31 r. 24, 130:1, 185 e. 7, 342 r. 14, LÚ.2-*e-šú* 91:14, LÚ.2-*i* 52 r. 8, 81:4, 245:1, LÚ.[2-*u* 328 r. 13, LÚ.2-*u* 26 r. 3, 50 r. 11, 57 r. 8, 86 r. 11, 166:3, 177:12, 205 r. 4, 239 r. 12, 243:1, 288 r. 7, 301 r. 10, 307:4, 308 r. 9, 309 r. 10, 310 r. 8, 315 r. 3, 316 r. 10, 317 r. 3, 318:1, 320 r. 3, 5, 321 r. 6, 323:4, 325:1, r. 17, 18, 329 r. 19, 332 r. 10, 335 r. 21, 339 r. 8, 10, LÚ.2-*u]* 324:10, LÚ.2-*[u* 314 r. 18, 321 r. 8, LÚ.2-*[u]* 312 r. 12, L]Ú.2-*u* 338 r. 15, LÚ].2-*u* 324:1, 328 r. 9, [LÚ.2-*u* 243:5, 313 r. 1, 330 r. 13, [L]Ú.2-*u* 296:4, LÚ.2-*ú* 123:1, 8, 193 r. 8, 247 r. 1, 287:3, 274 r. 19, 347 r. 12, 2-*e* 19 r. 13, 21 r. 14, 133:6, 2-*i* 31:12, r. 19, 127 r. 6, 2-*u* 210 r. 17, 288:7, 314:6, 335 r. 14, 2-*u]* 212 r. 8,

šaniu B "second, other, different": *šá-ni-u* 139:6,

šapal "under": KI.TA 11 r. 6, 87 r. 4, 98 r. 3, 302 r. 1, KI.[TA 251 r. 2,

šapartu "pledge": *šá-bar-te* 307:7, *šá-par-te* 91:13, 307:7, *šá-par-ti* 81:9, 95:2, 97 r. 5, 295 e. 8, *šá-par-ti]* 180:4, *šá-par-[ti]* 252 r. 8, *šá-pa[r-ti* 317:4, *šá]-par-ti* 146:7, 186 r. 3, [*šá-par-ti* 268:7, *ši-par-ti* 245 r. 2, see also *šapru,*

šapru "pledge": *šap-ri* 272:5, *šap-ri]* 272 r. 2,

šāpiru "administrator": LÚ.*šá-pi-ru* 101:14,

šāqiu "cupbearer": LÚ.KA[Š.LUL] 40 r. 16, LÚ.KAŠ.LUL 12 r. 3, 342 r. 13, LÚ.KAŠ.LU[L] 41 r. 8, LÚ.[KAŠ.LUL] 13 r. 1, 39 r. 9,

šarāpu "to burn": *i-šar-rap* 101 r. 6, 102 r. 9,

šarāqu "to steal": *is-si-riq* 265:4,

šarru "king": LUGAL 27 r. 4, 31 e. 30, r. 4, 29, 42:10, 55:4, 93 e. 9, r. 5, 115:6, 142 e. 13, 155 r. 9, 160 r. 16, 177 r. 20, 180:1, 206 r. 1, 225:1, 235 r. 1, 238:10, 257 r. 36, 287:17, 298 r. 5, 311:8, 315:10, 336:9, 339:4, 345:8, LUGA[L 317:5, LUG[AL 154 s. 3, LU[GAL] 317 r. 9, LU]GAL 121 e. 12, (LUGAL) 95 r. 5, [LUGAL 1 r. 22, MAN 11:9, 24 r. 4, 37:8, 38:4, 50:10, 59:7, 85:8, 88 r. 12, 90 r. 17, 138:10, 142 r. 12, 143:1, 151 r. 12, 152 e. 10, 153 r. 5, 156 r. 8, 167:1, 174 r. 17, 180 r. 2, 201 r. 14, 202 s. 1, 203 r. 4, 210 r. 18, 212 r. 7, 232:2, 233:4, 246 r. 2, 251:5, 6, 266 s. 1, 271:6, 275:13, 279 r. 10, 280 r. 10, 283 r. 4, 301:7, 9, 309:7, 313:8, 314:16, 317 r. 2, 326:16, r. 5, 328:10, 334 r. 3, 335:12, 339:2, 341 r. 2, 343:10, 344:7, 346:2, MAN] 51:5, 324:9, MA]N 130:10, M[AN 349:1, M[AN] 65:10, [MAN 48 s. 2, 57:8, [MAN] 245 r. 16,

šartinnu see *sartinnu,*

šattu "year": MU.12.KÁM 31 r. 29, MU.22.KAM 180 r. 1, MU.22.KÁM 177 r. 19, MU.23 90 r. 16, MU].25.[KÁM] 48 s. 1, MU.AN.NA 174 r. 16, 243:3, 285:3, 287 r. 3, MU.AN.NA] 287 r. 1, MU.AN.N]A 287 r. 2, MU.AN.[NA] 212 r. 6, MU.A]N.NA 287:18, [M]U.AN.NA 162 r. 6, MU.AN.NA.MEŠ 219:12, 223:8, 224 e. 8, 295 e. 9, r. 1, MU.AN.NA].MEŠ 271 r. 4, MU.AN.N[A.MEŠ] 226:13, MU.AN.N]A.MEŠ 65 r. 2, MU.A]N.NA.MEŠ 342:11, M[U.AN.NA.MEŠ] 266 r. 3, M[U.AN.NA].MEŠ 160:14, MU].AN.NA.MEŠ-*šú* 295 r. 3, MU.MEŠ 268:3,

šatû "to drink": *i-šat-ti* 31 r. 30, NAG 96:17, 101 r. 4, 102 r. 6, 201 r. 16, NAG] 20:3,

šazbussu "maintenance": *ša-az-bu-si* 123:6,

ša-epinni "plowman": LÚ.GIŠ.APIN 149:5,

ša-ginēšu "official in charge of the regular offering": *ša—gi-né-šú* 124 r. 4,

ša-huṭāri "staff-bearer": *ša—hu-ṭa-ru* 52 r. 16, LÚ.*ša—hu-ṭa-ri* 244 r. 7,

ša-kubšīšu "hatter": LÚ.*šá*—U.SAG.MEŠ-*šú* 342:4,

ša-muhhi-āli "city overseer": LÚ].*šá*—UGU—URU

86 r. 7, LÚ.*šá*—UGU—URU 31 r. 13, 166:5, 319 r. 7,
ša-muhhi-bētāni "chamberlain": LÚ.*šá*—UGU—É-*a-ni* 42:9, [L]Ú.*šá*—U[G]U—É-*a-ni* 42 r. 11,
ša-muhhi-bēti "overseer of the household": *šá*—UGU—É 63 r. 5, LÚ.*ša*—UGU—É 17:9, r. 11,
ša-muhhi-bēt-ilāni "overseer of the temple": [LÚ.*šá*—UG]U—É—DINGIR.MEŠ 86 r. 13,
ša-muhhi-nīnua "superintendent of Nineveh": LÚ.*šá*—UGU—NINA.KI 338 r. 14,
ša-muhhi-qanāti "overseer of reeds": LÚ.*šá*—UGU—*qa-*(*na*)*-a-te* 35 r. 2,
ša-mutqītišu "candy peddler": LÚ.*šá—mut-qi-ti-šú* 262:4,
ša-pān-dēnāni "president of the court": LÚ.*šá*—IGI—DI.KUD.MEŠ 265:14,
ša-pān-ekalli "palace superintendent": LÚ.*ša*—IGI—[É.GAL] 283 r. 19, LÚ.*šá*—IGI—É.GAL 305:2, LÚ.*šá*]—IGI—É.GAL 328 r. 7,
ša-pēthalli "cavalryman": LÚ.*ša*—BAD.[HAL.MEŠ 25:1, LÚ].BAD.HAL 132:2,
ša-qurbūti "royal bodyguard": *qur*-ZAG 133:5, r. 6, 7, 323 r. 7, *qur*-ZAG] 327 r. 2, 330 r. 5, LÚ.*qur-bu-te* 28 r. 2, LÚ.*qur-bu-*(*te*) 240 r. 5, LÚ].*qur-bu-ti* 253 r. 11, LÚ.*qur-bu-ti* 43:6, LÚ.*qu*[*r-bu-ti*] 19 r. 1, [LÚ].*qur-bu-ti* 116:7, LÚ.*qur-bu-tú* 36 r. 4, 164 r. 6, 221 r. 4, 238 r. 4, LÚ.*qur*-ZAG 44:5, 89 r. 6, 10, 133:6, 185 r. 10, 265 r. 9, 324 r. 8, 325 r. 19, 329 r. 10, LÚ.*šá—qur-*[*bu-ti*] 11 r. 15,
ša-rēši "eunuch": LÚ].SAG 92 r. 9, LÚ.SAG 22 r. 4, 23:6, 27 r. 4, 31 r. 14, 15, 120 r. 3, 152 r. 3, 7, 283 r. 4, 287:13, 309:3, 318 r. 2, LÚ.[SAG] 96 r. 4, L]Ú.SAG 30 r. 2, 318 r. 1, [LÚ].SAG 228:2, LÚ.SAG.MEŠ 96 r. 5,
ša-šēpi "(king's) personal guard": *ša*—GÌR.2 121 r. 10, 164 r. 14, 204 r. 9, 325 r. 20, LÚ.*šá*—GÌR.2 205 r. 1,
ša-šīmi "bought slave": *ša*—LÚ.ŠÁM 52 r. 9,
šēdu "genie": ^{d}ALAD 288 r. 6, ^{d}ALAD.MEŠ 288:21, LÚ.^{d}]ALAD 288:2, LÚ.^{d}ALAD 288:18,
šelappāiu "architect": LÚ.*še-*[*lap-pa-a-a*] 132 e. 13, L]Ú.*še-*[*l*]*ap-pa-a-*[*a*] 195 r. 1, LÚ.*še-la-pa-a-a* 158 r. 3,
šemû see *šamû*,
šēpu "foot": GÌR.2 20 r. 1, 2, 32 r. 5, 42 r. 1, 3, 66 r. 1, 87 r. 3, 92 r. 6, 200 r. 3, 251 r. 1, 253 r. 12, 308 r. 2, 325 r. 5, 326 r. 7, 8, 334 r. 14, 15, GÌR.2] 11 r. 5, 92 r. 5, GÌ[R.2 32 r. 3, see also *ša-šēpi*,
šibšu "straw tax": *še-e*[*b*]*-šú* 95:5, *ši-ib-ši*] 176 s. 1, ŠE.*ši-ib-še* 252 r. 4, ŠE.*ši-ib-še*] 326:3,
šību "witness": IGI 1 r. 10, 11, 12, 13, 14, 2 r. 1, 2, 3, 5 r. 1, 6 r. 9, 10, 11, 13, 14, 8 r. 3, 4, 10 r. 6, 15, 18, 19, 20, 12 r. 1, 2, 3, 4, 13 r. 1, 2, 3, 4, 5, 17 r. 7, 9, 10, 12, 13, 14, 15, 18 r. 2, 3, 4, 19 r. 7, 8, 9, 10, 14, 21 r. 5, 6, 7, 8, 9, 22 r. 2, 3, 4, 5, 6, 7, 8, 9, 10, 23 r. 4, 5, 6, 7, 8, 11, 24 r. 1, 26 e. 9, r. 1, 2, 3, 4, 5, 6, 9, 28 r. 4, 5, 6, 29 r. 4, 5, 6, 30 r. 2, 3, 4, 5, 7, 8, 10, 11, 12, 31 r. 12, 13, 14, 15, 16, 17, 18, 19, 20, 23, 25, 26, 32 r. 9, 10, 12, 13, 14, 15, 33 r. 1, 2, 4, 5, 7, 34 r. 6, 7, 8, 9, 10, 11, 12, 35 e. 7, r. 1, 3, 4, 36:5, 7, e. 8, r. 2, 4, 37 r. 11, 12, 13, 15, 39:4, r. 1, 2, 3, 4, 5, 7, 8, 40 r. 5, 6, 7, 8, 9, 10, 11, 12, 13, 15, 17, 41 r. 5, 7, 9, 10, 12, 13, 14, 15, 19, 42 r. 8, 9, 10, 11, 12, 13, 14, 17, 18, 19, 43:5, 6, 7, 8, 9, 44:4, 5, 6, 7, 45 r. 1, 2, 3, 4, 46 r. 1, 2, 3, 4, 5, 47 e. 7, r. 1, 2, 3, 4, 48 r. 10, 11, 12, 52 r. 8, 9, 10, 11, 53 r. 4, 5, 6, 7, 8, 55 r. 2, 4, 5, 6, 56 s. 1, 2, 57 r. 6, 11, 59 r. 1, 2, 3, 4, 5, 6, 7, 8, 9, 10, 11, 12, 13, 14, 15, 16, 61 r. 1, 2, 63 r. 2, 3, 4, 5, 64:5, e. 6, 66 r. 7, 8, 9, 10, 69:3, 5, 6, r. 1, 73 r. 3, 4, 81 r. 2, 3, 4, 5, 6, 7, 8, 9, 83:5, e. 7, r. 1, 84:5, e. 6, 7, r. 1, 85 r. 7, 8, 9, 10, 11, 86 r. 5, 6, 7, 8, 9, 10, 11, 12, 13, 87 r. 7, 8, 89 r. 6, 7, 8, 9, 10, 11, 12, 13, 14, 90 r. 8, 9, 10, 11, 12, 13, 14, 15, 91 r. 1, 2, 3, 4, 95 r. 6, 7, 8, 96 r. 3, 4, 6, 7, 8, 9, 10, 11, 12, 13, 14, 15, 16, 17, 97 r. 10, 98 r. 7, 8, 9, 100 r. 12, 13, 14, 16, 17, 18, 19, 20, 101 r. 10, 11, 102 r. 12, 13, 14, 15, 16, 104 r. 3, 4, 105 r. 1, 2, 3, 4, 5, 6, 7, 8, 9, 10, s. 2, 106:10, 11, 12, 13, r. 2, 3, 4, 5, 6, 107 r. 1, 2, 3, 4, 5, 108:5, 6, r. 1, 3, 110 r. 7, 8, 9, 10, 11, 12, 111 r. 4, 5, 6, 7, 8, 9, 112 r. 7, 113 r. 3, 4, 5, 116 r. 7, 8, 9, 118 r. 5, 6, 7, 8, 9, 10, 119 r. 11, 12, 13, 14, 15, 16, 17, 18, 19, 120 r. 4, 123 r. 7, 8, 124 r. 3, 4, 5, 6, 7, 8, 9, 10, 11, 12, 13, 125 r. 7, 8, 9, 12, 13, s. 1, 127 r. 3, 5, 11, 128 r. 2, 130 r. 1, 2, 3, 4, 5, 6, 7, 8, 9, 10, 11, 12, 131 r. 6, 7, 8, 10, 14, 133 r. 7, 8, 9, 10, 11, 12, s. 2, 134 r. 6, 7, 8, 9, 10, 11, 12, 13, 135 r. 4, 5, 138 r. 14, 15, 16, 17, 139 r. 1, 2, 3, 4, 5, 140 r. 2, 3, 4, 5, 6, 7, 9, 10, 141 r. 4, 5, 6, 7, 8, 9, 142 r. 12, 13, 14, 15, 16, 17, s. 2, 3, 143 r. 3, 4, 5, 6, s. 1, 145 r. 1, 147 r. 2, 3, 4, 5, 6, 148 r. 2, 150:8, 9, r. 1, 2, 3, 151 r. 6, 8, 9, 152 r. 1, 2, 4, 5, 6, 7, 8, 153 r. 1, 2, 154 r. 10, s. 1, 2, 155 r. 1, 2, 3, 4, 5, 6, 7, 156 r. 2, 3, 4, 5, s. 1, 157 r. 3, 4, 5, 7, 8, 158 r. 1, 2, 3, 4, 5, 6, 159 r. 1, 2, 160 r. 4, 5, 6, 7, 8, 9, 10, 11, 12, 13, 14, 161 r. 10, 11, 12, 13, 14, 15, 16, 17, 162 r. 1, 2, 3, 4, 164 r. 3, 5, 6, 11, 13, 15, 16, 19, 166 r. 2, 3, 4, 5, 6, 7, 8, 167 e. 7, 8, r. 1, 2, 3, 4, 5, 170 r. 1, 2, 3, 4, 173 r. 1, 2, 3, 6, 174 r. 12, 13, 177 r. 1, 3, 4, 5, 6, 7, 8, 9, 10, 11, 13, 14, 15, 178 r. 4, 5, 6, 180 r. 3, 4, 5, 6, 181 r. 3, 4, 5, 6, 182 r. 4, 5, 6, 7, 183 r. 3, 184:5, 6, 7, r. 1, 2, 4, 187 r. 2, 3, 4, 5, 188 r. 2, 3, 4, 7, 8, 9, 189 r. 2, 3, 4, 5, 190:8, 9, r. 1, 2, 3, 4, 192 r. 2, 3, 4, 5, 6, 7, 8, 9, 193 r. 8, 194 r. 5, 6, 7, 8, 9, 10, 11, 12, 13, 14, 15, 195 r. 4, 5, 6, 9, 10, 196 r. 2, 3, 4, 5, 6, 7, 197 r. 2, 3, 4, 5, 6, 7, 198 r. 2, 3, 4, 199 r. 2, 3, 4, 5, 6, 7, 8, 9, 10, 11, 12, 201 r. 5, 6, 7, 8, 9, 10, 11, 12, 202 r. 11, 12, 13, 14, 15, 16, 17, 204 r. 2, 3, 4, 5, 6, 7, 8, 9, 10, 11, 12, 206 r. 4, 5, 9, 207 r. 7, 208 r. 1, 2, 3, 4, 5, 210 r. 5, 6, 7, 9, 10, 11, 12, 13, 14, 15, 214 r. 4, 5, 6, 7, 215 e. 8, 9, r. 1, 2, 3, 4, 5, 216:9, e. 10, 217 r. 9, 10, 11, 12, 14, 15, 218 r. 1, 2, 3, 4, 5, 6, 219 r. 13, s. 1, 220 r. 9, 12, 13, 221 r. 2, 3, 4, 5, 222 r. 2, 3, 4, 223 r. 5, 6, 7, 8, 224 r. 1, 2, 3, 4, 5, 226 r. 3, 4, 5, 6, 7, 8, 9, 10, 227 r. 1, 2, 3, 4, 5, 6, 7, 8, 9, 229 r. 5, 6, 7, 8, 9, 10, 11, 12, 231:5, 232 r. 1, 2, 3, 4, 5, 233:8, 9, r. 1, 234 r. 1, 2, 3, 4, 5, 235 e. 9, r. 1, 2, 3, 4, 236 r. 2, 3, 4, 237 r. 1, 2, 3, 4, 5, 6, 7, 238 r. 1, 2, 3, 5, 6, 7, 8, 9, 239 r. 6, 7, 8, 9, 240 r. 1, 2, 3, 4, 241 r. 5, 6, 243 e. 10, r. 1, 2, 3, 7, 8, 244 r. 2, 3, 4, 5, 6, 8, 11, 245 r. 11, 12, 246 r. 1, 3, 4, 5, 247:7, e. 8, 9, r. 1, 2, 3, 4, 5, 6, 7, 248 e. 11, r. 1, 2, 3, 249 r. 1, 2, 3, 4, 5, 6, 7, 8, 250 r. 7, 8, 9, 10, 252 r. 12, s. 1, 253 r. 8, 254 r. 2, 3, 4, 5, 6, 7, 257 r. 24, 25, 26, 27, 29, 30, 31, 32, 258 r. 1, 2, 3, 4, 5, 259 r. 2, 3, 4, 5, 6, 260 r. 2, 3, 4, 5, 6, 7, 8, 262 r. 1, 2, 3, 4, 5, 6, 263 r. 1, 2, 3, 4, 264 r. 7, 8, 9, 10, 265:13, 14, r. 2, 3, 4, 5, 6, 7, 9, 10, 11, 266 r. 4, 5, 6, 7, 8, 9, 10, 11, 267 r. 1, 2, 3, 4, 268 r. 1, 2, 3, 4, 7, 8, 9, 269 r. 4, 5, 6, 7, 8, 9, 10, 11, 12, s. 1, 3, 270 r. 1, 3, 272:9, r. 6, 273:6, 7, e. 8, r. 1, 2, 3, 274 r. 7, 8, 9, 10, 12, 13,

14, 15, 16, 275 r. 22, 23, 27, s. 1, 3, 277 r. 1, 2, 3, 4, 5, 6, 7, 8, 9, 278 r. 8, 9, 10, 11, 12, 13, 14, 15, 16, 279 r. 1, 2, 3, 4, 5, 6, 280 r. 2, 3, 4, 5, 6, 8, 9, 10, 11, 12, 13, 14, 281:6, 7, 282 r. 1, 283 r. 14, 15, 16, 17, 18, 19, 20, 21, 22, 284 r. 12, 13, 14, 15, 286 r. 1, 2, 3, 4, 5, 6, 7, 8, 9, 10, 287 r. 8, 9, 11, 12, 13, 14, 15, 288 r. 6, 7, 8, 9, 10, 11, 12, 14, 289 r. 11, 291 e. 9, 10, r. 1, 2, 3, 4, 5, 292:2, r. 1, 2, 3, 293 r. 8, 294 r. 2, 3, 4, 5, 6, 296 r. 5, 6, 7, 8, 297 r. 2, 3, 4, 5, 6, 9, 10, 12, 13, 298 r. 6, 7, 8, 9, 299 r. 1, 2, 3, 4, 5, 6, 7, 301 r. 7, 8, 9, 10, 11, 12, 14, 16, 302 r. 13, 303 r. 3, 4, 304 r. 1, 2, 3, 4, 5, 9, 307 r. 1, 2, 3, 4, 5, 6, 308 r. 5, 6, 7, 8, 9, 10, 309 r. 6, 7, 8, 9, 11, 12, 13, 14, 15, 310 r. 6, 7, 8, 9, 10, 11, 12, 14, 15, 16, 311 r. 5, 7, 312 r. 14, 15, 314 r. 8, 9, 10, 11, 16, 17, 18, 19, 20, 21, 22, 23, 24, 28, s. 1, 315 r. 3, 4, 5, 6, 7, 317 e. 12, r. 1, 2, 3, 9, 318 r. 2, 3, 319 r. 5, 6, 7, 8, 9, 10, 11, 12, 13, 14, 15, 320 r. 2, 3, 4, 5, 6, 7, 8, 321 r. 1, 2, 3, 4, 323 r. 3, 4, 5, 6, 7, 8, 9, 10, 324 r. 4, 11, 325 r. 8, 9, 10, 11, 12, 13, 14, 15, 16, 17, 18, 19, 20, 21, 22, 326 r. 14, 15, 16, 17, 18, 20, 21, 22, 23, 327 r. 7, 328 r. 12, 13, 14, 15, 329 r. 8, 9, 11, 12, 13, 15, 16, 17, 18, 19, 20, 330 r. 4, 5, 6, 7, 8, 9, 10, 11, 12, 13, 14, 331 r. 2, 3, 4, 5, 6, 332 r. 6, 7, 8, 9, 10, 11, 12, 13, 14, 334 r. 27, 28, 30, 335 r. 14, 16, 17, 19, 20, 338 r. 7, 8, 12, 13, 339 r. 6, 11, 341 s. 4, 342 r. 11, 12, 13, 14, 15, 348 r. 3, 5, 6, 7, 8, 350 r. 9, 10, IGI] 50 r. 14, 105 s. 1, 119:18, 188 r. 1, 324 r. 7, IG[I 7 r. 10, 8 r. 7, 22 r. 1, 96 r. 2, 104 r. 2, 254 r. 5, 292 r. 5, IG[I] 254 r. 4, IG]I 324 r. 6, 332 r. 12, I[GI 7 r. 9, 11, 12, 55 r. 1, 96 r. 1, 174 r. 15, 305 r. 6, 331 r. 1, I[G]I 42 r. 16, I]GI 224:2, (IGI) 97 r. 9, [IGI 1 r. 13, 14, 16, 18, 6 r. 16, 7 r. 8, 10 r. 7, 8, 9, 10, 11, 11 r. 10, 11, 12, 13, 14, 15, 16, 13 r. 6, 15 r. 7, 8, 9, 16 r. 4, 5, 6, 19 r. 1, 2, 3, 4, 21 r. 11, 24 r. 1, 2, 28 r. 2, 3, 31 r. 22, 23, 32 r. 10, 35 r. 5, 6, 7, 37 r. 7, 8, 9, 39:19, 20, 21, 48 r. 8, 9, 13, 14, 15, 16, 50 r. 11, 12, 13, 14, 52 r. 16, 17, 18, 57 r. 1, 2, 3, 4, 6, 8, 9, 58 r. 8, 61 r. 9, 65 r. 7, 8, 9, 10, 11, 12, 13, 14, 69 r. 2, 86 r. 3, 14, 15, 16, 17, 92 r. 9, 10, 11, 12, 98 r. 10, 11, 99 r. 7, 8, 9, 10, 11, 12, 13, 100 r. 8, 9, 10, 11, 103 r. 1, 2, 3, 4, 5, 6, 7, 105 s. 1, 2, 109 r. 3, 4, 5, 7, 10, 112 r. 3, 4, 6, 8, 9, 10, 11, 114 r. 3, 115 r. 1, 2, 3, 6, 116 r. 1, 2, 119 r. 14, 121 e. 13, 14, 15, r. 3, 4, 5, 10, 11, 122 r. 2, 3, 123 r. 5, 6, 7, 8, 9, 10, 11, 12, 125 r. 6, 126 r. 7, 8, 9, 10, 11, 127 r. 2, 129 r. 1, 2, 135 r. 2, 138 r. 11, 12, 13, 18, 140 r. 1, 11, 144 r. 1, 2, 145 r. 1, 2, 146 r. 5, 6, 7, 147 r. 1, 2, 9, 148 r. 1, 149:1, 2, 3, 4, 5, 6, 163 r. 6, 7, 8, 9, 10, 11, 12, 13, 14, 164 r. 9, 10, 165 r. 6, 7, 8, 9, 166 r. 6, 168 r. 1, 2, 3, 169 r. 7, 13, 14, 171 r. 5, 172 r. 2, 174 r. 8, 10, 176 r. 12, 13, 14, 181 r. 5, 182 r. 3, 185 r. 11, 12, 186 r. 7, 8, 9, 10, 12, s. 1, 187 r. 2, 3, 4, 5, 192 r. 1, 193 r. 3, 4, 5, 6, 194 s. 1, 195 r. 2, 3, 4, 5, 198 r. 5, 6, 7, 200 r. 7, 8, 9, 10, 11, 12, 205 r. 1, 3, 4, 5, 206 r. 6, 7, 209 r. 1, 2, 3, 4, 5, 7, 211 r. 7, 8, 212 r. 2, 3, 4, 5, 220 r. 14, 222 s. 1, 224 r. 2, 3, 5, 225 r. 4, 5, 6, 7, 8, 9, 10, 11, 12, 226 r. 3, 230 r. 7, 231:1, 2, 3, 238 r. 1, 2, 3, 4, 10, 239 r. 3, 4, 5, 240 r. 5, 6, 250 r. 11, 252 r. 13, s. 1, 2, 3, 253 r. 9, 10, 11, 12, 254 r. 8, 255 r. 1, 2, 261 r. 1, 2, 3, 268 r. 11, 269 s. 1, 3, 271 r. 7, 8, 9, 10, 11, 12, 13, 15, 18, 272:10, r. 6, 7, 275 r. 25, 26, s. 1, 2, 276 r. 1, 2, 3, 4, 284 r. 16, 17, 18, 19, s. 1, 285 r. 4, 5, 6, 7, 8, 9, 10, 288 r. 15, 289 r. 8, 9, 10, 12, 293 s. 1, 294 r. 1, 295 r. 6, 300 r. 2, 3, 4, 5, 6, 7, 305 r. 7, 8, 9, 10, 11, 14, 15, 306 r. 5, 6, 7, 8, 9, 10, 309 s. 2, 310 r. 4, 311 r. 1, 2, 3, 4, 312 r. 7, 8, 9, 10, 11, 12, 313 r. 2, 3, 314 r. 12, 13, 14, 15, 26, 27, 28, 315 r. 1, 316 r. 3, 9, 10, 11, 12, 13, 14, 317 r. 6, 7, 318:7, e. 8, 9, r. 1, 321 r. 5, 6, 9, 323 s. 2, 324 r. 5, 6, 7, 8, 9, 10, 327 r. 1, 2, 3, 4, 5, 6, 328 r. 6, 7, 8, 9, 10, 11, 332 r. 3, 4, 334 r. 20, 21, 22, 33, 34, 35, 335 r. 13, 14, 15, 16, 17, 19, 20, 21, 22, 23, 338 r. 10, 11, 13, 14, 15, 16, 17, 339 r. 2, 3, 4, 5, 6, 7, 8, 9, 10, 11, 12, 13, 340 r. 4, 5, 6, 7, 8, 9, 10, 11, 12, 341 s. 3, 342 r. 3, 4, 5, 6, 7, 8, 9, 345 r. 4, 5, 6, 8, 9, 10, 347 r. 8, 14, 348 r. 9, 349 r. 7, 8, 9, 350 r. 2, [IGI] 1 r. 11, 19 r. 5, 21 r. 10, 42 r. 15, 61:16, r. 3, 4, 86 r. 4, 87 r. 10, 11, 88 r. 10, 101 r. 12, 13, 103 r. 8, 104 r. 5, 106 r. 1, 116 r. 3, 4, 5, 6, 12, 120 r. 3, 121 r. 6, 133 r. 10, s. 1, 146 r. 4, 147 r. 3, 4, 5, 151 s. 1, 157 r. 7, 164 r. 7, 171 r. 4, 174 r. 9, 11, 14, 179 r. 4, 5, 7, 8, 9, 185 r. 10, 186 s. 2, 193 r. 10, 199 r. 13, 206 r. 8, 220 r. 11, 12, 13, 221 r. 1, 230 r. 1, 2, 3, 4, 5, 6, 238 s. 1, 251 r. 5, 266 r. 12, 272:9, 275 r. 24, 302 r. 8, 9, 10, 11, 303 r. 1, 310 r. 5, 19, 315 r. 2, 316 r. 4, 5, 7, 8, 320 r. 1, 321 r. 8, 323 s. 1, 324 r. 11, 325 r. 15, 326 r. 19, 327 r. 7, 332 r. 5, 334 r. 25, 32, 338 r. 8, 12, 342 r. 10, 17, 345 r. 7, 347 r. 9, 12, 13, 350 r. 3, [IG]I 2 r. 6, 7 r. 7, 10 r. 12, 13, 14, 15, 16, 19 r. 6, 39:16, 17, 40 r. 4, 52 r. 13, 14, 83:6, 97 r. 10, 11, 120 r. 5, 121 r. 7, 143 s. 2, 146 r. 3, 154 r. 11, 157 r. 6, 163 r. 15, 171 r. 3, 179 r. 3, 6, 203 r. 1, 211 r. 6, 220 r. 10, 231:4, 245 r. 7, 8, 9, 10, 251 r. 6, 7, 8, 9, 10, 265 r. 1, 269 r. 13, 282 r. 2, 283 r. 13, 289 r. 16, 292 s. 3, 297 r. 1, 7, 8, 9, 10, 300 r. 8, 302 r. 5, 6, 7, 309 r. 10, 316 r. 2, 6, 317:8, 9, 10, e. 11, r. 4, 5, 319 r. 15, 323 r. 2, 334 r. 26, 31, 347 r. 10, 11, 350 r. 4, 6, 11, [I]GI 2 r. 5, 7 r. 5, 18 r. 1, 52 r. 12, 61:15, 73 s. 1, 87 r. 9, 125 r. 11, 171 r. 1, 2, 319 r. 16, 334 r. 29, 350 r. 5, 7, 8, [I]G[I 280 r. 1, [I]G[I] 39:18, 347 r. 6, IGI.ME[Š 314 r. 23, IGI.MEŠ 1 r. 17, 12 r. 1, 30 r. 6, 9, 32 r. 11, 96 r. 5, 274 r. 11, 303 r. 2, 311 r. 6, 339 r. 12, IGI].MEŠ 1 r. 15, LÚ.IGI.MEŠ-*e* 105 r. 5,

šiddu "along": *ši-di* 125:5,

šikāru "beer": KAŠ.MEŠ 21:6,

šīmu see *ša-šīmi,*

šinip "two thirds": 2:3 42:5, 124:9,

šinšerāti "twelvefold": 12.A.TA.AN 101 r. 7, 1[2.T]A-*a-a* 102 r. 9, 12.TA-*a*]-*a* 100 r. 6,

šiqlu "shekel": GÍN 23:6, 43:1, 44:1, 47:4, 80:1, 97:6, 108:4, 118:6, 127:7, 133:4, e. 10, 144:4, 172 r. 6, 189:1, 208:1, 240:1, 241 s. 2, 244:6, 272:2, 273:1, 285:4, 293:1, G]ÍN 284 s. 2, [GÍN 196:7, 292:1, GÍN-*šú* 36:4, 234:7, 293 r. 2, GÍN.MEŠ 36:1, 98:7, 104:6, 107:4, 109:7, 113:6, 139:4, 140:2, 150:6, 154 r. 2, 156:1, 160:13, 161:11, 174:5, 201:9, 216:2, 217:13, 227:5, 229:8, 234:1, 235:6, 268:7, 295:7, 345:10, GÍN.[MEŠ 226:12, 236:2, GÍ]N.MEŠ 239:8, [GÍN.MEŠ 286:6,

šīqu "irrigation": *ši-qi* 334 r. 7, 335:9, 336:6, *ši-qi*] 336 r. 1, 9, *ši-q*[*i* 334:3, *ši-*[*qi* 337:4, *ši*]-*qi* 163:4, 336:1,

šû "he": *šu-u* 188 r. 7,

šuātu "that": *šu-a-te* 37:14, 48:8, 89:10, 154 r. 4, 176 r. 2, 177:10, 207:4, 213:4, 244:8, *šu-a-te*] 39:5, *šu-a-t*[*e* 169 r. 2, *šu-a-t*[*e*] 45:8, *šu-a-*[*te*

251:8, 286:8, *šu-a-[te]* 310 r. 13, *šu]-a-te* 347:11, *šu-a-ti* 127:9, 185 r. 5, *šu-a-tu* 14 r. 3, 87:3, 98:9, 125:12, 185:3, 336 r. 2, 10, *šu-a-tu]* 348:4, *šu-a-[tu]* 315:15, *šu-[a-tu* 164:10, *šu-a-tum* 219:8, *šu-a-tú* 6:8, 8:2, 9:1, 15:2, 32:11, 34:11, 42:12, 55:7, 82:3, 85:11, 88:10, 93 r. 7, 96:8, 110:11, 138:12, 144:7, 161 e. 15, 174 r. 1, 201:11, 202:14, 227:7, 228:7, 229:10, 250 e. 12, 253:10, 257:11, 283 r. 6, 289:8, 290:6, 299:3, 301:10, 312:14, *šu-a-tú]* 50:12, 124:10, 246:6, 322:2, *šu-a-[tú]* 17 e. 15, 51:8, *šu]-a-t[ú]* 284:9, *š]u-a-tú* 3:6, 309:9, 313:12, *[šu-a-tú* 217:15, 341 r. 6, *[šu-a-tú]* 102:5, *šu-u-a-te* 56:7, *šú-a-te* 52:12, 305:10, *šú-a-t[e* 49:5, *šú-[a-te* 197:7, *šú-[a-te]* 239:12, *šú]-a-te* 99:11, *šú-a-tu* 346:6, *šú-a]-tu* 345:11, *šú]-a-tu* 19:10, *šú-a-tú* 4:6, 7:7, 10 e. 21, 38:6, 57:10, 118:8, 119 r. 2, 126 e. 12, 142 r. 5, 191 r. 4, 287 r. 5, 306:7, 314:19, 326:21, 329:16, 335 r. 1, 342:8, *šú-a-tú]* 218:9, *šú-a-[tú]* 61:8, *šú-a]-tú* 344:12, *šú]-a-tú* 334 r. 7, UR$_5$-*tú* 130:12, UR$_5$.MEŠ 274:8,

šulmu "(judicial) peace": DI-*mu* 238:8, 288:6,

šumma "if": *šum-ma* 46:5, 63:5, 67:5, 97:5, 143:6, 150:6, 156:6, 214:6, 226 r. 13, 248:8, 276:7, 281:4, 296 e. 8, 323 e. 11, *šum]-ma* 324 r. 3, *[šum-ma* 206:6, 222 e. 6, *[šum-ma]* 282:1, *[šum]-ma* 158:6, 180:8, 208:5, *šúm-ma* 167:5, 234:6, 240:5, *šúm-mu* 21 r. 1, 29 r. 1, 157 e. 8, 181:6, 241 r. 2, 266 s. 1, *šúm-mu]* 243:8, *[šúm-mu]* 182:6, *[šúm-m]u* 242:6, *[šúm]-mu* 221:6, *[šú]m-mu* 241 s. 1, 293 e. 7, r. 4, BE 22 r. 3, BE-*ma* 215:1, 216:6, 232:5, 235:6, 236:6, 272:7, r. 4, [BE-*ma* 318:6,

šunnāia "two each": 2-*a-a* 241:2,

šunu "they": *šú-nu* 25:4, 101:11, *šú-nu]* 25 e. 8,

šunūti "these": *šu-nu-ti* 17:12, *šu-nu-tú* 275 r. 16,

tabriu (a type of field): *tab-ri-ʾu* 93 r. 7, *tab-ri-u* 275 r. 9, *tab-ri-u]* 93 r. 1, *tab-ri-[u]* 275:3, 277:3,

tadānu "to give": *ad-din* 106:4, 7, *id-dan]* 281:3, *[i]d-dan* 42 r. 5, *[i]d-dan-šú-nu* 25 r. 2, *id-dan-u-ni* 265:8, *[i]d-dan-u-ni* 317:7, *id-dan.an* 214:5, *id-din* 156:6, 234:6, 281:4, 324 r. 3, *id-din-nu* 241 r. 2, *[id-din-nu* 243 e. 9, *[id-din-nu]* 242:6, *id-din-nu-ni* 150:6, *id-di-ni* 214:6, *id]-di-nu* 276:7, *id-du-nu* 150:5, 241 r. 3, 242:5, 243:8, *id-du-nu]* 243 e. 9, *id-du-[nu]* 241 r. 1, *it-ti-din* 35:5, 178:5, 265:7, *i[t-ti-din]* 25 r. 3, *[i]t-ti-din* 80:3, *i-dan* 40 r. 1, 63:5, 140:11, 154 r. 9, 167:4, 232:5, 234:5, 235:5, 293 e. 6, *i-dan]* 41 r. 2, *i-[dan]* 275 r. 21, *i-dan-u-ni* 271 r. 6, *i-dan.an* 293 r. 3, *i-da-[an]* 157 e. 7, *i-da-na* 236 e. 7, *i-da-nu-u-ni* 264 r. 5, *i-din* 143:6, 167:5, 215:4, 232:5, 266 s. 2, 282:1, *i-[din]* 208:5, *i-din-nu* 221:6, 222 e. 6, *i-di-na* 293 r. 1, *i-di-ni* 181:6, *i-[d]i-ni* 182:6, *i-di-nu-ni* 186 r. 11, *i-du-nu* 221:5, *i-tan-nu]* 132:8, *i-ti-din* 259:4, 260:4, 293 r. 4, *la—din* 240 e. 6, *ta-ad-[da-ni]* 41:3, *ta-ad-din* 34:10, 41:13, 42:11, 51:7, 85:10, 88:9, 100 r. 2, 102:4, 111 r. 1, 118:7, 127:8, 201:10, 227:7, 274:7, 290:6, 301:10, 306:7, 311:11, 313:11, 329:16, 340:10, 346:5, *ta-ad-din]* 50:11, 269:11, 312:13, *ta-ad-d[in]* 101:19, *ta-ad-[din* 39:5, *ta-ad-[di]n* 315:14, *ta-a]d-din* 339:6, *ta-[ad-din]* 40:11, *ta]-ad-din* 15:2, *[ta-ad-din]* 144:7, *[ta]-ad-din* 98:8, *ta-dan-a-ni* 105:5, *ta-dan-ni* 115:2, *ta-da-an* 245:3, *ta-da-a-ni* 121:3, 227:2, 287:6, 312:3, 313:3, 329:3, 334:3, *ta-da-a-n[i]* 331:3, *ta-da-a-[ni]* 48:2, 275:3, *ta-da-ni* 23:3, 31:4, 61:3, 91:3, 110:2, 138:2, 168:2, 209:4, 210:2, 255:3, 258:2, 280:2, 347:3, *ta-da-ni]* 116:2, 302:2, 332:1, *ta-da]-ni* 128:2, *ta-d[a-ni]* 53:2, 126:3, *ta-[da-ni]* 145:5, *t[a-da-ni]* 34:2, *[ta-da-ni]* 179:2, 330:3, *[t]a-da-[ni]* 321:3, *ta-din* 6:8, 7:7, 14 r. 2, 17 e. 15, 23:7, 27 r. 7, 31 r. 6, 32:10, 37:13, 53:9, 56:7, 57:10, 58:3, 61:8, 87:3, 89:9, 93 r. 6, 96:8, 99:10, 102 r. 4, 103:10, 110:10, 119 r. 1, 123:9, 124:10, 138:12, 140:3, 142 r. 4, 169 r. 1, 174:7, 176 r. 1, 177:9, 185 r. 4, 5, 197:7, 213:3, 217:14, 218:9, 228:7, 229:9, 244:7, 246:6, 250 e. 12, 251:8, 253:9, 257:11, 278:11, 284:8, 305:10, 308:3, 309:9, 319:7, 326:20, 328:12, 341 r. 5, *ta-din]* 10:20, 48:7, 59:10, 82:2, 152:2, 210:12, 239:12, 286:7, 288:21, 349:3, *ta-[din* 33:4, 314:18, *ta-[din]* 55:6, 161 e. 14, 283 r. 5, *ta]-din* 22:11, 130:11, 185:2, 342:8, *t[a-din]* 4:5, 207:3, *t]a-din* 27 r. 8, *[ta-din* 19:10, 45:8, 90:16, 101:6, 299:2, *[ta-din]* 8:1, 125:12, 347:10, *[t]a-din* 49:5, 348:4, *ta-din-ni* 219:7, 289:7, 322:2, 335 e. 16, 336 r. 1, 9, 344:11, *ta-din]-ni* 334 r. 6, *ta-di]n-ni* 109:9, *ta-di-ni* 3:5, 126 e. 11, 275 r. 16, *ta*-SUM-*ni* 154 r. 4, 200:3, SUM 241 s. 1, SUM] 1:2, SU[M] 192:2, [SUM 56 r. 8, SUM-*an* 3:13, 6 r. 2, 4, 17 r. 6, 23 e. 14, 34 r. 2, 37:4, r. 5, 39:13, 46:5, 52:5, r. 6, 61:12, 63:4, 89:2, r. 3, 95 r. 4, 97:4, 127:3, 129:2, 142:5, r. 11, 143:6, 146 r. 1, 152:7, 158:7, 163 r. 4, 169:2, 177 e. 14, 181:5, r. 1, 182:5, e. 8, 197:14, 202 r. 5, 206:5, 6, r. 1, 216:6, 232 e. 7, 233:6, 236:5, r. 5, 238 e. 11, 240:5, 254:10, 257 r. 21, 272:7, r. 4, 283 r. 10, 288 r. 4, 5, 289 r. 5, 305 r. 3, 323 e. 10, 324 r. 3, 342:17, 347 r. 5, SUM-*an]* 14 r. 9, 20 r. 3, 32 r. 2, 6, 306 r. 1, SUM-*a[n]* 208:4, SU[M-*an]* 95 r. 4, S[UM-*an]* 131 r. 2, 210 r. 1, 211 r. 2, S]UM-*an* 349 r. 5, [SUM-*an* 11 r. 8, [SUM-*a]n* 194 r. 2, [S]UM-*an* 272:7, [S]UM-*an]]* 189:5, SUM-*an-ni* 274:2, SUM-*an-u-ni* 180 e. 10, SUM-*an-[u-ni]* 132:9, SUM-*a-ni* 244:2, 261:2, 278:2, SUM-*in* 229:2, SUM-*na* 125:3, 158:5, SUM-*ni* 2 e. 8, 10:2, 12:3, 13:2, 28:2, 30:3, 35:6, 38:5, 40:2, 42:2, 46:5, 52:14, 67:5, 85:3, 88:2, 90:4, 96:2, 97:5, 98:2, 103:2, 109:2, 111:2, 113:3, 118:2, 119:2, 122:2, 123:8, 124:2, 130:2, 132:4, 148:3, 149:1, 153:2, 154:2, 158:6, 163:2, 166:2, 172:2, 173:3, 177:2, 180:8, 191:3, 195:2, 196:2, 197:2, 201:1, 202:3, 204:2, 216:6, 226:2, 228:2, 235:6, 239:3, 252:3, 257:4, 277:4, 297:5, 300:4, 301:3, 305:3, 311:3, 316:2, 319:2, 323 e. 11, 325:12, 328:2, 343:4, SUM-*ni]* 24:3, 32:2, 59:1, 188:2, 248:8, 256:2, 286:2, SUM-*n]i* 120:2, SUM-[*ni]* 45:2, 160:4, SUM]-*ni* 114:2, 157 e. 8, SU[M-*ni]* 161:4, 193:2, 338:4, SU]M-*ni* 320:1, S[UM-*ni]* 50:2, 135:3, S[UM]-*ni* 250:2, [SUM-*ni]* 151:2, 203:5, 217:3, 218:3, 304:3, 309:2, 310:2, 314:3, 345:2, [SUM-*n]i* 187:3, [SU]M-*ni* 202:14, SUM-*nu* 65:3, 222:5, 267:2, 318:5, SUM-[*nu]* 296 e. 7, SU[M-*nu]* 296 e. 8, SU]M-*nu* 318:6, SUM-*nu-ni* 1 r. 8, SUM-*nu]-ni* 65 r. 3, [SUM-*nu-ni]* 307 e. 9, SUM-*nu-u-ni* 259 r. 1, SUM-*u-ni* 81 e. 11, 286 s. 1, SUM-*u-n]i* 186 r. 5, SUM-*u-[ni]* 260 e. 7,

tahūmu "border, territory": *ta-hu-me* 326:5, *ta-hu-[me* 326:4,

talpittu (reading uncert.) "barnyard(?)": *t]al-pi-ta-a-te* 334:31, *tal-pi-te* 200:4, *ta]l-pi-tu* 316:9, *tal-pi-tú* 21:8, 315:2, 332:7, 336:4, *tal-pi-tú]* 316:4, *tal-pi-t[ú]* 315:7,

tamkāru "merchant": DAM.QA[R].M[EŠ] 133 r.

12, LÚ.*tam*-QAR 111 r. 4, LÚ].DAM.QAR 127 r. 2, 246 r. 1, LÚ.DAM.QAR 13 r. 5, 27 r. 6, 42 r. 12, 86 r. 9, 10, 96:7, 105 s. 2, 124:7, 134 r. 9, 10, 166 r. 2, 192 r. 10, 204 r. 12, 210 r. 14, 239 r. 5, 285 r. 5, 309 r. 9, 319 r. 11, LÚ.DAM.QAR] 348 r. 7, LÚ.DAM.Q[AR] 97:1, LÚ.DAM.[QAR] 140 r. 11, 297 r. 10,

tamû "to swear; (D) to administer oath": *ú-ta-me* 238:5,

tamūzu (Tammuz, name of the 4th month): ITI.ŠU 67 r. 1, 68 r. 1, 152:8, 153 r. 3, 166 r. 9, 179 r. 10, 202 r. 8, 240:4, 312 r. 17, 313 r. 4, 329 r. 21, 330 r. 15, [IT]I.ŠU 53 r. 9,

tarammu "corn heap": *ta-ra-m[e* 160 r. 2, [*ta-r*]*a-me* 287 r. 4, ŠE.*ta-ra-me* 146 r. 1, 223 r. 2, ŠE.*ta-ra-mi* 252 r. 11, ŠE.SU$_7$] 226:16,

tarbāṣu "courtyard, pen": *tar-ba-ṣu* 277:4, TÙR 105:7, 124:2, 142:7, 154:3, TÙR-*šú* 42:4,

tarṣu "reach, time of": *tar-iṣ* 257 r. 36, *tar-ṣi* 1 r. 21, 201 r. 14, 202 s. 1, 210 r. 18, 266 s. 1, *ti-ri-ṣi* 203 r. 3,

tašlīšu (reading uncert.) "third man": LÚ.3-*si-šú* 323:6, r. 2, LÚ.[3-*šú* 321 r. 7, 332 r. 3, LÚ.[3-*šú*] 86 r. 16, LÚ.3-*šú* 26 r. 1, 2, 36:7, 42 r. 18, 46 r. 1, 52:2, 57 r. 8, 103:4, 110 r. 9, 142:4, r. 13, 164 r. 11, 192 r. 2, 205 r. 4, 283 r. 15, 287:4, r. 9, 314 r. 9, s. 1, 317 r. 1, 2, 320 r. 1, 324 e. 12, r. 4, 325 r. 15, 329 r. 16, 332 r. 8, 339 r. 2, 340 r. 7, 10, LÚ.3-*šú*] 305 r. 6, 321 r. 9, 334 r. 26, LÚ.3-*š*[*ú* 285 r. 10, LÚ.3-*š*[*ú*] 320 r. 4, LÚ.3-[*šú* 283 r. 17, LÚ.3-[*šú*] 86 r. 15, 193 r. 3, 320 r. 6, 7, 327 r. 5, LÚ.3]-*šú* 334 r. 20, L[Ú.3-*šú* 330 r. 10, L]Ú.3-*šú* 285 r. 8, 9, 306 r. 5, L]Ú.3-[*š*]*ú* 321 r. 4, [LÚ.3-*šú*] 327 r. 6, LÚ.3.U$_5$ 1 r. 12, 44:4, 53 r. 5, 127:6, r. 6, 177 r. 2, 7, 199 r. 6, 210 r. 7, 242:3, 253 r. 8, 294 r. 3, 310 r. 4, 316 r. 8, 324:3,325:4, r. 10, 21, 339 r. 3, 342 r. 3, 345 r. 4, 5, LÚ.3.U$_5$] 243:7, 326 r. 14, 20, 21, 350 r. 3, LÚ.3.[U$_5$ 41 r. 9, LÚ.3.[U$_5$] 185 r. 11, 199 r. 3, 342 r. 4, 5, L[Ú.3.U$_5$] 315 r. 1, [LÚ.3.U$_5$] 350 r. 2, [LÚ.3].U$_5$ 295:5, LÚ.3.U$_5$-*šú* 310 r. 15, 3-*si-šú* 323:9, s. 1, 324 r. 1, 335 r. 14, 16, 3-*s*]*i-šú* 335 r. 17, 3-*šú* 43:5, 9, 324 r. 11,

tašrītu (Tishri, name of the 7th month): ITI.DUL 25 r. 1, 47:5, 103 r. 9, 104 e. 8, 111 r. 10, 143:5, 155 r. 8, 156 r. 6, 172 r. 3, 189 e. 6, 262:6, 277 r. 11, ITI.D[UL 237 r. 8, I[TI.DUL 293 r. 6, [ITI].DUL 120 r. 6, 204 r. 13, [IT]I.DUL 208:4, 263:6, 292 s. 1, [I]TI.DUL 122 r. 4, ITI.DU$_6$ 37 r. 16, 72 r. 3, 97:4, 157 r. 9, 241 r. 3, 273:4,

tibnu "straw": ŠE.IN.NU-*šú* 287 r. 6,

tidintu "gift": *ti-din-tú* 269:6,

tillu "tell": DU$_6$ 14:5, D]U$_6$ 194 s. 4,

tillutu "vine": *til-lit* 37:5, 253:6, 332:3, 5, 334:31, *til-lit-te* 188:3, *til-li-te* 186:1, [*til-li-te* 186 r. 6, GI]Š.*til-lit* 330:5, GIŠ.*til-lit* 50:3, 97:7, 201:2, 314:4, 6, 326:7, 20, 329:5, 333:2, 334:24, 336:1, 6, GIŠ.*til-lit*] 314:8, GIŠ.*til-l*[*it* 331:5, GIŠ.*til-*[*lit* 326:7, GIŠ.*t*[*il-lit* 112:5, GIŠ.[*til-lit* 336:2, GIŠ.*til-lit-te* 120:3, [GIŠ.*til-lit-te* 120:2, GIŠ.*til-lit-ti* 202:4, GIŠ.*til-lit-*[*ti*] 202:3, GIŠ.*til-lit*.MEŠ 314:12,

titurru "bridge": *ti-tu-ri* 204:4,

tuāru "to turn; revocation": *i-tu-ra* 238:4, 264 r. 6, *t*[*u*]*-a-ri* 274:9, *tu-a-ru* 6:10, 7:8, 14 r. 3, 15:3, 17 r. 2, 23:9, 27 r. 8, 31 r. 6, 32:12, 34:12, 37:15, 40:13, 41 e. 15, 42:13, 48:9, 50 r. 1, 51:10, 52:14, 61:9, 82:4, 85:12, 87:4, 88:12, 89:11, 90:17, 93 r. 8, 96:9, 98:10, 101:8, 110:12, 111 r. 2, 118:9, 119 r. 3, 123:11, 130:13, 138:14, 142 r. 6, 144:8, 152:3, 161 e. 16, 174 r. 2, 207:5, 210:13, 213:5, 219:9, 229:11, 244:9, 250 e. 14, 251:9, 253:11, 257:12, 283 r. 6, 311:12, 312:15, 319:8, 322:3, 329:17, 334 r. 8, 335 r. 1, 336 r. 3, 340:2, 346:7, *tu-a-ru*] 55:7, 58:4, 164:11, 298:1, 308:3, 348:5, *tu-a-r*[*u* 218:10, *tu-a-r*]*u* 57:11, *tu-a-*[*ru* 124:11, *tu-a-*[*ru*] 126 r. 1, *tu-a*]*-ru* 313:13, *tu-*[*a-ru* 39:6, *tu-*[*a-ru*] 10 e. 21, *tu*]*-a-ru* 309:10, 341 r. 6, *t*[*u-a-ru* 288:22, *t*[*u-a*]*-ru* 275 r. 18, [*tu-a-ru* 4:6, 19:11, 22:12, 100:12, 163 r. 1, 185:4, 198:1, 284:10, 342:9, 344:13, [*tu-a-ru*] 33:5, 99:12, 299:3, [*tu-a-r*]*u* 3:7, 301:11, 347:12, [*tu-a*]*-ru* 53:11, 127:10, 254:1, [*tu*]*-a-ru* 8:3, 9:2, 38:7, 169 r. 3, [*t*]*u-a-ru* 103:11, *tu-u-a-ru* 56:8, *tú-a-ru* 154 r. 6, 201:12, 202 e. 15, 227:8, 228:8, 246:7, 278:12, 305:11, 306:8, 314:20, *tú-a-*[*ru*] 326:21, *tú-a*]*-ru* 328:13, *tú-*[*a-ru* 49:6, [*t*]*ú-a-ru* 102:5, *u*-GUR 289 r. 2, *ú-tar* 32 r. 8, *ú-*[*tar*] 225 r. 1, *ú*]*-tar-ra* 349 r. 6, *ú-ta-a-ra* 194 r. 4, *ú-ta-ra* 40 r. 2, 86 r. 1, 106:9, 110 r. 4, 298 r. 3, *ú-ta-r*[*a*] 335 r. 11, *ú-t*[*a-ra*] 6 r. 5, *ú-*[*ta-ra*] 8 e. 9, 193 r. 2, [*ú-ta-ra*] 41 r. 3, [*ú-ta*]*-ra* 310 r. 3, *ú*-GUR 48 r. 4, 308 r. 3, *ú*-GU[R] 211 r. 3, *ú*-[GUR] 126 r. 5, 210 r. 2, *ú*-GUR-*r*[*a*] 151 r. 4, GUR 50 r. 9, 90 r. 6, 140:12, 164 r. 2, 165 r. 4, 198:6, 202 r. 6, 220 r. 7, 250 r. 5, 253 r. 7, 254 r. 1, 289:9, 290:7, 309 r. 4, 328 r. 5, 340 r. 2, GUR] 10 r. 4, 20 r. 4, 27 r. 11, 96:20, 112 r. 1, 113 r. 1, 124 r. 1, 169 r. 5, 179 r. 1, 274 r. 5, 284 r. 8, 332 r. 1, 345 r. 1, GU[R 130 e. 17, [GUR 134 r. 2, 239 r. 2, 246:15, 334 r. 19, 346 r. 8, [GUR] 131 r. 4, GUR-*ár* 3:14, 301 r. 5, GUR-*ra* 11 r. 8, 15 r. 5, 16 r. 2, 23 r. 2, 31 r. 11, 34 r. 4, 39:14, 42 r. 6, 53 r. 2, 85 r. 3, 87 r. 5, 92 r. 2, 98 r. 5, 101 r. 8, 102 r. 10, 118 r. 4, 138 r. 9, 161 r. 8, 201 r. 3, 219 r. 10, 229 r. 3, 278 r. 6, 283 r. 11, 299:14, 325 r. 6, 329 r. 6, 348 r. 1, GUR-*ra*] 93 r. 12, 119 r. 9, 141 r. 1, 302 r. 3, 314 r. 6, 319 r. 3, 330 r. 2, GUR-*r*[*a* 269 r. 1, GU[R-*ra*] 51 r. 8, GU]R-*ra* 326 r. 11, GU]R-[*r*]*a* 212:7, G[UR-*ra*] 7 r. 2, 123 r. 4, 342 r. 1, [GUR-*ra* 99 r. 5, [GUR-*ra*] 100 r. 6, 174 r. 6, 176 r. 9, 238 e. 12, [GUR]-*ra* 338 r. 7, 339 e. 12, [G]UR-*ra* 58 r. 6, [GUR-*r*]*a* 9:8,

turtānu "commander-in-chief": LÚ.*tur-tan* 29 r. 7, 89 r. 16, 107 e. 7, 169 r. 16, LÚ.*tur-*[*tan* 24:8, L[Ú.*tur-ta*]*n* 338 r. 9, LÚ.*tur-tan-nu* 70 r. 3, 166 r. 10, [LÚ.*tur-t*]*a-a-nu* 168 r. 6, LÚ.*tur-ta-ni* 86 r. 16, LÚ.*tur-t*[*a-ni*] 22:3, LÚ.*t*]*ur-ta-ni* 1:7, LÚ.*tur-ta-nu* 96 r. 10, 163 r. 18, LÚ.*tur-ta-*[*nu*] 161 r. 19, 164 r. 17, LÚ.*tur-t*[*a-nu*] 256 r. 2, LÚ.*tur-*[*ta-nu*] 1 r. 20, [L]Ú.*tur-ta-*[*nu*] 325 r. 23,

ṭābihu "butcher": LÚ.GÍR.LÁ 6 r. 9, 10,

ṭēhi (reading uncert.) "adjoining": SUHUR 10:4, 5, 6, 7, 9, 10, 12, 14, 15, 11:1, 2, 3, 4, 6, 7, 14, 12:5, 7, 9, 10, 11, 13:3, 4, 5, 14:1, 2, 3, 4, 7, 8, 16:3, 17:8, 9, 27:1, 2, 3, 4, 5, 7, 8, 10, e. 12, 13, 28:3, 4, 30:7, 31:6, 8, 9, 10, 11, 12, 14, 15, 18, 20, 22, 23, 24, e. 26, r. 1, 2, 32:3, 5, 6, 7, 93:2, 3, 6, 7, e. 11, 97 e. 8, 9, r. 1, 99:5, 119:4, 5, 7, 8, 10, 11, 12, 14, 124:4, 5, 6, 125:5, 6, 7, 8, 142:8, 9, 10, 155:5, 6, 159:5, 160:7, 8, 9, 10, 11, 161:6, 7, 8, 9, 169:3, 8, 176:2, 3, 4, 6, 7, 186:6, 194:7, 201:3, 4, 5, 6, 202:6, 7, 8, 204:5, 6, 7, 210:6, 7, 211:3, 5, 217:9, 10, 218:6, 226:6, 7, 8, 245:8, 9, 252:5, 6, 268:4, 5, 6, 271:3, 4, 7, 11, 18, 275:6, 8, 9, 10, 11, 12, 13, 14, 15, 16, 17, e. 20, 21, r. 1, 7, 8, 9, 10, 277:5, 278:5, 6, 7, 8, 283:1, 3, 4, 5, 10, 14, 15, 287:9, 10, 11, 12, s. 1, 288:5, 10, 12, 16, 314:5, 320:2, 4, 7, 321:5, 6,

7, 9, 326:4, 5, 6, 328:5, 6, 7, 8, 329:9, 10, 11, 331:7, 332:3, 4, 5, 6, 7, 334:4, 6, 8, 17, 18, 19, 20, 24, 25, 335:2, 3, 4, 6, 7, SUHUR] 11:1, 93 e. 11, 271:14, 321:9, SUHU[R 275:7, SUHU]R 11:8, SUH[UR 251:2, SUH]UR 11:12, 13:7, 126:6, 251:2, 271:4, 334:23, SU[HUR 27:9, 186:5, 283:5, SU[HUR] 11:5, S[UHUR 332:6, S]UHUR 271 e. 21, 321:4, [SUHUR 10:13, 15, 11:5, 13:8, 27:6, e. 11, 31:10, 65:5, 93:5, 6, e. 8, 119:6, 126:5, 7, 146:5, 6, 159:6, 169:6, 188:5, 6, 194:10, 200:6, 7, 252:7, 271:13, 15, 16, 18, 275 e. 19, 283:2, 288:5, 320:5, 6, 332:8, 334:15, 19, 20, 335:3, [SUHUR] 10:11, 13:7, 16:1, 27:10, 28:4, 30:8, 31 e. 27, 194:9, 302:7, 8, 331:8, 338:6, [SUHU]R 10:8, 10, 13:5, 218:5, 275 r. 11, [SUH]UR 10:7, 9, 12, 13:6, 24:7, 27:9, 245:6, 271:5, 8, 9, [SU]HUR 24:5, 6, 194:8, 211:2, [S]UHUR 245:7, SUHUR.MEŠ 176:8, see also *gabdi*,

ṭuppu "tablet": *ṭup-pi* 17 r. 16, 18 r. 5, 30 r. 12, 100 r. 21, 105 r. 11, 121 r. 8, 135 r. 5, 173 r. 7, 294 r. 7, 302 r. 14, [*ṭup-pi*] 96 r. 17, 164 r. 20, DUB.IM 23 r. 12, IM 13 r. 6, 34 r. 13, 41 r. 20, 114 r. 3, 159 r. 3, 212 r. 5, 257 r. 33, 265 r. 7, IM] 1 r. 18, 59 r. 16, [IM] 40 r. 19,

ṭupšar ekalli "palace scribe": LÚ.A.BA—É.GAL 86 r. 11, LÚ.A.B]A—KUR 334 r. 34,

ṭupšarru "scribe, secretary": A.BA 63 r. 4, 64 r. 2, 73 s. 2, 95 r. 8, 148 r. 2, 163 r. 15, 252 s. 3, 310 r. 19, A.B]A 138 r. 18, A.[BA 59 r. 16, LÚ].A.BA 57 r. 1, 115 r. 6, 328 r. 6, LÚ.A.BA 1 r. 18, 10 r. 18, 12 r. 4, 13 r. 6, 17 r. 16, 18 r. 5, 22 r. 10, 26 r. 9, 28 r. 10, 29 r. 6, 31 r. 4, 12, 16, 26, 32 r. 15, 34 r. 6, 13, 37 r. 15, 39:18, 20, 40 r. 6, 7, 8, 10, 11, 19, 41 r. 20, 42 r. 17, 43:7, 44:5, 45 r. 5, 52 r. 18, 57 r. 7, 65 r. 13, 80:5, 81 r. 2, 86 r. 8, 89 r. 9, 90 r. 8, 15, 91 r. 4, 96 r. 15, 105 r. 10, 109 r. 4, 10, 119 r. 21, 122 r. 3, 123 r. 10, 11, 124 r. 11, 13, 125 s. 2, 127 r. 3, 9, 134 r. 13, 141 s. 1, 142:11, 143 r. 7, 145 r. 2, 147 r. 9, 151 s. 1, 160 r. 14, 161 r. 17, 163 r. 7, 13, 173:2, r. 7, 174 r. 15, 177 r. 12, 14, 15, 180 r. 7, 193 r. 10, 195 r. 6, 201 r. 12, 202:2, 208 r. 6, 209 r. 3, 4, 5, 210 r. 5, 6, 12, 227 r. 9, 235 r. 4, 243 r. 4, 244 r. 11, 247 e. 8, 253:7, r. 10, 255 r. 1, 2, 257 r. 32, 264 r. 7, 265:13, r. 2, 7, 11, 267 r. 4, 272:10, r. 7, 278 r. 17, 282 r. 2, 283 r. 23, 285 r. 4, 287 r. 12, 15, 289 r. 16, 301 r. 16, 305 r. 15, 309 s. 2, 311 r. 7, 315 r. 7, 316 r. 14, 317 r. 9, 319 r. 16, 323:5, 324:2, 325:2, 329:2, r. 20, 331:2, 334:19, 345 r. 7, LÚ.A.BA] 162 r. 4, 194 s. 1, 302 r. 13, 304 r. 9, LÚ.A.B[A 310 r. 14, LÚ.A.B[A] 84 r. 1, 96 r. 17, 128 r. 2, 248 r. 3, 310 r. 12, LÚ.A.B]A 39 r. 2, 246 r. 5, LÚ.A.[BA] 100 r. 20, 137 r. 5, 172 r. 2, 243 r. 1, 331:1, LÚ.A].BA 39:21, r. 3, LÚ.[A.BA 314 r. 24, LÚ.[A.BA] 55 r. 6, 140 r. 10, 266 r. 10, L[Ú].A.[BA] 159 r. 2, L[Ú.A.BA] 239 r. 9, 331 r. 6, L[Ú.A.B]A 271 r. 18, L]Ú.A.BA 39:19, 118 r. 10, 269 s. 1, 324:11, [LÚ].A.BA 53 r. 11, [LÚ.A.BA] 61 r. 10, 218 r. 6, 249 r. 8, 266 r. 11, 314 s. 1, 330:2, r. 14, [L]Ú.A.BA 121 r. 8, LÚ.DUB.SAR 31 r. 14,

u "and": *u* 11 r. 2, 91:13, 98:11, 102 r. 2, 142 r. 6, 9, 201:19, 238:10, 246:12, 283:13, 15, 287:12, 295:2, 317:3, 328 e. 14, 15, 16, 17, r. 1, 347 r. 2, [*u* 212:5, 328 r. 2, *ú* 334:13, *ù* 32:16, 38 r. 6, 7, 40:20, 42:15, 82:11, 96:15, 100:7, 101:3, 17, 161 r. 5, 176 s. 1, 210 e. 18, 217 r. 3, 219 r. 6, 251:13, 14, 253:12, 254:3, 6, 257 r. 19, 265:10, 281:1, 288 r. 1, 299:10, 301:18, 314:13, 319:13, 325 r. 1, 326:23, 336 r. 7, 342:15, 349 r. 2, [*ù* 38 r. 6, 7, 100:21, 220 r. 3, [*ù*] 305 r. 1,

ubālu "to bring": *ub-bu-lu* 288:15, *ú-ba-la* 156:5,

ugāru "field": *ú-gar-ru* 173:4, A.QAR 210:4, A.QAR.MEŠ 65:7,

ulādu "to give birth": *ú-lu-du* 323 e. 11, 324 r. 4,

ūmâ "now": *ú-ma-a* 100 r. 5,

ummi šarri "queen mother": AMA—LUGAL 252 r. 7, AMA—MAN 253 r. 8, 255:2, AMA—[MAN] 325:2, MÍ.AMA—LUGAL 253:7, MÍ.AMA—MAN 143:2,

ummu "mother; side road(?)": *um-me* 24:5, 27 e. 12, 211:2, 271:8, *um-mi* 31 e. 27, 28, AMA 10:5, 10, 11:4, 6, 13, 12:8, 13:8, 27:10, 226:6, AMA] 271:13, A]MA 10:13, [AMA]-*šu* 313:5, AMA-*šu-nu* 343:7, AMA-*šú* 90:5, 91:6, 7, AMA-*šú-nu* 315:6, AMA-*šú-nu*] 316:7, [AM]A-*šú-nu* 344:4, MÍ.AMA 288:21, MÍ.AMA-*šú* 53:3, 110:3,

ūmu "day": U[D 259 s. 2, UD-*me* 3:8, 6 r. 7, 48 r. 6, 61:13, 81 e. 11, 85 r. 5, 97 r. 6, 100:13, 102:8, 103:12, 174 r. 3, 4, 180 e. 9, 219:11, 259 e. 6, 260 e. 7, 272:6, r. 3, 301 r. 5, 306 r. 3, UD-*me*] 164:13, 266 r. 2, UD-*m*[*e*] 48 r. 7, [UD-*me*] 101:9, UD-*me*-10.[KAM] 126 r. 13, UD-*mu* 65 r. 3, 89 r. 4, 123:13, 295 r. 3, 307 e. 9, [UD-*mu* 271 r. 6, UD-*mu*.MEŠ 201 r. 15, UD-*mu*-16.KÁM 110 r. 13, U[D-*x* 256 r. 1, UD-*x*]*x* 137 r. 6, UD-*x*-KAM 106 r. 7, 149:8, 270 s. 1, 276 r. 5, 328 r. 16, UD-*x*-KAM] 159 r. 3, 218 r. 7, 302 r. 14, UD-*x*-K]AM 115 r. 4, 183 r. 1, 280 r. 15, UD-[*x*-KAM] 131 r. 11, 151 r. 10, 153 r. 3, [UD-*x*-KAM 141 s. 2, 162 r. 5, [UD-*x*-KAM] 41 r. 16, 279 r. 7, UD-*x*-KÁM 173 r. 4, 243:8, UD-*x*-KÁM] 168 r. 4, UD-*x*]-KÁM 13 r. 7, 129 r. 3, 146 r. 8, UD-[*x*-KÁM] 74 r. 1, 309 r. 16, U[D-*x*]-KÁM 104 e. 8, [UD-*x*-KÁM 217 r. 16, [UD-*x*-KÁM] 96 r. 18, 179 r. 10, UD-*x*]4.KÁM 317 r. 8, UD.MEŠ 61:14, 85 r. 6, 89 r. 5, 134 r. 4, 5, 156:5, 185:6, 289 r. 7, 306 r. 4, 334 r. 17, 18, 342:10, UD.MEŠ] 305 r. 4, UD.[MEŠ] 284 r. 6, U]D.MEŠ 186 r. 4, [UD.MEŠ] 305 r. 5, UD.MEŠ-*te* 6 r. 8, UD.[MEŠ-*te* 301 r. 6, U]D.1 296 r. 3, UD.1.KAM 81 r. 9, 232:4, 241 e. 7, 242:4, 267 r. 5, U]D.1.KAM 316 r. 15, UD.1.KÁM 37 r. 16, 60 r. 1, 90 r. 16, 145 r. 3, 157:6, 166 r. 9, 216:7, 227 r. 10, 229 s. 1, 234:5, 268 r. 10, 273:4, 275 s. 2, 283 r. 23, 287 r. 16, 297 r. 11, 303 r. 5, 311 r. 8, 315 r. 8, UD.1.[KÁM] 33 r. 8, UD].1.KÁM 291:6, UD.2.KÁM 53 r. 9, 148 r. 3, U D.2.KÁ[M] 107:5, UD.3.KAM 331 r. 7, UD.3.KÁM 6 s. 1, 63 e. 7, 158 r. 7, 208 e. 7, 289 r. 13, UD.3.[KÁM] 5 r. 2, UD].3.KÁM 271 r. 16, UD.4.KAM 47:5, UD.4.KÁM 17 r. 17, 144 r. 3, 240 r. 7, 245 r. 13, UD.5 189 e. 6, UD.5.KAM 232 r. 6, 244 r. 9, UD.5.KÁM 61 r. 5, 128 r. 3, 197 r. 8, UD.6.KAM 23 r. 9, UD].6.KA[M] 21 r. 12, UD.6.KÁM 225 r. 13, 260 s. 2, UD].6.KÁM 69 r. 3, UD.7.KAM 127 r. 8, 255 r. 3, UD].7.KAM 109 r. 8, U]D.7.KAM 186 r. 13, UD.7.KÁM 98 r. 12, 160 r. 15, 161 r. 18, 178 r. 2, 243 r. 5, 272:11, r. 8, UD.7.[KÁM] 190 r. 5, UD.8.KAM 177 r. 16, UD.8.KÁM 105 r. 11, UD].8.KÁM 175 r. 1, UD.9.KAM 164 r. 18, UD.9.KÁM 85 r. 12, 97 r. 8, UD.9.K[ÁM 2 r. 7, UD.10-[*x*-KÁM] 78 r. 6, UD.10.KAM 215:6, UD.10.KÁM 42 r. 20, 43:10, 76 r. 1, 83 r. 2, 84 r. 2, 119 r. 19, 236 r. 1, 248:10, 257 r. 34, 265 r. 8, 314 r. 25, 319 r. 17, UD.10.KÁ]M 44 r. 1, UD.10.K[ÁM] 307 r. 7, UD.10.[KÁM] 100 r. 21, UD.11.KAM 191 r. 2, 214 r. 2, UD.11.KÁM 252 s. 3, UD.11.

KÁM] 237 r. 8, UD.12.KAM 223 r. 9, UD.12.KÁM 36 r. 5, 103 r. 9, 169 r. 15, 193 r. 11, 226 r. 2, UD.12.[KÁM 226 r. 11, UD].12.KÁM 139:7, UD.13.KÁM 31 r. 27, 194 s. 2, 204 r. 13, UD.14.KAM 59 r. 17, 241 r. 3, UD.14.KÁM 147 r. 7, 196 r. 8, UD.15.KAM 30 r. 13, 163 r. 16, UD.15.KÁM 123 r. 13, 134 r. 14, 152:8, 155 r. 8, 206 r. 2, UD.15.K[ÁM] 32 r. 16, UD].15.KÁM 132 s. 1, UD.16.KAM 142 s. 1, UD.16.KÁM 10 r. 17, 170:5, 171:2, 259 r. 7, 310 r. 17, UD.17.KAM 29 r. 8, 274 r. 17, UD.17.KÁM 22 r. 11, 269 s. 2, 320 r. 9, UD.18.KAM 89 r. 15, 156 r. 6, UD.18.KÁM 62 r. 1, 122 r. 4, 202 r. 8, UD].18.KÁM 130 r. 13, UD.19.KÁM 18 r. 6, UD.2[*x*-KAM] 116 r. 10, UD.20.[KAM] 138 r. 19, UD.20.KÁM 34 r. 14, 157 r. 9, 167 r. 6, 174 s. 1, 236 r. 5, 240:4, 301 r. 18, 312 r. 17, UD.20.[KÁM] 304 r. 6, [UD.2]0.KÁM 313 r. 5, UD.21 263:6, UD.21.KAM 26 r. 6, UD.21.KÁM 46:7, 63:4, 73 r. 1, 75 r. 4, 124 r. 14, 262:6, 281:5, 342 r. 16, UD.21.K[ÁM 207 s. 1, UD].21.KÁM 305 r. 12, UD.22 154 s. 3, UD.22.KAM 24 r. 3, 120 r. 6, UD.22.KÁM 88 r. 11, 261 r. 4, 294 r. 8, 318 r. 4, UD.23 68 r. 1, UD].23.KAM 65 r. 5, UD.23.K[ÁM] 292 s. 1, UD].23.KÁM 293 r. 6, UD.24.KAM 210 r. 16, UD.24.KÁM 133 s. 3, UD.24.[KÁM] 187 r. 6, UD.25 181 r. 2, UD.25.KAM 45 r. 5, 113 r. 6, 180 r. 1, 325 r. 23, UD.25.[KAM] 239 r. 10, UD.25.KÁM 108 r. 2, 150 r. 4, 172 r. 3, 188 r. 5, 195 r. 7, 212 r. 6, 278 r. 18, UD.25.[KÁM] 77:9, UD].25.KÁM 182 r. 1, UD.26.KAM 1 r. 19, 330 r. 15, UD.26.KÁM 19 r. 12, 282:3, 329 r. 21, UD.26.K[ÁM] 284 r. 21, UD.27.KAM 125 r. 15, UD.27.KÁM 71 r. 1, 91 r. 5, 114 r. 1, 264 s. 1, UD.28.KAM 300 r. 9, UD.28.KÁM 28 r. 8, 201 r. 13, 258 r. 6, 327 r. 8, UD.29.KÁM 70 r. 1, 135 r. 6, 143 r. 1, 234 r. 6, 235:8, UD.30.KAM 35 r. 8, UD.30.KÁM 118 r. 11, UD].30.KÁM 288 r. 21, 2.KÁM 121 r. 9, 5.KÁM 212 r. 6, 20.[KAM 162 r. 6, 25.KÁM 323 r. 1,

unūtu "utensils, equipment": *a-nu-tú* 133:4, *a-nu-u-ti* 275 r. 13,

unzarhu "domestic slave": *un-zar₄-hi* 283 e. 20, 21,

uppu "paid (mng. uncert.)": *u*]*p-pu* 164:10,

urda ekalli "palace servant": LÚ.ARAD—É.GAL 27:5,

urdu "servant, subject": ARAD 30 r. 7, 8, 31:12, r. 25, 42 r. 11, 55:2, 85 r. 7, 96 r. 7, 10, 12, 13, 193:2, 201 r. 8, 257:7, 265:2, 284 r. 14, 289 r. 10, 304:2, 305:10, 306:7, AR[AD 116 r. 6, ARAD-*su-nu*] 132:5, ARAD-*šu* 132:10, 227:3, 301:5, ARAD-*šú* 118:3, 174:2, 196:3, 219:1, 244:3, 265:9, 267:3, 274:3, 289:3, 290:3, 305:4, 345:3, ARAD-[*šú* 89:3, ARAD]-*šú* 306:1, [ARAD-*šú*] 246:2, ARAD-*šú-nu* 257:5, ARAD-*šú-n*[*u*] 347:4, AR]AD-*šú-nu* 56:1, ARAD.MEŠ 31 r. 24, 39:1, 50:6, 51:1, 90:3, 109:4, 110:6, 130:7, 265:3, 284:3, ARAD.MEŠ] 112:3, 138:6, 266:8, 294:3, ARAD.[MEŠ 54:4, AR[AD.MEŠ 33 r. 6, AR]AD.MEŠ 40:6, 229:2, [ARAD.MEŠ 41:7, 343:8, [ARAD.M]EŠ 313:6, ARAD.MEŠ-*ni* 85:5, 257:3, ARAD.MEŠ]-*ni* 86:5, [ARAD.M]EŠ-*ni* 38:1, ARAD.ME[Š-*šú*] 116:5, ARAD.MEŠ-*šú* 57:2, 4, 229:5, LÚ.ARAD 6 r. 12, 15, 28 r. 4, 29 r. 7, 31 r. 18, 19, 20, 22, 39 r. 7, 40 r. 17, 52 r. 17, 140 r. 8, 191 r. 1, 199 r. 8, 301 r. 14, LÚ.ARAD] 342 r. 12, LÚ.AR[AD 121 r. 11, LÚ.ARAD-*šú* 5:2, 7:3, 127:4, 309:4, [LÚ.ARAD]-*šú* 305:2, LÚ.ARAD-*šú-nu* 300:5, LÚ].ARAD.MEŠ 53:4, LÚ.ARAD.MEŠ 1 r. 17, 6:3, 90:10, 111:7, 297:8, 319:4, 341 r. 1, LÚ.[ARAD.MEŠ] 344:4, LÚ.ARAD.ME[Š-*ni*] 195:4, LÚ.ARAD.MEŠ-*ni* 96:4, [LÚ.ARAD.MEŠ]-*ni* 317:3, LÚ.ARAD.MEŠ-*šú* 317:7,

urhu "month": ITI 21:7, r. 3, 47:4, 184 r. 3, 215:1, 288 r. 3, ITI-*šu* 150:7, ITI-*šú* 97:6, 107:4, 108:4, 139:5, 235:7, IT]I-*šú* 104:6,

urki "after": EGIR 21 r. 3, 101:9, 123:13, 134 r. 5, 185:6, 186 r. 4, 259 s. 1, 260 s. 1, 286 r. 11, [EGIR 287 r. 3, [EGI]R 221 s. 1,

urkīu "successor": EGIR-*šú* 82:11, 96:15,

urkiš "in the future": *ur-kiš* 3:8, 6:12, 7:9, 8:4, 9:3, 14 r. 4, 17 r. 3, 22:12, 27 r. 9, 31 r. 6, 32:13, 34:13, 37:16, 40:14, 42:14, 50 r. 2, 52 r. 1, 55:9, 56 e. 10, 82:5, 85:14, 87:5, 88:13, 96:10, 98:11, 106:2, 110:13, 119 r. 5, 125 r. 2, 127:11, 138 e. 15, 140:5, 142 r. 7, 152:4, 161 r. 1, 163 r. 2, 176 r. 3, 177:11, 185:5, 201:13, 213 r. 1, 219 r. 1, 246:8, 251:10, 253:12, 257:13, 278:14, 283 r. 7, 288:23, 289:10, 298:3, 305:12, 306:9, 308:5, 311:13, 314:21, 319:9, 322:4, 326:22, 328 e. 14, 329:18, 334 r. 9, 338 r. 1, 341 r. 8, 344:14, 346:8, 347 r. 2, *ur-kiš*] 57:12, 90 r. 1, 92:6, 124:12, 284:11, 299:4, 301:12, 313:14, 340:3, *ur-ki*[*š*] 15:4, 342:11, *ur-ki*]*š* 19:12, 130:14, 312:16, *ur-k*[*iš*] 48:11, 339:7, *ur-*[*kiš* 20:1, 51 e. 12, 274:10, 348:7, *ur-*[*kiš*] 210:14, 227:9, 254:2, *ur-*[*k*]*iš* 38 r. 1, *ur*]*-kiš* 169 r. 4, 202 r. 1, 228:10, *u*[*r-kiš* 212:1, *u*[*r-kiš*] 39:7, 61:10, *u*[*r-ki*]*š* 91:13, *u*[*r*]*-kiš* 118:11, 207 e. 7, *u*]*r-kiš* 49:8, 218:11, 290:8, *ur-kiš-ši* 93 r. 9, 335 r. 2, 336 r. 3, *ur-ki-i*]*š* 99:13,

urkīu "later, junior": EGIR-*at* 164:13,

urqu "vegetable": Ú.SAR 113:4, 173:5, 187:3, 204:3, 271:17, 326:8, Ú.SAR] 326:20, Ú.SAR.MEŠ 335:9,

ursutu "parcel(?)": *ur-su-tu* 190:1,

urû "team": *u-rat* 239 r. 6,

ūru "roof": *ú-ri* 21 e. 10,

uṣû "to emerge; (Š) to redeem": *u-še-ṣa* 259 r. 1, 260 r. 1, *ú-ṣa* 1 r. 7, *ú-še-aṣ* 257 r. 22, *ú-še-eṣ-ṣi* 37 r. 6, *ú-še-ṣa* 1 r. 9, 81 r. 1, 97 r. 8, 132:10, 146 r. 2, 163 r. 5, 197 r. 1, 223 r. 3, 252 r. 11, 264 r. 6, 265:9, 287 r. 5, *ú-še-ṣa*] 226 r. 1, *ú-še*]*-ṣa* 186 r. 6, 295 r. 5, *ú-*(*še*)*-ṣa* 271 r. 6, *ú-*[*še-ṣa*] 61:12, 317:7, *ú-še-ṣi* 245 r. 6, 275 r. 21, *ú-še-ṣu-u* 65 r. 4, *ú-še-ṣu-*[*u*] 160 r. 3, *ú-*[*še-ṣu-u*] 307 e. 10, *ú-še-*[*ṣu-ú-n*]*i* 288:13,

ušābu "to sit, dwell": *a-šib* 6 r. 2, 11 r. 5, 14 r. 9, 32 r. 2, 56 r. 7, 58 r. 4, 92 r. 4, 96:19, 98 r. 4, 131 r. 2, 140:10, 198:4, 220 r. 6, 250 r. 4, 283 r. 9, 284 r. 5, 299:13, 301 r. 2, 325 r. 4, [*a-šib* 200 r. 4, [*a-š*]*ib* 16 r. 1, *a-ši-bat* 7 e. 16, 50 r. 8, 53 e. 15, 87 r. 2, 110 r. 2, 163 r. 4, 201 r. 1, 219 r. 9, 229 r. 1, 278 r. 4, 309 r. 3, 326 r. 10, 329 r. 4, 330 r. 1, 335 r. 10, *a-ši-bat*] 51 r. 6, 118 r. 1, 314 r. 5, *a-ši*]*-bat* 328 r. 4, *a-*[*ši-bat* 251:16, 274 r. 4, [*a-ši-bat* 99 r. 3, 253 r. 6, 334 r. 17, 349 r. 5, [*a-ši-bat*] 202 r. 5, *a-ši-*[*b*]*i* 298 r. 1, *a-ši-pat* 176 r. 7, 210 r. 1, 211 r. 2, *ú-šab* 295 r. 2,

ušallu "meadow": *ú-šal-li* 29 r. 2, 100:4, 119:9, 11, 288:4, *ú-šal-lu* 329:7, *ú-*[*šal-lu*] 330:7,

ušandû "fowler": LÚ.MUŠEN.DÙ 257 r. 24, [LÚ].MUŠEN.DÙ 52 r. 15,

utāru "to exceed": *ut-ru-te* 201 r. 16,

uttartu "large-wheeled chariot": GIŠ.*ut-tar*.MEŠ 37 r. 10,

uṭṭutu "barley": ŠE.BAR 94 r. 1, 288:13,

uzuzzu "to stand, to be present": GUB-*u-ni* 123:8,
zakāru "to pronounce, call": *iz-zak-ru* 149:4,
zakû "to be clean, exempt": *za-a-ku* 3:6, *za*]-*ka-šá* 149:4, *za-ku-te* 223 r. 4, 224:5, 226:4, 252 r. 4, *za-*[*ku-te* 326:3, *za-ku-u* 194 s. 4,
zakūtu "exemption": *za-ku-ti* 271:9,
zammāru "singer": [LÚ.*za-ma-r*]*i* 313:2,
zamru "fruit": *za-mar* 90:9,
zaqāpu "to plant, erect, impale; to attack, lodge a complaint": *iz-qa-pu-u-ni* 35:2, *i-zaq-qa*[*p* 251 e. 18, *i-zaq-qup-an-ni* 15:5, 34:14, 42:15, 201:14, 246:9, 253 r. 2, 299:5, 311: 14, 329:19, *i-zaq-qup-an-ni*] 314:21, *i-zaq-qup-an-n*[*i* 39:8, *i-zaq-qup-an-*[*ni* 301:13, *i-zaq-qup-an-*[*ni*] 326:23, *i-zaq-qup-*[*an-ni*] 254:3, *i-zaq-qu-pan-ni* 87:6, *i-zaq-qu-pa-ni* 37:17, 319:11, *i-za-qa-p*[*a-ni* 274:11, *i-za-qup-an-ni* 56 e. 11, 161 r. 2, *i-za-qup-an-ni*] 88 r. 1, *i-za-qu*]*p-an-ni* 212:4, 213 r. 4, *i-za-q*[*up-an-ni* 322:5, *i-*[*za-qup-an-ni* 338 r. 2, [*i-za-qup-an-ni*] 90 r. 2, *i-za-qu*]-*ban-ni* 341 r. 8, *i-za-qu-ba-ni* 152:5, *i-za-qu-pan-ni* 31 r. 8, *i-za-qu-pa-an-ni* 40:15, 346:9, *i-za-qu-pa-an-ni*] 41 r. 1, *i-za-qu-*[*pa-an-ni*] 91:16, [*i-za-qu-pa*]-*an-ni* 99 e. 14, [*i-z*]*a-q*[*u-pa-an-ni*] 227:10, *i-za-qu-pa-a-ni* 7:10, 257:14, 298: 4, 334 r. 9, 335 r. 3, 347 r. 3, *i-za-qu-pa-a-ni*] 312: 17, *i-za-qu-pa-a-*[*ni*] 61:11, *i-za-q*[*u*]-*pa-a-*[*ni*] 48:12, [*i-za-qu-p*]*a-a-*[*ni*] 284:12, [*i-z*]*a-qu-pa-a-ni* 9:4, *i-za-qu-pa-ni* 32:13, 110:14, 197:8, 202 r. 2, 251:10, *i-za-qu-p*[*a-ni*] 98:12, *i-za-qu-*[*pa-ni*] 123:13, *i-za-q*]*u-pa-ni* 138 r. 1, [*i-za-qu-pa-ni* 127: 12, [*i-za-qu-pa-ni*] 218:12, [*i-za-qu-pa-n*]*i* 85:15, [*i-za*]-*qu-pa-*[*ni* 344:15, [*i-z*]*a-qu-pa-ni* 38 r. 2, *zaq-pu* 97:7, 201:2,
zarāpu "to purchase": *i-za-rip* 52:12, *i-zi-rip* 32:9, 161:13, 174:6, 219:6, 305:9, 306:6, *i-*[*zi-rip*] 103:8, *i-*[*z*]*i-rip* 58:2, [*i-zi-rip*] 284:7, [*i-z*]*i-rip* 3:5, *zar-pat* 88:11, 228:8, 272:8, r. 5, *zar-pat*] 197:7, *zar-p*[*at* 82:3, *zar-*[*pa*]*t* 98:9, *zar-pu* 34:11, 39:6, 100:11, 169 r. 2, 185:3, 250 e. 13, 274:8, 329:16, 341 r. 6, *zar-pu*] 4:6, 9:1, 101 r. 1, 251:8, 314:19, *zar-*[*pu* 345:11, *z*[*ar-p*]*u* 38:6, [*zar-pu* 57: 11, 101:8, [*zar-p*]*u* 299:3, *zar*$_4$*-pu* 110:11, 138:13, 177:10, 253:10, *za-ar-pa* 336 r. 2, 10, *za-ar-pat* 17 r. 1, *za-ar-pat*] 49:5, *za-ar-pi* 154 r. 5, 219:8, 339:7, *za-a*[*r-pi* 14 r. 3, *za-ar-pu* 6:9, 40:12, 53:10, 87:4, 89:10, 96:9, 119 r. 3, 123:11, 229:10, 335 r. 1, *za-ar-pu*] 41:13, 340:11, *za-ar-p*[*u* 284:9, *za-ar-*[*pu* 8:2, *za-a*[*r-pu* 50:13, 342:8, *za-a*[*r-p*]*u* 130: 12, *za-*[*ar-pu*] 140:3, [*za-a*]*r-pu* 315:16, [*za*]-*ar-pu* 348:5, *za-ár-pat*] 286:8, *za-ár-pi* 213:4, *za-ár-pu* 51:9, 52:13, 85:11, 319:7, 322:3, 326:21, 340:1, *za-ár-p*[*u*] 334 r. 7, *za-ár-p*]*u* 312:14, *za-á*[*r-p*]*u* 313:12, [*za-á*]*r-pu* 58:4, [*za-á*]*r-p*[*u* 298:1, [*za*]-*ár-pu* 344:12, *za-rip* 3:6, 7:8, 10 e. 21, 19:10, 22:11, 23:8, 32:11, 33:5, 37:14, 42:12, 55:7, 56:8, 99:11, 102:5, r. 5, 118:8, 124:11, 125 r. 5, 126 e. 12, 127:9, 142 r. 5, 161 e. 15, 164:10, 174 r. 1, 201:11, 210:12, 217:15, 218:10, 227:7, 244:8, 246:7, 257:12, 278:12, 289:8, 290:6, 301:10, 306: 7, 311:12, 328:12, 346:6, 347:11, *za-r*[*ip*] 207:4, 275 r. 17, *za-*[*rip* 103:10, [*za-rip* 15:3, 90:17, 144:8, 309:10, [*za-rip*] 305:10, [*za-ri*]*p* 61:9, 125: 13, 202 e. 15, *za-rip-pu* 93 r. 7, *za-ri-i*[*p*] 176 r. 2, *za-r*[*i-ip*] 48:8,
zar'u "seed, sown field": ŠE.NUMUN 258 s. 1, 287 r. 1, 288:15, ŠE.NUMUN-*šú* 287:8, ŠE.NUMUN.MEŠ]š 330:8, ŠE.NUMUN.MEŠ 245:13, 329:7,
ziblu "dung, manure": *zi-ib-li* 28:4, 271:3,
zizibu "milk": GA 112:3, G[A] 57:1,

Index of Names

Personal Names

Adūnai-izzī (candy peddler): ^{m}*a-du-na—iz* 262:4, 263:3, ^{m}*a-du-na—i-zi* 262:1,
Adūnī-ṭūrī: ^{m}*a-du-ni—ṭu-*[*ri* 41:5,
Adūru: ^{m}*a-du-ru* 283:19, ^{m}*a-du-ú-ri* 105 s. 1,
Aginu: ^{m}*a-gi-nu* 283:13,
Agru: ^{m}*ag-ru* 198 r. 3, ^{m}*ag-*[*ru*] 197 r. 3,
Ahabu: ^{m}PAB—*a-bi* 262 r. 4, ^{m}PAB—*a-bu* 215 e. 9,
Ahabû (chief scribe 268): ^{m}PAB-*bu-u* 26:4, 268 r. 2, ^{m}PAB]-*bu-u* 58 r. 8, ^{m}PAB-*bu-ú* 138:3, ^{m}PAB—*a-bu-u* 134 r. 7,
Ahāssunu: [M]Í.NIN-[*s*]*u-nu* 293:5,
Ahātī-immâ: MÍ.NIN—*im-ma-a* 239:5,
Ahī-bāštu (head porter): ^{m}*a-hi—ba-as-tú* 248 e. 11, see also *Habāsti,*
Ahī-Iāʾu: ^{m}PAB-*ia-u* 61:4,
Ahī-iābaba (farmer 109): ^{m}PAB—*ia-ba-ba* 123:5, e. 14, ^{m}PAB—*ia*]*-ba-ba* 109 r. 7,
Ahī-iaqar (deputy of Arrapha 123): ^{m}PAB—*ia-qar* 123:1, 246 r. 3,
Ahī-ia[...]: ^{m}PAB—*ia-*[*x* 252:5,
Ahī-immê (farmer 37): ^{m}PAB—*im-me-e* 94:3, ^{m}PAB—*im-*[*me* 14:8, ^{m}PAB-*me-e* 37:8,
Ahī-milki: ^{m}PAB—*mil-ki* 274:5, r. 1,
Ahī-nadbi: ^{m}PAB—*na-ad-bi* 85 r. 9,
Ahī-nūrī (scribe 40): ^{m}PAB—ZALÁG 40 r. 7, 46 r. 3, 148:2, 243 r. 3, ^{m}ŠEŠ—*nu-ri* 52:6,
Ahī-pāda: ^{m}PAB—*pa-da* 334:27,
Ahī-qām (merchant 246): ^{m}PAB-*i—qa-m*[*u* 246 r. 1, ^{m}PAB—*qa-mu* 283:8, 12, 15, 18, 19, ^{m}PAB—*q*[*a-mu*] 283:3, r. 21,
Ahī-rām (scribe): ^{m}PAB-*i—ra-me* 34 r. 7,
Ahī-ṭāba: ^{m}*a*]*-hi—ṭa-ba* 305 r. 14, ^{m}PAB—DÙG.GA 10 r. 15, 12:7,
Ahī-ṭallī: MÍ.*a-hi—ṭar-li* 93 r. 3, MÍ.PAB—*ṭal-li* 88:5, MÍ.PAB—*ṭ*]*al-li* 90:11, M]Í.PAB—*ṭar-li* 92:2, MÍ.PAB—*ṭa-li* 89:6,
Ahūa-[...]: ^{m}PAB-[*u*]*-a—x* 275:2,
Ahūʾa: ^{m}PAB-*u-a* 192:3,
Ahūʾāia: ^{m}PAB-*u-a-a* 238:6, ^{m}PAB-*u-a-a* 12 r. 2, ^{m}PAB-[*u-a*]*-a* 69:3,
Ahūʾa-āmur (horse trainer 309, ditto of the open chariotry 325, 338): ^{m}PAB-*u-a—a-mur* 31:20, ^{m}PAB-*u-*[*a—a-mur*] 31 e. 26, ^{m}PAB-*u—a-mur* 309 r. 11, 325 r. 22, 332 r. 12, 338 r. 16,
Ahūʾa-erība: ^{m}PAB-*ú-a*—SU 301 r. 11, ^{m}PAB-*u-a*—SU 13 r. 5, 200 r. 10, ^{m}PAB-*u-a*—S[U] 15:6,
Ahūnî: ^{m}*a-hu-ni-i* 192 r. 8, ^{m}PAB-*u-ni-i* 78:9,
Ahūnu: ^{m}*a-hu-ni* 216:1, 4, ^{m}*a-hu-nu* 237 r. 5, ^{m}PAB-*ú-nu* 268 r. 8,
Ahusītu: MÍ.*a-hu-si-te* 233:2,
Ahūšina (weaver): ^{m}PAB-*ši-na* 301:4,
Ahu-damqu: ^{m}PAB—SIG 160:7, ^{m}PAB—SIG$_5$ 251:3,
Ahu-dūrī (son of PN 294): ^{m}]PAB—BÀ[D] 230 r. 7, ^{m}PAB—BÀD 223 r. 5, 224 r. 1, 229 r. 11, 232 r. 4, 233 r. 1, 238 r. 6, 281:6, 314 r. 23, ^{m}PA]B—BÀD 225 r. 6, 294 r. 1, ^{m}P]AB—BÀD 163:1, 261 r. 2,
Ahu-ēreš: ^{m}PAB—APIN-*eš* 104 r. 3, ^{m}PAB—APIN.EŠ 329:11, ^{m}PAB—KAM-*eš* 252 s. 1,
Ahu-erība (royal horse trainer 235): ^{m}PAB—SU 95 e. 9, 235 r. 2,
Ahû-erība: ^{m}PAB-*u*—SU 139:3,
Ahu-iddina: ^{m}PAB—AŠ 105 r. 3, 160 r. 8, 161 r. 10,
Ahu-ilāʾī: ^{m}PAB—DINGIR-*a-a* 120:1, 133 s. 1, 204 r. 9, 319 r. 15, ^{m}ŠEŠ—DI[NGIR-*a-a*] 21:3,
Ahu-illika (royal bodyguard 89, servant of PN 96): ^{m}PAB—DU 89 r. 6, ^{m}PAB—DU-*ka* 202:6, 281:7, ^{m}PAB—DU—*ka* 96 r. 12,
Ahu-ittabši: ^{m}PAB—*i-tab-ši* 22 r. 7,
Ahu-lāmur (eunuch 309, horse trainer 347, priest 59, son of PN 195): ^{m}PAB—*la-mur* 59 r. 5, 309:3, 314 r. 20, ^{m}[PAB—*la-m*]*ur* 347 r. 13, ^{m}PAB—IGI.LAL 195 r. 10,
Ahu-lā-amašši (farmer 28, servant 31, son of PN 332, 'third man' 315, 316, 326, [of the prince] 317, of ditto 334): ^{m}]PAB—*la-maš-ši* 315 r. 1, ^{m}PAB—*la-maš-ši* 28 r. 5, 6, 161 r. 12, 316 r. 8, 317 r. 2, 325 r. 15, 332 r. 8, ^{m}PAB—*la-maš-*[*ši*] 160 r. 6, ^{m}PAB—*la-m*[*aš-ši* 326 r. 20, ^{m}PAB—*la-*[*maš*]*-ši* 93 e. 8, ^{m}PAB—*l*[*a-maš-ši* 334 r. 26, ^{m}PAB—*la—a-maš-ši* 31 r. 20,
Ahu-lēʾītī (servant 219): ^{m}PAB—*le-ʾi-ti* 289:3, 290:2, [^{m}PA]B—*li-ti* 219:1,
Ahu-lēšir: ^{m}PAB—SI.SÁ 150:9,
Ahu-uqur (servant 5): ^{m}PAB—*ú-qur* 5:2, 160:10,
Ahu-[...]: ^{m}PAB-[*x* 69:3, ^{m}PAB—[*x*]*x* 314 s. 1,
Aiābu-ahi: ^{m}]*a-a-bu*—PAB 268 r. 11,
Aia-ahhē (farmer 116): ^{m}]*a-a*—PAB.MEŠ 116 r. 2, ^{m}*a-a*—PAB.MEŠ 263 r. 3,
Aia-metūnu: ^{m}*a-a—me-tu-nu* 146:6,
Aia-milki: ^{m}*a-a—mì-il-ki* 275 s. 3,
Aia-nērī: ^{m}*a-a—ni-iʾ-ri* 64:5,
Aia-ṭūrī (servant): ^{m}*a-a—ṭu-ri* 227:3,
Aia-[...]: ^{m}*a-a—x*[*x* 79:2, 332:8,
Ainê: ^{m}*a-a-né-e* 10 r. 20,
Ai-sūrī: ^{m}*a-i—su-ú-ri* 236 r. 4,
Akakua: ^{m}*a-ka-ku-a* 291 r. 2,
Akbarâ: MÍ.*ak-ba-ra-a* 85:4,
Akbaru (servant 7): *mak-bar* 7:3, *mak-ba-ru* 246:1,
Akburu: ^{m}*ak-bu-ru* 300:3,
Akisu: ^{m}]*a-ki-su* 288:5,
Akkullanu: ^{m}]*a-kul-la-a-nu* 345 r. 9,
Akpalu: ^{m}*ak-pa-lu* 271:14,
Āl-tuklātūʾa: ^{m}URU—*tuk-la-a-tú-u-a* 2:3,
Amat-Suʾla: MÍ.*a-mat—*^{d}*su-uʾ-la* 142:3, MÍ.*a-mat—su-uʾ-la* 142 r. 3,
Ameqi: ^{m}*a-me-qi* 116 r. 9,
Ammâ: ^{m}*am-ma-a* 47 r. 4,
Ammīni-[...]: ^{m}*am-me-n*[*i—x* 334 r. 28,
Amsî: ^{m}*am-si-i* 264 r. 10,
Amurrî (servant): ^{m}IM.4-*i* 89:3,
Āmur-ilu: ^{m}*a-mu*]*r*—DINGIR 252:2,
Am-iateʾ: ^{m}*am—ia-te-eʾ-ú* 111 r. 5,
Am-rām (tailor of the palace): ^{m}*am—ra-mu* 91 r. 2,
Am-[...]: ^{m}*a*[*m-x* 2:1,
Anāku: ^{m}*ana-ku* 120 r. 5,
Ana-abi-dallāti: [M]Í.*a-na*—AD—*da-la-ti* 88:3,
Ana-Aššūr-taklāk: ^{m}*a-n*]*a—aš-šur—tak-lak* 35 r. 7,
Andarānu: ^{m}*an-da-ra-nu* 81 r. 6,
Andiāiu: ^{m}*an-di-a-a* 190:9,
Apladad-dalâ: ^{m}]A.10—*dàl-*[*a*] 76:1,
Apladad-hutnī: ^{m}A.10—*hu-ut-ni* 107 r. 4,
Apladad-ilāʾī: ^{md}A.10—DINGIR-*a-a* 146 r. 4,
Aplāia (son of PN 188, 'third man' 103): ^{m}A-*a-a* 102 r. 1, ^{m}A-*a-a*] 102:2, ^{m}A-[*a-a*] 104:3, ^{m}A-*ia* 328:8, ^{m}A-*iá* 103:4, ^{m}]DUMU.UŠ-*a-a* 100:21, ^{m}DUMU.UŠ-*a-a* 101:17, 108:3, 188 r. 8, 243 r. 3, 329:11, ^{m}DUMU.UŠ-*a*]*-a* 101:4, ^{m}[DUMU.UŠ-*a-a*] 100:7, ^{m}DUMU.UŠ-*ia* 107:2,
Aplî: ^{m}A-*i* 12:5, 14:3, 7, 201 r. 6, ^{m}DUMU.UŠ-*i*

266 r. 10, ^{m}a-zi—DIN[GIR 280 r. 14,
Ba'al-immī (servant): ^{m}ba-la—im-me 116 r. 6,
Ba'al-sūrī (gardener): ^{m}b]a-al—su-ri 314:9,
Bābāia: MÍ.ba-ba-a-a 116:4,
Babānu (wheelwright): ^{m}ba-ba-a-nu 124 r. 9,
Bābilāiu (seller 96): ^{m}KÁ.DINGIR-a-a 96:2, 4, 6, 11, ^{m}KÁ.DINGIR-a-[a] 19 r. 6, ^{m}KÁ.DINGIR-[a-a 22 r. 2, ^{m}KÁ.DINGIR.KI-a-a 160 r. 8, ^{m}K]Á.DINGIR.KI-a-a 271 e. 22, ^{m}K]Á.DINGIR.K[I-a-a] 144:5,
Babiri: ^{m}ba-bi-ri 133:1,
Bābu-ahhē-iddina: ^{md}BA.Ú—PAB.MEŠ—A[Š] 100 r. 19,
Bābu-[...]: ^{md}BA.Ú—[x 155:7,
Bāb-Tinūrāiu (temple steward): ^{m}KÁ—ti-nu-ra-a-a 59 r. 3,
Baddudu (reading uncert.): ^{m}ba-du_8-du_8 130 r. 5,
Badia: MÍ.ba-di-a 111:4,
Bahî: ^{m}ba-hi-i 278 r. 15,
Bahiānu (village manager of the stewardess 66): ^{m}ba-hi-a-ni 60:3, 62:3, 66:1, 67:2, 70:5, 71:2, 72:4, 73:2, 74:2, 75:2, 76:2, 77:6, 79:8, 200:6, ^{m}ba-hi-a-n[i 78 r. 4, ^{m}ba-[hi-a-ni] 69:2, ^{m}ba-hi-a-nu 61:5, 63:3, 64:2, ^{m}ba-hi-a-[nu] 80:1, 190 r. 2, ^{m}b]a-hi-a-nu 65:9, 311 r. 4,
Balasî: ^{m}ba-la-si-i 29:3, ^{m}ba-la-[si-i] 296 r. 7,
Balāssu (royal delegate 150): ^{m}]ba-la-su 195 r. 5, ^{m}ba-la-su 150:2,
Balāṭu-ēreš (seller 7): ^{m}TI.LA—APIN-eš 8:5, ^{m}TI.LA—KAM-eš 7:2, 11, ^{m}TI.L[A—KAM-eš] 7:5,
Bālti-[...]: ^{m}bal-t[i—x 100 r. 18,
Balṭāia (scribe 202): ^{m}bal-ṭa-a-a 157 r. 6, 202:1, 10, ^{m}ba]l-ṭa-a-a 163:7, ^{m}b[a]l-ṭa-ia 130:8,
Bānāia (gate-guard of the palace 59, son of PN 265): ^{m}ba-na-a-a 59 r. 14, ^{m}DÙ-a-a 265 r. 10, 11, ^{m}DÙ-iá 246 r. 4,
Banbâ (vizier 210, 212, 226, vizier of the deputy 239, 274): ^{m}]ban-ba-a 240 r. 8, ^{m}ban-ba-a 214 r. 3, 215:7, 239 r. 11, 274 r. 18, ^{m}ban-ba-a] 226 r. 2, 11, ^{m}ban-b[a-a 212 r. 8, ^{m}ba-an-ba-a 210 r. 17, 273:5,
Bānî (physician 309, deputy 307, ditto of the chief physician 320-328, 339, scribe 90, 124): ^{m}ba-ni-i 90 r. 15, 124 r. 13, 321 r. 8, 325 r. 18, 328 r. 9, ^{m}ba-ni-i] 339 r. 8, ^{m}ba-ni-[i 184:6, ^{m}ba-n[i-i 341:6, ^{m}ba-n[i-i] 309 r. 8, ^{m}ba-ni]-i 307:4, ^{m}ba]-ni-i 317 r. 7, ^{m}DÙ-i 268 r. 7, 320 r. 5,
Bānūnu (cohort commander): ^{m}ba-nu-nu 164 r. 5, ^{m}ba]-nu-nu 165 r. 8,
Barīku (chief [...] 314): ^{m}ba-ri-ki 314:1, 17, 22, 319 r. 14, ^{m}ba-ri-k[i 314:13,
Barruqu (seller 22, chariot driver 318, 324, 326-327, 335, 350, [of the prince] 317, scribe 272): ^{m}bar-ruq 198 r. 4, 323 r. 5, 324 r. 6, 325 r. 14, 326 r. 19, 335 r. 19, 338 r. 12, 339 r. 6, 350 r. 6, ^{m}bar-r[uq] 197 r. 2, ^{m}bar-ruq-qu 150:8, 317:10, ^{m}bar-r]uq-q[u 327 r. 1, ^{m}bar-[r]uq-qu 347 r. 11, ^{m}bar]-ruq-qu 272 r. 7, ^{m}b]ar-ruq-qu 272:10, [^{m}]bar-ruq-q[u] 106:12, ^{m}bar-ru-qu 22:1, 316 r. 6, ^{m}bar-ru]-qu 318:7,
Barsipītu: MÍ.BÁR.SIPA.KI-i-tú 96:5, 15,
Bar-ahu: br'ḥ] 59 r. 19, ^{m}ba-ra-a-hu 59:2,
Bar-hatê: ^{m}bar—ha-a[t-e] 51 e. 13, ^{m}bar—ha-te 50 r. 3, ^{m}bar—ha]-te-e 50:7, ^{m}bar—h[a-te-e] 51:1, ^{m}bar—(ha)-te-[e] 51:4, ^{m}bar—[ha-te-e] 50:1, ^{m}b]ar—ha-te-e 50:9,
Bar-zaqê: ^{m}bar—za-qe-e 195 r. 5,
Bar-zikūtu: ^{m}bar-zi-ku-tú 314 r. 22,
Basû'a: ^{m}ba-su-u-a 297 r. 9,
Batīti (architect): ^{m}ba-ti-i-ti 158 r. 2,
Batû'a: ^{m}ba-tú-'a-a 113:5, ^{m}ba-tu-'a-a 113:2,
Baṭuṭānu (scribe): ^{m}ba-ṭu-ṭa-[nu] 243 r. 1,
Bauiâ: MÍ.ba-ú-ia-a 266:4,
Bēlet-ēreš: ^{md}GAŠAN—APIN-eš 108:1, 3,
Bēlu-halūṣu: ^{m}bé-e-lu—ha-lu-ṣu 334:26,
Bēltu-uṣur: MÍ.GAŠAN—PAB 94:1,
Bēl-abu-uṣur (seller): ^{m}EN—AD—PAB 59:1, ^{m}EN—A[D—PAB 59:9,
Bēl-ahhē: ^{m}EN—PAB.MEŠ 158:3,
Bēl-ahhēšu (chariot driver): ^{m}EN—PAB.MEŠ-šú 41 r. 10, ^{m}EN—PAB.[MEŠ-šú] 40 r. 13, ^{m}[EN—PAB.MEŠ-šú] 39 r. 5,
Bēl-ahu-iddina (trainer of reserve horses): ^{m}]EN—PAB—AŠ 193 r. 6,
Bēl-ahu-uṣur (cohort commander): ^{md}EN—PAB—PAB 46 r. 2,
Bēl-āli: ^{m}EN—U[RU] 19 r.3, 5,
Bēl-aplu-iddina (governor 319, chief singer of Til-Barsip 312, 313): $^{md+}$[E]N—A—SUM-na 319 r. 12, ^{md}EN]—A—AŠ 313:1, ^{m}[^{d}EN]—A—AŠ 312:1, [^{md}EN]—A—AŠ 313:9, ^{md}EN—A—SUM-na 313:6, ^{m}EN—A—AŠ 312 e. 18, [^{m}]EN—A—S[UM-na 104:4, ^{m}EN—DUMU.UŠ—SUM-na 319 r. 5,
Bēl-ašarēd: ^{m}EN—MAŠ 44:3, ^{m}EN—SAG.KAL 43:3, 44:1,
Bēl-dān (prefect of Calah 19): ^{m}EN—KALAG-an 19 r. 12, 21 r. 13,
Bēl-dūrī (village manager 61, 'third man' 142): ^{m}EN—BAD 142 r. 3, ^{m}EN—BÀD 142:4, 210 r. 11, ^{m}EN—B[ÀD] 106:11, [^{m}]EN—BÀD 61:15,
Bēl-ēlī: ^{m}EN—U[RU] 19 r. 3, 5,
Bēl-ēmuranni (commander-in-chief 89-169): ^{md}EN—IGI.LAL-an-ni 166 r. 9, ^{m}EN.IGI.LAL-a-ni 161 r. 19, ^{m}EN—IGI-a-ni 61 r. 1, 70 r. 2, 167 r. 7, ^{m}EN—IGI.LAL-an-ni 34 r. 10, ^{m}EN—IGI].LAL-an-ni 168 r. 5, ^{m}EN—I]GI.LAL-an-ni 169 r. 16, [^{m}]EN—IGI.LAL-[an-ni 2 r. 8, ^{m}EN—IGI.LAL-a-ni 89 r. 16, 107 e. 6, 163 r. 17, 164 r. 17, ^{m}E[N—IG]I.LAL-a-ni 139 r. 1, ^{m}EN—IGI.LAL-ni] 162 r. 5,
Bēl-ēpuš: ^{md}E]N—DÙ-uš 66:4,
Bēl-ēreš (guarantor 221, 222): [^{m}EN—AP]IN 221 e. 8, [^{m}E]N—APIN 222 r. 1, ^{m}EN—APIN-eš 259 r. 3, ^{m}EN—KAM-eš 260 r. 5,
Bēl-ēṭir: ^{m}EN—KAR-ir 215:2,
Bēl-Harrān-bēlu-uṣur: ^{m}EN—KASKAL—U—PAB 23 r. 10,
Bēl-Harrān-dūrī (singer 196): ^{m}EN—KASKAL—BÀD 167 e. 8, 196 r. 5, 277 r. 1, 278 r. 12,
Bēl-Harrān-issē'a (seller 40, 41): $^{md+}$EN—KASKAL—KI-[ia 132:6, ^{m}EN—KASKAL—KI-ia 40:16, 132:1, ^{m}EN—KASKAL—KI-ia] 39:1, 4, 8, 41:7, ^{m}EN—KASKAL—KI-i[a 40:10, ^{m}EN—KASKAL—K]I-ia 40:2, ^{m}EN—KAS[KAL—K]I-[i]a 40:6, ^{m}EN—K[ASKAL—KI-ia 41:2, ^{m}EN—[KASKAL—KI-ia] 41:11,
Bēl-Harrān-kuṣuranni: ^{m}EN—KASKAL—k[u-ṣur]-a-ni 196:1, ^{m}E]N—KASKAL—[ku]-ṣur-a-ni 196:6,
Bēl-Harrān-šarru-uṣur (information officer 37, major-domo 254): ^{md}EN—URU.KASKAL—MAN—PAB 254 r. 2, 297 r. 5, ^{m}EN]—KASKAL—MAN—PAB 37 r. 8,
Bēl-Harrān-taklāk: ^{m}EN—KASKAL—tàk-lak 111:5, ^{m}EN—KASKAL—tak-lak 52:4,
Bēl-Harrān-[...]: ^{md}EN—KASKAL—[x 32 r. 14, ^{m}EN—KASKAL-x-[x 14:2, ^{m}EN—KASKAL—[x 184:5,

Hanṭušu: ^{m}*ha-an-ṭu-šú* 52 r. 10,
Hanūnu: ^{m}*ha-nu-nu* 237 r. 6,
Hara-Dādi: ^{m}*ha-ra*—MAN 245 r. 9, ^{m}*ha-ra*—U.U 244 r. 5,
Harhandâ ('genie'): ^{m}*har-ha-an-da-a* 288:18, r. 1,
Hāri-ahhē: ^{m}*ha-a-ri*—PAB.MEŠ 105 r. 9,
Harmāku: ^{m}*har-ma-ki* 189 r. 5,
Harmāṣu (chief boatman 142, 'third man' 142): ^{m}*har-ma-ṣa* 142 r. 13, 16,
Harurānu: ^{m}*ha-ru-ra-a-nu* 101:3, 10, ^{m}*ha-ru-ra-*[*a-nu*] 100:1, ^{m}*ha-ru-*[*ra-a-nu*] 100:14, ^{m}*h*[*a-ru-ra-a-nu*] 100:6,
Haruṣâ: ^{m}*ha-ru-ṣa-a* 196 r. 4,
Hasabu: ^{m}*ha-sa-bu* 218:8, ^{m}*ha-sa-b*[*u* 218:2, [^{m}*ha-sa-bu*] 218:12,
Hasāiu: ^{m}*ha-sa-a-a* 275:7, ^{m}KUR.*ha-sa-a-a* 275:1,
Hasusî (son of PN): ^{m}[*h*]*a-su-si-i* 98 r. 9,
Hašānu (information officer 36): ^{m}*ha-šá-na* 36 e. 8, 50:4,
Hatiānu: ^{m}*ha-ti-a-nu* 113 r. 5,
Hattāiu: ^{m}*ha-ta-a-a* 244:1, 5,
Hazālâ: MÍ.*ha-za-la-a* 239:4,
Hazā-il: ^{m}*ha-za*—DINGIR 257:1, 3,
Himārî: ^{m}*hi-ma-ri-i* 131 r. 6, 244 r. 3,
Hinnumu: ^{m}*hi-nu-mu* 192 r. 5,
Hiri-ahhē (chariot driver 325): ^{m}*hi-ri*—PAB 277 r. 9, ^{m}*hi-ri*—PAB.MEŠ 325:3,
Hubašāti (driller): ^{m}*h*]*u-ba-šá-a-te* 345 r. 8,
Huhabašu: ^{m}*hu-ha-ba-šu* 47 r. 2,
Humamāti (scribe 105): ^{m}*hu*—*ma-ma-a-ti* 105 r. 10, ^{m}*hu*—*ma-ma-te* 177 r. 13, ^{m}PAB—*ma-ma-a-te* 106 r. 3,
Hunnî: ^{m}*hu-ni-*[*i*] 93:4,
Hurāia: ^{m}*hu-ra-a-a* 229 r. 12,
Hurubisa[...]: ^{m}*hu-ru-bi-sa-*[*x*] 326:10,
Ia'lâ: ^{m}*ia-a'-la-a* 44:7,
Iāda'-il (Itu'ean): ^{m}*ia-da*—DINGIR 30 r. 5,
Iāda'-[...]: ^{m}*ia-da-*[*x* 309 r. 15,
Iadānu: ^{m}*ia-da-nu* 201 r. 11,
Iādi': ^{m}*ia-di-i'* 277 r. 8,
Iādi'-il: ^{m}*ia-a-di*—DINGIR 175:1,
Iahūṭu (deputy of Raṣappa 243): ^{m}*ia-hu-ṭi* 243:1, 5, ^{m}*ia-hu-ṭu* 241:4, 242:1, ^{m}*ia-hu-u-ṭu* 105 r. 2,
Iāia: ^{m}*ia-a-a* 1 r. 14,
Iākê: ^{m}*ia-a-ke-e* 150:5,
Ianuqu: ^{m}*ia-nu-qu* 266:2,
Iaqar-ahhē: MÍ.*ia-qar*—PAB.MEŠ 250:3,
Ia-ahhē: ^{m}*ia*—PAB.MEŠ 326:9, ^{m}*ia*—P[AB.MEŠ] 179 r. 7,
Ia-dādu: ^{m}*ia*—*da-du* 157 r. 5,
Ibašši-ilāʾī (servant of the commander-in-chief): ^{m}Ì.GÁL—DINGIR-*a-a* 29 r. 6,
Ibašši-ilu (president of the court): ^{m}GÁL-*ši*—DINGIR 265:14,
Ibnāia (son of PN): ^{m}*ib-n*]*a-a-a* 239 r. 3,
Ibni-Ēa (scribe): ^{m}*ib-ni-ia* 173:2,
Iddāti-Bēl-allaka: ^{m}*de-ti*—EN—DU-*k*[*a*] 298:6, ^{m}*i*—*da-a-te*—EN—*a-la-ka* 297:1, see also *Dāt-Bēl-allak*,
Iddî see *Addî*,
Iddināia: ^{m}SUM-*na-a* 320:5,
Iddin-ahhē (prefect 68, of Dur-Šarruken 40, 41, 106, of Ṣimirra 67, 69): ^{m}*id-di*[*n*]—*a-*[*hi*] 138 r. 20, ^{m}]AŠ—PAB.MEŠ 139:8, ^{m}AŠ—PAB.MEŠ 69 r. 4, 106 r. 7, ^{m}AŠ—PAB.[MEŠ] 275:12, ^{m}AŠ—[PAB.MEŠ] 64 r. 1, ^{m}SUM-*na*—PAB.MEŠ 67 r. 2, 68 r. 2, 150 r. 4, ^{m}SUM-*na*—PAB.M[EŠ] 137 r. 6, ^{m}SUM-[*na*—PAB.MEŠ] 41 r. 17, ^{m}SUM-*ni*—PAB.MEŠ 97 r. 9, ^{m}SUM—PAB.MEŠ 40 r. 18, 66 r. 11,
Iddin-Ēa: ^{m}SUM-*ni-*[*ia*] 321:6,
Idrīa (seller): ^{m}*ad-ra-iá* 201:9, ^{m}*ad-ri-iá* 201:14, ^{m}]*id-ri-iá* 201:1,
Idu'a (village manager): ^{m}*i-du-u-a* 255:1, ^{m}*i-du-*[*u-a*] 256:1,
Iglî (servant): ^{m}*ig-li-i* 31 r. 18, ^{m}*i*]*g-li-i* 31:10,
Ikkāru: ^{m}]*ik-ka-ru* 147 r. 2, ^{m}*i-ka-ri* 326:19, ^{m}*i-ka-ru* 326 e. 25,
Ilâ (bought man): ^{m}*i-la-a* 52 r. 9,
Ilāʾī-[...]: ^{m}DING]IR-*a-*[*a*—*x* 252:7,
Ilī-pāda: ^{m}]DINGIR—*pa-a-di* 65 r. 10,
Illû: ^{m}*il-lu-u* 180 r. 4,
Illuknu: ^{m}*il-lu-uk-nu* 47 r. 1,
Iltappa: ^{m}*il-tap-pa* 259 r. 2, 260 r. 3,
Ilumma-lēʾi (son of PN): ^{m}DINGIR-*ma*—ZU 19 r. 8,
Ilumma-lidgul (butcher): ^{m}DINGIR-*ma*—*lid-g*[*u*]*l* 6 r. 10,
Ilu-dēnī-amur (son of PN): ^{m}DINGIR—*de-ni*—IGI.LAL 319 r. 12,
Ilu-ēreš (gate-guard of the palace 59, seller 227): ^{m}DINGIR—APIN-*eš* 31:10, 11, 15, 17, 22, r. 1, 2, ^{m}DINGIR—KAM-*eš* 59 r. 12, 227:1, 4,
Ilu-erība: ^{m}DINGIR—SU 121:2,
Ilu-ibni (scribe 96): ^{m}[D]INGIR—*ib-ni* 96 r. 17, ^{m}DINGIR—DÙ 42 r. 9,
Ilu-iqbi: ^{m}DINGIR—*iq-bi* 29:4,
Ilu-issēʾa (prefect 39, of Damascus 37, 81, 134, 135): ^{m}DINGIR—KI-*e-a* 83 r. 3, 84 r. 3, ^{m}DINGIR—KI-*ia* 37 r. 16, 39 r. 10, 81 r. 10, 103 r. 10, 133 s. 4, 134 r. 15, 135 r. 6, ^{m}DINGIR—KI-*i*[*a*] 136 r. 1, (^{m})DINGIR—KI-*ia* 142:9,
Ilu-iṣbatanni (king's eunuch): ^{m}DINGIR—DIB-*an-ni* 283 r. 4,
Ilu-iṣṣur (servant of the crown prince from Illat 257, ditto of the commander-in-chief 96): ^{m}DINGIR—PAB 96 r. 10, 100 r. 18, 257:7, r. 19,
Ilu-kēnu-uṣur (son of PN 242, 243): ^{m}DINGIR—GIN—PAB 242:2, 297:6, ^{m}DINGIR—GIN—P[AB 243:6, ^{m}DINGIR—GIN—[PAB] 241:5,
Ilu-lēʾi (scribe): ^{m}DINGIR—ZU 195 r. 6,
Ilu-liphur: ^{m}DINGIR—*lip-hur* 135 r. 4,
Ilu-mušēzib (horse trainer of the open chariotry): ^{m}DINGIR—*mu-še-zib* 310 r. 10, 331 r. 5,
Ilu-mutaqqin: ^{m}DINGIR—*mu*-LAL 188 r. 4,
Ilu-pīa-uṣur: ^{m}DINGIR—KA—PAB 138 r. 14,
Ilu-pīa-[...]: ^{m}DINGIR—KA-*ia-a*—[*x* 266 r. 9,
Ilu-tapputi: ^{m}DINGIR—*tap-*[*pu-ti* 33 r. 7,
Ilu-udaʾʾinanni: ^{m}DINGIR—*ú*-KALAG-*an-ni* 84:5, ^{m}DINGIR—*ú*-KALAG-*ni* 83:6,
Ilu-[...]: [^{m}DINGIR-*x* 343:6, ^{m}DINGIR—*lu-*[*x* 249 r. 2,
Il-amara (chief of granaries): ^{m}DINGIR—*a-mar* 37:2, 18, ^{m}]DINGIR—*a-mar-ra* 38:1, ^{m}DINGIR—*a-ma*[*r*]*-ra* 38 r. 2, ^{m}DINGIR—*a-ma-*[*ra* 37:12,
Il-dalâ ('third man'): ^{m}DINGIR—*dàl-a* 323:7, ^{m}DINGIR—*dàl-a*] 324:4, e. 13,
Il-gabbê: ^{m}DINGIR—*gab-e* 196 r. 6,
Il-hanāni: ^{m}DIN]GIR—*ha-na-ni* 104 r. 2,
Il-ia[...]: ^{m}DINGIR—*i*[*a-x* 252:6,
Il-immī: ^{m}DINGIR—*im-me* 83:5, 199 r. 11,
Il-kabar: ^{m}DINGIR—*ka-bar* 160:9, 161 r. 14,
Il-mādi: ^{m}[DINGIR—*m*]*a-a-di* 187 r. 5,
Il-malak: *'lmlk* 217 s. 1, ^{m}DINGIR—*ma-la-k*[*u*] 217:12, ^{m}DINGIR—[*ma-la-ku*] 217:2,

arba-ìl 202:9, ^{m}man-nu—ki-i—[arba-ìl] 208:2, 299 r. 7, ^{m}m[an-nu—ki-i—arba-ìl] 226 r. 7, ^{m}man-nu—ki-i—arba-ìl.KI 150 r. 3, ^{m}man-nu—ki-i—arba-ìl.K[I] 283:1, ^{m}man-nu—ki-i—URU.arba-ìl 201:7, 18, 216: 3, 247:7, ^{m}man-nu—ki-i—URU.arba-[ìl] 268 r. 1, ^{m}man-nu—ki-i—UR]U.arba-ìl 213 r. 5, ^{m}man-nu—ki—arba-ìl 156:2, 214:3, 215:3, 220 r. 3, 223 r. 7, ^{m}man-nu—ki—arba-[ìl] 204:8, ^{m}man-nu—ki—ar[ba-ìl 249 r. 1, ^{m}man-nu—ki—ar[ba-ìl] 212:4, ^{m}man-nu—ki—a[rba-ìl] 207 r. 2, ^{m}man-nu—ki]—arba-ìl 224 r. 3, [^{m}man-nu—ki—arba-ìl 213:1, ^{m}man-nu—ki—URU.arba-ìl 61:4, 219:2, r. 5, 325:8, ^{m}man-nu—ki—URU.[arba-ìl] 157:4, ^{m}man-nu—ki—[URU.arba-ìl] 218:7, ^{m}man-nu—k[i—URU.arba-ìl] 210 e. 17, 217:11, ^{m}man-n]u—ki—URU.arba-ìl 210:8, ^{m}m[an-nu—ki—URU.arba-ìl] 217 r. 2, ^{m}man-nu—GIM—URU. arba-ìl 66 r. 8, 206:2,

Mannu-kī-Aššūr (chariot driver 300, ditto of the crown prince 329-330, 335): ^{m}man-nu—ki-i—aš-šur 329 r. 15, ^{m}man-nu]—ki-i—aš-šur 102:9, [^{m}man-nu]—ki-i—aš-[šur 102:1, ^{m}man-nu—ki—aš-šur 330 r. 9, 335 r. 17, ^{m}man-nu]—ki—aš-šur 300 r. 4,

Mannu-kī-aššur-lē'i (prefect of Tillê): ^{m}man-nu—ki-i—aš-šur—ZU 34 r. 14, ^{m}man-nu—ki—aš-šur—ZU 31 r. 28,

Mannu-kī-Harrān (horse trainer 347, ditto of the open chariotry 310, 315, 316, 335, 338): ^{m}man-nu—ki-i—URU.KASKAL 315 r. 4, ^{m}man-nu—ki—KASKAL 325 r. 22, ^{m}man-nu—ki—KASKAL] 338 r. 17, ^{m}man-nu—ki]—KASKAL 347 r. 14, ^{m}man-nu—ki—URU. KASKAL 310 r. 9, 332 r. 13, 335 r. 23, ^{m}man]-nu—ki—URU.KASKAL 316 r. 11,

Mannu-kī-Issār: ^{m}]man-nu—ki-i—^{d}15 137:2, ^{m}man-nu—ki-0—15 84 e. 7,

Mannu-kī-Issarān: ^{m}man-nu—ki—AN.GAL 183:4,

Mannu-kī-Issār-lē'i (cohort commander 177, of the queen 164): ^{m}man-nu—ki—^{d}15—ZU 177 r. 5, ^{m}man-n]u—ki—^{d}15—ZU 165 r. 9, ^{m}man-nu—ki—15—ZU 164 r. 3,

Mannu-kī-Libbāli (scribe 287): ^{m}man-nu—ki—URU.ŠÀ—URU 294 r. 6, ^{m}man-nu—ki—ŠÀ—URU 287 r. 12, 293 r. 8,

Mannu-kī-metīna: ^{m}man-nu—ki—me-ti-i-na 105 r. 3,

Mannu-kī-Nabû: ^{m}man-nu—ki—^{d}PA 63 r. 3,

Mannu-kī-Nīnua: ^{m}man-nu—a-ki—NINA.KI 180: 3, ^{m}man-nu—ki-i—URU.NINA 326:18, ^{m}man-nu—ki—NINA.KI 52:7, 182:2, ^{m}man-nu—ki—N[INA.KI] 181:3, ^{m}man-nu—ki—URU.NINA 158 r. 5, 326 e. 24,

Mannu-kī-ṣābi (brother of PN 320): ^{m}man-nu—ki-i—ERIM 10 r. 20, ^{m}man-nu—ki—ERIM.MEŠ 236 r. 2, 320 r. 8, ^{m}man]-nu—GIM—ERIM.MEŠ 48 r. 13,

Mannu-kī-šarri (chariot driver 300): ^{m}man-nu—ki-i—LUGAL 319 r. 18, ^{m}man-nu—ki—MAN 318 r. 4, ^{m}man-nu]—ki—MAN 300 r. 5,

Mannu-kī-[...] (cavalryman 132): ^{m}man-nu—ki-i—^{d}x 97 r. 9, ^{m}man-nu—ki-i—[x 302 r. 6, ^{m}man-nu—ki-[x 41 r. 12, ^{m}man-nu—ki—x] 132:6, ^{m}man-nu—ki—[x 132:2,

Mannu-limmī (son of PN): ^{m}man-nu—li-im-me 284 r. 15,

Mannu-lū-ahū'a: ^{m}man-nu—lu—PAB-u-a 31:3, 6, 15, 25, ^{m}man-nu—lu—P[AB-u-a] 31:18,

Mannu-lū-same: ^{m}man-nu—li-s[a-me] 161:1, ^{m}man-nu—lu-sa-me 160:1,

Mannu-[...]: ^{m}man-nu-[x 140 r. 2,

Manzarnê (governor 177, prefect of Kullania 59): ^{m}man-za-ár-né-e 43:11, ^{m}[man-za-ár-né-e] 59 r. 17, [^{m}man-za-ár]-né-e 44 r. 2, ^{m}man-za-ar-né-e 177 r. 17, ^{m}ma-an-za-né-e 74 r. 2, ^{m}ma-za-ar-né-e 73 r. 2,

Man-kî (bronzesmith): ^{m}ma-an—ki-i 26 r. 5,

Mardâ: ^{m}mar-da-[a] 275 r. 11,

Mardānu: ^{m}m]ar-da-a-na 195 r. 4, ^{m}mar-da-ni 119 r. 13, ^{m}mar-da-[ni] 122:1,

Mardî (priest 59): ^{m}mar-di-i 59 r. 8, 90:2, 10, 254:4, 278 r. 8,

Mardû (village manager): ^{m}mar-d]u-ú 164:1,

Mardua (scribe): ^{m}mar-du-u-a 239 r. 9,

Marduk: ^{m}mar-duk 222:4, 240 r. 4,

Mardukia: ^{m}]^{d}ŠÚ-ia 225 r. 11,

Marduk-abu-uṣur: ^{md}AMAR.UTU—AD—PAB 292 s. 3,

Marduk-bēlu-uṣur ('third man' of Ša-Nabû-šû 295): ^{md}AMAR.UTU—EN—PAB 295:4, ^{md}AMAR.UTU—EN—PAB] 295 r. 2, ^{md}ŠÚ—EN—PAB 12:10,

Marduk-ēreš (recruitment officer 86): ^{md}]AMAR. UTU—APIN-eš 86 r. 3, ^{md}AMAR.UTU—APIN-eš 125:5, 280:1, [^{m}]^{d}KU—APIN-eš 119 r. 12, ^{md}KU—KAM-eš 28: 4, ^{md}ŠÚ—APIN-eš 275:16, e. 21, r. 7,

Marduk-erība: ^{md}AMAR.UTU—SU 336:7, r. 4, ^{md}]ŠÚ—SU 166 r. 7, ^{md}ŠÚ—SU 210 r. 13, 234:4,

Marduk-ibni: ^{md}ŠÚ—DÙ 161 r. 10, ^{m}ŠÚ—DÙ 160 r. 6,

Marduk-iddina (chariot fighter 90, scribe 12): ^{md}AMAR.UTU—AŠ 12 r. 4, ^{md}ŠÚ—AŠ 90 r. 12,

Marduk-iqbi: ^{md}MES—iq-bi 273:7,

Marduk-rēmanni: ^{md}ŠÚ—rém-a-ni 311 r. 5,

Marduk-šākin-šumi (chief exorcist): ^{md}AMAR. UTU—GAR—M[U 330 r. 7, ^{md}ŠÚ—GAR—MU 329 r. 12,

Marduk-šarrāni (oil master): ^{md}AMAR.UTU—MAN-a-ni 287 r. 13,

Marduk-šarru-uṣur (chariot driver of the queen 329, 330, 332, scribe 64, son of PN 321, 324, 327, 335): ^{md}AMAR.UTU—MAN—PAB 329 r. 13, 330 r. 8, ^{md}AMAR.UTU—MAN—P[AB] 121 r. 2, ^{md}A[MAR. UTU—MAN—PAB] 321 r. 2, ^{md}MES—MAN—PAB 332 r. 5, ^{md}ŠÚ—MAN—PAB 64 r. 2, 324 r. 11, 347:1, 5, ^{md}ŠÚ—MA]N—PAB 327 r. 4, 335 r. 15, ^{md}ŠÚ]—MAN—PAB 323 s. 2,

Marduk-šumu-iddina (horse trainer of the royal guard 53): ^{md}AMAR.UTU—MU—AŠ 101 r. 13, [^{m}]^{d}AMAR.[UTU—MU—AŠ 100 r. 12, ^{md}MES—MU—AŠ 53 r. 8,

Marduk-šumu-uṣur (chief haruspex 339, scribe 227): ^{md}AMAR.UTU—M]U—PAB 339 r. 7, ^{md}MES—MU—PAB 221:4, ^{md}ŠÚ—MU—PAB 227 r. 9,

Marduk-zēru-ibni (scribe 329-331): ^{md}AMAR. UTU—NUMUN—DÙ 330 r. 14, 331 r. 6, ^{md}ŠÚ—NUMUN—DÙ 97 r. 10, 329 r. 20,

Marduk-[...]: ^{md}MES—[x 59:6, ^{md}ŠÚ—la-[x 334 r. 27,

Mari': ^{m}]ma-ri-i' 200 r. 9,

Marqihitâ: mrqḥt' 284 r. 11, MÍ.mar-qi-hi-t[a]-a 284:2,

Marṣiš-adallal: ^{m}GIG—a-[da-lal 155 r. 5, ^{m}[GIG]—a-da-la-l[i] 343:5, [^{m}GI]G—a-da-la-li 344:2,

Martu' (village manager of the queen 90): ^{m}mar-tú-[x 94:8, ^{m}mar-tú-u' 90:1, ^{m}[mar-t]ú-u' 90: 10, see also Mardû,

Mār-bi'dī: ^{m}mar—bi-i'-di 79:4,

Mār-iate': ^{m}mar—ia-te-e' 109:3,

266 r. 7, ^{md}PA—PAB—[AŠ] 246:3, ^{m}]^{d}PA—PAB—[SUM]-*na* 57 r. 4,
Nabû-ahu-uṣur (farmer 334, postmaster 124, royal bodyguard 43, 44): ^{md}PA—PAB—PAB 43:6, 44: 5, 63 r. 2, 83 e. 7, 84 e. 6, 108 r. 1, 124 r. 10, 196 r. 7, 334:27, ^{md}PA—PAB—[PAB 179 r. 8,
Nabû-aiālī (servant): [^{m}]^{d}PA—*ia-a-li* 347:4,
Nabû-aplu-iddina (scribe 265, scribe of the queen 310): ^{md}AG—A—AŠ 310 r. 19, ^{md}PA—A—AŠ 265 r. 11, ^{m}]^{d}PA—A—SUM-*na* 345:9, ^{md}PA—A—SUM-*na*] 345:1,
Nabû-ašarēd (scribe 177): ^{md}PA—MAŠ 19:2, 85 r. 11, 177 r. 14, 318:2, [^{md}P]A—SAG.KAL 254 r. 2,
Nabû-balāssu-iqbi (scribe): ^{m}]^{d}PA—TI.L[A-*su*—E] 53 r. 10,
Nabû-bāni: ^{md}PA—*ba-ni* 229 r. 10, 230 r. 6,
Nabû-bāni-ahhē: ^{md}PA—DÙ—PAB.MEŠ 262 r. 2, 263 r. 2,
Nabû-bāni-apli (scribe): ^{md}PA—DÙ—A 160 r. 14, 161 r. 17,
Nabû-bēlu-ka''in (cohort commander 270): ^{md}PA—EN—GIN 220 r. 13, 270 r. 1,
Nabû-bēlu-uṣur (baker 305, 306, mayor of Nineveh 86, 87, prefect 282, ditto of Dur-Šarrukku 283): *nbw*[*blṣr*] 284 e. 17, ^{md}PA—EN—PAB 86 r. 5, 87 r. 7, 234 r. 7, 244 r. 10, 282 e. 4, 305:4, ^{m}[^{d}PA—EN—PAB] 284:3, ^{m}[^{d}PA]—EN—[PAB] 284:5, [^{md}PA—EN—PAB 306:1, [^{md}PA—EN—PAB] 283 r. 23, [^{md}P]A—[EN—PAB] 284:1, ^{md}PA—U—PAB 245 r. 14,
Nabû-bēl-ilī: ^{md}PA—EN—DINGIR.MEŠ 158 r. 6,
Nabû-bēl-šumāti (gate-guard 167, scribe 42): ^{md}PA—EN—MU.MEŠ 167 r. 5, ^{md}PA—EN—MU.MEŠ-*te* 42 r. 17,
Nabû-da''inanni (commander-in-chief 1): ^{md}PA—KALAG-*in-an-ni* 247:1, [^{md}P]A—KALAG-*in-an-ni* 1 r. 20,
Nabû-dalâ: ^{md}AG—*da-*[*la-a*] 147 r. 2,
Nabû-dammiq (deputy of the palace scribe 86): ^{md}PA—SIG$_5$ 173:6, ^{md}PA—[SIG$_5$]-*iq* 86 r. 11,
Nabû-damqi-ilāni: ^{md}PA—SIG$_5$—DINGIR.MEŠ 260 r. 2, ^{md}PA—SIG—DINGIR.MEŠ 259 r. 2,
Nabû-dannaka-lāmur: ^{md}PA—*dan-na-ka*—IGI 119 r. 20,
Nabû-dēnī-amur (deputy): ^{md}PA—*de-ni*—*a-mur* 247 r. 1,
Nabû-dēnī-epuš: ^{md}PA—*de-e-nu*—DÙ-*uš* 60 r. 2, ^{md}PA—*de-ni*—[DÙ-*uš* 94:2,
Nabû-dūru-kuṣur (eunuch): ^{md}PA—BÀD—*ku-ṣur* 228:1, 4, 5, 11,
Nabû-dūru-uṣur (eunuch 152, ditto of the palace cook 31, horse raiser 142, scribe 45): ^{md}PA—BÀD—PAB 31 r. 15, 45 r. 4, 102:8, 124:4, 127 r. 7, 142 r. 15, 152 r. 7, ^{md}PA—BÀ[D—PAB] 126:14,
Nabû-ēmuranni ('third man'): ^{md}P]A—IGI.LAL-*an* 345 r. 5,
Nabû-erība (deputy 301, 347, deputy of the team commander 308-342, scribe 163, 174): ^{md}AG—SU 177:1, 6, 193:1, ^{m}]^{d}PA—SU 163 r. 13, 174 r. 15, 316 r. 10, 321 r. 6, ^{md}PA—SU 167 r. 4, 177:12, 301 r. 10, 308 r. 9, 309 r. 10, 314 r. 18, 315 r. 3, 317 r. 3, 320 r. 3, 325 r. 17, 328 r. 13, 329 r. 19, 330 r. 13, 332 r. 10, 335 r. 21, 338 r. 15, 342 r. 14, ^{md}PA—SU] 339 r. 10, ^{md}P]A—SU 312 r. 12, ^{md}[PA—SU] 347 r. 12, ^{m}[^{d}P]A—SU 310 r. 8,
Nabû-ēṭir (chariot driver 297, scribe 218, ditto of the vizier 265): ^{md}PA—KAR 52:8, 338 r. 12, ^{md}PA—KAR-*ir* 143 r. 6, 218 r. 6, 265:13, 297 r. 10, ^{md}PA—KAR-[*ir*] 297 r. 1,
Nabû-ēṭiranni: ^{md}PA—KAR-*ir-an-ni* 202 r. 12, ^{md}PA—KA[R-*ir-a*]*n*-[*ni*] 216 e. 10, ^{md}PA—KAR-*ir-a-ni* 215 e. 8, ^{md}PA—KAR-*ir-a*-[*ni* 59 r. 1,
Nabû-ēṭir-napšāti (son of PN 173, scribe 173, 209, ditto of the chief eunuch 31): ^{md}PA—KAR-*ir*—ZI.MEŠ 173:1, ^{md}PA—[KA]R-*ir*—ZI.MEŠ 173 r. 6, ^{md}PA]—KAR-*ir*—ZI.MEŠ 209 r. 4, ^{md}PA—KAR—ZI.MEŠ 31 r. 16, 208 r. 5,
Nabû-ēṭir-[...]: ^{md}PA—KA[R-*x* 280 r. 12,
Nabû-hussanni (chariot driver 39, 40): ^{md}PA—*hu-sa-an-ni* 40 r. 5, ^{md}PA—*hu-sa-a-ni* 66 r. 9, ^{md}PA—*hu-us-sa-an-ni* 39:17,
Nabû-iddina: ^{md}PA—MU 52:8,
Nabû-iqīša (palace superintendent 283): ^{m}]^{d}AG—BA-*šá* 285:5, ^{md}PA—BA-*šá* 283 r. 19,
Nabû-iqīšanni (Kişirtean 119): ^{md}PA—BA-*šá-an-ni* 106 r. 2, ^{md}PA—BA-*šá-ni* 119 r. 18,
Nabû-iṣṣur: ^{md}PA—PAB 124 r. 4, 346 r. 1,
Nabû-ka''in-aplu (scribe): ^{md}PA—GIN—A 163 r. 15,
Nabû-ka''in-šarru (chief [...]): ^{md}P[A]—*ka-in*—MAN 130 r. 3,
Nabû-kabti-ahhēšu (scribe of the palace of Sargon): ^{md}PA—IDIM—PAB.MEŠ-*šú* 31 r. 4, 9,
Nabû-kāšir (overseer of reeds): ^{md}PA—*ka-šir* 35 r. 1,
Nabû-kēnu-dugul (chariot fighter): ^{md}PA—GIN—*du-gul* 204:5,
Nabû-kēnu-uṣur (prefect of Samaria 147, 148): ^{md}AG—GIN—PAB 147 r. 7, ^{m}]^{d}PA—GIN—PAB 104 r. 1, ^{md}PA—GIN—PAB 105 r. 12, 148 r. 4,
Nabû-kibsī-uṣur: ^{md}PA—*kib-si*—(PAB) 291 r. 5,
Nabû-killanni: ^{md}PA—*kil-la-an-ni* 265 r. 5,
Nabû-kuṣuranni: ^{md}PA—KÀD-*an-ni* 45 r. 3,
Nabû-la-tuššaranni: ^{md}PA—*la*—*tú-šar-a-ni* 221 r. 1,
Nabû-lē'āni ('third man' 177): ^{md}AG—ZU-*a-ni* 177 r. 1, ^{md}PA—ZU-*a-ni* 43:9, 44:6,
Nabû-lē'i (prefect of Arbela 114, 115, son of PN 284): ^{m}]^{d}PA—ZU 114 r. 2, 284 r. 16, ^{md}PA—ZU 113 r. 7, 278:1, e. 15, ^{md}PA—ZU] 115 r. 5,
Nabû-lēšir: ^{md}PA—GIŠ 286 r. 6,
Nabû-malik: ^{md}]PA—*ma-li-ik* 328 e. 15,
Nabû-mudammiq: ^{md}PA—*mu*-SIG$_5$ 59 r. 2,
Nabû-na'id (horse trainer 199): ^{m}]^{d}AG—I 115 r. 2, ^{md}PA—I 19:3, 85:4, 110 r. 11, 199 r. 5, ^{md}P]A—I 165 r. 7,
Nabû-nādin-ahhē (scribe 61, 301, 305): ^{m}]^{d}[A]G—SUM—PAB.MEŠ 61 r. 9, ^{md}PA—AŠ—PAB.ME[Š 253:4, ^{md}PA—MU—PAB.MEŠ 301 r. 16, ^{md}PA]—SUM—PAB.MEŠ 305 r. 15,
Nabû-nādin-ahi: ^{md}AG—AŠ—PAB 147 r. 4, ^{md}PA—AŠ—PAB 84:4,
Nabû-nādin-šumi: ^{md}PA—SU]M—MU 314 r. 14,
Nabû-nammir: ^{md}PA—*nam-mir* 199 r. 7, ^{m}]^{d}PA—ZALÁG-*ir* 105:9, ^{md}PA—ZALÁG-*ir* 145:4,
Nabû-nashir: ^{md}PA—*n*[*a-as-hir*] 181 r. 4, ^{md}PA—*na-sa-hir* 182 r. 4,
Nabû-nāṣir (farmer 28, 115, scribe 331, son of PN 119): ^{md}]PA—PAB-*ir* 125 r. 14, ^{md}PA—PAB-*ir* 28 r. 5, 90 r. 14, 115 r. 2, 119 r. 15, 124:6, 277 r. 7, 331:2,
Nabû-natkil (royal bodyguard): ^{m}]^{d}PA—*nat-kil* 240 r. 5,

Nātan: ^{m}*na-tan* 195 r. 4,
Nātunu: ^{m}*na-tú-nu* 227 r. 6,
Nazi[...]: ^{m}*na-zi-*[*x* 118 r. 7,
Nergal-abu-uṣur: ^{m}U.GUR—AD—PAB 273:6,
Nergal-ahu-uṣur (commander-of-fifty 124): ^{md}U.GUR—PAB—PAB 124 r. 6, 254 r. 4, ^{md}U].GUR—PAB—PAB 93:6,
Nergal-ašarēd: ^{md}U.GUR—MAŠ 37 r. 14, ^{m}U.GUR—MAŠ 77:3, 161 r. 12, 223 r. 8, ^{m}U.GUR]—MAŠ 224 r. 5,
Nergal-ēṭir: ^{md}]MAŠ.MAŠ—KAR-*ir* 240 r. 6, ^{md}U.GUR—KAR-*ir* 103:3,
Nergal-ibni (scribe 63, 'third man' 193): ^{m}]^{d}U.GUR—D[Ù 10 r. 9, ^{md}U.GUR—DÙ 32 r. 12, ^{m}]U.GUR—DÙ 193 r. 3, ^{m}U.GUR—DÙ 167 r. 1, 291 r. 3, ^{m}U.GUR—DÙ-*ni* 63 r. 4,
Nergal-iddina: ^{md}U.GUR—SUM-*na* 86:5,
Nergal-ilā'ī (governor 287, scribe 345): ^{md}U.GUR—DINGIR-*a-a* 143:4, 287:1, 345 r. 7,
Nergal-ilī: ^{m}U.GUR—DINGIR 177 r. 13,
Nergal-mušēzib: ^{md}MAŠ.MAŠ—*mu-še-zib* 7 r. 5,
Nergal-na'id: ^{m}U.G[UR]—I 273 r. 3,
Nergal-nāṣir: ^{md}U.GUR—PAB-*ir* 125 r. 9,
Nergal-šallimanni (chief [...] 100): ^{md}U.GUR—*šal-lim-a-ni* 101 r. 10, ^{m}U.GUR—*š*]*al-lim-an-ni* 100 r. 8,
Nergal-šarru-uṣur (chariot driver 349, chief cupbearer 255, 271, city overseer 319, horse trainer 239, son of PN 258, son of emissary 312-314, 'third man' 305-350, ditto of the crown prince 321): ^{m}]^{d}MAŠ.MAŠ—MAN—PAB 324 r. 4, 350 r. 2, ^{md}MAŠ.MA]Š—M[AN—PAB 305 r. 6, ^{md}MAŠ.MAŠ—MAN—PAB 258 r. 4, 306 r. 5, 314 r. 9, 323 r. 2, 325 r. 10, 332 r. 8, ^{md}MAŠ.MAŠ—MAN—P[AB 326 r. 14, ^{md}MAŠ].MAŠ—MAN—PAB 332 r. 3, 342 r. 3, 349 r. 7, ^{md}U.GUR—LUGAL—PAB 319 r. 7, ^{m}]^{d}U.GUR—MAN—PAB 313 r. 3, ^{md}U.GUR—MAN—PAB 312 r. 15, 320 r. 4, 334 r. 20, ^{md}U.GUR—MAN—P[AB 30 r. 2, ^{md}U.GUR—MAN]—PAB 339 r. 2, ^{md}U.GUR]—MAN—PAB 327 r. 5, [^{md}U.GUR]—MAN—PAB 271 r. 17, ^{m}U.GUR—MAN—PAB 270:1, 321 r. 7, 323 s. 1, 324 r. 11, 325 r. 16, ^{m}U.GUR—MAN—PAB] 207 s. 1, ^{m}U.GUR—[MAN]—PAB 239 r. 6, ^{m}U.G[UR—MAN—PAB] 208 e. 7, ^{m}U].GUR—MAN—PAB 255 r. 4,
Nergal-šumu-ibni: ^{md}U.GUR—MU—DÙ 186 e. 9,
Nergal-šumu-[...] (prince): ^{md}U.GUR—MU—[*x*] 41 r. 6,
Nergal-uballiṭ: ^{md}U.GUR—*ú-ba*[*l-liṭ*] 251:3,
Nihrammu ('third man' of the crown prince): ^{m}*ni-ih-ra-mu* 283 r. 17,
Nīnuāiu (mayor 96): ^{m}*ni-nu-a-a* 2 r. 5, 319 r. 14, ^{m}NINA.KI-*a-a* 215 r. 2, ^{m}URU.NINA-*a-a* 47:3, 96 r. 6,
Nīnu'ītu: MÍ.UR]U.NINA.KI-*i-*[*tú*] 163:8,
Nuhšāia (gate-guard 177, 247, 249, cohort commander of the chief eunuch 174): ^{m}HÉ.NUN-*a-a* 10:9, 55 r. 5, 160 r. 11, 161:8, r. 16, 174 r. 9, 177 r. 6, 247 r. 7, 248 r. 2, 278 r. 14, ^{m}HÉ.NUN-[*a-a* 249 r. 3, ^{m}HÉ.NU]N-*a-a* 99 r. 11, ^{m}HÉ.N[UN-*a-a* 13:7, ^{m}[HÉ].NUN-*a-a* 11:3,
Nunu'a: ^{m}*nu-nu-a* 118 r. 8,
Nūrāia (son of PN 284): ^{m}*nu-ra-a-a* 52:9, ^{m}ZALÁG-*a-a* 284 r. 13,
Nūrānu (cohort commander 177, herald 98): ^{m}*nu-ra-a-ni* 221 r. 2, ^{m}ZALÁG-*a-nu* 98 r. 8, 177 r. 4, 277 r. 6,
Nūr-Adad: ^{m}ZALÁG—^{d}IM 194 r. 5,
Nūr-ilā'ī: ^{m}ZALÁG—DINGIR-[*a-a*] 218 r. 5,
Nūr-Ṣē': ^{m}ZALÁG—*se-e* 23 r. 8,
Nūr-Šamaš: ^{m}ZALÁG—^{d}*šá-maš* 238 r. 6,
Nūr-[...]: ^{m}ZALÁG—[*x* 341:3,
Nušhu-sallihanni (horse trainer of the open chariotry): ^{md}*nu-uš-hu—sa-lìh-an-*[*ni*] 316:1, ^{md}*nu-uš-hu—sa-l*[*ìh-an-ni*] 315:11,
Nušku-ilā'ī: ^{m}]^{d}PA.TÚG—DINGIR-*a-a* 225 r. 5, ^{md}PA.TÚG—DINGIR-*a-a* 167 r. 3, 229 r. 5, 232 r. 1, 233:8, ^{md}PA.TÚG—DINGIR-[*a-a*] 230 r. 1, 231:4, ^{md}PA.TÚG—DI[NGIR-*a-a*] 131 r. 14, ^{m}*nu-uš-ku*—DINGIR-*a-a* 221 r. 5, 238 r. 5,
Nušku-nāṣir: ^{md}]PA.TÚG—PAB 272:2,
Palhu-šēzib: ^{m}*pal-hu—še-zib* 192 r. 9,
Palhu-ušēzib: ^{m}*pal-h*]*u—ú-še-zib* 252 r. 13,
Pān-Nabû-ṭēmī: ^{m}IGI—^{d}PA—*ṭ*[*è-mì*] 279:1,
Papâ: MÍ.*pa-pa-a* 315:6, MÍ.*p*[*a-pa-a* 316:7,
Paqaha (village manager): ^{m}*pa-qa-ha* 34 r. 8, ^{m}*pa-qa-*[*ha*] 40 r. 12, ^{m}*pa-*[*q*]*a-ha* 41 r. 13,
Paršidu: ^{m}*par-ši-di* 30:2, ^{m}*par-ši-du* 17:5, ^{m}*par-*[*ši-d*]*u* 18 r. 3,
Partāma: ^{m}*par-ta-a-ma* 182:3, ^{m}*par-t*[*a-a-ma*] 181:1, ^{m}*pa*[*r*]*-ta-a-ma* 181:4,
Paruṭṭu: ^{m}*pa-ru-ṭi* 253:9, ^{m}*pa-ru-ṭu* 166 r. 3, 253 r. 1,
Pilaqqâ: ^{m}GIŠ.BAL-*a* 91:5,
Pilaqqu-lipirê: ^{m}GIŠ.BAL—*li-pi-re-e* 206:3,
Piqāqu: ^{m}*pi-qa-qi* 120:4,
Piri'-Ea (scribe): ^{m}NUNUZ-*a-a* 59 r. 16,
Pišarmu (recruitment officer): ^{m}*pi-ša-ar-mu* 36 r. 2,
Pudupiāti: ^{m}*pu-du-pi-ia-ti* 236:3, 6,
Pūlu (tanner 134): ^{m}*pu-ú-lu* 134 r. 8, ^{m}*pu-u-*[*lu* 32 r. 13,
Qâ (bought man): ^{m}*qa-a* 52 r. 10,
Qabal-hurdāti: ^{m}MURUB$_{4}$—*hur-da-a-te* 288 r. 12,
Qalunzu (shepherd): ^{m}*qa-lu-un-zu* 42 r. 15,
Qaqâ: ^{m}*qa-q*[*a-a*] 151 r. 8,
Qarhâ (farmer 315, 316): ^{m}*qar-ha-a* 315:4, [^{m}*qar-ha-a* 316:6, ^{m}*qa-ra-ha-a* 194:9,
Qāribu: ^{m}*qa-ri-bu* 147 r. 3,
Qausu: ^{m}*qa-ú-su* 37:7,
Qibinnî (weaver): ^{m}*qí-bi-ni-i* 13 r. 3, see also *Qibitnê,*
Qibitnê: ^{m}*qí-bit-né-e* 10 r. 14, ^{m}*qi-bit-*[*né*]*-e* 10:15, ^{m}*qi-*[*bit-né-e*] 11:7, see also *Qibinnî,*
Qibīt-Aššūr: ^{m}*qí-bit—aš-šur* 188 r. 4, 273 e. 8,
Qibīt-ili: ^{m}*qí-bit*—DINGIR 273 r. 2,
Qibīt-Issār: ^{m}*qí-bit*—15 170:3,
Qidinu: ^{m}*qi-di-ni* 176:7,
Qīti-ilāni: ^{m}*qi-ti*—DINGIR.MEŠ 274 r. 7,
Qīti-Illil: ^{m}*qi-ti*—BE 189 r. 3,
Quaqua: ^{m}*qu-a-qu-a* 288 r. 10,
Qū'a: ^{m}*qu-u-a* 214 r. 5,
Qūia: ^{m}*qu-u-ia* 157 r. 7,
Qulî: ^{m}*qu-li-i* 23 r. 6,
Ququa (outrider): ^{m}*qu-qu-u-a* 257 r. 29,
Qurbu-abū'a: ^{m}*q*[*ur-b*]*u*—AD-*u-a* 158:2,
Qurbu-ilu: ^{m}*qur-bu*—DINGIR 21 r. 6,
Qurdî: ^{m}*qur-di-i* 277 r. 2,
Qurdi-Adad (team commander 65, scribe 31): ^{m}*qur-di*—^{d}IM 31 r. 26, 81:7, ^{m}*qur-d*]*i*—^{d}IM 65 r. 8, ^{m}*qur-di*—10 120 r. 4,
Qurdi-Harrān: ^{m}*qu*[*r-d*]*i*—URU.KASKAL 139 r. 2,
Qurdi-Issār (cohort commander 204, 247, 249): ^{m}*qur-di*—^{d}15 204 r. 4, 220 r. 9, 247 r. 3, 249 r. 6,

^{m}qur-di—15 32:6, 78 r. 1,
Qurdi-Issār-lāmur: ^{m}qur-di—15—la-mur 191:1,
Qurdi-Nergal: ^{m}qur-di—^{d}U.GUR 2 r. 1,
Qurdi-[...]: ^{m}qur-di—^{d}[x 2 r. 6,
Quwāiu (son of PN): ^{m}qu-u-a-a 188:1,
Radimu: ^{m}ra-di-mu 196 r. 3,
Rahīmî: ^{m}ra-hi-mì-i 227 r. 7,
Rahīm-Dādi (merchant): ^{m}ri-hi-me—MAN 319 r. 11,
Rahīm-il: ^{m}ra]-hi-me—DINGIR 122 r. 2,
Rāma-iâ: MÍ.ra-ma-a—[ia-a 286:3, MÍ.ra-ma-a]—ia-a 286 s. 1,
Rammān-dalâ (from Ša-Zabini 195): ^{md}ra-man—dàl-a 195 r. 9, ^{md}ra-man—dal-a 261:1,
Ranqira[...]: ^{m}ra-an-qi-ra-[x] 126:6,
Rapaia: ^{m}ra-pa-ia 50 r. 14,
Rapi' ('third man'): ^{m}ra-pi-i' 287 r. 9,
Rasu' (chief boatman): ^{m}ra-su-u' 142 r. 14,
Rēmanni-Adad (carpenter 96, chariot driver [of the king] 297-347): ^{m}rém-an-ni—^{d}]IM 340:7, ^{m}rém-an-ni—^{d}IM 301:6, 17, 311:7, 318:4, 319:5, 13, 326:15, r. 4, 329:13, 334 r. 2, 339:3, 342:5, 15, ^{m}rém-an-ni—^{d}IM] 314 r. 2, 339:9, 348:9, ^{m}rém-an-ni—^{d}[IM 314:15, ^{m}rém-an-ni—[^{d}IM] 337:5, ^{m}rém-an-n[i—^{d}IM] 297:9, [^{m}rém-an-ni—^{d}IM] 329:21, ^{m}rém-an-[ni]—^{d}10 299:9, ^{m}rém-a-na—^{d}IM 309:5, ^{m}rém-a-ni—^{d}IM 298:9, 308 e. 9, 313:7, 315:9, 323:3, 324:8, 325 r. 1, 328:9, 334 r. 13, 335:11, r. 7, 336:8, 344:6, r. 6, 346 r. 3, ^{m}rém-a-ni—^{d}IM] 312 r. 1, 317:4, ^{m}rém-a-ni—^{d}I]M 328 r. 1, ^{m}rém-a-ni—^{d}[IM] 347:6, ^{m}rém-a-n]i—^{d}IM 349 r. 2, ^{m}rém-a-[ni—^{d}IM 322:8, ^{m}rém-[a-ni—^{d}IM] 317:6, ^{m}rém]-a-ni—^{d}IM 336:11, 343:9, ^{m}ré]m-a-ni—^{d}IM 307:3, 336 r. 7, ^{m}ré]m-a-ni—[^{d}IM] 338 r. 4, [^{m}rém-a-ni—^{d}IM 300:7, [^{m}rém-a-ni—^{d}IM] 316:10, [^{m}rém-a-ni]—^{d}IM 345:7, [^{m}r]ém-a-ni—^{d}IM 333 e. 5, ^{m}rém-a-ni—^{d}10 306:12, ^{m}rém-a]-ni—^{d}10 306:3, ^{m}rém-a-ni—10 96 r. 9, 305:15, 341 r. 2, 9, ^{m}rém-a-ni—[10] 305:6, ^{m}[ré]m-a-ni—10 296:3,
Rēmanni-Aššūr: ^{m}rém-a-ni—aš-šur 52 r. 11,
Rēmanni-Illil (confectioner): ^{m}rém-a-ni—BE 204 r. 11, 205 r. 5,
Rēmanni-ilu: ^{m}rém-a-ni—DINGIR 14 r. 5, 22 r. 6, 97 r. 12, ^{m}rém-ni—DINGIR 66 r. 10,
Rēmanni-[...]: ^{m}rém-an-ni—[x 155 r. 3, ^{m}rém-a-ni—[x 140 r. 6,
Rēmutti-ili: ^{m}re-mut-ti—DINGIR 77:4,
Rēmuttu: MÍ.ri-mu-t[ú 138:5, ^{m}rém-ut 192 r. 7,
Rēmūt-Bābu: ^{m}rém-ut—^{d}BA.Ú 178 r. 6,
Rēmūt-ilāni: ^{m}rém-ut—DINGIR.MEŠ 90:5,
Rēmūt-ili: ^{m}]rém-u[t—DINGIR] 181 r. 5, ^{m}rém-ut—DINGIR 30 r. 4, 182 r. 5,
Rēmūt-[...]: ^{m}rém-ut-[x 269 r. 8,
Rībāia: ^{m}ri-ba-a-a 158 r. 1,
Rībāti: ^{m}ri-ba-a-[te] 161:10, ^{m}ri-ba-te 160:12, ^{m}SU.MEŠ-t[e] 161 r. 4,
Rība-ahhē (cohort commander 125, delegate of Kar-Šamaš 188, from Goldsmith Town 19): ^{m}SU—PAB.MEŠ 19 r. 9, 125 r. 11, 188 r. 7, 336:7, r. 4, ^{m}S[U—PAB—MEŠ] 336 r. 4,
Rībā-ilāni (merchant 124): ^{m}SU—DINGIR.MEŠ-ni 78:8, 124:7, ^{m}S[U—DINGIR.MEŠ-ni 124:15,
Rihāti: ^{m}]ri-ha-te 198 r. 5, ^{m}ri-ha-[te] 197 r. 7,
Rīsāia (bodyguard 116): ^{m}ri-sa-a-a 177 r. 10, ^{m}ri-sa-[a-a] 116:6,
Rīšat-abīša: MÍ.ri-šá-0—AD-šá 257:2, MÍ.r[i-šá—A]D-šá 257:15,
Ruradidi (eunuch of the harem governess): ^{m}ru-ra-di-di 152 r. 2,
Sa'īlu: ^{m}sa-i-li 178:3, ^{m}sa-i-lu 178:4, ^{m}se-'i-lu 35 r. 4, ^{m}si-i-lu 207 e. 8,
Sa'īru ('third man' 199, 310, 345): ^{m}sa-']i-ru 345 r. 4, ^{m}sa-e-ru 178 r. 4, 199 r. 3, ^{m}sa-i-ru 310 r. 15,
Sa'uti: ^{m}sa-'u-ú-ti 300:1,
Sagab: ^{m}sa-gab 18:2, 262 r. 5,
Saggil-bi'dī (servant of the vizier): ^{m}sa-gi-i[l]—bi-i'-di 6 r. 11,
Sagībî (gate-guard 81, ditto of the palace 96, weaver 294): ^{m}sa-gíb-i 81 r. 8, ^{m}sa-gi-bi-i 96 r. 16, 272:9, r. 6, 294:1,
Sahār-ili: ^{m}NIGIN-ár—DINGIR 277 r. 9,
Sahhî: ^{m}sa-ah-hi-i 25 r. 4,
Sakā': ^{m}sa-ka-a[' 302 r. 10,
Sakkannu (chariot driver): ^{m}sak-kan 324 r. 7, ^{m}sa-ak-kan 316 r. 7, 317 e. 11, ^{m}sa-a]k-kan 327 r. 3, ^{m}s]a-ak-kan 338 r. 13, ^{m}sa-[a]k-k[an-n]u 347 r. 10, ^{m}sa-kan 310 r. 6, ^{m}sa-k]an 318 e. 8, ^{m}sa-kan-nu 323 r. 6, 325 r. 14, ^{m}sa-kan-[nu 328 r. 14, 350 r. 5, ^{m}sa-kan]-nu 349 r. 9, ^{m}sa-ka]n-nu 312 r. 11, ^{m}sa-ka-nu 332 r. 7,
Salamame (royal bodyguard 221): ^{m}sa-la-ma-me 221 r. 4, ^{m}sa-la-[ma-me] 231:3,
Salāmu: ^{m}]sa-la-me 268:1,
Salām-Adad: ^{m}sa-la-ma—^{d}IM 94:9,
Salilānu: ^{m}sa-li-la-a-nu 100:2, 101:11, ^{m}sa-l]i-la-a-nu 100:15, ^{m}sa-l]i-la-a-[nu] 101:3, [^{m}sa-li-la-a-nu 100:7,
Salsali (scribe): ^{m}sal-sa-li 267 r. 4,
Sama' (horse raiser of the crown prince 37-40, ditto of PN 41): ^{m}sa-ma-a' 39:16, 40 r. 4, ^{m}s[a-m]a-a' 41 r. 5, ^{m}s]a-ma-a' 37 r. 7,
Same': ^{m}sa-me-e' 108 r. 1, 202 r. 13, ^{m}sa-me-[e' 203 r. 1,
Samsī: ^{m}sa-am-si 133 s. 2,
Sanānu: ^{m}]sa-na-a-nu 182 r. 3, ^{m}sa-na-nu 181 r. 3,
Sanā-il (messenger of the major-domo): ^{m}sa-na—DINGIR 95 r. 7,
Sangî: ^{m}sa-an-gi-i 111 r. 6,
Sangû-Issār (scribe 32, 65, 283): ^{m}SANGA—^{d}15 32 r. 15, 262:3, 265:3, 8, 284 r. 14, ^{m}SANGA—^{d}1[5] 283 r. 22, ^{m}SANGA—15 263:2, ^{m}SAN]GA—15 65 r. 13,
Sanî (chief [...]): ^{m}]sa-ni-i 112 r. 4,
Sarru-kīna: ^{m}]sa-ru—ki-na 225 r. 10,
Sar-uarri: ^{m}sar-ú-ar-ri 166:1,
Sasallû (deputy): ^{m}sa-s[a]-lu-u 288 r. 7,
Sasî (mayor 338): ^{m}sa-a-si-i 160:11, ^{m}sa-si-i 90:6, 314 r. 10, ^{m}sa-si-[i 251 r. 5, ^{m}sa-si-[i] 296 r. 5, ^{m}]sa-si-i' 338 r. 10,
Sâ-abu: ^{m}sa-a-AD 274:1, 4,
Sâ-ṣidqi ('genie'): ^{m}sa-[a—ṣi]-id-qi 288 r. 6,
Sē'-abī: ^{m}]se—AD 120 r. 1,
Sē'-barakki: ^{m}se-e'—ba-rak-ki 97 e. 9,
Sē'-dalâ (horse trainer of the open chariotry 310): ^{m}se-e'—dàl-a$_{4}$ 315 r. 5, ^{m}se]-e'—dàl-a$_{4}$ 316 r. 12, ^{m}se-e'—da-la-a 310 r. 16, [^{m}]se—dàl-a 23:4, ^{m}se—da-l[a-a] 23:1,
Sē'-dūrī: ^{m}se—BÀD 111 r. 8,
Sē'-gabba: ^{m}se—gab-a 111:5,
Sē'-gabbāri: ^{m}se-e'—gab-ba-ri 87:7,
Sē'-hāri ('third man' 315): ^{m}]se-e'—ha-ri 316 r. 9, ^{m}se-e'—ha-ri 315 r. 2,
Sē'-hāti (city overseer): ^{m}se-e—ha-ti 166:5,

Sēʾ-hutnī (horse trainer): ^{m}*se-eʾ—hu-ut-ni* 110 r. 10,
Sēʾ-ilāʾī: ^{m}*se-e*]ʾ—DINGIR-*a-a* 311 r. 3,
Seʾīlu see *Saʾīlu*
Sēʾ-immī: ^{m}*se-eʾ—im-me* 109:3,
Sēʾ-maʾādī (village manager 109, ditto of the crown prince 110, 112): ^{m}*se-eʾ—ma-aʾ-du* 110:7, ^{m}*s*[*e-eʾ—ma-a-di*] 112:7, [^{m}*se-eʾ—ma*]-*ʾa-di* 109:6, ^{m}*se—ma-a-di* 111:9,
Sēʾ-matiʾ: ^{m}*se—ma-ti-iʾ* 23 r. 4,
Sēʾ-nātan: ^{m}*se—na-tan* 319:1, 4, 10,
Sēʾ-na[...]: ^{m}*se—na-x*[*x* 179 r. 5,
Sēʾ-nūrī (major-domo 166): ^{m}*se-eʾ—nu-ri* 223 r. 5, 224 r. 2, 294:2, ^{m}*se-e*—NU 166:4, ^{m}]*se-e*—ZALÁG 112 r. 6,
Sēʾ-parakka: ^{m}*se-eʾ—pa-rak-ka* 199 r. 10,
Sēʾ-sakâ (major-domo): ^{m}*se-e—sa-ka-a* 267:1, ^{m}*se-e—sa*]-*ka-a* 267:4,
Sēʾ-šumkī: ^{m}*se-e—šúm-ki* 267 r. 3,
Sēʾ-ṭūrī (smith): ^{m}*se-eʾ—ṭu-ri* 26 r. 4,
Sēʾ-zabadī: ^{m}*se-eʾ—za-ba-di* 98:1, ^{m}*se-eʾ—za-ba-*[*di*] 98:4, ^{m}*se-eʾ—za-b*[*a*]-*di* 98:6,
Sēʾ-[...]: ^{m}*s*]*e-eʾ—*[*x* 11 r. 15,
Sebetti-ilāʾī (servant of the crown prince): ^{m}UD.7.KÁM—DINGIR-*a-a* 201 r. 8,
Silim-Aššūr (ša [...] 238, vizier 308-338): ^{m}*si-lim—aš-šur* 221:2, 222:1, 223:2, 6, 224:2, 6, 226:11, 227:5, 228:5, 229:7, 232:2, 233:4, 234:3, 235:4, 237:4, 308 r. 5, 316 r. 2, 325 r. 9, 329 r. 8, 332 r. 6, 338 r. 8, ^{m}*si-lim—aš-šu*]*r* 335 r. 13, ^{m}*si-lim—aš-*[*šur* 330 r. 4, ^{m}*si-lim—*[*aš-šur* 132:8, ^{m}*s*[*i-lim—aš-šur*] 226 r. 13, [^{m}*s*]*i-lim—aš-šur* 238:6, ^{m}*si-lim—*^{d}*aš-šur* 312 r. 7, ^{m}*si-lim*—AN.ŠÁR 236:5, [^{m}*si-lim*—AN.ŠÁR] 236:2,
Silim-Dādi: ^{m}*si-lim*—U.U 334:28,
Silim-ili (priest 250): ^{m}*si-lim*—DINGIR 237 r. 1, 250 r. 7, 252 r. 12, 303 r. 3,
Silim-Issār (gate-guard): ^{m}*si-lim*—^{d}15 6 r. 14,
Silim-Sēʾ: ^{m}*si-lim—se* 180 r. 6,
Silim-[...]: ^{m}*si-lim—x*[*x* 179 r. 3,
Simesīme (village manager): ^{m}*si-me-s*[*i-i*]-*me* 233:5, ^{m}*s*]*i-me-*[*s*]*i-me* 233:1,
Sinâ: ^{m}*si-na-a* 170 r. 3, 171 r. 3,
Sinqi-Issār: ^{m}*si-qi*—^{d}15 241 r. 5,
Sīn-abu-uṣur (gate-guard 174, scribe 159): ^{m}]^{d}30—AD—PAB 174 r. 10, ^{md}30—AD—PAB 159 r. 2, 319 r. 6,
Sīn-ahhē-rība (king of Assyria): ^{md}[30—PAB.MEŠ.SU] 153 r. 4, ^{md}30—PAB.ME[Š—SU 59:7, ^{md}30—PAB.MEŠ—SU 57:7, 88 r. 12, 90 r. 16, 154 s. 3, 158 r. 8, 177 r. 19, 180 r. 2, ^{md}30—PAB.MEŠ—SU] 155 r. 8, 162 r. 6, ^{md}30—PAB.M[EŠ—SU] 48 s. 1, ^{md}3[0—PAB.MEŠ—SU] 159 r. 4, ^{md}[30—PAB.MEŠ—SU] 151 r. 11, [^{md}]30—PAB.MEŠ—SU 251:5, ^{m}30—PAB.MEŠ—SU 152 e. 9, 156 r. 7, 160 r. 15, 174 r. 16, ^{m}30—PAB.MEŠ—[SU] 157 r. 10,
Sīn-ahu-iddina: ^{md}30—PAB—SUM-*na* 239:1, ^{m}30—PAB—AŠ 73 r. 3,
Sīn-ālik-pāni: ^{m}*si-in*—DU—IGI 342:1,
Sīn-ašarēd ('third man' 317, ditto of the crown prince 320-325): ^{md}30—MAŠ 317 r. 1, 320 r. 1, 325 r. 21, ^{md}30—[MAŠ 321 r. 4,
Sīn-balāssu-iqbi (chariot fighter): ^{md}3[0—TI-*s*]*u*—E 130 r. 12,
Sīn-bēlu-uṣur (cohort commander 192, ditto of the palace 287): ^{md}30—EN—PAB 192 r. 4, ^{m}30—EN—PAB 287 r. 8, [^{m}3]0—EN—[P]AB 267 r. 1,
Sīn-ēreš: ^{md}30—APIN-[*eš*] 93:6,
Sīn-erība: ^{md}30—SU 96 r. 12,
Sīn-iddina ('third man'): ^{md}30—AŠ 1 r. 12,
Sīn-ilāʾī: ^{md}30—DINGIR-*a-a* 227 r. 1,
Sīn-kāšir (scribe): ^{m}*si-in—ka-šir* 148 r. 2,
Sīn-mutaqqin: ^{md}30—LAL-*in* 199 r. 9,
Sīn-naʾdi (brother of PN 23, cohort commander 53, seller 5, tanner of coloured leather 29): ^{md}30—I 22 r. 6, 53 r. 7, 348 r. 6, ^{m}30—I 5:1, 23:2, 4, 29 r. 4,
Sīn-nādin-ahhē: ^{md}30—SUM-*na*—PAB.MEŠ 243 r. 7,
Sīn-nādin-ahi: ^{m}30—SUM—PAB 140:6,
Sīn-nāṣir (herald): ^{md}30—PAB-*ir* 166 r. 4, 8,
Sīn-rēmanni: ^{md}30*—rém-*[*an-ni*] 301 r. 7, ^{md}30*—rém-a-ni* 338 r. 12, ^{md}30*—rém-ni* 183:3, ^{md}30*—re-man-ni* 185 r. 1, ^{md}30—[*re-man-ni*] 184:3,
Sīn-ṣalla: ^{md}30*—ṣa-la-a* 266 r. 5,
Sīn-šallimani (prefect of Raṣappa): ^{md}30*—šal-*(*lim*)*-a-ni* 17 s. 1,
Sīn-šarru-uṣur (chariot driver 235, deputy 287, prefect 139): ^{m}]^{d}30—MAN—PAB 77:2, 146 r. 6, ^{md}30—MAN—PAB 142 r. 17, 235 e. 9, 287:3, ^{m}30—[LUG]AL.PAB 140:7, ^{m}3[0—LUGAL—PAB] 140:1, ^{m}30—MAN—PAB 139:2,
Sīn-šar-ilāni (seller 258): ^{md}30—LUGAL—DINGIR.MEŠ 86 r. 15, ^{md}30—MAN—DINGIR.MEŠ 258:1,
Sīn-taklāk (treasurer): ^{m}30*—tak-lak* 18 r. 7,
Sīn-zāqipī (fowler): ^{m}30*—za-qi-pi* 52 r. 14,
Sīn-zēru-ibni ('third man' 44): ^{md}30—NUMUN—DÙ 43:5, 44:4,
Sīn-zēru-iddina: ^{m}30—NUMUN—SUM-*na* 267 r. 2,
Sīn-[...]: ^{md}3[0*—x* 342 r. 17, ^{md}30—MU—[*x*] 326:18, ^{md}3[0—MU*—x*] 326 e. 24,
Siprānu (tanner of coloured leather 1): ^{m}*si-ip-ra-a-nu* 146 r. 3, ^{m}*si-ip-*[*ra-a-nu*] 192:1, ^{m}*si-par-a-nu* 156 s. 1, ^{m}*si-pa-ra-nu* 1 r. 10,
Sīri: ^{m}*si-i-ri* 143 r. 5,
Sitirkānu: *š*(*t*)*rkn* 59 r. 19, [^{m}*s*]*i-ti-ir-ka-a-nu* 59:4,
Sitir[...]: ^{m}*si-t*[*i-ir-x* 86:4,
Suhiru: ^{m}*su-hi-ru* 17 r. 12,
Suhuramû (merchant of the crown prince): ^{m}*su-hu-ra-mu-u* 210 r. 14,
Sukkāia (weaver 13, servant 342): ^{m}*suk-ka-a-a* 12 r. 1, 13 r. 2, ^{m}*suk-ka-a-*[*a* 342 r. 12, ^{m}*suk-ku-a-a* 167:3, ^{m}*su-ka-a-a* 107:3, ^{m}TE-*a-a* 10 r. 15, 291 e. 9, 334:23,
Sukkūia see *Sukkāia*,
Sūrāiu: ^{m}*su-r*[*a-a-a*] 145:2,
Surarāti: ^{m}*su-ra-*[*ra*]*-a-te* 66 r. 7, ^{m}*s*]*u-ra-ra-a-te* 65 r. 12, ^{m}*su-ra-ra-te* 262 r. 3,
Sūsî (tailor): ^{m}*su-si-i* 31 r. 23,
Sūsīa (goldsmith of the vizier, son of PN): ^{m}*su-si-ia* 19 r. 7, 8,
Susû: ^{m}*su-su-ú* 2 r. 2,
Ṣabbutānu: ^{m}*ṣab-ta-a-nu* 70:4, ^{m}*ṣa-bu-ta-a-nu* 72:1,
Ṣābu-damqu: ^{m}*ṣa-bu*—SIG_5 17:1, ^{m}ERIM.MEŠ—SIG 9:4,
Ṣadduru: ^{m}*ṣa-du-ru* 274 r. 10,
Ṣaiādu (chief carpenter): ^{m}*ṣa-a-a-di* 265 r. 6,
Ṣalam-ahhē (horse trainer 257, seller 28): ^{m}*ṣal-mu*—PAB.MEŠ 28:2, 257 r. 26,
Ṣalam-šarri-iqbi: ^{md}]NU—LUGAL*—iq-bi* 317:1, ^{md}NU—LUG[AL*—iq-bi* 317:3, ^{md}NU—MAN*—iq-*[*bi* 302 r. 8, ^{m}*ṣal-mu*—MAN*—iq-bi* 264 r. 8, ^{m}NU—MAN*—iq-bi*

Šarru-uṣur: ^{m}MAN—PAB 238 s. 1,

Šār-Aššūr: ^{m}IM—*aš-šur* 87 r. 9,

Šār-Nabû-allak: ^{m}IM—^{d}PA—*a-la-ka* 270 r. 3,

Ṣaulānu (scribe): ^{m}*ṣa-ú-la-a-nu* 17 r. 15,

Ša-Adad-anīnu: ^{m}*šá*—^{d}IM—*a-ni-nu* 247:6,

Ša-Aššūr-anīnu: ^{m}*ša—aš-šur—a-*[*ni-ni*] 19 r. 2,

Ša-Aššūr-dubbu: ^{m}*šá—aš-šur—*[*du-bu*] 32 r. 17,

Ša-Issār-dubbu (servant 174): ^{m}*šá*—^{d}15—*du-bu* 85 r. 8, ^{m}*ša*—15—*du-*[*b*]*u* 174:2,

Ša-lā-mašāʾ**e** (mayor): ^{m}*šá—la—ma-šá-e* 274 r. 8,

Ša-lā-mašê: ^{m}*šá—la—maš* 143 s. 1, ^{m}*šá—la*]*—ma-še-e* 275 s. 1, ^{m}*šá—la*]*—ma-ši-i* 186 r. 8,

Ša-Nabû-šû: ^{m}*šá*—^{d}PA—*su-u* 295:5,

Ša-[...]-anīnu: ^{m}*šá*—^{d}[*x—a-ni*]*-ni* 17 r. 9,

Šēlebu: ^{m}*še-li-pi* 210:1, ^{m}*še*]*-li-pi* 210:9,

Šemahu: ^{m}*še-ma-hu* 126:8,

Šēp-Adad: ^{m}GÌR.2—^{d}IM 157:3, ^{m}GÌR.2—10 30 r. 11,

Šēp-Aššūr (royal bodyguard 265): ^{m}GÌR.2—*aš-šur* 158 r. 3, 265 r. 9, 273:3, ^{m}GÌ]R.2—*aš-šur* 220 r. 14,

Šēp-Ēa (son of PN 284): ^{m}]GÌR.2-[*a*]*-a* 284 r. 18, ^{m}GÌR.2-*a-a* 105 r. 7,

Šēp-Issār (scribe 210, seller 302, servant of the governor of Birtu 31): ^{m}]GÌR.2—^{d}15 31 r. 22, ^{m}GÌR.2—^{d}15 12 r. 2, 302:2, ^{m}GÌR.2—[^{d}15 302:11, ^{m}GÌR.2—15 210 r. 5, 334:4,

Šēp-[...]: ^{m}GÌR.2—[*x* 24:7, 184 r. 2,

Šēr-idrī (seller): ^{m}*še-er-ri—id-ri* 10:2, ^{m}*še-er-id-ri* 10:19,

Šēr-ilāʾī: ^{m}]^{d}*šér*—DINGIR-*a-a* 224 r. 2, ^{md}*šér*—DINGIR-*a-a* 223 r. 6,

Šēr-nūrī (son of PN): ^{md}*šér—nu-ri* 13 r. 4,

Šēr-uāri (coffer-master 201): ^{md}*šér—ú-a-ri* 201 r. 7, ^{m}*šér*]*—ú-a-ri* 267:5,

Šimānu (merchant 297): ^{m}*ši-ma-a-nu* 105 r. 4, ^{m}*ši-ma-nu* 297 r. 10,

Šulmānu-ašarēd (king of Assyria): [^{m}]DI-*ma-nu*—MAŠ 24 r. 4,

Šulmu-ahhē (archer 258): ^{m}DI-*mu*—PAB.MEŠ 153:1, 236 r. 3, 258 r. 3, ^{m}]DI-*mu*—ŠEŠ.MEŠ 52 r. 16,

Šulmu-Bēli (farmer 326, village manager 110, prefect of Talmusa 128): ^{m}DI-*mu*]*—be-lí* 129 r. 4, ^{m}DI-*mu*—EN 62 r. 2, 110 r. 8, 138:1, 9, r. 2, 326:8, ^{m}DI-*mu*]—EN 130 r. 14, ^{m}DI-*m*[*u*—EN] 138:7, ^{m}DI-*m*[*u*]—EN 128 r. 4,

Šulmu-Bēli-lāmur ('third man' 177): ^{m}DI-*mu*—EN—*la-mur* 177 r. 3, 328:7,

Šulmu-Bēli-lašme (chariot driver 163, cook 204, 205, prefect of Der 289, 301, 'third man' 185): ^{m}DI-*mu*—EN—*la-áš-me* 167 r. 2, 204 r. 10, 287 r. 17, 300 r. 10, ^{m}DI-*mu*—EN—*la-*[*áš-me*] 289 r. 14, ^{m}DI-*mu*—EN]—*la-áš-me* 205 r. 3, ^{m}DI-*mu*—E[N]—*la-áš-me* 236 r. 1, ^{m}DI-*mu*]—EN—*la-áš-me* 163 r. 9, ^{m}DI-*m*]*u*—EN—*la-áš-me* 291:7, ^{m}D[I-*mu*—EN—*la-áš-me*] 218 r. 1, ^{m}D]I-*mu*—EN—*la-áš-*(*me*) 185 r. 11, ^{m}DI-*mu*—EN—HAL 301 r. 18, ^{m}DI-*mu*—EN—H[AL] 237 r. 9,

Šulmu-lāmur: ^{m}DI-*mu—l*[*a-mur*] 79:3,

Šulmu-šarri (prefect of Halziatbar 123, 125): ^{m}DI-*mu*—LUGAL 100 r. 22, 122 r. 5, 123 r. 14, 125 r. 16, 150 r. 1, ^{m}DI]-*mu*—LUGAL 138 r. 11, ^{m}DI-*mu*—MAN 26:3, 118 r. 12, 121 r. 9, ^{m}DI—MAN 241 r. 5,

Šulmu-[...]: ^{m}DI-*m*[*u—x* 135 r. 2, ^{m}DI-*mu—x*[*x* 279:4,

Šumāia (son of PN 284, 314): ^{m}*šu-ma-a* 192 r. 6, ^{m}*šu-ma-a-a* 113 r. 3, ^{m}MU-*a-a* 284 r. 12, ^{m}M]U-*a-a* 314 r. 13,

Šumma-Adad: ^{m}*šum-ma*—^{d}I[M 253:2, ^{m}BE-*ma*—^{d}IM 281:7,

Šumma-ahhē: ^{m}BE-[*ma*—P]AB.MEŠ 139 r. 3,

Šumma-Aššūr (governor): ^{m}*šum-ma*—^{d}*aš-šur* 314 r. 8,

Šumma-ibašši-kettu: ^{m}*šum-ma—i-ba-ši*—ZI 229:6, ^{m}*šum-ma—i-b*[*a-ši*—Z]I 229:1,

Šumma-ilāʾī: ^{m}*šúm-ma*—DINGIR-*a-a* 17 r. 11, ^{m}]*šum-mu*—DINGIR-*a-a* 137 r. 2,

Šumma-ilāni (chariot driver 34-42, 54, 324, 347, ditto of the crown prince 317): ^{m}*šúm-ma*—DINGIR.MEŠ 35:2, 5, 49:3, ^{m}*šúm-m*]*a*—DINGIR.ME[Š] 48:5, ^{m}*šúm-ma*—DINGIR.ME]Š-*ni* 37:10, ^{m}*šúm-ma*—DINGIR.MEŠ-*ni* 37 r. 2, ^{m}*šúm-mu*—DINGIR.MEŠ 52:10, r. 4, ^{m}*šúm-mu*—DINGIR.MEŠ-*ni* 47:2, 50:8, r. 5, ^{m}*šúm-m*[*u*—DINGIR.MEŠ-*ni*] 51 r. 2, ^{m}*šum-ma*—DINGIR.MEŠ 40:19, 48:14, 55:3, 323 r. 6, 324 r. 7, ^{m}*šum-ma*—DI[NGIR].ME[Š] 40:7, [^{m}*šum-ma*—DINGIR.MEŠ] 41:8, ^{m}*šum-ma*—DINGIR.MEŠ-*ni* 36:2, 38:3, 45:5, 46:4, 316 r. 5, ^{m}*šum-ma*—DINGIR.MEŠ-[*n*]*i* 38 r. 5, ^{m}*šum-ma*—DINGIR.M[EŠ]-*ni* 42:18, ^{m}*šum-ma*—[DINGIR.MEŠ-*ni* 347 r. 9, ^{m}*šum-ma*—[DINGIR.MEŠ-*ni*] 299 r. 6, ^{m}*šum-ma*]—DINGIR.MEŠ-*ni* 56 r. 4, ^{m}*š*]*um-ma*—DINGIR.MEŠ-*ni* 56:3, ^{m}*šum-mu*—DINGIR.MEŠ-*ni* 43:2, 44:2, 53:5, ^{m}*šum-*[*mu*—DINGIR.MEŠ-*ni*] 51:3, ^{m}BE-*ma*—DINGIR.MEŠ 34:5, 18, 39:11, 154 s. 2, ^{m}BE-*ma*—DINGIR.MEŠ] 39:2, ^{m}BE-*ma*—DINGIR.MEŠ-*ni* 42:8, 317:9, ^{m}BE-*m*[*a*—DINGIR.MEŠ-*ni*] 54:5,

Šumma-ilu (cohort commander 283, 307, 308, merchant 42, priest 160, 161): ^{m}*šúm-ma*—DINGIR 42 r. 12, 161 r. 11, ^{m}*šúm-ma*—[DINGIR 160 r. 4, ^{m}*šúm-mu*—DINGIR 307 r. 6, 308 r. 6, ^{m}*šum-ma*—DINGIR 328 e. 15, ^{m}BE-*ma*—DINGIR 283 r. 13,

Šumma-tašēzib (servant): ^{m}*šum-ma—ta-še-zib* 301 r. 14,

Šumma-[...]: ^{m}*šúm-ma*—[*x* 279 r. 3,

Šumu-lēšir (recruitment officer): ^{m}MU—GIŠ 19:7, 20:2,

Šuriha-ilāʾī: ^{md}*šu-ri-ha*—DINGIR-*a-a* 81 r. 3,

Šūsanqu: ^{m}*šu-sa-an-qu* 142 r. 12,

Tâ: ^{m}*ta-a* 133:3, ^{m}[*ta*]*-a* 133 r. 1,

Tabālāiu ('third man' of the crown prince 283): ^{m}*tab*-URU-*a-a* 234 r. 5, 283 r. 18, ^{m}*ta-bal-a-a* 170 r. 4, ^{m}*ta-bal-a-*[*a*] 171 r. 4,

Tabnî (scribe): ^{m}*tab-ni-i* 34 r. 12, 264 r. 7,

Tabni-Issār: ^{m}*tab-ni*—^{d}15 197:5, 12,

Tabni-[...]: ^{m}*tab-ni*—^{d}[*x* 302 r. 13,

Takali: ^{m}*ta-ka-li* 133:2,

Takkulu: ^{m}*tak-ku-*[*lu*] 45 r. 2,

Taklāk-ana-Bēl (prefect of Nisibin): ^{m}*tàk-lak—a-na*—[^{d}]EN 12 r. 6,

Taklāk-ana-Bēlīa (overseer of the household of PN): ^{m}*tàk-la*[*k*]*—a-na*—EN-*ia* 17 r. 10,

Taqīsu (brewer 282): ^{m}*ta-qis* 282 r. 1, ^{m}*ta-qi-su* 291 r. 1,

Tardīʾa: ^{m}*tar-di-ia-a* 174 r. 12,

Tardītu-ahhē: ^{m}*tar-di-tú*—PAB.M[EŠ] 188 r. 1,

Tardītu-Aššūr ('third man' of the crown prince): ^{m}*tar-di-it—aš-šur* 330 r. 10, ^{m}*tar-di-tú—aš-šur* 329 r. 16,

Tarhundapî: ^{m}*ta*]*r-hu-da-pi-i* 117:2, ^{m}*tar-hu-un-dáp-pi-i* 169:12, ^{m}*tar-hu-un-da-pi-i* 118:5, 17,

Tarība-Issār (tailor 124, cook 138): ^{m}*ta-ri-bi*—^{d}15 96:3, ^{m}*ta*-SU—15 146:2, ^{m}]SU—^{d}15 138 r. 12, ^{m}SU—^{d}15 124 r. 8,

driver 300, ditto of the crown prince 299): ^{m}]^{d}za-ba$_4$-ba$_4$—SU 327 r. 6, ^{m}]^{d}za-ba$_4$-[ba$_4$—SU 321 r. 9, ^{md}za-ba$_4$-ba$_4$—SU 299 r. 2, 320 r. 6, 325 r. 15, ^{md}za-ba$_4$-ba$_4$—[SU] 301 r. 8, ^{md}za-[ba$_4$-ba$_4$—SU 326 r. 21, ^{md}z]a-ba$_4$-ba$_4$—SU 300 r. 2,

Zābāiu (from Barhalzi 116): ^{m}za-ba-a-a 116 r. 7, 176:6, ^{m}za-ba-a-a-u 176 r. 5,

Zabdâ (chariot driver): ^{m}za-ab-da-a 244 r. 4

Zabīnâ: ^{m}za-bi-na-a 235:1,

Zabīnu (chariot driver 287, gardener 90, tailor 81): ^{m}za-bi-ni 10:4, 7, 9, 12, r. 16, 13:4, 5, 14:4, [^{m}za-bi-ni 11:6, [^{m}za-bi-ni] 11:4, [^{m}za-b]i-ni 11:2, ^{m}za-bi-nu 81 r. 6, 90:8, 287:5,

Zabūdu: ^{m}za-bu-du 23 r. 5,

Zahaṭuṭu (tailor): ^{m}za-ha-ṭu-ṭu 124 r. 7,

Zaibdānu: ^{m}za-ib-da-a-ni 245 r. 12,

Zakkūru: ^{m}za-ku-ri 61:6, ^{m}za]-ku-ri 61:2,

Zanzānu (cohort commander): ^{m}za-an-za-nu 294 r. 4,

Zārî: ^{m}NUMUN-i 173:5, 219:3, r. 2,

Zārūtî (physician 271, chariot driver 321, 342, 348, [of the crown prince] 283, 309, 312, 323, ditto of the chief cook 36, cohort commander 304-306, 320, 326, [of the crown prince's bodyguard] 312, 321-325, scribe 124, son of PN 237): ^{m}za-ru-ti-i 36:5, 124 r. 11, 237:5, ^{m}]NUMUN-ti-i 271 r. 15, ^{m}NUMUN-ti-i 304 r. 4, 348 r. 3, ^{m}NUMUN-ut-i 283 r. 16, ^{m}]NUMUN-ut-ti-i 271:10, ^{m}NUMUN-ut-ti-i 320 r. 2, 326 r. 17, ^{m}NUMUN-ú-t]i-i 342 r. 6, ^{m}NUMUN-u-te-i 325 r. 19, ^{m}NUMUN-u-ti-i 306 r. 9, 309 r. 6, 312 r. 8, 9, 323 r. 8, 9, 324 r. 9, ^{m}NUMUN-u-ti-i] 305 r. 10, ^{m}NUMUN-u-t[i-i 321 r. 3, ^{m}NUMUN-u]-ti-i 321 r. 5, ^{m}NUMUN-[u-t]i-i 299 r. 7, ^{m}NU[MUN]-u-tú 139 r. 5,

Zār-Issār (chief weaver 90, keeper of the contract 284): ^{m}]NUMUN—^{d}15 212 r. 4, 284 s. 1, ^{m}NUMUN—^{d}15 210 r. 9, ^{m}NUMUN—15 90 r. 10, 182 r. 6, 259 r. 5, 260 r. 8, ^{m}NUMUN—15] 181 r. 6,

Zazāia (prefect of Arpad 42, 142): ^{m}za-za-a 142 s. 1, ^{m}za-za-a-a 143 r. 2, ^{m}za-z]a-a-a 65 r. 6, [^{m}za-za-a-a] 42 r. 20, [^{m}za-za]-a-a 146 r. 9, ^{m}za-za-ia 144 r. 4, ^{m}za-ze-e 141 s. 2, see also Zazakku,

Zazakku: ^{m}za-za-ku 145 r. 4, see also Zazāia,

Zāzî (chariot driver 39, 40, 41, 53, king's eunuch 27): ^{m}za-a-zi-i 39 r. 8, 40 r. 15, ^{m}za-zi-i 26:2, 41 r. 7, 53 r. 4, ^{m}za-zi]-i 27 r. 11, ^{m}za-z]i-i 27 r. 4, ^{m}za-[zi]-i 85 r. 13,

Zermāhu: ^{m}zer-ma-hu 147 r. 5,

Zēru-lēšir: ^{m}NUMUN—SI.SÁ 65:2,

Zēru-ukīn (chariot fighter 325, chariot driver 329, 330, 335): ^{m}]NUMUN—GIN 335 r. 20, ^{m}NUMUN—GIN 325:9, 329 r. 18, 330 r. 12,

Zēr-ketti-lēšir: ^{m}NUMUN—kit-ti—GIŠ 55 r. 4, ^{m}NUMUN—ZI—GIŠ 46 r. 4,

Zēr-[...]: ^{m}NUMUN-[x 137 r. 2,

Zibāti (mayor): ^{m}zi-ba-a-te 22 r. 5,

Zibdî: ^{m}zib-di-i 98 r. 9,

Zilî: I-zi-[li-i] 344:9, ^{m}zi-l[i-i] 343:1, [^{m}zi-li-i] 343:12, 344 r. 1,

Zitti: ^{m}zi-it-t[i] 142 r. 17,

Zīzî (gate-guard of the palace 59, information officer 57, merchant 166): ^{m}zi-zi-i 166 r. 2, ^{m}z]i-zi-i 57 r. 9, ^{m}zi-zi-ia 59 r. 11, 152 r. 5,

Zunbu: ^{m}zu-un-b[i] 103:6, ^{m}zu-un-bu 103:1,

broken: MÍ.da-hi-x[x 54:2, MÍ.hi-[x 124 r. 5, MÍ.hu-d[a-x 239:4, MÍ.man-nu—[x 344:3, [MÍ.man-nu—x-x-x] 343:7, MÍ.sa-an-x[x 266:7, MÍ.sa-ma-[x 283:9, MÍ.su-u-[x 86:1, MÍ.ú-a-r[i-x 326:9, MÍ.ú-n[u-x 34:3, MÍ.x 86:6, 94 r. 3, 99 r. 1, MÍ.[x 116:3, 128:4, 266:2, [MÍ.x 99:7, 193:6, 345:4, 5, MÍ.x[x 266:3, MÍ.x]-da-ta 209:2, ^{m}aš-šur—[x 326 r. 22, ^{m}aš]-šur—[x 144:2, ^{m}a-[x 173 r. 1, ^{m}a-[x]-ʾu-ú 118 r. 5, ^{m}ba-qu-[x 100 r. 16, ^{m}ba-[x 141 r. 7, 314 r. 21, 344:2, ^{m}(blank) 111 r. 9, 265 r. 1, ^{m}bur-x[x 135:2, ^{m}b[u-x 314 r. 22, ^{m}dan-[x 277 r. 3, ^{m}da-ha-[x 350 r. 11, ^{m}da-[x 130 r. 11, ^{m}]^{d}[x 334 r. 33, ^{md}x 226 r. 12, 328 r. 10, ^{md}[x 102 r. 14, 119 r. 13, 132 r. 2, 133 r. 9, 151:1, 188 r. 3, 194:3, 226 r. 4, 251 r. 9, 280 r. 3, 294:4, 302:7, 341:5, ^{md}x[x 105 r. 1, ^{m}]^{d}[x]x[x 112 r. 8, ^{md}x]x—SUM-na 115 r. 1, ^{md}x—b]a-ni 27:6, e. 11, ^{md}x]—ka-ši[r] 133 r. 10, ^{md}[x]—šal-lim 237 r. 2, ^{md}x]—še-zib 209 r. 7, ^{md}x—ú-pa-hí]r 306 r. 10, ^{md}x]—ú-pa-hír 305 r. 11, ^{md}x]—AŠ 252 s. 3, ^{md}x]—PAB—AŠ 109 r. 10, ^{md}x]—PAB—PAB 65 r. 7, ^{md}[x]—ZALÁG-i[r] 125 s. 1, ^{md}AG—[x 159:6, ^{md}AMA[R.UTU—x 184 r. 4, ^{md}EN—[x] 106 r. 4, ^{md}E[N—x 226 r. 8, ^{m}]^{d}IM—[x 10 r. 8, ^{md}]IM—[x 21 r. 11, ^{md}IM—[x 301 r. 9, 348 r. 8, ^{md}I[M—x 186 s. 2, ^{md}MAŠ—[x 116 r. 12, ^{md}P[A-x 280 r. 8, ^{md}]PA—[x 130:4, 186 s. 1, ^{md}PA—[x 5 r. 1, 21 r. 10, 162 r. 4, 173 r. 2, 204 r. 2, 269 r. 4, 9, 10, 284 r. 16, 286 r. 2, ^{md}P[A—x 226 r. 5, 246 r. 5, 334 r. 32, ^{md}UTU—x 123 r. 8, ^{md}U[TU—x 184:7, 284 r. 12, ^{md}30—x[x 121 r. 1, ^{m}ga-x-[x 130 r. 1, ^{m}ha-an-[x 203:3, ^{m}ha-a[n-x]-ti 283:10, ^{m}ha-x[x 45 r. 1, ^{m}hu[m-x 194 r. 11, ^{m}hu-ul-li 97 r. 4, ^{m}hu-[x 284 r. 13, ^{m}hu-x[x 179 r. 6, ^{m}ia-bur-x[x 286 r. 5, ^{m}ia-[x 277 r. 2, ^{m}im-[x 286 r. 10, ^{m}ina-[x 203:1, ^{m}it-ta-[x 155 r. 4, ^{m}ka[b-x 269:7, ^{m}k[i-x 126:2, ^{m}la-[x 173 r. 3, ^{m}lu-x 321:6, ^{m}lu-[x 277 r. 4, 320:4, ^{m}mar-[x 155 r. 2, ^{m}ma[r-x]x 187 r. 3, ^{m}ma-[x 288:10, ^{m}na-[x 126:1, ^{m}pa-[x 294 r. 1, ^{m}p]a-x[x 311 r. 1, ^{m}pu-ṭi-[x 226:8, ^{m}pu-ṭ[u-x 226 r. 9, ^{m}qi-[x 284 r. 18, ^{m}r[ém-x 199:1, ^{m}si-x 207 r. 7, ^{m}s[i-x 280 r. 6, 302:8, ^{m}si-x[x 303 r. 1, ^{m}su-[x 226 r. 6, ^{m}ṣil-[x 251 r. 8, ^{m}šá—^{d}[x 341:4, ^{m}še-x[x 78:3, ^{m}ši-[x 94:1, 135:1, ^{m}šu-[x 18 r. 2, ^{m}tab-li-[x 131 r. 10, ^{m}ta[b-x 141 r. 8, ^{m}tak-li-[x 190 r. 4, ^{m}ta-ab-[x 33:3, ^{m}tu-[x 217 r. 11, ^{m}ú-ṣa-[x 342:3, ^{m}ú-[x 55 r. 2, ^{m}ú-x[x 91 r. 1, ^{m}za-[x 157 r. 7, ^{m}ze-e-[x 304:1, ^{m}]x 135 r. 2, 140 r. 1, 207:2, 275 r. 25, ^{m}x 1:2, 2:1, 3:9, 7 r. 8, 9, 10, 11, 12, 8 r. 7, 10 r. 7, 11 r. 10, 11, 12, 16, 13 r. 6, 15 r. 9, 19 r. 2, 3, 4, 21:2, 22 r. 1, 24 r. 1, 27:9, 28 r. 2, 3, 31:2, 3, 32 r. 9, 10, 39:19, 20, 21, 48 r. 9, 15, 16, 50 r. 12, 13, 52:1, 2, r. 17, 18, 53 r. 9, 54:4, 55 r. 1, 56:2, 57 r. 1, 2, 3, 4, 6, 8, 65 r. 9, 69 r. 2, 78:1, 79:1, 86 r. 14, 15, 16, 17, 92:4, 7, r. 9, 10, 11, 12, 95 r. 6, 96 r. 1, 2, 99 r. 8, 9, 13, 100 r. 9, 102:10, 103 r. 1, 2, 3, 4, 5, 6, 7, 105 s. 1, 2, 109 r. 3, 4, 5, 114:2, 115:1, r. 3, 6, 116:1, 121 e. 13, 14, 15, r. 4, 11, 123 r. 5, 6, 7, 8, 9, 10, 11, 12, 126 r. 10, 11, 127 r. 2, 128:1, 129 r. 1, 2, 132 r. 5, 7, 138:3, r. 4, 18, 140 r. 3, 4, 5, 11, 141:1, 144 r. 1, 145 r. 1, 2, 147 r. 9, 149:1, 2, 3, 4, 5, 6, 155:9, 162:3, 4, 5, 163 r. 6, 7, 8, 165 r. 6, 168 r. 1, 2, 3, 169 r. 7, 13, 14, 172 r. 2, 176 r. 12, 13, 14, 185 e. 7, r. 12, 186 r. 7, 9, 10, 187 r. 2, 3, 4, 5, 192 r. 1, 194:1, 195 r. 2, 3, 196:5, 200 r. 7, 8, 9, 10, 11, 12, 205 r. 1, 4, 209:1, r. 1, 2, 5, 210:7, 217 r. 16, 220 r. 1, 226 r. 3, 231:1, 238:2, r. 1, 2, 3, 239 r. 4, 5, 243:6, 252:1, s. 1, 253 r. 9, 10, 11, 12, 254 r. 5, 255 r. 1, 256 r. 1, 261 r. 1, 269:8, s. 1, 3, 271:1, r. 7, 8, 9, 10, 11, 12, 13, 272:4, 275 r. 24, 26, 276 r. 1, 2, 280:1, r. 1, 284

Place Names

Bīrtu: URU.HAL.ṢU 31 r. 22,
Bīt-Zamāni (Assyrian province around mod. Diyarbakir): KUR.É—*za-ma-a-ni* 158:5,
Bīt- see *also Bēt-*,
Burrim (town near Qatna): URU.*bur-ri-im* 335:10,
Buruqu: URU.*bu-ru-qa*]-*a-a* 31:4, URU.*bu-ru-qi* 31 r. 3,
Dadiualla (town in the province of Talmusu): URU.*da-di-ú-al-la* 91:10,
Dannānu (town near Šura): URU.*dan-na-a-ni* 146:5,
Darigu (town in northern Babylonia): URU.*da-ri-g*[*i*] 337:3,
Dēru (city in Babylonia, now Badrah): *de-ri* 287 r. 18, BÀD.DINGIR.KI 301 r. 19, URU.*d*[*e-e-r*]*i* 289 r. 15, UR]U.*de-*[*e-ri*] 290 r. 1,
Dimašqa (Damascus): KUR.*d*[*im-maš-qa*] 39 r. 11, URU.*dim-maš-qa* 37 r. 17, URU.*di-maš-qa* 81 r. 10, 134 r. 16, 135 r. 7,
Duʾūʾa: URU.*du-ʾu-ú-a* 17:7, URU.*du-ʾu-*[*ú-a*] 17 r. 8,
Dunnu: URU.*du-ni* 115:3,
Dūr-Katlimmu (city on the Khabur, now Tell Šeh Hamad): URU.BÀD—*a-du-ku*—1-*lim* 335:8,
Dūr-Nanāia: URU.BÀD—ᵈ*na-na-a* 245:9,
Dūr-Šarrukēn (city in Assyria, now Khorsabad): BÀD—MAN—GIN 282 e. 5, K[UR.BÀD—MAN—GIN] 41 r. 18, URU.BÀD—LUGA]L—*ú-k*[*in*] 106 r. 8, URU.BÀD—MAN—GIN 310:2, URU.BÀD—MAN—GIN] 40 r. 18, U]RU.BÀD—[MAN—GIN] 144:3, URU.BÀD—MAN—GIN-*a-a* 287:11, URU.BÀD—ᵐMAN—GIN 340 r. 4, URU.BÀD—ᵐMAN—GI[N] 320 r. 10,
Dūr-Šarrukku (city in Babylonia, now Tell ed-Der): URU.BÀD—ᵐMAN-*uk-*[*ku*] 283 r. 24,
Elamtu (Elam): KUR.NIM.MA-*a-a* 287 r. 14,
Gargamis (Carchemish, mod. Kargamis/Jarablus): *gar-gar-mis* 45:6, *gar-ga-mis* 110:9, 183:2, 306:5, *gar-ga-*[*mis*] 263:1, *gar-*[*ga-mis*] 108:2, 305:8, *gar-*[*g*]*a-mis* 273:1, KUR.*gar-gá-mis* 235:2, KUR. *gar-ga-mis* 26:1, 158:1, 219:5, URU.*gar-gar-mis* 107:1, URU.*gar-ga-mis* 34:9, 39:4, 46:2, 53:7, 81:2, 91:12, 99:9, 103:8, 104:2, 119:19, 177:8, 202:12, 210:11, 223:1, 224:1, 234:2, 239:9, 250:10, 251:7, 257:10, 262:2, 274:6, 275 r. 15, 284:7, 307:2, 311:10, 315:13, 318:3, 323:1, 326:17, 329:15, 335 e. 13, 342:7, 346:4, URU.*gar-ga-mis*] 269:10, 299:1, URU.*gar-ga-mi*]*s* 196:8, URU.*gar-ga-*[*mis*] 245 e. 15, URU.*gar-ga*]-*mis* 324:6, URU. *gar-g*[*a-mis*] 347:9, URU.*gar-g*]*a-mis* 57:9, 312:12, URU.*g*]*ar-ga-mis* 313:10, URU.[*gar-ga-mis*] 40:9, 334 r. 4, 344:8, UR[U.*gar-ga-mis*] 41:10, UR]U. *gar-ga-m*[*is*] 90:14, U[RU.*gar-ga-mis*] 17 e. 13, 54:7, U[RU.*g*]*ar-ga-mis* 248:2, U]RU.*gar-ga-mis* 343:11, [URU.*gar-ga-mis* 333 r. 2,
Gasupu: K]UR.*ga-su-pi* 288:3,
Gilzānu (country S of Lake Urmia): KUR.*g*]*il-za-a-nu* 92 r. 11,
Gimir (Bibl. Gomer, Cimmerians): *gi-mir-a-a* 204 r. 8,
Habrūri (or Kirrūri, mod. Herir plain NE of Erbil): KUR.*hab-ru-ri* 5 r. 4,
Habūr (Khabur): ÍD.*h*[*a*]*-bur* 335:3,
Halina: URU].*hal-i-na* 92 r. 4,
Halzi-atbāri (district N of Halahhu): URU.*hal-zi*—AD.BAR 125 r. 17, [UR]U.*hal-zi*—[AD.BAR] 123 r. 15,
Hamê: URU.*ha-me-*[*e*] 217:8, *ḥmc* 217 s. 1,
Hanūri: URU.*ha-nu-ri* 27 r. 3,
Harrānu (Carrhae, mod. Harran): URU.KASKAL 98 r. 4, 333 e. 4, URU.K]ASKAL 334 r. 15, URU. [KASKAL] 140:10, URU.KASKAL-*a-a* 172:2,
Hataiāte: URU.*ha-ta-ia-te* 200 r. 11,
Hatarikka (city near Damascus, Bibl. Hadrach): URU.*ha-ta-r*]*ik-ka* 149:9,
Hatpina[...]: URU.*ha-at-pi-na-x* 122 r. 2,
Hattâ: URU.*hat-ta-a* 268:2, URU.*ha-ta-a* 223:5, 224:5, 226:5,
Hazzat (Gaza): KUR.*ha-zi-te* 252:1,
Iarānu: URU.*ia-ra-nu* 271:8,
Ibla (Ebla, mod. Tell Mardikh near Aleppo?): URU.*ib-ʾa-la* 271:16, URU.*ib-li* 271:4,
Ilabbiašu (a river): ÍD].*i-lab-bi-a-šú* 332:6, ÍD.*i-lab-b*[*i-a-šú*] 332:3,
Illat: URU.*il-lat-a-a* 257:7,
Imgur-Illil (city in central Assyria, mod. Balawat): URU.*im-gúr*—ᵈBE 301 r. 17,
Irria: URU.*ir-ri* 120 r. 2,
Isana (city in the upper Khabur area): U[RU].*i-sa-na* 61 r. 8,
Ispallurê (town in Izalla): URU.*is-pal-lu-ra-a-a*] 314 r. 23, URU.*is-pal-lu-r*[*e-e* 314:14,
Issēte (town in NE Assyria, reading uncert.): URU.1-*te* 275:10, URU.1-*tú* 238:7,
Ituʾu (Aram. tribe): LÚ.*i-tú-ʾa-a-a* 30 r. 5,
Izalla (class. Izala mons, part of Tur Abdin): KUR.*i-za-li* 314:13, KUR.*i-za-li*] 314:4,
Kaldu (Chaldea): LÚ.*kal-da-a* 12:8,
Kalgurig: URU.*kal-gu-rig* 113:4,
Kalhu (Calah, mod. Nimrud): URU.*kàl-ha* 10:7, 11:8, 265:15, URU.*kàl-ha*] 11:2, U]RU.*kàl-ha* 10:4, URU.*kàl-hi* 13:4, 5, 28:7, 131 r. 2, 220 r. 6, 284 r. 5, 298 r. 1, 299:13, URU.*kàl*]-*hi* 11 r. 5, URU.*kal-ha*] 10:15, URU.*kal-*[*ha*] 151 r. 7, U]RU.*kal-ha* 164 r. 8, URU.*kal-hi* 6 r. 2, 19 r. 13, 31:9, 14, r. 12, 13, 24, 25, 26, URU.*kal-*[*hi* 32 r. 2, URU.*kal-*[*hi*] 6 s. 2, [URU.*k*]*al-hi* 6 r. 15, [UR]U.*kal-hi* 31:11,
Kannuʾ (city in Assyria, Bibl. Kanneh): URU. *kan-nu-uʾ* 169:9, UR]U.*kan-nu-uʾ* 169:5, URU.*ka-an-nu-*[*uʾ*] 211:2, UR]U.*ka-a*[*n-nu-uʾ*] 211:1,
Kapar Ahī-iaqar (village in Babylonia): URU. ŠE—ᵐPAB—*ia-qar* 287:12,
Kapar Ahūni: URU.ŠE—ᵐ*a-hu-u-ni* 238:7,
Kapar Andarāni (village near Darigu): URU. ŠE—ᵐ*an-da-ra-ni* 337:2,
Kapar Armāia (village in central Assyria): [URU.ŠE—ᵐ]*ar-ma-a-a* 10:5,
Kapar Bahāia (village in Babylonia): URU.ŠE—ᵐ*ba-ha-a-a* 287:7,
Kapar Bēl-ahhē: URU.ŠE—ᵐEN—PAB.MEŠ 97 e. 8,
Kapar Bēt-balāṭi: [URU.ŠE]—É—*bala-*[*ṭ*]*i* 119:3,
Kapar Dannāia (village in the district of Arrapha 336, near Qatna 320): URU.ŠE—*dan-a-a* 336:3, URU.ŠE—*da-na-ia* 30 r. 9, URU.ŠE—ᵐ[*dan-na-a*] 320:2, 321:4, UR]U.ŠE—ᵐ*dan-na-a* 320:6, 321:7, see also *Āl Dannāia*,
Kapar Ildiši: URU.ŠE—ᵐ*il-di-ši* 320:3, [URU.ŠE—ᵐ*il-di-ši* 321:5,
Kapar ili (village near Kannu'): URU.ŠE—DINGIR 169:8,
Kapar Kaldu: URU.ŠE—*kal-du* 283 e. 21,
Kapar Kīni (village near Qatna): URU.ŠE—ᵐ*ki-i-*

ni 335:6,
Kapar Kiluhti: URU.ŠE—*ki-luh-te* 119:16,
Kapar Lā-qēpi: URU.ŠE—ᵐ*la—qé-pi* 30 r. 6, URU. ŠE—ᵐ*la—qé-pu* 30:6,
Kapar Milki-[...]: URU.ŠE—ᵐ*mil-ki-x*[*x*] 186 r. 7,
Kapar rabûti: URU.ŠE—GAL.MEŠ 30:7,
Kapar Ṣilli-Bēl (village in Babylonia): URU.ŠE—ᵐ*ṣil*—EN 287:10, 12,
Kapar Šamaš: URU.ŠE—ᵈUTU 271:15,
Kapar Tapha-ari[...] (village in Babylonia): URU.ŠE—ᵐ*tap-ha—a-ri*-[[*x*]] 287:9,
Kapar Tēmanāie (village near Ibla): URU.ŠE—*te-ma-na-a-a* 271:13, [URU.ŠE—*t*]*e-ma-na-a-a* 271: 12,
Kapar Ṭuba (village in northern Assyria): URU. ŠE—*ṭu-ba* 275 r. 3,
Kapar Zīzî (village in central Assyria): URU. ŠE—ᵐ*zi-zi*-[*i*] 10:13, URU.ŠE—ᵐ*zi-z*[*i-i*] 11:4, URU. ŠE—ᵐ*z*]*i-zi-i* 13:8, URU.ŠE—ᵐ[*zi-zi-i*] 11:6, URU.ŠE—[ᵐ*zi-zi-i*] 10:10,
Kapar Zumbi (village in the district of Arrapha): URU.Š]E—ᵐ*zu-um-bi* 336:4,
Kapar [...]: URU.ŠE—ᵐ*x* 321:8,
Kaprabu: URU.ŠE—*ra-bu* 109 r. 6,
Kār-Apladad: URU.*kar*—A.10 260:2, UR]U.*kar*—A.10 259:2,
Kār-Issār: URU.*kar*—ᵈ15 119:6,
Kār-Mullissi (city in central Assyria, now Keremlis): URU.*kar*—ᵈNIN.LÍL 216:2,
Kār-Nergal (town in Babylonia, near Cutha): URU.*kar*—ᵈU.GUR 288:2,
Kār-Šamaš (town on the Tigris S of Samarra): URU.*kar*—ᵈUTU 188 r. 7,
Kāšiēri (hilly area in NW Assyria, mod. Ṭur Abdin): KUR.*kaš-ie*-[*e-ri*] 288 r. 13,
Kilizi (city in central Assyria, now Qasr Shamamok): URU.*kàl-zi* 247:5, 289 r. 1,
Kipšūna (town in northern Assyria, now Gefše): URU.*kip-šu-na* 202:5, URU.*kip-šu-u-ni* 201:4,
Kiṣirtu (town in Mazamua): URU.*ki-ṣir*-[*t*]*a-a-a* 119 r. 18,
Kullania (city in Syria, Bibl. Calneh, now Tell Tacyinat): KUR.*kul-la-ni-a* 177 r. 18, URU.*ku-l*[*a-ni-a*] 59 r. 18,
Kuluna: URU.*ku-lu-na* 28:6,
Kummuhi (Commagene): URU.*k*[*u-mu-hi*] 327 r. 9,
Kurbail (city in Assyria): URU.*kur-ba-ìl* 120 r. 7, 124 r. 15,
Lahīru (city in Babylonia): KUR.*la-hi-ra* 216:8, KUR.*la-hi-ri* 287:2, UR]U.*la-hi-ra* 255:2, URU.*la-h*[*i-ri*] 280 r. 16,
Libbi āli ("Inner City," an appellative of Assur): URU.ŠÀ—URU 86 r. 13, URU.ŠÀ—URU-*a-a* 42 r. 10, ŠÀ-*bi*—URU 93:3,
Li[...]gama: URU.*li-x-gam-a-a* 120 r. 4,
Maganuba (city in central Assyria, near Dur-Šarruken): URU.*ma-ga-ni-ib* 200:2, URU.*ma-g*[*a-ni-ib*] 200:9, URU.*ma-ga-nu-ba* 37:3, URU.*m*[*a-g*]*a-nu-ba* 50 r. 11,
Maliāti (town in central Assyria): U]RU.*ma-li-ia-ti* 169:4,
Manṣuāti (city in Syria, mod. Maṣyat?): KUR. *man-ṣu-a-te* 259 r. 9, URU.*man-ṣu-a-te* 202 r. 10, URU.*man-ṣu*.MEŠ 257 r. 35,
Marqāsa (capital of Gurgum, now Maraş): *mar-qa-sa* 197 r. 10, URU.*mar-ha-si* 45 r. 7, URU.*mar-qa-sa* 258 r. 8, U]RU.*mar-qa-sa* 192 s. 2, URU.*mar-qa-si* 98 r. 14, 188 r. 5, 191 r. 3, URU.*mar-qa*-[*si*] 190 r. 7,
Maškarit: UR[U.*maš-ka-r*]*i-ta-a-a* 32 r. 11,
māt Aššūr (Assyria): KUR—*aš-šur* 31 r. 29, 88 r. 12, 156 r. 8, 202 s. 1, 210 r. 18, 245 r. 16, 251:5, 309:7, 328:10, 341 r. 2, KUR—*aš-šur*] 57:8, 154 s. 3, 349:1, KUR]—*aš-šur* 334 r. 3, KUR—*aš-šur-ma* 251:6, KUR—*aš-šur*].KI 339:4, KUR—*aš-šur*.KI 90 r. 17, 152 e. 10, 174 r. 17, 177 r. 20, 201 r. 14, 257 r. 36, 266 s. 1, 311:8, 324:9, 326:16, r. 5, 335:12, 336:9, 343:10, KUR—*aš-šur*.KI] 1 r. 22, 59:7, KUR—*aš-šur*.K[I] 31 r. 4, 160 r. 16, 315:10, KUR—*aš-šur*.[KI] 314:16, KUR—*aš-š*[*ur*.KI] 346:2, KUR—*a*[*š-šur*.KI] 153 r. 5, KUR—[*aš-šur*.KI] 151 r. 12, 155 r. 9, 203 r. 4, 344:7, KUR]—*aš-šur*.K[I] 48 s. 2, [KUR—*aš-šur*.KI] 24 r. 4, 279 r. 10, KUR—AN.ŠÁ[R.KI] 212 r. 7,
Medun: URU.*me-du-un* 120:3,
Mera: URU.*me-ra* 28 r. 7, URU.*me-ra-a-a* 115 r. 3,
Mulu[...]: URU.*mu-lu-x*[*x*] 275:4,
Musīna-aplu-iddina (town in the district of Arpad, near Nerab): URU.*mu-si-na*—A—AŠ 326:12, URU.*mu-si-na*—A—[AŠ 326:1,
Muṣru (Egypt): LÚ.*mu-ṣur-a-a* 311:2, LÚ.*mu-ṣu-ra-a-a* 142 e. 12,
Nabur (city near Naṣibina): URU.*na-bu-ur* 90:9,
Napihu: URU.*na-pi-hi* 31:7, 13, URU.*n*[*a-pi-hi*] 31:21, URU.[*na-pi-hi*] 31:10, [URU.*na-pi-hi*] 31:19,
Naṣībina (class. Nisibin/s, mod. Nuṣaibin): URU. *na-ṣi-bi*-[*na*] 12 r. 7,
Nēmed-Issār (city in Assyria, Tell Afar?): URU. *né-med*—ᵈ15 328:5,
Nērubu (town S of Aleppo, mod. Nerab): URU. *né-ri-bi* 326:6, 13,
Nihut: URU.*ni-hu-ut-a-a* 30 r. 11,
Nīnua (Nineveh): DUMU—NINA 12 r. 1, DUMU—URU.NINA 81 r. 2, NINA 328 r. 4, 346 r. 6, NINA.KI 51 r. 7, 52 r. 7, 118 r. 2, 133:8, 181:5, 182 e. 7, 250 r. 4, 278 r. 5, 342:17, N[INA.KI 330 r. 1, N[INA.KI] 310 r. 1, URU.*ni-nu-u* 142:8, URU-*ni-nu*-[*a*] 86 r. 6, URU].*ni-na-a* 99 r. 3, URU].*ni-nu-a* 149:3, URU.*ni-nu-a* 53 e. 15, 86 r. 5, 12, 17, 181 e. 1, 185 r. 7, 202 r. 5, 204:3, 211 r. 2, URU.*ni-nu*-[*a*] 86 r. 7, URU.*ni-n*[*u-a*] 93 r. 4, U]RU.*ni-nu-a* 182:5, URU]. NINA 253 r. 6, URU.NINA 31 r. 10, 85 r. 1, 87 r. 2, 110 r. 3, 165 r. 1, 201 r. 2, 254:10, 314 r. 6, URU.NIN]A 326 r. 10, URU.[NINA] 50 r. 8, URU. [NI]NA 6 r. 13, UR]U.NINA 92:3, U]RU.NINA 158:7, 163 r. 4, [UR]U. NINA 229 r. 2, URU.NINA-*a* 121 r. 3, URU.NINA.KI 90:12, 154:5, 232 e. 7, 251:16, 309 r. 3, 325 r. 4, 335 r. 10, 349 r. 5, URU.NINA.KI] 329 r. 4, URU. NINA.[KI] 302 r. 12, URU.NI[NA.KI] 11 r. 12, 332 r. 11, URU.N[INA.KI 301 r. 2, URU.N[INA.KI] 100 r. 15,
Nuhub (town in Assyria): URU.*nu-hu-bi* 211:3,
Pāqutu (town in Babylonia): URU.*pa-qu-tú* 287: 11,
Parsua (Assyrian province): URU.*par-s*[*u-a* 25 e. 8,
Pilistu (Philistia): *pi-li-is-ta*-[*a-a*] 268:6,
Qatna (city on the Khabur, now Tell Fadghami?): [UR]U.*qat-ta-na-a-a* 321:2, URU.*qa-di-né-e* 335:6, 7, 10, URU.*q*[*a-di-né-e* 335:2,
Qubāti: URU.*qu-ba-a-te* 245:5,

Qudāru: URU.*qu-da-ru* 130 r. 10,
Que (country in Asia Minor, Bibl. Coa): KUR.*qu-e* 172 r. 5,
Raṣappa (Bibl. Rezeph, class. Risafe, mod. Riṣafa?): KUR.*ra-ṣap-pa*] 243:5, KUR.*ra-ṣ*[*ap-pa*] 243:1, KUR.*ra-ṣa-pi* 17 s. 2, KUR.*ru-ṣa-pa* 242:5, URU.*ra-ṣa-pa* 245:2,
Sairi: URU.*sa-i-ri* 278:5,
Samʾalla (city in SE Anatolia, now Zencirli): *sa-ma-*[*al-la*] 193 r. 13, URU.*sam-al-li* 196 r. 10, URU.*sa-am-al-la* 91 r. 6, URU.*sa-am-a-al-l*[*a* 194 s. 3, URU.*sa-ma-al-la* 46:8,
Sāmirīna (Samaria): URU.*sa-mir-i-na* 147 r. 8, URU.*sa-mir-*[*n*]*a* 148 r. 5,
Sasuka: URU.*sa-su-ka* 92 r. 10,
Siʾimmê (Ass. provincial capital in the upper Khabur area): URU.*si-me-e* 26 r. 8,
Singāra (Jebel Sinjar): KUR.*si-in-ga-ra* 329:4, 331:4, KUR.*si-i*[*n-ga-ra* 330:4,
Sumurūnu: URU.*su-mur-u-nu* 271:5,
Supūri-eddeti: URU.*su-pu-ri—e-de-te* 293:4, URU.*su-pu-ri—e-de-te*] 292:4,
Ṣāb-Adad: URU.ERIM.MEŠ—^{d}IM 311:6,
Ṣalli-ibši: URU.*ṣal-li—ib-ši* 27:2,
Ṣimirra (city in Phoenicia, class. Simyra): URU.*ṣi-me-er* 68 r. 3, 69 r. 5, URU.*ṣi-me-ra* 66 r. 12, 67 r. 3,
Ṣirina: URU.*ṣi-ri-na* 23 r. 7,
Ṣūpat (city in the Beqaa valley, Bibl. Zobah, mod. Homs?): URU].*ṣu-ba-te* 109 r. 9, URU.*ṣu-pi-te* 90 r. 18, 108 r. 3,
Šadikanni (city on the Khabur, now Tell Ajajah): URU.*šá-di-kan-ni* 286:2,
Šahuppa (capital city of Katmuhi in NW Assyria): [URU.*šá-hup-pa*] 131 r. 13, U[RU.*šá-hu-up-pa*] 96 r. 20,
Šamaš-rīqa (town in the district of Arrapha): URU.^{d}UTU*—ri-qa* 336:5, URU.^{d}UTU*—r*[*i-qa*] 336:7,
Ša-Zabīni: URU.*šá—za-bi-na-a-a* 195 r. 9,
Šibanība (city in central Assyria, now Tell Billa): URU.*ši-ba-ni-ba* 163:4,
Šiddi-hirīti (town near Maganuba); URU.UŠ*—hi-ri-ṭi* 37:6,
Šūru (city in NE Assyria, now Savur): URU.*šú-ra* 146:4, URU.*šu-r*[*i* 226:6, 7,
Talmūsa (Assyrian city, mod. Jerahiya?): URU.*tal-mu-si* 91:2, 11, 128 r. 5,
Tarqana URU.*tar-qa-na-a-a* 188:2,
Tiʾi: URU.*ti-ʾi-i* 50:7, URU.*ti-ʾi-*[*i*] 51:2,
Tillê (city in the Khabur triangle): URU.*til-e* 31 r. 28,
Til-Barsip (city near Carchemish, now Tell Ahmar): URU.*tar-bu-si-ba* 312:2, UR]U.*tar-bu-si-ba* 312 r. 16, URU.*tar-bu-si-e* 313:2, r. 4,
Til-hawar: URU.*til—ha-ú-ar* 277 s. 2, URU.*til—ha-ú-a*[*r*] 277:2,
Til-Inurta: URU.DU$_6$—^{d}MAŠ-*a-a* 1 r. 15,
Til-kurgarrê: URU.DUL—LÚ.KUR.GAR.RA 27:10,
Til-nahīri: URU.DUL*—na-hi-ri* 316:5, URU.DUL*—na-h*[*i-ri*] 315:3,
Til-rahaiāti: URU.*til—ra-ha-ia-te* 245:6,
Tursāna (city on the Lower Zab, now Tell Mahuz): URU.*tu-ur-sa-na* 188 r. 10, UR]U.*tu-ur-s*[*a-na* 188:4,
Tušhan (city in northern Assyria, mod. Kurh or Tepe): URU.*tú-uš-hi* 340 r. 6,
Ṭāb-ṣil-[...]: URU.DÙG.GA—GIŠ.MI—[*x* 326:5,
Ulāia (river in Elam, class. Eulaios, mod. Karkheh?): ÍD.*ú-la-ia* 288:16,
Upî (city in Babylonia, class. Opis): URU].*ú-pe-e* 276:4,
Urakka (city in Assyria, mod. Tell Amuda?): URU.*ú-rak-ka* 96:19,
Urulli: URU.*ur-ul-li* 201:3,
Zakūtu: URU.*za-ku-u-te* 288:17,
Zidada: URU.*zi-da-da* 210:4,
broken: Í[D.*x* 332:4, KUR.[*x* 193 s. 1, KUR.*x*[*x* 250 r. 14, 288 r. 11, URU.*a-mu-x*[*x* 112 r. 11, URU.*hi-x*[*x* 193:7, URU.*n*[*i-x* 218:4, [U]RU.*ši-*[*x*] 252 r. 1, URU.*tu-x*[*x* 24:5, URU.*zi-*[*x* 112 r. 5, URU.*x* 14 r. 9, 56 r. 7, 101:1, 283 r. 20, 326:4, 334:8, 15, r. 17, URU.*x*] 274 r. 4, URU.[*x* 16 r. 1, 24:4, 58 r. 4, 100:4, 112:6, 116 r. 8, 9, 126:4, 169:11, 283 r. 3, 288:16, r. 9, UR[U.*x* 302 r. 16, 314 r. 10, U[RU.*x* 25:3, 120 r. 1, URU.*x*[*x* 304 r. 8, URU.*x*]*x-hi-li* 334:18, URU.*x-hu-ú-te* 176:4, URU.BÀD—[*x* 303 r. 6, URU.É—*x*[*x* 27:3, URU.ŠE—[*x* 30:8, URU.Š[E—*x* 155:6, 287 s. 1, UR[U.ŠE—*x* 155:5, URU.ŠE—*x*[*x* 247:4, URU.Š[E]—^{m}[*x*]*-x-ha* 169:7,

God and Temple Names

Adad (weather god): ^{d}IM 58 r. 4, 198:4, 285 r. 2, 289 r. 1, ^{d}I[M] 96:18, ^{d}10 126 r. 4,
Aššūr (national god of Assyria): *aš-šur* 87 r. 3, 188 r. 6, 200 r. 3, 265:10, 283 r. 9, 308 r. 2, 325 r. 5, 326 r. 7, 334 r. 14, *aš-š*[*ur*] 95 r. 3, ^{d}*aš-šur*] 32 r. 3, 42 r. 1, 251 e. 17, ^{d}[*aš-šur* 20 r. 1, [^{d}*aš-šur* 11 r. 6, 251 r. 1,
Bēlat ṣēri (an underworld deity): *be-lit*—^{d}EDIN 101 r. 6, 102 r. 8,
Bēlet Nīnua ("Lady of Nineveh," Ištar of Nineveh): ^{d}GAŠAN—NINA.[KI 319 r. 2,
Bēt kidmūri (temple of Ištar in Calah): É*—kad-mu-ri* 11 r. 10,
Esaggil (main shrine of Marduk): É.SAG.Í[L 348:2,
Ešarra (main shrine of Aššur): É.ŠÁR.RA 283 r. 9, É.ŠÁR.RA] 200 r. 4,
Gula (goddess of healing): ^{d}ME.ME 59 r. 9,
Inurta (Ninurta, Assyrian war god): ^{d}]MAŠ 131 r. 2, ^{d}MAŠ 6 r. 1, 32 r. 2, 185 r. 9, 220 r. 6, 299:13, ^{d}MAŠ] 284 r. 4, [^{d}]MAŠ 298 r. 1, [^{d}MAŠ 11 r. 5,
Issār (Ištar, Assyrian war goddess): ^{d}]IŠ.TAR 309 r. 2, ^{d}IŠ.TAR 7 e. 16, 50 r. 8, 87 r. 2, 99 r. 2, 110 r. 2, 201 r. 1, 210 r. 1, 211 r. 2, 219 r. 8, 229 r. 1, 251:16, 278 r. 4, 325 r. 4, 334 r. 16, 335 r. 10, 349 r. 4, ^{d}IŠ.T[AR 314 r. 5, 326 r. 10, ^{d}IŠ.[TAR 51 r. 6,

Subject Index

List of Text Headings

Index of Texts

By Publication Number

By Museum Number

82-5-22,29	319
82-5-22,31	176
82-5-22,32	155
82-5-22,33	302
82-5-22,34	90
82-5-22,36	118
82-5-22,38	264
82-5-22,41	263
82-5-22,47	35
82-5-22,139	340
82-5-22,151	58
83-1-18,163	56
83-1-18,201	221
83-1-18,259	348
83-1-18,269	212
83-1-18,291+	10
83-1-18,323	78
83-1-18,328	267
83-1-18,330	84
83-1-18,331	100
83-1-18,333	216
83-1-18,334	59
83-1-18,335	32
83-1-18,337	210
83-1-18,338	284
83-1-18,339	52
83-1-18,340	274
83-1-18,341	300
83-1-18,342	160
83-1-18,343	39
83-1-18,344	45
83-1-18,345	196
83-1-18,348	341
83-1-18,350+	334
(83-1-18,352+)	305
83-1-18,353	298
83-1-18,357	290
83-1-18,359	57
83-1-18,360	277
83-1-18,362	270
83-1-18,364	156
83-1-18,365	47
83-1-18,366	215
83-1-18,367	238
83-1-18,370	108
83-1-18,371	262
83-1-18,372	128
83-1-18,373	236
83-1-18,374	237
83-1-18,379	14
83-1-18,382	324
83-1-18,387	334
83-1-18,390	279
83-1-18,391	165
83-1-18,393	180
83-1-18,405	73
83-1-18,406	70
83-1-18,407	67
83-1-18,408	68
83-1-18,460	201
83-1-18,461B	311
(83-1-18,484+)	283
83-1-18,560	289
83-1-18,579	349
83-1-18,688	11
83-1-18,689	343
83-1-18,698	280
83-1-18,723	327
83-1-18,770	211
83-1-18,900	162
Bu 89-4-26,7	317
Bu 89-4-26,10	233
Bu 89-4-26,22	228
Bu 89-4-26,32	222
Bu 89-4-26,33	149
Bu 89-4-26,120	103
Bu 89-4-26,122	87
Bu 89-4-26,128	112
Bu 89-4-26,131	185
Bu 91-5-9,4	150
Bu 91-5-9,10	206
Bu 91-5-9,27	281
Bu 91-5-9,40	49
Bu 91-5-9,41	339
Bu 91-5-9,59	106
Bu 91-5-9,84	38
Bu 91-5-9,94	227
Bu 91-5-9,95	169
Bu 91-5-9,121	122
Bu 91-5-9,123	254
Bu 91-5-9,138	272
Bu 91-5-9,162	330
Bu 91-5-9,166+	305
Bu 91-5-9,173	269
Bu 91-5-9,179	309
Bu 91-5-9,197	93
Bu 91-5-9,209	161
Ki 1904-10-9,13	105
Ki 1904-10-9,21	328
Ki 1904-10-9,29	268
Ki 1904-10-9,31	308
Ki 1904-10-9,43	23
Ki 1904-10-9,44	219
Ki 1904-10-9,46	229
Ki 1904-10-9,56	62
Ki 1904-10-9,62	94
Ki 1904-10-9,98	28
Ki 1904-10-9,133	119
Ki 1904-10-9,139+	174
Ki 1904-10-9,147+	22
Ki 1904-10-9,148	137
(Ki 1904-10-9,150+)	22
Ki 1904-10-9,161+	125
Ki 1904-10-9,162	115
Ki 1904-10-9,180	247
Ki 1904-10-9,181	338
Ki 1904-10-9,182	170
Ki 1904-10-9,183	171
Ki 1904-10-9,189	257
Ki 1904-10-9,192+	275
Ki 1904-10-9,198	129
(Ki 1904-10-9,230+)	22
(Ki 1904-10-9,236+)	22
(Ki 1904-10-9,238+)	174
(Ki 1904-10-9,240+)	22
Ki 1904-10-9,292+	69
(Ki 1904-10-9,299+)	275
(Ki 1904-10-9,310+)	69
(Ki 1904-10-9,314+)	69
(Ki 1904-10-9,316+)	69
(Ki 1904-10-9,386+)	125
(Ki 1904-10-9,388+)	22
(Ki 1904-10-9,391+)	22
(Ki 1904-10-9,393+)	174
(Ki 1904-10-9,395+)	22
(Ki 1904-10-9,401+)	174
(Ki 1904-10-9,404+)	174
Th 1905-4-9,43	207
Th 1905-4-9,49	29
Th 1905-4-9,353	18
BM 121054	147
BM 121104	148
BM 123360	133
BM 128026+	194
(BM 128146+)	194
BM 134582	114
N. III 3157	31

List of Joins

List of Illustrations

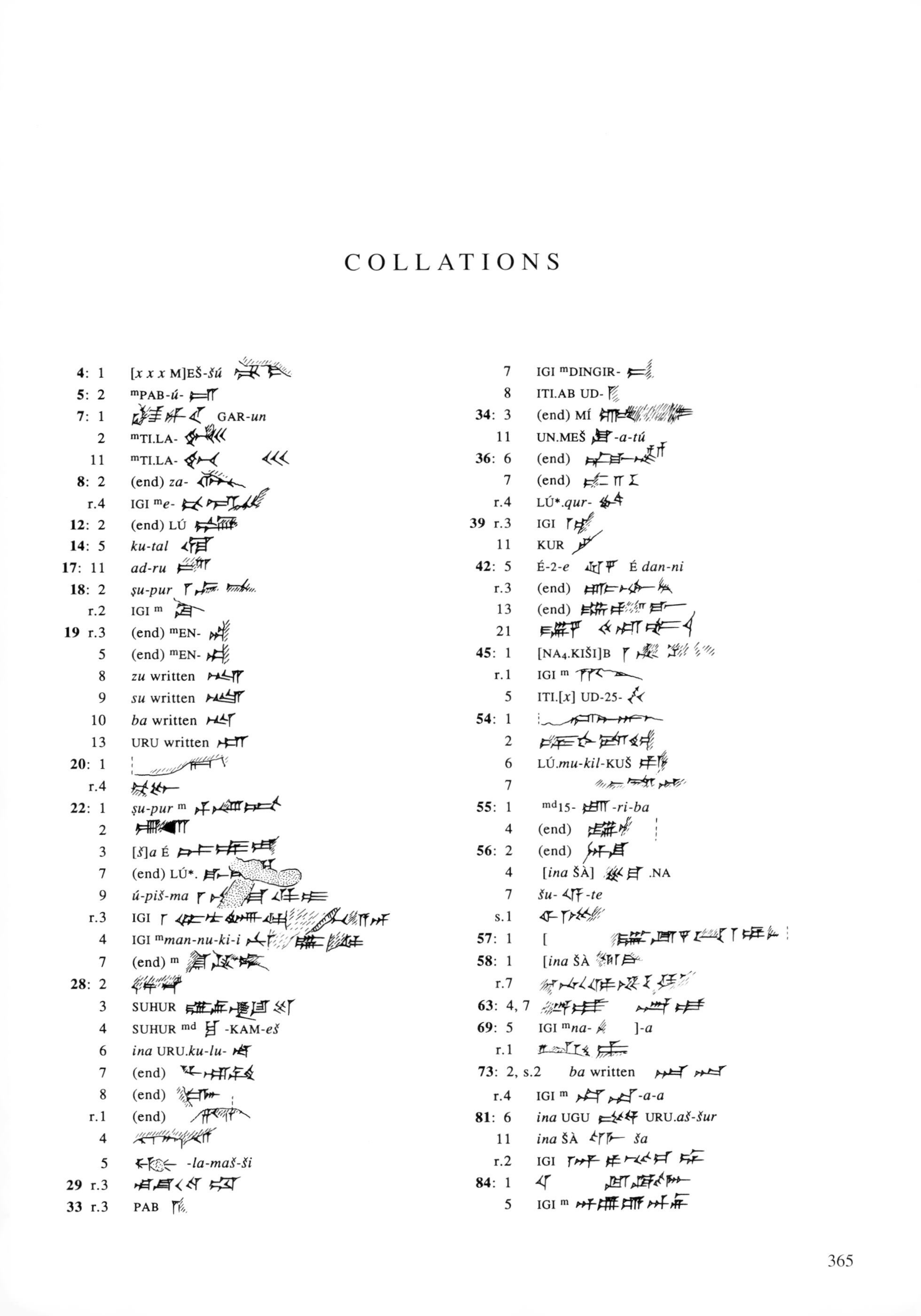

COLLATIONS

4: 1 [*x x x* M]EŠ-*šú*
5: 2 ^{m}PAB-*ú*-
7: 1 GAR-*un*
2 ^{m}TI.LA-
11 ^{m}TI.LA-
8: 2 (end) *za*-
r.4 IGI ^{m}*e*-
12: 2 (end) LÚ
14: 5 *ku-tal*
17: 11 *ad-ru*
18: 2 *ṣu-pur*
r.2 IGI ^{m}
19 r.3 (end) ^{m}EN-
5 (end) ^{m}EN-
8 *zu* written
9 *su* written
10 *ba* written
13 URU written
20: 1
r.4
22: 1 *ṣu-pur* ^{m}
2
3 [*š*]*a* É
7 (end) LÚ*.
9 *ú-piš-ma*
r.3 IGI
4 IGI ^{m}*man-nu-ki-i*
7 (end) ^{m}
28: 2
3 SUHUR
4 SUHUR ^{md} -KAM-*eš*
6 *ina* URU.*ku-lu*-
7 (end)
8 (end)
r.1 (end)
4
5 -*la-maš-ši*
29 r.3
33 r.3 PAB
7 IGI ^{m}DINGIR-
8 ITI.AB UD-
34: 3 (end) MÍ
11 UN.MEŠ -*a-tú*
36: 6 (end)
7 (end)
r.4 LÚ*.*qur*-
39 r.3 IGI
11 KUR
42: 5 É-2-*e* É *dan-ni*
r.3 (end)
13 (end)
21
45: 1 [NA$_4$.KIŠI]B
r.1 IGI ^{m}
5 ITI.[*x*] UD-25-
54: 1
2
6 LÚ.*mu-kil*-KUŠ
7
55: 1 ^{md}15- -*ri-ba*
4 (end)
56: 2 (end)
4 [*ina* ŠÀ] .NA
7 *šu*- -*te*
s.1
57: 1 [
58: 1 [*ina* ŠÀ
r.7
63: 4, 7
69: 5 IGI ^{m}*na*-]-*a*
r.1
73: 2, s.2 *ba* written
r.4 IGI ^{m} -*a-a*
81: 6 *ina* UGU URU.*aš-šur*
11 *ina* ŠÀ *ša*
r.2 IGI
84: 1
5 IGI ^{m}

7 IGI m
88: 3
4
13 [*man-*
r.2
3
90: 10 LÚ.ARAD.MEŠ *šá* m[
17 [*x x x* -*a-ru*
r.17 *lim-me* m*man-nu-ki-*
91: 6 DUMU-*šú* m -*te-e*
92: 1 (end)
2 (end)
4
5
r.4
7
8
11
12
93: 1
6 [SUHUR
8 [*x x x*] *ša*
9 [*x x x*]
r.1 A.ŠÀ
3 MÍ.GAR-
10 *lu-u* DUMU.MEŠ
94: 1
4
10
11 (end) *ina*
r.1 PAB 31
2 (end)
97: 1 (end) *ma-né-e ša*
4 ITI
7 GIŠ.SAR *ša*
9 (end) m*se-e*ʾ*-ba-rak-*
r.9 (end) m*man-nu-ki-i-*
10 mdŠÚ- -DÙ
11 LÚ*.ZADIM BAN.
98: 5 *ú-piš-ma*
103: 9 *i-* -*qi*
11 [*t*]*u-a-ru*
12
105 r.2 (end)
3 (end)
4 IGI m*ha-*
5 IGI *lu-u-* -*i*
s.2 [*x x x* m -*bu-za-a*ʾ
109: 9 [*kas-pu gam-mur ta-*
r.8 UD- -KAM
115: 4 [*x x* *mi-šil bu-ri*

6 (end) *ša*
r.1 [IGI md
2 [IGI m
3
5 mdPA-ZU
6 [IGI m*x x x x* LÚ*
117: 2 [*šá* m
119: 2 *ṣu-*[*pur*] m
16 *ša* PÚ
r.3 *za-ar-pu*
15 IGI md
16 (end)
18 (end)
19
122 r.1 [IGI MÁ.DU.DU.MEŠ
2 URU.*ha-at-*
124: 1 (end)
125: 5 (end) *ši-di*
6 (end) SUHUR
8 SUHUR mdPA-
9 [*x x x x x*
r.3 (end) -*ú-ni*
4 (end)
13 IGI m*e-ṣi-di-a-a*
126: 4
6
7
8 [*ú-pi*]*š-ma*
9
r.4 [*ina bur-ki*]
128: 3 (end)]
129: 1 [NA₄.KIŠIB m -dAMAR.UTU
2 [EN É GIŠ
r.2 (end)
4 [*lim-mu* mDI-*mu*
131 r.14 IGI m
134 r.5 IGI m*ab-da-a*
137: 2 (end) 1 ANŠE
4 É 1 ANŠE
r.5 IGI m
6 *lim-me* mSUM-*na*-PAB
141 r.4
7
8
143: 6 *la i-din*
r.1 ITI.KIN
3 IGI md*a-a-*
4 IGI
s.1 IGI m*šá-*
144: 2 [
5 [

r.1
2 [IGI ^{m}]
145: 3 ^{m}KUR.*gar-ga-* … *-a-a*
r.1
150: 3 (end)
4 (end)
5 (end)
151 r.4
8 (end) IGI ^{m}
9 (end) IGI ^{m}
153 r.1
2 IGI ^{md}PA-
156 r.14
158: 2
160: 1 ^{m}*man-nu-lu*
2 ^{md}IM-
6
13
r.15 ITI.AB UD- … -KÁM
161: 1 ^{m}*man-nu-*
162: 1 NA$_4$
164: 1 [NA$_4$.KIŠIB ^{m}*mar*?-
10 (end)
15
r.3 ^{m}*man-nu-ki-*
10 [IGI ^{m}]
166: 4 ^{m}*se-e-*
6 ^{m} … *-hi-ra-*
r.5 ^{m}*ab-di-a-* … *zi*
170: 1 MA.NA
r.2 IGI
171 r.2 [I]GI … *-bu-nu*
174: 2
r.6
7 DUG$_4$.DUG$_4$
9 (end) *ša*
s.1 ^{m}*aš-šur-*
2 (blank)
178 r.5
180: 3 ^{m}*man-nu-* … *-ki-*NINA.KI
r.9 (end) GUR-
10 (end) *e-*
184: 6 IGI … *-ni-[i*
r.1
197: 3 MÍ.^{d}*na-na-*TUK-
201: 1 [NA$_4$.KIŠIB ^{m}] … *-ri-iá*
10 *kas-pu*
14 *lu-u* ^{m} … *-ri-iá*
r.7 (end)
204 r.3 ^{m}*aš-šur-*MU-
4 ^{m}*qur-di-*^{d}

206: 1
3 *ina* IGI
7
r.3 TA written
7 [IGI ^{m} … *-ba-bu-*DINGIR*-a-a*
207: 1
2
3
r.2 ^{m}*man-nu-*
208: 3 *ina* IGI
r.1 IGI
210: 4 A.QAR
r.3 (end) *la*
212: 1
4 (end)
5 [
6 [*ub-ta-*
r.2 (end)
3 (end)
6 [ITI.BAR]AG
7 (end)
216: 1
218: 4 (end) URU
219: 9 *tu-a-ru*
11 [
r.9 (end)
12 *di-in-šú*
s.1
220 r.8
14 [
222: 7
225 r.7 (end)
8 (end)
9 (end)
226: 6 (end) URU.*šu-*
7 (end) URU.*šu-*
r. 5 IGI ^{m}
8 IGI ^{m}
9 IGI ^{m}*pu-*
227: 2, 7 TUR written
228: 12 *lu-u*] … MEŠ*-šú*
229: 1 ^{m}*šum-ma-*
6 ^{m}*šum-ma-i-*
r.2 *kas-pu ina*
236 r.3 IGI ^{m} … ; cf. … obv.3
4 IGI ^{m} … *-ú-ri*
246: 4 IGI ^{m} … …]
r.5 (end)
247: 3 ANŠE
250: 2 E[N] M[Í … S[UM-*ni*]
251: 1 [*x x x x x x*]

4 [
5
17
18
253 r.5 [*x* GÚ
254: 1 [
5 TA written
r.2 (end)
3 (end)
7
8
257: 7 (end)
258: 3 É [A.ŠÀ GIŠ
s.1 (end)
264: 10
r.6 *hur-sa-an*
267 r.1 IGI
2 IGI [m]30- -SUM-*na*
6 [m]AD-*ra*-
268: 1 [*x x x*
5 SUHUR [m]
6 SUHUR
7 *ku-um*
270 r.1 (end)
271: 6 *i-kar-ri-ka*
14 (end)
21 [d]PA-*u-a*
22 (end)
r.6 (end)
9 (end)
275: 1 NA$_4$.K[IŠIB]
22 É 6BÁN
r.1 É 4BÁN
10 (end) SUHUR [m]*ur*-
s.1 [IGI [m]*šá-la*]-*ma-še-e* [L]Ú*
2 [IGI [m]
3 IGI [m]*a-a*-
4 (blank)
277 r.1 IGI [m]EN-KASKAL-
4 IGI -*ta-a*
5 (end) [m]AD-
6 (end)
8 (end)
9 IGI [m] -*ár*-DINGIR : [m]*hi-ri*
11 DUL written
278: 5 SUHUR [m]
10 *ina* ŠÀ MA.NA
r.13 IGI
16 IGI [md]PA-*šá*-
282: 5
r.1 (end)
285: 1
2
4
5
r.1 (end)
5 (end) DAM.QAR
8
9
286: 6 *ina* ŠÀ-*bi*
r.1 IGI [m]
5 IGI
287: 8 *a*- ŠE.NUMUN-*šú*
9 URU.ŠE
11 (end)
r.2 [*x x x x* *kar-ap-hi*
13 (end)
289: 7 *i-si*-
r.4
10 ARAD *šá*
11 (end) LÚ*
13 ITI
291: 4 (end)
r.2 [m]*a-ka*-
295: 3 [*x x* *i-sa-he*-
300: 4
r.2
3
307: 6 [m]*di-*[*d*]*i-i* LÚ*
r.7 ITI.GUD UD-
311: 2 [D]UMU [m] -*ši-e-šu*
4 É
10 4 MA.NA KUG.UD
15
r.1
2
3
4
5
318: 1 (end) LÚ.2-*u*
320: 1
325: 2 NA$_4$.KIŠIB [m]*as*- -*di* LÚ*.A.BA *ša*
8 (end)
10 NA$_4$.KIŠIB [m]
r.20 IGI [md]PA-
22 IGI
22 (end) IGI [m]*man-nu*-
23 *lim-me* [m]
327 r.9 [L]Ú*.GAR.KUR URU
328: 6 (end)·SUHUR [m]
8 SUHUR É
15 [*lu-u* [md]

r.1 [TA ^{m}*rém-a-ni-*^{d} 

7 (end) -É.GAL 

9 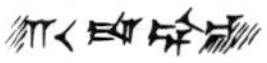

14 IGI ^{m} 

329: 9 GIŠ.SAR  SUKKAL

13 (end) LÚ 

r.19 LÚ.2-*u*  LÚ.GAL-*ú-rat*

330: 2 [LÚ.A.BA 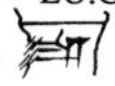

r.1 

333: 1 [

3 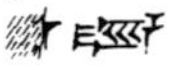

r.2 (end) 

343: 1 (end) NA_4.KIŠIB ^{m} 

7 (end)  ZI.MEŠ

344: 1
2
3
4 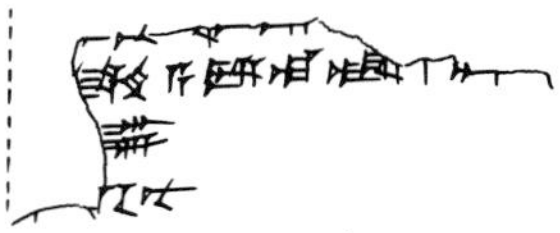

8 5 MA.NA 

14 (end) *man-nu ša* ]

r.3 [*lu-u*] 

348: 2 

349: 1 [

r.3 [DUMU-DUMU.MEŠ 

6 (end) 

8
9 

350: 1 [*ina de-* 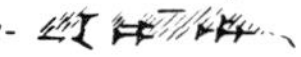

PLATES

PLATE I. N. III 3157 (= No. 31), Obverse

PLATE II. N. III 3157 (= No. 31), Reverse

STATE ARCHIVES OF ASSYRIA

VOLUME I
THE CORRESPONDENCE OF SARGON II, PART I
Letters from Assyria and the West
Edited by Simo Parpola
1987

VOLUME II
NEO-ASSYRIAN TREATIES AND LOYALTY OATHS
Edited by Simo Parpola and Kazuko Watanabe
1988

VOLUME III
COURT POETRY AND LITERARY MISCELLANEA
Edited by Alasdair Livingstone
1989

VOLUME IV
QUERIES TO THE SUNGOD
Divination and Politics in Sargonid Assyria
Edited by Ivan Starr
1990

VOLUME V
THE CORRESPONDENCE OF SARGON II, PART II
Letters from the Northern and Northeastern Provinces
Edited by Giovanni B. Lanfranchi and Simo Parpola
1990

VOLUME VI
LEGAL TRANSACTIONS OF THE ROYAL COURT OF NINEVEH, PART I
Tiglath-Pileser III through Esarhaddon
Edited by Theodore Kwasman and Simo Parpola
1991